HARRAP'S
FRENCH AND ENGLISH DICTIONARY OF

Slang
and
Colloquialisms

HARRAP'S
FRENCH AND ENGLISH DICTIONARY OF

Slang
and
Colloquialisms

by
GEORGETTE A. MARKS
Special Lecturer, University of Manchester

and

CHARLES B. JOHNSON M.A.

ENGLISH-FRENCH
FRENCH-ENGLISH

HARRAP LONDON
1981

First published in this edition in Great Britain 1980
by GEORGE G. HARRAP & CO. LTD
182 High Holborn, London WC1V 7AX

Fifth Impression: 1981

ISBN 0 245-53602-7 (Great Britain)
ISBN 0 245-53601-9 (France)

Printed in Great Britain by offset lithography by
Biddles Ltd, Guildford, Surrey

PART ONE

ENGLISH—FRENCH

FOREWORD

The present work is the second part (English-French) of *Harrap's French-English Dictionary of Slang and Colloquialisms* by Joseph Marks, and has been planned along the same lines. It is not intended only for the specialist. An ever-increasing number of French-speaking people travel in countries where English and American English are spoken; they like to be able to understand the man in the street, and are interested in English and American novels, plays and films. Our purpose is to enable them to cope with the English slang and colloquialisms they are likely to come across, and also to help English speakers to find the French equivalents of current words and expressions in non-standard English.

No dictionary can claim to be exhaustive. This one contains what is hoped to be a far-reaching and, at the same time, a judicious selection (subjective though it must be) of colloquial, popular and even vulgar words and phrases with appropriate French renderings. Admittedly some entries are rarely encountered outside certain contexts and *milieux*, but even so they are, we feel, of sufficient frequency to justify their inclusion.

Compiling a dictionary of slang may be regarded as a form of lexicographical heroism, for nothing is more subject to change than popular speech; at the same time, nothing is more succulent, vehement or picturesque. Plato, who did not care for the common people, nevertheless called them "my masters in language"; and Montaigne sought an approach to language "not so much delicate and well-groomed as vigorous, terse and concentrated, typical of the barrack-room rather than of pedantry". And so, however ephemeral some expressions may be, they have a span of life—a vogue— while others become common enough to pass into everyday language and literature.

In France, since the Second World War, a number of works, research studies and dictionaries have been devoted to *l'argot*, and, to take but one notable example, in the latest Supplement to the Robert dictionary it plays an important part. In Great Britain, on the other hand, linguists seem on the whole to disdain slang and there are very few, apart from Eric Partridge, who have spent many years of research on it. And yet slang has a long and fascinating history. As far back as in the reign of Elizabeth I, Thomas Harman, a worthy gentleman who set out to combat vagrancy, published a lexicon of vagabond terms. Dekker did likewise some fifty years later. Shakespeare, Beaumont and Fletcher, and Ben Jonson used beggars' cant in their plays. At length, in 1785, a certain Captain Francis Grose published his large *Classical Dictionary of the Vulgar Tongue*, more comprehensive than that of Hautel on the low French language which appeared in 1808. But who better to defend slang than G. K. Chesterton: "Good slang is the one stream of poetry which is constantly flowing. Every day some nameless poet weaves some fairy tracery of popular language. The world of slang is a kind of topsy-turvydom of poetry".

The origin of the word *slang* is obscure; it is supposed to have first applied to the language of nomads and gipsies, and it was not until the end of the eighteenth century that its meaning was broadened to include thieves' cant and the language of the underworld. The vocabulary of thieving and deception, of prostitution and sexual intercourse still figures among its richest elements. The secret language of criminals, tramps and beggars was known as *cant*—now understood as a mode of expression confined to members of a particular profession, trade, age-group or social stratum. *Jargon* is more restricted in that it is too technical in its terminology to be comprehensible to the uninitiated—i.e. to anyone outside the group in which it is spoken. As cant and jargon terms, in the course of time, filter through to a wider sector of the public they become known as *slang* or *popular language*.

At the other end of the spectrum are *colloquialisms*, words and expressions typical of everyday conversation but not regarded as being formal enough for "polite" conversation, business correspondence or the like. One of the major problems in the compilation of a dictionary of slang and colloquialisms is to determine which words and expressions are eligible for inclusion and which are to be omitted because they have reached the stage where they can rightly be regarded as "standard" or "approved" English. The problem is further complicated by the widespread use of figurative speech in English. The decision whether to include this or that word or expression must, in the end, be an arbitrary one, since there is no ultimate authority to which one can turn for guidance. One of the chief aims of this dictionary has been, so far as is possible, to elucidate a very broad range of terms, from the colloquial bordering on standard English to the very vulgar.

But not only does the dictionary contain a comprehensive cross-section of terms in use at the present time, but also a representative selection of those which, to the modern generation, will seem "dated"; yet they owe their place in this work to the fact that, over a period of time, they have established themselves sufficiently to find their way into the literature and other art-forms of this country and of other English-speaking countries. They are included, however, not only on account of their historical importance but also because such expressions have a habit of being reintroduced after a lapse of time, either for novel effect to a new generation or because the various alternatives tried are rejected in their favour. The fact is that, English being a living language, it is never static but for ever self-regenerating, and words are created and discarded practically every day—especially since the advent of mass-media.

Because of all these considerations it is very difficult to determine what is colloquial and what is popular or vulgar, but, to serve as a guide to the uninitiated, every head-word in the dictionary is followed by one of the following abbreviations:

> *F:* = familiar; colloquial
> *P:* = popular; slang
> *V:* = vulgar
> *VV:* = very vulgar; "taboo"

It is impossible to be squeamish, for the coarse, the violent and the obscene are part and parcel of popular expression. To call a spade a spade presents no problem nowadays. It is precisely when a spade is no longer a spade that the lexicographer's interest awakens. It may be added that the popular mentality was never greatly concerned with spades as such. It has moved in other fields, as has been noted above, with vigour and inventiveness, but with scant regard for social or moral conventions. We have not deemed it necessary to avoid printing in full English or French words that are often considered taboo.

The foreign student of English generally finds himself attracted by popular speech and is often tempted to use it, feeling that it gives the impression of a greater familiarity with the spoken language. But one has only to think of the many pitfalls *l'argot* offers in French—and not merely to foreigners—for one to be very cautious before attempting to use some of the expressions found in this dictionary. Slang, it should be remembered, is linked, even more than *l'argot*, not only with a particular *milieu* but often with specific circumstances. It is also characterized by forms of pronunciation and grammar peculiar to itself. Used "out of situation" and so away from its proper context it can appear ludicrous if not offensive.

In order to keep the work within a reasonable compass, a number of space-saving devices have been used. Where in an example a head-word is repeated in exactly the same form it is represented by the initial letter, though plural nouns or verb conjugations in which the form differs from the infinitive are written in full:

e.g. **stack** (*noun*) . . . **to have a s.** (*or* **stacks**) **of money,** être très riche*...
     give (to) . . . **don't g. me that!** ne me raconte pas d'histoires!... **to know what gives,** être à la page. . .

Similarly, compound words appearing in examples are represented by the two initial letters:

e.g. **milk-train** (*noun*) . . . **to catch the m.-t.,** rentrer au petit matin.

This method of abbreviation also applies to the English compound verbs where the infinitive form remains intact in the example:

e.g. **doll up (to)** . . . **to d. oneself u.,** s'orner, se bichonner...

If, however, the form differs from the infinitive the components are given in full:

e.g. **doll up (to)** . . . **to get all dolled up,** se mettre sur son trente et un...

Irregular plural forms of nouns have been given only where it was felt they might present special difficulties for non-English users of the dictionary.

It should be noted that, for maximum convenience, the dictionary is arranged in strict alphabetical order; hence words which rightly belong together may be separated:

e.g. **goofball, goofed (up), goofer, go-off, go off, goof off.**

Entries labelled (*U.S.*) (Americanisms) or (*Austr.*) (Australianisms), though numerous, are restricted to such terms as would be unlikely to be understood in Great Britain in the context given. These labels are not used for words which have passed into English colloquial or popular usage, whatever their origin.

Popular language is so rich in synonyms that, in order to save space and avoid repetition, it has been decided to give the generic term followed by an asterisk (*e.g.* **mitt,** main*). The asterisk indicates that the word so marked is given as a head-word in the *Répertoire alphabétique de synonymes argotiques et populaires* at the end of the dictionary; there will be found a list of familiar and popular synonyms and closely related words from which a choice can be made. Most key-words in the dictionary itself are followed by one or more of these synonyms which approximate most closely in register. In the case of drugs (*drogues**) the reader is being referred to a wider group than the synonyms for a specific word.

To facilitate reference, nouns have normally been taken as key-words, and the first noun serves this purpose if a phrase contains two or more nouns (*e.g.* **like a dose of salts** will be found under **dose**). Cross-references are frequently given in cases where it was thought useful to do so.

The authors are indebted to all those who helped to make the publication of this dictionary possible: first and foremost to Mrs Jean Johnson, who provided the inestimable support of an understanding wife, and Mr David Marks, whose filial support was matched by his valuable collaboration; to Mr R. P. L. Ledésert, Director of the Modern Languages Department of Messrs Harrap, and to his wife Margaret—the Curies of lexicography—for their encouragement and help, and also to a number of his colleagues, especially Mr P. H. Collin, for their advice; to Mr F. White, whose knowledge and unflagging interest were extremely helpful; to Miss Gillian Seymour, who typed much of the material; and to everyone who, wittingly or unwittingly, contributed to this work.

G.A.M.
C.B.J.

AVANT-PROPOS

Cet ouvrage se présente comme la deuxième partie anglaise-française du *Harrap's French-English Dictionary of Slang and Colloquialisms* de Joseph Marks et a été conçu dans le même esprit. Il ne s'adresse pas seulement au spécialiste. Un nombre toujours croissant de touristes francophones voyagent dans les pays de langue anglaise et américaine; ils veulent comprendre l'homme de la rue et s'intéressent aux romans, aux pièces de théâtre, aux films anglais et américains. Notre but est de leur permettre d'assimiler les éléments populaires et argotiques de cette langue, et aussi d'aider l'anglophone curieux de la transposition en français des expressions courantes et vivantes de l'anglais non-académique.

Aucun dictionnaire ne peut prétendre être complet. Celui-ci veut présenter une sélection — personnelle peut-être — mais aussi étendue et judicieuse que possible de phrases et de mots familiers, populaires et même vulgaires et de leur équivalent en français. Certaines expressions sónt peut-être rares et ne se rencontrent que dans certains contextes et certains milieux mais semblent cependant assez fréquentes pour justifier leur inclusion.

Présenter un dictionnaire d'argot est une sorte d'héroïsme lexicographique car rien n'est plus fluide, changeant, incertain que la langue populaire; mais rien non plus n'est aussi succulent, véhément et pittoresque. Platon, qui n'aimait pas le peuple, l'appelait cependant «mon maître de langue»; et Montaigne recherchait «un parler non tant délicat et peigné comme nerveux, court et serré, non pédantesque mais plutôt soldatesque.» Donc, même si certaines expressions sont éphémères, elles ont vécu et d'autres deviennent assez usuelles pour passer dans la langue de tous les jours et dans la littérature.

En France, depuis l'après-guerre, plusieurs ouvrages, études et dictionnaires ont été consacrés à *l'argot* et il est très caractéristique que le dernier Supplément du Dictionnaire de Robert lui fasse une large place. En Grande-Bretagne, au contraire, les linguistes semblent dédaigner le *slang* et il n'y a guère qu'Eric Partridge qui lui ait voué de longues années de recherches. Pourtant le slang a une longue et fascinante histoire. Dès le règne de la première Elizabeth, Thomas Harman, un digne homme qui voulait combattre le vagabondage, publia un lexique de sa langue. Dekker fit de même quelque cinquante années plus tard. Shakespeare, Beaumont et Fletcher, Ben Jonson employèrent le *cant* des mendiants dans leurs pièces. Enfin, en 1785, un capitaine Francis Grose publia un gros dictionnaire classique de la langue vulgaire plus compréhensif que celui d'Hautel sur le bas langage français qui parut à Paris en 1808. Mais qui peut mieux défendre le slang que G. K. Chesterton: «Le bon *slang* est un des ruisseaux de la poésie qui constamment s'écoule. Chaque jour quelque poète anonyme tisse quelque réseau féerique de la langue populaire. Le monde du *slang* est un royaume renversé de la poésie.»

L'origine du mot *slang* est obscure; on pense qu'il s'appliquait d'abord à la langue des nomades et des romanichels et ce ne fut qu'à la fin du dix-huitième siècle qu'il s'étendit à la langue de la pègre et du milieu. Le vocabulaire des voleurs et des escrocs, celui de la prostitution et des rapports sexuels lui procure encore ses plus riches éléments. Le langage secret des truands et des larrons d'autrefois s'appelait le *cant*, mot qui aujourd'hui désigne surtout le mode d'expression d'un métier, d'une profession, d'une génération ou d'une classe sociale. Le *jargon* a un sens plus restreint car il est trop technique pour être compris par le non-initié, c'est-à-dire quiconque n'appartient pas au groupe où on le parle. On peut donc dire qu'aujourd'hui le *slang* ou *langue populaire* couvre tous les termes de *cant* et de *jargon* qui se sont infiltrés dans un usage plus courant.

A l'autre bout de la gamme se trouve la langue familière et les locutions de la langue de tous les jours mais qu'on ne considère pas suffisamment convenables pour une conversation polie ou des rapports épistolaires. Un des grands problèmes de la composition d'un dictionnaire d'argot et de langue familière est de savoir déterminer quels termes peuvent y figurer et quels autres doivent être rejetés du fait qu'ils sont devenus de l'anglais «correct» et accepté. L'emploi en anglais du figuré et de la métaphore rend ce problème encore plus compliqué. Dans ce choix la décision finale ne peut être qu'arbitraire puisqu'on ne peut être guidé par aucun principe directeur. Autant que possible le but de ce dictionnaire a été de présenter un vaste déploiement de termes qui partent du familier touchant au correct, pour aller jusqu'à l'obscène et l'ordurier.

Ce dictionnaire contient non seulement un assortiment étendu de mots et expressions d'aujourd'hui mais aussi une sélection représentative de termes que les jeunes pourraient qualifier de «périmés». Ils ont leur place dans cet ouvrage car pendant un laps de temps ils ont vécu et ont pénétré dans l'expression littéraire orale ou écrite en Grande-Bretagne ou en Amérique. Et ce n'est pas seulement à cause de leur importance historique qu'ils ont été retenus, mais aussi parce qu'après un certain temps, souvent ils réapparaissent, sonnant neufs aux oreilles d'une nouvelle génération ou peut-être simplement exprimant mieux l'idée que ce qui les avait remplacés. L'anglais, parlé par tant de millions d'individus, est en vérité une langue vivante, jamais statique mais se renouvelant sans cesse; chaque jour des mots naissent et meurent, surtout depuis l'apparition du mass-media.

Du fait de toutes ces considérations il est donc fort difficile de déterminer le familier, le populaire, le vulgaire, mais pour guider le lecteur non averti chaque terme est suivi d'une des abréviations suivantes:

F   pour familier
P   pour populaire et argotique
V   pour vulgaire et trivial
VV pour le très vulgaire, l'obscène, l'ordurier

Il est impossible de se montrer pudibond; le grossier, le violent et l'obscène font partie intégrante de l'expression populaire. On est habitué aujourd'hui à appeler les choses par leur nom: *un chat un chat, et Rolet un fripon*, mais c'est précisément quand un chat n'est plus un chat que l'intérêt du lexicographe s'éveille. D'ailleurs, la mentalité populaire a surtout tendance à broder sur le côté *fripon* avec vigueur et pittoresque sans se soucier des conventions sociales et morales. Il ne nous a donc pas semblé nécessaire d'éviter d'écrire en toutes lettres les mots anglais et français que certains déclarent tabous.

Quiconque apprend l'anglais semble attiré par le parler populaire et essaie de s'en servir, ayant ainsi l'impression qu'il se familiarise avec le langage courant du pays. Mais il suffit de penser à tous les traquenards que rencontre même le francophone s'il veut parler argot pour n'employer qu'avec beaucoup de précautions les expressions que l'on trouvera dans ce dictionnaire. Le *slang*, plus encore que l'*argot*, appartient non seulement à un milieu déterminé mais aussi dépend de circonstances précises. Il est accompagné d'une prononciation particulière et enrobé d'une grammaire spéciale. Si on le sort hors de son cadre et de son contexte normal, il devient grotesque et même choquant.

Afin que ce volume soit commode et maniable, on s'est servi de plusieurs moyens pour gagner de la place. Lorsque dans un exemple le mot de tête (ou entrée) est répété sans changement orthographique il est représenté par sa lettre initiale, mais les noms pluriel et les verbes conjugués dont la forme diffère de l'infinitif sont en toutes lettres :

ex. **stack** (*noun*) . . . **to have a s.** (*or* **stacks**) **of money,** être très riche*...
    give (to) . . . **don't g. me that!** ne me raconte pas d'histoires!... **to know what gives,** être à la page...

De même, les mots composés qui se trouvent dans un exemple sont représentés par leurs deux lettres initiales :

ex. **milk-train** (*noun*) . . . **to catch the m.-t.,** rentrer au petit matin.

Cette méthode d'abréviation s'applique aussi aux verbes composés anglais lorsque la forme infinitive est conservée dans l'exemple :

ex. **doll up (to)** . . . **to d. oneself u.,** s'orner, se bichonner...

Mais si cette forme diffère de l'infinitif le verbe est alors donné en toutes lettres :

ex. **doll up (to)** . . . **to get all dolled up,** se mettre sur son trente et un...

Les pluriels irréguliers de certains noms ont été indiqués là où ils pourraient offrir quelques difficultés au lecteur non-anglais.

On remarquera aussi que, pour plus de commodité, ce dictionnaire est arrangé en suivant strictement un ordre alphabétique, ce qui explique pourquoi certains mots apparentés sont séparés les uns des autres :

ex. **goofball, goofed (up), goofer, go-off, go off, goof off.**

Les entrées indiquées (*U.S.*) (américanismes) ou (*Austr.*) (australienismes) sont assez nombreuses mais limitées à des termes qui seraient difficilement compris en Grande-Bretagne dans un contexte donné. Ces termes ne sont pas employés lorsque les mots, quelle que soit leur origine, sont passés dans la langue anglaise courante.

La langue populaire est si riche en synonymes que, pour économiser de la place et éviter les répétitions, il a été décidé de donner le terme générique suivi d'un astérisque (*ex.* **mitt,** main*). L'astérisque indique que le mot ainsi marqué figure comme entrée dans le *Répertoire alphabétique de synonymes argotiques et populaires* à la fin du dictionnaire, où l'on peut trouver une liste de synonymes et de termes apparentés et ainsi faire un choix. D'ailleurs, dans le corps du dictionnaire, ces entrées sont suivies d'un ou plusieurs synonymes qui semblent les plus proches de l'expression anglaise. Dans le cas des *drogues** le lecteur trouvera une liste plus complète de termes affiliés.

Pour faciliter l'emploi du dictionnaire, les noms sont pris comme mots-clefs dans une phrase. Si la phrase contient plus d'un nom c'est le premier nom qui sert de repère (*ex.* **like a dose of salts** se trouvera sous **dose**). Certains renvois peuvent aussi aider le lecteur à relier des expressions similaires.

Les auteurs tiennent à remercier tous ceux qui ont rendu possible la publication de ce dictionnaire.

Tout d'abord leurs proches: Mrs Jean Johnson qui apporta l'appui inestimable d'une épouse compréhensive, et Mr David Marks qui sut combiner le soutien filial à une collaboration précieuse.

Mr R. P. L. Ledésert, Directeur de la Section de Langues vivantes de la Maison Harrap et sa femme Margaret, les Curie de la Lexicographie, qui, avec générosité, prodiguèrent aide et encouragements.

Mr P. H. Collin et ses collaborateurs, dont les conseils furent fort appréciés.

Mr F. White qui allia connaissances et dévouement.

Miss G. Seymour, à qui l'on doit la dactylographie d'une grande partie du manuscrit.

Enfin tous les parents et amis qui ont, par leurs offrandes, contribué à cet ouvrage.

G.A.M.
C.B.J.

ABBREVIATIONS—ABRÉVIATIONS

abbr.	abbreviation	abréviation
adj.	adjective	adjectif
adv.	adverb; adverbial	adverbe; adverbial
attrib.	attributive	attributif
Austr.	Australianism	australienisme
av.	aviation	aviation
c.	circa	circa
cf.	refer to	conferatur
conj.	conjunction	conjonction
c.p.	catchphrase	locution populaire
euph.	euphemism	euphémisme
excl.	exclamation	exclamation
f	feminine	féminin
F:	familiar; colloquial	familier; style de la conversation
fig.	figurative(ly)	figuratif, figurativement
iron.	ironical(ly)	ironique(ment)
m	masculine	masculin
mf	masculine or feminine	masculin ou féminin
mil.	military	militaire
P:	popular; slang	expression populaire; argot
pej.	pejorative	sens péjoratif
pl.	plural	pluriel
p.p.	past participle	participe passé
prep.	preposition	préposition
pres. part.	present participle	participe présent
pr. noun	proper noun	nom propre
pron.	pronoun	pronom
qch.	something	quelque chose
qn	someone	quelqu'un
R.S.	Rhyming Slang	mots composés qui ont leur sens non pas en eux-mêmes mais dans le mot avec lequel ils riment

sing.	singular	singulier
s.o.	someone	quelqu'un
sth.	something	quelque chose
th.	theatre	théâtre
T.V.	television	télévision
U.S.	United States; Americanism	États-Unis; américanisme
V:	vulgar	trivial; vulgaire
VV:	very vulgar; "taboo"	très vulgaire; obscène; ordurier
W.W. II	Second World War	deuxième guerre mondiale
*	see Appendix	voir le Répertoire alphabétique de synonymes argotiques et populaires

PRONUNCIATION

The phonetics of every word listed are given, using the notation of the International Phonetic Association. Colloquial language and slang have a wide diversity of pronunciations which even have a tendency sometimes to produce a specialized form of expression. The best-known example is perhaps Cockney, the vernacular of Londoners, the features of which are too diverse to describe here. Moreover, the same words are pronounced in different ways in various English-speaking countries. Hence the task has not been an easy one, but the phonetics provided should at least serve as a useful—even if not an infallible—guide, particularly to non-English-speaking users of the work.

The following points call for special attention:

(1) Symbols appearing between round brackets, *e.g.* **empty** [ˈem(p)ti], show that there are alternative and equally acceptable pronunciations with or without the corresponding sound.

(2) Words such as **whip, whistle, white** have been shown with the optional initial h-sound [(h)wip, ˈ(h)wisl, (h)wait], though in practice the h is rarely sounded in colloquial or popular speech.

(3) Word-stress is indicated by a stress mark [ˈ] preceding the stressed syllable, *e.g.* **junky** [ˈdʒʌŋki], **connect** [kəˈnekt]. Secondary stress is not indicated.

(4) The sound [r] does not usually occur before consonants or before a pause; the italicized symbol [*r*] is used at the end of such words as **banger, door, here** [ˈbæŋər, dɔːr, ˈhiər] to show that the r-sound may occur there if, and only if, the following word in the phrase begins with a vowel and there is no intervening pause, as in **here and now** [ˈhiərəndˈnau].

TABLE OF PHONETIC SYMBOLS

VOWELS

[æ]	bat, gander, ack-ack
[ɑː]	cart, bar, nark, hoo-ha(a)
[e]	get, jelly, dead
[i]	bit, diddies, system, breeches, dimwitted
[iː]	bee, peter, tea, spiel
[ɔ]	hot, what, cough, Aussie
[ɔː]	all, haul, rorty, jaw, war
[u]	put, wool, pull
[uː]	shoes, move, loo, jew
[ʌ]	nut, bun, ton, some, cover, rough
[ə]	china, goner, balon(e)y
[əː]	burn, learn, herb, whirl

DIPHTHONGS

[ai]   aisle, high, kite, fly, hypo, buy, eye
[au]   down, mouse, kraut
[ei]   mate, lay, trey, bait, weight
[ɛə]   bear, spare, there, airy-fairy
[iə]   queer, gear, real, here
[ɔi]   boil, boy
[ou]   go, snow, soap, dope, dough
[ʊə]   poor, sure

CONSONANTS

[b]   bat, job, boob, grabbed
[d]   dab, bad, under, griddle
[f]   fat, fifty, riff, laugh, rough, elephants
[g]   gag, gherkin, guide, agony, egg
[h]   hat, behind
[k]   cat, ache, kitten, make, plonk, quick, septic
[l]   lid, all, tumble, chisel, dilly
[m]   mug, ram, jism, jammy
[n]   nab, bun, tenner, pancake, knob, gnashers
[p]   pan, nap, napper
[r]   rat, around, jerry
[ɾ]   driver, finger, gear
     (*sounded only when final and carried on to the*
     next word, as in later on)
[s]   sausage, scene, mouse, sassy, psycho, whistle, cement
[t]   top, pot, batter, trip, Thames
[v]   vine, ever, rave, savvy
[z]   zip, quiz, buzz, lousy, pansy, breeze, business, eggs

[dz]   reds, odds
[dʒ]   ginger, age, edge, jelly
[ks]   extras, expect, accident, mixer
[kʃ]   ructions
[lj]   million
[nj]   onion
[tʃ]   chat, hatch, search, chick, rich
[θ]   thatch, tooth, methhead
[ð]   that, the, other, with
[ʃ]   shark, dish, chassis, machine
[ʒ]   usual
[ŋ]   bang, sing, conk, anchors
[ŋg]   finger, angle

SEMI-CONSONANTS

[j]   yack, yob, cute, putrid, used, euchre, few, queue
[w]   wad, wind, swipe, away

PRONONCIATION

Chaque entrée du dictionnaire est suivie de sa transcription phonétique pour laquelle on a employé les signes de l'Association phonétique internationale.

La langue populaire et le *slang* ont une prononciation extrêmement fluide et diversifiée, qui tend même quelquefois à en faire un langage particulier. Le plus connu est peut-être le *cockney* qui est la prononciation londonienne vulgaire, et il n'est pas question ici de le décrire. D'autre part, les mêmes mots sont prononcés différemment dans les pays si variés qui constituent le monde anglophone. Toutes ces considérations ont rendu notre tâche phonétique difficile, et notre but a été d'offrir un guide utile (et non infaillible) au lecteur étranger.

Il est quelques points sur lesquels nous nous permettons d'attirer l'attention:

(1) Les symboles mis entre parenthèses, *ex.* **empty** [ˈem(p)ti], indiquent qu'il y a deux prononciations possibles, avec ou sans ce symbole.

(2) Dans les mots tels que **whip, whistle, white** le h initial a été indiqué comme possible [(h)wip, ˈ(h)wisl, (h)wait], alors qu'en règle générale le h n'est jamais prononcé en anglais familier et populaire.

(3) L'accent tonique est indiqué par un accent [ˈ] précédant la syllabe accentuée, *ex.* **junky** [ˈdʒʌŋki], **connect** [kəˈnekt]. L'accent secondaire n'est pas indiqué.

(4) Le son [r] ne s'entend généralement pas devant une consonne ou devant une pause. On emploie le symbole en italique [*r*] à la fin des mots tels que **banger, door, here** [ˈbæŋə*r*, dɔː*r*, ˈhiə*r*] pour indiquer que le son de r peut se faire entendre dans le cas, et uniquement dans le cas, où le mot suivant dans la phrase commence par une voyelle sans qu'il y ait de pause, *ex.* **here and now** [ˈhiərəndˈnau].

TABLEAU DES SYMBOLES PHONÉTIQUES EN ANGLAIS

VOYELLES

[æ] bat, gander, ack-ack
[ɑː] cart, bar, nark, hoo-ha(a)
[e] get, jelly, dead
[i] bit, diddies, system, breeches, dimwitted
[iː] bee, peter, tea, spiel
[ɔ] hot, what, cough, Aussie
[ɔː] all, haul, rorty, jaw, war
[u] put, wool, pull
[uː] shoes, move, loo
[ʌ] nut, bun, ton, some, cover, rough
[ə] china, goner, balon(e)y
[əː] burn, learn, herb, whirl

DIPHTONGUES

[ai] aisle, high, kite, fly, hypo
[au] down, mouse, kraut
[ei] mate, lay, trey, bait, weight
[ɛə] bear, spare, there, airy-fairy
[iə] queer, gear, real
[ɔi] boil, boy
[ou] go, snow, soap, dope, dough
[uə] poor, sure

CONSONNES

[b] bat, job, boob, grabbed
[d] dab, bad, under, griddle
[f] fat, fifty, riff, laugh, rough, elephants
[g] gag, gherkin, guide, agony, egg
[h] hat, behind
[k] cat, ache, kitten, make, plonk, quick, septic
[l] lid, all, tumble, chisel, dilly
[m] mug, ram, jism, jammy
[n] nab, bun, tenner, pancake, knob, gnashers
[p] pan, nap, napper
[r] rat, around, jerry
[ʀ] driver, finger, gear
     (*prononcé seulement lorsqu'il est final et en
     liaison avec le mot suivant, ex.* later on)
[s] sausage, scene, mouse, sassy, psycho, whistle, cement
[t] top, pot, batter, trip, Thames
[v] vine, ever, rave, savvy
[z] zip, quiz, buzz, lousy, pansy, breeze, business, eggs

[dz] reds, odds
[dʒ] ginger, age, edge, jelly
[ks] extras, expect, accident, mixer
[kʃ] ructions
[lj] million
[nj] onion
[tʃ] chat, hatch, search, chick, rich
[θ] thatch, tooth, methhead
[ð] that, the, other, with
[ʃ] shark, dish, chassis, machine, sugar
[ʒ] usual
[ŋ] bang, sing, conk, anchors
[ŋg] finger, angle

SEMI-CONSONNES

[j] yack, yob, cute, putrid, used, euchre, few
[w] wad, wind, away

A

A [ei] (*abbr.*), *P:* **1.** (=*amphétamine*) amphétamine *f* (*drogues**). **2.** = **acid**, 2. **3. A. over T.** (=*arse over tip* (*or tit*(*s*)), cul par-dessus tête; *cf.* **arse**, **4.**

a b [æb], **A.B.** [ˈeiˈbiː] (*abbr.* = *abscess*), *P:* (*abcès causé par une piqûre avec aiguille non stérilisée ou par des drogues impures*) caramel *m*, fondant *m*, puant *m*; *cf.* **ABC, 3.**

ABC [ˈeibiˈsiː] (*noun*). **1.** *F:* (**as**) **easy as ABC**, simple comme bonjour; *cf.* **easy**[1], **6. 2.** *F:* **the ABC of sth.**, le B.A. ba de qch. **3.** *P:* = **A.B.**

abdabs [ˈæbdæbz] (*pl. noun*), *P:* **to have the screaming a.**, piauler à la bit(t)ure, voir les rats bleus.

abo, Abo [ˈæbou] (*noun*) (*Austr.*), *F:* aborigène *mf.*

absoballylutely! [ˈæbsouˈbæliˈl(j)uːtli] (*excl.*), *F:* ça colle, Anatole! naturellement et comme de bien entendu!

absobloodylutely! [ˈæbsouˈblʌdiˈl(j)uːtli] (*excl.*), *P:* = **absoballylutely!**

abysmal [əˈbizməl] (*adj.*), *F:* d'une bêtise* noire, d'une ignorance crasse.

accident [ˈæksidənt] (*noun*), *F:* **to have an a.**, (*a*) avoir un avaro; (*b*) être pris d'un besoin pressant; s'oublier; **Guy has had an a.**, Guy a fait pipi dans sa culotte.

accidentally [æksiˈdentəli] (*adv.*), *F:* **a. on purpose**, exprès.

A.C.-D.C. (**ac-dc, ac/dc**) [ˈeisiˈdiːsiː] (*adj.*), *P:* = **ambidextrous.**

ace[1] [eis] (*adj.*), *F:* **1.** excellent*, épatant, formid(able), super. **2.** (*a*) agréable; (*b*) généreux.

ace[2] [eis] (*adv. & excl.*), *F:* d'accord*, dac, O.K.

ace[3] [eis] (*noun*). **1.** *F:* as *m*, crack *m*. **2.** *F:* **to have an a. up one's sleeve**, avoir un as dans sa manche, avoir plus d'un tour dans son sac. **3.** *F:* **to hold all the aces**, avoir tous les atouts en main. **4.** (*U.S.*) *P:* billet* d'un dollar. **5.** *F:* (*a*) individu* loyal, bon, généreux; épée *f*; (*b*) individu* épatant. **6.** *P:* **on**

one's a., tout seul, seulabre. **7.** *P:* **cigarette* de marijuana** (*drogues**), reefer *m*, stick *m*. **8.** *F:* **to be aces with s.o.**, prendre qn pour un crack, ne voir que par qn.

ace[4] [eis] (**to**), *P:* **a. it!** ça suffit! c'est marre!

ace in [ˈeisˈin] (**to**), *P:* **1.** jouer des coudes, se faufiler en haut de l'échelle. **2. to a. i. on s.o.'s conversation**, piger la conversation de qn.

acid [ˈæsid] (*noun*), *P:* **1. to put the a. on, to come the a.**, la faire à la pose; **don't come the a. with me**, (*a*) ne fais pas le zouave; (*b*) ne jardine pas, ne te paye pas ma fiole. **2.** *P:* LSD *m* (*drogues**), sucre *m*; **a. freak, a. head,** habitué(e) du LSD, acidulé(e); **a. cube,** morceau *m* de sucre trempé dans du LSD (*cf.* **cubehead**); **a. funk,** dépression due au LSD, trouille acidulée.

ack-ack [ˈækˈæk] (*noun*), *F:* (*mil.*) défense antiaérienne, défense contre-avions (D.C.A.).

ackamaraka [ˈækəməˈrækə] (*noun*), *P:* **don't give me the (old) a.**, ne me bourre pas le crâne, ne me monte pas le cou (*ou* le coup).

ack-emma [ˈækˈemə] (*adv.*), *F:* (*mil.*) avant midi.

ackers [ˈækəz] (*pl. noun*), *P:* argent*, pésettes *f.pl.*

acquire [əˈkwaiər] (**to**), *F:* voler*, faucher, subtiliser.

act [ækt] (*noun*), *F:* **1. to put on an a.** (*or a* **big a.**), frimer. **2. to get in on the a.**, se mettre dans le bain. **3. to let s.o. in on the a.**, mettre qn dans le coup. *Voir aussi* **sob-act.**

actress [ˈæktris] (*noun*), *F:* **as the a. said to the bishop**, *c.p.*, comme dit l'autre.

ad [æd] (*abbr.*). **1.** *F:* (=*advertisement*) annonce *f*; **small ads**, petites annonces; *cf.* **advert. 2.** *P:* = **A.D.**

A.D. [ˈeiˈdiː] (*abbr.*) (=*drug*) *addict*), *P:* drogué*, camé *m*, toxico *m*.

---

* L'astérisque indique que le mot marqué de ce signe figure comme entrée dans le Répertoire.

Adam [ˈædəm] (*pr. noun*), *F:* **1.** I don't know him from A., je ne le connais ni d'Ève ni d'Adam. **2.** the old A., le vieil Adam. **3.** A.'s ale, eau*, Châteaula-Pompe *m.* **4.** A. and Eve on a raft, œufs servis sur du toast.

add up [ˈædˈʌp] (to), *F:* it (just) doesn't a. u., cela n'a ni queue ni tête (*ou* ni sens ni raison).

adjourn [əˈdʒəːn] (to), *F:* (*a*) abandonner un travail; (*b*) passer autre part.

ad-lib[1] [ˈædˈlib] (*adj.*), *F:* (*a*) à volonté, à discrétion; (*b*) improvisé, impromptu.

ad-lib[2] [ˈædˈlib] (to), *F:* (*a*) dévider, palasser; (*b*) (*th.*) faire du texte, improviser.

ad-man [ˈædmæn] (*pl.* ad-men) (*noun*), *F:* agent *m* de publicité.

admirer [ədˈmaiərər] (*noun*), *F:* adorateur *m*, soupirant *m*.

adrift [əˈdrift] (*adv.*), *F:* **1.** to be (all) a., dérailler, perdre le nord. **2.** the button has come a., le bouton a lâché, le bouton est décousu. **3.** to be several hours a., avoir plusieurs heures de retard.

advert [ˈædvəːt] (*abbr.*) (=*advertisement*), *F:* annonce *f*; *cf.* ad, **1.**

aer(e)ated [ˈɛər(i)eitid] (*adj.*), *P:* fâché, vexé; don't get (all) a., ne prends pas la pique.

after [ˈɑːftər] (*prep.*), *F:* **1.** A. you, Claude. – No, a. you, Cecil, *c.p.*, Après vous, Marquis. – Non, après vous, Prince. **2.** what are you a.? qu'est-ce que tu cherches? où veux-tu en venir?

afters [ˈɑːftəz] (*pl. noun*), *F:* dessert *m.*

age [eidʒ] (*noun*), *F:* **1.** be (*or* act) your a.! fais pas l'enfant! **2.** it took us an a. (*or* ages) to get here, ça nous a pris un temps fou pour arriver ici; I saw that film ages ago, il y a une éternité que j'ai vu ce film. **3.** (*a*) the a. to catch 'em: *voir* bingo (**17**); (*b*) my a.?: *voir* bingo (**21**). *Voir aussi* awkward.

aggravate [ˈægrəveit] (to), *F:* exaspérer, assommer, taper sur le système à (qn).

aggravating [ˈægrəveitiŋ] (*adj.*), *F:* exaspérant, assommant, crispant.

aggravation [ˈægrəˈveiʃ(ə)n] (*noun*), *F:* agacement *m*, exaspération *f.*

aggro[1] [ˈægrou] (*noun*), *P:* provocation *f*, discorde *f*; to give s.o. the a. = to aggro s.o.

aggro[2] [ˈægrou] (to), *P:* agacer, tracasser (qn); provoquer (qn); embêter (qn).

agin [əˈgin] (*prep. & adv.*), *F:* contre.

agony [ˈægəni] (*noun*), *F:* **1.** it was a.! j'en ai bavé! **2.** to pile on the a., forcer la dose. **3.** a. column, rubrique *f* des annonces personnelles.

agreeable [əˈgriːəbl] (*adj.*), *F:* I'm a., je veux bien.

agro [ˈægrou] (*noun & verb*), *P:* = aggro[1,2].

ahead [əˈhed] (*adv.*), *F:* **1.** to come out a., (*a*) être en pointe; (*b*) sortir en tête (de liste). **2.** to be one jump a., avoir de l'avance, avoir une longueur d'avance (sur qn). *Voir aussi* go-ahead.

aid [eid] (*noun*), *F:* what's this (*or* that) in a. of? à quoi ça rime?

ain't [eint], *P:* = am not, is not, are not; a. got = has not (got), have not (got).

air[1] [ɛər] (*noun*). **1.** *F:* to go (straight) up in the a., se mettre en colère*, se mettre en rogne. **2.** *F:* to float on (or tread on *or* walk on) a., nager dans le bonheur, être au septième ciel, voir les anges, voir la vie en rose; planer; voyager. **3.** *F:* to live on (fresh) a., vivre d'amour et d'eau fraîche, vivre de l'air du temps. **4.** *F:* to take the a., prendre le large. **5.** *F:* on the a., sur les ondes, en diffusion. **6.** *P:* to give s.o. the a., se débarrasser* de qn. **7.** *P:* airs and graces (*R.S.* = faces), visages*. **8.** *F:* hot a., discours *m.pl.* vides, platitudes *f.pl.*; that's all hot a., tout cela n'est que du vent. **9.** *F:* none of your airs! pas tant de manières!; to give oneself airs, faire sa poire (anglaise).

air[2] [ɛər] (to), *P:* planter (là), plaquer (qn).

airy-fairy [ˈɛəriˈfɛəri] (*adj.*), *F:* vasouillard, du bidon.

aisle [ail] (*noun*). **1.** *F:* to walk down the a., se marier. **2.** *P:* that'll knock 'em (*or* have 'em rolling) in the aisles, cela fera crouler la baraque; *cf.* knock[2] (to), **5.**

akkers [ˈækəz] (*pl. noun*), *P:* = ackers.

alarming [əˈlɑːmiŋ] (*adv.*), *P:* she carried on a., elle se démena comme une furie; she went off at me (something) a., elle m'est tombée dessus (comme une furie).

Alec, alec(k) [ˈælik] (*noun*). **1.** *F:* smart

---

* An asterisk indicates that the word so marked is included as a head-word in the Appendix.

alf   21   angel

a., finaud *m*, combinard *m*, plastronneur *m*, m'as-tu-vu *m*, je-sais-tout *m*.
2. (*Austr.*) *P:* dupe *f*, cavé *m*, navet *m*;
cf. bunny[1], 8.
alf [ælf] (*noun*), *P:* mâle hétérosexuel.
alibi ['ælibai] (*noun*), *F:* bonne excuse.
alive [ə'laiv] (*adj.*), *F:* 1. a. and kicking,
en pleine forme. 2. look a.! réveille-toi!
secoue-toi! *Voir aussi* dead-and-alive;
Jack, 12.
alky ['ælki] (*noun*), *P:* 1. alcool*, gnôle *f*.
2. whisky *m* de mauvaise qualité *ou*
de contrebande. 3. (*a*) alcoolique *mf*;
(*b*) clochard* alcoolique.
all[1] [ɔ:l] (*adv.*), *F:* 1. to be a. for sth.,
en tenir pour qch., en être pour qch.
2. to go a. out for sth., (*a*) être emballé
par qch.; (*b*) mettre toute son énergie
à faire qch., se donner corps et âme
pour faire qch. 3. that's him a. over,
c'est lui tout craché; je le reconnais
bien là! 4. to be a. in, être fatigué*, être
exténué. 5. to be a. there, avoir les yeux
en face des trous; *voir aussi* there, 2. 6.
to be a. over s.o., faire de la lèche à qn.
Voir aussi all right; jump[2] (to), 11.
all[2] [ɔ:l] (*noun*), *F:* 1. it's a. over (*or* up)
with him, (*a*) il est fichu, c'est le bout
du rouleau pour lui; (*b*) il est liquidé;
(*c*) il est pigé; *voir aussi* up[2], 3. 2. I'm
tired. – Aren't we a.? Je suis fatigué.* –
Et nous donc! 3. a. but one: *voir* bingo
(89). *Voir aussi* bugger-all; damn-all;
fuck-all; know-all; sod-all; what-all.
all-clear [ɔ:l'kliər] (*noun*), *F:* to give
the a.-c., donner le feu vert.
alley ['æli] (*noun*). 1. *F:* that's right up
my a., c'est tout à fait mon rayon; *cf.*
street, 2. 2. *P:* a. cat, prostituée*,
racoleuse *f*. *Voir aussi* doodle-alley; tin-
pan alley.
allez oop! ['æli'(j)up, 'æli'(j)u:p] (*excl.*),
F: allez hop!
alligator ['æligeitər] (*noun*), *F:* See you
later, a.! – In a while, crocodile, *c.p.*,
A tout à l'heure, voltigeur! – A bientôt, mon oiseau.
all-nighter [ɔ:l'naitər] (*noun*), *P:* 1.
boum *f* du petit matin. 2. cille *m* de
nuit. 3. session *f* (*parlement, etc.*) qui
dure toute une nuit.
all-overish [ɔ:l'ouvəriʃ] (*adj.*), *P:* to be
(*or* feel) a.-o., être patraque (*ou* tout
chose).
all right[1] [ɔ:l'rait] (*adv.*), *F:* 1. d'accord*.

2. it's a. r. for you, you don't have to
get up early, cela t'est bien égal, tu
n'es pas obligé de te lever de bonne
heure. 3. don't worry about him, he's
a. r., t'en fais pas pour lui. 4. to see
s.o. a.r., (*a*) veiller à ce que qn ait
son dû, veiller à ce que qn ne soit
pas lésé; (*b*) promettre de l'aide à qn,
donner un coup de main à qn.
all right[2] [ɔ:l'rait] (*noun*), *P:* a bit of
a. r., une fille* séduisante, un beau
petit lot.
all-time [ɔ:l'taim] (*adj.*), *F:* sans précé-
dent, inouï; a.-t. high, record le plus
élevé. *Voir aussi* great[3].
almighty [ɔ:l'maiti] (*adj.*). 1. *F:* formidable; an a. crash, un fracas de tous
les diables. 2. *F:* the a. dollar, le dollar
tout-puissant. 3. *P:* God A.! Bon Dieu
de Bon Dieu!
alone [ə'loun] (*adj.*), *F:* 1. to go it a.,
y aller d'autor. 2. leave me a.! laisse-
moi tranquille!
Alphonse ['ælfɔns] (*pr. noun*) (*R.S.* =
ponce), *P:* souteneur*, Alphonse.
alright [ɔ:l'rait] (*adv. & noun*), *F:*
= all right,[1,2].
also-ran [ɔ:lsoutæn] (*noun*), *F:* perdant
m; to be an a.-r., être dans les choux.
altogether [ɔ:ltə'geðər] (*noun*), *F:*
in the a., nu*, à poil.
ambidextrous ['æmbi'dekstrəs] (*adj.*),
P: ambivalent, qui marche à voiles et
à vapeur.
ammo ['æmou] (*abbr.*) (=*ammunition*),
F: munitions *f.pl.*
amscray ['æm'skrei] (to) (*backslang* =
scram), *P:* partir*, décamper, se débiner, se tailler.
amster ['æmstər] (*noun*) (*Austr.*), *P:* =
shill (aber).
amy ['eimi] (*noun*), *P:* nitrite *m* d'amyle
(*drogues*).
amy-john ['eimi'dʒɔn] (*noun*), *P:* lesbienne* f, gougnot(t)e *f*.
anchors ['æŋkəz] (*pl. noun*), *F:* to put
the a. on, mettre les freins *m.pl.* (*ou*
les ripans *m.pl.*).
ancient ['einʃənt] (*adj.*), *F:* 1. she's a.,
elle n'est pas de première jeunesse.
2. that's a. history, c'est du réchauffé.
angel[1] ['eindʒəl] (*noun*). 1. *F:* you're an
a. (to do that for me), tu es un amour
(de faire cela pour moi); be an a. and . . .,
sois un amour,... 2. *F:* you're no a.!

* L'astérisque indique que le mot marqué de ce signe figure comme entrée dans le Répertoire.

ne te prends pas pour un enfant de chœur! tu n'es pas un prix de vertu! 3. *F:* **angels on horseback,** fricassée *f* d'huîtres au lard. 4. *P:* **white a.,** (*infirmière qui, à l'hôpital, fait passer des drogues à un toxicomane*) ange blanc. 5. *P:* (*a*) commanditaire *m* (*surtout* de théâtre); (*b*) (*U.S.*) commanditaire *m* d'un parti politique. 6. *P:* victime *f* d'un voleur *ou* d'un escroc. 7. *P:* pédéraste* qui tient le rôle de l'homme, rivette *f.* 8. *P:* cocaïne *f* (*drogues**), fée blanche. *Voir aussi* **hell, 15.**

angel² [ˈeindʒəl] (to), *P:* commanditer; (*th.*) bailler les fonds *m.pl.*

angel-face [ˈeindʒəlfeis], **angel-puss** [ˈeindʒəlpʊs] (*noun*), *F:* **1.** (*terme d'affection*) ma toute belle. **2.** gueule *f* d'amour, jolie frimousse.

angie [ˈeindʒi] (*noun*), *P:* = **angel¹, 8.**

angle [ˈæŋgl] (*noun*), *F:* **1. what's your a.?** (*a*) quel est ton point de vue?; (*b*) comment vois-tu la chose? **2. to figure out an a.,** chercher moyen (de se tirer d'affaire). **3. to know all the angles,** connaître la musique; la connaître dans les coins.

Anne [æn] (*pr. noun*), *F:* **Queen A.'s dead,** (*a*) ta combinaison passe; tu cherches une belle-mère?; *cf.* **Charl(e)y²**, **2;** (*b*) c'est du réchauffé.

another [əˈnʌðər] (*pron.*), *F:* **tell me a.!** allez! va conter ça ailleurs!; **ask me a.,** tu me fais rigoler; et après?

answer [ˈɑːnsər] (*noun*), *F:* **1. the a. to a maiden's prayer,** le mari rêvé. **2. to know all the answers,** avoir réponse à tout, être un Monsieur Je-sais-tout.

answer back [ˈɑːnsəˈbæk] (to), *F:* **don't a. b.!** pas de rouspétance!

ante [ˈænti] (*noun*) (*U.S.*), *F:* **to up** (*or* **raise**) **the a.,** (*a*) forcer la mise (*poker*); (*b*) augmenter le prix, donner le coup de pouce, allonger le tir.

ante up [ˈæntiˈʌp] (to), *F:* payer*, les lâcher, cracher.

anti [ˈænti, *U.S.:* ˈæntai] (*adv. & prep.*), *F:* **1. to feel a.,** avoir une âme de contestataire. **2. to be a.** (*s.o. or sth.*), être contre, être de l'opposition.

antics [ˈæntiks] (*pl. noun*), *F:* **to be up to one's a. again,** rejouer les mêmes tours *m.pl.*

ants [ænts] (*pl. noun*), *F:* **to have a. in**

one's pants, avoir la bougeotte, avoir le feu quelque part.

antsy [ˈæntsi] (*adj.*) (*U.S.*), *F:* énervé, agité, sur des charbons ardents, survolté.

any¹ [ˈeni] (*adj.*), *F:* **1. a. more for a. more?** qui veut du rabiot? **2. a. day,** n'importe quand; **I can do better than that a. day,** je peux faire mieux quand ça me chante.

any² [ˈeni] (*pron.*), *F:* **1. he wasn't having a.,** il n'a pas marché; **I'm not having a.!** rien à faire! cela ne prend pas! **2. a. to come,** (*turf*) report *m.* *Voir aussi* **without.**

anyhow [ˈenihau] (*adv.*), *F:* **1. to feel all a.,** se sentir tout chose. **2. to do sth. all a.,** faire qch. à la six-quatre-deux.

Anzac [ˈænzæk] (*noun*), *F:* soldat* australien ou néo-zélandais.

apart [əˈpɑːt] (*adj.*), *P:* déboussolé, désorienté.

ape¹ [eip] (*adj.*) (*U.S.*), *P:* **1.** époustouflant, formid(able). **2. to go a.,** (*a*) perdre les pédales; (*b*) se déchaîner. **3. to go a. over s.o.,** s'enticher (*ou* toquer) de qn.

ape² [eip] (*noun*), *F:* **you big a.!** grosse brute! espèce de gorille!

apology [əˈpɔlədʒi] (*noun*), *F:* **an a. for ...,** un vague semblant d'excuse pour...

apple [ˈæpl] (*noun*), *P:* **1. apples (and pears)** (*R.S. = stairs*), escalier *m.* **2.** (*U.S.*) individu*, type *m*, mec *m*; **smooth a.,** individu* suave, girofle *m*; **wise a.,** jeune effronté; **square a.,** (*a*) cave *m*; (*b*) individu* qui ne se drogue pas. **3.** (*U.S.*) **to polish the a.,** (*a*) flatter*, faire de la lèche; *cf.* **apple-polish** (to); **apple-polisher;** (*b*) agir comme si on était occupé. *Voir aussi* **toffee.**

apple-cart [ˈæplkɑːt] (*noun*), *F:* **to upset s.o.'s a.-c.,** chambarder les plans de qn.

apple-pie¹ [ˈæplˈpai] (*attrib. adj.*), *F:* **1. a.-p. bed,** lit *m* en portefeuille. **2. in a.-p. order,** en ordre parfait, soin-soin.

apple-pie² [ˈæplˈpai] (*noun*), *F:* **as American as a.-p.,** amerloc comme l'oncle Sam.

apple-polish [ˈæplˈpɔliʃ] (to) (*U.S.*), *P:* flatter*, lécher les bottes à (qn); *cf.* **apple, 3.**

---

* An asterisk indicates that the word so marked is included as a head-word in the Appendix.

apple-polisher [ˈæplˈpɒliʃər] (*noun*) (*U.S.*), *P:* flatteur *m*, lèche-bottes *m*.

apple-sauce [ˈæplˈsɔːs] (*noun*) (*U.S.*), *P:* **1**. bêtise*, foutaise *f*, bidon *m*. **2**. flatterie *f*, pommade *f*.

apple-tree [ˈæpl-triː] (*noun*), *P:* **to fall off the a.-t.**, (*d'une fille*) perdre sa virginité, voir le loup, casser sa cruche.

appro [ˈæprou] (*abbr.*) (= *approval*), *F:* **on a.**, à condition, à l'essai.

apron-strings [ˈeiprən-striŋz] (*pl. noun*), *F:* **tied to mother's a.-s.**, dans les jupons de sa mère.

arf [ɑːf] (*adj. & adv.*), *P:* = **half**.

arf-an'-arf [ˈɑːfɒnˈɑːf] (*adv. & noun*), *P:* = **half and half** (*voir* half[1], **5**; half[2]).

arge [ɑːdʒ] (*noun*), *P:* argent *m* (*métal*), blanc *m*, blanquette *f*.

argie-bargie [ˈɑːdʒiˈbɑːdʒi] (*noun*), *F:* = **argy-bargy**.

argle-bargle [ˈɑːglˈbɑːgl] (to), *F:* discutailler; discuter le coup.

argufy [ˈɑːgjuːfai] (to), *P:* discuter le bout de gras.

argy-bargy [ˈɑːdʒiˈbɑːdʒi] (*noun*), *F:* chicane *f*, prise *f* de bec.

aris [ˈæris] (*noun*), *P:* = **Aristotle**.

Aristotle [æriˈstɒtl] (*noun*) (*R.S.* = *bottle*), *P:* bouteille *f*.

arm [ɑːm] (*noun*). **1**. *F:* **to chance one's a.**, tenter le coup. **2**. *P:* **to put the a. on s.o.**, mettre le grappin sur qn. **3**. (*U.S.*) *P:* **on the a.**, (*a*) à crédit, à la gagne, à croum(e); (*b*) gratuit*, gratis, à l'œil. *Voir aussi* short[1], **3**; shot[2], **3**; strong-arm[1,2].

army [ˈɑːmi] (*noun*), *P:* **1**. . . . **you and whose a.?** (*réponse à une menace de coups*), toi et qui encore? **2**. **the** (**old**) **a. game**, escroquerie*, coup *m* d'arnac. *Voir aussi* Fred.

around [əˈraund] (*adv.*), *F:* **I've been a.** (**a bit**), je connais la vie, j'ai roulé ma bosse.

arse [ɑːs] (*noun*), *V:* **1**. cul*. **2**. **Twenty-five, my a.!** She's forty if she's a day, Vingt-cinq ans je t'en fiche, elle a quarante ans et mèche! **3**. **he doesn't know whether he's on his a. or his elbow**, (*a*) il ne sait pas où il en est; (*b*) c'est un vrai cul. **4**. **to go a. over tip** (*or* **tit(s)**), faire tête à cul; *cf.* **A. over T**. **5**. **to sit on one's a.** (**and do nothing**), ne pas se manier le cul. **6**. **you can kiss**

my a.! you can stick it up your a.! tu peux te le mettre au cul!; *voir aussi* shove (**to**); stick[2] (**to**), **3**. **7**. **a. about face**, sens devant derrière. **8**. **to be out on one's a.**, être flanqué (*ou* foutu) à la porte. **9**. **to shag one's a. off**, (*a*) coïter* fréquemment, bourriquer à gogo; (*b*) se vanner à la bourre. **10**. **to work one's a. off**, travailler* dur, en foutre un coup. *Voir aussi* ass[1]; kick[1], **5** (*b*); lead[1], **4**; pain (*c*); short-arse; split-arse; tear-arse.

arse about (*or* **around**) [ˈɑːsəˈbaut, ˈɑːsəˈraund] (to), *V:* traîner son cul; **don't go arsing about in there!** ne va pas te mêler là-dedans! va pas faire le con là-dedans!

arse-bandit [ˈɑːsbændit] (*noun*), *V:* pédéraste*, lopart *m*, enculé *m*.

arse-crawl [ˈɑːs-krɔːl] (to), *V:* lécher le cul à qn.

arse-crawler [ˈɑːs-krɔːlər] (*noun*), *V:* lèche-cul *mf*.

arse-crawling [ˈɑːs-krɔːliŋ] (*noun*), *V:* la lèche.

arse-creep [ˈɑːs-kriːp] (to), *V:* = **arse-crawl** (to).

arse-creeper [ˈɑːs-kriːpər] (*noun*), *V:* = **arse-crawler**.

arse-creeping [ˈɑːs-kriːpiŋ] (*noun*), *V:* = **arse-crawling**.

arsehole [ˈɑːs(h)oul] (*noun*), *V:* **1**. anus*, anneau *m*, troufignon *m*. **2**. **pissed as arseholes**, bourré à zéro, rond comme une bille.

arse-kisser [ˈɑːs-kisər] (*noun*), *V:* = **arse-crawler**.

arse-lick [ˈɑːs-lik] (to), *V:* = **arse-crawl** (to).

arse-licker [ˈɑːs-likər] (*noun*), *V:* = **arse-crawler**.

arse-licking [ˈɑːs-likiŋ] (*noun*), *V:* = **arse-crawling**.

arse-man [ˈɑːsmæn] (*noun*), *V:* = **arse-bandit**.

arse up [ˈɑːsˈʌp] (to), *V:* **1**. mettre en désordre, chambouler; foutre en l'air. **2**. abîmer*, amocher.

artillery [ɑːˈtiləri] (*noun*), *P:* **1**. (**light**) **a.**, attirail *m* de camé. **2**. revolver*; couteau*; armes *f.pl.* à main.

arty [ˈɑːti] (*adj.*), *F:* **to be a.**, se piquer de talent artistique.

arty-crafty [ˈɑːtiˈkrɑːfti] (*adj.*), *F:* artiste, bohème.

---

* L'astérisque indique que le mot marqué de ce signe figure comme entrée dans le Répertoire.

arvo [ˈɑːvou] (noun) (Austr.), F: après-midi m ou f.

ashes [ˈæʃiz] (pl. noun). 1. F: the A., trophée symbolique remporté par l'Angleterre ou l'Australie après leurs jeux de cricket. 2. (U.S.) P: to get one's a. hauled, coïter*, tirer un coup. Voir aussi green¹, 1.

ask [ɑːsk] (to). 1. P: to a. for it, chercher des embêtements m.pl.; you asked for it! tu l'as cherché! tu l'as voulu!; you're asking for it, and you'll get it if you're not careful! tu me cherches, et tu vas me trouver! 2. P: a. yourself! raisonne-toi un peu! 3. F: a. a silly question and you'll get a silly answer, c.p., à question idiote, réponse idiote. Voir aussi another.

ass¹ [æs] (noun) (U.S.), V: 1. = arse. (Pour tous les composés de ass voir arse.) 2. piece of a., (a) coït*, partie f de jambes en l'air; (b) femme* (péj.), gonzesse f, fendue f. 3. (parfois) vulve*. 4. on one's a., dans la gêne, dans le besoin. 5. to do sth. a. backwards, (a) faire qch. à rebours, brider l'âne par la queue; (b) faire un micmac. 6. to have one's a. in a sling, avoir le cafard, broyer du noir, être au sixième dessous. 7. (big) a. man, coureur m de jupons, cavaleur m. Voir aussi green-ass; kiss-ass; lead¹, 4; ream out (to); shit-ass; suckass.

ass² [ɑːs, æs] (noun), P: (you) silly a.! espèce d'idiot!

assy [ˈæsi] (adj.) (U.S.), P: 1. radin; entêté; vil; méchant. 2. (fond de pantalon) reluisant.

aste [eist] (to) (Austr.), P: to a. it, se tenir tranquille, s'appliquer.

at [æt] (prep.), F: where it's a., où ça boume, où ça ronfle.

attababy! [ˈætəbeibi] (excl.), F: vas-y, petit!

attaboy! [ˈætəbɔi] (excl.), F: vas-y, fiston! vas-y, Toto!

attagirl! [ˈætəgəːl] (excl.), F: vas-y, fifille! vas-y, Nénette!

attic [ˈætik] (noun), F: to be queer in the a., être fou*, yoyoter de la mansarde; cf. bat¹, 5.

aunt, Aunt [ɑːnt] (noun). 1. F: my A. Fanny! quelle bonne blague! et ta sœur! 2. F: A. Jane, W.C.*, goguenots m.pl. 3. F: A. Sally, jeu m de massacre. 4.

P: (a) patronne* d'un bordel, taulière f, mère-maquerelle, mère-maca f; (b) vieille prostituée*, tarte f, tarderie f, fromage m. 5. P: vieux pédéraste*, tante f, tata f, tantouse f. 6. P: A. Emma, morphine f (drogues*). 7. P: Aunt Maria (R.S. = fire), feu m, conflagration f. Voir aussi Bob².

auntie¹, aunty¹ [ˈɑːnti] (noun), P: pédéraste* qui prend de l'âge, tata f.

Auntie², Aunty² [ˈɑːnti] (noun), F: A. (Beeb), la BBC (British Broadcasting Corporation).

Aussie¹ [ˈɔsi] (adj.) (abbr. = Australian) F: Australien.

Aussie² (noun) (abbr. = Australian), F: Australien m, kangourou m.

away [əˈwei] (adv.), F: 1. (euph.) en prison*, au bloc. 2. well a., ivre*, pompette, parti. 3. he's well a., le voilà lancé, il est bien parti (ou bien en train). Voir aussi have (to), 1, 2, 3.

awful [ˈɔːful] (adj.), F: terrible, affreux; détestable; an a. bore, (a) (d'une chose) qch. d'assommant (ou de canulant); (b) (d'une personne) casse-burettes m, casse-pieds m; he's an a. bore, il est terriblement rasoir; a. weather, un temps de chien (ou de cochon). Voir aussi god-awful.

awfully [ˈɔːfli] (adv.), F: that's a. nice of you, c'est tout plein gentil de votre part; I'm a. glad about it, j'en suis ravi; thanks a., merci mille fois; a. funny, drôle comme tout.

awkward [ˈɔːkwəd] (adj.), F: the a. age, l'âge ingrat.

A.W.O.L. [ˈeiˈdʌbljuˈouˈel, ˈeiwɔl] (abbr. = absent without leave) (mil.), F: absent sans permission, avec fausse-perm(e).

ax¹ [æks] (U.S.), **axe¹** [æks] (noun), F: 1. to get the a., passer au couperet, se faire vider. 2. to give s.o. the a., se débarrasser* de qn, sacquer, vider, balancer qn. 3. to have an a. to grind, prêcher pour son saint. 4. the a., coupe f, réduction f dans un budget; diminution f de personnel. Voir aussi battle-axe.

ax² [æks] (U.S.), **axe²** [æks] (to), F: to a. expenditure, faire des coupes f.pl. sombres dans le budget; to a. s.o., porter la hache à qn.

---

* An asterisk indicates that the word so marked is included as a head-word in the Appendix.

B

b [biː] (abbr.), P: **1.** = **bloody. 2.** =**bastard. 3.** Benzédrine f (marque déposée). **4. B flats,** poux*, punaises f.pl., morpions m.pl.
babbling [ˈbæbliŋ] (adj.), F: **b. brook,** jacteuse f, tapette f, pie f borgne.
babe [beib] (noun), P: **1.** pépée f, poupée f, poule f; petite amie; **hello b.!** bonjour poupée! salut beauté (ou bébé)! **2. a hot b.,** une chaude de la pince, une chaude lapine, bandeuse f, tendeuse f.
baboon [bəˈbuːn] (noun), F: **he's a great b.,** c'est une espèce d'armoire à glace, c'est un vrai orang-outan.
baby[1] [ˈbeibi] (attrib. adj.). **1.** F: **b. doll,** bonbonnière f, poupée f, bébé f; voir aussi **baby-doll. 2.** P: **b. elephant,** femme* grosse, bonbonne f; **to walk around like a b. elephant,** marcher comme un chien dans un jeu de quilles.
baby[2] [ˈbeibi] (noun). **1.** P: = **babe, 1. 2.** P: **a hot b.** = **a hot babe (babe, 2). 3.** P: un homme*, un mec, un dur. **4.** F: **to be left holding the b.,** porter le chapeau, payer les pots cassés, être le dindon de la farce. **5.** F: **that's my b.,** c'est ma création, c'est mon blot. **6.** F: **that's your b.,** c'est ton business (ou tes oignons m.pl.); débrouille-toi tout seul. **7.** P: **to (nearly) have a b.,** (a) avoir peur*, chier dans son froc, être dans tous ses états; (b) être en colère*, être à cran. **8.** P: marijuana f (drogues*), douce f. Voir aussi **bathwater; cry-baby; jelly-baby; scare-baby.**
baby-doll [ˈbeibi-dɔl] (attrib. adj.), F: **b.-d. pyjamas,** mini-pyjama m.
baby-juice [ˈbeibi-dʒuːs] (noun), P: sperme*, jus m de cyclope, purée f.
baby-kisser [ˈbeibi-kisər] (noun), F: député m en période électorale.
baby-snatcher [ˈbeibi-snætʃər] (noun), (a) F: kidnappeur m, -euse f; (b) P: vieux marcheur, vieux barbeau.
baccy [ˈbæki] (noun), F: tabac*, pétun m.
bach[1] [bætʃ] (noun), F: **1.** (=bachelor)

célibataire m, vieux garçon. **2.** (Austr.) baraque f, cambuse f.
bach[2] [bætʃ] (to), F: **to b. it,** mener une vie de célibataire, vivre en vieux garçon.
bachelor [ˈbætʃələr] (attrib. adj.), F: **b. flat,** garçonnière f; **b. girl,** (a) jeune fille* indépendante, pucelle f de la première heure; (b) vieille fille, laissée pour compte.
back[1] [bæk] (adj.). **1.** F: **to take a b. seat,** être la cinquième roue du carrosse; voir aussi **backseat. 2.** F: **the b. end,** automne m; voir aussi **back-end. 3.** P: **b. door,** anus*, trou m de balle. Voir aussi **fed up,** (a).
back[2] [bæk] (noun). **1.** F: **to have one's b. up,** être en colère*; **to get s.o.'s b. up,** mettre qn en colère*, prendre (ou frotter) qn à rebrousse-poil, braquer qn. **2.** P: **get off my b.!** fous-moi la paix! **3.** F: **to be on s.o.'s b.** (about sth.), (a) tomber sur le dos (ou le râble) de qn; (b) talonner qn. **4.** F: **you scratch my b. and I'll scratch yours,** passe-moi la rhubarbe, je te passe le séné; cf. **backscratcher. 5.** F: **to put one's b. into sth.,** donner un coup de collier, en mettre un coup. **6.** F: **to break one's b.,** se fatiguer, s'échiner. **7.** F: **to have one's b. to the wall,** avoir le dos au mur, tirer ses dernières cartouches, être acculé dans ses derniers retranchements. **8.** F: **the b. of beyond,** la brousse, en plein bled, au diable vauvert; **he lives at the b. of beyond,** il habite au delà des poules. **9.** F: **to be (laid) on one's b.,** (a) être malade*, être mal fichu; (b) être faible, être impuissant. **10.** F: **to break the b. of sth.,** faire le plus dur de qch. **11.** P: **she earns her living on her b.,** elle fait l'horizontale. Voir aussi **greenback; greybacks; piggyback; shellback.**
backasswards [bækˈæswədz] (adv.) (U.S.), P: = **ass backwards (ass**[1], **5).**
backbone [ˈbækboun] (noun), F: courage m, persévérance f, cran m.

---

backchat[1] [ˈbæktʃæt] (*noun*), *F:* 1. (*a*) insolence *f*; (*b*) réplique cinglante. 2. (*th.*) baratin *m* d'acteur.

backchat[2] [ˈbæktʃæt] (**to**), *F:* répliquer.

back down [ˈbækˈdaʊn] (**to**), *F:* caler, caner, lâcher pied.

back-end [ˈbækend] (*noun*), *F:* **she looks like the b.-e. of a bus**, c'est une mocheté. *Voir aussi* back[1], 2.

backfire [ˈbækˈfaɪər] (**to**), *F:* rater, mal tourner, faire fausse route.

backhanded [ˈbækˈhændɪd] (*adj.*), *F:* **b. compliment**, compliment *m* à double tranchant.

backhander [ˈbækˈhændər] (*noun*), *P:* 1. revers *m* de main, baff(r)e *f*, torgnole *f*. 2. graissage *m* de patte, pot-de-vin *m*.

backlash [ˈbæklæʃ] (*noun*), *F:* retour *m* de flamme, effet *m* de boumerang.

back-number [ˈbæknʌmbər] (*noun*), *F:* 1. objet démodé. 2. croulant *m*, périmé *m*.

back off [ˈbækˈɔf] (**to**), *P:* **b. o.!** fiche-moi la paix!

back out [ˈbækˈaʊt] (**to**), *F:* 1. se dédire, se dérober, se défiler. 2. sortir d'une position difficile, faire marche arrière.

back-pedal [ˈbækˈpedl] (**to**), *F:* faire marche arrière, faire machine arrière.

backroom [ˈbækruːm] (*attrib. adj.*), *F:* confidentiel, secret; **b. boy**, (*a*) technicien employé à des recherches secrètes; (*b*) = boffin.

backscratcher [ˈbæk-skrætʃər] (*noun*), *F:* flatteur *m* (*flatter**), lèche-cul *m*, lèche-bottes *m*, lécheur *m*; *cf.* back[2], 4.

backscratching [ˈbæk-skrætʃiŋ] (*noun*), *F:* flagornerie *f*.

back-scuttle [ˈbæk-skʌtl] (**to**), *V:* pratiquer la pédérastie active sur (qn) (*coït* anal); aller aux fesses de (qn), encaldosŝer.

backseat [ˈbæksiːt] (*attrib. adj.*), *F:* **b. driver**, passager *m* donnant des conseils au chauffeur.

backside[1] [ˈbæksaid] (*attrib. adj.*), *P:* **b. special**, spé *m*, spécial *m*.

backside[2] [ˈbækˈsaid] (*noun*), *F:* = **behind**.

backslang [ˈbæk-slæŋ] (*noun*), *F:* verlan *m*, code *m* verlan.

backslapper [ˈbæk-slæpər] (*noun*), *F:* **to be a b.**, être à tu et à toi avec qn.

backslapping [ˈbæk-slæpiŋ] (*noun*), *F:* bruyante démonstration d'amitié.

backstairs [ˈbæk-stɛəz] (*attrib. adj.*), *F:* **b. influence**, protection *f* en haut lieu; **he succeeded through b. influence**, il est arrivé à coups de piston; **b. gossip**, cancan *m* de domestiques; **b. politics**, intrigues *f.pl.* politiques, politique *f* de sous-main.

backtrack [ˈbæk-træk] (**to**). 1. *F:* (*a*) rebrousser chemin; (*b*) faire marche arrière, se dégonfler, se défiler, caner. 2. *P:* = **back up** (**to**), 2 (*b*).

backtracker [ˈbæk-trækər] (*noun*), *F:* caneur *m*.

back-up [ˈbækʌp] (*noun*). 1. *F:* appui *m*, soutien *m*, aide *f*. 2. *P:* (*a*) piqûre *f* (dans une veine déjà gonflée); (*b*) poussette *f*. 3. *P:* enculage (hétérosexuel).

back up [ˈbækˈʌp] (**to**). 1. *F:* **to b. s.o. u.**, seconder qn, prendre (*ou* porter) les patins pour qn. 2. *P:* (*a*) dilater la veine avant une piqûre de drogues; gonfler; (*b*) aspirer le sang dans la seringue pendant une piqûre; (*c*) faire poussette. 3. *F:* faire marche arrière.

backward [ˈbækwəd] (*adj.*), *F:* **he's not b. in coming forward**, il n'est pas le dernier à se pousser, il n'a pas froid aux yeux.

backwards [ˈbækwədz] (*adv.*), *F:* 1. **to lean over b. for s.o.**, se mettre en quatre pour qn, faire son possible pour aider qn; *cf.* fall (**to**), 3. 2. **to know sth. b.**, comprendre qch. parfaitement, savoir (*ou* connaître) qch. par cœur.

backwoodsman [ˈbækwʊdzmən] (*noun*), *F:* 1. rustre *m*, rustaud *m*, péquenaud *m*. 2. un Pair qui fréquente peu la Chambre des Lords.

bacon [ˈbeikən] (*noun*), *F:* 1. **to bring home the b.**, (*a*) faire bouillir la marmite, gagner sa croûte (*ou* son bifteck); (*b*) remporter le pompon. 2. **to save one's b.**, sauver sa peau (*ou* ses côtelettes *f.pl.*). *Voir aussi* bonce.

bad[1] [bæd] (*adj.*). 1. *F:* **that's too b.!** (*a*) dommage! manque de pot!; (*b*) tant pis pour lui (eux, *etc.*)! 2. *F:* **a b. lot** (*or* **'un** *or* **hat** *or* **egg**), sale* individu, canaille *f*, salaud *m*. 3. *F:* **to turn up like a b. penny**, se présenter comme un mauvais sou; venir comme un cheveu (*ou* des cheveux) sur la soupe. 4. *F:* **that's not b.!** c'est pas de la gnognot(t)e! 5. *F:* **in b. shape** (*or* **in a b. way**), mal

---

* An asterisk indicates that the word so marked is included as a head-word in the Appendix.

parti, en fichu état. **6.** *F:* **to give sth. up as a b. job,** laisser tomber qch. **7.** *F:* **to have a b. time of it,** passer un mauvais moment (*ou* quart d'heure). **8.** *F:* **to make it b. for s.o.,** (*a*) jouer un mauvais tour à qn; (*b*) en faire baver à qn. **9.** *F:* **he's as b. as they make 'em** (*or* **as they come**), il est mauvais comme une teigne. **10.** *F:* **b. form,** mauvaises manières; ce qui ne se fait pas. **11.** *P:* **b. news,** facture *f*, note *f*, addition *f* (*surtout* dans une boîte de nuit). **12.** *P:* **excellent***, super, terrible.

bad[2] [bæd] (*adv.*) (=*badly*), *P:* mal; **to have it b. for s.o.,** aimer* qn, être épris de qn.

bad[3] [bæd] (*noun*), *F:* **1. to go to the b.,** être sur la mauvaise pente, mal tourner, tourner au sur. **2. to the b.,** en arriérages, en moratoire.

baddie, baddy ['bædi] (*noun*), *F:* **1.** vaurien*, affreux *m*, canaille *f*. **2.** (*film, pièce de théâtre*) le vilain, le méchant; *cf.* **goodies,** 2.

badge [bædʒ] (*noun*), *P:* quantité de drogues insuffisante pour le prix payé

badger ['bædʒər] (*noun*). **1.** (*Austr.*) *P:* reçu maquillé, quittance maquillée. **2.** *P:* **the b. game,** (*a*) moyens employés pour compromettre un homme avec une femme pour lui tirer de l'argent; (*b*) escroquerie*, chantage *m*; tromperie *f*, duperie *f* dans un but personnel ou politique. **3.** (*U.S.*) *F:* habitant *m* de l'état de Wisconsin.

bad-looking ['bæd'lukiŋ] (*adj.*), *F:* **she's not b.-l.,** elle n'est pas mal, c'est un beau petit lot.

bad-mouth ['bædmauθ] (**to**) (*U.S.*), *F:* dire du mal de (qn, qch.), casser du sucre sur le dos de (qn).

bag[1] [bæg] (*noun*). **1.** *P:* (**old**) **b.,** femme* (*péj.*); vieille pouffiasse, mocheté *f*. **2.** *P:* **overnight b.,** baise-en-ville *m*. **3.** *F:* **b. of wind,** (*a*) vantard*, hâbleur *m*; (*b*) bavard*, baratineur *m*. **4.** *F:* **there's bags of it,** il y en a en abondance*, il y en a à gogo, il y en a une charibotée. **5.** *F:* **it's in the b.,** c'est dans le sac, c'est du tout cuit. **6.** *F:* **the whole b. of tricks,** tout le Saint-Frusquin. **7.** *V:* **b. (of tricks),** testicules*, bijoux *m.pl.* de famille. **8.** *F:* **she's a b. of bones,** elle est maigre*,

elle n'a que la peau et (*ou* sur) les os. **9.** *F:* **bags of mystery,** saucisses *f.pl.,* bifteck *m* de pan(n)é. **10.** *P:* parachute *m*, pépin *m*. **11.** (*pl.*) *F:* pantalon*, falzar(d) *m*. **12.** (*U.S.*) *P:* **to have** (*or* **tie**) **a b. on,** (*a*) faire la bombe, faire ribote; (*b*) être ivre*, être en ribote. **13.** *P:* humeur *f*, état *m* d'esprit; **to have sad bags,** être triste sur les bords. **14.** (*U.S.*) *P:* occupation *f*, marotte *f*, dada *m*. **15.** (*U.S.*) *P:* milieu social, entourage *m*, ambiance *f*, clique *f*, groupe *m*. **16.** *P:* provision *f* de drogues d'un usager; plaquette *f*. **17.** *P:* **the bottom of the b.,** (*a*) la dernière ressource; (*b*) atout gardé en réserve. **18.** *F:* **to be left holding the b. = to be left holding the baby** (**baby**[2], 4). **19.** *P:* **to empty the b.,** vider son sac. **20.** *P:* **to give s.o. the b. = to give s.o. the sack** (**sack**[1], 1). **21.** (*U.S.*) *P:* **to set one's b.,** tout mettre en œuvre pour avoir un poste politique *ou* une promotion. **22.** *P:* (*a*) capote (anglaise); (*b*) pessaire *m* en caoutchouc, calotte *f*. **23.** *F:* **it's not my b. = it's not my scene** (**scene,** 7). *Voir aussi* **cat,** 12; **fag,** 2 (*c*); **fleabag; gasbag; haybag; moneybags; nosebag; ragbag; ratbag; scumbag; shagbag.**

bag[2] [bæg] (**to**), *P:* **1.** arrêter*, agrafer. **2.** mettre le grappin sur (qch.). **3.** voler*, piquer, chauffer. **4.** descendre, piffer (un avion). **5. b.** (*or* **bags**) **I the first go!** pour bibi (*ou* mézigue) le premier tour!

baggage ['bægidʒ] (*noun*), *F:* **1.** fille* effrontée, garce *f*, gisquette *f*. **2.** prostituée*, chamelle *f*.

bagged [bægd] (*adj.*) (*U.S.*), *P:* ivre*, blindé, chargé.

bagman ['bægmæn] (*noun*), *P:* **1.** commis voyageur *m*. **2.** fourgueur *m* de drogues.

bag-snatcher ['bæg-snætʃər] (*noun*), *F:* piqueur *m* (*ou* faucheur *m*) de sacs à main.

bail out ['beil'aut] (**to**), *P:* **to b. s.o. o.,** (*a*) aider qn à remonter le courant; (*b*) tendre une main secourable à qn.

bait [beit] (*noun*), *P:* (*a*) homme beau et efféminé qui attire, malgré lui, les pédérastes*; un Antinoüs; (*b*) femme belle mais masculine; une Diane chasseresse. *Voir aussi* **dream-bait; jail-bait.**

---

* L'astérisque indique que le mot marqué de ce signe figure comme entrée dans le Répertoire.

baksheesh ['bækʃi:ʃ] (*noun*), *P:* bak-chich(e) *m*.

baldheaded ['bɔːld'hedid] (*adv*.), *P:* **to go for s.o., sth., b.**, foncer sur qn, qch., tête baissée, ne pas y aller de main morte.

baldie, baldy ['bɔːldi] (*noun*), *P:* personne chauve*, tête *f* de veau.

ball[1] [bɔːl] (*noun*). **1.** *F:* **to be on the b.**, (*a*) être là pour un coup; (*b*) être dans le coup, savoir nager, être sous la gouttière; (*c*) être malin*, être dégourdi. **2.** *P:* **to have (oneself) a b.**, se goberger, s'en payer une tranche, se marrer. **3.** *F:* **to play b. with s.o.**, coopérer avec qn, être de mèche avec qn, être en tandem avec qn, faire le chemin à deux. **4.** *F:* **to set the b. rolling**, mener la danse (*ou* le branle). **5.** *P:* pilule *f ou* portion *f* d'une drogue; *cf.* **goofball, 3, 4, 5; speedball. 6.** *F:* **b. of fire**, individu* du tonnerre; *cf.* **fireball. 7.** *P:* **b. and chain**, épouse*, boulet *m*. **8.** *F:* **the b. is in your court**, c'est à votre tour, c'est maintenant votre initiative. **9.** *P:* **that's the way the b. bounces**, c'est comme ça et pas autrement, voilà d'où vient le vent; *cf.* **cookie, 2; mop; onion, 1. 10.** *V:* testicule*, bille *f*, balloche *f*; *cf.* **ballock**[1], **1; balls.** *Voir aussi* **chalk, 4; eight, 2; fly-ball; oddball**[2]; **pat-ball; pinball; screwball**[2]; **snowball**[1].

ball[2] [bɔːl] (**to**). **1.** *P:* = **to have (oneself) a ball (ball**[1], 2). **2.** *V:* coïter* avec (une femme), égoïner, bourrer. *Voir aussi* **jack, 6; snowball**[2] (**to**).

ball-breaker ['bɔːl-breikər], **ball-buster** ['bɔːl-bʌstər] (*noun*) (*U.S.*), *P:* tâche *f* extrêmement difficile, casse-gueule *m*; *cf.* **balls, 10.**

balling out ['bɔːliŋ'aut] (*noun*), *P:* engueulade *f*, savon *m*.

ballock[1] ['bɔlək] (*noun*), *V:* **1.** testicule*, balloche *f*. **2. to drop a b.**, s'attirer des crosses *f.pl.*, s'emmouscailler. *Voir aussi* **ballocks**[1].

ballock[2] ['bɔlək] (**to**), *V:* réprimander*, enguirlander, engueuler.

ballocking ['bɔləkiŋ] (*noun*), *V:* **to get a b.**, recevoir un abattage (*ou* une engueulade).

ballock-naked ['bɔlək'neikid] (*adj*.), *V:* nu*, à poil, le cul à l'air.

ballocks[1] ['bɔləks] (*pl. noun*), *V:* **1.** testicules*, balloches *f.pl.* **2. b. (to**

you)! mon cul! **3. to make a b. of sth.**, faire cafouiller qch., foutre la pagaille. *Voir aussi* **ballock**[1].

ballocks[2] ['bɔləks] (**to**), *V:* **1.** esquinter, bousiller. **2. to be (*or* get) ballocksed**, se faire contrer ; *cf.* **ballock**[2] (**to**).

ball-off ['bɔːlɔf] (*noun*), *V:* branlage *m*; **to have a b.-o.**, se masturber*, se branler.

ball off ['bɔːl'ɔf] (**to**), *V:* = **to have a ball-off.**

balloon [bə'luːn] (*noun*), *F:* **1. when the b. goes up . . .**, quand on découvrira le pot aux roses... **2.** ballon *m* d'essai.

balloon-head [bə'luːnhed] (*noun*), *F:* individu bête*, ballot *m*, baluchard *m*.

ball out ['bɔːl'aut] (**to**), *P:* injurier*, enguirlander (qn).

balls [bɔːlz] (*pl. noun*), *V:* **1.** testicules*, couilles *f.pl.* **2. to have s.o. by the b.**, avoir qn à la pogne. **3. to get one's b. chewed off**, se faire réprimander*, en prendre pour son grade; *voir aussi* **chew off (to). 4. b. (to you)!** mon cul!; espèce de couillon! **5. b. to that!** tête de con!; con à ressort! **6. it's all (*or* a load of) b.**, c'est de la couille (*ou* des couilles) en barre. **7. what b.!** quelle connerie!; quelle couillonnade! **8. it's cold enough to freeze the b. off a brass monkey**, ça caille; il fait un froid de canard; on se les gèle. **9.** (*U.S.*) courage *m*, cran *m*. **10. to break one's b.**, se casser les couilles; *cf.* **ball-breaker. 11.** = **balls-up.**

balls-ache ['bɔːlzeik] (*noun*), *V:* **you give me (the) b.-a.**, tu me casses les couilles, tu me fais mal aux couilles.

ballsey ['bɔːlzi] (*adj*.) (*U.S.*), *P:* agressif, impulsif, emplumé.

balls-up ['bɔːlzʌp] (*noun*), *V:* **to make a (right) b.-u. of it**, en faire une couillonnade (*ou* une connerie).

balls up ['bɔːlz'ʌp] (**to**), *V:* embrouiller, chambouler, bousiller.

ball up ['bɔːl'ʌp] (**to**). **1.** *V:* = **balls up** (to). **2.** *P:* **to be (all) balled up**, être embrouillé, vasouiller.

bally ['bæli] (*adj*.), *F:* (*euph. pour* **bloody**) satané, sacré.

ballyhoo ['bæli'huː] (*noun*), *F:* **1.** grosse publicité, battage *m*, tamtam *m*. **2.** mensonge*, bourrage *m* de crâne, boniment *m*.

---

* An asterisk indicates that the word so marked is included as a head-word in the Appendix.

balmy [ˈbɑːmi] (adj.), P: = **barmy**.

balon(e)y [bəˈlouni] (noun), F: bêtises*, sornettes f.pl.; b.! c'est du bidon! Voir aussi **load, 2.**

bam [bæm] (noun), P: 1. amphétamine f (drogues*). 2. mélange m de stimulant et de calmant (drogues).

bambalacha [ˈbæmbəˈlɑːtʃə] (noun), P: marijuana f (drogues*), bambalouche f.

bamboo [bæmˈbuː] (noun), P: pipe f à opium, bambou m; **to suck the b.**, tirer sur le bambou; b. **puffer**, tireur m de dross.

bamboozle [bæmˈbuːzl] (to), F: duper*, empaumer, embobeliner, embobiner.

banana [bəˈnɑːnə] (noun). 1. V: **to have one's b. peeled**, coïter*, arracher un copeau. 2. F: b. **shot**, (football) balle f en courbe. 3. F: **I haven't just come in on the b. boat**, je ne suis pas de la dernière couvée; je ne suis pas tombé de la dernière pluie. 4. (U.S.) F: comédien m, acteur m burlesque; **top b.**, vedette f; **second b.**, acteur m de second rôle.

bananas [bəˈnɑːnəz] (adj.), P: fou*, maboul, toqué.

band [bænd] (noun), F: **Big B.**, grand orchestre de jazz comportant vingt éléments. Voir aussi **one-man**.

bandit [ˈbændit] (noun), F: **one-armed b.**, machine f à sous. Voir aussi **arse-bandit; beef-bandit.**

bandwagon [ˈbændwægən] (noun), F: **to jump** (or **climb** or **hop**) **on the b.**, prendre le train en marche, se mettre du côté du manche.

bandy-chair [ˈbændi-tʃɛər] (noun), F: **to make a b.-c.**, faire la chaise.

bang[1] [bæŋ] (adj.), F: **the whole b. lot** (or **shoot**), tout le tremblement, le train et l'arrière-train.

bang[2] [bæŋ] (adv.), F: 1. **to arrive b. on time**, arriver pile (ou recta). 2. **to be caught b. to rights**, être pris sur le fait, être pris en flagrant délit; cf. **dead**[2], 8 (b). Voir aussi **slap-bang(-wallop); wallop**[1].

bang[3] [bæŋ] (noun). 1. P: coït*, partie f de jambes en l'air; **gang b.**, coït* d'une femme avec plusieurs hommes; dérouillage m en bande. 2. F: coup*, gnon m. 3. F: accrochage m, avaro m. 4. F: **to go with a b.**, aller comme sur des roulettes, gazer. 5. P: **I got a real b. out of it**, ce truc m'a remué les boyaux.

6. P: **to have a b. at sth.**, tenter (ou risquer) le coup. **7.** P: b. (**in the arm**), piquouse f; **to give oneself a b.**, se charger. **8.** P: impression f de plénitude qui suit une injection intraveineuse de drogue; flash m. **9.** (Austr.) P: bordel*, claque m. Voir aussi **whizz-bang.**

bang[4] [bæŋ] (to). 1. P: battre*, cogner, encadrer (qn). 2. P: coïter* avec (une femme), envoyer en l'air. 3. F: tamponner, entuber (une voiture). 4. F: **to b. into s.o.**, se taper dans qn. 5. P: piquouser.

banger [ˈbæŋər] (noun). 1. F: voiture*, guimbarde f. 2. F: saucisse f, bifteck m de pan(n)é. 3. P: queutard m, bourriqueur m. 4. F: mensonge* énorme, bateau m.

bang-on [ˈbæŋˈɔn] (adv.), F: b.-o.! recta!; it's b.-o., c'est au poil, c'est extra.

bangster [ˈbæŋstər] (noun), P: piquouseur m, chevalier m de la poussette.

bang-up [ˈbæŋʌp] (adj.), F: excellent*, soin-soin, du tonnerre; **a b.-u. meal**, un repas à tout casser, de la grande bouffe; cf. **slap-up.**

banjax [ˈbændʒæks] (to), P: démolir, bousiller, foutre en l'air.

banjo [ˈbændʒou] (noun), P: 1. miche de pain coupée en deux formant un grand sandwich. 2. nourriture* volée aux cuisines de prison. Voir aussi **Irish**[1], 4.

bankroll [ˈbæŋkroul] (attrib. adj.), P: b. **man**, qn qui finance une affaire de jeu; directeur m d'une salle de jeux, bouleur m.

bar [bɑːr] (noun). 1. F: **to be behind bars**, être emprisonné*, être derrière les barreaux m.pl., être bouclé. 2. P: billet* d'une livre. 3. V: **to have a b. (on)**, être en érection*, avoir la trique. Voir aussi **handlebar; nosh-bar.**

barber [ˈbɑːbər] (to), P: **to b. a joint**, voler* dans une chambre alors que qn y dort, grincher à l'endormage.

barbs [bɑːbz] (pl. noun) (abbr. = barbiturates), P: barbituriques m.pl. (drogues*), barbitos m.pl.

bare-arsed [ˈbɛərˈɑːst], U.S.: **bare-ass(ed)** [ˈbɛərˈɑːs(t)] (adj.), P: nu*, le cul à l'air, en Jésus.

bareback [ˈbɛəbæk] (adv.), P: **to ride b.**, cracher dans le bénitier, jouer sans blanc.

---

* L'astérisque indique que le mot marqué de ce signe figure comme entrée dans le Répertoire.

barf [bɑːf] (**to**) (*U.S.*), *P:* vomir*, dégueuler.

bar-fly [ˈbɑːflai] (*noun*), *F:* 1. pilier *m* de bistrot. 2. ivrogne* qui se fait offrir des tournées.

barge in [ˈbɑːdʒˈin] (**to**), *F:* 1. to b. i. on a party, (*a*) arriver en trouble-fête; (*b*) arriver en pique-assiette. 2. to b. i. on s.o.'s conversation, mettre son grain de sel. 3. to b. i. where you're not wanted, piétiner les bégonias, marcher sur les plates-bandes de qn.

barge into [ˈbɑːdʒˈintu] (**to**), *F:* to b. i. s.o., se taper dans qn, bousculer qn, entrer dans qn.

barge out [ˈbɑːdʒˈaut] (**to**), *F:* partir* en claquant la porte.

barge-pole [ˈbɑːdʒpoul] (*noun*), *F:* I wouldn't touch it with a b.-p., je ne le prendrais pas avec des pincettes *f.pl.*

bar-girl [ˈbɑːɡəːl] (*noun*), *P:* hôtesse *f*, entraîneuse *f.*

bar-happy [ˈbɑːˈhæpi] (*adj.*) (*U.S.*), *F:* (légèrement) ivre*, éméché.

bark [bɑːk] (**to**), *F:* 1. tousser bruyamment. 2. to b. up the wrong tree, se mettre le doigt dans l'œil (jusqu'au coude), tirer sur ses propres troupes. *Voir aussi* dog[1], 7.

barker [ˈbɑːkər] (*noun*), *P:* revolver*, pétard *m*, flingue *m.*

barmy [ˈbɑːmi] (*adj.*), *P:* fou*, toqué, loufoque; to put on the b. stick, faire le cinglé.

barn [bɑːn] (*noun*), *F:* 1. it's a b. of a place, c'est une grande baraque (*ou* un vrai hangar); it's like a b. in here, c'est ouvert à tout vent, c'est comme chez Frisco et Cie. 2. were you born (*U.S.*: raised) in a b.? t'es né sous les ponts?

Barnaby Rudge [ˈbɑːnəbiˈrʌdʒ] (*pr. noun*) (*R.S.* = judge), *P:* juge *m*, gerbier *m.*

barnet [ˈbɑːnit] (*noun*), *P:* = **Barnet Fair.**

Barnet Fair [ˈbɑːnitˈfɛər] (*pr. noun*) (*R.S.* = hair), *P:* cheveux*, tiffes *m.pl.*

barney[1] [ˈbɑːni] (*noun*), *P:* 1. a (bit of a) b., querelle*, prise *f* de bec, accrochage *m.* 2. arrangement *m* malhonnête, entourloupette *f.*

barney[2] [ˈbɑːni] (**to**), *P:* discuter pour le bout de gras.

baron [ˈbærən] (*noun*), 1. *P:* prisonnier *m* qui a de l'argent, du tabac, *etc.*; baron *m*; *cf.* **snout, 2.** 2. *F:* magnat *m*, gros bonnet (de l'industrie, *etc.*).

barrack-room [ˈbærək-ruːm] (*attrib. adj.*), *F:* b.-r. lawyer, chicaneur *m*, râleur *m*, mauvais coucheur, emmerdeur *m.*

barrel[1] [ˈbærəl] (*noun*), *P:* 1. to be over a b., être dans le pétrin (*ou* dans la merde). 2. to get (*or* have) s.o. over a b., avoir qn dans sa poche (*ou* à sa pogne). 3. to make a b., gagner des mille et des cents; to have a b. of money, être riche*. *Voir aussi* scrape[2] (to), 1.

barrel[2] (**ass**) [ˈbærəl(æs)] (**to**) (*U.S.*), *P:* aller vite*, rouler à plein tube, gazer.

barrelhouse [ˈbærəlhaus] (*noun*) (*U.S.*), *P:* cabaret *m* populaire dans un quartier noir.

barrelled up [ˈbærəldˈʌp] (*adj.*), *P:* ivre*, bit(t)uré.

barrow [ˈbærou, ˈbærə] (*noun*). 1. *P:* to fall right into (*or* land right in) one's b., tomber tout frit (*ou* tout rôti). tomber dans le bec. 2. *F:* b. boy, marchand *m* à la sauvette, estampeur *m.*

base [beis] (*noun*), *F:* 1. he won't even make first b., il claquera au départ. 2. he went b. over apex, il a fait une belle culbute; *cf.* **arse, 4.**

bash[1] [bæʃ] (*noun*), *P:* 1. coup*, châtaigne *f.* 2. to have a b. at sth., to give sth. a b., tenter le coup (*ou* sa chance).

bash[2] [bæʃ] (**to**), *P:* 1. battre*, cogner. 2. to b. it = to hit the bottle (bottle[1], 1). *Voir aussi* **bishop; square-bash** (**to**).

basher [ˈbæʃər] (*noun*), *P:* cogneur *m*, pugiliste *m*, raton *m*, chasseur *m*; *cf.* **pak(k)i-basher; queer-basher; spud-basher; square-basher.**

bash in [ˈbæʃˈin] (**to**), *P:* to b. i. s.o.'s face, abîmer le portrait à qn.

bashing [ˈbæʃiŋ] (*noun*), *P:* 1. coup(s)*, peignée *f*, raclée *f*, trempe *f.* 2. the platoon took a b., la section se fit amocher. *Voir aussi* **pak(k)i-bashing; queer-bashing; spud-bashing; square-bashing.**

bash on [ˈbæʃˈɔn] (**to**), *P:* to b. o. (regardless), aller envers et contre tout.

bash out [ˈbæʃˈaut] (**to**), *P:* to b. o. a tune, tapoter un air.

bash up [ˈbæʃˈʌp] (**to**), *P:* battre*, filer une avoine à (qn).

basinful [ˈbeisnful] (*noun*), *P:* 1. to

* An asterisk indicates that the word so marked is included as a head-word in the Appendix.

have (had) a b., en avoir marre, en
avoir ras le bol. 2. O.K., I'll have a b.,
O.K., je veux!
basket ['bɑːskit] (noun), P: 1. (euph.
pour bastard) vaurien*, salaud m. 2.
= bread-basket. Voir aussi fruit-basket.
bastard ['bɑːstəd, 'bæstəd] (noun), V:
1. vaurien*, fils m (ou fan m) de pute,
canaille f. 2. that's a b., ça c'est couille;
quelle mouscaille! quel emmerdement!
bat¹ [bæt] (noun), 1. P: an old b., (a) une
vieille bique; (b) (U.S.) prostituée*,
grue f. 2. F: like a b. out of hell, vite*,
comme un zèbre. 3. F: right off the b.,
illico-presto. 4. P: réjouissances*, noce
f, bombe f; to be on the (or a) b., faire
la nouba. 5. F: to have bats in the
belfry (or attic), être fou*, avoir une
araignée au plafond, yoyoter de la
mansarde.
bat² [bæt] (to). 1. P: battre*, frapper,
rosser. 2. F: he didn't b. an eyelid, il
n'a pas sourcillé (ou pipé). 3. F: to b.
first, tirer le premier. Voir aussi
sticky, 4.
bat along ['bætə'lɔŋ] (to), P: aller
vite*, filer à pleins gaz, rouler à tout
berzingue.
bat around ['bætə'raʊnd] (to), F: to b.
an idea a., tournicoter une idée.
batch [bætʃ] (to), F: to b. it = to bach
it (bach² (to)).
bathwater ['bɑː:θ-wɔːtər] (noun), F: to
throw the baby out with the b., envoyer
tout promener, balancer le manche
après la cognée.
bats [bæts] (adj.), P: 1. fou*, timbré;
to go b., devenir fou*, perdre la boule.
2. to be b. about s.o., sth., aimer* (ou
être toqué de) qn, qch.
batter¹ ['bætər] (noun), P: to be on the
b., (a) racoler*, aller aux asperges,
faire le tapin; (b) = to be on the bat
(bat¹, 4); (c) être échappé de prison*,
déballonner de la taule. Voir aussi
belt² (to), 4.
batter² ['bætər] (to), P: mendier*, taper
qn (argent), faire la manche.
batter on ['bætə'rɔn] (to), P: se batailler,
piocher de l'avant.
battleaxe ['bætl-æks] (noun), F: femme*
(péj.), harpie f, dragon m.
battledress ['bætldres] (noun), F:
pyjama m.
battler ['bætlər] (noun), F: bagarreur m,

battant m, chercheur m de cognes.
batty ['bæti] (adj.), P: = bats, 1, 2.
bawling out ['bɔːliŋ'aʊt] (noun), P: =
balling out.
bawl out ['bɔːl'aʊt] (to), P: = ball out
(to).
bayonet ['beiənit] (noun), P: pénis*,
arbalète f; to have b. practice, coïter*,
tirer un coup.
bazooka [bə'zuːkə] (noun), P: 1. pénis*,
arbalète f. 2. (pl.) seins*, doudounes
f.pl.
bazookaed [bə'zuːkəd] (adj.), P: coulé,
sabordé, bousillé.
bazooms [bə'zuːmz] (pl. noun), P: =
bazookas (bazooka, 2).
beach [biːtʃ] (noun), F: 1. to be on the
b., être sur le sable, être à la côte. 2.
you're not the only pebble on the b.,
tu n'es pas unique dans ton genre;
t'es pas l'oiseau rare.
beak [biːk] (noun), P: 1. magistrat m
(du commissariat de police), chat m,
curieux m. 2. nez* (crochu), pif m,
tarin m. Voir aussi stickybeak.
beam [biːm] (noun), F: 1. on the b., (a)
sur la même longueur d'ondes; (b)
dans la bonne direction, sur la bonne
route. 2. to be off the b., (a) ne pas
comprendre, ne rien piger, être sur
une autre longueur d'ondes; (b) faire
fausse route, changer de cap. 3. to be
broad in the b., être joufflu du pétard.
beam-ends ['biːm'endz] (pl. noun), F:
to be on one's b.-e., être pauvre*, être
dans la dèche.
bean [biːn] (noun). 1. P: tête*, caboche f.
2. F: old b., mon vieux pote, ma vieille
branche. 3. F: he hasn't a b., il n'a
pas le sou*, il n'a pas un radis. 4. F:
it's not worth a b., cela ne vaut pas
chipette (ou tripette). 5. F: he knows
how many beans make five, c'est un
malin*, il en connaît un rayon. 6. F:
to spill the beans, (a) vendre (ou
éventer) la mèche, vider son sac; (b)
avouer*, manger le morceau. 7. F: to
be full of beans, (a) être d'attaque;
(b) être plein d'entrain, péter le feu.
8. P: Benzédrine f (marque déposée)
(drogues*). 9. P: jolly beans, amphétamine f (drogues*). 10. (U.S.) P: (péj.)
un Mexicain. Voir aussi string-bean.
beano ['biːnou] (noun), F: réjouissances*,
bamboula f.

bean-pole ['biːnpoʊl], bean-stick ['biːn-stik] (noun), F: (d'une personne) une grande perche, une asperge (montée).

bear [bɛər] (noun) (U.S.), P: 1. femme laide*, mocheté f, tartignole f. 2. qch. de très difficile*, duraille f. Voir aussi sore, 2.

beard ['biəd] (noun), V: = beaver, 2.

bear-garden ['bɛəgɑːdn] (noun), F: foire f, pétaudière f; to turn the place into a b.-g., mettre le désordre partout, foutre la pagaille.

beat¹ [biːt] (adj.), F: 1. (dead) b., très fatigué*, claqué, vanné. 2. découragé, lessivé, vidé. 3. the b. generation, la génération beat (ou sacrifiée). Voir aussi downbeat; off-beat; upbeat.

beat² [biːt] (noun). 1. P: beatnik m. 2. F: (jazz) temps fort de la mesure, le beat. 3. F: that's off my b., ce n'est pas mon rayon. 4. V: to have a b. on, être en érection*, avoir le gourdin. Voir aussi deadbeat.

beat³ [biːt] (to). 1. P: to b. it, s'enfuir*, se tirer; now then, b. it! file! décampe! fiche le camp! débine-toi! 2. F: that beats everything (or the band), c'est le comble, c'est plus fort que de jouer aux bouchons. 3. F: can you b. it! ça alors! 4. F: it beats me, cela me dépasse. Voir aussi dummy, 5; meat, 4.

beat off ['biːt'ɔf] (to), V: se masturber*, s'en battre une.

beat-up ['biːtʌp] (adj.), F: a b.-u. old car, une vieille voiture*, tacot m.

beat up ['biːt'ʌp] (to), F: 1. battre*, rosser. 2. to b. it u., mener une vie de patachon, faire les quatre cents coups.

beaut¹ [bjuːt] (adj.) (Austr.), F: beau*, bath.

beaut² [bjuːt] (noun) (=beauty). 1. F: qch. de beau*; she's a b.! quelle belle poupée! 2. F: coup bien envoyé par un boxeur. 3. P: two (or a pair of) beauts, seins*, une paire de rotoplots m.pl.

beaver ['biːvər] (noun). 1. F: barbe*, barbouze f. 2. (U.S.) V: (d'une femme) poils m.pl. du pubis, le barbu. Voir aussi eager.

bed¹ [bed] (noun), F: 1. b. of roses, la vie de château; it's not a b. of roses, c'est pas tout miel. 2. you got out of (U.S.: you got up on) the wrong side of the b. this morning, tu t'es levé du pied gauche ce matin. 3. b. and breakfast: voir bingo (26). Voir aussi breakfast; feather-bed.

bed² [bed] (to), P: to b. s.o., coïter* avec qn; she's all right for bedding, c'est une bonne baiseuse.

bed down ['bed'daʊn] (to), F: se coucher*, se bâcher.

bed-house ['bedhaʊs] (noun) (mainly U.S.), P: bordel*, boxon m.

bed-sit ['bed'sit] (noun) (=bed-sitter), F: garni m, meublé m.

bedworthy ['bedwəːði] (adj.), P: belle de nuit, prix m de Diane.

bee [biː] (noun), 1. F: he thinks he's the b.'s knees, il ne se prend pas pour de la petite bière (cf. cat, 8). 2. P: bees and honey (R.S. = money), argent*, flouse m, fric m. 3. F: to have a b. in one's bonnet, (a) être un peu fou*, avoir une araignée au plafond; (b) avoir une idée fixe. 4. P: to put the b. on s.o., taper qn (argent). Voir aussi bird, 7; queen, 3.

Beeb [biːb] (noun), F: the B. = Auntie².

beef¹ [biːf] (noun). 1. F: to have plenty of b., être fort* comme un bœuf, être costaud. 2. P: réclamation f, rouspétance f. Voir aussi corned beef.

beef² [biːf] (to), P: grogner*, rouspéter, ronchonner.

beef-bandit ['biːfbændit] (noun), V: = arse-bandit.

beefcake ['biːfkeik] (noun), F: pin-up masculin; cf. cheesecake.

beefer ['biːfər] (noun), P: rouspéteur m.

beef up ['biːf'ʌp] (to), P: corser (qch.).

been [biːn] (p.p.), P: he's b. and gone and done it! il en a fait de belles! il a fait du joli! Voir aussi has-been.

beer [biər] (noun), P: to go on the b., boire*, picoler.

beer-up ['biərʌp] (noun), P: beuverie f de bière.

beer up ['biər'ʌp] (to), P: boire* de la bière en grande quantité.

beetle-crushers ['biːtl-krʌʃəz] (pl. noun), F: grosses chaussures*, écrase-merde m.pl.; cf. crushers.

beetle off ['biːtl'ɔf] (to), F: partir*, déguerpir, se déhotter.

beezer¹ ['biːzər] (adj.), F: = spiffing.

beezer² ['biːzər] (noun), P: 1. nez*, blair m. 2. visage*; tête*, fiole f.

beggar ['begər] (noun) (euph. pour

---

* An asterisk indicates that the word so marked is included as a head-word in the Appendix.

bugger), *F:* individu*; **silly b.!** espèce d'imbécile (*ou* d'abruti)!; **poor b.!** pauvre diable!

beggar-my-neighbour [ˈbegəmiˈneibər] (*noun*) (*R.S.* = *Labour* (*Exchange*)), *P:* on the b.-m.-n., au chômage.

begorra! [biˈgɔrə] (*excl.*), *F:* nom d'un chien!

behind [biˈhaind, bəˈhaind] (*noun*), *F:* fesses*; postérieur *m*; **to sit on one's b.** (and do nothing), ne pas se manier le cul; **he does nothing but sit on his b.**, il ne bouge pas d'une semelle.

be-in [ˈbiː(j)in] (*noun*), *F:* réunion *f* d'individus pour participer à des activités spontanées.

bejesus![1] [biˈdʒiːzəs, biˈdʒeizəs] (*excl.*), *F:* = **begorra!**

bejesus[2] [biˈdʒiːzəs, biˈdʒeizəs] (*noun*), *P:* **to knock the b. out of s.o.**, battre* qn comme plâtre, envoyer dormir qn.

belch [beltʃ] (to), *P:* avouer*, dégorger.

bell [bel] (*noun*), *F:* 1. **it rings a b.**, ça me dit quelque chose. 2. **pull the other one** (=*leg*), **it's got bells on,** *c.p.*, à d'autres! cela ne prend pas! *Voir aussi* **dumb-bell.**

bell-bottoms [ˈbelbɔtəmz] (*pl. noun*) (=*bell-bottomed trousers*), *F:* pantalon* à pattes d'éléphant.

bell-hop [ˈbelhɔp] (*noun*) (*U.S.*), *F:* garçon *m* d'hôtel.

bell-rope [ˈbelroup] (*noun*), *V:* pénis*, berdouillette *f*.

belly [ˈbeli] (*noun*), *F:* ventre*, panse *f*, bedaine *f*; **my b. thinks** (*or* **is beginning to think**) **my throat's cut,** j'ai faim*, j'ai l'estomac dans les talons. *Voir aussi* **yellow-belly.**

belly-ache[1] [ˈbeli-eik] (*noun*), *F:* mal *m* au ventre.

belly-ache[2] [ˈbeli-eik] (to), *P:* grogner*, réclamer, ronchonner, rouspéter; **he's always belly-aching,** il râle toujours.

belly-acher [ˈbeli-eikər] (*noun*), *P:* râleur *m*.

belly-aching [ˈbeli-eikiŋ] (*noun*), *P:* rouspétance *f*.

belly-button [ˈbelibʌtn] (*noun*), *F:* nombril *m*, bouton *m* du milieu.

belly-flop [ˈbeliflɔp] (*noun*), *F:* **to do a b.-f.,** (*natation*) faire un plat (ventre).

bellyful [ˈbeliful] (*noun*), *P:* **to have (had) a b.,** (*a*) en avoir une gavée, en

être gavé, en avoir tout son soûl; (*b*) en avoir assez*, en avoir marre, en avoir ras le bol; *cf.* **gutful.**

belly-laugh[1] [ˈbelilɑːf] (*noun*), *F:* rigolade *f*, marrade *f*; **it's a b.-l.,** c'est très amusant*, c'est bidonnant (*ou* boyautant).

belly-laugh[2] [ˈbelilɑːf] (to), *F:* se tordre de rire*, se bidonner, se boyauter.

belly-wash [ˈbeliwɔʃ] (*noun*), *F:* bibine *f*, vinasse *f*.

belt[1] [belt] (*noun*). 1. *P:* **to give s.o. a b.,** battre* qn, donner (*ou* filer) une raclée à qn. 2. *F:* **to hit s.o. below the b.,** donner un coup bas à qn. 3. *F:* **to tighten one's b.,** se serrer la ceinture, se l'accrocher. 4. *F:* **to have sth. under one's b.,** (*a*) avoir mangé*, avoir qch. dans le fusil; (*b*) avoir une réussite à son acquis. 5. *P:* coït*, baisage *m*. 6. *P:* bang *m* aux anges. 7. *P:* (endless) **b.,** fille* *ou* femme* de mœurs faciles. 8. *P:* **to have a b. at sth.,** s'attaquer à qch., tenter l'aventure. *Voir aussi* **bracket.**

belt[2] [belt] (to). 1. *P:* attaquer*, violenter (qn), sauter dessus. 2. *P:* battre*, filer une rossée à (qn). 3. *P:* coïter* avec (qn), bourrer, bourriquer. 4. *V:* **to b. one's batter,** se masturber*, se taper sur la colonne. 5. (*U.S.*) *P:* **to b. the grape,** boire* abondamment, picoler, siroter.

belt around [ˈbeltəˈraund] (to), *P:* 1. voyager, circuler. 2. faire bombance.

belting [ˈbeltiŋ] (*noun*), *P:* 1. volée *f* de coups*, raclée *f*, dérouillée *f*. 2. défaite écrasante.

belt off [ˈbeltˈɔf] (to), *P:* s'enfuir*, se carapater, se tirer.

belt out [ˈbeltˈaut] (to), *P:* 1. gueuler, brailler, beugler (une chanson). 2. **to b. o. a tune** = **to bash out a tune.**

belt up [ˈbeltˈʌp] (to), *P:* se taire*, la boucler.

bend[1] [bend] (*noun*), *P:* 1. (*a*) **to go round the b.,** devenir fou*, perdre la boule, déménager, piquer le coup de bambou; (*b*) **that kid drives me round the b.,** ce gosse me rend fou*; **I'm driven round the b. by her incessant chatter,** son bavardage incessant me fait perdre la boule. 2. **to go on a b.** = **to go on a bender (bender,** 1).

bend[2] [bend] (to), *F:* 1. **to b. the rules,**

faire un passe-droit. **2. to b. over back-**
wards to please s.o., se mettre en quatre
pour qn. **3. to catch s.o. bending,**
surprendre qn en mauvaise posture.
4. to b. to it, faire qch. contre son gré,
rechigner. *Voir aussi* **bent**[1]; **elbow,**
6.

bender [ˈbendər] (*noun*), *P:* **1. to go on**
a b., faire la noce (*ou* la bringue);
cf. **hell-bender. 2. to be on one's bend-**
ers (=*bended knees*), (*a*) être très
fatigué*, être sur les genoux *m.pl.* (*ou*
sur les rotules *f.pl.*); (*b*) être dans le
pétrin, être foutu. **3.** pédéraste*, emmanché *m. Voir aussi* **mind-bender.**

bennie, benny [ˈbeni] (*noun*), *P:* (*a*)
Benzédrine *f* (*marque déposée*)
(*drogues**), bennie *f*; (*b*) cachet *m* de
Benzédrine.

bent[1] [bent] (*adj.*), *P:* **1.** pauvre*,
fauché. **2. a b. copper**, un flic véreux.
3. (*U.S.*) **b. (out of shape)**, déraison-
nable, dérangé. **4.** drogué*, camé. **5.**
homosexuel.

bent[2] [bent] (*noun*), *P:* pédéraste*,
travesti *m.*

benz [benz] (*noun*) (*abbr.* = *Benzedrine*),
Benzédrine *f* (*marque déposée*)
(*drogues**); *cf.* **bennie.**

berk [bəːk] (*noun*), *P:* individu bête*,
gourde *f*, tourte *f*, cornichon *m.*

bernice [ˈbəːnis] (*noun*), **bernies** [ˈbəː-
niz] (*pl. noun*), *P:* cocaïne *f* (*drogues**),
topette *f.*

berth [bəːθ] (*noun*). **1.** *F:* **to give s.o. a**
wide b., passer au large de qn. **2.** *P:*
soft (*or* **safe**) **b.**, emploi *m* pépère,
planque *f*, filon *m.*

bet [bet] (**to**), *F:* **1. you b.!** pour sûr! tu
parles! (il) y a des chances! **2. I b.**
you don't! chiche (que tu ne le feras
pas)! **3. b. you I will!** chiche (que je
le fais)! **4. I'll b. you anything you like,**
j'en mettrais ma tête à couper (*ou* ma
main au feu). **5. you can b. your boots**
(*or* **your bottom dollar**), tu peux y
aller; **I'll b. my boots** (*or* **my bottom**
dollar) **that . . .**, je mettrais ma tête à
couper que..., je vous parie la lune que
..., je te fous mon billet que..., chiche
que... **I b.!** je t'en fiche mon billet!
7. want to b.? tu t'alignes? *Voir aussi*
sweet[1], **2.**

better [ˈbetər] (*adj.*), *F:* **b. half**, épouse*,
moitié *f.*

betty [ˈbeti] (*noun*), *P:* passe-partout *m*,
crochet *m*, rossignol *m.*

betwixt [biˈtwikst] (*adv.*), *F:* **b. and**
between, ni chèvre ni chou; mi-figue,
mi-raisin.

bevvy [ˈbevi] (*noun*), *P:* un pot, un verre
(de bière, vin, *etc.*); **we had a b. in the**
bar, on a été boire un coup (*ou* siffler
un verre) au bistrot.

b. f., B. F. [ˈbiːˈef] (*abbr.*), *F: euph. pour*
bloody fool (*voir* **bloody**[1]).

B.-girl [ˈbiːgəːl] (*noun*), *P:* = **bar-girl.**

bhang [bæŋ] (*noun*), *P:* **baby b., b.**
ganjah, marijuana *f* (*drogues**).

bi [bai] (*adj.*) (=*bisexual*), *P:* = **ambi-**
dextrous.

bib [bib] (*noun*), *F:* **best b. and tucker,**
beaux vêtements*; **in one's best b. and**
tucker, sur son trente et un, tiré à
quatre épingles.

bible-basher [ˈbaiblbæʃər], **bible-**
puncher [ˈbaibl-pʌntʃər] (*noun*), *F:*
évangéliste *m* de carrefour, prêcheur
agressif.

biddy [ˈbidi] (*noun*), *F:* **1.** jeune fille*,
femme*. **2.** servante *f*, femme de
chambre, cambreline *f*, bonniche *f.* **3.**
an old b., une vieille poule, une chipie.
4. red b., vin* rouge de mauvaise
qualité, gros *m* rouge, décapant *m*,
casse-pattes *m.* **5.** (*U.S.*) poule *f*
(*oiseau*). **6.** (*Austr.*) institutrice *f*,
maîtresse *f* (d'école).

biff[1] [bif] (*noun*), *F:* coup*, gnon *m*,
beigne *f.*

biff[2] [bif] (**to**), *F:* **to b. s.o.**, battre* qn,
flanquer un gnon à qn; **to b. s.o. on**
the nose, abîmer le portrait à qn,
encadrer qn.

big[1] [big] (*adj.*), *F:* **1. b. noise** (*or* **bug**
or **cheese** *or* **gun** *or* **pot** *or* **shot**), grosse
légume, grossium *m*, gros bonnet, ponte
m. **2. b. pot**, (*a*) = **big noise** (**big**[1], **1**);
(*b*) = **pot**[1], **2** (*a*). **3. he has b. ideas**, il
voit grand. **4. he earns b. money**, il
gagne gros. **5. what's the b. idea?** à
quoi ça rime? **6. the b. time**, le haut
de l'échelle; **to be in the b. time**, être
en haut de l'échelle, être parmi les
huiles, tenir le haut du pavé. **7. to**
give s.o. a b. hand, applaudir qn à
tour de bras (*ou* à tout rompre). **8.**
b. mouth, vantard*, gueulard *m*, grande
gueule. **9. b. stiff**, (*a*) gros bêta; (*b*)
individu prétentieux*, gros plein de

---

* An asterisk indicates that the word so marked is included as a head-word in the Appendix.

soupe. **10. B. Brother,** le grand Frère. **11. b. man,** le cerveau, la grosse tête. **12. Mr B.,** le grand manitou, le gros bonnet. **13. b. talk,** grande gueule. **14. b. top,** (*a*) grande tente d'un cirque; (*b*) (vie *f* de) cirque *m*. **15.** (*U.S.*) **B. House,** prison*, grande marmite. *Voir aussi* **bloke, 3; chief, 1; stick**[1], **2; way**[2], **2.**

big[2] [big] (*adv.*), *F:* **1. to talk b.,** faire l'important, battre la grosse caisse. **2. to come** (*or* **go**) **over b.,** boumer, réussir. **3. to hit it b.,** mettre du foin dans ses bottes, attraper le haut de l'échelle.

big-bellied [ˈbigˈbelid], **big-gutted** [ˈbigˈgʌtid] (*adj.*), *P:* ventru, pansu, gros du bide.

biggie, biggy [ˈbigi] (*noun*), *F:* = **big-wig.**

big-head [ˈbighed] (*noun*), *P:* **1.** bouffi *m*, enflé *m*. **2.** gros plein de soupe.

big-headed [ˈbigˈhedid] (*adj.*), *P:* prétentieux*, vaniteux, suffisant.

big-note[1] [ˈbigˈnout] (*attrib. adj.*) (*Austr.*), *F:* **b.-n. man,** richard *m*, rupin *m*.

big-note[2] [ˈbigˈnout] (**to**) (*Austr.*), *F:* louanger, porter (qn) aux nues, empommader.

big-time [ˈbigˈtaim] (*adj.*), *F:* **1. b.-t. operator,** gros trafiquant. **2. b.-t. racketeer,** chef *m* de bande, caïd *m*; *cf.* **small-time.** *Voir aussi* **big**[1], **6.**

big-timer [ˈbigˈtaimər] (*noun*), *F:* **1.** = **big noise (big**[1], **1); to be a b.-t.,** être sur la lancée; *cf.* **small-timer. 2.** joueur (pour de l'argent) professionnel.

bigwig [ˈbigwig] (*noun*), *F:* personnage important, gros bonnet, grosse légume.

bike [baik] (*noun*). **1.** *F:* bicyclette *f*, vélo *m*; *cf.* **push-bike. 2.** *F:* motocyclette *f*, moto *f*, pétrolette *f*. **3.** (*Austr.*) *P:* cavaleuse *f*, Marie-couche-toi-là *f*.

bilge [bildʒ], (*noun*) *P:* **1.** bêtise*, foutaise *f*, eau *f* de bidet, sornette *f*. **2. to talk b.,** dire des bêtises*, sortir des foutaises. **3.** boisson *f* insipide, pipi *m* de chien (*ou* de chat *ou* de singe), pissat *m* d'âne.

bilge-water [ˈbildʒwɔːtər] (*noun*), *P:* = **bilge, 3.**

bill [bil] (*noun*). **1.** *F:* (*a*) **top of the b.,** tête *f* d'affiche; (*b*) **to top the b.,** to be top of the b.,** être en vedette; (*c*) **it**

tops the b., c'est le comble. **2.** *F:* **to draw úp a stiff b.,** saler la note. **3.** *F:* **to stick it on the b.,** laisser monter l'addition; **stick it on the b.!** collez ça sur la note! **4.** *F:* **to fit** (*or* **fill**) **the b.,** remplir toutes les conditions, faire l'affaire. **5.** *P:* **nez***, pif *m*, blair *m*. *Voir aussi* **foot**[2] (**to**), **2.**

billet [ˈbilit] (*noun*), *F:* **to get a safe b.,** s'embusquer.

Billingsgate [ˈbiliŋzgeit] (*pr. noun – marché aux poissons de Londres*), *P:* **1.** langage *m* de poissarde. **2. B. pheasant,** gendarme*, sauret *m*.

billio [ˈbiliou] (*noun*), *F:* = **billy-ho.**

Billjim, billjim [ˈbildʒim] (*noun*), *F:* Australien *m*.

billy [ˈbili] (*noun*). **1.** *P:* mouchoir*, blave *m*. **2.** (*Austr.*) *F:* (*a*) (=*billy-can*) gamelle *f*, bouilloire *f* (à thé); (*b*) eau*, flotte *f*.

billy-ho [ˈbilihou] (*noun*), *F:* **to go like b.-h.,** (*a*) aller vite*, foncer à tout berzingue; (*b*) gazer à bloc.

bim [bim] (*noun*), *P:* agent* de police, flic *m*.

bin [bin] (*noun*), *P:* = **loony-bin.**

bind [baind] (*noun*), *F:* **1.** (*d'une personne*) crampon *m*, casse-pieds *m*. **2.** (*d'une chose*) scie *f*; **it's an awful b.,** quelle corvée! **3. to be in a bit of a b.,** être dans le pétrin.

binder [ˈbaindər] (*noun*), *F:* **1.** coup *m* de l'étrier. **2.** = **bind, 1, 2.** *Voir aussi* **highbinder; spellbinder.**

bindle [ˈbindl] (*noun*) (*U.S.*), *P:* **1.** baluchon *m*. **2.** cornet *m* de stups. **3. b. stiff,** (*a*) clochard*, clodo(t) *m*; (*b*) drogué*, camé *m*, toxico *m*.

bing [biŋ] (*noun*), *P:* **1.** = **bindle, 2. 2.** piquouse *f*. **3. b. room,** trou *m* à came. **4.** (*U.S.*) cachot *m* (de prison), mitard *m*.

binge [bindʒ] (*noun*), *F:* réjouissances*, bombe *f*, ribouldingue *f*; **to go on the b.,** faire la ribouldingue; **to be on the b.,** faire une virée.

bingo [ˈbiŋgou] (*noun*), sorte de loto public. *Les termes suivants sont employés dans ce jeu:* **Kelly's eye** *or* **Little Jimmy** *or* **Willie's whatsit** = **1; buckle my shoe** *or* **dirty old Jew** *or* **Little Boy Blue** *or* **one little duck** = **2; dearie me!** = **3; knock at the door** = **4; Jack's alive** = **5; Tom Mix** = **6; lucky seven**

---

* L'astérisque indique que le mot marqué de ce signe figure comme entrée dans le Répertoire.

= 7; one fat lady = 8; doctor's orders = 9; Downing Street = 10; legs eleven = 11; one doz. = 12; unlucky for some = 13; she's lovely or never been kissed = 16; the age to catch 'em = 17; key of the door or my age? = 21; all the twos or dinky-doo or two little ducks or toodle-oo = 22; bed and breakfast or half-a-crown = 26; you're doing fine = 29; all the threes or feathers = 33; dirty whore = 34; all the steps = 39; life begins = 40; life's begun = 41; all the fours or droopy-drawers or open the door = 44; half-way = 45; bullseye or bung-hole = 50; all the varieties or Heinz = 57; Brighton line = 59; old-age pension = 65; clickety-click = 66; any way round = 69; was she worth it? = 76; crutches or sunset strip or walking-sticks = 77; two fat ladies = 88; all but one or nearly there or spot below = 89; top of the shop or as far as we go = 90; bingo! jeu! gagné!

bint [bint] (*noun*), *P:* 1. femme*, gonzesse *f.* 2. petite amie, poule *f.*

bird [bə:d] (*noun*). 1. *F:* individu*, type *m*, oiseau *m*, moineau *m*; who's that old b.? qu'est-ce que c'est que ce vieux type? 2. *F:* (*a*) fille*, gamine *f*; (*b*) petite amie, poule *f*, souris *f*; (*c*) pépée *f.* 3. *F:* to get the b., se faire siffler. 4. *F:* to give s.o. the b., (*a*) envoyer promener qn, envoyer qn au bain (*ou* sur les roses); (*b*) (*th.*) huer qn, siffler qn. 5. *P:* to do b., faire de la prison*, faire du trou (*ou* de la taule); first b., première fois en prison*. 6. *F:* it's (strictly) for the birds, c'est seulement pour les cruches, c'est de la roupie de sansonnet. 7. *F:* the birds and the bees, éléments sexuels de base, l'histoire *f* du chou. 8. *P:* red birds = reds (red[2], 5). *Voir aussi* dicky-bird; dolly-bird; early; feather[1], 1; gallows-bird; home-bird; jail-bird; jay-bird; lovebird; night-bird; snowbird; whirly-bird; yardbird.

bird-brain [bə:dbrein] (*noun*), *F:* 1. individu bête*, crâne *m* de piaf. 2. = scatterbrain.

bird-brained [bə:dbreind] (*adj.*), *F:* 1. bête*. 2. = scatterbrained.

bird-cage [bə:dkeidʒ] (*noun*), *P:* 1. cellule *f* de prison*, cellote *f.* 2. dortoir *m* dans un asile de nuit.

bird-fancier [bə:dfænsiər] (*noun*), *P:* juponnard *m*, coureur *m* de filles, dragueur *m* de mines.

birdie [bə:di] (*adj.*), *P:* fou*, dingue, givré.

birdie-powder [bə:di-paudər] (*noun*), *P:* mélange *m* d'héroïne et de morphine (*drogues**).

bird-lime [bə:dlaim] (*noun*) (*R.S.* = *time*), *P:* 1. how's the b.-l.? quelle heure est-il? 2. = bird, 5.

birdlimed [bə:dlaimd] (*adj. & p.p.*) (*Austr.*), *P:* condamné pour le crime d'un autre, gerbé sans fleurs.

bird's-eye [bə:dzai] (*noun*), *P:* 1. dix grammes de drogue. 2. chiffe *f* de came.

bird-watcher [bə:dwɔtʃər] (*noun*), *P:* = bird-fancier.

bird-wood [bə:dwud] (*noun*), *P:* cigarettes* de marijuana (*drogues**).

birk [bə:k] (*noun*), *P:* = berk.

birthday [bə:θdei] (*noun*), *F:* 1. to be in one's b. suit (*U.S.:* clothes), être nu*, être à poil, être en Jésus. 2. (*sports*) to have a b., avoir un bon match, avoir un jour de fête.

biscuit [biskit] (*noun*), *F:* to take the b., avoir le pompon; you take the b., à toi le pompon.

biscus [biskəs] (*noun*) (*Austr.*), *P:* in the b., dans le pétrin, dans de mauvais draps.

bish[1] [biʃ] (*noun*), *F:* bévue*, bourde *f*, gaffe *f.*

bish[2] [biʃ] (to), *F:* gaffer, faire une bourde.

bishop [biʃəp] (*noun*), *V:* to flog (*or* bash) the b., se masturber*, se secouer le bonhomme. *Voir aussi* actress.

bit[1] [bit] (*adj.*), *F:* (*th.*) a b. part, un rôle secondaire, une panne; a b. player, un figurant.

bit[2] [bit] (*noun*). 1. *P:* a nice b. of stuff (*or* crackling *or* fluff *or* skirt), un beau petit lot, un prix de Diane. 2. *F:* a b. much, (*a*) un peu cher*; (*b*) un peu exagéré, dépassant la dose; it was all a b. of a laugh really, c'était plutôt une rigolade; he's a b. of a liar, il est menteur sur les bords. 3. (*U.S.*) *F:* two bits, pièce *f* de 25 cents; *voir aussi* two-bit. 4. (*U.S.*) *P:* condamnation* à la prison, purge *f.* 5. *F:* to do a b. of fishing, taquiner le goujon (*ou* l'ablette *f*); a b. of news, une nouvelle. 6. *P:* activité *f,* ligne *f* de conduite. **7.** *F:* **to be thrilled to bits**, être ravi (*ou* rayonnant); exulter. *Voir aussi* **side, 1, 2; spare**[2]; **stray; threepenny-bits; trey-bits.**

bitch[1] [bitʃ] (*noun*), *P:* **1.** femme* (*péj.*), salope *f*, ordure *f*, chameau *m*, chipie *f*. **2.** pédéraste* cancanier. **3.** plainte *f*, rouspétance *f*. **4.** tâche *f ou* chose *f* désagréable, saloperie *f*. **5.** **to be (as) drunk as a fiddler's bitch**, être saoul comme une bourrique. *Voir aussi* **s.o.b., 2; son-of-a-bitch.**

bitch[2] [bitʃ] (**to**), *P:* **1.** grogner*, rouspéter, bougonner, râler. **2.** tromper*, entuber, rouler (qn); **to b. s.o. out of** **sth.**, roustir qn à propos de qch. **3.** = **bitch up (to).**

bitchiness [ˈbitʃinis] (*noun*), *P:* méchanceté *f*, saloperie *f*, coup *m* en vache.

bitch up [ˈbitʃˈʌp] (**to**), *P:* saboter, bousiller (qch.).

bitchy [ˈbitʃi] (*adj.*), *P:* moche, rosse, vache.

bite[1] [bait] (*noun*). **1.** *P:* **to put the b. on s.o.**, (*a*) emprunter* à qn; (*b*) faire chanter qn. **2.** *F:* **to have a b. to eat**, manger* un morceau, casser la croûte. *Voir aussi* **cherry, 2; fleabite.**

bite[2] [bait] (**to**). **1.** *F:* (*fig.*) se faire avoir, mordre à l'hameçon. **2.** *F:* **I've been badly bitten** (*fig.*), (*a*) j'ai été roulé; (*b*) on m'a mis dedans. **3.** *F:* **what's biting you?** quelle mouche te pique? qu'est-ce qui te prend? **4.** *P:* **to b. s.o. for money**, taper qn. *Voir aussi* **dust**[1], **4.**

bite off [ˈbaitˈɔf] (**to**), *F:* **1. to b. s.o.'s head o.**, injurier* qn, rembarrer qn. **2. to b.o. more than one can chew**, avoir les yeux plus grands que le ventre.

bitsy-witsy [ˈbitsiˈwitsi] (*noun*), *F:* **a b.-w.**, un peu*, un chouia.

bitter-ender [ˈbitərˈendər] (*noun*), *F:* jusqu'auboutiste *mf*; *cf.* **end, 3.**

bitty [ˈbiti] (*adj.*), *F:* (livre, pièce, *etc.*) décousu, hétéroclite, de bric et de broc.

bivvy [ˈbivi] (*noun*), *P:* **1.** bière *f*; *cf.* **bevvy. 2. to have a b.**, tailler une bavette, faire un brin de causette.

biz [biz] (*noun*), *P:* **the b.** (=*the business*), le bis(e)ness, le truc. *Voir aussi* **showbiz.**

blab (off) [ˈblæb(ˈɔf)] (**to**), *P:* **1.** révéler un secret, lâcher le morceau. **2.** bavarder*, jacter, papoter.

black[1] [blæk] (*adj.*). **1.** *F:* **a b. mark**, un mauvais point. **2. b. spot**, (*a*) *F:* endroit dangereux; (*b*) *P:* fumerie *f* d'opium. **3.** *P:* **b. stuff**, opium *m* (*drogues**), noir *m*. **4.** *P:* **b. and white**, amphétamine *f* (*drogues**), durophet *m*, bonbon *m*; *voir aussi* **bomber** (*a*); **minstrel. 5. b. and tan**, (*a*) *F:* panaché *m* de bière brune et blonde; (*b*) *P:* amphétamine *f* (*drogues**), rouquine *f*; (*c*) *F:* **B. and Tans**, milice chargée de l'ordre en Irlande (*c.* 1920). **6.** *F:* **B. Maria**, car* de police, panier *m* à salade, poulailler ambulant. **7.** *F:* **b. diamonds**, (*a*) charbon *m*; (*b*) truffes *f.pl. Voir aussi* **book**[1], **2; dog**[1], **19; velvet, 2.**

black[2] [blæk] (*noun*). **1.** *F:* nègre*, bougnoul *m*. **2.** *F:* **to put up a b.**, faire une gaffe. **3.** *P:* chantage *m*; **to put the b. on s.o.**, faire du chantage. **4.** *F:* **in the b.**, à l'actif *m* de qn. **5.** *F:* **in b. and white**, en noir et blanc.

black[3] [blæk] (**to**), *F:* = **blacklist (to).**

blackbirding [ˈblækbəːdiŋ] (*noun*), *P:* trafic *m* d'esclaves noirs.

blackbirds [ˈblækbəːdz] (*pl. noun*), *P:* esclaves noirs.

blackie [ˈblæki] (*noun*), *P:* = **black**[2], **3.**

blackleg[1] [ˈblækleg] (*noun*), *F:* briseur *m* de grèves, renard *m*, jaune *m*, traître *m*.

blackleg[2] [ˈblækleg] (**to**), *F:* faire le briseur de grèves.

blacklist [ˈblæklist] (**to**), *F:* mettre sur la liste noire.

black-out [ˈblækaut] (*noun*), *F:* **1.** évanouissement *m*. **2.** (*a*) panne *f* d'électricité; (*b*) camouflage *m* des lumières.

black out [ˈblækˈaut] (**to**), *F:* **1.** s'évanouir*, tomber dans le cirage. **2.** être en panne d'électricité, se trouver dans le noir.

blag [blæg] (**to**), *P:* voler*, chiper, chaparder.

blah(-blah) [ˈblɑː(ˈblɑː)] (*noun*), *F:* bla-bla(-bla) *m*, baratin *m*.

blank [blæŋk] (*noun*), *F:* **to draw a b.**, faire chou blanc.

blankety(-blank) [ˈblæŋkiti(ˈblæŋk)] (*adj. & noun*), *F:* euph. *pour* **damn(ed), bloody,** *etc.*

blank out [ˈblæŋkˈaut] (**to**), *F:* = **black out (to), 1.**

* L'astérisque indique que le mot marqué de ce signe figure comme entrée dans le Répertoire.

blarney[1] [ˈblɑːni] (*noun*), *F:* flatterie *f*, cajolerie *f*, boniment *m*.
blarney[2] [ˈblɑːni] (to). **1.** *F:* flatter*, cajoler, bonimenter. **2.** (*U.S.*) *P:* crocheter une serrure.
blast[1] [blɑːst] (*noun*), *P:* **1.** réjouissances*, boum *f*. **2.** = **bang**[3], **7. 3.** longue bouffée de cigarette* de marijuana. **4.** effet puissant d'une drogue, flash *m*. **5.** attaque verbale, engueulade *f*, déblatérage *m*; **to put the b. on s.o.**, critiquer* qn, dénigrer, débiner qn.
blast[2] [blɑːst] (to), *P:* **1.** (*sports*) battre à plate(s) couture(s). **2.** avoir des injections de drogues, se piquouser; **to b. a joint** (*or* **a stick**), fumer la marijuana, tirer sur un stick. **3. b. (it)!** zut!; **b. you!** va au diable!; **damn and b.!** bordel de Dieu!
blasted [ˈblɑːstid] (*adj.*), *P:* **1.** = damned. **2.** drogué*, chargé, envapé.
blasting [ˈblɑːstiŋ] (*noun*), *P:* **to give s.o. a b.**, réprimander* qn, passer une bonne engueulade à qn.
blast off [ˈblɑːstˈɔf] (to), *P:* **1.** s'enfuir*, décamper, mettre les bouts. **2. to b.o. at s.o.**, donner le bal à qn.
blather[1] [ˈblæðər] (*noun*), *F:* bêtises*, fadaises *f.pl.*
blather[2] [ˈblæðər] (to), *F:* dire des bêtises*, dire des inepties *f.pl.*
blazes [ˈbleiziz] (*pl. noun*), *F:* **1. go to b.!** allez au diable! va te coucher! **2. what the b. . . .**, que diable. . . **3. to run like b.**, courir très vite*, comme si on avait le feu au derrière.
bleat [bliːt] (to), *P:* gémir, geindre, ronchonner.
bleeder [ˈbliːdər] (*noun*), *P:* **1. poor b.!** pauvre bougre! **2. wait till I catch the little b.!** le petit morveux ne perd rien pour attendre!
bleeding [ˈbliːdiŋ, ˈbliːdn] (*adj.*), *P:* = **bloody**[1,2].
bleep out [ˈbliːpˈaut] (to), *F:* **to b. sth. o.**, laisser échapper une bourde.
blessed [ˈblesid] (*adj.*), *F:* **what a b. nuisance!** quel fichu contretemps!; **that b. boy!** ce sacré gamin!; **the whole b. day**, toute la sainte journée.
blest [blest] (*p.p.*), *F:* **well I'm b.!** par exemple!; **I'm (**or** I'll be) b. if I know**, que le diable m'emporte si je le sais.
blether [ˈbleðər] (*noun & verb*) (*Scottish*), *F:* = **blather**[1,2].

blew [bluː] (to), *P:* = **blue**[3] (to).
blighter [ˈblaitər] (*noun*), *F:* individu*, type *m*, zèbre *m*; **poor b.!** pauvre hère! pauvre diable!; **you lucky b.!** veinard!; **you b.!** espèce de fripouille!
Blighty [ˈblaiti] (*noun*) (*mil.*), *F:* l'Angleterre *f*, retour *m* au foyer.
blimey! [ˈblaimi] (*excl.*), *P:* zut alors!; *cf.* **cor!** (*b*); **gorblimey!**
blimp [blimp] (*noun*) (*aussi:* **Colonel Blimp**), *F:* vieille culotte de peau.
blind[1] [blaind] (*adj.*). **1.** *F:* **b. date**, rendez-vous* (*ou* rancart *m*) fantôme (*ou* à l'aveuglette). **2.** *P:* = **blinders**. *Voir aussi* **eye**, **13**.
blind[2] [blaind] (*noun*). **1.** *F:* couverture*, couverte *f*, couvrante *f*. **2.** *P:* = **blinder**, **2. 3.** *P:* **to put the blinds on s.o.**, mettre un bandeau sur les yeux de qn.
blind[3] [blaind] (to), *P:* **1.** jurer, sacrer. **2.** conduire avec insouciance; **b. and brake driver**, chauffard *m*.
blinder [ˈblaindər] (*noun*), *P:* **1.** jeu époustouflant. **2.** réjouissances*, bamboche *f*.
blinders [ˈblaindəz] (*adj.*), *P:* (**Harry**) **b.**, complètement ivre*, rétamé, blindé.
blink [bliŋk] (*noun*), *F:* **on the b.**, qui ne marche pas, qui foire, qui fait des siennes; **my phone is on the b.**, mon téléphone débloque.
blinkers [ˈbliŋkəz] (*pl. noun*), *F:* yeux *m.pl.* (*œil**), quinquets *m.pl.*
blinking [ˈbliŋkiŋ] (*adj.*), *F:* *euph. pour* **bloody**[1,2].
blister [ˈblistər] (*noun*), *P:* **1.** sommation *f*, faf(f)iot *m* à promont. **2.** prostituée*, pute *f*. *Voir aussi* **skin**[1], **11**.
blithering [ˈbliðəriŋ] (*adj.*), *F:* **b. idiot**, bougre *m* d'idiot, connard *m*.
blob [blɔb] (*noun*), *F:* zéro *m*; **to score a b.**, ne pas marquer de points.
block [blɔk] (*noun*), *P:* **1.** tête*, caboche *f*; **to knock s.o.'s b. off**, battre* qn, rentrer dans le chou (*ou* dans le lard) à qn. **2. to do one's b.**, se mettre en colère*, se mettre en rogne. **3.** (*a*) cornet *m* de morphine; (*b*) boulette *f* de hachisch (*drogues**). **4. to put the blocks on**, serrer la vis. **5. to put the b. on sth.**, mettre un frein à qch. *Voir aussi* **chip**[1], **6**.
blockbuster [ˈblɔkbʌstər] (*noun*), *P:* **1.** bombe très puissante, marmite *f*. **2.** coup *m* de poing très puissant, direct

m. 3. réussite *f* fantastique, coup *m* de Trafalgar.

blocked [blɔkt] (*adj.*), *P:* drogué*, chargé.

bloke [blouk] (*noun*), 1. *F:* individu*; **a good b.**, un brave type, un bon zigue. 2. *F:* **the B.**, (*Marine*) le Patron. 3. *P:* **big b.**, cocaïne *f* (*drogues**).

blood [blʌd] (*noun*). 1. *F:* **to be after s.o.'s b.**, vouloir la peau de qn. 2. *F:* **to get s.o.'s b. up**, mettre qn en colère*, faire fulminer qn. 3. *F:* **to have one's b. up**, être en colère*, voir rouge. 4. *F:* **to make s.o.'s b. run cold**, glacer le sang à qn. 5. *F:* **it makes my b. boil**, ça me fait voir rouge. 6. **to sweat b.**, suer sang et eau, travailler* dur, bûcher, turbiner. 7. *P:* = **soul-brother.** *Voir aussi* **Nelson.**

bloody[1] [ˈblʌdi] (*adj.*), *P:* sacré, satané, fichu, foutu; **you b. fool!** bougre *m* d'idiot! bon sang d'imbécile!; **to play the b. fool**, faire le con; **stop that b. row!** assez de chahut!; **they're all the b. same**, c'est du pareil au même; **the b. limit**, la fin des haricots. *Voir aussi* **Mary, 4.**

bloody[2] [ˈblʌdi] (*adv.*), *P:* vachement, bougrement; **How do you feel? – B!** Comment ça va? – Vachement mal!; **not b. likely!** pas de danger! non mais chez qui!; **it's b. hot!** qu'est-ce qu'il fait chaud!

bloody-minded [ˈblʌdimaindid] (*adj.*), *P:* pas commode; **a b.-m. fellow**, un mauvais coucheur.

bloody-mindedness [ˈblʌdiˈmaindid- nis] (*noun*), *P:* sale caractère *m*, caractère de cochon, disposition *f* peu commode.

bloomer [ˈbluːmər] (*noun*), *F:* bévue*, gaffe *f*, bourde *f*.

blooming [ˈbluːmiŋ, ˈbləmin] (*adj. & adv.*), *F: euph. pour* **bloody**[1,2].

blot out [ˈblɔtˈaut] (to), *P:* tuer*, effacer, dézinguer (qn).

blotto [ˈblɔtou] (*adj.*), *F:* complètement ivre*, rétamé, noir.

blow [blou] (to). 1. *F: euph. pour* **blast**[2] (to), 3; **b. the expense!** je me moque de la dépense!; **b. me!** zut alors!; **well I'm blowed!** j'en bave! j'en reste comme deux ronds de flan!; *cf.* **blest.** 2. *F:* **generous be blowed, he's as mean as they come**, généreux? mon œil! il est

radin comme tout. 3. *P:* = **buzz off** (to). 4. *P:* (s)chnouffer, prendre une reniflette; **to b. hay** (*or* **a stick**), fumer de la marijuana, tirer sur un stick. 5. *F:* **to b. one's own trumpet** (*U.S.:* **horn**), se vanter, se faire mousser, s'envoyer des fleurs. 6. *P:* (*a*) dénoncer*, balanstiquer (qn); (*b*) révéler un secret, éventer la mèche. 7. *P:* exposer publiquement un scandale, lâcher les grandes orgues. 8. *V:* faire un coït* buccal à (qn), sucer, pomper. 9. *P:* bousiller, saboter, louper; **we should have won but we blew it**, on aurait dû gagner mais on a tout loupé; **to b. a chance**, louper l'occasion. 10. *P:* = **blue**[3] (to). 11. *P:* se masturber*, se faire mousser. 12. *P:* **to b. down s.o.'s ear**, donner un tuyau à qn. 13. *P:* **blown pack**, paquet *m* de cigarettes vide. 14. *F:* **to b. hot and cold**, souffler le chaud et le froid, n'être ni chair ni poisson. 15. *P:* **to b. one's mind**, (*a*) = **to blow one's top** (**top**[1], 2); *cf.* **cool**[3], 2; **fuse; gasket;** (*b*) être profondément ému; **b. your mind!** branche-toi!; (*c*) s'effondrer sous l'émotion. *Voir aussi* **gaff, 3; lid, 2; stack, 2; tank, 1.**

blowens [ˈblouənz] (*noun*), *P:* = **bob- tail.**

blower [ˈblouər] (*noun*), *P:* téléphone*, ronfleur *m*, tube *m*; **to get on the b. to s.o.**, passer un coup de fil à qn. *Voir aussi* **mind-blower.**

blow in [ˈblouˈin] (to), *P:* 1. = **blue**[3] (to), 1, 2. 2. arriver* en coup de vent, s'amener à l'improviste.

blow-job [ˈblouˈdʒɔb] (*noun*), *V:* coït* buccal, taillage *m* de plume.

blow off [ˈblouˈɔf] (to), *P:* 1. péter*, cloquer. 2. **to b. one's mouth o.**, parler* trop, dégoiser, dévider. *Voir aussi* **steam, 1.**

blow-out [ˈblouˈaut] (*noun*), *F:* 1. gueuleton *m*, ripaille *f*; **to have a good b.-o.**, manger* abondamment, se taper la cloche, s'en mettre plein la fusil. 2. éclatement *m* de pneu. 3. (*électricité*) **there's been a b.-o.**, les plombs *m.pl.* ont sauté.

blow out [ˈblouˈaut] (to), *P:* rejeter, envoyer paître (qn).

blow over [ˈblouˈouvər] (to), *F:* se passer, se dissiper.

blow-through [ˈblouθruː] (*noun*), *V:*

---

* L'astérisque indique que le mot marqué de ce signe figure comme entrée dans le Répertoire.

to have a b.-t., coïter*, foutre un coup de brosse.

blow-up [ˈblou-ʌp] (*noun*), *F:* **1.** (accès *m* de) colère*. **2.** agrandissement *m* de photo.

blow up [ˈblouˈʌp] (to), *F:* **1.** se mettre en colère*, exploser. **2.** réprimander*, sonner les cloches à (qn). **3.** agrandir (une photographie), faire un agrandissement. **4.** survenir, arriver.

blub [blʌb] (to), *F:* pleurer*, chialer, pleurnicher.

blubberhead [ˈblʌbəhed] (*noun*), *F:* individu bête*, baluchard *m*, gourde *f.*

bludge¹ [blʌdʒ] (*noun*) (*Austr.*), *P:* **to have a b.**, (*a*) se reposer, tirer sa flemme; (*b*) travailler lentement, flânocher.

biudge² [blʌdʒ] (to) (*Austr.*), *P:* flâner, fainéanter, traîner, battre l'asphalte, flemmarder.

bludger [ˈblʌdʒər] (*noun*) (*Austr.*), *P:* **1.** fainéant *m*, flemmard *m*, batteur *m* de pavé. **2.** souteneur*, mangeur *m* de brioche. **3.** agent* de police, cogne *m*, flic *m*.

blue¹ [bluː] (*adj.*). **1.** *F:* (*a*) sale*, osé, cochon; (*b*) **b.** film (*or* movie), film bleu. **2.** *F:* **to scream** (*or* yell) **b.** murder, crier* (*ou* gueuler) au charron. **3.** *F:* **once in a b. moon**, la semaine des quatre jeudis; tous les 36 du mois. **4.** *F:* mélancolique, triste, cafardeux; *cf.* devil¹, 23. **5.** *P:* **b. ruin**, alcool*, tord-boyaux *m.* **6.** *F:* **true b.**, (*en politique*) Conservateur, de la droite. *Voir aussi* funk¹, 1; velvet, 1.

blue² [bluː] (*noun*). **1.** *P:* (*drogues*) la bleue; **double b.**, mélange *m* d'amphétamine et de barbiturique; **French b.**, cachet *m* d'amphétamine et de barbiturique; bleuet *m*, bleuette *f*; (*pl.*) bleues *f.pl.*; préparation artisanale d'amphétamines; **heavenly blues**, graines *f.pl.* de volubilis (employées comme drogues); *cf.* pearly gates. **2.** *F:* **to turn up out of the b.**, arriver* à l'improviste, venir comme un cheveu sur la soupe. **3.** *F:* **to have the blues**, avoir le cafard, broyer du noir. **4.** *P:* = bluebottle. **5.** (*pl.*) *F:* chant *m* populaire négro-américain; **country blues**, forme primitive du blues, blues rural. **6.** (*Austr.*) *P:* une perte, qch. de paumé.

blue³ [bluː] (to), *P:* **1. to b. one's money**, dépenser*, bouffer son argent. **2.** he

blued his lot, il a tout paumé, il a mangé la ferme.

blue-arsed [ˈbluːˈɑːst] (*adj.*), *P:* **to rush around like a b.-a. fly**, se manier le popotin.

bluebottle [ˈbluːbɔtl] (*noun*), *P:* agent* de police, flic *m*, poulet *m.*

blue-eyed [ˈbluːaid] (*adj.*), *F:* innocent, candide; **to be s.o.'s b.-e. boy**, être le chouchou (*ou* le favori) de qn.

bluenose [ˈbluː-nouz], **bluenoser** [ˈbluː-nouzər] (*noun*), *F:* **1.** (*U.S.*) habitant *m* de l'est des États-Unis. **2.** (*Canada*) habitant *m* de la Nouvelle-Écosse.

bluey [ˈbluːi] (*noun*), *P:* = French blue (blue², 1).

b.o., **B.O.** [ˈbiːˈou] (*abbr.* = *body odour*), *F:* odeur corporelle.

bo [bou] (*noun*) (*U.S.*), *F:* **1.** clochard*, chemineau *m*, clodot *m.* **2.** jeune garçon, gosse *m.* **3.** homme*, camarade *m*, Jules.

boat [bout] (*noun*). **1.** *F:* **to push the b. out**, (*a*) payer* une tournée; (*b*) partir* en virée. **2.** *F:* **to miss the b.**, passer à côté, manquer le coche. **3.** *F:* **to be in the same b.**, être sur le même bateau, être logé(s) à la même enseigne, être du même convoi. **4.** (*pl.*) *F:* grandes chaussures*, bateaux *m.pl.* **5.** *P:* (*R.S.* = *boat-race* = *face*) visage*. **6.** *P:* **the (little) man in the b.**, clitoris*, bouton *m* (de rose), clicli *m. Voir aussi* dream-boat; gravy, 1; pig-boat; rock² (to), 2.

bob¹ [bɔb] (*noun*), *F:* cinq pence; **ten b.**, cinquante pence. *Voir aussi* fly-bob.

Bob² [bɔb] (*pr. noun*), *P:* **B.'s your uncle (and Fanny's your aunt)**, ça y est, ça roule, c'est dans le sac.

bobbish [ˈbɔbiʃ] (*adj.*), *F:* en forme.

bobby [ˈbɔbi] (*noun*), *F:* agent* de police, flic *m.*

bobby-dazzler [ˈbɔbi-dæzlər] (*noun*), *F:* **1.** qch. de voyant (*ou* de clinquant *ou* de tapageur). **2.** fille* tape-à-l'œil.

bobbysock [ˈbɔbisɔk] (*noun*), *F:* socquette *f.*

bobbysoxer [ˈbɔbisɔksər] (*noun*), *F:* fille* dans le vent, fille à l'âge ingrat.

bo-bo [ˈboubou] (*noun*), *P:* marijuana *f* (*drogues**), kif *m*; *cf.* bush, 3.

bobtail [ˈbɔbteil] (*noun*), *P:* femme* atteinte de maladie vénérienne (*malade**), nazicotée *f*, plombée *f*, pourrie *f.*

* An asterisk indicates that the word so marked is included as a head-word in the Appendix.

bob up [ˈbɔbˈʌp] (to), *F:* apparaître, émerger, surgir.
bod [bɔd] (*noun*), *F:* individu*; **an odd b.**, un drôle de type; **a few odd bods**, quatre pelés et un tondu.
bodge¹(-up) [ˈbɔdʒ(ʌp)] (*noun*), *F:* gâchis *m*, cafouillage *m*.
bodge²(up) [ˈbɔdʒ(ˈʌp)] (to), *F:* gâcher, cafouiller.
bodgie [ˈbɔdʒi] (*noun*) (*Austr.*), *P:* jeune voyou *m*.
bodywork [ˈbɔdiwɔːk] (*noun*), *P:* = **shelf-kit.**
boffin [ˈbɔfin] (*noun*), *F:* scientifique *m* qui fait de la recherche.
bog [bɔg] (*noun*), *P:* **1.** W.C.*, goguenots *m.pl.*, chiottes *f.pl.*; **to go to the b.**, aller chier. **2. to make a b. of sth.**, cafouiller qch., gâcher qch.; **what an awful b.!** quelle belle gaffe!
bogey, bogie [ˈbougi] (*noun*), *P:* **1.** policier* en civil, perdreau *m*. **2.** agent* de police, poulet *m*.
bogue [boug] (*adj.*), *P:* (*a*) en manque de drogues; (*b*) souffrant du sevrage de drogues.
bog-up [ˈbɔgʌp] (*noun*), *P:* = **bog, 2.**
bog up [ˈbɔgˈʌp] (to), *P:* = **bodge²(up)** (to).
bogy [ˈbougi] (*noun*), *P:* = **bogey, 1, 2.**
bohunk [ˈbouhʌŋk] (*noun*) (*U.S.*), *P:* **1.** immigrant *m* d'Europe centrale. **2.** individu bête* et gauche, empoté *m*, patate *f*.
boil¹ [bɔil] (*noun*), *F:* **to go off the b.**, perdre son enthousiasme, se dégonfler.
boil² [bɔil] (to), *P:* **go (and) b. your head!** va te faire voir! *Voir aussi* **blood, 5.**
boiled [bɔild] (*adj.*), *P:* ivre*, rétamé. *Voir aussi* **hard-boiled; shirt, 5.**
boiler [ˈbɔilər] (*noun*). **1.** *P:* vieille femme* (*péj.*), vieille poule, rombière *f*. **2.** *F:* poule *f* au pot. *Voir aussi* **potboiler.**
boiling [ˈbɔiliŋ] (*noun*), *P:* **the whole b.**, (*a*) toute la bande*; (*b*) tout le bazar, toute la ribambelle, tout le tremblement; *cf.* **caboodle; shebang, 1; shoot¹, 1; shooting-match.**
boilout [ˈbɔilaut] (*noun*), *P:* déchargeage *m* (cure de toxicomane).
boing! [bɔiŋ] (*excl.*), *F:* boum (badaboum)! pan! vlan!
boko [ˈboukou] (*noun*), *P:* grand nez*.

tarin *m*.
bollock [ˈbɔlək] (*noun & verb*), *V:* = **ballock** [1,2].
bollocking [ˈbɔləkiŋ] (*noun*), *V:* = **ballocking.**
bolon(e)y [bəˈlouni] (*noun*), *F:* = **balon(e)y.**
bolshie, bolshy¹ [ˈbɔlʃi] (*adj.*), *F:* **1.** bolcho, communo, communard. **2.** = **bloody-minded.**
bolshie, bolshy² [ˈbɔlʃi] (*noun*), *F:* = **commie** [2].
bomb [bɔm] (*noun*). **1.** *F:* **to cost a b.**, coûter cher*, coûter les yeux de la tête. **2.** *F:* **to make a b.**, gagner* beaucoup d'argent, faire du fric, tomber sur un champ d'oseille. **3.** *F:* **to go like a b.**, ronfler, gazer, boumer. **4.** (*U.S.*) *P:* échec*, fiasco *m*, four *m*. **5.** (*Austr.*) *F:* vieille voiture*, guimbarde *f*. *Voir aussi* **sex-bomb; stink-bomb.**
bombed (out) [ˈbɔmd(ˈaut)] (*adj.*), *P:* = **stoned** (*b*).
bomber [ˈbɔmər] (*noun*), *P:* (*a*) **black b.**, bonbon *m* (*drogues*); **brown b.** = **black and tan** (*b*) (*voir* **black¹, 5**); (*b*) cigarette* de marijuana (*drogues**), reefer *m*.
bombita [bɔmˈbiːtə], **bombito** [bɔmˈbiːtou] (*noun*), *P:* amphétamine *f* pour injection (*drogues**).
bombshell [ˈbɔmʃel] (*noun*), *F:* **1. a blonde b.**, une blonde, un coup de foudre. **2. the news was a b.**, la nouvelle tomba comme une bombe.
bonaroo [ˈbɔnəˈruː] (*adj.*) (*U.S.*), *P:* excellent*, foutral, du tonnerre, bolide.
bonce [bɔns] (*noun*), *P:* tête*, caboche *f*; **bacon b.**, une andouille.
bone¹ [boun] (*noun*). **1.** *F:* **to make no bones about sth.**, ne pas y aller par quatre chemins. **2.** *F:* **to pick a b. with s.o.**, chercher querelle* à qn, chercher noise (*ou* des noises) à qn; **to have a b. to pick with s.o.**, avoir maille à partir avec qn. **3.** *F:* **to have a b. in one's leg**, avoir la cosse. **4.** *V:* **to have a b.**, être en érection*, bander. **5.** (*pl.*) *F:* dés*; **to roll the bones**, pousser les bobs *m.pl.* **6.** *P:* **pick the bones out of that!** va en tirer quelque chose! extirpe ce que tu peux! *Voir aussi* **dry, 1; marrow-bones; sawbones.**
bone² [boun] (to), *P:* **1.** voler*, chiper. **2.** (*U.S.*) ennuyer*, barber, canuler

(qn). **3. to b.** (**up on**) a subject, piocher (*ou* potasser *ou* bûcher) un sujet. **4.** interroger (un suspect), cuisiner.

bonehead [ˈboʊnhed] (*noun*), *F:* ignorant *m*, tête *f* de bois, bûche *f*.

bone-on [ˈboʊnɔn] (*noun*), *V:* = **hard-on**; *cf.* **bone**[1], 4.

bone-orchard [ˈboʊn-ɔːtʃəd], **bone-park** [ˈboʊnpɑːk] (*noun*), *P:* cimetière* parc *m* des cronis *m.pl.*

boner [ˈboʊnər] (*noun*). **1.** *F:* bévue*, bourde *f*, gaffe *f*. **2.** *V:* = **bone**[1], 4.

bone-rattler [ˈboʊnrætlər], **bone-shaker** [ˈboʊnʃeikər] (*noun*), *F:* vieille voiture*, tape-cul *m*.

bone-yard [ˈboʊnjɑːd] (*noun*), *P:* = **bone-orchard**.

bonk[1] [bɔŋk] (*noun*), *F:* coup*, gnon *m*.

bonk[2] [bɔŋk] (**to**), *F:* **to b. s.o. on the head**, donner un coup* (*ou* un gnon) sur le crâne de qn, assommer qn.

bonkers [ˈbɔŋkəz] (*adj.*), *P:* **stark raving** (*or* **staring**) **b.**, Harry **b.**, fou* à lier, archifou.

bonzer [ˈbɔnzər] (*adj.*) (*Austr.*), *F:* excellent*, sensas(s), super.

boo [buː] (*noun*), *P:* marijuana *f* (*drogues**), kif *m*.

boob[1] [buːb] (*noun*). **1.** *F:* (*a*) individu bête*, ballot *m*; (*b*) individu crédule, gogo *m*, nave *m*, gobe-mouches *m*. **2.** *F:* bévue*, gaffe *f*, boulette *f*. **3.** (*pl.*) *P:* = **boobies** (**booby**, 2).

boob[2] [buːb] (**to**), *F:* faire une bévue* (*ou* une gaffe *ou* une boulette).

booboo [ˈbuːbuː] (*noun*). **1.** *F:* = **boob**[1], **2.** *2.* (*pl.*) *P:* testicules*, clopinettes *f.pl.*

booby [ˈbuːbi] (*noun*). **1.** *F:* = **boob**[1], **1.** *2.* (*pl.*) *P:* seins*, doudounes *f.pl.*

booby-hatch [ˈbuːbihætʃ] (*noun*), *P:* maison *f* de fous, cabanon *m*.

boodle [ˈbuːdl] (*noun*), *P:* butin*, fade *m*, taf(fe) *m*.

boodler [ˈbuːdlər] (*noun*) (*Austr.*), *P:* homme (politique) qui se pousse, arriviste *m*.

boofhead [ˈbuːfhed] (*noun*) (*Austr.*), *F:* individu bête*.

boogie [ˈbuːgi] (*noun*) (*U.S.*) (*pej.*), *P:* nègre*, bougnoul(l)e *m*.

book[1] [bʊk] (*noun*), *F:* **1. to throw the b. at s.o.**, donner la peine maximum à qn, saper qn au maxi; **he got the b. thrown at him**, il a attrapé le maxi. **2. to be in**

s.o.'s good books, être dans les petits papiers de qn; **to be in s.o.'s bad** (*or* **black**) **books**, ne pas être en odeur de sainteté auprès de qn. **3. it suits my b.**, ça me va, ça me botte. **4. to make a b.**, organiser un sweepstake, *etc.* *Voir aussi* **cook**[2] (**to**), **2**; **turn-up**, **1**.

book[2] [bʊk] (**to**), *F:* **1. to b. s.o.**, (*a*) farguer qn; (*b*) mettre un P.V. (= procès-verbal) à qn. **2. to get booked**, (*a*) se faire farguer; (*b*) coller un biscuit; (*c*) (*sports*) recevoir un avertissement.

bookie [ˈbʊki] (*noun*), *F:* book *m*.

book in [ˈbʊkˈin] (**to**), *F:* s'inscrire à l'arrivée.

book out [ˈbʊkˈaʊt] (**to**), *F:* s'inscrire au départ.

booky [ˈbʊki] (*noun*), *F:* = **bookie**.

boong [bʊŋ] (*noun*) (*Austr.*), *F:* aborigène *mf.*

boost [buːst] (**to**), *P:* voler* à l'étalage (*ou* à la détourne).

booster [ˈbuːstər] (*noun*), *P:* **1.** fourgue *m*. **2.** voleur* à l'étalage (*ou* à la détourne), voleur* des grands magasins. **3. b.** (**pill**), cachet *m* d'amphétamine (*drogues**), survolteur *m*.

boot [buːt] (*noun*). **1.** *P:* **to give s.o. the** (**order of the**) **b.**, congédier* qn, mettre (*ou* flanquer) qn à la porte; **to get the b.**, être congédié*, se faire sa(c)quer. **2.** *P:* **an old b.**, femme* (*péj.*), une vieille bique. **3.** *P:* bang *m*. **4.** *P:* **to put the b. in**, donner (*ou* filer *ou* flanquer) un coup de pied vicieux; *cf.* **boot-boy**, **5**. *P:* **a boots and shoes**, un défoncé. **6.** *F:* **to be too big for one's boots**, péter plus haut que son derrière. **7.** *P:* **to splash one's boots**, uriner*, lancequiner. **8.** *P:* **a new set of boots**, quatre pneus de voiture neufs. **9.** *F:* **like old boots**, avec vigueur *f*, d'attaque. **10.** *F:* **to lick s.o.'s boots**, lécher les bottes *f.pl.* (*ou* les pieds *m.pl. ou* les genoux *m.pl.*) de qn; *cf.* **boot-licker**. *Voir aussi* **bet** (**to**), **5**; **bovver-boots**; **slyboots**.

boot-boy [ˈbuːtbɔi] (*noun*), *P:* jeune gouape *f* qui se bat à coups de chaussures.

bootleg [ˈbuːtleg] (**to**), *F:* faire la contre-bande de l'alcool *ou* des boissons alcooliques.

bootlegger [ˈbuːtlegər] (*noun*), *F:* contre-bandier *m* de boissons alcooliques.

---

* An asterisk indicates that the word so marked is included as a head-word in the Appendix.

bootlicker ['buːtlikər] (noun), F: lèche-bottes m, lèche-cul m.

boot out ['buːt'aut] (to), P: se débarrasser* de (qn), sacquer, vider, virer (qn).

booze[1] [buːz] (noun), P: alcool*, cric m; to be on the (or to hit the) b., boire* beaucoup, picoler, bit(t)urer.

booze[2] [buːz] (to), P: = to be on the booze.

boozed (up) ['buːzd('ʌp)] (adj.), P: ivre*, saoul.

boozer ['buːzər] (noun), P: 1. ivrogne*, poivrot m. 2. café*, bistrot m, troquet m.

booze-up ['buːzʌp] (noun), P: bringue f, bamboche f, bordée f.

boozing ['buːziŋ] (noun), P: ivresse*, soûlerie f, bit(t)ure f.

boozy ['buːzi] (adj.), P: ivrogne, soûlard, riboteur; a b. evening, un soir de nouba (ou de cuite).

bo-peep ['bou'piːp] (noun) (R.S. = sleep), P: dodo m.

boracic[1]]bə'ræsik, 'bræsik] (adj.) (R.S. = boracic lint = skint): voir skint.

boracic[2] [bə'ræsik, 'bræsik] (noun), P: = ackamaraka.

born [bɔːn] (p.p. & adj.), F: 1. never in all my b. days, au grand jamais. 2. I wasn't b. yesterday, je ne suis pas né d'hier, je ne suis pas tombé de la dernière pluie, je ne suis pas de la dernière couvée. Voir aussi one, 7.

borrow ['bɔrou] (to), F: to live on borrowed time, vivre sur le rabiot.

bosh [bɔʃ] (noun), F: bêtises*, boniments m.pl., sornettes f.pl.

boss[1] [bɔs] (adj.) (U.S.), P: = groovy.

boss[2] [bɔs] (noun), F: patron*, singe m, boss m.

boss[3] [bɔs] (to), P: 1. mener, diriger; to b. the show (or the outfit), contrôler, conduire, être le manitou de l'affaire, tenir la barre, faire marcher la machine, faire la pluie et le beau temps. 2. vouloir tout diriger, faire preuve d'autorité. 3. bâcler, saboter, louper.

boss about ['bɔsə'baut] (to), boss around ['bɔsə'raund] (to), F: to b. s.o. a., mener qn par le bout du nez, faire marcher qn.

boss-eyed ['bɔsaid] (adj.), P: qui louche,* qui boite des calots.

boss-man ['bɔsmæn] (noun), F: = boss[2].

bossy ['bɔsi] (adj.), P: autor(itaire); he's (too) b., c'est un Monsieur Jordonne.

bossy-boots ['bɔsi-buːts] (noun), F: individu* autoritaire, grand manitou.

bot [bɔt] (noun), F: = bottom[2], 1.

bottle[1] ['bɔtl] (noun), P: 1. to hit (or be on) the b., caresser la bouteille, pomper à la bouteille. 2. black b. = knockout drops (voir knockout[1], 1). Voir aussi bluebottle; milk-bottles; titty-bottle.

bottle[2] ['bɔtl] (to), P: taper (qn) à coups de bouteille.

bottled ['bɔtld] (adj.), P: ivre*, plein comme une bourrique.

bottle-holder ['bɔtlhouldər] (noun), P: assistant m d'un boxeur.

bottle-nose ['bɔtlnouz] (noun), P: nez* rouge, betterave f, pif communard.

bottler ['bɔtlər] (noun), P: = palm-tree; cf. square-wheeler.

bottle-washer ['bɔtlwɔʃər] (noun): voir cook[1], 2.

bottom[1] ['bɔtəm] (adj.), F: to bet one's b. dollar, risquer le paquet; voir aussi bet (to), 5.

bottom[2] ['bɔtəm] (noun), F: 1. fesses*, derrière m, dédé m. 2. bottoms up! videz vos verres! cul sec! à la pomponnette! Voir aussi bell-bottoms; heap, 2 (b); rock[1], 4; scrape[2] (to), 1.

botty ['bɔti] (noun), F: 1. = bottom[2], 1. 2. biberon m. Voir aussi smack-botty.

bounce [bauns] (to). 1. P: congédier*, flanquer (qn) à la porte (du cabaret, etc.), vider. 2. F: to b. a cheque, renvoyer un chèque sans provision (chèque en bois).

bouncer ['baunsər] (noun), P: 1. videur m. 2. chèque m en bois. 3. (pl.) seins*, globes m.pl., rotoplots m.pl.

bovver-boots ['bɔvə'buːts] (pl. noun), P: chaussures* des boot-boys.

bovver-boy ['bɔvəbɔi], bovvie ['bɔvi] (noun), P: = boot-boy.

bowler-hat[1] ['boulə'hæt] (noun), F: to give s.o. his b.-h. = to bowler-hat s.o.

bowler-hat[2] ['boulə'hæt] (to), P: renvoyer (qn) à la vie civile, limoger (qn).

bowl over ['boul'ouvər] (to), F: 1. épater, sidérer. 2. chambouler.

bowser ['bauzər] (noun) (Austr.), F: poste m d'essence.

bow-sow ['bausau] (noun), P: drogues*, stups m.pl.

bow-window ['bou'windou] (noun), F:

---

* L'astérisque indique que le mot marqué de ce signe figure comme entrée dans le Répertoire.

box   44   break

ventre* protubérant, bedaine *f*, brioche *f*.

box[1] [bɔks] (*noun*). **1.** *V:* vagin*, boîte *f* à ouvrage; **to go down for a b. lunch**, faire un coït* buccal. **2.** *F:* poste *m* de télé; **what's on the b.?** qu'est-ce qu'il y a à la télé?; *cf.* **goggle-box; idiot-box. 3.** *F:* barre *f* (de témoins). **4.** *F:* (*football*) zone *f* de pénalisation. **5.** *P:* cercueil*, boîte *f* à dominos; **to go home in a b.**, mourir*, partir les pieds en avant. **6.** *P:* coffre-fort *m*, coffiot *m*. **7.** *P:* **to make a b. of = box up** (to). *Voir aussi* **brain-box; domino-box; jack-in-the-box; saucebox; soapbox; squeezebox; think-box.**

box[2] [bɔks] (to), *F:* **to b. clever**, faire le malin, bien manœuvrer.

boxed [bɔkst] (*adj.*), *P:* **1.** (*a*) ivre*, rétamé à l'alcool; (*b*) drogué*, camé. **2.** emprisonné*, bloqué, bouclé, coffré.

box up [ˈbɔksˈʌp] (to), *F:* bousiller, gâcher, saboter, louper.

boy![1] [bɔi] (*excl.*), *F:* **1. oh b.! b. oh b.!** chouette alors! **2. b., did she tear me off a strip!** mes enfants! qu'est-ce qu'elle m'a passé!

boy[2] [bɔi] (*noun*), *F:* **hello, old b.!** salut, vieille branche (*ou* vieux pote)! *Voir aussi* **backroom; barrow, 2; bootboy; bovver-boy; bum-boy; cornerboy; doughboy; glamour-boy; jay-boy; J-boy; jewboy; job, 15; K-boy; loverboy; old-boy; playboy; sandboy; wide, 1.**

boyo [ˈbɔijou] (*noun*), *P:* fiston *m*, mon gars.

bra [brɑː] (*noun*) (*abbr.* = *brassière*), *F:* soutien(-gorge) *m*, soutien-loloches *m*.

bracelets [ˈbreislits] (*pl. noun*), *F:* menottes*, bracelets *m.pl.*, cadènes *f.pl.*

bracer [ˈbreisər] (*noun*), *F:* coup *m* de fouet; **to have an early-morning b.**, tuer le ver.

bracket [ˈbrækit] (*noun*), *P:* **to give s.o. a belt up the b.**, abîmer le portrait à qn. *Voir aussi* **upper**[1], **2.**

braille [breil] (*noun*), *P:* **a (bit of) b.**, renseignement*, rancard *m*, tuyau *m*.

brain[1] [brein] (*noun*), *F:* **1.** individu de grande intelligence, grosse tête. **2. to be the brains of the outfit**, être le ressort de la machine. **3. to have s.o., sth., on the b.**, être obsédé par qn, qch., l'avoir sur le ciboulot. *Voir aussi* **bird-brain; featherbrain; lame-brain; scatterbrain.**

brain[2] [brein] (to), *F:* battre*, rosser, assommer, bourrer de coups*.

brain-box [ˈbreinbɔks] (*noun*), *F:* crâne *m*; **to have a b.-b.**, en avoir dans le ciboulot.

brain-drain [ˈbreinˈdrein] (*noun*), *F:* fuite *f* (*ou* exode *m*) des cerveaux, émigration *f* des savants.

brain-storming [ˈbreinstɔːmiŋ] (*noun*), *F:* remue-méninges *m*.

brainy [ˈbreini] (*adj.*), *F:* intelligent, calé, débrouillard.

brass[1] [brɑːs] (*attrib. adj.*), *F:* **b. tacks**, faits *m.pl.*, réalités essentielles; **to get down to b. tacks**, se concentrer sur l'essentiel, s'en tenir aux faits. *Voir aussi* **balls, 8.**

brass[2] [brɑːs] (*noun*), **1.** *P:* argent*, pépettes *f.pl.*, pognon *m*. **2.** *P:* toupet *m*, culot *m*. **3.** *F:* **top b.**, (*mil.*) les galonnards *m.pl.* **4.** *P:* prostituée*, roulure *f*, tapin *f*; *cf.* **half-brass.**

brassed off [ˈbrɑːstˈɔf] (*adj.*), *P:* de mauvaise humeur, de mauvais poil.

brass-hat [ˈbrɑːsˈhæt] (*noun*) (*mil.*), *F:* galonné *m*, galonnard *m*.

brass up [ˈbrɑːsˈʌp] (to), *P:* payer*, abouler, casquer.

brassy [ˈbrɑːsi] (*adj.*), *P:* effronté, culotté.

bread [bred] (*noun*). **1.** *P:* (*a*) argent*, galette *f*, blé *m*; (*b*) salaire *m*, gages *m.pl.* **2.** *P:* **to be on the b. line**, claquer du bec, danser devant le buffet. **3.** *F:* **that's his b. and butter**, c'est son gagne-pain, c'est avec ça qu'il gagne sa croûte.

bread-and-butter [ˈbredən(d)ˈbʌtər] (*attrib. adj.*), *F:* **1. b.-a.-b. issues**, (*politique*) le prix du bifteck. **2. b.-a.-b. letter**, lettre *f* de remerciement (*ou* de château). *Voir aussi* **bread, 3.**

bread-basket [ˈbredbɑːskit] (*noun*), *F:* ventre*, bedaine *f*, brioche *f*; **to get one in the b.-b.**, recevoir un coup* dans le gésier.

break[1] [breik] (*noun*), *F:* **1. a lucky b.**, de la chance*, coup *m* de pot; *cf.* **tough**[1], **4. 2. to give s.o. a b.**, (*a*) mettre qn à l'essai, donner sa chance à qn; (*b*) tendre la perche à qn. **3.** récréation *f*; **a b. for lunch**, une pause pour le déjeuner. **4.** évasion *f* de prison*, décarrade *f*.

---

* An asterisk indicates that the word so marked is included as a head-word in the Appendix.

break² [breik] (to), *F:* to b. even, rentrer dans son argent* (*ou* sa galette), faire ses frais, retomber sur ses pattes. *Voir aussi* neck¹, 9.

breakfast [ˈbrekfəst] (*noun*), *V:* to have b. in bed, faire un coït* buccal. *Voir aussi* bingo (26); hell, 13.

break-in [ˈbreikin] (*noun*), *F:* cambriolage *m*, cambriole *f*, casse *m*, fric-frac *m*.

break-out [ˈbreikaut] (*noun*), *F:* = break¹, 4.

break up [breikˈʌp] (to), *F:* 1. b. it u.! arrêtez de vous battre! arrêtez de vous disputer! 2. that's right, b. u. the happy home!, *c.p.*, faites chauffer·la colle!

breather [ˈbriːðər] (*noun*), *F:* moment *m* de répit (*ou* de repos); to go out for a b., sortir prendre l'air.

breeches [ˈbritʃiz] (*pl. noun*), *F:* 1. to wear the b., porter la culotte. 2. to be too big for one's b. = to be too big for one's boots (boot, 6). *Voir aussi* fussy-breeches.

breeze¹ [briːz] (*noun*), *P:* 1. (*a*) to get the b. up, avoir peur*, avoir la trouille; (*b*) to put the b. up s.o., faire peur* à qn, ficher la frousse à qn. 2. there was a bit of a b. when he got home, il y a eu du grabuge (*ou* de la houle) quand il est rentré. 3. it was a b., c'était facile, c'était l'enfance de l'art. *Voir aussi* shoot² (to), 7.

breeze² [briːz] (to), *P:* = breeze off (to).

breeze in [ˈbriːzˈin] (to), *F:* 1. entrer en coup de vent. 2. gagner (une course) dans un fauteuil.

breeze off [ˈbriːzˈɔf] (to), *F:* partir*, se barrer, se débiner.

breezy [ˈbriːzi] (*adj.*), *F:* (all) bright and b., plein d'entrain (*ou* d'attaque).

brekker [ˈbrekər] (*noun*), *F:* (*langage enfantin*) petit déjeuner.

brick [brik] (*noun*), *F:* 1. he's been a (real) b., c'est le meilleur des potes. 2. to drop a b., faire une bévue*, lâcher le pavé dans la mare. *Voir aussi* come down (to), 3; drop² (to), 1; goldbrick¹; wall, 5, 6, 7.

bride [braid] (*noun*), *P:* 1. fille*, gamine *f*, môme *f*. 2. la petite amie, la nénette.

bridge [bridʒ] (*noun*) (*Austr.*), *P:* boniment *m* plausible, bonne excuse.

bridgewater [ˈbridʒwɔːtər] (*noun*) (*Austr.*), *P:* objet truqué, article falsifié.

Brighton line [ˈbraitnˈlain], *F:* voir bingo (59).

bring-down [ˈbriŋdaun] (*noun*), *P:* qn *ou* qch. qui a un effet déprimant, rabat-joie *m*.

bring down [ˈbriŋˈdaun] (to), *P:* déprimer, attrister, rendre cafardeux; he looked really brought down, il avait l'air d'avoir un cafard noir. *Voir aussi* brought down; house, 3.

bring up [ˈbriŋˈʌp] (to), *P:* = back up (to), 2.

brinkmanship [ˈbriŋkmənʃip] (*noun*), *F:* la politique du bord de l'abîme.

briny [ˈbraini] (*noun*), *F:* the b., l'océan *m*, la Grande Tasse, la Grande Baille.

bristlers [ˈbrisləz] (*pl. noun*), *P:* seins*, rondins *m.pl.*, nénés *m.pl.*

Bristol-fashion [ˈbristəl-fæʃən] (*adv.*), *F:* (ship-shape and) B.-f., parfait en tout, nec plus ultra, parfaitement comme il faut.

Bristols, bristols [ˈbristəlz] (*pl. noun*) (*R.S.* = *Bristol City's* = *titties*), *P:* (pair of) b., seins*, nichons *m.pl.*; *cf.* fit², 4; tale, 3; threepenny-bits; treybits.

broad [brɔːd] (*noun*), *P:* 1. (*U.S.*) (*a*) fille*, femme*, gonzesse *f*; (*b*) prostituée*, grue *f*. 2. (*pl.*) cartes* à jouer; to fake the broads, truquer les cartes, maquiller les brèmes.

broadsman [ˈbrɔːdzmən] (*pl.* broadsmen) (*noun*), *P:* tricheur* aux cartes, empalmeur *m*, biseauteur *m*.

brodie, brody [ˈbroudi] (*noun*) (*U.S.*), *P:* 1. échec*, four *m*, fiasco *m*; balourdise *f*, gaffe *f*. 2. to throw (*or* do) a b., tomber en digue-digue.

broke [brouk] (*adj.*), *F:* 1. to be b. (*or* stony b. *or* dead b. *or* flat b.), être pauvre*, être sans un (sou); to be b. to the wide, être fauché (comme les blés). 2. to go for b., risquer tout, risquer le paquet.

broker [ˈbroukər] (*noun*), *P:* trafiquant *m*, fourgue *m*.

brolly [ˈbrɔli] (*noun*), *F:* 1. parapluie*, pépin *m*, riflard *m*. 2. parachute *m*, pépin *m*.

bronco [ˈbrɔŋkou] (*noun*) (*U.S.*), *F:* cheval non dressé.

bronco-buster [ˈbrɔŋkou-bʌstər] (*noun*) (*U.S.*), *F:* cowboy qui dresse les chevaux.

broth [brɔθ] (noun), F: a b. of a boy, (irlandais) un rude gars, un fameux gaillard.

brought down [ˈbrɔːtˈdaun] (p.p. & adj.), P: déprimé après le flash des drogues. Voir aussi bring down (to).

brown [braun] (adj.), P: to be done b., se faire entuber, être chocolat; b. job, coït anal, baisage m à la riche.

brown-hatter [ˈbraunˈhætər] (noun), V: pédéraste*, tante f, tantouse f.

brown-nose [ˈbraun-nouz] (to), V: lécher le cul à (qn).

brown off [ˈbraunˈɔf] (to), P: décourager (qn); to be browned off, avoir le cafard, broyer du noir.

bruiser [ˈbruːzər] (noun), F: pugiliste m, boxeur m, cogneur m.

Brum [brʌm] (pr. noun), F: (habitant m de) Birmingham.

brumby [ˈbrʌmbi] (noun) (Austr.), F: = bronco.

brunch [brʌntʃ] (noun), F: petit déjeuner et déjeuner ensemble.

brush [brʌʃ] (noun). 1. P: = brush-off, 1. 2. (Austr.) P: fille*, jeune femme*, mistonne f. 3. F: moustache*, balai m. 4. V: pubis féminin, barbu m. Voir aussi tar 2 (to); tar-brush.

brush-off [ˈbrʌʃɔf] (noun), F: 1. rebuffade f, soufflet m; to give s.o. the b.-o. = to brush s.o. off (brush off (to), (a), (b)). 2. coup m de balai.

brush off [ˈbrʌʃˈɔf] (to), F: to b. s.o. o., (a) snob(b)er qn, faire un affront à qn; (b) se débarrasser* de qn, laisser choir qn, larguer qn.

bubbies [ˈbʌbiz] (pl. noun), P: seins*, nichons m.pl.

bubble [ˈbʌbl] (to), P: =squeak2 (to).

bubble-and-squeak [ˈbʌblən(d)ˈskwiːk] (noun). 1. F: mauvaise nourriture*, réchauffé m. 2. P: (R.S. = Greek) un Grec. 3. P: (R.S. = beak = magistrate): voir beak, 1.

bubbly [ˈbʌbli] (noun), F: (vin m de) champagne m, champ(e) m, roteuse f; cf. champers.

bubbly-jock [ˈbʌbli-dʒɔk] (noun), F: dindon m.

bubs [bʌbz] (pl. noun), P: = bubbies.

buck1 [bʌk] (noun). 1. P: old b., (a) vieux birbe; (b) insolence f. 2. (U.S.) F: dollar m; fast b., argent* obtenu rapidement, facilement et sans scrupule,

fric m de tripotage. 3. F: to pass the b., faire porter le chapeau.

buck2 [bʌk] (to), F: to b. (against), résister (à), s'opposer (à); ruer dans les brancards.

bucked [bʌkt] (adj.), F: ragaillardi, content; enchanté, fier.

buckaroo, bucker (oo) [ˈbʌkər(ˈuː)] (noun) (U.S.), F: cowboy m.

bucket [ˈbʌkit] (noun), F: 1. to kick the b., mourir*, lâcher la rampe, casser sa pipe. 2. it's raining buckets, il pleut à seaux (ou à torrents).

bucket down [ˈbʌkitdaun] (to), F: it's bucketing down = it's raining buckets (bucket, 2).

buckle [ˈbʌkl] (to), P: 1. b. my shoe: voir bingo (2). 2. (Austr.) arrêter*, ceinturer, cravater.

bucko [ˈbʌkou] (adj.), P: (a) vantard, bravache, fanfaron; (b) crâneur, crosson.

buckshee1 [ˈbʌkˈʃiː] (adj.), F: gratuit*, gratis, à l'œil.

buckshee2 [ˈbʌkˈʃiː] (noun), F: 1. rabiot m, rabe m. 2. de la resquille, de l'affure.

buck up [ˈbʌkˈʌp] (to), F: 1. (a) remonter le moral à (qn); (b) se ravigoter. 2. se dépêcher*, se grouiller.

bud [bʌd] (noun), F: 1. (U.S.) = buddy, 1. 2. to nip sth. in the b., tuer (ou étouffer) qch. dans l'œuf.

buddy [ˈbʌdi] (noun), F: 1. ami*, copain m, pote m; they're great buddies, ils sont comme cul et chemise. 2. associé m, assoce m.

buddy-buddy [ˈbʌdi-bʌdi] (adj.), F: to be b.-b., être amis comme cochons, s'entendre comme des larrons en foire.

buff [bʌf] (noun), F: in the b., tout nu*, à poil.

buffalo [ˈbʌfəlou] (to) (U.S.), F: intimider, bluffer, entortiller, entourlouper (qn).

bug1 [bʌg] (noun). 1. F: écoute clandestine. 2. F: enthousiaste m, mordu m. 3. F: a b. in the machine, accroc m, pépin m. 4. P: b. doctor, psychiatre m. 5. F: obsession f, marotte f. 6. F: microbe m ou bactérie f (rhume, infection). 7. (U.S.) P: to have a b. on, être de mauvaise humeur, être de mauvais poil. 8. (U.S.) P: (a) = hot rod (hot, 22); (b) chauffeur m d'un bolide de course. 9. P: love bugs = crabs (voir crab1, 2). 10. F: as snug as a b. in a

---

rug, *c.p.*, tranquille comme Baptiste. *Voir aussi* big[1], **1**; doodle-bug; firebug; jitterbug; litter-bug.

bug[2] [ˈbʌg] (to). **1**. *F:* installer des écoutes clandestines dans (une salle, *etc.*), sonoriser. **2**. *P:* to b. s.o., ennuyer* qn, empoisonner qn. **3**. *(U.S.) P:* faire un examen psychologique *ou* psychiatrique à (qn).

bug-eyed [ˈbʌgaid] (*adj.*), *F:* **1**. to be b.-e., (*a*) avoir les yeux* en boules de loto; (*b*) ouvrir les yeux* comme des portes cochères. **2**. b.-e. monster, monstre *m* atomique.

bugger[1] [ˈbʌgər] (*noun*), *V:* **1**. don't play silly buggers with me! ne te paye pas ma tête! ne fais pas l'idiot avec moi! **2**. I don't give (*or* care) a b., je m'en fous (comme de l'an quarante). **3**. that's a b.! ça, c'est couillon! **4**. you silly b.! espèce de couillon! **5**. you dirty little b.! sale petite lope! **6**. poor b.! pauvre bougre!

bugger[2] [ˈbʌgər] (to), *V:* **1**. b. him! (*or* he can go and b. himself), qu'il aille se faire foutre. **2**. (*a*) faire échouer, faire avorter; (*b*) = bugger up (to); it's buggered, c'est foutu. **3**. well I'm buggered! j'en rote des ronds de chapeau! ça m'en bouche un coin!

bugger about (*or* around) [ˈbʌgərəˈbaut, ˈbʌgərəˈraund] (to), *V:* **1**. traîner (la savate), flâner, flânocher. **2**. balocher, feignasser, se la couler (douce). **3**. avoir la main baladeuse; to b. a. with s.o., peloter qn. **4**. to b. s.o. a., faire tourner qn en bourrique.

bugger-all [ˈbʌgəˈrɔːl] (*noun*), *V:* rien*, des clous, que dalle.

buggeration![1] [ˈbʌgəˈreiʃən] (*excl.*), *V:* tonnerre de Dieu! bordel de Dieu!

buggeration[2] [ˈbʌgəˈreiʃən] (*noun*), *V:* **1**. fouterie *f*. **2**. emmerdement *m*.

buggered [ˈbʌgəd] (*adj.*), *V:* fatigué*, foutu. *Voir aussi* bugger[2] (to), 3.

bugger off [ˈbʌgəˈrɔf] (to), *V:* partir*, foutre le camp.

bugger up [ˈbʌgəˈrʌp] (to), *V:* bousiller, saboter, cochonner, louper.

buggery [ˈbʌgəri] (*noun*), *V:* **1**. can she cook? can she b.! et quant à la cuisine? que dalle!; et pour la bouffe? mon cul! **2**. (all) to b., complètement, jusqu'au trognon, en brise-tout. **3**. like b., (*a*) bougrement, à corps et à cris, sadique-

ment; (*b*) certainement pas; comme mon cul! comme la peau!

bugging [ˈbʌgiŋ] (*noun*), *F:* installation *f* de microphones clandestins.

buggy [ˈbʌgi] (*adj.*), *P:* **1**. fou*, timbré, louftingue. **2**. névrosé, malade des nerfs, détraqué.

bug-house[1] [ˈbʌghaus] (*adj.*) *(U.S.)*, *P:* = bugs.

bug-house[2] [ˈbʌghaus] (*noun*), *P:* asile *m* de fous, maison *f* de dingues, cabanon *m*.

bug-hunter [ˈbʌghʌntər] (*noun*), *F:* entomologiste *mf*.

bugle [ˈbjuːgl] (*noun*), *P:* nez*, pif *m*, blair *m*.

bugler [ˈbjuːglər] (*noun*) *(Austr.)*, *F:* **1**. bavard*, baratineur *m*, jacasseur *m*. **2**. vantard*, fanfaron *m*, crâneur *m*, crosseur *m*.

bug out [ˈbʌgˈaut] (to) *(U.S.)*, *P:* **1**. se dégonfler, retirer ses marrons du feu. **2**. s'enfuir*, déguerpir, foncer dans le brouillard.

bugs [bʌgz] (*adj.*) *(U.S.)*, *P:* fou*, cinglé, dingo.

bug-trap [ˈbʌgtræp] (*noun*), *P:* lit*, pucier *m*.

build-up [ˈbildʌp] (*noun*), *F:* campagne *f* publicitaire, battage *m*, tam-tam *m*.

bulge [bʌldʒ] (*noun*), *F:* the battle of the b., la bataille du bide, la lutte pour la ligne.

bull [bul] (*noun*), *P:* **1**. policier*, condé *m*, bourre *m*; *cf.* fly-bull. **2**. = bullshit[1], **1,2**. **3**. b. and cow *(R.S. = row)* querelle*. *Voir aussi* rag[1], 4; shoot[2] (to), 7.

bulldagger [ˈbul-dægər] (*noun*), *P:* = bull-dyke.

bulldoze [ˈbuldouz] (to), *F:* brutaliser (qn) (pour lui faire faire qch.).

bull-dyke [ˈbuldaik] (*noun*), *P:* lesbienne* qui tient le rôle de l'homme, vrille *f*; *cf.* dyke.

bullet [ˈbulit] (*noun*), *P:* **1**. capsule *f* de drogues. **2**. to give s.o. the b., (*a*) se débarrasser* de qn, sacquer qn, virer qn; (*b*) refuser d'avoir affaire à qn, couper les ponts avec qn.

bullion-fringe [ˈbuljənˈfrindʒ] (*noun*), *F:* = scrambled eggs (egg, 4).

bullseye [ˈbulzai] (*noun*), *F:* voir bingo (50).

bullshine [ˈbulʃain] (*noun*), *F:* euph. *pour* bullshit[1], **1**.

bullshit[1] [ˈbulʃit] (*noun*), *P:* 1. service-service *m.* 2. bêtises*, boniments *m.pl.*, sornettes *f.pl.*; b. artist = bullshitter, 1,2. 3. propos peu importants, balivernes *f.pl.*, bagatelles *f.pl.*
bullshit[2] [ˈbulʃit] (**to**), *P:* baratiner, dévider, jaspiner.
bullshitter [ˈbulʃitər] (*noun*), *P:* 1. baratineur *m,* jaspineur *m.* 2. esbrouffeur *m,* plastronneur *m.*
bully[1] [ˈbuli] (*adj.*), *F:* 1. (*U.S.*) fameux, épatant, bœuf. 2. b. for you! bravo!
bully[2] [ˈbuli] (*noun*), *P:* souteneur*, maquereau *m,* Alphonse.
bum[1] [bʌm] (*adj.*) (*U.S.*), *F:* laid*, piètre, misérable, moche; b. steer, faux renseignement*, tuyau crevé. *Voir aussi* kick[1], 3.
bum[2] [bʌm] (*noun*), *P:* 1. fesses*, postérieur *m.* 2. qui paresse*, fainéant *m,* crossard *m;* ski b., qn qui passe ses journées à skier, et ne travaille pas; fana *mf* du ski. 3. (*U.S.*) (*a*) clochard*, chemineau *m;* (*b*) purotin *m.* 4. (*U.S.*) to give s.o. the b.'s rush, balancer qn; to get the b.'s rush, être flanqué à la porte. *Voir aussi* touch-your-bum.
bum[3] [bʌm] (**to**), *P:* 1. emprunter* (qch.), taper (qn). 2. to b. a lift, se faire emmener en voiture; to b. a dinner off s.o., se faire payer à dîner par qn. 3. vivre aux crochets de qn. 4. = bum around (to), 1, 2. 5. vivre en clochard*, faire le clodo(t).
bum around [ˈbʌməˈraund] (**to**) (*mainly U.S.*), *P:* 1. paresser*, fainéanter. 2. flânocher, traîner son cul.
bum-boy [ˈbʌmbɔi] (*noun*), *P:* pédéraste*, enculé *m.*
bumf [bʌmf] (*noun*) (=*bum-fodder*), *F:* 1. papier *m* hygiénique, torche-cul *m.* 2. paperasserie *f.* 3. papillons *m.pl.*, tracts *m.pl.*
bum-fodder [ˈbʌmfɔdər] (*noun*), *P:* = bumf, 1.
bum-freezer [ˈbʌmfriːzər] (*noun*), *P:* pet-en-l'air *m,* rase-pet *m.*
bum-hole [ˈbʌm(h)oul] (*noun*), *V:* anus*, anneau *m,* rond *m.*
bummer[1] [ˈbʌmər] (*adj.*), *P:* bousillé.
bummer[2] [ˈbʌmər] (*noun*), *P:* 1. bousillage *m.* 2. fainéant *m,* écornifleur *m,* mendigot *m.* 3. désappointement *m,* déception *f,* sale expérience *f.* 4.

mauvais voyage à la drogue. 5. = brown-hatter.
bummy [ˈbʌmi] (*adj.*), *P:* sale*, cracra, merdeux.
bumper [ˈbʌmpər] (*adj.*), *F:* excellent*, formid(able), à tout casser.
bumph [bʌmf] (*noun*), *F:* = bumf.
bump off [ˈbʌmpˈɔf] (**to**), *F:* assassiner*, but(t)er, zigouiller.
bum-rubber [ˈbʌmrʌbər] (*noun*), *P:* pédéraste*, pédé *m.*
bum-sucker [ˈbʌmsʌkər] (*noun*), *P:* lèche-cul *m,* lécheur *m.*
bun [bʌn] (*noun*). 1. *P:* to have a b. in the oven, être enceinte*, avoir un polichinelle dans le tiroir. 2. (*U.S.*) *P:* to have a b. on, (*a*) être ivre*, être saoul; (*b*) être défoncé (par les drogues). 3. *F:* to take the b. = to take the biscuit. *Voir aussi* currant-bun.
bunce [bʌns] (*noun*), *F:* affure *f,* bénef *m.*
bunch [bʌntʃ] (*noun*). 1. *F:* a b. of idiots, une bande* d'idiots. 2. *P:* a b. of fives, main*, pince *f,* pogne *f. Voir aussi* honeybunch; pick.
bunco [ˈbʌŋkou] (**to**), *P:* rouler (qn) au jeu (*surtout* aux cartes).
bundle [ˈbʌndl] (*noun*). 1. *F:* grande somme d'argent*, une liasse, un paquet; to make a b., faire sa pelote. 2. *P:* une belle fille*, une bath pépée, un beau petit lot. 3. *P:* to have a b., coïter*, se mélanger. 4. *F:* to go a b., parier gros, y mettre beaucoup d'argent* (*ou* le paquet). 5. *P:* I don't go a b. on that, ça ne m'emballe pas, ça ne me botte pas. 6. *F:* a b. of nerves, un paquet de nerfs.
bung[1] [bʌŋ] (*noun*), *P:* (*a*) pourboire*, bouquet *m;* (*b*) graissage *m* de patte.
bung[2] [bʌŋ] (**to**), *P:* 1. jeter*, envoyer dinguer. 2. donner*, abouler, allonger. 3. payer*, les abouler, les allonger, arroser.
bung-ho! [ˈbʌŋˈhou] (*excl.*), *F:* 1. au revoir! ciao! salut! 2. à la tienne!
bung-hole [ˈbʌŋ(h)oul] (*noun*). 1. *V:* anus*, anneau *m.* 2. *F:* voir bingo (50).
bunhead [ˈbʌnhed] (*noun*), *P:* individu bête*, pomme *f,* tourte *f.*
bunk [bʌŋk] (*noun*). 1. *F:* =bunkum. 2. *P:* to do a b., s'enfuir*, filer, déguerpir.
bunk off [ˈbʌŋkˈɔf] (**to**), *P:* = to do a bunk (bunk, 2).

bunkum [ˈbʌŋkəm] (*noun*), *F:* bêtises*, fariboles *f.pl.*; **that's (all) b.!** tout ça c'est des histoires *f.pl.* (*ou* des balivernes *f.pl. ou* du bidon)!

bunk-up [ˈbʌŋkʌp] (*noun*). **1.** *V:* **to have a b.-u.,** coïter*, coucher avec qn. **2.** *P:* **to give s.o. a b.-u.,** (*a*) faire la courte échelle à qn, aider qn dans une escalade; (*b*) pistonner qn.

bunny[1] [ˈbʌni] (*noun*). **1.** *P:* hôtesse *f*, entraîneuse *f*. **2.** *P:* femme* de petite vertu. **3.** *P:* prostituée* pour lesbiennes*, chatte *f* jaune. **4.** *P:* prostitué mâle pour pédérastes*, chien *m* jaune. **5.** *F:* lapin *m*, Jeannot Lapin. **6.** (*U.S.*) *F:* **lost b.,** ahuri *m*; **helpless b.,** abruti *m*. **7.** *P:* bavardage *m*, déblatérage *m*, bavette *f*. **8.** (*Austr.*) *P:* = **Alec, 2.** *Voir aussi* **dumb, 1** (*b*); **jungle, 3.**

bunny[2] [ˈbʌni] (**to**), *P:* = **rabbit**[2] (**to**).

bunny-fuck [ˈbʌni-fʌk] (**to**), *VV:* coïter* avec rapidité, fourailler à la une.

bunter [ˈbʌntər] (*noun*), *P:* prostituée*, radeuse *f*.

burk(e) [bə:k] (*noun*), *P:* = **berk.**

burl [bə:l] (*noun*) (*Austr.*), *F:* **to give sth. a b., to have a b. at sth.,** faire un essai à qch., tenter le coup.

burn[1] [bə:n] (*noun*), *P:* **1.** (*a*) cigarette*, cibiche *f*; **to twist a b.,** rouler une cigarette*; (*b*) cigarette* de marijuana (*drogues**), joint *m*. **2.** (*Austr.*) allumette *f*, bûche *f*, soufrante *f*.

burn[2] [bə:n] (**to**), *P:* **1.** (*a*) escroquer*, arnaquer, empiler; (*b*) voler*, barboter, chaparder. **2.** avcir une grosse déception. **3.** (*U.S.*) être exécuté par électrocution. **4.** (*a*) se mettre en colère*, fulminer; (*b*) mettre en colère*, mettre en boule. **5.** aller vite*, foncer, gazer. **6.** attraper *ou* donner une maladie vénérienne (*malade**), être fadé (*ou* faisandé *ou* nazicoté). **7.** fumer*, brûler, bouffarder.

burned out [ˈbə:ndˈaut] (*p.p. & adj.*), *P:* **1.** fatigué*, pompé, flapi. **2.** ennuyé*, embêté, assommé. **3.** défoncé.

burnese [bəˈni:z] (*noun*), *P:* = **bernice.**

burn-up [ˈbə:nʌp] (*noun*), *P:* **to have a b.-u.,** lutter de vitesse en auto *ou* en moto; *cf.* **burn up (to), 2.**

burn up [ˈbə:nˈʌp] (**to**), *P:* **1.** être très en colère*, voir rouge. **2. to b. u. the**

road, aller très vite*, brûler le pavé (*ou* la route); *cf.* **burn-up.**

burp[1] [bə:p] (*noun*), *F:* rot *m*, soupir *m* de Bacchus.

burp[2] [bə:p] (**to**), *F:* roter, avoir une fuite de gaz.

burp-gun [ˈbə:pgʌn] (*noun*), *P:* mitraillette*, sulfateuse *f*, moulinette *f*.

burton [ˈbə:tn] (*noun*), *F:* **to go for a b.,** disparaître, s'évanouir (dans la nature); (*av.*) faire un trou dans l'eau; (*mil.*) mourir*; être manquant, être porté disparu.

bus [bʌs] (*noun*), *F:* **1.** (*a*) véhicule motorisé; (*b*) avion *m*, coucou *m*; tacot *m*. **2. to miss the b.,** manquer le coche, rater l'occasion. **3. to get on the b.,** se laisser graisser la patte. *Voir aussi* **back-end.**

bush [buʃ] (*noun*). **1.** *V:* mousse *f*, gazon *m*, fourrure *f*. **2.** (*Austr.*) *P:* fille* *ou* jeune femme*, gonzesse *f*. **3.** *P:* **bo-bo** (*or* **righteous**) **b.,** marijuana *f* (*drogues**), foin *m*. **4.** *F:* **b. telegraph,** téléphone *m* arabe. *Voir aussi* **mulberry-bush.**

bushed [buʃt] (*adj.*), *P:* **1.** désorienté, interdit. **2.** fatigué*, vanné, fourbu.

bushel and peck [ˈbuʃələn(d)ˈpek] (*noun*), *P:* (*R.S.* = *neck*) cou*.

bushwa(h) [ˈbuʃwɑ:] (*noun*) (*U.S.*), *P:* = **bunkum.**

bush-whacker [ˈbuʃwækər] (*noun*) (*Austr.*), *F:* qn qui habite au fin fond du bled.

business [ˈbiznis] (*noun*). **1.** *F:* **to mean b.,** prendre les choses au sérieux, ne pas rigoler. **2.** *F:* **to do one's b.,** déféquer*, débourrer. **3.** *F:* **what a b.!** quelle affaire! **4. the b.,** (*a*) *P:* (i) traitement brutal; (ii) assassinat *m*, buttage *m*; (iii) réprimande *f*, savon *m*; (*b*) *V:* (i) pénis*, tracassin *m*; (ii) vagin*, didi *m*; (iii) coït*, truc *m*; (*c*) *P:* le business; (*d*) *P:* attirail *m* de camé; (*e*) *P:* poussette *f*. **5.** *F:* **what he paid for it is nobody's b.,** Dieu seul sait ce qu'il l'a payé. *Voir aussi* **funny**[1], **2.**

busk [bʌsk] (**to**). **1.** *F:* (*musiciens*) (*a*) jouer dans les rues; (*b*) improviser. **2.** (*th.*) *F:* jouer dans une troupe ambulante. **3.** *P:* vendre des livres obscènes à la sauvette.

busker [ˈbʌskər] (*noun*). **1.** *F:* (*a*)

---

musicien *m* qui joue dans les rues; (*b*) improvisateur *m*. **2.** *F:* comédien ambulant. **3.** *P:* fourgueur *m* de livres obscènes.

busman [ˈbʌsmən] (*noun*), *F:* **to take a b.'s holiday,** faire du métier en guise de congé ou de loisirs.

bust[1] [bʌst] (*adj.*), *F:* **1.** cassé, esquinté. **2.** (*a*) sans le sou, dans la purée; (*b*) **to go b.,** faire faillite, boire un bouillon.

bust[2] (bʌst] (*noun*), *P:* **1.** (*th.*) fiasco *m*, four *m*. **2.** bamboche *f*, bringue *f*, bordée *f*. **3.** faillite *f*, binelle *f*. **4.** **to do a b.,** s'évader de prison, sauter le mur. **5.** rafle *f* de police.

bust[3] [bʌst] (to), *P:* **1.** casser (un sergent, un racket, *etc.*). **2.** (*a*) prendre sur le fait (*ou* en flagrant délit); (*b*) arrêter*, agrafer. **3.** battre*, frapper, rosser. *Voir aussi* gut; shit[4] (to), 3.

buster [ˈbʌstər] (*noun*), *P:* **1.** homme* fort*, malabar *m*, costaud *m*. **2.** = **whopper, 1, 2.** *Voir aussi* **ball-buster; blockbuster; bronco-buster; jawbuster.**

bust in [ˈbʌstˈin] (to), *P:* **1.** entrer en coup de vent. **2.** **to b. s.o.'s face i.,** casser la figure* à qn, abîmer le portrait à qn. **3.** **to b. i. on s.o.,** arriver* comme un chien dans un jeu de quilles. **4.** **to b. i. on s.o.'s conversation,** s'injecter dans la conversation.

bust open [ˈbʌstˈoupən] (to), *P:* **to b. o. a safe,** casser un coffre-fort.

bust out [ˈbʌstˈaut] (to), *P:* **1.** s'évader, en jouer un air. **2.** **she's busting out all over,** elle a des seins* plantureux, il y a du monde au balcon.

bust-up [ˈbʌstʌp] (*noun*), *F:* **1.** querelle*, attrapade *f*. **2.** rupture *f*, mallette et paquette *f*; **they've had a b.-u.,** ils ont rompu.

bust up [ˈbʌstˈʌp] (to). *F:* **1.** esquinter (une pièce de machine, *etc.*). **2.** rompre (une amitié), briser (un mariage).

busty [ˈbʌsti] (*adj.*), *F:* avec une poitrine proéminente, avec de l'avant-scène, mamelue.

busy [ˈbizi] (*noun*), *P:* agent* *ou* inspecteur *m* de la Sûreté; policier*.

butch [butʃ] (*noun*) *P:* Miss Mec *f*, viriliste *f*.

butchers [ˈbutʃəz] (*noun*) (*R.S.* = *butcher's hook* = *look*), *P:* coup d'œil*;

to give sth. a b., to take a b. at sth., regarder* qch., reluquer qch.

butt [bʌt] (*noun*) (*U.S.*). **1.** *F:* fesses*, derrière *m*. **2.** *P:* (*a*) **dusty b.,** trois pouces et le cul tout de suite; (*b*) mocheté *f* de trottoir, (vieux) passe-lacet.

butter [ˈbʌtər] (*noun*), *F:* **to look as though b. wouldn't melt in one's mouth,** faire la Sainte-Nitouche, faire la sucrée, ne pas avoir l'air d'y toucher. *Voir aussi* **bread, 3; bread-and-butter.**

buttercup [ˈbʌtəkʌp] (*noun*), *P:* pédéraste*, joconde *f*.

butterfingers [ˈbʌtəfiŋgəz] (*noun*), *F:* malagauche *mf*, malapatte *mf*; **to have b., to be a b.,** avoir la main malheureuse, être brise-tout.

butterflies [ˈbʌtəflaiz] (*pl. noun*), *F:* **to have b. (in the tummy),** avoir peur*, avoir les jetons.

butter up [ˈbʌtəˈ(r)ʌp] (to), *F:* flatter*, pommader, embobiner, passer à la pommade.

button[1] [ˈbʌtn] (*noun*). **1.** *P:* menton *m*, bichonnet *m*. **2.** *V:* clitoris*, bouton *m*. **3.** *F:* **on the b.,** à point, recta. *Voir aussi* **belly-button; panic, 2.**

button[2] [ˈbʌtn] (to), *P:* **b. your mouth** (*or* **lip**)! (ferme) ton bec!

buttoned up [ˈbʌtndˈʌp] (*p.p. & adj.*), *P:* **1.** peu communicatif, constipé. **2.** cadenassé. **3.** **it's all b. u.,** c'est dans le sac (*ou* dans la poche).

buttonhole [ˈbʌtnhoul] (to), *F:* agrafer, cramponner (qn).

buy[1] [bai] (*noun*), *F:* achat *m*; **a good b.,** une bonne occase.

buy[2] [bai] (to). **1.** *F:* (*a*) (**go on,**) **I'll b. it,** vas-y, déballe!; je donne ma langue au chat; (*b*) **I'll b. that,** je marche, je suis d'acc. **2.** *P:* **he bought it** (*or* **a packet**), il a écopé.

buyer [ˈbaiər] (*noun*), *P:* receleur*, fourgue *m*.

buzz[1] [bʌz] (*noun*). **1.** *F:* bruit *m*, on-dit *m*. **2.** *F:* **to give s.o. a b.,** donner (*ou* passer) un coup de fil à qn. **3.** *P:* plaisir violent, transport *m*, animation *f*, émoi *m*.

buzz[2] [bʌz] (to). **1.** *F:* **to b. s.o. = to give s.o. a buzz** (buzz[1], 2). **2.** *P:* voler* à la tire (*ou* à la fourche *ou* à la fourchette). **3.** *F:* (*d'un avion ou d'une* *voiture*) coller (un autre avion ou une autre voiture). **4.** *P:* être aux anges. **5.** *P:* essayer d'acheter des drogues*, bibeloter.

buzzing [ˈbʌziŋ] (*noun*), *P:* interrogatoire* sévère (par la police), blutinage *m*, cuisine *f*.

buzz off [ˈbʌzˈɔf] (**to**), *F:* s'enfuir*,

décamper, filer, se tailler; **b.o.!** débarrasse! de l'air!

bye(-bye)! [ˈbai(ˈbai)] (*excl.*), *F:* salut! ciao!

bye-byes [ˈbaibaiz] (*pl. noun*), *F:* (*langage enfantin*) dodo *m*; **to go to b.-b.,** aller faire dodo.

---

* L'astérisque indique que le mot marqué de ce signe figure comme entrée dans le Répertoire.

C

C, c [si:] (*abbr.* = *cocaine*), *P:* (**big**) **c.**, cocaïne *f* (*drogues**).

cabbage ['kæbidʒ] (*noun*), *P:* argent*, galette *f*; *cf.* **kale; lettuce.**

cabbage-head ['kæbidʒhed] (*noun*), *F:* individu bête*, gourde *f*.

cabbie, cabby ['kæbi] (*noun*), *F:* 1. cocher *m*, collignon *m*. 2. chauffeur *m* de taxi*, rongeur *m*.

caboodle [kə'bu:dl] (*noun*), *F:* the whole (**kit and**) **c.**, tout le Saint-Frusquin, tout le bataclan; *cf.* **boiling; shebang,**[1]; **shoot**[1], 1; **shooting-match.**

cack[1] [kæk] (*noun*), *P:* étron*, caca *m*.

cack[2] [kæk] (**to**), *P:* déféquer*, caguer, faire caca.

cackhanded ['kæk'hændid] (*adj.*), *F:* balourd, empoté.

cackle ['kækl] (*noun*), *P:* **cut the c.!** assez bavardé! assez jacté!

cacky ['kæki] (*adj.*), *P:* merdeux.

cactus ['kæktəs] (*noun*), *P:* mescaline *f* (*drogues*), cactus *m* du Mexique.

cadet [kə'det] (*noun*), *P:* nouvel initié à la drogue.

cadge[1] [kædʒ] (*noun*), *F:* **he's always on the c.**, c'est un tapeur chronique (*ou* professionnel).

cadge[2] [kædʒ] (**to**), *F:* emprunter*, repasser le burlingue; **to c. a thousand francs from s.o.**, taper (*ou* torpiller) qn de mille francs.

cadger ['kædʒər] (*noun*), *F:* tapeur *m*, torpilleur *m*.

cadging ['kædʒiŋ] (*noun*), *F:* tapage *m*, relance *f*.

cadie ['keidi] (*noun*), *P:* chapeau*.

cafe [kæf, keif], **caff** [kæf] (*noun*), *P:* café* (*débit*), troquet *m*.

cag(e)y ['keidʒi] (*adj.*), *F:* malin*, futé; **to play c.**, se boutonner, jouer serré.

cahoot(s) [kə'hu:t(s), kɑ:'hu:t(s)] (*noun*), *F:* **to be in c. with s.o.**, être de mèche (*ou* en cheville) avec qn; **to go c. with s.o.**, partager avec qn.

Cain [kein] (*pr. noun*), *P:* 1. **to raise C.**, faire du bruit*, gueuler au charron. 2. **C. and Abel** (*R.S.* = *table*), table *f*.

cake [keik] (*noun*), 1. *F:* **a piece of c.**, du gâteau, du nanan. 2. *F:* **that takes the c.**, c'est le comble (*ou* le bouquet). 3. (*U.S.*) *P:* **to grab a piece of c.**, coïter*, faire un carton. 4. *F:* **you can't have your c. and eat it, you can't eat your c. and have it**, on ne peut pas être à avoir été, on ne peut pas avoir le drap et l'argent. *Voir aussi* **beefcake; cheesecake; cup-cakes; fruitcake; hot,** 18; **pancakes.**

cakehole ['keik(h)oul] (*noun*), *P:* bouche*, bec *m*; **shut your c.!** ferme ça! la ferme!

cake-walk ['keik-wɔ:k] (*noun*), *F:* 1. = **piece of cake** (**cake,** 1); **it's a c.-w.**, c'est dans le sac. 2. cake-walk *m* (*danse*).

calaboose, calaboosh [kælə'bu:s, kælə'bu:ʃ] (*noun*), *P:* prison*, bloc *m*, violon *m*.

calf [kɑ:f] (*noun*), *P:* 1. cinquante pence; *cf.* **cow,** 4. 2. **in c.** = **in pig** (**pig**[1], 5).

call [kɔ:l] (*noun*), *P:* 1. **to pay a c.**, uriner*, aller faire sa petite commission. 2. **it was a close c.**, il était moins une.

call down ['kɔ:l'daun] (**to**) (*U.S.*), *F:* réprimander*, attraper.

calling-down ['kɔ:liŋ'daun] (*noun*) (*U.S.*), *F:* attrapade *f*, savon *m*; **to get a c.-d.**, être réprimandé*, recevoir un savon, en prendre pour son grade.

camp[1] [kæmp] (*adj.*), *F:* 1. affecté, poseur. 2. répugnant, véreux, à l'estoc. 3. chichiteux. 4. gommeux, gandin. 5. rococo, vieux jeu. 6. tartavelle, tocard. 7. (*a*) efféminé; (*b*) homosexuel; (*c*) lesbienne.

camp[2] [kæmp] (*noun*), *F:* manières efféminées (*souvent* d'homosexuel), tantouserie *f*.

camp[3] [kæmp] (**to**), *P:* être pédéraste* *ou* lesbienne*, être de la bague *ou* de la maison tire-bouton.

---

* An asterisk indicates that the word so marked is included as a head-word in the Appendix.

camp about [ˈkæmpəˈbaut] (**to**), *F:* faire des simagrées *f.pl.*

camp up [ˈkæmpˈʌp] (**to**), *F:* **to c. it u.**, (*a*) jouer la comédie; (*b*) se montrer efféminé, faire la persilleuse; (*c*) prendre part à une partouse (*ou* à une surboum); (*d*) avoir une liaison homosexuelle; passer un week-end en pédale.

can[1] [kæn] (*noun*). **1.** *P:* prison*, bloc *m*; **to be in the c.**, être emprisonné*, être bloqué; **to put s.o. in the c.**, mettre qn dedans, fourrer qn au bloc. **2.** *F:* **in the c.**, en boîte. **3.** *F:* **to carry the c.** (**for s.o.**), écoper pour qn, porter le chapeau. **4.** *F:* pot *m*, chope *f*, chopotte *f.* **5.** *P:* (*a*) opium *m* (*drogues**), noir *m*; (*b*) deux grammes de n'importe quelle drogue. **6.** (*U.S.*) *P:* W.C.*, pissotière *f.* **7.** (*U.S.*) *P:* fesses*, montre *f*; **to kick s.o. in the c.**, botter les fesses* à qn. **8.** (*U.S.*) *P:* voiture*, auto *f*, bagnole *f.* **9.** (*U.S.*) (*pl.*) *P:* seins*, boîtes *f.pl.* à lait. *Voir aussi* **oil-can.**

can[2] [kæn] (**to**). **1.** *P:* emprisonner*, fourrer dedans. **2.** *P:* se débarrasser* de (qn), sacquer, flanquer à la porte. **3.** *F:* enregistrer (de la musique, *etc.*), mettre en conserve; *cf.* **canned, 2. 4.** *P:* **c. it!** ferme ça! *Voir aussi* **shitcan** (**to**).

canapa [ˈkænəpə] (*noun*), *P:* canapa *f*, marijuana *f* (*drogues**).

canary [kəˈnɛəri] (*noun*), *P:* dénonciateur*, chevreuil *m.*, donneur *m.*

cancer-stick [ˈkænsə-stik] (*noun*), *P:* cigarette*, cibiche *f.*

candle [ˈkændl] (*noun*), *F:* bougie *f* (*automobile*). *Voir aussi* **Roman, 1.**

candy [ˈkændi] (*noun*). **1.** *P:* (*drogues*) (*a*) cocaïne *f*, bigornette *f*; (*b*) hachisch *m*; (*c*) cube sucré de LSD; (*d*) drogues* en général; **c. man**, fourgueur *m* de drogues. **2.** (*U.S.*) *F:* bonbons *m.pl.*, friandises *f.pl.*; **like taking c. from a child** (*or* **blind man**), comme si on lui retirait la nourriture de la bouche. *Voir aussi* **needle-candy; nose-candy; rock-candy.**

cane[1] [kein] (*noun*), *P:* pince-monseigneur*, rossignol *m.* *Voir aussi* **varnish**[2] (**to**).

cane[2] [ˈkein] (**to**), *P:* **to c. s.o.**, (*a*) faire payer* trop cher à qn, fusiller qn; (*b*) battre qn à plate(s) couture(s).

canful [ˈkænful] (*noun*), *P:* **to have (had) a c.**, être ivre*, avoir une cuite.

caning [ˈkeiniŋ] (*noun*), *F:* victoire *f* facile (*ou* les doigts dans le nez).

canned [kænd] (*adj.*). **1.** *P:* (*a*) ivre*, saoul; (*b*) drogué*, camé. **2.** *F:* **c. music**, musique *f* en conserve (*disques, bandes, cassettes, etc.*). **3.** (*U.S.*) *P:* balancé, viré.

canoe [kəˈnuː] (*noun*), *F:* **to paddle one's own c.**, mener seul sa barque, voler de ses propres ailes.

canoodle [kəˈnuːdl] (**to**), *F:* (se) bécoter, (se) peloter.

canoodling [kəˈnuːdliŋ] (*noun*), *F:* pelotage *m*, mamours *m.pl.*

Canuck [ˈkænʌk] (*noun*), *F:* Canadien français.

cap[1] [kæp] (*noun*), *P:* capsule *f* de narcs. *Voir aussi* **Dutch**[1], **3**; **feather**[1], **2**; **Red-cap**; **thinking-cap.**

cap[2] [kæp] (**to**), *P:* **1.** ouvrir *ou* consommer une capsule de narcotique. **2.** acheter des narcotiques.

caper [ˈkeipər] (*noun*). **1.** *F:* (*a*) escapade *f*, farce *f*; (*b*) affaire*, fric-frac *m.* **2.** *P:* **. . . and all that c.**, entourloupe et compagnie. **3.** *P:* truc *m*, ficelle *f.*

carat [ˈkærət] (*noun*), *F:* **a twenty-two c. chap**, un vrai de vrai.

carcase, carcass [ˈkɑːkəs] (*noun*), *F:* **plant your c. there!** assieds-toi! pose ton pont arrière!; **drag your c. over here!** radine! amène ta viande!; **move your c.!** (*a*) bouge-toi! remue ta graisse!; (*b*) débarrasse!

card [kɑːd] (*noun*), *F:* **1.** drôle d'individu*, drôle de numéro (*ou* de phénomène). **2.** **to get one's cards**, être renvoyé, se faire virer; **to give s.o. his cards**, renvoyer qn, virer qn. **3.** **to put one's cards on the table**, jouer cartes sur table. **4.** **it's on the cards**, c'est du possible (*ou* probable). **5.** **to show one's cards**, abattre son jeu. **6.** **house of cards**, château *m* de cartes. **7.** **to play one's trump c.**, jouer sa meilleure carte (*ou* son atout); **to hold the trump c.**, avoir les atouts en main. **8.** **to throw in one's cards**, abandonner la partie. *Voir aussi* **mark**[2] (**to**), **1.**

cardy [ˈkɑːdi] (*noun*) (*abbr.* = *cardigan*), *F:* paletot *m* de laine, cardigan *m.*

carpet[1] [ˈkɑːpit] (*noun*). **1.** *F:* **on the c.** (=*under consideration*), sur le tapis. **2.** *F:* **to put s.o. on the c.**, tenir qn sur

la sellette. 3. *P:* trois mois de taule.
Voir aussi dirt[1], 4; red[1], 2.
carpet[2] [ˈkɑːpit] (to), *F:* to c. s.o. =
to put s.o. on the carpet (carpet[1], 2).
carpetbagger [ˈkɑːpitbæɡər] (*noun*)
(*U.S.*), *F:* candidat parachuté, aven-
turier *m* politique.
carrier [ˈkæriər] (*noun*), *F:* contact *m*,
intermédiaire *m* (pour les drogues).
carrot(s) [ˈkærət(s)], carrot-top
[ˈkærəttɔp] (*noun*), *F:* rouquin *m*,
poil *m* de carotte, poil *m* de brique.
carry [ˈkæri] (to), *F:* 1. avoir en magasin.
2. avoir, posséder de la drogue. 3. to
c. s.o., garder du bois mort. 4. he's
had as much as he can c., il a son
compte, il en a tout son soûl.
carryings-on [ˈkæriiŋzˈɔn] (*pl. noun*),
F: simagrées *f.pl.*, pitreries *f.pl.*
carry off [ˈkæriˈɔf] (to), *F:* to c. it o.
(well), bien s'en tirer, réussir le coup.
carry-on [ˈkæriˈɔn] (*noun*), *P:* what a
c.-o.! quel cirque! quelle comédie!
carry on [ˈkæriˈɔn] (to), *F:* 1. continuer,
persister, aller jusqu'au bout; c. o.
regardless! continue envers et contre
tout! 2. to c. o. with s.o., fréquenter
qn, sortir avec qn, flirter. 3. don't
c. o. like that! ne fais pas l'idiot! *Voir
aussi* alarming.
cart [kɑːt] (*noun*), *F:* to land s.o.
(right) in the c., mettre qn dans le
pétrin. *Voir aussi* apple-cart; dog-cart.
cart about [ˈkɑːtəˈbaut] (to), *F:* trim-
bal(l)er (qn, qch.).
cartload [ˈkɑːtloud] (*noun*), *F:* a c. of
trouble, toute une accumulation de
malheurs.
cart off [ˈkɑːtˈɔf] (to). 1. *F:* to get
carted off to hospital, être transbahuté
à l'hôpital*. 2. *P:* c. yourself o.! fiche
le camp!
cartwheel [ˈkɑːt-wiːl] (*noun*). 1. *F:* to
do a c., faire un tonneau (*ou* une
roue). 2. *P:* = brodie, 1. 3. (*pl.*) *P:*
amphétamines *f.pl.* (*drogues**), topette *f.*
carve-up [ˈkɑːvʌp] (*noun*), *P:* 1. escroquerie*, arnaquage *m.* 2. distribe *f.*
carve up [ˈkɑːvʌp] (to), *P:* 1. massacrer,
charcuter (qn). 2. partager, décarpiller.
carzy [kɑːzi] (*noun*), *P:* = karzy.
Casanova [ˈkæsəˈnouvə] (*noun*), *F:* Casanova *m*, cavaleur *m*, godilleur *m*.
case[1] [keis] (*noun*). 1. *F:* he's a hard c.,
c'est un dur, c'est une mauvaise tête.

2. *P:* to go c. with s.o., coïter* avec
qn, godiller avec qn. 3. *P:* casse *f,*
fric-frac *m*; to have (*or* do) a c., voler*,
faire un fric-frac. *Voir aussi* nut-
case.
case[2] [keis] (to), *P:* 1. to c. s.o., coïter*
avec qn, godiller avec qn. 2. to c. a
joint, aller examiner une maison, *etc.*,
avant de la cambrioler*; faire une
ballade au fric-frac. 3. guetter*, broquer, se rencarder. 4. to get cased,
être inculpé (*ou* fargué).
cash in [ˈkæʃˈin] (to). 1. *P:* to c. i.
one's chips, mourir*, lâcher la rampe,
poser sa chique. 2. *F:* to c. i. on sth.,
tirer profit de qch.
cast-iron [ˈkɑːstˈaiən] (*adj.*), *F:* 1. c.-i.
case, affaire *f* inattaquable. 2. c.-i.
constitution (will, *etc.*), santé *f* (volonté
f, etc.) de fer; c.-i. stomach, estomac
m d'autruche (*ou* de fer); c.-i. alibi,
alibi *m* irréfutable.
cast-offs [ˈkɑːstɔfs] (*pl. noun*), *F:* 1.
vieux vêtements*, vieilles frusques. 2.
laissés-pour-compte *m.pl.*
casual [ˈkæzjuəl] (*noun*), *F:* 1. client *m*
de passage. 2. (*pl.*) mocassins *m.pl.*,
chaussures* pour tout aller.
cat [kæt] (*noun*). 1. *P:* (a) qn qui est de
l'avant-garde en musique, art ou
littérature, (b) qn qui s'habille à la
dernière mode, minet *m.* 2. *P:* musicien *m* de jazz; *voir aussi* hot, 7. 3. *P:*
homme*, zèbre *m.* 4. *P:* coureur *m* de
jupons. 5. *F:* an old c., femme* (*péj.*),
une vieille chipie. 6. *P:* chapardeur *m*,
chipeur *m.* 7. (=cat-o'-nine-tails) *F:*
fouet *m*, chat *m* à neuf queues. 8. *P:*
he thinks he's the c.'s whiskers (*or*
pyjamas), il ne se prend pas pour de
la crotte; *cf.* bee, 1. 9. *F:* to lead a c.
and dog life, vivre comme chien et
chat. 10. *F:* to play c. and mouse with
s.o., jouer au chat et à la souris avec
qn. 11. *F:* to be raining cats and dogs,
pleuvoir des hallebardes. 12. *F:* to
let the c. out of the bag, éventer la
mèche. 13. *P:* pédéraste*, pédoque *m.*
Voir aussi copycat; fraidy; hell-cat;
hep-cat; hoity, 1; night[1], 5; scaredy-cat;
she-cat; shoot[2] (to), 6; wildcat.
catch[1] [kætʃ] (*attrib. adj.*), *F:* 1. a c.
question, une question-piège. 2. a
snappy c. answer, une réponse bien
envoyée (*ou* désinvolte).

* An asterisk indicates that the word so marked is included as a head-word in the Appendix.

catch[2] [kætʃ] (*noun*). **1.** *F:* (=*love-con-quest*) prise *f*, chopin *m*. **2.** *P:* pédé-raste* qui tient le rôle de femme, chouquette *f*.

catch[3] [kætʃ] (**to**), *F:* **1.** **c. me doing that!** pas de danger qu'on m'y prenne! **2. you'll c. it!** tu en prendras pour ton grade! **3. caught napping**, pris au pied levé (*ou* au dépourvu *ou* sans vert). **4. the age to c. 'em:** *voir* **bingo** (**17**). *Voir aussi* **cold**[2], **1**; **packet**, **1**.

catch on [ˈkætʃˈɔn] (**to**), *F:* **1.** com-prendre, piger, entraver. **2.** prendre, être en vogue (*ou* dans le vent).

catch out [ˈkætʃˈaut] (**to**), *F:* **1.** prendre en défaut. **2.** coincer.

cathouse [ˈkæthaus] (*noun*), *P:* **1.** bordel*, claque *m*, boxon *m*. **2.** (*U.S.*) = **barrelhouse**.

cat-lap [ˈkætlæp] (*noun*), *F:* bibine *f*, jus *m* de chaussette (*ou* de serpil-lière).

cat-lick [ˈkætlik] (*noun*), *F:* bout *m* de toilette.

catty [ˈkæti] (*adj.*), *F:* rosse, vache.

cauliflower [ˈkɔli-flauər] (*noun*), *F:* **1. c. ear**, oreille *f* en chou-fleur. **2.** trèfle *f* (*cartes*), herbe *f* à la vache.

caution [ˈkɔːʃ(ə)n] (*noun*), *F:* **a c.**, un drôle de numéro, un phénomène; **she's a** (**proper**) **c.**, elle est formid(able).

cave-man [ˈkeivmæn] (*noun*), *F:* grosse brute; **c.-m. stuff**, brutalités *f.pl.*

cazz [kæz] (*adj.*), *F:* (=*casual*) **in a very c. voice**, sans avoir l'air d'y toucher; **c. clothes**, vêtements* de sport.

Cecil, cecil [ˈsesl, ˈsisl] (*noun*), *P:* cocaïne *f* (*drogues**), cécile *m*. *Voir aussi* **after**, **1**.

cee [siː] (*noun*), *P:* cocaïne *f* (*drogues**), la c.

ceiling [ˈsiːliŋ] (*noun*), *F:* **to go through** (*or* **hit**) **the c.**, se mettre en colère*, sortir de ses gonds, monter à l'échelle.

cement [siˈment] (*noun*), *P:* (=*illicit narcotics*) ciment *m*.

century [ˈsentʃuri, ˈsentʃəri] (*noun*), *P:* cent livres sterling.

cert [səːt] (*abbr.* = *certainty*), *F:* **it's a** (**dead**) **c.**, c'est du nougat, c'est du tout cuit, c'est affiché; (*courses aux che-vaux*) c'est un gagnant sûr.

certifiable [səːtiˈfaiəbl] (*adj.*), *F:* bon pour le cabanon.

cha [tʃɑː] (*noun*), *F:* = **char**, **1**.

chain-gang [ˈtʃeingæŋ] (*noun*), *P:* =

daisy chain (*voir* **daisy**[2], **6**).

chair [ˈtʃɛər] (*noun*), *F:* **1.** (*U.S.*) chaise *f* électrique; **to go to the c.**, être grillé. **2. c. warmer**, rond-de-cuir *m*, gratte-papier *m*. **3. to be in the c.**, (*au café*) être celui qui offre une tournée. *Voir aussi* **bandy-chair**.

chalk [tʃɔːk] (*noun*). **1.** *F:* **better by a long c.**, de bien loin le meilleur; **not by a long c.**, il s'en faut de beaucoup. **2.** *F:* **they're like** (*or* **as different as**) **c. and cheese**, c'est le jour et la nuit. **3.** *P:* amphétamine *f* (*drogues**), to-pette *f*. **4.** *P:* **ball** (*or* **penn'orth**) **of c.** (*R.S.* = *walk*), promenade *f*.

chalk up [tʃɔːkˈʌp] (**to**). **1.** *F:* porter sur l'ardoise. **2.** *P:* **to c.u. a score** = **score**[2] (**to**), **1, 2**.

champ[1] [tʃæmp] (*noun*) (*abbr.* = *cham-pion*), *F:* as *m*, crack *m*.

champ[2] [tʃæmp] (**to**), *F:* ronger son frein.

champers [ˈʃæmpəz] (*noun*), *F:* (vin *m* de) champagne *m*, champ(e) *m*.

champion[1] [ˈtʃæmpjən] (*adj.*), *F:* (**pro-per**) c., excellent*, de première, impec; *voir aussi* **gate-crasher**.

champion[2] [ˈtʃæmpjən] (*adv.*), *F:* excel-lemment, soin-soin.

chancer [ˈtʃɑːnsər] (*noun*), *F:* risque-tout *m*, tête brûlée.

chancy [ˈtʃɑːnsi] (*adj.*), *F:* chanceux, glandilleux.

change [tʃeindʒ] (*noun*), *F:* **you won't get much c. out of him**, tu n'en tireras pas grand-chose, tu perds tes peines avec lui. *Voir aussi* **ring**[2] (**to**), **2**.

chant [tʃɑːnt] (**to**), *P:* chanter* dans les rues, pousser la goualante.

chap [tʃæp] (*noun*), *F:* individu*, type *m*; **he's a queer c.**, c'est un drôle de bonhomme; **hello, old c.!** salut, vieux pote (*ou* vieille branche)!

char [tʃɑːr] (*noun*), *F:* **1.** thé *m*; **a cup of c.**, une tasse de thé. **2.** (=*charwoman*) femme de ménage, torche-pot *m*, bonniche *f*.

character [ˈkæriktər] (*noun*), *F:* drôle d'individu*, un numéro.

charas [tʃæˈræs], **charash** [tʃæˈræʃ] (*noun*), (*drogues**), *F:* cannabis *m*, marijuana *f* (*drogues**), dagga *m*.

charge [tʃɑːdʒ] (*noun*), *P:* **1.** marijuana *f* (*drogues**). **2.** piquouse *f*; **to go on the c.**, se camer. **3.** plaisir *m*, émotion *f*; **to get a c. out of sth.**, tirer plaisir de

qch., s'en payer une tranche; I got a
c. out of it, ça m'a fait quelque chose.
Voir aussi depth-charge.
charged (up) [ˈtʃɑːdʒd(ˈʌp)] *(p.p. &*
adj.), *P:* drogué*, bourré, camé; to
get c., se camer.
charl(e)y¹, charlie [ˈtʃɑːli] *(adj.*), *P:*
qui a peur*, flubé, foireux.
Charl(e)y², charl(e)y, Charlie,
charlie [ˈtʃɑːli] *(noun)*, *P:* 1. a right
(or **proper)** C., un vrai gugusse. 2. C.'s
dead, ton jupon passe; tu pavoises;
cf. Anne *(a)*. 3. *(pl.)* seins*, roberts
m.pl. 4. *(pl.)* testicules*, balloches *f.pl.*
5. cocaïne *f (drogues*)*; C. coke, un
Jules de la c. 6. race-horse C., morphine
f (drogues)*. 7. lesbienne*, gouchotte *f.*
8. *(U.S.)* un blanc *(terme employé par*
les nègres). 9. *(U.S.)* un dollar. *Voir*
aussi good-time, 2.
charms [tʃɑːmz] *(pl. noun)*, *F:* seins*,
appas *m.pl.*, doudounes *f.pl.*
chart [tʃɑːt] *(noun)*, *F:* 1. arrangement musical *(par ex.* pour orchestre de jazz). 2. to be in the charts,
être au palmarès, être dans le hit-
parade.
charver [ˈtʃɑːvər] *(noun)*, *V:* coït*,
tringlage *m*; to have a c., coïter*,
tringler.
chase [tʃeis] (to), *F:* (go) c. yourself!
va te faire fiche!
chase around [ˈtʃeisəˈraund] (to), *F:*
to c. a. after women, courir les filles
(ou les jupons).
chaser [ˈtʃeisər] *(noun)*, *F:* 1. rince-
cochon *m*, rince-gueule *m*. 2. lettre *f*
qui fait suite à une autre. *Voir aussi*
petticoat-chaser; skirt-chaser; woman-
chaser.
chassis [ˈʃæsi] *(noun)*, *F:* (d'une femme)
châssis *m*, académie *f.*
chat [tʃæt] *(noun)*, *P:* 1. = backchat¹,
1 *(a)*. 2. pou*, galopard *m*.
chat up [ˈtʃætˈʌp] (to), *F:* baratiner;
to c. u. a bird, faire du rentre-dedans
(ou du gringue) à une fille*, faire du
rambin à une fille*.
cheapjack [ˈtʃiːpdʒæk] *(noun)*, *F:* camelot *m*, batousard *m*.
cheapskate [ˈtʃiːp-skeit] *(noun)*, *F:* 1.
avare*, grippe-sou *m*. 2. vaurien*,
bon-à-rien *m*.
cheat [tʃiːt] (to) *(U.S.)*, *F:* cocufier,
doubler, faire porter des cornes (à).

cheaters [ˈtʃiːtəz] *(pl. noun)*, *F:* 1. =
falsies, 2. 2. lunettes*, berniches *f.pl.*
check! [tʃek] *(excl.)*, oui*, d'acc! banco!
check in [ˈtʃekˈin] (to), *F:* = book in (to).
check out [ˈtʃekˈaut] (to). 1. *P:* mourir*,
déposer le bilan, plier bagage. 2. *F:*
= book out (to). 3. *P:* partir*, filer.
4. *F:* se vérifier. 5. *F:* to c. s.o., sth., o.
= to check up on s.o., sth.
checks [tʃeks] *(pl. noun)*, *P:* to hand
in one's c., mourir*, dévisser son
billard.
check-up [ˈtʃekʌp] *(noun)*, *F:* 1. (personne) contrôle *m*, examen médical.
2. *(mécanique)* révision *f.*
check up [ˈtʃekˈʌp] (to), *F:* to c. u. on
s.o., sth., se rencarder sur qn, qch.
cheek¹ [tʃiːk] *(noun)*, *F:* toupet *m*,
culot *m*; he's got plenty of c. *(or* a
hell of a c. *or* the c. of the devil), il a
un culot monstre, il en a un souffle;
c.! *(or* the c. of him, *etc.*!), quel culot!
ce culot!; don't give me any of your c.!
(ne) te fiche pas de moi!; it's a damned
c.! c'est se fiche(r) du monde!
cheek² [tʃiːk] (to), *F:* se payer la tête
de (qn), dire des impertinences à (qn),
manquer de respect à (qn), faire l'insolent avec (qn).
cheeky [ˈtʃiːki] *(adj.)*, *F:* effronté, culotté, soufflé.
cheerio! [ˈtʃiəriˈou] *(excl.)*, *F:* 1. =
cheers! 2. à bientôt! bon courage! ciao!
cheers! [tʃiəz] *(excl.)*, *F:* (a) à la bonne
vôtre! à la tienne (Étienne)!; (b) *(par-*
fois) merci.
cheerybye! [ˈtʃiəriˈbai] *(excl.)*, *F:* au
revoir! salut!
cheese [tʃiːz] *(noun)*. 1. *P:* big c.,
lourdaud *m*, butor *m*, rustre *m*; *voir*
aussi big¹, 1. 2. *P:* old c., du réchauffé.
3. *P:* hard c.! pas de chance*! pas de pot!
quelle guigne! 4. *P:* c. and kisses *(R.S.)*
= missis. 5. *F:* say c.! souriez! regardez
le petit oiseau! *Voir aussi* chalk, 2.
cheesecake [ˈtʃiːzkeik] *(noun)*, *F:* pin-up
f.
cheesed (off) [ˈtʃiːzd(ˈɔf)] *(p.p. & adj.)*,
P: to be *(or* feel) c., avoir le cafard,
en avoir marre.
cheese it [ˈtʃiːzit] (to), *P:* partir*, se
calter; c. i.! ça va! barca! fiche le camp!
cheesy [ˈtʃiːzi] *(adj.)*, *P:* miteux, à la
manque, toc.
chef [ʃef] *(noun)*, *P:* 1. opium *m (drogues*)*,

* An asterisk indicates that the word so marked is included as a head-word in the Appendix.

boue verte. **2.** *(dans une fumerie d'opium)* chef *m*, caïd *m*.

cherry ['tʃeri] *(noun).* **1.** *P:* virginité *f*, pucelage *m*, fleur *f*, primeur *f*, coquille *f*, coquillage *m*; **to lose one's c.**, sa fleur; **to pick a girl's c.**, déflorer une fille. **2.** *F:* **to take two bites at the c.**, **to have another bite at the c.**, s'y prendre à deux fois, y remordre.

cherry-ripe ['tʃeri'raip] *(noun) (R.S.)*, *P:* (a) (=*pipe*) pipe *f*; (b) (=*tripe*) bêtises*, sornettes *f.pl.*

chest [tʃest] *(noun), F:* **to get sth. off one's c.**, déballer ce qu'on a sur le cœur, vider son sac. *Voir aussi* **close**[2]; **hair, 5.**

chestnut ['tʃesnʌt] *(noun).* **1.** *F:* histoire rabâchée, rengaine *f*, blague éventée. **2.** *(pl.) P:* seins*, pelotes *f.pl.* **3.** *(pl.) P:* testicules*, olives *f.pl.*

chesty ['tʃesti] *(adj.), F:* **1.** délicat des bronches. **2.** *(U.S.)* vaniteux, faraud.

chevy (chase) ['tʃevi('tʃeis)] *(noun) (R.S. = face)*, *P:* visage*, bouille *f*.

chew [tʃu:] **(to),** *P:* **to c. the fat** *(or* **the rag),** bavarder*, jacter, discuter le bout de gras, ragoter. *Voir aussi* **bite off (to), 2.**

chewbacon ['tʃu:-beikən] *(noun), F:* paysan*, cul-terreux *m*.

chew off ['tʃu:'ɔf] **(to),** *F:* **to c. s.o.'s head** *(U.S.:* **ears**) o., réprimander* qn, passer un savon à qn. *Voir aussi* **balls, 3.**

chew out ['tʃu:'aut] **(to)** *(U.S.),* *P:* = **ball out (to); to get (one's ass) chewed out,** se faire engueuler.

chew over ['tʃu:'ouvər] **(to),** *F:* **to c. it o.,** réfléchir, ruminer.

chi [tʃai] *(noun), F:* = **char, 1.**

chichi ['ʃi:ʃi:] *(adj.), F:* chichiteux, collet monté.

chick [tʃik] *(noun), F:* **1.** enfant*, môme *mf*. **2.** fille*, poulette *f*. **3.** *(U.S.)* **to play c.** = **to lay chickie** *(voir* **chickie**). *Voir aussi* **head, 12.**

chickabiddy ['tʃikəbidi] *(noun), F:* cocotte *f*.

chicken[1] ['tʃikin] *(adj.), P:* poltron, capon; *cf.* **chicken**[2], **4; to turn c.** = **chicken out (to).**

chicken[2] ['tʃikin] *(noun).* **1.** *F:* **she's no (spring) c.!** c'est pas un poulet de grain! **2.** *F:* **to get up with the chickens,** se lever avec les poules. **3.** *F:* **to count one's chickens before they are hatched,**

vendre la peau de l'ours (avant de l'avoir tué). **4.** *P:* poltron*, caneur *m*, dégonfleur *m*, flubard *m*, froussard *m*, poule mouillée. **5.** *P:* mineur(e), gamin(e), poulet *m* de grain, poulette *f*; **to have a c. dinner,** faire l'amour avec un(e) mineur(e), déplumer le poulet. **6.** *F:* **when the chickens come home to roost,** quand arrivera le règlement des comptes, au moment venu de la rétribution.

chicken-feed ['tʃikinfi:d] *(noun), F:* **1.** quelques sous*, mitraille *f.* **2.** rien*, des clopinettes *f.pl.*; **it's just c.-f.,** c'est de la gnognot(t)e.

chicken-hearted ['tʃikin'hɑːtid], **chicken-livered** ['tʃikin'livəd] *(adj.)*, *F:* **to be c.-h., c.-l.,** avoir du sang de poulet *(ou* de navet).

chicken out ['tʃikin'aut] **(to),** *P:* se dégonfler.

chicken-roost ['tʃikinru:st] *(noun) (th.)*, *F:* poulailler *m*; *cf.* **pigeon-roost.**

chickie ['tʃiki] *(adv.) (U.S.)*, *F:* **to lay c.,** faire le guet, arçonner, faire le gaffe.

chief [tʃi:f] *(noun).* **1.** *F:* **the (big white) c.,** le patron*, le grand manitou. **2.** *P:* **the c.,** (a) LSD *m (drogues*)*; (b) mescaline *f (drogues).*

chill [tʃil] *(noun), P:* **1. to put the c. on s.o.,** battre froid à qn, faire la frime à qn. **2.** *(U.S.)* **to have the chills,** avoir peur*, avoir la tremblote.

chimbley ['tʃimbli] *(noun), F:* (=*chimney*) cheminée *f*, bouffardière *f*.

chime in ['tʃaim'in] **(to),** *F:* couper la parole, placer son mot, mettre son grain de sel.

chimney ['tʃimni] *(noun), F:* **to smoke like a c.,** fumer comme un pompier.

chin [tʃin] *(noun), F:* **1.** **to take it on the c.,** encaisser un sale coup, ne pas se laisser abattre. **2. c. up!** du courage! tiens bon!; **to keep one's c. up,** tenir bon, tenir le coup.

china ['tʃainə] *(noun), P:* ami(e)*, pote *m*, copain *m*, copine *f*.

Chinaman ['tʃainəmən] *(noun), P:* **1.** **to have a C. on one's back,** souffrir des symptômes du sevrage de drogues. **2. not to have a C.'s chance (in hell),** ne pas avoir l'ombre d'une chance.

chin-chin! ['tʃin'tʃin] *(excl.), F:* **1.** au revoir! adieu! **2.** à la vôtre! à la tienne!

chinfest [ˈtʃinfest] (noun), P: = chinwag[1].
chink[1] [tʃiŋk] (noun), P: argent*, fric
m.
Chink[2] [tʃiŋk] (noun), P: Chinois m,
Chinoise f, Chinetoc m.
chinky, Chinky [ˈtʃiŋki] (adj.), P:
chinois, chinetoque; c. nosh, nourriture*
chinoise, bouffe f chinetoque.
chin-music [ˈtʃinmjuːzik] (noun), P: =
chinwag[1].
chino [ˈtʃainou] (noun), P: Chinois m
fourgueur m de drogues.
chintzy [ˈtʃintsi] (adj.), F: rococo.
chinwag[1] [ˈtʃinwæg] (noun), P: bavette
f, causette f.
chinwag[2] [ˈtʃinwæg] (to), P: bavarder*,
jaboter, tailler une bavette.
chip[1] [tʃip] (noun). 1. P: cinq pence.
2. P: to be in the chips, être plein aux
as. 3. F: he's had his chips, il est cuit
(ou fichu). 4. F: when the chips are
down, quand les dés sont jetés, en cas
de coup dur. 5. F: to have a c. on one's
shoulder, chercher la bagarre (ou des
crosses f.pl.). 6. F: he's a c. of(f) the
old block, c'est bien le fils de son père.
7. P: to hand out the chips, donner*
de l'argent* avec largesse, abouler le
fric. Voir aussi cash in (to), 1; chips.
chip[2] [tʃip] (to), P: 1. faire l'insolent, se
payer la tête de (qn). 2. chiner, blaguer,
charrier (qn).
chip at [ˈtʃip-æt] (to), P: critiquer*,
bêcher, éreinter (qn, qch.).
chip in [ˈtʃipˈin] (to), P: 1. payer* sa
part. 2. placer son mot, y aller de son
grain de sel.
chipper[1] [ˈtʃipər] (adv.), P: to feel c.,
être en forme.
chipper[2] [ˈtʃipər] (noun), P: bavardage
m, commérages m.pl., jacasserie f.
chippy[1] [ˈtʃipi] (adj.), P: 1. aride, fade,
sans intérêt, barbant. 2. patraque, mal
fichu.
chippy[2] [ˈtʃipi] (noun), P: 1. (a) prostituée*, grue f, radeuse f; (b) allumeuse f,
dragueuse f. 2. receveuse f d'autobus. 3. (a) (= mild narcotic) herbe f
(drogues); (b) usager m de drogues à
faibles doses et par intervalle. 4.
menuisier m, copeau m.
chippy[3] [ˈtʃipi] (to), P: prendre des
drogues* irrégulièrement ou pour se
montrer initié, barboter dans la came.

chips [tʃips] (noun), P: = chippy[2], 4.
chirpy [ˈtʃəːpi] (adj.), F: gai, de bonne
humeur.
chirrupy [ˈtʃirəpi] (adj.), F: éveillé,
joyeux, bavard.
chisel[1][ˈtʃiz(ə)l] (noun), P: escroquerie*,
filouterie f, sale coup m.
chisel[2] [ˈtʃiz(ə)l] (to), P: voler*, rouler,
carotter (qn); to c. a fiver out of s.o.,
to c. s.o. out of a fiver, taper qn d'un
gros faffiot.
chiseller [ˈtʃiz(ə)lər] (noun), P: escroc*,
carotteur m.
chiselling [ˈtʃiz(ə)liŋ] (noun), P: escroquerie*, resquille f.
chit [tʃit] (noun), F: petit enfant*, bout
m de zan.
chiv[1] [ʃiv] (noun), P: 1. couteau*,
surin m. 2. rasoir*, rasibe m.
chiv[2] [ʃiv] (to) (p.p. chiv(v)ed [ʃivd]),
P: 1. taillader, larder, suriner (qn).
2. marquer, faire la croix des vaches à
(qn).
chive [ʃiv] (noun & verb), P: = chiv[1,2].
chive-man [ˈ(t)ʃivmæn, ˈtʃaivmæn],
chive-merchant [ˈ(t)ʃivməːtʃənt,
ˈtʃaivməːtʃənt] (noun), P: surineur m.
chivey [ˈʃivi] (noun), P: = chiv[1], 1, 2.
chiv(v)y up (or along)([ˈtʃiviˈʌp, əˈlɔŋ])
(to), F: relancer, poursuivre, harceler
(qn).
chock-a-block [ˈtʃɔkəˈblɔk] (adj.), F:
plein à craquer, archi-plein, plein comme
un œuf.
chocker [ˈtʃɔkər] (adj.). 1. F: = chock-
a-block. 2. P: to be c., en avoir assez*,
en avoir marre; cf. dead[2], 5.
chock-full [ˈtʃɔkˈful] (adj.), F: = chock-
a-block.
chocolate [ˈtʃɔklit] (noun), P: c. lover =
dinge queen (voir queen, 2); cf. coal-
burner.
choke [tʃouk] (noun), P: = chok(e)y,
2.
choked [tʃoukt] (p.p. & adj.), P: 1.
déçu, chocolat. 2. = chocker, 2.
choke off [ˈtʃoukˈɔf] (to), F: envoyer
balader (qn).
choker [ˈtʃoukər] (noun), P: that's a c.,
ça vous la bouche.
chok(e)y [ˈtʃouki] (noun), P: 1. bar-
rière f de péage. 2. prison*, clou m.
3. mitard m, trou m.
choo-choo [ˈtʃuːtʃuː] (noun), F: (langage
enfantin) teuf-teuf m.

---

* An asterisk indicates that the word so marked is included as a head-word in the Appendix.

chook(ie) [ˈtʃuːk(i)] (*noun*) (*Austr.*), *F:* poule *f*, poulet *m*.

choosy [ˈtʃuːzi] (*adj.*), *F:* chipoteur.

chop¹ [tʃɔp] (*noun*), *P:* 1. (*a*) **to give s.o. the c.**, se débarrasser* de qn, sacquer qn; *cf.* **sack**¹, 1; (*b*) **he's for the c.**! qu'est-ce qu'il va prendre! son affaire est bonne! 2. **to smack s.o. round the chops**, donner une bonne claque à qn. 3. **nourriture***, fricot *m*. *Voir aussi* **lamb**, 1; **lick**² (to), 3; **slobberchops**.

chop² [tʃɔp] (to). 1. *P:* guillotiner, raccourcir. 2. *P:* pendre*, béquiller; *cf.* **top**² (to). 3. *P:* (*sports*) donner un coup de pied dans les jambes de (qn). 4. *F:* **to c. and change**, changer d'idée comme de chemise.

chop-chop [ˈtʃɔpˈtʃɔp] (*adv.*), *F:* vite*, presto, dare-dare; **c.-c.**! dépêchez*-vous! vite!

chop down [ˈtʃɔpˈdaʊn] (to), *F:* **to c. s.o. d.** (to size), faire descendre qn `d'un cran, rapetisser qn.

chophouse [ˈtʃɔphaʊs] (*noun*), . *F:* restaurant chinois, gargot(t)e *f* chinetoque.

chopper [ˈtʃɔpər] (*noun*). 1. *V:* pénis*, défonceuse *f*. 2. *P:* mitraillette*, moulinette *f*. 3. *P:* hélicoptère *m*, battoir *m*, moulin *m*. 4. (*pl.*) *P:* dents*, croquantes *f.pl.* 5. *P:* vieille voiture* reprise pour une neuve. 6. *P:* (*a*) moto modifiée, sans chrome; (*b*) minivélo *m*.

chop-up [ˈtʃɔpʌp] (*noun*), *P:* partage *m* d'un butin, décarpillement *m*.

chouse [ˈtʃaʊz] (to), *P:* **to c. sth. out of s.o.**, carotter qch. à qn.

chow [tʃaʊ] (*noun*), *F:* nourriture*, mangeaille *f*, boustifaille *f*; **c. time**, l'heure *f* de la bouffe.

chowderhead [ˈtʃaʊdəhed] (*noun*) (*U.S.*), *F:* = **chucklehead**.

Christ [kraist] (*pr. noun*), *P:* 1. **C. (Almighty)**! bon Dieu (de bon Dieu)! Christi! 2. **for C.'s sake**! pour l'amour de Dieu! *Voir aussi* **Jesus** (**Christ**)!

Christmas-tree [ˈkrisməs-triː] (*noun*), *P:* drinamyl *m* (*drogues**), arbre *m* de Noël.

chromo [ˈkroʊmoʊ] (*noun*) (*Austr.*), *P:* 1. fille*, môme *f*; femme*, gonzesse *f*. 2. fille *ou* femme facile (*ou* de petite vertu).

chronic¹ [ˈkrɔnik] (*adj.*), *F:* insupportable, empoisonnant.

chronic² [ˈkrɔnik] (*adv.*), *P:* à haute dose; **I've got guts-ache something c.**, j'ai un mal de ventre carabiné; **she went off at me something c.**, elle m'a fait une scène du tonnerre.

chronic³ [ˈkrɔnik] (*noun*), *P:* drogué*, toxico(mane) *mf*.

chubb in [ˈtʃʌbˈin] (to), *P:* boucler, enfermer, coffrer (un prisonnier, *etc.*); *cf.* **miln** (to); **unchubb** (to).

chuck¹ [tʃʌk] (*noun*), *P:* 1. nourriture*, bectance *f*. 2. **c. habit**, gavage *m*. 3. **c. horrors**, dégoût *m* de la nourriture pendant le sevrage de drogues. 4. **to give s.o. the c.**, se débarrasser* de qn, balancer qn.

chuck² [tʃʌk] (to). 1. *F:* jeter*, lancer (qch.). 2. *P:* se débarrasser* de (qn), envoyer dinguer (qn). 3. *P:* (*a*) manger*, bouffer; (*b*) se gaver. 4. *F:* **c. it**! en voilà assez*! ça va comme ça! 5. *P:* **to get chucked**, être acquitté, être défargué. *Voir aussi* **dummy**, 4.

chuck about (*or* **around**) [ˈtʃʌkəˈbaʊt, ˈtʃʌkəˈraʊnd] (to), *F:* 1. **to c. one's money a.**, jeter son argent* par les fenêtres, gaspiller son argent*. 2. **to c. one's weight a.**, faire l'important, faire valoir son autorité, faire du volume (*ou* de l'esbrouf(f)e *f*).

chucker-out [ˈtʃʌkəˈraʊt] (*noun*), *F:* videur *m*.

chuck in [ˈtʃʌkˈin] (to), *F:* 1. **to c. i. one's job**, lâcher son travail* (*ou* son boulot). 2. **to c. it i.**, y renoncer, quitter la partie, lâcher les dés.

chucklehead [ˈtʃʌklhed] (*noun*) (*U.S.*), *F:* individu bête*, andouille *f*.

chuckleheaded [ˈtʃʌklhedid] (*adj.*) (*U.S.*), *F:* bête*, bas de plafond.

chuck out [ˈtʃʌkˈaʊt] (to), *F:* se débarrasser* de (qn), flanquer (qn) à la porte, balancer, vider (qn).

chuck up [ˈtʃʌkˈʌp] (to). 1. *F:* = **chuck in** (to), 1, 2. 2. *F:* **to c. s.o. u.**, lâcher qn, plaquer qn (comme une crêpe). 3. *P:* vomir*, dégobiller.

chuff [tʃʌf] (*noun*), *P:* 1. nourriture*, la soupe, le rata; *cf.* **honk** (to), 1. 2. anus*, anneau *m*. 3. fesses*, postérieur *m*.

chuffed [tʃʌft] (*adj.*), *F:* **to be c.**, (*a*) être ravi(e), être aux anges; (*b*) en

---

* L'astérisque indique que le mot marqué de ce signe figure comme entrée dans le Répertoire.

avoir assez*, en avoir marre (ou ras le bol); (c) être furibard (ou furax).

chum [tʃʌm] (noun), F: 1. ami*, pote m. 2. you've said it, c.! comme de juste (ou tout juste), Auguste! Voir aussi have (to), 4.

chummy [ˈtʃʌmi] (adj.), F: amical, bon copain.

chump [tʃʌmp] (noun). 1. P: tête*, caboche f; off one's c., fou*, timbré, loufoque. 2. F: a (silly) c., un individu bête*, un nigaud, une cruche.

chum up [ˈtʃʌmˈʌp] (to), F: copiner.

chunder [ˈtʃʌndər] (to) (Austr.), P: vomir*, dégueuler.

chunks [tʃʌŋks] (pl. noun), P: hachisch m (drogues*), griffs m.pl.

chunky [ˈtʃʌŋki] (adj.), F: 1. trapu. 2. (ameublement) encombrant, lourdaud. 3. c. jewellery, bijoux m.pl. mastoc.

chunner [ˈtʃʌnər] (to), P: grogner*, radoter.

churchy [ˈtʃəːtʃi] (adj.), F: calotin, tala; c. old women, vieilles punaises de sacristie.

churchyard [ˈtʃəːtʃjɑːd] (attrib. adj.), F: a c. cough, une toux de déterré (ou qui sent le sapin).

churn out [ˈtʃəːnˈaut] (to), F: produire beaucoup de (qch.), confectionner en quantité.

chute [ʃuːt] (noun). 1. P: up the c., (d'une personne) bête*, navet, con(n)asse. 2. P: to go up the c. = to go up in smoke (smoke¹, 1). 3. F: (=parachute) parachute m, pépin m.

chyack [ˈtʃaijæk] (to), P: se montrer très insolent envers (qn), narguer (qn).

cig(gy) [ˈsig(i)] (noun), F: cigarette*, cibiche f.

cinch [sintʃ] (noun), F: certitude f; it's a c., (a) c'est certain, c'est couru d'avance, c'est du tout cuit; (b) c'est facile; she's a c., c'est une femme facile.

circs [səːks] (pl. noun) (abbr. = circumstances), F: in (or under) the c., dans ce cas-là.

circus [ˈsəːkəs] (noun). 1. F: le cirque, une rigolade. 2. = brody, 2. Voir aussi Piccadilly Circus.

cissy [ˈsisi] (noun), F: 1. femmelette f, chiffe(niolle) f 2. poltron*, vessard m, poule mouillée.

civvies [ˈsiviz] (pl. noun), F: in c., en civelot, en bourgeois; (police) en pékin.

Voir aussi civvy².

civvy¹ [ˈsivi] (adj.), F: civil, pékin; in c. street, dans le civil.

civvy² [ˈsivi] (noun), F: bourgeois m, civil m. Voir aussi civvies.

clack¹ [klæk] (noun), P: caquet m; stop your c.! tais*-toi, la ferme! ferme ça! ferme ton clapet!

clack² [klæk] (to), P: bavarder*, caqueter, jacasser.

clackety-clack [ˈklækətiˈklæk] (noun), F: caquetage m, jacasserie f; cf. yackety-yack.

clamp-down [ˈklæmpdaun] (noun), F: contrainte f, vissage m, étouffage m.

clamp down [ˈklæmpˈdaun] (to), F: contraindre par la force; to c. d. on sth., s.o., serrer la vis à qch., qn, visser qch., qn.

clamps [klæmps] (pl. noun), F: to put the c. on sth., s.o. = to clamp down on sth., s.o.

clam up [ˈklæmˈʌp] (to), F: se taire*, la boucler.

clanger [ˈklæŋər] (noun), F: to drop a c., faire une bévue*.

clanked [klæŋkt] (adj.) (U.S.), P: 1. fatigué*, éreinté. 2. déprimé, cafardeux.

clap [klæp] (noun), P: blennorragie*, gonorrhée f, chaude-pisse f, coulante f.

clapped out [ˈklæptˈaut] (p.p. & adj.). 1. P: atteint de maladie vénérienne (malade*), nazicoté. 2. F: fatigué*, avachi.

clapper [ˈklæpər] (noun), F: 1. langue*, clapette f. 2. to go like the clappers, filer comme un zebre; to work like the clappers, travailler dur.

claret [ˈklærət] (noun), P: sang m, résiné m; to have one's c. tapped, saigner du nez*, pavoiser.

class(y) [ˈklɑːs(i)] (adj.), F: (a) chic, bon genre; (b) beau*, badour; to be c., avoir de la classe.

clean [kliːn] (adj.), F: 1. to be c. (as a whistle), (a) être tout beau (ou tout propre); (b) être sans condamnation*, être blanc; (c) être pauvre*, être à blanc; (d) être sans arme; (e) ne pas prendre de drogues, être sur le blanc. 2. to make a c. breast of it, tout avouer*, se mettre à table. 3. to come c., avouer*, lâcher le paquet. Voir aussi nose, 3; sweep¹, 3.

---

* An asterisk indicates that the word so marked is included as a head-word in the Appendix.

cleaners [ˈkliːnəz] (*pl. noun*), *P:* **to take s.o. to the c.**, mettre qn à sec.

clean-out [ˈkliːnaʊt] (*noun*), *F:* lessive *f*, coup *m* de balai.

clean out [ˈkliːnˈaʊt] (**to**), *F:* **to c. s.o. o.**, prendre l'argent* à qn, lessiver qn; **to get cleaned out**, perdre son argent*, être rincé, boire un bouillon, se faire plumer.

clear¹ [kliər] (*adj.*), *F:* **it's (as) c. as mud**, c'est la bouteille à l'encre, c'est clair comme du jus de boudin (*ou* de chique).

clear² [kliər] (*noun*), *F:* (*a*) **to be in the c.**, (i) être tiré d'affaire (*ou* sorti de l'auberge); (ii) être blanc (*ou* défargué); (*b*) **to put s.o. in the c.**, (i) tirer qn d'affaire; (ii) défarguer qn. *Voir aussi* **all-clear.**

clear off [ˈkliərˈɔf] (**to**), *F:* partir*, prendre le large (*ou* la tangente); **c. o.!** file! fiche le camp! décampe!

clear-out [ˈkliəraʊt] (*noun*): **to have a c.-o.**, (*a*) *F:* faire du triage, désencombrer; (*b*) *P:* déféquer*, déflaquer.

clear out [ˈkliərˈaʊt] (**to**), *F:* **1. = clear off** (**to**). **2. to c. s.o. o. of sth.**, débarrasser qn de qch., nettoyer qn.

cleavage [ˈkliːvidʒ] (*noun*), *F:* (*a*) naissance *f* des seins*; (*b*) décolleté très ouvert.

cleft [kleft] (*noun*), *V:* vagin*, crac *m*, fente *f*.

clever-clever [ˈklevəklevər] (*adj.*), *F:* malin*, débrouillard.

cleverclogs [ˈklevəklɔgz], **cleverguts** [ˈklevəgʌts] (*noun*), *P:* **= clever Dick** (**dick, 3**).

click [klik] (**to**), *F:* **to c. with s.o.**, (*a*) sympathiser (*ou* accrocher) avec qn; (*b*) faire une touche.

clickety-click [ˈklikətiˈklik], *F:* *voir* **bingo (66).**

cliffhanger [ˈklifhæŋər] (*noun*), *F:* (*film*) drame-feuilleton *m*; suspense *m*.

climb [klaim] (**to**), *P:* coïter* avec (une femme), chevaucher. *Voir aussi* **bandwagon.**

clinch [klintʃ] (*noun*), *F:* embrassade *f*, étreinte amoureuse, enlacement *m*.

clincher [ˈklintʃər] (*noun*), *F:* argument définitif; **that's a c.**, (*a*) ça lui a fermé le bec; (*b*) c'est le mot de la fin.

clinger [ˈkliŋər] (*noun*), *F:* crampon *m*.

clink [kliŋk] (*noun*), *P:* prison*, violon

m; **to be in c.**, faire de la grosse caisse; **to put s.o. in c.**, mettre qn au bloc; **to go to c.**, être emprisonné*, être fourré au bloc.

clinker [ˈkliŋkər] (*noun*), *P:* **1.** coup*, gnon *m*. **2.** mensonge*, crac *m*. **3.** vieille voiture*, tacot *m*. **4.** type *m ou* chose *f* formidable.

clip¹ [klip] (*noun*), *F:* **1.** coup*, beigne *f*, taloche *f*. **2.** pas *m* rapide.

clip² [klip] (**to**). **1.** *F:* flanquer une taloche à (qn). **2.** *P:* voler*, écorcher, plumer, estamper (qn). **3.** *P:* aller à vive allure (*ou* à toute bride).

clip-game [ˈklipgeim] (*noun*), *P:* filouterie *f*.

clip-joint [ˈklipdʒɔint] (*noun*), *F:* boîte *f*, tripot *m*, maison *f* tire-pognon.

clipper [ˈklipər] (*noun*), *F:* individu *ou* chose remarquable, du tonnerre.

clippie [ˈklipi] (*noun*), *F:* receveuse *f* d'autobus.

clit [klit] (*noun*), *V:* clitoris*, clicli *m*.

cloak-and-dagger [ˈkloʊk(ə)nˈdægər] (*attrib. adj.*), *F:* de cape et d'épée.

clobber¹ [ˈklɔbər] (*noun*), *P:* vêtements*, frusques *f.pl.*, hardes *f.pl.*

clobber² [ˈklɔbər] (**to**), *P:* **1.** battre*, matraquer, rosser; **to get clobbered**, être rossé, se faire arranger. **2.** écraser, battre à plate(s) couture(s).

clobbering [ˈklɔbəriŋ] (*noun*), *P:* **to give s.o. a c.**, donner une rossée à qn.

clock¹ [klɔk] (*noun*). **1.** *P:* visage*, poire *f*. **2.** *F:* **to beat the c.**, arriver* avant l'heure. **3.** *F:* **round the c.**, vingt-quatre heures sur vingt-quatre; **to sleep round the c.**, **to sleep the c. round**, faire le tour du cadran.

clock² [klɔk] (**to**), *P:* **1.** battre*, calotter (qn), abîmer le portrait à (qn). **2.** guetter*, mater, gaffer (qn).

clock up [ˈklɔkˈʌp] (**to**), *F:* **to c. u. the miles**, rouler vite*, avaler les kilomètres.

clock-watcher [ˈklɔkwɔtʃər] (*noun*), *F:* tire-au-flanc *m*.

clod [klɔd] (*noun*), *F:* **= clodhopper, 1.**

clod-crushers [ˈklɔdkrʌʃəz] (*pl. noun*), *P:* **= clodhoppers** (**clodhopper, 3**).

clodhopper [ˈklɔdhɔpər] (*noun*), *P:* **1.** paysan*, plouc *m*. **2.** déguingandé *m*. **3.** (*pl.*) grosses chaussures*, tatanes *f.pl.*

clogging [ˈklɔgiŋ] (*noun*) (*football*), *F:* jeu déloyal, barbouillage *m*.

---

* L'astérisque indique que le mot marqué de ce signe figure comme entrée dans le Répertoire.

cloghead [ˈklɔghed] (*noun*), *P:* individu bête*, gourde *f.*

clomp about [ˈklɔmpəˈbaʊt] (**to**), *F:* = **clump about** (**to**).

clonk¹ [klɔŋk] (*noun*), *P:* coup*, ramponneau *m*; **to fetch s.o. a c.**, filer un ramponneau à qn.

clonk² [klɔŋk] (**to**), *P:* battre*, frapper; **to c. s.o. one**, filer un gnon à qn; **to c. s.o. on the head**, assommer qn, envoyer dormir qn.

clonk about [ˈklɔŋkəˈbaʊt] (**to**), *F:* = **clump about** (**to**).

close¹ [klous] (*adj.*), *P:* excellent*, foutral. *Voir aussi* **shave**.

close² [klous] (*adv.*), *F:* **to play it c.** (**to the chest**), y aller mollo, jouer serré.

close-fisted [ˈklousˈfistid] (*adj.*), *F:* avare*, radin, dur à la détente.

clot [klɔt] (*noun*), *F:* personne bête*, clope *m*, cave *m*; **you clumsy c.!** espèce d'empoté! **what a c.!** qu'est-ce qu'il trimbal(l)e!

cloth-ears [ˈklɔθ-iəz] (*noun*), *F:* sourd*, dur *m* de la feuille.

clothes-horse [ˈklouðzhɔːs] (*noun*), *P:* femme* tape-à-l'œil, mannequin ambulant.

cloth-head [ˈklɔθhed] (*noun*), *F:* = **clot**.

cloud [klaʊd] (*noun*), *F:* **1. to have one's head in the clouds**, être dans la lune. **2. to be (up) in the clouds**, être aux anges. **3. to be on c. nine**, être au septième ciel.

cloud-cuckoo-land [ˈklaʊdˈkʊkuːlænd] (*noun*), *F:* pays *m* des rêves, pays des Châteaux en Espagne.

clout¹ [klaʊt] (*noun*). **1.** *F:* coup*, calotte *f*; **to give** (*or* **fetch**) **s.o. a c.**, filer une calotte à qn. **2.** *V:* vagin*, motte *f.* *Voir aussi* **dishclout**.

clout² [klaʊt] (**to**), *F:* filer une calotte à (qn).

clover [ˈklouvər] (*noun*), *F:* **to be in c.**, être comme un coq en pâte.

club [klʌb] (*noun*). **1.** *F:* **to join the c.**, s'acoquiner avec qn. **2.** *P:* **to join the** (**pudding**) **c.**, être enceinte*.

cluck [klʌk] (*noun*), *P:* **dumb c.**, individu bête*, gourde *f*, cruchon *m.*

clue [kluː] (*noun*), *F:* **he hasn't a c.**, (*a*) il n'a pas la moindre idée; (*b*) il n'est bon à rien.

clueless [ˈkluːlis] (*adj.*), *F:* **1.** qui est

dans le noir (*ou* dans le brouillard). **2.** qui n'a pas trouvé le joint.

clue up [ˈkluːˈʌp] (**to**), *F:* **to c. s.o. u.**, mettre qn sur la piste (*ou* au parfum *ou* à la page); **to be clued up**, être au parfum; **to get clued up**, se faire rencarder.

clump¹ [klʌmp] (*noun*), *F:* coup*, beigne *f.*

clump² [klʌmp] (**to**), *F:* battre*, tabasser (qn).

clump about [ˈklʌmpəˈbaʊt] (**to**), *F:* marcher lourdement.

clunk [klʌŋk] (*noun & verb*), *P:* = **clonk¹,²**.

clunkhead [ˈklʌŋkhed] (*noun*) (*U.S.*), *P:* = **chucklehead**.

clutch up [ˈklʌtʃˈʌp] (**to**) (*U.S.*), *F:* s'énerver, se monter le ciboulot.

cly [klai] (*noun*), *P:* poche*, fouille *f.*

coal-burner [ˈkoulbəːnər] (*noun*), *P:* = **dinge queen** (*voir* **queen**, 2); *cf.* **chocolate**.

coalie, coaly [ˈkouli] (*noun*), *F:* charbonnier *m*, carbi *m.*

coast along [ˈkoustəˈlɔŋ] (**to**), *F:* **1.** aller en roue libre. **2.** se la couler douce, ne pas se fouler.

coasting [ˈkoustiŋ] (*noun*). **1.** *F:* (*d'une personne, d'un véhicule*) marche *f* en roue libre. **2.** *P:* état *m* d'animation dû à la drogue, bang *m.*

cob [kɔb] (*noun*), *P:* miche *f* de pain* (*en prison*), demi-boule *f.*

cobber [ˈkɔbər] (*noun*) (*Austr.*), *F:* ami*, copain *m*, pote *m.*

cobbler [ˈkɔblər] (*noun*), *P:* faussaire *m*, homme *m* de lettres. *Voir aussi* **cobblers**.

cobblers [ˈkɔbləz] (*pl. noun*) (*R.S.* = *cobblers' awls* = *balls*), *P:* **it's a load of c.** = **it's all balls** (**balls**, 6).

cock [kɔk] (*noun*). **1.** *V:* (*a*) pénis*, queue *f*; (*b*) mâle (*considéré sexuellement*). **2.** *P:* bêtise*, coq-à-l'âne *m*; **to talk c.**, déconner; *voir aussi* **load**, 2; **poppycock**. **3.** *P:* **all to c.**, de traviole. **4.** *P:* **well, old c.**, eh bien, mon colon!; **wotcher, c.!** comment ça gaze, ma vieille branche? **5.** *P:* **c. and hen** (*R.S.* = *ten*), billet* de dix livres; **half a c.**, billet* de cinq livres, un gros talbin. *Voir aussi* **half-cock**.

cock-a-hoop [ˈkɔkəˈhuːp] (*adj.*), *F:* fier comme Artaban.

---

* An asterisk indicates that the word so marked is included as a head-word in the Appendix.

cockalorum [kɔkəˈlɔːrəm] (noun), F: petit* individu plein de prétention, astèque plastronneur.

cockatoo(er) [ˈkɔkəˈtuː(ər)] (noun) (Austr.), P: compère m qui fait le guet, arçonneur m, gaffe m, gâfe m.

cocked [kɔkt] (adj.), F: to knock sth. into a c. hat, démantibuler qch.; to knock s.o. into a c. hat, (a) battre* qn à plate(s) couture(s), pulvériser qn; (b) abasourdir qn.

cocker [ˈkɔkər] (noun), P: = cock, 4.

cockeyed [ˈkɔkaid] (adj.), P: 1. très bête*, noix, à la manque. 2. ivre*, rétamé à bloc. 3. de travers, de guingois. 4. qui louche*, qui a un œil qui dit zut à l'autre. 5. inexact, biscornu.

cock-handler [ˈkɔkhændlər], cock-pusher [ˈkɔkpuʃər] (noun), V: pédéraste*, empaffé m.

cock-shy [ˈkɔkʃai] (adj.), V: (d'une femme) qui a peur des rapports sexuels.

cock-sparrow [ˈkɔkˈspærou, ˈkɔkˈspærə] (noun). 1. F: = cockalorum. 2. P: wotcher, me old c.-s.! = wotcher, cock! (cock, 4).

cock-stand [ˈkɔk-stænd] (noun), V: érection*, bandoche f, coliques cornues.

cock-sucker [ˈkɔk-sʌkər] (noun), V: 1. pédéraste*, lope f. 2. salaud m, fumier m. 3. lèche-bottes m, lèche-cul m.

cock-sucking [ˈkɔk-sʌkin] (noun), V: coït* buccal, prise f de pipe.

cock-teaser [ˈkɔk-tiːzər] (noun), V: = prick-teaser.

cock-up [ˈkɔkʌp] (noun), V: = balls-up.

cock up [ˈkɔkˈʌp] (to). 1. V: = balls up (to). 2. F: to c. u. one's eyes, faire des yeux de merlan frit.

cocky [ˈkɔki] (adj.), F: culotté, qui a du toupet; suffisant.

coco(a) [ˈkoukou] (to), P: 1. (R.S. = say so) I should c.! et comment donc! tu parles! 2. croire*, couper dedans; you wouldn't c. it! tu ne t'en fais pas la moindre idée!

cod [kɔd] (to), P: duper*, emmener (qn) en bateau, faire marcher (qn).

codger [ˈkɔdʒər] (noun), F: 1. (drôle de) coco m. 2. old c., vieux décati.

cods [kɔdz] (pl. noun), P: testicules*, burettes f.pl., burnes f.pl.

codswallop [ˈkɔdzwɔləp] (noun), F: 1. bêtises*, tissu m d'âneries. 2. bière f de mauvaise qualité, bibine f.

co-ed [ˈkouˈ(w)ed] (noun), F: élève mf d'une école mixte.

coffin [ˈkɔfin] (noun). 1. (U.S.) P: mitard m, (s)chtard m. 2. F: c. nail, cigarette*, cibiche f.

cog [kɔg] (to), P: tricher* (surtout aux dés), biseauter; cogged dice, dés* pipés.

coin [kɔin] (to), F: to c. it, to be coining it, devenir riche*, faire des affaires d'or, tomber sur un champ d'oseille.

coke [kouk] (noun). 1. F: Coca-Cola m (marque déposée). 2. P: cocaïne f (drogues*), coco f; c. fiend, cocaïnomane mf, (s)chnouffé(e); c. oven, clandé m. cf. charl(e)y², 5.

coked (up) [ˈkoukt(ˈʌp)] (adj.), P: drogué*, chargé, bourré (à la cocaïne).

cokehead [ˈkoukhed] (noun), P: = coke fiend (coke, 2).

cokernut [ˈkoukənʌt] (noun). 1. F: (=coco(a)nut) noix f de coco. 2. P: tête*, coco m.

cokey, cokie [ˈkouki], cokomo [kou-ˈkoumou] (noun), P: = coke fiend (coke, 2).

cold¹ [kould] (adj.), F: 1. to be out (stone) c., être dans les pommes; to pass out c., s'évanouir*, tourner de l'œil; to knock s.o. out c., mettre qn sur le tapis, étendre raide qn. 2. that leaves me c., ça me laisse froid. 3. to give s.o. the c. shoulder, battre froid à qn, faire la tête à qn; cf. cold-shoulder (to). 4. c. feet, peur*, frousse f; to get c. feet, caner, caponner. 5. c. fish, pisse-froid m. 6. (a) c. potato = c. fish (voir 5); (b) c. potatoes, du réchauffé. 7. to put in c. storage, (a) (fig.) mettre au frigidaire; (b) économiser*, mettre à gauche; (c) emprisonner*, mettre au bloc. Voir aussi blood, 4; meat, 5; stone-cold; sweat¹, 4; turkey, 1; water, 1.

cold² [kould] (noun), F: 1. to catch a c., écoper. 2. to be left out in the c., être mis de côté, rester sur le carreau.

cold-shoulder [ˈkouldˈʃouldər] (to), F: battre froid à (qn), faire grise mine à (qn); cf. cold¹, 3.

colin [ˈkɔlin] (noun), P: érection*, bambou m, trique f.

collar¹ [ˈkɔlər] (noun), F: to get one's c. felt (or touched), être arrêté*, se faire alpaguer. Voir aussi dog-collar; hot, 5; white-collar.

collar² [ˈkɔlər] (to), F: 1. arrêter*, cravater. 2. (a) plaquer; (b) saisir, pincer, mettre la main sur (qn, qch.).

collywobbles [ˈkɔliwɔblz] (pl. noun), F: to have the c., (a) avoir des borborygmes m.pl.; (b) avoir la diarrhée*, avoir la chiasse.

colour [ˈkʌlər] (noun), F: let's see the c. of your money, prouve que tu as de l'argent*; où est l'auréole de ton Saint-Fric? Voir aussi horse¹, 3; off⁴, 1.

column-dodger [ˈkɔləmˈdɔdʒər] (noun), F: tire-au-flanc m; cf. to dodge the column (dodge² (to), 1).

combo [ˈkɔmbou] (noun), P: orchestre m de jazz.

comb-out [ˈkoumaut] (noun), F: ratissage m.

come¹ [kʌm] (noun), P: sperme*, jus m.

come² [kʌm] (to). 1. P: avoir un orgasme*, jouir, juter. 2. F: as dim (or daft) as they c., bête* comme ses pieds. 3. F: you'll get what's coming to you! tu ne perds rien pour attendre! 4. F: to c. it (a bit) strong, exagérer*, y aller fort, attiger (la cabane). 5. P: to c. it over s.o., faire la loi à qn. 6. P: don't (you) c. it with me! charrie pas avec moi! 7. F: to c. over funny (or queer), se sentir tout chose. Voir aussi acid, 1; clean, 3; soldier¹, 3; think¹.

come-back [ˈkʌmbæk] (noun), F: 1. to make a c.-b., se remettre sur pied, se retaper, se refaire. 2. réplique pertinente ou pleine de sel.

come-down [ˈkʌmdaun] (noun). 1. F: what a c.-d.! quelle dégringolade! quelle douche! 2. P: retour m à l'état hors drogue, descente f.

come down [ˈkʌmˈdaun] (to). 1. F: revenir à l'état hors drogue, redescendre. 2. V: to c. d. on s.o. = eat (to), 7; cf. go down (to), 5. 3. F: to c. d. on s.o. (like a ton of bricks), réprimander* qn, enguirlander qn. 4. P: to c. d. in the world, déchoir, descendre plusieurs échelons. Voir aussi peg¹, 2 (b).

comedy [ˈkɔmidi] (noun), F: cut the c.! finie la comédie!

come-hither [ˈkʌmˈhiðər] (adj.), F: a c.-h. look, les yeux* doux, œillade* en lousdoc.

come off [ˈkʌmˈɔf] (to), P: 1. = come² (to), 1. 2. c. o. it! (a) change de disque! arrête ton char!; (b) pas tant de ma-

nières!

come-on [ˈkʌmɔn] (noun), P: to give s.o. the c.-o., encourager les avances sexuelles de qn.

come on [ˈkʌmˈɔn] (to), P: 1. commencer à ressentir les effets d'une drogue, partir. 2. flirter, faire des avances. 3. to c. o. (a bit) = to come it (a bit) strong (come² (to), 4).

come up [ˈkʌmˈʌp] (to), F: gagner, affurer; to c. u. on the horses, gagner aux courses; prendre un paquet aux courtines.

come-uppance [ˈkʌmˈʌpəns] (noun), F: coup m de caveçon; to get one's c.-u., recevoir un coup de caveçon, se faire dire ses quatre vérités.

comfy [ˈkʌmfi] (adj.) (=comfortable), F: confortable, douillet. Voir aussi nice and . . .

comic [ˈkɔmik] (adj.), F: c. cuts, (a) bandes dessinées; (b) bille f de clown, gugusse m; (c) rapport confidentiel.

commercial [kəˈməːʃəl] (noun), P: to have a right old c., faire du bruit*, faire du barouf.

Commie¹, commie [ˈkɔmi] (adj.), F: communiste, bolcho, communo.

Commie², commie [ˈkɔmi] (noun), F: communiste mf, communo m.

common [ˈkɔmən] (noun), F: sens commun, du chou.

compos [ˈkɔmpɔs] (adj.) he doesn't seem c. to me, je le trouve un peu cinglé.

compree [kɔmˈpriː] (verbal form), F: compris, pigé.

con¹ [kɔn] (noun). 1. F: (=convict) taulard m; cf. ex. 2. (U.S.) P: pédéraste*, lope f. 3. F: escroquerie*, carottage m; c. game, combine f louche, attrape-couillons m; c. man (or artist), escroc*, arnaqueur m, estampeur m. Voir aussi pro, 3.

con² [kɔn] (to), F: escroquer*, empaumer (qn); to c. s.o. into doing sth., entortiller qn.

conchie, conchy [ˈkɔntʃi] (noun), F: (=conscientious objector) objecteur m de conscience.

confab [ˈkɔnfæb] (noun), F: bavette f, causette f; there's a family c. going on, toute la famille est en train de conférer.

confab(ulate) [kənˈfæb(juleit)] (to), F: bavarder*, tailler une bavette;

conférer.

conflab [ˈkɔnflæb] (*noun*), *F:* = confab.

Congo Mataby [ˈkɔŋgouˈmætəbi] (*noun*), *F:* cannabis *m* (*drogues**).

conk[1] [kɔŋk] (*noun*), *P:* 1. nez*, pif *m*. 2. tête*, caboche *f*, ciboulot *m*. 3. coup*, gnon *m*.

conk[2] [kɔŋk] (to), *P:* to c. s.o., flanquer un gnon à qn, matraquer qn.

conker [ˈkɔŋkər] (*noun*). 1. *F:* marron *m* d'Inde. 2. (*pl.*) *F:* jeu *m* de marrons. 3. (*pl.*) *P:* argent*, flouze *m*. 4. (*pl.*) *P:* testicules*, olives *f.pl.*

conk out [ˈkɔŋkˈaut] (to). 1. *F:* tomber en rade, claquer, caler. 2. *P:* s'évanouir*, tomber dans les pommes. 3. *P:* mourir*, caner, cadancher.

Connaught ranger [ˈkɔnɔːtˈreindʒər] (*noun*) (*R.S.* = *stranger*), *P:* inconnu *m*, étranger *m*.

connect [kəˈnekt] (to), *P:* 1. faire un boum. 2. faire une touche. 3. acheter des drogues.

connection [kəˈnekʃ(ə)n], **connector** [kəˈnektər], **connexion** [kəˈnekʃ(ə)n] (*noun*), *F:* contact *m*, inter *m*, fourgue *m*.

conshie, conshy [ˈkɔnʃi] (*noun*), *F:* = conchie, conchy.

contract [ˈkɔntrækt] (*noun*), *P:* engagement *m* à tuer* qn, dessoudage *m*; to have a c. on s.o., s'être engagé à tuer* qn.

coo! [kuː] (*excl.*), *F:* tiens! mazette! c'est pas vrai!

cook[1] [kuk] (*noun*). 1. *P:* = chef, 2. 2. *F:* to be head (*or* chief) c. and bottle-washer, être l'homme à tout faire, être le lampiste (*ou* le sous-fifre en chef).

cook[2] [kuk] (to). 1. *F:* what's cooking? quoi de neuf? qu'est-ce qui se mijote? qu'est-ce qui se goupille? 2. *F:* to c. the books, trafiquer (*ou* tripoter *ou* cuisiner *ou* maquiller) les comptes *m.pl.* 3. *F:* to c. s.o.'s goose, faire son affaire à qn, régler son compte à qn. 4. *P:* = cook up (to), 2 (*b*).

cooked [kukt] (*adj.*). 1. *F:* très fatigué*, exténué. 2. *F:* to be c., (*d'une personne*) cuire dans son jus. 3. *P:* = cooked up.

cooked up [ˈkuktˈʌp] (*adj.*), *P:* drogué*, camé. *Voir aussi* cook up (to), 2.

cooker [ˈkukər] (*noun*). 1. *F:* (=*cooking apple*) pomme *f* à cuire. 2. *P:* = cookie, 4.

cookie [ˈkuki] (*noun*). 1. *F:* that's the

way the c. crumbles = that's the way the mop flops (*voir* mop). 2. *P:* cocaïne *f* (*drogues**), coco *f*. 3. *P:* toxico *m*, cocaïnomane *mf.* 4. *P:* = chef, 2. 5. (*U.S.*) *F:* individu*, type *m*. 6. *P:* hot c. = hot babe (babe, 2). 7. (*U.S.*) *V:* = cooze, 2.

cook up [ˈkukˈʌp] (to). 1. *F:* to c. u. an excuse, combiner une excuse. 2. *P:* (*a*) cuire (de l'opium); (*b*) dissoudre une drogue à la chaleur avant la piqûre. *Voir aussi* cooked up.

cool[1] [kuːl] (*adj.*). 1. *F:* détendu, relax. 2. *F:* beau*, bath; bien, satisfaisant. 3. *F:* a c. £1000, £1000 au minimum. 4. *F:* distant, peu abordable, peu émotif, cool. 5. *F:* passionnant, palpitant. 6. *F:* dans le vent, avant-garde. 7. (*jazz*) *F:* sobre (dans l'expression musicale), cool; *cf.* hot, 7. 8. *P:* to be c., (*drogués*) planer calmement.

cool[2] [kuːl] (*adv.*), *F:* to play it c., ne pas s'énerver, y aller la tête froide.

cool[3] [kuːl] (*noun*), *F:* 1. to keep one's c. = to play it cool (cool[2]). 2. to lose (*or* blow) one's c., se mettre en colère*, piquer une crise. 3. le cool (*type de jazz*).

cool[4] [kuːl] (to), *F:* to c. it, se relâcher, se calmer; c. it! ne t'emballe pas! laisse courir! *Voir aussi* heel, 2.

cooler [ˈkuːlər] (*noun*), *P:* 1. prison*, taule *f*, tôle *f*. 2. mitard *m*, (s)chtard *m*.

coon [kuːn] (*noun*), *P:* 1. nègre*, bougnoule *m*. 2. individu*, mec *m*.

co-op [ˈkou(w)ɔp] (*noun*), *F:* (=*cooperative stores*) société coopérative, coopé *f*.

coop [kuːp] (*noun*), *P:* prison*; to fly the c., s'évader*, (se) calter.

coot [kuːt] (*noun*). 1. *P:* individu bête*, gourde *f*. 2. *F:* bald as a c., chauve* comme un genou (*ou* un œuf *ou* une bille).

cootie [ˈkuːti] (*noun*), *P:* pou*, morbac *m*.

cooty [ˈkuːti] (*adj.*), *P:* pouilleux, plein de poux*.

cooze [kuːz], **coozie** [ˈkuːzi] (*noun*) (*U.S.*), *V:* 1. coït*, coup *m* de tringle. 2. vulve*, baba *m*. 3. femelle *f*, bout *m* de con.

cop[1] [kɔp] (*noun*). 1. *F:* = copper, 1; speed (*or* courtesy) c., motard *m*; *cf.* fly-cop. 2. *P:* it's a fair c., on est fait, rien à dire. 3. *P:* **no (great) c.**, **not much c.**, sans valeur, pacotille. 4. (*Austr.*) *P:* (bon) filon, affure *f.*

cop[2] [kɔp] **(to),** *P:* 1. arrêter*, pincer (qn); **to get copped,** se faire pincer. 2. **to c. it,** (*a*) écoper; (*b*) être réprimandé*, recevoir un savon. 3. affurer, agricher. 4. **to c. hold of sth.,** choper, attraper (le bout de qch.). 5. obtenir *ou* acheter des drogues, se fournir. *Voir aussi* **dose,** 1; **needle**[1], 1 (*c*); **packet,** 1; **spike**[1], 2.

copilot [ˈkouˈpailət] (*noun*), *P:* Benzédrine *f* (*marque déposée*) (*drogues**), topette *f.*

cop out [ˈkɔpˈaut] **(to),** *P:* 1. se retirer, se dégager. 2. se désolidariser, s'esquiver. 3. éluder (une question, *etc.*). 4. ne pas tenir une promesse. 5. vendre la mèche, lâcher le paquet. 6. avouer*, accoucher, déballonner.

copper [ˈkɔpər] (*noun*). 1. *P:* agent* de police, flic *m.* 2. *P:* **to come c.,** devenir indicateur* de police, y aller du coup de casserole. 3. *F:* gros sou*.

copper-nob [ˈkɔpənɔb], **copper-top** [ˈkɔpətɔp] (*noun*), *P:* rouquin(e), poil *m* de carotte.

cop-shop [ˈkɔp-ʃɔp] (*noun*), *P:* commissariat *m* de police, burlingue *m* de quart.

cop-wagon [ˈkɔpwægən] (*noun*), *P:* = **Black Maria.**

copycat [ˈkɔpikæt] (*noun*), *F:* **to be a c.,** faire le singe; **c.!** perroquet!.

cor! [kɔːr] (*excl.*), (*a*) *F:* ça alors!; **c., she's a smasher!** bon Dieu, ce qu'elle est bath!; **c. love a duck!** grands dieux!; (*b*) *P:* **c. blimey!** = **gorblimey!**

corked [kɔːkt] (*adj.*), *P:* ivre* mort.

corker [ˈkɔːkər] (*noun*), *F:* 1. (*a*) individu* formidable; (*b*) une belle fille. 2. gros mensonge*, bourrage *m* de crâne. 3. **that's a c.,** ça vous la bouche, ça vous en bouche un coin.

corking [ˈkɔːkiŋ] (*adj.*), *F:* excellent*, foutral, formid(able).

corky [ˈkɔːki] (*adj.*), *F:* plein d'allant, éveillé, animé.

corn [kɔːn] (*noun*), *F:* 1. vieille rengaine. 2. vieux jeu. 3. guimauve *f.* 4. **to step** (*or* **tread**) **on s.o.'s corns,** toucher qn à l'endroit sensible, marcher sur les pieds de qn; froisser qn. *Voir aussi* **popcorn.**

corned beef [ˈkɔːn(d)ˈbiːf] (*noun*), *P:* (*R.S.* = *thief*) voleur*; *cf.* **tea-leaf.**

corner [ˈkɔːnər] (*noun*), *F:* (*a*) part *f*, portion *f*; **to pay one's c.,** payer* sa part; (*b*) part *f* de butin*, fade *m.* *Voir aussi* **cut**[3] **(to),** 7, 8; **hole-and-corner.**

corner-boy [ˈkɔːnəbɔi] (*noun*), *P:* batteur *m* de pavé, traîne-cul *m*, traînelattes *m.*

cornhole[1] [ˈkɔːnhoul] (*noun*) (*U.S.*), *V:* anus*, trou *m* de balle.

cornhole[2] [ˈkɔːnhoul] **(to)** (*U.S.*), *V:* empaffer (*coït* anal).

cornholer [ˈkɔːnhoulər] (*noun*) (*U.S.*), *V:* pédéraste*, qui est de la bague.

corn-stalk [ˈkɔːn-stɔːk] (*noun*) (*U.S.*), *F:* (*d'une personne*) grande perche.

corny [ˈkɔːni] (*adj.*), *F:* 1. banal, rebattu. 2. vioque. 3. à l'eau de rose.

'cos [kɔz] (*conj.*), *F:* (=*because*) parce que, pasque, bicause.

cosh[1] [kɔʃ] (*noun*), *F:* matraque *f*, assommoir *m*, cigare *m.*

cosh[2] [kɔʃ] **(to),** *F:* matraquer, assommer (qn).

cost [kɔst] **(to),** *F:* **I can get it but it'll c. you,** je peux l'avoir mais ça sera chérot (*ou* ça ira chercher loin).

cotics [ˈkɔtiks] (*pl. noun*) (=*narcotics*), *P:* drogues*, narcs *m.pl.*

cotton[1] [kɔtn] (*noun*), *P:* 1. amphétamines *f.pl.* (*drogues**). 2. tout ce qui est saturé d'une drogue qui peut être inhalée; **c. freak,** drogué* par inhalation.

cotton[2] [kɔtn] **(to),** *F:* **to c. to s.o.,** être attiré par qn, avoir qn à la bonne.

cotton on [ˈkɔtnˈɔn] **(to),** *F:* 1. comprendre, piger, entraver. 2. **I can't c. o. to him,** sa tête ne me revient pas, ça ne biche pas avec lui.

cotton-picking [ˈkɔtnˈpikiŋ] (*adj.*) (*U.S.*), *F:* 1. commun, vulgaire. 2. sacré, satané. 3. gnognot(t)eux, navet.

cotton-wool [ˈkɔtnˈwul] (*noun*), *F:* **to wrap s.o. in c.-w.,** mettre qn dans du coton, garder qn sous cloche.

couch [kautʃ] (*noun*), *F:* **casting c.,** lit *m* par où doit passer une actrice pour avoir un rôle.

couch-doctor [ˈkautʃdɔktər] (*noun*), *F:* psychanalyste *mf.*

cough-drop [ˈkɔfdrɔp] (*noun*), *F:* 1. dur *m* à cuire. 2. drôle *m* de numéro.

cough up [ˈkɔfˈʌp] **(to),** *F:* 1. payer*,

---

* An asterisk indicates that the word so marked is included as a head-word in the Appendix.

cracher, abouler. 2. parler*, dévider, dégoiser.

count [kaunt] (noun), F: to be out for the c., (a) avoir son compte, aller au tapis, être K.O.; (b) être profondément endormi.

counter ['kauntər] (noun), F: to sell sth. under the c., vendre qch. en cachette. Voir aussi under-the-counter.

count in ['kaunt'in] (to), F: you can c. me i., je marche, je suis partant.

count out ['kaunt'aut] (to), F: you can c. me o., je ne marche pas, je ne suis pas partant.

county ['kaunti] (adj.), F: (a) the c. set, l'aristocratie provinciale, la haute bourgeoisie provinciale; (b) qui appartient au beau monde.

courage ['kʌridʒ] (attrib. adj.), P: c. pills, comprimé m d'héroïne (drogues*).

cove [kouv] (noun), F: individu*; a queer c., un drôle de pistolet.

Coventry ['kovəntri] (noun), F: to send s.o. to C., mettre qn en quarantaine.

cover¹ ['kʌvər] (noun), F: couverture*, couverte f, prétexte m.

cover² ['kʌvər] (to), P: 1. accepter un pari. 2. faire un pari, parier, mettre une mise.

cover-girl ['kʌvəgə:l] (noun), F: pin-up f, cover-girl f.

cover up ['kʌvər'ʌp] (to), F: to c. u. for s.o., couvrir qn, prendre les patins pour qn.

cow [kau] (noun). 1. P: an (old) c., femme* (péj.), une vieille bique, une vache. 2. P: poor c.! pauvre pute! 3. (Austr.) P: loquedu m, teigne f; it's a fair c., que c'est moche!; he's a fair c., qu'il est moche! 4. P: une livre sterling; a c. and calf, une livre cinquante pence; cf. calf, 1. 5. P: till the cows come home, dans la semaine des quatre jeudis, jusqu'à la Saint-Glinglin, quand les poules auront des dents, jusqu'à plus soif. Voir aussi bull, 3; holy, 1; moo-cow.

cow-juice ['kaudʒu:s] (noun), F: lait m, lolo m.

cow-poke ['kaupouk], cow-puncher ['kaupʌntʃər] (noun) (U.S.), F: cowboy m.

cozzer ['kɔzər] (noun), P: policier*, condé m.

cozzy ['kɔzi] (noun), P: = karzy.

crab¹ [kræb] (noun), P: 1. grognon m, rouscailleur m; she's an old c., elle est une vieille emmerdeuse (ou râleuse). 2. (pl.) poux* du pubis, morpions m.pl.

crab² [kræb] (to), P: 1. grogner*, râler. 2. to c. the act (or deal), mettre des bâtons dans les roues.

crabber ['kræbər] (noun), P: grognon m, rouspéteur m.

crack¹ [kræk] (noun). 1. V: vagin*, fente f, crac m. 2. F: blague f, vanne f. 3. F: to have a c. (at sth.), tenter le coup (ou sa chance). 4. F: to have a c. at s.o., (a) filer une taloche à qn; (b) se moquer* de qn; cf. wisecrack¹. Voir aussi paper² (to), 2; whip¹, 1.

crack² [kræk] (to). 1. P: filer un coup* à (qn). 2. F: to get cracking, (a) commencer, embrayer; (b) aller vite*, se grouiller. 3. F: craquer, flancher. 4. to c. it, (a) F: réussir, l'avoir belle; (b) P: (d'un homme) coïter*, avoir réussi un exploit amoureux, tringler. Voir aussi crib¹, 1; nut¹, 6; whip¹, 4.

crack down ['kræk'daun] (to), F: 1. to c. d. on s.o., (a) tomber sur le paletot à qn; (b) serrer la vis à qn. 2. to c. d. on sth., mettre le frein à qch.

cracked [krækt] (adj.), P: fou*, fêlé.

cracker ['krækər] (noun), F: 1. mensonge*, craque f. 2. she's a c., elle est formid(able). Voir aussi crib-cracker; whipcracker.

crackerjack¹ ['krækədʒæk] (adj.), F: excellent*, formid(able), sensas.

crackerjack² ['krækədʒæk] (noun), F: 1. as m, crack m. 2. du tonnerre.

crackers ['krækəz] (adj.), P: fou*, cinglé.

cracking ['krækiŋ] (adj.), F: 1. to be in c. form, être en pleine forme. 2. at a c. pace, très vite*, en quatrième vitesse.

crackle ['krækl] (noun), P: billets*, gros faf(f)iots m.pl.

crackling ['krækliŋ] (noun), P: a nice bit of c., une croquignole, un prix de Diane.

crack on ['kræk'ɔn] (to), P: 1. faire semblant, frimer. 2. faire savoir, répandre, semer la nouvelle (que...); don't c. o.! ne crache pas le morceau!

crackpot ['krækpɔt] (adj. & noun), F: fou*, fada (m), louf(oque) (m).

cracksman ['kræksmən] (noun), P: cambrioleur*, casseur m.

---

* L'astérisque indique que le mot marqué de ce signe figure comme entrée dans le Répertoire.

crack-up ['krækʌp] (noun), F: 1. accident m d'avion très sérieux. 2. dépression nerveuse.

crack up ['kræk'ʌp] (to), F: 1. vanter, pommader, porter aux anges. 2. prendre un coup de vieux, craquer. 3. flancher, se détraquer, s'effondrer. 4. faire une dépression nerveuse.

cradle ['kreidl] (noun), F: to rob the c., les prendre au berceau.

cradle-robber ['kreidl-rɔbər], cradle-snatcher ['kreidl-snætʃər] (noun), F: = baby-snatcher (b); cf. cradle.

crafty ['krɑ:fti] (adj.), F: to have a c. smoke, en griller une en loucedoc. Voir aussi arty-crafty.

crank up ['kræŋk'ʌp] (to), P: piquer, pousser.

cranky ['kræŋki] (adj.), P: 1. malade*, patraque. 2. mal boumé.

crap¹ [kræp] (noun), V: 1. étron*. 2. bêtise*; don't give me that c., ne me sers pas ces conneries. 3. it's a lot (or load) of c., tout ça c'est de l'eau de bidet. 4. full of c., fort en gueule. 5. héroïne f (drogues*) de qualité inférieure. Voir aussi shoot² (to), 7.

crap² [kræp] (to), V: 1. déféquer*, chier. 2. don't c. about like that! fais pas le con!

craphouse ['kræphaʊs], crapper ['kræpər] (noun), V: W.C.*, chiottes f.pl., goguenots m.pl.

crappy ['kræpi] (adj.), V: sale*, cracra, dégueulasse.

crash [kræʃ] (to), P: 1. = gate-crash (to). 2. roupiller, pioncer, en écraser.

crashed [kræʃt] (adj.) (U.S.), P: ivre*, rétamé.

crashing ['kræʃiŋ] (adj.), F: c. bore, casse-pieds m (ou raseur m) de première classe.

crash-out ['kræʃaʊt] (noun), F: = break¹, 4; cf. break-out.

crash-pad ['kræʃpæd] (noun), P: asile m temporaire.

crate [kreit] (noun), F: 1. coucou m, zinc m. 2. vieille voiture*, tacot m.

crawl [krɔ:l] (to), F: 1. s'aplatir, faire des courbettes f.pl.; to c. round s.o., ramper devant qn; to c. all over s.o., faire de la lèche. 2. the place was crawling with police, l'endroit grouillait de policiers*. Voir aussi arse-crawl (to); pub-crawl² (to).

crawler ['krɔ:lər] (noun), F: 1. lécheur

m de bottes. 2. = pub-crawler. 3. tortillard m. Voir aussi arse-crawler.

crazy ['kreizi] (adj.), F: 1. are you c.? t'es pas fou*? 2. terrible, formid(able). 3. enthousiaste, fervent, passionné. Voir aussi man-crazy; sex-crazy; woman-crazy.

crazyhouse ['kreizihaʊs] (noun), P: maison f de fous, asile m de dingues.

cream¹ [kri:m] (noun), P: sperme*, blanc m, jus m. Voir aussi ice-cream.

cream² [kri:m] (to) (U.S.), P: 1. battre*, filer une raclée à (qn). 2. tuer*, repasser, descendre (qn). 3. éjaculer*, cracher son venin; to c. one's jeans, juter dans son froc.

cream off ['kri:m'ɔf] (to), P: faire jouir (qn).

creampuff ['kri:m'pʌf] (noun), P: 1. amusette f, qch. de facile. 2. femmelette f, mollasson m.

crease¹ [kri:s] (noun), V: = crack¹, 1.

crease² [kri:s] (to), P: 1. tuer*, effacer (qn). 2. assommer, aplatir (qn). 3. ennuyer*; you c. me, tu me cours. 4. to feel creased, (a) être déprimé (ou cafardeux); (b) être fatigué* (ou vanné). 5. you c. me! tu me fais tordre de rire!

create ['kri:eit] (to), P: faire une scène, grogner*, rouscailler; voir aussi hell, 3.

creature ['kri:tʃər] (noun). 1. F: femme* (péj.), créature f, femelle f. 2. P: the c., whisky m, scotch m.

creek [kri:k] (noun), F: to be up the c. (or V: up shit c.) (without a paddle), être embêté (ou emmouscaillé); V: être dans les emmerdements m.pl.

creep¹ [kri:p] (noun). 1. F: vaurien*, salaud m, fripouille f. 2. F: lèche-bottes m, lèche-cul m, flagorneur m. 3. P: chapardeur m, chipeur m. Voir aussi creeps.

creep² [kri:p] (to). 1. F: ramper (devant les grands), s'aplatir. 2. P: c. away and die! fous-moi le camp! va te faire fiche! Voir aussi arse-creep (to).

creeper ['kri:pər] (noun). 1. F: = creep¹, 2. 2. P: monte-en-l'air m. 3. (pl.) F: espadrilles f.pl. Voir aussi arse-creeper; jeepers!

creeps [kri:ps] (pl. noun), F: he gives me the c., il me fait peur*, il me donne la chair de poule; it gives me the c., ça me met les nerfs en pelote.

creepy-crawly¹ ['kri:pi'krɔ:li] (adj.), F:

---

* An asterisk indicates that the word so marked is included as a head-word in the Appendix.

c.-c. feeling, (a) fourmillement m; (b) chair f de poule.

creepy-crawly[2] [ˈkriːpiˈkrɔːli] (noun), F: vermine f; insecte etc. rampant.

cretin [ˈkretin] (noun), F: individu absolument bête*, crétin m.

cretinous [ˈkretinəs] (adj.), F: (remarque, etc.) bête* (ou crétine).

crib[1] [krib] (noun). 1. P: = pad[1], 1; to crack a c., cambrioler*, faire un fric-frac, casser un coffiot; voir aussi **crib-cracker.** 2. F: antisèche f. 3. P: rouspétance f.

crib[2] [krib] (to). 1. F: tricher, bidocher. 2. P: voler*, chaparder. 3. to c. at sth., tiquer sur qch., regimber.

crib-cracker [ˈkribkrækər] (noun), P: cambrioleur*, casseur m; voir aussi **crib**[1], 1.

crib-cracking [ˈkribkrækiŋ] (noun), P: cambriolage m, casse(ment) m.

cricket [ˈkrikit] (noun), F: it's not c., c'est pas de jeu.

crikey! [ˈkraiki] (excl.), F: c. (Moses)! mince alors! fichtre! mazette!

crimp [krimp] (noun), F: to put a c. in s.o.'s style, couper les effets à qn.

cripes! [kraips] (excl.), F: = **crikey!**

croak [krouk] (to), P: 1. tuer*, descendre (qn), liquider (qn). 2. mourir*, cronir, cadancher.

croaker [ˈkroukər] (noun), P: docteur m, toubib m; right c., toubib à la gauche.

crock[1] [krɔk] (noun). 1. P: (a) pipe f à opium, bambou m; (b) fourneau m (de pipe). 2. F: old c., (a) vieille voiture*, tacot m, bagnole f; (b) croulant m, vieux birbe, vieux jeton. 3. F: cheval*, rosse f, carne f. 4. (U.S.) F: individu* peu sympathique, arsouille m, sale coco m. 5. (U.S.) P: c. of shit, (a) mensonges*, boniments m.pl.; (b) menteur m, bourreur m de crâne, fumiste m.

crock[2] [krɔk] (to), F: to get crocked, (a) se blesser*, s'amocher; (b) s'enivrer, se (faire) rétamer.

crockery [ˈkrɔkəri] (noun), F: dentier m, tabourets m.pl.

crock up [ˈkrɔkˈʌp] (to), F: 1. tomber malade*, se décatir. 2. blesser*, abîmer, amocher.

crocky [ˈkrɔki] (adj.), F: abîmé, claqué.

crocodile [ˈkrɔkədail] (noun), F: élèves marchant deux à deux, en rang(s)

d'oignons (ou à la queue leu-leu). Voir aussi **alligator.**

crombie [ˈkrɔmbi] (noun), P: pardessus*, lardingue m.

cronk[1] [krɔŋk] (adj.) (Austr.), F: 1. = **crook**[1], 2. 2. camelote, tocard. 3. défavorable, adverse, anti.

cronk[2] [krɔŋk] (noun), F: old c. = old crock (**crock**[1], 2 (a)).

crook[1] [kruk] (adj.). 1. P: malhonnête, louche. 2. (Austr.) F: malade*, patraque. 3. (Austr.) F: to go c. at s.o., se mettre en colère* contre qn, fulminer contre qn.

crook[2] [kruk] (noun), F: 1. escroc*, arnaqueur m. 2. voleur*, doubleur m, faiseur m.

cropper [ˈkrɔpər] (noun), F: to come a c., (a) tomber*, prendre une pelle, ramasser une bûche; (b) tomber sur un bec, faire un bide.

crop up [ˈkrɔpˈʌp] (to), F: survenir à l'improviste, surgir.

cross[1] [krɔs] (noun), P: on the c., malhonnêtement, en filouterie. Voir aussi **white**[1], 1.

cross[2] [krɔs] (to), F: 1. tromper*, trahir, posséder (qn); cf. **double-cross** (to). 2. to c. one's heart, jurer ses grands dieux; c. my heart (and hope to die), (enfants) croix de bois, croix de fer (, si je meurs j'irai en enfer).

crotch [krɔtʃ] (noun), P: 1. vulve*, cramouille f. 2. c. **crickets** = **crabs** (voir **crab**[1], 2).

crow [krou] (noun). 1. P: guetteur m, gaffeur m. 2. P: prêtre*, corbeau m, ratichon m. 3. F: old c., femme* (péj.), vieille bique, vieux trumeau. 4. (U.S.) F: to eat c., avaler des couleuvres. Voir aussi **Jim Crow.**

crowd[1] [kraud] (noun), F: bande*, équipe f, soce f.

crowd[2] [kraud] (to), P: casser les pieds à (qn), s'en prendre à (qn), chercher noise à (qn).

crown [kraun] (to), F: 1. flanquer un coup* à la tête de (qn), assommer (qn). 2. **and to c. everything . . .,** le comble c'est . . .

crow's-feet [ˈkrouzfiːt] (pl. noun), F: pattes f.pl. d'oie (sur le visage).

crud [krʌd] (noun), P: 1. = **turd,** 2. 2. **Bombay cruds,** diarrhée*, riquette f.

cruiser ['kru:zər] (noun), P: prostituée*, marcheuse f, péripaticienne f.
crumb [krʌm] (noun), P: vaurien*, salaud m.
crumbs! [krʌmz] (excl.), F: = **crikey!**
crummy ['krʌmi] (adj.), F: sale*, miteux.
crump [krʌmp] (noun), P: gros obus, (grosse) marmite.
crumpet ['krʌmpit] (noun). 1. V: vulve*, framboise f; **to have a bit of c.**, to have (or get) one's c., coïter*, se farcir (ou s'envoyer) une femme*. 2. P: **she's a nice bit of c.**, c'est une môme bath. 3. F: tête*, caboche f; **off one's c.**, fou*, maboul, loufoque; (Austr.) **to bow the c.**, plaider coupable, se péter bon (ou propre), larguer le blanc.
crunch [krʌntʃ] (noun), F: **the c.**, le moment critique; **when it comes to the c....**, quand on est au pied du mur...
crush [krʌʃ] (noun), F: 1. béguin m; **to have a c. on s.o.**, aimer* qn, en pincer pour qn. 2. boum surpeuplée, moutonnaille f.
crushers ['krʌʃəz] (pl. noun), F: grosses chaussures*, godasses f.pl.; cf. **beetle-crushers; clod-crushers.**
crust [krʌst] (noun), F: 1. **the upper c.**, la haute, le gratin, le dessus du panier. 2. **to be off one's c.**, être fou*, être parti du ciboulot. 3. **to have plenty of c.**, être très culotté.
crutch [krʌtʃ] (noun). 1. P: béquille f (allumette fendue qui permet de fumer une cigarette de marijuana jusqu'au bout). 2. (pl.) F: voir **bingo** (77).
cry-baby ['krai-beibi] (noun), F: chialeur m, pleurnicheur m.
cry off ['krai'ɔf] (to), F: lâcher les dés, caner.
cry out ['krai'aut] (to), F: **for crying out loud!** c'est le bouquet!
crystal ['kristəl] (adj.), F: **to gaze into the c. ball**, prédire l'avenir, lire dans le marc du café (ou dans la boule de cristal).
crystals ['kristəlz] (pl. noun), P: méthédrine cristallisée (drogues*).
C.T., c.t. ['si:'ti:] (abbr.), P: = **cockteaser;** cf. **P.T.**
cube [kju:b] (noun), P: 1. un gramme de hachisch m, un cube; voir aussi **acid, 2.** 2. (pl.) dés*, bouts m.pl. de sucre,

doches m.pl., bobs m.pl.
cubehead ['kju:bhed] (noun), P: consommateur m de morceaux de sucre imprégnés de LSD.
cuckoo ['kuku:] (adj.), P: fou*, loufoque.
cuddlesome ['kʌdlsəm], **cuddly** ['kʌdli] (adj.), F: bien capitonné(e), qu'on aimerait bichot(t)er, gentil(le) à croquer.
cuff [kʌf] (noun). 1. P: **to buy sth. on the c.**, acheter qch. à crédit (ou à croume). 2. F: **to say sth. off the c.**, dire qch. au pied levé, improviser. 3. F: **for the c.**, confidentiel(lement), sous cape. 4. F: (pl.) (=handcuffs) menottes*, bracelets m.pl. 5. P: = **soul-brother.**
cum [kʌm] (noun & verb), P: = **come**[1], **come**[2], 1.
cunt [kʌnt] (noun), VV: 1. vulve*, con m. 2. femme* (péj.), fumelle f, garce f; **a nice bit of c.**, une gonzesse qui a du chien. 3. **he's a prize** (or **first-class**) **c.**, il est archi-con.
cunt-lapper ['kʌnt-læpər] (noun), VV: brouteur m de cresson.
cunt-struck ['kʌnt-strʌk] (adj.), VV: queutard, porté sur la bagatelle.
cup [kʌp] (noun). 1. F: **that's not my c. of tea**, (a) ça ne me dit rien, ce n'est pas à mon goût; (b) ce n'est pas dans mes cordes. 2. P: **to have a c. of tea**, coïter* entre pédérastes* dans des toilettes publiques. 3. F: **in one's cups**, dans les Vignes du Seigneur.
cup-cakes ['kʌpkeiks] (pl. noun), P: testicules*, croquignoles f.pl., olives f.pl.
cuppa, cupper ['kʌpə] (noun), F: tasse f (ou bol m) de thé.
curfuffle [kə'fʌfl] (noun), F: = **kerfuffle.**
curl up ['kə:l'ʌp] (to), F: 1. **I just want to c. u. and die**, j'ai envie de tout lâcher (ou de tout planter là). 2. **he simply curled up**, on l'aurait fait rentrer dans un trou de souris. 3. **to c. u. laughing**, rire*, se rouler.
curly ['kə:li] (noun). 1. F: frisé(e). 2. P: **to have s.o. by the short and curlies**, avoir qn à sa merci (ou à sa pogne).
currant-bun ['kʌrənt'bʌn] (noun) (R.S. = son), P: fils m.
curse [kə:s] (noun), F: **the c.**, menstrues*, argagnasses f.pl.
curtains ['kə:tnz] (pl. noun), F: **it'll be**

c. for you if ..., votre compte est bon si...

curvaceous [kə:ˈveiʃəs] (adj.), F: (d'une femme) bien balancée (ou carrossée ou capitonnée), plantureuse.

cushy [ˈkuʃi] (adj.), F: a c. time (or number), une planque, un filon; to have a c. time (of it), l'avoir pépère; a c. life, une vie pépère; c. job, prébende f, sinécure f.

cuss[1] [kʌs] (noun), F: 1. individu*, client m; an awkward c., un mauvais coucheur. 2. it's not worth a (tinker's) c., ça ne vaut pas un clou; voir aussi tinker, 2.

cuss[2] [kʌs] (to), F: 1. sacrer, jurer. 2. réprimander*, enguirlander (qn).

cussed [ˈkʌsid] (adj.), F: damné, sacré.

customer [ˈkʌstəmər] (noun), F: 1. individu*, type m; a queer c., un drôle de client (ou de numéro); an awkward c., un type pas commode; voir aussi rough[1], 4; tough[1], 2. 2. (de prostituée) clille m.

cut[1] [kʌt] (adj.). 1. P: (légèrement) ivre*, pompette, éméché; cf. half-cut. 2. F: c. and dry (or dried), tout fait, tout taillé.

cut[2] [kʌt] (noun), F: 1. fade m, taf(fe) m; to get one's c., prendre son fade, avoir sa gratte. 2. a c. above..., un cran (ou un échelon) au-dessus de... 3. a short c. (to riches, etc.), un raccourci. 4. (cartes) to slip the c., faire sauter la coupe.

cut[3] [kʌt] (to). 1. P: partir*; to c. and run, se tirer. 2. P: adultérer, couper (une drogue). 3. F: to c. it fine, (a) compter (ou calculer) trop juste; (b) ne pas laisser beaucoup de temps, arriver* à la dernière minute (ou tout juste). 4. F: to c. no ice (with s.o.), demeurer sans effet. 5. F: to c. s.o. dead, snober qn, tourner le dos à qn. 6. F: to c. a class, sécher la classe. 7. F: to c. a corner, (auto) prendre un virage à la corde. 8. F: to c. corners, économiser*, couper un sou en quatre. 9. F: it cuts both ways, c'est à double tranchant. 10. F: to c. a dash, faire de l'épate. 11. F: to c. loose, (a) s'évader*, se cavaler; (b) être déchaîné, mener une vie de patachon, envoyer son bonnet par-dessus les moulins. Voir aussi cackle; comedy; rug, 1; throat, 2.

cut-back [ˈkʌtbæk] (noun), F: 1. retour m en arrière, flash-back m. 2. économie f (sur les dépenses).

cut back [ˈkʌtˈbæk] (to), F: 1. économiser*, mettre à gauche. 2. revenir sur ses pas.

cut down [ˈkʌtˈdaun] (to), F: = cut back (to), 1. Voir aussi size, 1.

cute [kju:t] (adj.), F: 1. (de personnes) (a) charmant, gentil; what a c. little baby! quel mignon petit bébé!; (b) malin*, déluré; he's a c. one, il a le nez creux. 2. (de choses) mignon, savoureux, délicat. 3. to play a c. trick on s.o., faire une entourloupette à qn.

cutey, cutie [ˈkju:ti] (noun), F: 1. charmante jeune personne, mignonne poupée. 2. petite maligne.

cut in [ˈkʌtˈin] (to), F: to c. s.o. i., mettre qn dans le coup.

cut out [ˈkʌtˈaut] (to). 1. P: = cut[3] (to), 1. 2. F: c. it o.! ça suffit! basta! rideau! 3. F: to have one's work c. o. (to do sth.), avoir de la besogne sur les bras, avoir de quoi faire, avoir du pain sur la planche. 4. F: I'm not c. o. for that sort of work, je ne suis pas taillé pour ce genre de travail. 5. F: souffler la place à (qn), couper l'herbe sous les pieds de (qn). Voir aussi fancy[1], 4.

cut-throat [ˈkʌtθrout] (attrib. adj.), F: 1. c.-t. competition, concurrence acharnée. 2. c.-t. razor, rasoir*, grattoir m, coupe-chou m.

cutty(-pipe) [ˈkʌti(paip)] (noun), F: pipe*, brûle-gueule m.

cut up [ˈkʌtˈʌp] (to), F: 1. to be (or feel) c. u., être démonté (ou affecté ou affligé). 2. éreinter, mettre en morceaux (un livre, etc.). 3. to c. u. nasty (or rough ou rusty or savage or ugly), (a) se mettre en colère* (ou en rogne), se rebiffer, regimber; (b) mal prendre les choses, faire le méchant. 4. to c. u. rich, mourir* riche*, claquer plein aux as.

cylinder [ˈsilindər] (noun), F: to fire (or hit) on all cylinders, (a) rouler très vite*, rouler à pleins tubes; (b) rouler comme un charme, tourner rond; to miss on two cylinders, avoir des ratés.

---

* L'astérisque indique que le mot marqué de ce signe figure comme entrée dans le Répertoire.

D

d [di:] (*abbr.* = *decent*), *F:* gentil, chic, chouette; **that's jolly d of you,** c'est joliment chic de ta part; *cf.* **decent, 1.**

D [di:] (*abbr.*), *P:* **1.** (=*LSD*) D *m*, acide *m* (*drogues**). **2.** (=*diamond*) diamant*, diame *m*. **3.** (=*detective*) agent* de la Sûreté. *Voir aussi* **D-racks.**

D.A. [ˈdi:ˈei] (*abbr.* = *drug addict*), *P:* drogué*, toxico(mane) *mf*, camé *m*.

da [dɑ:] (*noun*), *F:* père*, papa, daron *m*; *cf.* **dar.**

dab¹ [dæb] (*adj.*), *F:* capable, calé, fort(iche); **a d. hand = dab³, 4.**

dab² [dæb] (*adv.*), *F:* **(right) d. in the middle,** en plein dans le mille.

dab³ [dæb] (*noun*). **1.** *F:* **a d.,** un peu*, une miette, un (petit) bout, un chouia. **2.** *F:* **poor d.!** pauvre type! pauvre diable! **3.** *F:* (petite) tape, tapette *f*, rampognon *m*. **4.** *F:* expert *m*, as *m*, épée *f*, crack *m*. **5.** (*pl.*) *P:* empreintes digitales; **to have one's dabs taken,** passer au piano; *voir aussi* **mug¹, 1.** **6.** *F:* = **dash¹, 2.**

dab⁴ [dæb] (**to**), *F:* **to d. one's nose,** se poudrer le nez, faire un raccord.

dabble [ˈdæbl] (**to**), *F:* se droguer* irrégulièrement, (s)chnouffailler.

dabbler [ˈdæblər] (*noun*), *F:* drogué* par intermittence, toxico *m* du dimanche, (s)chnouffailleur *m*.

dab down [ˈdæbˈdaun] (**to**), *P:* donner* de l'argent*, les allonger, les abouler.

dabster [ˈdæbstər] (*noun*), *F:* = **dab³, 4.**

dad [dæd] (*noun*), *F:* **1.** père*, papa, daron *m*. **2.** un vieux, un pépère.

dad(d)a [ˈdædə] (*noun*), *F:* (*langage enfantin*) père*, papa, papy.

daddio [ˈdædiou] (*noun*), *P:* **1.** = **dad, 2.** **2.** chef *m* d'un groupe de beatniks, moré *m*.

daddle [ˈdædl] (*noun*), *P:* main*, paluche *f*, pince *f*.

daddy [ˈdædi] (*noun*), *F:* **1.** = **dad, 1.** **2. the d. of them all,** l'ancien, le maestro; **he's the d. (of them all),** il les coiffe tous. **3.** = **sugar-daddy.**

daffodil [ˈdæfədil] (*noun*), *P:* jeune homme* efféminé, minet *m*.

daffy [ˈdæfi] (*adj.*), *P:* **1.** (*a*) bête*, cruche; (*b*) fou*, timbré, toqué. **2. to be d. about s.o.** = **to be daft about s.o.** (daft¹, 2).

daft¹ [dɑ:ft] (*adj.*), *F:* **1. (as) d. as a brush** (*or* **as they come** *or* **as they make 'em**), (*a*) bête* comme ses pieds; (*b*) fou* à lier. **2. to be d. about s.o.,** être toqué de qn. *Voir aussi* **plain.**

daft² [dɑ:ft] (*adv.*), *P:* **don't talk d.!** ne sors pas des inepties!

daftie, dafty [ˈdɑ:fti] (*noun*), *P:* individu bête*, cruche *f*, crétin *m*.

dag [dæg] (*noun*) (*Austr.*), *F:* rigolo *m*, excentrique *m*.

dagga [ˈdægə] (*noun*), *P:* cannabis *m* (*drugues**), dagga *m*.

dagged [dægd] (*adj.*)(*U.S.*), *P:* ivre*, saoul.

dago [ˈdeigou] (*noun*), *P:* **1.** (*péj.*) métèque *m*. **2. d. red,** vin* rouge ordinaire, pivois *m*.

daily [ˈdeili] (*noun*), *F:* femme de journée.

dairies [ˈdɛəriz] (*pl. noun*), *P:* seins*, boîtes *f.pl.* à lait, lolos *m.pl.*

daisy¹ [ˈdeizi] (*adj.*), *F:* excellent*, super; **a d. day,** une belle journée.

daisy² [ˈdeizi] (*noun*). **1.** *F:* qn *ou* qch. d'excellent* (*ou* d'épatant *ou* d'impec); **she's a d.,** c'est une perle; elle est bath. **2.** *P:* pot *m* de chambre, Jules. **3.** *F:* **to be kicking** (*or* **pushing**) **up the daisies,** être enterré, bouffer les pissenlits par la racine. **4.** (*pl.*) *P:* = **daisy roots** (*voir* **5**). **5.** *P:* **d. roots** (*R.S.* = *boots*), chaussures*, godillots *m.pl.* **6.** *P:* pédéraste*; **d. chain,** partouze *f* à la bague. **7.** *F:* **as fresh as a d.,** frais et rose (*ou* dispos). *Voir aussi* **knee-high; oops-a-daisy!; ups-a-daisy!; upsy-daisy!; whoops-a-daisy!**

dallop [ˈdɔləp] (*noun*), *F:* = **dollop.**

dam [dæm] (*noun*), *F:* **1.** = **damn³.** **2. that's water over the d.,** c'est de l'eau sous le pont.

damage [ˈdæmidʒ] (*noun*), *F:* **what's**

the d.? ça fait combien?; to stand the d., payer* l'addition, régler la douloureuse.

damaged [ˈdæmidʒd] (adj.), P: d. goods, une ex-vierge, cruche cassée, branche défleurée, fille* qui a vu le loup.

dame [deim] (noun), F: femme*, baronne f, gonzesse f; cf. dizzy, 2.

damfool¹ [ˈdæmˈfuːl] (adj.), F: bête*, stupide, idiot.

damfool² [ˈdæmˈfuːl] (noun), F: individu bête*, sacré idiot, imbécile m, crétin m.

damfoolery [ˈdæmˈfuːləri], damfoolishness [ˈdæmˈfuːliʃnis] (noun), F: sacrée imbécillité.

dammit! [ˈdæmit] (excl.), F: 1. sacrebleu! nom d'un chien! sacristi! 2. it was as near as d., il était moins une; as quick (or soon) as d., aussi sec, illico.

damn¹ [dæm] (adj. & adv.) = damned¹,².

damn!² [dæm] (excl.) = dammit!, 1; voir aussi damn⁴ (to), 4, 5, 6.

damn³ [dæm] (noun), F: I don't give (or care) a d. (or a tinker's d. or a tupp'ny d.), je m'en moque pas mal, je m'en fiche (ou je m'en soucie) comme de ma première chemise (ou comme de colin-tampon); cf. tuppenny.

damn⁴ [dæm] (to), F: 1. d. you! (or you be damned!), va te faire pendre! 2. well I'm (or I'll be) damned! ça c'est (trop) fort! 3. I'll see him damned first! qu'il aille au diable! 4. d. it! zut! 5. d. and blast! nom de Dieu! bordel (de Dieu)! 6. d. it all! nom de nom! nom d'un chien!

damnable [ˈdæmnəbl] (adj.), F: maudit, exécrable.

damnably [ˈdæmnəbli] (adv.), F: diablement, bigrement.

damn-all [ˈdæmˈɔːl] (noun), F: he's doing d.-a., il ne fiche rien; he's done d.-a. today, il n'a fichu que dalle aujourd'hui, il n'a pas fichu un coup de la sainte journée.

damnation! [ˈdæmˈneiʃ(ə)n] (excl.), F: sacrebleu!; d. take it! le diable l'emporte!

damned¹ [dæmd] (adj.), F: 1. sacré, satané. 2. what a d. nuisance! quel empoisonnement! 3. he's a d. nuisance! quel enquiquineur! 4. it's a d. shame!

c'est une sacrée honte! 5. a d. sight better than . . ., bigrement mieux que .., fichtrement meilleur que...

damned² [dæmd] (adv.), F: 1. diablement, bigrement, vachement; it's d. hard, c'est vachement difficile. 2. . . . and a d. good job! ...et c'est pas malheureux! 3. he knows d. well he mustn't, il sait pertinemment bien qu'il ne doit pas; voir aussi damned-well. 4. you're d. right there! là tu as joliment raison! 5. pretty d. quick! au trot! et que ça saute! 6. it'll be d. useful, ça va nous rendre rudement service.

damnedest [ˈdæmdist] (noun), F: to do (or try) one's d., se décarcasser, travailler* d'achar.

damned-well [ˈdæmdˈwel, ˈdæmˈwel] (adv.), F: 1. it d.-w. serves you right! c'est bougrement bien fait! 2. you can do what you d.-w. like! fais ce que tu veux, je m'en fous!

damp [dæmp] (noun), F: to keep the d. out, boire* un alcool, se rincer le gosier, tuer le ver.

damper [ˈdæmpər] (noun), F: 1. rabat-joie m. 2. to put the d. on sth., (a) donner un coup de frein à qch.; (b) refroidir l'enthousiasme, défriser qch. 3. to put the d. on s.o., faire taire* qn, boucler la trappe à qn, clouer le bec à qn.

dance [dɑːns, U.S.: dæns] (noun), F: to lead s.o. a d., donner du fil à retordre à qn, en faire voir (des vertes et des pas mûres) à qn. Voir aussi song, 1.

dander [ˈdændər] (noun), F: to get one's d. up, se mettre en colère*, s'emballer.

dandruff [ˈdændrʌf] (noun), P: walking d., poux*, morpions m.pl.

dandy¹ [ˈdændi] (adj.), F: excellent*, sensas, super, de première.

dandy² [ˈdændi] (adv.), F: excellemment; to get along (just) d. with s.o., s'entendre épatamment avec qn.

dandy³ [ˈdændi] (noun), F: chose excellente* (ou épatante).

dang¹ [dæŋ] (noun) (mainly U.S.), F: = damn³.

dang² [dæŋ] (to) (mainly U.S.), F: = damn⁴ (to).

danglers [ˈdæŋgləz] (pl. noun), V: testicules*, balloches f.pl.

daphne [ˈdæfni] (*noun*) (*Austr.*), *P:* femme* hétérosexuelle.

dar [dɑːr] (*noun*), *F:* père*, daron *m*; *cf.* da.

darb [dɑːb] (*noun*) (*U.S.*), *P:* chose excellente* (*ou* remarquable).

darbies [ˈdɑːbiz] (*pl. noun*), *P:* 1. menottes*, fichets *m.pl.*, bracelets *m.pl.* 2. empreintes digitales, piano *m*.

Darby and Joan [ˈdɑːbiən(d)ˈdʒoʊn] (*pr. noun*). 1. *F:* un vieux ménage; **D. and J. club**, club *m* du troisième âge. 2. *P:* (*R.S.* = *telephone*) téléphone*, bigophone *m*. 3. *P:* on one's D. and J. (*R.S.* = *alone*), seul(abre).

dare [dɛər] (to), *F:* I d. you! chiche!

dark¹ [dɑːk] (*adj.*), *F:* to keep it d., cacher*, étouffer; keep it d.! motus! *Voir aussi* horse¹, 1.

dark² [dɑːk] (*noun*). 1. *F:* to be in the d. about sth., ne pas être dans le coup. 2. *P:* (*mil.*) in the d., au cachot, à l'ombre. *Voir aussi* shot², 7.

darkey, darkie, darky [ˈdɑːki] (*noun*) (*often pej.*), nègre*, moricaud *m*, bougnoul(l)e *m*.

darling [ˈdɑːliŋ] (*adj.*), *F:* that is d. of you! c'est chou(ette) de ta part.

darn¹ [dɑːn] (*adj.* & *adv.*), *F: euph. pour* damned¹,²; *cf.* darned.

darn!² [dɑːn] (*excl.*), *F: euph. pour* damn!².

darn³ [dɑːn] (to), *F: euph. pour* damn⁴ (to).

darnation! [dɑːˈneiʃ(ə)n] (*excl.*), *F: euph. pour* damnation!; *cf.* tarnation!

darned [dɑːnd] (*adj.* & *adv.*), *F: euph. pour* damned¹,²; *cf.* darn¹.

darnedest [ˈdɑːndist] (*noun*), *F: euph. pour* damnedest.

darry [ˈdæri] (*noun*), *P:* coup *m* d'œil, coup de sabords; to have a d. at sth., regarder* qch., reluquer qch.

dash¹ [dæʃ] (*noun*), *F:* 1. (=*dashboard*) tableau *m* (*ou* panneau *m*) de bord. 2. tentative *f*, essai *m*; to have a d. at sth., tenter le coup, risquer sa chance. *Voir aussi* cut³ (to), 10.

dash² [dæʃ] (to), *F:* partir* rapidement, filer, se débiner; (I) must d., il faut que je file.

dash(ed) [dæʃ(t)] (*adj.* & *adv.*), *F: euph. pour* damned¹,².

dasher [ˈdæʃər] (*noun*), *F:* 1. (*a*) individu élégant*; (*b*) individu gommeux (*ou*

miché). 2. prétentieux *m*, crâneur *m*, épateur *m*. 3. dragueur *m*.

date¹ [deit] (*noun*), *F:* 1. individu bête*, cruche *f*, crétin *m*; you soppy d.! espèce de gourde! 2. rendez-vous*, rambour *m*; to break a d., poser un lapin. 3. personne (du sexe opposé) avec qui on a rendez-vous*.

date² [deit] (to), *F:* to d. s.o., donner rendez-vous* à qn, sortir régulièrement avec qn. *Voir aussi* blind¹, 1.

daughter [ˈdɔːtər] (*noun*) (*R.S.* = *quarter*), *P:* 25 livres sterling; four and a d., £425.

day [dei] (*noun*), *F:* 1. that'll be the d.! on fera une croix à la cheminée! 2. to name the d., fixer le jour du mariage. 3. to pass the time of the d., bavarder*, jacasser, tailler une bavette. 4. to win the d., gagner, emporter le morceau. 5. to know the time of d., la connaître (dans les coins). 6. to call it a d., débrayer (à la fin de la journée), dételer. 7. to have seen better days, avoir connu des jours meilleurs, être décati, avoir fait son temps. 8. it's not my d., aujourd'hui le sort est contre moi, rien ne tourne rond aujourd'hui. 9. I've had my d., mes beaux jours sont passés. 10. at the end of the d., à la fin, en fin de compte. *Voir aussi* rainyday.

daylight¹ [ˈdeilait] (*adj.*), *F:* it's d. robbery! c'est du vol manifeste! on est volé comme au coin d'un bois!

daylight² [ˈdeilait] (*noun*), *F:* 1. to be able to see d., apercevoir la fin d'un long travail, commencer à en voir le bout, sortir du tunnel. 2. to knock (*or* beat *or* bash) the (living) daylights out of s.o., battre* qn comme plâtre, envoyer dormir qn.

dazzler [ˈdæzlər] (*noun*), *F:* 1. diamant*, diame *m*, éclair *m*. 2. une journée très ensoleillée, où le bourguignon tape. 3. un(e) m'as-tu-vu; époustoufleur *m*, époustoufleuse *f*, qn qui en met plein la vue. *Voir aussi* bobby-dazzler.

dead¹ [ded] (*adj.*), *F:* 1. a d. loss, (*a*) une nullité, un propre à rien; (*b*) une perte sèche; a d. cert (*or* cinch), une certitude absolue; a d. liberty, une sacrée audace; *cf.* diabolical; to come to a d. stop, s'arrêter pile, stopper net. 2. d. man (*or* 'un *or* soldier *or* marine), bouteille*

---

* An asterisk indicates that the word so marked is included as a head-word in the Appendix.

vide, cadavre *m*; *voir aussi* **soldier**[1], **2** (*b*). **3. drop d.**! écrase·! ta gueule! **4. a d. duck**, une chose *ou* personne fichue, ruinée, finie; échec*, faillite *f*, four complet. **5. d. from the neck up**, bête*, bouché à l'émeri. **6. the d. spit of s.o.**, l'image crachée de qn; **he's the d. spit of his father**, c'est son père tout craché. **7. d. to the world** (*or* **to the wide**), (*a*) ivre* mort, bourré à bloc; (*b*) profondément endormi, dans les bras de Morphée. **8.** (*d'un moteur, etc.*) à plat, mort; **to go d.**, lâcher. **9. to be waiting for d.** **men's shoes**, attendre la dépouille de qn. **10. I wouldn't be seen d. with him**, à aucun prix je ne veux être vu(e) avec lui. **11.** très fatigué*, claqué, crevé. **12.** ennuyeux*, barbant, canulant. *Voir aussi* **Anne**; **Charl(e)y**[2], **2**; **cut**[3] (**to**), **5**; **dead-and-alive**; **horse**[1], **4**; **ringer**, **1**; **set**[2].

dead[2] [ded] (*adv*.), *F:* **1. d. broke**, archi-pauvre*, fauché, sans le sou. **2. d. easy**, facile comme bonjour, bête comme chou. **3. d. scared**, mort de peur*; **d. drunk**, ivre* mort. **4. d. innocent**, innocent comme l'enfant qui vient de naître. **5. d. chocker** (*or* **choked**), ennuyé* à mourir, en ayant ras le bol. **6. d. chuffed**, (*a*) =**d. chocker** (*voir* **5**); (*b*) aux anges. **7. d. on**, dans le mille. **8.** (*a*) **d. to rights**, absolument; (*b*) **to catch s.o. d. to rights**, prendre qn sur le fait (*ou* la main dans le sac), épingler qn sur le tas; *cf.* **bang**[2], **2. 9. to be d. (set) against sth.**, être braqué (*ou* monté *ou* buté) contre qch.

dead-and-alive [ˈdedəndəˈlaiv] (*adj*.), *F:* **a d.-a.-a. place**, un endroit mort (*ou* triste *ou* sans animation), un trou, un bled.

dead-beat [ˈdedˈbiːt] (*adj*.), *F:* très fatigué*, épuisé, vanné.

deadbeat [ˈdedbiːt] (*noun*), *P:* **1.** paresseux*, fainéant *m*, parasite *m*. **2.** (*U.S.*) mauvais payeur, filou *m*.

dead-end [ˈdedˈend] (*adj*.), *F:* **1. d.-e. job**, travail* (*ou* boulot *m*) sans avenir. **2. d.-e. kid**, blouson noir.

deader [ˈdedər] (*noun*), *P:* cadavre*, croni *m*, refroidi *m*.

deadhead [ˈdedhed] (*noun*), *P:* **1.** individu bête*, déplafonné *m*. **2.** ennuyeux*, casse-pieds *m*, crampon *m*. **3.** (*th.*)

personne qui entre avec un billet de faveur.

deadly[1] [ˈdedli] (*adj*.), *F:* ennuyeux*, mourant.

deadly[2] [ˈdedli] (*adv*.), *F:* archi-, très; **d. dull**, mortellement ennuyeux*.

deadneck [ˈdednek] (*noun*), *P:* = **deadhead, 1**.

deadpan [ˈdedpæn] (*adj*.), *F:* (visage) impassible, de pierre, de marbre; **to give s.o. the d. treatment**, battre froid à qn.

deal [diːl] (*noun*). **1.** *F:* **to clinch a d.**, s'assurer une vente, boucler une affaire; **to make a d.**, décrocher une affaire; **a new d.**, un nouveau départ; **a phoney** (*or* **rigged**) **d.**, une affaire véreuse; **to get the short end of the d.**, recevoir une petite partie des bénéfices, tenir le mauvais bout, n'avoir que les clopinettes; **dirty d.**, mauvais tour, sale coup *m*, vacherie *f*; *voir aussi* **raw**[1], **1**; **square**[1], **1. 2.** *F:* **big d.**! belle affaire! et mon œil!; **no d.**! pas mèche! rien à faire! **3.** *P:* petite dose (d'une drogue).

dealer [ˈdiːlər] (*noun*), *F:* fourgueur *m* (de drogues), trafiquant *m*. *Voir aussi* **wheeler-dealer**.

dearie, deary [ˈdiəri] (*noun*), *F:* **1.** (mon petit) chéri, (ma petite) chérie. **2.** (oh) **d. me**! (*a*) mes enfants! douce Mère!; (*b*) *voir* **bingo** (**3**). *Voir aussi* **hello-dearie**.

death [deθ] (*noun*), *F:* **1. to feel like d.** (**warmed up**), se sentir mortibus (*ou* fricassé); **to look like d.** (**warmed up**), avoir l'air cadavérique (*ou* d'un cadavre ambulant). **2. to die the d.**, (*d'un acteur*) tomber à vide. **3. to do sth. to d.**, faire qch. jusqu'à la lie (*ou* jusqu'à en vomir). **4. to bore s.o. to d.**, faire mourir* qn d'ennui, barber qn jusqu'à la gauche. **5. I'm frozen to d.**, je meurs de froid. *Voir aussi* **flog** (**to**), **3**; **hang on** (**to**), **2**; **sudden**; **tickle**[2] (**to**), **3**.

deb [deb] (*abbr.* = *debutante*), *F:* débutante *f*.

debag [diːˈbæg] (**to**), *F:* déculotter.

debt [det] (*noun*), *F:* **to pay the last d.**, mourir*, avaler sa chique.

debug [diːˈbʌg] (**to**), *F:* **1.** réparer, mettre au point, réviser. **2.** désonoriser, neutraliser des micros clandestins.

debunk [diːˈbʌŋk] (**to**), *F:* déboulonner, dégonfler, faire descendre d'un cran.

---

* L'astérisque indique que le mot marqué de ce signe figure comme entrée dans le Répertoire.

decent [ˈdiːs(ə)nt] (adj.), F: 1. passable, acceptable, correct; **a d. chap**, un brave type, un bon gars. 2. **to be d.**, être habillé décemment, être convenable.

decently [ˈdiːs(ə)ntli] (adv.), F: généreusement, abondamment.

deck [dek] (noun). 1. F: **to hit the d.**, (a) se lever du lit, se dépager, se dépieuter; (b) tomber à plat ventre. 2. F: **to clear the decks**, tout préparer, se préparer à agir, être sur le point d'attaquer, faire le branle-bas. 3. F: jeu m de cartes*; **to play with a stacked d.**, (a) jouer avec des cartes biseautées (ou maquillées); (b) avoir l'avantage sur qn, tenir le bon bout. 4. P: (a) petite quantité de drogues, prise f, boulette f; (b) petite dose d'héroïne ou de cocaïne (drogues*).

decker [ˈdekər] (noun), P: chapeau*, doulos m. Voir aussi **double-decker**.

decko [ˈdekou] (noun), P: = **dekko**.

deck out [ˈdekˈaut] (to), F: **to be all decked out**, être sur son trente et un, être tout flambé.

decoke [ˈdiːˈkouk] (to), F: décalaminer, décarburer.

decorators [ˈdekəreitəz] (pl. noun), P: **to have the d. in**, avoir ses menstrues*, repeindre sa grille en rouge; cf. **painter, 2.**

dee-jay (noun) (abbr. = disc-jockey), F: présentateur m de disques, disquaire m.

deep[1] [diːp] (adj.), F: 1. malin*, fin, matois, retors. 2. **to put sth. in the d.** freeze, mettre qch. au frigidaire, mettre qch. sur la planche. Voir aussi **end, 5, 13; jump[2] (to), 12.**

deep[2] [diːp] (noun), P: **to plough the d.** (R.S. = to sleep), dormir*, pioncer.

degree [diˈgriː] (noun), F: 1. **to be** (or feel) **one d. under**, être légèrement malade*, être patraque, ne pas être dans son assiette. 2. **third d.**, tortures f.pl. pour faire avouer*, cuisinage m; **to give s.o. the third d.**, cuisiner qn, griller qn.

dekko [ˈdekou] (noun), P: **let's have a d.!** fais-moi voir! juste un coup d'œil*!; **have** (or **take**) **a d. out of the window**, jette un coup d'œil* par la fenêtre.

delicate [ˈdelikət] (adj.), F: **to be in a d. condition**, être enceinte*, être dans une situation intéressante.

demo [ˈdemou] (noun), F: manifestation f politique, manif f.

demob[1] [ˈdiːˈmɔb] (noun) (abbr. = demobilization), F: libération f militaire, décarrade f, la quille; **to be due for d.**, être de la classe.

demob[2] [ˈdiːˈmɔb] (to) (abbr. = demobilize), F: libérer, décarrer, renvoyer dans ses foyers.

demolish [diˈmɔliʃ] (to), F: manger*, boulotter.

den [den] (noun), F: repaire m, clandé m.

dense [dens] (adj.), F: bête*, bouché.

dent [dent] (noun), F: **to make a d.** (in sth.), commencer à mordre.

depth-charge [ˈdepθtʃɑːdʒ] (noun), étouffe-chrétien m.

Derby Kel(1) or Kelly [ˈdɑːbiˈkel(i)] (noun) (R.S. = belly), P: ventre*, bide m.

dern [dəːn] (adj. & adv.), F: euph. pour damned[1,2]; cf. **darn**.

derry [ˈderi] (noun), P: baraque f, cambuse f.

deuce [djuːs] (noun). 1. F: diable m; **to raise the d.** = **to raise the devil** (devil[1], 15). 2. F: **to get the d.** = **to get the devil** (devil[1], 17). 3. F: **to give s.o. the d.**, réprimander* qn, lessiver la tête à qn. 4. P: deux livres sterling; (U.S.) deux dollars.

deuced[1] [djuːst] (adj.), F: satané, sacré.

deuced[2] [djuːst] (adv.), F: diablement, diantrement, bigrement.

devil[1] [ˈdevl] (noun), F: 1. **I had the d. of a job** (or **the d.'s own job**) **to . . .**, c'était la croix et la bannière pour . . .; **it's the very d. to wake him up in the morning**, c'est la croix et la bannière pour le réveiller le matin. 2. **he's an absolute d.!** il est infernal! 3. **he's a d. with women**, il est terrible avec les femmes; il les tombe toutes. 4. **who the d. are you?** qui, diable, êtes-vous?; **who the d. do you think you are?** pour qui, diable, te prends-tu? 5. **how the d. . . .?** comment diable...? 6. **go to the d.!** (allez) au diable! 7. **poor d.!** pauvre hère! pauvre diable! 8. **to send s.o. to the d.**, envoyer qn au diable (ou sur les roses). 9. **to go to the d.**, mal tourner, tomber dans la mélasse, piquer une tête. 10. **he has the d. of a temper**, il est mauvais coucheur, il a un caractère de cochon. 11. **there'll be the d. to**

---

* An asterisk indicates that the word so marked is included as a head-word in the Appendix.

pay, ça nous (vous) coûtera cher (ou chaud); vous ne perdez rien pour attendre. **12. be a d. and have another drink,** laisse-toi tenter (ou faire) et reprends un verre. **13. to play the d. with sth.,** mettre la confusion dans qch., mettre la pagaille; **to play the d. with s.o.,** maltraiter qn, malmener qn, être chien (ou vache) avec qn. **14. to work like the d.,** travailler* avec acharnement, trimer comme un nègre (ou un forçat). **15. to raise the d.,** faire du bruit*, faire un potin du diable. **16. to beat the d. out of s.o.,** battre* qn comme plâtre, secouer les puces à qn. **17. to get the d.,** se faire réprimander* (ou enguirlander). **18. give the d. his due,** à chacun son dû; rendons justice à... **19. between the d. and the deep blue sea,** entre l'enclume et le marteau. **20. the D.'s Bible** (or **playthings),** cartes* à jouer. **21. to be a d.,** avoir le diable au corps. **22. red devils = reds** (red[2], 5). **23. blue devils,** le cafard, le bourdon.

devil[2] [ˈdevl] (to), *F:* **to d. the life out of s.o.,** tourmenter qn, faire suer qn, empoisonner qn.

devil-dodger [ˈdevldɔdʒər] (noun), *F:* prêtre*, ratichon *m.*

devilish(ly) [ˈdevliʃ(li)] (adv.), *F:* diablement, diantrement, extrêmement.

dewdrop [ˈdjuː-drɔp] (noun), *F:* la goutte au nez, chandelle *f.*

dex [deks], **dexie** [ˈdeksi], **dexo** [ˈdeksou], **dexy** [ˈdeksi] (noun), *P:* cachet *m* de dexamphétamine, dexo *m* (drogues); (pl.) amphétamines *f.pl.* (drogues*).

dhobying [ˈdoubiːiŋ] (noun), *P:* lessive *f,* blanchissage *m,* savonnage *m.*

diabolical [daiəˈbɔlik(ə)l] (adj.), *F:* diabolique, satané, affreux, odieux; **it's a d. liberty!** c'est un sacré culot!

diabolically [daiəˈbɔlikli] (adv.), *F:* = **devilish(ly).**

dial(-piece) [ˈdaiəl(piːs)] (noun), *P:* visage*, museau *m,* margoulette *f,* bobine *f.*

dib [dib] (noun), *P:* **1.** part *f,* fade *m.* **2.** (pl.) argent*, fric *m;* **to have the dibs,** être riche* (ou bourré), avoir du fric, être au pèze.

dice[1] [dais] (pl. noun), *F:* **1. no d.!** pas mèche! je ne marche pas! rien à

faire! **2. to throw in the d.,** lâcher les dés (ou la partie), jeter l'éponge, mettre les pouces.

dice[2] [dais] (to), *F:* (automobiles) se poursuivre, gratter; *cf.* **dicing; to d. with death,** faire la course à la mort, jouer avec la mort.

dicey [ˈdaisi] (adj.), *F:* hasardeux, au flanc; **it's a bit d.,** c'est du risqué, c'est pas du tout cuit.

dicing [ˈdaisiŋ] (noun), *F:* (automobiles) course *f* entre deux chauffeurs, grattage *m; cf.* **dice**[2] (to).

dick [dik] (noun), *P:* **1.** pénis*, Charles-le-Chauve, Popaul *m.* **2.** policier*, détective *m,* poulet *m,* bourre *m; cf.* **fly-dick.** **3. clever D.,** un petit (ou gros) malin, affranchi *m.* **4. dirty D.,** sale dégoûtant, sale coco *m.* **5.** (pl.) poux*, morpions *m.pl.* **6.** déclaration *f,* serment *m;* **to take one's d.,** prêter serment, salbiner. **7. up to d. = up to scratch; to keep s.o. up to d.,** serrer les côtes à qn. **8.** dictionnaire *m,* dico *m;* **to swallow the d.,** avoir avalé le dico. **9.** (U.S.) **to buy the d.,** (a) s'attirer des ennuis, s'amocher; (b) mourir*, dévisser son billard. *Voir aussi* **Tom, 1.**

dickens [ˈdikinz], **the** (noun), *F:* **1.** le diable. **2. the d. of a noise,** un bruit* (ou un potin) du diable. **3. it's the d. of a job,** c'est le diable à confesser. **4. to give s.o. the d. = to give s.o. the deuce** (deuce, 3); **to get the d. = to get the devil** (devil[1], 17); **to raise the d. = to raise Cain** (Cain, 1).

dickey [ˈdiki] (noun), *F:* = **dicky**[2], 3.

dickory-dock [ˈdikəriˈdɔk] (noun), *P:* **1.** (R.S. = clock) horloge *f,* toquante *f.* **2.** (R.S.) = **cock, 1.**

dicky[1] [ˈdiki] (adj.), *F:* **1.** malade*, patraque, pas dans son assiette; *cf.* **ticker,1. 2.** déchard, frisant la faillite.

dicky[2] [ˈdiki] (noun). **1.** *P:* = **dick, 1. 2.** *F:* = **dicky-bird, 1. 3.** *F:* plastron *m* (de chemise) mobile, bavoir *m* à liquette.

dicky-bird [ˈdikibəːd] (noun), *F:* **1.** (R.S. = word) mot *m.* **2.** oiseau *m,* zozio *m.*

dicky-dido [ˈdikiˈdaidou] (noun), *V:* vulve*, cramouille *f.*

dicky-dirt [ˈdikiˈdəːt] (noun) (R.S. = shirt), *P:* chemise *f,* liquette *f.*

---

* L'astérisque indique que le mot marqué de ce signe figure comme entrée dans le Répertoire.

dicy ['daisi] (*adj.*), *F:* = dicey.
diddies ['didiz] (*pl. noun*), *P:* seins*, nénés *m.pl.*
diddle ['didl] (to). 1. *F:* voler*. 2. *F:* duper*, rouler, carotter (qn). 3. *P:* coïter* avec (une femme), calecer. 4. (*U.S.*) *P:* se masturber*, se branler. 5. *F:* = piddle[2] (to).
diddle around ['didl-ə'raʊnd] (to), *P:* flânocher, baguenauder.
diddle away ['didl-ə'wei] (to), *F:* to d. a. one's time, flâner.
diddler ['didlər] (*noun*), *F:* 1. voleur*. 2. escroc*, carotteur *m*, estampeur *m*. 3. bricoleur *m*, baguenaudeur *m*.
diddling ['didliŋ] (*noun*), *F:* 1. vol *m*, estampage *m*. 2. escroquerie*
diddy ['didi], **didekei, didikai** ['didikai], **didlo** ['didloʊ] (*noun*), *P:* romanichel *m*, romani *m*, rabouin *m*.
dido ['daidoʊ] (*noun*) (*U.S.*), *P:* farce *f*, niche *f*, frasque *f*, fredaine *f*. *Voir aussi* dicky-dido.
dig[1] [dig] (*noun*). 1. *F:* fouilles *f.pl.* (archéologiques). 2. *P:* d. in the grave (*R.S.* = shave), rasage *m*, raclage *m*. 3. (*pl.*) *F:* logement*, garni *m*, crèche *f*. 4. *F:* to have a d. at s.o., to get a d. in at s.o., lancer (*ou* filer) un vanne (*ou* un coup de patte) à qn. 5. *P:* piqûre *f*, piquouse *f*.
dig[2] [dig] (to). 1. *F:* (*a*) I d. that, ça me plaît, ça me botte; (*b*) comprendre, piger, entraver (qch.). 2. *F:* aimer*, gober (qn), avoir à la bonne. 3. *P:* taper sur les nerfs (*ou* le système) à (qn). 4. *P:* coïter* avec (une femme), piquer, bourrer. 5. *F:* se moquer* de, bêcher, lancer des vannes à. 6. *P:* faire gaffe, se débrider l'esgourde. 7. *F:* travailler* dur, trimer, bosser. 8. *F:* habiter*, crécher.
digger ['digər] (*noun*). 1. *F:* (*a*) Australien *m*; (*b*) Néo-zélandais *m*. 2. (*pl.*) *P:* groupe de hippies qui veulent abattre le système capitaliste en donnant au lieu de vendre; les sapeurs *m.pl.* 3. (*mil.*) *P:* the d., trou *m*, taulerie *f*. 4. (*pl.*) (*cartes*) *P:* pique *m*, croque-mort *m*, piche *m*. *Voir aussi* gold-digger.
diggings ['digiŋz] (*pl. noun*), *F:* logement*, crèche *f*, carrée *f*.
dig in ['dig'in] (to), *F:* 1. manger*, s'empiffrer, bouffer. 2. travailler* soigneusement. 3. rester sur ses positions, ne pas broncher.

dig into ['dig'intuː] (to), *F:* creuser (une question, *etc.*), pinocher.
digit ['didʒit] (*noun*), *F:* to extract the d.: *euph. pour* to pull one's finger out. (finger[1], 2).
digums ['daigəms] (*pl. noun*), *P:* bouts *m.pl.* des seins*, fraises *f.pl.*
dig up ['dig'ʌp] (to), *F:* where did you d. that u.? d'où l'as-tu tiré? où l'as-tu déniché (*ou* pêché *ou* cueilli)?
dike [daik] (*noun*), *P:* 1. W.C.*, chiottes *f.pl.*; to do a d., déféquer*, aller à la débourre. 2. = dyke.
dikey ['daiki] (*adj.*), *P:* = dykey.
dildo ['dildoʊ] (*noun*), *P:* gode(miché) *m*.
dill [dil] (*noun*) (*Austr.*), *P:* = alec, 2.
dilly[1] ['dili] (*adj.*), *F:* chouette, bath, mignon.
dilly[2] ['dili] (*noun*), *F:* 1. she's a d., elle est mignonne (à croquer). 2. qch. de chouette. 3. star *f*, as *m*, vedette *f*, starlette *f*.
dim [dim] (*adj.*), *F:* 1. to take a d. view of sth., avoir une piètre opinion de qch. 2. a d. type (*or* character), (*a*) individu bête*, espèce d'idiot, buse *f*; (*b*) nullité *f*, mocheté *f*, perte sèche; *cf.* come[2] (to), 2.
dime [daim] (*noun & attrib. adj.*) (*U.S.*), *F:* dîme *f* (dix cents); d. novel, roman feuilleton (*ou* de deux sous); a d. a dozen, qui ne vaut pas cher (*ou* deux sous *ou* pipette *ou* peau de balle); d.-a-dance palace, bal musette, bastringue *m*, guinche *f*.
dimmock ['dimək] (*noun*), *P:* argent*, artiche *m*.
dimp [dimp] (*noun*), *P:* mégot*, clope *m*.
dimwit ['dimwit] (*noun*), *F:* individu bête*, andouille *f*, ballot *m*.
dimwitted ['dimwitid] (*adj.*), *F:* bête*, bas de plafond, baluche.
dinch [dintʃ] (*noun*), *P:* = dimp.
din-dins ['dindinz] (*pl. noun*), *F:* (*language enfantin*) repas *m*, dînette *f*.
dine out ['dain'aʊt] (to), *F:* danser devant le buffet, claquer du bec, la sauter, manger avec les chevaux de bois.
ding [diŋ] (*noun*), *P:* to have a d. with a girl, fréquenter une fille, sortir avec une fille.
ding-dong ['diŋdɒŋ] (*adj.*), *F:* d.-d. battle, lutte acharnée, luttanche *f*, pétard *m*.

dinge[1] [dindʒ] (*noun*), *P:* nègre* (*péj.*), bougnoule *m*. *Voir aussi* queen, 2.

dinge[2] [dindʒ] (to), *P:* amocher, esquinter, bosseler, cabosser.

dinger [ˈdiŋər] (*noun*), *P:* = humdinger.

dinghiyen [ˈdiŋgiˈjen] (*noun*), *P:* = dripper.

dingle-dangle [ˈdiŋglˈdæŋgl] (*noun*), *P:* pénis*, berdouillette *f*, queue *f*.

dingus [ˈdiŋ(g)əs] (*noun*), 1. *F:* truc *m*, machin *m*, chose *f*, fourbi *m*. 2. *P:* = dripper.

dinkum [ˈdiŋkəm] (*adj.*) (*Austr.*), *F:* 1. (fair) **d.**, régulier, réglo, aux petits oignons, vrai de vrai. 2. **the d.** article, (*a*) de l'authentique, du vrai; (*b*) l'homme qu'il faut. 3. **a d.** Aussie, Australien *m* de naissance, kangourou *m*.

dinky [ˈdiŋki] (*adj.*), *F:* 1. mignon, menu, joliet, croquignole. 2. (*Austr.*) sûr et certain.

dinky-doo [ˈdiŋkiˈduː], *F:* *voir* bingo (22).

dinlow [ˈdinlou] (*noun*), *F:* = dimwit.

dip[1] [dip] (*noun*). 1. *P:* voleur* à la tire (*ou* à la fourche *ou* à la fourchette). 2. *P:* drogué*, camé *m*, toxico *m*. 3. *P:* diphtérie *f*. 4. *P:* individu bête*, nigaud *m*, ballot *m*. 5. *F:* une petite baignade, une trempette. 6. *F:* lucky **d.**, (*a*) loterie *f*; (*b*) au petit bonheur la chance. 7. *P:* chapeau*, bada *m*, doulos *m*.

dip[2] [dip] (to), *P:* 1. mettre en gage, mettre au Mont (de Piété) (*ou* chez ma tante). 2. voler* à la tire (*ou* à la fourche *ou* à la fourchette). *Voir aussi* lid, 1; wick, 2.

dipper [ˈdipər] (*noun*), *P:* 1. = dip[1], 1. 2. baptiste *m* (qui croit au baptême par immersion).

dippy [ˈdipi] (*adj.*), *P:* 1. fou*, maboul, timbré, loufoque, dingo. 2. **to be d.** about s.o., être entiché de qn, avoir le béguin pour qn.

dipso [ˈdipsou] (*abbr.* = *dipsomaniac*), *F:* dipsomane *mf*, ivrogne*, soûlot *m*, poivrot *m*.

dirt[1] [dəːt] (*noun*). 1. *F:* porno(graphie) *f*, obscénité *f*, cochonnerie *f*. 2. *P:* ragots *m.pl.*, cancans *m.pl.*, potins *m. pl.*; **to dish out the d.**, ragoter, cancaner, potiner; **to throw d. at s.o.**, déblatérer contre qn, débiner qn, dauber sur qn;

to have the d. on s.o., savoir des choses peu relevées sur qn. 3. *F:* to treat s.o. like **d.**, traiter qn plus bas que terre. 4. *F:* to sweep the **d.** under the carpet (*U.S.*: under the rug), couvrir la vérité, tirer le rideau, mettre la lumière sous le boisseau. 5. *F:* to eat **d.**, avaler son amour-propre, avaler des couleuvres. 6. *P:* to do **d.** on s.o., to do s.o. **d.**, faire un sale coup (*ou* une crasse *ou* une vacherie) à qn; *cf.* dirty[2]. 7. *P:* yellow **d.**, or*, jonc *m*, quart *m* de beurre. 8. *P:* argent*, braise *f*. *Voir aussi* dicky-dirt; grass[1], 2.

dirt[2] [dəːt] (to), *P:* duper*, rouler, carotter (qn).

dirt-cheap [ˈdəːtˈtʃiːp] (*adj. & adv.*), *F:* à vil prix, pour rien*, pour des prunes (*ou* des haricots).

dirt-track [ˈdəːttræk] (*attrib. adj.*), *P:* **d.-t.** rider, pédéraste* qui est de la bague (*ou* du zéro).

dirty[1] [ˈdəːti] (*adj.*). 1. *F:* to have a d. mind, avoir l'esprit cochon (*ou* mal tourné); how d.-minded she is! comme elle est cochonne! 2. *F:* d. dog, sale type *m*; d. trick, sale tour *m*; d. weather, sale temps *m*; d. look, sale coup d'œil; d. rat, bordille *f*. 3. (*a*) *F:* he does the d. work, il fait la grosse besogne, à lui la sale besogne; (*b*) d. work at the crossroads, (i) *F:* sale coup *m*, crasse *f*, saloperie *f*; (ii) *P:* coït*. 4. *P:* (*intensif*) a d. great lorry, un camion maous(se); a d. big suitcase, une valise qui se pose là. 5. *F:* a d. old man, un vieux barbeau, un vieux marcheur. 6. *P:* (*a*) d. old Jew: *voir* bingo (2); (*b*) d. whore: *voir* bingo (34). 7. *F:* a d. weekend, un week-end de débauche. 8. *P:* d. money, (*a*) argent* mal acquis, gratte *f*, tour *m* de bâton; (*b*) prime *f* (de travail). 9. *F:* to have a d. mouth, parler comme un charretier, être mal embouché. 10. *P:* (*jazz*) grinçant, agressif. *Voir aussi* linen; mac[2].

dirty[2] [ˈdəːti] (*noun*), *P:* to do the d. on s.o., jouer un tour de cochon à qn, chier dans les bottes de qn; *cf.* dirt[1], 6.

disappearing [disəˈpiəriŋ] (*adj.*), *F:* to do a d. act, (*a*) partir*, s'esquiver, jouer rip; (*b*) déménager à la cloche de bois.

dischuffed [ˈdisˈtʃʌft] (*adj.*), *P:* dé-

---

* An asterisk indicates that the word so marked is included as a head-word in the Appendix.

courage, dégoûté, qui n'a pas le moral;
cf. **chuffed,** (b).
disco [ˈdiskou] (*noun*), *F:* **1.** discothèque
f. **2.** club *m* de discophiles.
dish[1] [diʃ] (*noun*). **1.** *F:* belle* fille;
what a d.! quelle beauté! un vrai
régal!; *cf.* **dishy. 2.** *P:* fesses*, arrière-
boutique *f*, dédé *m*. **3.** *P:* visage*,
fiole *f*, binette *f*.
dish[2] [diʃ] (**to**), *P:* **1.** enfoncer (ses
adversaires), prendre de court, couper
l'herbe sous le pied à (qn); **to be dished,**
être coulé (*ou* enfoncé *ou* flambé). **2.**
duper*, rouler (qn). **3.** confondre,
dérouter, frustrer. **4.** (*U.S.*) bavarder*,
potiner.
dishclout [ˈdiʃ-klaut] (*noun*), *P:* salope
f, souillon *f*.
dish out [ˈdiʃˈaut] (**to**), *F:* **1. to d. o.
money** (*or* **the lolly**), payer*, casquer
(*ou* abouler *ou* cracher) de l'argent*.
2. to d. it o., réprimander*, faire
une semonce, passer un savon. **3. to
d. o. punishment,** (*d'un boxeur*) as-
sener des coups* à son adversaire, envoyer les marrons. *Voir aussi* **dirt**[1], **2**;
porridge.
dishrag [ˈdiʃræg] (*noun*), *F:* **to feel like
a d.,** se sentir très fatigué*, être éreinté
(*ou* sur les genoux).
dish up [ˈdiʃˈʌp] (**to**). **1.** *F:* bien arranger
(*ou* trousser), pomponner, requinquer.
2. *P:* **to be dished up,** être fatigué*
(*ou* éreinté *ou* pompé *ou* à bout).
dishwater [ˈdiʃwɔːtər] (*noun*), *F:* **1.**
lavasse *f*; bibine *f*; **to taste of d.,**
(*nourriture*) sentir le graillon. **2. dull as
d.** = **dull as ditchwater** (*voir* **ditchwater**).
dishy [ˈdiʃi] (*adj.*), *F:* qui a du chien;
cf. **dish**[1], **1.**
dismals [ˈdizməlz] (*pl. noun*), *F:* **to have
the d.,** broyer du noir, avoir le cafard.
distance [ˈdist(ə)ns] (*noun*), *F:* **to go the
d.,** (*boxe, lutte*) aller à la limite.
ditch[1] [ditʃ] (*noun*), *F:* **1. to die in the
last d.,** mourir* dans l'impénitence
finale (*ou* à la dernière extrémité). **2.
the D.,** (*a*) la Manche *ou* la mer du
Nord; (*b*) Shoreditch (*banlieue-est de
Londres*); **the big d.,** l'océan *m*, la
Grande Tasse, la baille. *Voir aussi*
last-ditch.
ditch[2] [ditʃ] (**to**), *F:* **1.** jeter par-dessus
bord, larguer. **2. to d. a car,** (*a*) verser

une automobile dans un fossé, la faire
entrer dans les décors; (*b*) abandonner*
une voiture, la larguer. **3. to d. a plane,**
amerrir en catastrophe, faire un amer-
rissage forcé. **4.** (*a*) abandonner* (une
femme, idée, *etc.*), plaquer, laisser
tomber; (*b*) se débarrasser* de, sacquer,
balancer. **5.** faire dérailler.
ditchwater [ˈditʃwɔːtər] (*noun*), *F:* **dull
as d.,** ennuyeux* comme la pluie;
he's as dull as d., c'est un robinet d'eau
tiède.
dither [ˈdiðər] (*noun*), *F:* **to be all of a d.,
to have the dithers,** être dans tous ses
états, ne plus savoir où donner de la
tête.
dithery [ˈdiðəri] (*adj.*), *F:* agité, nerveux, tout chose.
ditto[1] [ˈditou] (*noun*), *F:* **1.** un complet,
un ensemble. **2. to say d.,** opiner du
bonnet.
ditto[2] [ˈditou] (**to**), *F:* faire *ou* dire la
même chose.
dive[1] [daiv] (*noun*), *F:* **1.** café*, bouge
m, tripot *m*, gargote *f*, boui-boui *m*.
2. to take a d., (*a*) (*boxe*) se coucher;
(*b*) faire le plongeon. *Voir aussi* **nose-
dive**[1].
dive[2] [daiv] (**to**). **1.** *F:* **to d. into a shop,**
s'engouffrer dans un magasin. **2.** *V:*
to d. (into the bushes) = **muff**[2] (**to**),
3; *cf.* **pearl-dive** (**to**). *Voir aussi* **nose-
dive**[2] (**to**).
divi [ˈdivi] (*noun*), *F:* = **divvy.**
divine [diˈvain] (*adj.*), *F:* excellent*,
divin.
divvy [ˈdivi] (*noun*), *F:* intérêt *m*,
divi(dende) *m*, fade *m*.
divvy up [ˈdiviˈʌp] (**to**), *F:* partager,
aller au fade, faire la motte.
dizzy [ˈdizi] (*adj.*), *F:* **1.** = **scatterbrained. 2. a d. blonde,** une blonde
tape-à-l'œil; **a d. dame,** une femme*
bête*, cruche *f*, bourrique *f*, gourde *f*.
3. it's the d. limit, c'est le comble,
c'est la fin des haricots. **4. to go the
d. round,** faire la noce (*ou* la bamboche),
faire la tournée des grands-ducs.
D.J., d.j. [ˈdiːˈdʒei] (*abbr.* = *disc-jockey*),
F: voir **dee-jay.**
do[1] [duː] (*noun*). **1.** *F:* réjouissances*,
boum *f*, bombance *f*. **2.** *P:* filouterie *f*,
sale tour *m*, attrape *f*. **3.** *F:* affaire(s)
f. (*pl.*), événement *m*. **4.** (*pl.*) *F:* partage *m*, portion *f*, taf *m*; **fair d.'s,**

---

* An asterisk indicates that the word so marked is included as a head-word in the Appendix.

une juste part; **to give s.o. fair d.'s,** jouer franc jeu avec qn. **5.** *P:* réussite *f;* **to make a d. of sth.,** se bien tirer de qch. **6.** *P:* bataille *f* entre jeunes voyous; rififi *m. Voir aussi* **hair-do;** **shaky.**

do[2] [duː] **(to). 1.** *P:* coïter* avec (qn), tomber, brosser (qn). **2.** *P:* sodomiser, caser, empaffer (*coït* anal). **3.** *F:* **to d. sth. no one else can d. for you,** déféquer*, aller où le Roi va à pied. **4.** *P:* escroquer*, refaire; **to be** (*or* **get**) **done,** se faire avoir; *voir aussi* **eye, 5. 5.***P:* cambrioler*, caroubler; *cf.* **drum, 1** (*b*). **6.** *P:* battre*, passer (qn) à tabac. **7.** *P:* arrêter*, épingler; **to get done,** se faire paumer (*ou* fabriquer). **8.** *F:* visiter; **to d. Venice,** faire Venise. **9.** *F:* **that'll d.,** ça suffit; **that'll d.!** assez!* c'est marre! classe! **10.** *F:* botter (qn); **he'll d. me,** il me va, ça fait mon blot. **11.** *F:* **that won't d.,** cela ne prend pas (*ou* ne passe pas). **12.** *F:* **have nothing to d. with it!** ne vous y frottez pas! **13.** *F:* **nothing doing!** rien à faire! **14.** *F:* **it** (simply) **isn't done, it's** (simply) **not done,** ça ne se fait pas, c'est pas canonique. **15.** *F:* **done!** d'accord!* dac! **16.** *F:* **that's done it!** = **that's torn it!** (*tear*[2] (**to**)). **17.** *F:* **d. or die,** marche ou crève. *Voir aussi* **done** *et les verbes composés* **to do down, for, in, out, over, up, with, without.**

dobeying [ˈdoubiːiŋ] (*noun*), *P:* = **dhobying.**

dob in [ˈdɔbˈin] (**to**) (*Austr.*), *F:* trahir, vendre, moutonner (qn).

doc [dɔk] (*abbr.* = *doctor*), *F:* docteur *m,* toubib *m.*

dock[1] [dɔk] (*noun*), *F:* **in d.,** (*a*) à l'hôpital, à l'hosto; (*b*) (*d'une voiture*) au garage, en réparation. *Voir aussi* **dickory-dock.**

dock[2] [dɔk] (**to**), *F:* **to d. s.o.'s pay,** diminuer (*ou* rogner) le salaire de qn.

doctor[1] [ˈdɔktər] (*noun*), *F:* **1.** just what the d. ordered, exactement ce qu'il (me) faut. **2. d.'s orders:** *voir* **bingo** (9). *Voir aussi* **couch-doctor; horse-doctor.**

doctor[2] [ˈdɔktər] (**to**), *F:* **1.** châtrer, couper. **2.** frelater (vin, *etc.*), tripatouiller. **3.** truquer, maquiller (comptes).

doctor up [ˈdɔktərˈʌp] (**to**), *F:* rac-

commoder, remettre en état, rafistoler, retaper.

do-da [ˈduːdɑː] (*noun*), *F:* = **doo-da.**

dodderer [ˈdɔdərər] (*noun*), *F:* (old) **d.,** vieux* gaga, croulant *m,* gâteux *m,* ramolli *m.*

doddle[1] [dɔdl] (*noun*), *F:* = **cinch.**

doddle[2] [dɔdl] (**to**), *F:* **to d. it,** gagner les doigts dans le nez, gagner dans un fauteuil.

dodge[1] [dɔdʒ] (*noun*), *F:* **1.** ruse *f;* **to be up to all the dodges,** connaître tous les trucs (*ou* toutes les ficelles), la connaître dans les coins. **2.** a clever d., un bon truc, une astuce.

dodge[2] [dɔdʒ] (**to**), *F:* **1. to d. the column,** tirer au flanc, se défiler, couper à qch.; *cf.* **column-dodger. 2. to d. the draft,** (*a*) éviter d'être envoyé outremer, se défiler; (*b*) déserter, faire chibis à la grive; *cf.* **draft-dodger.**

dodger [ˈdɔdʒər] (*noun*): **artful d.,** (*a*) *F:* malin *m,* dégourdi *m,* débrouillard *m;* (*b*) *P:* (*R.S.* = *lodger*) locataire *mf. Voir aussi* **column-dodger; devil-dodger; draft-dodger.**

dodgy [ˈdɔdʒi] (*adj.*). **1.** *F:* **d. business,** affaire louche (*ou* douteuse *ou* qui sent mauvais). **2.** *P:* **d. grub,** nourriture* volée, boustifaille ratiboisée. **3.** *F:* difficile*, coton, duraille. **4.** *F:* malin*, débrouillard, roublard, madré.

dodo [ˈdoudou] (*noun*), *F:* vieux* rabâcheur, vieux croûton; **old d.,** vieux* bonze (*ou* birbe), son-et-lumière *m;* **dead as a d.,** mort et enterré.

do down [ˈduːˈdaun] (**to**), *F:* l'emporter sur (qn), rouler (qn).

do for [ˈduːˈfɔːr] (**to**). **1.** *P:* tuer*, descendre, dégommer, zigouiller. **2.** *P:* faire le ménage pour (qn). **3.** *F:* **to be done for,** (*a*) être ruiné (*ou* fauché *ou* flambé *ou* fichu *ou* fini *ou* cuit); **he's done for,** ses carottes sont cuites; (*b*) être à la mort (*ou* foutu); (*c*) être fatigué* (*ou* pompé *ou* à bout de forces).

dog[1] [dɔg] (*noun*), *F:* **1.** it's a d.'s life, c'est une vie de chien. **2. to be dressed up** (*or* **got up**) **like a d.'s dinner,** être en grand tralala (*ou* sur son trente et un *ou* tout fringué). **3. to try** (sth.) **out on the d.,** utiliser comme cobaye. **4. to take a hair of the d.** (that bit you), reprendre du poil de la bête. **5. he doesn't stand a d.'s chance,** il n'a pas l'ombre d'une chance. **6. d.'s nose,** boisson *f* de bière et de gin. **7.** (*pl.*) pieds*, nougats *m.pl.*; **to have dogs that bite** (*or* **barking dogs**), avoir mal aux pattes. **8.** vaurien*, sale type *m*, fripouille *f*, canaille *f*. **9. a gay d.**, un gai luron, un joyeux drille, un noceur. **10. a sly d.**, un fin renard. **11. the dogs,** courses *f.pl.* de lévriers. **12. to go to the dogs,** mal tourner, aller à sa ruine. **13. to be top d.**, être vainqueur, avoir le dessus. **14. d. in the manger,** le chien du jardinier. **15. hot d.**, hot dog *m*, (*saucisse chaude dans du pain*). **16. let sleeping dogs lie,** ne réveillez pas le chat qui dort. **17. to put on (the) d.**, faire le paon, en étaler, poser pour la galerie. **18. = dog-end. 19. to have a black d. on one's back,** broyer du noir, avoir le bourdon, être au 36ème dessous. **20. to see a man about a d.**, aller aux W.C.*, aller changer son poisson d'eau. **21. to work like a d.**, travailler* dur, trimer. **22. in a d.'s age,** il y a belle lurette (*ou* un bail *ou* une paye). **23. to call off the dogs,** cesser les hostilités. **24.** (*a*) pleutre *m*; (*b*) camelote *f*, gnognot(t)e *f*. **25. there's life in the old d. yet,** il n'est pas près de sa fin, il a encore du ressort. **26. spotted d.**, (*a*) chien *m* de Dalmatie; (*b*) pudding *m* aux raisins. *Voir aussi* **cat, 9, 11; dirty¹, 2; dumb, 2; hot, 26; hound-dog; shaggy-dog; sheep-dog; yard-dog.**

dog² [dɔg] (**to**), *F:* **to d. it**, négliger son travail, traîner les patins.

dog-cart [ˈdɔgkɑːt] (*noun*) (*Austr.*), *P:* = **trawler**.

dog-collar [ˈdɔgkɔlər] (*noun*), *F:* faux-col *m* d'ecclésiastique, col romain; **the d.-c. brigade,** le clergé, les prêtres*, la ratiche.

dog-end [ˈdɔgend] (*noun*), *F:* mégot*, clope *m*.

dog-fashion [ˈdɔgfæʃ(ə)n] (*adv.*), *P:* = **dogways.**

dog-fight [ˈdɔgfait] (*noun*), *F:* combat aérien; mêlée *f*.

doggie [ˈdɔgi] (*noun*), *F:* = **doggy², 1.**

doggo [ˈdɔgou] (*adv.*), *F:* caché*, planqué; **to lie d.**, faire le mort, se tenir peinard.

doggone [ˈdɔgɔn] (*adj.*) (*U.S.*): *euph. pour* **goddamned. d. it!** sacré bordel!

doggy¹ [ˈdɔgi] (*adj.*), *F:* **1.** amateur de chiens, père à chiens. **2.** élégant*, flambard.

doggy² [ˈdɔgi] (*noun*), *F:* **1.** chien*, chien-chien *m*, toutou *m*, azor *m*. **2.** officier secondant un amiral.

dog-hole [ˈdɔghoul] (*noun*), *P:* logement* sale, piaule *f*, bouge *m*, porcherie *f*.

dog-house [ˈdɔghaus] (*noun*), *F:* **in the d.-h.,** mis de côté, en quarantaine, mal en cour.

dogie [ˈdoudʒi] (*noun*), *P:* héroïne *f* (*drogues**), cheval *m*.

do-gooder [ˈduːgudər] (*noun*), *F:* redresseur *m* de torts, dame patronesse.

dogsbody [ˈdɔgzbɔdi] (*noun*), *F:* subordonné(e), sous-fifre *m*, lampiste *m*.

dog-tag [ˈdɔgtæg] (*noun*), *F:* plaque *f* d'identité.

dog-tired [ˈdɔgˈtaiəd] (*adj.*), *F:* très fatigué*, crevé, claqué, fourbu, vanné.

dogways [ˈdɔgweiz] (*adv.*), *P:* **to have** (*or* **do**) **it d.**, coïter* par enculage, enculer (*coït** *anal*).

do in [ˈduːˈin] (**to**), *P:* **1.** tuer, assassiner*; **to d. oneself i.**, se suicider*, se buter, se flanquer en l'air. **2.** fatiguer, éreinter; **done in,** très fatigué*, claqué. **3.** démolir, saboter, bousiller. **4.** dépenser*, claquer, bouffer (de l'argent*).

doing! [ˈdɔiŋ] (*excl.*), *F:* = **boing!;** *cf.* **doink!**

doings [ˈduiŋz] **the** (*pl. noun*), *F:* **1.** machin *m*, truc *m*, fourbi *m*. **2.** (*a*) raclée *f*, dérouillée *f*; (*b*) réprimande *f*, savon *m*, engueulade *f*. **3.** tout le bataclan, tout le fourbi; **I've got the d.,** j'ai de quoi, j'ai ce qu'il faut.

doink! [ˈdɔiŋk] (*excl.*), *F:* = **boing!;** *cf.* **doing.**

do-it-yourself [ˈduitjəˈself] (*noun*). **1.** *F:* (*a*) bricolage *m*, la bricole; (*b*) attirail *m* de bricoleur. **2.** *V:* masturbation *f*, branlage *m* maison.

do-it-yourselfer [ˈduitjəˈselfər] (*noun*), *F:* bricoleur *m*.

dojee, dojie [ˈdoudʒi] (*noun*), *P:* = **dogie.**

dokka [ˈdɔkə] (*noun*), *P:* cigarette*, cibiche *f*, sèche *f*.

doldrums [ˈdɔldrəmz] (*pl. noun*), *F:* **to be in the d.,** (*a*) avoir le cafard, broyer du noir; (*b*) être dans le marasme.

doll [dɔl] (*noun*), *F:* **1.** fille* *ou* jeune

---

* An asterisk indicates that the word so marked is included as a head-word in the Appendix.

femme*, poupée *f.* 2. tête *f* de linotte, poupée *f. Voir aussi* baby[1], 1; baby-doll.
dollop [ˈdɔləp] (*noun*), *F:* morceau *m* informe, flanquée *f*, plâtrée *f*; a good d. of jam, une bonne tapée de confiture.
doll up [ˈdɔlˈʌp] (to), *F:* to d. oneself u., se pomponner, se bichonner; to get all dolled up, se mettre sur son trente et un.
dolly[1] [ˈdɔli] (*adj.*), *F:* 1. that's real d.! c'est du nanan! 2. (*cricket, etc.*) d. catch, balle facilement prise de volée.
dolly[2] [ˈdɔli] (*noun*). 1. *F:* poupée *f*, pépée *f.* 2. *F:* = dolly-bird, 1. 3.*P:* méthadone *f* (dolophine) (*drogues*). 4. (*pl.*) *P:* seins*, rotoplots *m.pl.*
dolly-bird [ˈdɔlibə:d], dolly-girl [ˈdɔligə:l] (*noun*). 1. *F:* (belle) poupée, prix *m* de Diane. 2. *P:* fille facile, pépée *f*, nana *f.*
dolly-shop [ˈdɔliʃɔp] (*noun*), *P:* (a) officine *f* de prêteur sur gage; (b) boutique *f* de chiffonnier, friperie *f.*
dome [doum] (*noun*), *F:* tête*, caboche *f*, boule *f. Voir aussi* double, 4; ivory.
domino-box [ˈdɔminoubɔks] (*noun*), *P:* = box of dominoes (dominoes, 3).
dominoes [ˈdɔminouz] (*pl. noun*), *P:* 1. capsules *f.pl.* de durophet, dominos *m.pl.* (*drogues*). 2. it's d. with (*or* for) him, il est fichu (*ou* foutu). 3. dents* jaunies, dominos *m.pl.*; box of d., bouche*, boîte *f.*
dona(h) [ˈdounə] (*noun*), *P:* la petite amie, sa régulière, sa particulière.
done [dʌn] (*adj. & p.p.*), *P:* = done up, 1, 2. *Voir aussi* do[2] (to); frazzle, 1.
done up [ˈdʌnˈʌp] (*adj. & p.p.*), *P:* 1. très fatigué*, crevé. 2. ruiné*, fauché, nettoyé. 3. (a) maquillée, emplâtrée; (b) habillé élégamment, bien fringué, tiré à quatre épingles. *Voir aussi* do up (to).
dong [dɔŋ], donker [ˈdɔŋkər] (*noun*), *V:* = donkey, 5.
donkey [ˈdɔŋki] (*noun*). 1. *F:* to talk the hind leg off a d., être bavard* comme une pie, être un moulin à paroles. 2. *F:* d. work, travail *m* de routine. 3. *F:* d.'s years, une éternité, un bail, une paye; d.'s years ago, il y a belle lurette. 4. *F:* âne bâté, imbécile *mf.* 5. *V:* (gros) pénis*, gros bout; to flog one's d., se masturber*, s'astiquer la colonne.
donnybrook [ˈdɔnibruk] (*noun*) (*U.S.*), *F:* querelle*, bagarre *f*, badaboum *m*, corrida *f.*

doo-da [ˈduːdɑː], doodad [ˈduːdæd], doodah [ˈduːdɑː] (*noun*), *F:* 1. truc *m*, machin *m*, fourbi *m.* 2. agitation *f*, énervement *m*; to be all of a d., être aux cent coups, être démonté.
doodle [ˈduːdl] (*noun*), *P:* 1. individu bête*, nouille *f.* 2. pénis*, verge *f.*
doodle-alley [ˈduːdlˈæli] (*adj.*), *P:* (a) qui a une case de vide, demeuré; (b) fou*, tapé, cinoque.
doodle-bug [ˈduːdlbʌg] (*noun*), *F:* 1. vieille voiture*, tacot *m.* 2. (*W.W.II*) bombe volante.
doofer [ˈduːfər] (*noun*), *P:* 1. moitié *f* de cigarette*, un ça suffit. 2. = whatcha-(ma)callit.
doohickey [ˈduːˈhiki] (*noun*) (*U.S.*), *F:* = doo-da, 1.
doojee [ˈduːdʒiː], doojer [ˈduːdʒər], dooji [ˈduːdʒiː] (*noun*), *P:* = dogie.
doojigger [ˈduːdʒigər] (*noun*) (*U.S.*), *F:* = doo-da, 1.
dooks [duːks] (*pl. noun*), *P:* = dukes.
doolally (tap) [ˈduːˈlæli(ˈtæp)] (*adj.*), *P:* = doodle-alley.
door [dɔːr] (*noun*), *F:* 1. to show s.o. the d., mettre (*ou* flanquer) qn à la porte. 2. you make a better d. than a window, tu n'es pas transparent. 3. (a) knock at the d.: *voir* bingo (4); (b) key of the d.: *voir* bingo (21); (c) open the d.: *voir* bingo (44). *Voir aussi* back[1], 3.
doormat [ˈdɔːmæt, ˈdɔəmæt] (*noun*), *F:* individu* qui se laisse marcher dessus, paillasson *m.*
door-nail [ˈdɔːneil, ˈdɔəneil] (*noun*), *F:* dead as a d.-n., mort et enterré.
doorstep [ˈdɔːstep, ˈdɔəstep] (*noun*), *F:* quignon *m* de pain.
do out [ˈduːˈaut] (to), *F:* 1. débarrasser, lessiver. 2. to d. s.o. o. of sth., escroquer* qn, arnaquer, rouler, carotter qn, souffler qch. à qn.
do over [ˈduːˈouvər] (to). 1. *F:* recouvrir, retaper (peinture, *etc.*). 2. *P:* = do[2] (to), 3. 3. *P:* (a) voler* (qn); (b) tromper*, estamper (qn). 4. *P:* fouiller (un suspect).
dope[1] [doup] (*noun*). 1. *F:* (a) renseigne-ment* (confidentiel *ou* préalable), tuyau *m*, tubard *m*; the latest d., les dernières nouvelles, les derniers renseignements*; to give s.o. the latest d., mettre qn à la page, affranchir qn; (b) renseignements* exacts; (c) faux renseignements*;

---

* L'astérisque indique que le mot marqué de ce signe figure comme entrée dans le Répertoire.

bourrage *m* de crâne; (*d*) tuyaux *m.pl.* sur les courses de chevaux; **d. sheet**, journal *m* hippique, le papier. **2.** *F:* what a d. he is! quel crétin (*ou* quelle nouille) que ce type! qu'il est bête*! **3.** *F:* potion *f*, remède *m.* **4.** *P:* essence *f*, jus *m.* **5.** *F:* doping *m* (administré à un cheval), dopage *m.* **6.** *P:* stup(éfiant) *m*, narc(otique) *m* (*drogues**); **d.** hop, défonce *f*, planète *f*; **d. fiend**, morphinomane *mf*, drogué*, toxico(mane) *mf*; **d. habit**, toxicomanie *f*; **d. peddler** (*or* **pedlar** *or* **merchant** *or* **runner**), fourgueur *m* de came, trafiquant *m* (en stupéfiants); **d. den**, fumerie *f* d'opium, repaire *m* de drogués*, clandé *m*; **to hit the d.**, se droguer*, se schnouffer; **to be on d.**, être un usager de drogues, marcher à la drogue; **d. racket**, trafic *m* de drogues; **d. ring**, bande* de trafiquants, flèche *f* de la came. **7.** (*U.S.*) *P:* = **dopehead.**

dope² [doup] (**to**). **1.** *F:* (*a*) administrer un narcotique à (qn), droguer, doper; (*b*) mêler un narcotique à (un verre de vin), narcotiser (une cigarette), doper; (*c*) **to d. oneself**, prendre des stupéfiants *m.pl.*, se droguer*; **doped (up) to the eyebrows**, schnouffé à bloc. **2.** *F:* doper (un cheval). **3.** *F:* ajouter de l'alcool à une boisson non alcoolisée, corser. **4.** *F:* calmer, tranquilliser. **5.** *P:* tromper*, refaire, rouler (qn).

dopehead [ˈdouphed] (*noun*), *P:* drogué*, camé *m*, toxico *m.*

dope out [ˈdoupˈaut] (**to**), *P:* (*a*) découvrir*, dénicher; (*b*) trouver le joint.

doper [ˈdoupər] (*noun*), *P:* = **dopehead.**

doperie [ˈdoupəri] (*noun*), *P:* = **dope den** (**dope¹, 6**).

dopester [ˈdoupstər] (*noun*), *P:* **1.** = **dopehead. 2.** marchand *m* de tuyaux (*courses hippiques*), tuyauteur *m*, tubardeur *m.*

dope up [ˈdoupˈʌp] (**to**), *P:* (*a*) se droguer*, se camer; (*b*) droguer, schnouffer (qn).

dopey¹ [ˈdoupi] (*adj.*), *F:* **1.** bête*, bêta, empoté. **2.** abruti (de fatigue). **3.** stupéfié, hébété (par un narcotique); léthargique.

dopey², **dopie** [ˈdoupi] (*noun*), *P:* = **dopehead.**

dopium [ˈdoupiəm] (*noun*), *P:* opium *m* (*drogues**), op *m*, noir *m.*

dopy [ˈdoupi] (*adj. & noun*) = **dopey¹,².**

do-re-mi [ˈdouˈreiˈmiː] (*noun*), *P:* argent*, pépettes *f.pl.*, picaillons *m.pl.*

dorm [dɔːm] (*abbr.* = *dormitory*), *F:* dortoir *m*, dorto *m.*

dose [dous] (*noun*). **1.** *P:* **to get** (*or* **catch** *or* **cop**) **a d.**, attraper une maladie* vénérienne, ramasser la chtouille, se faire poivrer (*ou* fader *ou* plomber *ou* nazicoter). **2.** *F:* **like a d. of salts**, comme une lettre à la poste.

dose up [ˈdousˈʌp] (**to**), *P:* contaminer (qn) avec une maladie* vénérienne, fader, poivrer, plomber (qn); **to be dosed up** (**to the eyebrows**), (*a*) souffrir d'une maladie* vénérienne, être (bien) poivré (*ou* fadé); (*b*) être drogué* (*ou* camé *ou* chargé) jusque-là.

dosh [dɔʃ] (*noun*), *P:* argent*, fric *m*, pèze *m.*

doss¹ [dɔs] (*noun*), *P:* **1.** lit* (dans une pension peu relevée), plumard *m* de garno (*ou* de bustingue). **2.** un somme, une dorme; **to do a d.**, dormir*, piquer un roupillon.

doss² [dɔs] (**to**), *P:* dormir*, pioncer.

doss down [ˈdɔsˈdaun] (**to**), *P:* **1.** se coucher*, se lâcher. **2.** arranger un lit de dépannage.

dosser [ˈdɔsər] (*noun*), *P:* **1.** clochard*, clodo *m.* **2.** drogué*, junkie *m*, camé *m.*

doss-house [ˈdɔshaus] (*noun*), *F:* asile *m* de nuit, dorme *m*, piaule *f* à clodos.

dot¹ [dɔt] (*noun*). **1.** *F:* **on the d.**, à l'heure, à pic, pile, recta. **2.** *P:* **off one's d.**, fou*, timbré. **3.** *F:* **in the year d.**, il y a longtemps; **it goes back to the year d.**, cela remonte au déluge, c'est antédiluvien. **4.** *P:* clitoris*, bouton *m*, grain *m* de café.

dot² [dɔt] (**to**). **1.** *P:* **to d. s.o.** (**one**), battre* qn, flanquer un gnon à qn. **2.** *F:* **to d. and carry one**, boiter (en marchant), béquiller, faire cinq et trois font huit, clopiner.

dottiness [ˈdɔtinis] (*noun*), *F:* toquade *f*, loufoquerie *f*, détraquage *m.*

dotty [ˈdɔti] (*adj.*), *F:* fou*, cinglé, tapé, toqué; **to go d.**, perdre la boule (*ou* la boussole).

double [ˈdʌbl] (*adj.*), *F:* **1. to do a d. take**, regarder* par deux fois. **2. d. talk**, propos *m.pl.* à endormir les gens,

---

* An asterisk indicates that the word so marked is included as a head-word in the Appendix.

double parler m. 3. d. think, croyance f au pour et au contre, double penser m. 4. d. dome, intellectuel m, mandarin m, grosse tête. 5. to do the d. act, se marier. Voir aussi Dutch³, 1.

double-cross¹ [ˈdʌblˈkrɔs] (noun), F: entubage m, roustissure f.

double-cross² [ˈdʌblˈkrɔs] (to), F: tromper*, entuber, doubler.

double-crosser [ˈdʌblˈkrɔsər] (noun), F: faux jeton, entubeur m, fourbe m.

double-decker [ˈdʌblˈdekər] (noun), F: 1. autobus m à impériale. 2. sandwich m à deux étages.

double-quick [ˈdʌblˈkwik] (adv.), F: au pas de course, en cinq secs. Voir aussi quick.

double-sheet [ˈdʌblˈʃiːt] (to) (U.S.), F: = short-sheet (to).

double-tongued [ˈdʌblˈtʌŋd] (adj.), F: qui a deux paroles.

double up [ˈdʌblˈʌp] (to), F: 1. to d. u. (or to be doubled up) with laughter, pain, se tordre de rire*, de douleur, être plié en deux. 2. to d. u. on a horse, doubler la mise. 3. to d. u. with s.o., partager une chambre avec qn.

douche [duːʃ] (noun), F: surprise f désagréable, douche f.

dough [dou] (noun), F: argent*, galette f, fric m; to be in the d. (or rolling in d.), être riche*, rouler dans le fric, être bourré à bloc; to throw one's d. around, dépenser* sans compter, jeter son argent* par les fenêtres.

doughboy [ˈdoubɔi], doughfoot [ˈdoufut] (noun) (U.S.), F: soldat* (de 2ème classe) de l'infanterie américaine, biffin m, troufion m.

doughy [ˈdou(w)i] (adj.), F: 1. (teint) pâle, pâteux, de papier mâché. 2. riche*, galetteux, bourré aux as.

do up [ˈduːˈʌp] (to). 1. P: fatiguer, éreinter, crever. 2. P: battre*, arranger, tabasser. 3. F: raccommoder, remettre en état. 4. F: ficeler (un paquet), boutonner (un vêtement). Voir aussi done up.

dove [dʌv] (noun), F: qn qui s'oppose à la guerre, colombe f; cf. hawk¹.

do with [ˈduːwið] (to), F: 1. supporter, tolérer, encaisser. 2. I could d. w. a drink, je prendrais bien un verre, un verre ne serait pas de refus.

do without [ˈduːwiðˈaut] (to), F: se

l'accrocher, se serrer la ceinture, se brosser, se taper.

down¹ [daun] (adj.), F: d. drugs, drogues tranquillisantes; cf. up¹.

down² [daun] (adv.), F: 1. to be d. and out, être très pauvre*, être dans la dèche (ou la mouise). 2. to be d. on s.o. = to have a d. on s.o. (down³, 1). 3. to be d. for the count, (a) (boxe) être knock-out, être k.o.; (b) être ruiné*, être sur le pavé. 4. to be d. on one's luck, avoir de la malchance* (ou de la guigne ou la poisse). 5. d. under, aux antipodes. 6. to be d., (drogues) redescendre, avoir la gueule de bois. Voir aussi ground, 2; mouth, 2.

down³ [daun] (noun), F: 1. to have a d. on s.o., avoir une dent contre qn, avoir qn dans le nez. 2. = downer, 1, 2.

down⁴ [daun] (to), F: 1. faire tomber, descendre (qn), envoyer (qn) à terre. 2. boire*; to d. a pint, s'envoyer un coup, s'en jeter un derrière la cravate. 3. to d. tools, se mettre en grève. Voir aussi dust¹, 3.

down-and-out¹ [ˈdaunəndˈaut] (adj.), F: vrai; a d.-a.-o. cad, une canaille achevée; a d.-a.-o. liar, un fieffé menteur. Voir aussi down², 1.

down-and-out² [ˈdaunəndˈaut] (noun), F: fauchemane m, déchard m, bat-la-dèche m.

downbeat [ˈdaunbiːt] (adj.), F: calme, tête froide, sans avoir l'air d'y toucher; cf. upbeat.

downer [ˈdaunər] (noun), F: 1. tranquillisant m, sédatif m; cf. up(per). 2. situation déprimante, déconfiture f. Voir aussi up-and-downer.

downhill [ˈdaunhil] (adv.), F: to go d., dégringoler, être sur le déclin (ou sur la mauvaise pente).

downie [ˈdauni] (noun), P: = downer, 1.

Downing Street [ˈdauniŋstriːt] (pr. noun), F: voir bingo (10).

downy¹ [ˈdauni] (adj.), F: malin*, marloupin, roublard.

downy² [ˈdauni] (noun), P: lit*, plumard m, pageot m.

doxy [ˈdɔksi] (noun), F: garce f, salope f, boudin m, pouffiasse f.

doz. [dʌz] (noun) (abbr. = dozen), F: one d.: voir bingo (12).

dozen [ˈdʌzn] (noun), F: 1. a baker's

d., treize à la douzaine. 2. **daily d.**, culture *f* physique. 3. **dozens of . . .**, une abondance* de..., une flop(p)ée de..., une tripotée de..., une tapée de ... *Voir aussi* **dime; nineteen; six,** 3.

dozy [ˈdouzi] (*adj.*), *F:* **1.** abruti, endormi, demeuré. **2.** paresseux*, flemmard, cossard.

dozy-arsed [ˈdouzi-aːst] (*adj.*), *P:* bête*; **d.-a. bastard,** cucul *m*, connasse *m*.

D-racks [ˈdiːræks] (*pl. noun*), *P:* cartes* à jouer.

draft-dodger [ˈdrɑːftdodʒər] (*noun*), *F:* tire-au-flanc *m*, insoumis *m*; (*mil.*) déserteur *m*; *cf.* **dodge²,** 2.

drag¹ [dræg] (*noun*). **1.** *F:* (*a*) vêtements* de travelo; **in d.,** en travelo; **d. queen,** travelo *m*; (*b*) boum *f* de travelo, partouse *f* de bague. **2.** *F:* individu ennuyeux*, casse-pieds *m*, raseur *m*. **3.** *P:* voiture*; camion *m*; **d. race,** course *f* de vieilles voitures*; *voir aussi* **hot,** 9. **4.** *P:* (*a*) cigarette*, cibiche *f*, sèche *f*; *voir aussi* **spit,** 2; (*b*) bouffée *f* de tabac; **to take a d.,** tirer une bouffée; **give us a d.,** donne une bouffée; (*c*) bouffée *f* (*drogues*). **5.** (*U.S.*) *P:* piston *m*, pistonnage *m*. **6.** (*U.S.*) *P:* **the main d.,** la grand-rue.

drag² [dræg] (**to**), *F:* **to d. one's feet,** se faire tirer l'oreille, renâcler, marcher à contre-cœur.

drag-ass [ˈdrægæs] (**to**) (*U.S.*), *P:* **1.** être abattu, être à plat. **2.** partir*, se barrer, se carapater.

dragged out [ˈdrægdˈaut] (*adj.*) (*U.S.*), *P:* fatigué*, crevé, éreinté. *Voir aussi* **drag out** (to).

dragger [ˈdrægər] (*noun*), *P:* voleur* de voitures*, leveur *m* de bagnoles.

dragging [ˈdrægiŋ] (*noun*), *P:* (*a*) vol *m* de voitures*; (*b*) vol *m* à la roulotte.

draggy [ˈdrægi] (*adj.*), *P:* ennuyeux*, canulant, rasoir.

drag in [ˈdrægˈin] (**to**), *F:* amener (qch.) comme les cheveux sur la soupe.

dragnet [ˈdrægnet] (*noun*), *F:* rafle *f*, descente *f* de police, coup *m* de filet (*ou* de raclette), quadrillage *m*.

drag on [ˈdrægˈon] (**to**), *F:* tirer en longueur.

dragon [ˈdrægən] (*noun*). **1.** *F:* (*personne féroce, chaperon sévère*) dragon *m*. **2.** *F:* **d.'s teeth,** défenses *f.pl.* anti-tank. **3.** *P:* **green d.,** amphétamine *f* (*drogues**),

serpent vert; **to chase the d.,** avoir la toxicomanie, fonctionner à la drogue, marcher à la topette.

drag out [ˈdrægˈaut] (**to**), *F:* **1.** éterniser, faire traîner. **2. to d. sth. o. of s.o.,** extirper qn, délier la langue à qn. *Voir aussi* **dragged out.**

dragsman [ˈdrægzmən] (*noun*), *P:* voleur* de train.

drag up [ˈdrægˈʌp] (**to**). **1.** *F:* **to d. u. s.o.'s past,** faire ressortir (*ou* déterrer) le passé de qn. **2.** *P:* **where were you dragged up?** où as-tu été élevé? d'où sors-tu?; **dragged up,** élevé à la va-comme-je-te-pousse.

drain¹ [drein] (*noun*), *F:* **1. to go down the d.,** échouer*, tomber dans le lac; **it's money down the d.,** c'est jeter l'argent* par les fenêtres. **2. to laugh like a d.,** rire* de bon cœur, se boyauter, se bidonner, se tordre comme une baleine. **3. up the d.,** (*a*) dans le pétrin, dans ses petits souliers; (*b*) dans le lac. *Voir aussi* **brain-drain.**

drain² [drein] (**to**), *F:* **to d. s.o. dry,** saigner qn à blanc, tondre la laine sur le dos à qn.

drainpipe [ˈdreinpaip] (*noun*), *F:* **1.** individu* grand et mince, échalas *m*, asperge *f*, grande perche. **2.** (*pl.*) (=*drainpipe trousers*) pantalon* étroit, tuyau *m* de poêle, fuseau *m*.

drape¹ [dreip] (*noun*), *F:* toilette tapageuse (*ou* outrée), grand tralala; **a set of drapes,** un complet, un ensemble.

drape² [dreip] (**to**), *F:* **to d. oneself,** se draper dans sa dignité, se carrer, poser pour la galerie.

drappie, drappy [ˈdræpi] (*noun*), *F:* **a wee d.,** un petit verre (*ou* un petit coup) d'alcool* (*ou* de gnôle).

drat [dræt] (**to**), *F:* (*a*) **d. the child!** sacré gosse! au diable ce gosse! maudit mioche!; (*b*) **d. (it)!** sacré nom! nom de nom! bon sang!

dratted [ˈdrætid] (*adj.*), *F:* maudit, sacré, satané.

draught [drɑːft] (*noun*), *F:* **to feel the d.,** être touché à mal par qch., le sentir passer.

draw¹ [drɔː] (*noun*), *F:* **1. to be quick on the d.,** (*a*) être rapide à dégainer son arme, être rapide à la détente, avoir la détente facile; (*b*) piger au quart de tour, avoir de bonnes reprises.

* An asterisk indicates that the word so marked is included as a head-word in the Appendix.

2. **to be slow on the d.,** (a) être lent à la détente; (b) avoir la comprenette lente (ou difficile). **draw**[2] [drɔ:] **(to),** F: 1. être le point de mire. 2. **to d. s.o.,** faire parler* qn, le travailler, lui tirer les vers du nez. 3. taquiner, faire enrager (ou bisquer). 4. **to d. it mild,** modérer ses propos, mettre de l'eau dans son vin. 5. **to d. the long bow,** exagérer*, faire du pallas, cherrer dans les bégonias. **drawers** [ˈdrɔ:z] (pl. noun), P: culotte f; **to let one's d. down, to drop one's d.,** (d'une femme) permettre des rapports sexuels, laisser tomber la culotte. Voir aussi **droopy-drawers.**

dream[1] [dri:m] (attrib. adj.), F: rêvé, de rêve; **to live in a d. world,** nager dans le bleu.

dream[2] [dri:m] (noun). 1. F: **she's a d.,** (a) c'est la femme rêvée; (b) elle est dans les nuages (ou dans la lune). 2. F: **wet d.,** carte f (de France). 3. (pl.) P: opium m (drogues*); **d. wax,** opium m (drogues*); **d. stick,** (a) bambou m, pipe f à rêves; (b) pilule f d'opium.

dream-bait [ˈdri:mbeit], **dream-boat** [ˈdri:mbout] (noun), F: = **dream**[2], 1 (a).

dreamer [ˈdri:mər] (noun), P: opiomane mf, noircicot m.

dream up [ˈdri:mˈʌp] **(to),** F: imaginer, inventer, gamberger.

dreamy [ˈdri:mi] (adj.), F: exquis, charmant.

dreck [drek] (noun), P: 1. camelote f, gnognot(t)e f. 2. clinquant m, tape-à-l'œil m.

dress down [ˈdresˈdaun] **(to),** F: 1. battre*, filer une raclée à (qn). 2. réprimander*, enguirlander, assaisonner (qn). Voir aussi **dressing-down.**

dressed [drest] (p.p. & adj.), F: **d.** (fit) **to kill,** élégant*, habillé sur son trente et un, en grand tralala, tiré à quatre épingles; cf. **dress up (to),** 2.

dress-house [ˈdreshaus] (noun), P: bordel*, maison bancale, boxon m.

dressing-down [ˈdresiŋˈdaun] (noun), F: 1. volée f de coups*, raclée f. 2. réprimande f, abattage m, savon m. Voir aussi **dress down (to).**

dress up [ˈdresˈʌp] **(to),** F: 1. **all dressed up and nowhere to go,** laissé(e) pour compte (ou en plan). 2. **dressed up to**

the nines (or to the teeth or to the knocker) = dressed (fit) **to kill** (voir **dressed**). Voir aussi **dog**[1], 2.

dressy [ˈdresi] (adj.), F: élégant*, chic, ridère.

dribs [dribz] (pl. noun), F: **in d. and drabs,** petit à petit, au compte-gouttes.

drift[1] [drift] (noun), F: **to catch the d.,** tenir (ou piger) le fil, entraver, saisir; **get the d.?** tu piges? tu saisis?

drift[2] [drift] **(to),** F: 1. se laisser aller (à vau-l'eau ou à la dérive). 2. baguenauder, flâner, flânocher.

drifter [ˈdriftər] (noun), F: personne qui se laisse aller, gnangnan m.

drill [dril] (noun), F: **to know the d.,** connaître les rouages m.pl. (ou la musique), s'y connaître. Voir aussi **pack-drill.**

drin [drin] (noun), P: comprimé m de Benzédrine (marque déposée) (drogues*).

drink [driŋk] (noun), F: **the d.,** la mer, la Grande Tasse, la flotte.

drinkies [ˈdriŋkiz] (pl. noun), F: boissons f.pl., consommations f.pl.

drip [drip] (noun), F: nouille f, empoté m.

dripper [ˈdripər] (noun), F: goutte-à-goutte m (seringue faite avec un compte-gouttes et une épingle).

drippy [ˈdripi] (adj.), F: 1. bête*, empoté. 2. fadasse, larmoyant, vieux jeu.

driver [ˈdraivər] (noun). 1. F: **to be in the d.'s seat,** être en position de force, tenir les rênes, diriger les opérations. 2. P: amphétamine f (drogues*); cf. **truckdriver.** Voir aussi **backseat; niggerdriver; pile-driver; slave-driver.**

drizzle-puss [ˈdrizlpus] (noun) (U.S.), F: rabat-joie m, peau f de vache, vieux chameau.

drome [droum] (noun) (=aerodrome), F: aérodrome m, terrain m (d'aviation).

drongo [ˈdrɔŋgou] (noun) (Austr.), F: individu bête*, buse f.

droob [dru:b] (noun) (Austr.), F: 1. un chouia; **he didn't get a d.,** il n'a rien* eu, il n'a eu que dalle. 2. = **drube.**

drool [dru:l] **(to),** F: **to d. over sth., s.o.,** baver (d'admiration, de plaisir) sur qch., qn.

droop [dru:p] (noun), P: 1. = **drip.** 2. **brewer's d.,** affaissement m du pénis dû à l'alcool, les six heures de l'alcoolique.

---

* L'astérisque indique que le mot marqué de ce signe figure comme entrée dans le Répertoire.

drooper [ˈdruːpər] (*noun*), 1. *F:* moustache* tombante, ramasse-miettes *m*. 2. (*pl.*) *P:* seins* tombants, blagues *f.pl.* à tabac, pendants *m.pl.*, tétasses *f.pl.*
droopy-drawers [ˈdruːpidrɔː(ə)z] (*noun*), *P:* 1. individu dont la culotte tombe, nu-fesses *f*. 2. *voir* bingo (44).
drop[1] [drɔp] (*noun*). 1. *P:* = dropsy, 1, 2. 2. *F:* at the d. of a hat, tout de suite, illico. 3. *P:* cache *f*, planque *f*. 4. *P:* to get the d. on s.o., sortir son arme (*ou* gagner de vitesse) avant l'adversaire; tenir qn à merci, tenir le bon bout. 5. *F:* a d. in the ocean, une goutte d'eau dans la mer. 6. *P:* to have a d. in the eye, être ivre*, avoir chaud aux plumes. 7. *F:* petit verre d'alcool*, une goutte, un doigt, un fond de verre. 8. *P:* on the d., (achat *m*) à tempérament. *Voir aussi* cough-drop.
drop[2] [drɔp] (to). 1. *F:* to d. s.o. (like a hot potato *or* a hot brick), abandonner* qn, lâcher qn, plaquer qn comme une crêpe. 2. *F:* abattre, descendre (qn), envoyer (qn) à terre. 3. *F:* (*comme cycliste*) semer. 4. *P:* donner un pourboire*; did he d.? a-t-il lâché le pourliche? a-t-il donné la pièce? 5. *P:* (*jeu*) perdre, paumer de l'argent*. 6. *F:* d. it! c'est marre! arrête les frais! laisse tomber! 7. *F:* fit to d., très fatigué*, crevé, éreinté; he's fit to d., il a (reçu) le coup de bambou. 8. *F:* to d. s.o. a line, envoyer (*ou* mettre *ou* griffonner) un mot à qn. 9. *F:* to d. the matter, to let it d., laisser courir. 10. *P:* prendre des pilules *f.pl.* (*ou* capsules *f.pl.*) par voie buccale. *Voir aussi* brick, 2; clanger; mire; shit[3], 2; stumer, 3.
drop in [ˈdrɔpˈin] (to), *F:* to d. i. on s.o., rendre visite à qn en passant, passer chez qn.
drop off [ˈdrɔpˈɔf] (to), *F:* 1. s'endormir, piquer un roupillon, baisser la vitrine. 2. baisser, décliner, être sur la pente. 3. to d. s.o. o., déposer qn (à un certain endroit).
drop-out [ˈdrɔpaut] (*noun*), *F:* 1. qn qui refuse la société (*ou* le système), qn qui vit en marge de la société; hors-la-loi *mf*. 2. qn qui se retire d'un jeu, *etc*.
drop out [ˈdrɔpˈaut] (to), *F:* 1. refuser

la société (*ou* le système), vivre en marge de la société. 2. tirer son épingle du jeu, reprendre ses billes.
dropper [ˈdrɔpər] (*noun*). 1. *F:* = dripper. 2. *P:* passeur *m* de faux chèques, pastiqueur *m*. *Voir aussi* name-dropper.
dropsy [ˈdrɔpsi] (*noun*), *P:* 1. pot-de-vin *m*, graissage *m* de patte, dessous-de-table *m*. 2. pourboire*, pourliche *m*, pièce *f*.
dross [drɔs] (*noun*). *P:* argent*, fric *m*, pèze *m*.
drown [draun] (to), *F:* 1. to d. a drink, mettre trop d'eau dans une boisson, inonder (*ou* noyer) une boisson. 2. to d. in a teacup, se noyer dans un crachat (*ou* dans un verre d'eau). 3. to d. one's sorrows, noyer ses chagrins.
drube [druːb] (*noun*) (*Austr.*), *F:* individu bête*, nouille *f*.
drum [drʌm] (*noun*). 1. *P:* logement*, bocal *m*, cambuse *f*; to have one's d. done, (*a*) avoir une perquisition, avoir une descente dans sa piaule; (*b*) être cambriolé*, en être d'un baluchonnage; *cf.* gaff, 1; screw[2] (to), 3. 2. *P:* un paradis pour les voleurs, un bon casse. 3. *F:* to beat the drums (*or* the big d.) for s.o., faire du battage pour qn, faire du tamtam, battre la grosse caisse pour qn. 4. *P:* route*, antif(fe) *f*, ruban *m*.
drummer [ˈdrʌmər] (*noun*), *P:* commis voyageur, roulant *m*, hirondelle *f*.
drumming [ˈdrʌmiŋ] (*noun*). 1. *F:* (*d'une auto*) ferraillement *m*. 2. *P:* vol *m* après avoir sonné à la porte pour s'assurer qu'il n'y a personne, vol *m* au bonjour.
drumstick [ˈdrʌm-stik] (*noun*), *F:* 1. pilon *m* (de poulet). 2. (*pl.*) jambes* maigres, allumettes *f.pl.*, flûtes *f.pl.*; d. cases, pantalon*, fourreau *m*, fendard *m*.
drum up [ˈdrʌmˈʌp] (to), *F:* 1. to d. u. one's friends, rassembler (*ou* réunir *ou* racoler) ses amis, battre le rappel de ses amis. 2. to d. u. business, faire de la réclame, chauffer une affaire.
drunk [drʌŋk] (*noun*), *F:* 1. ivrogne*, saoulard *m*. 2. ivresse*, cuite *f*, soûlerie *f*, bit(t)ure *f*; ribote *f*.
dry [drai] (*adj.*). 1. *F:* to be d., avoir

---

* An asterisk indicates that the word so marked is included as a head-word in the Appendix.

soif*, avoir la pépie; **d. as a bone**, sec comme un clou. **2.** *F:* **not d. behind the ears**, blanc-bec, morveux, qui a le lait qui sort du nez; *cf.* **wet**[1], **5. 3.** *F:* **the d. facts**, les faits tout purs. **4.** **d. run**, *(a)* *P:* coït* avec emploi d'un contraceptif, dérouillage *m* à sec; *(b)* *F:* (*th.*) répétition *f* d'essai; *(c)* *F:* (*av.*) manœuvre *f* d'essai. *Voir aussi* **drain**[2] (to); **high**[1], **2; home, 1; suck (to), 2.**

dry out ['draɪ'aʊt] (to), *P:* **1.** couver son vin, déboiser sa gueule, se dépoivrer. **2.** se désintoxiquer (des drogues).

dry up ['draɪ'ʌp] (to), *F:* **1. d. u.!** tais-toi! (*se taire**), ferme-la! écrase! **2.** (*th.*) oublier son rôle, sécher, avoir un trou.

D.T.'s ['di:'ti:z] (*pl. noun*), *F:* delirium *m* tremens, les rats bleus.

dub[1] [dʌb] (*noun*). **1.** *F:* (*th.*) doublure *f*, double *m*. **2.** (*U.S.*)' *P:* nourriture*, boustifaille *f*. **3.** (*pl.*) *P:* W.C.*, chiottes *f.pl.*

dub[2] [dʌb] (to), *F:* **1. to d. for s.o.**, remplacer qn, suppléer qn. **2. to d. s.o.**, qualifier qn, donner un sobriquet à qn. **3. to d. (in)**, doubler.

dubee ['d(j)u:bi:] (*noun*), *P:* cigarette* de marijuana (*drogues**), reefer *m*.

dub up ['dʌb'ʌp] (to), *P:* **1.** enfermer (un prisonnier), boucler (la lourde sur...). **2.** payer*, douiller, décher.

duby ['d(j)u:bi:] (*noun*), *P:* = **dubee.**

duchess ['dʌtʃis] (*noun*), *F:* **1.** grande dame, marquise *f.* **2. my old d.** = my old Dutch (**Dutch**[3], **2**).

duck[1] [dʌk] (*noun*), *F:* **1.** (*terme d'affection*) mon poulet, mon chou; *voir aussi* **ducks; ducky**[2]. **2. (Lord) love a d.!** grands dieux! **3. a sitting d.**, une cible facile. **4. to behave like a dying d. (in a thunderstorm)**, faire la carpe pâmée, faire des yeux de merlan frit. **5. to have d.'s disease**, avoir le cul bas, traîner le derrière. **6. lame d.**, *(a)* une épave, un(e) éclopé(e); **to help a lame d.**, aider un canard boiteux; *(b)* (*U.S.*) fonctionnaire public qui arrive à terme sans être réélu; *(c)* (*Bourse*) défaillant *m*, agent *m* en défaut; *(d)* bateau endommagé. **7.** (*mil.*) véhicule *m* amphibie. **8. it's like water off a d.'s back**, c'est comme si on chantait. **9. to play ducks and drakes with one's money**, jeter son argent* par les fenêtres.

10. like a d. takes to water, comme un poisson dans l'eau. **11. d. (egg)**, zéro (pointé), chou blanc; **to break one's d.**, retrouver sa veine. **12.** (*U.S.*) **to have** (*or* **throw**) **a d. fit**, se mettre en colère*, piquer une crise. **13.** (*U.S.*) **d. soup**, qch. de très facile, du cousu-main, bête comme chou. **14. a nice day for ducks**, beau temps pour les grenouilles. **15. one little d.** (=2), two little ducks (=22): *voir* bingo. *Voir aussi* **dead**[1], **4; fuck**[2] (to), **3; knee-high.**

duck[2] [dʌk] (to), *F:* éviter (qn, qch.); *voir aussi* **duck out** (to); **scone.**

duckie ['dʌki] (*noun*), *F:* = **ducky**[2].

duck out ['dʌk'aʊt] (to), *F:* **to d. o. of (doing) sth.**, s'esquiver, se tirer, se débiner; se dérober, sécher; *voir aussi* **duck**[2] (to).

ducks [dʌks] (*noun*), *F:* chéri(e), chou *m*; *voir aussi* **duck**[1], **1; ducky**[2].

ducky[1] ['dʌki] (*adj.*), *F:* excellent*, très satisfaisant, chouette, bath.

ducky[2] ['dʌki] (*noun*), *F:* mon poulet, ma petite chatte, ma poupoule, ma cocotte, mon chou; **she's a dear little d.**, c'est un amour.

dud[1] [dʌd] (*adj.*), *F:* mauvais*, toc(ard), à la manque.

dud[2] [dʌd] (*noun*), *F:* **1.** obus non éclaté. **2.** échec*, four *m*, un(e)...à la manque. **3.** faux billet; chèque *m* sans provision. **4.** un raté, un zéro, une nullité, un cancre. **5.** (*pl.*) vêtements*, frusques *f.pl.*, nippes *f.pl.*

dude [d(j)u:d] (*noun*) (*U.S.*), *F:* **1.** gommeux *m*, miché *m*, freluquet *m*. **2. d. ranch**, ranch-hôtel *m* de vacances (*ou* pour vacanciers).

dud up ['dʌd'ʌp] (to), *F:* **1.** maquiller (la marchandise, la vérité, *etc.*). **2.** se bichonner, se pomponner.

duff[1] [dʌf] (*adj.*), *F:* faux, truqué, à la manque, gnognot(t)eux; *voir aussi* **gen.**

duff[2] [dʌf] (*noun*). **1.** *P:* dessert *m* (de prison). **2.** *F:* pudding anglais. **3.** *F:* poussière *f* de charbon. **4.** *P:* agent* de police, flic *m*.

duff[3] [dʌf] (to), *F:* **1.** (*golf, etc.*) cogner une balle de travers, louper une balle. **2.** rater, bousiller, louper. **3.** maquiller, camoufler. **4.** truquer, frauder.

duffer ['dʌfər] (*noun*), *F:* individu bête*, cancre *m*; **a d. at maths**, une nullité en maths.

---

* L'astérisque indique que le mot marqué de ce signe figure comme entrée dans le Répertoire.

dugout [ˈdʌgaut] (noun), P: **1.** drogué*, junkie m. **2.** officier m à la retraite rappelé en service, rempilé m, naphtalinard m.

duke off [ˈdjuːkˈɔf] (to), P: filer en poussant l'adversaire.

dukes [djuːks] (pl. noun), P: mains*, poings m.pl., paluches f.pl., pognes f.pl.

dullsville [ˈdʌlzvil] (noun), F: comble f de la monotonie.

dumb [dʌm] (adj.). **1.** (a) F: bête*, bouché, stupide; (b) P: **d. bunny** (or **cluck** or **jerk**), individu bête*, cruchon m, gourde f; (c) F: **to act** (or **play**) **d.**, faire l'idiot; (d) F: **d. blonde** (or **Dora**), blonde évaporée, bécasse f; voir aussi **plain. 2.** F: **d. dog**, personne f taciturne, bonnet m de nuit.

dumb-bell [ˈdʌmbel], **dumbhead** [ˈdʌmhed] (noun), F: individu bête*, baluche f, andouille f.

dumb-lick [ˈdʌmlik] (noun) (U.S.), P: vaurien*, canaille f.

dumbo [ˈdʌmbou], **dummox** [ˈdʌməks] (noun), P: = **dumb-bell.**

dummy [ˈdʌmi] (noun). **1.** P: sourd-muet m, sourde-muette f. **2.** P: un ballot, un empoté, un empaillé. **3.** P: = **flash Harry** (flash[1], **1**). **4.** P: **to chuck a d.**, (a) s'évanouir*, tomber dans le cirage (ou dans les vapes); (b) simuler un évanouissement dans une foule pour faciliter le travail des pickpockets. **5.** V: **to beat** (or **flog**) **the d.**, se masturber*, se secouer le bonhomme, se branler. **6.** P: portefeuille*, lazingue m.

dummy up [ˈdʌmiˈʌp] (to), P: se taire*, boucler la trappe, la boucler.

dump[1] [dʌmp] (noun), F: **1.** endroit m sordide, dépotoir m, taudis m. **2.** gargote f, boui-boui m, bouge m. **3.** **to be fit for the d.**, être bon pour la casse. **4.** **to be (down) in the dumps**, avoir le cafard, être dans le cirage (ou dans le 36ème dessous).

dump[2] [dʌmp] (to), F: **1.** abandonner*, larguer, laisser choir. **2.** délaisser, planter, plaquer.

dumpling [ˈdʌmpliŋ] (noun). **1.** F: patapouf m, pot m à tabac, bouboule m. **2.** (pl.) P: seins*, rondins m.pl.

dun [dʌn] (noun), P: tueur m à gages, homme m de main.

dunk [dʌŋk] (noun), F: **to take a quick d.**, prendre un bain rapide, faire trempette.

dunno [dəˈnou] (=don't know), P: sais pas!

duros [ˈduːrɔs] (noun) (U.S.), P: marijuana f (drogues*).

durries [ˈdʌriz] (pl. noun), P: amphétamines f.pl. (drogues*), bonbons m.pl.

dust[1] [dʌst] (noun). **1.** F: **you couldn't see him for d.**, il courait comme s'il avait le feu au derrière, il a filé comme l'éclair. **2.** P: (a) (**foo-foo** or **happy** or **heaven** or **reindeer**) **d.**, narcotiques m.pl. en poudre, poudrette f; (b) **gold** (or **heaven**) **d.**, cocaïne f (drogues*), coco f, talc m, neige f. **3.** P: argent*, pépettes f.pl., picaillons m.pl.; **to down the d.**, payer*, casquer, les allonger; **to raise the d.**, se procurer de l'argent*. **4.** F: **to bite** (or **kiss**) **the d.**, mordre la poussière. **5.** F: **to lick the d.**, s'aplatir, lécher les bottes à qn. **6.** F: **to shake the d. off one's feet**, secouer la poussière de ses souliers. **7.** F: **to throw d. in s.o.'s eyes**, jeter de la poudre aux yeux de qn. **8.** F: **to make s.o. eat one's d.**, dépasser qn (en véhicule ou au figuratif), faire sentir ses gaz, faire la pige à qn. Voir aussi **kick up** (to), 2 (b); **stardust.**

dust[2] [dʌst] (to), F: **to dust s.o.'s jacket for him**, battre* qn, flanquer une raclée à qn, tanner le cuir à qn.

dustbin [ˈdʌs(t)bin] (noun), P: **d. lids** (R.S. = **kids**), enfants*, mioches m.pl.; cf. **godfer.**

duster [ˈdʌstər] (noun), P: **1.** (=knuckleduster) coup-de-poing américain, sortie f de bal. **2.** (Austr.) (pl.) testicules*, roupignolles f.pl.

dusting [ˈdʌstiŋ] (noun), F: coups*, raclée f, tabassée f, trempe f.

dustman [ˈdʌs(t)mən] (noun), F: **the d.**, sommeil m, le marchand de sable; cf. **sandman.**

dust off [ˈdʌstˈɔf] (to), F: **1.** **to d. s.o. o.**, abandonner* qn, se débarrasser* de qn, laisser qn en carafe. **2.** **to d. sth. o.**, faire qch. rapidement, enlever un travail; bâcler, torcher qch.

dust-up [ˈdʌstʌp] (noun), F: bagarre*, coup m de chien.

dusty [ˈdʌsti] (adj.). **1.** F: **not so d.**, pas si moche, pas tarte (du tout).

2. *F:* **to get a d. answer,** se faire rembarrer. *Voir aussi* **butt, 2.**
Dutch[1] [dʌtʃ] (*adj.*), *F:* **1. D. courage,** courage puisé dans la bouteille *ou* dans les stupéfiants. **2. D. auction,** enchère *f* au rabais, vente *f* à la baisse. **3. D. cap,** pessaire *m*, capote anglaise. **4. D. comfort,** consolation qui n'en est pas une, piètre consolation. **5. to talk to s.o. like a D. uncle,** dire ses quatre vérités à qn. **6. D. treat,** sortie *f* où chacun paye son écot, sortie en Suisse; *cf.* **Dutch**[2]. **7. to do the D. act,** se suicider*, se faire sauter la caisse, se flanquer en l'air. **8. to take D. leave,** filer à l'anglaise.
Dutch[2] [dʌtʃ] (*adv.*), *F:* **to go D.,** payer son écot; *cf.* **Dutch**[1], **6.**
Dutch[3] [dʌtʃ] (*noun*). **1.** *F:* **to talk double D.,** baragouiner, parler une langue inintelligible; **that's double D. to me,** pour moi c'est de l'hébreu. **2.** *F:* **my (old) D.,** mon épouse*, ma bourgeoise. **3.** *F:* **that beats the D.!** c'est

le comble! c'est le bouquet! **4.** *P:* **to be in D.,** avoir de la malchance*, être dans le pétrin (*ou* dans la panade).
Dutchman [ˈdʌtʃmən] (*noun*), *F:* **1. if that's so then I'm a D.,** si c'est ainsi j'y perds mon latin (*ou* je veux bien être pendu). **2. to have a D.'s headache,** avoir la gueule de bois.
duty [ˈdjuːti] (*noun*), *F:* **to do one's d.,** déféquer*, faire sa grande commission.
dyke [daik] (*noun*), *P:* lesbienne*, gouine *f*, gousse *f*; *cf.* **bull-dyke; dike, 2.**
dykey [ˈdaiki] (*adj.*), *P:* lesbienne*, gavousse, aillée; *cf.* **dikey.**
dynamite [ˈdainəmait] (*noun*). **1.** *P:* (*a*) stupéfiant très fort, dynamite *f*; (*b*) stupéfiant *m* de haute qualité; (*c*) marijuana *f* (*drogues**); (*d*) héroïne *f* (*drogues**). **2.** *F:* **she's d.!** elle est explosive! **3.** *F:* **don't touch it, it's d.!** n'y touche pas, c'est de la dynamite (*ou* c'est explosif *ou* c'est jouer avec le feu)!

E

eager [ˈiːgər] (*adj.*), *F:* e. beaver, bourreau *m* de travail*, turbineur *m*, bûcheur *m*; to be an e. beaver, faire du zèle.

ear [iər] (*noun*). **1.** *F:* to be all ears, être tout oreilles, être tout ouïe. **2.** *F:* up to one's ears (*in debt, etc.*), jusqu'au cou, par-dessus la tête; up to one's ears in work, accablé (*ou* débordé) de travail*. **3.** *F:* to play it by e., jouer d'oreille, y aller d'instinct, voir venir, aller au pif(f)omètre. **4.** *P:* to throw s.o. out on his e., se débarrasser* de qn, flanquer (*ou* foutre) qn dehors; to get thrown out on one's e., se faire flanquer dehors. **5.** *F:* to give s.o. a thick e., donner des coups* à qn, abîmer le portrait à qn, donner une paire de gifles *f.pl.* (*ou* de taloches *f.pl.*) à qn. **6.** *F:* to pin s.o.'s ears back, réprimander* qn, enguirlander qn, passer un savon à qn. *Voir aussi* blow (to), **12**; cloth-ears; dry, **2**; flea, **2**; pig[1], **4**; wet[1], **5**.

earful [ˈiəful] (*noun*), *P:* **1.** tas *m*, tapée *f*, séquelle *f* (de nouvelles, potins, *etc.*). **2.** to give s.o. an e., (*a*) réprimander* qn, enguirlander qn; (*b*) dire son fait à qn.

earhole [ˈiəroul] (*noun*), *P:* to clip s.o. round the e. = to give s.o. a thick ear (ear, **5**). *Voir aussi* plug[1], **2**.

early [ˈəːli] (*adj.*), *F:* to be an e. bird, se lever tôt (*ou* avec les poules).

earners [ˈəːnəz] (*pl. noun*), *P:* (*a*) argent*, pognon *m*; (*b*) aumônes *f.pl.*, truches *f.pl.*, trunes *f.pl.*

earth [əːθ] (*noun*), *F:* **1.** to come back to e., revenir sur terre, (re)tomber des nues. **2.** to cost the e., coûter cher*; to pay the e. for sth., payer les yeux de la tête pour qch. **3.** to be down to e., avoir les pieds sur terre, être terre à terre. **4.** where on e....? où diable...? où diantre...?; why on e....? pourquoi diable...? *Voir aussi* end, **4**.

earthly[1] [ˈəːθli] (*adj.*), *F:* no e. use,

sans aucune (*ou* la moindre) utilité, comme un cautère sur une jambe de bois; for no e. reason, à propos de bottes.

earthly[2] [ˈəːθli] (*noun*), *F:* he hasn't an e., il n'a pas l'ombre d'une chance, il n'a pas la moindre chance (de réussir). .

earwig [ˈiəwig] (*noun*), *F:* qn qui écoute aux portes, esgourdeur *m* de lourdes.

ease off [ˈiːzˈɔf] (to), *F:* se détendre, se relaxer, se relâcher.

East-ender [ˈiːstˈendər] (*noun*), *F:* habitant *m* de la banlieue-Est de Londres, faubourien *m*.

easy[1] [ˈiːzi] (*adj.*), *F:* **1.** to be on e. street, être riche*, rouler sur l'or, être tombé sur un champ d'oseille. **2.** e. money, argent* gagné facilement, affure *f*, fleur *f*. **3.** e. mark, personne bête* et crédule, dupe *f*, jobard *m*, andouille *f*. **4.** to take the e. way out, (*a*) sortir par la première porte, ne pas s'en faire, s'en tirer à bon compte; (*b*) se suicider*, se déramer. **5.** e. meat, (*a*) individu* complaisant (*ou* facile *ou* de bonne composition); (*b*) adversaire peu dangereux, une bouchée (de pain). **6.** e. as pie, simple comme bonjour, bête comme chou, qui est du billard; *cf.* ABC, **1**. **7.** e. rider, souteneur*, mangeur *m* de brioche.

easy[2] [ˈiːzi] (*adv.*), *F:* **1.** to take it e., ne pas se fouler la rate, en prendre à son aise; take it e., (*a*) ne te tracasse* pas, ne t'en fais pas; (*b*) laisse-toi vivre. **2.** e. now! doucement! piano! **3.** e. does it! vas-y doucement (*ou* mou *ou* chouia)! **4.** e. come, e. go, vite gagné, vite perdu; ce qui vient avec le flot s'en retourne avec la marée. **5.** go e. on it! vas-y mollo (*ou* en peinard)!

easy-going [ˈiːziˈgouiŋ] (*adj.*), *F:* facile à vivre, du bois dont on fait les flûtes.

eat [iːt] (to). **1.** *F:* what's eating him? quelle mouche l'a piqué? qu'est-ce

---

* An asterisk indicates that the word so marked is included as a head-word in the Appendix.

qui le tracasse? qu'est-ce qui le turlupine? 2. *F:* to e. one's words, se rétracter, revenir sur ses paroles. 3. *F:* to e. one's heart out, se ronger le cœur, sécher sur pied. 4. *F:* to e. s.o. out of house and home, coûter plus qu'on est gros, ruiner qn. 5. *F:* to e. out of s.o.'s hand, manger dans la main de qn. 6. *F:* to e. s.o.'s head off, réprimander* qn, avaler qn. 7. *V:* sucer, brouter (qn) (*coït* buccal*). *Voir aussi* dirt[1], 5.

eatery ['i:təri] (*noun*), *P:* café* (*débit*), bistroquet *m.*

eats [i:ts] (*pl. noun*), *P:* nourriture*, boustifaille *f;* an e. joint, une gargote.

edge[1] [edʒ] (*noun*). 1. (*U.S.*) *P:* to have an e., être légèrement ivre*, être parti (*ou* éméché). 2. (*Austr.*) *F:* over the e., qui dépasse les limites.

edge[2] [edʒ] (to) (*Austr.*), *P:* to e. it = to aste it.

edged [edʒd] (*adj.*) (*U.S.*), *P:* ivre*, rétamé, blindé.

edgy ['edʒi] (*adj.*), *F:* crispé, ayant les nerfs en pelote (*ou* à fleur de peau).

educated ['edʒukeitid] (*adj.*), *F:* malin*, marloupin.

egg [eg] (*noun*). 1. *F:* individu*, mec *m,* zigue *m;* bad (*or* rotten) e., vaurien*, sale type *m,* bon à rien. 2. *F:* good e.! épatant! bravo! 3. *F:* golden eggs, gros bénéfices*, grosse gratte, beau velours. 4. *F:* (*mil.*) scrambled eggs, feuilles *f.pl.* de chêne, graine *f* d'épinards, sardines *f.pl.* 5. *F:* as sure as eggs is eggs, couru d'avance, aussi vrai qu'il fait jour, comme un et un font deux. 6. *F:* don't put all your eggs in one basket, ne mettez pas vos œufs dans le même panier. 7. *F:* to teach one's grandmother to suck eggs, apprendre aux vieux singes à faire la grimace. 8. *P:* to lay an e., avoir un échec*, faire four. *Voir aussi* nest-egg.

egghead ['eghed] (*noun*), *F:* intellectuel *m,* mandarin *m,* grosse tête.

eight [eit] (*numeral adj. & noun*), *F:* 1. to have one over the e., être ivre*, boire un coup de trop; *voir aussi* one, 1. 2. (*U.S.*) to be behind the e. ball, être en mauvaise posture (*ou* dans le pétrin *ou* mal en point).

eighteen-pence ['eiti:n'pens] (*noun*) (*R.S.* = (*common*) *sense*), *P:* bon sens,

sens commun, du chou; ain't you got no e.-p.? as-tu perdu la tête* (*ou* la boussole)?

elbow ['elbou] (*noun*), *F:* 1. at one's e., à portée de la main. 2. out at e., miteux, déguenillé, loqueteux. 3. to rub elbows with s.o., fréquenter qn, s'acoquiner avec qn. 4. e. room, du champ, du large, les coudées franches. 5. e. grease, huile *f* de coude (*ou* de bras), énergie *f,* de la moelle. 6. to bend (*or* lift) the e., boire*, lever le coude; e. bender, ivrogne*, picoleur *m;* e. bending, ivresse*, bit(t)ure *f,* cuite *f.* 7. more power to your e.! vas-y! bonne chance! la meilleure des chances! *Voir aussi* arse, 3.

elbow out ['elbou'aut] (to), *F:* écarter, évincer, envoyer dinguer (qn); to be elbowed out, être délogé.

elephant ['elifənt] (*noun*). 1. *F:* white e., possession inutile et coûteuse, éléphant blanc, attrape-poussière *m.* 2. *F:* pink elephants, rats bleus (vus par les alcooliques). 3. (*U.S.*) *P:* to see the e., se rincer l'œil, s'en mettre plein les mirettes. 4. *P:* she's seen the e., elle a vu le loup (*ou* la lune). *Voir aussi* baby[1], 2.

elephants ['elifənts] (*adj.*) (*R.S.* = *elephant's trunk* = *drunk*), ivre*.

elevenses [i'levnziz] (*pl. noun*), *F:* pause-café *f.*

'em [əm] (*pron.*), *F:* = *them; cf.* daft[1], 1; lick[2] (to), 1 (*c*); make[2] (to), 2; pack in (to), 3; set up (to), 1; stick up (to), 2.

empty ['em(p)ti] (*adj.*), *F:* to feel e., avoir faim*, avoir un creux, claquer du bec.

end [end] (*noun*). 1. *P:* fesses*, l'arrière-train *m; cf.* rear (end). 2. *V:* pénis*, queue *f,* le (gros) bout; to get one's e. in (*or* away), coïter*, mettre la cheville dans le trou. 3. *F:* (*a*) to the bitter e., jusqu'au bout des bouts; to go on to the bitter e., boire le calice jusqu'à la lie; *cf.* bitter-ender; (*b*) he's the (bitter) e., il est au-dessous de tout. 4. *F:* to go to the ends of the earth (to do sth.), se mettre en quatre, se démener, se donner un mal fou (pour faire qch.). 5. *F:* to go off the deep e., (*a*) se mettre en colère*, sortir de ses gonds, piquer une crise, monter sur ses grands chevaux; (*b*) prendre les choses au

---

* L'astérisque indique que le mot marqué de ce signe figure comme entrée dans le Répertoire.

tragique, broyer du noir. **6.** _F:_ **to keep one's e. up,** _(a)_ résister, se défendre, tenir bon; _(b)_ faire sa part, y mettre du sien. **7.** _F:_ **at a loose e.,** désœuvré, traînant les patins, s'endormant sur le mastic; **to be at a loose e.,** se tourner les pouces, avoir du temps à perdre. **8.** _F:_ **to make ends meet,** joindre les deux bouts, boucler son budget. **9.** _F:_ **no e. of...,** une abondance* **de...,** une infinité _(ou_ flopée _ou·_ tapée _ou_ bardée) de...; **it'll do you no e. of good,** ça vous fera un bien fou _(ou_ énormément de bien); **no e. of money,** un argent* fou; **he thinks no e. of himself,** il est prétentieux*, il se gobe, il s'en croit. **10.** _F:_ **on e.,** _(a)_ debout, tout droit; _(b)_ sans relâche; **three weeks on e.,** trois semaines d'affilée. **11.** _F:_ _(a)_ **to get hold of the wrong e. of the stick,** prendre qch. à contre-sens, saisir le mauvais bout, comprendre de travers; _(b)_ **to have the right e. of the stick,** être dans la bonne voie, tenir le bon bout. **12.** _F:_ **to beat s.o. all ends up,** battre qn à plate(s) couture(s). **13.** _F:_ **to be thrown in at the deep e.,** être mis en pleine eau, être tout de suite dans le bain. _Voir aussi_ **back**[1], **2; back-end; beam-ends; dead-end; dog-end; fag-end; jump**[2] **(to), 12; tab-end; tail-end.**

enders [ˈendəz] _(noun),_ _P:_ **to go e. with a woman, to have (Harry) e.,** coïter* avec une femme*, mettre une femme* au bout.

enemy [ˈenəmi] _(noun),_ _F:_ **the e.,** l'heure _f_ qui tourne. **how's the e.?** t'as l'heure?

erk [əːk] _(noun),_ _F:_ conscrit _m,_ bleu _m,_ recrue _f._

euchre [ˈjuːkər] **(to),** _P:_ duper*, entuber (qn); **to be euchred,** être dans le pétrin _(ou_ dans une impasse).

even[1] [ˈiːvən] _(adj.),_ _P:_ **e. Steven** _(or_ **Stephen),** quitte; **to call it e. Steven,** être quitte; **to go e. Steven,** aller fifty-fifty.

even[2] [ˈiːvən] _(adv.),_ _F:_ **to get e. (with s.o.),** se venger, aller à la rebiffe, rendre la pareille, attraper qn au tournant. _Voir aussi_ **break**[2] **(to).**

evens [ˈiːvənz] _(pl. noun),_ _F:_ **to lay e.,** parier à égalité.

even up on [ˈiːvənˈʌpˈɔn] **(to),** _F:_ = **get even with (to)** _(voir_ **even**[2]).

ever [ˈevər] _(adv.),_ _F:_ **1. e. so...,** tellement...; **e. so much,** beaucoup*,

bougrement. **2. did you e.!** époustouflant! renversant!

ex [eks] _(prefix & noun),_ _F:_ **ex(-mari,** _etc.);_ **ex-con,** ex-prisonnier _m,_ relargué _m,_ guéri _m._

exhibition [eksiˈbiʃ(ə)n] _(noun),_ _F:_ **to make an e. of oneself,** faire la comédie, se donner en spectacle.

expect [eksˈpekt] **(to),** _F:_ **1.** penser, supposer; **I e. you're right,** tu as sans doute raison. **2. to be expecting,** être enceinte*, être dans une situation intéressante.

experience [eksˈpiəriəns, iksˈpiəriəns] _(noun),_ _F:_ voyage _m (drogues)._

extras [ˈekstrəz] _(pl. noun),_ _F:_ à-côtés _m.pl._

extra-special [ˈekstrəˈspeʃ(ə)l] _(adj.),_ _F:_ excellent*, super, sensas(s).

eye [ai] _(noun)._ **1.** _F:_ **easy on the e.,** agréable à regarder _(ou_ à l'œil), de quoi se rincer l'œil. **2.** _F:_ **to have an e. for sth.,** s'y connaître, avoir l'œil américain _(ou_ le coup d'œil). **3.** _F:_ **all my e. (and Betty Martin),** bêtises*, foutaises _f.pl.,_ balivernes _f.pl._ **4.** _F:_ **my e.!** _(a)_ mon œil! mon zob!; _(b)_ mince alors! **5.** _P:_ **to do s.o. in the e.,** duper* qn, empiler qn. **6.** _F:_ **glad e.,** œillade*; **to give s.o. the (glad) e.,** faire de l'œil à qn, lancer des coups de châsse à qn. **7.** _F:_ **to keep an e. on s.o.,** surveiller qn, avoir qn à l'œil. **8.** _F:_ **to keep one's eyes open** _(or_ **skinned),** allumer ses lampions, ouvrir l'œil et le bon, ne pas avoir ses yeux dans sa poche. **9.** _F:_ **sheep's eyes,** des yeux de carpe pâmée. **10.** _F:_ **to make eyes at s.o.,** couver qn des yeux, faire les yeux doux _(ou_ en coulisse _ou_ en tirelire). **11.** _F:_ **to open s.o.'s eyes (to sth.),** éclairer la lanterne à qn, nettoyer les lucarnes à qn. **12.** _F:_ **to see e. to e. (with s.o.),** être d'accord, voir du même œil. **13.** _F:_ **to turn a blind e. (to sth.),** fermer les yeux (sur qch.). **14.** _F:_ **to be up to the** _(or_ **one's) eyes in sth.,** être plongé jusqu'aux yeux _(ou_ pardessus les yeux _ou_ jusqu'au cou); _cf._ **ear, 2. 15.** _F:_ **a sight for sore eyes,** un régal pour les yeux. **16.** _F:_ **there's more in this than meets the e.,** il y a quelque anguille sous roche. **17.** _F:_ **to have eyes for s.o.,** aimer* qn, être entiché, avoir le pépin pour qn. **18.**

F: to have an e. to the future, avoir des visées d'avenir. **19.** *F:* to have an e. to the main chance, s'attacher à ses intérêts, viser au solide. **20.** *F:* to see with half an e., voir du premier coup, sauter aux yeux. **21.** *F:* private e., détective privé, fileur *m.* **22.** *F:* to get one's e. in, s'habituer à une situation, être rodé. **23.** *P:* that's one in the e. for him! il a été mouché de belle façon! **24.** *V:* round e., anus*, œil de bronze. *Voir aussi* bird's-eye; drop[1], 6; four-eyes; Kelly, 2; mud, 1; red-eye; shut-eye; slap[2], 1; snake-eyes.

eyebrows [ˈai-brauz] (*pl. noun*), *F:* he's hanging on by his e., il se maintient tout juste, il est sur la corde raide, il tient à un fil. *Voir aussi* dose up (to); poxed (up).

eye-eye! [ˈaiˈ(j)ai] (*excl.*), *P:* ouvre l'œil! fais gaffe!

eyeful [ˈaifʊl] (*noun*), *P:* **1.** jolie fille*, chouette pépée. **2.** to get an e., voir qch. de très beau* (*ou* de très intéressant), se rincer l'œil, s'en mettre plein les mirettes.

eye-opener [ˈai(j)oup(ə)nər] (*noun*), *F:* **1.** révélation *f,* surprise *f;* it was an e.-o. for me, ça a déclenché mes clignotants. **2.** boisson forte prise à jeun, rince-cochon *m,* réveil-matin *m.*

Eyetie [ˈaiˈtai, ˈaitai] (*noun*), *P:* Italien *m,* rital *m,* macaroni *m.*

eyewash [ˈaiwɔʃ] (*noun*), *F:* **1.** flatterie *f,* bourrage *m* de crâne, frime *f.* **2.** baratin *m,* foutaise *f,* boniment *m.* **3.** explications *f.pl.* miton mitaine.

F

f.a. [ˈefˈei] (*abbr.*) = **fuck-all; sweet f.a.** (*or* **F.A.**) = **sweet fuck-all** *or* **sweet Fanny Adams** (**sweet**[1], **4**).

fab(ulous) [ˈfæb(jʊləs)] (*adj.*), *F:* excellent*, fabuleux, sensas(s), du tonnerre.

face[1] [feis] (*noun*). **1.** *P:* **shut** (*or* **button up**) **your f.!** ferme ta boîte (*ou* ton clapet *ou* ta gueule)! **2.** *F:* **to have the f. to do sth.**, avoir le culot (*ou* l'audace *f ou* le toupet) de faire qch. **3.** *F:* **to show one's f.**, montrer (le bout de) son nez. **4.** *F:* **to feed one's f.**, manger*, s'empiffrer. **5.** *F:* **to paint one's f.**, se maquiller*, se badigeonner; *cf.* **face-paint.** *Voir aussi* **angel-face; fungus; laugh**[2] (**to**), **2; pudding-face; pushface; slap**[2], **1; stare** (**to**); **turn-about-face.**

face[2] [feis] (**to**), *F:* **1. let's f. it**, il faut regarder les choses en face. **2.** (*Austr.*) = **dud up** (**to**), **1.** *Voir aussi* **music.**

face-ache [ˈfeiseik] (*noun*), *P:* **tête** *f* **à claques; hello, f.-a.!** salut, corniaud!

face-lift [ˈfeislift] (*noun*), *F:* (*a*) chirurgie *f* esthétique, lifting *m*; (*b*) (*fig.*) embellissement *m*, rénovation *f*, retapage *m*.

face off [ˈfeisˈɔf] (**to**), *F:* tenir tête à qn.

face out [ˈfeisˈaut] (**to**), *F:* **to f. it o.** = **to face the music** (*voir* **music**).

face-paint [ˈfeis-peint] (*noun*), *F:* badigeon *m*; *cf.* **face**[1], **5; war-paint.**

facer [ˈfeisər] (*noun*), *F:* **1.** coup* au visage, torgnole *f.* **2.** pépin *m*, tuile *f.* **3.** carte* (à jouer) qui baise.

face up [ˈfeisˈʌp] (**to**), *F:* **to f. u. to s.o.**, affronter qn.

facings [ˈfeisiŋz] (*pl. noun*), *F:* **to put s.o. through his f.**, (*a*) éprouver le savoir de qn, voir ce qu'il a dans le crâne (*ou* dans le ventre); (*b*) injurier* qn comme il faut, dire son fait à qn.

factory [ˈfæktəri] (*noun*), *P:* **1.** = **artillery, 1.** **2.** commissariat *m* de police. *Voir aussi* **glue-factory.**

fade [feid] (**to**), *P:* s'enfuir*, s'éclipser, en jouer un air.

fag [fæg] (*noun*). **1.** *F:* cigarette*, sèche *f*, cibiche *f.* **2.** *P:* (*a*) pédéraste*, fiotte *f*, lope(tte) *f*; (*b*) homme efféminé, chouquette *f*; (*c*) **f. bag**, femme* qui recherche la compagnie des pédérastes*, fagoteuse *f.* **3.** *F:* **what a f.!** quelle corvée!

fag-end [ˈfægend] (*noun*), *F:* mégot*, clope *m*.

fageroo [fægəˈruː] (*noun*), *P:* = **fag, 1.**

fagged (out) [ˈfægd(ˈaut)] (*adj.*), *F:* très fatigué*, vanné, éreinté.

faggot [ˈfægət] (*noun*). **1.** *P:* pédéraste*, fagot *m.* **2.** *F:* **old f.**, vieille femme* (*péj.*), fumelle *f*, vieille pouffiasse.

fainites! [ˈfeinaits] (*excl.*), *F:* (*langage enfantin*) pouce!; *cf.* **pax!**

fair[1] [fɛər] (*adj.*), *F:* **1. f. enough!** ça va! d'accord!* **2. it's f. and square,** c'est de bonne guerre (*ou* à la loyale). **3. it's a f. swindle,** c'est une pure escroquerie*, c'est un vrai (*ou* sacré) coup d'arnac. *Voir aussi* **cow, 3; do**[1], **4; middling; shake**[1], **3; whip**[1], **1.**

fair[2] [fɛər] (*adv.*), *P:* très, bougrement; **I'm f. knackered,** je suis complètement à plat; **this f. stumped me,** du coup je n'ai su que répondre.

fair[3] [fɛər] (*noun*), *F:* **to arrive the day after the f.,** arriver trop tard, manquer le coche.

fair-haired [ˈfɛəˈhɛəd] (*adj.*) (*U.S.*), *F:* = **blue-eyed.**

fair-looking [ˈfɛə-lukiŋ] (*adj.*), *F:* beau*, bath, badour.

fair-weather [ˈfɛəweðər] (*adj.*), *F:* **f.-w. friends,** amis *m.pl.* des beaux jours.

fairy [ˈfɛəri] (*noun*), *P:* **1.** pédéraste*, tapette *f*; **f. hawk** = **queer-basher; f. lady** (*or* **queen**), lesbienne*, vrille *f*, gougne(tte) *f.* **2.** (*football*) joueur ramollo, mou *m. Voir aussi* **airy-fairy.**

fairyland [ˈfɛərilænd] (*noun*), *P:* le monde des pédérastes*, les familles *f.pl.* tuyau de poêle, la pédale; *cf.* **pansyland.**

fake[1] [feik] (*adj.*), *F:* bidon, toc.

---

* An asterisk indicates that the word so marked is included as a head-word in the Appendix.

fake² [feik] (noun), F: 1. = faker. 2. imposteur m.

fake³ [feik] (to), F: 1. cuisiner (des comptes, etc.), truquer. 2. (th.) faire du texte.

faker [ˈfeikər] (noun), F: faisan m, estampeur m.

fall [fɔːl] (to), F: 1. to f. for a trick, gober, tomber dans un piège. 2. to f. for s.o., se toquer de qn, s'amouracher de qn. 3. to f. all over oneself to please s.o., se mettre en quatre (ou en trente-six) pour plaire à qn; cf. backwards, 1.

fall down [ˈfɔːlˈdaun] (to), F: 1. to f. d. on a job, échouer*, louper, faire la culbute (ou un four), foirer. 2. it's falling down, ça flotte dur, ça dégringole à seaux.

fall-guy [ˈfɔːlgai] (noun), F: bouc m émissaire, âne m de moulin, dindon m de la farce, lampiste m.

fall through [ˈfɔːlˈθruː] (to), F: foirer; it fell through at the last moment, ça m'a claqué dans la main.

false [fɔls] (adj.), F: f. money, (chèque, etc.) cavalerie f de Saint Georges.

falsies [ˈfɔlsiz] (pl. noun), F: 1. fausses dents*, râtelier m, clavier m. 2. seins* artificiels, roberts m.pl. de chez Michelin, flotteurs m.pl.

family [ˈfæm(i)li] (attrib. adj.). 1. F: in the f. way, enceinte*, cloquée, dans une situation intéressante. 2. P: f. jewels, testicules*, bijoux m.pl. de famille, précieuses f.pl.

famished [ˈfæmiʃt], famishing [ˈfæmiʃiŋ] (adj.), F: to be f., avoir très faim*, la crever, avoir la dent.

famous [ˈfeiməs] (adj.), F: excellent*, sensas(s), fameux.

famously [ˈfeiməsli] (adv.), F: fameuse-ment, épatamment; to get on f., s'entendre à merveille.

fan [fæn] (noun), F: fanatique mf, fan m, fana m, mordu m, emballé m; f. club, club m des fanas; f. mail, courrier m des admirateurs (ou des fanas).

fancy¹ [ˈfænsi] (adj.). 1. P: f. man, (a) amant m de cœur, gigolo m; (b) souteneur*. 2. P: f. woman, (a) prosti-tuée*, mousmé(e) f; (b) maîtresse f. 3. P: f. pants, coco m, joli-cœur m. 4. F: to cut out the f. stuff, déblayer, élaguer; cut out the f. stuff! pas d'en-jolivures, au fait!

fancy² [ˈfænsi] (noun), P: (a) = fancy man (fancy¹, 1); (b) = fancy woman (fancy¹, 2). Voir aussi tickle² (to), 1.

fancy³ [ˈfænsi] (to), F: 1. f. (now)! (or f. that!), figurez-vous ça! comme ça se trouve! 2. f. meeting you! quelle bonne rencontre! quel hasard de vous rencontrer! 3. to f. oneself, être infatué de sa petite personne, se gober, s'en croire, faire sa poire, croire que c'est arrivé. 4. a little of what you f. does you good, c.p., un chouia de ce qui ragail-lardit, ça fait du bien par où ça passe. 5. do you f. her? elle te dit?

fandangle [fænˈdæŋgl] (noun), F: ori-peau m, clinquant m, broquille f, zinzin m.

fanny [ˈfæni] (noun). 1. V: vagin*, minou m; f. tickler, lesbienne*, gou-chotte f. 2. (U.S.) P: fesses*, baba m, pétrousquin m. 3. P: bêtises*, sornettes f.pl.; a lot (or load) of f., un tas de foutaises. Voir aussi aunt, 1; Bob²; sweet¹, 4.

fanzine [ˈfænziːn] (noun) (U.S.), F: magazine m des fans, fanzine m.

far [fɑːr] (adv.), F: 1. f. gone, (a) fou* à lier; (b) ivre* mort; cf. gone, 1. 2. as f. as we go: voir bingo (90).

far-out [ˈfɑːrˈaut] (adj.), F: 1. loufoque, branquignole. 2. intellectuel, avant-garde. 3. emballant, enthousiasmant. 4. éloigné (de la réalité), perdu en soi. 5. fervent du jazz far-out (jazz extra-moderne).

fart¹ [fɑːt] (noun), V: 1. pet*, cloque f, vesse f. 2. = turd, 2. 3. I don't care a f. (or two farts), je m'en bats l'œil, je m'en fiche comme de ma première chemise (ou culotte). 4. to stand as much chance as a f. in a wind-storm, ne pas avoir la moindre chance de réussir, avoir autant d'effet que pisser dans la mer. 5. like a f. in a bottle, agité, nerveux. Voir aussi sparrow-fart.

fart² [fɑːt] (to), V: péter*, cloquer, en écraser un.

fart(-arse) around (or about) [ˈfɑːt(ɑːs)əˈraund, əˈbaut] (to), V: 1. traîner son cul. 2. faire le con.

fart-catcher [ˈfɑːtkætʃər] (noun), V: pédéraste*, enculé m.

fart-hole [ˈfɑːt(h)oul] (noun), V: anus*, trou m de balle, troufignon m.

fast¹ [fɑːst] (adj.), F: dévergondé; to

---

* L'astérisque indique que le mot marqué de ce signe figure comme entrée dans le Répertoire.

lead a f. life, mener une vie de bâtons de chaise, faire les quatre cents coups. *Voir aussi* buck[1], 2; one, 4.

fast[2] [fɑːst] (*adv.*), *F:* to play f. and loose, jouer double jeu.

fastie ['fɑːsti] (*noun*), *P:* cavaleur *m*, juponneur *m*.

fat[1] [fæt] (*adj.*). I. *P:* bête*, ballot, enflé, lourdaud. 2. *P:* a f. lot, (*a*) abondance*, tas *m*, tapée *f*; (*b*) rien*, des clous, nix; a f. lot of good that'll do you! cela vous fera une belle jambe!; a f. lot I care! je m'en fiche pas mal! je m'en soucie comme de l'an quarante (*ou* comme de ma première chemise)!; a f. lot you know about it! comme si vous en saviez quelque chose!; a f. lot of difference it makes to you! pour ce que ça vous coûte! 3. *P:* a f. chance he's got! il n'a pas l'ombre d'une chance. 4. *F:* a f. salary, de gros appointements. 5. *F:* to cut up f. = to cut up rich (cut up (to), 4). 6. *F:* one f. lady (=8), two fat ladies (=88): *voir* bingo.

fat[2] [fæt] (*noun*), *F:* I. (*a*) (*th.*) premier rôle, rôle en or; (*b*) bonne réplique, une percutante. 2. the f. is in the fire, le feu est aux poudres; le torchon brûle. 3. to live off the f. of the land, vivre grassement, mener la vie de château, vivre comme un coq en pâte. 4. to live on one's f., vivre sur ses réserves (*ou* sur sa graisse). *Voir aussi* chew (to); puppy, I.

fathead ['fæthed] (*noun*), *F:* individu bête*, enflé *m*, empaqueté *m*, bas *m* de plafond.

fatheaded ['fæthedid] (*adj.*), *F:* bête*, ballot, baluchard.

fatso ['fætsou], fatty ['fæti] (*noun*), *P:* personne grosse*, bouboule *mf*, patapouf *m*, gravos(se) *m*(*f*), gros plein de soupe.

favourite (*U.S.:* favorite) ['feiv(ə)rit] (*adj.*), *F:* excellent*, bœuf, chouette.

faze [feiz] (to) (*U.S.*), *F:* gêner (qn), casser les pieds à (qn), courir sur l'haricot (*ou* le haricot) à qn.

fear [fiər] (*noun*), *F:* no f.! pas de danger! sois sans crainte!

fearful ['fiəful] (*adj.*), *F:* I. terrible, formidable; f. bore, emmerdeur *m*, emmerdement *m*, casse-pieds *m*. 2. en abondance*; a f. lot, une tapée, une flopée.

fearfully ['fiəfəli] (*adv.*), *F:* terriblement, fichtrement, bigrement.

feather[1] ['feðər] (*noun*). I. *F:* birds of a f., du pareil au même, du même acabit (*ou* bateau *ou* bord). 2. *F:* a f. in one's cap, une perle à sa couronne, un bon point. 3. *F:* in high f., en pleine forme, plein d'entrain. 4. *F:* to show the (white) f., laisser voir qu'on a peur*, caner, caler. 5. *F:* you could have knocked me down with a f.! j'ai pensé tomber de mon haut! 6. (*pl.*) *P:* lit*, plumard *m*; to hit the feathers, se coucher*, se plumer. 7. *F:* to make the feathers fly = to make the fur fly (*voir* fur). 8. (*pl.*) *F:* voir bingo (33).

feather[2] ['feðər] (to), *F:* to f. one's nest, faire ses choux gras, faire sa pelote (*ou* son beurre), mettre du foin dans ses bottes.

feather-bed ['feðəbed] (*noun*), *F:* traitement *m* de faveur, fromage *m*.

featherbrain ['feðəbrein] (*noun*), *F:* individu bête*, tête *f* de linotte; she's a f., c'est une petite évaporée.

featherbrained ['feðəbreind] (*adj.*), *F:* bête*, à tête de linotte, écervelé, évaporé; to be f., avoir une cervelle de moineau.

fed[1] [fed] (*adj.*), *P:* = fed up.

fed[2], Fed [fed] (*noun*) (*abbr.* = *Federal Agent*) (*U.S.*), *F:* I. fonctionnaire fédéral de l'ordre judiciaire. 2. agent *m* de la Brigade fédérale des Stupéfiants.

fed up ['fed'ʌp] (*adj.*), *F:* (*a*) to be f. u. (to the back teeth), en avoir assez*, en avoir sa claque, en avoir ras le bol, en avoir (plus que) marre; (*b*) I'm f. u. with him, il me tape sur le système, il m'enquiquine, j'ai soupé de lui.

feed [fiːd] (*noun*), *F:* to be off one's f., être malade*, n'être pas dans son assiette. *Voir aussi* chicken-feed.

feeding ['fiːdiŋ] (*adj.*), *P:* ennuyeux*, barbe, canulant.

feel[1] [fiːl] (*noun*), *P:* attouchement *m*, tripotage *m*, pelotage *m*.

feel[2] [fiːl] (to). I. *P:* caresser, peloter (une femme); aller aux renseignements, mettre la main au panier. 2. *F:* do you f. like it? est-ce que cela te chante? est-ce que le cœur t'en dit?

feel up ['fiːl'ʌp] (to), *P:* = feel[2] (to), I.

feet [fiːt] (*pl. noun*): *voir* foot[1].

---

* An asterisk indicates that the word so marked is included as a head-word in the Appendix.

feeze[1] [fi:z] *(noun) (U.S.)*, *P:* potin *m*, chichis *m.pl.*, histoires *f.pl.*

feeze[2] [fi:z] **(to)** *(U.S.)*, *P:* en faire un plat, faire des histoires *(ou* des chichis *ou* des arias).

feisty [ˈfaisti] *(adj.) (U.S.)*, *F:* hargneux, irritable, de mauvais poil.

feller [ˈfelər] *(noun)*, *F:* (=*fellow*) *(a)* individu*, type *m*, mec *m*, coco *m*; *(b)* prétendant *m*, soupirant *m*, amoureux *m*.

fem [fem] *(noun)*, *P:* 1. femme*. 2. lesbienne* (qui tient le rôle de la femme), gavousse *f*.

female [ˈfi:meil] *(noun)*, *F:* femme* *(péj.)*, femelle *f*, fumelle *f*.

fence[1] [fens] *(noun)*, *F:* 1. receleur*, fourgueur *m*, lessiveur *m*. 2. **to sit on the f.**, ménager la chèvre et le chou, nager entre deux eaux, ne pas se mouiller. 3. *(Austr.)* **over the f.** = **over the edge (edge**[1], 2).

fence[2] [fens] **(to)**, *F:* receler, fourguer.

fencing [ˈfensiŋ] *(noun)*, *F:* recelage *m*, fourgage *m*, lessivage *m*, fourgue *f*.

fest [fest] *(noun)*, *F:* fête *f*, festival *m*, gala *m*; *voir aussi* **chinfest**; **eatfest**; **gabfest**; **popfest**; **slugfest**.

fetch[1] [fetʃ] *(noun)*, *F:* ruse *f*, attrape *f*, truc *m*, attrape-couillons *m*.

fetch[2] [fetʃ] **(to)**, *F:* séduire, emballer, taper dans l'œil. *Voir aussi* **clonk**[1]; **clout**[1], 1; **one**, 3.

fetching [ˈfetʃiŋ] *(adj.)*, *F:* beau*, chic, chouette.

fetch up [ˈfetʃˈʌp] **(to)**, *F:* vomir*, refiler, dégobiller.

few [fju:] *(pl. noun)*, *F:* **to have (had) a f.**, être ivre*, avoir bu un coup de trop, avoir un verre dans le nez.

fib[1] [fib] *(noun)*, *F:* mensonge*, craque *f*.

fib[2] [fib] **(to)**, *F:* mentir*, en conter.

fibber [ˈfibər] *(noun)*, *F:* menteur *m*, craqueur *m*.

fiddle[1] [ˈfidl] *(noun)*, *F:* 1. violon *m*, crincrin *m*, frémillon *m*. 2. combine *f* (à la gomme); *cf.* **work**[2] **(to)**, 1. 3. fricotage *m*; **to be on the f.**, fricoter. 4. **to be as fit as a f.**, se porter comme un charme. 5. **to play second f.**, jouer en sous-fifre.

fiddle[2] [ˈfidl] **(to)**, *F:* 1. violoner, racler du violon. 2. **to f. the income tax**, rouler le percepteur, maquiller sa feuille d'impôts. 3. combiner, fricoter, trafiquer. 4. barboter, écornifler.

fiddle about [ˈfidl-əˈbaut] **(to)**, *F:* *(a)* aller et venir, traînasser, flânocher; *(b)* bricoler.

fiddle-arse about [ˈfidlˈɑ:sə ˈbaut] **(to)**, *P:* = **fiddle about (to)**, *(b)*.

fiddle-arsed [ˈfidl-ɑ:st] *(adj.)*, *P:* insignifiant, cucul, camelote.

fiddlede(e)dee! [ˈfidldi(:)ˈdi:] *(excl.)*, *F:* = **fiddlesticks!**

fiddle-faddle[1] [ˈfidlfædl] *(noun)*, *F:* bêtise*, baliverne *f*.

fiddle-faddle[2] [ˈfidlfædl] **(to)**, *F:* musarder, baguenauder, tatillonner, chercher midi à quatorze heures.

fiddler [ˈfidlər] *(noun)*, *F:* 1. racleur *m* de violon. 2. fricoteur *m*, combinard *m*. 3. écornifleur *m*, pique-assiette *m*. 4. *(a)* baguenaudeur *m*; *(b)* bricoleur *m*.

fiddlestick [ˈfidl-stik] *(noun)*, *F:* 1. archet *m* *(ou* baguette *f)* de violon. 2. un rien, un brin, une vétille.

fiddlesticks! [ˈfidl-stiks] *(excl.)*, *F:* balivernes! quelle bêtise*! quelle blague!

fiddling[1] [ˈfidliŋ] *(adj.)*, *F:* insignifiant; **f. queries**, questions oiseuses *(ou* futiles *ou* agaçantes).

fiddling[2] [ˈfidliŋ] *(noun)*, *F:* 1. raclage *m* de violon. 2. combine *f*, fricotage *m*. 3. écorniflage *m*, manche *f*. 4. *(a)* baguenaudage *m*, tripotage *m*; *(b)* bricolage *m*.

fiddly [ˈfidli] *(adj.)*, *F:* **a f. job**, un travail délicat, un sac de nœuds.

fidgets [ˈfidʒits] *(pl. noun)*, *F:* **to have the f.**, avoir la bougeotte, ne pas tenir en place, être assis sur une pile électrique.

fiend [fi:nd] *(noun)*, *F:* amateur passionné, fana *m*, emballé *m*, mordu *m*; **fresh-air f.**, pleinairiste *mf*, fervent du plein air; **sex f.**, coureur *m* de jupon, queutard *m*; **dope f.**, toxico(mane) *mf*, drogué*, morphinomane *mf*.

fierce [fiəs] *(adj.)*, *F:* affreux, détestable, épouvantable; **f. weather**, temps *m* de chien.

fifty-fifty [ˈfiftiˈfifti] *(adj. & adv.)*, *F:* à parts égales, moitié-moitié, afanaf; **to go f.-f.**, se mettre de moitié; **a f.-f. chance**, une chance sur deux; *cf.* **half**[1], 5 *(b)*.

fig[1] [fig] *(noun)*. 1. *V:* vagin*, figue *f*.

---

* L'astérisque indique que le mot marqué de ce signe figure comme entrée dans le Répertoire.

2. *F:* **I don't care a f.,** je m'en moque pas mal, je m'en fiche éperdument. **3.** *F:* **full f.,** tenue *f* de soirée, queue de pie; **in full f.,** sur son trente et un.

fig[2] [fig] **(to),** *P:* doper (un cheval).

figure [ˈfigə] **(to),** *F:* **I.** compter (sur qch.), penser; **they don't f.** he'll live, on ne pense pas le sauver. **2.** **that figures,** ça va de soi, ça va sans dire. **3.** **I f. that's O.K.,** ça m'a l'air régulier (*ou* O.K.), ça a l'air d'aller.

figure out [ˈfigərˈaut] **(to),** *F:* **I.** calculer, supputer, chiffrer. **2.** comprendre; **he can't f. it o.,** ça le dépasse. *Voir aussi* **angle, 2.**

file [fail] *(noun),* *P:* **I.** malin *m,* roublard *m,* matois *m.* **2.** tireur *m,* fourchette *f.*

fill-in [ˈfilin] *(noun),* *F:* **I.** sommaire *m,* tuyautage *m,* mise *f* au courant. **2.** suppléant *m,* intérim *m,* volant *m.*

fill in [ˈfilˈin] **(to),** *F:* **I.** **to f. s.o. i.** **(on sth.),** affranchir qn, mettre qn au courant (*ou* au parfum), faire le point pour qn. **2.** faire le remplaçant; **to f. i. for s.o.,** suppléer, remplacer qn.

filly [ˈfili] *(noun),* *F:* jeune fille* fringante, jolie pouliche.

filter [ˈfiltər] **(to),** *P:* déserter, faire chibis à la grive.

filthy [ˈfilθi] *(adj.),* *F:* **I.** (*a*) sale*, cradingue; **f. weather,** temps *m* de chien (*ou* de cochon), bougre *m* de temps; (*b*) **don't be f.!** ne sors pas d'ordures!; **you've got a f. mind,** tu es mal embouché. **2.** riche*; **the f. rich,** les (sales) rupins, les pleins aux as, les cousus d'or. **3.** (*sport*) **f. player,** joueur salaud. *Voir aussi* **lucre.**

fin [fin] *(noun),* *P:* **I.** main*, pince *f,* patte *f;* **tip us your f.,** serre-moi la pince; on y va de cinq; *cf.* **flipper. 2.** bras*, aile *f,* nageoire *f.*

finagle [finˈeigl] **(to),** *F:* manigancer, resquiller; (*cartes*) renoncer.

finagler [finˈeiglər] *(noun),* *F:* manigancer *m,* fricoteur *m,* resquilleur *m.*

fine[1] [fain] *(adj.),* *F:* **I.** chic, parfait; **it's all very f. but . . .,** tout cela est bien joli (*ou* bel et bien) mais... **2.** **one f. day,** un beau matin, un de ces quatre matins.

fine[2] [fain] *(adv.),* *F:* **I.** **I'm doing f.!** je me débrouille bien! **2.** **you're doing f.:** *voir* **bingo (29).** *Voir aussi* **cut**[3] **(to), 3.**

finger[1] [ˈfingər] *(noun).* **I.** *P:* indicateur*,

mouchard *m,* donneur *m;* **to put the f. on s.o.,** (*a*) balancer qn, enfoncer qn; (*b*) dénoncer* qn, donner qn (à la police), balanstiquer qn, cafarder qn. **2.** *F:* **to pull one's f. out,** se secouer, se dégrouiller; **pull your f. out! finger(s) out!** secoue tes puces! **3.** *F:* **to put one's f. on it** (*the real issue, etc.*), mettre le doigt dessus. **4.** *P:* **fingers to you!** je t'emmerde!; *cf.* **fingers-up. 5.** *F:* **to have a f. in the pie,** (*a*) y être mêlé, y être pour quelque chose; (*b*) en être. **6.** *F:* **to lay a f. on s.o.,** toucher qn, amocher qn. **7.** *F:* **not to lift a f. (to help s.o.),** ne pas se remuer, ne pas lever le petit doigt (pour aider qn). **8.** *F:* **to twist s.o. round one's little f.,** entortiller qn, faire tourner (et virer) qn (en bourrique), faire de qn tout ce qu'on veut. **9.** (*U.S.*) *P:* **to give s.o. the f.,** (*a*) faire une crasse à qn; (*b*) snober qn, bazarder qn; **she was giving me the polite f.,** elle me snobait, elle me donnait le signal du départ. **10.** *F:* **to keep one's fingers crossed,** toucher du bois. **11.** *F:* **to lift (or raise) the little f.,** boire*, lever le coude. **12.** *P:* **f. artist,** lesbienne*, gouchotte *f. Voir aussi* **but**[t]**fingers; fruit-basket; green**[1]**, 5; sticky, 3; thumb, 1.**

finger[2] [ˈfingər] **(to). I.** *P:* (*a*) fouiller (qn); (*b*) dénoncer*, moucharder, balancer (qn). **2.** *P:* **to f. sth.,** (*a*) chaparder, chiper, griffer qch.; (*b*) receler, fourguer qch. **3.** *V:* **to f. oneself,** (*d'une femme*) se masturber*, s'astiquer le boilton.

finger-fuck[1] [ˈfingəfʌk], **finger-job** [ˈfingədʒɔb] *(noun),* *VV:* (*d'une femme*) masturbation *f,* gerbe *f.*

finger-fuck[2] [ˈfingəfʌk] **(to),** *VV:* (*d'une femme*) (*a*) se masturber*; (*b*) mettre la main au panier.

fingers-up [ˈfingəzˈʌp] *(noun),* *V:* geste *m* obscène de défi et de mépris.

finisher [ˈfiniʃər] *(noun),* *F:* knock-out *m,* coup* de la fin, coup d'assommoir.

fink[1] [fiŋk] *(noun)* (*mainly U.S.*), *P:* **I.** briseur *m* de grèves, jaune *m,* faux frère, traître *m.* **2.** clochard*, clodo *m.* **3.** vaurien*, fripouille *f,* ordure *f,* fumier *m;* *cf.* **ratfink. 4.** détective privé, policier*, poulet *m,* perdreau *m.* **5.** indicateur*, indic *m,* donneur *m,*

---

cafard *m.* 6. des rossignols *m.pl.*, de la pacotille.

fink[2] [fiŋk] **(to)** (*mainly U.S.*), *P:* 1. dénoncer* (à la police), cafarder, balancer. 2. se dégonfler, se déballonner, foirer.

fire[1] [ˈfaiər] (*noun*), *F:* 1. between two fires, entre deux feux. 2. to hang f., traîner, faire long feu. 3. to play with f., jouer avec le feu. 4. running f., feu roulant (de questions). 5. under f., sur la sellette. 6. where's the f.? il y a le feu sur le pont? *Voir aussi* sure-fire; Thames.

fire[2] [ˈfaiər] **(to)**, *F:* balancer, sacquer, dégommer (qn).

fire away [ˈfaiərəˈwei] **(to)**, *F:* commencer (à parler), se lancer; f. a.! allez-y! dites toujours! à vous d'ouvrir le feu!

fireball [ˈfaiəbɔːl] (*noun*), *F:* = ball of fire (ball[1], 6).

fire-bug [ˈfaiəbʌg] (*noun*), *F:* incendiaire *mf*, boutefeu *m*.

fire-eater [ˈfaiəriːtər] (*noun*), *F:* matamore *m*.

fire off [ˈfaiəˈrɔf] **(to)**, *F:* lancer, décocher.

fire up [ˈfaiəˈrʌp] **(to)**. 1. *F:* se mettre en colère*, s'emporter, voir rouge. 2. *P:* fumer la marijuana (*drogues**).

fire-water [ˈfaiəwɔːtər] (*noun*), *F:* alcool*, casse-gueule *m*, tord-boyaux *m*.

fireworks [ˈfaiəwɔːks] (*pl. noun*), *F:* 1. éclat *m* de colère, pétard *m*, grabuge *m*. 2. if you do that again there'll be f.! si tu recommences, ça va barder (*ou* il y aura du grabuge)!

first [fəːst] (*adj.*), *F:* I'll do it f. thing, c'est ce que je ferai en premier; je le ferai avant tout.

first-class [ˈfəːstˈklɑːs], **first-rate** [ˈfəːstˈreit] (*adv.*), *F:* excellemment, au poil, de première; it's going f.-c., f.-r., ça marche à merveille.

first-rater [ˈfəːstˈreitər] (*noun*), *F:* as *m*, crack *m*.

first-timer [ˈfəːstˈtaimər] (*noun*), *F:* prisonnier *m* pour la première fois, un nouveau de la lourde.

fish[1] [fiʃ] (*noun*). 1. *F:* individu*, zèbre *m*; a queer f., un drôle d'oiseau (*ou* de client); a poor f., un paumé. 2. *F:* to cry stinking f., se dénigrer, se déprécier. 3. *F:* to feed the fishes, (*a*) avoir le mal

de mer, donner à manger aux poissons; (*b*) se noyer, boire le bouillon. 4. *F:* to have other f. to fry, avoir d'autres chiens (*ou* chats) à fouetter. 5. *F:* to be like a f. out of water, ne pas être dans son élément; like a f. out of water, comme un poisson hors de l'eau. 6. *F:* to drink like a f., boire* comme un trou (*ou* un tonneau). 7. *P:* a fresh f., (*a*) un nouveau, un bleu; (*b*) qn arrêté pour la première fois, un ramassé de preu. *Voir aussi* cold[1], 5; jellyfish; kettle, 2; tin[1], 4.

fish[2] [fiʃ] **(to)**, *F:* 1. aller à la pêche, tirer les vers du nez à qn; to f. for compliments, quêter des compliments. 2. to f. in troubled waters, pêcher en eau trouble.

fish-bowl [ˈfiʃboul] (*noun*) (*U.S.*), *P:* = tank, 2.

fish-pond [ˈfiʃpɔnd], **fish-shop** [ˈfiʃʃɔp] (*noun*), *P:* vulve*, boîte *f* à ouvrage, bénitier *m*.

fish-tank [ˈfiʃtæŋk] (*noun*) (*U.S.*), *P:* = tank, 2.

fish-wrapper [ˈfiʃræpər] (*noun*), *F:* journal*, canard *m*.

fishy [ˈfiʃi] (*adj.*), *F:* douteux, louche, équivoque, véreux; it looks f., ça ne dit rien de bon (*ou* rien qui vaille).

fist [fist] (*noun*), *P:* main*, pogne *f*, paluche *f*. *Voir aussi* hand[1], 2.

fistful [ˈfistful] (*noun*), *F:* a f. of money, un tas d'argent*, le sac, flouze *m* à la pelle.

fit[1] [fit] (*adj.*), *F:* are you f.? es-tu prêt? tu te sens d'attaque? *Voir aussi* dressed; drop[2] **(to)**, 7; dump[1], 3.

fit[2] [fit] (*noun*). 1. *F:* to have (*or* throw) a f., (*a*) piquer une colère*, se mettre à cran; (*b*) avoir peur*, avoir les foies. 2. *F:* to have s.o. in fits, faire rire* qn, faire boyauter qn, donner le fou-rire à qn. 3. *P:* instance judiciaire qui peut être retournée contre un criminel; beurre *m*. 4. *P:* fainting fits (*R.S.* = *tits*), seins*, tétons *m.pl.*; *cf.* Bristols; tale, 3; threepenny-bits; trey-bits. 5. *P:* attirail *m* de camé.

fit-out [ˈfitaut] (*noun*), *F:* attirail *m*, équipement *m*, barda *m*.

five [faiv] (*numeral adj. & noun*), *F:* 1. take f.! arrêt buffet! dételez un peu! 2. to give f., en écraser cinq, y aller de cinq; *cf.* bunch, 2.

---

* L'astérisque indique que le mot marqué de ce signe figure comme entrée dans le Répertoire.

fiver [ˈfaivər] (*noun*), *F:* (*a*) cinq livres *f.pl.* sterling; gros faffiot; (*b*) billet* de cinq livres *ou* de cinq dollars.

five-spot [ˈfaivspɔt] (*noun*) (*U.S.*), *F:* 1. billet* de cinq dollars. 2. emprisonnement *m* de cinq années, cinq longes *f.pl.* (*ou* berges *f.pl.*). 3. le cinq.

fix¹ [fiks] (*noun*). 1. *P:* (*a*) le fixe, la piquouse, le joint; **to take a f.**, se piquer; (*b*) quantité *f* de drogue vendue en sac *ou* en paquet; fixe *m*. 2. *P:* **the f.**, (*a*) pot-de-vin *m*, dessous-de-table *m*; (*b*) graissage *m* de patte (de la police, *etc.*). 3. *F:* difficulté *f*, mauvais pas; **to be in a f.**, être dans une situation embarrassante; **to get into a f.**, se mettre dans le pétrin. 4. *F:* éléments *m.pl.* et données *f.pl.* qui permettent de déterminer la position d'un bateau *ou* d'un avion.

fix² [fiks] (**to**). 1. *F:* arranger, mettre en ordre. 2. *F:* réparer, retaper, rabibocher. 3. *F:* préparer, décider (d'un jour, d'une heure); **I'm fixing to go to London**, je compte aller à Londres. 4. *F:* soudoyer, suborner. 5. *P:* rendre la pareille à (qn); **I'll f. him!** je lui ferai son affaire! je l'aurai au tournant! 6. *F:* **how are you fixed (for money)?** es-tu paré côté argent? 7. *F:* **to f. a fight**, truquer un combat. 8. *P:* s'injecter une drogue, avoir un fixe, faire une piquouse.

fixer [ˈfiksər] (*noun*), *P:* 1. avocat* véreux, arrangeur *m*, faisan *m*. 2. pourvoyeur *m* de drogues, fourgue(ur) *m*, porteur *m*.

fixings [ˈfiksiŋz] (*pl. noun*), *F:* fourniture *f*, équipement *m*, garniture *f*.

fixture [ˈfikstʃər] (*noun*), *F:* 1. **to be a (permanent) f.**, (*d'une personne*) faire partie des meubles, être fixé en permanence. 2. **I've got a full f. list**, j'ai un programme bien rempli. 3. voiture* ventouse.

fix-up [ˈfiksʌp] (*noun*), *P:* = **fix¹**, 1.

fix up [ˈfiksˈʌp] (**to**), *F:* 1. **to f. u. accommodation for s.o.**, caser qn. 2. **to f. s.o. u. with a job**, trouver un emploi à qn. 3. **they got fixed up**, (*a*) ils se sont fait mettre en règle; (*b*) ils se sont casés. 4. réparer, rapetasser, rafistoler.

fizz [fiz] (*noun*), *F:* champagne *m*, champ(e) *m*.

fizzer [ˈfizər] (*noun*), *F:* 1. qch. d'excellent* (*ou* de super), du tonnerre. 2. balle rapide lancée à toute vitesse. 3. (*mil.*) **to be on a f.**, être consigné au rapport.

fizzle¹ [ˈfizl] (*noun*), *P:* 1. échec*, bide *m*. 2. raté *m*, fruit sec.

fizzle² [ˈfizl] (**to**), *F:* échouer*, se casser le nez, faire chou blanc.

fizzle out [ˈfizlˈaut] (**to**), *F:* ne pas aboutir, finir en queue de poisson, foirer, s'en aller en eau de boudin.

flabbergast [ˈflæbəgɑːst] (**to**), *F:* épater; **I was flabbergasted**, j'en suis resté baba.

flabby [ˈflæbi] (*adj.*), *F:* avachi, mou comme une chique.

flag¹ [flæg] (*noun*). 1. *F:* **to show the f.**, faire acte de présence, faire une apparition. 2. *P:* faux nom*, blaze *m*, alias *m*. 3. *F:* **to lower one's f.**, baisser pavillon. 4. *F:* **to keep the f. flying**, tenir bon, se défendre. 5. *P:* **to fly the f.**, avoir ses menstrues*, repeindre sa grille en rouge.

flag² (down) [ˈflægˈdaun)] (**to**), *F:* arrêter (une voiture, *etc.*) au drapeau.

flag-pole [ˈflægpoul] (*noun*), *F:* = **beanpole**.

flag-wagger [ˈflægwægər], **flag-waver** [ˈflægweivər] (*noun*), *F:* 1. cocardier *m*, chauvin *m*. 2. signaleur *m*.

flag-wagging [ˈflægwægiŋ], **flag-waving** [ˈflægweiviŋ] (*noun*), *F:* le chauvinisme, la cocarde.

flake [fleik] (*noun*), *P:* cocaïne *f* (*drogues**), poudrette *f*.

flaked (out) [ˈfleikt(ˈaut)] (*adj.*), *F:* = **flakers.**

flake out [ˈfleikˈaut] (**to**), *F:* 1. s'évanouir*, tourner de l'œil. 2. être très fatigué*, avoir le coup de barre (*ou* de pompe).

flakers [ˈfleikəz] (*adj.*), *P:* (**Harry**) **f.**, très fatigué*, crevé, esquinté, claqué.

flam¹ [flæm] (*noun*), *F:* 1. histoire *f*, chiqué *m*, trompe-l'œil *m*, salades *f.pl.* 2. (*U.S.*) escroquerie*, arnaque *f*, blague *f*; *cf.* **flimflam¹**. 3. lèche-cul *m*, eau bénite (de cour).

flam² [flæm] (**to**), *F:* 1. escroquer*, arnaquer, refaire, rouler; *cf.* **flimflam²** (**to**). 2. flirter avec (qn). 3. se rebiffer.

flame [fleim] (*noun*), *F:* béguin *m*, flamme *f;* **an old f.**, une de mes anciennes (amours). *Voir aussi* **shoot down** (**to**).

---

flaming [ˈfleimiŋ] (adj.), F: (a) a f.
temper, un caractère infernal; (b) a f.
row, une querelle* du tonnerre, un
barouf de tous les diables; (c) a f.
idiot, un satané crétin, un imbécile
achevé.

flannel¹ [ˈflæn(ə)l] (noun), F: flatterie f,
huile (versée sur les rouages), pommade
f, lèche f, eau bénite.

flannel² [ˈflæn(ə)l] (to), F: acheter les
bonnes grâces de (qn); verser de l'huile
sur les rouages, passer la pommade.

flanneller [ˈflænələr] (noun), F: flatteur
m, bonimenteur m, lèche-bottes m.

flannelling [ˈflænəliŋ] (noun), F: =
flannel¹.

flap¹ [flæp] (noun). 1. F: affolement m,
panique f; to be in a f., être dans tous
ses états; to get into a f., paniquer,
s'affoler. 2. (pl.) P: oreilles*, pavillons
m.pl., anses f.pl.

flap² [flæp] (to), F: = to get into a flap
(flap¹, 1).

flapdoodle [ˈflæpˈduːdl] (noun), F:
bêtise*, bidon m, salades f.pl.; baratin m.

flapjaw [ˈflæpdʒɔː] (noun), F: 1. bavardage m, bavette f, papotage m. 2.
bavard*, jacteur m, tapette f.

flapper [ˈflæpər] (noun). 1. F: jeune
fille*, gamine f, loulou f. 2. P: = fin, 1;
cf. flipper.

flare-up [ˈflɛərʌp] (noun), F: (a) une
colère bleue; (b) altercation f, scène f;
(c) bagarre *, grabuge m.

flare up [ˈflɛərʌp] (to), F: se mettre en
colère*, s'emporter.

flash¹ [flæʃ] (adj.). 1. F: voyant, tapageur; F. Harry (or Jimmy), Fredo
l'Esbrouf(f)e, minet m, un m'as-tu-vu.
2. P: contrefait, toc, bidon. 3. qui est
du milieu, de la pègre.

flash² [flæʃ] (noun). 1. F: (a) épate f,
esbrouf(f)e f; (b) clinquant m, tape-à-
l'œil m. 2. F: a f. in the pan, un feu
de paille. 3. P: le flash, le bang (des
drogués); cf. rush¹. 4. P: argot* des
voleurs, arguemuche m du milieu,
jars m. 5. P: œillade*, clin m d'œil,
coup m de sabord. 6. F: pensée-éclair
f, idée-éclair f.

flash³ [flæʃ] (to), P: 1. arborer, étaler.
2. crâner, plastronner. 3. exhiber ses
organes génitaux (ou ses parties f.pl.).

flasher [ˈflæʃər] (noun), P: qn qui exhibe
ses parties f.pl.; satyre m.

flashy [ˈflæʃi] (adj.), F: (a) = flash¹, 1;
(b) qui jette du jus.

flat¹ [flæt] (adj.). 1. F: net, catégorique;
that's f.! c'est clair et net! c'est mon
dernier mot! 2. P: ruiné*, fauché,
raide, à la côte. Voir aussi spin, 1.

flat² [flæt] (adv.), F: 1. entièrement,
tout à fait; f. broke, fauché comme les
blés, grand schlem. 2. exactement, au
poil. 3. carrément, catégoriquement.
4. to go f. out, (a) se mettre en quatre;
(b) aller bille en tête, mettre le paquet;
(c) aller à fond de train (ou à plein gaz).
5. to fall f. (on its face), (a) (plaisanterie)
manquer son effet, rater; (b) (pièce)
faire four. Voir aussi nothing, 2.

flat³ [flæt] (noun). 1. P: individu m bête*,
nouille f, cave m. 2. F: pneu m à plat.

flat-backer [ˈflætbækər] (noun), P:
prostituée*, bourrin m.

flatfoot [ˈflætfut] (noun), F: agent* de
police, poulet m.

flatfooted [ˈflætˈfutid] (adj.), P: 1.
bête*, lourdaud, pied, empoté. 2. to
be caught f., être pris la main dans le
sac, être piqué sur le tas.

flathead [ˈflæthed] (noun), P: = flat³, 1.

flatheaded [ˈflætˈhedid] (adj.), P: bête*,
bas de plafond.

flatten [ˈflætn] (to), F: 1. mettre (qn)
knock-out, knockouter (qn). 2. aplatir,
déconcerter, déconfire (qn).

flattener [ˈflætnər] (noun), F: coup*
d'assommoir, knock-out m, un K.O.

flattie, flatty [ˈflæti] (noun), P: 1. =
flatfoot. 2. femme aux seins* plats,
une planche à repasser.

flea [fliː] (noun), F: 1. individu ennuyeux*, barbe f, crampon m, raseur
m. 2. to send s.o. away with a f. in his
ear, secouer les puces f.pl. à qn, dire
à qn ses quatre vérités.

fleabag [ˈfliːbæg] (noun), P: 1. (a) sac
m de couchage; (b) lit*, pucier m;
(c) matelas m. 2. pouilleux m, sac m à
puces. 3. mauvais cheval* de course,
tocard m, bourrin m, bique f. 4. =
fleapit, (a).

fleabite [ˈfliːbait] (noun), F: un rien,
une bagatelle, une vétille, une broutille.

flea-bitten [ˈfliːbitn] (adj.), F: sale*,
pouilleux, miteux, craspouillard.

flea-house [ˈfliːhaus] (noun), P: 1.
hôtel m borgne, hôtel des Trois Canards.
2. = fleapit (b).

---

flea-market [ˈfliː-mɑːkit] (*noun*), *F:* marché *m* aux puces.

fleapit [ˈfliː-pit], **flea-trap** [ˈfliː-træp] (*noun*), *F:* (*a*) piaule *f*, taudis *m*, nid *m* (*ou* trou *m*) à puces, bouge *m*; asile *m* de nuit; (*b*) cinéma *m*.

fleece [ˈfliːs] (to), *F:* estamper, plumer, écorcher (qn).

flesh-peddler [ˈfleʃpedlər] (*noun*), *F:* 1. souteneur*, mangeur *m* de blanc, maquereau *m*. 2. prostituée*, marcheuse *f*, raccrocheuse *f*.

flick [flik] (*noun*), *F:* 1. film *m*, ciné *m*, cinoche *m*. 2. cinéma *m*; **to go to a f.** (*or* **to the flicks**), aller au cinetoche. *Voir aussi* **skin-flick**.

flier [ˈflaiər] (*noun*), *F:* **to take a f.**, (*a*) risquer le paquet; (*b*) tomber*, ramasser une bûche, prendre une pelle. *Voir aussi* **high-flier**.

flim [flim] (*noun*), *P:* 1. billet* de cinq livres; *cf.* **flimsy, 2.** 2. cinq longes *f.pl.* (*ou* berges *f.pl.*) en taule.

flimflam[1] [ˈflimflæm] (*noun*) (*U.S.*), *F:* escroquerie*, filouterie *f*, entubage *m*.

flimflam[2] [ˈflimflæm] (to) (*U.S.*), *F:* escroquer*, filouter, entuber.

flimflammer [ˈflimflæmər] (*noun*) (*U.S.*), *F:* escroc*, entôleur *m*, filou *m*.

flimsy [ˈflimzi] (*noun*). 1. papier-pelure *m*. 2. *F:* billet* de banque, faf(f)iot *m*, faffe *m*. 3. *P:* télégramme *m*, petit bleu.

fling [fliŋ] (*noun*), *F:* 1. réjouissances*, bamboche *f*, foire *f*. 2. boum *f*, coup *m* de bastringue, guinche *f*. 3. **to take a f.**, tenter sa chance; **to have a f. at sth.**, tenter le coup. 4. **to have one's f.**, jeter sa gourme. 5. **to have a f. at s.o.**, envoyer (*ou* lancer) un trait à qn.

flip[1] [flip] (*adj.*). 1. *P:* impudent, désinvolte, culotté, qui a du toupet. 2. *P:* mordu pour qch., qui en pince. 3. *F:* **f. side** (**of a record**), revers *m* (d'un disque).

flip[2] [flip] (*noun*). 1. *F:* un petit tour, une virée (en auto, *etc.*). 2. *P:* faveur *f*, gracieuseté *f*; **do me a f.**, fais-moi une fleur. 3. *P:* rigolade *f*, bonne blague. 4. *P:* fervent *m*, fana(tique) *mf*, mordu *m*. 5. *P:* peur*, délire *m* des drogués.

flip[3] [flip] (to). 1. *P:* s'emballer, tiquer, entraver. 2. *P:* **to f. one's top** (*or* **lid** *or* (*U.S.*) **noodle** *or* **raspberry** *or* **wig**), être très en colère*, sortir de ses gonds,

piquer une crise. 3. (*U.S.*) *P:* rouler dans un train sans payer, brûler le dur. 4. *P:* faire rire* (*ou* gondoler *ou* bidonner) (qn). 5. *P:* emballer, botter (qn). 6. *P:* **to f. one's lip,** (*a*) bavarder*, jacasser, baver; (*b*) dire des bêtises*, dégoiser, radoter. 7. *F:* **to f. a coin,** jouer à pile ou face. 8. *P:* faire une dépression émotive, être claqué. 9. *P:* dénoncer*, bourdiller.

flip out [ˈflipˈaut] (to), *P:* = **freak out** (to), 1, 2, 3.

flipper [ˈflipər] (*noun*), *P:* = **fin**, 1.

flipping [ˈflipiŋ] (*adj.*), *F:* satané, fichu; **it's a f. nuisance,** c'est un fichu embêtement.

flit[1] [flit] (*noun*). 1. *F:* **to do a moonlight f.**, déménager à la cloche de bois. 2. *F:* fuite *f*, enlèvement *m*. 3. *P:* pédéraste*, lope *f*.

flit[2] [flit] (to), *F:* 1. = **to do a moonlight flit** (**flit**[1], 1). 2. s'enfuir* (avec un amant, *etc.*), se faire enlever.

fliv [fliv] (*noun*), *P:* = **flivver**, 1.

flivver [ˈflivər] (*noun*), *P:* 1. vieille voiture*, guimbarde *f*, tinette *f*. 2. échec*, bide *m*, fiasco *m*, four *m*. 3. supercherie *f*, farce *f*, fumisterie *f*, canular(d) *m*. 4. porte-guigne *m*, porte-poisse *m*.

float[1] [flout] (*noun*), *P:* client qui sort pendant que le marchand cherche l'article; volant *m*.

float[2] [flout] (to), *P:* **to f. one,** (*a*) toucher un chèque; (*b*) prêter de l'argent*. *Voir aussi* **air**[1], 2.

float about (*or* **around**) [ˈfloutəˈbaut, ˈfloutəˈraund] (to), *F:* **to f. names a.**, lancer des noms*.

floater [ˈfloutər] (*noun*), *F:* 1. un prêt, argent* prêté *ou* emprunté*, tapage *m*, sonnage *m*. 2. bévue*, faux pas, gaffe *f*, bourde *f*. 3. (*a*) vagabond*, vacant *m*; (*b*) ouvrier itinérant.

floating [ˈfloutiŋ] (*adj.*) (*U.S.*), *F:* (*a*) ivre*, dans les vapes; (*b*) high, flippé par la drogue.

flog [flɔg] (to). 1. *P:* bazarder, trafiquer, troquer, lessiver. 2. *P:* voler*, barboter, choper. 3. *F:* **to f. sth. to death**, éreinter qch.; **to f. s.o. to death**, matraquer qn; **to f. oneself to death**, se fatiguer à l'extrême, se crever. *Voir aussi* **bishop; donkey, 5; dummy, 5; horse**[1], 4.

floor[1] [flɔːr, ˈflɔər] (*noun*). 1. *F:* **to take the f.,** (*a*) ouvrir le bal; (*b*) prendre la parole. **2.** *F:* **to hold the f.,** tenir le crachoir. **3.** *P:* **to be on the f.,** être pauvre*, être sur le pavé, traîner la savate. *Voir aussi* **wipe**[2] **(to), I.**

floor[2] [flɔːr, ˈflɔər] **(to),** *F:* **1.** terrasser (qn), envoyer (qn) à terre. **2.** coller (un adversaire), réduire (qn) à quia, désarçonner (qn). **3.** secouer (qn), laisser (qn) baba.

floorer [ˈflɔːrər, ˈflɔərər] *(noun), F:* une colle; **that's a f. for you!** ça te la coupe!

floosie, floosy, floozie, floozy [ˈfluːzi] *(noun) (mainly U.S.), F:* **1.** une mémère, une fille* quelconque, une fille pot-au-feu. **2.** aguicheuse *f*, cocotte *f*, mousmé(e) *f*. **3.** prostituée*, roulure *f*.

flop[1] [flɔp] *(adv.), F:* **1. to fall f.,** faire patapouf. **2. to go f.** = **flop**[3] **(to), 1, 2.**

flop[2] [flɔp] *(noun).* **1.** *F:* (a) échec*; (b) raté *m*, laissé *m* pour compte; four noir, chou blanc. **2.** *P:* (a) asile *m* de nuit, abri *m*, guérite *f*; (b) lit*, bâche *f*, paddock *m. Voir aussi* **belly-flop.**

flop[3] [flɔp] **(to),** *F:* **1.** échouer*, faire faillite, ramasser une veste. **2.** s'affaisser, s'affaler; **to f. into an armchair,** s'effondrer dans un fauteuil. *Voir aussi* **mop, 1.**

flop about [ˈflɔpəˈbaut] **(to),** *F:* faire des sauts *m.pl.* de carpe.

flop-house [ˈflɔphaus] *(noun), P:* **1.** hôtel *m* borgne (*ou* des Trois Canards). **2.** asile *m* de nuit.

flop out [ˈflɔpˈaut] **(to),** *P:* s'évanouir*, tomber dans les pommes.

flopperoo [ˈflɔpəˈruː] *(noun) (U.S.), P:* = **flop**[2], **I.**

floppy [ˈflɔpi] *(adj.), F:* (d'une personne) mollasse, veule.

floral [ˈflɔːrəl] *(adj.), P:* **f. arrangement** = **daisy chain (daisy**[2], 6).

flossie, flossy [ˈflɔsi] *(adj.), F:* (a) archi-élégant*, riflo, urf(e); (b) tape-à-l'œil.

flounder[1] [ˈflaundər] *(noun), P:* **f. (and dab)** (*R.S.* = (taxi-)cab), taxi*.

flounder[2] [ˈflaundər] **(to),** *F:* cafouiller, patauger.

flower [ˈflauər] *(noun).* **1.** *F:* **F. people,** enfants-fleur *m.pl.*; **F. power,** règne *m* de la fleur (*vocable hippy pour le retour à la nature*). **2.** *(pl.) P:* menstrues*, carlets *m.pl.*, affaires *m.pl.* **3.** *P:* pédéraste*, chouquette *f. Voir aussi* **wallflower.**

flowery (dell) [ˈflau(ə)ri(ˈdel)] *(noun)* (*R.S.* = (*prison*) *cell*), *P:* cellule *f* (de prison), bloc *m*, trou *m*; *cf.* **Peter (Bell) (peter, 2).**

flu [fluː] *(noun)* (*=influenza*), *F:* grippe *f.*

flue [fluː] *(noun).* **1.** *V:* vagin*, cheminée *f*, bonbonnière *f*. **2.** *V:* **you can stick it up your f.,** tu peux te le mettre quelque part; *cf.* **stick**[2] **(to), 3. 3.** *P:* (*R.S.* = *screw*) gardien* de prison, gaffe *m*, matuche *m*. **4.** (*U.S.*) *F:* **to go up the f.,** échouer*, foirer.

fluence [ˈfluːəns] *(noun), F:* **1.** influence délicate et subtile. **2. to put the f. on s.o.,** (a) persuader qn; (b) hypnotiser qn.

fluey [ˈfluːi] *(adj.), F:* **to feel f.,** se sentir grippé; *cf.* **flu.**

fluff[1] [flʌf] *(noun).* **1.** *F:* (a) jeune femme*, une jeunesse, mousmé(e) *f*; (b) **a nice piece** (*or* **bit) of f.,** un beau petit lot. **2.** *F:* (a) cuir *m*, pataquès *m*; (b) boulette *f*. **3.** *P:* **to give s.o. the f.,** remettre qn à sa place, snober qn, asseoir qn, rabattre le caquet à qn.

fluff[2] [flʌf] **(to),** *F:* **1.** (*th.*) rater (*ou* louper) son entrée, bouler (son rôle). **2.** saboter, bousiller, louper, rater.

fluff off [ˈflʌfˈɔf] **(to),** *P:* **to f. s.o. o.** = **to give s.o. the fluff (fluff**[1], 3).

fluke[1] [fluːk] *(noun), F:* coup *m* de chance*, veine *f*, fion *m*, bol *m*, pot *m*.

fluke[2] [fluːk] **(to),** *F:* **1.** avoir un coup de chance*, avoir une veine de cocu. **2.** gagner par raccroc.

fluky [ˈfluːki] *(adj.), F:* **1.** incertain, hasardeux. **2.** par raccroc.

flummery [ˈflʌməri] *(noun), F:* **1.** bêtises*, balivernes *f.pl.*, blagues *f.pl.*, sornettes *f.pl.* **2.** flatterie *f*, boniment *m*, panade *f*, du plat.

flummox [ˈflʌməks] **(to),** *F:* démonter, épater, éberluer (qn).

flump[1] [flʌmp] *(noun), F:* coup sourd, plouf *m*, floc *m*.

flump[2] [flʌmp] **(to),** *F:* **1.** tomber avec un bruit sourd, s'affaisser. **2.** laisser tomber lourdement, flanquer par terre.

flunk [flʌŋk] **(to),** *F:* **1.** se dérober, se défiler, tirer au flanc. **2.** être recalé (*ou* collé *ou* étendu) à un examen. **3.** recaler, coller, étendre.

flurry [ˈflʌri] *(noun), F:* **all in** (*or* **of) a f.,** en catastrophe.

---

flush[1] [flʌʃ] (*adj.*), *F:* riche*, plein aux as.

flush[2] [flʌʃ] (**to**), *P:* faire monter le sang dans une seringue hypodermique, rougir la poussette. *Voir aussi* **four-flush** (**to**).

flute [fluːt], **fluter** [ˈfluːtər] (*noun*), *P:* pédéraste*, tapette *f*, lope(tte) *f*. *Voir aussi* **whistle**[1], 2.

flutter [ˈflʌtər] (*noun*), *F:* 1. to be in a (*or* all of a) f., être tout chose, être dans tous ses états. 2. to have a f. on the gee-gees, jouer aux courtines, avoir une petite flambée, faire le thunard. *Voir aussi* **ring**[1], 1.

fly[1] [flai] (*adj.*), *F:* 1. malin*, roublard, mariole. 2. agile, leste, preste.

fly[2] [flai] (*noun*), *F:* 1. there are no flies on him, c'est un malin, il n'est pas né d'hier, il n'est pas tombé de la dernière pluie, il n'est pas manchot. 2. (*sing. ou pl.*) braguette *f*. 3. a f. in the ointment, une ombre au tableau, un cheveu (dans la soupe), un hic. 4. (*Austr.*) to have a f. at sth. = to have a stab at sth. *Voir aussi* **bar-fly**.

fly[3] [flai] (**to**). 1. *F:* to f. in the face of sth., braver qch., tenir tête à qch., lancer un défi à qch. 2. (*a*) *F:* to f. high, voler (*ou* voir *ou* viser) haut; (*b*) *P:* flying high, camé, envapé. 3. to let f., (*a*) *F:* lâcher une volée d'injures; (*b*) *P:* cracher*, glavioter; (*c*) *P:* uriner*, lâcher un fil (*ou* l'écluse). *Voir aussi* **coop**; **flag**[1], 4, 5; **fur**; **handle**, 1.

fly-ball [ˈflaibɔːl], **fly-bob** [ˈflaibɔb], **fly-bull** [ˈflaibul] (*noun*), *P:* policier* en civil, hambourgeois *m*, perdreau *m*.

fly-by-night[1] [ˈflaibainait, ˈflaibənait] (*adj.*), *F:* irréfléchi, évaporé.

fly-by-night[2] [ˈflaibainait, ˈflaibənait] (*noun*), *F:* 1. déménageur *m* à la cloche de bois. 2. évaporé *m*, huluberlu *m*, tête *f* de linotte, oiseau *m* des îles. 3. noctambule *m*, oiseau *m* de nuit.

fly-cop [ˈflaikɔp], **fly-dick** [ˈflaidik], **fly-mug** [ˈflaimʌg] (*noun*), *P:* = **fly-ball**.

fly out [ˈflaiˈaut] (**to**), *F:* = **to fly off the handle** (**handle**, 1).

fly-pitch [ˈflaipitʃ] (**to**), *F:* vendre à la sauvette, cameloter.

fly-pitcher [ˈflaipitʃər] (*noun*), *F:* camelot *m* à la sauvette.

fly-pitching [ˈflaipitʃiŋ] (*noun*), *F:* vente *f* à la sauvette.

fob [fɔb] (**to**), *P:* duper*, rouler, empiler, embobiner.

fob off [ˈfɔbˈɔf] (**to**), *F:* to f. sth. o. on s.o., refarcir qch. à qn; to get fobbed off with sth., se faire refiler qch.

fog [fɔg] (*noun*), *F:* to be in a f., être dans le brouillard (*ou* le cirage), perdre les pédales.

fogey [ˈfougi] (*noun*), *F:* (old) f., vieille baderne, croulant *m*, périmé *m*.

foggiest [ˈfɔgiist] (*adj.*), *F:* I haven't the f. (idea), je n'ai pas la moindre idée.

fog up [ˈfɔgˈʌp] (**to**), *F:* brouiller (les cartes), embrouiller.

fogy [ˈfougi] (*noun*), *F:* = **fogey**.

fold (**up**) [ˈfould(ˈʌp)] (**to**), *F:* 1. s'effondrer, lâcher, caner, se dégonfler. 2. échouer*, faire faillite.

folks [fouks] (*pl. noun*), *F:* 1. les gens, le populo, populmiche *m*. 2. (old) f., les parents*, les vieux, les dab(e)s *m.pl.*

folksy [ˈfouksi] (*adj.*), *F:* 1. populo. 2. folklore, campagnard, à la bonne franquette. 3. sociable, populaire, sympa.

Follies [ˈfɔliz] (*pl. noun*), *P:* the F., les Assises trimestrielles, les grands carreaux, les Assiettes *f.pl.*, les Assottes *f.pl.*; to be weighed off at the F., être jugé aux Assises trimestrielles, passer aux Assises; *cf.* **weigh off** (**to**).

fooey! [ˈfuːi] (*excl.*), *F:* la barbe! flûte!

foo-foo [ˈfuːfuː] (*adj.*), *P:* f.-f. dust: *voir* **dust**[1], 2 (*a*); *cf.* **fu**.

fool[1] [fuːl] (*adj.*), *F:* bête*, idiot, imbécile; *cf.* **damfool**[1].

fool[2] [fuːl] (*noun*), *F:* to play the f. = **fool**[3] (**to**), 1.

fool[3] [fuːl] (**to**), *F:* 1. faire le bête*, faire des bêtises*. 2. to f. s.o., (*a*) se payer la tête de qn; (*b*) escroquer* qn, empiler qn.

fool around [ˈfuːləˈraund] (**to**), *F:* 1. flânocher, lanterner, vadrouiller, baguenauder. 2. taquiner, asticoter, faire enrager qn. 3. flirter, faire des avances (*ou* les yeux doux) à qn.

foot[1] [fut] (*noun*) (*pl.* feet), *F:* 1. my f.! quelle blague! et ta sœur! 2. to fall on one's feet, (re)tomber sur ses pieds (*ou* pattes). 3. to find one's feet, voler de ses propres ailes, (re)trouver son aplomb. 4. to have one f. in the grave,

---

* An asterisk indicates that the word so marked is included as a head-word in the Appendix.

avoir un pied dans la tombe. **5. to put one's f. down,** faire acte d'autorité, mettre bon ordre, mettre le holà. **6. to put one's best f. forward,** (*a*) allonger le pas; (*b*) faire de son mieux. **7. to put one's f. in it,** mettre les pieds dans le plat; **he's always putting his f. in it!** il n'en rate pas une! **8. to put one's feet up,** se reposer, s'allonger, se relaxer, poser ses fesses. **9. to be carried out feet first,** mourir*, partir les pieds devant. **10. to be out on one's feet,** être très fatigué*, être à plat. *Voir aussi* cold[1], 4; crow's-feet; doughfoot; drag[2] (to); flatfoot; pussyfoot[1]; six, 1; sweep[2] (to), 1; tanglefoot.

foot[2] [fut] **(to),** *F:* **1.** donner un coup de pied* à (qn). **2. to f. the bill,** payer* la note, douiller, casquer, cigler, arroser la douloureuse. **3. to f. it,** marcher*, aller à pattes, arquer. *Voir aussi* **hotfoot (to); pussyfoot[2] (to).**

football [ˈfutbɔːl] (*noun*), *P:* mélange *m* de dextroamphétamine et amphétamine (*drogues**), football *m*.

footer [ˈfutər] (*noun*), *F:* **1.** le football. **2.** baby-foot *m*.

footle[1] [ˈfuːtl] (*noun*), *F:* bêtise*, fadaise *f*.

footle[2] [ˈfuːtl] **(to),** *F:* **1.** (*a*) traînasser, flemmarder, baguenauder; (*b*) bricoler. **2.** (*a*) faire des bêtises*; (*b*) dire des sornettes *f.pl.*, bavasser.

footless [ˈfutlis] (*adj.*) (*U.S.*), *F:* maladroit, impuissant, empoté, empaillé.

footling [ˈfuːtliŋ] (*adj.*), *F:* **1.** bête*, stupide. **2.** futile, insignifiant, négligeable. **3.** tatillon, mesquin, chichiteux.

footman [ˈfutmən] (*noun*), *F:* pédicure *m*.

footsies [ˈfutsiz] (*pl. noun*), *F:* = footsy.

foot-slog [ˈfut-slɔg] **(to),** *F:* marcher* péniblement, cheminer, se traîner, arquer, trimarder, battre le bitume.

foot-slogger [ˈfut-slɔgər] (*noun*), *F:* marcheur *m*, pousse-cailloux *m*; (*mil.*) biffin *m*.

footsy [ˈfutsi], **footums** [ˈfutəmz], **footy-footy** [ˈfuti¹futi] (*noun*), *F:* **to play f. (with s.o.) (under the table),** faire du pied* à qn; *cf.* **kneesies; tootsy-footsy.**

foozle[1] [ˈfuːzl] (*noun*), *P:* **1.** coup raté. **2.** vieux tableau, vieille rombière, vieille barbe. **3.** parent*, dab(e) *m*.

foozle[2] [ˈfuːzl] **(to),** *P:* patauger, louper, bousiller, rater son coup.

for [fɔːr] (*prep.*), *F:* **to be f. it,** (*a*) être pour...; **I'm all f. it,** je suis pour, je suis partisan de cela, j'en suis très partisan; (*b*) être bon pour...; **you'll be f. it!** ton affaire est bonne! qu'est-ce que tu vas prendre!; *cf.* **what-for.**

fork [fɔːk] (*noun*), *P:* (*a*) main*, croche *f*, grappin *m*; (*b*) (*pl.*) doigts*, fourchettes *f.pl.*

fork out [ˈfɔːkˈaut] **(to),** *F:* payer*, les allonger, les aligner; **to f. o. again,** redouiller. *Voir aussi* **needful.**

fork up [ˈfɔːkˈʌp] **(to),** *F:* = fork out **(to).**

form [fɔːm] (*noun*), *F:* **1. to know the f.,** savoir ce qu'il faut faire; **what's the f.?** qu'est-ce qu'il faut faire? **2.** casier *m* judiciaire, blase *m*, faffes *f.pl.*; **to have f.,** avoir ses faffes. **3. to be off f.,** ne pas tenir la forme, n'avoir pas la patate.

forrader [ˈfɔrədər] (*adv.*), *F:* plus en avant; **that doesn't get us any further f.,** ça ne nous avance pas.

fort [fɔːt] (*noun*), *F:* **to hold the f.,** garder la baraque.

forty [ˈfɔːti] (*numeral adj.*), *F:* **to have f. winks,** dormir*, faire un petit somme, piquer une ronflette (*ou* un roupillon).

forty-four (*noun*) (*R.S.* = *whore*), *P:* prostituée*, putain *f*.

forward [ˈfɔːwəd] (*noun*), *P:* amphétamine *f* (*drogues**).

fossick [ˈfɔsik] **(to),** *F:* **1.** fureter, fouiller, farfouiller. **2.** (*Austr.*) marauder dans les mines d'or.

fossil [ˈfɔsl] (*noun*), *F:* **1.** (old) f., vieux birbe, un fossile, un périmé, un vestige. **2.** le vieux, le dab(e).

foul [faul] (*adj.*), *F:* **1.** dégueulasse, dégoûtant, infect. **2. to fall f. of s.o.,** se brouiller avec qn, se prendre de querelle* avec qn.

foul-mouth [ˈfaulmauθ] (*noun*), *F:* grossier personnage.

foul up [ˈfaulˈʌp] **(to),** *F:* amocher, bousiller, saloper; **to f. u. the works,** esquinter le mécanisme; **to f. u. s.o.'s plans,** faire louper (*ou* saboter) les projets de qn; **all fouled up,** (*a*) emberlificoté; (*b*) amoché; *voir aussi* **snafu.**

four-eyes [ˈfɔːraiz] (*noun*), *P:* qn qui porte des lunettes*, binoclard *m*, bésiclard *m*.

---

* L'astérisque indique que le mot marqué de ce signe figure comme entrée dans le Répertoire.

four-flush [ˈfɔːflʌʃ] (to), P: 1. bluffer*, se gonfler, se monter le job. 2. ne pas payer ses dettes, ne pas essuyer (ou laisser) une ardoise. 3. écornifler, vivre aux crochets de qn.

four-flusher [ˈfɔːflʌʃər] (noun), P: vantard*, bluffeur m, chiqueur m.

four-letter [ˈfɔːletər] (adj.), F: f.-l. word, les cinq lettres, le mot de Cambronne (=merde), un gros mot.

fourpenny [ˈfɔːpni] (adj.), P: to give s.o. a f. one, donner un coup* de poing (ou un gnon ou un marron) à qn, filer une châtaigne maison à qn.

fox [fɔks] (to), F: (a) duper*, avoir, posséder, rouler (qn); (b) mystifier (qn).

frabjous [ˈfræbdʒəs] (adj.), F: pharamineux.

fracture [ˈfræktʃər] (to), P: 1. you f. me!, (a) tu me fais tordre de rire*! tu me boyautes!; (b) tu m'écœures! tu me fais mal (aux tripes)! 2. battre*, tabasser (qn).

fractured [ˈfræktʃəd] (adj.), P: ivre*, mâchuré, rétamé.

fraidy [ˈfreidi] (adj.), F: to be a f. cat, être un poltron* (ou un couard ou une poule mouillée), avoir peur*, avoir les jetons (ou les copeaux ou la colique).

frail[1] [freil] (adj.), P: f. job, (a) femme* de petite vertu, femme facile, nénette f, gonzesse f; (b) coït*, chique f, partie f de jambes en l'air.

frail[2] [freil] (noun), P: = frail job (frail[1] (a)).

frame[1] [freim] (noun), P: hétérosexuel m qui attire les homosexuels, une amorce; cf. bait (a).

frame[2] [freim] (to), F: to f. s.o., farguer qn, faire porter le bada à qn, poser un gluau à qn, monter un coup contre qn.

frame-up [ˈfreimʌp] (noun), F: complot m, machination f, coup monté.

frat [fræt] (to), F: fraterniser.

frazzle [ˈfræzl] (noun), F: 1. to be done to a f., (a) F: être trop cuit, être carbonisé; (b) P: se faire empiler (dans les grandes largeurs). 2. F: to be worn to a f., être très fatigué*, être à plat (ou à bout ou rendu). 3. F: to beat s.o. to a f., battre* qn à plate(s) couture(s).

frazzled [ˈfræzld] (adj.), P: ivre*, blindé, qui a une cuite, noir.

freak[1] [friːk] (adj.), F: bizarre, fantaisiste, hors-circuit, hors-série.

freak[2] [friːk] (noun). 1. F: drôle m de numéro, phénomène m, curiosité f. 2. P: pédéraste*, lopette f. 3. P: usager m d'un narcotique; voir aussi acid,2. 4. P: fervent m, fana m, mordu m. 5. P: hippy m.

freak out [ˈfriːkˈaut] (to), P: 1. se dévergonder. 2. devenir farfelu. 3. perdre tout contrôle mental après l'usage de drogues; être défoncé.

freaky [ˈfriːki] (adj.), F: = freak[1].

Fred [fred] (pr. noun), F: F. Karno's army, cafouillis m, gâchis m, loufoquerie f.

Freddy [ˈfredi] (noun), P: comprimé m d'éphédrine (drogues*), Freddie m.

free [friː] (adj.), F: f., gratis and for nothing (or for f.), gratuit*, gratis (pro Deo), pour la peau. Voir aussi show[1], 1.

free-for-all [ˈfriːfərɔːl] (noun), F: mêlée générale, barouf m, corrida f, castagne f.

free-load [ˈfriːˈloud] (to) (U.S.), P: écornifler, écumer la marmite, vivre aux crochets de qn.

free-loader [ˈfriːˈloudər] (noun) (U.S.), P: parasite mf, écornifleur m, tapeur m.

free-loading [ˈfriːˈloudiŋ] (noun) (U.S.), P: vie f aux crochets des autres (ou de pique-assiette).

free-wheeling [ˈfriː(h)wiːliŋ] (adj.), F: 1. qui dépense* sans compter, qui les fait valser. 2. sans gêne, en roue libre.

freeze[1] [friːz] (noun), P: to put the f. on s.o. = to put the chill on s.o. (chill, 1). Voir aussi deep[1], 2.

freeze[2] [friːz] (to), F: 1. mettre en quarantaine, boycotter. 2. (a) avoir peur*, avoir le sang qui gèle, se glacer; (b) être figé sur place, se figer. 3. it's freezing cold, ça caille; cf. balls, 8.

freeze out [ˈfriːzˈaut] (to), F: (a) = freeze[2] (to), 1; (b) supplanter (un rival), évincer (qn).

freeze-up [ˈfriːzʌp] (noun), F: 1. gel m à pierre fendre. 2. statue f de glace, frigorification f.

French[1] [frentʃ] (adj.). 1. F: F. kiss, baiser lingual, patin m, saucisse f, langouse f. 2. F: F. letter (U.S.: F. safe), capote anglaise, imperméable m à Popaul (ou Popol). 3. F: F. fries, pommes frites. 4. F: to take F. leave, filer à l'anglaise, brûler la politesse à qn. 5. V: the F. way, coït* buccal, (a)

---

* An asterisk indicates that the word so marked is included as a head-word in the Appendix.

broutage *m*; (*b*) suçage *m*, taillade *f* de plume. *Voir aussi* blue², 1.

French² [frentʃ] (*noun*), *F:* that goddamned . . . – pardon my F.! ce sacré... – excusez mon latin!

french³ [frentʃ] (to), *V:* faire un coït* buccal à (qn), prendre (qn) en poire.

frenchie, frenchy [ˈfrentʃi] (*noun*), *P:* = French letter (French¹, 2).

fresh¹ [freʃ] (*adj.*), *F:* 1. légèrement ivre*, gris, paf, parti. 2. effronté; **don't get f. with me!** ne la ramène pas avec moi! 3. bleu, en herbe; **young man f. down from university,** jeune homme frais émoulu de l'université. 4. flirt(eur), coureur. *Voir aussi* air¹, 3.

fresh² [freʃ] (*adv.*), *F:* **to be f. out of sth.,** être complètement vidé de qch.

fresher [ˈfreʃər] (*noun*), *F:* étudiant de première année, bizut *m*.

friar [ˈfraiər] (*noun*), *P:* **holy f.** (*R.S.* = liar), menteur *m*.

fridge [fridʒ] (*noun*) (*abbr.* = refrigerator), *F:* réfrigérateur *m*, frigo *m*.

frig¹ [frig] (*noun*), *V:* coït*, bourre *f*, tronche *f*.

frig² [frig] (to). 1. *V:* coïter* avec (une femme), baiser, bourrer, troncher. 2. (*U.S.*), *P:* escroquer*, carotter, baiser, entuber.

frigger [ˈfrigər] (*noun*). 1. *V:* baiseur *m*, tringleur *m*, troncheur *m*. 2. (*U.S.*) *P:* escroc*, empileur *m*, carotteur *m*.

frigging¹ [ˈfrigiŋ] (*adj.*), *P:* sacré, satané.

frigging² [ˈfrigiŋ] (*noun*). 1. *V:* coït*, partie *f* de balayette, bourre *f*. 2. (*U.S.*) *P:* escroquerie*, entubage *m*, filouterie *f*.

fright [frait] (*noun*), *F:* individu laid*, mocheté *f*, tarte *f*, caricature *f*, carnaval *m*.

frightful [ˈfraitful] (*adj.*), *F:* affreux, effroyable.

frightfully [ˈfraitfəli] (*adv.*), *F:* bougrement, fichtrement, vachement; **it's f. good of you,** c'est extrêmement aimable à vous; **I'm f. sorry,** mille excuses!

frill [fril] (*noun*), *P:* jeune fille* *ou* femme*, frou-frou *f*, mousmé(e) *f*, tartavelle *f*.

frippet [ˈfripit] (*noun*), *P:* = talent.

frisk [frisk] (to), *F:* fouiller (un suspect *ou* un local), barboter.

Fritz [frits] (*pr. noun*), *P:* Allemand*, fritz *m*, fridolin *m*, frizou *m*.

frog¹ [frɔg] (*noun*), *P:* f. (and toad) (*R.S.* = road), route*. *Voir aussi* knee-high; pond, 2.

Frog² [frɔg], **frog-eater** [ˈfrɔgiːtər], **Froggie, Froggy** [ˈfrɔgi] (*noun*), *P:* Français *m*, Fransquillon *m*.

front¹ [frʌnt] (*adj.*), *F:* 1. **f. runner,** candidat *m* en tête, la tête de liste (*ou* de peloton), le major. 2. **to have a f. seat,** être aux premières loges.

front² [frʌnt] (*noun*), *F:* 1. couverture *f*, parapluie *m*, homme *m* de paille. 2. culot *m*, toupet *m*. 3. **to put on a f.,** faire le prétentieux*, crâner, faire de l'esbrouf(f)e. 4. **t o put on a bold f.,** faire bonne contenance (*ou* figure). 5. **to come to the f.,** émerger, percer, se pousser (en avant).

frost [frɔst] (*noun*), *F:* échec*, four *m* (complet *ou* noir), fiasco *m*, bouchon *m*.

frowst [fraust] (*noun*), *F:* 1. renfermé *m*, odeur *f* de renfermé. 2. qn qui se confine (*ou* qui aime se quat' murs).

frowsty [ˈfrausti] (*adj.*), *F:* qui sent le renfermé.

frowsy, frowzy [ˈfrauzi] (*noun*), *F:* femme* mal torchée.

fruit [fruːt] (*noun*). 1. *P:* pédéraste*, fagot *m*; **frozen f.,** pédéraste* frigide, fruit rafraîchi; **f. fly** = fag bag (fag, 2 (*c*)). 2. (*U.S.*) *P:* prostituée*, grue *f*, morue *f*. 3. *F:* **hello, old f.!** salut, vieux pote (*ou* vieille branche)!

fruit-basket [ˈfruːtbɑːskit] (*noun*), *V:* vagin*, boîte *f* à ouvrage, bonbonnière *f*; **to have one's fingers in the f.-b.,** mettre la main au panier.

fruit-cake [ˈfruːtkeik] (*noun*). 1. (*U.S.*) *P:* pédéraste*, tapette *f*. 2. *F:* **nutty as a f.-c.,** fou* à lier, complètement dingue.

fruit-salad [ˈfruːtˈsæləd] (*noun*), *F:* 1. rangée *f* de médailles et décorations, batterie *f* de cuisine, bananes *f.pl.* 2. (*d'une machine à sous*) embrouillamini *m*.

fruity [ˈfruːti] (*adj.*). 1. *F:* salace, épicé, pimenté, corsé. 2. *F:* (voix) chaude, moelleuse. 3. *F:* homosexuel, tapette. 4. *P:* = horny (*b*).

fruity-pie¹ [ˈfruːtipai] (*adj.*), *P:* = fruity, 3.

fruity-pie² [ˈfruːtipai] (*noun*), *P:* = fruit, 1.

fry [frai] (to) (*U.S.*), *F:* (a) électrocuter

(qn) (dans la chaise), griller (qn); (b) être grillé (ou épuré). Voir aussi **fish¹**, **4**.

fu [fuː] (noun), P: marijuana f (drogues*); cf. **foo-foo**.

fuck¹ [fʌk] (noun), VV: **1.** coït*, baisage m, baisade f. **2. I don't give a f.**, je m'en fous et m'en contrefous. **3. what the f.!** quelle espèce de connerie! qu'est-ce que c'est que ce con! . Voir aussi **finger-fuck¹**; **honey-fuck(ing)**.

fuck² [fʌk] (to), VV: **1.** (a) coïter*; (b) coïter avec (qn), baiser. **2. f. me!** [ˈfʌkˈmiː], mon cul! merde alors!; **f. you!** [ˈfʌkˈjuː], go **f. yourself!** je t'emmerde! tiens mes deux! va te faire foutre! **3. f. a duck!** sacré nom de Dieu! **4. f. it!** [ˈfʌkit], (a) merde (alors)!; (b) c'est marre! change de disque! **5.** (U.S.) escroquer*, empiler, carotter, baiser. Voir aussi **bunny-fuck (to)**; **finger-fuck²** (to); **honey-fuck (to)**.

fuckable [ˈfʌkəbl] (adj.), VV: bonne à baiser.

fuck about (or **around**) [ˈfʌkəˈbaut, ˈfʌkəˈraund] (to), VV: **1.** traîner son cul, couillonner. **2.** faire tourner (qn) en bourrique.

fuck-all [ˈfʌkˈɔːl] (noun), VV: **(sweet) f.-a.**, rien*, peau de balle (et balai de crin), que dalle, des prunes; cf. **f. a.**

fucked (out) [ˈfʌkt(ˈaut)] (adj.), VV: fatigué*, foutu, rendu, vidé, vanné.

fucking¹ [ˈfʌkiŋ] (adj.), VV: **1.** sacré, satané, foutu. **2. what the f. hell!** Bon Dieu de merde! **3.** difficile*, coton, glandilleux. **4.** dégueulasse, dégueulbif. **5.** couillonnant, emmouscaillé. Voir aussi **motherfucking**.

fucking² [ˈfʌkiŋ] (adv.), VV: **it's f. cold,** il fait bougrement froid; **a f. awful film,** une vraie connerie de film; **it's a f. long way,** c'est vachement loin.

fucking³ [ˈfʌkiŋ] (noun), VV: coït*, baisage m, dérouillage m, tronche f. Voir aussi **honey-fuck(ing)**.

fuck off [ˈfʌkˈɔf] (to), VV: **1.** s'enfuir*, se tirer, se tailler, mettre les bouts; **f. o.!** va te faire foutre! **2.** se masturber*, se branler (la colonne), se tirer un coup. **3.** (U.S.) faire le con, déconner.

fuck over [ˈfʌkˈouvər] (to) (U.S.), VV: (police) fouiller, décarpiller (qn).

fuckster [ˈfʌkstər] (noun), VV: baiseur

m, qn porté sur l'article (ou sur la bagatelle).

fuckstress [ˈfʌkstris] (noun), VV: baiseuse f, chaude f de la pince.

fuck up [ˈfʌkˈʌp] (to), VV: cochonner, massacrer, torcher, bousiller. Voir aussi **snafu**.

fuddy-duddy [ˈfʌdi-dʌdi] (noun), F: vieux croulant, vieux rococo, périmé m.

fudge [ˈfʌdʒ] (to) (U.S.). **1.** F: raconter des blagues f.pl. (ou des craques f.pl.). **2.** V: faire jouir au toucher, faire mousser.

fudge out [ˈfʌdʒˈaut] (to), P: caner.

fug [fʌg] (noun), F: forte odeur de renfermé, schlingage m.

full [ful] (adj.), P: **1.** ivre*, plein (comme une bourrique), rond. **2.** intoxiqué par la drogue, chargé, bourré. Voir aussi **chock-full**.

fume [fjuːm] (to), F: se mettre en colère*, fumer, fulminer.

fuming [ˈfjuːmiŋ] (adj.), F: **to be in a f. temper**, être en colère*, être à cran (ou en rogne), vouer rouge.

fun¹ [fʌn] (attrib. adj.), F: **it's the f. thing to do**, c'est la chose bath à faire; **f. clothes**, vêtements* psychédéliques.

fun² [fʌn] (noun), F: **1. like f.**, (a) pas du tout; (b) très vite*, à toute barre, en moins de deux. **2. f. and games**, (a) farces et attrapes; (b) grabuge m; (c) (toute la) musique.

funeral [ˈfjuːnərəl] (noun), F: **that's your f.**, c'est votre affaire; mêle-toi de tes oignons; **it's not my f.**, ce n'est pas mon affaire, c'est pas mon rayon, c'est pas mes oignons.

fungus [ˈfʌŋgəs] (noun), P: **(face) f.**, barbe*, moustache*, poils m.pl. au menton.

funk¹ [fʌŋk] (noun), F: **1.** peur*, frousse f, trac m, trouille f; **to be in a (blue) f.**, avoir une peur* bleue, avoir la frousse (ou le trac); voir aussi **acid, 2**. **2.** froussard m, trouillard m, mouilleur m.

funk² [fʌŋk] (to), F: **to f. it**, caner, se dégonfler, les mouiller.

funked out [ˈfʌŋktˈaut] (adj.), P: sous l'influence des drogues, chargé, défoncé.

funky [ˈfʌŋki] (adj.). **1.** F: froussard. **2.** P: bath, badour, jojo, chouctose, nickel. **3.** P: (jazz) manière virile de jouer les blues.

funny¹ [ˈfʌni] (adj.). **1.** F: **don't be f.!**

---

* An asterisk indicates that the word so marked is included as a head-word in the Appendix.

ne fais pas l'imbécile (*ou* le zigoto)!
2. *F:* **f. business,** affaire *f* louche,
fricotage *m*; **none of your f. tricks!**
I don't want any f. business! (*a*) pas de
blagues! (*b*) je ne veux pas d'histoires!
3. *F:* **I came over all f.,** je me suis senti
tout chose. **4.** *P:* **f. farm,** asile *m*
d'aliénés, maison *f* de loufoques.
funny[2] [ˈfʌni] (*noun*) (*pl.* **funnies**), *F:* **1.
a f.,** plaisanterie *f*, blague *f*, rigolade *f*.
2. (*pl.*) (*a*) bandes dessinées; (*b*) dessins
animés.
fur [fəːr] (*noun*), *F:* **to make the f. fly,**
(*a*) se battre* avec acharnement, se
crêper le chignon; (*b*) se quereller avec
fracas, tempêter.
furburger [ˈfəːbəːgər] (*noun*), *VV:* =
hairburger.
furniture [ˈfəːnitʃər] (*noun*), *F:* **1. to be
part of the f.** = **to be a (permanent)
fixture (fixture,** 1). **2.** (*U.S.*) **a nice
little piece of f.,** une fille* qui a du
chien, un beau petit lot.
furphy [ˈfəːfi] (*noun*) (*Austr.*), *P:* fausse
rumeur, clabaud *m*, canular(d) *m*.
fury [ˈfjuːri] (*noun*), *F:* **like f.,** (*a*)
déchaîné, en (pleine) fureur; (*b*) très
vite*, à toute pompe, à tout berzingue.

fuse [fjuːz] (*noun*), *F:* **to blow a f.,** se
mettre en colère*, piquer une crise.
fuss [fʌs] (*noun*), *F:* chichis *m.pl.*,
chinoiseries *f.pl.*; **to make a f.,** faire
des arias; **it's nothing to make a f.
about,** il n'y a pas de quoi fouetter un
chat.
fusspot [ˈfʌspɔt], **fussy-breeches**
[ˈfʌsi-britʃiz] (*noun*), *F:* individu* qui
fait des histoires (*ou* des embarras),
chichiteux *m*.
future [ˈfjuːtʃər] (*noun*). **1.** *F:* **there's
no f. in it,** ça n'a pas d'avenir *m* (*ou*
de débouchés *m.pl.*). **2.** *P:* testicules*,
sac *m* à roupes.
futz[1] [fʌts] (*noun*), *V:* vagin*, fente *f*,
chagatte *f*.
futz[2] [fʌts] (**to**) (*U.S.*), *V:* = **fuck**[2] (**to**),
1.
fuzz [fʌz] (*noun*), *P:* **1.** policier*, détective *m*, flic *m*, roussin *m*. **2.** la police*,
flicaille *f*, rousse *f*. **3.** gardien* de prison,
matuche *m*, maton *m*. **4.** (*U.S.*) Brigade
fédérale des Stupéfiants.
fuzzled [ˈfʌzld] (*adj.*), *P:* ivre*, asphyxié,
bit(t)uré, chargé.

G

G [dʒiː], P: **1. to put in the G**, (a) agir sur
qn, serrer la vis (ou les pouces) à qn;
(b) dénoncer*, cafarder, moutonner,
moucharder, donner qn. **2.** = **grand.**
Voir aussi **G-man.**

gab[1] [gæb] (*noun*). **1.** P: blabla *m*,
jactage *m*. **2.** F: **to have the gift of the
g.**, (a) avoir du bagout, savoir baratiner,
avoir une bonne tapette; (b) savoir
vendre sa salade. **3.** P: = **gob[1], 1.**

gab[2] [gæb] (**to**), P: parler* trop,
bavarder*, bavasser, blablater, jacter,
jacasser, tenir le crachoir.

gabber [ˈgæbər] (*noun*), P: bavard*,
baratineur *m*, jacteur *m*, tapette *f*.

gabby [ˈgæbi] (*adj.*), P: bavard, qui a la
langue bien pendue.

gabfest [ˈgæbfest] (*noun*), P: bavette *f*,
causette *f*.

gad, Gad [gæd] (*noun*), F: **by g.!** sacrebleu! sapristi! mes aïeux!

gad about [ˈgædəˈbaʊt] (**to**), F: **1.**
vadrouiller, être par voies et par
chemins (ou par monts et par vaux).
2. courir le jupon, courir la prétentaine.

gadie [ˈgeidi] (*noun*), P: gadjé *m* (celui
qui n'est pas bohémien ou manouche).

gaff [gæf] (*noun*), P: **1.** logement*,
piaule *f*, taule *f*, crèche *f*; **they did him
in his g.**, ils l'ont piqué dans sa piaule;
cf. **drum, 1**; *voir aussi* **screw[2] (to), 3.
2. gambling g.**, maison *f* de jeu, tripot
m. **3. to blow the g.**, vendre la mèche;
to blow the g. on s.o., dénoncer* qn,
donner qn. **4.** (*U.S.*) **to stand the g.**,
être brave, encaisser les coups durs,
en avoir dans le ventre, être gonflé.
5. = **guff. 6.** café-concert *m*, beuglant *m*.

gaffed [gæft] (*adj.*) (*U.S.*), P: **g. dice** =
shapes.

gaffer [ˈgæfər] (*noun*), F: patron*,
taulier *m*, singe *m*.

gag[1] [gæg] (*noun*), F: **1.** plaisanterie *f*,
blague *f*, rigolade *f*. **2. to pull a g. on
s.o.**, (a) mettre qn en boîte; (b) faire
une entourloupe à qn. **3.** (*cinéma, etc.*)
gag *m*.

gag[2] [gæg] (**to**), F: (*th.*) enchaîner.

gaga [ˈgɑːgɑː] (*adj.*), F: **1.** gaga. **2.**
fou*, cinglé, timbré. **3. to go g. over
s.o.**, s'enticher de qn, se toquer de qn.

gage [geidʒ] (*noun*) (*mainly U.S.*), P:
1. whisky *m*, alcool* bon marché,
tord-boyaux *m*. **2.** tabac*, cigarettes*,
cigares*, chique *f*; **stick of g.**, cigarette*

(tabac *ou* marijuana), la fume. **3.**
marijuana *f* (*drogues**). **4. to get one's
g. up**, (a) se mettre en colère*, sortir
de ses gonds; (b) être ivre*, se piquer
le nez, se bit(t)urer, avoir sa cuite.

gaged [geidʒd] (*adj.*) (*U.S.*), P: ivre*,
bit(t)uré, noir, rond, schlass.

gal [gæl] (*noun*), F: jeune fille*, môme *f*,
gonzesse *f*.

galah [ˈgɑːlə] (*noun*) (*Austr.*), F: individu
bête*, buse *f*.

gall [gɔːl] (*noun*), F: culot *m*, toupet *m*.

gallows-bird [ˈgæloʊzbəːd] (*noun*), F:
gibier *m* de potence.

galluses [ˈgæləsiz] (*pl. noun*), P: bretelles *f.pl.*

galoot [gəˈluːt] (*noun*), P: **1.** individu*,
type *m*, mec *m*, client *m*. **2.** lourdaud *m*,
empoté *m*, godiche *m*.

galumph [gəˈlʌmf] (**to**), F: caracoler,
galoper lourdement.

gam[1] [gæm] (*noun*). **1.** V: = **gamaroosh[1].
2.** (*pl.*) P: jambes*, guibolles *f.pl.*,
gambettes *f.pl.* **3.** (*U.S.*) F: bavette *f*,
causette *f*.

gam[2] [gæm] (**to**). **1.** V: = **gamaroosh[2]
(to). 2.** (*U.S.*) P: se vanter, esbrouffer,
en installer. **3.** (*U.S.*) P: flirter.

gamaroosh, gamar(o)uche[1] [ˈgæmə-
ˈruːʃ] (*noun*), V: coït* buccal, suçage *m*,
taillade *f* de plume.

gamaroosh, gamar(o)uche[2] [ˈgæmə-
ˈruːʃ] (**to**), V: faire un coït* buccal,
sucer; faire minette, prendre la pipe,
souffler dans la canne (ou dans le
mirliton).

game[1] [geim] (*adj.*), F: **1. I'm g.!** dac!
ça botte! je veux! **2.** crâne; **to be
dead g.**, avoir beaucoup de courage, en
avoir dans le ventre. **3.** = **gammy.**

game[2] [geim] (*noun*). **1.** P: **to be on the
g.**, racoler* (*prostituée*), turfer, turbiner.
2. F: **I know your little g.!** je vois votre
manigance (*ou* votre petit jeu)! **3.** F:
to have the g. sewn up, avoir la partie
belle (*ou* en main), tenir le bon bout.
Voir aussi **army, 2; badger, 2; clip-
game; fun[2], 2; play[2] (to), 2; sack[1], 4;
skin[1], 5** (a); **up[2], 3.**

gamesmanship [ˈgeimzmənʃip] (*noun*),
F: l'art *m* de gagner.

gammer [ˈgæmər] (*noun*), F: grand-
mère, la vieille.

gammon[1] [ˈgæmən] (*noun*), P: bobards
m.pl., boniments *m.pl.*

---

* An asterisk indicates that the word so marked is included as a head-word in the Appendix.

II2

gammon² [ˈgæmən] **(to)**, *P:* **1.** duper*, monter un bateau à (qn), emmener (qn) en bateau. **2.** emberlificoter.

gammy [ˈgæmi] *(adj.)*, *F:* boiteux, bancal, banban, béquillard.

gamp [gæmp] *(noun)*, *F:* parapluie*, riflard *m*, pébroc *m*.

gander¹ [ˈgændər] *(noun)*, *P:* **to have a g.**, jeter un coup d'œil,* bigler, zyeuter; **just take a g.! mate-moi ça!**

gander² [ˈgændər] **(to)**, *P:* regarder*, lorgner, reluquer.

ganga [ˈgændʒər] *(noun)*, *P:* marijuana *f (drogues*)*, gania *m*.

gangster [ˈgæŋstər] *(noun)*, *P:* (a) marijuana *f (drogues*)*; (b) habitué(e) de la marijuana; (c) cigarette* de marijuana, reefer *m*, stick *m*.

gang up [ˈgæŋˈʌp] **(to)**, *F:* **to g. u. on s.o.**, former équipe (*ou* se liguer) contre qn, s'acoquiner pour tomber qn.

ganjah [ˈgændʒɑː], **ganji** [ˈgændʒi] *(noun)*, *P:* marijuana *f (drogues*)*; *cf.* **bhang; ganga; gunji.**

gannet [ˈgænit] *(noun)*, *F:* goinfre*, bouffe-tout *m*, bec *m* à tout grain.

garbage [ˈgɑːbidʒ] *(noun)*. **1.** *F:* camelote *f*, rossignols *m.pl.* **2.** *P:* boniments *m.pl.*, bobards *m.pl.*, bidon *m*. **3.** *P:* mauvaise nourriture*, ragougnasse *f*. **4.** *P:* drogue *f* de mauvaise qualité, foin *m*. **5.** *P:* résidu *m* après cuisson d'une drogue, fond *m* de culot. **6.** *P:* amphétamines *f.pl. (drogues*)*.

garbo [ˈgɑːbou] *(noun)* (*Austr.*), *F:* boueur *m*.

garden [ˈgɑːdn] *(noun)*, *F:* **1. to lead s.o. up the g. path**, faire marcher qn, faire voir des étoiles en plein midi, emmener qn en bateau. **2. everything in the g. is lovely**, tout va comme sur des roulettes, tout baigne dans le beurre. *Voir aussi* **bear-garden.**

gas¹ [gæs] *(adj.)*, *P:* **1.** excellent*, terrible, super. **2.** très amusant*, à crever de rire*, marrant, boyautant, astap.

gas² [gæs] *(noun)*. **1.** *F:* bavardage *m* vide, palas(s) *m*, baratinage *m*, bidon *m*; **his talk is all g.**, il parle pour ne rien dire, tout ça c'est du vent. **2.** (*U.S.*) *F:* (=*gasoline*) essence *f*, jus *m*; **to step on the g.**, (a) appuyer sur le champignon, donner plein gaz; (b) se dépêcher*, se grouiller; **to run out of g.**, (a) être en panne d'essence (*ou* en

manque de jus); (b) devenir fatigué* (*ou* vidé), être à bout de souffle. **3.** *P:* du tonnerre, qch. de foutral.

gas³ [gæs] **(to)**. **1.** *F:* bavarder*, baratiner, jacter. **2.** *P:* bonimenter, bourrer le crâne, avoir (qn) au baratin. **3.** *P:* entourlouper, épater, époustoufler.

gasbag [ˈgæsbæg] *(noun)*, *F:* moulin *m* à paroles, beau parleur, phraseur *m*.

gash¹ [gæʃ] *(adj.)*, *P:* de rechange, en surplus, en rab(iot). *Voir aussi* **lob¹**, 3.

gash² [gæʃ] *(noun)*. **1.** *P:* rab(iot) *m*. **2.** *P:* femme*, fendue *f*, fumelle *f*. **3.** *V:* vagin*, fente *f*, crevasse *f*; (b) coït*, giclée *f*.

gash-hound [ˈgæʃhaund] *(noun)*, *P:* coureur *m* de jupons, chaud lapin.

gasket [ˈgæskit] *(noun)*, *F:* **to blow a g.** = **to blow a fuse** (*voir* **fuse**).

gas-meter [ˈgæsmiːtər] *(noun)*, *F:* **to lie like a g.-m.**, mentir* comme un arracheur de dents.

gasp [gɑːsp] *(noun)*, *F:* **to be at one's last g.**, être à bout (*ou* au bout de son rouleau).

gasper [ˈgɑːspər] *(noun)*, *P:* cigarette*, cibiche *f*, sèche *f*.

gassed [gæst] *(adj.)*, *P:* **1.** ivre*, asphyxié, allumé. **2.** tordu de rire*, époustouflé, renversé.

gasser [ˈgæsər] *(noun)*, *P:* **1.** baratineur *m*, fort *m* en gueule. **2.** une merveille, du bath, du badour. **3.** éteignoir *m*, vieux jeu, périmé *m*. **4.** rigolade *f*, franche marrade.

gassy [ˈgæsi] *(adj.)*, *P:* **1.** bavard, baratineur, esbrouffeur. **2.** = **groovy.**

gas up [ˈgæsˈʌp] **(to)** (*U.S.*). **1.** *F:* se fournir d'essence, faire son plein. **2.** *P:* animer, exciter, stimuler, émoustiller.

gat [gæt] *(noun)* (*U.S.*), *P:* revolver*, pistolet *m*, calibre *m*.

gate-crash [ˈgeitkræʃ] **(to)**, *F:* se rendre à une réception (*fête, etc.*) sans être invité, resquiller.

gate-crasher [ˈgeitkræʃər] *(noun)*, *F:* passe-volant *m*, resquilleur *m*; **champion g.-c.**, roi *m* des resquilleurs.

gate-post [ˈgeitpoust] *(noun)*, *F:* **between you and me and the g.-p.**, entre quat'zyeux, entre quat'murs, de toi z'à moi.

gauge [geidʒ] *(noun)*, *P:* = **gage**, 3.

Gawd [gɔːd] *(noun)* (=*God*), *P:* **oh my G.!** ah mon Dieu!

---

* L'astérisque indique que le mot marqué de ce signe figure comme entrée dans le Répertoire.

gawk [gɔ:k] (noun), F: 1. godiche mf.
2. big g., grand escogriffe.

gawky [ˈgɔ:ki] (adj.), F: dégingandé.

gay¹ [gei] (adj.), F: 1. g. deceivers =
falsies, 2. 2. homosexuel, qui sent la
pédale. Voir aussi dog¹, 9.

gay² [gei] (noun) (Austr.), P: = alec, 2.

gazump [gəˈzʌmp] (to), F: 1. escroquer*
en faisant monter le prix d'une pro-
priété au dernier moment; faire valser
les prix. 2. escroquer*, carotter.

gazumper [gəˈzʌmpər] (noun), F: escroc*
en propriétés immobilières.

gear¹ [giər] (adj.), P: excellent*, du
tonnerre, formid, bath.

gear² [giər] (noun). 1. F: biens m.pl.,
possessions f.pl.; cf. marriage. 2. F:
attirail m, barda m, bataclan m.
3. F: vêtements*, nippes f.pl., frusques
f.pl. 4. P: attirail m de drogué*, la
popote. 5. P: butin*, rafle f, fade m.
6. F: to be in high g., être survolté,
péter le feu; to be in low g., ne pas
être en forme, être déprimé. 7. P:
grand spectacle, gala m. 8. (Austr.) P:
fausses dents*, râtelier m.

geared up [ˈgiədˈʌp] (p.p. & adj.), F:
to be g. u. for sth., être fin prêt, être
conditionné pour qch.

geck¹ [gek] (noun), P: = git².

geck² [gek] (to), P: zyeuter, filer un
coup de sabord.

gee!¹ [dʒi:] (excl.), F: g. (whiz(z))! ah,
dis donc! mince! bigre!

gee² [dʒi:] (noun), P: 1. = G, 1, 2.
2. (U.S.) individu*, mec m; front g.,
homme m de paille, couverture f; a
hip g., un mec à la coule; un pote, un
régulier.

gee³ [dʒi:] (to), P: voler*, chiper.

geed up [ˈdʒi:dˈʌp] (adj.), P: sous
l'effet des drogues*, chargé, défoncé.

gee-er [ˈdʒi:ər] (noun), P: cafardeur m,
faiseur m de crosses, mauvais coucheur.

gee-gee [ˈdʒi:dʒi:] (noun), F: 1. cheval*,
dada m. 2. to follow the gee-gees,
jouer aux courtines, suivre les gails
(ou les canassons). Voir aussi flutter,
2.

gee-up [ˈdʒi:ʌp] (noun), F: = gip, 2.

gee up [ˈdʒi:ˈʌp] (to). 1. F: (à un cheval)
g. u.! hue! au trot! 2. he gee-ed them
up, (a) P: il les a montés l'un contre
l'autre; (b) F: il les a fait se dégrouiller.
Voir aussi geed up.

Geez(e)! [dʒi:z] (excl.), P: bon Dieu!
tonnerre de Dieu!; cf. Jeeze!

geezed up [ˈdʒi:zdˈʌp] (adj.), P: 1.
ivre*, bit(t)uré, blindé, rétamé. 2. =
geed up.

geezer [ˈgi:zər] (noun), P: 1. (a) homme*,
type m, mec m; (b) femme*, souris f.
2. an old g., (a) un vieux*, un vieux
birbe (ou bonze); (b) une carabosse,
une vieille rombière.

gefuffle [gəˈfʌfl] (noun), F: = kerfuffle.

gel [gel] (noun), F: = gal.

gelt [gelt] (noun), P: argent*, pognon m,
soudure f.

gen [dʒen] (noun), F: renseignements*,
tuyaux m.pl.; duff g., faux renseignements, canard m, du bidon; pukka g.,
renseignement* sûr, bon tuyau, tuyau
increvable, de l'officiel, de l'authentique,
bath rencard m.

genned up [ˈdʒendˈʌp] (adj. & p.p.),
F: to get g. u., se mettre au courant,
se rencarder; to be g. u., être rencardé,
être à la page (ou dans le bain ou au
parfum).

gent [dʒent] (noun) (=gentleman), F:
1. un monsieur, un type bien. 2. to go
to the gents, aller aux W.C.*, aller
chez les messieurs.

geography [dʒiˈɔgrəfi] (noun), F: to
show s.o. the g. of the house, (a) faire
le tour du propriétaire; (b) montrer les
W.C.* à qn.

Geordie [ˈdʒɔ:di] (noun), F: originaire
de la région de Tyneside.

George¹ [dʒɔ:dʒ] (pr. noun), F: 1.
by G.! sapristi! mince alors! 2. (av.)
pilote m automatique, Georges m.

george² [dʒɔ:dʒ] (to), P: émoustiller,
échauffer, allumer (qn).

gerdoing! gerdoying! [gəˈdɔiŋ] (excl.),
F: boum (badaboum)! pan! vlan!; cf.
doing!; kerdoing!

gessein [geˈsi:n] (to), P: = con² (to).

gesseiner [geˈsi:nər] (noun), P: 1. tout
le bataclan, les cliques et les claques.
2. (Marine marchande) poubelle f,
boîte f à ordures.

gessump [geˈsʌmp] (to), P: voler*,
barboter, empiler; emberlificoter; to g.
the gesseiner, s'affurer, chauffer, faire
une cambriole.

get [get] (to). 1. F: comprendre; I don't
g. you, je ne pige pas; g. me? tu y es?
tu saisis? 2. F: I'll g. you for that!

j'aurai ta peau, je t'aurai au tournant; **I've got him,** je le tiens. **3.** *F:* **it gets me when . . .,** ça m'énerve (*ou* ça me crispe *ou* ça m'agace) lorsque… **4.** *F:* **to g. it in the neck,** écoper, en prendre pour son grade (*ou* son compte), se faire aplatir. **5.** *P:* **we got trouble** (=*we have trouble*), on a des ennuis; **I got rhythm** (=*I have rhythm*), j'ai du swing; **(you) got a light?** (=*do you have a light?*), t'as du feu? **6.** *F:* **to g. ten years,** attraper (*ou* piger) dix berges. **7.** *F:* **you've got me there,** tu m'as, tu me colles; je donne ma langue au chat. **8.** *F:* émouvoir, secouer, emballer. **9.** *F:* tuer*, bousiller, zigouiller. **10.** *F:* arrêter*, épingler. **11.** *F:* **to g. there,** réussir, arriver, se débrouiller; **not to g. anywhere,** n'aboutir à rien. **12.** *F:* **to g. going,** (*a*) se dépêcher*, se magner, se dégrouiller; **g. going!** en route!; (*b*) se mettre au travail*, se mettre en branle. **13.** *P:* **to g. behind it,** (*a*) (*drogues*) être défoncé, être high; (*b*) être possédé (par qch.).

get across [ˈgətəˈkrɔs] (to), *F:* (*a*) faire comprendre, faire piger, éclairer; (*b*) communiquer, faire passer la rampe.

get along [ˈgetəˈlɔŋ] (to), *F:* **1. I must be getting along,** il faut que je m'en aille (*ou* que je me mette en route). **2. g. a. with you!** (*a*) va te promener! débarrasse (le plancher)!; (*b*) vas-y voir! tu charries!; (*c*) je n'en crois rien; allons donc!; pour qui me prends-tu? **3. to g. a. with s.o.,** bien s'entendre avec qn. **4.** se défendre, pouvoir faire.

get around [ˈgetəˈraund] (to), *F:* **1. it's getting around that . . .,** le bruit court que… **2.** rouler sa bosse, circuler. **3.** = **get round** (to). **4. to g. a. to doing sth.,** arriver à faire qch. **5.** circonvenir, surmonter (une difficulté, *etc.*).

get at [ˈget-æt] (to), *F:* **1.** acheter, soudoyer, graisser la patte à (qn). **2.** découvrir (la vérité, *etc.*). **3. what are you getting at?** où voulez-vous en venir? **4.** asticoter, chercher des crosses à (qn). **5.** tripoter, tripatouiller, trifouiller.

get-at-able [ˈgetˈætəbl] (*adj.*), *F:* accessible, d'accès facile.

getaway [ˈgetəwei] (*noun*), *F:* évasion *f*, la belle, la cavale; **to make a g.,**

s'éclipser, faire un plongeon; **g. car,** voiture* de fuite, bagnole *f* de cavale.

get away [ˈgetəˈwei] (to). **1.** *F:* **g. a. (with you)!** (*a*) laisse tomber! fiche-moi la paix! barca!; (*b*) je ne mords pas! ça ne prend pas! **2.** *F:* **to g. a. with it,** s'en tirer à bon compte; **he won't g. a. with it,** il ne l'emportera pas au paradis. **3.** *F:* **there's no getting away from it,** il n'y a pas moyen d'en sortir. **4.** *P:* **to g. it a.** = **to get it off** (get off (to), 4 (*b*)).

get by [ˈgetˈbai] (to), *F:* s'en tirer, en être quitte, s'en contenter.

get down [ˈgetˈdaun] (to), *F:* **1. to g. s.o. d.,** irriter, déprimer, déconcerter qn; taper sur le système à qn, coller le cafard à qn; **what gets me down is . . .,** ce qui est cafardeux, c'est… **2. to g. d. to it,** s'y mettre, en mettre un coup.

get off [ˈgetˈɔf] (to). **1.** *F:* **to g. o. lightly,** s'en tirer à bon compte, bien s'en sortir. **2.** *P:* **g. o.!** fous-moi la paix! arrête le char! **3.** *F:* **to g. o. with s.o.,** faire une touche. **4.** *V:* **to g. it o.,** (*a*) avoir un orgasme*, lâcher le jus; (*b*) coïter*, s'envoyer en l'air; (*c*) se masturber*, se branler. **5.** *P:* se doper, s'enfoncer (avec la drogue). **6.** *F:* **g. it o. your chest!** vide ton sac! **7.** *F:* **to tell s.o. where to g.o.,** réprimander* sévèrement qn, dire à qn ses quatre vérités. **8.** *P:* **to g. o. on sth.,** être transporté par qch.; **we got off on that music,** cette musique nous a remués (*ou* nous a secoué les entrailles *ou* nous a pris au ventre).

get on [ˈgetˈɔn] (to), *F:* **g. o. with you!** = **get along with you!** (get along (to), 2).

get on to [ˈgetˈɔntuː] (to), *F:* **1.** découvrir*. **2.** se mettre en rapport avec (qn), contacter (qn).

get-out [ˈgetaut] (*noun*), *F:* **1.** esquive *f*, moyen *m* de sortie. **2.** (*U.S.*) = **get-up, 1.**

get out [ˈgetˈaut] (to), *P:* **to g. o. from under** = **to find an out** (out[2]).

get over [ˈgetˈouvər] (to), *F:* **I can't g. o. it!** je n'en reviens pas, j'en reste baba!

get-rich-quick [ˈgetˈritʃˈkwik] (*adj.*), *F:* véreux; **g.-r.-q. plan,** projet *m* qui promet la lune.

get round [ˈgetˈraund] (to), *F:* cajoler,

---

* L'astérisque indique que le mot marqué de ce signe figure comme entrée dans le Répertoire.

enjôler; **you can't g. r. me like that,** tu ne m'auras pas comme ça.
get through [ˈgetˈθruː] **(to). 1.** F: contacter, avoir la communication. **2.** F: **to g. t. to s.o.,** faire comprendre qch. à qn, faire piger qn. **3.** F: **to g. t. the month,** boucler son mois, joindre les deux bouts. **4.** P: obtenir des drogues*, se garnir, trouver la cheville (ou le joint ou le contact). **5.** F: **to g. t. some work,** abattre du travail*; **to g. t. a lot of money,** dépenser* beaucoup d'argent*, croquer beaucoup de fric.
get-together [ˈgettəgeðər] (noun), F: réunion amicale, retrouvaille f.
get together [ˈgettəˈgeðər] (to), F: **to g. it t.,** (a) se préparer à partir d'un endroit, prendre ses cliques et ses claques; (b) s'éclaircir les idées, éclairer sa lanterne.
get-up [ˈgetʌp] (noun), F: **1.** vêtements*, fripes f.pl., nippes f.pl., loques f.pl., accoutrement m. **2.** tenue f, présentation f.
get up [ˈgetˈʌp] (to), V: **to g. it u.,** coïter*, s'envoyer en l'air.
get-up-and-go [ˈgetʌpən(d)ˈgou] (adj.), F: plein d'allant, plein d'entrain, dynamique.
ghastly [ˈgɑːstli] (adj.), F: abominable, hideux, **the weather's g.,** il fait un temps de chien; **what a g. woman!** quelle femme* abominable! quelle sale chipie!
gherkin [ˈgəːkin] (noun), P: pénis*, gourdin m, gourde f à poils; **to jerk one's g.,** se masturber*, se tirer son coup.
ghost [goust] (to), F: **to g. (for)** s.o., remplacer qn, faire le nègre.
G.I. [ˈdʒiːˈlai] (abbr.) (U.S.), F: **1.** (= government issue) ce qui vient de l'intendance militaire américaine. **2.** soldat* américain; **G.I. Joe,** le type du biffin américain pendant la deuxième guerre mondiale.
giddy up [ˈgidiˈʌp] (to), F: = **gee up** (to), 1.
gift [gift] (noun), F: qch. de pas difficile*, du beurre, du nougat.
gig[1] [gig] (noun) (mainly U.S.). **1.** F: joujou m quelconque, sucette f. **2.** V: anus*, rondibé m, trou m; **up your g.!** mon cul! **3.** V: vagin*, baba m, crac m. **4.** F: réjouissances*, surboum f,

bamboche f. **5.** F: festival m de jazz. **6.** F: engagement m d'un soir (th., jazz, etc.). **7.** P: (a) vieille voiture*, guimbarde f; (b) bolide m. **8.** P: emploi* bouche-trou, placarde f. **9.** P: qn qui regarde* avec curiosité, reluqueur m, zyeuteur m. **10.** P: détective privé, condé m. **11.** P: (prize) g., individu bête*, gourde f, crétin m de première. **12.** F: passe-temps m, dada m, hobby m.
gig[2] [gig] (to). **1.** (U.S.) F: jouer dans un groupe de jazz. **2.** P: regarder*, reluquer, zyeuter. **3.** (Austr.) P: taquiner, tourmenter, faire enrager (qn).
giggle [ˈgigl] (noun). **1.** F: **we did it (just) for a g.,** c'était pour rigoler. **2.** F: **we had a right g.,** on s'est tordu de rire*; **what a g.!** quelle bonne rigolade! **3.** F: **to get the giggles,** attraper un fou-rire. **4.** P: **g. smoke** (or **weed**), cigarette* de marijuana (drogues*), joint m, stick m, reefer m. **5.** (U.S.) F: **g. water,** champagne m.
gigi [ˈʒiːʒiː] (noun) = **gig**[1], 1, 2, 3.
gills [gilz] (pl. noun), P: **to be stewed to the g.,** être complètement ivre*, avoir sa cuite, être bourré à bloc.
gimme [ˈgimi] (abbr.) (= give me), F: donne! aboule!; cf. **skin**[1], 10.
gimmick [ˈgimik] (noun), F: **1.** attrape f, tour m, combine f, astuce f, truc m. **2.** attrape-couillons m, truc m publicitaire. **3.** gadget m, truc m, machin m.
gimmickry [ˈgimikri] (noun), F: truquage m.
gimmicky [ˈgimiki] (adj.), F: rempli de trucs m.pl.
gin [dʒin] (noun), P: **1.** (U.S.) prostituée* nègre*, pépée cirée, frangine f bamboula. **2.** (Austr.) femme aborigène. **3.** cocaïne f (drogues*).
ginger [ˈdʒindʒər] (noun), F: **1.** rouquin(e) m(f), poil m de carotte. **2.** boisson gazeuse au gingembre. **3.** **to have (a lot of) g.,** avoir de l'entrain m (ou de l'allant m ou de l'abattage m). **4. g. group,** groupe m de pression. Voir aussi **stone-ginger.**
ginger up [ˈdʒindʒərˈʌp] (to), F: émoustiller, mettre de l'entrain dans, donner un coup de fouet à.
gink [giŋk] (noun), P: (a) (terme de mépris pour un individu) plouc m, rustre m, pataud m, drôle de parois-

---

* An asterisk indicates that the word so marked is included as a head-word in the Appendix.

sien *m*; (*b*) pauvre type *m*, couillon *m*,
tartempion *m*, zigomar *m*.

gin-mill [ˈdʒinmil] (*U.S.*), **gin-palace**
[ˈdʒinpæləs] (*noun*), *F:* bar *m* de basse
classe, boui-boui *m*, bouge *m*, assommoir *m*.

ginormous [dʒaiˈnɔːməs] (*adj.*), *F:* colossal, maous(se), bœuf.

gip [dʒip] (*noun*), *F:* **1. to give s.o. g.**,
tomber sur qn à bras raccourcis, tomber
sur le paletot à qn. **2. my rheumatism
is giving me g.**, mes rhumatismes me
font voir trente-six chandelles.

giped [ˈgaiped] (*adj.*) (*mainly Scottish*),
P: fou*, toqué, timbré.

gippo [ˈdʒipou] (*noun*), *P:* **1.** romanichel
m, romani *m*, manouche *m*. **2.** (*mil.*)
la soupe, le rata.

girl [gəːl] (*noun*), *P:* **1.** cocaïne *f*
(*drogues**), fillette *f*, coco *f*. **2.** pédé-
raste*, chouquette *f*, tante *f*. **3. working
g.**, prostituée*, persilleuse *f*, gagneuse
f. *Voir aussi* **bar-girl; B-girl; cover-
girl; dolly-girl; glamour-girl; playgirl;
sweater-girl; yes-girl.**

girlie [ˈgəːli] (*noun & attrib. adj.*). **1.** *F:*
fillette *f*, girl *f*; **g. show**, spectacle *m*
de girls; **g. magazines**, presse *f* de
charme.. **2.** *P:* (*mainly U.S.*) prosti-
tuée*, fille *f*.

git![1] [git] (*excl.*), *P:* file! fiche le camp!
décolle!

git[2] [git] (*noun*), *P:* individu bête*,
crétin *m*, con *m*.

give [giv] (**to**), *F:* **1. don't g. me that!**
ne me raconte pas d'histoires! **2. to g.
it to s.o.**, réprimander* qn, passer un
savon à qn. **3. g. it all you've got!** faites
le maximum! donne un (bon) coup de
collier! **4. to know what gives**, être à
la page (*ou* dans le vent *ou* à la coule).
5. what gives?, (*a*) salut!; (*b*) qu'est-ce
qui se fricote?; (*c*) quoi de neuf? *Voir
aussi* **vocals.**

give-away[1] [ˈgivəwei] (*adj.*), *F:* **to sell
sth. at a g. price**, vendre qch. à un
prix défiant toute concurrence.

give-away[2] [ˈgivəwei] (*noun*), *F:* **1.**
article sacrifié. **2. a (dead) g.**, geste *m*
(mot, *etc.*) qui en dit long.

give over [ˈgivˈouvər] (**to**), *F:* renoncer
à (qch.), dételer, remiser; **g.o., will
you?** laisse tomber, veux-tu?

glad [glæd] (*adj.*), *F:* **g. rags**, les plus
beaux vêtements* de sa garde-robe,

des nippes *f.pl.* baths, les fourgues *f.pl.*
du dimanche; **to put on one's g. rags**,
se mettre sur son trente et un. *Voir
aussi* **eye, 6.**

glamour-boy [ˈglæməbɔi] (*noun*), *F:*
(*a*) séducteur *m*, joli cœur, jeune premier; (*b*) un beau mâle.

glamour-girl [ˈglæməgəːl] (*noun*), *F:*
(*a*) ensorceleuse *f*, vamp *f*; (*b*) beau
morceau, prix *m* de Diane.

glamour-puss [ˈglæməpus] (*noun*), *F:*
pin-up *f*, ensorceleuse *f*.

glass[1] [glɑːs] (*adj.*), *F:* **to have a g. jaw**,
(*d'un boxeur*) avoir la mâchoire en verre.

glass[2] [glɑːs] (*noun*), *P:* bimbeloterie *f*,
verroterie *f*, strass *m*.

glass[3] [glɑːs] (**to**), *P:* taillader (qn)
avec du verre cassé (dans une rixe).

glasshouse [ˈglɑːshaus] (*noun*), *P:* (*mil.*)
prison* militaire, grosse lourde.

glassy-eyed [ˈglɑːsiˈaid], **glazed** [gleizd]
(*adj.*), *F:* ivre*, blindé, blindezingue.

gleep [gliːp] (**to**), *P:* injurier*, agoniser
(qn).

glims [glimz] (*pl. noun*), *P:* **1.** yeux*,
quinquets *m.pl.*, lanternes *f.pl.* **2.**
lumières *f.pl.*, ca(le)bombe *f*, calbiche
f; **to douse the g.**, étouffer la cabombe.
3. phares *m.pl.* (d'une voiture). **4.**
lunettes*, bernicles *f.pl.*, carreaux
m.pl.

glitch [glitʃ] (*noun*), *F:* **1.** (*a*) anicroche
f, accroc *m*, hic *m*; (*b*) panne *f*, os *m*
(*mécanique*, *etc.*). **2.** (*astronautique*) per-
turbations *f.pl.* atmosphériques.

globes [gloubz] (*pl. noun*), *P:* seins*,
globes *m.pl.*, ballons *m.pl.*

glory [ˈglɔːri] (*noun*), *F:* **1. he's got the
g.**, il tombe dans la bondieuserie. **2. to
go to g.**, (*a*) mourir*; (*b*) se délabrer,
dégringoler, aller à dame.

glory-hole [ˈglɔːrihoul] (*noun*), *F:*
capharnaüm *m*, cagibi *m*.

glossies [ˈglɔsiz] (*pl. noun*), *F:* **the g.**,
revues *f.pl.*, magazines *m.pl.*, les glossies
m.pl.

glow [glou] (*noun*), *F:* **to have** (*or* get) **a
g. on**, être légèrement ivre*, être gris
(*ou* pompette *ou* éméché).

glue-factory [ˈgluːfæktəri], **glue-pot**
[ˈgluːpɔt] (*noun*), *V:* vagin*, baveux
m.

G-man [ˈdʒiːmæn] (*noun*) (*U.S.*), *F:*
agent *m* du Deuxième Bureau
américain.

---

* L'astérisque indique que le mot marqué de ce signe figure comme entrée dans le Répertoire.

gnashers [ˈnæʃəz] (*pl. noun*), *P:* dents*, croquantes *f.pl.*

go[1] [gou] (*adj.*), *F:* en bon ordre, O.K.; **all systems are g.**, on a le feu vert.

go[2] [gou] (*noun*), *F:* **1.** (*a*) **no g.!** = **no dice!** (dice[1], 1); (*b*) **it's no g.**, rien à faire, cela ne prend pas, c'est nib, c'est midi (sonné). **2. to have a g. at s.o.**, s'en prendre à qn, dire deux mots à qn. **3. to be always on the g.**, avoir la bougeotte, être toujours (*ou* tout le temps) sur la brèche, avoir toujours un pied en l'air; **it's all g.!** on n'a pas une minute à soi! **4. have a g.!** tente la chance!; **have another g.!** remets ça! **5. he's got no g. in him**, il n'a pas d'allant, il est ramollo. **6. to put some g. into it**, y mettre de l'entrain (*ou* de l'animation). **7. to give sth. a g.**, tenter le coup, s'attaquer à qch. **8. at one g.**, d'un seul coup (*ou* trait), tout d'une haleine. **9. to be all the g.**, faire rage, faire fureur. **10. (right) from the word g.**, dès le départ, tout au début. *Voir aussi* **bag**[2] (to), 5; **little**, 1; **touch**[1], 2.

go[3] [gou] (to). **1.** *F:* **how goes it?** ça va-t-il comme vous voulez? **2.** *F:* **g. it!** lance-toi! fonce! **3.** *P:* **to be gone**, être défoncé, planer (*drogues*). *Voir aussi* **gone** *et les verbes composés* **to go along with, down, for, off, on, out, over, through, up.**

go-ahead[1] [ˈgouəhed] (*adj.*), *F:* **a g.-a. young man with g.-a. ideas**, un garçon entreprenant qui voit loin; un jeune loup.

go-ahead[2] [ˈgouəhed] (*noun*), *F:* **to get the g.-a.**, avoir le feu vert.

goalie [ˈgouli] (*noun*) (=*goalkeeper*), *F:* gardien *m* de but, goal *m.*

go along with [ˈgouəˈlɒŋwið] (to), *F:* accepter (qch.) en tout et pour tout; **I'll g. a. w. that**, je suis pleinement d'accord; **I can't g. a. w. that**, je ne suis pas d'accord; je ne marche pas.

goat [gout] (*noun*), *F:* **1. to get s.o.'s g.**, ennuyer* qn, déconcerter, irriter, ahurir qn; faire bisquer qn; **he gets my g.**, il me sort par les narines. **2. old g.**, vieux* birbe, vieille bique, vieille baderne.

gob[1] [gɔb] (*noun*), *P:* **1.** bouche*, gueule *f*; **to keep one's g. shut**, se taire*; **shut your g.!** la ferme! **2.** crachat*, glaviot *m*, mollard *m.* **3.** (*U.S.*) marin*,

cachalot *m*, mataf *m.* **4. gobs of . . .**, une abondance* de..., une flopée (*ou* tapée) de...

gob[2] [gɔb] (to), *P:* cracher*, mollarder; *cf.* **gob**[1], 2.

gobbledegook [ˈgɔbldiguːk] (*noun*), *F:* jargon *m*, charabia *m*, baragouin *m.*

gobble up [ˈgɔblˈʌp] (to) (*Austr.*), *P:* arrêter*, agrafer, coffrer (qn).

gobstruck [ˈgɔb-strʌk] (*adj.*), *P:* ahuri, abasourdi, estomaqué; **I'm g.!** je suis comme deux ronds de flan!

goby [ˈgoubi] (*noun*) (=*go-between*), *P:* messager *m*, matignon *m.*

go-by [ˈgoubai] (*noun*), *F:* **to give s.o. the g.-b.**, battre froid à qn, snober qn, faire grise mine à qn; **to give sth. the g.-b.**, dépasser qch., esquiver qch.

God, god [gɔd] (*noun*). **1.** *F:* **by G.!** (sacré) nom de Dieu! grands dieux!; **my G.!** bon Dieu (de bon Dieu)!; **G. Almighty!** Dieu Tout-Puissant!; **G. only knows**, Dieu seul le sait. **2.** *P:* **the G. man**, prêtre*, l'homme du bon Dieu, cureton *m.* **3.** (*th.*) *F:* **the gods**, le poulailler, la poulaille, le paradis, le paradou, les titis *m.pl. Voir aussi* **tin**[1], 3.

god-awful [ˈgɔdˈɔːful] (*adj.*), *P:* répugnant, dégueulasse, puant, infect.

goddam [ˈgɔdæm], **goddamned** [ˈgɔdæmd] (*adj.*), *P:* sacré, satané; **this g. idiot**, ce sacré bon Dieu d'idiot.

goddammit! goddamnit! [ˈgɔdˈdæmit] (*excl.*), *P:* sacré nom (de nom)!

godfer [ˈgɔdfər] (*noun*) (*R.S.* = *God forbid* = *kid*), *P:* enfant*, gosse *mf*, môme *mf*; *cf.* **dustbin.**

God-forbid [ˈgɔdfəbid] (*noun*) (*R.S.* = *kid*), *P:* = **godfer.**

go down [ˈgouˈdaun] (to). **1.** *F:* (*a*) finir ses études universitaires; (*b*) partir en vacances. **2.** *F:* tomber malade*. **3.** *F:* **my dinner won't g. d.**, mon dîner a du mal à passer. **4.** *F:* **it goes down well with the public**, le public l'avale tout rond; **that won't g. d. with me**, ça ne prend pas avec moi. **5.** *V:* faire un coït* buccal; **to g. d. on s.o.**, manger, sucer, pomper qn; *cf.* **box**[1], 1; **come down** (to), 2.

goer [ˈgouər] (*noun*), *P:* **1. she's a g.**, c'est une chaude de la pince, c'est une chaude lapine; elle en veut. **2. expert** *m*, calé *m*, fortiche *m.*

go for [ˈgoufɔːr, ˈgoufər] (to), *F:* **1. to**

---

* An asterisk indicates that the word so marked is included as a head-word in the Appendix.

g. f. s.o., rentrer dans le chou à qn, tomber sur le poil à qn. **2.** aller chercher, essayer d'obtenir. **3.** marcher pour, être entiché de; **I don't g. f. that**, cela ne m'emballe pas beaucoup.

go-getter ['gougetər] (*noun*), *F:* arriviste *m*, homme qui a les dents longues.

go-getting ['gougetiŋ] (*adj.*), *F:* opportuniste, ambitieux, arriviste.

goggle-box ['gɔglbɔks] (*noun*), *F:* télé *f*, boîte *f* à images, petit écran; *cf.* **box¹, 2; idiot-box; idiot's lantern** (*voir* **lantern**).

goggle-eyed ['gɔgl'aid] (*adj.*), *F:* avec les yeux en boules de loto (*ou* qui sortent de la tête).

goggles ['gɔglz] (*pl. noun*), *P:* lunettes*, pare-brise *m.pl.*

going ['gouiŋ] (*noun*), *F:* **to get out while the g.'s good**, partir*.pendant que c'est possible (*ou* que la voie est libre *ou* qu'on a le vent en poupe *ou* qu'on en a l'occase).

going-over ['gouiŋ'ouvər] (*noun*), *F:* **1. to give s.o. a g.-o.**, (*a*) battre* qn, donner une raclée à qn; (*b*) réprimander* qn, attraper qn; (*c*) fouiller qn, faire la barbote à qn. **2.** fignolage *m*, révision *f*.

goings-on ['gouiŋz'ɔn] (*pl. noun*), *F:* conduite *f*, manège *m*, manigances *f.pl.*; **such g.-o.!** en voilà des façons!; **I've heard of your g.-o.**, j'en ai appris de belles sur vous.

gold [gould] (*noun*), *P:* **1.** argent*, pèze *m*, flouze *m*. **2.** (**Acapulco**) **g.**, marijuana *f* (*drogues**) de bonne qualité, gold *m*. *Voir aussi* **dust¹, 2** (*b*).

goldbrick¹ ['gouldbrik] (*noun*) (*U.S.*), *P:* **1.** paresseux*, tire-au-flanc *m*, ramier *m*. **2.** une fille* tartignole.

goldbrick² ['gouldbrik] (**to**) (*U.S.*), *P:* **1.** paresser à son travail, tirer au cul (*ou* au flanc), se défiler. **2.** duper*, estamper (qn).

goldbricker ['gouldbrikər] (*noun*) (*U.S.*), *P:* **1.** = **goldbrick¹, 1. 2.** escroc*, estampeur *m*.

gold-digger ['goulddigər] (*noun*), *F:* croqueuse *f* de diamants, gigolette *f*.

golden ['gould(ə)n] (*adj.*), *F:* **1. g. disc**, disque *m* d'or (le millionième). **2. g. opportunity**, affaire *f* d'or, occasion rêvée. **3.** doré, beurré, en or. **4.** excellent*, superbe, doré sur tranche. *Voir aussi* **handshake**.

goldfish-bowl ['gouldfiʃboul] (*noun*), *F:* maison *f* de verre, place *f* publique.

goldmine ['gouldmain] (*noun*), *F:* situation lucrative, mine *f* d'or, filon *m*.

gollion ['gɔliən] (*noun*) (*Austr.*), *P:* crachat*, graillon *m*.

golly! ['gɔli] (*excl.*), *F:* (**by**) **g.!** mince alors! flûte! bigre!

goma ['goumə] (*noun*), *P:* opium brut (*ou* vert), goma *m* (*drogues*).

gone [gɔn] (*adj.*), *P:* **1.** parti (sous l'influence de l'alcool* ou du hachisch, *etc.*); *cf.* **go³** (**to**), **3. 2.** du nanan, du cool. *Voir aussi* **far; go on** (**to**), **6.**

goner ['gɔnər] (*noun*), *F:* **1.** (*a*) type fini; (*b*) chose perdue. **2. almost a g.**, crevard *m*, crevetant *m*, qui a son compte.

gong [gɔŋ] (*noun*). **1.** *F:* médaille *f*, pastille *f*, banane *f*, méduche *f*. **2.** *P:* pipe *f* à opium, bambou *m*; **to kick the g. around**, tirer sur le bambou.

gonga ['gɔŋgə] (*noun*), *P:* anus*, anneau *m*, troufignon *m*; (**you can**) **stick it up your g.!** tu peux te le mettre (*ou* te le fourrer) quelque part!; *cf.* **stick²** (**to**), **3.**

gonif¹ ['gɔnif] (*noun*), *P:* **1.** voleur*, chapardeur *m*, barboteur *m*. **2.** pédéraste*, pédé *m*.

gonif² ['gɔnif] (**to**), *P:* voler*, chaparder, barboter.

gonna ['gɔnə], *P:* = **going to**.

goo [gu:] (*noun*), *F:* **1.** sentimentalité excessive (*ou* à la guimauve *ou* à l'eau de rose). **2.** bouillabaisse *f*, ratatouille *f*, colle *f*. **3.** flatterie *f*, pommade *f*, lèche *f*. *Cf.* **gooey.**

good [gud] (*adj.*), *F:* **1. g. God** (*or* **Lord**)! bondieu! **2. g. heavens!** ciel! **3. g. grief!** zut alors! **4. g. gracious!** fichtre! **5. g. egg!** bath! super! bravo! *Voir aussi* **hiding, 1; job, 6, 7; no-good; thing, 9.**

goodies ['gudiz] (*pl. noun*), *F:* **1.** gourmandises *f.pl.*, du nanan. **2.** les bons, les bien-pensants; *cf.* **baddie, 2.**

goodish ['gudiʃ] (*adj.*), *F:* **1.** assez bon. **2. a g. while**, assez longtemps, une paie; **it's a g. way** (*or* **step**) **from here**, c'est à un bon bout de chemin d'ici.

goodness ['gudnis] (*noun & excl.*), *F:* **g.!** Dieu! bigre!; **g. me!** bonté divine!; **g. gracious** (**me**)! miséricorde!; **for g. sake!** pour l'amour de Dieu! **thank g.!**

---

* L'astérisque indique que le mot marqué de ce signe figure comme entrée dans le Répertoire.

Dieu merci!; g. (only) knows what I
must do, Dieu sait ce que je dois faire.
Voir aussi honest-to-goodness.
goodo! [ˈgudou] (*excl.*), *F:* chic alors!
parfait! épatant!
goods [gudz] (*pl. noun*), *P:* **1. a nice
bit of g.**, une fille* bien balancée, un
beau petit châssis, une jolie poupée;
voir aussi damaged. **2. it's the g.**,
c'est ce qu'il faut, ça tombe pile. **3. to
deliver the g.**, remplir ses engagements,
tenir parole. **4.** chose promise, chose
due. **5. to have the g.**, être capable.
6. preuves *f.pl.* de culpabilité; **to have
the g. on s.o.**, tenir le bon bout contre
qn. **7.** drogues* en général, stups *m.pl.*,
came *f. Voir aussi* sample (to).
good-time [ˈgudˈtaim] (*adj.*), *P:* **1.
g.-t. girl**, fille* rigolote (*ou* qui en prend
une bosse). **2. g.-t. Charley**, (joyeux)
viveur *m*, noceur *m*, bambocheur *m*.
goody [ˈgudi] (*noun*), *F: voir* goodies.
goody-goody[1] [ˈgudigudi] (*adj.*), *F:*
bien-pensant; d'une vertu suffisante;
to be g.-g., faire le saint, faire sa Sophie,
recevoir le bon Dieu sans confession.
goody-goody![2] [ˈgudiˈgudi] (*excl.*), *F:*
chic de chic!
goody-goody[3] [ˈgudigudi] (*noun*), *F:*
he's a little g.-g., c'est un petit saint (de
bois).
gooey [ˈguːi] (*adj.*), *F:* **1.** collant,
visqueux, poisseux. **2.** mièvre, à l'eau
de rose. *Cf.* goo.
goof[1] [guːf] (*noun*) (*mainly U.S.*). **1.** *F:*
individu bête*, couillon *m*, cavé *m*,
empoté *m*. **2.** *F:* fou *m*, timbré *m*. **3.**
F: homme*, mec *m*, type *m*. **4.** *P:*
drogué*, camé *m*, toxico *m*. **5.** *F:*
bévue*, boulette *f*, gaffe *f*, bourde *f*.
goof[2] [guːf] (**to**). **1.** *F:* gaffer, faire une
bourde (*ou* une boulette); *cf.* goof off
(to), **1. 2.** *F:* se trahir, se vendre, se
couper. **3.** *F:* rêvasser, être dans les
nuages. **4.** *F:* duper*, endormir, engourdir (qn). **5.** *P:* rater (*ou* louper)
une piquouse. **6.** *P:* se droguer*) se
camer; *cf.* goofed (up).
goof at [ˈguːfˈæt] (**to**), *P:* regarder*,
reluquer, mirer, mater.
goofball [ˈguːfbɔːl] (*noun*) (*mainly U.S.*),
P: **1.** = goof[1], **1. 2.** individu* bizarre,
drôle d'oiseau, drôle de paroissien. **3.**
barbiturique *m* (*drogues**), schnouff
m, balle *f* de copaille (*cf.* ball[1], **5**). **4.**

marijuana *f* (*drogues**), kif *m*. **5.** (*a*)
dose *f* de narcotique, boulette *f* de
narcs, un fade; (*b*) mélange *m* de
cocaïne et d'héroïne; panaché *m*;
(*c*) mélange *m* de barbituriques et
d'amphétamines. **6.** drogué*, camé *m*,
toxico *m*. **7.** calmant *m*, tranquillisant
m.
goofed (up) [ˈguːft(ˈʌp)] (*adj.*), *P:*
sous l'influence d'un narcotique ou d'un
barbiturique; bourré, chargé, défoncé;
cf. goof[2] (to), **6.** *Voir aussi* goof up (to).
goofer [ˈguːfər] (*noun*), *P:* qn qui prend
des pilules.
go-off [ˈgouˈɔf] (*noun*), *F:* **at the first
g.-o.**, au premier coup, au départ.
go off [ˈgouˈɔf] (**to**), **1.** *F:* détériorer,
s'abîmer, tourner. **2.** *F:* **to g. o. s.o.**,
ne plus aimer* qn, ne plus en pincer,
en revenir de qn. **3.** *F:* s'évanouir*,
perdre connaissance. **4.** *P:* avoir un
orgasme*, décharger, jouir. **5.** *F:* **how
did it g. o.?** comment cela a-t-il tourné?
comment cela s'est-il passé? *Voir aussi*
alarming; end, **5**; rails.
goof off [ˈguːfˈɔf] (**to**) (*U.S.*), *P:* **1.** faire
une bévue*, gaffer, mettre les pieds
dans le plat; *cf.* goof[2] (to), **1. 2.** traînasser, flemmarder, ne rien faire de ses
dix doigts.
goof up [ˈguːfˈʌp] (**to**) (*mainly U.S.*), *P:*
mal exécuter, rater, saboter, louper.
Voir aussi goofed (up).
goofy [ˈguːfi] (*adj.*) (*mainly U.S.*), *F:*
1. bête*, stupide, sot, gourde. **2. to be
g. over s.o.**, être toqué de qn; **to be g.
over sth.**, être enthousiasmé pour qch.,
être mordu pour qch.
goog [gug] (*noun*) (*Austr.*), *F:* **1.** œuf *m*.
2. individu bête*, ballot *m*.
goo-goo [ˈguːguː] (*adj.*), *F:* **to make g.
eyes at s.o.**, faire les yeux doux à qn.
gook[1] [guk] (*adj.*) (*mainly U.S.*), *P:* du
toc, de la camelote.
gook[2] [guk] (*noun*) (*mainly U.S.*), *P:*
1. saleté*, saloperie *f*, crasse *f*. **2.** sauce
ou assaisonnement visqueux; graille *f*.
3. moricaud *m*, café *m* au lait.
gooky [ˈguki] (*adj.*) (*mainly U.S.*), *P:*
gras, collant, poisseux.
gool(e)y [ˈguːli] (*noun*) (*pl.* goolies), *P:*
1. (*pl.*) testicules*, pendeloques *f.pl.*,
balloches *f.pl.* **2. to drop a g.**, faire une
gaffe, gaffer.
goon [guːn] (*noun*). **1.** *F:* individu

---

* An asterisk indicates that the word so marked is included as a head-word in the Appendix.

bête* et grotesque, clown *m*, cornichon *m*, enflé *m*. **2.** (*U.S.*) *P:* anti-gréviste *m*, jaune *m*, renard *m*. **3.** (*U.S.*) *P:* gorille *m*, cogneur *m*, casseur *m* de gueules. **4.** (*U.S.*) *P:* un(e) laissé(e) pour compte, un hotu.

go on [ˈgouˈɔn] (**to**), *F:* **1.** **that's enough to g. o.** **with** (*or* **to be going on with**), voilà du pain sur la planche, assez pour le quart d'heure. **2.** **I don't g. much o.** that, ça ne me chante pas, je ne suis pas d'accord. **3.** **g. o.!**, (*a*) dis toujours!; (*b*) **g. o.** (**with you**)! à d'autres! n'en jetez plus! **4.** discuter le bout de gras; **she does g. o.!** impossible de lui boucler la trappe!; **to g. o.** **and on** (**about sth.**), déblatérer (sur qch.). **5.** **to be going on for forty**, friser la quarantaine, aller sur ses quarante ans. **6.** **to be gone on s.o.**, aimer* qn, être entiché (*ou* pincé) de qn. **7.** = **go for** (**to**), 3.

goop [guːp] (*noun*) (*mainly U.S.*), *F:* **1.** = **goof**[1],1. **2.** bêtise*, foutaise *f*, connerie *f*.

goose[1] [guːs] (*noun*), *F:* **1.** individu bête*, oie *f*. **2.** **all his geese are swans**, tout ce qu'il fait tient du prodige. *Voir aussi* **cook**[2] (**to**), 3.

goose[2] [guːs] (**to**), *P:* **1.** mignoter, faire des papouilles (*ou* des pattes d'araignée) à (qn). **2.** pincer les fesses* à (qn). **3.** duper*, faisander, pigeonner, englander (qn).

gooseberry [ˈguzb(ə)ri] (*noun*). **1.** *F:* **to play g.**, faire le chaperon, tenir le chandelier. **2.** *P:* les fils barbelés, les barbelouses *f.pl.* **3.** *P:* corde *f* à linge.

goosegog [ˈguzgɔg] (*noun*) (=*gooseberry*), *P:* groseille verte (*ou* à maquereau).

gooser [ˈguːsər] (*noun*), *P:* pédéraste*, empapaouté *m*.

go out [ˈgoˈaut] (**to**), *F:* **to g. o.** **like a light**, s'évanouir*, tourner de l'œil, tomber dans les pommes.

go over [ˈgouˈouvər] (**to**), passer la rampe, faire son petit effet.

gope [goup] (**to**), *F:* regarder* fixement, zyeuter; béer, être bouche bée, bayer aux corneilles; **to g. at sth.**, regarder* qch. d'un air hébété.

gorblimey! [ˈgɔːˈblaimi] (*excl.*), *P:* zut de zut! sacré nom (de nom)!; *cf.* **blimey!**

gorgeous [ˈgɔːdʒəs] (*adj.*), *F:* excellent*, super(be), terrible, bath.

gorilla [gəˈrilə] (*noun*). **1.** *F:* brute *f*, gorille *m*. **2.** *P:* gangster *m*, tueur *m*, malfrat *m*. **3.** *P:* mille livres sterling; *cf.* **monkey**, 2.

gormless [ˈgɔːmlis] (*adj.*), *F:* bouché, gourde.

gosh! [gɔʃ] (*excl.*), *F:* (**by**) **g.!** mince! zut! bigre!

gospeller [ˈgɔspələr] (*noun*), *F:* **hot g.**, évangéliste outré, bigot *m* à tous crins.

go through [ˈgouˈθruː] (**to**). **1.** *F:* **he's gone through a lot**, il en a vu des vertes et des pas mûres. **2.** (*Austr.*) *P:* = **tommy** (**to**).

gotta [ˈgɔtə], *P:* **1.** (=*got to*) **when you've g. go you've g. go**, quand l'heure est venue il faut partir. **2.** (=*got a*) **you've g. lot to go through**, tu en verras des vertes et des pas mûres.

go up [ˈgouˈʌp] (**to**), *P:* s'envoyer en l'air, s'envoyer haut (*dû à la drogue*). *Voir aussi* **air**[1], 1.

gov [gʌv], **governor** [ˈgʌvnər], **the** (*noun*), *F:* **1.** le patron*, le singe; dirlot *m*. **2.** père*, le vieux, le paternel.

gow [gau] (*noun*), *P:* **1.** opium *m* (*drogues**), chandoo *m*. **2.** came *f*. **3.** cigarette* de marijuana, stick *m*, reefer *m*. **4.** le voyage (*expérience psychédélique*). **5.** = **cheesecake**. *Voir aussi* **hoosegow**.

gowed up [ˈgaudˈʌp] (*adj.*), *P:* **1.** drogué*, camé. **2.** survolté.

gowster [ˈgaustər] (*noun*), *P:* fumeur *m* de marijuana, amateur *m* de stick, pipeur *m*.

goy, Goy [gɔi] (*noun*), *F:* non-Juif *m*, Gentil *m*, goy(e) *m*.

grab[1] [græb] (*noun*), *P:* **1.** paye *f*, salaire *m*; **g. day**, jour *m* de paye, la Sainte-Touche. **2.** **up for grabs**, sur le marché, à vendre.

grab[2] [græb] (**to**). **1.** *P:* arrimer (qn, qch.). **2.** *F:* accrocher (qn), prendre (qn) aux entrailles. **3.** *F:* **how does that g. you?** qu'est-ce que tu en dis? **4.** *F:* **to g. a bite of sth. to eat**, avaler un casse-croûte (*ou* un morceau) (sur le pouce). **5.** *P:* arrêter*, agrafer, agriffer (qn).

grabber [ˈgræbər] (*noun*), *P:* **1.** qch. qui accroche. **2.** qn qui intéresse et stimule.

---

* L'astérisque indique que le mot marqué de ce signe figure comme entrée dans le Répertoire.

grade [greid] (*noun*), *F:* **to make the g.,** réussir, être à la hauteur.

graft [grɑ:ft] (*noun*). **1.** *F:* pot-de-vin *m*, graissage *m* de patte, gratte *f*, tour(s) *m* (*pl.*) de bâton. **2.** *F:* (**hard**) **g.**, travail*, boulot *m*, turbin *m*. **3.** *P:* logement* et nourriture*, pension *f*; **good g.,** bon gîte, bonne bouffe.

grafter [ˈgrɑ:ftər] (*noun*), *F:* **1.** tripoteur *m*, rapineur *m*, trafiquant *m*. **2.** politicien véreux, affairiste *m*, politicard *m*. **3.** bûcheur *m*, turbineur *m*, boulot *m*.

grand [grænd] (*noun*), *F:* (*a*) mille livres sterling; (*b*) (*U.S.*) mille dollars; un gros faf(f)iot.

grannie, granny [ˈgræni] (*noun*). **1.** *F:* grand-mère, mémé(e), mémère, bonnemaman. **2.** *P:* négoce légal qui couvre des activités condamnables; couvert *m*, couverture *f*, paravent *m*. **3.** *P:* **to strangle one's g.,** se masturber*, s'astiquer la colonne.

grapes [greips] (*pl. noun*), *P:* hémorroïdes *f.pl.*, grappillons *m.pl.*

grapevine [ˈgreipvain] (*noun*), *F:* renseignements* (de vive voix), téléphone *m* arabe.

grappler [ˈgræplər] (*noun*). **1.** *F:* lutteur *m*, catcheur *m*, tombeur *m*. **2.** (*pl.*) *P:* mains*, agrafes *f.pl.*, grappins *m.pl.*

grappling [ˈgræpliŋ] (*attrib. adj.*). **1.** *F:* **g. fan,** amateur *m* de lutte, fervent *m* du catch. **2.** *P:* **g. hooks = grapplers** (**grappler, 2**).

grass[1] [grɑ:s] (*noun*), *P:* **1. = grasser. 2.** (**dirt**) **g.,** marijuana *f* (*drogues**), thé vert. **3.** (*Austr.*) **to be on the g. = reign** (**to**).

grass[2] [grɑ:s] (**to**), *P:* cafarder, moutonner; **to g. on s.o.,** dénoncer* qn.

grasser [ˈgrɑ:sər] (*noun*), *P:* dénonciateur*, cafardeur *m*, mouton *m*, donneur *m*.

grasshopper [ˈgrɑ:shɔpər] (*noun*), *P:* **1.** (*a*) usager *m* de la marijuana; (*b*) habitué(e) de la marijuana; *cf.* **grass**[1], **2. 2.** (*R.S. = copper = policeman*) agent* de police, perdreau *m*. *Voir aussi* **knee-high.**

grassroots[1] [ˈgrɑ:sˈru:ts] (*adj.*), *F:* qui vient de la masse (*ou* d'en bas); **g. political movement,** mouvement *m* politique populaire; **g. democracy,** le populisme.

grassroots[2] [ˈgrɑ:sˈru:ts] (*pl. noun*), *F:*

1. région *f* agricole, la brousse. **2.** le gros (de la troupe), la masse, la base (d'un parti, d'une société, *etc.*). **3.** raisonnements *m.pl.* de grosse caisse. **4.** fondation *f*, source *f*, base *f*.

grass-widow [ˈgrɑ:sˈwidou] (*noun*), *F:* **1.** femme dont le mari est absent pendant un laps de temps. **2.** (*parfois*) femme séparée ou divorcée.

graveyard [ˈgreivjɑ:d] (*attrib. adj.*), *F:* **1. a g. cough,** une toux qui sent le sapin. **2. g. shift,** équipe *f* (de travailleurs) de nuit.

gravy [ˈgreivi] (*noun*), *P:* **1.** bénéfice*, butin*, bénef *m*, affure *f*, gratte *f*; **the g. train** (*or* **boat**), l'assiette *f* au beurre, bon filon; **to ride the g. train,** taper dans l'assiette au beurre. **2.** l'Atlantique *m*, la Grande Tasse. **3. to dish out the g. = to dish out the porridge** (*voir* **porridge**).

grease[1] [gri:s] (*noun*), *P:* **1.** (*a*) petit cadeau, glissage *m* de pièce, pommade *f*; (*b*) achat *m* de conscience, prix *m* du silence, amende *f*; *cf.* **palm-grease. 2. g. monkey,** garagiste *m*, mécanicien *m*, mécano *m*.

grease[2] [gri:s] (**to**). **1.** *P:* acheter, soudoyer; *voir aussi* **palm, 1. 2.** *F:* **like greased lightning,** (rapide) comme l'éclair.

greaser [ˈgri:sər] (*noun*), *P:* **1.** soudoyeur *m*, graisseur *m*, chien couchant. **2.** (*U.S.*) (*péj.*) Mexicain *m*, Sud-Américain *m*, café au lait.

greasie, greasy[1] [ˈgri:si] (*noun*), *P:* **= smarmer.**

greasy[2] [ˈgri:si, gri:zi] (*adj.*), *P:* **1.** flagorneur, lèche-bottes. **2. g. spoon,** bistrot *m*, gargote *f*.

great[1] [greit] (*adj.*), *F:* excellent*, terrible, du tonnerre; **it's g. to be alive,** c'est bon d'être au monde et d'y voir clair; **he's a g. guy,** (*a*) c'est un chic type; (*b*) c'est un type sensas(s); **he's g. at tennis,** il est fort(iche) au tennis. *Voir aussi* **gun**[1], **3, 4; shake**[1], **5.**

great[2] [greit] (*adv.*), *F:* **I feel g.,** je suis bien dans ma peau.

great[3] [greit] (*noun*), *F:* **he's one of the all-time greats,** il est un des grands de toujours (*ou* un des plus fameux de tous les temps).

greedy-guts [ˈgri:diɡʌts] (*noun*), *P:* goinfre*, glouton *m*, (béni-)bouftou(t) *m*.

greefa [ˈgriːfə] (*noun*), *P:* cigarette* de marijuana *f* (*drogues**), reefer *m*, stick *m*.

greefo [ˈgriːfou] (*noun*), *P:* marijuana *f* (*drogues**), kif *m*, herbe *f*.

Greek¹ [griːk] (*adj.*), *P:* the G. way, coït* anal, baisage *m* à la riche.

Greek² [griːk] (*noun*), *F:* it's all G. to me, c'est de l'hébreu, c'est du chinois.

Greek³ [griːk] (to), *P:* pratiquer le coït* anal, casser coco.

green¹ [griːn] (*adj.*). 1. *P:* g. mud (*or* ashes), opium *m* (*drogues**), dross *m*, boue verte. 2. *P:* g. and blacks, capsules *f.pl.* barbituriques, vert et noir. 3. *F:* to give s.o. the g. light, donner le feu vert à qn. 4. *F:* (*a*) novice, inexpérimenté; (*b*) crédule, naïf, béjaune, blanc-bec. 5. *F:* to have a g. thumb (*or* g. fingers), être un habile jardinier, avoir la main verte. *Voir aussi* dragon, 3.

green² [griːn] (*noun*), *F:* do you see any g. in my eye? tu ne m'as pas regardé? je ne suis pas né d'hier! *Voir aussi* greens.

green-ass [ˈgriːnæs] (*adj.*) (*U.S.*), *P:* = green¹, 4 (*a*), (*b*).

greenback [ˈgriːnbæk] (*noun*), *F:* (*a*) billet* d'une livre sterling; (*b*) billet* de banque américain.

greenie [ˈgriːni] (*noun*), *P:* 1. novice *m*, bleu *m*, blanc-bec *m*, serin *m*. 2. = green dragon (dragon, 3).

greens [griːnz] (*pl. noun*). 1. *F:* légumes verts. 2. *P:* to like one's g., être porté sur l'article (*ou* sur la bagatelle).

grefa [ˈgriːfə] (*noun*), *P:* = greefo.

gremlin [ˈgremlin] (*noun*), *F:* 1. lutin *m* de malheur, pépin *m*, eau *f* dans le gaz. 2. crampon *m*, casse-pieds *m*, enquiquineur *m*.

greta [ˈgriːtə] (*noun*), *P:* = greefo.

greybacks [ˈgrei-bæks] (*pl. noun*), *P:* poux*, grains *m.pl.* de blé, mies *f.pl.* de pain.

griddle¹ [ˈgridl] (*noun*), *P:* (*th.*) cabotin *m*, théâtreux *m*.

griddle² [ˈgridl] (to), *P:* faire du théâtre ambulant, cabotiner.

griff(in) [ˈgrif(in)] (*noun*), *F:* the g., renseignement* utile, bon tuyau, bon rencart; to get the g. on sth., être affranchi (*ou* mis à la page), s'être rencardé sur qch.

grift [grift] (to), *P:* escroquer*, empiler, estamper.

grifter [ˈgriftər] (*noun*), *P:* escroc*, estampeur *m*, empileur *m*.

grill¹ [gril] (*noun*), *F:* mixed g. = fruit-salad, 2.

grill² [gril] (to), *F:* to g. s.o., serrer les pouces *m.pl.* à qn (pour obtenir un aveu), cuisiner qn.

grilled [grild] (*adj.*) (*U.S.*), *P:* ivre*, noir, noiricot.

grim [grim] (*adj.*), *F:* mauvais*, désagréable, de mauvais augure; things look g., ça la fout mal, ça s'annonce mal. *Voir aussi* hang on (to), 2.

grind¹ [graind] (*noun*). 1. *F:* travail* dur et monotone; the daily g., la routine, le train-train quotidien, le métro-boulot-dodo; to go back to the old g., reprendre le collier, se remettre au turbin. 2. *F:* (*a*) course *f* difficile; (*b*) steeple *m*. 3. *P:* coït*, fouraillage *m*, dérouillade *f*.

grind² [graind] (to). 1. *F:* travailler* dur; trimer, bûcher, bosser. 2. *P:* coïter*, fourailler, dérouiller. *Voir aussi* axe¹, 3.

grinder [ˈgraindər] (*noun*), *F:* 1. to put s.o. through the g., faire passer un mauvais quart d'heure à qn. 2. (*pl.*) dents*, croquantes *f.pl.*, piloches *f.pl.*

grip¹ [grip] (*noun*). 1. to get a g. on oneself, (*a*) *F:* se contenir, se retenir, se contrôler; (*b*) *V:* = grip² (to). 2. *F:* to lose one's g., perdre la tête (*ou* les pédales *f.pl.*), déménager.

grip² [grip] (to), *V:* se masturber*, se taper la colonne, se pogner.

gripe¹ [graip] (*noun*), *F:* 1. plainte *f*, rouspétance *f*; to have the gripes, (*a*) = gripe² (to), 1; (*b*) avoir la diarrhée* (*ou* la courante). 2. geignard *m*, râleur *m*, bâton merdeux.

gripe² [graip] (to), *F:* 1. grogner*, rouspéter, ronchonner, râler. 2. ennuyer*, tourmenter, barber, raser (qn).

griper [ˈgraipər] (*noun*), *F:* râleur *m*, rouspéteur *m*.

grit [grit] (*noun*), *F:* cran *m*, battant *m* ; *cf.* sand.

gritty [ˈgriti] (*adj.*), *F:* qui est brave*, qui a du cran, qui a qch. dans le ventre.

grizzle [ˈgrizl] (to), *F:* 1. pleurnicher, geindre. 2. grogner*, rouspéter.

---

grizzleguts ['grizlgʌts], **grizzler** ['grizlər] (*noun*), *F:* 1. pleurnicheur *m*, chialeur *m*. 2. geignard *m*, chignard *m*.

groaty ['grouti] (*adj.*), *F:* = **grotty**, 1.

groggy ['grɔgi] (*adj.*), *F:* 1. un peu malade*, patraque, mal fichu. 2. (*boxe*) groggy, sonné. 3. ivre*, paf, éméché, parti. 4. **a g. old table**, une vieille table bancale.

groin [grɔin] (*noun*), *P:* bande* noire de parieurs sur un champ de courses.

grooby ['gru:bi] (*adj.*), *F:* = **groovy**.

groove [gru:v] (*noun*), *F:* 1. spécialité *f*, dada *m*, rayon *m*; **that's my g.**, ça, c'est mon blot. 2. **it's a g.**, c'est chic. 3. **in the g.**, en pleine forme, en plein boum; (*jazz*) (orchestre) donnant son plein, faisant des étincelles. 4. **to get into a g.**, s'encroûter, être dans l'ornière, s'enroutiner.

groovy ['gru:vi] (*adj.*), *F:* excellent*, bath, en bon ordre.

grope [group] (**to**), *P:* (*a*) = **feel**[2] (**to**), 1; (*b*) palper les «parties» de qn sous ses vêtements.

grotty ['grɔti] (*adj.*), *F:* 1. laid*, moche, tocard, tarte. 2. outré et inutile.

grouch[1] [grautʃ] (*noun*), *F:* 1. ronchonnage *m*, rouspétance *f*. 2. râleur *m*, ronchonneur *m*.

grouch[2] [grautʃ] (**to**), *F:* grogner*, râler, ronchonner.

groucher ['grautʃər] (*noun*), *F:* = **grouch**[1], 2.

ground [graund] (*noun*), *F:* 1. **to run s.o. into the g.**, débiner, démolir qn. 2. **that suits me down to the g.**, cela me convient parfaitement, ça me botte, ça fait mon affaire. 3. **to get** (**a scheme**, *etc.*) **off the g.**, faire démarrer (un projet, *etc.*); **it'll never get off the g.**, cela ne verra jamais le jour, cela ne démarrera jamais. *Voir aussi* **stamping-ground**.

groupie ['gru:pi] (*noun*). 1. *F:* fervente des pop-groups, groupette *f*. 2. *P:* fille* qui fait l'amour en groupe, groupe-sexuelle.

grouse[1] [graus] (*noun*), *F:* 1. grogne(rie) *f*, bougonnement *m*. 2. rouscailleur *m*, marronneur *m*.

grouse[2] [graus] (**to**), *F:* grogner*, marronner, rouscailler.

grouser ['grausər] (*noun*), *F:* = **grouse**[1], 2.

grub [grʌb] (*noun*), *P:* 1. nourriture*,

boustifaille *f*, mangeaille *f*; g. **up!** la bouffe! la soupe! 2. enfant sale*, petite vermine, petit morveux.

grubby ['grʌbi] (*adj.*), *F:* sale*, pouilleux, cracra, crado; g. **hands**, mains douteuses.

gruel ['gru:əl] (*noun*), *F:* 1. réprimande *f*, attrapade *f*, engueulade *f*, trempe *f*. 2. **to give s.o. his g.**, (*a*) battre* qn (comme plâtre); (*b*) éreinter, échiner qn. 3. **to take** (*or* get) **one's g.**, avaler sa médecine, encaisser.

gruelling ['gru:əliŋ] (*noun*), *F:* (*a*) passage *m* à tabac, dérouillée *f*, raclée *f*; (*b*) épreuve éreintante.

Grundy ['grʌndi] (*pr. noun*), *F:* **not to care about Mrs. G., not to care what Mrs. G. says**, se moquer du qu'en-dira-t-on.

grunt-and-groan ['grʌntən(d)'groun] (*noun*), *F:* la lutte, le catch.

grunt-and-groaner ['grʌntən(d)'grounər] (*noun*), *F:* lutteur *m*.

grunter ['grʌntər] (*noun*), *F:* porc *m*.

G-string ['dʒi:-striŋ] (*noun*), *F:* cache-sexe *m*, feuille *f* de vigne, cache-fri-fri *m*, cache-truc *m*.

gubbins ['gʌbinz] (*noun*), *F:* 1. nourriture*, becquetance *f*. 2. gadget *m*, bidule *m*, truc *m*, machin *m*. 3. = **muggins**.

guess [ges] (**to**) (*mainly U.S.*), *F:* croire, penser; **I g. that...**, il y a des chances pour que...; **you're right, I g.**, oui, il me semble que vous avez raison.

guesstimate[1] ['gestimət] (*noun*), *F:* conjecture *f*, estimation bien pesée.

guesstimate[2] ['gestimeit] (**to**), *F:* estimer, évaluer soigneusement.

guest [gest] (*noun*), *F:* **be my g.!** c'est à vous! prends! emporte!

guff [gʌf] (*noun*), *F:* bêtise*, blague *f*, foutaise *f*.

guide [gaid] (*noun*), *P:* drogué* endurci qui entraîne les autres, guide *m* de neufs.

guinea ['gini] (*noun*), *F:* **it's a g. a minute**, c'est très amusant*, c'est impayable.

guiver[1] ['gaivər] (*noun*) (*Austr.*), *F:* baratin *m*; **to sling the g.** = **guiver**[2] (**to**).

guiver[2] ['gaivər] (**to**) (*Austr.*), *F:* baratiner, faire du baratin.

gum [gʌm] (*noun*), *F:* **by g.!** mince alors! *Voir aussi* **gum-tree**.

---

* An asterisk indicates that the word so marked is included as a head-word in the Appendix.

gump [gʌmp] (*noun*), *F:* individu bête*, nouille *f*, oie *f*.

gumption [ˈgʌm(p)ʃ(ə)n] (*noun*), *F:* débrouillardise *f*, entregent *m*; **to have g.**, avoir de la jugeot(t)e; **he's got plenty of g.**, c'est un débrouillard.

gumshoe [ˈgʌmʃuː] (*noun*) (*U.S.*), *F:* agent* de police habillé en civil, poulet *m*, ham(bourgeois) *m*, condé *m*.

gum-tree [ˈgʌmtriː] (*noun*), *F:* **up a g.-t.**, dans une impasse, dans le pétrin, dans de beaux draps.

gum up [ˈgʌmˈʌp] (**to**), *F:* **to g. u. the works**, encrasser les rouages, mettre des bâtons dans les roues.

gun[1] [gʌn] (*noun*). **1.** *P:* seringue *f* hypodermique, poussette *f*, lance *f*. **2.** *F:* **to jump the g.**, brûler le feu, marcher avant les violons. **3.** *F:* **to go great guns**, prospérer, faire boum. **4.** *F:* **to blow great guns**, (*du vent*) souffler en tempête (*ou* à décorner les bœufs*). **5.** *F:* **to stick to one's guns**, soutenir son opinion, s'accrocher, tenir bon, ne pas en démordre. **6.** (*U.S.*) *P:* (*a*) voleur*, caroubleur *m*, casseur *m*; voleur *m* à la tire; (*b*) bandit *m*, gangster *m*, malfrat *m*, porte-flingue *m*. **7.** *F:* **to give sth. the g.**, accélérer qch., mettre les gaz, mettre la gomme. **8.** *P:* **to get behind the g.**, risquer la prison* (*ou* la taule). *Voir aussi* **big**[1], **1**; **burp-gun**; **spike**[2] (**to**), **3**.

gun[2] [gʌn] (**to**), *F:* **to be (out) gunning for s.o.**, pourchasser qn pour se venger de lui, aller à la rebiffe.

gun down [ˈgʌnˈdaun] (**to**), *F:* fusiller, flinguer, descendre (qn).

gunge [gʌndʒ] (*noun*), *F:* saleté*, saloperie *f*, crotaille *f*.

gunji [ˈgʌndʒi], **gunny** [ˈgʌni] (*noun*), *P:* marijuana *f* (*drogues*), kif *m*; *cf.* **ganjah**.

gunsel [ˈgʌnzl] (*noun*) (*U.S.*), *P:* **1.** gangster *m*, malfrat *m*, dur *m*, poisse *m*. **2.** faux jeton, faux frère, bordille *f*. **3.** mignon *m*, giton *m*, lopette *f*. **4.** blanc-bec *m*, béjaune *m*, dadais *m*.

gunslinger [ˈgʌn-slinər] (*noun*), *F:* vaurien* armé, porte-flingue *m*.

gup [gʌp] (*noun*), *P:* potin *m*, ragots *m.pl.*, foutaise *f*, cancans *m.pl.*

gurk [gəːk] (**to**), *P:* roter, avoir une fuite de gaz.

gussie [ˈgʌsi] (*noun*) (*Austr.*), *P:* pédéraste*, lopaille *f*.

gut [gʌt] (*noun*), *P:* **to bust a g. to do sth.**, se sortir les tripes pour faire qch. *Voir aussi* **guts**; **rot-gut**.

gutful [ˈgʌtful] (*noun*), *P:* (*a*) ventrée *f*, gavée *f*; (*b*) **to have (had) a g.**, en avoir ras le bol, en avoir son compte; *cf.* **bellyful**.

gutless [ˈgʌtlis] (*adj.*), *P:* **to be g.**, être poltron, ne rien avoir dans le bide; **a g. character**, un type mou, un trouillard, une lavette.

gut-rot [ˈgʌt-rɔt] (*noun*), *F:* = **rot-gut**.

guts [gʌts] (*pl. noun*). **1.** *F:* **to have g.**, être brave*, avoir du cran (*ou* de l'estomac), en avoir dans le bide; **to lose one's g.**, perdre courage, avoir les foies *m.pl.*, ne pas en avoir dans le bidon. **2.** *P:* **to hate s.o.'s g.**, détester* qn, avoir qn dans le nez, ne pas pouvoir blairer qn. **3.** *V:* **to drop one's g.**, péter*, en lâcher un, vesser. **4.** *P:* **to knife s.o. in the g.**, éventrer qn, mettre les tripes à l'air à qn, crever la paillasse à qn. **5.** *P:* **put some g. into it!** mets-en un (bon) coup! magne-toi le train! dépêche! **6.** *P:* **to sweat one's g. out**, travailler* dur, en foutre un coup, se casser les reins, pisser du sang. **7.** *P:* **to heave** (*or* **spew**) **one's g. up**, vomir*, dégoupillonner. **8.** (*Austr.*) *P:* **to hold one's g.**, se taire*, poser sa chique. **9.** (*Austr.*) *P:* **to spill one's g.**, avouer*, vider son sac. **10.** *P:* **I'll have your g. for garters!** j'aurai ta peau! je me ferai un porte-monnaie avec tes couilles! **11.** *P:* du charnu, de l'étoffe *f*, de la substance. **12.** *P:* engrenages *m.pl.*, rouages *m.pl.*, boyaux *m.pl.*, entrailles *f.pl.* **13.** *P:* = **greedy-guts**. *Voir aussi* **cleverguts**; **grizzleguts**; **gut**; **worryguts**.

guts-ache [ˈgʌts-eik] (*noun*), *P:* **1.** mal *m* au ventre*. **2.** casse-pieds *m*, casse-burettes *m*.

gut-scraper [ˈgʌt-skreipər] (*noun*), *P:* racleur *m* de cordes, joueur *m* de crincrin.

gutsy [ˈgʌtsi] (*adj.*), *P:* **1.** percutant, qui a du cran (*ou* des entrailles *f.pl.*). **2.** goinfre*, goulu. **3.** passionné, jouisseur.

gutter [ˈgʌtər] (*noun*), *F:* **to be in the g.**, être dans la pauvreté* (*ou* dans le ruisseau *ou* sur la paille).

gutty [ˈgʌti] (*adj.*), *P:* **1.** qui prend aux entrailles (*ou* aux tripes), qui empoigne.

---

* L'astérisque indique que le mot marqué de ce signe figure comme entrée dans le Répertoire.

2. fondamental, substantiel, qui vient du tréfonds. 3. bolide, puissant.

gutzer [ˈgʌtsər] (*noun*) (*Austr.*), *P:* to come a g. = to come a cropper (cropper (*a*)).

guv [gʌv], **guv'nor** [ˈgʌvnər], the (*noun*), *F:* = gov, governor, the.

guy[1] [gai] (*noun*). 1. *F:* homme*, type *m*, loustic *m*, zigoto *m*; **a wise g.**, (*a*) un crâneur, un je-sais-tout; (*b*) un roublard, un mariol(e). 2. *P:* to do a g., (*a*) = **slope off** (**to**); (*b*) donner un faux nom*, filer le faux blaze (*ou* le faublas). *Voir aussi* **fall-guy; great**[1]; **right**, 3; **tough**[1], 1.

guy[2] [gai] (**to**), *P:* = to do a guy (**guy**[1], 2 (*a*)).

guzunder [gəˈzʌndər] (*noun*), *F:* pot *m* de chambre, Jules *m*, Thomas *m*, Colin *m*.

gyp[1] [dʒip] (*noun*). 1. *F:* domestique dans un collège, larbin *m*. 2. *F:* = **gip**, 1, 2. 3. (*U.S.*) *P:* escroc*, filou *m*, carotteur *m*. 4. (*U.S.*) *P:* escroquerie*, tromperie *f*, arnaque *f*, carottage *m*. 5. *P:* **g. joint** = **clip-joint.**

gyp[2] [dʒip] (**to**) (*U.S.*), *P:* **to g. s.o.**, (*a*) escroquer* qn, tirer une carotte à qn, estamper qn, empiler qn; (*b*) écorcher qn; **to be gypped**, être pigeonné.

gyve [dʒaiv] (*noun*), *P:* cigarette* de marijuana (*drogues**), stick *m*, reefer *m*.

---

* An asterisk indicates that the word so marked is included as a head-word in the Appendix.

H

H [eitʃ] (*abbr.* = *heroin*), *P:* héroïne *f* (*drogues**), H *f*.

habit [ˈhæbit] (*noun*). **1.** *F:* usage *m* des drogues; **to kick the h.**, se décamer, lâcher le pied; **off the h.**, décamé, désintoxiqué. **2.** *P:* dose habituelle de drogues.

hack around [ˈhækəˈraʊnd] (**to**), *F:* flâner, flânocher.

hack down [ˈhækˈdaʊn] (**to**), *F:* assaillir, faire des crocs-en-jambe *m.pl.* à (qn).

hacked (off) [ˈhækt(ˈɔf)] (*adj.*), *P:* **1.** en colère*, à cran. **2.** qui en a assez*, qui en a soupé.

haddock [ˈhædək] (*noun*), *F:* **limp h.**, main* molle et flasque.

hair [hɛər] (*noun*). **1.** *F:* **to get in s.o.'s h.**, irriter qn, taper sur les nerfs à qn. **2.** *F:* **to let one's h. down**, se laisser aller, ne pas faire de chichis. **3.** *P:* **keep your h. on!** calme-toi! ne t'emballe pas! **4.** *F:* **to split hairs**, couper les cheveux en quatre. **5.** *F:* **get some h. on your chest!** conduis-toi en homme! sors de tes langes! **6.** *P:* **to have s.o. by the short hairs** = **to have s.o. by the short and curlies** (**curly**, **2**). *Voir aussi* **dog**[1], **4**; **long-hair**[2].

hairburger [ˈhɛəbə:gər] (*noun*) (*U.S.*), *VV:* vagin*, barbu *m*.

haircut [ˈhɛəkʌt] (*noun*), *P:* courte période en prison*.

hair-do [ˈhɛədu:] (*noun*), *F:* **I'm going to have a h.-d.**, je vais me faire coiffer.

hairpie [ˈhɛəˈpai] (*noun*) (*U.S.*), *VV:* = **hairburger**.

hairy [ˈhɛəri] (*adj.*), *P:* **1.** périlleux, épineux, provocateur. **2.** vieux*, passé, rengaine. **3.** piètre, miteux, moche.

half[1] [hɑ:f] (*adv.*), *F:* **1.** **not h.!** et comment! tu peux y aller! tu parles! **2.** **she didn't h. laugh**, elle s'est bien tordue de rire. **3.** **you won't h. catch it!** qu'est-ce que tu vas prendre! **4.** **he hasn't h. changed**, il a drôlement décollé. **5.** (*a*) **h. and h.**, moitié-moitié; (*b*) **to go h. and h.**, faire (*ou* marcher)

afanaf; *voir aussi* **fifty-fifty**; **half**[2]. **6.** **to be only h. there**, être un peu fou*, être toqué. *Voir aussi* **shift**[2] (**to**), **1**.

half[2] [hɑ:f] (*noun*), *F:* **h. and h.**, panaché *m* de bière brune et blonde. *Voir aussi* **better**; **half**[1], **5**.

half-a-crown [ˈhɑ:fəˈkraun] (*noun*), *F:* *voir* **bingo** (**26**).

half-assed [ˈhæfˈæst] (*adj.*) (*U.S.*), *V:* **1.** margoulin, sabreur, sabot. **2.** mal fait, torché, bousillé.

half-baked [ˈhɑ:fˈbeikt] (*adj.*), *F:* **1.** inexpérimenté, blanc-bec. **2.** bête*, niais, bêta.

half-brass [ˈhɑ:fˈbrɑ:s] (*noun*), *P:* femme facile qui ne fait pas payer ses faveurs; *cf.* **brass**[2], **4**.

half-cock [ˈhɑ:fˈkɔk] (*noun*), *F:* **to go off at h.-c.**, mal partir, mal démarrer.

half-cut [ˈhɑ:fˈkʌt] (*adj.*), *P:* légèrement ivre*, gris; *cf.* **cut**[1], **1**.

half-inch [ˈhɑ:fˈintʃ] (**to**) (*R.S.* = *pinch* = *steal*), *P:* voler*, chiper, chaparder.

half-iron [ˈhɑ:fˈaiən] (*noun*), *P:* qn qui fréquente les homosexuels sans en être; *cf.* **iron hoof** (**hoof**[1], **2**).

half-pint [ˈhɑ:fˈpaint], **half-portion** [ˈhɑ:fˈpɔ:ʃən] (*noun*), *F:* petit* individu, personne insignifiante, demi-portion *f*.

half-screwed [ˈhɑ:fˈskru:d], **-seasover** [-ˈsi:zˈouvər], **-shaved** [-ˈʃeivd], **-shot** [-ˈʃɔt], **-slewed** [-ˈslu:d], **-snaped** [-ˈsneipt], **-sprung** [-ˈsprʌŋ] (*adj.*), *P:* légèrement ivre*, paf.

half-squarie [ˈhɑ:fˈskwɛəri] (*noun*) (*Austr.*), *P:* fille* *ou* jeune femme* de petite vertu, Marie-couche-toi-là *f*.

half-stewed [ˈhɑ:fˈstju:d], **-under** [-ˈʌndər] (*adj.*), *P:* = **half-screwed**.

half-way [ˈhɑ:fˈwei] (*adv.*), *F:* **1.** **to meet s.o. h.-w.**, couper la poire en deux. **2.** *voir* **bingo** (**45**).

halls [hɔ:lz] (*pl. noun*), *F:* **the h.**, théâtres *m.pl.* vaudeville.

halvers [ˈhɑ:vəz], **halvo(e)s** [ˈhɑ:vouz] (*adv.*), *F:* **to go h.**, y aller moitié-

---

moitié.

ham¹ [hæm] (adj.), F: 1. amateur. 2. inférieur, de basse qualité; **h. joint**, gargote f.

ham² [hæm] (noun), F: 1. **pure h.**, (th.) pièce pleine de clichés et d'emphase; cagnade f. 2. acteur amateur. 3. mauvais acteur, cabotin m, crabe m. 4. radio-téléphoniste amateur.

ham³ [hæm] (to), F: 1. (th.) mal jouer un rôle, cabotiner. 2. déclamer, jouer pour la galerie.

ham-fisted ['hæm'fistid], **ham-handed** ['hæm'hændid] (adj.), F: maladroit, empoté, lourdaud, balourd.

hammer ['hæmər] (to). 1. F: (Bourse) déclarer (un agent) en défaut (ou défaillant). 2. F: **to h. s.o. into the ground**, vaincre qn, battre qn à plate(s) couture(s), tailler qn en pièces. 3. P: **to h. (and nail)** (R.S. = trail), traîner, suivre.

hammering ['hæməriŋ] (noun), F: 1. volée f de coups*. 2. (sports) défaite f, raclée f.

hammocks ['hæməks] (pl. noun), P: seins* opulents, balcons m.pl.

hammy ['hæmi] (adj.), F: outré, chargé, exagéré.

Hampton ['hæmptən] (noun) (= Hampton Wick, R.S. = prick), V: pénis*; **it gets on my H.**, ça me tape sur les couilles; cf. wick, 1, 2.

hand¹ [hænd] (noun), F: 1. **to keep one's h. in**, conserver le pied à l'étrier. 2. **to make money h. over fist**, gagner* beaucoup d'argent*, remuer (ou ramasser) du fric à la pelle, faire des affaires d'or. Voir aussi big¹, 7; dab¹.

hand² [hænd] (to). 1. F: **you've got to h. it to him!** devant lui, chapeau! 2. P: **don't h. me that!** ne me raconte pas cela! ne me fais pas accroire cela! Voir aussi sweet¹, 3.

handful ['hændful] (noun). 1. P: condamnation* à cinq ans* de prison*, cinq longes f.pl. de taule. 2. P: cinq livres sterling; **a couple of handfuls**, dix livres sterling. 3. F: **to be a h.**, donner du fil à retordre, être une teigne.

hand-job ['hænd-dʒɔb] (noun), V: **to give s.o. a h.-j.**, masturber* qn, pogner qn.

handle ['hændl] (noun), F: 1. **to fly off the h.**, se mettre en colère*, sortir de

ses gonds. 2. **to have a h.**, avoir un titre, avoir un nom à charnière. 3. nom* de famille, prénom m, surnom m, blaze m.

handlebar ['hændlbɑ:r] (attrib. adj.), F: **h. moustache**, moustache* à la gauloise, bacchantes f.pl. en guidon.

hand-me-downs ['hændmidaunz] (pl. noun), F: vêtements* usagés ou bon marché; frusques f.pl.; décrochez-moi-ça m; cf. reach-me-downs.

hand-out ['hændaut] (noun), F: 1. prospectus m, circulaire m publicitaire. 2. aumône f, charité f.

handshake ['hændʃeik] (noun), F: **golden h.**, cadeau m d'adieu, indemnité f de départ.

handsome ['hænsəm] (adv.), F: **to come down h.**, être généreux, être large.

hang¹ [hæŋ] (noun), F: 1. **to get the h. of sth.**, saisir le truc pour faire qch.; **when you've got the h. of things**, quand vous serez au courant. 2. **I don't give a h.**, je m'en moque, je m'en fiche, je m'en fous; **it's not worth a h.**, cela ne vaut pas tripette.

hang² [hæŋ] (to), F: **h. it!** flûte! mince alors!; **h. the expense!** = blow the expense! (blow (to), 1). Voir aussi hung.

hang about (or **around**) ['hænə'baut, 'hænə'raund] (to), F: 1. flâner, flânocher, rôdailler; **to keep s.o. hanging a.**, faire (ou laisser) poireauter qn. 2. **to h. a. s.o.**, fréquenter qn, se coller à qn.

hanger-on ['hænər'ɔn] (pl. hangers-on) (noun), F: 1. dépendant m, parasite m. 2. crampon m, pique-assiette m.

hang on ['hæŋ'ɔn] (to). 1. F: (a) attendre*; **h. o.!** une seconde! un moment!; (b) poireauter. 2. F: **to h. o. like grim death**, s'agrafer, se cramponner, s'accrocher. 3. F: tenir bon. 4. (U.S.) P: **to h. one o.**, s'enivrer, se piquer le nez.

hang-out ['hæŋaut] (noun), F: 1. logement*, chez-soi m. 2. rendez-vous*, lieu m de réunion; repaire m de gangsters.

hang out ['hæŋ'aut] (to), F: 1. **to h. o. for sth.**, réclamer, contester qch. 2. habiter*, crécher, nicher; **where do you h. o.?** où perchez-vous?

hangover ['hæŋouvər] (noun), F: **to have a h.**, avoir la gueule de bois, avoir mal aux cheveux.

hang-up ['hæŋʌp] (noun), F: 1. ennui

---

* An asterisk indicates that the word so marked is included as a head-word in the Appendix.

mental, trouble *m* psychique. **2**. dada *m*, combine *f*. **3**. embêtement *m*, enquiquinement *m*, scie *f*.

hang up [ˈhæŋˈʌp] (**to**), *F:* **1**. (*téléphone*) raccrocher (l'appareil). **2**. **he wants to h. u. his hat**, il a envie de se marier. **3**. **to h. s.o. u. = to stand s.o. up**. *Voir aussi* **hung up**.

hankie, hanky [ˈhæŋki] (*noun*) (= *handkerchief*), *F:* mouchoir*, blave *m*.

hanky-panky [ˈhæŋkiˈpæŋki] (*noun*), *F:* **1**. supercherie *f*, tour *m* de passe-passe, coup fourré. **2**. (*a*) adultère*, carambolage *m* en douce; (*b*) flirt *m*. **3**. manigance *f*.

happen[1] [ˈhæp(ə)n] (*adv*.), *F:* peut-être; **h. he will, h. he won't**, peut-être bien que oui, peut-être bien que non.

happen[2] [ˈhæp(ə)n] (**to**), *F:* **it's all happening**, tout est en marche, tout roule.

happen along [ˈhæp(ə)nəˈlɔŋ] (**to**), *F:* arriver* au hasard, entrer en passant.

happenings [ˈhæp(ə)niŋz] (*pl. noun*), *F:* drogues*, narcotiques *m.pl.*, came *f*.

happenstance [ˈhæp(ə)nstæns] (*noun*) (*U.S.*), *F:* événement fortuit.

happy [ˈhæpi] (*adj*.), *F:* **1**. légèrement ivre*, paf. **2**. **h. days!** à la bonne vôtre! *Voir aussi* **bar-happy; dust**[1], **2** (*a*); **shag-happy; slap-happy; trigger-happy**.

hard[1] [hɑːd] (*adj*.). **1**. *F:* **a drop of the h. stuff**, une goutte d'alcool*, un petit coup de gnôle. **2**. *F:* **h. drugs**, drogues toxiques majeures (opiacés et cocaïne); *cf.* **soft**[1], **4**. **3**. *F:* **h. lines**, malchance*, guigne *f*, poisse *f*; *cf.* **cheese**, **3**. **4**. *F:* **h. tack**, biscuits *m.pl.* de marin. **5**. *F:* **h. sell**, battage *m* publicitaire, vente *f* au sabot; *cf.* **soft**[1], **5**. **6**. *F:* **to play h. to get**, faire la difficile, faire la Sainte-Nitouche. **7**. *P:* excellent*, super. *Voir aussi* **hat**, **6**.

hard[2] [hɑːd] (*noun*). **1**. *P:* (=*hard labour*) travaux forcés; **fifteen years' h.**, quinze longes *f.pl.* des durs. **2**. *V:* = **hard-on**.

hard-baked [ˈhɑːdˈbeikt] (*adj*.), *F:* endurci, dur(aille).

hard-bitten [ˈhɑːdˈbitn] (*adj*.), *F:* = **hard-boiled**, **2**.

hard-boiled [ˈhɑːdˈbɔild] (*adj*.), *F:* **1**. malin*, coriace; **a h.-b. businessman**,

un homme d'affaires consommé. **2**. dur (à cuire). **3**. peu susceptible.

hard-liner [ˈhɑːdˈlainər] (*noun*), *F:* **1**. intransigeant *m* (en politique), dur *m* (d'un parti). **2**. toxicomane majeur (opium et dérivés).

hard-on [ˈhɑːdɔn] (*noun*), *V:* **to have a h.-o.**, être en érection*, bander.

hard up [ˈhɑːdˈʌp] (*adj*.), *F:* pauvre*, dans la gêne, dans la dèche, fauché; **to be h. u.**, tirer le diable par la queue.

hardware [ˈhɑːdweər] (*noun*), *F:* armes *f.pl.*, outils *m.pl.*

hare[1] [hɛər] (*noun*), *F:* **1**. plan *m ou* projet *m* impraticable. **2**. **to raise a h.**, donner un nouveau tour à la discussion.

hare[2] (**off**) [ˈhɛərˈɔf] (**to**), *F:* s'enfuir*, se sauver à toutes jambes; **to h. back home**, regagner la maison à toutes jambes.

Harley [ˈhɑːli] (*noun*), *P:* **a H.**, un club.

harnessed [ˈhɑːnist] (*adj. & p.p.*), *F:* **to get h.**, se marier, sauter le fossé.

harp[1] [hɑːp] (*noun*), *F:* un Irlandais. *Voir aussi* **jew's-harp**.

harp[2] [hɑːp] (**to**), *F:* **he's always harping on the same string**, il récite toujours la même litanie; il rabâche toujours la même chose.

Harry [ˈhæri] (*pr. noun*). **1**. *F:* **old H.**, le diable; **it's giving me old H.**, cela me fait un mal du diable. **2**. *F:* **to play old H. with s.o.**, engueuler, enguirlander qn. **3**. *P:* **H. preggers = preggers**, *q.v.*; **H. blinders = blinders; H. bonkers = bonkers**, *etc*. *Voir aussi* **flash**[1], **1**; **Tom**, **1**.

has-been [ˈhæzbiːn] (*noun*), *F:* **1**. individu* vieux-jeu; vieux ramolli; **he's a h.-b.**, il est déchu (*ou* démodé); **it's better to be a h.-b. than a never-was**, il vaut mieux ne plus être que n'avoir jamais été. **2**. chose périmée (ayant perdu son utilité).

hash[1] [hæʃ] (*adj*.), *P:* formid(able), super, cool.

hash[2] [hæʃ] (*noun*), *F:* **1**. nourriture*, boustifaille *f*, bectance *f*. **2**. (*U.S.*) nouvelles *f.pl.*, potins *m.pl.*, cancans *m.pl.* **3**. hachisch *m* (*drogues**). **4**. pagaille *f*, embrouillamini *m*, gâchis *m*; **to make a h. of it**, bousiller l'affaire. **5**. du rebattu, du rabâché. **6**. **to settle s.o.'s h.**, (*a*) régler son compte à qn; (*b*) rabattre le caquet à qn.

---

* L'astérisque indique que le mot marqué de ce signe figure comme entrée dans le Répertoire.

hash³ [¹hæʃ] (to), F: gâcher, bousiller, bâcler.

hashery [¹hæʃəri], hash-house [¹hæʃ-haus] (noun), F: gargote f.

hash over [¹hæʃ¹ouvər] (to) (U.S.), F: discuter, ramener, rabâcher.

hash-slinger [¹hæʃsliŋər] (noun), F: 1. mauvaise cuisinière, Marie-graillon f. 2. serveur m de gargote, loufiat m. 3. marmiton m, coq m, gargot m.

hash-up [¹hæʃʌp] (noun), F: réchauffé m, ripopée f (de vieux contes, etc.).

hash up [¹hæʃ¹ʌp] (to), F: =hash³ (to).

hassle¹ [¹hæsl] (noun) (U.S.), F: querelle*, bagarre*, barabille f.

hassle² [¹hæsl] (to) (U.S.), F: 1. se quereller, se battre*, se bagarrer. 2. se tracasser*, se faire de la bile.

hat [hæt] (noun), F: 1. old h., vieux jeu; that's old h., c'est du déjà vu, c'est vieux comme le monde. 2. to talk through one's h., parler* à tort et à travers, radoter. 3. to keep it under one's h., tenir qch. en secret (ou sous cape), garder qch. pour soi. 4. to pass the h. round, faire la quête. 5. my h.! mince alors! mes aïeux! 6. hard h., turbineur m de la brique, boulot m de la duraille; the hard hats, les gens du bâtiment. 7. high h., cymbale f. Voir aussi bowler-hat¹; brass-hat; cocked; drop¹, 2.

hatch [hætʃ] (noun), F: down the h.! à la vôtre!; to put one down the h., en mettre un à l'abri de la pluie. Voir aussi booby-hatch.

hatchet [¹hætʃit] (noun), F: 1. to bury the h., se réconcilier, se rabibocher. 2. h. man, (a) bandit m, gangster m; (b) militant m, dur m (politique).

haul [hɔ:l] (to), F: to h. s.o. over the coals, réprimander* qn; to get hauled over the coals, prendre qch. pour son rhume. Voir aussi ashes, 2.

haul-ass [¹hɔ:læs] (to) (U.S.), P: partir* en vitesse, se tailler.

hauler [¹hɔ:lər] (noun), F: auto f très rapide, bolide m.

haul in [¹hɔ:l¹in] (to), F: arrêter*, agrafer, épingler.

have [hæv] (to). 1. P: to h. it, coïter*, faire l'amour; to h. s.o., to h. it away (or off) with s.o., coïter* avec qn. 2. F: to h. it away with sth., voler* qch., chiper qch. 3. F: to h. it away,

s'échapper; he's had it away over the wall, il a fait le mur (de la prison). Voir aussi 1, 2 ci-dessus. 4. F: to h. had it, (a) rater sa chance, rater le coup; (b) mourir*, claquer; (c) être fatigué* (ou crevé); (d) être ruiné* (ou à plat); you've had it, chum! (a) tu es fait, mon vieux!; (b) tu es foutu, mon vieux! 5. F: to let s.o. h. it, (a) battre* qn, frapper qn, flanquer un coup* à qn; (b) critiquer* qn; (c) réprimander* qn, éreinter qn; (d) dire son fait à qn; (e) régler son compte à qn. 6. F: duper*, avoir (qn). 7. F: vaincre, défaire (qn). 8. F: to h. it out with s.o., vider une querelle* avec qn, s'expliquer avec qn. 9. F: to h. it in for s.o., en vouloir à qn, avoir une dent contre qn. Voir aussi any², 1.

have in [¹hæv¹in] (to), F: inviter (qn), donner l'hospitalité à (qn). Voir aussi have (to), 9.

have-nots [¹hæv¹nɔts] (pl. noun), F: les dépourvus m.pl., les miséreux m.pl., les déshérités m.pl.; the haves and the h.-n., les riches* et les pauvres*, les rupins m.pl. et les purotins m.pl.

have on [¹hæv¹ɔn] (to), F: 1. duper*, faire marcher (qn); he's having you on, il te fait marcher. 2. to h. sth. o., être occupé, être pris.

have up [¹hæv¹ʌp] (to), F: traduire (qn) en justice.

hawk¹ [hɔ:k] (noun), F: qn qui pousse à la guerre et au chauvinisme; un faucon; cf. dove. Voir aussi fairy, 1; news-hawk.

hawk² [hɔ:k] (to), F: graillonner.

hay [hei] (noun). 1. F: to hit the h., se coucher*, se pieuter. 2. P: to get in the h. with s.o., coïter* avec qn; voir aussi roll¹, 2. 3. P: (Indian) h., marijuana f (drogues*), chanvre (indien). 4. F: peu d'argent*, gnognot(t)e f. 5. F: to make h. (while the sun shines), battre le fer pendant qu'il est chaud. 6. F: to make h. of sth., chambarder, bouleverser qch.

haybag [¹heibæg] (noun), P: (a) femme* (péj.), tarderie f, vieille moukère; (b) prostituée* de basse classe, pute f.

hayhead [¹heihed] (noun), P: (a) usager m de la marijuana; (b) habitué(e) de la marijuana; cf. hay, 3.

haymaker [¹hei-meikər] (noun), F: coup*

---

* An asterisk indicates that the word so marked is included as a head-word in the Appendix.

puissant (mettant l'adversaire hors de combat).

hayseed [ˈheisiːd] (*noun*) (*U.S.*), *F:* paysan*, cul-terreux *m*.

haywire [ˈheiwaiər] (*adj.*), *F:* 1. confus, embrouillé, vasouillard. 2. emballé, excité, cinglé. 3. to go h., (*a*) (*d'une personne*) ne pas tourner rond; (*b*) (*d'un projet, etc.*) être loupé, finir en queue de poisson.

haze [heiz] (to) (*U.S.*), *F:* brimer (à l'école), faire des brimades *f.pl.* à (un nouvel élève).

head [hed] (*noun*). 1. *F:* mal *m* de tête; to have a (bad) h., to have a h. on one, (*a*) avoir mal à la tête; (*b*) avoir la gueule de bois. 2. *F:* to yell one's h. off, gueuler. 3. *F:* to be h. over heels in love, aimer* qn, être toqué de qn, être éperdument amoureux de qn. 4. *P:* usager *m* de drogues; drogué(e)*, camé(e); *voir aussi* acid, 2; cokehead; cubehead; dopehead; hayhead; hophead; juicehead; methhead; pillhead; pothead; teahead; weedhead. 5. *F:* to go off one's h., devenir fou*, perdre la boule. 6. *P:* W.C.*, chiottes *f.pl.* 7. *F:* I need it like a hole in the h., j'ai pas besoin de ça, c'est aussi souhaitable qu'une jambe cassée. 8. *F:* not to (be able to) make h. or tail of sth., ne comprendre goutte à qch., n'y comprendre que couic. 9. *F:* I could do it (standing) on my h., c'est simple comme bonjour. 10. *F:* to talk s.o.'s h. off, étourdir qn; rompre les oreilles* à qn. 11. *P:* la guêpe, la guenon. 12. *P:* fana *mf*. 13. *V:* h. job, coït buccal, prise *f* de pipe; h. chick, femme qui pratique le coït* buccal, rogneuse *f* d'os. *Voir aussi* balloon-head; big-head; blubber-head; bonehead; boofhead; bunhead; cabbagehead; chew off (to); chowder-head; chucklehead; cloghead; cloth-head; clunkhead; deadhead; dumbhead; eat (to), 6; egghead; fathead; flathead; jughead; knock² (to); knothead; knucklehead; lughead; lunkhead; meat-head; muscle-head; muttonhead; nail¹, 2; pea-head; pinhead; puddinghead; pumpkinhead; redhead; rockhead; sap-(head); screw² (to), 6; shithead; skin-head; sleepyhead; snap off (to); sore, 2; sorehead; squarehead; thickhead; turniphead; water, 2; wet-head.

headache [ˈhedeik] (*noun*), *F:* ennui *m*, embêtement *m*, casse-tête *m*. *Voir aussi* **Dutchman, 2.**

header [ˈhedər] (*noun*), *F:* to take a h., tomber* par terre, ramasser une bûche.

heading [ˈhediŋ] (*noun*), *F:* coup *m* de tête (sur la figure).

headlights [ˈhedlaits] (*pl. noun*), *P:* 1. seins*, amortisseurs *m.pl.*, pare-chocs *m.pl.* 2. gros diamants*, bouchons *m.pl.* de carafe.

headlines [ˈhedlainz] (*pl. noun*), *F:* to hit the h., devenir fameux, faire la une.

head-merchant [ˈhedmə:tʃ(ə)nt] (*noun*), *F:* = **head-shrinker.**

head-piece [ˈhedpiːs] (*noun*), *F:* tête*, cerveau *m*, ciboulot *m*.

head-shrinker [ˈhedʃriŋkər] (*noun*), *F:* psychiatre *mf*, psychanalyste *mf*; *cf.* shrink.

health [helθ] (*noun*), *F:* I don't do that for my h., je ne fais pas cela pour mon bon plaisir.

heap [hiːp] (*noun*), *F:* 1. to be (struck) all of a h., rester comme deux ronds de flan. 2. (*a*) to come out at the top of (*or* on top of) the h., être au premier rang, tenir le haut du pavé; (*b*) to stay at the bottom of the h., être le dernier des derniers, être au fin fond. 3. a h. of nonsense, un tissu d'âneries. 4. nouille *f*, andouille *f*, nullité *f*. 5. vieille voiture*, bagnole *f*. 6. heaps of..., une abondance* de..., un tas de..., une tripotée de..., une flopée de... *Voir aussi* scrap-heap.

heart [hɑːt] (*noun*), *F:* have a h.! (ne) parle pas de malheur! *Voir aussi* purple.

heart-throb [ˈhɑːtθrɔb] (*noun*), *F:* objet *m* de l'amour, béguin *m*.

hearty [ˈhɑːti] (*noun*), *F:* 1. un athlète (opposé à un esthète). 2. (*pl.*) camarades *m.pl.*, copains *m.pl.*

heat [hiːt] (*noun*). 1. *F:* pression *f*, feu *m*; to turn on the h., (*a*) s'enflammer, s'échauffer; (*b*) faire pression sur qn, lui mettre le feu au derrière. 2. *F:* interrogatoire* poussé, saignement *m* de nez. 3. (*U.S.*) *P:* fonctionnaire *m* de l'ordre judiciaire. 4. (*U.S.*) *P:* = heater.

heater [ˈhiːtər] (*noun*), *P:* revolver*, calibre *m*.

heave-ho [ˈhiːvˈhou] (*noun*), *P:* renvoi *m*, expulsion *f*; to get the h.-h., être

---

* L'astérisque indique que le mot marqué de ce signe figure comme entrée dans le Répertoire.

congédié*, être flanqué à la porte;
to give s.o. the h.-h., se débarrasser*
de qn, larguer, sacquer, virer qn.
heaven [ˈhevn] (*noun*), *F:* **1.** grand
plaisir, ravissement *m*; **it's h. to relax**,
c'est divin de pouvoir se reposer.
2. good heavens! juste ciel! bonté du
ciel! bonté divine!; **heavens above!** nom
d'une pipe!; **for h.'s sake!** pour l'amour
de Dieu! *Voir aussi* dust¹, 2 (*a*), (*b*).
heavenly [ˈhevnli] (*adj.*), *F:* divin,
ravissant, délectable. *Voir aussi* blue², 1.
heaves [hi:vz] (*pl. noun*), *F:* **to have the
h.**, avoir des nausées *f.pl.*
heavy¹ [ˈhevi] (*adj.*). **1.** *F:* passionné,
sexy; impudique, vicieux; **h. necking**,
pelotage *m*, tripotage *m*. **2.** *F:* **h. date**,
rendez-vous* sentimental important.
3. *F:* **to make h. weather of sth.**, faire
toute une affaire de qch. **4.** *P:* (butin)
de valeur; **the h. mob**, bande* de
voleurs* de grande envergure. **5.** *F:*
h. stuff, renforts motorisés dans une
descente de police. **6.** *P:* en grande
quantité; **h. dough**, des tas de fric. **7.**
P: malhonnête, louche. **8.** *F:* (*th.*) **h.
rôle**, rôle *m* du vilain de la pièce; rôle
pompeux. **9.** *P:* sale*, dégueulbif. **10.**
P: super-beat, maxi-beat. **11.** *P:* ex-
cellent*, très agréable. **12.** *P:* enceinte*.
heavy² [ˈhevi] (*noun*). **1.** *F:* (*boxe*) (=
heavyweight) poids lourd. **2.** *P:* (*a*)
apache *m*, bandit *m*; (*b*) assassin*;
on the h., sur le chemin du crime,
goupinant à la dure. **3.** *F:* le vilain
dans une pièce *ou* un film. **4.** *P:* **to be
in the h.**, avoir beaucoup d'argent*,
être riche*, rouler dans le fric. **5.** *F:*
the Hollywood heavies, les durs *m.pl.*
de Hollywood.
hebe [ˈhi:bi] (*noun*). **1.** *P:* = heeb. **2.** *F:*
serveuse *f*, loufiate *f*.
heck [hek] (*noun & excl.*) (*euph. pour
hell*), *F:* **1. h.!** sapristi! la barbe!
morbleu!; **what the h. . . . !** que diable...!
2. a h. of a lot, une abondance*, une
grande quantité, une foultitude, une
bardée.
hedge [hedʒ] (**to**), *F:* **1. to h. one's
bets**, étaler *ou* protéger ses paris.
2. chercher des échappatoires *f.pl.* (*ou*
des faux-fuyants *m.pl.*), s'échapper par
la tangente.
hedge-hop [ˈhedʒhɔp] (**to**), *F:* (*av.*)
faire du rase-mottes *m.pl.*

hedge-hopping [ˈhedʒhɔpiŋ] (*noun*), *F:*
(*av.*) vol *m* en rase-mottes.
heeb [hi:b] (*noun*), *P:* Juif *m*, Youpe *m*,
Youpin *m*.
heebie-jeebies [ˈhi:biˈdʒi:biz] (*pl. noun*),
F: **1.** delirium *m* tremens, les rats
bleus. **2.** angoisse *f*, nervosité *f* extrême,
peur bleue; **to give s.o. the h.-j.**,
donner un choc nerveux à qn.
heebies [ˈhi:biz] (*pl. noun*), *F:* (*leaping*)
h. = heebie-jeebies, 1, 2.
heel [hi:l] (*noun*). **1.** *F:* individu*
méprisable, gouape *f*; **to feel a (bit
of a) h.**, friser la canaille. **2.** *P:* **to have
round heels**, avoir la cuisse hospitalière;
cf. roundheel(s). **3.** *F:* **to cool (or kick)
one's heels**, se morfondre, croquer le
marmot, faire le pied de grue, poireauter. *Voir aussi* head, 3; kick up
(to), 4; shitheel.
heeled [hi:ld] (*adj.*) (*U.S.*), *P:* **1.** =
well-heeled. **2.** armé d'un revolver*,
flingué.
heesh [hi:ʃ] (*noun*), *P:* = hash², 3.
heft [heft] (**to**), *F:* soulever, soupeser
(qch.).
hefty [ˈhefti] (*adj.*), *F:* **1.** fort*, costaud,
malabar. **2.** gros, important; **a h. bill**,
une note de taille (*ou* d'un montant
élevé); **a h. chunk**, un morceau im-
posant.
heifer [ˈhefər] (*noun*), *F:* jeune fille*.
he-ing and she-ing [ˈhi:iŋˈʃi:iŋ]
(*noun*), *P:* coït*, baisage *m*.
Heinie, heinie [ˈhaini] (*noun*), *P:* (*a*)
Allemand*, boche *m*; (*b*) soldat allemand, hun *m*.
Heinz 57 [ˈhainzˈfiftiˈsevn] (*noun*), *F:*
chien* bâtard. *Voir aussi* bingo (57).
heist¹ [haist] (*noun*) (*mainly U.S.*), *F:*
1. cambriolage *m*, casse *m*, fric-frac *m*
(par professionnels). **2.** = heister. **3.**
amélioration *f*, augmentation *f*.
heist² [haist] (**to**) (*mainly U.S.*), *F:*
1. cambrioler*, faire un casse. **2.**
arrêter (un camion, *etc.*) pour le voler,
pirater. **3.** améliorer, augmenter, ren-
forcer. **4.** se débarrasser* de (qch.),
se défarguer de (qch.).
heister [ˈhaistər] (*noun*) (*mainly U.S.*),
F: cambrioleur*, bandit *m*, casseur *m*.
hell [hel] (*noun*). **1.** *P:* (*a*) **go to h.!**
va au diable!; **to h. with it!** au diable
que tout cela!; **get the (or to) h. out
of here!** nom de Dieu débarrasse le

---

* An asterisk indicates that the word so marked is included as a head-word in the Appendix.

plancher!; **oh h.!** merde alors!; **h.'s
bells (and buckets of blood)!** sacré nom
de nom!; **would he go? would he h.!**
partir? le bougre ne bougeait pas!;
h., I don't know, diable, je n'en sais
rien; (b) **what the h. does it matter?**
qu'est-ce que ça peut bien faire?;
who the h. are you? mais diable qui
êtes-vous?; **who the h. do you think
you are (anyway)?** tu te prends pour
qui, que diable!; **what the h. do you
think you're doing** (or **playing at)?**
que diable es-tu en train de fabriquer?;
what in h. (or **h.'s name) is that?**
qu'est-ce que c'est que ce satané truc?;
why the h. doesn't he belt up? pourquoi
diable ne la ferme-t-il pas? **2.** F: **to
give s.o. h.,** faire passer un mauvais
quart d'heure à qn, en faire voir (de
toutes les couleurs) à qn; **to get h.,
to have h. to pay,** être réprimandé* ou
puni, être engueulé (ou incendié),
prendre qch. pour son rhume. **3.** F:
like (all) h. let loose, comme les damnés
en enfer; **to create** (or **raise) (merry) h.,**
(a) faire du boucan, faire un chambard
du diable; (b) rouscailler, râler (comme
un enragé). **4.** P: **in a** (or **one) h. of a
mess** (or **state),** dans une pagaille
infernale (ou du tonnerre); **a h. of a
nice fellow,** un bien brave type;
you've got a h. of a nerve (or **cheek)!**
tu as un culot du diable!; **it's a h. of a
bore** (or **bind),** c'est diablement embêtant; **a h. of a row,** (a) un bruit* d'enfer,
un vacarme infernal; (b) une engueulade
maison. **5.** F: **to do sth. for the h. of it,**
faire qch. histoire de rire (ou pour s'en
payer une tranche). **6.** F: **to play h.
with s.o., sth.,** en faire voir à qn,
cabosser qch. **7.** F: **to feel like h.,** se
sentir au cent mille dessous. **8.** P:
sure as h., sûr et certain, dans la fouille.
9. P: **to knock h. out of s.o.,** battre*
qn comme plâtre, bourrer qn de coups.
10. P: **all to h.,** démoli, gâché, coulé.
11. F: **to go h. for leather,** galoper ventre
à terre, courir avec le feu au derrière.
12. F: **till h. freezes over,** jusqu'à la
Saint-Glinglin. **13.** (U.S.) F: **from h. to
breakfast,** entièrement, totalement, de
A à Z. **14.** (U.S.) F: **to h. and gone,**
(a) disparu, passé à l'as, évanoui; (b)
aux antipodes, chez les damnés. **15.** F:
h.'s angels, jeunes voyous m.pl. en

moto. **16.** F: tripot m, boui-boui m.
17. F: **come h. or high water,** advienne
que pourra. Voir aussi **Chinaman, 2;
kick up (to), 3; snowball[1], 2; stink[1], 1.**
hell-bender [ˈhel-bendər] (noun), P:
1. bamboche infernale; cf. **bender, 1.**
2. débauché m, noceur m.
hell-cat [ˈhel-kæt] (noun), F: **1.** jeune
fille* pleine d'entrain et de témérité.
2. vieille sorcière, carabosse f.
hell-hole [ˈhelhoul] (noun), F: endroit
mal famé, coupe-gorge m.
hellion [ˈheljən] (noun) (U.S.), F: **1.**
vaurien*, sale type m, fripouille f.
2. enfant* terrible, petit diable.
hellishly [ˈheliʃli] (adv.), F: diablement,
diaboliquement.
hello-dearie [ˈhəlouˈdiəri] (noun), P:
prostituée*, frangipane f.
hell-raiser [ˈhelreizər] (noun), P: **1.**
individu* déchaîné, téméraire mf. **2.** débauché m, noceur m.
helluva [ˈheləvə] (=**hell of a**), P: voir
hell, 4.
he-man [ˈhiːmæn] (noun) (pl. **he-men**),
F: (a) homme fort* et viril, malabar m;
(b) un beau mâle.
hemp [hemp] (noun), F: **(Indian) h.,**
cannabis m (drogues*), chanvre (indien).
hen [hen] (noun), F: (a) femme* (péj.),
mégère f, rombière f, vieille dinde;
(b) jeune femme*, une petite poule; **h.
party,** réunion f de femmes seules,
volière f; cf. **stag[1], 1.**
Henry, henry [ˈhenri] (noun), F:
héroïne f (drogues*).
hep [hep] (adj.), F: (a) qui apprécie la
musique swing; (b) qui est au courant
(ou à la coule ou dans le vent); **a h.
guy,** un affranchi; **to put s.o. h.,**
mettre qn à la page, affranchir qn.
hep-cat [ˈhepkæt] (noun), F: **1.** (a)
musicien m faisant partie d'un orchestre
swing; (b) fanatique mf de la musique
swing; (c) danseur m swing. **2.** individu*
nouvelle vague (ou dans le vent).
hepped up [ˈheptˈʌp] (adj.), F: **1.** en
colère*, à cran. **2.** très enthousiasmé,
emballé.
herb [həːb] (noun), F: **(the) h.,** cannabis
m (drogues*), herbe f.
here [ˈhiər] (adv.), F: **1. that's neither
h. nor there,** cela ne fait ni chaud ni
froid, cela n'a aucune importance.
2. h. goes! ça démarre! ça va barder!

---

* L'astérisque indique que le mot marqué de ce signe figure comme entrée dans le Répertoire.

3. **h. you are**, tenez, prenez-le, et voilà. 4. **from h. on in**, à partir de ce moment.
heron [ˈherən] (*noun*), *P: héroïne f (drogues*).
herring [ˈheriŋ] (*noun*), *F:* 1. **red h.**, procédé servant à détourner l'attention. 2. **the H. Pond**, l'océan *m* Atlantique, la Grande Tasse.
he-she [ˈhiːʃiː] (*noun*), *P:* prostituée*, catin *f*.
het up [ˈhetʌp] (*adj.*), *F:* 1. énervé, agité, tracassé. 2. en colère*, en rogne.
hex [heks] (*noun*), *F:* (*a*) malchance*; (*b*) porte-guigne *m*.
hex² [heks] (to), *F:* porter la guigne (*ou* la poisse) à (qn).
hi! [hai] (*excl.*), *F:* (*a*) salut! bonjour!; (*b*) **h.! you there!** eh! dites donc, là-bas!
hick¹ [hik] (*adj.*) (*U.S.*), *P:* 1. rustique, campagnard; **a h. town**, un patelin. 2. ignorant, rustaud.
hick² [hik] (*noun*) (*U.S.*), *P:* 1. paysan*, péquenaud *m*. 2. innocent *m*, couillon *m*, niguedouille *m*. 3. cadavre*, croni *m*.
hickey [ˈhiki] (*noun*) (*U.S.*), *F:* marque sur la peau faite par un baiser ardent; suçon *m*.
hide [haid] (*noun*), *F:* 1. peau *f* (de l'homme), cuir *m*; **to tan the h. off s.o.**, battre* qn, carder le cuir à qn. 2. **to have a thick h.**, avoir la peau dure; *cf.* **thick-skinned**.
hiding [ˈhaidiŋ] (*noun*), *F:* 1. (**good) h.**, volée *f* de coups*, dérouillée *f*, passage *m* à tabac. 2. **to be on a h. to nothing**, avoir tout à perdre sans rien à gagner.
hi-fi [ˈhaiˈfai] (=*high fidelity*), *F:* de haute fidélité.
high¹ [hai] (*adj.*), *F:* 1. **to be for the h. jump**, en être pour de la casse, être dans de mauvais draps; **he's for the h. jump**, qu'est-ce qu'il va prendre!; son affaire est bonne. 2. **to leave s.o. h. and dry**, laisser qn en plan. 3. **h. and mighty**, prétentieux*, poseur, bêcheur. 4. **to be h.**, (*a*) être ivre* (*ou* parti *ou* rétamé); (*b*) avoir un sentiment de bien-être; être dans un état d'euphorie dû aux drogues*; high; *voir aussi* **fly³** (to), 2 (*b*); **kite**, 4. 5. (*U.S.*) **h. on sth.**, s.o., qui a une haute opinion de qch., de qn. 6. **to have a h. old time**, faire la fête* (*ou* la noce *ou* la riboul-

dingue). *Voir aussi* **hat, horse¹, 5; jinks; knee-high.**
high² [hai] (*noun*), *F:* **to have a h.** = **to be high** (**high¹, 4** (*b*)).
highbinder [ˈhaiˈbaindər] (*noun*) (*U.S.*), *F:* 1. gangster *m*, assassin*, bandit *m*. 2. escroc*, filou *m*, empileur *m*. 3. politicien corrompu.
highbrow¹ [ˈhaiˈbrau] (*adj.*), *F:* intellectuel, calé.
highbrow² [ˈhaiˈbrau] (*noun*), *F:* intellectuel *m*, mandarin *m*, ponte *m*, grosse tête.
highfalutin [ˈhaifəˈluːtin] (*adj.*), *F:* prétentieux*, déclamatoire, ronflant.
high-flier [ˈhaiˈflaiər] (*noun*), *F:* ambitieux *m*, qn qui va aux extrêmes; *cf.* **fly³** (to), 2 (*a*).
high-muck-a-muck [ˈhaiˈmʌkəmʌk] (*noun*), *F:* personnage important, grosse légume.
highspots [ˈhaiˈspɒts] (*pl. noun*), *F:* **to hit the h.**, exceller, toucher les hauteurs *f.pl.*
hightail [ˈhaiteil] (to), *F:* **to h. it**, se dépêcher*, se magner le train.
high-ups [ˈhaiʌps] (*pl. noun*), *F:* hauts fonctionnaires, gros bonnets.
highway [ˈhaiwei] (*attrib. adj.*), *F:* **it's h. robbery!** c'est du vol manifeste!
hijack [ˈhaidʒæk] (to), *F:* détourner; **to h. a vehicle**, s'emparer de force d'un véhicule et de son contenu; **to h. a plane**, pirater un avion.
hijacker [ˈhaidʒækər] (*noun*), *F:* détourneur *m*; pirate *m* (de l'air), voleur* de voiture*.
hike¹ [haik] (*noun*), *P:* augmentation *f*, hausse *f*.
hike² [haik] (to), *F:* **to h. a cheque**, falsifier un chèque.
hike up [ˈhaikʌp] (to), *F:* augmenter, hausser (le prix), allonger le tir.
hillbilly [ˈhilˈbili] (*noun*) (*U.S.*), *F:* 1. petit fermier de montagne. 2. rustre *m*, rustaud *m*. 3. chanson montagnarde et rustique.
hinge [hindʒ] (*noun*), *P:* **to get** (*or* **take**) **a h.**, jeter un coup d'œil*, lancer un coup de châsse.
hip¹ [hip] (*adj.*). 1. *F:* = **hep**, (*a*), (*b*). 2. *F:* = **cool¹**, 1. 3. *P:* qui a été initié(e) à la drogue. *Cf.* **hipster**.
hip² [hip] (to), *F:* rendre morose et cafardeux.

---

* An asterisk indicates that the word so marked is included as a head-word in the Appendix.

hipped [hipt] (*adj.*), *P:* 1. **to be h. on sth.**, (*a*) être obsédé (*ou* hypnotisé) par qch.; (*b*) être au courant, être bien renseigné sur qch. 2. crevé d'ennui.

hippie, hippy [ˈhipi] (*noun*), *F:* hippie *mf*, hippy *mf*, yippie *mf*.

hipster [ˈhipstər] (*noun*). 1. *F:* = **hep-cat**, 2. 2. *F:* membre d'un groupe de cools. 3. *F:* membre de la génération beat (*ou* sacrifiée). 4. *P:* initié(e) à la drogue. *Cf.* **hip**[1].

hister [ˈhaistər] (*noun*) (*U.S.*), *F:* = **heister**.

hit[1] [hit] (*noun*). 1. *F:* pièce *f*, chanson *f*, *etc.*, à succès. 2. *F:* succès *m* populaire; **to make a h.**, faire un boum. 3. *F:* acteur *m*, chanteur *m*, *etc.*, en vogue. 4. *P:* réussite sexuelle, partie *f* de piquet. 5. *P:* rendez-vous* de contre-bande; moyens *m.pl.* de contrebande. 6. *P:* plaquette *f* de drogues. 7. *P:* injection *f* de drogues, piquouse *f*. 8. *P:* meurtre prémédité. *Voir aussi* **smash-hit**.

hit[2] [hit] (**to**). 1. *F:* **to h. the hundred mark**, (*auto*) taper le 160. 2. *P:* pro-voquer une forte réaction (*drogues*); **to h. s.o.**, pourvoir un usager avec de la drogue. *Voir aussi* **bottle**[1], 1; **ceiling**; **deck**, 1; **feather**[1], 6; **hay**, 1; **highspots**; **jackpot**; **pad**[1], 4; **pipe**[1], 2; **road**, 2; **sack**[1], 3; **sauce**[1], 2; **track**[1], 4; **trail**.

hitch[1] [hitʃ] (*noun*), *F:* promenade *f* en voiture (*souvent* auto-stop).

hitch[2] [hitʃ] (**to**), *F:* 1. **to h. one's wag(g)on to a star**, être dévoré d'ambi-tion, viser très haut. 2. **to get hitched**, se marier, se maquer; *cf.* **unhitched**. 3. **to h. a ride**, se faire conduire en voiture.

hit off [ˈhitˈɔf] (**to**), *F:* **to h. it o. with s.o.**, bien s'entendre avec qn; **they don't h. it o.**, il y a du tirage entre eux.

hit-parade [ˈhitpəreid] (*noun*), *F:* hit-parade *m*.

hit up [ˈhitˈʌp] (**to**), *F:* **to h. it u.**, avoir une conduite déchaînée, faire la vie.

hive off [ˈhaivˈɔf] (**to**), *F:* 1. mettre de côté, mettre à l'écart. 2. s'enfuir*, se cavaler.

hiya! [ˈhaijə] (*excl.*), *F:* salut!; *cf.* **hi!** (*a*).

hock[1] [hɔk] (*noun*). 1. *F:* **in h.**, (*a*) en gage, chez ma tante; (*b*) en prison*, en taule. 2. (*Austr.*) *P:* pédéraste*, lope *f*.

hock[2] [hɔk] (**to**), *F:* mettre en gage, mettre au clou.

hocker [ˈhɔkər] (*noun*) (*U.S.*), *P:* cra-chat*, graillon *m*.

hockshop [ˈhɔkʃɔp] (*noun*), *F:* mont-de-piété *m*, chez ma tante, le clou.

hocky [ˈhɔki] (*noun*) (*U.S.*), *P:* 1. mensonges*, exagération *f*, blagues *f.pl.* 2. merde *f*, caca *m*. 3. sperme*, blanc *m*. 4. nourriture* peu appétis-sante, boustifaille *f*, graille *f*.

ho-dad(dy) [ˈhouˈdæd(i)] (*noun*) (*U.S.*), *F:* 1. individu* farfelu, m'as-tu-vu *m*. 2. individu* qui aime fréquenter les sportifs sans en être un lui-même. 3. pète-sec *m*, collet monté, constipé *m*.

hoedown [ˈhoudaun] (*noun*) (*U.S.*), *F:* 1. danse *f* rustique; bal animé, guinche boumée. 2. querelle*, engueulade *f*. 3. bagarre*, rixe *f*, rififi *m*.

hog[1] [hɔg] (*noun*), *F:* 1. goinfre*, porc *m*. 2. **to go the whole h.**, aller jusqu'au bout, tout risquer, mettre le paquet; *cf.* **whole-hogger**; **whole-hoggism**. *Voir aussi* **road-hog**; **speed-hog**.

hog[2] [hɔg] (**to**), *F:* 1. goinfrer. 2. **to h. the limelight**, accaparer la vedette. 3. **to h. the road**, conduire au milieu de la route; *cf.* **road-hog**. 4. **to h. it**, vivre comme un cochon.

hog-tie [ˈhɔgtai] (**to**), *F:* réduire à l'impuissance.

hogwash [ˈhɔgwɔʃ] (*noun*), *F:* 1. bibine *f*, rinçure *f*, lavasse *f*. 2. bêtise*, sottise *f*, absurdité *f*. 3. boniments *m.pl.*, baratinage *m*.

hoist[1] [hɔist] (*noun*), *P:* 1. vol *m*, chouravage *m*, attaque *f* à main armée, hold-up *m*. 2. enquilleuse *f*. 3. vol *m* à l'étalage.

hoist[2] [hɔist] (**to**), *P:* 1. cambrioler*, voler*, carburer; *cf.* **heist**[2] (*v*.), 1, 2. 2. voler* à l'étalage, acheter à la foire d'empoigne. 3. (*Austr.*) procéder à une arrestation, coffrer.

hokey-pokey [ˈhoukiˈpouki] (*noun*), *F:* 1. = **hokum**, 1. 2. (*U.S.*) glace *f* *ou* bonbon *m* de mauvaise qualité.

hokum [ˈhoukəm] (*noun*), *F:* 1. bêtises*, blagues *f.pl.* 2. sensiblerie *f*, mélo-(drame) *m*.

hokus [ˈhoukəs] (*noun*), *P:* drogues*, came *f*, narcs *m.pl.*

hold [hould] (**to**). 1. *F:* **h. everything!** arrêtez! attendez! 2. *P:* (*a*) fourguer

des drogues; (b) posséder des drogues.
3. P: se masturber*, se branler.
hold out on [ˈhoʊldˈaʊtɔn] (to), F:
faire des cachotteries f.pl. à (qn).
hold-up [ˈhoʊldʌp] (noun), F: **1.** arrêt
m, embarras m de voitures, embouteillage m. **2.** vol m à main armée, braquage
m, hold-up m.
hold up [ˈhoʊldˈʌp] (to), F: **1.** voler* à
main armée, braquer. **2.** entraver,
gêner, embarrasser, immobiliser. Voir
aussi wash¹, **1.**
hole [hoʊl] (noun). **1.** F: bouge m,
bastringue m, caboulot m. **2.** F: taudis
m, gourbi m, piaule f; cf. dog-hole.
3. F: embarras m, pétrin m, impasse f;
to be in a h., être dans une situation
difficile, être en rade. **4.** F: **to make a
h. in one's capital,** écorner (ou ébrécher)
son capital. **5.** F: **to pick holes in sth.**,
trouver à redire à qch. **6.** V: vagin*,
fente f; cf. manhole. **7.** V: anus*,
trou m (de balle); cf. arsehole; bum-
hole; bung-hole, **1**; cornhole¹; fart-
hole; shit-hole. **8.** (U.S.) P: the h.,
cachot m (disciplinaire), mitard m.
9. F: h. in the wall, petite maison ou
lieu m de commerce, trou m. **10.** F:
to burn a h. in one's stomach, manger*
ou boire* qch. de très fort, se brûler
l'estomac m. **11.** (U.S.) P: **to go in
the h.,** s'endetter, s'encroumer. **12.** F:
to put a h. through s.o., to drill a h.
(or holes) in s.o., assassiner* qn,
butter, démolir, fusiller, flinguer qn,
transformer qn en passoire. **13.** F:
h. in the heart, (a) communication f
inter-ventriculaire; (b) communication
f inter-auriculaire. Voir aussi cakehole;
dog-hole; earhole; glory-hole; head, **7**;
hell-hole; keyhole; lugholes; nineteenth;
square¹, **7**; top-hole.
hole-and-corner [ˈhoʊlən(d)ˈkɔːnər]
(adj.), F: fait en sous-main (ou sous
la table); **h.-a.-c. work,** manigances
f.pl.
hole away [ˈhoʊləˈweɪ] (to), F: cacher*,
mettre à gauche.
hole up [ˈhoʊlˈʌp] (to), F: **1.** s'installer,
faire son nid (d'un soir). **2.** se cacher*,
se terrer, se planquer.
holier-than-thou [hoʊliəðænðaʊ]
(noun), F: personne f hypocrite qui
donne l'apparence de dévotion; Sainte-
Nitouche f.

holler [ˈhɔlər] (to), P: **1.** crier*, gueuler,
beugler. **2.** moucharder, cafarder.
holler-wag(g)on [ˈhɔləwægən] (noun),
P: voiture-radio f de la police.
hollow [ˈhɔloʊ, ˈhɔlə] (adv.), F: **to beat
s.o. h.,** battre qn à plate(s) couture(s).
holly-golly [ˈhɔliˈgɔli] (noun) (U.S.),
F: **1.** bêtises*, sornettes f.pl. **2.** tintamarre m, vacarme m, remue-ménage m.
Hollywood [ˈhɔliwʊd] (adj.), F: **1.**
(articles, vêtements) clinquant, criard.
2. (personnes) artificiel, maniéré, affecté.
hols [hɔlz] (pl. noun) (abbr. = holidays),
F: vacances f.pl. (scolaires), vacs f.pl.
holy [ˈhoʊli] (adj.). **1.** F: h. cow! (or
cats! or mackerel! or Moses! or smoke!),
sapristi! saperlotte! saperlipopette!
crénom de nom! **2.** P: (péj.) h. Joe,
(a) prêtre*, pasteur m; étudiant m
en théologie, ratichon m; (b) personne
dévote, grenouille f de bénitier. **3.** F:
h. terror, (a) enfant* malicieux, petit
diable; (b) individu* canulant; colique
f; (c) individu* qui fait peur, épou-
vantail m. **4.** H. Ghost (R.S. = winning
post), poteau m (d'arrivée). Voir aussi
friar.
home [hoʊm] (adv.), F: **1.** h. and dry,
à bon port, sain et sauf. **2.** my suit is
going h., mon costume est usé. **3.**
nothing to write h. about, rien qui
vaille la peine, rien d'époustouflant.
home-bird [ˈhoʊmbɔːd] (noun), F:
casanier m, casanière f.
homestretch [ˈhoʊmˈstretʃ] (noun), F:
dernière étape, dernier échelon.
homework [ˈhoʊmwɔːk] (noun). **1.** to
do one's h., (a) F: faire une préparation
attentive; (b) P: remplir ses obligations conjugales (rapports sexuels). **2.**
P: (a) pelotage m, baisage m; (b) a
nice bit of h., une fille* à la cuisse
hospitalière.
homie [ˈhoʊmi] (noun), P: = homo².
homo¹ [ˈhoʊmoʊ] (adj.), P: homo-
(sexuel).
homo² [ˈhoʊmoʊ] (noun), P: pédéraste*,
homosexuel m, pédé m.
honest-to-goodness [ˈɔnist(t)əˈgʊdnis]
(adj.), F: vrai, réel, authentique.
honey [ˈhʌni] (noun), F: **1.** petit(e)
ami(e), chéri(e), bien-aimé(e). **2.** as m,
crack m; a h. of an acrobat, un as
d'acrobate. **3.** qch. d'excellent* (ou de
bath ou de chouette). **4.** un vrai chou,

---

* An asterisk indicates that the word so marked is included as a head-word in the Appendix.

un amour, un trognon. *Voir aussi* bee, 2.

honeybunch [ˈhʌnibʌntʃ] (*noun*), *F :* = honey, 1, 4.

honey-fuck [ˈhʌnifʌk] (to), *VV :* 1. coïter* d'une manière romantique (*ou* à la douce). 2. coïter* avec une fille très jeune, baiser la petite fleur.

honey-fuck(ing) [ˈhʌnifʌk(iŋ)] (*noun*), *VV :* 1. coït* (*ou* crampette *f*) à la douce. 2. coït* lent et agréable, soupe délayée à la quéquette. 3. coït* avec une fille très jeune, baisage *m* de petite fleur.

honk [hɔŋk] (to). 1. *P :* to h. (one's chuff), vomir*, dégobiller. 2. *P :* to get honked, s'enivrer, se paffer. 3. (*Austr.*) *F :* = hoot² (to), 2.

honkers [ˈhɔŋkəz] (*adj.*), *P :* (Harry) h., ivre*, rétamé, saoul.

honky-tonk [ˈhɔŋkiˈtɔŋk] (*noun*) (*U.S.*), *F :* 1. cabaret *m* de basse classe, caboulot *m*, boui-boui *m*. 2. petit théâtre de province. 3. bordel*, bobinard *m*.

hooch [huːtʃ] (*noun*) (*U.S.*), *F :* (*a*) alcool*, gnôle *f* (de contrebande); (*b*) alcool* très fort, casse-gueule *m*; whisky *m*.

hood [hud] (*noun*), *P :* 1. = hoodlum. 2. religieuse *f*, bonne sœur, bibine *f*.

hoodlum [ˈhuːdləm] (*noun*), *F :* vaurien*, chenapan *m*, jeune apache *m*.

hooey [ˈhuːiː] (*noun*), *P :* = balon(e)y.

hoof¹ [huːf] (*noun*). 1. *F :* pied*, ripaton *m*; to pad the h., aller à pied, aller à patte; *voir aussi* pad² (to). 2. *P :* iron h. (*R.S.* = poof), pédéraste*; *cf.* half-iron.

hoof² [huːf] (to), *F :* to h. it = to pad it (pad² (to)).

hoof out [ˈhuːfˈaut] (to), *F :* 1. sortir (qn) à coups de pied, expulser. 2. congédier*, mettre à la porte, envoyer dinguer (qn).

hoo-ha(a) [ˈhuːhɑː] (*noun*), *F :* 1. bruit*, boucan *m*. 2. querelle*, barabille *f*. 3. embarras *m.pl.*, chichis *m.pl.*

hook¹ [huk] (*noun*). 1. *F :* on the h., dans une mauvaise passe, dans le pétrin. 2. *F :* to get off the h., se débrouiller*, se tirer d'embarras (*ou* d'affaire); that lets me off the h., cela m'a tiré d'affaire; to get s.o. off the h., tirer qn d'affaire, sortir qn de

mauvais draps. 3. *P :* to go off the hooks, (*a*) devenir fou*, dérailler, partir du ciboulot; (*b*) mourir*. 4. *F :* on one's own h., sans appui, à son propre compte. 5. *P :* to sling one's h., partir*, s'enfuir, décamper, mettre les bouts. 6. (*pl.*) *F :* mains*, croches *f.pl.*; to get one's hooks on s.o., sth., mettre le grappin sur qn, qch.; *cf.* grappling, 2; meat-hooks. 7. *P :* drogue narcotique (héroïne *f*). 8. (*U.S.*) *V :* to put the hooks to s.o., coïter* avec qn, fourailler qn. 9. *P :* voleur*, leveur *f*.

hook² [huk] (to). 1. *P :* voler*, grappiner, enquiller. 2. *P :* arrêter*, agrafer. 3. *P :* to get hooked for X pounds, être estampé de X livres (au jeu). 4. *F :* to be hooked on drugs, se droguer*, se camer, se (s)chnouffer. 5. *F :* to be hooked on s.o., être épris de qn, avoir le béguin pour qn. 6. *F :* to h. a husband, crocheter (*ou* agrafer) un mari. 7. *F :* agripper, empoigner. 8. *F :* trouver*, dégot(t)er. 9. *P :* to h. it, s'enfuir*, décamper.

hooker [ˈhukər] (*noun*), *P :* 1. prostituée*, poule *f*, raccrocheuse *f*. 2. dupeur *m*, entôleur *m*, roustisseur *m*; fourgueur *m* de drogues, joueur professionnel, *etc.* 3. (*U.S.*) verre *m* d'alcool* *ou* de whisky.

hookey [ˈhuki] (*noun*) (*U.S.*), *F :* to play h., faire l'école buissonnière.

hook-shop [ˈhukʃɔp] (*noun*), *P :* bordel*, clandé *m*, maison bancale.

hook up [ˈhukˈʌp] (to), *F :* to be hooked up with s.o., être le complice* de qn, être de mèche (*ou* de cheville) avec qn.

hoop [huːp] (*noun*), *F :* to go through the h., (*a*) passer un mauvais moment (*ou* quart d'heure); (*b*) être puni, en prendre pour son grade.

hooper-dooper [ˈhuːpəˈduːpər] (*adj.*), *F :* = super-duper.

hoop-la [ˈhuːplɑː] (*noun*), *F :* 1. tapage *m*, chahut *m*, boucan *m*. 2. publicité exagérée.

hoosegow [ˈhuːsgau] (*noun*) (*U.S.*), *F :* 1. commissariat *m* de police, burlingue *m* de quart. 2. prison*, bloc *m*, taule *f*.

hoot¹ [huːt] (*noun*), *F :* 1. rigolade *f*, blague *f*. 2. I don't care (*or* give) a h., je m'en moque, je m'en balance. 3.

---

* L'astérisque indique que le mot marqué de ce signe figure comme entrée dans le Répertoire.

it's not worth a h., ça ne vaut rien*, ça ne vaut pas chipette.

hoot[2] [huːt] (to), F: 1. rire* aux éclats, se bidonner. 2. (Austr.) sentir* mauvais, puer.

hootch [huːtʃ] (noun) (U.S.), F: = hooch.

hooter ['huːtər] (noun), P: grand nez*, trompette f.

hop[1] [hɔp] (noun). 1. F: danse f, sauterie f, surboum f. 2. F: a short h., une courte distance, un pas, un saut; it's only a h., skip and a jump away, c'est à deux pas d'ici, ce n'est qu'à trois enjambées d'ici. 3. F: to catch s.o. on the h., surprendre qn, prendre qn au pied levé. 4. F: to be full of hops, (a) raisonner comme une grosse caisse, sortir des sornettes f.pl.; (b) avoir sa cuite de bière. 5. F: to be on the h., être toujours en mouvement, être toujours affairé, avoir la bougeotte. 6. P: opium m (drogues*); h. fiend = hophead. Voir aussi bell-hop.

hop[2] [hɔp] (to). 1. F: h. in! allez hop! saute dedans! 2. F: h. it! file! fiche le camp! 3. F: to h. on a bus, sauter dans un autobus; to h. off a bus, sauter d'un autobus. 4. F: hopping mad, très en colère*, en rogne. 5. P: to h. into bed with s.o., se foutre au lit avec qn. 6. P: to h. the twig, (a) mourir*, sauter le pas; (b) s'esquiver, échapper à ses créanciers. Voir aussi hedge-hop (to); lorry-hop (to); wag[1].

hophead ['hɔphed] (noun), P: morphinomane mf.

hop-joint ['hɔpdʒɔint] (noun), P: 1. gargote f, boui-boui m. 2. fumoir m d'opium, touffianerie f.

hopped up ['hɔpt'ʌp] (adj.), P: 1. stimulé par la drogue, dopé, chargé. 2. = souped up. 3. surexcité, survolté.

hoppite ['hɔpait] (noun), P: fou*, aliéné (de l'asile de Broadmoor).

horn [hɔːn] (noun). 1. V: érection f; to have the h., être en érection*, bander. 2. (U.S.) F: (jazz) trompette f. Voir aussi blow (to), 5.

horn in ['hɔːn'in] (to), F: s'immiscer; to h. i. on s.o.'s conversation, fourrer le nez dans la conversation.

hornswoggle ['hɔːnswɔgl] (to) (U.S.), F: = hose (to), 2.

horny ['hɔːni] (adj.), V: to be h., (a) être en érection*, avoir le bambou

(ou la canne ou le gourdin); (b) être lascif (ou libidineux ou allumé).

horror ['hɔrər] (noun), F: 1. qch. de laid* et ridicule, horreur f, monstruosité f. 2. individu* abominable, une horreur. 3. (a) h. film, film m d'épouvante; (b) h. comic, bandes dessinées à thème d'épouvante. 4. to have the horrors, (a) grelotter de peur*; être en proie au delirium tremens; (b) avoir des troubles mentaux dus aux amphétamines; (c) faire une dépression due au manque de drogues; (d) avoir des symptômes dus au sevrage d'héroïne. Voir aussi chuck[1], 3.

horse[1] [hɔːs] (noun). 1. F: he's a dark h., il cache son jeu, il n'a pas l'air d'y toucher. 2. F: it's straight from the h.'s mouth, (a) ça vient de la source, tu l'as de première main; (b) c'est un tuyau increvable; to have it straight from the h.'s mouth, ne pas l'envoyer dire. 3. F: a h. of another colour, une autre paire de manches. 4. F: to flog a dead h., faire des pas m.pl. inutiles, se dépenser en pure perte, enfoncer des portes ouvertes. 5. F: to get on one's high h., monter sur ses grands chevaux, le prendre de haut. 6. F: a willing h., un bûcheur, un turbineur. 7. F: hold your horses! (a) ne t'emballe pas! du calme!; (b) attendez! arrêtez! 8. (U.S.) F: h. opera, film m western. 9. P: héroïne f (drogues*), cheval m; cf. Charl(e)y, 6. 10. P: to water the horses, uriner*, changer son poisson d'eau. Voir aussi clothes-horse; one-horse; switch[2] (to); war-horse.

horse[2] [hɔːs] (to) (U.S.). 1. F: = horse about (to). 2. P: coïter* en adultère, biquer.

horse about ['hɔːsə'baut] (to), horse around ['hɔːsə'raund] (to), F: faire le plaisant, batifoler, faire le zouave.

horse-doctor ['hɔːsdɔktər] (noun), F: 1. vétérinaire mf. 2. médecin peu compétent, toubib m marron.

horseplay ['hɔːs-plei] (noun), F: jeu brutal, jeu de mains, badinerie grossière.

horse-shit ['hɔːsʃit] (noun) (mainly U.S.), V: 1. mensonges*. 2. conneries f.pl., battages m.pl.

horse-trading ['hɔːs-treidiŋ] (noun), F: manigance f.

---

* An asterisk indicates that the word so marked is included as a head-word in the Appendix.

hose [houz] (**to**). 1. *V:* coïter* avec (qn), fourailler (qn). 2. *P:* duper*, frauder, monter le coup à (qn).

hoss [hɔs] (*noun*) (*U.S.*) (=*horse*), *F:* cheval *m*.

hot [hɔt] (*adj.*). 1. *P:* chaud(e) de la pince (*ou* de la pointe); **to have h. pants**, (*a*) avoir le feu aux fesses*; (*b*) avoir le feu au pantalon; **to be a h. skirt**, avoir le feu au jupon; **to be h. for s.o.**, bander pour qn; **h. mama**, femme* passionnée; *cf.* **red-hot**, 2; *voir aussi* **baby**[2], 2; **cookie**, 6; **number**, 3; **patootie**. 2. *F:* **h. pants**, les shorts *m.pl.* 3. **h. stuff**, (*a*) *P:* un(e) chaud(e) lapin(e); (*b*) *P:* jeux provocants; (*c*) *F:* butin* facilement identifiable; (*d*) *F:* **he's h. stuff at tennis**, c'est un as du tennis. 4. *F:* expert, as, crack. 5. *F:* **to be h. under the collar**, être en colère*, fulminer, être en rogne. 6. *F:* (*a*) énervé, excité, qui a les nerfs en pelote; (*b*) agité, effaré, en émoi; **to get all h. and bothered**, s'échauffer, se faire du mauvais sang. 7. *F:* (*jazz*) improvisé avec passion, joué avec chaleur, hot; *cf.* **cool**[1], 7; **h. music**, le jazz, le swing; **h. cat**, fana(tique) *mf* du jazz *ou* du swing. 8. *F:* très récent, sensationnel; **h. tip**, renseignement* sûr, tuyau *m* increvable; **h. from the press**, dernier cri. 9. *P:* (*a*) (*objets volés*) recherché par la police, difficile à écouler; **h. drag**, auto volée*; **h. money**, argent* volé; **h. rock**, bijou fauché; (*b*) criminel recherché par la police pour crime. 10. *P:* dangereux, scandaleux, chiant. 11. (*a*) (*U.S.*) *F:* **h. seat**, *P:* **h. squat**, chaise *f* électrique; (*b*) *F:* **to be in the h. seat**, être dans le fauteuil directorial. 12. *F:* **to make it h. for s.o.**, faire des difficultés *f.pl.* à qn, être vache avec qn. 13. *F:* **to give it to s.o.** (*or* **to let s.o. have it**) **h.** (**and strong**), passer un bon savon à qn, donner une belle engueulade à qn. 14. *F:* **to be in h. water**, être dans de mauvais draps (*ou* dans la mélasse); **to get into h. water**, se mettre dans de vilains draps. 15. *F:* **that's not so h.**, c'est pas formidable. 16. *F:* **h. on the scent** (*or* **track**) **of . . .**, aux trousses *f.pl.* de... 17. *F:* (*jeux*) **you're getting h.**, tu brûles. 18. *F:* **to sell like h. cakes**, se vendre comme des petits pains.

19. *F:* **to hold a h. hand**, avoir en main des cartes* maîtresses (au jeu); **to have a h. streak**, avoir une chance* persistante (au jeu). 20. *F:* **a h. one**, (*a*) qch. *ou* qn de renversant; (*b*) une bonne blague. 21. *F:* **h. war**, la guerre sanglante (*contraire de* la guerre froide). 22. *F:* **h. rod**, bolide *m* (de course) (*automobile*). 23. *F:* **h. spot**, (*a*) cabaret *m*, boîte *f* de nuit; (*b*) mauvaise passe, pétrin *m*. 24. **h. shot**, (*a*) *F:* = **big shot** (**big**[1], 1); (*b*) *P:* injection *f* de drogues qui devient fatale. 25. *F:* radio-actif; **h. laboratory**, laboratoire *m* traitant des matières radio-actives. 26. (*U.S.*) *F:* **h.** (**diggety**) **dog!** hourra! vivat! bravo! *Voir aussi* **air**[1], 8; **blow (to)**, 14; **dog**[1], 15; **drop**[2] (**to**), 1; **gospeller**; **potato**, 3; **red-hot**.

hotfoot [ˈhɔtˈfut] (**to**), *F:* **to h. it**, se dépêcher*, mettre les bouts.

hothouse [ˈhɔthaus] (*attrib. adj.*), *F:* **h. plant**, personne délicate.

hot-rod [ˈhɔtrɔd] (**to**) (*U.S.*), *V:* se masturber*, faire cinq contre un; *cf.* **rod**, 1. *Voir aussi* **hot**, 22.

hots [hɔts] (*pl. noun*) (*U.S.*), *P:* **the h.**, (*a*) amour *m*; (*b*) désir sexuel.

hotsie-totsie, hotsy-totsy [ˈhɔtsi-ˈtɔtsi] (*adj.*) (*U.S.*), *F:* = **hunky-dory**.

hotted up [ˈhɔtidˈʌp] (*adj.*), *F:* 1. **h. u. food**, du réchauffé. 2. **h. u. car**, voiture* au moteur poussé (*ou* gonflé).

hottie, hotty [ˈhɔti] (*noun*) (=*hot-water bottle*), *F:* bouillotte *f*.

hound-dog [ˈhaunddɔg, *U.S.* ˈhaunddɔːg] (*noun*), *F:* 1. homme à femmes, cavaleur *m*, juponneur *m*. 2. = **tripehound**.

house [haus] (*noun*), *F:* 1. (*a*) **like a h. on fire**, vite*, à toute pompe, à pleins gaz; (*b*) **to get on like a h. on fire**, sympathiser, s'entendre comme les larrons en foire. 2. **on the h.**, gratuit*, à l'œil, aux frais *m.pl.* de la princesse. 3. **to bring the h. down**, faire crouler la salle (sous les applaudissements), casser la baraque. *Voir aussi* **barrelhouse**; **big**[1], 15; **bug-house**[1,2]; **cathouse**; **chophouse**; **craphouse**; **crazyhouse**; **dog-house**; **doss-house**; **dress-house**; **flea-house**; **flop-house**; **glasshouse**; **hash-house**; **hot-house**; **jag-house**; **joy-house**; **kip-house**; **madhouse**; **meat-house**; **nut-house**; **pisshouse**; **power-house**; **rough-house**; **shit-house**; **whore-house**.

---

* L'astérisque indique que le mot marqué de ce signe figure comme entrée dans le Répertoire.

how[1] [haʊ] (*adv.*), *F:* **1. any old h.**, n'importe comment, à la va-comme-je-te-pousse. **2. h. come?** comment est-ce possible? pourquoi? pour quelle raison? **3. and h.!** et comment! **4. all you know h.**, aussi bien que possible. *Voir aussi* **nohow.**

how![2] [haʊ] (*excl.*), *F:* comment va? ça va?

how-do-you-do [ˈhaʊdjuːduː:,ˈhaʊdjə-duː:] (*noun*), *F:* = **how-d'ye-do.**

howdy! [ˈhaʊdi] (*excl.*) (*U.S.*), *F:* = **how!**[2].

how-d'ye-do [ˈhaʊdjədu:] (*noun*), *F:* **it's a fine (old)** (*or* **a right old) h.**, (*a*) c'est une mauvaise passe, c'est une sale affaire; (*b*) c'est une drôle d'histoire; nous voilà bien! en voilà du joli!

howl [haʊl] (*noun*), *F:* = **scream**[1], **1**, (*a*), (*b*).

how's-your-father [ˈhaʊzjəˈfɑːðər] (*noun*), *F:* = **how-d'ye-do.**

hubba-hubba [ˈhʌbəˈhʌbə] (*adv.* & *excl.*), *F:* **vite***, à toute barde.

hubby [ˈhʌbi] (*noun*) (=*husband*), *F:* mari *m*, le légitime.

huddle [ˈhʌdl] (*noun*), *F:* **1.** séance secrète; **to go into a h.**, tenir une séance secrète. **2.** période *f* de réflexion personnelle.

hugsome [ˈhʌgsəm] (*adj.*), *F:* = **cuddle-some.**

hully-gully [ˈhʌliˈgʌli] (*noun*) (*U.S.*), *F:* = **holly-golly, 1, 2.**

hum [hʌm] (**to**), *F:* **1. to be humming**, être en pleine activité, boumer. **2.** sentir* mauvais, schlinguer.

humdinger [ˈhʌmˈdiŋər] (*noun*), *F:* qn *ou* qch. d'excellent*, du tonnerre.

hummy [ˈhʌmi] (*adj.*), *F:* **1.** excellent*, admirable, épatant. **2.** heureux, content, insouciant. **3.** puant, cocotant.

hump[1] [hʌmp] (*noun*). **1.** *F:* **to get over the h.**, surmonter le plus dur (d'un problème, *etc.*). **2.** *F:* **to have the h.**, être de mauvaise humeur, broyer du noir; **to give s.o. the h.**, donner le cafard à qn. **3.** *V:* (*a*) coït*; **to like one's h.**, aimer la crampette; (*b*) femme*, femelle *f*, garce *f*, gonzesse *f*; **she's good h.**, c'est une rude baiseuse, c'est une Marie-jambe(s)-en-l'air. **4.** (*U.S.*) *F:* **to get a h. on**, se dépêcher*, se dégrouiller. **5.** *P:* vaurien*, rien-du-tout *m*.

hump[2] [hʌmp] (**to**). **1.** *V:* coïter* avec (qn), pinocher (qn). **2.** *F:* porter sur le dos (avec difficulté), trimbal(l)er. **3.** *F:* = **to get a hump on** (**hump**[1], **4**).

humpity [ˈhʌmpiti] (*adj.*), *F:* = **humpy.**

humpty-dumpty [ˈhʌm(p)tiˈdʌm(p)ti] (*noun*), *P:* **to do a h.-d.**, se casser la figure, être capout.

humpy [ˈhʌmpi] (*adj.*), *F:* = **umpit(t)y.**

Hun, hun[1] [hʌn] (*adj.*), *F:* allemand*, boche.

Hun, hun[2] [hʌn] (*noun*), *F:* (*a*) Allemand*, boche *m.*; (*b*) soldat* allemand, hun *m*, doryphore *m*.

hunch [hʌntʃ] (*noun*), *F:* intuition *f*, pressentiment *m*; **to have a h. that ...,** soupçonner que...; **to play a h.**, agir par intuition.

hundred [ˈhʌndrəd] (*numeral noun*), *F:* **1. a h.**, cent livres sterling; **half a h.**, cinquante livres sterling; *cf.* **century. 2. a h. proof**, le meilleur, vrai, authentique, cent pour cent.

hundred-percenter [ˈhʌndrədpəˈsentər] (*noun*), *F:* = **whole-hogger.**

hung [hʌŋ] (*adj.*), *P:* **1.** fâché, irrité, embêté. **2.** fatigué*, vanné. *Voir aussi* **well-hung.**

hunger [ˈhʌŋgər] (*noun*) (*U.S.*), *F:* **to be from h.**, être miteux (*ou* pouilleux *ou* toc).

hung up [ˈhʌŋˈʌp] (*adj.*), *F:* **1.** collet monté, vieux jeu. **2.** retardé, retenu. **3.** trouvant des obstacles, tombant sur un accroc (*ou* un os). **4.** en manque de drogues*. **5.** obsédé, frustré, agité. *Voir aussi* **hang up** (to).

hunkers [ˈhʌŋkəz] (*pl. noun*), *F:* **on one's h.**, accroupi, à croupeton.

hunks [hʌŋks] (*noun*), *F:* **1.** vieux birbe. **2.** avare *m*, vieux grigou.

hunky[1] [ˈhʌŋki] (*adj.*) (*U.S.*), *F:* **1.** = **chunky, 1. 2.** = **hunky-dory.**

hunky[2] [ˈhʌŋki] (*noun*) (*U.S.*), *P:* immigrant *m* de l'Europe centrale; *cf.* **bohunk, 1.**

hunky-dory [ˈhʌŋkiˈdɔːri] (*adj.*), *F:* parfait, ronflant, satisfaisant.

hurry-up[1] [ˈhʌriˈʌp] (*attrib. adj.*), *F:* **h.-u. wag(g)on** = **Black Maria.**

hurry-up[2] [ˈhʌriˈʌp] (*noun*), *P:* **to have it away for the h.-u.**, partir* en hâte, décamper.

hush [hʌʃ] (*noun*), *F:* **let's have some**

---

* An asterisk indicates that the word so marked is included as a head-word in the Appendix.

(*or* **a little bit of**) **h.**, un peu de silence, s'il vous plaît.

hush-hush [ˈhʌʃˈhʌʃ] (*adj.*), *F:* très secret, confidentiel.

hush up [ˈhʌʃˈʌp] (**to**), *F:* étouffer, supprimer (par la censure).

hustle[1] [ˈhʌsl] (*noun*), *F:* **1.** tromperie *f*, arnaquage *m*, faisage *m* de graisse. **2.** bousculade *f*, grouillement *m*; **to get a h. on**, se dépêcher*, se grouiller. **3.** investigation *f*, recherche *f*.

hustle[2] [ˈhʌsl] (**to**), *P:* **1.** mendier*, mangaver. **2.** racoler*, faire le trottoir, faire le business. **3.** vendre (qch.), bazarder. **4.** gagner sa vie par des méthodes louches, fourguer, lessiver de la marchandise.

hustler [ˈhʌslər] (*noun*), *P:* **1.** qn qui gagne sa vie par des moyens louches, débrouillard *m*, brasseur *m* d'affaires. **2.** prostituée*, bisenesseuse *f*. **3.** souteneur*, marlou(pin) *m*.

hyp(e) [haip] (*noun*), *P:* **1.** (=*hypodermic needle*) aiguille *f* hypodermique. **2.** piqûre *f* de drogues*, piquouse *f*. **3.** fourgueur *m* de drogues*.

hyped up [ˈhaipdˈʌp] (*adj.*) drogué*, camé.

hype-stick [ˈhaip-stik] (*noun*), *P:* = **hyp(e)**, **1**.

hypo [ˈhaipou] (*noun*), *P:* **1.** (*a*) (=*hypochondria*) hypocondrie *f*; (*b*) (=*hypochondriac*) hypocondriaque *mf*. **2.** = **hyp(e)**, **1,2**. **3.** drogué*, camé *m*, usager *m* de la drogue.

I

I-am [ai'(j)æm] (*noun*), *F:* **he thinks he's the big I-am,** il se croit le bon Dieu en personne; il se prend pour Dieu le Père.

ice¹ [ais] (*noun*). 1. *P:* diamant(s)*, diam *m*; **green i.,** émeraude(s) *f.* (*pl.*); **i. palace,** bijouterie *f*, brocaillerie *f*. 2. *F:* **to break the i.,** rompre la glace. 3. *F:* **to cut no i. with s.o.,** ne pas impressionner qn, ne pas faire d'effet sur qn. 4. *F:* **to put on i.,** mettre au frigidaire (*ou* sur la planche). 5. *F:* **to skate on thin i.,** marcher sur des œufs. 6. *P:* **to be on i.,** (*a*) être assuré d'avance, être du tout cuit, être affiché; (*b*) = **to be iced** (**ice²** (to), 4). 7. *P:* **to have i. in one's shoes,** avoir peur de se donner à la drogue, avoir la hantise des drogues.

ice² [ais] (to), *P:* 1. tuer*, refroidir (qn). 2. feindre d'ignorer qn, ne pas s'occuper de qn, négliger qn. 3. se taire*, la boucler. 4. **to be iced,** être emprisonné* au secret, être quasi-mort.

iceberg ['aisbə:g] (*noun*), *F:* (*d'une personne*) glaçon *m*, bloc *m* de glace.

ice-cream ['ais'kri:m] (*noun*), *P:* opium *m* (*drogues**), boue *f*.

iceman ['aismæn, 'aismən], *P:* voleur* de bijoux, chopeur *m* de joncaille; *cf.* **ice¹,** 1.

icky ['iki] (*adj.*), *P:* 1. vieux jeu, rococo. 2. poisseux, visqueux.

idiot-board ['idiətbɔ:d] (*noun*), *F:* (*T.V.*) pancarte cachée des cameras qui «souffle» aux acteurs, pense-bête *m*.

idiot-box ['idiətbɔks] (*noun*), *F:* = **goggle-box**; *cf.* **box¹,** 2; **idiot's lantern** (*voir* **lantern**).

iffy ['ifi] (*adj.*), *F:* douteux, plein de «si», avec des «si» et des «mais».

Ikey (Mo) ['aiki('mou)] (*pr. noun*), *P:* (*péj.*) Juif *m*, Youpin *m*, Youpe *m*.

imp [imp] (*noun*), *F:* petit diable, polisson *m*.

in¹ [in] (*attrib. adj.*), *F:* **i. joke,** plaisanterie *f* de coterie.

in² [in] (*adv.*). 1. *P:* **to get (it) i.,** coïter*, mettre la cheville dans le trou. 2. *F:* **to be (well) i. with s.o.,** être bien avec qn, être dans les petits papiers de qn. 3. *F:* **to be i.,** (*a*) être dans le vent (*ou* à la page), être dans la rage du moment; (*b*) être accepté dans la bonne société, savoir nager, faire partie du Gotha. 4. *F:* **to have it i. for s.o.,** (*a*) en vouloir à qn, avoir une dent contre qn; (*b*) détester* qn, avoir qn dans le nez. 5. *F:* **to be i. on sth.,** être dans le bain (*ou* dans le coup). 6. *F:* **he's i. for it!** son affaire est bonne! le voilà dans de beaux draps! il va écoper! 7. *F:* **to be all i.,** être fatigué* (*ou* claqué *ou* vidé).

in³ [in] (*noun*), *F:* 1. **to have an i.,** avoir de l'influence, avoir le bras long; *cf.* **out².** 2. **the ins and outs,** les coins et recoins (d'une affaire), les tenants et les aboutissants.

include out [in'klu:d'aut] (to), *F:* exclure, mettre de côté; **you can i. me o.,** tu peux compter que je n'y serai pas; compte sur tout sauf moi.

incy(-wincy) ['insi('winsi)] (*adj.*), *F:* **an i. bit of...,** un petit peu* de..., un chouia de...

India, india ['indiə] (*noun*), *P:* cannabis *m* (*drogues**), chanvre indien.

Indian ['indiən] (*adj.*), *P:* 1. **I. gift,** cadeau-hameçon *m*, cadeau-bidon *m*; **I. giver,** donneur *m* de cadeaux-hameçons. 2. **I. hay** (*or* **hemp**) = **India.**

indigo ['indigou] (*adj.*), *F:* **i. mood,** idées noires, cafard *m*, bourdon *m*.

influence ['influəns] (*noun*), *F:* **under the i.,** sous l'empire de la boisson, dans les vignes (du Seigneur).

info ['infou] (*abbr.* = *information*), *F:* renseignement*, tuyau *m*.

infra dig ['infrə'dig] (*adv. phrase*), *F:* indigne, au-dessous de soi.

ink-slinger ['iŋk-sliŋər] (*noun*), *F:* gratte-papier *m*, rond-de-cuir *m*.

in-laws ['inlɔ:z] (*pl. noun*), *F:* belle-

---

* An asterisk indicates that the word so marked is included as a head-word in the Appendix.

famille *f*; les beaux-parents *m.pl.*, les beaux-dabs *m.pl.*

innards ['inədz] (*pl. noun*), *F:* ventre*, boyaux *m.pl.*, tripes *f.pl.*

inner ['inər] (*adj.*), *F:* the i. man, appétit *m*, ventre*; to look after the i. man, se remplir le buffet.

innings ['ininz] (*noun*), *F:* 1. to have (had) a good i., vivre vieux*, avoir couvert pas mal de chemin. 2. your i.! à vous de jouer! à vous le tour!

inside[1] ['insaid] (*adj.*), *F:* 1. i. information (*or* dope), tuyaux confidentiels. 2. the i. story, l'histoire *f* authentique (*ou* véridique). 3. an i. job, un crime attribué à une personne de l'entourage de la victime, un coup fourré (*ou* monté).

inside[2] [in'said, 'insaid] (*adv.*), *F:* 1. en prison*, à l'ombre. 2. i. out, (*a*) à fond; to know sth. i. out, connaître qch. comme sa poche (*ou* sur le bout du doigt); to know Paris i. out, connaître Paris dans ses tours et ses détours; (*b*) to turn everything i. out, mettre tout sens dessus dessous. 3. to be i. on sth., connaître les dessous d'une affaire, être bien tuyauté.

inside[3] [in'said] (*noun*), *F:* 1. =innards; I laughed so much my insides were all sore, j'ai ri jusqu'à en avoir mal aux côtes. 2. to be on the i., être dans le coup, être du bâtiment.

inside[4] ['insaid] (*prep.*), *F:* to do sth. i. (of) an hour, faire qch. en moins d'une heure.

instrument ['instru:mənt] (*noun*), *P:* pénis*, instrument *m*.

intended [in'tendid] (*noun*), *F:* un(e) futur(e).

into ['intu:] (*prep.*), *F:* absorbé par (qch.), en proie à (qch.); I'm i. Russian novels this week, je suis plongé dans les romans russes cette semaine.

invite ['invait] (*noun*), *F:* invitation *f*, invite *f*, appât *m*.

Irish[1] ['airiʃ] (*adj.*), *F:* 1. biscornu; the whole sentence sounds a bit I., toute la phrase ne tient pas debout. 2. I. coffee, café* noir au whisky (couronné de crème Chantilly). 3. I. confetti, briques *f.pl.* 4. I. banjo, pelle *f*. 5. I. grape, pomme *f* de terre, patate *f*. 6. I. wedding, soûlerie générale.

Irish[2] ['airiʃ] (*noun*), *F:* to get one's I. up, se mettre en colère* (*ou* en rogne), voir rouge.

iron ['aiən] (*noun*). 1. *P:* to carry i., être armé (*ou* enfouraillé); *voir aussi* shooting-iron. 2. *F:* (eating) irons, couteau *m*, fourchette *f* et cuiller *f*; les couverts *m.pl. Voir aussi* cast-iron; half-iron; hoof[1], 2.

issue ['isju:, 'iʃu:] (*noun*), *P:* the whole (bloody) i., tout le bataclan, toute la sacrée bande.

it [it] (*pron.*). 1. *F:* du sex-appeal, du chien. 2. *F:* vermouth (italien). 3. *F:* you've had i.! t'as ton compte! tu l'as voulu! tu es fichu! 4. to give i. to s.o., (*a*) *P:* coïter* avec qn, baiser (*ou* ramoner) qn; (*b*) *F:* battre* qn; (*c*) *F:* réprimander* qn. 5. *P:* to make i. with s.o., (*a*) coïter* avec qn, faire l'amour avec qn; (*b*) plaire à qn, faire une touche, avoir un ticket. 6. *F:* to step on i. = to step on the gas (gas[2], 2).

itch[1] [itʃ] (*noun*), *F:* 1. the seven-year i., l'écueil *m* des sept ans* de mariage, la démangeaison de la septième année*; le démon de midi. 2. to have an i. to do sth., mourir (*ou* crever) d'envie de faire qch.

itch[2] [itʃ] (to), *F:* to i. to do sth. = to have an itch to do sth. (itch[1], 2); he's itching for trouble, la peau lui démange, ça le démange.

itchy ['itʃi] (*adj.*), *F:* qui brûle de faire qch. *Voir aussi* palm, 2.

itsy-bitsy ['itsi'bitsi] (*adj.*), *F:* = bitty.

ivories ['aivəriz] (*pl. noun*), *F:* 1. dents*, clavier *m*; *voir aussi* sluice[2] (to). 2. boules *f.pl.* de billard. 3. dés*, doches *m.pl.*, bobs *m.pl.* 4. touches *f.pl.* d'un piano, clavier *m*; to tickle the i., jouer du piano, taquiner les touches.

ivory ['aivəri] (*adj.*), *F:* i. dome, intellectuel *m*, grosse tête.

* L'astérisque indique que le mot marqué de ce signe figure comme entrée dans le Répertoire.

J

J [dʒei] = jay, 1.

jab¹ [dʒæb] (noun), F: (a) inoculation f, vaccin m, piqûre f; **have you had your jabs?** tu les a eues, tes piqûres?; (b) piqûre f de drogues, piquouse f, shoot m.

jab² [dʒæb] (to), F: (a) inoculer, faire une piqûre à (qn); (b) piquer, piquouser, shooter.

jabber [ˈdʒæbər] (noun), F: aiguille f hypodermique, poussette f, shooteuse f.

jab-off [ˈdʒæbɔf] (noun), P: (a) piqûre f, piquouse f (de narcotique); (b) effet m de la piqûre, le bang, le flash.

jack¹, Jack [dʒæk] (noun). 1. P: on one's j., tout seul, seulabre, esseulé. 2. F: every man j., tout un chacun. 3. VV: fuck you (or F: pull the ladder up), J., I'm all right, ça tourne rond pour bibi, bibi lui il s'en tire; cf. ladder. 4. V: to get the j., être en érection*, avoir le bambou (ou la canne). 5. P: cachet m d'héroïne (drogues*), cheval m. 6. (U.S.) F: to ball the j., (a) se dépêcher*, s'activer, se magner; (b) jouer son va-tout (ou le tout pour le tout), mettre le paquet. 7. F: j., J. Tar, marin*, matelot m, mathurin m. 8. F: before you can (or could) say J. (Robinson), en un clin d'œil, avant de pouvoir dire ouf, en moins de deux (ou de rien). 9. (U.S.) P: argent*, galette f; a nice piece of j., une somme rondelette. 10. P: J. the Ripper (R.S. = kipper), hareng saur, kipper m. 11. P: policier*, condé m. 12. P: J.'s alive, (a) (billet* de) cinq livres sterling; (b) voir bingo (5). 13. F: yellow j., fièvre f jaune, godiche f jaune.

jack² [dʒæk] (to), P: 1. = jack in (to), 1. 2. = jack up (to), 3.

jackaroo [ˈdʒækəˈruː] (noun), P: 1. (Austr.) colon immigrant sans expérience. 2. (U.S.) cowboy m.

jack around [ˈdʒækəˈraund] (to), P: 1. traîner, lambiner, flemmarder. 2. faire le zouave (ou le con), couillonner.

jacked up [ˈdʒæktˈʌp] (adj.), P: 1. sous l'influence d'un stimulant. 2. excité, tendu, énervé. Voir aussi jack up (to), 1.

jackeroo [ˈdʒækəˈruː] (noun), P: = jackaroo.

jacket [ˈdʒækit] (to), P: battre*, sauter sur le paletot à; cf. dust² (to).

jack in [ˈdʒækˈin] (to), P: 1. abandonner*, lâcher, balancer, plaquer. 2. to j. it i., se taire*, la boucler, la fermer.

jack-in-office (noun), F: fonctionnaire plein de son importance, Monsieur Lebureau.

jack-in-the-box [ˈdʒækinðəbɔks] (noun), F: 1. diablotin m, qn qui a un ressort au derrière. 2. fantoche m.

jack-knife [ˈdʒæknaif] (to) (U.S.), F: suriner (qn).

jack off [ˈdʒækˈɔf] (to), V: se masturber*, s'astiquer le manche, se taper la colonne, se tirer son coup.

jackpot [ˈdʒækpɔt] (noun), F: to hit the j., gagner le gros lot, décrocher la timbale, taper dans le mille.

jack-priest [ˈdʒækˈpriːst] (noun), P: prêtre*, ratichon m.

jacksie [ˈdʒæksi] (noun), P: 1. fesses*, postérieur m; you can stick it up your j.! tu peux te le mettre quelque part!; cf. stick² (to), 3; to boot s.o. up the j., donner un coup de pied dans le derrière de qn. 2. (Austr.) bordel*, tringlodrome m.

jack up [ˈdʒækˈʌp] (to). 1. P: se faire piquouser, se faire shooter; voir aussi jacked up, 1. 2. P: = jack in (to), 1. 3. P: to j. u. the price, corser (ou fader) le prix, saler la note. 4. F: to j. s.o. u., encourager qn, donner du cœur au ventre à qn. 5. (Austr.) F: protester, se regimber, piaffer. 6. (Austr.) P: plaider innocent, se dire blanc, blanchir.

jacky [ˈdʒæki] (noun) (Austr.), P: arrangement m louche.

---

* An asterisk indicates that the word so marked is included as a head-word in the Appendix.

jacob [ˈdʒeikəb] (*noun*), *P:* échelle *f*, montante *f*, lève-pieds *m*.

jade [dʒeid] (*noun*), *F:* she's a real (*or* right) j., c'est une vraie rosse (*ou* carne).

jag¹ [dʒæg] (*noun*), *P:* **1.** piqûre *f*, piquouse *f*. **2.** état prolongé d'intoxication par une drogue. **3.** to have a j. on, (*a*) être drogué* (*ou* camé); (*b*) être ivre* (*ou* rond *ou* noir *ou* rétamé). **4.** to go on a j., (*a*) se camer à bloc; (*b*) faire la noce (*ou* la bombe), se saouler, prendre une cuite; (*c*) faire une orgie de...; **to go on a culture j.**, se lancer dans une débauche culturelle, prendre une indigestion de culture. **5.** coup *m* de chance*, du pot.

Jag² [dʒæg] (*noun*), *F:* Jag(uar) *f* (*automobile; marque déposée*).

jagged [dʒægd] (*adj.*), *P:* **1.** ivre*, rond, noir, rétamé. **2.** drogué*, camé, (s)chnouffé.

jag-house [ˈdʒæghaus] (*noun*), *P:* bordel* de pédérastes*, musée *m* à jocondes.

jag off [ˈdʒægˈɔf] (to), *V:* = jack off (to).

jail-bait [ˈdʒeilbeit] (*noun*), *P:* fille* de moins de seize ans, faux-poids *m*.

jailbird [ˈdʒeilbəːd] (*noun*), *F:* individu* qui est souvent en prison*, cheval *m* de retour, bois dur.

jake¹ [dʒeik] (*adv.*) (*U.S.*), *P:* **1.** d'accord*, dac, O.K.; things are (*or* everything is) j., ça marche bien, ça biche, ça roule. **2.** excellent*, impec, de première.

jake² [dʒeik] (*noun*), *F:* **1.** (*U.S.*) valet *m*, valdingue *m* (*cartes*); *cf.* jock, 4. **2.** (*pl.*) W.C.*, goguenots *m.pl.*

jalop(p)y [dʒəˈlɔpi] (*noun*), *F:* **1.** voiture*, bagnole *f*, tacot *m*. **2.** avion *m* de transport, coucou *m*.

jam¹ [dʒæm] (*adj.*), *P:* hétérosexuel, sexuellement normal.

jam² [dʒæm] (*noun*), *F:* **1.** it's money for j., c'est de l'argent* facile, c'est donné. **2.** to be in a j., être dans le pétrin (*ou* dans la mélasse). **3.** a bit of j., un coup de chance*, du pot, du bol. **4.** pacotille *f*, bibelots *m.pl.* **5.** do you want j. on it? et quoi encore? tu le veux doré sur tranches? **6.** that's real j.! c'est du nanan! *Voir aussi* jim-jams; session, 1.

jam³ [dʒæm] (to), *F:* (*jazz*) improviser.

jamboree [dʒæmbəˈriː] (*noun*), *F:* réjouissances*, bamboche *f*, foire *f*.

jam-jar [ˈdʒæmdʒɑːr] (*noun*), *P:* **1.** (*R.S.* = *car*) auto *f*. **2.** œillet *m* (des fleuristes).

jammed up [ˈdʒæmdˈʌp] (*adj.*), *P:* ayant dépassé une dose normale de drogue.

jammy [ˈdʒæmi] (*adj.*), *P:* **1.** facile comme bonjour. **2.** qui a de la chance*, veinard, bidard. **3.** de premier ordre, de prem(ière).

jam-packed [ˈdʒæmˈpækt] (*adj.*), *F:* au grand complet, bourré à craquer.

jam-pot [ˈdʒæm-pɔt] (*noun*), *F:* col romain, col à manger de la tarte.

jam-sheet [ˈdʒæmʃiːt] (*noun*), *P:* = shit-list.

jam up [ˈdʒæmˈʌp] (to), *F:* to j. u. the works = to gum up the works. *Voir aussi* jammed up.

jane, Jane [dʒein] (*noun*). **1.** *F:* fille* *ou* femme*, nénette *f*, nana *f*; a plain J., une laidasse, une pas-jolie. **2.** *P:* la petite amie, la nénette. **3.** *P:* W.C.* pour femmes, chiottes *f.pl.* à poules; *cf.* john, 1. **4.** Calamity J., Cassandre *f*, rabat-joie *m*. *Voir aussi* lady.

jankers [ˈdʒæŋkəz] (*pl. noun*) (*mil.*), *F:* punitions *f.pl.*, la pelote, le bal; to be on j., être au piquet des punis.

Jap¹ [dʒæp] (*adj.*), *F:* japonais, nippon.

Jap² [dʒæp] (*noun*), *F:* Japonais *m*, Nippon *m*.

jar [dʒɑːr] (*noun*). **1.** *F:* to have (*or* down) a few jars, boire*, s'envoyer quelques verres, se jeter des jattes. **2.** *P:* faux diamant*, faux diam(e), caillou *m*. *Voir aussi* jam-jar.

jarred [dʒɑːd] (*adj.*), *P:* **1.** ivre*, rétamé. **2.** = jarred off.

jarred off [ˈdʒɑːdˈɔf] (*adj.*), *P:* cafardeux; to be j. o., avoir le cafard, en avoir ras le bol.

jasper [ˈdʒæspər] (*noun*), *P:* **1.** lesbienne*, gavousse *f*. **2.** puce *f*.

java [ˈdʒɑːvə] (*noun*) (*U.S.*), *P:* café*, caoua *m*, jus *m*.

jaw¹ [dʒɔː] (*noun*). **1.** *P:* bavardage *m*; to have a good j., tailler une bonne bavette; hold your j.! not so much of your j.! tais-toi! ta gueule! la ferme!; to be full of j., être fort en gueule; *cf.* flapjaw. **2.** *P:* pi j., bondieuseries *f.pl.*, sermon *m*, prêche *m*, paroles *f.pl.* de

curé. 3. *F:* his j. dropped, il fit une
sale (*ou* une drôle de) tête. *Voir aussi*
stickjaw.
jaw² [dʒɔ:] (to), *P:* (*a*) bavarder*,
jaspiner; (*b*) engueuler (qn).
jaw-breaker [ˈdʒɔ:-breikər], jawbuster [ˈdʒɔ:-bʌstər] (*noun*), *F:* 1. nom
m ou mot *m* à coucher dehors (*ou* à vous
décrocher la mâchoire). 2. bonbon dur.
jawing [ˈdʒɔ:iŋ] (*noun*), *P:* 1. bavardage
m. 2. to give s.o. a j., réprimander*
qn, passer un savon à qn, sonner les
cloches à qn.
jaw out [ˈdʒɔ:ˈaut] (to) (*U.S.*), *P:* to j.s.o.
o. = to give s.o. a jawing (jawing, 2).
jaw-twister [ˈdʒɔ:-twistər] (*noun*), *F:* =
jaw-breaker.
jay [dʒei] (*noun*). 1. *P:* cigarette* de
marijuana (*drogues**), joint *m*, stick *m.*
2. (*U.S.*) *F:* individu bête*, nouille *f.*
jaybird [ˈdʒeibə:d] (*noun*) (*U.S.*). 1. *F:*
paysan*, plouc *m*, péquenot *m.* 2. *F:* =
jailbird. 3. *P:* Juif *m*, Youpin *m.*
jayboy [ˈdʒeibɔi] (*noun*) (*U.S.*), *F:* =
jake², 1.
jaywalk [ˈdʒeiwɔ:k] (to), *F:* traverser
en dehors des clous.
jaywalker [ˈdʒeiwɔ:kər] (*noun*), *F:*
piéton imprudent.
jazz¹ [dʒæz] (*noun*). 1. *F:* (*a*) garniture
f, fioritures *f.pl.*, tape-à-l'œil *m*, fan-
freluches *f.pl.*; (*b*) ... and all that j.,
et tout et tout, et tout ce qui s'ensuit.
2. (*U.S.*) *V:* (*a*) coït*; (*b*) vagin*,
grippette *f*, chatte *f.* 3. (*U.S.*) *P:*
emballement *m*, entrain *m.*
jazz² [dʒæz] (to). 1. (*U.S.*) *V:* coïter*,
tirer un coup, godiller. 2. (*U.S.*) *P:*
mettre en train, donner le branle à
(qch.), aiguillonner. 3. *P:* (*a*) mentir*,
bourrer le crâne; (*b*) exagérer*, en
rajouter.
jazzed up [ˈdʒæzdˈʌp] (*adj.*). 1. *F:*
élégant*, endimanché. 2. *P:* animé,
survolté. 3. *P:* drogué*, camé, chargé,
bourré.
jazz up [ˈdʒæzˈʌp] (to), *F:* émoustiller,
échauffer, ravigoter, requinquer. *Voir
aussi* jazzed up.
jazzy [ˈdʒæzi] (*adj.*). 1. *F:* tape-à-l'œil,
psychédélique. 2. *P:* vieux-jeu, périmé.
J-boy [ˈdʒeibɔi] (*noun*) (*U.S.*), *F:* =
jake², 1; *cf.* jayboy.
jeepers (creepers)! [ˈdʒi:pəz(ˈkri:pəz)]
(*excl.*) (*U.S.*), *F:* mon Dieu! sapristi!

jeez(e)! Jeez(e)! [dʒi:z] (*excl.*) (*euph.
pour* Jesus!), *P:* mazette! (tonnerre de)
Dieu!
jeff [dʒef] (*noun*), *P:* corde *f*, fil *m.*
jell [dʒel] (to). 1. (*d'idées, etc.*) (se)
cristalliser. 2. bien s'entendre, sympathiser, être sur la même longueur
d'ondes.
jelly [ˈdʒeli] (*noun*), *F:* 1. gélignite *f*,
gelée *f.* 2. to pound s.o. into a j.,
battre* qn comme plâtre, mettre qn
en capilotade.
jelly-baby [ˈdʒeli-beibi] (*noun*), *P:*
amphétamine *f* (*drogues**).
jellyfish [ˈdʒeli-fiʃ] (*noun*), *F:* larve *f*,
mollasson *m.*
jelly-roll [ˈdʒeli-roul] (*noun*) (*U.S.*). 1.
V: vagin*, baveux *m*, millefeuille *m.*
2. *P:* homme *m* à femmes, conassier
m, queutard *m.* 3. *P:* amant *m.* 4. *P:*
collage *m*, baisage *m*, conasserie *f.*
jemima [dʒəˈmaimə] (*noun*), *F:* pot *m*
de chambre, Jules *m*, Thomas *m.*
jerk¹ [dʒə:k] (*noun*). 1. *P:* individu
bête*, petit con, enflé *m*, emplâtré *m*,
déplombé *m*; *voir aussi* dumb, 1 (*b*).
2. *P:* novice *m*, bleu *m.* 3. *F:* put a j.
in(to) it! et que ça saute! 4. *F:* physical
jerks, mouvements *m.pl.* de gymnas-
tique.
jerk² [dʒə:k] (to), *V:* coïter* avec (qn),
bourrer, bourriquer (qn). *Voir aussi*
gherkin.
jerk off [ˈdʒə:kˈɔf] (to), *V:* = jack off (to).
jerkwater [ˈdʒə:kwɔ:tər] (*noun*) (*U.S.*),
P: = one-horse town (*voir* one-
horse).
jerky [ˈdʒə:ki] (*adj.*) (*U.S.*), *F:* bête*,
cavé.
jerry¹ [ˈdʒeri] (*adj.*), *F:* inférieur, à la
manque, à la noix, de carton, en
papier mâché.
jerry,² Jerry [ˈdʒeri] (*noun*), *F:* 1. pot
m de chambre, Thomas *m*, Jules *m.*
2. soldat* allemand*, Fritz, fridolin *m*,
frizou *m.* 3. les Allemands*, les boches
m.pl. 4. avion (char, *etc.*) allemand.
jerry-go-nimble [ˈdʒerigouˈnimbl]
(*noun*), *P:* diarrhée*, courante *f.*
Jesus (Christ)! [ˈdʒi:zəs(ˈkraist)] (*excl.*),
P: nom de Dieu! grands dieux!; *cf.*
Jeez(e)!; Christ.
jet [dʒet] (*attrib. adj.*), *F:* 1. the j. set,
les bringueurs *m.pl.* cosmopolites, la
jet-set. 2. j. job, bolide *m.*

---

* An asterisk indicates that the word so marked is included as a head-word in the Appendix.

Jew[1] [ˈdʒuː] (*noun*), *P:* **dirty old J.:** *voir* **bingo** (2).

jew[2] [dʒuː] (to), *P:* duper* (qn), mettre (qn) dedans.

jewboy, Jewboy [ˈdʒuːbɔi] (*noun*) (*péj.*), *P:* Juif *m*, Youpin *m*.

jew down [ˈdʒuːˈdaun] (to), *P:* marchander, chipoter, regratter (qn).

jew's-harp [ˈdʒuːzˈhɑːp] (*noun*), *F:* peigne recouvert de papier de soie qui sert d'harmonica; guimbarde *f*.

jiff [dʒif], **jiffy** [ˈdʒifi] (*noun*), *F:* **in (half) a j.,** dans un instant, en un clin d'œil, en moins de deux; *cf.* **mo; sec; shake**[1], 1, 2; **tick**[1], 3.

jig [dʒig] (*noun*). 1. *P:* gigolo *m*, lustucru *m*, frère mironton. 2. (*U.S.*) *P:* (*a*) nègre*, bougnoule *m*, bamboula *m*; (*b*) moricaud *m*, café *m* au lait. 3. *F:* **the j. is up,** c'est fichu, c'est dans le lac. 4. *F:* bal public, guinche *f*, pince-cul *m*.

jigamaree [dʒigəməˈriː] (*noun*), *F:* = **thingamy.**

jigger [ˈdʒigər] (*noun*). 1. *F:* truc *m*, machin *m*. 2. (*mil.*) *P:* prison*, bloc *m*. 3. *P:* pénis*, queue *f*.

jigger (up) [ˈdʒigər(ˈʌp)] (to), *F:* abîmer*, bousiller.

jiggered [ˈdʒigəd] (*adj.*), *F:* étonné*, estomaqué; **well I'm j.!** j'en suis comme deux ronds de flan!

jiggered up [ˈdʒigədˈʌp] (*adj.*), *F:* fatigué*, à bout, claqué.

jiggery-pokery [ˈdʒigəriˈpoukəri] (*noun*), *F:* manigance *f*, attrape *f*, tour *m* de passe-passe.

jiggumbob [ˈdʒigəmbɔb] (*noun*), *F:* = **thingamy.**

jig-jig [ˈdʒigˈdʒig] (*noun*), *P:* coït*, criquon-criquette *m*.

Jim Crow [ˈdʒimˈkrou] (*noun*) (*U.S.*), *F:* (*a*) nègre*, bamboula *m*; (*b*) la ségrégation raciale et tout ce qui s'y rapporte.

jiminy! [ˈdʒimini] (*excl.*), *F:* **(by) j.!** mince! pitchoun!

jim-jams [ˈdʒimdʒæmz] (*pl. noun*), *P:* (*a*) les nerfs *m.pl.* en boule, la chair de poule; (*b*) delirium tremens *m*, les rats bleus.

Jimmy [ˈdʒimi] (*pr. noun*), *P:* 1. **J. Riddle** (*R.S.* = **piddle**), pipi *m*; **to have a J. Riddle,** uriner*, faire pipi. 2. **J. Rix** (*or* **Hix**) (*R.S.* = *fix*) = **fix**[1], 1.

3. **J. Prescott** (*R.S.* = *waistcoat*), gilet *m*. 4. **Little J.:** *voir* **bingo** (1). 5. (*Marine*) **J.** (**the one**), officier *m* qui commande en second à bord d'un navire (de guerre). *Voir aussi* **flash**[1], 1.

jingbang [ˈdʒiŋbæŋ] (*noun*), *F:* **the whole j.** = **the whole shooting-match.**

jing-jang [ˈdʒiŋdʒæŋ] (*noun*) (*U.S.*), *V:* 1. pénis*, zizi *m*. 2. vagin*, didi *m*. 3. coït*, zizi-panpan *m*.

jinks [dʒiŋks] (*pl. noun*), *F:* **high j.,** réjouissances*, noce *f*, bamboche *f*.

jinx[1] [dʒiŋks] (*noun*), *F:* 1. malchance*, guigne *f*, poisse *f*. 2. porte-poisse *m*, porte-guigne *m*.

jinx[2] [dʒiŋks] (to), *F:* porter malchance* (*ou* la guigne *ou* la poisse) à (qn).

jism [ˈdʒizm], **jissom** [ˈdʒis(ə)m] (*noun*) (*mainly U.S.*). 1. *V:* sperme*, jus *m*, came *f*. 2. *P:* dynamisme *m*, tonus *m*.

jitney[1] [ˈdʒitni] (*adj.*) (*U.S.*), *P:* camelote, piètre, piteux.

jitney[2] [ˈdʒitni] (*noun*) (*U.S.*), *F:* 1. pièce *f* de cinq cents. 2. microbus *m*. 3. **j. bag,** porte-monnaie*, artiche *m*, morlingue *m*.

jitter [ˈdʒitər] (to), *F:* (*a*) **to j. s.o.** = **to give s.o. the jitters;** (*b*) se trémousser, s'exciter, se démener.

jitterbug [ˈdʒitəbʌg] (*noun*), *F:* défaitiste *mf*, paniquard *m*.

jitters [ˈdʒitəz] (*pl. noun*), *F:* **to have the j.,** avoir les nerfs à fleur de peau, avoir la tremblote; **to give s.o. the j.,** flanquer la trouille à qn.

jittery [ˈdʒitəri] (*adj.*), *F:* crispé, à cran; **to feel j.,** avoir les nerfs en pelote, avoir la venette, serrer les fesses.

jive[1] [dʒaiv] (*noun*). 1. *F:* = **jazz**[1], 1 (*a*), (*b*); 2. (*a*); 3. 2. *P:* marijuana *f* (*drogues**).

jive[2] [dʒaiv] (to) (*U.S.*), *P:* 1. trouver les maillons de la chaîne, éclairer la lanterne. 2. bavarder*, bavasser, jacter, dévider le jars.

jizz [dʒiz] (*noun*) (*mainly U.S.*), *V:* = **jism,** 1.

joanna [dʒouˈænə] (*noun*) (*R.S.* = *piano*), *P:* (vieux) piano, chaudron *m*.

job [dʒɔb] (*noun*). 1. *F:* tout article façonné, manufacturé ou fabriqué; *cf.* **jet,** 2. 2. *P:* (*a*) réparation *f*; (*b*) boulot *m*. 3. *P:* vol *m*, coup *m*, fric-

---

* L'astérisque indique que le mot marqué de ce signe figure comme entrée dans le Répertoire.

frac *m*. **4.** *P:* crime *m*, méfait *m*, coup *m*, combine *f*. **5. to be on the j.**, (*a*) *F:* être sur le boulot; (*b*) *P:* être en train de coïter* (*ou* de besogner). **6.** *F:* **it's a good j. that . . .**, heureusement que... **7.** *F:* **. . . and a good j. too!** c'est pas malheureux! **8.** *F:* **just the j.!** juste ce qu'il faut! c'est au poil! **9.** *F:* défécation *f*, la grande commission; (*langage enfantin*) **to do small jobs**, faire sa petite commission; **to do big jobs**, faire sa grosse commission; *cf.* **number, 7. 10.** *P:* colis *m* de drogues*, la charge. **11.** *F:* **to lie** (*or* **lay** *or* **fall**) **down on the j.**, paresser*, tirer au flanc, s'endormir sur le mastic. **12.** *F:* **the blonde j. sitting over there**, la petite blonde assise là-bas. **13.** *P:* (*taxi*) client *m*, griot *m*. **14.** *F:* **to make a clean j. of sth.**, faire qch. à fond (*ou* de fond en comble). **15.** *F:* **jobs for the boys**, l'assiette *f* au beurre, distribution *f* des planques, partage *m* du même gâteau. **16.** *F:* **to have a j. to do sth.**, avoir du mal à faire qch. *Voir aussi* **bad¹, 6; blow-job; brown; finger-job; frail¹; hand-job; head, 13; pipe-job; put-up; shack-up; skull-job; snow-job; soup up (to)**, (*a*).

jock [dʒɔk] (*noun*), *P:* **1.** pédéraste*, emmanché *m*. **2.** (*pl.*) testicules*, roustons *m.pl*. **3.** *F:* = **jock-strap. 4.** *F:* valet (*cartes*); *cf.* **jake², 1. 5.** *F:* Écossais *m*.

jocker [ˈdʒɔkər], **jockey** [ˈdʒɔki] (*noun*), *P:* = **jock, 1.**

jock-strap [ˈdʒɔk-stræp] (*noun*), *F:* suspensoir *m*, soutien-couilles *m*.

joe, Joe [dʒou] (*noun*), *P:* **1.** (*U.S.*) café*, cao *m*, jus *m*. **2.** (*U.S.*) homme*, un Julot, un bon zigue. **3.** (*U.S.*) soldat*, pioupiou; *cf.* **G.I. Joe. 4.** (*a*) prêtre*, cureton *m*; *cf.* **holy, 2;** (*b*) aumônier *m* militaire. **5. J. Soap**, Père Tartempion. **6. J. Blake** (*R.S.* = *cake*), gâteau *m*. **7. J. Gurr** (*R.S.* = *stir* = *prison*), prison*, bloc *m*. **8.** *F:* **not for j.**, pour rien au monde, dans aucun cas. *Voir aussi* **sloppy, 2.**

joey [ˈdʒoui] (*noun*). **1.** *F:* clown *m*, gugusse *m*, pierrot *m*. **2.** *P:* paquet passé en fraude. **3.** (*Austr.*) *P:* fraude *f*, tartignole *f*, carotte *f*. **4.** *P:* menstrues*, les anglais *m.pl*. **5.** (*Austr.*) *F:* jeune kangourou *m*.

john, John [dʒɔn] (*noun*). **1.** *F:* **the j.**, W.C.* pour hommes, azor *m*, gogues *m.pl.*; *cf.* **jane, 3. 2.** *P:* **J. Thomas**, pénis*, Popaul, Charles-le-Chauve. **3.** *F:* **J. Barleycorn**, le whisky. **4.** *P:* **the johns**, la police*, les flics *m.pl*. **5.** (*U.S.*) *F:* **J. Doe**, l'Américain moyen (= Monsieur Blot, Monsieur Dupont-Durand). **6.** *F:* **long Johns**, caleçon long, caneçon *m*. **7.** *P:* client d'une prostituée*, miché *m*, michet *m*, micheton *m*. *Voir aussi* **amy-john.**

johnnie, Johnnie, johnny, Johnny [ˈdʒɔni] (*noun*). **1.** *P:* jeune homme*, zigoto *m*, zigue *m*, loulou *m*. **2.** *P:* homme élégant*, miche(ton) *m*, minet *m*. **3.** *P:* capote (anglaise). **4.** *P:* **J. Horner** (*R.S.* = *corner*), coin *m* (*surtout* un coin de rue *et souvent* le bistrot du coin). **5.** *F:* **J. Raw**, bleu *m*, morveux *m*. **6.** *F:* = **john, 1.**

Johnny-come-lately [ˈdʒɔnikʌmˈleitli] (*noun*), *F:* blanc-bec *m*, bleu *m*, serin *m*.

Johnny-on-the-spot [ˈdʒɔniɔnðəˈspɔt] (*noun*) (*U.S.*), *F:* **1.** qn qui tombe à pic. **2.** qn qui arrive au poil.

joint [dʒɔint] (*noun*), *P:* **1.** logement*, cambuse *f*, piaule *f*; **a nice j.**, un beau petit coin; *voir aussi* **barber (to); case², (to), 2. 2.** bouge *m*, foutoir *m*; **gambling j.**, tripot *m*. **3.** cigarette* de marijuana *f* (*drogues*), joint *m*, stick *m*. **4.** attirail *m* pour s'injecter des drogues, la popote. **5.** pénis*, queue *f*, gourdin *m*. *Voir aussi* **clip-joint; eats; hop-joint.**

joke¹ [dʒouk] (*noun*), *F:* **1. it was no j. (I can tell you)**, c'était pas rigolo (je t'assure). **2. he must have his little j.**, il aime à plaisanter.

joke² [dʒouk] (**to**), *F:* **you must be** (*or* **you've got to be**) **joking!** c'est pas sérieux! c'est pas vrai! tu veux rire!

joker [ˈdʒoukər] (*noun*), *F:* **1.** homme*, type *m*, client *m*. **2.** malin *m*, loustic *m*, lascar *m*.

jollies [ˈdʒɔliz] (*pl. noun*), *F:* tout ce qui emballe et passionne.

jolly¹ [ˈdʒɔli] (*adj.*), *F:* **1.** agréable, drôle, bath, rigolo. **2.** légèrement ivre*, gris, éméché. **3. J. Roger**, drapeau *m* des pirates, le pavillon noir. *Voir aussi* **bean, 9.**

jolly² [ˈdʒɔli] (*adv.*), *F:* **1. it's a j. good**

job that ..., bien heureusement que... **2. it serves him j. well right!** c'est rudement bien fait pour lui! c'est pain bénit! **3. she's j. nice**, elle est joliment bien. **4. I should j. well think so!** c'est bien ce qui me semble! à qui le dis-tu?

jolly along [ˈdʒɔliəˈlɔŋ] (to), *F:* (a) dérider, ragaillardir (qn); (b) faire marcher (qn) (pour en obtenir qch.).

jolt[1] [dʒoult] (noun), *P:* 1. cigarette* de marijuana (*drogues**), stick *m.* 2. effets *m.pl.* primaires d'une drogue *ou* d'une cigarette* de marijuana. 3. (a) piqûre *f* d'un narcotique; (b) piqûre *f* d'héroïne. 4. un petit coup d'alcool*, une lampée. *Voir aussi* **overjolt**.

jolt[2] [dʒoult] (to), *P:* se faire une piqûre d'héroïne dans le bras.

jonah [ˈdʒounə] (noun), *F:* porte-guigne *m*, porte-poisse *m*, bonnet *m* de nuit.

Joneses [ˈdʒounziz] (pl. pr. noun), *F:* **to keep up with the J.**, imiter ses voisins, vivre au-dessus de ses moyens pour donner l'illusion d'un standing élevé.

jordan [ˈdʒɔːdn] (noun), *P:* pot *m* de chambre, Jules *m*, Thomas *m.*

josh[1] [dʒɔʃ] (noun), *F:* plaisanterie *f*, blague *f.*

josh[2] [dʒɔʃ] (to), *F:* taquiner, chiner, blaguer, mettre (qn) en boîte.

josher [ˈdʒɔʃər] (noun), *F:* blagueur *m*, chineur *m.*

joskin [ˈdʒɔskin] (noun) (U.S.), *F:* = **rube**, 1, 2.

josser [ˈdʒɔsər] (noun), *P:* individu*, type *m*, mec *m.*

Jove [dʒouv] (noun), *F:* **by J!** bon sang! sacrebleu!; **by J. it's cold!** bigre, qu'il fait froid!

joy [dʒɔi] (noun), *F:* chance*, veine *f*, pot *m*; **any j.?** ça a marché?; **no j.!** pas de chance*! tant pis!

joy-girl [ˈdʒɔi-gəːl] (noun), *P:* prostituée*, fille *f* de joie.

joy-house [ˈdʒɔihaus] (noun), *P:* bordel*, maison *f* de passe, maison bancale.

joy-pop [ˈdʒɔi-pɔp] (noun), *P:* emploi intermittent (*ou* pour le plaisir) d'une drogue par un non-initié; piqûre *f* de remonte-pente; *cf.* **pop**[1], 5.

joy-popper [ˈdʒɔi-pɔpər] (noun), *P:* 1. qn qui se drogue* (*surtout* marijuana) pour la première fois; un neuf. 2. qn qui ne se drogue* pas régulièrement; un saccadeur.

joy-powder [ˈdʒɔi-paudər] (noun), *P:* morphine *f* (*drogues**).

joy-ride [ˈdʒɔi-raid] (noun). 1. *F:* (a) promenade *f* en voiture sans la permission du propriétaire; balade *f* à la sauvette; (b) promenade *f* à toute vitesse; (c) partie *f* de plaisir. 2. *P:* expérience de drogues faite par un non-initié; une saccade.

joy-rider [ˈdʒɔi-raidər] (noun), 1. *F:* qn qui se promène en voiture (a) sans la permission du propriétaire, (b) en allant à toute vitesse, (c) pour son plaisir. 2. *P:* = **joy-popper**, 1, 2.

joy-smoke [ˈdʒɔi-smouk] (noun), *P:* (a) marijuana *f* (*drogues**); (b) hachisch *m* (*drogues**).

joystick [ˈdʒɔi-stik] (noun), *P:* 1. pénis*, cigare *m* à moustache, l'instrument *m.* 2. (a) pipe *f* à opium, bambou *m*; (b) = **joint**, 3.

juana [dʒuˈɑːnə, ˈhwɑːnə], **juane** [dʒuːˈlɑːn, hwɑːn], **juanita** [dʒuəˈniːtə, hwɑːˈniːtə] (noun), *P: abréviations pour* «*marijuana*» (*drogues**), *surtout la cigarette;* juana *f; cf.* **marjie**.

judy [ˈdʒuːdi] (noun), *P:* 1. fille*, femme*, nénette *f*, nana *f.* 2. **to make a j. of oneself**, faire le guignol (*ou* le polichinelle).

jug[1] [dʒʌg] (noun), *P:* 1. prison*, tôle *f*, coffre *m*; **to go to j.**, aller en tôle (*ou* au coffre). 2. (pl.) seins*, boîtes *f.pl.* à lait. 3. récipient *m* contenant une drogue liquide, flacon *m*, fiole *f.* 4. banque *f.*

jug[2] [dʒʌg] (to), *P:* emprisonner*, coffrer, mettre en tôle, boucler.

jugful [ˈdʒʌgful] (noun), *F:* **not by a j.!** tant s'en faut! il s'en faut de beaucoup!

juggins [ˈdʒʌginz] (noun), *F:* = **muggins**.

jughead [ˈdʒʌghed] (noun), *F:* individu bête*, cruche *f*, cruchon *m.*

juice [dʒuːs] (noun). 1. *F:* courant *m* électrique, jus *m.* 2. *F:* essence *f*, coco *m*; **to step on the j.**, mettre les gaz *m.pl.*; 3. *P:* sperme*, jus *m*; *cf.* **baby-juice**. 4. *F:* **the J.**, la mer du Nord, le Bouillon. 5. *P:* alcool*,

---

* L'astérisque indique que le mot marqué de ce signe figure comme entrée dans le Répertoire.

surtout whisky *m*; gnôle *f*. **6.** *P:* tonus *m*, force *f*, vigueur *f*. *Voir aussi* **cow-juice; stew**[2] **(to).**

juiced (up) [ˈdʒuːstˈʌp] (*adj.*). **1.** *P:* (*a*) ivre*, chargé, fadé; (*b*) aiguillonné, survolté. **2.** *F:* (*auto*) = **hotted up, 2.**

juicehead [ˈdʒuːshed] (*noun*) (*U.S.*), *P:* ivrogne*, soûlard *m*, poivrot *m*.

juicer [ˈdʒuːsər] (*noun*) (*U.S.*), *F:* (*th.*) électricien *m*, projectionniste *m*, électro *m*.

juicy [ˈdʒuːsi] (*adj.*), *F:* **1.** juteux, savoureux, risqué. **2.** lucratif, qui rapporte, bien beurré.

juju, ju-ju [ˈdʒuːdʒuː] (*noun*), *P:* cigarette* de marijuana (*drogues**), juju *f*.

jumbo[1] [ˈdʒʌmbou] (*adj.*), *F:* de grande taille, maouss(e), mastodonte; **j. screen**, écran géant; **j. jet** (avion), gros porteur.

Jumbo, jumbo[2] [ˈdʒʌmbou] (*noun*), *F:* nom donné à un éléphant, Babar.

jumbuck [ˈdʒʌmbʌk] (*noun*) (*Austr.*), *F:* mouton *m*.

jump[1] [dʒʌmp] (*noun*). **1.** *P:* coït*, partie *f* de jambes en l'air; **to have a j., to give a woman a j.** = **jump**[2] **(to),** **1** (*a*). **2.** *P:* **go (and) take a running j. (at yourself)!** va te faire voir! va te faire foutre!; *cf.* **jump**[2] **(to), 6. 3.** *F:* **to have the jumps,** ne pas rester en place, avoir la bougeotte, être sur une pile électrique. **4.** *P:* **on the j.,** en plein coup de feu. *Voir aussi* **ahead, 2; high**[1], **1.**

jump[2] [dʒʌmp] **(to). 1.** *P:* (*a*) coïter*, faire une partie de jambes en l'air; (*b*) coïter* avec (qn), sauter, enjamber (qn). **2.** *P:* voler*, faire sauter, faucher, gauler; **to j. a drag,** voler* une voiture*, faucher une tire. **3.** *F:* **to j. bail,** se dérober à la justice. **4.** *F:* **to j. ship,** tirer une bordée. **5.** *F:* **to j. the queue,** passer avant son tour; *cf.* **queue-jumper. 6.** *F:* **go (and) j. in the lake!** va te coucher! va te faire voir!; *cf.* **jump**[1], **2. 7.** *F:* **j. to it!** et que ça saute! **8.** *F:* **to j. on s.o.,** réprimander* qn, passer un savon à qn. **9.** *P:* attaquer*, sauter sur le paletot à (qn), agrafer. **10.** *F:*

boumer, être en plein boum, ronfler, gazer. **11.** *F:* **to j. down s.o.'s throat, to j. all over s.o.,** tirer dans les pattes à qn, bouffer le nez à qn, rabrouer qn. **12.** *F:* **to j. off the deep end,** y aller d'autor, foncer. **13.** *F:* **to j. the hurdle,** se marier, sauter le pas, se passer la corde au cou. *Voir aussi* **bandwagon; gun**[1], **2.**

jumped up [ˈdʒʌmptˈʌp] (*adj.*), *F:* **1.** prétentieux*, crâneur, esbrouffeur. **2.** parvenu, nouveau-riche. **3.** bâclé, fait à la six-quatre-deux.

jumper [ˈdʒʌmpər] (*noun*). **1.** *P:* **(you can) stick it up your j.!** colle (*ou* fous) ça dans ta poche (et ton mouchoir par-dessus)!; *cf.* **stick**[2] **(to), 3. 2.** *P:* receveur *m*, -euse *f* (*autobus ou métro*). **3.** *F:* **counter j.,** vendeur *m*, -euse *f*, camelotier *m*. *Voir aussi* **queue-jumper.**

jungle [ˈdʒʌŋgl] (*noun*). **1.** *F:* la jungle, endroit *m* de mauvaises mœurs. **2.** *P:* lieu *m* de refuge des vagabonds, la zone, la cloche. **3.** *P:* **j. bunny** (*péj.*), nègre*, bougnoul(e) *m*.

junk[1] [dʒʌŋk] (*noun*). **1.** *F:* articles variés sans grande valeur, pacotille *f*, camelote *f*, gnognote *f*. **2.** *P:* (*a*) drogues*, stupéfiants *m.pl.*, stups *m.pl.*; **to be on the j.,** se droguer*, se camer; (*b*) héroïne *f* (*drogues**). **3.** *F:* bêtises*, balivernes *f.pl.* **4.** *F:* ferraille *f*; **heap of j.,** vieille voiture*, tacot *m*. **5.** *P:* ordures *f.pl.*, de la cochonnerie. **6.** *P:* bijoux *m.pl.* (comme butin*), joncaille *f*, broquille *f*.

junk[2] [dʒʌŋk] **(to),** *P:* mettre au rebut (*ou* au rencart *ou* à la casse).

junked up [ˈdʒʌŋktˈʌp] (*adj.*), *P:* drogué*, camé, junké, junkie; *cf.* **junk**[1], **2.**

junker [ˈdʒʌŋkər] (*noun*), *P:* **1.** = **junkie. 2.** trafiquant *m* de drogues*, fourgueur *m*, agent *m* de voyage.

junkie, junky[1] [ˈdʒʌŋki] (*noun*), *P:* toxico(mane) *mf*, junkie *mf*, camé(e).

junky[2] [ˈdʒʌŋki] (*adj.*), *F:* qui n'a pas de valeur, bon à foutre en l'air, camelote, toc.

---

* An asterisk indicates that the word so marked is included as a head-word in the Appendix.

K

kale [keil] (noun) (U.S.), P: = cabbage.

kangaroo [ˈkæŋgəruː] (noun), F: 1.
k. court, tribunal illégal, guignol m à
l'estoc. 2. (pl.) titres m.pl. de bourse
australiens, des mous m.pl.

kaput(t) [kæˈput] (adj.), F: cassé,
fichu, flingué; to be k., être à plat
(ou rousti).

karzy [ˈkɑːzi] (noun), P: W.C.*, le petit
coin; k. paper, papier m hygiénique,
torche-cul m.

kayo[1] [ˈkeiˈjou] (noun), F: = k.o.[1].

kayo[2] [ˈkeiˈjou] (to), F: = k.o.[2] (to).

kazoo [kəˈzuː] (noun), P: mirliton m de
jazz.

K-boy [ˈkeibɔi] (noun) (U.S.), P: roi m
(cartes), le papa.

keef [kiːf] (noun), P: marijuana f
(drogues*), kif m.

keel over [ˈkiːlˈouvər] (to), F:
s'évanouir*, tourner de l'œil, tomber
dans le cirage.

keep [kiːp] (to), F: 1. to k. the party
clean, ne pas dire de bêtises* et ne
pas faire de bêtises. 2. to k. oneself to
oneself, faire bande à part. 3. to k. at
it, persévérer, s'accrocher à qch., en
vouloir; to k. s.o. at it, serrer les côtes
(ou la vis) à qn. Voir aussi hat, 3.

keep in [ˈkiːpˈin] (to), F: to k. i. with
s.o., rester bien avec qn, cultiver qn,
peaufiner (une relation); to k. i. with
both sides, ménager la chèvre et le
chou, nager entre deux eaux.

keep on [ˈkiːpˈɔn] (to), F: to k. o. at
s.o., seriner qn, être sur le dos de qn.

keep out [ˈkiːpˈaut] (to), F: you k. o.
of this! mêle-toi de ce qui te regarde!
occupe-toi de tes oignons!

keeps [kiːps] (pl. noun), F: for k., pour
de bon, pas pour la frime, à perpète,
jusqu'à plus soif.

keep up [ˈkiːpˈʌp] (to), F: k. it u.!
vas-y! continue! tu l'auras! Voir aussi
end, 6; Joneses.

keester [ˈkiːstər] (noun) (U.S.), P: 1.
fesses*, postérieur m, derche m. 2.

poche* arrière de pantalon, fouille(tte)
f, profonde f. 3. valise f de camelot,
valdingue f, valoche f. 4. coffre-fort
m, coffiot m.

kef [keif, kef] (noun), P: = keef.

kefuffle [kəˈfʌfl] (noun), F: = kerfuffle.

keister [ˈkiːstər] (noun) (U.S.), P: =
keester.

Kelly, kelly [ˈkeli] (noun). 1. P:
chapeau*, galurin m, bada m, doulos m.
2. F: K.'s eye: voir bingo (1). Voir
aussi Derby Kelly.

kerdoying! [kəˈdɔiŋ] (excl.), F: = gerdoing!

kerflooie [kəˈfluːi] (adv.) (U.S.), F:
to go k., échouer*, foirer, finir en
queue de poisson.

kerfuffle [kəˈfʌfl] (noun), F: commotion
f, agitation f, perturbation f.

kerplunk [kəˈplʌŋk] (adv.), F: to go k.,
tomber*, partir à dame, ramasser un
gadin.

kettle [ˈketl] (noun). 1. P: montre*
(en ou *); k. and piece, montre et chaîne,
toccante et pendante. 2. F: here's a
nice (or fine or pretty) k. of fish! (a) en
voilà une affaire! en voilà des histoires!;
(b) nous voilà dans de beaux draps (ou
dans un beau gâchis ou dans un bel
embrouillamini)!

key [kiː] (noun), F: k. of the door:
voir bingo (21).

keyed up [ˈkiːdˈʌp] (p.p. & adj.), F:
gonflé à bloc.

keyhole [ˈkiːhoul] (noun). 1. P: to play
K. Kate, faire le voyeur, fouiner à la
serrure. 2. one of the k. brigade,
fouinard m de location.

keyster [ˈkiːstər] (noun) (U.S.), P: =
keester.

khazi [ˈkɑːzi] (noun), P: = karzy.

Khyber [ˈkaibər] (noun) (R.S. = Khyber
Pass = arse), P: he can stick it up his
K., il peut se le mettre (ou se le fourrer)
quelque part; cf. stick[2] (to), 3.

ki [kai] (noun), P: cacao m ou chocolat m
de prison.

---

* L'astérisque indique que le mot marqué de ce signe figure comme entrée dans le Répertoire.

kibitz [ˈkibits] (to), F: 1. suivre une partie de cartes en donnant son avis. 2. se mêler de ce qui ne regarde pas, mettre son grain de sel, canuler, ramener sa fraise.

kibitzer [ˈkibitsər] (noun), F: individu qui donne des conseils non sollicités, qui se mêle de tout; canule f, canulard m.

kibosh [ˈkaibɔʃ] (noun), F: 1. = bosh. 2. to put the k. on sth., mettre fin (ou son veto ou le holà) à qch., étouffer qch.

kick[1] [kik] (noun). 1. F: frisson m (de plaisir), piquant m (d'une chose); le fade; to get a k. out of sth., prendre (ou éprouver du) plaisir à qch.; to do sth. for kicks, faire ce qui botte (ou ce qui chante). 2. F: (d'une boisson) du goût, une certaine force alcoolique; it's got a k. in it, c'est une boisson qui remonte. 3. F: (d'une drogue) le pied, le râle, la renaude, l'extase f; to go on a k., se lancer dans la drogue*, prendre le pied, aller à la défonce; bum kicks, mauvaise expérience d'un drogué*, flippage m, mauvais voyage. 4. F: he's got no k. left in him, il est à plat, il est vide (ou pompé). 5. (a) F: that's better than a k. in the pants, ça vaut mieux qu'un coup de pied au derrière, ça vaut mieux que de se casser la jambe, ça vaut mieux qu'une jambe cassée; (b) P: he's had a k. in the arse (U.S. ass) (or pants), il s'est fait botter le cul, il s'est fait asseoir; voir aussi pants, 3. 6. F: the k., sacquage m; to get the k., recevoir son paquet, être boulé. 7. P: poche* (surtout de pantalon), fouille f. 8. P: grogne f, rouspétance f, rouscaille f. Voir aussi sidekick.

kick[2] [kik] (to). 1. P: grogner*, bougonner, rouspéter, ronchonner, râler. 2. F: résister, ruer dans les brancards. Voir aussi alive, 1; bucket, 1; habit, 1; heel, 3.

kick along [ˈkikəˈlɔŋ] (to), F: se maintenir, se défendre.

kick around [ˈkikəˈraund] (to), F: 1. retourner, ruminer, ergoter sur (une idée, etc.). 2. to k. s.o. a., mener qn à la trique, être chien (ou vache) avec qn. 3. rouler sa bosse, bourlinguer. 4. there are lots of people like that

kicking around, des gens comme ça, ce n'est pas ce qui manque. 5. I've lost my gloves, but they must be kicking around somewhere, j'ai perdu mes gants, mais ils doivent traîner quelque part. Voir aussi gong, 2.

kickback [ˈkikbæk] (noun). 1. F: réaction violente, coup m de boomerang, retour m de manivelle. 2. P: ristourne f, dessous-de-table m. 3. P: récidive f dans la drogue, rebranchage m.

kicker [ˈkikər] (noun) (U.S.), P: piège m, hic m, os m, cactus m. Voir aussi shitkicker.

kick in [ˈkikˈin] (to), F: payer sa part, payer son écot.

kickman [ˈkikmæn] (noun), P: approvisionneur m (ou fourgueur m) de drogues.

kick-off [ˈkikɔf] (noun), F: coup m d'envoi, démarrage m.

kick off [ˈkikˈɔf] (to). 1. F: donner le départ (ou le coup d'envoi), démarrer. 2. P: partir*, lever l'ancre, se tirer, se tailler. 3. P: mourir*, claquer, clamser.

kick out [ˈkikˈaut] (to), F: (a) flanquer (qn) à la porte, balancer, larguer (qn); (b) congédier* (qn), sacquer (qn).

kick-stick [ˈkik-stik] (noun), P: = joint, 3.

kick-up [ˈkikʌp] (noun), F: 1. chahut m, tapage m, chambard m. 2. réjouissances*, bamboche f, bamboula f, ribouldingue f.

kick up [ˈkikˈʌp] (to). 1. F: to k. u. a fuss, faire des chichis m.pl. (ou des embarras m.pl.). 2. F: (a) to k. u. a row (or a racket or a shindig or a shindy or a hullabaloo), faire beaucoup de bruit*, faire du boucan (ou du chambard); (b) to k. u. a dust, mener grand bruit*, faire de la musique, faire une scène; voir aussi rumpus. 3. P: to k. u. hell, faire un scandale du diable. 4. F: to k. u. one's heels, sauter de joie. Voir aussi stink[1], 1.

kick upstairs [ˈkikʌpˈstɛəz] (to), F: to k. s.o. u., donner de l'avancement à qn pour s'en débarrasser*, souvent donner un titre de noblesse, faire un limogeage doré.

kid[1] [kid] (adj.), F: 1. jeunet, cadet; a k. sister, une sœur cadette. 2. enfantin, puéril; k. stuff, enfantillage m, gaminerie *f*; **it's k. stuff,** c'est du primaire, c'est une amusette. **3. to handle** (*or* **treat**) **s.o. with k. gloves,** (*a*) ménager qn, traiter qn avec ménagement, manier qn comme du verre cassé; (*b*) dorloter, chouchouter qn.

kid[2] [kid] (*noun*), *F:* **1.** enfant*, gosse *mf*, môme *mf*. **2.** farce *f*, blague *f*; **no k.?** = **are you kidding?** (**kid**[3] (**to**), **2**); **no k.!** = **no kidding!** *Voir aussi* **whiz**(**z**)[1], **2.**

kid[3] [kid] (**to**), *F:* **1.** en conter à (qn), faire marcher (qn); **don't k. yourself!** ne te fais pas d'illusion!; **who are you trying to k.?** tu te fiches de moi? **2.** plaisanter; **are you kidding?** tu me fais marcher? tu veux me mener en bateau?; **stop kidding!** arrête ton char!; *cf.* **kidding.**

kid along [ˈkidəˈlɔŋ] (**to**), *F:* bourrer le crâne à (qn), emberlificoter (qn).

kidder [ˈkidər] (*noun*), *F:* farceur *m*, blagueur *m*, loustic *m*.

kiddie [ˈkidi] (*noun*), *F:* = **kiddy.**

kidding [ˈkidiŋ] (*noun*), *F:* blague *f*, mise *f* en boîte, charriage *m*; **no k?** = **are you kidding?** (**kid**[3] (**to**), **2**); **no k.!** sans blague! blague à part! sans char!; *cf.* **kid**[3] (**to**), **2.**

kiddy [ˈkidi], **kiddywink**(**y**) [ˈkidiwiŋk(i)] (*noun*), *F:* petit enfant*, mioche *mf*; *cf.* **kid**[2], **1.**

kidology [kiˈdɔlədʒi] (*noun*), *F:* l'art *m* de faire gober les gens.

kief [kiːf], **kif** [kif] (*noun*), *P:* = **keef.**

kike [kaik] (*noun*), *P:* (*péj.*) Juif *m*, Youpe *m*, Youpin *m*.

kill[1] [kil] (*noun*), *F:* **1.** assassinat *m*, butage *m*, saignage *m*. **2.** (*a*) descente *f* (d'avion ennemi), inscription *f* au tableau de chasse; (*b*) coulée *f* (d'un navire ennemi). **3. a k. or cure,** un remède de cheval. *Voir aussi* **set up** (**to**), **2.**

kill[2] [kil] (**to**), *F:* **1. to k. a bottle,** sécher une bouteille, faire cul sec, tout avaler. **2.** ruiner, enfoncer, couler (qn *ou* qch.). **3.** (*th.*) **to k. an audience,** brûler les planches, casser la baraque, faire un emportage. **4.** éteindre, écraser (une cigarette, *etc.*). **5. to k. time,** paresser*, flemmarder. *Voir aussi* **dressed.**

killer [ˈkilər] (*noun*), *P:* **1.** flambard *m*, enjôleur *m*. **2.** tombeur *m* (de femmes),

dénicheur *m* de fauvettes; *cf.* **ladykiller. 3.** = **lulu. 4.** qch. qui émoustille *ou* transporte *ou* ragaillardit. **5.** cigarette* de marijuana (*drogues**), stick

killing[1] [ˈkiliŋ] (*adj.*), *F:* **1.** très amusant*, tordant, crevant; **it's too k. for words,** c'est à mourir de rire. **2.** emballant, fascinant. **3.** fatigant, tuant, crevant.

killing[2] [ˈkiliŋ] (*noun*), *F:* **to make a k.,** faire de gros profits, affurer.

kind [kaind] (*noun*), *F:* **1. I don't have that k. of money,** je n'ai pas des sommes pareilles. **2. these k. of things annoy me,** ce genre de choses m'agace. *Voir aussi* **kind of.**

kinda [ˈkaində] (*adv.*) *F:* = **kind of.**

kind of [ˈkaindəv] (*adv.*), *F:* **1. he's k. o. careful with money,** il est radin sur les bords. **2. I k. o. expected it,** je m'en doutais presque. **3. it's k. o. chilly,** il fait passablement froid (*ou* frisquet).

kingdom-come [ˈkiŋdəmˈkʌm] (*noun*). **1.** *F:* le paradis, le paradouze. **2.** *P:* **to knock s.o. to k.-c.,** foutre une trempe à qn. **3.** *P:* (*R.S.* = *rum*) rhum *m*; *cf.* **Tom, 4; touch-your-bum.**

king-pin [ˈkiŋpin] (*noun*), *F:* personne (la plus) importante, caïd *m*, magnat *m*, grand manitou.

king-size(**d**) [ˈkiŋsaiz(d)] (*adj.*), *F:* (*a*) = **jumbo**[1]; (*b*) gros* et long; **k.-s. cigarettes,** cigarettes* grand format.

kink [kiŋk] (*noun*), *F:* **1.** truc *m*, lubie *f*, manie *f*, dada *m*; **he's got a k.,** il est un peu timbré. **2. to be in kinks,** se tordre de rire.

kinky[1] [ˈkiŋki] (*adj.*). **1.** *F:* fantasque, excentrique, fada. **2.** *F:* bizarre, équivoque. **3.** *P:* inverti. **4.** *P:* louche, injuste, inique. **5.** *P:* volé*, chipé, chopé, barboté.

kinky[2] [ˈkiŋki] (*noun*), *P:* **1.** pédéraste*, fagot *m*, empapaouté *m*. **2.** lesbienne*, goudou *f*, gouchotte *f*.

kip[1] [kip] (*noun*), *P:* **1.** lit*, pieu *m*, plumard *m*. **2.** pension *f* de famille, chambre meublée, garno *m*, crèche *f*. **3.** sommeil *m*; **to have a k.,** dormir*, piquer un roupillon.

kip[2] [kip] (**to**), *P:* **1.** se coucher*, se pieuter. **2.** dormir*, pioncer, roupiller. **3.** coucher sur la dure.

---

* L'astérisque indique que le mot marqué de ce signe figure comme entrée dans le Répertoire.

kip down ['kip'daʊn] (to), P: = kip² (to), 1.
kipe [kaip] (to), P: = kype (to).
kip-house ['kiphaʊs] (noun), P: = doss-house.
kipper ['kipər] (noun), P: individu*, type m, client m.
kip-shop ['kipʃɔp] (noun), P: bordel*, bocard m, boxon m.
kiss¹ [kis] (noun), F: the k. of death, le coup de grâce. Voir aussi French¹, 1; tongue-kiss.
kiss² [kis] (to), F: 1. to k. sth. goodbye, faire ses adieux à qch., tirer un trait sur qch., en faire son deuil. 2. never been kissed: voir bingo (16). 3. to k. and be friends, se réconcilier, se rebonneter, faire ami-ami. Voir aussi arse, 6; dust¹, 4.
kiss-ass ['kisæs] (noun) (U.S.), V: = arse-kisser.
kisser ['kisər] (noun), P: 1. bouche*, museau m, margoulette f. 2. lèvres*, baiseuses f.pl., babines f.pl. 3. visage*, binette f, fiole f; one right in the k., une pêche en pleine poire. Voir aussi arse-kisser; baby-kisser.
kiss-off ['kisɔf] (noun) (U.S.), P: 1. mort f, crève f, crevaison f. 2. sacquage m, limogeage m.
kiss off ['kis'ɔf] (to) (U.S.), P: 1. tuer*, effacer (qn). 2. se débarrasser* de (qn), sacquer, balancer, débarquer.
kissy ['kisi] (adj.), P: servile, flagorneur.
kit [kit] (noun), F: (a) barda m, bataclan m, Saint-Frusquin m; voir aussi caboodle; (b) effets m.pl. (de voyageur). Voir aussi shelf-kit.
kitchen-sink¹ ['kitʃin'siŋk] (attrib. adj.), F: k.-s. novel, etc., roman m, etc., boîte à ordures.
kitchen-sink² ['kitʃin'siŋk] (noun), F: everything but the k.-s., tout sans exception, y compris la cage aux serins.
kite [kait] (noun), 1. F: avion m, coucou m. 2. F: to fly a k., (a) mettre une fausse traite en circulation; (b) tâter le terrain, lancer un ballon d'essai; (c) (finances) tirer en l'air, tirer en blanc. 3. P: chèque m; k. man, faussaire m, mornifleur m. 4. F: high as a k., (a) ivre*, parti, rétamé; (b) drogué*, chargé, bourré à zéro, défoncé. 5. P: prostituée*, roulure f, radeuse f.

kitsch [kitʃ] (noun), F: bêtises* prétentieuses, sornettes f.pl., esbrouf(f)e f.
kittens ['kitnz] (pl. noun), F: to (nearly) have k., (a) être très en colère*, piquer une crise, avoir le coup de sang; (b) avoir peur*, avoir les foies m.pl., avoir chaud aux fesses f.pl. Voir aussi sex-kitten.
kitty ['kiti] (noun). 1. F: chaton m, petit(e) chat(te). 2. F: (a) cagnotte f; (b) magot m. 3. P: prison*, trou m, tôle f.
Kiwi, kiwi ['ki:wi:] (noun), F: 1. Néo-Zélandais m, Kiwi m. 2. employé d'un aéroport affecté à terre; rampant m.
klink [kliŋk] (noun), P: = clink.
k-man ['keimæn] (abbr.), P: = kick-man.
knacker ['nækər] (to), P: 1. châtrer, abélarder. 2. réduire à quia, démonter. Voir aussi knackered.
knackered ['nækəd] (p.p. & adj.), P: to be k., (a) être fatigué*, être éreinté (ou vanné); (b) se trouver en mauvaise posture, être emmerdé, ne pas savoir sur quel pied danser.
knackers ['nækəz] (pl. noun), P: testicules*, balloches f.pl.
knap [næp] (to), P: voler*, barboter.
knee [ni:] (noun), F: 1. housemaid's k., épanchement m de synovie, genou m en compote. 2. gone at the knees, décrépit, décati, avachi, vachement amorti. Voir aussi bee, 1.
knee-high ['ni:'hai] (adj.), F: to be k.-h. to a bumble-bee (or a daisy or a duck or a frog or a grasshopper or a mosquito or a sparrow), être une courtebotte (ou un petit poucet) (petit* individu).
kneesies ['ni:ziz] (pl. noun), F: to play k. (under the table), faire du genou; cf. footsy.
knees-up ['ni:zʌp] (noun), F: gambade f, cabriole f, trémoussements m.pl.
knee-trembler ['ni:-tremblər] (noun), V: to do a k.-t., coïter* debout, sabrer à la verticale.
knickers ['nikəz] (pl. noun), P: don't get your k. in a twist, ne te mets pas dans tous tes états.
knicks [niks] (pl. noun), F: (=knickers) culotte f (de femme).
knife [naif] (noun), F: 1. to get one's k. into s.o., to have one's k. in s.o., avoir

une dent contre qn, s'acharner sur qn.
2. to put the k. in, entamer le morceau.
knob [nɔb] (*noun*). **1.** *V:* pénis*, (gros)
bout, polard *m*, zob *m*. **2.** *P:* = **nob¹, 1.**
3. *P:* **with knobs on,** et le pouce, et
mèche, et le rab.
knob-gobbler [ˈnɔbgɔblər] (*noun*), *V:* =
cock-sucker, 1.
knobstick [ˈnɔb-stik] (*noun*), *P:* ouvrier
non-syndiqué, jaune *m*.
knock¹ [nɔk] (*noun*). **1.** *F:* critique *f*,
éreintement *m*, abattage *m*. **2.** *P:* ennui
m, pépin *m*, os *m*, cactus *m*. **3.** *P:* coït*,
bourre *f*, carambolage *m*. **4.** *F:* **to
take a k.,** essuyer un échec* (*ou* une
déception), recevoir un coup dans les
gencives. **5.** *F:* **it's your k.,** c'est ton
tour, c'est ta passe.
knock² [nɔk] (**to**). **1.** *F:* critiquer*,
trouver à redire à (qn, qch.), éreinter,
débiner. **2.** *F:* **to k. sth. on the head,**
battre qch. en brèche, mettre le holà,
arrêter les frais. **3.** *F:* **to be knocking
60,** friser la soixantaine. **4.** *P:*
escroquer*, refaire, carotter; **to k. s.o.
for sth.,** écorcher qn de qch. **5.** *P:* **to
k. 'em,** épater la galerie, époustoufler;
that'll k. 'em cold, cela va leur en
boucher un coin; *cf.* **aisle, 2. 6.** (*Austr.*)
P: violer, riper. **7.** *P:* coïter* avec
(une femme), bourrer, caramboler.
8. *F:* **to k. s.o. silly** (*or* **for six**), battre
qn à plate(s) couture(s), donner une
tabassée à qn, démolir qn, ébouzer qn.
9. *F:* **k. at the door:** *voir* **bingo** (4).
Voir aussi **sideways; week.**
knock about *or* **around** [ˈnɔkəˈbaut,
ˈnɔkəˈraund] (**to**), *F:* **1.** = **kick around**
(**to**), **3. 2. to k. a. with s.o.,** s'acoquiner
avec qn, sortir avec qn, fréquenter qn.
knock back [ˈnɔkˈbæk] (**to**), *F:* **1. to
k. b. a drink,** boire*, lamper un verre,
s'en jeter un derrière la cravate; **k. it
b.!** cul sec!. **2.** coûter, peser; **it knocked
him back a packet,** ça lui a pesé un
sac. **3.** renvoyer, faire rebondir; **he
knocked it back at me,** il me l'a balans-
tiqué.
knocked out [ˈnɔktˈaut] (*p.p.* & *adj.*),
P: **1.** = **knocked up, 2. 2.** épaté,
estomaqué, médusé. **3.** = **jagged, 2.**
Voir aussi **knock out** (**to**).
knocked up [ˈnɔktˈʌp] (*p.p.* & *adj.*),
P: **1.** malade*, patraque. **2.** très
fatigué*, éreinté, claqué. **3.** enceinte*,

engrossée, en cloque. *Voir aussi* **knock
up** (**to**).
knocker [ˈnɔkər] (*noun*). **1.** *F:* critique
m sévère, éreinteur *m*, esquinteur *m*,
abatteur *m*. **2.** *P:* personne importante
(ou qui se croit telle), gros bonnet,
grosse légume. **3.** (*pl.*) *P:* seins*,
nichons *m.pl.*, rondins *m.pl.* **4.** *P:* **on
the k.,** à crédit, à tempérament, au
croum(e), au crayon. *Voir aussi* **dress
up** (**to**), **2.**
knock in [ˈnɔkˈin] (**to**), *F:* (*football*)
to k. it i., marquer un but, envoyer
dans le filet. *Voir aussi* **tooth, 5.**
knocking [ˈnɔkiŋ] (*adj.*), *P:* **1. k. company,** maison *f* de ventes à crédit,
croumiers *m.pl.* **2. k. shop,** bordel*,
maison *f* d'abattage.
knockings [ˈnɔkiŋz] (*pl. noun*), *P:* **to
be on the last k.,** être à la dernière
étape (*ou* au dernier échelon).
knock-kneed [ˈnɔkˈniːd] (*adj.*), *F:* pol-
tron*, froussard, péteux.
knock-off [ˈnɔkɔf] (*noun*), *P:* **to have
a k.-o.,** coïter*, avoir un carambolage.
knock off [ˈnɔkˈɔf] (**to**). **1.** *P:* **to k. it o.
with a woman,** coïter*, caramboler.
2. *P:* **k. it o.** (**will you**)! basta! écrase!
passe la main! **3.** *F:* **to k. o. a pint,**
étouffer (*ou* étrangler) un demi, s'envoyer un coup. **4.** *P:* voler*, faucher.
5. *F:* finir de travailler, débrayer,
boucler, dételer. **6.** *F:* finir vite,
exécuter avec rapidité, liquider, expédier. **7.** *P:* arrêter*, agrafer. **8.** *P:*
tuer*, démolir, dessouder. **9.** *F:* faire
un rabais (*ou* un avantage *ou* une
ristourne) de... *Voir aussi* **block,
1.**
knockout¹ [ˈnɔkaut] (*adj.*), *F:* **1. k.
drops,** stupéfiant *m* qu'on met dans la
boisson de la victime pour lui faire
perdre connaissance (dans le but de
la dépouiller), coup *m* d'assommoir.
2. mirobolant, transcendant.
knockout² [ˈnɔkaut] (*noun*), *F:* **1.** une
merveille, un phénomène, qch. *ou* qn
de mirifique. **2.** (*d'une femme*) prix *m*
de Diane. *Voir aussi* **k.o.¹**
knock out [ˈnɔkˈaut] (**to**), *F:* **1. to k.
oneself o.,** travailler* dur, s'éreinter,
s'esquinter. **2.** époustoufler, éblouir,
fasciner, épater. *Voir aussi* **knocked out;
k.o.² (to).**
knock-over [ˈnɔkouvər] (*noun*), *P:*

---

* L'astérisque indique que le mot marqué de ce signe figure comme entrée dans le Répertoire.

cambriolage *m*, caroublage *m*, mise *f* en l'air.

knock over [ˈnɔkˈouvər] **(to)**, *P:* **1.** cambrioler*, caroubler, mettre en l'air. **2.** faire une descente (de police) dans…, rafler.

knock together [ˈnɔktəˈgeðər] **(to)**, *F:* = **knock up (to)**, **1.**

knock up [ˈnɔkˈʌp] **(to)**. **1.** *F:* préparer, concocter, combiner. **2.** *F:* (*a*) réveiller, secouer; (*b*) tambouriner à une porte à une heure tardive. **3.** *P:* rendre enceinte*, engrosser, mettre en cloque. **4.** *P:* abîmer*, amocher, saboter. **5.** *F:* **to k. u. £100 a week**, se faire cent livres par semaine.

knot [nɔt] **(noun)**, *F:* **1. to tie the k.**, se marier, se mettre la corde au cou. **2. to get tied (up) in knots**, s'embrouiller, s'emberlificoter, ne pas s'en sortir. *Voir aussi* **top-knot.**

knothead [ˈnɔthed] **(noun)**, *F:* = **knucklehead.**

knotted [ˈnɔtid] (*p.p. & adj.*), *P:* **get k.!** va te faire voir!

know¹ [nou] **(noun)**, *F:* **to be in the k.**, être affranchi, être au parfum, être dans le coup.

know² [nou] **(to)**, *F:* **1. I don't want to k.**, rien à juter, je ne marche pas. **2. not that I k. of**, pas que je sache. **3. for all I k.**, autant que je sache. **4.** (*a*) **what do you k.?** quoi de neuf?; (*b*) **well, what do you k.!** sans blague! sans char! **5. don't I k. it!** à qui le dites-vous! **6. not if I k. (anything about) it!** pour rien au monde! **7. I wouldn't k.**, je ne saurais dire. **8. he knows a good thing when he sees one** (*or* **it**), c'est un connaisseur, il sait ce qui est bon. **9. you k. what you can do with that, you k. where you can put** (*or* **stick** *or* **shove**) **that**, tu peux te le mettre quelque part. **10. to k. a thing or two, to k. what's what**, être malin*, être à la coule.

know-all [ˈnouwɔːl] (*noun*), *F:* je-sais-tout *m*; **Mr K.**, Monsieur Je-sais-tout.

know-how [ˈnouhau] (*noun*), *F:* (*a*) savoir-faire *m*, habileté *f*; (*b*) savoir-faire (technique), connaissances *f.pl.* techniques, mise *f* en pratique.

knuckle [ˈnʌkl] (*noun*), *F:* **near the k.**, scabreux, grivois.

knuckle down [ˈnʌklˈdaun] **(to)**, *F:* se ranger des voitures, s'y mettre, avoir du plomb dans la tête.

knucklehead [ˈnʌklhed] (*noun*), *F:* individu bête*, niguedouille *m*, empoté *m*.

knuckle under [ˈnʌklˈʌndər] **(to)**, *F:* se soumettre, filer doux, baisser pavillon.

k.o., K.O.¹ [ˈkeiˈjou] (*abbr. = knockout*), *F:* (*boxe, lutte*) K.O. *m*, knock-out *m*.

k.o., K.O.² [ˈkeiˈjou] **(to)** (*abbr. = knock out*), *F:* **1.** (*boxe, lutte*) mettre K.O., knockouter. **2.** = **to knock on the head** (**knock²** (to), 2).

kokomo [kouˈkoumou] (*noun*), *P:* = **cokomo.**

kook [kuːk] (*noun*), *P:* excentrique *m*, braque *m*, branquignol(le) *m*, louftingue *m*.

kooky [ˈkuːki] (*adj.*), *F:* **1.** un peu fou*, braque, louftingue. **2.** (*vêtements*) sophistiqué, raffiné.

kosher [ˈkouʃər] (*adj.*), *F:* au poil, impec, réglo.

kowtow [ˈkautau] **(to)**, *F:* **to k. to s.o.**, s'aplatir (*ou* se mettre à genoux) devant qn.

kraut, Kraut [kraut], **krauthead** [ˈkrauthed] (*noun*), *P:* (*péj.*) Allemand*, fridolin *m*, frizou *m*.

kudos [ˈkjuːdɔs] (*noun*), *F:* panache *m*, gloriole *f*.

kybo [ˈkaibou] (*noun*), *P:* W.C.*, goguenots *m.pl.*

kype [kaip] **(to)**, *P:* voler* (de petites choses), chiper, chaparder.

---

* An asterisk indicates that the word so marked is included as a head-word in the Appendix.

L

lab [læb] (abbr. = laboratory), F: labo m.
lace [leis] (to), F: alcooliser,. corser,
arroser; laced coffee, café* au rhum.
lace around ['leisə'raund] (to), F:
foncer, se précipiter.
lace into ['leis'intu:] (to), F: 1. to l. i.
s.o., (a) battre*, rosser qn; (b) critiquer*,
éreinter, dégrainer qn. 2. to l. i. sth.,
y aller de tout son cœur (ou avec
ardeur), y mettre toute la sauce.
lacy ['leisi] (adj.), P: efféminé, homosexuel sur les bords.
lad [læd] (noun), F: 1. he's a bit of a l.
(with the women), c'est un tombeur
de filles, c'est un chaud lapin. 2. one
of the lads, un gai luron, un joyeux
compère.
ladder ['lædər] (noun), F: pull the l. up
(, Jack), take the l. away (, Jack),
c.p., après nous le déluge (ou la fin du
monde); cf. Jack, 3.
laddie ['lædi] (noun), F: (petit) gars,
gamin m.
la-de-da, la-di-da, ladidah ['lɑ:di'dɑ:]
(adj.), F: 1. élégant*, (super-)chic, à
grand tralala; it was a very l. gathering,
tout le gratin se trouvait là. 2. (péj.)
she's so l.! elle fait la prétentieuse*,
elle jette du jus; she's got such a l.
accent, elle parle avec affectation, elle
veut mousser du claque-merde.
lady ['leidi] (noun), P: L. Jane, vagin*,
mimi m, pâquerette f. Voir aussi fat¹,
6; lollipop-lady; old, 4.
lady-killer ['leidi-kilər] (noun), F: bourreau m des cœurs, tombeur m de filles;
cf. killer, 2.
lag¹ [læg] (noun), F: (a) forçat m,
bagnard m, fague m; (b) forçat libéré,
fagot affranchi; old l., cheval m de
retour, forçat chevronné.
lag² [læg] (to), F: (a) arrêter*, épingler;
(b) emprisonner*, bloquer, boucler.
lah-de-dah ['lɑ:di'dɑ:] (adj.), F: =
la-de-da.
laid up ['leid'ʌp] (p.p. & adj.), F:
malade*, alité, mal fichu.

lair ['lɛər] (noun) (Austr.), F: élégant m,
tape-à-l'œil m.
lairy ['lɛəri] (adj.) (Austr.), F: voyant,
tapageur.
lake [leik] (noun), F: go (and) jump in
the l.! va te faire pendre! va te faire
voir!
lam¹ [læm] (noun) (U.S.), P: on the l.,
(a) en fuite, en cavale; (b) en déplace-
ment, en voyage, par monts et par vaux.
lam² [læm] (to), P: 1. battre*, rosser,
étriller. 2. (U.S.) partir* précipitam-
ment, mettre les bouts, décambuter.
lamb [læm] (noun). 1. P: l. (chop),
piqûre f de narcotique, piquouse f,
fixe m. 2. F: (a) (d'un enfant) lapin m,
agneau m; (b) (terme d'affection) poulet
m, coco m. 3. (U.S.) F: individu*
crédule, gobeur m, cave m, pigeon m.
4. F: he took it like a l., il s'est laissé
faire, il n'a pas rouspété.
lambaste ['læm'beist] (to), F: (a)
battre*, dérouiller; (b) critiquer*, éreinter.
lambasting ['læm'beistiŋ] (noun), F:
(a) raclée f, frottée f; (b) critique f,
éreintage m, abattage m.
lame [leim] (adj.), P: = square¹, 4 (a).
Voir aussi duck¹, 6.
lame-brain ['leim'brein] (noun) (U.S.),
F: individu bête*, imbécile m, sot m.
lam into ['læm'intu:] (to), P: = lam²
(to), 1.
lamming ['læmiŋ] (noun), P: = lambasting.
lam out ['læm'aut] (to) (U.S.), P: =
lam² (to), 2.
lamp [læmp] (to), P: regarder*, zyeuter,
reluquer, mater.
lamp-post ['læmppoust] (noun), F: between you and me and the l.-p., tout à
fait entre nous, entre quat'zyeux; cf.
gate-post.
lamps [læmps] (pl. noun), P: (a) yeux*,
quinquets m.pl., lanternes f.pl., lampions m.pl.; (b) yeux* pochés, coquards
m.pl.

land [lænd] (to), *F:* 1. gagner, obtenir, dénicher, dégot(t)er. 2. arriver*, débarquer, s'abouler. 3. to l. s.o. a blow, filer (*ou* flanquer) à qn un coup* (*ou* une taloche *ou* une baffe). 4. that will l. you in prison, cela vous vaudra de la prison*, ça va vous faire entôler. *Voir aussi* mire; muck, 3; shit³, 2.

landed [ˈlændid] (*p.p. & adj.*), *F:* dans le pétrin; to be l. with s.o., avoir qn sur les bras, être empêtré de qn.

land up [ˈlændˈʌp] (to), *F:* (a) to l. u. with nothing, n'aboutir à rien, finir en queue de poisson; (b) to l. u. somewhere, aboutir quelque part; aboutir à qch.; (c) to l. u. in a bar, atterrir finalement dans un bar.

language [ˈlæŋgwidʒ] (*noun*), *F:* to speak s.o.'s l., parler la même langue, être sur la même longueur d'ondes.

lantern [ˈlæntən] (*noun*), *F:* idiot's l. = goggle-box; *cf.* box¹, 2; idiot-box.

lap [læp] (*noun*), *F:* 1. to lay sth. in s.o.'s l., coller qch. sur le dos de qn; it fell right into his l., ça lui est tombé tout rôti. 2. in the l. of luxury, en plein luxe, au sein de l'abondance. *Voir aussi* cat-lap.

lap it up [ˈlæpitˈʌp] (to), *F:* 1. gober, avaler qch., boire du petit lait. 2. boire* beaucoup, picoler, biberonner.

lark [lɑːk] (*noun*), *F:* 1. talk about a l.! quelle rigolade! quelle bonne blague! 2. he did it for a l., il l'a fait pour rigoler (*ou* histoire de rigoler); *cf.* skylark (to).

lark about [ˈlɑːkəˈbaut] (to), *F:* folichonner, rigoler, faire le pitre.

larrikin [ˈlærikin] (*noun*) (*Austr.*), *F:* gavroche *m*, gamin *m* des rues; petit voyou.

larrup [ˈlærəp] (to), *F:* 1. battre*, frapper, rosser. 2. battre (un adversaire) à plate(s) couture(s).

larruping [ˈlærəpiŋ] (*noun*), *F:* (a) volée *f* de coups*, rossée *f*, raclée *f*, roulée *f*; (b) victoire *f* facile (*ou* les doigts dans le nez).

larry up [ˈlæriˈʌp] (to), *P:* blesser*, amocher, abîmer* (qch.).

lash [læʃ] (*noun*) (*Austr.*), *F:* to have a l. at sth., tenter sa chance, tenter le coup.

lashings [ˈlæʃiŋz] (*pl. noun*), *F:* une abondance* de..., des tas *m.pl.* de...; l. of sauce, une tapée de sauce.

lash out [ˈlæʃˈaut] (to), *F:* 1. lâcher un coup*, décocher des coups*. 2. dépenser, larguer son fric; I lashed out on a new coat, je me suis lancée dans la dépense: j'ai acheté un manteau neuf. 3. invectiver, se déchaîner.

lash-up [ˈlæʃˈʌp] (*noun*), *P:* (a) expédient *m*, échappatoire *f*, moyen *m* de fortune; (b) réunion *f* intime (*ou* à la bonne franquette).

last [lɑːst] (*adj.*), *F:* the l. word, le dernier cri; the l. word in socks, des chaussettes dernier cri. *Voir aussi* leg¹, 9; straw, 1, 2.

last-ditch [ˈlɑːstˈditʃ] (*adj.*), *F:* a l.-d. effort, un dernier effort, un baroud d'honneur.

latch on [ˈlætʃˈɔn] (to), *F:* comprendre, piger, entraver.

latch onto (*or* on to) [ˈlætʃˈɔntuː] (to), *F:* obtenir, agrafer, mettre le grappin sur (qch.).

latest [ˈleitist] (*noun*), *F:* to be up on the l., être à la page, être au courant, être dans le vent.

lather¹ [ˈlɑːðər] (*noun*), *F:* to work oneself (up) into a l., (a) se mettre en colère*, fulminer, sortir de ses gonds; (b) s'inquiéter, se faire du mauvais sang.

lather² [ˈlɑːðər] (to), *F:* battre*, rosser, tabasser.

laugh¹ [lɑːf] (*noun*), *F:* 1. that's a l.! quelle blague! c'est marrant! 2. to go sth. for laughs, faire qch. pour rigoler (*ou* à la rigolade). *Voir aussi* belly-laugh¹.

laugh² [lɑːf] (to), *F:* 1. don't make me l.! ne me fais pas rire* (*ou* marrer)! 2. to l. on the other side of one's face, rire jaune; I soon made him l. on the other side of his face, je lui ai bientôt fait passer son envie de rire*. 3. to be laughing, se la couler douce, vivre pépère; if you win the pools you'll be laughing, si vous gagnez à la loterie vous aurez le filon (*ou* les poches bien garnies). 4. to l. to oneself, rire* aux anges. *Voir aussi* belly-laugh² (to); drain¹, 2.

launching-pad [ˈlɔːntʃiŋpæd] (*noun*), *P:* = shooting-gallery.

lav [læv] (*noun*) (*abbr.* = *lavatory*), *F:*

---

* An asterisk indicates that the word so marked is included as a head-word in the Appendix.

W.C.*, cabinets *m.pl.*, cabinces *f.pl.*; **to go to the l.**, aller aux vécés *m.pl.*

lavatorial ['lævəˈtɔːriəl] (*adj.*), *F:* ordurier, cochon.

law, Law [lɔː] (*noun*), *F:* **the l.**, (*a*) la police*, la rousse; (*b*) policier*, flic *m*; **I'll have the l. on you**, je vais vous poursuivre en justice.

lay[1] [lei] (*noun*). **1.** *P:* **to have a l.**, coïter*, coucher avec une femme, fourailler. **2.** *P:* femelle *f*, fendue *f*; **an easy l.**, une môme facile, une cavaleuse, une tombeuse, une baiseuse. **3.** *P:* projet *m*, ligne *f* de conduite, résolution *f*. **4.** *P:* besogne délictueuse, bis(e)ness *m*, turbin *m*. **5.** *F:* pari *m*, mise *f*. **6.** *F:* **to get the l. of the land**, tâter le terrain, se rencarder sur qch.

lay[2] [lei] (**to**), *P:* **1. to l. a woman**, coïter* avec une femme, coucher avec une femme, sch(e)nailler une femme. **2. to l. one on s.o.**, battre* qn, flanquer une taloche à qn. **3. to l. for s.o.**, attendre qn au tournant.

lay down ['leiˈdaun] (**to**), *F:* **1.** (*=lie down*) se coucher*, s'étendre. **2.** renvoyer (qn) avec détention provisoire.

lay-in ['leiˈin] (*noun*), *F:* = **lie-in**.

lay into ['leiˈintuː] (**to**), *F:* (*a*) attaquer*, agrafer, serrer (qn); (*b*) critiquer*, éreinter (qn).

lay off ['leiˈɔf] (**to**). **1.** *P:* lâcher, larguer, plaquer (qn). **2.** *P:* **l. o., will you?** laisse tomber! c'est marre! écrase! **3.** *F:* **to l. a ball o. to s.o.**, (*football*) faire une passe à qn. **4.** *P:* **to l. o. s.o.**, (*a*) ficher (*ou* foutre) la paix à qn; (*b*) congédier*, bouler, virer qn. **5.** (*Austr.*) *P:* **to l. o. with a woman** = **to lay a woman** (lay[2] (to), **1**).

lay on ['leiˈɔn] (**to**), *F:* **1. to l. it o. thick** (*or* **with a shovel** *or* **with a trowel**), (*a*) flatter*, passer la pommade, casser le nez à coups d'encensoir; (*b*) exagérer*, y aller fort, charrier, broder, forcer la dose. **2.** arranger, préparer, amarrer, arnaquer; **it's all laid on**, tout est bien branché.

layout ['leiaut] (*noun*), *P:* **1. to be sick of the whole l.**, en avoir assez* (de tout le fourbi), en avoir ras le bol. **2.** = **fit**[2], **5.**

lay out ['leiˈaut] (**to**), *F:* **1.** assommer, étendre (qn) sur le carreau. **2. to l. oneself o.** (**to do sth.**), se mettre en

quatre, se démener, se décarcasser (pour faire qch.).

lay up ['leiˈʌp] (**to**), *F:* se la couler douce, se prélasser. *Voir aussi* **laid up**.

lazybones ['leizibounz] (*noun*), *F:* paresseux*, cossard *m*.

lead[1] [led] (*noun*). **1.** *F:* **to fill s.o. with l.**, **to pump s.o. full of l.**, fusiller, flinguer, truffer qn, transformer qn en passoire; *cf.* **lead-poisoning**. **2.** *F:* **to swing the l.**, tirer au flanc (*ou* au cul); *cf.* **lead-swinger**. **3. to have l. in one's pencil**, (*a*) être en érection*, avoir la canne (*ou* le bambou); (*b*) *P:* être prêt à ouvrir l'allumage (*coïter**); (*c*) *F:* avoir de l'allant, péter le feu. **4.** *P:* (*a*) **to get the l. out of one's arse** (*U.S.:* **ass**) (*or* **pants**), se dépêcher*, se magner (le derrière), se démerder; (*b*) **to have l. in one's arse** (*U.S.:* **ass**) (*or* **pants**), paresser*, tirer au cul.

lead[2] [liːd] (*noun*), *F:* (*a*) **to have a l. on sth.**, avoir des renseignements* sur qch., avoir un tuyau (*ou* un rencart); (*b*) **to have a l. on s.o.**, avoir barre (*ou* le pas) sur qn.

lead-off ['liːdɔf] (*noun*), *F:* démarrage *m*, point *m* de départ.

lead off ['liːdˈɔf] (**to**), *F:* **to l. o. at s.o.**, passer un abattage à qn, redresser qn.

lead-poisoning ['ledˈpɔizniŋ] (*noun*), *F:* **to have l.-p.**, être fusillé, être farci (*ou* bourré) de plomb; *cf.* **lead**[1], **1**.

lead-swinger ['ledˈswiŋər] (*noun*), *F:* paresseux*, tire-au-flanc *m*; *cf.* **lead**[1], **2**.

league [liːg] (*noun*), *F:* **not to be in the same l. as s.o.**, ne pas être dans la même catégorie, ne pas arriver à la cheville de qn.

leak[1] [liːk] (*noun*). **1.** *P:* **to go for a l.**, (*U.S.*) **to spring a l.**, uriner*, lansquiner, égoutter son cyclope (*ou* sa sardine). **2.** (*a*) *P:* donneur *m*, macaron *m*, passoire *f*; (*b*) *F:* fuite *f* (de secrets, nouvelles, *etc.*), divulgation *f*, macaronage *m*.

leak[2] [liːk] (**to**), *F:* divulguer, laisser filtrer (nouvelles, *etc.*); cabasser, faire du ragoût.

lean and lurch ['liːnənˈləːtʃ] (*noun*) (*R.S.* = *church*), *P:* église *f*.

lean on ['liːnˈɔn] (**to**), *F:* faire pression sur (qn), serrer la vis à (qn), passer (qn) à la casserole.

leap [liːp] (*noun*), *F:* **to take the big l.**,

---

* L'astérisque indique que le mot marqué de ce signe figure comme entrée dans le Répertoire.

se marier, se maquer, se mettre la corde au cou.

leaper ['li:pər] (*noun*), *P:* amphétamine *f* (*drogues**).

learn [lə:n] (to), *P:* **I'll l. you!** je t'apprendrai!

leary ['liəri] (*adj.*), *F:* = **leery**.

leather[1] ['leðər] (*noun*), *P:* 1. **to put the l. in,** flanquer un coup de pied (à qn). 2. **voleur* à la tire** (*ou* à la fourche); **to snatch l.,** voler* (*ou* piquer) un portefeuille à la tire. *Voir aussi* **hell,** 11.

leather[2] ['leðər] (to), *F:* battre*, carder le cuir à (qn), étriller.

leather-man ['leðəmæn] (*noun*), *P:* = **leather**[1], 2.

leatherneck ['leðənek] (*noun*) (*U.S.*), *F:* fusilier marin, marsouin *m.*

lech[1] [letʃ] (*noun*), *P:* 1. (=*lecher*) débauché *m,* paillard *m,* noceur *m.* 2. (*a*) (=*lechery*) paillardise *f,* lubricité *f;* (*b*) = **yen**[1], 1.

lech[2] [letʃ] (to), *P:* **to l. for s.o.,** en pincer pour qn, en mouiller pour qn.

leery ['liəri] (*adj.*), *F:* méfiant; **to be l. of s.o.,** se méfier de qn.

leftfooter ['left'futər] (*noun*), *P:* catholique *mf.*

left-handed ['left'hændid] (*adj.*), *P:* homosexuel, emmanché.

leftover ['leftouvər] (*noun*), *F:* 1. laissé(e) pour compte. 2. (*pl.*) restes *m.pl.,* arlequins *m.pl.,* rogatons *m.pl.*

lefty ['lefti] (*noun*), *F:* gaucher *m.*

leg[1] [leg] (*noun*). 1. *F:* **to show a l.,** se lever, sortir du lit. 2. *F:* **l. show,** spectacle *m* avec de la fesse. 3. *F:* **to shake a l.,** (*a*) danser*, gambiller; (*b*) se dépêcher*, se grouiller; (*c*) jouer des guibolles *f.pl.* 4. *F:* **he hasn't a l. to stand on,** on lui a rivé son clou. 5. *F:* **to pull s.o.'s l.,** faire marcher qn, mettre qn en boîte, monter un bateau à qn; *cf.* **leg-pull.** 6. *F:* **to have l. room,** être au large. 7. *F:* **to give s.o. a l. up,** (*a*) faire la courte échelle à qn; (*b*) dépanner qn, donner un coup de main à qn. 8. *F:* **to get (up) on one's hind legs,** se mettre debout. 9. *F:* **to be on one's last legs,** (*a*) filer un mauvais coton, avoir un pied dans la tombe, battre de l'aile; (*b*) être très fatigué*, être à bout de course (*ou* au bout de son rouleau), tirer à sa fin, être crevé. 10. *F:* **to have**

a l. up on s.o., avoir barre (*ou* le pas) sur qn. 11. *F:* **to stretch one's legs,** se dérouiller (*ou* se dégourdir) les jambes. 12. *P:* **middle** (*or* **third**) **l.,** pénis*, jambe *f* du milieu. 13. *P:* **to get one's l. over,** (*pour un homme*) coïter*, enjamber. 14. *F:* **legs eleven:** *voir* **bingo** (11). *Voir aussi* **donkey,** 1; **open**[2] (to), 1; **peg-leg; show**[1], 1.

leg[2] [leg] (to), *F:* 1. faire trébucher (qn). 2. **to l. it,** marcher*, courir*, s'enfuir*, se cavaler, jouer des flûtes *f.pl.*

leggo! ['le'gou] (*excl.*) (=*let go!*), *F:* lâche (tout)!

legit [le'dʒit] (*adj.*) (=*legitimate*), *F:* vrai, authentique; **on the l.,** officiel, légal.

legman ['legmæn] (*noun*), *F:* 1. reporter *m,* envoyé spécial. 2. celui qui travaille activement, turbineur *m; cf.* **legwork.**

leg-pull ['legpul] (*noun*), *F:* blague *f,* mise *f* en boîte; *cf.* **leg**[1], 5.

legwork ['legwə:k] (*noun*), *F:* travail* actif, turbin *m; cf.* **legman,** 2.

lemon ['lemən] (*noun*). 1. *F:* **the answer's a l.,** rien à faire! des clous! berique! 2. *F:* **to feel a (right) l.,** se sentir un peu bête*, être comme deux ronds de flan. 3. *P:* femme* laide, tartignole *f,* mocheté *f,* remède *m* d'amour. 4. *P:* coup monté, doublage *m,* fumisterie *f.* 5. *P:* **to squeeze the l.,** uriner*, ouvrir les écluses *f.pl.*

length [leŋ(k)θ] (*noun*), *P:* 1. **to go one's l.,** chercher des embêtements *m.pl.;* **you're going your l.!** tu le cherches! 2. **to give** (*or* **slip**) **(a woman) a l.,** coïter* avec une femme, filer un coup (d'arbalète *ou* de patte) (à une femme). *Voir aussi* **wavelength.**

lergi ['lə:dʒi] (*noun*) (=*allergy*), *P:* allergie *f.*

les[1] [lez] (*adj.*) (=*lesbian*), *P:* lesbienne, qui aime (*ou* tape) l'ail.

les[2] [lez] (*noun*) (=*lesbian*), *P:* lesbienne*, gougnote *f,* goudou *f.*

lesbie ['lezbi], **lesbo** ['lezbou] (*noun*), *P:* = **les**[2]; **they're a couple of lesbies, lesbos,** c'est deux marchandes d'ail.

let [let] (to), *P:* **to l. one** = **let (one) off** (to).

letch [letʃ] (*noun & verb*), *P:* = **lech.**

let-down ['letdaun] (*noun*), *F:* déception *f,* déboire *m.*

let down ['let'daun] (to), *F:* 1. décevoir (qn), laisser (qn) en panne, faire faux

---

* An asterisk indicates that the word so marked is included as a head-word in the Appendix.

bond à (qn). 2. **to l. s.o. d.** gently (or lightly), contrecarrer qn avec ménagement.

let in on [ˈletˈinɔn] (**to**), F: **to l. s.o. i. o. sth.**, mettre qn dans le coup (ou au parfum).

let off [ˈletˈɔf] (**to**), P: **to l. (one) o.**, péter*, en lâcher un, en écraser un. Voir aussi **steam, 1**.

let on [ˈletˈon] (**to**), F: **1. to l. o. (about sth.) to s.o.**, mettre qn au courant (ou à la page); **don't l. o.!** bouche cousue! **2.** prétendre, frimer, chiquer.

let-out [ˈletaʊt] (noun), F: (a) porte f de sortie; (b) alibi m, parapluie m.

lettuce [ˈletis] (noun), P: argent*, galette f; billets*, faf(f)iots m.pl.; cf. **cabbage**; **kale**.

letty [ˈleti] (noun), P: lit*, plumard m.

let-up [ˈletʌp] (noun), F: **with no l.-u.**, sans cesse (ou pause ou relâche), sans débrider.

let up [ˈletˈʌp] (**to**). **1.** F: cesser, diminuer, relâcher, ralentir. **2.** P: **to l. u. on s.o.**, ficher (ou foutre) la paix à qn.

level¹ [ˈlevəl] (adj.), F: **to do one's l. best**, faire de son mieux, en mettre un bon coup, mettre le paquet. Voir aussi **pegging**.

level² [ˈlevəl] (noun), F: **on the l.**, honnête, régulier, réglo.

level³ [ˈlevəl] (**to**), F: **to l. with s.o.**, (a) parler franchement, vider son sac; (b) rendre la pareille, garder un chien de sa chienne.

lez [lez], **lezo** [ˈlezoʊ] (noun), P: = **les²**.

lick¹ [lik] (noun). **1.** F: démarrage m, coup m de vitesse (ou de collier). **2.** P: coup*, torgnole f, raclée f. **3.** F: **a l. and a promise**, un bout (ou brin) de toilette, une toilette de chat; cf. **cat-lick**. **4.** F: **to get a l. at sth.**, tenter de faire qch., tâter de qch., se faire la main à qch. Voir aussi **dumblick**.

lick² [lik] (**to**), F: **1.** (a) venir à bout de (qch.), vaincre, enfoncer, maîtriser, écraser (un problème, une difficulté, etc.); (b) **to l. s.o. = to give s.o. a licking**, (a), (b); (c) **if you can't l. them (or 'em) join them (or 'em)**, c.p., si tu ne peux pas les mettre pattes en l'air, serre-leur la pince. **2. to l. sth. into shape**, finir un travail, boucler une affaire; **to l. s.o. into shape**, former qn,

dégrossir qn. **3. to l. one's chops**, (a) faire des gorges chaudes de qn; (b) s'en lécher (ou pourlécher) les babouines f.pl. Voir aussi **arse-lick** (**to**); **boot, 10**; **dust¹, 5**; **pants, 6**.

licketysplit [ˈlikətiˈsplit] (adv.) (U.S.), F: très vite*, à plein gaz, à fond de train.

licking [ˈlikiŋ] (noun), F: **to give s.o. a l.**, (a) donner une volée de coups* (ou une rossée ou une raclée) à qn; (b) vaincre, écraser, griller qn. Voir aussi **arse-licking**.

lid [lid] (noun). **1.** F: chapeau*, galurin m, casquette*, bâche f; **to dip one's l.**, soulever son bibi. **2.** F: **to take (or blow) the l. off sth.**, faire éclater (ou exposer) un scandale. **3.** F: **to put the l. on sth.**, interdire qch., mettre le holà à qch.; **that puts the l. on it!** c'est le comble! **4.** P: deux grammes de marijuana. **5.** F: capote f (d'une voiture). Voir aussi **dustbin**; **flip³ (to), 2**; **skid-lid**; **tin¹, 1, 2**.

lid-popper [ˈlidpɔpər] (noun), P: amphétamine f (drogues*).

lie-in [ˈlaiˈin] (noun), F: **to have a l.-i.**, faire la grasse matinée.

life [laif] (noun), F: **1. for the l. of me I can't remember**, j'ai beau chercher à me souvenir, je n'y arrive pas. **2. to worry the l. out of s.o.**, tourmenter, asticoter qn. **3. he turned up the next day as large as l.**, il reparut le lendemain comme si de rien n'était; **as large as l. and twice as natural**, dans toute sa beauté, grandeur nature. **4. to see l.**, rouler sa bosse, en voir des vertes et des pas mûres. **5. not on your l.!** pas de danger! rien à faire! **6. to get l.**, être condamné* à perpétuité, être gerbé à perpète. **7. to get another l.**, repartir à zéro, avoir une autre possibilité. **8.** (a) **l. begins**: voir **bingo (40)**; (b) **l.'s begun**: voir **bingo (41)**. Voir aussi **dog¹, 25**; **Riley**; **sweet¹, 2**.

lifemanship [ˈlaifmənʃip] (noun), F: l'art m de se montrer supérieur aux autres, l'art de se faire mousser.

lifer [ˈlaifər] (noun), F: (a) prisonnier m à perpétuité, enchetibé m à perpète (ou à perte de vue); (b) gerbement m à perpète.

lifesaver [ˈlaifseivər] (noun), F: planche f de salut.

---

* L'astérisque indique que le mot marqué de ce signe figure comme entrée dans le Répertoire.

lift¹ [lift] (*noun*), F: **to give s.o. a l.**, (*a*) faire monter qn (en voiture) avec soi, épargner à qn une partie de la route; (*b*) remonter le moral à qn; **l. pill**, amphétamine *f* (*drogues**). *Voir aussi* **face-lift.**

lift² [lift] (**to**), F: **1.** voler*, chiper, faucher. **2.** plagier, démarquer. **3.** augmenter, hausser. *Voir aussi* **elbow, 6.**

lifter [¹liftər] (*noun*), F: voleur*, faucheur *m*. *Voir aussi* **shirt-lifter.**

light¹ [lait] (*adj.*), F: **to be sth. l.**, (*a*) avoir qch. qui manque; (*b*) être à court d'argent*.

light² [lait] (*noun*). **1.** F: (*a*) **to be out like a l.**, (i) être ivre*, être éteint (*ou* cuit); (ii) dormir*, en écraser, être occis; (*b*) **to go out like a l.**, s'évanouir*, tomber dans les pommes (*ou* dans le cirage); **... and then the lights went out**, ...et puis je me suis évanoui* (*ou* j'ai tourné de l'œil). **2.** (*pl.*) P: yeux (*œil**), lanternes *f.pl.*, quinquets *m.pl.* **3.** F: **the l.**, compréhension *f*, comprenette *f*; **to see the l.**, comprendre, entraver, piger. **4.** F: **to see the red l.** (**flashing**), flairer le danger. *Voir aussi* **green¹, 3; headlights; red-light; strike (to), 1; tosh-light.**

light-footed [¹lait¹futid] (*adj.*), P: homosexuel, chochotte, chouquette.

light into [¹lait¹intu:] (**to**), F: **to l. i. s.o.**, (*a*) attaquer* qn, tomber (à bras raccourcis) sur qn, agrafer qn; (*b*) réprimander* qn sévèrement, enguirlander, engueuler qn.

lightweight [¹lait-weit] (*noun*), F: individu* qui ne fait pas le poids, un minus.

like¹ [laik] (*adv.*), F: **1.** comme qui dirait; **you're one of the family, l.**, vous êtes comme qui dirait de la famille. **2. very l.**, (**as**) **l. as not, l. enough**, probablement, vraisemblablement.

like² [laik] (*conj.*), F: **1.** (=*as if*) **he treated me l. I was dirt**, il m'a traité comme si j'étais de la crotte; **seems l. it works**, on dirait que ça marche. **2.** (=*as*) **l. I said**, comme je l'ai (si bien) dit; **I can't knit l. mother does**, je ne sais pas tricoter comme le fait maman.

like³ [laik] (*noun*), F: **the likes of us**, des gens comme nous, nos semblables.

like⁴ [laik] (**to**), F: (**well,**) **I l. that!** elle est bien bonne, celle-là! en voilà une bonne! par exemple!

likely [¹laikli] (*adj.*), F: **1. a l. lad**, un joyeux gaillard, un gars qui promet. **2. as l. as not**, vraisemblablement, il y a beaucoup de chance (que...). **3. not l.!** pas de danger! jamais de la vie!; *voir aussi* **bloody².**

lily [¹lili] (*noun*) (*U.S.*), P: pédéraste*, tapette *f*.

lily-livered [¹lililivəd] (*adj.*), F: = **yellow-bellied.**

lily-white [¹liliwait] (*adj.*), F: = **snow-white; she's not so l.-w.!** ce n'est pas un prix de vertu!

limb [lim] (*noun*), F: **out on a l.**, en plan, sur la corde raide, le bec dans l'eau.

limey [¹laimi] (*noun*), P: **1.** Anglais *m*, Angliche *m*. **2.** matelot *m* britannique (*ou* engliche).

limit [¹limit] (*noun*). **1.** F: **that's the l.!** c'est le comble! c'est le bouquet!; **she's the l.!** elle est marrante (*ou* impayable)! **2. to go the l.**, (*a*) F: y aller à fond, mettre le paquet; (*b*) P: (*d'une femme*) coïter*, lever la jambe. **3.** F: **the sky's the l.**, vers monts et merveilles!

limy [¹laimi] (*noun*), P: = **limey, 1, 2.**

line [lain] (*noun*), F: **1. what's your l.** (**of business**)? quel est votre genre d'affaires? quelle est votre partie?; **that's not in my l., that's not my l.** (**of country**), ce n'est pas mon rayon (*ou* mon blot); **that's more in his l.**, c'est plus dans son genre (*ou* dans ses cordes); **a rice pudding or something in that l.**, du riz au lait ou quelque chose dans ce genre-là. **2.** (*a*) **to get a l. on sth.**, reconnaître*, retapisser, reconnoïr qch.; (*b*) **to get a l. on s.o.**, se renseigner* sur qn, se rencarder sur qn. **3. to win all along the l.**, gagner sur toute la ligne. **4. to toe the l.**, rentrer dans les rangs, marcher au pas. **5. to read between the lines**, lire entre les lignes. **6. to put it on the l.**, dire en toutes lettres, ne pas mâcher les mots. **7. to be in l.**, se conformer (aux idées, *etc.*); **to be out of l.**, être rebelle. **8. to come to the end of the l.**, mourir*, lâcher la rampe. *Voir aussi* **drop² (to), 8; hard¹, 3; headlines; main-line¹;**

pipeline; punch-line; shoot² (to), 5;
sweet¹, 3; top-line.

linen ['linin] (*noun*). **1.** *F:* **to wash one's
dirty l. in public,** laver son linge sale
en public. **2.** *P:* **l. draper** (*R.S.* =
newspaper), journal*.

line-shooter ['lainʃuːtər] (*noun*), *F:*
vantard*, esbrouf(f)eur *m*, baratineur
m, rambineur *m*; *cf.* shoot² (to), 5.

line-shooting ['lainʃuːtiŋ] (*noun*), *F:*
rambin *m*, esbrouf(f)e *f*, baratin *m*;
cf. shoot² (to), 5.

lingo ['liŋgou] (*noun*). **1.** *F:* langue
étrangère, baragouin *m*. **2.** *P:* argot*;
to shoot (*or* **sling**) **the l.,** parler l'argot*,
dévider (*ou* bagouler *ou* rouler) le jars.

lip [lip] (*noun*). **1.** *P:* effronterie *f*;
don't give me (*or* **I don't want**) **any of
your l.!** ne te fiche pas de moi! ne te
paye pas ma tête! ne la ramène pas!
2. *F:* **to keep a stiff upper l.,** ne pas
broncher, garder son courage et faire
contre mauvaise fortune bon cœur,
serrer les dents. *Voir aussi* flip³ (to), 6.

lippy ['lipi] (*adj.*), *P:* **1.** effronté, culotté.
2. bavard*, bavasseur, jacasseur.

liquidate ['likwideit] (to), *F:* tuer*,
liquider, effacer.

liquored up ['likəd'ʌp] (*p.p. & adj.*),
F: ivre*, qui a pris une bit(t)ure (*ou*
une cuite).

listed ['listid] (*adj.*), *P:* aliéné.

lit [lit] (*p.p. & adj.*), *F:* = lit up.

literally ['litərəli] (*adv.*), *F:* absolument; **l. speaking,** à proprement parler.

litter-bug ['litəbʌg], **litter-lout** ['litə-
laut] (*noun*), *F:* qn qui fait des ordures
f.pl., ordurier *m*.

little ['litl] (*adj.*), *F:* **1.** **l. go,** (*a*) examen
m propédeutique à l'Université de
Cambridge; (*b*) (*U.S.*) banalité *f*, trivia-
lité *f*. **2.** **the l. woman,** mon épouse*, ma
moitié.

lit up ['lit'ʌp] (*p.p. & adj.*), *F:* (*a*)
légèrement ivre*, éméché; **well l. u.,**
ivre*, noir; (*b*) drogué*, camé, bourré.

live it up ['livit'ʌp] (to), *F:* faire la
noce, faire bombance.

lively ['laivli] (*adj.*), *F:* **look l. (about it)!**
et que ça saute!

liver ['livər] (*noun*), *F:* **to have a l.,**
(*a*) être malade* du foie; (*b*) être de
mauvaise humeur (*ou* d'humeur massacrante), être en rogne.

liverish ['livəriʃ] (*adj.*), *F:* qui a le foie

dérangé; **to feel l.,** se sentir mal en train
(*ou* détraqué).

livid ['livid] (*adj.*), *F:* blême de colère*,
à cran.

lizard ['lizəd] (*noun*) (*U.S.*), *P:* pénis*,
frétillard *m*; **to stroke the l.,** se masturber*, s'astiquer.

lizzie ['lizi] (*noun*). *F:* **1.** (tin) l., vieille
voiture*, tinette *f*. **2.** *P:* pédéraste*,
tantouse *f*.

load [loud] (*noun*). **1.** *P:* **get a l. of that!**
écoutez ça! regardez* ça! vise! **2.** *P:*
a l. of baloney (*or* **balls** *or* **cobblers** *or*
cock *or* **codswallop** *or* **crap**), un tissu
d'âneries *f.pl.*, un tas de foutaises *f.pl.*;
cf. muck, 2; swill¹, 3. **3.** *P:* **to drop
one's l.,** déféquer*, lâcher un
colombin. **4.** *P:* stock illégal de drogues,
charge *f*. **5.** *F:* **loads of . . .,** une
abondance* de..., une bardée (*ou* une
flopée) de... **6.** *F:* **take the l. off your
feet!** asseyez-vous! pose tes fesses!
7. *F:* **he's a l. of wind,** il parle pour ne
rien dire. **8.** *P:* sperme*, jus *m*; **to
shoot one's l.,** éjaculer*, lancer son jus.
Voir aussi cartload; tie on (to).

loaded ['loudid] (*adj.*). **1.** *P:* riche*,
plein aux as; **to be l.,** être à l'as, avoir
du foin dans ses bottes. **2.** *P:* ivre*
ou drogué*, chargé, bourré. **3.** *F:* (*d'un
discours, d'une entreprise*) explosif.

loaf [louf] (*noun*) (*R.S.* = *loaf of bread* =
head), *F:* tête*, caboche *f*; **use your l.!**
fais travailler tes méninges!

lob¹ [lɔb] (*noun*), *P:* **1.** pénis*, zob *m*.
2. oreille*, pavillon *m*. **3.** paye *f*,
gages *m.pl.*; **gash l.,** économies *f.pl.*,
care *f*, bas *m* de laine. **4.** (*U.S.*) gourde *f*,
andouille *f*. **5.** tiroir-caisse *m*.

lob² [lɔb] (to), *P:* **1.** jeter, envoyer
dinguer; **l. it over!** balance-moi ça!
2. (*Austr.*) **to l. somewhere,** arriver*,
s'abouler quelque part; **to l. back,**
revenir, rabouler, radiner.

local ['loukəl] (*noun*), *F:* café* de
quartier, bistrot *m* du coin.

lock-up ['lɔkʌp] (*noun*), *F:* prison*,
violon *m*, taule *f*.

lock up ['lɔk'ʌp] (to), *F:* emprisonner*,
mettre au violon.

loco ['loukou] (*adj.*), *F:* fou*, maboul,
dingo.

lofty ['lɔfti] (*noun*), *F:* **1.** individu* grand,
une grande perche. **2.** (*iron.*) petit*
individu, un astèque.

lollie [ˈlɔli] (*noun*), *F:* = lolly, 5.

lollipop-man, -lady [ˈlɔlipɔpˈmæn, -ˈleidi] (*nouns*), *F:* contractuel(le) qui fait traverser la rue aux enfants.

lollop [ˈlɔləp] (to), *F:* 1. marcher* lourdement, se traîner. 2. sauter, rebondir, faire des sauts de carpe. 3. paresser*, flânocher.

lolly [ˈlɔli] (*noun*). 1. *F:* argent*, flouze *m*; **lay off the l.!** (ne) touchez pas au grisbi! 2. *P:* agent* de police, flic *m*, cogne *m*. 3. (*Austr.*) *P:* un timide, un tiède, un frileux. 4. (*Austr.*) *P:* = alec, 2. 5. *F:* (=*lollipop*) sucette *f*; **ice(d) l.**, sucette glacée.

loner [ˈlounər] (*noun*), *F:* homme qui fait bande à part (*ou* qui fait cavalier seul).

lonesome [ˈlounsəm] (*noun*), *F:* **(all) on one's l.**, tout seulabre; *cf.* ownsome.

long[1] [lɔŋ] (*adj.*), *F:* **to be l. on sth.**, avoir des masses *f.pl.* de qch., déborder de qch. *Voir aussi* draw[2] (to), 5; shot[2], 5; tooth, 2; vac.

long[2] [lɔŋ] (*noun*), *F:* 1. **the l. and short of it is . . .**, le fin mot de l'histoire c'est que... 2. **the L.**, (*écoles*) les grandes vacances.

long-hair[1] [ˈlɔŋhɛər] (*adj.*), *F:* = long-haired.

long-hair[2] [ˈlɔŋhɛər] (*noun*). 1. *F:* intellectuel *m*, grosse tête, ponte *m*. 2. contestataire *m*.

long-haired [ˈlɔŋhɛəd] (*adj.*), *F:* intellectuel, calé.

long-tailed [ˈlɔŋteild] (*adj.*), *P:* **l.-t. 'uns**, billets* de banque.

loo [luː] (*noun*), *F:* W.C.*, ouatères *m.pl.*; **l. paper** = bumf, 1.

look[1] [lʊk] (*noun*), *F:* **to take a long, hard l. at sth.**, examiner qch. sur toutes les coutures.

look[2] [lʊk] (to), *F:* 1. **to l. like a million dollars**, être très élégant*, être très chic. 2. **here's looking at you!** à la tienne! à la bonne vôtre! 3. **l. here!** dis donc! *Voir aussi* nose, 7.

looker [ˈlʊkər] (*noun*), *F:* **a (good) l.**, une beauté, un prix de Diane, un joli lot.

look-in [ˈlʊkˈin] (*noun*), *F:* 1. belle occasion, beau jeu. 2. chances *f.pl.* de succès; **he won't get a l.-i.**, il n'a pas la moindre chance. 3. coup *m* d'œil rapide. 4. visite-éclair *f*.

look-out [ˈlʊkaut] (*noun*), *F:* 1. guet-

teur *m*, vigie *f*, gaffe *m*, gaffeur *m*. 2. **that's your l.-o.!** c'est ton affaire! c'est tes oignons!

look-see [ˈlʊkˈsiː] (*noun*), *F:* coup *m* d'œil*, coup de sabord.

look up [ˈlʊkˈʌp] (to), *F:* **business is looking up**, les affaires reprennent; **things are looking up with him**, ses affaires s'améliorent.

looloo [ˈluːluː] (*noun*), *F:* = lulu.

loony [ˈluːni] (*noun & adj.*), *F:* fou*, tapé (*m*), cinglé (*m*), dingue (*m*).

loony-bin [ˈluːnibin] (*noun*), *P:* maison *f* de fous, cabanon *m*, asile *m* de dingues; **to be fit for the l.-b.**, être bon (*ou* mûr) pour Sainte-Anne.

looped [luːpt] (*adj.*), *P:* ivre*, plein, rond; **l. to the eyeballs**, plein comme une bourrique.

loop-the-loop [ˈluːpðəˈluːp] (*noun*) (*R.S.* = *soup*), *P:* soupe *f*, rata *m*.

loopy [ˈluːpi] (*adj.*), *F:* fou*, dingo, tapé, cinglé, maboul.

loose [luːs] (*noun*), *F:* **to be (out) on the l.**, (*a*) être déchaîné, faire les quatre cents coups; (*b*) être en bordée, mener une vie de bâtons de chaise.

loosen up [ˈluːsənˈʌp] (to), *F:* se détendre, se relaxer.

loot [luːt] (*noun*), *P:* (*a*) argent*, artiche *m*, flouse *m*; (*b*) bénéfice* financier, gratte *f*, gratouille *f*.

lorry-hop [ˈlɔrihɔp] (to), *F:* faire de l'auto-stop *m* (dans les camions).

lose [luːz] (to). 1. *P:* **get lost!** va te faire fiche (*ou* foutre)! va te faire voir! au bout du quai les ballots! 2. *F:* **you've lost me!** je n'y suis plus, j'ai perdu le fil.

lose out [ˈluːzˈaut] (to), *F:* perdre, paumer.

lotties [ˈlɔtiz] (*pl. noun*), *P:* seins*, boîtes *f.pl.* à lolo, nénés *m.pl.*

loud [laud] (*adv.*), *F:* **for crying out l.!** (sacré) nom d'un chien! nom de nom!

loudmouth [ˈlaudmauθ] (*noun*), *F:* gueulard *m*, va-de-la-gueule *m*.

loudmouthed [ˈlaudmauðd] (*adj.*), *F:* gueulard, fort en gueule.

louse [laus] (*noun*), *F:* vaurien*, saligaud *m*, salope *f*.

louse around [ˈlausəˈraund] (to), *P:* traîner, traînasser, lambiner.

louse up [ˈlausˈʌp] (to), *P:* bousiller, gâcher, saloper, louper.

lousy [ˈlauzi] (*adj.*). 1. *F:* mauvais*,

moche; miteux, pouilleux; **a l. trick**, un tour de cochon, une vacherie. **2.** *P:* **l. with . . .**, plein de...; **the place was l. with cops**, ça grouillait de flics.

love [lʌv] (*noun*), *F:* **hello, l.!** salut!; **thanks, l.!** merci mon pote! *Voir aussi* **bug**[1], **9**; **puppy, 2**; **smother-love**.

lovebird [ˈlʌvbəːd] (*noun*), *F:* amoureux *m*, amoureuse *f*, soupirant(e) *m(f)*.

love-in [ˈlʌvin] (*noun*), *F:* festival *m* hippie.

lovely[1] [ˈlʌvli] (*adj.*), *F:* **1. it's been (just) l. seeing you again**, ça a été charmant de vous revoir. **2. she's l.:** *voir* **bingo (16)**.

lovely[2] [ˈlʌvli] (*noun*), *F:* belle* fille*, une vénus.

lover-boy [ˈlʌvəbɔi] (*noun*), *F:* **1.** beau* gars, un Adonis, un Apollon, un jeune premier. **2.** un don Juan, coureur *m* de jupons, cavaleur *m*.

love-up [ˈlʌvʌp] (*noun*), *P:* caresses *f.pl.* intimes, papouilles *f.pl.*

love up [ˈlʌvˈʌp] (**to**), *P:* caresser (qn) en palpant, peloter (qn).

love-weed [ˈlʌvwiːd] (*noun*), *P:* marijuana *f* (*drogues**), herbe douce.

lovey [ˈlʌvi] (*noun*), *F:* chéri(e), petit chou.

lovey-dovey [ˈlʌviˈdʌvi] (*adj.*), *F:* **1.** affectueux, amoureux, sentimental. **2.** à la guimauve, à l'eau de rose.

lowbrow[1] [ˈlou-brau] (*adj.*), *F:* (*a*) sans prétentions intellectuelles, terre à terre; (*b*) faubourien, populo.

lowbrow[2] [ˈlou-brau] (*noun*), *F:* (*a*) prolétaire *m*, prolo *m*, inculte *mf*, simplet *m*; (*b*) qn qui ne s'intéresse pas aux choses intellectuelles, individu* peu relevé.

lowdown[1] [ˈlouˈdaun] (*adj.*), *F:* méprisable, moche, dégueulasse.

lowdown[2] [ˈloudaun] (*noun*). **1.** *F:* (*a*) renseignements* privés; tuyau *m*, rencart *m*; (*b*) renseignements* généraux, pleins tubes. **2.** *P:* tour *m* de cochon, coup fourré, sale coup.

lube [luːb] (*noun*), *P:* huile *f* de graissage.

lubricate [ˈluːbrikeit] (**to**), *F:* **1.** graisser la patte à (qn). **2.** enivrer, soûler (qn).

luck [lʌk] (*noun*), *F:* **you never know your l.**, on ne sait jamais ce qui vous pend au nez. *Voir aussi* **push**[2] (**to**), **2**; **pot-luck**.

lucre [ˈluːkər] (*noun*). *F:* argent*, lucre *m*; bénéfice*, bénef *m*; **filthy l.**, (*a*) gain *m*, gratte *f*; (*b*) argent*, carbure *m*; **to do sth. for filthy l.**, faire qch. par amour du lucre.

lucy [ˈluːsi] (*noun*), *P:* sweet l., marijuana *f* (*drogues**), herbe *f*, kif *m*.

lug[1] [lʌg] (*noun*), *P:* **1.** (*a*) oreille*, esgourde *f*; *cf.* **lugholes**; (*b*) visage*; menton *m*; gueule *f*; (*c*) (*pl.*) (*U.S.*) mains*, paluches *f.pl.* **2.** (*a*) homme*, mec *m*; (*b*) ballot *m*, baluchard *m*. **3.** (*U.S.*) (*a*) demande *f* d'argent*, botte *f*; (*b*) dessous-de-table *m*, gratte *f*, tour *m* de bâton.

lug[2] [lʌg] (**to**) (*Austr.*), *P:* **to l. s.o. for money**, emprunter* de l'argent à qn, taper qn, bottiner qn.

lughead [ˈlʌghed] (*noun*), *P:* individu bête*, ballot *m*, cruche *f*.

lugholes [ˈlʌg(h)oulz] (*pl. noun*), *P:* oreilles*; **pin back your l.!** dessable tes portugaises! écarquille tes esgourdes!; *cf.* **lug**[1], **1** (*a*).

lulu [ˈluːluː] (*noun*), *F:* (*a*) as *m*, vedette *f*; (*b*) fille* bath, môme formid(able); (*c*) qch. de sensas(s) (*ou* de super).

lumber [ˈlʌmbər] (**to**). **1.** *P:* arrêter*, agrafer, épingler; **to get lumbered**, se faire agrafer (*ou* épingler). **2.** *F:* **to get lumbered with s.o., sth.**, être chargé (*ou* encombré) de qn, de qch.

lumme! [ˈlʌmi] (*excl.*), *F:* mon Dieu! mince alors!

lummox [ˈlʌməks] (*noun*) (*U.S.*), *P:* individu bête*, cornichon *m*, niguedouille *m*.

lummy! [ˈlʌmi] (*excl.*), *F:* = **lumme!**

lump[1] [lʌmp] (*noun*), *F:* **1.** personne bête*, crétin *m*, cruche *f*. **2. a big l. of a girl**, une grosse dondon, une godiche.

lump[2] [lʌmp] (**to**), *F:* **1.** porter, trimbal(l)er. **2. like it or l. it**, que ça plaise ou non, c'est le même prix; **you'll have to l. it**, il faudra l'avaler, il faut passer par là.

lunch [lʌntʃ] (*noun*), *P:* **to be out to l.**, se mettre le doigt dans l'œil. *Voir aussi* **box**[1], **1**.

lunkhead [ˈlʌŋkhed] (*noun*), *P:* = **lughead**.

lush[1] [lʌʃ] (*adj.*), *F:* chouette, badour; **she's a l. piece**, elle est bath (*ou* juteuse).

lush[2] [lʌʃ] (*noun*) (*U.S.*), *F:* **1.** ivrogne*, poivrot *m*, soûlard *m*. **2.** soûlerie *f*, bringue *f*. **3.** alcool*, gnôle *f*.

---

* L'astérisque indique que le mot marqué de ce signe figure comme entrée dans le Répertoire.

lush³ [lʌʃ] (to) (U.S.), F: boire* de
l'alcool*, biberonner, siffler.
lush-hound [ˈlʌʃhaʊnd] (noun) (U.S.),
F: = lush², 1.
lush-roller [ˈlʌʃroʊlər] (noun) (U.S.),
P: voleur* d'ivrognes, poivrier m.

lush-rolling [ˈlʌʃroʊliŋ] (noun) (U.S.),
P: vol m au poivrier.
lush up [ˈlʌʃˈʌp] (to) (U.S.), F: soûler,
charger, bourrer.
luv [lʌv] (noun), F: = love.

M

M [em] (*abbr.*), *P:* (*a*) morphine *f* (*drogues**), morph *f*; (*b*) marijuana *f* (*drogues**), Maria *f*, Marie *f*.

ma [mɑː] (*noun*), *F:* mère*, maman.

Mac¹ [mæk] (*noun*). 1. *F:* Écossais *m*. 2. *P:* = mack¹, 3.

mac² [mæk] (*noun*) (*abbr.* = *mackintosh*), *F:* imper(méable) *m*; the dirty m. brigade, individus qui vont voir des films, *etc.*, orduriers; pornos *m.pl.*

macaroni [mækəˈrouni] (*noun*), *P:* Italien *m*, macaroni *m*, Rital *m*.

mace [meis] (to), *P:* obtenir qch. pour rien, faire de la resquille.

machine [məˈʃiːn] (*noun*), *P:* seringue *f* hypodermique, poussette *f*, shooteuse *f*.

machinery [məˈʃiːnəri] (*noun*), *P:* attirail *m* de camé.

mack¹ [mæk] (*noun*). 1. *F:* = mac². 2. *P:* souteneur*, maquereau *m*, mac *m*. 3. *P:* mec *m*, zigoto *m*.

mack² [mæk] (to), *P:* rabattre le client (pour une prostituée*), maquereauter.

Mackay [məˈkai] (*noun*), *F:* the real M., (*a*) boisson *f* de bonne qualité; de la vraie (de vraie); (*b*) tout à fait ce qui convient; de l'authentique; (*c*) marchandise *f* irréprochable.

mackerel [ˈmækərəl] (*noun*), *P:* = mack¹, 2. *Voir aussi* holy, 1.

macking [ˈmækiŋ] (*noun*), *P:* maquereautage *m*.

mackman [ˈmækmən] (*noun*), *P:* = mack¹, 2.

mad¹ [mæd] (*adj.*), *F:* 1. en colère*; to be m. at s.o., être à cran contre qn. 2. to be m. about s.o., sth., raffoler de qn, de qch. 3. like m., (*a*) comme un enragé, comme un perdu; (*b*) très vite*; to run like m., foncer, gazer. *Voir aussi* man-mad; sex-mad; woman-mad.

mad² [mæd] (*adv.*), *F:* m. keen on sth., s.o., emballé par (*ou* entiché de) qch., qn.

madam¹ [ˈmædəm] (*noun*). 1. *P:* it's a load of old m., c'est de la foutaise; *cf.*

load, 2. 2. *P:* don't come the old m. with me! ne monte pas sur tes grands chevaux! ne la ramène pas! 3. *F:* patronne* (de maison de tolérance), madame, taulière *f*, maquerelle *f*.

madam² [ˈmædəm] (to), *P:* 1. mentir*, bourrer le crâne. 2. = to tell the tale (tale, 1).

madame [mæˈdɑːm] (*noun*) (*pl.* madames [mæˈdɑːmz]), *F:* = madam¹, 3.

made [meid] (*p.p.*): *voir* make (to).

madhouse [ˈmædhaʊs] (*noun*), *F:* maison *f* de fous, Charenton; this place is like a m., on se croirait à Charenton, chez les fous.

mag [mæg] (*abbr.*), *F:* 1. (=*magazine*) magazine *m*, revue *f*. 2. (=*magneto*) magnéto *f*.

main-line¹ [ˈmeinˈlain] (*noun*), *P:* veine apparente (pour piqûre intraveineuse).

main-line² [ˈmeinˈlain] (to), *P:* se piquer, se piquouser.

main-liner [ˈmeinˈlainər] (*noun*), *P:* drogué* qui se fait des piqûres intra-veineuses, piquouseur *m*.

make¹ [meik] (*noun*). 1. *P:* easy m., femme* facile (*ou* à la cuisse hos-pitalière); *cf.* lay¹, 2. 2. on the m., (*a*) *F:* âpre au gain, chercheur d'affure; (*b*) *P:* en quête d'aventures amoureuses, dragueur. 3. *P:* to get a m. on (a criminal, *etc.*), identifier, détrancher, tapisser (un criminel, *etc.*). 4. *P:* fade *m*, bouquet *m*, taf *m*.

make² [meik] (to). 1. (*a*) *F:* to m. it, réussir, gagner le cocotier, l'avoir belle; (*b*) *P:* to m. (it with) a woman, avoir les faveurs *f.pl.* d'une femme*, lever une fille*. 2. *F:* he's as sharp as they m. 'em, c'est un malin s'il en est. 3. *F:* gagner*; how much do you m.? qu'est-ce que tu gagnes comme pèze? 4. *P:* voler*, faire, fabriquer (qch.). 5. *P:* = to get a m. on (make¹, 3). 6. *P:* comprendre, piger, entraver (qn, qch.). 7. *F:* arriver à, débarquer à (un endroit). 8. *F:* do you

---

* L'astérisque indique que le mot marqué de ce signe figure comme entrée dans le Répertoire.

want to m. sth. (out) of it? veux-tu chercher noise (*ou* du grabuge) ? veux-tu en faire toute une histoire ? **9.** *F:* **to have it made,** se la couler douce, avoir le filon. **10.** *F:* **I just made my train,** j'ai eu mon train mais au poil. *Voir aussi* **daft**[1], **1**; **side, 1.**
make out [ˈmeikˈaut] **(to). 1.** *F:* prospérer, faire des progrès; aller, marcher (bien *ou* mal); **how do your children m.o. at school?** comment vos enfants se débrouillent-ils à l'école? **2.** *F:* subsister; **I can m. o. on bread and water,** je peux vivre de pain et d'eau. **3.** *F:* faire semblant. **4.** *P:* s'étreindre, s'enlacer passionnément.
make up [ˈmeikˈʌp] **(to),** *F:* **1.** inventer (une histoire, *etc.*). **2. to m. it u.,** se rabibocher.
malark(e)y [məˈlɑ:ki] (*noun*), *F:* **1.** flatteries *f.pl.*, boniment *m.* **2.** balivernes *f.pl.*
mammie, mammy [ˈmæmi] (*noun*) (*U.S.*), *F:* **1.** mère*, maman. **2.** nourrice *f*, nounou noire. **3. m. boy,** homme faible, femmelette *f*, chiffe molle.
man [mæn] (*noun*). **1.** *F:* **why, m., you're crazy!** mais mon pauvre vieux, tu es fou*! **2.** *F:* **come here, young m.!** viens ici, mon petit bonhomme!; **good m.!** bravo! **3.** *F:* **he's a big m.,** c'est quelqu'un; *cf.* **big**[1], **1. 4.** *F:* **her m.,** son mari, son homme. **5.** *F:* **my young m.,** (*a*) mon bon ami; (*b*) mon futur, mon promis, mon fiancé. **6.** *P:* **the m., the M.,** (*a*) la police*, ces Messieurs *m.pl.*; (*b*) fourgueur *m* (de drogues); **to make the m.,** acheter des drogues, brancher; (*c*) patron*, dab *m*, chef *m. Voir aussi* ad-man; arse-man; boss-man; busman; cave-man; chive-man; dead[1], 2, 9; dog[1], 20; dustman; G-man; he-man; ice-man; kickman; k-man; leatherman; legman; lollipop-man; mackman; media-man; middleman; muscle-man; old, 1; one-man; penman; peterman; prop-man; rod-man; sandman; screwsman; showman; sideman; snowman; spiderman; swagman; swordsman; tailman; trigger-man; yes-man.
manage [ˈmænidʒ] **(to),** *F:* **can you m. a few more cherries?** peux-tu manger encore quelques cerises ?
man-crazy [ˈmænˈkreizi] (*adj.*), *F:* nymphomane; *cf.* **woman-crazy.**

manhole [ˈmænhoul] (*noun*), *V:* vulve*, fente *f*, con(n)asse *f.*
man-mad [ˈmænˈmæd] (*adj.*), *F:* = man-crazy; *cf.* woman-mad.
manor [ˈmænər] (*noun*), *P:* (*a*) territoire *m*, champ *m* d'action (d'un criminel); (*b*) secteur couvert par un commissariat de police; *cf.* **patch, 2**; morguey m., quartier farci (*ou* pourri) de flics. *Voir aussi* mystery.
man-size(d) [ˈmænsaiz(d)] (*adj.*), *F:* (*a*) gros*, de taille; (*b*) costaud, maousse; **a m.-s. meal,** un repas copieux (*ou* abondant *ou* solide).
map [mæp] (*noun*). **1.** *F:* **to put on the m.,** populariser, mettre en vedette. **2.** *F:* **off the m.,** inaccessible, au diable vauvert. **3.** (*Austr.*) *P:* **to throw a m.,** vomir*, aller au refil(e). **4.** *P:* visage*, boule *f*, bobine *f.* **5.** (*U.S.*) *P:* chèque *m.*
maracas [məˈrækəz] (*pl. noun*), *P:* seins*, ropoplots *m.pl.*, rotoplots *m.pl.*
marbles [ˈmɑːblz] (*pl. noun*), *P:* **1. to pass in one's m.,** mourir*, passer l'arme à gauche. **2. go and play m.!** va te faire cuire un œuf! **3. to lose one's m.,** devenir fou*, perdre le nord, perdre la boule, déménager. **4.** testicules*, billes *f.pl.*
marching [ˈmɑːtʃiŋ] (*noun*), *F:* **to give s.o. his m. orders,** se débarrasser* de qn, flanquer qn à la porte.
mare [meər] (*noun*), *P:* femme* méprisable, carne *f*, vache *f.*
marge [mɑːdʒ] (*noun*). **1.** *F:* (=*margarine*) margarine *f.* **2.** *P:* lesbienne*, goudou *f.*
Marine [məˈriːn] (*noun*), *F:* **tell that to the Marines!** à d'autres! allez conter ça ailleurs! *Voir aussi* **dead**[1], **2.**
marjie [ˈmɑːdʒi], **marjorie** [ˈmɑːdʒəri] (*noun*), *P:* marijuana *f* (*drogues**), kif *m*, Marie-Jeanne *f; cf.* juana.
mark[1] [mɑːk] (*noun*), *F:* **to feel up to the m.,** être en train, être en pleine forme; **I don't feel up to the m.,** je ne suis pas dans mon assiette. *Voir aussi* **easy**[1], **3**; tide-mark.
mark[2] [mɑːk] **(to),** *P:* **1. to m. s.o.'s card,** mettre qn sur ses gardes, faire ouvrir l'œil à qn. **2.** chercher *ou* trouver un cave (*ou* un bon casse).
marker [ˈmɑːkər] (*noun*), *P:* reconnaissance *f* de dette.
mark up [ˈmɑːkˈʌp] **(to),** *F:* donner un

---

* An asterisk indicates that the word so marked is included as a head-word in the Appendix.

bon point pour (qch.); **to m. it u. to s.o.**, mettre (qch.) au crédit de qn.

marm [mɑːm] (*noun*), *F:* madame; *cf.* **schoolmarm**.

marriage ['mærɪdʒ] (*attrib. adj.*), *P:* **m. gear** (*or* **prospects**), testicules*, bijoux *m.pl.* de famille.

marrow-bones ['mæroʊboʊnz, 'mærəbəʊnz] (*pl. noun*), *P:* genoux *m.pl.*, coussinets *m.pl.*

marshmallows ['mɑːʃmæloʊz] (*pl. noun*), *P:* **1.** seins*. **2.** testicules*.

marvellous ['mɑːv(ə)ləs] (*adj.*), *F:* excellent*, super; **isn't it m.!** (*iron.*), voilà bien le bouquet!

Mary, mary ['mɛəri] (*noun*). **1.** *P:* pédéraste* (qui joue le rôle de femme), persilleuse *f.* **2.** *P:* lesbienne*, gouine *f.* **3.** *P:* = **Mary-Ann(e)**. **4.** *F:* **bloody M.**, cocktail *m* ɑe vodka et jus de tomate.

Mary Ann(e) ['mɛəri'æn], **Mary-Jane** ['mɛəri'dʒein], **Mary Warner** ['mɛəri'wɔːnər] (*pr. nouns*), *P:* (*a*) marijuana *f* (*drogues**), Marie-Jeanne; (*b*) cigarette* de marijuana, juju *f*, joint *m*.

masher ['mæʃər] (*noun*), *F:* **1.** gigolo *m*, gommeux *m*, coco-bel-œil *m*. **2.** (*pl.*) dents*, croquantes *f.pl.*

mat [mæt] (*noun*), *F:* **on the m.** = **on the carpet** (**carpet**[1], **2**). *Voir aussi* **doormat; welcome-mat**.

mate [meit] (*noun*), *F:* **1.** ami*, copain *m*, pote *m*. **2.** mec *m*, zigoto *m*; **that's too bad, m.!** tant pis pour toi, vieux frère!

matey[1] ['meiti] (*adj.*), *F:* **to be m.**, être à tu et à toi, copiner.

matey[2] ['meiti] (*noun*), *F:* = **mate, 1, 2**.

mateyness ['meitinis] (*noun*), *F:* copinage *m*.

matlo(w) ['mætloʊ] (*noun*), *F:* marin*, matelot *m*.

maverick[1] ['mævərik] (*adj.*) (*U.S.*), *F:* indépendant, n'appartenant à aucun parti, réfractaire, hors série.

maverick[2] ['mævərik] (*noun*) (*U.S.*), *F:* homme politique indépendant, franctireur *m*.

maxi ['mæksi] (*adj. & noun*), *F:* (manteau, jupe, *etc.*) maxi (*m*); lèche-trottoir *m*; *cf.* **midi; mini**.

maybe ['meibiː] (*adv.*), *F:* **. . . and I don't mean m.!** ...et je ne plaisante (*ou* rigole) pas!

mazuma [mə'zuːmə] (*noun*), *P:* argent*, pognon *m*, fric *m*.

McCoy [mə'kɔi] (*pr. noun*), *F:* = **Mackay**.

meal-ticket ['miːl-tikit] (*noun*), *F:* gagne-pain *m*, vache *f* à lait.

mealy-mouthed ['miːli'maʊðd] (*adj.*), *F:* mielleux, benoît.

mean [miːn] (*adj.*). **1.** *F:* **m. weather**, mauvais (*ou* sale) temps; **m. job**, travail* désagréable, fichu boulot. **2.** *P:* formid(able), du tonnerre.

meanie, meany ['miːniː] (*noun*), *F:* grigou *m*, rapiat *m*, minable *m*.

measly ['miːzli] (*adj.*), *F:* **1.** misérable, insignifiant. **2.** avare*, constipé du crapaud, radin, pingre.

meat [miːt] (*noun*). **1.** *F:* fond *m*, moelle *f*, substance *f.* **2.** *P:* **to love one's m.**, être porté sur l'article *m* (*ou* sur la chose). **3.** *V:* pénis*; **small m.**, un petit pénis*, petit bout; **to beat the m.** = **to beat the dummy** (**dummy, 5**). **4.** *P:* (*a*) mâle (considéré sexuellement); (*b*) jouissance *f* (d'un pédéraste*), nanan *m*. **5.** *F:* **to make cold m. of s.o.**, tuer* qn, refroidir qn. *Voir aussi* **easy**[1], **5**; **mincemeat; pig-meat; plate**[1], **2**.

meathead ['miːthed] (*noun*), *P:* individu bête*, saucisse *f*, gourde *f.*

meat-hooks ['miːthʊks] (*pl. noun*), *P:* grandes mains*, battoirs *m.pl.*, croches *f.pl.*; *cf.* **hook**[1], **6**.

meat-house ['miːthaʊs] (*noun*), *P:* bordel*, maison *f* d'abattage.

meat-show ['miːtʃoʊ] (*noun*), *P:* spectacle *m* du nu, parade *f* de fesses.

meat-wag(g)on ['miːt-wægən] (*noun*), *P:* **1.** ambulance *f.* **2.** corbillard*, roulotte *f* à refroidis, trottinette *f* à macchabs. **3.** car* de police, panier *m* à salade.

mebbe ['mebi] (*adv.*), *P:* (=*maybe*) ça se peut, des fois.

medals ['med(ə)lz] (*pl. noun*), *F:* **your m. are showing**, ta braguette est ouverte; n'expose pas tes bijoux.

media-man ['miːdiəmæn] (*noun*), *F:* agent *m* publicitaire.

medic(o) ['medik(oʊ)] (*noun*), *F:* **1.** médecin *m*, toubib *m*. **2.** étudiant *m* en médecine, carabin *m*.

meemies ['miːmiːz] (*pl. noun*) (*U.S.*), *P:* **the screaming m.** = **the screaming abdabs** (*voir* **abdabs**).

meet [miːt] (*noun*), *P:* **1.** = **gig**[1], **5**. **2.** rendez-vous*, rancart *m*. **3. to make**

---

* L'astérisque indique que le mot marqué de ce signe figure comme entrée dans le Répertoire.

a m. = to make the man (man, 6
(b)).

mental ['ment(ə)l] (adj.), F: to go m.,
devenir fou*; you must be m.! t'es pas
fou* (ou dingue ou maboul)?

merchant ['mɔːtʃənt] (noun), F:
individu*, type m, mec m. Voir aussi
chive-merchant; speed-merchant.

merry ['meri] (adj.), F: légèrement ivre*,
pompette, éméché. Voir aussi hell,
3.

mess [mes] (noun). 1. P: andouille f,
gourdichon m, tourte f. 2. F: isn't she a
m.! ce qu'elle est tarte! 3. F: what a m.!
quel gâchis! quelle pagaille! 4. F: to be
in a (bit of a) m., être dans le pétrin (ou
dans de mauvais draps); to help s.o. out
of a m., repêcher qn. 5. P: to make a m.
of s.o., battre* qn, tabasser, amocher
qn. 6. F: to make a m. of things (or it),
tout gâcher; he always makes a m. of
things, il n'en rate pas une. Voir aussi
right, 1.

mess about (or around) ['mesə'baut,
'mesə'raund] (to). 1. F: patauger (dans
la boue). 2. F: traîner, bricoler,
lambiner. 3. F: to m. s.o. a., tourmenter,
turlupiner qn. 4. P: to m. a. with s.o.,
(a) peloter, pelotailler qn; (b) s'acoquiner
avec qn.

message ['mesidʒ] (noun), F: to get the
m., comprendre, piger, entraver.

mess-up ['mesʌp] (noun), F: 1. gâchis m,
méli-mélo m, pagaille f. 2. malentendu
m, embrouillamini m, cafouillage m.

mess up ['mes'ʌp] (to), F: 1. salir,
bousiller, saloper. 2. abîmer*, amocher,
saboter; he's messed his face up, il s'est
abîmé le portrait.

metal-spiv ['met(ə)l-spiv] (noun), P:
marchand m (ou trafiquant m) en ferraille; cf. spiv.

meth [meθ] (noun) (abbr.). 1. P: (=methe-
drine) méthédrine f (drogues), meth f.
2. (pl.) F: (=methylated spirits) alcool
m à brûler.

methhead ['meθhed] (noun), P: habitué
m de la méthédrine.

mezz [mez] (noun) (mainly U.S.), P:
cigarette* de marijuana (drogues*),
stick m.

miaow! [miː'au, mjau] (excl.), F: oh
(que) t'es rosse!

mick, Mick [mik] (noun), P: 1. (a)
Irlandais m; (b) qn d'origine irlandaise.

2. to take the m. = to take the mick(e)y
(mick(e)y, 2).

mick(e)y, Mick(e)y ['miki] (noun). 1.
P: = mick, Mick, 1. 2. F: to take the
m. out of s.o., faire marcher qn, se
payer la tête de qn; stop taking the m.!
ne charrie pas! n'attige pas!; cf.
mick(e)y-taker. 3. P: pomme f de terre,
patate f. 4. F: M. (Finn), (a) boisson
droguée; (b) casse-pattes m. 5. P: to do
a m. = slope off (to). Voir aussi Mickey
Mouse².

Mickey Mouse¹ ['miki'maus] (adj.), P:
1. camelote, inférieur. 2. simple, facile,
pas dif. 3. routinier, train-train. 4.
louche, toc.

Mickey Mouse² ['miki'maus] (noun)
(R.S. = house), P: maison f.

mick(e)y-taker ['miki-teikər] (noun), F:
moqueur m, railleur m, lardeur m,
gouailleur m; cf. mick(e)y, 2.

middleman ['midlmæn] (noun), F: =
carrier.

middle-of-the-road ['midl-əvðəroud]
(adj.), F: modéré; the Party has a
m.-o.-t.-r. policy, le parti poursuit une
politique modérée ou centriste.

middling ['midliŋ] (adv.), F: fair to m.,
pas mal, couci-couça, entre les deux.

midi ['midi] (adj. & noun), F: (vêtement
m, etc.) de longueur moyenne, midi (m);
cf. maxi; mini.

miff¹ [mif] (noun), F: (a) mauvaise
humeur, cran m, rogne f; (b) pique f,
brouille f.

miff² [mif] (to), F: 1. (a) offenser, vexer;
(b) se draper dans sa dignité. 2. rater,
louper.

mighty ['maiti] (adv.), F: bigrement,
bougrement, fichtrement, vachement;
it's m. cold, il fait bougrement froid;
I'm m. glad to see you, je suis vachement
content de te voir. Voir aussi high¹, 3.

mike¹ [maik] (noun). 1. P: = mick, 1.
2. F: to take the m. = to take the
mick(e)y (mick(e)y, 2). 3. F: (=micro-
phone) micro(phone) m. 4. P: to take a
m. at sth., regarder* qch., lorgner qch.
5. P: to do a m. = slope off (to). 6. P: to
have a m. = mike² (to). 7. P: M.
Malone (R.S. = telephone), téléphone*.

mike² [maik] (to), P: paresser*, se
tourner les pouces, tirer sa cosse.

mile [mail] (noun), F: 1. you're a m. (or
miles) out, tu en es à mille lieues, tu n'y

* An asterisk indicates that the word so marked is included as a head-word in the Appendix.

es pas du tout; **you're miles too slow,** tu es mille fois trop lent. **2. I'd go a m.** (*or* **miles**) **for that,** je ferais des kilomètres pour cela. **3. a miss is as good as a m.,** but manqué, fût-ce de peu, n'est pas atteint. **4. to be miles away,** être ailleurs, rêvasser, décoller. **5. it sticks out a m.** = **it sticks out like a sore thumb (thumb,** 4).

milk [milk] (**to**). **1.** *F:* traire (qn, qch.). **2.** *V:* masturber*, allonger (qn).

milk-bottles [¹milkbɔtlz] (*pl. noun*), **milk-shop**[¹milkʃɔp] (*noun*), *P:* seins*, boîtes *f.pl.* à lolo.

milk-train [¹milk-trein] (*noun*), *F:* **to catch the m.-t.,** rentrer au petit matin.

milk-wag(g)on [¹milk-wægɔn] (*noun*), *P:* car* de police, panier *m* à salade.

milky [¹milki] (*adj.*), *F:* **to turn m.,** avoir peur*, avoir le trac (*ou* la trouille).

mill¹ [mil] (*noun*), *F:* **1.** bagarre*, empoignade *f*, rixe *f*. **2. to go through the m.,** en voir de toutes les couleurs, en baver; **to put s.o. through the m.,** faire passer qn par la filière. *Voir aussi* **run-of-the-mill.**

mill² [mil] (**to**), *F:* bourrer de coups*, tabasser.

milling [¹miliŋ] (*noun*), *F:* **to give s.o. a m.,** donner une raclée (*ou* une rossée) à qn.

million [¹miljən] (*numeral adj. & noun*), *F:* **1.** **thanks a m.!** merci mille fois! **2. to feel like a m. (dollars),** être au septième ciel, être aux anges.

miln [miln] (**to**), *P:* = **chubb in** (**to**); *cf.* **unchubb** (**to**); **unmiln** (**to**).

min [min] (*noun*), *P:* agent* de police, flic *m*.

mince (*noun*), *F:* **at a fast m.,** vite*, à toute barde.

mincemeat [¹mins-mi:t] (*noun*), *F:* **to make m. (out) of s.o.,** mettre qn en bouillie, mettre qn dans sa poche.

mince on [¹mins¹ɔn] (**to**), *P:* **to m. o.,** to go mincing on, radoter, rabâcher.

mince-pies [¹mins¹paiz] (*pl. noun*) (*R.S.* = *eyes*), *P:* yeux (*œil**), mirettes *f.pl.*

mincers [¹minsəz] (*pl. noun*), *P:* = **mince-pies.**

mind-bender [¹maindbendər] (*noun*), *P:* **1.** drogue *f* qui affine l'intelligence; euphorisant *m*. **2.** qn ou qch. qui élargit l'esprit et l'approfondit.

mind-blower [¹maindblouər] (*noun*), *P:* (*a*) expérience inaccoutumée; (*b*) choc

soudain, coup *m* de massue; (*c*) drogue *f* hallucinogène extatique, bonbon *m* à kick.

minge [mindʒ] (*noun*), *V:* vulve*, barbu *m*; **m. fringe,** (*d'une femme*) poils *m.pl.* du pubis, paquet *m* de tabac.

mingy [¹mindʒi] (*adj.*), *F:* = **measly, 1, 2.**

mini [¹mini] (*adj. & noun*), *F:* (vêtement, *etc.*) très court, mini (*m*); rase-pet *m*; *cf.* **maxi, midi.**

minstrel [¹minstrəl] (*noun*), *P:* **black and white** (*or* **nigger**) **m.,** amphétamine *f* (*drogues**), capsule *f* «Durophet», speed *m*.

mint [mint] (*noun*), *F:* **to cost a m.** (of money), coûter les yeux de la tête.

mintie, minty¹ [¹minti] (*adj.*), *P:* homosexuel, tata, chochotte.

mintie, minty² [¹minti] (*noun*), *P:* lesbienne* masculine et agressive.

mire [¹maiər] (*noun*), *F:* **to land** (*or* **drop**) **s.o. in the m.,** mettre qn dans la mouscaille (*ou* dans le pétrin).

mischief [¹mis-tʃif] (*noun*), *F:* enfant* espiègle, petit diable.

mish-mash [¹miʃmæʃ] (*noun*), *F:* méli-mélo *m*.

miss [mis] (*noun*), *F:* **to give sth. a m.,** laisser passer qch., laisser courir qch.; sécher (un cours). *Voir aussi* **mile, 3.**

missis [¹misiz] (*noun*), *F:* **the** (*or* **my**) **m.,** mon épouse*, la bourgeoise; **I'll have to ask the m.,** faut demander à mon gouvernement.

miss out on [¹mis¹autɔn] (**to**), *F:* manquer, louper, rater (qch.); **I missed out on my best chance,** j'ai raté ma meilleure occasion.

missus [¹misiz] (*noun*), *F:* = **missis.**

missy [¹misi] (*noun*), *F:* mademoiselle.

mistake [mis¹teik] (*noun*), *F:* **. . . and no m.!** ...et tu peux en être sûr!, ...je t'en réponds.

mitt [mit] (*noun*), *P:* **1.** main*, patte *f*; **keep your mitts off!** (à) bas les pattes! **2.** gant *m* de boxe, mitaine bourrée. **3.** (*pl.*) menottes*, pinces *f.pl.* **4. to put one's mitts on sth.,** voler* qch., faire main basse sur qch.

mitten [¹mitn] (*noun*), *F:* **to give s.o. the m.** = **to walk out on s.o. (walk out (to),** 2).

mitt-reader [¹mit-ri:dər] (*noun*), *P:* diseur *m* (diseuse *f*) de bonne aventure (*ou* de bonne ferte), chiromancien *m*, chiromancienne *f*.

---

* L'astérisque indique que le mot marqué de ce signe figure comme entrée dans le Répertoire.

mix [miks] (to), F: to m. it with s.o., se battre* avec qn, se bagarrer, se tabasser.

mixer ['miksər] (noun), F: he's a good m., il est sociable, il se lie facilement, il a de l'entregent; he's a bad m., c'est un ours, il est sauvage.

mix-up ['miksʌp] (noun), F: 1. confusion f, pagaille f. 2. (U.S.) bagarre*, mêlée f.

miz (z) [miz] (adj.), P: malheureux, tout chose, cafardeux.

mizzers ['mizəz] (pl. noun), P: to have the m., avoir le cafard (ou le bourdon), être dans le 36ème dessous.

mizzle ['mizl] (to), P: 1. s'enfuir*, se cavaler, mettre les bouts. 2. rouspéter, râler.

mizzler ['mizlər] (noun), P: geignard m, pleurnicheur m.

mo [mou] (noun) (=moment), F: half a m.! une seconde!; cf. jiff(y); sec; shake1, 1, 2; tick1, 3.

moan1 [moun] (noun), F: to have a (good) m. = moan2 (to).

moan2 [moun] (to), F: grogner*, ronchonner, rouscailler.

moaner ['mounər] (noun), F: ronchonneur m, rouscailleur m, râleur m.

moaning ['mouniŋ] (adj.), F: a m. Minnie, une geignarde, une rouspéteuse.

mob [mɔb] (noun), F: bande* de criminels, flèche f, gang m, soce f; voir aussi heavy1, 4; swell1, 3.

mobile ['moubail] (adj.), F: to get m., (a) travailler* plus vite, se décarcasser, se démancher; (b) se dépêcher*, se magner, se grouiller.

mobster ['mɔbstər] (noun) (U.S.), F: homme* du milieu, dur m, truand m.

mockers ['mɔkəz] (pl. noun), F: to put the m. on s.o., sth., jeter un sort sur qn, qch., enguignonner qn, qch.

mockie, mocky ['mɔki] (noun), P: (péj.) Juif m, Youpin m.

mod1 [mɔd] (adj.), F: moderne.

mod2 [mɔd] (noun), F: scootériste m, blouson noir; cf. rocker, 1.

mog [mɔg], moggie, moggy ['mɔgi] (noun), F: chat m, matou m, griffard m.

mojo ['moudʒou] (noun), P: stupéfiant(s) m (pl.) (en poudre), stups m.pl. (drogues*).

moke [mouk] (noun), F: âne m, bourricot m, martin m.

mola ['moulə] (noun) (U.S.), P: pédéraste*, pédé m.

moll [mɔl] (noun). 1. P: jeune femme*, gonzesse f, mousmé(e) f. 2. P: prostituée*, catin f. 3. F: la poule (ou la môme) d'un gangster.

molly-shop ['mɔli-ʃɔp] (noun), P: = meat-house.

Molotov cocktail ['mɔlɔtɔv'kɔkteil] (noun), F: bouteille remplie d'essence servant de bombe, cocktail m molotov.

mom [mɔm] (noun) (U.S.), F: mère*, mam(an).

moments ['moumənts] (pl. noun), F: I've had my m., j'ai eu mes bons moments; j'ai fait mes entourloupettes f.pl.

Monday ['mʌndi] (noun), F: that M. morning feeling = that Mondayish feeling.

Mondayish1 ['mʌndiiʃ] (adj.), F: that M. feeling, l'humeur f du lundi, l'après-week-end m.

Mondayish2 ['mʌndiiʃ] (adv.), F: to feel M., être dans les vapes du lundi, avoir le cafard du lundi.

money ['mʌni] (noun), F: 1. to be in the m., être riche*, rouler sur l'or, avoir le sac. 2. he's the man for my m., c'est juste l'homme qu'il me faut; il a tous mes suffrages. 3. to throw good m. after bad, (a) jouer à quitte ou double; (b) remplir le tonneau des Danaïdes, lancer l'argent* par les fenêtres. 4. I'm not made of m., je ne suis pas cousu d'or; je ne roule pas sur l'or.

moneybags ['mʌnibægz] (noun), F: individu très riche*, rupin m, richard m.

moniker ['mɔnikər] (noun), P: nom*, blaze m, centre m.

monkey ['mʌŋki] (noun). 1. F: to get one's m. up, se mettre en colère*, prendre la mouche; to get s.o.'s m. up, mettre qn en colère (ou en rogne). 2. P: billet* (ou faf(f)iot m) de cinq cents livres, un gros talbin. 3. P: I don't give a m.'s! je m'en fous et contrefous! 4. F: to make a m. (out) of s.o., se payer la tête de qn. 5. F: m. business, (a) affaire peu sérieuse (ou peu loyale), fricotage m; (b) conduite f malhonnête, procédé irrégulier; (c) coup fourré, goupinage m; (d) fumisterie f. 6. F: to stand there like a stuffed m., rester là comme une souche. 7. F: right m.! à bon entendeur,

---

salut! **8.** *P:* habitude *f* de la drogue, la guêpe, la guenon; **to get the m. off,** se désintoxiquer, chasser la guenon; **to have a m. on one's back,** (*a*) être drogué* (*ou* camé); (*b*) avoir une dent contre qn. **9.** *F:* **m. jacket,** veste courte, spencer *m.* **10.** *F:* **m. suit,** uniforme *m* de gala. *Voir aussi* **balls, 8; grease**[1], **2.**

monkey about (*or* **around**) [ˈmʌŋkiə-ˈbaut, ˈmʌŋkiəˈraund] (**to**), *F:* **to m. a. with s.o., sth.,** tripoter, tripatouiller qn, qch.

monniker [ˈmɔnikər] (*noun*), *P:* = **moniker.**

monthlies [ˈmʌnθliz] (*pl. noun*), *F:* **the m.,** menstrues*, histoires (mensuelles).

moo [muː] (*noun*), *P:* **1. she's a (right old) m.,** c'est une belle vache; **silly (old) m.!** espèce de vieille bique! **2.** = **moola(h).**

moocah [ˈmuːkɑː, ˈmuːkə] (*noun*), *P:* marijuana *f* (*drogues**), Marie-Jeanne *f.*

mooch [muːtʃ] (**to**), *P:* **1.** mendier*, mendigoter. **2.** voler*, chaparder. **3.** flâner, traîner ses lattes *f.pl.* (*ou* ses patins *m.pl.*), baguenauder. **4.** emprunter*, taper, sonner.

moocher [ˈmuːtʃər] (*noun*), *P:* **1.** mendiant*, mendigot *m.* **2.** voleur*, chapardeur *m.* **3.** baguenaudeur *m,* traîne-patins *m.* **4.** tapeur *m,* torpilleur *m.*

mooching [ˈmuːtʃiŋ] (*noun*), *P:* **1.** mendicité*, mendiche *f.* **2.** vol *m,* chaparderie *f.* **3.** baguenaudage *m.* **4.** tapage *m,* sonnage *m.*

moo-cow [ˈmuː-kau] (*noun*). **1.** *F:* (*langage enfantin*) vache *f,* meu-meu *f.* **2.** *P:* = **cow, 1.**

moody [ˈmuːdi] (*noun*), *P:* flatterie *f,* boniment *m;* **cut out the m.!** assez de baratin! suffit les boniments!

moola(h) [ˈmuːlɑː, ˈmuːlə] (*noun*), *P:* argent*, pognon *m,* fric *m.*

moon [muːn] (*noun*). **1.** *P:* **a m.,** un mois de prison, un marqué. **2.** *F:* **over the m.,** au septième ciel, aux nues. *Voir aussi* **blue**[1], **3; shoot**[2] (**to**), **9.**

moon about (*or* **around**) [ˈmuːnəˈbaut, ˈmuːnəˈraund] (**to**), *F:* lambiner, musarder, cueillir les pâquerettes.

moonlight [ˈmuːnlait] (**to**), *F:* faire le travail noir, cumuler.

moonlighter [ˈmuːnlaitər] (*noun*), *F:* cumulard *m;* **he's a m.,** il cumule.

moonshine [ˈmuːnʃain] (*noun*), *F:* **1.** alcool* illicitement distillé (*ou* en

contrebande), gnôle *f* sous les fagots. **2.** bêtises*, fariboles *f.pl.,* balivernes *f.pl.*

moony [ˈmuːni] (*adj.*), *P:* un peu fou*, toqué.

moosh [muʃ] (*noun*), *P:* = **mush**[2], **1, 2.**

mooters [ˈmuːtəz] (*pl. noun*), *P:* = **muggles, 3.**

mop [mɔp] (*noun*), *F:* **1. that's the way the m. flops,** c'est comme ça que tombent les dés (*ou* les bobs); c'est ainsi que la roue tourne; c'est comme ça et pas autrement; *cf.* **cookie, 1; onion, 1. 2.** tignasse *f,* tête *f* de loup; **m. top,** chichis *m.pl.,* moumoute *f.*

moppy [ˈmɔpi] (*adj.*), *P:* ivre*, paf, dans le cirage.

mop up [ˈmɔpˈʌp] (**to**). **1.** *F:* exterminer, nettoyer, liquider. **2.** *P:* aplatir, rouler (qn).

more-ish [ˈmɔːriʃ] (*adj.*), *F:* **these sweets are m.,** ces bonbons ont un goût de revenez-y.

morguey [ˈmɔːgi] (*adj.*), *P:* *voir* **manor.**

mosey along [ˈmouziəˈlɔŋ] (**to**), *F:* aller son petit bonhomme de chemin, aller mollo.

mosey off [ˈmouziˈɔf] (**to**), *F:* s'enfuir*, décamper, les mettre, se barrer.

moss [mɔs] (*noun*), *P:* cheveux*, crins *m.pl.,* cresson *m.*

mostest [ˈmoustist] (*noun*), *P:* **the m.,** le super, l'archi(bien).

mota [ˈmoutɑː, ˈmoutə] (*noun*), *P:* marijuana *f* (*drogues**) de haute qualité.

mote [mout] (**to**) (*Austr.*), *F:* filer à toute allure, brûler le pavé.

mother [ˈmʌðər] (*noun*). **1.** *F:* **to be m.,** servir le thé. **2.** *P:* **m.'s ruin** (*R.S.* = *gin*), genièvre *m,* gin *m.*

motherfucker [ˈmʌðəfʌkər] (*noun*) (*U.S.*), *VV:* **1.** (belle) saloperie, (espèce de) con *m,* empaffé *m,* (tas de) fumier *m.* **2.** (*terme vulgaire et familier employé entre hommes*) cucul *m* (la praline), connard *m* (à la crème).

motherfucking [ˈmʌðəfʌkiŋ] (*adj.*) (*U.S.*), *VV:* **1.** charognard, pourri, saligaud, chiasseux. **2.** emmerdant, canulant.

mother-in-law [ˈmʌðərinlɔː] (*noun*), *F:* mélange *m* de *stout* (bière brune forte) et de *bitter* (bière amère); panaché *m* nègre.

motor-bike (*attrib. adj.*), *F:* **m.-b. boys** = **rockers** (**rocker, 1**).

---

moula [ˈmuːlɑː, ˈmuːlə] (*noun*), *P:* = **moola(h)**.

mouldy [ˈmouldi] (*adj.*), *F:* moche(ton), toc(ard), tarte, tartignol(l)e.

mount[1] [maunt] (*noun*), *P:* **to do a m.**, coïter*, grimper, bourrer une femme; *cf.* **mounties.**

mount[2] [maunt] (**to**), *P:* = **to do a mount.**

mountain [ˈmauntin] (*noun*), *F:* **1. to make a m. out of a molehill**, faire d'un œuf un bœuf, se noyer dans un verre d'eau. **2. a m. of a man**, un homme* fort (*ou* bien baraqué), une armoire à glace. **3. a m. of work**, un tas de travail*; un boulot du diable.

mounties [ˈmauntiz] (*pl. noun*), *P:* **to join the m.**, coïter*, pousser sa pointe; *cf.* **mount**[1,2].

mourning [ˈmɔːniŋ] (*noun*), *F:* **to have one's (finger-)nails in m.**, avoir les ongles sales (*ou* en deuil).

mouse [maus] (*noun*) (*pl.* **mice**), *F:* **1. are you a man or a m.?** *c.p.*, t'es un homme ou une bûche? t'en as ou t'en as pas? **2.** fille* *ou* jeune femme* piquante, gisquette *f*, gosseline *f*. *Voir aussi* **cat, 10; Mickey Mouse**[1,2]; **rat**[1], **11.**

mouth [mauθ] (*noun*), *F:* **1. to have a big m.**, être une grande gueule; *cf.* **big**[1], **8; blow off (to), 2; loudmouth; shoot off (to), 2. 2. to be down in the m.**, avoir le cafard, être abattu (*ou* défrisé), être au 36ème dessous. *Voir aussi* **foul-mouth; horse**[1], **2.**

mouthful [ˈmauθful] (*noun*), *F:* **you've said a m.!** tu as parlé d'or! tu l'as dit bouffi!

mouth on [ˈmauðˈɔn] (**to**), *F:* discutailler, pinailler, titiller.

mouthpiece [ˈmauθpiːs] (*noun*), **1.** *F:* porte-parole *m.* **2.** *P:* avocat*, débarbot *m*, débarbotteur *m.*

move[1] [muːv] (*noun*), *F:* **1. to get a m. on**, se dépêcher*, se magner. **2. to be up to every m.**, la connaître dans les coins.

move[2] [muːv] (**to**), *P:* voler*, lever, piquer.

movie [ˈmuːvi] (*noun*) (*mainly U.S.*), *F:* film *m*; **the movies**, le cinéma; **to go to the movies**, aller au cinoche.

much [mʌtʃ] (*adv.*), *F:* **1. that's a bit m.!** (*a*) c'est un peu beaucoup*; (*b*) c'est le comble! c'est le bouquet! **2. m. of a muchness**, kif-kif, bonnet blanc et blanc bonnet, jus vert et verjus, du pareil au même.

muchly [ˈmʌtʃli] (*adv.*) (*emploi humoristique de* **much**), *F:* beaucoup*, bézef.

muck [mʌk] (*noun*), *P:* **1. to make a m. of sth.**, abîmer*, gâcher, bousiller qch.; *voir aussi* **right, 1. 2. it's a load of m.**, (*a*) c'est un tas de conneries; (*b*) c'est de la saleté* (*ou* de la cochonnerie). **3. to land (or drop) s.o. in the m.** = **to land s.o. in the mire** (*voir* **mire**). **4. common as m.** = **common as mud** (**mud 6** (*b*)). **5. dog m.**, crotte *f* de chien. **6.** confusion *f*, pagaille *f.* **7. Lord M.**, Monsieur J'en-fous-plein-la-vue. *Voir aussi* **high-muck-a-muck.**

muck about (*or* **around**) [ˈmʌkəˈbaut, ˈmʌkəˈraund] (**to**). **1.** *F:* traîner, lambiner, bricoler. **2.** *F:* flâner, flânocher, traîner ses lattes. **3.** *F:* **to m. s.o. a.**, faire tourner qn en bourrique. **4.** *P:* **to m. a. with s.o.** = **to mess about with s.o.** (**mess about (to), 4** (*a*)).

mucker [ˈmʌkər] (*noun*), *P:* **1.** qn qui est sale* (*ou* crasseux). **2.** ami*, copain *m*, pote *m*, aminche *m.* **3.** (*U.S.*) rustre *m*, grossier personnage. **4.** chute *f*, culbute *f*, bûche *f*; **to come a m.**, tomber*, ramasser un billet de parterre.

muck in [ˈmʌkin] (**to**), *F:* **1. to m. i. with s.o.**, chambrer avec qn, faire gourbi ensemble. **2. to m. i. together**, (*a*) partager, fader, décarpiller; (*b*) s'actionner (*ou* s'escrimer *ou* se dépatouiller) ensemble.

muck-raker [ˈmʌk-reikər] (*noun*), *F:* (*journalisme*) fouille-merde *m.*

muck up [ˈmʌkʌp] (**to**), *F:* **1.** emberlificoter. **2.** abîmer*, gâcher, bousiller, cochonner.

mucky [ˈmʌki] (*adj.*), *F:* **1. a m. eater**, qn qui mange comme un cochon. **2. a m. pup**, un enfant qui fait des saletés *ou* qui se tient mal; un petit goret.

mud [mʌd] (*noun*). **1.** *F:* **here's m. in your eye!** à votre santé! à la bonne vôtre! **2.** *P:* (*drogues**) (*a*) opium brut; (*b*) opium, dross *m*, boue *f*; *voir aussi* **green**[1], **1. 3.** (*U.S.*) *P:* café* (*boisson*), jus *m* (de chaussette). **4.** (*U.S.*) *P:* pudding *m* au chocolat. **5.** (*U.S.*) *P:* signes télégraphiques brouillés, brouillage *m.* **6.** *F:* **common as m.**, (*a*) du tout-venant, chemin battu; (*b*) qui traîne partout (*ou* dans les ornières),

---

* An asterisk indicates that the word so marked is included as a head-word in the Appendix.

qui sent le pavé. **7.** *F:* cancan *m*, déblatérage *m*, débinage *m*; **to throw** (*or* **sling**) **m. at s.o.**, éclabousser qn, traîner qn dans la boue (*ou* dans la fange). **8.** *F:* **his name is m.**, sa réputation est moins que rien. *Voir aussi* **clear**[1]; **stick-in-the-mud**[1,2].

muddler[ˈmʌdlər] (*noun*), *F:* brouillon *m*, pagailleur *m*.

mudslinger [ˈmʌd-slinər] (*noun*), *F:* calomniateur *m*, médisant *m*, débineur *m*, casseur *m* de sucre.

mudslinging [ˈmʌd-sliniŋ] (*noun*), *F:* attaque calomnieuse, médisance *f*, bêche *f*.

muff[1] [mʌf] (*noun*). **1.** *F:* échec*, loupage *m*, coup raté. **2.** *V:* vulve*, barbu *m*, chatte *f*, chagatte *f*.

muff[2] [mʌf] (**to**). **1.** *F:* faire une erreur, commettre une faute, louper. **2.** *F:* bousiller, bâcler, rater, gâcher. **3.** *V:* exécuter un cunnilingus, faire minette; *cf.* **pearl-dive** (**to**).

muff-diver [ˈmʌfdaivər] (*noun*), *V:* cunnilinguiste *mf*, buveur *m* de bénitier, lécheur *m* de minette; *cf.* **pearl-diver**.

mug[1] [mʌg] (*noun*). **1.** *P:* visage*, fiole *f*; **ugly m.**, gueule *f* d'empeigne; **m. and dabs**, photo et empreintes digitales; **to have one's m. and dabs taken**, passer au pied et au sommier. **2.** *F:* dupe *f*, cavé *m*, bonnard *m*; **mugs wanted**, on cherche des poires *f.pl.*; **to be a m.**, être poire; **to be the m.**, être le dindon de la farce; **mugs' tax**, impôt *m* sur le revenu, l'impôt des poires. *Voir aussi* **fly-mug**; **thunder-mug**.

mug[2] [mʌg] (**to**), *F:* attaquer* (les passants) à main armée, tabasser, voler*.

mugger [ˈmʌgər] (*noun*), *F:* **1.** voleur* à main armée, cogneur *m*. **2.** (*U.S.*) acteur *m* qui grimace pour faire rire; farineux *m*.

mugging [ˈmʌgiŋ] (*noun*), *F:* attaque *f* (de passants) à main armée.

muggins [ˈmʌginz] (*noun*), *P:* individu bête*, gourde *f*, cruche *f*.

muggles [ˈmʌglz] (*noun*), *P:* **1.** (*drogues**) (*a*) marijuana *f*; (*b*) cigarette* de marijuana, kif *m*. **2.** habitué(e) de la marijuana. **3.** hachisch *m* (*drogues**), merde *f*.

mug up [ˈmʌgˈʌp] (**to**), *F:* bûcher, piocher, potasser.

mularky [məˈlɑːki] (*noun*), *F:* = **malark(e)y.**

mulberry-bush [ˈmʌlbəribuʃ] (*noun*), *F:* **to go (all) round the m.-b.**, tourner en rond, tourner autour du pot.

muldoon [mʌlˈduːn] (*noun*), *P:* goinfre*, bâfreur *m*, gueulard *m*.

mule [mjuːl] (*noun*), *P:* passeur *m* (de drogues), mule *f* (à came).

mullarky [məˈlɑːki] (*noun*), *F:* = **malark(e)y.**

mulligans [ˈmʌligənz] (*pl. noun*)(*Austr.*), *P:* cartes* à jouer, brèmes *f.pl.*, cartons *m.pl.*

mull over [ˈmʌlˈouvər] (**to**), *F:* ruminer, ressasser, gamberger.

mum [mʌm] (*adj.*), *F:* **to keep m.**, se taire*, ne pas moufter; **m.'s the word!** motus et bouche cousue!

murder[1] [ˈməːdər] (*noun*), *F:* **1.** **it's (sheer) m. in the rush-hour**, c'est (absolument) épouvantable (*ou* monstrueux) aux heures de pointe. **2.** **to get away with m.**, s'en tirer à bon compte, tirer les marrons du feu. *Voir aussi* **blue**[1,2].

murder[2] [ˈməːdər] (**to**). **1.** *P:* battre* (qn) comme plâtre, tabasser (qn). **2.** *F:* massacrer, écorcher, estropier (un morceau de musique, *etc.*).

Murphy [ˈməːfi] (*noun*), *P:* = **spud (Murphy).**

muscle-head [ˈmʌslhed] (*noun*), *F:* individu bête*, bûche *f*, truffe *f*.

muscle in [ˈmʌslˈin] (**to**), *F:* **1.** se pousser, jouer des coudes. **2.** **he muscled his way in**, il s'introduisit de force, il força la porte. **3.** **to m. i. on a conversation**, s'injecter dans une conversation.

muscle-man [ˈmʌslmæn] (*noun*), *F:* homme fort*, malabar *m*, costaud *m*, homme à pogne.

mush[1] [mʌʃ] (*noun*), *F:* **1.** propos *m.pl.* bêtes*, niaiseries *f.pl.* **2.** flatterie *f*. **3.** cafouillage *m*. **4.** amourette *f*.

mush[2] [muʃ] (*noun*), *P:* **1.** (*a*) visage*, frime *f*; (*b*) bouche*, goule *f*. **2.** (*a*) individu*, type *m*, mec *m*; (*b*) corniaud *m*, cornichon *m*, con *m*.

mushy [ˈmʌʃi] (*adj.*), *F:* à l'eau de rose, à la guimauve.

music [ˈmjuːzik] (*noun*), *F:* **to face the m.**, (*a*) tenir le coup, payer d'audace; (*b*) braver l'orage, payer les pots cassés,

---

* L'astérisque indique que le mot marqué de ce signe figure comme entrée dans le Répertoire.

avaler la pilule. *Voir aussi* **chin-music.**

mutt [mʌt] (*noun*), *P:* **1. poor m.!** le pauvre (*ou* pauv') mec! **2.** chien* (bâtard), clebs *m*, cabot *m*.

mutton [ˈmʌtn] (*noun*), *F:* **m. dressed up as lamb,** vieux tableau, vieille poupée.

mutton-fancier [ˈmʌtnfænsiər] (*noun*), *P:* pédéraste*, enviandé *m*.

muttonhead [ˈmʌtnhed] (*noun*), *F:* individu bête*, andouille *f*, saucisse *f*.

muzzle [ˈmʌzl] (*noun*), *P:* **1.** chance*, veine *f*, pot *m*. **2.** visage*, museau *m*, frimousse *f*.

muzzy [ˈmʌzi] (*adj.*), *F:* légèrement ivre*, paf, éméché.

mystery [ˈmist(ə)ri] (*noun*), *P:* femme* inconnue dans le pays; **a m. in the manor,** une nouvelle venue dans le coin. *Voir aussi* **bag¹, 9.**

---

* An asterisk indicates that the word so marked is included as a head-word in the Appendix.

N

nab¹ [næb] (*noun*), *P:* agent* de police, flic *m*.

nab² [næb] (to), *P:* 1. (*a*) arrêter*, pincer, agrafer, cueillir (qn); the police nabbed the lot, la police les a tous ratissés (*ou* cueillis *ou* embarqués); to get nabbed, se faire pincer (*ou* piger), se faire faire; (*b*) prendre (qn) sur le fait (*ou* la main dans le sac); *cf.* nip³ (to), 4. 2. (*a*) voler*, chiper, chaparder (qch.); (*b*) saisir, escamoter (qch.).

nadgers [ˈnædʒəz] (*pl. noun*), *P:* to put the n. on s.o., donner la malchance* à qn, foutre la poisse à qn.

nadget [ˈnædʒit] (*noun*) (*Austr.*), *P:* tête*, caboche *f*, gadin *m*.

nag [næg] (*noun*), *F:* cheval*, bidet *m*, canasson *m*; to follow the nags = to follow the gee-gees.

nagsbody [ˈnægzbɔdi] (*noun*), *P:* rouspéteur *m*, rouscailleur *m*.

nail¹ [neil] (*noun*), *F:* 1. to pay (cash) on the n., payer cash (*ou* recta *ou* rubis sur l'ongle). 2. to hit the n. on the head, mettre le doigt dessus. *Voir aussi* coffin, 2; doornail; tooth, 6.

nail² [neil] (to), *P:* 1. filer un coup* à (qn), frapper. 2. (*a*) intercepter (qn); (*b*) arrêter*, coincer (qn). 3. demander un prix exorbitant à (qn), fusiller (qn), extorquer de l'argent* à (qn). 4. coïter* avec (qn), aiguiller (qn). *Voir aussi* hammer (to), 3.

nailer [ˈneilər] (*noun*), *F:* as *m*, épée *f*, crack *m*.

name [neim] (*noun*), *F:* to call s.o. names, injurier* qn. *Voir aussi* pack-drill; what's-(h)er-name; what's-(h)is-name.

name-dropper [ˈneimdrɔpər] (*noun*), *F:* qn qui a la langue trop longue, boîte *f* à cancans.

nana [ˈnɑːnə] (*noun*), *P:* he's a right n.! c'est un vrai gugusse!; to feel a right n., se sentir tout bête* (*ou* ballot *ou* gourdiflot); you silly great n.! espèce de grande gourde!

nance [næns], nancy(-boy) [ˈnænsi(bɔi)] (*noun*), *P:* 1. pédéraste* (qui tient le rôle de la femme), persilleuse *f*, joconde *f*, chouquette *f*. 2. homme* efféminé, femmelette *f*, mauviette *f*.

nanna [ˈnænə] (*noun*), *F:* grand-mère, mémé *f*.

nap¹ [næp] (*noun*), *F:* to go n. on sth., être sûr et certain de qch., en mettre sa main au feu, foutre son billet.

nap² [næp] (to), *F:* to be caught napping, (*a*) être pris au dépourvu; (*b*) être pris en faute.

napoo¹ [næˈpuː] (*adj.*), *P:* fini, fichu, foutu, rétamé.

napoo² [næˈpuː] (*noun*), *P:* (*a*) la fin, le bout du rouleau; to n., jusqu'à la gauche, jusqu'à plus soif; (*b*) la mort, la canne, la crève.

napper [ˈnæpər] (*noun*), *P:* tête*, caboche *f*.

nappy [ˈnæpi] (*noun*) (=(*baby's*) napkin), *F:* couche *f*.

narc(o) [ˈnɑːk(ou)] (*noun*), *P:* agent *m* de la Brigadeféd érale des Stupéfiants.

nark¹ [nɑːk] (*noun*), *P:* 1. qn qui sert de piège, coqueur *m*. 2. indicateur* de police, mouton *m*, bordille *m*, mouchard *m*. 3. = narc(o).

nark² [nɑːk] (to), *P:* 1. mettre en colère, braquer, mettre en rogne, prendre à rebrousse-poil. 2. to get narked, (*a*) être en colère*, fulminer; (*b*) se faire arrêter* (*ou* agrafer *ou* pincer). 3. moucharder, bourriquer, en croquer, en manger. 4. n. it! écrase! la ferme! fous-moi la paix!

narky [ˈnɑːki] (*adj.*), *P:* 1. en colère*, en rogne, de mauvais poil. 2. = sarky.

natch! [nætʃ] (*excl.*), *P:* naturellement! naturliche!

natter¹ [ˈnætər] (*noun*), *F:* baratinage *m*, jactage *m*, tapette *f*; to have a n. = natter² (to), 1.

natter² [ˈnætər] (to), *F:* 1. bavarder*, baver, jacter. 2. gronder, criailler.

---

* L'astérisque indique que le mot marqué de ce signe figure comme entrée dans le Répertoire.

natural ['nætʃrəl] (noun), F: 1. never
(or not) in all my n., jamais de la vie.
2. a n., qui est né pour ça, tout trouvé
pour..., qui va comme un gant.

naughty ['nɔːti] (to) (Austr.), P: coïter*
avec (qn), godiller avec (qn).

n.b.g., N.B.G. ['en'biː'dʒiː] (abbr. =
no bloody good), P: bon à rien*, bon à nib.

nearly ['niəli] (adv.), F: n. there: voir
bingo (89).

necessary ['nesəsəri] (noun), F: the n.,
argent*, galette f, beurre m, blé m,
carbure m; to do the n., payer* la note,
casquer.

neck¹ [nek] (noun), F: 1. to get it in the
n., écoper, en avoir pour son compte
(ou son grade), trinquer. 2. you've
got a n.! quel toupet! quel culot!
3. to stick one's n. out, prendre des
risques, se mouiller. 4. it's n. or nothing,
il faut risquer (ou jouer) le tout pour
le tout. 5. to be up to one's n. in work,
être débordé de travail*, en avoir
jusque-là. 6. to be in sth. up to one's n.,
être submergé, y être jusqu'au cou.
7. to have a n. (with s.o.) = neck² (to),
1. 8. to be thrown out on one's n. (or
n. and crop), être flanqué dehors avec
perte(s) et fracas. 9. to break (or be
breaking) one's n. (to spend a penny),
mourir d'envie d'aller au petit coin.
Voir aussi deadneck; leatherneck; pain;
roughneck; rubberneck¹; stiffneck;
wood, 3.

neck² [nek] (to), F: 1. s'embrasser, se
bécoter, se peloter; rouler une pelle.
2. boire*, pinter, picoler. Voir aussi
rubberneck² (to).

necking ['nekiŋ] (noun), F: = petting.

necktie ['nektai] (noun) (U.S.), F: corde
f du gibet, cravate f; to throw a n.
party, lyncher, pendre*, béquiller.

needful ['niːdful] (noun), F: the n. =
the necessary.

needle¹ ['niːdl] (noun), P: 1. (a) to give
s.o. the n. = to needle s.o. (needle²
(to), 1–5); (b) to have the (dead) n.
for s.o., avoir une (sacrée) dent contre
qn; (c) to get (or cop) the n., se mettre
en colère*, piquer une crise. 2. to be
on the n., (a) être de la piquouse, tenir
à la poussette; (b) être drogué* (ou
camé ou toxico). 3. n. and pin (R.S. =
gin), gin m. Voir aussi pins, 2; piss² (to),
2.

needle² ['niːdl] (to). 1. F: agacer, asticoter, enquiquiner (qn); to be needled,
être de mauvais poil. 2. F: aiguillonner,
inciter, tanner. 3. F: harceler, bassiner.
4. F: taquiner, canuler, chiner. 5. P:
inoculer, vacciner. 6. P: extirper des
renseignements* de (qn), pomper (qn).

needle-candy ['niːdl-kændi] (noun), P:
(a) stupéfiant pris par injection, liqueur
f de shooteuse; (b) héroïne f (drogues*),
cheval m, jus m.

nellie, Nellie, nelly, Nelly ['neli]
(noun). 1. P: pédéraste*, persilleuse f.
2. F: not on your n.! jamais de la vie!
rien à faire! tu peux courir!

Nelson ['nelsən] (pr. noun), F: N.'s
blood, rhum m. Voir aussi tear¹, 2.

nerve [nəːv] (noun), F: 1. to get on
s.o.'s nerves, courir (ou taper) sur les
nerfs m.pl. (ou le système) à qn.
2. you've got a n.! quel culot! quel
toupet!; what a n. you've got! t'as un
rude toupet!; I like your n.! t'es
culotté! 3. to have the n. to do sth.,
avoir de l'audace (ou du ventre ou du
poil au cul) pour faire qch. Voir aussi
bundle, 6.

nest-egg ['nesteg] (noun), F: économies
f.pl., argent* mis de côté; to have a
nice little n.-e. (tucked away), avoir un
bas de laine bien garni.

never ['nevər] (adv.), F: 1. well I n.! pas
possible! ça par exemple! je n'en reviens
pas! 2. n. been kissed: voir bingo (16).
3. n. fear (R.S. = beer), bière f.

never-never ['nevər'nevər] (noun), F:
to buy sth. on the n.-n., acheter qch. à
crédit (ou à croume).

Newfie ['njuːfi] (pr. noun) (U.S.), F:
Terre-neuvien m.

news-hawk ['njuːzhɔːk], news-hound
['njuːzhaund] (noun), F: journaliste
mf, reporter m, chasseur m de copie.

newt [njuːt] (noun), F: tight as a n.,
ivre* mort.

newy ['njuːi] (noun) (Austr.), F: 1.
novice m, bleu m. 2. qch. de nouveau,
nouveauté f.

next [nekst] (adv.), P: 1. to get n. to s.o.,
se mettre bien avec qn, se mettre dans
les petits papiers de qn. 2. n. off, puis,
après, alors.

nibble ['nibl] (noun), P: to have a n.,
coïter*, faire un carton.

nibs, Nibs [nibz] (noun), F: his n.,

---

* An asterisk indicates that the word so marked is included as a head-word in the Appendix.

(a) gros bonnet, grosse légume, milord;
(b) individu élégant*, type bien sapé
(ou bien frusqué); (c) cézig(ue) m.
nice and... [ˈnaisənd] (adv.), F: fort
bien...; **n. a. handy,** bien commode;
n. a. comfy, bien à l'aise, tout bien.
nick¹ [nik] (noun). **1.** P: (a) prison*,
bloc m, taule f; (b) commissariat m de
police, le quart. **2.** P: **in good n.,** (a) en
bon état; (b) en forme, d'attaque. **3.** F:
Old N., le diable, le Malin, le barbet.
nick² [nik] (to), P: **1.** voler*, faucher,
chiper. **2.** arrêter*, agrafer, cravater,
épingler; **to get nicked,** se faire pincer
(ou pingler). **3.** faire payer*, extorquer,
étriller.
nickel [ˈnikl] (noun) (U.S.), F: pièce f de
5 cents.
nicker [ˈnikər] (noun), P: **1.** billet* d'une
livre sterling **2.** mégot*, clope m.
niff¹ [nif] (noun), P: **1.** (a) puanteur f,
(s)chlingage m; (b) odeur f, effluve m;
to catch a n. of perfume, prendre une
bouffée de parfum. **2.** reniflette f;
take a n. at that, renifle-moi ça.
niff² [nif] (to), P: puer, (s)chlinguer,
cocoter.
niffy [ˈnifi] (adj.), P: = **nifty, 3.**
nifty [ˈnifti] (adj.). **1.** F: beau*, pimpant,
bath, choucard. **2.** P: malin*, débrouillard. **3.** P: qui sent* mauvais, puant.
nig [nig] (abbr.), P: (péj.) = **nigger, 1.**
nigger [ˈnigər] (noun), P: (péj.) **1.**
nègre*, bougnoul(e) m, bamboula m.
2. there's a n. in the woodpile, il y a
anguille sous roche; **that's the n. in
the woodpile,** voilà le fin mot de
l'histoire. **3. to work like a n.,** travailler*
comme un nègre (ou comme une brute
ou comme quatre), trimer comme un
forçat. Voir aussi **minstrel.**
nigger-driver [ˈnigə-draivər] (noun), P:
négrier m, garde-chiourme m.
nigger-lover [ˈnigə-lʌvər] (noun) (U.S.),
P: (péj.) anti-ségrégationiste mf, protecteur m du noir.
niggly [ˈnigli] (adj.), F: de mauvaise
humeur, ronchonnard.
night-bird [ˈnaitbəːd] (noun), F: =
fly-by-night, 3.
nightie [ˈnaiti] (noun), F: = **nighty.**
nightspot [ˈnaitspɔt] (noun), F: night-
club m, boîte f (de nuit).
nighty [ˈnaiti] (noun) (=night-dress), F:
chemise f (ou liquette f) de nuit.

nighty-night! [ˈnaitiˈnait] (excl.), F:
bonne nuit!
nignog [ˈnignɔg] (noun), P: **1.** individu
bête*, niguedouille mf. **2.** (péj.) nègre*,
bougnoul(e) m.
nineteen [ˈnaintiːn] (numeral adj. &
noun), F: **to talk n. to the dozen,**
(a) parler* vite, faire couler le crachoir;
(b) bavarder* (ou bavasser ou jaser)
comme une pie borgne.
nineteenth [ˈnaintiːnθ] (numeral adj.),
F: **the n. hole,** le bar d'un club de golf.
ninnies [ˈniniz] (pl. noun), P: seins*,
nénés m.pl., tétons m.pl.
nip¹ [nip] (noun), F: **1. there's a n. in
the air,** ça pince; le fond de l'air est
froid. **2. a n. of gin,** une rincette de gin.
3. to make a n. for it, se trotter,
décaniller, prendre la poudre d'escampette. **4.** =**nipper, 1.**
Nip² [nip] (noun), P: Jap(onais) m.
nip³ [nip] (to), **1.** F: **to n. round** (or
along or **over) to s.o.'s house,** faire un
saut chez qn. **2.** P: **to n. s.o. for money,**
emprunter* de l'argent à qn, taper qn.
3. P: voler*, barboter, faucher. **4.** P:
prendre (qn) la main dans le sac,
prendre (qn) en flag, faire marron sur
le tas.
nip along [ˈnipəˈlɔŋ] (to), F: se dépêcher*, se décarcasser; voir aussi **nip³**
(to), **1.**
nip in [ˈnipˈin] (to), F: **1.** entrer (leste-
ment). **2. to n. i. (smartly),** tirer avantage d'une situation.
nip off [ˈnipˈɔf] (to), F: partir*, jouer
des flûtes, prendre le large.
nipper [ˈnipər] (noun). **1.** F: (a) gamin m,
gavroche m, loupiot m; (b) **I've got
two nippers,** j'ai deux enfants*. **2.** (pl.)
P: menottes*, bracelets m.pl.
nippy¹ [ˈnipi] (adj.), F: **1.** froid, frisquet,
frisco. **2.** rapide, alerte, vif; **to be n.,**
se dépêcher*, se grouiller.
nippy² [ˈnipi] (noun), P: serveuse f,
loufiate f.
nishte [ˈniʃtə] (noun), P: rien*, nib.
nit [nit] (noun), F: **1.** individu bête*,
crétin m; **a steaming n.,** un couillon
fini, un duschnock achevé, un triple
crétin. **2.** (Austr.) **to keep n.,** monter
la garde, faire le pet; cf. **cockatoo(er);**
voir aussi **nit-nit!**
nitery [ˈnaitəri] (noun) (U.S.), F: =
nightspot.

---

* L'astérisque indique que le mot marqué de ce signe figure comme entrée dans le Répertoire.

nit-nit! [ˈnitˈnit] (excl.), P: tais-toi!
(se taire*), boucle-la! gare! vingt-deux!
acré!

nitty [ˈniti] (adj.), F: bête*, baluchard.

nitty-gritty [ˈnitiˈgriti] (noun), F: the
n.-g., le (fin) fond, le tréfonds (d'une
affaire), le substratum.

nix¹ [niks] (excl.), P: pas mèche! rien
à faire!

nix² [niks] (noun), P: rien*, nib, nix.

no¹ [nou] (adj.), F: long time n. see!
une éternité qu'on s'est vu! Voir
aussi fear; go², 1.

no² [nou] (adv.), F: n. can do, compte
pas sur bibi.

nob¹ [nɔb] (noun). 1. P: tête*, coco m,
caboche f, nénette f; so much a n.,
tant par tête de pipe; cf. copper-nob.
2. P: aristo(crate) m, gommeux m; the
nobs, les rupins m.pl. 3. V: = knob, 1.

nob² [nɔb] (to), P: assommer, étourdir
(qn).

nobble [ˈnɔbl] (to). 1. F: doper, écloper
(un cheval); acheter (un jockey, etc.).
2. P: affurer, faucher, rafler. 3. P:
duper*, entôler. 4. P: enlever,
kidnapper.

nobby [ˈnɔbi] (adj.), P: élégant*, chic,
flambard.

nobody [ˈnoubɔdi] (noun), F: a n.,
une nullité, un zéro, un rien-du-tout.

nod [nɔd] (noun), P: 1. on the n., (a)
ahuri par la drogue, envapé; (b) (U.S.)
à crédit, à crôme, à la gagne. 2. to get
the n., être choisi (ou élu). 3. to give
the n., donner le feu vert.

noddle [ˈnɔdl] (noun), F: tête*, ciboulot
m, caboche f; use your n.! = use your
loaf!

nod off [ˈnɔdˈɔf] (to), F: s'endormir,
piquer un roupillon.

nog [nɔg] (noun), F: = noggin, 2.

noggin [ˈnɔgin] (noun), F: 1. = noddle.
2. verre m de bière, pot m, demi m.

no-good [ˈnouˈgud] (adj.), F: bon à
rien.

no-gooder [ˈnouˈgudər], nogoodnik
[ˈnouˈgudnik] (noun), F: vaurien*,
bon-à-rien m, loquedu m.

nohow [ˈnouhau] (adv.), P: en aucune
façon.

noise [nɔiz] (noun), F: to make the right
noises, savoir se tirer d'affaire. Voir
aussi big¹, 1.

non-com [ˈnɔnˈkɔm] (abbr. = non-com-

missioned officer) (mil.), F: sous-off m,
sous-officier m.

non-starter [ˈnɔnˈstɑːtər] (noun), F:
(a) non-partant m; (b) projet, etc.,
fichu d'avance.

noodle [ˈnuːdl] (noun), F: 1. individu
bête*, nouille f, andouille f. 2. (U.S.)
tête*, tronche f; voir aussi flip³ (to), 2.

nookie, nooky [ˈnuki] (noun), P: coït*,
crampe f, crampette f.

nope [noup] (adv.) (=no), P: non*.

norgies [ˈnɔːgiz], norgs [nɔːgz], norkers
[ˈnɔːkəz], norks [nɔːks] (pl. noun)
(Austr.), P: seins*, rotoplots m.pl.

north and south [ˈnɔːθən(d)ˈsauθ,
ˈnɔːfənˈsauf] (R.S. = mouth), P:
bouche*, goule f.

nose [nouz] (noun). 1. F: to poke one's
n. in (where it's not wanted), fourrer
son nez*, mettre son grain de sel.
2. F: to pay through the n. for sth.,
payer* les yeux de la tête pour qch.,
acheter qch. au poids de l'or. 3. P:
to keep one's n. clean, se tenir à carreau, ne pas se mouiller. 4. P: indicateur* de police, mouton m. 5. F:
to put s.o.'s n. out of joint, faire une
contrecarre à qn, contrer qn. 6. F:
to turn one's n. up (at sth.), faire le
dégoûté, faire la petite bouche. 7. F:
to look down one's n. at s.o., sth.,
toiser qn, qch., regarder* qn, qch.,
de haut (en bas). 8. F: to have a n.
(for sth.), avoir le nez creux, avoir du
pif. 9. F: he gets up my n., il me fait
monter la moutarde au nez. 10. F:
the parson's n., le croupion (d'une
volaille), as m de pique. Voir aussi
bottle-nose; dog¹, 6; skin¹, 2, 3;
toffee-nose.

nose about (or around) [ˈnouzəˈbaut,
ˈnouzəˈraund] (to), F: fureter, fouiner.

nosebag [ˈnouzbæg] (noun), P: to put
(or tie) on the n., manger*, casser la
croûte, se remplir le bocal.

nose-candy [ˈnouzkændi] (noun), P:
cocaïne f (drogues*), neige f.

nosedive¹ [ˈnouzdaiv] (noun), F: baisse
f (de prix, etc.), plongeon m.

nosedive² [ˈnouzdaiv] (to), F: (prix,
etc.) tomber à pic, dégringoler, s'effondrer.

nose on [ˈnouzɔn] (to), P: dénoncer*,
moutonner, bourdiller (qn).

nose-rag [ˈnouzræg], nose-wipe [ˈnouz-

* An asterisk indicates that the word so marked is included as a head-word in the Appendix.

waip], **nose-wiper** [ˈnouz-waipər]
(*noun*), P: mouchoir*, tire-jus *m*.

nosey [ˈnouzi] (*adj.*), F: = nosy.

nosh[1] [nɔʃ] (*noun*), P: 1. nourriture*,
boustifaille *f*. 2. repas *m*, boulottage *m*;
voir aussi chinky.

nosh[2] [nɔʃ] (to), P: 1. manger*, boulotter,
croûter. 2. mettre la main sur (qch.).

nosh-bar [ˈnɔʃbɑːr] (*noun*), P: snack
(-bar) *m*.

nosher [ˈnɔʃər] (*noun*), P: mangeur *m*,
bouffeur *m*.

nosh-up [ˈnɔʃʌp] (*noun*), P: bon repas,
noce *f*, bombe *f*.

nostrils [ˈnɔstrilz] (*pl. noun*), F: he
gets up my n. = he gets up my nose
(**nose, 9**).

nosy [ˈnouzi] (*adj.*), F: fureteur, fouinard;
n. parker, fouine *f*, fouille-merde *mf*.

nothing [ˈnʌθiŋ] (*noun*). 1. F: n. doing!
rien à faire! macache! 2. F: to do sth.
in n. flat, faire qch. très vite* (*ou*
illico *ou* en cinq secs). 3. P: you don't
know (from) n., tu es ignorant*, tu n'y
piges que dalle, tu es en retard d'une
rame. *Voir aussi* sweet[1], 5; write (to).

nowt [naut] (*noun*), F: rien*, nib, que
dalle; *cf.* owt.

nubbies [ˈnʌbiz] (*pl. noun*) (*Austr.*),
P: = bubbies.

number [ˈnʌmbər] (*noun*), F: 1. your
n.'s up, ton compte est bon. 2. to look
after n. one, penser à mézigue, soigner
bibi, tirer la couverture à soi. 3. a
hot n., (*a*) une chaude lapine, une
chaude de la pince; (*b*) morceau de
musique enlevé avec fougue; (*c*) article
m qui se vend bien, article-réclame *m*.
4. to have s.o.'s n., en savoir long sur
qn, être rencardé sur qn. 5. to have the
wrong n., être sur la mauvaise piste,
se gour(r)er. 6. (*langage enfantin*) to do
n. one = to do small jobs (**job, 9**);
to do n. two = to do big jobs (**job, 9**).
7. (*Marine*) n. one, officier *m* qui commande en second à bord d'un navire (de
guerre). *Voir aussi* back-number;
cushy.

nunky [ˈnʌŋki] (*noun*), F: 1. (*langage
enfantin*) oncle *m*, tonton *m*. 2. =
uncle, 5.

nurd [nəːd] (*noun*) (*U.S.*), P: = jerk[1],
1.

nut[1] [nʌt] (*noun*). 1. P: tête*, caboche *f*,

ciboulot *m*; use your n.! = use your
loaf!; (*Austr.*) to nod the n. = to
bow the crumpet (**crumpet, 3**); off one's
n., fou*, dingue, dingo; to go off one's
n., devenir fou*, perdre la boule; *cf.*
nuts[1]. 2. P: = nut-case. 3. P: to do
one's n., se mettre en colère*, sortir de
ses gonds. 4. F: he's a hard n. (to
crack), c'est un têtu (*ou* un cabochard
ou une bourrique *ou* une tête de mule);
cf. tough[1], 1. 5. F: she can't play (sing,
etc.) for nuts, elle joue (chante, *etc.*)
comme un pied; he can't drive for nuts,
il conduit comme un manche; *cf.*
toffee. 6. (*pl.*) V: testicules*, noix *f.pl.*;
to get hot nuts, être en érection*,
bander; to get one's nuts off, éjaculer*,
vider ses burettes; to have one's nuts
cracked, coïter*, tirer sa chique. 7. P:
to talk nuts, dire des bêtises* (*ou* des
conneries *f.pl.*). *Voir aussi* peanut.

nut[2] [nʌt] (to). 1. P: donner un coup
de tête* (*ou* de caboche *ou* de ciboulot)
à (qn). 2. (*U.S.*) V: coïter* avec (qn),
buriner (qn).

nut-case [ˈnʌtkeis] (*noun*), P: he's a
n.-c., c'est un cas.

nut-house [ˈnʌthaus] (*noun*), P: maison *f*
de fous, asile *m* de dingues, cabanon *m*,
Charenton.

nuts[1] [nʌts] (*adj.*), P: 1. = off one's
nut (nut[1], 1). 2. to be n. about (*or* on)
s.o., sth., être toqué (*ou* fana) de qn,
de qch.; être mordu pour qn, qch.; he's
n. about basket-ball, il raffole (*ou* c'est
un mordu) du basket; *cf.* nutty, 2.

nuts![2] [nʌts] (*excl.*), P: n. (to you)!
zut! merde!

nutter [ˈnʌtər] (*noun*), P: = nut-case.

nutters [ˈnʌtəz] (*adj.*), P: = off one's
nut (nut[1], 1).

nuttiness [ˈnʌtinis] (*noun*), P: folie *f*,
loufoquerie *f*, maboulisme *m*.

nutting [ˈnʌtiŋ] (*noun*), P: = heading.

nutty [ˈnʌti] (*adj.*), P: 1. loufoque,
maboul(e). 2. fou* (à lier), cinglé;
voir aussi fruit-cake, 2. 3. to be n.
about s.o., sth. = to be nuts about s.o.,
sth. (nuts[1], 2).

nymphet [nimˈfet] (*noun*), F: petite
poule, nénette *f*.

nympho [ˈnimfou] (*noun*), F: (=*nympho-
maniac*) nymphomane *f*, femme* à
passions.

---

* L'astérisque indique que le mot marqué de ce signe figure comme entrée dans le Répertoire.

O

O [ou] (abbr. = opium), P: op(ium) m (drogues*), boue f.

oats [outs] (pl. noun). 1. P: to get one's o., être satisfait sexuellement, ne pas mettre ses chaussettes à la fenêtre. 2. F: to feel one's o., (a) se sentir important, se monter du collet; (b) avoir de l'entrain (ou de l'allant). 3. F: to be off one's o., se sentir patraque (ou tout chose ou pas dans son assiette).

obstropolous [ɔbˈstrɔpələs] (adj.), F: bruyant, tapageur.

ochre [ˈoukər] (noun) (mainly U.S.), P: argent*, osier m, blanc m.

O.D. [ˈouˈdiː] (abbr. = overdose), F: dose trop forte (de narcotiques), (a) dose nuisible; (b) dose mortelle.

oddball¹ [ˈɔdbɔːl] (adj.), P: 1. excentrique, loufoque, farfelu. 2. gaffeur.

oddball² [ˈɔdbɔːl] (noun), P: 1. excentrique mf, drôle m de zigoto, farfelu m. 2. flagorneur m. 3. dissident(e) m(f). 4. pédéraste*.

odds [ɔdz] (pl. noun). 1. P: o. and sods, petits bouts, bibelots m.pl., bribes et morceaux. 2. F: over the o., beaucoup trop, bien plus. 3. F: what o. does it make? what's the o.? qu'est-ce que ça fait? 4. P: to shout the o., se vanter, faire de la gloriole. 5. F: to be within the o., être bien possible. 6. F: volumes dépareillés; livres m.pl. supplémentaires.

odds-on [ˈɔdzɔn] (adj.), F: to have an o.-o. chance, jouer gagnant; it's an o.-o. chance he'll get arrested, il y a bien des chances qu'il se fasse arrêter*.

off¹ [ɔf] (adj.), F: to have an o. day, se sentir un peu malade*, ne pas être en train.

off² [ɔf] (adv.), F: that's a bit o., (a) c'est un peu de travers, ce n'est pas tout à fait ça; (b) ça dépasse les bornes; (c) ça commence à être mauvais.

off³ [ɔf] (noun), F: ready for the o., prêt à partir*, sur le départ.

off⁴ [ɔf] (prep.). 1. F: o. colour, (a) un peu malade*, patraque, mal fichu; (b) (U.S.) scabreux, osé, salé, pimenté. 2. P: o. (of)..., de...; I got it o. (of) my brother, je le tiens de mon frère. Voir aussi go off (to), 2.

off-beat [ˈɔfˈbiːt] (adj.), F: original, qui sort de l'ordinaire.

office [ˈɔfis] (noun), P: signal particulier, œillade f. Voir aussi jack-in-office.

offish [ˈɔfiʃ] (adj.), F: (a) distant, hautain; (b) mal en train.

off-putting [ˈɔfputiŋ, ɔfˈputiŋ] (adj.), F: déconcertant, déroutant.

offy [ˈɔfi] (noun) (=off-licence), F: débit m (où on vend des boissons à emporter).

oh-be-joyful [ˈoubiːˈdʒɔifəl] (noun), F: bouteille f de rhum.

oil [ɔil] (noun), F: 1. flatterie f, boniment m, pommade f; cf. palm-oil. 2. pot-de-vin m, dessous-de-table m. 3. to strike o., gagner* beaucoup d'argent, trouver un bon filon.

oil-can [ˈɔil-kæn] (noun) (U.S.), P: échec*, four m, fiasco m.

oiled [ɔild] (adj.), F: (well) o., ivre*, fadé, bituré, cuit, dans le cirage.

oil-painting [ˈɔil-peintiŋ] (noun), F: she's no o.-p., elle est laide*, c'est un vieux tableau.

oily [ˈɔili] (adj.), F: (péj.) onctueux. Voir aussi rag¹, 10.

oink [ɔiŋk] (noun) (U.S.), P: policier*, condé m.

O.K.¹, o.k., okay [ˈouˈkei] (adj.), F: O.K., impec, au poil; an O.K. guy, un type bien. Voir aussi scene, 3 (a).

O.K.², o.k., okay [ˈouˈkei], oke [ouk], okey-doke [ˈoukiˈdouk], okey-dokey [ˈoukiˈdouki] (adv.), F: d'accord*, dac, O.K., banco; it's O.K. by me, quant à moi c'est d'accord.

O.K.³, o.k., okay [ˈouˈkei] (noun), F: accord m, conciliation f, approbation f, O.K. m; to give s.o. the O.K., donner le feu vert à qn.

O.K.⁴, o.k., okay [ˈouˈkei] (to), F: être

---

* An asterisk indicates that the word so marked is included as a head-word in the Appendix.

d'accord avec, approuver; opiner du bonnet.

old [ould] (*adj.*), 1. **the o. man**, (*a*) *F:* mari *m*, l'homme *m*, le vieux; (*b*) *F:* le père*, papa; **my o. man**, mon homme, mon vieux; (*c*) *F:* le patron*, le singe; (*d*) (*majuscules initiales*) *F:* le capitaine d'un navire; (*e*) *P:* pénis*, le petit frère. 2. *F:* **hello, o. man!** salut, vieille branche (*ou* vieux pote)!; *cf.* **thing, 8.** 3. *F:* **o. woman**, (*a*) épouse*, la moitié; (*b*) mère*, la vieille; (*c*) individu* qui fait des manières, chichiteux *m*. 4. *F:* **o. lady** = **old woman** (*voir* **old**, 3 (*a*) *ci-dessus*); *voir aussi* **white**[2], 4. 5. *F:* **the same o. story** (*or* **tune**), la même rengaine. 6. *F:* **I met o. Smith the other day**, j'ai rencontré l'ami Smith l'autre jour. 7. *F:* **it's a funny o. world (we live in)**, *c.p.*, tout est bizarre autant qu'étrange. 8. *F:* **put them down any o. where**, pose-les n'importe où. *Voir aussi* **army, 2; bean, 2; boot, 9; boy**[2]; **chap; crock**[1], **2; fruit, 3; Harry, 1, 2; hat, 1; high**[1], **6; how**[1], **1; how-d'ye-do; nick**[1], **3; rare; soldier**[1], **3; stick**[1], **9** (*b*); **thing, 8.**

old-boy [¹ould¹bɔi] (*attrib. adj.*), *F:* **the o.-b. network**, la franc-maçonnerie des anciens (d'une école, *etc.*).

oldie [¹ouldi] (*noun*), *F:* 1. vieux*, viocard *m*, vioque *m*. 2. vieillerie *f*, antiquaille *f*.

old-timer [ould¹taimər] (*noun*), *F:* un vieux de la vieille.

oldy [¹ouldi] (*noun*) = **oldie.**

Oliver (Twist) [¹ɔlivə(¹twist)] (*noun*) (*R.S.* = *fist*), *P:* poing*.

on[1] [ɔn] (*adj.*). 1. *V:* (pénis) en érection*, en l'air. 2. *P:* (*a*) euphorisé par la drogue, high; (*b*) habitué des drogues, branché; *cf.* **switched on, 2.**

on[2] [ɔn] (*adv.*), *F:* 1. **it's o.**, ça marche, ça va; **it's not o.**, rien à faire, pas mèche. 2. **I'm o.**, j'en suis. 3. **to be always o. at s.o.**, être toujours sur le dos de qn.

on[3] [ɔn] (*prep.*), *F:* **the drinks are o. me, this one's o. me**, j'offre la tournée, c'est moi qui régale.

once [wʌns] (*adv.*), *P:* **o. a week** (*R.S.* = *cheek*) = **cheek**[1,2].

once-over [¹wʌnsouvər] (*noun*), *F:* **to give sth., s.o., the o.-o.**, regarder*, reluquer, mirer qch., qn.

oncer [¹wʌnsər] (*noun*), *P:* billet* d'une livre, faf(f)iot *m*.

one [wʌn] (*pron.*). 1. *F:* un verre, un coup; **to have (had) o. too many**, avoir (pris) un coup de trop; **o. for the road** (*or* **for the swing of the gate**), le coup du départ (*ou* de l'étrier); *voir aussi* **eight, 1; quick, 1.** 2. *F:* (=*plaisanterie*) **that's a good o.!** elle est bien bonne celle-là! 3. *F:* (=*coup**) **he landed** (*or* **fetched**) **him o. on the nose**, il lui a donné un ramponneau sur le nez*; *voir aussi* **fourpenny.** 4. *F:* **he pulled a fast o. on me**, il m'a eu (*ou* fait *ou* refait), il m'a joué un tour (de cochon). 5. *F:* **you are a o.!** tu me la copieras! 6. *F:* **to be a o. for sth.**, être un fana (*ou* un mordu) de qch. 7. *F:* (= *nigaud*) **there's o. born every minute**, *c.p.*, on pend les andouilles sans les compter; *cf.* **sucker**[2], **1.** 8. *F:* **my o. and only**, mon cher et tendre, ma chère et tendre. 9. *F:* **it's** (*or* **that's**) **a new o. on me!** ça m'en bouche un coin! 10. *P:* **ones and twos** (*R.S.* = *shoes*), chaussures*, croquenots *m.pl. Voir aussi* **eye, 23; number, 7; stick**[2] (to), **11.**

one-eyed [¹wʌnaid] (*adj.*), *P:* insignifiant, de rien du tout, pitoyable, piètre; **a o.-e. town**, un patelin insignifiant, un bled. *Voir aussi* **trouser-snake.**

one-horse [¹wʌnhɔ:s] (*adj.*), *F:* **a o.-h. town**, une petite ville de province, un trou (perdu).

one-man [¹wʌn¹mæn] (*adj.*), *F:* **o.-m. band**, homme-orchestre *m* (=*amant parfait* ou *qn qui fait tout lui-même*).

one-nighter [¹wʌn¹naitər] (*noun*), *P:* = **one-night stand** (**stand**[1], **1**).

one-off [¹wʌnɔf] (*adj.*), *F:* (*a*) (*T.V.*) **o.-o. film**, film *m* en exclusivité; (*b*) **o.-o. book**, livre *m* à tirage limité.

oner [¹wʌnər] (*noun*), *F:* 1. sommité *f*, ongle *m*, as *m*, crack *m*. 2. un expert, un calé. 3. coup* de la fin, assommoir *m*.

one-two [¹wʌn¹tu:] (*noun*), *F:* coup* sec de gauche suivi d'un direct de droite.

one-upmanship [¹wʌn¹ʌpmənʃip] (*noun*), *F:* refus *m* de se laisser jeter la poudre aux yeux, l'escalade *f*, l'art *m* des raménoïdes; **to practise o.-u.**, renchérir, avoir la dragée haute.

onion [¹ʌnjən] (*noun*). 1. *F:* **that's the way the o. peels** = **that's the way the mop flops** (*voir* **mop, 1**); *cf.* **cookie, 1.** 2. *F:* **to know one's onions**, connaître son

---

* L'astérisque indique que le mot marqué de ce signe figure comme entrée dans le Répertoire.

sujet à fond, être à la coule (*ou* à la hauteur). **3.** *P:* tête*, poire *f*; **off one's o.**, fou*, maboul(e).

oodles [ˈuːdlz] (*pl. noun*), *F:* **o. of ...**, beaucoup de..., une abondance* de..., des tas de...

oof [uːf] (*noun*), *P:* argent*, fric *m*.

oojamaflip [ˈuːdʒəməflip], **oojie** [ˈuːdʒi] (*noun*), *F:* machin *m*, chose *mf*, machin-chose *m*.

oo-la-la! [ˈuːlɑːˈlɑː] (*excl.*), *F:* ho-la-la!

oomph [umf] (*noun*), *F:* charme *m*, personnalité *f*, sex-appeal *m*, chien *m*, allant *m*.

oops-a-daisy! [ˈupsəˈdeizi] (*excl.*), *F:* hop-là! youp-là (boum)!

oozer [ˈuːzər] (*noun*), *P:* = **boozer, 2.**

open[1] [ˈoup(ə)n] (*adj.*), *F:* **it's an o. and shut case**, c'est sûr et certain, c'est du tout cuit, c'est couru, c'est dans le sac.

open[2] [ˈoup(ə)n] (**to**). **1.** *P:* **to o. one's legs (for s.o.)**, (*d'une femme*) coïter*, faire une partie de jambes en l'air. **2.** *F:* **o. the door:** *voir* **bingo** (44).

openers [ˈoup(ə)nəz] (*pl. noun*), *F:* **for o.**, pour commencer, comme hors-d'œuvre.

open up [ˈoup(ə)nˈʌp] (**to**), *F:* **1.** (*a*) avouer*, dégorger, manger le morceau; (*b*) parler franchement, vider son sac. **2.** se déchaîner, y aller de tout son saoul. **3.** (*fusil, revolver*) tirer*, flinguer.

operator [ˈɔpəreitər] (*noun*), *P:* **1.** voleur* (à la tire), escroc*, filou *m*, empileur *m*. **2.** fourgueur *m* (*ou* pourvoyeur *m*) de drogues. *Voir aussi* **smooth, 2.**

organize [ˈɔːgənaiz] (**to**), *P:* = **wangle (to)**.

ornery [ˈɔːnəri] (*adj.*) (*U.S.*), *P:* d'humeur maussade, de mauvais poil.

Oscar [ˈɔskər] (**to**), *V:* pratiquer le coït* anal sur (qn), emproser (qn).

other [ˈʌðər] (*noun*), *P:* **to have a bit of**

the **o.**, coïter*, faire un peu de truc. *Voir aussi* **tother.**

out[1] [aut] (*adv.*). **1.** *F:* **o. on one's feet**, fatigué*, flapi, flagada. **2.** *F:* (*a*) **to be o. of it**, (i) ne pas être de connivence; (ii) être laissé à l'écart; (*b*) **to feel o. of it**, (i) se sentir dépaysé; (ii) se sentir de trop. **3.** *P:* **o. of sight**, bœuf, du tonnerre. *Voir aussi* **light, 1.**

out[2] [aut] (*noun*), *F:* **to find an o.**, se tirer d'affaire, se débrouiller*, se dépatouiller, se trouver une porte de sortie; *cf.* **get out (to)**; **in**[3], **1.** *Voir aussi* **in**[3], **2.**

out-and-abouter [ˈautəndəˈbautər] (*noun*), *F:* vadrouilleur *m*.

outfit [ˈautfit] (*noun*), *F:* **1.** équipe *f*, groupement *m*. **2.** firme *f*, (maison *f* de) travail *m*.

outside[1] [ˈautˈsaid] (*noun*), *F:* **to be on the o. looking in**, ne pas faire partie d'une société *ou* d'un groupe; être un outsider.

outside[2] [ˈautˈsaid] (*prep.*), *F:* **get o. that!** enfile-toi ça!

overcoat [ˈouvəkout] (*noun*), *F:* **wooden** (*or* **pine**) **o.**, cercueil*, paletot *m* (*ou* redingote *f*) de sapin, pardessus *m* sans manches.

overjolt [ˈouvə-dʒoult] (*noun*), *F:* dose trop forte (d'une drogue).

overspill [ˈouvə-spil] (*noun*), *F:* ville *f* satellite.

ownsome [ˈounsəm], **owny-o** [ˈouniou] (*noun*), *F:* **on one's o.**, tout seul, seulabre; *cf.* **lonesome.**

owt [aut] (*noun*), *F:* quelque chose; **I don't do o. for nowt**, je ne fais rien pour rien; *cf.* **nowt.**

oyster [ˈɔistər] (*noun*), *P:* **1.** crachat*, glaviot *m*. **2.** bouche*, boîte *f*.

ozzy [ˈɔzi] (*noun*), *P:* hôpital*, host(e)au *m*, hosto *m*.

---

* An asterisk indicates that the word so marked is included as a head-word in the Appendix.

P

p [pi:], *F:* **1. to mind** (*or* **watch**) **one's p's and q's,** (*a*) bien se tenir, se tenir convenablement; (*b*) s'occuper de ses affaires (*ou* de ses oignons) **2. to know one's p's and q's,** être débrouillard (*ou* démerdeur).

pa [pɑ:] (*noun*), *F:* perè*, papa *m.*

pace [peis] (*noun*), *F:* **to go the p.,** mener la vie à grandes guides; mener un train d'enfer.

pack[1] [pæk] (*noun*). **1.** *P:* pochette *f* d'héroïne (*drogues*). **2.** *F:* **p. of lies,** tissu *m* (*ou* tas *m*) de mensonges*.

pack[2] [pæk] (**to**), *F:* **1. to p. a gun,** être armé (*ou* chargé). **2. to p. a punch,** (*a*) boxer dur, perloter; (*b*) (*boisson*) être corsé. **3. to send s.o. packing,** envoyer dinguer qn, envoyer promener qn, envoyer qn sur les roses.

pack-drill [ˈpækdril] (*noun*), *F:* **no names, no p.-d.,** *c.p.,* pas de nom, pas de démon.

packet [ˈpækit] (*noun*). **1.** *P:* **to catch** (*or* **cop**) **a p.,** (*a*) écoper, en prendre pour son grade; (*b*) être bouclé, être envoyé en villégiature; (*c*) = **to get a dose** (**dose, 1**). **2.** *F:* **to cost a p.,** coûter cher*, être salé (*ou* lerche). **3.** *F:* (*a*) **to make a p.,** gagner* beaucoup d'argent, prendre le paquet, en ramasser, se sucrer, faire son beurre; (*b*) **to lose a p.,** perdre beaucoup d'argent*, ramasser une culotte, être paumard. **4.** *F:* un sale coup, une bonne dose. *Voir aussi* **buy**[2] (**to**), **2.**

pack in [ˈpækˈin] (**to**). **1.** *P:* **to p. s.o. i.,** cesser de voir qn, débarquer, plaquer, envoyer bouler qn. **2.** (*a*) *F:* **to p. sth. i.,** cesser de faire qch., larguer, laisser choir qch.; (*b*) *P:* **p. it i.!** (i) arrête!; (ii) ta gueule! la ferme! **3.** *F:* **to p. them** (*or* **'em**) **i.,** faire salle comble (*théâtre, cinéma, etc.*).

pack up [ˈpækˈʌp] (**to**). **1.** *P:* **to p. s.o. u.** = **to pack s.o. in** (**pack in** (**to**), **1**). **2.** *F:* **to p. sth. u.** = **to pack sth. in** (**pack in** (**to**), **2** (*a*), (*b*)). **3.** *F:* arrêter le travail, débrayer. **4.** *F:* se détraquer, sombrer, s'effondrer. **5.** (*a*) *F:* partir*, plier bagage, prendre ses cliques et ses claques; (*b*) *P:* mourir*, lâcher la rampe, se laisser glisser.

pad[1] [pæd] (*noun*). **1.** *F:* logement*, piaule *f*, case *f*, pied-à-terre *m*; *cf.* **crash-pad; pill-pad; tea-pad. 2.** *P:* **the pads** = **paddy, 2. 3.** *P:* route*, tire *f*; **to be on the p.,** être sur le trimard. **4.** *P:* lit*, pieu *m*; **to hit the p.,** se coucher*, se pieuter. *Voir aussi* **launching-pad.**

pad[2] [pæd] (**to**), *F:* marcher* (péniblement), trimarder; **to p. it,** aller à pied, affûter des pinceaux, prendre le train onze; *voir aussi* **hoof**[1], **1; hoof**[2] (**to**).

paddler [ˈpædlər] (*noun*) (*Austr.*), *P:* agent* de police, tige *f*.

paddles [ˈpædlz] (*pl. noun*) (*Austr.*), *F:* pieds*, péniches *f.pl.*, ripatons *m.pl.*

pad down [ˈpædˈdaun] (**to**), *F:* dormir*, roupiller.

paddy [ˈpædi] (*noun*). **1.** *F:* (*a*) mauvaise humeur; (*b*) éclat *m* de colère, coup *m* de sang. **2.** *P:* cellule matelassée, cabanon *m*. **3.** Irlandais *m*.

paddy-wag(g)on [ˈpædiwægən] (*noun*) (*U.S.*), *F:* = **Black Maria** (**black**[1], **6**).

paddywhack [ˈpædi(h)wæk] (*noun*), *F:* **1.** = **paddy, 1. 2.** (*langage enfantin*) fessée *f*.

pain [pein] (*noun*), (*a*) *F:* **a p. in the neck,** individu ennuyeux* *ou* antipathique, raseur *m*, casse-pieds *m*; (*b*) *F:* **he gives me a p. in the neck,** il me tape sur le système; (*c*) *P:* **a p. in the arse,** un emmerdeur.

paint [peint] (**to**), *F:* **to p. a picture,** faire le point. *Voir aussi* **red**[1], **3.**

painter [ˈpeintər] (*noun*). **1.** *F:* **to slip the p.,** mourir*, lâcher la rampe. **2.** *P:* **to have the painters in,** avoir ses menstrues*, repeindre sa grille en rouge; *cf.* **decorators.**

pak(k)i-basher [ˈpæki-bæʃər] (*noun*), *P:* chasseur *m* de Pakistanais.

---

pak(k)i-bashing [ˈpæki-bæʃiŋ] (*noun*), *P:* chasse *f* aux Pakistanais.

pal [pæl] (*noun*), *F:* ami*, copain *m*, pote *m*; *cf.* pal up (to).

palaver[1] [pəˈlɑːvər] (*noun*), *F:* **1.** bavardages *m.pl.*, palabres *f. pl.* **2.** embarras *m.pl.*, chichis *m.pl.* **3.** flagornerie *f*, baratin *m*.

palaver[2] [pəˈlɑːvər] (to), *F:* **1.** parler*, palabrer. **2.** flagorner, baratiner.

pally [ˈpæli] (*adj.*), *F:* (*a*) liant; (*b*) **to be p. with s.o.**, être copain (*ou* lié) avec qn.

palm [pɑːm] (*noun*), *F:* **1. to grease** (*or* **oil**) **s.o.'s p.**, graisser la patte à qn. **2. to have an itchy** (*or* **itching**) **p.**, être grippe-sou (*ou* grigou), les avoir crochues.

palm-grease [ˈpɑːmɡriːs] (*noun*), *P:* graissage *m* de patte.

palm off [ˈpɑːmˈɔf] (to), *F:* **to p. sth. o. on to s.o.**, colloquer, refiler, pastiquer, coller qch. à qn.

palm-oil [ˈpɑːmɔil] (*noun*), *P:* = **palm-grease**.

palm-tree [ˈpɑːmtriː] (*noun*), *P:* voiture *f* difficile à vendre, un rossignol; *cf.* bottler; square-wheeler.

palooka [pəˈluːkə] (*noun*), *P:* **1.** joueur peu compétent, nullité *f*, nouille *f*. **2.** un gros plein de soupe.

palsy-walsy [ˈpælziˈwælzi] (*adj.*), *F:* **to be** (**all**) **p.-w.** (**with s.o.**), être bons amis*, être à tu et à toi, être comme cul et chemise.

pal up [ˈpælˈʌp] (to), *F:* **to p. u. with s.o.**, copiner, se lier avec qn.

pan[1] [pæn] (*noun*). **1.** *P:* **to go down the p.** = **to go down the drain** (drain[1], **1**). **2.** *P:* visage*, burette *f*, fiole *f*. **3.** *F:* compte-rendu *m* défavorable, éreintage *m*, abattage *m*. *Voir aussi* flash[2], **2**.

pan[2] [pæn] (to), *F:* **1.** critiquer*, éreinter (qn, qch.). **2.** panoramiquer (une vue).

pancake[ˈpænkeik] (to), *F:* (*av.*) atterrir en crash (*ou* sur le gésier).

pancakes [ˈpænkeiks] (*pl. noun*), *P:* seins* aplatis, blagues *f.pl.* à tabac, tétasses *f.pl.*

panhandle [ˈpænhændl] (to) (*U.S.*), *F:* mendier*, pilonner, torpiller.

panhandler[ˈpænhændlər] (*noun*) (*U.S.*), *F:* mendiant*, mendigot *m*, torpilleur *m*.

panic [ˈpænik] (*noun*). **1.** *F:* **p. stations**, (*fig.*) postes *m.pl.* de combat, garde-à-vous *m*. **2.** *F:* **to push** (*or* hit) **the p. button**, (*a*) appuyer sur l'accélérateur, mettre les gaz; (*b*) être pris de panique, paniquer, avoir les foies. **3.** *P:* manque *m* (de drogues).

panicky [ˈpæniki] (*adj.*), *F:* (*a*) paniqué, paniquard; **don't get p.**, ne t'affole pas!; (*b*) (*d'un journal, etc.*) alarmiste.

panning [ˈpæniŋ] (*noun*), *F:* = **pan**[1], **3**.

pan out [ˈpænˈaut] (to). **1.** *F:* finir, se terminer, aboutir. **2.** *P:* rapporter (de l'argent), donner. **3.** *P:* **to p. o. about sth.**, s'étendre sur un sujet.

pansified [ˈpænzifaid], **pansy**[1] [ˈpænzi] (*adj.*), *F:* **1.** homosexuel, pédé. **2.** efféminé.

pansy[2] [ˈpænzi] (*noun*), *F:* **1.** pédéraste*, lopette *f*. **2.** homme efféminé, chochotte *f*, femmelette *f*, mauviette *f*.

pansyland [ˈpænzilænd] (*noun*), *F:* **1.** le monde des pédérastes*, la pédale, les tuyaux *m.pl.* de poêle; *cf.* fairyland. **2. in p.**, au pays des contes de fées.

panties [ˈpæntiz] (*pl. noun*), *F:* culotte *f* de femme, culbute *f*.

pants [pænts] (*pl. noun*). **1.** *F:* (*a*) pantalon*, falzar *m*; (*b*) caleçon *m*, slip *m*; (*c*) = **panties**. **2.** *P:* **to be caught with one's p. down**, être pris au dépourvu (*ou* la main dans le sac *ou* sur le tas), se trouver en mauvaise posture. **3.** *F:* **to get a kick in the p.**, être réprimandé* sévèrement, recevoir un coup de pied aux fesses* (*ou* quelque part); *voir aussi* kick[1],**5**. **4.** *P:* **to scare the p. off s.o.**, faire peur* à qn, donner (*ou* foutre) la pétoche à qn, les mouiller. **5.** *P:* **to tear the p. off s.o.**, prendre qn à partie, habiller qn, secouer les puces à qn. **6.** *P:* **to beat** (*or* **lick**) **the p. off s.o.**, battre qn à plate(s) couture(s), écraser qn. **7.** (*U.S.*) *F:* **to wear the p.** = **to wear the trousers** (*voir* trousers). *Voir aussi* ants; fancy[1], **3**; hot, **1**, **2**; lead[1], **4**; smarty(-pants).

paper[1] [ˈpeipər] (*noun*), *P:* (*th.*) billets *m.pl.* de faveur, bif(fe)tons *m.pl.*

paper[2] [ˈpeipər] (to). **1.** *P:* (*th.*) **to p. the house**, jouer à la bif(fe)tonnade. **2.** *F:* **to p. over the cracks**, essayer de rafistoler les choses.

paper-hanger [ˈpeipehæŋər], **paper-pusher** [ˈpeipə-puʃər] (*noun*), *P:* faux-monnayeur *m*, faux-mornifleur *m*.

---

* An asterisk indicates that the word so marked is included as a head-word in the Appendix.

paralytic [ˈpærəˈlitik] (adj.), F: ivre*
mort, bituré.

pard [pɑːd], **pardner** [ˈpɑːdnər] (noun)
(U.S.), F: (a) associé m, assoce m,
baron m; (b) ami*, pote m.

park [pɑːk] (to), F: to p. oneself somewhere, se mettre (ou s'installer) quelque part; **p. it over there!** mets-le (ou
colle le) là! Voir aussi **ticket, 2.**

parky [ˈpɑːki] (adj.), F: (du temps)
frais, frisco, frisquet.

parney [ˈpɑːni] (noun), P: pluie*, flotte
f, saucée f.

party [ˈpɑːti] (noun), F: **a certain p.**,
un certain individu*, un loustic, un
numéro. Voir aussi **hen; keep (to), 1;
stag¹; tea-party.**

pash [pæʃ] (noun), F: **to have a p. on
s.o.**, aimer* qn, avoir le béguin pour
qn, en pincer pour qn, être mordu
pour qn.

pass [pɑːs] (noun), F: **to make a p. at
s.o.**, essayer de séduire qn, flirter, faire
du boniment à qn.

passenger [ˈpæsindʒər] (noun), F: un
poids mort.

pass up [ˈpɑːsˈʌp] (to), F: se passer de
(qch.), sauter, supprimer (qch.).

past [pɑːst] (prep.), F: **I wouldn't put
it p. him**, il en est bien capable.

paste [peist] (to), F: battre*, rosser,
dérouiller, étriller.

pasting [ˈpeistiŋ] (noun), F: **to give
s.o. a p.**, (a) coller une raclée à qn,
passer une peignée à qn; (b) (sports,
etc.) battre qn à plate(s) couture(s).

pasture [ˈpɑːstjər] (noun), F: **to be put
out to p.**, être mis à la retraite (ou au
vert).

pat-ball [ˈpætbɔːl] (noun), F: tennis
mal joué, jeu m à la raquette.

patch [pætʃ] (noun). **1.** F: **she's not a p.
on him**, elle n'est pas de taille, elle ne
lui arrive pas à la cheville. **2.** P:
(argot du milieu) territoire m, champ m
d'action, chasse gardée; cf. **manor.
3.** F: **bad p.**, malchance*, guigne f,
pétrin m. **4.** P: devise inscrite sur le
dos des blousons de cuir des «Hell's
Angels».

patch up [ˈpætʃˈʌp] (to), F: **to p. u. a
quarrel**, rabibocher (ou replâtrer) une
querelle*.

pathetic [pəˈθetik] (adj.), F: **it's p.!**
c'est de la gnognot(t)e! c'est lamentable!

patootie [pəˈtuːti] (noun) (U.S.), P:
hot p., petite amie; blonde incendiaire.

patsy [ˈpætsi] (noun) (U.S.), P: **1.** dupe
f, victime f, gogo m, jobard m. **2.**
pleutre m, poule mouillée.

patter [ˈpætər] (noun), F: bavardage m,
causette f, jaserie m, baratinage m.

patteran [ˈpætəræn] (noun), P: langage
m par signes des bohémiens, manouche
muet.

paw¹ [pɔː] (noun), P: main*, patte f,
paluche f; **paws off! keep your paws
to yourself!** (à) bas les pattes! pas
touche! Voir aussi **southpaw.**

paw² [pɔː] (to), F: peloter, tripoter
(une femme); patouiller (qn, qch.).

pax! [pæks] (excl.), F: (langage enfantin)
pouce!; **end of p.**, pouce cassé.

pay [pei] (to), P: battre*, rosser, tabasser,
étriller. Voir aussi **call, 1; visit.**

pay-off [ˈpeiˈɔf] (noun), F: **1.** règlement
m de comptes. **2.** le bouquet, le comble
(qch. de tout à fait inattendu). **3.** pot-
de-vin m, dessous-de-table m. **4.** (a)
facteur décisif; (b) le fin mot (de
l'histoire).

pay off [ˈpeiˈɔf] (to), F: avoir du succès,
être rentable, faire un boum, boumer.

payola [peiˈjoulə] (noun), F: ristourne
f, gratte f, gant m.

payroll [ˈpeiroul] (noun), F: **to be on
the p.**, faire partie de la bande*, être
du même bâtiment.

p.d.q. [ˈpiːˈdiːˈkjuː] (abbr. = pretty damn
quick), P: très vite*, en cinq secs.

peach¹ [piːtʃ] (noun). **1.** F: belle* fille,
jolie pépée, bath petit lot; **she's a p.
of a girl**, c'est un beau brin de fille,
c'est une belle petite caille. **2.** F: qch. de
super (ou de sensass), un délice; **it's
a p. of a party**, c'est une super boum,
c'est une bath surboum. **3.** P: amphétamine f (drogues*).

peach² [piːtʃ] (to), P: dénoncer*,
moucharder, cafarder, bourdiller; **to p.
on s.o.**, trahir, vendre, moutonner qn.

peachy [ˈpiːtʃi] (adj.), F: agréable, jojo,
juteux.

pea-head [ˈpiːhed] (noun), P: individu
bête*, tête f de linotte.

peanut [ˈpiːnʌt] (noun). **1.** P: barbiturique m (drogues*). **2.** (pl.) F: presque
rien*, de la gnognot(t)e, des clous, des
prunes. **3.** (U.S.) F: (th.) **p. gallery** =
chicken-roost.

---

* L'astérisque indique que le mot marqué de ce signe figure comme entrée dans le Répertoire.

pearl-dive ['pə:l-daiv] (to), V: = **muff**[2] (to), 3.

pearl-diver ['pə:l-daivər] (noun), V: = **muff-diver.**

pearlies ['pə:liz] (pl. noun), F: dents*, dominos m.pl.

pearls [pə:lz] (pl. noun), P: = amy.

pearly ['pə:li] (adj.), P: **p. gates,** graines f.pl. de volubilis (drogue hallucinogène); cf. **heavenly blues (blue**[2], 1).

pea-shooter ['pi:-ʃu:tər] (noun), P: revolver*, rigolo m; cf. **shooter.**

pea-souper ['pi:'su:pər] (noun), F: brouillard m (à couper au couteau), purée f de pois.

peck [pek] (to), F: manger* du bout des dents; **to p. at one's food,** pignocher, mangeotter son repas.

pecker ['pekər] (noun). 1. P: pénis*, goupillon m, chibre m. 2. F: courage m, cran m; **to keep one's p. up,** ne pas se laisser abattre, tenir bon, tenir le coup.

peckish ['pekiʃ] (adj.), F: **to be** (or **feel) p.,** avoir faim*, claquer du bec.

pedigree ['pedigri:] (noun), P: casier m judiciaire d'un criminel, faffes m.pl., blase m.

pee[1] [pi:] (noun), P: urine f, pipi m; **to have a p.,** uriner*; **to go for a p.,** aller faire pipi.

pee[2] [pi:] (to), P: 1. uriner*, pisser. 2. pleuvoir à torrent, flotter, pisser.

peed off ['pi:d'ɔf] (adj.), P: = **pissed off.**

pee down ['pi:'daun] (to), P: = **pee**[2] (to), 2.

peek [pi:k] (noun), P: **the p.** = **the peep.**

peeker ['pi:kər] (noun), P: curieux m, indiscret m, voyeur m.

peel (off) ['pi:l('ɔf)] (to), F: se déshabiller*, se décarpiller, se dénipper. Voir aussi **banana,** 1; **onion,** 1.

peeler ['pi:lər] (noun), P: strip-teaseuse f, effeuilleuse f.

peenie ['pi:ni] (noun), P: pénis*, pine f.

pee off ['pi:'ɔf] (to), P: = **piss off** (to).

peep [pi:p] (noun). 1. P: **the p.,** cellule f (ou cellot(t)e f) de remouchage, cage f à poules. 2. F: **I don't want to hear another p. out of you,** tâche de ne pas piper.

peepers ['pi:pəz] (pl. noun), F: yeux m.pl. (œil*), mirettes f.pl., châsses m.pl.

pee-slit ['pi:-slit] (noun), V: vagin*, fente f.

peeve[1] [pi:v] (noun), F: ennui m, barbe f, crampon m, emmerdement m; **pet p.,** barbe f de premier ordre, poison violent.

peeve[2] [pi:v] (to), F: ennuyer*, barber, canuler, empoisonner.

peeved [pi:vd] (adj.), F: fâché, irrité, ennuyé.

peg[1] [peg] (noun), F: 1. **off the p.,** prêt à porter, confection. 2. (a) **to take s.o. down a p.,** rabattre le caquet à qn, rogner les ailes à qn, faire déchanter qn; (b) **to come down a p.,** en rabattre, baisser le ton, baisser d'un cran, déchanter. 3. doigt m (de whisky, etc.). 4. (pl.) jambes*, bâtons m.pl., cannes f.pl. Voir aussi **square**[1], 7.

peg[2] [peg] (to), F: **to have s.o., sth., pegged** = **to have s.o., sth., taped (tape**[2] (to)).

peg away ['pegə'wei] (to), F: travailler* dur, turbiner, piocher.

peg back ['peg'bæk] (to), F: stabiliser, maintenir (le prix, etc., de qch.).

peg-leg ['pegleg] (noun), F: (a) jambe f de bois, pilon m; (b) pilonneur m.

peg out ['peg'aut] (to), F: 1. mourir*, lâcher la rampe, casser sa pipe. 2. **to be pegged out,** être très fatigué* (ou éreinté ou fourbu).

pen [pen] (noun), F: (=penitentiary) prison*, taule f, ballon m.

pen and ink ['penənd'iŋk] (to), P: 1. (R.S. = to stink) puer, schlinguer. 2. (R.S. = to drink) boire*.

pencil ['pensl] (noun), P: pénis*, le bout, la pointe; cf. **lead**[1], 3.

penguin ['peŋgwin] (noun), F: 1. (av.) = **ground walla(h) (walla(h),** 2). 2. **p. suit,** habit m (de soirée), queue f de pie.

penman ['penmən] (noun), P: faussaire m, homme m de lettres, maquilleur m.

penny ['peni] (noun), F: 1. **then the p. dropped,** alors on a compris (ou pigé). 2. **to spend a p.,** aller aux W.C.*, aller au petit coin. 3. **a p. for your thoughts,** c.p., à quoi penses-tu? 4. **she cost me a pretty p.,** elle m'en a fait écosser. Voir aussi **bad**[1], 3.

penny-pincher ['peni-pintʃər] (noun), F: avare m, radin m, rapiat m.

penny-pinching[1] ['peni-pintʃiŋ] (adj.), F: avare*, constipé du morlingue, grippe-sou.

---

* An asterisk indicates that the word so marked is included as a head-word in the Appendix.

penny-pinching[2] [ˈpeni-pintʃiŋ] (noun),
  F: avarice f, radinerie f.
pen-pusher [ˈpenpuʃər] (noun), F:
  gratte-papier m, rond-de-cuir m.
pension [ˈpenʃ(ə)n] (noun), F: old-age p.:
  voir **bingo** (65).
pen-yen [ˈpenˈjen] (noun) (U.S.), P:
  opium m (drogues*), op m, touffiane f.
people [ˈpiːpl] (pl. noun), F: **1**: the
  income-tax p., les gens du fisc, les
  dégraisseurs m.pl. **2. to know the right
  p.**, avoir des relations f.pl. (utiles),
  avoir le bras long. **3.** famille f, parents*,
  smala f.
pep [pep] (noun), F: **1. to be full of p.**,
  être plein d'entrain, péter le feu.
  2. p. pill, stimulant m, topette f,
  remontant m, excitant m. **3. p.
  talk**, paroles encourageantes qui remontent
  le moral et émoustillent, petit discours*
  d'encouragement.
pepper-upper [ˈpepəˈrʌpər] (noun), F:
  apéritif m, remontant m, coup m de
  fouet, stimulant m; cf. **pep up (to)**.
peppy [ˈpepi] (adj.), F: plein d'allant et
  de vitalité.
pep up [ˈpepˈʌp] (to), F: **1.** émoustiller,
  ravigoter (qch.). **2.** remonter, ragaillardir (qn).
Perce [pəːs], **Percy** [ˈpəːsi] (noun), P:
  pénis*, cyclope m, Popaul; **to point P.
  at the porcelain**, uriner*, égoutter son
  cyclope.
perch [pəːtʃ] (noun), F: **to knock s.o.
  off his p., to make s.o. come down
  from his p.**, faire descendre qn de son
  perchoir, déboulonner qn; **to come off
  one's p.**, jeter du lest.
perfect [ˈpəːfikt] (adj.), F: vrai, absolu;
  he's a p. idiot, c'est un idiot fini; **he's
  a p. menace**, c'est une vraie menace.
perform [pəˈfɔːm] (to), P: **1.** déféquer*,
  déballer. **2.** coïter*, niquer.
period [ˈpiəriəd] (noun), F: **He's no
  good at maths. – He's no good, period,**
  Il est nul en math. – Il est nul, tout
  court.
perished [ˈperiʃt] (adj.), F: exténué de
  froid ou de faim, rétamé, plombé.
perisher [ˈperiʃər] (noun), F: sale type
  m, chameau m, saligaud m.
perishing [ˈperiʃiŋ] (adj.), F: **1. it's p.**,
  il fait un froid de loup; **I'm p.**, je suis
  transi de froid. **2.** sacré, satané, maudit.
perks [pəːks] (pl. noun = perquisites),

F: gratte f, affure f, grinche f, tour m
  de bâton; les petits à-côtés, les petits
  bénefs.
perk up [ˈpəːkˈʌp] (to), F: (a) ravigoter,
  requinquer (qn); (b) se ravigoter, se
  requinquer.
perm[1] [pəːm] (noun), F: **1.** (=permanent
  wave) indéfrisable f, permanente f,
  modelling m. **2.** (=permutation) permutation f (au tiercé du football).
perm[2] [pəːm] (to), F: **1. to have one's
  hair permed**, se faire faire une indéfrisable. **2.** (tiercé du football) faire une
  permutation; permuter.
pernickety [pəˈnikəti] (adj.), F: vétilleux, pointilleux; **to be p. about one's
  food**, être difficile (ou délicat) sur la
  nourriture*.
persuader [pəˈsweidər] (noun), P: **1.**
  pénis*, baïonnette f. **2.** arme f, flingue m.
perve[1] [pəːv] (noun), P: perverti m;
  inverti m.
perve[2] [pəːv] (to) (Austr.), P: **to p. on
  s.o.**, se rincer l'œil (en regardant qn).
pesky [ˈpeski] (adj.) (U.S.), F: ennuyeux*,
  scie, rasoir.
pest [pest] (noun), F: enquiquineur m,
  poison mf, plaie f.
pet [pet] (to), F: se caresser, se peloter;
  cf. **petting**.
Pete [piːt] (pr. noun), F: **for P.'s sake!**
  au nom des Saints! pour l'amour de
  Dieu!
peter [ˈpiːtər] (noun), P: **1.** coffre-fort
  m, coffiot m. **2. P.** (or **P. Bell**) (R.S. =
  (prison) cell), cellule f de prison, cellot(t)e
  f; cf. **flowery (dell)**. **3.** pénis*, Charles-
  le-Chauve, Popaul.
peterman [ˈpiːtəmən] (noun), P: casseur
  m de coffre-fort (ou de coffiot).
petticoat-chaser [ˈpetikout-tʃeisər]
  (noun), F: coureur m de jupons.
petting [ˈpetiŋ] (noun), F: badinage
  amoureux, pelotage m; **p. party**, party
  f de pelote maison; **p. session**, séance f
  de bécotage m (ou de pelotage m);
  cf. **pet (to)**.
pew [pjuː] (noun), F: **to take a p.**,
  s'asseoir, poser ses fesses.
pewter [ˈpjuːtər] (noun), P: argent m
  (métal).
phenie [ˈfiːni] (noun), F: phénobarbital
  m; barbiturique m (drogues*).
phiz [fiz], **phizog** [ˈfizɔg] (noun), P:
  visage*, frime f, frimousse f.

---

* An asterisk indicates that the word so marked is included as a head-word in the Appendix.

phon(e)y[1] [ˈfouni] (*adj.*). **1.** *F:* faux*, chinetoque, bidon, toc(árd). **2.** (*a*) *F:* contrefait, falsifié; (*b*) *P:* **p. white**, fausses pièces d'argent*, mornifle truquée.

phon(e)y[2] [ˈfouni] (*noun*). **1.** *F:* charlatan *m*, bluffeur *m*, chiqueur *m*. **2.** *P:* qn qui fait des appels téléphoniques obscènes.

phooey! [ˈfuːi] (*excl.*), *F:* fi! fi donc! flûte!

phut [fʌt] (*adv.*), *F:* **to go p.**, échouer*, rater, louper, s'en aller en eau de boudin, claquer.

phy [fai] (*abbr.* = *physeptone*), *P:* physeptone *f* (*drogues*).

pi [pai] (*adj.*), *P:* papelard, cagot, bondieusard. *Voir aussi* **jaw**[1], 2.

Piccadilly Circus [ˈpikədiliˈsəːkəs] (*pr. noun*), *F:* **it's like P. C.!** quel embouteillage!

pick [pik] (*noun*), *F:* **the p. of the bunch**, le dessus du panier, la fleur des petits pois.

picker [ˈpikər] (*noun*) (*U.S.*), *P:* = **peeker**. *Voir aussi* **winkle-pickers**.

pickle [ˈpikl] (*noun*), *F:* **1. to be in a p.**, être dans le pétrin (*ou* dans de mauvais draps). **2.** petit diable, diablotin *m*.

pickled [ˈpikld] (*adj.*), *F:* ivre*, rétamé.

pick-me-up [ˈpikmi(ː)ʌp] (*noun*), *F:* cordial *m*, remontant *m*, stimulant *m*, coup *m* de fouet.

pick on [ˈpikɔn] (**to**), *F:* chercher noise à (qn).

pick-up [ˈpikʌp] (*noun*). **1.** *F:* rencontre *f* de fortune, femme dont on fait connaissance dans la rue. **2.** *F:* **to have a p.-u.**, être conduit quelque part en voiture. **3.** *F:* redressement *m*, relèvement *m*, reprise *f*. **4.** *P:* drogues* obtenues d'un pourvoyeur.

pick up [ˈpikˈʌp] (**to**). **1.** *F:* arrêter*, agrafer, pincer. **2.** *F:* (*d'une prostituée*) ramasser (un client), faire (un levage). **3.** *F:* ramasser, récolter (microbes, *etc.*). **4.** *F:* **to p. u. the pieces**, repartir à zéro, recoller les restes. **5.** *F:* reprendre, corriger (qn). **6.** *F:* **to p. u. with s.o.**, faire la connaissance de qn. **7.** *P:* obtenir des drogues* d'un pourvoyeur. **8.** *F:* **to p. u. on sth.**, assimiler, digérer qch. **9.** *F:* (*physiquement, financièrement*) se rebecter, se rebecqueter, se remplumer.

picky [ˈpiki] (*adj.*), *F:* méticuleux,

chichiteux; **to be p.**, chercher la petite bête.

picnic [ˈpiknik] (*noun*), *P:* **1.** occupation *f* agréable et facile, partie *f* de plaisir. **2.** rigolade *f*, un vrai cirque.

picture [ˈpiktʃər] (*noun*), *F:* **1. to put s.o. in the p.**, mettre qn au courant (*ou* à la page). **2. she's a real p.!** c'est une beauté! elle est ravissante! **3.** (*a*) **to step into the p.**, se montrer, se manifester; (*b*) **to step out of the p.**, s'effacer, se retirer. **4. get the p.?** tu comprends? tu piges? *Voir aussi* **paint** (**to**).

piddle[1] [ˈpidl] (*noun*), *F:* urine *f*, pipi *m*.

piddle[2] [ˈpidl] (**to**). *F:* **1.** uriner*, faire pipi. **2.** *P:* pleuvoter, pleuvasser.

piddle about (*or* **around**) [ˈpidl-əˈbaut, ˈpidl-əˈraund] (**to**), *P:* paresser*, flânocher, galvauder.

piddling [ˈpidliŋ] (*adj.*), *F:* bête*, niais, futile.

pidgin [ˈpidʒin] (*noun*), *F:* **1.** = **pigeon**, 2. **2. to talk p.**, parler petit nègre.

pie [pai] (*noun*), *F:* **p. in the sky**, le miel de l'autre monde. *Voir aussi* **apple-pie**[1,2]; **easy**[1], 6; **finger**[1], 5; **fruity-pie**[1,2]; **hairpie**; **mince-pies**; **resurrection pie**; **sweetie-pie**; **tongue-pie**; **tweety(-pie)**.

piece [piːs] (*noun*). **1.** *P:* fille*, femme*, un (beau) petit lot; *voir aussi* **lush**[1]. **2.** *F:* **to go to pieces**, (*d'un individu*) s'effondrer, se catastropher, s'écrouler. **3.** *P:* deux grammes d'héroïne *ou* de stupéfiant. **4.** *F:* **to pull s.o. to pieces**, déchirer qn à belles dents, mettre qn en capilotade, éreinter qn. **5.** (*U.S.*) *F:* arme *f*. *Voir aussi* **ass**[1], 2; **cake**, 1, 3; **head-piece**; **kettle**, 1; **mouth-piece**; **pick up** (**to**), 4; **ring-piece**; **sky-piece**; **tail**[1], 4; **think-piece**; **two-piece**; **work**[1].

pie-eyed [ˈpai-aid] (*adj.*), *F:* ivre*, gris, éméché.

piffle [ˈpifl] (*noun*), *F:* bêtises*, futilités *f.pl.*, balivernes *f.pl.*

piffling [ˈpifliŋ] (*adj.*), *F:* = **piddling**.

pig[1] [pig] (*noun*). **1.** *F:* goinfre*, gueulard *m*, morfalou *m*. **2.** *F:* salaud *m*, saligaud *m*, vache *f*. **3.** *P:* agent* de police, perdreau *m*. **4.** *P:* **p.'s ear** (*R.S.* = *beer*), bière *f*. **5.** *P:* **in p.**, enceinte*, en cloque. **6.** *F:* **to buy a p. in a poke**, acheter chat en poche.

pig² [pig] (**to**), *P.:* **1.** se goinfrer, s'empiffrer, bâfrer, manger comme un goret. **2. to p. it**, vivre comme un cochon, vivre dans une écurie. **3. to p. together**, partager la même chambre.

pig-boat [ˈpigbout] (*noun*), *P.:* sous-marin *m*, plongeant *m*.

pigeon [ˈpidʒin] (*noun*), *F.:* **1.** dupe *f*, dindon *m*, poire *f*, poireau *m*. **2. it's not my p.**, ça ne me regarde pas, c'est pas mes oignons; **that's your p.**, ça te regarde, c'est ton rayon (*ou* ton affaire). **3.** jeune fille*. *Voir aussi* **stool-pigeon**.

pigeon-roost [ˈpidʒinruːst] (*noun*), *F.:* (*th.*) le poulailler, le paradis; *cf.* **chicken-roost**.

piggy¹ [ˈpigi] (*adj.*), *F.:* goinfre*, goulu.

piggy² [ˈpigi] (*noun*), *F.:* **1.** cochonnet *m*, cochon *m* de lait, porcelet *m*. **2.** petit goret, petit goulu.

piggyback [ˈpigibæk] (*noun*), *F.:* **to give s.o. a p.**, porter qn sur le dos *ou* sur les épaules.

piggy-bank [ˈpigibæŋk] (*noun*), *F.:* tirelire *f*, boîte *f* à sous (en forme de cochon).

pig-meat [ˈpigmiːt] (*noun*), *P.:* **1.** prostituée*, bourrin *m*. **2.** la Veuve Montretout, une vieille paillasse. **3.** fille bête*, andouille *f*.

pigwash [ˈpig-wɔʃ] (*noun*), *F.:* = **hogwash, 1**.

pike¹ [paik] (*noun*), *P.:* route*, trime *f*.

pike² [paik] (**to**), *P.:* marcher*, trimarder, aller à pattes.

piker [ˈpaikər] (*noun*), *P.:* avare *m*, grigou *m*.

pile [pail] (*noun*), *F.:* **1.** (*a*) **to make a p. (of money)**, gagner* beaucoup d'argent, en amasser, faire sa pelote; (*b*) **to make one's p.**, devenir riche*, faire son beurre. **2. a p. of work**, un tas (*ou* un monceau *ou* une pile) de travail* (*ou* de boulot).

pile-driver [ˈpail-draivər] (*noun*), *F.:* coup* d'assommoir, direct *m*, marron *m*.

pile in [ˈpailˈin] (**to**), *F.:* s'empiler dans un véhicule.

pile into [ˈpailˈintuː] (**to**), *F.:* **to p. i. s.o.**, attaquer* qn, rentrer dedans, agrafer qn.

pile on [ˈpailˈɔn] (**to**), *F.:* **to p. it o.**, exagérer*, y aller fort, charrier. *Voir aussi* **agony, 2**.

pile-up [ˈpailʌp] (*noun*), *F.:* **1.** embouteillage *m*, bouchon *m*. **2.** carambolage *m*, emboutissage *m*.

pill [pil] (*noun*). **1.** *F.:* balle *f*, ballon *m*. **2.** (*pl.*) *P.:* testicules*, billes *f.pl.*, roupettes *f.pl.* **3.** *F.:* (**bitter**) **p.**, personne *f ou* chose *f* désagréable, pilule *f*, poison *mf*, colique *f*. **4.** capsule *f* de Nembutal (*drogues*). **5.** *P.:* boulette *f* d'opium (*drogues**); *cf.* **pill-pad. 6.** *F.:* **to be on the p.**, prendre la pilule.

pillhead [ˈpilhed] (*noun*), *P.:* habitué(e) des opiacés, opiomane *mf*.

pillow-talk [ˈpilou-tɔːk] (*noun*), *F.:* semonce conjugale, discours *m* sur l'oreiller, engueulade *f* entre deux draps.

pill-pad [ˈpil-pæd] (*noun*), *P.:* fumerie *f* d'opium, repaire *m* (*ou* turne *f*) de drogués*.

pimple [ˈpimpl] (*noun*), *P.:* **p. and blotch** (*R.S. = Scotch* (*whisky*)), whisky *m*.

pin [pin] (**to**), *F.:* **to p. sth. on s.o.**, rendre qn responsable, mettre qch. sur le dos de qn.

pinball [ˈpinbɔːl] (*noun*), *F.:* flipper *m*.

pinch¹ [pintʃ] (*noun*), *F.:* **1. to feel the p.**, tirer le diable par la queue. **2. at a p.**, au besoin.

pinch² [pintʃ] (**to**), *F.:* **1.** voler*, chiper, chaparder. **2.** arrêter*, agrafer; **to get pinched**, se faire épingler. **3. to be pinched for time** (*money, etc.*), être à court de temps (d'argent, *etc.*).

pinchers [ˈpintʃəz] (*pl. noun*), *P.:* menottes*, pinces *f.pl.*

pinching [ˈpintʃiŋ] (*noun*), *F.:* vol *m*, chapardage *m*. *Voir aussi* **pennypinching**².

pine [pain] (*noun*), *F.:* **p. overcoat = wooden overcoat** (*voir* **overcoat**).

pineapple [ˈpainæpl] (*noun*), *F.:* grenade *f* à main, poire *f*.

ping [piŋ] (*noun*), *P.:* piqûre *f* de drogue; **p. in the wing**, piquouse *f* dans l'aile.

pinhead [ˈpinhed] (*noun*), *F.:* **1.** petite tête*, tête d'épingle. **2.** qn d'ignorant*, tête *f* de linotte.

pink¹ [piŋk] (*adj.*), *F.:* à tendances socialistes, rose (*ou* rouge) sur les bords. *Voir aussi* **elephant, 2**; **strike (to), 1**; **tickle**² (**to**), **2**.

pink² [piŋk] (*noun*), *F.:* **to be in the p.**, se porter à merveille (*ou* comme un charme).

---

* L'astérisque indique que le mot marqué de ce signe figure comme entrée dans le Répertoire.

pinkie, pinky [ˈpiŋki] (*noun*). 1. *F:* le petit doigt, le riquiqui. 2. *P:* un (homme) blanc; *cf.* **whitie.**

pinny [ˈpini] (*noun*) (=*pinafore*), *F:* tablier *m*, bavette *f*.

pin-pricks [ˈpinpriks] (*pl. noun*), *F:* tracasseries *f.pl.*, asticotages *m.pl.*

pins [pinz] (*pl. noun*), *F:* 1. jambes*, fusains *m.pl.*, quilles *f.pl.* 2. **to be on p. and needles,** être sur des charbons ardents. *Voir aussi* piss² (to), 2.

pinta [ˈpaintə] (*noun*), *F:* bouteille *f* de lait; demi-litre *m* (de lait, *etc.*).

pint-size(d) [ˈpaint-saiz(d)] (*adj.*), *F:* **a p.-s. person,** individu *m* de petite* taille, courte-botte *f*, demi-portion *f*.

pin-up [ˈpinʌp] (*noun*), *F:* 1. belle fille*, pin-up *f*, prix *m* de Diane; **p.-u. mag(azine),** magazine *m* de pin-up.

pip¹ [pip] (*noun*), *F:* 1. **to give s.o. the p.,** déprimer qn, flanquer le cafard à qn. 2. (*mil.*) galon *m*, ficelle *f*; **to get one's p.,** recevoir ses galons, arborer la ficelle; **he's just got his third p.,** il vient d'avoir sa troisième ficelle. 3. jeune personne alléchante, charmeuse *f*.

pip² [pip] (**to**). 1. *P:* blackbouler (qn). 2. *F:* **the horse was pipped on the post,** le cheval a été battu au poteau d'arrivée. 3. *F:* **to p. an exam,** être recalé à un examen.

pipe¹ [paip] (*noun*). 1. *F:* **put that in your p. and smoke it!** mets ça dans ta poche et ton mouchoir par-dessus! 2. *P:* **to hit the p.,** fumer de l'opium, y aller du chilom. 3. *P:* = **gonga.** *Voir aussi* drainpipe; stove-pipe.

pipe² [paip] (**to**), *P:* laisser savoir, laisser transpirer, mettre au parfum.

pipe down [ˈpaipˈdaun] (**to**), *P:* (*a*) faire moins de bruit*, mettre un bémol (*ou* une sourdine) (à la clef); **p. d., will you!** baisse un peu ta musique!; (*b*) se taire*, la boucler.

pipe-job [ˈpaipdʒɔb] (*noun*), *V:* coït* buccal, prise *f* de pipe; *cf.* **blow-job.**

pipeline [ˈpaip-lain] (*noun*), *F:* 1. **to be in the p.,** être en cours (*ou* en voie *ou* en train). 2. **to have a p.,** avoir une filière.

pipe up [ˈpaipˈʌp] (**to**), *F:* se faire entendre, l'ouvrir tout d'un coup.

pip out [ˈpipˈaut] (**to**), *P:* mourir*, faire couic.

pippins [ˈpipinz] (*pl. noun*), *P:* seins*, nénés *m.pl.*

pipsqueak¹ [ˈpip-skwi:k] (*adj.*), *F:* petit, minuscule, insignifiant.

pipsqueak² [ˈpip-skwi:k] (*noun*), *F:* 1. gringalet *m*, minus *m*, minable *m*. 2. mobylette *f*, pétrolette *f*.

piss¹ [pis] (*noun*), *P:* 1. urine *f*, pisse *f*. 2. **to take the p. (out of s.o.),** faire marcher qn, se payer la tête de qn; *cf.* **piss-taker.** 3. **a long streak of p.,** (*a*) une perche, un échalas, un individu long comme un jour sans pain; (*b*) un gros plein de soupe. 4. bêtises*, foutaises *f.pl.*, conneries *f.pl.* 5. **cat's (or gnat's) p.,** pipi *m* de chat. 6. **to be full of p. and wind,** être comme une bulle de savon. 7. **to be full of p. and vinegar,** être plein d'entrain, péter le feu. 8. **to beat the p. out of s.o.,** battre* qn comme plâtre, tabasser qn.

piss² [pis] (**to**), *P:* uriner*, pisser, lansquiner. 2. **to p. pins and needles,** être atteint de gonorrhée* (*ou* de chaude-pisse), pisser des lames de rasoir (en travers). 3. **to p. oneself laughing,** se tordre les côtes de rire, rire* à s'en mouiller. 4. **to p. blood,** suer sang et eau, s'échiner. 5. = **piss down** (to).

piss-artist [ˈpis-ɑːtist] (*noun*) (*Austr.*), *P:* ivrogne*, poivrier *m*.

piss away [ˈpisəˈwei] (**to**), *P:* dépenser* sans compter, bouffer, claquer (de l'argent*).

piss down [ˈpisˈdaun] (**to**), *P:* = **pee²** (to), 2.

pissed [pist] (*adj.*), *P:* ivre*; **to get p.,** s'enivrer, prendre une cuite (*ou* une bit(t)ure); *voir aussi* arsehole, 2.

pissed off [ˈpistˈɔf] (*adj.*), *P:* 1. **to be p. o.,** en avoir assez* (*ou* ras le bol *ou* plus que marre). 2. (*U.S.*) très en colère*, en rage.

pisser [ˈpisər] (*noun*), *P:* **to pull s.o.'s p.,** faire marcher qn, monter un bateau à qn, faire monter qn à l'échelle.

pisshouse [ˈpishaus] (*noun*), *P:* W.C.*, pissotière *f*.

piss off [ˈpisˈɔf] (**to**), *P:* s'enfuir*, se tirer, se trisser; **p. o.!** fous le camp! *Voir aussi* pissed off.

piss on [ˈpisɔn] (**to**), *P:* dénigrer, débiner (qn), traiter (qn) comme du poisson pourri.

---

* An asterisk indicates that the word so marked is included as a head-word in the Appendix.

piss-poor [ˈpisˈpɔːr] (adj.), P: 1. très pauvre*, purotin, déchard, dans la purée noire. 2. de mauvaise qualité, tocard, camelote.

pisspot [ˈpispɔt] (noun), P: 1. pot m de chambre, Jules, Thomas. 2. saligaud m, salaud m. 3. ivrogne*, sac m à vin.

piss-taker [ˈpis-teikər] (noun), P: blagueur m, persifleur m; cf. mick(e)y-taker; piss¹, 2.

piss-tank [ˈpis-tæŋk] (noun), P: = piss-pot, 3.

pit [pit] (noun), P: 1. lit*, pageot m. 2. poche* intérieure d'un vêtement, profonde f. Voir aussi fleapit.

pitch¹ [pitʃ] (noun), P: 1. «paroisse» f d'une prostituée*, chasse gardée. 2. le «mâle» dans un couple homosexuel, chauffeur m. 3. discours*, boniment m, speech m; laïus m; to make a p., bonimenter, pleurer misère. Voir aussi queer³ (to), 1.

pitch² [pitʃ] (to), F: to be in there pitching, y aller de tout son saoul, se décarcasser. Voir aussi fly-pitch (to); yarn¹.

pitcher [ˈpitʃər] (noun) (Austr.), F: = bugler, 1. Voir aussi fly-pitcher.

pitch in [pitʃˈin] (to), F: 1. s'empiffrer, s'en mettre plein la lampe. 2. se mettre au travail*, embrayer, rentrer dans le mastic, s'y mettre. 3. donner de l'argent*, les abouler, filer à la manche.

pitch into [pitʃˈintuː] (to), F: 1. attaquer*, tomber sur le poil de (qn), rentrer dans le lard à (qn). 2. réprimander*, attraper, secouer les puces à (qn).

pix¹ [piks] (noun) (U.S.), P: pédéraste*, lope f.

pix² [piks] (pl. noun) (=pictures) (U.S.), F: (a) film m; cinéma m, cinoche m; (b) images f.pl., illustrations f.pl.

pixil(l)ated [ˈpiksileitid] (adj.), F: 1. un peu fou*, cinglé. 2. (U.S.) ivre*, bit(t)uré, rétamé.

place¹ [pleis] (noun), F: 1. to go places, (a) voir du pays et du monde; (b) réussir dans la vie, monter les échelons, faire un boum. 2. come and lunch at our p., venez déjeuner chez nous.

place² [pleis] (to), F: I can't p. him, je ne le remets pas.

plain [plein] (adv.), F: p. daft (or dumb), bête* comme chou, complètement borné.

plank [plæŋk] (to), F: = plonk² (to).

plant¹ [plɑːnt] (noun), P: 1. faux-frère m, pisteur m, chevilleur m. 2. piège m, amarre f, duperie f, roustissure f. 3. fabrication f de faux témoignage, boucanade f. 4. planque (voulue ou délibérée). 5. cachette*, lieu sûr, planque f, planquouse f.

plant² [plɑːnt] (to). 1. F: to p. s.o., planter qn, laisser qn en plan. 2. F: to p. sth., cacher* qch., mettre qch. en planque. 3. P: enterrer, mettre dans le royaume des taupes, faire manger les pissenlits par la racine. 4. P: donner, flanquer, foutre (un coup* à qn). 5. F: to p. oneself in front of s.o., se planter devant qn; to p. oneself on s.o., s'implanter chez qn.

plaster [ˈplɑːstər] (to), P: 1. battre*, rosser, rouer de coups*, filer une pâtée à (qn). 2. battre (un adversaire) à plate(s) couture(s). 3. bombarder, tabasser.

plastered [ˈplɑːstəd] (adj.), P: ivre*, rétamé, blindé, fadé.

plastering [ˈplɑːstəriŋ] (noun), F: 1. volée f de coups*, pâtée f, raclée f. 2. défaite f, raclée f. 3. (mil.) bombardement m d'artillerie lourde, artiflottage m. 4. (mil.) bombardement m de saturation.

plate¹ [pleit] (noun). 1. F: to have plenty (or a lot) on one's p., avoir du pain sur la planche, avoir de quoi faire. 2. P: plates (of meat) (R.S. = feet), pieds*. 3. F: to give (or hand) s.o. sth. on a p., le servir sur un plateau, l'offrir tout rôti.

plate² [pleit] (to), V: manger, sucer (coït buccal*).

play¹ [plei] (noun), F: to make a p. for s.o., sth., user de tout son talent (ou de tout son charme) pour obtenir qch. ou pour séduire qn, faire du gringue (ou du palass), faire du charme. Voir aussi horseplay.

play² [plei] (to), F: 1. to p. with oneself, se masturber*, jouer de la mandoline, faire cinq contre un. 2. don't p. games with me! ne te paye pas ma tête! ne me fais pas marcher! ne me fais pas tourner en bourrique! n'essaie pas de me rouler! Voir aussi ball¹, 3; cool²; fool²; Harry, 2; safe²; sucker², 1.

play about (or around) [ˈpleiəˈbaut,

ˈpleiəˈraund] (to), F: 1. to p. a. with
women, courir le jupon, juponner.
2. don't p. a. with me! = don't play
games with me! (play² (to), 2).

play-act [ˈplei-ækt] (to), F: faire du
théâtre, jouer la comédie (fig.).

play along [ˈpleiəlɔŋ] (to), F: to p. a.
with s.o., être de mèche (ou en cheville)
avec qn, aller de barre avec qn.

playboy [ˈpleibɔi] (noun), F: homme
riche* qui aime s'amuser, grand viveur,
noceur m, playboy m.

played out [ˈpleidˈaut] (adj.). 1. F:
très fatigué*, vanné, éreinté. 2. F:
vieux jeu, démodé. 3. F: banal, usé,
rebattu. 4. P: très pauvre*, sans le sou,
dans la purée, décavé, à sec.

playgirl [ˈpleigəːl] (noun), F: femme*
qui aime s'amuser, bambocheuse f,
noceuse f.

play up [ˈpleiˈʌp] (to), F: 1. my rheumatism is playing me up, mes douleurs me
font mal. 2. ennuyer*, asticoter, enquiquiner. 3. to p. sth. u., monter qch. en
épingle, faire ressortir qch. 4. to p. u.
to s.o., (a) flatter* qn, lécher les
bottes à qn, pommader qn; (b) collaborer avec qn, baronner qn.

pleb¹ [pleb], plebby [ˈplebi] (adj.), P:
vulgaire, populo, populmiche.

pleb² [pleb] (noun), P: faubourien m,
prolo m.

plenty [ˈplenti] (adv.), F: it's p. good
enough, ça suffit grandement; it's p.
big enough, c'est bien assez gros.

plonk¹ [plɔŋk] (noun), F: vin* ordinaire,
gros rouge, vinasse f, décapant m.

plonk² [plɔŋk] (to), F: (a) mettre,
flanquer, coller, ficher; to p. money
on a horse, miser sur un cheval*;
(b) laisser tomber lourdement.

plonker [ˈplɔŋkər] (noun), P: pénis*,
défonceuse f, dardillon m; to pull
one's p., se masturber*, s'astiquer (la
colonne).

plonko [ˈplɔŋkou] (noun), P: ivrogne*,
sac m à vin; cf. wino.

plonk out [ˈplɔŋkˈaut] (to), P: (a)
payer*, les allonger, les abouler; (b)
placer de l'argent*.

plough¹ [plau] (noun), F: échec m (à
un examen), recalade f, recalage m.

plough² [plau] (to), F: to p. an exam-
(ination), échouer*, être recalé (ou
collé) à un examen. Voir aussi deep².

ploughed (U.S.: plowed) [plaud] (adj.),
P: ivre*, blindé, bourré (à zéro).

plough (U.S.: plow) into [ˈplauˈintuː]
(to), F: to p. i. s.o. = to pitch into s.o.

ploy [plɔi] (noun), F: stratagème m,
roublardise f.

plug¹ [plʌg] (noun). 1. F: publicité f,
battage m, postiche f, coup m de pouce.
2. P: to give s.o. a p. (in the earhole),
donner* (ou foutre) une beigne (ou une
baffe) à qn. 3. P: balle* (arme à feu),
bastos f, pastille f. 4. (U.S.) F: cheval*
médiocre, canasson m, bourrin m.
5. F: to pull the p. on sth., faire échouer*
qch.; to pull the p. on s.o., couler qn
(à fond).

plug² [plʌg] (to). 1. F: (a) faire de la
réclame (ou du battage); (b) promouvoir
(qch.). 2. P: coïter* avec (une femme),
fourrer, égoïner. 3. P: battre*, frapper,
rosser (qn). 4. F: = plug away (to),
1, 2. 5. P: fusiller, flinguer, flingoter (qn).

plug away [ˈplʌgəˈwei] (to), F: 1.
travailler* dur, turbiner, bûcher. 2.
s'acharner, s'obstiner.

plugger [ˈplʌgər] (noun), F: 1. agent m
de publicité, posticheur m, promoteur
m de vente. 2. trimeur m, turbineur
m, bûcheur m, coltineur m.

plug-ugly [ˈplʌgʌgli] (noun) (U.S.), F:
vaurien*, affreux m, charogne f, dur m.

plum [plʌm] (noun), F: 1. travail* facile
et bien rétribué, boulot m en or (ou
aux petits oignons), filon m. 2. assiette
f au beurre, vache f à lait.

plumb [plʌm] (adv.), F: p. crazy, fou* à
lier.

plumbing [ˈplʌmiŋ] (noun), F: to have
a look at the p., aller aux W.C.*, faire
pipi.

plummy [ˈplʌmi] (adj.), F: 1. (travail,
etc.) agréable, bien payé, bath, en or.
2. (voix) profonde, caverneuse.

plunge¹ [plʌndʒ] (noun), F: to take the
p., prendre le taureau par les cornes,
plonger au large.

plunge² [plʌndʒ] (to), F: jouer gros jeu,
se mouiller.

plunger [ˈplʌndʒər] (noun), F: joueur
m de grosse mise, ponte m.

plunk¹ [plʌŋk] (noun) (U.S.), P: 1.
dollar m. 2. coup* bien asséné, une
bonne beigne.

plunk² [plʌŋk] (to) (U.S.), P: = plug²
(to), 5.

---

* An asterisk indicates that the word so marked is included as a head-word in the Appendix.

plushy [ˈplʌʃi] (*adj.*), *F:* riche*, rupin, époustouflant.

plute [pluːt] (*abbr.* = *plutocrat*), *F:* plutocrate *m*, rupin(os) *m*.

po [pou] (*noun*), *F:* pot *m* de chambre, Jules; *cf.* **po-faced**.

pock [pɔk] (*noun*), *P:* **the p.** = (the) pox.

pod [pɔd] (*noun*), *P:* 1. (*a*) marijuana *f* (*drogues**), thé vert; (*b*) cigarette* de marijuana, stick *m*. 2. **to be in p.**, être enceinte*, être en cloque; *cf.* **pod up** (**to**). 3. ventre*, bidon *m*, bide *m*; *cf.* **podge, 2** (*b*).

podge [pɔdʒ] (*noun*), *F:* 1. individu gros*, bouboule *m*, patapouf *m*. 2. (*a*) graisse *f*, gras-double *m*, pneu *m* Michelin; (*b*) bedaine *f*, panse *f*.

pod up [ˈpɔdˈʌp] (**to**), *P:* cloquer (*femme enceinte*); *cf.* **pod, 2**.

po-faced [ˈpouˈfeist] (*adj.*), *P:* avec une figure* d'enterrement (*ou* de bedeau).

point [pɔint] (*noun*), *P:* shooteuse *f* (*piqûre de drogues*).

poison [ˈpɔizn] (*noun*), *F:* 1. **name your p.!** qu'est-ce que tu veux boire? 2. **to put the p. in**, empoisonner l'esprit de qn (contre qn), semer le venin. *Voir aussi* **rat**¹, **5**.

poke¹ [pouk] (*noun*), *P:* 1. coït*, bourre *f*, coup *m* d'arbalète. 2. **to take a p. at s.o.**, donner (*ou* filer *ou* foutre) une taloche à qn. 3. portefeuille*, lazingue *m*. *Voir aussi* **cow-poke; pig**¹, **6; slowpoke.**

poke² [pouk] (**to**), *P:* 1. coïter* avec (une femme), bourrer, filer un coup d'arbalète à (une femme). 2. **to p. s.o.** = **to take a poke at s.o.** (**poke**¹, **2**). *Voir aussi* **nose, 1**.

poke around (*or* **about**) [ˈpoukəˈbaut, ˈpoukəˈraund] (**to**), *F:* fouiller, farfouiller.

poker [ˈpoukər] (*noun*), *P:* (*université*) (*a*) masse *f* universitaire; (*b*) massier *m*, appariteur *m*. *Voir aussi* **strip**¹, **2**.

pokey [ˈpouki] (*noun*) (*U.S.*), *F:* prison*, trou *m*, boîte *f*, coffre *m*. *Voir aussi* **hokey-pokey.**

pole [poul] (*noun*), *F:* 1. **to go up the p.**, devenir fou*, partir du ciboulot, perdre la boule (*ou* la boussole). 2. **to drive s.o. up the p.**, rendre qn fou*, lui faire perdre la boule (*ou* le ciboulot *ou* le nord). 3. **I wouldn't touch it with a ten-foot p.** = **I wouldn't touch it with a**

barge-pole, *q.v. Voir aussi* **bean-pole; flag-pole.**

polisher [ˈpɔliʃər] (*noun*) (*Austr.*), *P:* échappé *m* de prison*, gibier *m* de potence. *Voir aussi* **apple-polisher.**

polish off [ˈpɔliʃˈɔf] (**to**), *F:* 1. tuer*, dégommer, démolir, liquider. 2. terminer, liquider, boucler. 3. achever (un plat, une bouteille), solder, nettoyer.

pom [pɔm] (*noun*). 1. *F:* (*abbr.* = *Pomeranian*) loulou *m* (de Poméranie). 2. (*Austr.*) *P:* (*péj.*) = **pommy**².

pommy¹ [ˈpɔmi] (*adj.*) (*Austr.*), *F:* anglais, engliche.

pommy², **Pommy** [ˈpɔmi] (*noun*) (*Austr.*), *F:* Anglais *m*, Engliche *m*.

ponce¹ [pɔns] (*noun*), *P:* souteneur*, marle *m*, marlou *m*, marloupin *m*.

ponce² [pɔns] (**to**), *P:* 1. se conduire comme un souteneur*. 2. mendier*, taper, torpiller, pilonner; **to p. a smoke from s.o.**, taper qn d'une cigarette*.

ponce off [ˈpɔnsˈɔf] (**to**), *P:* partir*, plaquouser, se trotter; **p. o.!** fous le camp! décampe! file!

ponce up [ˈpɔnsˈʌp] (**to**), *P:* **to get ponced up**, **to p. oneself u.**, se mettre sur son trente et un.

poncy [ˈpɔnsi] (*adj.*), *P:* **a p. individual**, un individu* qui semble se faire entretenir par les femmes, maquereau *m* sur les bords.

pond, Pond [pɔnd] (*noun*), *F:* 1. **the P.** = **the Herring Pond** (**herring, 2**). 2. **the frog p.**, caste enrichie de la société, les B.O.F.'s, les deux cents familles. *Voir aussi* **fish-pond.**

pong¹ [pɔŋ] (*noun*), *P:* ce qui sent* mauvais; puanteur *f*, (s)chlingage *m*.

pong² [pɔŋ] (**to**), *P:* sentir* mauvais; puer, (s)chlinguer, cocoter.

pongo [ˈpɔŋgou] (*noun*), *P:* (*argot de la Marine*) soldat*, bidasse *m*; fusilier marin, chie-dans-l'eau *m*.

ponk¹ [pɔŋk] (*noun*), *P:* = **pong**¹.

ponk² [pɔŋk] (**to**), *P:* = **pong**² (**to**).

pontoon [pɔnˈtuːn] (*noun*), *P:* 21 mois de prison.

pony [ˈpouni] (*noun*), *P:* 1. 25 livres sterling. 2. petit verre de liqueur, bourgeron *m*.

poo¹ [puː] (*noun*), *F:* excrément *m*, caca *m*.

---

* L'astérisque indique que le mot marqué de ce signe figure comme entrée dans le Répertoire.

poo² [pu:] (to), *F:* déféquer*, faire caca.

pooch [pu:tʃ], **poochy** ['pu:tʃi] (*noun*), *P:* (*a*) chien* (bâtard), cabot *m*; (*b*) chien* favori, toutou *m*.

poodle on ['pu:dl'ɔn] (to), *F:* bavasser, jacasser, jaspiner.

poof [puf, pu:f] (*pl.* **poofs** *or* **pooves** [pufs, pu:fs, pu:vz]), **poofdah** ['pufdɑ:], **poofter** ['puftər], **poofty** ['pufti] (*noun*), *P:* pédéraste*, empaffé *m*, empapaouté *m*.

poofy ['pufi, 'pu:fi] (*adj.*), *P:* à tendance homosexuelle, pédé sur les bords.

pooh! [pu:] (*excl.*), *F:* **1.** ça pue! **2.** (*expression de dédain*) quelle affaire! la belle affaire!

poop [pup, pu:p] (*noun*). **1.** *P:* individu bête*, ballot *m*, baluchard *m*. **2.** *P:* excrément *m*, merde *f*. **3.** (*U.S.*) *F:* renseignement*, rencard *m*; **to know the (latest) p.**, être dans le vent (*ou* à la coule); **p. sheet**, formulaire *m* de renseignements, rencardage *m*.

pooped (out) ['pu:pt('aut)] (*adj.*), *P:* très fatigué*, éreinté, épuisé, exténué.

poor [puər, pɔər, pɔ:r] (*adj.*), *F:* **to take a p. view (of sth.)** = **to take a dim view (of sth.)** (**dim**, **1**). *Voir aussi* **piss-poor**.

poorly ['puəli, 'pɔəli, 'pɔ:li] (*adj.*), *F:* malade*, patraque, pas dans son assiette; *voir aussi* **proper**.

poove [pu:v] (*noun*), *P:* = **poof**.

poovy ['pu:vi] (*adj.*), *P:* = **poofy**.

pop¹ [pɔp] (*noun*). **1.** *F:* (*a*) **p. (music)**, musique *f* pop, yé-yé *m*; **p. singer**, chanteur *m* de pop; **p. song**, chanson *f* en vogue (*ou* du moment); **top of the pops**, palmarès *m* de la chanson, hit-parade *m*; **p. art**, le pop'art. **2.** *F:* père*, papa; vieux *m*, croulant *m*. **3.** *F:* boisson pétillante. **4.** *P:* = **poppy**. **5.** *P:* piqûre (de drogue) intermittente *ou* pour le plaisir; *cf.* **joy-pop; joy-popper. 6.** (*Austr.*) *F:* **to give sth. a p.**, s'attaquer à qch., faire un essai. **7.** *F:* **to be in p.**, être chez ma tante (*ou* au clou).

pop² [pɔp] (to). **1.** *P:* injecter (une drogue), shooter; *cf.* **joy-pop; skin-pop** (to). **2.** *F:* **to p. the question**, proposer le mariage* (à une femme). **3.** *P:* avoir un orgasme*, décharger, dégorger. **4.** *F:* mettre en gage (*ou* chez ma tante *ou* au clou).

pop along ['pɔpə'lɔn] (to), *F:* **1.** aller voir qn, faire un saut (chez qn). **2.** = **pop off** (to), **1**.

popcorn ['pɔpkɔ:n] (*noun*), *F:* = **corn**, **1, 2, 3**.

pop-eyed ['pɔpaid] (*adj.*), *F:* (*a*) aux yeux protubérants (*ou* saillants); (*b*) aux yeux en boules de loto.

pop in ['pɔp'in] (to), *F:* (*a*) entrer en passant; (*b*) entrer à l'improviste.

pop off ['pɔp'ɔf] (to), *F:* **1.** partir*, filer, déguerpir. **2.** mourir* (subitement); **he just popped off**, il n'a pas fait couic. **3.** tuer*, but(t)er, estourbir; **to get popped off**, se faire tuer*. **4. to p. o. a gun**, lâcher un coup de fusil.

pop out ['pɔp'aut] (to), *F:* sortir (de la maison, *etc.*) pour peu de temps, faire un saut dehors; **I saw him p. o. of the house**, je l'ai vu sortir.

pop outside ['pɔpaut'said] (to), *F:* aller faire pipi.

pop over ['pɔp'ouvər] (to), *F:* = **pop along** (to), **1**.

poppa ['pɔpə] (*noun*) (*U.S.*), *F:* = **pop**¹, **2**.

popper ['pɔpər] (*noun*). **1.** *P:* = **amy. 2.** *F:* bouton *m* (à) pression. *Voir aussi* **joy-popper; lid-popper; skin-popper.**

poppet ['pɔpit] (*noun*), *F:* (*a*) petit(e) chéri(e), petit chou; (*b*) enfant* adorable, chérubin *m*.

popping ['pɔpin] (*noun*), *P:* (**skin**) **p.**, piqûre subcutanée de drogue.

poppy ['pɔpi] (*noun*), *P:* opium *m* (*drogues**), pavot *m*, fée brune.

poppycock ['pɔpikɔk] (*noun*), *F:* bêtises*, idioties *f.pl.*, fadaises *f.pl.*

pop round ['pɔp'raund] (to), *F:* faire une petite visite à qn.

popsy ['pɔpsi] (*noun*). **1.** *F:* petite amie, petite chérie. **2.** *P:* = **amy.**

pop up ['pɔp'ʌp] (to), *F:* apparaître, surgir, émerger.

porky ['pɔ:ki] (*adj.*), *F:* **1.** gros* et gras, gravos. **2.** (*U.S.*) très mauvais*, blèche, loquedu. **3.** (*U.S.*) en colère*, ronchonnant.

porn [pɔ:n], **porno** ['pɔ:nou] (*noun*), *F:* porno(graphie) *f*.

porn-shop ['pɔ:n-ʃɔp] (*noun*), *F:* boutique* érotique, sex(e)-shop *f*.

porridge ['pɔridʒ] (*noun*), *P:* **to dish out the p.**, ne pas y aller avec le dos de la cuiller, y aller carrément; (*d'un juge*) condamner au maximum; **to eat** (*or* **do**)

---

* An asterisk indicates that the word so marked is included as a head-word in the Appendix.

p., purger sa peine en prison*, être mis au frais.

port [pɔːt] (*noun*) (*Austr.*), *F:* valise *f*, valoche *f*.

posh¹ [pɔʃ] (*adj.*), *F:* élégant*, chic.

posh² [pɔʃ] (*adv.*) **to talk p.**, faire des phrases.

posh up [ˈpɔʃˈʌp] (**to**), *F:* **to p. oneself u.**, se pomponner, se bichonner; **all poshed up**, sur son trente et un.

possum [ˈpɔsəm] (*noun*) (=*opossum*), *F:* **to play p.**, (*a*) faire le mort; (*b*) se tenir coi.

posted [ˈpoustid] (*p.p.*), *F:* **to keep s.o. p.**, tenir qn au courant (*ou* au parfum).

pot¹ [pɔt] (*noun*), *F:* **I.** (*a*) marijuana *f* (*drogues**), pot *m*; (*b*) cigarette* de marijuana, joint *m*, kif *m*; (*c*) hachisch *m* (*drogues**); **p. party**, séance collective au hachisch *ou* à la marijuana. **2. a big p.**, (*a*) (=*pot-belly*) ventre*, bide *m*, bedaine *f*, brioche *f*; (*b*) = **big noise** (**big¹**, **I**). **3. to go to p.**, tomber en décrépitude, aller à la ruine, aller à la dérive; **he's gone to p.**, il est fichu; **his plans went (all) to p.**, ses projets sont tombés à l'eau. **4. pots of money**, une abondance* (*ou* une tapée) d'argent*; **to make pots of money**, gagner gros, gagner des mille et des cents. **5.** trophée *m*, coupe *f*. **6.** (*pl.*) (=*potatoes*) pommes *f.pl.* de terre, patates *f.pl.* **7.** = **kitty, 2** (*a*). *Voir aussi* **fusspot; glue-pot; jackpot; pisspot; sexpot; shitpot; stinkpot; swillpot; tinpot; toss-pot.**

pot² [pɔt] (**to**), *F:* **I. to p. a child**, asseoir un enfant sur le pot de chambre. **2. to p. at sth.**, tirer sur une cible peu éloignée.

potato [pəˈteitou, pəˈteitə] (*noun*). **I.** *P:* trou *m* dans une chaussette, patate *f*. **2.** *F:* **small potatoes**, (*a*) de la petite bière; (*b*) personnes *ou* choses insignifiantes, racaille *f*, gnognot(t)e *f*. **3.** (*U.S.*) **hot p.**, (*a*) *F:* casse-tête (chinois); (*b*) *F:* affaire épineuse; (*c*) *P:* = **hot patootie** (*voir* **patootie**). *Voir aussi* **cold¹, 6; drop² (to), I; sack¹, 2.**

pot-boiler [ˈpɔtbɔilər] (*noun*), *F:* abattage *m*, ticket *m* de pain.

pothead [ˈpɔthed] (*noun*), *P:* habitué(e) de la marijuana; amateur *m* de hachisch; *cf.* **pot¹, I.**

pot-luck [ˈpɔtˈlʌk] (*noun*), *F:* **to take**

p.-l., choisir au hasard (*ou* à l'aventure), y aller au petit bonheur.

pot-shot [ˈpɔtʃɔt] (*noun*), *F:* (*a*) **to take a p.-s. at sth.**, faire qch. au petit bonheur; (*b*) **to take a p.-s. at s.o.**, *s.o.*, lâcher à l'aveuglette un coup de fusil à qch., qn.

potted¹ [ˈpɔtid] (*adj.*), *F:* abrégé, épitomé.

potted² (**up**) [ˈpɔtid(ˈʌp)] (*adj.*) (*U.S.*), *P:* **I.** ivre*, rond, rondibé, rétamé. **2.** drogué*, camé, chargé.

pottie [ˈpɔti] (*noun*), *F:* = **potty².**

potty¹ [ˈpɔti] (*adj.*), *F:* **I. to go p.**, devenir fou* (*ou* maboul(e)). **2. to be p. about** (*or* **on**) **s.o., sth.**, être mordu pour (*ou* toqué de) qn, qch., en pincer pour qn, qch. **3.** minable, insignifiant.

potty² [ˈpɔti] (*noun*), *F:* pot *m* de chambre (d'enfant).

poufdah [ˈpufdɑː], **pouff** [puf] (*noun*), *P:* = **poof.**

pound [paund] (**to**), *P:* (*a*) coïter*, aller à la bourre, bourriquer; (*b*) coïter* avec (une femme), bourrer, dérouiller.

powder [ˈpaudər] (*noun*), *P:* **I. to do** (*or* **take**) **a p.**, (*a*) déserter (de l'armée), faire chibis; (*b*) s'enfuir*, prendre la poudre d'escampette. **2.** cocaïne *f* (*drogues**), poudrette *f*. *Voir aussi* **birdie-powder; joy-powder.**

powder-room [ˈpaudəˈruːm] (*noun*), *F:* W.C.*, toilette *f*.

power-house [ˈpauəhaus] (*noun*), *F:* individu* dynamique.

pow-wow [ˈpauwau] (*noun*), *F:* = **palaver¹, I.**

pox [pɔks] (*noun*), *P:* (**the**) **p.**, syphilis*, (s)chtouille *f*, lazziloffe *f*.

poxed (**up**) [ˈpɔkst(ˈʌp)] (*adj.*), *P:* **p. (u.) (to the eyebrows)**, naze(broque) poivré, plombé.

prance about (*or* **around**) [ˈprɑːnsəˈbaut, ˈprɑːnsəˈraund] (**to**), *F:* **I.** caracoler, trépigner de colère*, piaffer. **2.** se pavaner, poser.

prang¹ [præŋ] (*noun*), *F:* **I.** exploit *m*, coup fumant. **2.** raid *m* de bombardement. **3.** collision *f*, crash *m*, emboutissage *m*.

prang² [præŋ] (**to**), *F:* **I.** bombarder, tabasser. **2.** emboutir, bousiller (un avion, une auto, *etc.*).

prat [præt] (*noun*), *P:* **I.** fesses*, derche *m*, popotin *m*. **2.** vagin*, con *m*,

---

* L'astérisque indique que le mot marqué de ce signe figure comme entrée dans le Répertoire.

conasse *f*, cramouille *f*. 3. individu bête*, couillon *m*.

preachify ['priːtʃifai] (to), *F*: sermonner.

preachy ['priːtʃi] (*adj*.), *F*: sermonneur, tartuffeur.

preggers ['pregəz] (*adj*.), *P*: (**Harry**) p., enceinte*, en cloque.

pretty-pretty ['priti-priti] (*adj*.), *F*: tout plein coquet, fanfreluché, affété.

previous ['priːvjəs] (*adv*.), *F*: trop tôt, trop vite*; **you're a bit p., aren't you?** tu y vas un peu fort?

priceless ['praislis] (*adj*.), *F*: 1. très amusant*, impayable. 2. très bête*, unique.

pricey ['praisi] (*adj*.), *F*: cher*, chérot, coûteux, salé.

prick [prik] (*noun*), *V*: 1. pénis*, pine *f*. 2. vaurien*, sale coco *m*, couillon *m*. 3. **a spare p.**, un pas grand-chose, un bon à rien, un cautère sur une jambe de bois; **to feel like a spare p. at a wedding,** *c.p.*, être un onguent miton mitaine. *Voir aussi* **pin-pricks**.

prick-tease ['prik-tiːz], **prick-teaser** ['prik-tiːzər] (*noun*), *V*: allumeuse *f*, bandeuse *f*, aguicheuse *f*; *cf.* **cockteaser; tease; teaser, 2.**

printed ['printid] (*p.p.*), *P*: **to get p.,** se faire prendre les empreintes digitales, jouer du piano, passer au piano.

printers ['printəz] (*pl. noun*), *P*: **to have the p. in = to have the painters in (painter, 2).**

prissy ['prisi] (*adj*.), *F*: bégueule, collet monté, guindé, chochotte.

prize [praiz] (*adj*.), *F*: **a p. idiot,** un ballot de premier ordre, une andouille enracinée. *Voir aussi* **swill[1], 3.**

pro [prou] (*noun*). 1. *P*: (=*prostitute*) prostituée*, catin *f*, pute *f*. 2. *F*: (=*professional*) professionnel *m*; **he's a real p.,** il n'a rien d'un amateur. 3. *F*: **the pros and cons,** le pour et le contre.

pronto ['prɔntou] (*adv*.), *F*: vite*, illico, presto.

prop [prɔp] (*noun*), *P*: épingle *f* de cravate. *Voir aussi* **props.**

proper ['prɔpər] (*adv*.), *F*: vraiment, extrêmement; **p. poorly,** vraiment malade*. *Voir aussi* **champion, 1.**

prop-man ['prɔpmæn] (*noun*), *F*: = **props, 2.**

proposition [prɔpə'ziʃ(ə)n] (to), *F*: 1.

proposer un plan ou un projet à (qn). 2. **to p. a woman,** faire des propositions indécentes à une femme, proposer la botte à une femme.

props [prɔps] (*noun*), *F*: 1. (*pl.*) (*th.*) accessoires *m.pl.*, bouts *m.pl.* de bois. 2. (*sing.*) accessoiriste *mf*. *Voir aussi* **prop.**

prop up ['prɔp'ʌp] (to), *F*: **to p. u. the bar,** boire dans un bar, être accoudé au zinc.

pross [prɔs], **prossie, prossy** ['prɔsi], **prostie, prosty** ['prɔsti] (*noun*), *P*: prostituée*, pute *f*, putain *f*.

proud [praud] (*adv*.), *F*: 1. **to do s.o. p.,** (*a*) recevoir qn comme un roi, traiter qn à la hauteur; (*b*) se mettre en frais pour qn. 2. **to do oneself p.,** (*a*) faire un bon travail*, se montrer à la hauteur; (*b*) se bien soigner, ne se priver de rien.

prowl [praul] (*noun*), *F*: **to be on the p.,** chercher les aventures (amoureuses), chercher les bonnes fortunes.

prowl-car ['praul-kɑːr] (*noun*), *F*: voiture *f* de police, voiture-pie *f*.

pseudo ['sjuːdou] (*adj*.), *F*: pseudo, insincère, faux.

psycho[1] ['saikou] (*adj*.), *P*: fou*, dérangé, détraqué, dévissé.

psycho[2] ['saikou] (*noun*), *F*: 1. psycho-(pathe) *mf*. 2. (*a*) psychanalyste *mf*; (*b*) psychiatre *mf*.

p.t., P.T. ['piː'tiː] (*abbr*.), *P*: = **prick-tease(r)**; *cf.* **C.T.**

pub [pʌb] (*noun*), *F*: bistro(t) *m*, pub *m*.

pubbing ['pʌbiŋ] (*verbal noun*), *F*: **to go p.,** faire la tournée des bistro(t)s, godailler.

pub-crawl[1] ['pʌbkrɔːl] (*noun*), *F*: tournée *f* des bistro(t)s.

pub-crawl[2] ['pʌbkrɔːl] (to), *F*: = **to go pubbing.**

pub-crawler ['pʌbkrɔːlər] (*noun*), *F*: coureur *m* de bistro(t)s, vadrouilleur *m*.

pud [pud] (*noun*) (*abbr.* = *pudding*), *F*: 1. pudding *m*. 2. dessert *m*.

pudding ['pudiŋ, 'pudn] (*noun*), *P*: **to pull one's p.,** se masturber*, se l'allonger, s'astiquer (la colonne). *Voir aussi* **club, 2.**

pudding-face ['pudiŋfeis, 'pudnfeis] (*noun*), *F*: visage* empâté, pleine lune.

puddinghead ['pudiŋhed, 'pudnhed]

---

* An asterisk indicates that the word so marked is included as a head-word in the Appendix.

(*noun*), *F:* individu bête*, gourde *f*, empoté *m*.

puff[1] [pʌf] (*noun*), *F:* **1. to be out of p.**, être hors d'haleine, être essoufflé. **2. never in all my p.!** jamais de la vie! **3.** critique *f* favorable, battage *m*, puffisme *m*. *Voir aussi* **creampuff**.

puff[2] [pʌf] (**to**), *F:* prôner, vanter.

puffer(-train) [ˈpʌfər(trein)], **puff-puff** [ˈpʌfpʌf] (*noun*), *F:* (*langage enfantin*) teuf-teuf *m*.

pug [pʌg] (*noun*), *P:* pugiliste *m*, boxeur *m*.

puka [ˈpuːkə] (*noun*) (*U.S.*), *P:* vulve*, fente *f*, crac *m*.

puke [pjuːk] (*noun*), *P:* vomissement *m*, dégobillade *f*, fusée *f*, dégueulis *m*.

pukka [ˈpʌkə] (*adj.*), *F:* **p. sahib** [sɑːb], un vrai monsieur, un vrai gentleman. *Voir aussi* **gen**.

pull[1] [pul] (*noun*). **1.** *P:* coït*, carambolage *m*. **2.** *F:* influence *f*, piston *m*, bras long. *Voir aussi* **leg-pull**.

pull[2] [pul] (**to**). **1.** *P:* coïter* avec (une femme), caramboler; *voir aussi* **train**. **2.** *F:* **to p. a gun**, sortir un revolver*. *Voir aussi* **bell, 2; leg**[1], **5; one, 4; plonker; pudding; rank; wire, 2, 8; yarn**[1].

pull-in [ˈpulin] (*noun*), *F:* café* des routiers.

pull in [ˈpulˈin] (**to**), *F:* **1.** arrêter*, embarquer, choper. **2.** exécuter, réaliser. **3.** s'arrêter, faire une étape.

pull off [ˈpulˈɔf] (**to**). **1.** *F:* **to p. o. a deal**, réussir une opération, boucler une affaire. **2.** *P:* se masturber*, s'astiquer (la colonne).

pull out [ˈpulˈaut] (**to**), *F:* **1.** partir*, se (re)tirer. **2.** (*U.S.*) se dérober, tirer son épingle du jeu. **3. to p. o. all the stops**, donner un coup de collier, donner le maximum, mettre le paquet. *Voir aussi* **finger**[1], **2**.

pump [pʌmp] (**to**), *F:* **to p. s.o.**, pomper qn (pour avoir des renseignements*). *Voir aussi* **lead**[1], **1**.

pumpkinhead [ˈpʌmpkinhed] (*noun*) (*U.S.*), *F:* individu bête*, nouille *f*, andouille *f*.

punch[1] [pʌntʃ] ⟨*noun*⟩, *F:* **1.** allant *m*, énergie *f*, dynamisme *m*. **2. he didn't pull his punches**, il n'a pas ménagé son adversaire, il n'a pas pris de gants. *Voir aussi* **pack**[2] (**to**), **2**.

Punch[2] [pʌntʃ] (*pr. noun*), *F:* (*a*) (**as**) **proud as P.**, fier comme Artaban; (*b*) (**as**) **pleased as P.**, heureux comme un roi, aux anges.

punch-drunk [ˈpʌntʃˈdrʌŋk] (*adj.*), *F:* ivre de coups, ahuri, hébété (par des coups reçus), groggy.

punch-line [ˈpʌntʃ-lain] (*noun*), *F:* phrase-clef *f* (dans une histoire), astuce *f*, mot *m* de la fin.

punch-up [ˈpʌntʃʌp] (*noun*), *F:* échange *f* de coups de poing, raclée *f*, tabassée *f*.

pundit [ˈpʌndit] (*noun*), *F:* ponte *m*.

punk[1] [pʌŋk] (*adj.*), *P:* de basse qualité, moche, tocard, tarte.

punk[2] [pʌŋk] (*noun*), *P:* **1.** tordu *m*, tête *f* de lard, face *f* de rat, bille *f* de clown. **2.** débutant *m*, novice *m*, bleu *m*, blanc-bec *m*. **3.** pédéraste*, fiotte *f*, tapette *f*. **4.** jeune vaurien*, bizet *m*, fias *m*. **5.** jeune animal *m*, jeune bestiole *f*. **6.** qch. de toc(ard) (*ou* de moche), pacotille *f*, camelote *f*.

punk out [ˈpʌŋkˈaut] (**to**), *P:* se dégonfler, caner.

pup [pʌp] (*noun*), *F:* **to sell s.o. a p.**, escroquer*, faisander, rouler qn. *Voir aussi* **mucky, 2**.

puppy [ˈpʌpi] (*attrib. adj.*), *F:* **1. p. fat**, grassouille *f* du bébé. **2. p. love**, premier amour, amour juvénile.

purler [ˈpəːlər] (*noun*), *F:* **to come a p.**, tomber*, ramasser une bûche, prendre un gadin.

purple [ˈpəːpl] (*adj.*), *P:* **p. hearts**, barbituriques *f.pl.* (*drogues**), mélange barbituré.

purty [ˈpəːrti] (*adj.*) (*mainly U.S.*), *F:* joli, mignon.

push[1] [puʃ] (*noun*). **1.** *P:* bande*, gang *m*, flèche *f*. **2.** *F:* **to give s.o. the p.**, flanquer qn à la porte, sacquer qn; *cf.* **sack**[1], **1. 3.** *F:* **at a p.**, au moment critique, en cas de besoin; **when it comes to the p.**, quand il est question d'agir, au moment de l'exécution.

push[2] [puʃ] (**to**), *F:* **1. to p. drugs**, fourguer des drogues. **2. to p. one's luck**, pousser, aller trop loin, attiger, aller un peu fort. *Voir aussi* **queer**[3], **4**.

push around [ˈpuʃəˈraund] (**to**), *F:* **to p. s.o. a.**, malmener, maltraiter qn, être vache (*ou* chien) avec qn.

push-bike [ˈpuʃbaik] (*noun*), *F:* = **bike, 1**.

---

* L'astérisque indique que le mot marqué de ce signe figure comme entrée dans le Répertoire.

pusher [ˈpuʃər] (*noun*), *F:* 1. fourgueur *m* (*on* pourvoyeur *m*) (de drogues); *cf.* **push**[2] (**to**), 1. 2. ambitieux *m*, arriviste *m*, joueur *m* de coudes. *Voir aussi* **cock-pusher; paper-pusher; pen-pusher.**

pushface [ˈpuʃfeis] (*noun*), *P:* gueule *f* en coin (de rue), gueule de raie, tête *f* de pipe.

push off [ˈpuʃˈɔf] (**to**), *P:* partir*, déguerpir, décamper; **p. o.!** file! débarrasse (le plancher)! fous le camp!

push on [ˈpuʃˈɔn] (**to**), *F:* 1. pousser en avant, activer, faire avancer. 2. pousser, exciter (qn). 3. **to p. o. with sth.**, chauffer une affaire.

pushover [ˈpuʃouvər] (*noun*), (*a*) *F:* qch. de facile, du tout cuit, du tout rôti, du gâteau; (*b*) *P:* femme* facile (*ou* à la cuisse hospitalière *ou* qui donne dans le panneau).

pushy [ˈpuʃi] (*adj.*), *F:* arriviste, plastronneur, poseur.

puss [pus] (*noun*). 1. *F:* chat *m*, minou *m*, minet *m*. 2. *P:* visage*, frime *f*, frimousse *f*. 3. *P:* bouche*, gueule *f*, goule *f*, margoulette *f*. 4. *P:* = **pussy**, 2. *Voir aussi* **angel-puss; drizzle-puss; glamour-puss; sourpuss.**

pussy [ˈpusi] (*noun*). 1. *F:* = **puss**, 1. 2. *P:* vulve*, chat *m*, chatte *f*. 3. *F:* (=*cat-o'-nine-tails*) fouet *m* (à neuf cordes), garcette *f*.

pussyfoot[1] [ˈpusifut] (*noun*) (*U.S.*), *F:* prohibitionniste *m*, partisan *m* du sec.

pussyfoot[2] [ˈpusifut] (**to**) (*U.S.*), *F:* 1. marcher* à pas étouffés (*ou* sur la pointe des pieds). 2. faire patte de velours. 3. ne pas se mouiller, ménager la chèvre et le chou, nager entre deux eaux, zigzaguer.

pussyfooter [ˈpusifutər] (*noun*) (*U.S.*), *F:* qn qui ne veut pas se compromettre (*ou* qui tourne autour du pot), ennemi *m* du oui et du non.

pussyfooting [ˈpusifutiŋ] (*noun*) (*U.S.*) *F:* l'art *m* de ne pas se mouiller.

puta [ˈpuːtə] (*noun*) (*U.S.*), *P:* prostituée*, pute *f*.

put across [ˈputəˈkrɔs] (**to**), *F:* 1. **to p. it a. s.o.**, tromper*, refaire, rouler qn. 2. **to p. it a. to s.o.**, faire comprendre (*ou* piger) à qn, éclairer la lanterne à qn.

put away [ˈputəˈwei] (**to**). 1. *P:* (*boxe*) mettre (qn) knock-out. 2. *F:* **to p. it a. = to tuck it away (tuck away** (**to**), 2). 3. *F:* emprisonner*, faire enfermer, boucler, bloquer. 4. *P:* tuer*, descendre, dessouder, dézinguer. 5. *F:* mettre à côté; *cf.* **rainy.**

put-down [ˈputdaun] (*noun*), *F:* jugement *m* défavorable, éreintage *m*, sabrage *m*.

put-on [ˈputɔn] (*noun*), *F:* bateau *m*, boniment *m*, pilule *f*.

put on [ˈputˈɔn] (**to**), *F:* 1. **to p. it o.**, (*a*) prétendre, en installer, faire de la graisse, faire sa poire; (*b*) exagérer*, charrier, y aller fort; **he puts it on a bit**, il est un peu crâneur. 2. interloquer (qn), brouiller les idées à (qn). 3. **who p. you o. to it?** qui vous a donné le tuyau? *Voir aussi* **ritz.**

put out [ˈputˈaut] (**to**). 1. *F:* déconcerter, décontenancer, embarrasser (qn). 2. (*U.S.*) *P:* (*d'une femme*) avoir la cuisse hospitalière, être tombeuse (*ou* paumée).

putrid [ˈpjuːtrid] (*adj.*), *F:* dégueulasse, dégueulbif, débectant.

put-up [ˈputʌp] (*adj.*), *F:* **a p. u. job**, un coup monté, une affaire bricolée, un micmac.

putz [puts] (*noun*) (*U.S.*), *P:* pénis*, pine *f*, paf *m*.

pyjies [ˈpidʒiz] (*pl. noun*), *F:* pyjama *m*, pyj *m*.

python [ˈpaiθ(ə)n] (*noun*), *P:* **to siphon the p.**, uriner*, égoutter son cyclope.

---

* An asterisk indicates that the word so marked is included as a head-word in the Appendix.

Q

q.t., Q.T. [ˈkjuːˈtiː] (abbr.), F: 1. (= quiet time) petite prière, méditation f. 2. on the (strict) q.t. (=quiet), en douce, discrètement, en sourdine, en confidence; to do sth. on the q.t., faire qch. en cachette (ou à la dérobée); I am telling you on the q.t., je vous dis ça entre nous (ou entre quat'zyeux).

quack [kwæk] (noun), P: the q., le médecin, le toubib, le charlatan.

quack-quack [ˈkwækˈkwæk] (noun), F: (langage enfantin) canard m, coin-coin m.

quad [kwɔd] (noun). 1. F: (=quadrangle) cour carrée (d'une école, université, etc.). 2. P: prison*, boîte f, bloc m, taule f; in q., au bloc, à l'ombre. 3. F: (=quadruplet) quadruplé(e). 4. (U.S.) P: auto f à quatre phares m.pl.; (pl.) les quatre phares d'une auto.

quail [kweil] (noun), P: 1. femme*, fille*, fumelle f, souris f. 2. (U.S.) élève (fille) d'une école mixte.

quarter [ˈkwɔːtər] (noun) (U.S.), F: pièce f de 25 cents.

quean [kwiːn] (noun) P: = queen, 1, 2.

queen [kwiːn] (noun). 1. F: fille* ou femme* séduisante, une beauté, une (petite) reine. 2. P: pédéraste* qui joue le rôle de femme, persilleuse f; an old q., une vieille pédale; dinge q., pédéraste* blanc qui s'accouple de préférence avec des nègres. 3. F: q. bee, femme* active, maîtresse-femme. 4. F: Q. Mary, long véhicule.

queenie [ˈkwiːni] (noun), P: = queen, 2.

queer[1] [kwiər] (adj.). 1. F: homosexuel, pédé. 2. F: to be in q. street, être dans la mélasse, tirer le diable par la queue. 3. F: un peu fou*; q. in the head, maboul(e), loufoque; voir aussi attic; fish[1], 1. 4. P: criminel, suspect, louche. 5. P: faux, contrefait. 6. F: to feel q., se sentir tout chose (ou patraque ou pas dans son assiette).

queer[2] [kwiər] (noun). 1. F: (a) pédéraste*, tante f; (b) lesbienne*, gouine f; voir aussi quim. 2. P: in q.,

dans le pétrin, dans la mélasse. 3. P: on the q., par des moyens louches (ou peu honnêtes). 4. (U.S.) P: monnaie contrefaite, fausse mornifle; to push the q., passer de la fausse monnaie, faire la fournaise.

queer[3] [kwiər] (to), P: 1. déranger, détraquer; to q. the pitch, mettre des bâtons dans les roues, mettre des chaînes dans les engrenages; to q. s.o.'s pitch, contrecarrer qn. 2. to q. oneself with s.o., perdre l'estime de qn, se brouiller avec qn, ne plus être dans les petits papiers de qn. 3. to q. for sth., aimer* qch., en mordre pour qch.

queer-basher [ˈkwiə-bæʃər] (noun), P: chasseur m de pédés.

queer-bashing [ˈkwiə-bæʃiŋ] (noun), P: chasse f aux pédés.

quencher [ˈkwentʃər] (noun), F: boisson f, consommation f; let's have a q., on va boire*, on va se rincer la dalle (ou se mouiller la meule).

queue-jumper [ˈkjuː-dʒʌmpər] (noun), F: qn qui passe avant son tour, resquilleur m.

quick [kwik] (adj.), F: 1. a q. one = quickie, 1, 2. 2. to do sth. in q. order, faire qch. vite* (ou à la hâte ou en cinq secs). Voir aussi double-quick; draw[1], 1; p.d.q.; uptake (a).

quickie, quicky [ˈkwiki] (noun). 1. F: un (petit) verre (ou un (petit) coup) bu en vitesse; to have a q., s'en envoyer un; have a q.? tu prendras vite qch.? 2. P: coït* hâtif; to have a q., s'en envoyer un petit coup. 3. P: prostituée* rapide, pute f à la grouille. 4. F: qch. fait rapidement (ou à la six-quatre-deux); du vite-fait. 5. F: question-éclair f (dans un jeu de devinette). 6. (U.S.) F: grève soudaine et irrationnelle.

quid [kwid] (noun), F: 1. une livre sterling. 2. to be quids in, avoir de la marge, marcher comme sur des roulettes; he's quids in, il a de la chance* (ou du pot).

---

* L'astérisque indique que le mot marqué de ce signe figure comme entrée dans le Répertoire.

quiet[1] [ˈkwaiət] (*adj.*), *F:* **anything for a q. life!** tout ce que tu voudras, mais fiche-moi (*ou* fous-moi) la paix!

quiet[2] [ˈkwaiət] (*noun*), *F:* **on the q.** = **on the q.t. (q.t., 2).**

quiff [kwif] (*noun*). 1. *P:* argent*, pèze *m.* 2. *P:* prostituée* bon marché, pute *f* de la basse. 3. *P:* bon tour, tour de passe-passe. 4. *V:* vulve*, baba *m*, didi *m.* 5. *P:* conseil *m*, avis *m*, tuyau *m.*

quill [kwil] (**to**), *P:* s'efforcer de gagner les bonnes grâces de (qn), lécher les bottes à (qn).

quim [kwim] (*noun*), *VV:* vagin*, grippette *f*, millefeuille *m*; **q. queer,** lesbienne*, goudou *f.*

quin [kwin] (*noun*), *F:* (=*quintuplet*) quintuplé(e).

quince [kwins] (*noun*), *P:* pédéraste*, fiotte *f.*

quit [kwit] (**to**). 1. *F:* abandonner*, lâcher, débarquer, déposer. 2. *P:* **to q. it,** mourir*, se laisser glisser. 3. *P:* **to q. the scene,** (*a*) mourir*, lâcher la rampe; (*b*) partir*, lever l'ancre.

quitter [ˈkwitər] (*noun*), *P:* lâcheur *m*, tire-au-flanc *m.*

quod [kwɔd] (*noun*), *P:* = **quad, 2.**

quote [kwout] (*noun*), *F:* 1. citation *f* (*d'un auteur, etc.*). 2. (*pl.*) guillemets *m.pl.* qui indiquent la citation.

---

* An asterisk indicates that the word so marked is included as a head-word in the Appendix.

R

rab [ræb] (noun), P: tiroir-caisse m.

rabbit[1] ['ræbit] (noun), 1. P: salade f, crudités f.pl. 2. P: bavardage m, jactance f; I never heard anyone with so much r., je n'ai jamais entendu une telle tapette. 3. F: r. punch, le coup du lapin.

rabbit[2] (on) ['ræbit('ɔn)] (to), P: avoir la langue bien pendue, jacter.

rabbity ['ræbiti] (adj.), P: insignifiant, toc, tocard, camelote.

racket[1] ['rækit] (noun), F: 1. to make a r., faire du bruit* (ou du tapage ou du vacarme ou du tintamarre); voir aussi kick up (to). 2. coup fourré, combine f, trafic m louche. 3. to stand the r., (a) payer* les frais m.pl., casquer, essuyer le coup de fusil, payer les pots cassés; (b) tenir le coup. 4. escroquerie*, arnaque f. 5. to go on the r. = to go on the razzle.

racket[2] (about) ['rækit(ə'baut)] (to) F: = to make a racket (racket[1], 1).

rag[1] [ræg] (noun). 1. F: vêtement*; I haven't a r. to wear, je n'ai rien à me mettre; the r. trade, l'industrie f du vêtement, la nipperie; voir aussi glad. 2. P: serviette f hygiénique, tampon m; to be on the r., to have the r. (or rags) on, to have the r. out, avoir ses menstrues*, avoir la rue barrée. 3. F: journal*, canard m, torchon m; local r., la feuille de chou du pays. 4. F: like a red r. to a bull, comme le rouge pour les taureaux. 5. P: to lose one's r., to get one's r. out, se mettre en colère*, voir rouge. 6. P: langue*, chiffe f, chiffon m rouge. 7. F: r., tag and bobtail, la canaille, la merdaille, la chienlit. 8. F: to be in rags and tatters, (fig.) être raté, être dans la mouscaille. 9. F: carnaval m, monôme m d'étudiants, canular m. 10. P: oily r. (R.S. = fag = cigarette), cigarette*, cibiche f. 11. F: to feel like a wet r., se sentir mou comme une chiffe, être une vraie loque. Voir aussi chew (to); dishrag; nose-rag; snitch-rag; snot-rag.

rag[2] [ræg] (to), F: 1. brimer (un camarade). 2. chahuter (un professeur). 3. faire du chahut, railler, persifler.

ragbag ['rægbæg] (noun), F: individu mal vêtu (ou mal ficelé ou mal fagoté), souillon mf, loqueteux m.

raggle ['rægl] (noun) (U.S.), P: pin-up f, allumeuse f.

rag-top ['rægtɔp] (noun), F: voiture f décapotable.

railroad ['reilroud] (to) (U.S.), F: 1. bousculer, tarabuster (qn). 2. se débarrasser* de (qn), faire dinguer (qn) à la boucanade. 3. pousser, bouler (qch.).

rails [reilz] (pl. noun), F: to go off the r., dérailler, être détraqué.

rain [rein] (to), F: it never rains but it pours, c.p., un malheur n'arrive jamais seul.

rainbows ['reinbouz] (pl. noun), P: tuinal m (drogues) barbiturique, tricolore m.

raincheck ['rein-tʃek] (noun) (U.S.), F: invitation remise, partie remise.

rainy ['reini] (adj.), F: to put sth. away (or by) for a r. day, garder une poire pour la soif.

rainy-day ['reinidei] (attrib. adj.), P: r.-d. woman, cigarette* de marijuana (drogues*), joint m, stick m.

rake in ['reik'in] (to), F: to r. it i., gagner* beaucoup d'argent, (le) ramasser à la pelle, faire du pèze.

rake-off ['reikɔf] (noun), F: commission f, ristourne f, pot-de-vin m.

raker ['reikər] (noun) (Austr.), F: to go a r., tomber*, ramasser une bûche (ou un gadin), se casser la figure.

ram[1] [ræm] (noun), P: 1. (Austr.) = shill(aber). 2. individu porté sur le sexe, chaud lapin.

ram[2] [ræm] (to), V: 1. coïter* avec (une femme), égoïner, bourrer. 2. avoir un coït* anal avec (qn), empaffer, enculer (qn). Voir aussi throat, 1.

rambunctious [ræm'bʌŋkʃəs] (adj.), F: tapageur, chahuteur.

---

* L'astérisque indique que le mot marqué de ce signe figure comme entrée dans le Répertoire.

ramp [ræmp] (*noun*), *F:* = **racket**[1], 2.

randy [ˈrændi] (*adj.*), *P:* = **horny** (*b*).

rangoon [rænˈguːn] (*noun*), *P:* cannabis naturel (*drogues**).

rank [ræŋk] (*noun*), *F:* **to pull r.** (**on s.o.**), user et abuser de son rang *ou* de sa position.

rap[1] [ræp] (*noun*), *F:* **1.** réprimande *f*, punition *f*, attrapage *m*, engueulade *f*; **to take the r.**, payer les pots cassés. **2.** condamnation*, gerbage *m*, sape(ment) *m*, sucrage *m*; **murder r.**, accusation *f* de meurtre, dévidage *m* de but(t)e; **to beat the r.**, se faire acquitter (en justice), se soustraire à une amende, déjouer la loi, faire un coup de nib; **to square a r.**, faire enlever une punition *ou* une amende, défarguer. **3. not to care a r.**, s'en ficher éperdument. **4. not to be worth a r.**, ne rien* valoir, ne pas valoir tripette. **5.** (*U.S.*) conversation *f*, bavardage *m*.

rap[2] [ræp] (**to**). **1.** *F:* critiquer*, tancer, bêcher. **2.** *P:* arrêter*, choper, épingler; gerber, sucrer. **3.** *P:* tuer*, but(t)er, bousiller.

rare [reər] (*adj.*), *F:* **we had a r. old time**, on s'en est payé, on s'en est donné à cœur joie.

rarin' [ˈreərin], **raring** [ˈreəriŋ] (*adj.*), *F:* **to be r. to go**, piaffer d'impatience *ou* d'anticipation, être prêt à ruer, attendre le gong.

raspberry [ˈrɑːzb(ə)ri] (*noun*), *P:* **1.** (*a*) pet*, pastille *f*, perlouse *f*; (*b*) bruit *m* avec les lèvres qui imite un pet. **2.** désapprobation *f*, engueulade *f*. **3.** rebuffade *f*, défargage *m*, vidage *m*. **4.** (*a*) **to give s.o. a** (*or* **the**) **r.**, dire zut à qn, faire nargue à qn, envoyer chier qn; (*b*) **to get a r.** (**from s.o.**), se faire rabrouer. *Voir aussi* **flip**[3] (**to**), 2.

rat[1] [ræt] (*noun*). **1.** *F:* sale type *m*, salopard *m*, peau *f* de vache; *cf.* **dirty**[1], 2. **2.** *F:* indicateur*, chacal *m*, chevreuil *m*. **3.** *F:* briseur *m* de grève, jaune *m*, faux frère, gâte-métier *m*. **4.** *F:* **to smell a r.**, sentir qch. de louche, soupçonner anguille sous roche, avoir la puce à l'oreille. **5.** *F:* **r. poison**, alcool* de mauvaise qualité, casse-gueule *m*, camphre *m*, mort-aux-rats *f*. **6.** *F:* **the r. race**, la course au bifteck. **7.** *F:* **to have the rats**, (*a*) être en colère* (*ou* en rogne); (*b*) être en proie au delirium

tremens, voir les rats bleus. **8.** *F:* **rats to you!** zut! va-t-en voir! va donc! sans blague! **9.** *F:* (*mil.*, *W.W.II*) **the Desert Rats**, les Rats du Désert (7ᵉ division blindée en Afrique du Nord). **10.** *P:* logement*, piaule *f*, niche *f*. **11.** *P:* **r. and mouse** (*R.S.* = *house*), maison *f*.

rat[2] [ræt] (**to**), *F:* **1. to r. on s.o.**, (*a*) revenir sur un marché; (*b*) dénoncer*, cafarder, bourdiller qn. **2.** abandonner* ses complices, les lâcher (*ou* plaquer), les laisser en carafe; judasser, renarder.

ratbag [ˈrætbæg] (*noun*), *P:* **1.** vaurien*, sale coco *m*, salaud *m*. **2.** (*Austr.*) excentrique *mf*, original *m*.

rate [reit] (**to**), *F:* **1.** avoir un dû, recevoir son dû, empocher la monnaie de sa pièce. **2.** être coté (*ou* estimé *ou* considéré).

ratfink [ˈrætfiŋk] (*noun*), *P:* sale mouchard *m*, vieille gamelle; *cf.* **fink**[1], 3.

rat out [ˈrætˈaut] (**to**), *P:* partir*, déguerpir.

ratter [ˈrætər] (*noun*), *F:* = **rat**[1], 2, 3.

rattle [ˈrætl] (**to**), *F:* consterner, bouleverser, retourner (qn); **he never gets rattled**, il ne se laisse pas démonter, il ne s'épate jamais.

rattle on [ˈrætlˈɔn] (**to**), *F:* **she does r. o.!** c'est un moulin à paroles, elle a la langue bien pendue.

rattler [ˈrætlər] (*noun*), *F:* **1.** (*chemin de fer*) train *m*, dur *m*. **2.** (*=rattlesnake*) serpent *m* à sonnettes. **3.** personne *ou* chose excellente* (*ou* épatante *ou* super *ou* foutrale). *Voir aussi* **bone-rattler.**

rattling [ˈrætliŋ] (*adj.*), *F:* **1.** vif, déluré, d'attaque. **2.** excellent*, du tonnerre. **3. at a r. pace**, au grand trot.

rat-trap [ˈræt træp] (*noun*), *P:* bouche*, trappe *f*; *cf.* **trap**, 1.

ratty [ˈræti] (*adj.*). **1.** *F:* méchant*, chameau, teigne. **2.** *F:* râleur, ronchonneur, rouscailleur. **3.** (*U.S.*) *P:* (*a*) moche; (*b*) mal soigné; (*c*) délabré.

raunchy [ˈrɔːntʃi] (*adj.*) (*U.S.*), *F:* **1.** vieux*, croulant, bon pour la casse, esquinté. **2.** moche, toc, tocard. **3.** salingue, cracra. **4.** criard. **5.** ivre*, rondibé. *Cf.* **ronchie, ronchy.**

rave[1] [reiv] (*noun*), *F:* **1.** louange *f* enthousiaste, concert *m* de louanges, coup *m* d'encensoir; **r. review**, compte-rendu élogieux. 2. amoureux *m*. 3. béguin *m*, tocade *f*.

rave[2] [reiv] **(to)**, *F:* 1. être dans le vent (*ou* dans le mouvement). 2. s'extasier.

raver [ˈreivər] *(noun)*, *F:* 1. a **(little)** r., une beauté, un prix de Diane. 2. individu* à la mode (*ou* dans le vent).

rave-up [ˈreivʌp] *(noun)*, *F:* **to have a r.-u.**, se déchaîner, sortir de ses gonds.

raw[1] [rɔ:] *(adj.)*, *F:* 1. **it's a r. deal**, il y a de l'abus, c'est dur à avaler; **to give s.o. a r. deal**, en faire voir de dures à qn. 2. **nu***, à poil. 3. risqué, scabreux, cru. 4. **a r. hand**, un novice, un bleu, un mal dégrossi.

raw[2] [rɔ:] *(noun)*, *F:* 1. **to catch s.o. on the r.**, piquer qn au vif, toucher le point sensible de qn. 2. **in the r.**, (*a*) = **raw**[1], 2; (*b*) fruste, brut.

ray [rei] *(noun)*, *F:* **to be s.o.'s little r. of sunshine**, être le rayon de soleil de qn.

razz[1] [ræz] *(noun)* (*U.S.*), *F:* dérision *f*, ridicule *f*; huées *f.pl.*

razz[2] [ræz] **(to)** (*U.S.*), *F:* taquiner, narguer, railler, se moquer* de (qn), se payer la tête de (qn).

razzle [ˈræzl] *(noun)*, *F:* **on the r.**, en réjouissances*; **to go on the r.**, faire la bringue (*ou* la ribouldingue *ou* la noce).

razzle-dazzle[1] [ˈræzldæzl] *(noun)* (*U.S.*), *F:* 1. bouleversement *m*, chambardement *m*, remue-ménage *m*. 2. brouillamini (*ou* micmac) voulu. 3. fraude *f*, supercherie *f*, filouterie *f*, roustissure *f*. 4. agitation *f*, éclat *m*, clinquant *m*, tape-à-l'œil *m*. 5. réjouissances*, bombe *f*, nouba *f*.

razzle-dazzle[2] [ˈræzldæzl] **(to)** (*U.S.*), *F:* éblouir, en mettre plein la vue.

razzmatazz[1] [ˈræzməˈtæz] *(adj.)*, *F:* vieux jeu, usé, rococo, à l'eau de rose.

razzmatazz[2] [ˈræzməˈtæz] *(noun)*, *F:* brouillamini *m*, tape-à-l'œil *m*, clinquant *m*.

reach-me-downs [ˈriːtʃmidaunz] (*pl. noun*), *F:* prêt-à-porter *m*, décrochez-moi-ça *m*; *cf.* **hand-me-downs**.

read [riːd] **(to)**, *F:* 1. **I can r. him like a book**, je le connais comme (le fond de) ma poche, je le lis comme un livre. 2. comprendre, piger.

reader [ˈriːdər] *(noun)*, *P:* 1. (*argot des prisons*) livre *m*, revue *f*, journal *m*, de la lecture. 2. (*argot des drogués*)

ordonnance *f* pour des drogues. *Voir aussi* **mitt-reader**.

ready [ˈredi] *(noun)*, *F:* **the r.**, argent*, pèze *m*, fric *m*.

real [riəl] *(adv.)*, *F:* 1. **for r.**, (*a*) réel, vraisemblable, authentique; (*b*) trop beau pour y croire, incroyable. 2. réellement, véritablement, vraisemblablement, effectivement; **that's r. nice of you**, c'est très gentil de votre part.

ream [riːm] **(to)**, *P:* **to r. s.o.**, (*a*) rentrer qch. dans le rectum de qn; (*b*) = **ram**[2] **(to)**, 2.

ream out [ˈriːmˈaut] **(to)** (*U.S.*), *P:* **to r. s.o. o.**, to r. s.o.'s ass o., réprimander* qn sévèrement, enguirlander, engueuler qn.

rear(-end) [ˈriər(end)] *(noun)*, *F:* fesses*, postérieur *m*, popotin *m*; *cf.* **end, 1**.

recap[1] [ˈriːkæp] *(noun)*, *F:* (=*recapitulation*) résumé *m*, récapitulation *f*.

recap[2] [ˈriːˈkæp] **(to)**, *F:* (=*recapitulate*) récapituler, faire un résumé (de qch.).

recce[1] [ˈreki] *(noun)*, *F:* (=*reconnaissance*) exploration *f*, investigation *f*.

recce[2] [ˈreki] **(to)**, *F:* (=*reconnoitre*) faire une reconnaissance, éclairer le terrain.

red[1] [red] *(adj.)*. 1. *F:* communiste, communo, rouge. 2. *F:* **to roll out the r. carpet for s.o.**, faire les honneurs à qn, mettre les petits plats dans les grands. 3. *F:* **to paint the town r.**, être en réjouissances*, faire les quatre cents coups, faire la noce (*ou* la ribouldingue). 4. *P:* **r. birds** (*or* **devils** *or* **jackets**) = **reds** (**red**[2], 5). *Voir aussi* **herring**, 1; **light**[2], 4; **rag**[1], 4; **tape**[1].

red[2] [red] *(noun)*. 1. *F:* communiste *mf*, communo *m*, rouge *mf*. 2. *P:* or*, ioncaille *f*, dorure *f*. 3. *F:* **in the r.**, déficitaire, dans le rouge. 4. *F:* **to see r.**, voir rouge, piquer une colère*. 5. (*pl.*) *P:* diables *m.pl.* rouges (barbituriques) (*drogues**); *voir aussi* **red**[1], 4. 6. *P:* **to have the reds**, avoir ses menstrues*, repeindre sa grille en rouge.

red-cap [ˈredkæp] *(noun)*, *F:* 1. (*mil.*) soldat *m* de la police militaire. 2. (*U.S.*) porteur *m* (dans une gare).

reddite [ˈredait] *(noun)*, *F:* 1. bijoutier *m*, brocandier *m*. 2. qn qui s'occupe d'or*, marchand *m* de jonc; *cf.* **red**[2], 2.

red-eye [ˈredai] *(noun)* (*U.S.*), *P:* 1.

whisky *m* de contrebande, casse-pattes
m. 2. alcool*, tord-boyau(x) *m*, gnôle *f*.
redhead ['redhed] (*noun*), *F:* rouquin(e),
poil *m* de carotte, poil *m* de brique.
red-hot ['red'hɔt] (*adj.*), *F:* 1. plein de
nouvelles scandaleuses et de cancans; **a
r.-h. magazine,** un journal* à sensations.
2. (*a*) plein de sève (*ou* d'allant), qui
pète le feu; (*b*) avec du sex-appeal;
(*U.S.*) **a r.-h. mam(m)a,** (i) une petite
amie pétillante; (ii) vocaliste plantureuse, chanteuse de jazz. 3. **a r.-h.
communist,** un communiste à tous
crins. 4. très récent, tout chaud, tout
brûlant, dernière heure; **a r.-h. tip,** un
tuyau récent et sensationnel.
red-lamp ['red'læmp] (*attrib. adj.*), *F:* **a
r.-l. district,** un quartier à prostituées*.
red-letter ['red'letər] (*attrib. adj.*), *F:* **r.-
l. day,** jour *m* de fête, jour mémorable.
red-light ['red'lait] (*attrib. adj.*), *F:* =
red-lamp.
redneck ['rednek] (*noun*) (*U.S.*), *F:*
paysan*, plouc *m*, cul-terreux *m*.
reef[1] [ri:f] (*noun*), *F:* **to let out a r.,** se
desserrer, lâcher d'un cran.
reef[2] [ri:f] (**to**) (*Austr.*), *P:* prendre;
chaparder, faucher, ratiboiser.
reefer ['ri:fər] (*noun*). 1. *F:* cigarette* de
marijuana (*drogues**), reefer *m*. 2. *P:*
fumeur *m* de marijuana. 3. (*Austr.*) *P:*
complice *m* (d'un pickpocket), baron *m*.
re-entry [ri:'entri] (*noun*), *P:* fin *f* de
voyage d'un drogué.
ref[1] [ref] (*noun*), *F:* (*sports*) (=*referee*)
arbitre *m*.
ref[2] [ref] (**to**), *F:* (*sports*) (=*referee*)
arbitrer (un match).
reign [rein] (**to**) (*Austr.*), *P:* être en
liberté, profiter de la fraîche.
rent [rent] (*noun*), *P:* prostitué mâle.
rep [rep] (*abbr.*), *F:* 1. (=*representative*)
commis voyageur *m*, gaudissart *m*. 2.
(=*reputation*) réputation *f*. 3. (=*reper-
tory* (*theatre*)) théâtre *m* de province,
théâtre municipal; **to be in r.,** être
acteur/actrice au théâtre municipal.
repeaters [ri'pi:təz] (*pl. noun*), *P:* dés*
truqués, balourds *m.pl.*, matuches *m.pl.*
resurrection pie [rezə'rekʃ(ə)n'pai]
(*noun*), *F:* nourriture* réchauffée, arlequin *m*.
retread ['ri:tred] (*noun*) (*U.S.*), *F:*
rappelé *m* au service militaire; naphtalinard *m*.

revamp [ri:'væmp] (**to**), *F:* renouveler,
remettre à neuf, retaper.
reviver [ri'vaivər] (*noun*), *F:* remontant
m, apéritif *m*.
rhino ['rainou] (*noun*). 1. *F:* (=*rhinoceros*)
rhino(céros) *m*. 2. *P:* argent*, galette *f*;
paie *f*, salaire *m*, sonnettes *f.pl.*
rhubarb ['ru:bɑ:b] (*noun*), *P:* 1. bêtises*,
balivernes *f.pl.*, sornettes *f.pl.* 2. cacophonie *f*, tumulte *m*, chambard *m*. 3.
querelle*, chahut *m*, grabuge *m*.
rheumaticky [ru:'mætiki] (*adj.*), *F:*
rhumatisant.
rib[1] [rib] (*noun*), *P:* **on the ribs,** pauvre*,
fauché, dans la dèche.
rib[2] [rib] (**to**), *F:* taquiner, mettre en
boîte, chiner (qn).
ribbing ['ribiŋ] (*noun*), *F:* **to give s.o. a r.,**
taquiner qn.
rib-tickler ['ribtiklər] (*noun*), *F:*
plaisanterie *f*, rigolade *f*.
rich[1] [ritʃ] (*adj.*), *F:* 1. (*d'un incident*)
très divertissant, rigolo; épatant, impayable. 2. scabreux, osé, cochon. *Voir
aussi* **filthy, 2.**
rich[2] [ritʃ] (*adv.*), *F:* **to strike it r.,**
décrocher le gros lot.
Richard, richard ['ritʃəd] (*noun*), *P:* 1.
(*R.S.* = *Richard the Third* =) (*a*)
(*word*) mot *m*; *cf.* **dicky-bird;** (*b*) (*bird*)
oiseau *m*; (*c*) (*turd*) étron*, colombin *m*.
2. fille*, nénette *f*, pépée *f*. 3. (*U.S.*) =
dick, 2.
ride[1] [raid] (*noun*). 1. *P:* coït*, dérouillage
m, grimpage *m*. 2. *F:* **to take s.o. for a r.,**
(*a*) entraîner et tuer qn, aller dézinguer
qn; (*b*) tromper* qn, jouer un sale tour à
qn, mener qn en bateau. 3. *F:* **to go
along (just) for the r.,** suivre le gros de la
troupe, y aller pour y aller. *Voir aussi*
joy-ride.
ride[2] [raid] (**to**). 1. *P:* coïter* avec (une
femme), dérouiller, grimper. 2. (*U.S.*)
F: asticoter, canuler, enquiquiner. 3.
F: **to let sth. r.,** laisser courir qch.
riff [rif] (*noun*), *P:* 1. court motif mélo-
dique de jazz. 2. chicane *f*, chamaillerie
f.
rig[1] [rig] (*noun*), *P:* pénis*, colonne *f*.
rig[2] [rig] (**to**), *F:* arranger (*ou* manigancer) à son avantage.
right [rait] (*adj.*). 1. *P:* **to make a r. mess
(*or* muck) of it,** tout gâcher, tout
bousiller, foutre une vraie pagaille; *cf.*
balls-up; *voir aussi* **nana; so-and-so, 2;**

---

* An asterisk indicates that the word so marked is included as a head-word in the Appendix.

sucker[2], 1. 2. *F:* as r. as rain, en parfait état, comme un charme. 3. (*U.S.*) *F:* a r. guy, (*a*) un chic type, un mec bien; (*b*) un vrai de vrai, un régulo, un correct. 4. *F:* to get on the r. side of s.o., être bien vu de qn, se mettre dans les petits papiers de qn. *Voir aussi* noise; people, 2.

righteous [ˈraitʃəs] (*adj.*), *P:* 1. ivre*, raide. 2. tapageur, chahuteur.

right-ho! [ˈraitˈhou], right-o(h)! [ˈraitˈlou] (*excl.*), *F:* oui*, d'ac(cord)! O.K., entendu.

right on [ˈraitˈɔn] (*adv.*), *F:* au poil, impec.

righty-(h)o! [ˈraitiˈ(h)ou] (*excl.*), *F:* = right-ho!

rigid [ˈridʒid] (*adj.*), *P:* 1. to bore s.o. r., ennuyer* qn au plus haut point, emmerder qn jusqu'à la moelle. 2. (*U.S.*) ivre* mort, bituré.

rig-out [ˈrigaut] (*noun*), *F:* toilette *f*, tenue *f*, accoutrement *m*, attifage *m*.

rig out [ˈrigˈaut] (to), *F:* habiller*, accoutrer, attifer, fringuer, harnacher.

rig-up [ˈrigʌp] (*noun*), *F:* appareil improvisé, installation *f* de fortune.

rig up [ˈrigˈʌp] (to), *F:* 1. apprêter, préparer, concocter (un repas, une excuse, *etc.*). 2. = rig out (to).

Riley [ˈraili] (*noun*), *F:* to live the life of R., se la couler douce, se la faire belle, vivre comme un coq en pâte.

rim [rim] (to), *P:* = ream (to), (*a*).

ring[1] [riŋ] (*noun*). 1. *P:* anus*, anneau *m*, bague *f*; r. twitter (*or* flutter), peur*, la frousse. 2. *F:* to run (*or* make) rings round s.o., l'emporter sur qn, surpasser qn, remporter la palme, tenir la corde.

ring[2] [riŋ] (to). 1. *F:* it rings a bell, cela me dit quelque chose. 2. *F:* to r. the changes, (*a*) escroquer*, arnaquer, empiler; (*b*) écouler de la fausse monnaie, faire la fournaise; (*c*) ressasser (un sujet, *etc.*). 3. *F:* substituer un cheval pour un autre dans une course, aller de cheval à canasson. 4. *P:* maquiller des objets volés.

ringer [ˈriŋər] (*noun*), *F:* 1. to be a (dead) r. for s.o., être qn tout craché, être le portrait (tout) craché de qn. 2. qn qui substitue un cheval pour un autre dans une course.

ring-piece [ˈriŋpiːs] (*noun*), *P:* =ring[1], 1.

ringtail [ˈriŋteil] (*noun*) (*Austr.*), *F:* (*a*)

lâche *m*, caneur *m*, frileux *m*; (*b*) faux frère, macaron *m*, mouton *m*.

rinky-dink [ˈriŋkiˈdiŋk] (*noun*) (*U.S.*), *F:* 1. camelote *f*, pacotille *f*, saloperie *f*. 2. guinche *f*, boui-boui *m*.

riot [ˈraiət] (*noun*), *F:* 1. grand succès, boum *m* (du tonnerre), fureur *f*. 2. boute-en-train *m*, rigolo *m*, rigolboche *m*. 3. déchaînement *m*, tapage *m*, débauche *f*. 4. to read the R. Act to s.o., (*a*) avertir, menacer qn; (*b*) réprimander* qn, passer un savon à qn.

rip [rip] (to), *F:* to let r., exploser, vider son sac; let it r.! fonce! appuie sur le champignon!

ripe [raip] (*adj.*), *F:* 1. indécent, scabreux, osé. 2. ivre*, mûr, rétamé. 3. amusant*, gondolant, crevant.

rip into [ˈripˈintuː] (to), *F:* attaquer* (qn), rentrer dans le lard à (qn).

rip off [ˈripˈɔf] (to), *P:* 1. voler*, faucher; to get ripped off, être ratiboisé. 2. exploiter, arnaquer. 3. coïter* avec (une femme), égoïner. 4. tuer*, zigouiller.

ripped [ript] (*adj.*), *P:* 1. malheureux, piteux. 2. (*a*) (*drogues*) défoncé, très high; (*b*) très ivre*, rétamé.

ripping [ˈripiŋ] (*adj.*), *F:* excellent*, formid(able), super.

rip-roaring [ˈripˈrɔːriŋ] (*adj.*), *F:* (*a*) endiablé, piaffant, pétardant; (*b*) a r.-r. success, une réussite du tonnerre, une fureur de tous les diables, un succès fulgurant.

ripsnorter [ˈripˈsnɔːtər] (*noun*), *F:* personne *ou* chose remarquable, crack *m*, as *m*.

ripsnorting [ˈripˈsnɔːtiŋ] (*adj.*), *F:* excellent*, bœuf, du tonnerre.

rise[1] [raiz] (*noun*), *F:* to take a (*or* the) r. out of s.o., faire monter (*ou* mousser) qn.

rise[2] [raiz] (to), *F:* r. and shine! *c.p.*, debout les morts!

ritz [rits] (*noun*), *F:* to put on the r., être prétentieux*, se donner des airs, crâner, plastronner, faire du vent.

ritzy [ˈritsi] (*adj.*), *F:* 1. bariolé, tape-à-l'œil, voyant, clinquant; a r. tart, une pépée qui en jette, une minette. 2. élégant*, fastueux, ultra-chic. 3. crâneur, esbrouf(f)eur, plastronneur.

river [ˈrivər] (*noun*), *F:* 1. to sell s.o. down the r., trahir, vendre, moutonner qn. 2. to send s.o. up the r. = to send s.o. up (send up (to), 2).

roach [routʃ] (*noun*), *P:* mégot* de cigarette de marijuana.

road [roud] (*noun*), *F:* **1. to be on the r.**, vivre sur les grands chemins, vagabonder. **2. to hit the r.**, se mettre en route, prendre le large. *Voir aussi* **middle-of-the-road; one, 1.**

road-hog [ˈroudhɔg] (*noun*), *F:* chauffeur *m* qui conduit au milieu de la chaussée, chauffard *m*, écraseur *m*.

roast¹ [roust] (*noun*), *F:* (*a*) critique *f* défavorable, éreintage *m*, bêchage *m*; (*b*) calomnie *f*, débinage *m*, cassage *m* de sucre.

roast² [roust] (**to**), *F:* critiquer*, éreinter, bêcher, jardiner.

roasting [ˈroustiŋ] (*noun*), *F:* **to give (s.o.) a r.** = **roast²** (**to**).

rock¹ [rɔk] (*noun*). **1.** *F:* (*jazz*) rock *m*; *cf.* **rock-'n-roll. 2.** *F:* **on the rocks,** (*a*) (boisson) servie avec de la glace; (*b*) ruiné*, fauché, nettoyé, passé; (*c*) (mariage) en échec*, à (vau-)l'eau; (*d*) (*commerce*) en faillite, dans le bouillon. **3.** (*pl.*) *P:* diamants*, diames *m.pl.*, pierres *f.pl.*, cailloux *m.pl.*; *voir aussi* **hot, 9. 4.** *F:* **to touch r. bottom,** être arrivé au fin fond, être tout à fait à plat.

rock² [rɔk] (**to**). **1.** *F:* secouer, ébranler, alarmer. **2.** *F:* **to r. the boat,** secouer la barque (*ou* la baraque), secouer les puces, faire du grabuge. **3.** *P:* coïter* avec (une femme), biquer.

rock-candy [ˈrɔkˈkændi] (*noun*), *P:* = **rocks** (**rock¹, 3**).

rocker [ˈrɔkər] (*noun*), *F:* **1.** blouson noir sur grosse moto (*ou* trail bike); *cf.* **mod². 2. off one's r.,** fou*, timbré, loufoque, maboul(e), échappé de Charenton. **3.** rocking-chair *f*.

rocket [ˈrɔkit] (*noun*), *F:* **to give s.o. a r.,** réprimander* qn, passer un savon à qn. *Voir aussi* **sky-rocket.**

rockhead [ˈrɔkhed] (*noun*), *P:* individu bête*, buse *f*, bas-de-plafond *m*, ballot *m*.

rock-'n-roll¹ [ˈrɔkənroul] (*noun*), *F:* rock-and-roll *m*; *cf.* **rock¹, 1.**

rock-'n-roll² [ˈrɔkənroul] (**to**), *F:* faire le rock-and-roll.

rocky [ˈrɔki] (*adj.*), *F:* (*a*) vacillant, flageolant; **a r. marriage,** un mariage branlant; (*b*) chancelant, titubant (de boisson *ou* de fatigue).

rod [rɔd] (*noun*), *P:* **1.** pénis*, canne *f*, gourdin *m*; *cf.* **hot-rod** (**to**). **2.** revolver*, calibre *m*, flingue *m*. **3.** pardessus*, lardosse *m*. *Voir aussi* **hot, 22.**

rod-man [ˈrɔdmæn] (*noun*) (*U.S.*), *P:* gangster *m*, bandit *m*, voleur* armé.

Roger! roger!¹ [ˈrɔdʒər] (*excl.*), *F:* oui*, d'ac! O.K.!

roger² [ˈrɔdʒər] (**to**), *P:* coïter* avec (une femme), égoïner.

roll¹ [roul] (*noun*). **1.** *F:* liasse *f* de billets* (de banque), matelas *m* (de faf(f)iots). **2.** *P:* (*a*) coït*, giclée *f* du mâle; (*b*) **a r. in the hay,** coït*, couchage *m*, baisage *m*, une partie de jambes en l'air; *voir aussi* **hay, 2; jelly-roll; pay-roll; rock-'n-roll¹.**

roll² [roul] (**to**). **1.** *P:* voler*, rouler, roustir, ratiboiser. **2.** *F:* **to be rolling in it,** être très riche*, être plein aux as, rouler sur l'or. **3.** *F:* **to get rolling,** partir*, se déhotter, démarrer. **4.** *P:* coïter* avec (une femme), envoyer (une femme) en l'air. *Voir aussi* **aisle, 2; rock-'n-roll²** (**to**).

roll along [ˈroulǝˈlɔŋ] (**to**), *F:* avancer tranquillement, suivre son petit bonhomme de chemin.

rollicking [ˈrɔlikiŋ] (*noun*), *P:* engueulade *f*, savon *m*.

roll on [ˈroulˈɔn] (**to**), *F:* **r. o., Christmas!** vite Noël!

roll-ons [ˈroulɔnz] (*pl. noun*), *F:* gaine *f* (élastique).

roll out [ˈroulˈaut] (**to**), *F:* **they rolled out of the pub at closing time,** à la fermeture ils sortirent du café en titubant. *Voir aussi* **red¹, 2.**

roll-up [ˈroulʌp] (*noun*), *P:* cigarette* roulée (main), cibiche *f* maison; *cf.* **roll up** (**to**), **2.**

roll up [ˈroulʌp] (**to**). **1.** *F:* arriver*, s'abouler, débouler. **2.** *P:* faire une cigarette* de marijuana, rouler un reefer; *cf.* **roll-up.**

roll-your-own [ˈroul19ˈroun] (*noun*), *F:* (*a*) machine *f* à rouler les cigarettes*; (*b*) = **roll-up.**

roly-poly [ˈrouliˈpouli] (*noun*), *F:* individu* rondouillard, patapouf *m*, bouboule *m*, dondon *m*.

Roman [ˈroumən] (*adj.*), *P:* **1. R. candle,** catholique *mf*. **2.** (=*roaming*) (*a*) **R. hands,** mains caressantes (*ou* baladeuses); (*b*) **R. eyes,** yeux farfouilleurs.

---

* An asterisk indicates that the word so marked is included as a head-word in the Appendix.

romp[1] [rɔmp] (*noun*), F.: 1. **to have a r. on the sofa**, prendre ses ébats sur le canapé. 2. chose facile à réaliser, du nanan, du beurre, du nougat.

romp[2] [rɔmp] (**to**), F.: **to r. home**, (*d'un cheval*) gagner facilement, arriver dans un fauteuil.

ronchie, ronchy [ˈrɔntʃi] (*adj.*) (*U.S.*), F.: = **raunchy**.

roof [ruːf] (*noun*). 1. F.: **to go through** (*or* **hit**) **the r.**, piquer une colère, monter sur ses grands chevaux, sortir de ses gonds. 2. F.: **to raise the r.**, faire du chahut (*ou* du chambard *ou* du grabuge). 3. P.: **to fall off the r.**, avoir ses menstrues*, repeindre sa grille (en rouge).

rook [ruk] (**to**), F.: escroquer*, faisander, pigeonner.

rookie [ˈruki] (*noun*), F.: recrue *f*, débutant *m*, blanc-bec *m*.

rooking [ˈrukiŋ] (*noun*), F.: **to get a r.**, payer* trop cher, se faire empiler, être faisandé.

rooky [ˈruki] (*noun*), F.: = **rookie**.

room [ruːm] (*noun*), F.: **the smallest r.**, W.C.*, le petit endroit, le petit coin; *cf.* **throne-room**. *Voir aussi* **barrack-room**.

roost [ruːst] (*noun*), F.: 1. logement*, niche *f*, guitoune *f*. 2. **to hit the r.**, se coucher*, se zoner, aller au paddock. *Voir aussi* **chicken-roost; pigeon-roost**.

root[1] [ruːt] (*noun*), P.: 1. cigarette*, cibiche *f*. 2. amphétamine *f* (*drogues**). 3. pénis*, bout *m*, queue *f*.

root[2] [ruːt] (**to**). 1. (*Austr.*) P.: coïter* avec (une femme), fourrer, tringler. 2. (*Austr.*) P.: **get rooted!** = **get knotted!** 3. F.: **to r. for s.o.**, applaudir, encourager qn.

rooted [ˈruːtid] (*adj.*) (*Austr.*), P.: très fatigué*, vanné.

rooter [ˈruːtər] (*noun*), F.: partisan *m*, fana(tique) *mf* (d'une équipe, *etc.*).

rootie [ˈruːti] (*noun*), P.: nourriture*, repas *m*, bectance *f*, fricot *m*.

rootin'-tootin' [ˈruːtinˈtuːtin] (*adj.*) (*U.S.*), F.: bruyant, chahuteur, pétardier.

rooty [ˈruːti] (*adj.*), P.: = **horny**.

rope [roup] (*noun*). 1. F.: **it's money for old r.**, c'est donné pour une bouchée de pain. 2. P.: tabac* fort, perlot *m*, trèfle *m*. 3. P.: (*a*) marijuana *f* (*drogues**),

chanvre *m*; (*b*) cigarette* de marijuana (*drogues**), stick *m*. 4. F.: **to know the ropes**, être au courant (*ou* à la roue *ou* à la coule), savoir nager, connaître la combine (*ou* les tenants et les aboutissants). 5. F.: **to give s.o. plenty of r.**, lâcher la bride (*ou* la jambe) à qn. *Voir aussi* **bell-rope**.

rope in [ˈroupˈin] (**to**), F.: **to r. s.o. i.**, s'assurer le concours de qn.

rop(e)y [ˈroupi] (*adj.*), F.: camelote, toc, tocard, ordurier.

rort [rɔːt] (*noun*) (*Austr.*), F.: 1. coup monté (*ou* fourré), combine bien cuisinée. 2. boniment *m*, baratin *m*.

rorty [ˈrɔːti] (*adj.*), P.: 1. réjoui, de bonne humeur, guilleret, folichon. 2. = **horny** (*b*).

Rory (O'Moore) [ˈrɔːri(ouˈmɔər)] (*pr. noun*), P.: 1. (*R.S.* = *door*) porte *f*, lourde *f*. 2. **on the R.**, pauvre*, fauché, sans le sou.

Roscoe, roscoe [ˈrɔskou] (*noun*), P.: revolver*, pétoire *m*, rigolo *m*.

rosy [ˈrouzi] (*noun*), P.: 1. = **claret**. 2. vin* rouge, pinard *m*, rouquin *m*. 3. **ring around the r.** = **daisy chain** (**daisy**[2], 6). 4. **R. Lee** (*R.S.* = *tea*), thé *m*.

rot [rɔt] (*noun*), F.: bêtises*, sottises *f.pl.*, âneries *f.pl.*; (**what**) **r.!** allons donc! quelle blague!; **to talk** (**utter**) **r.**, dire des imbécillités *f.pl.*; *cf.* **tommy-rot**.

rot-gut [ˈrɔtɡʌt] (*noun*), F.: alcool* de mauvaise qualité, tord-boyau(x) *m*.

rotten [ˈrɔtn] (*adj.*), F.: 1. désagréable, dégueulasse, débectant, moche, lamentable; **r. weather**, temps *m* de chien; **r. luck!** quelle guigne! pas de veine! 2. toc, tocard, camelote, ordurier. 3. malade*, patraque. 4. ennuyeux*, barbant, emmerdant. *Voir aussi* **sod**[1], 2.

rotter [ˈrɔtər] (*noun*), F.: vaurien*, fripouille *f*, charogne *f*.

rough[1] [rʌf] (*adj.*), F.: 1. **r. diamond**, personne aux dehors grossiers mais bon enfant, un diamant dans sa gangue. 2. **that's r.!** c'est vache! c'est dur à avaler! 3. **he's had a r. deal**, il en a bavé, il a mangé de la vache enragée, il en a vu (des vertes et des pas mûres). 4. **they're a r. lot**, c'est une bande* de sales types; **a r. customer**, un mauvais coucheur, un dur à cuire. 5. **r. and ready**, (*a*) **a r. and ready person**, une personne nature (pas très fine ni distinguée), un pecnaud sur

---

* L'astérisque indique que le mot marqué de ce signe figure comme entrée dans le Répertoire.

les bords; (b) **a r. and ready method,** une méthode peu précise mais pratique; (c) **a r. and ready piece of work,** un ouvrage grossièrement fait. 6. **r. stuff,** brutalités *f.pl.,* vacheries *f.pl.* 7. **to give s.o. a r. time,** maltraiter qn, être chien (*ou* vache) avec qn.

rough² [rʌf] (*adv.*), *F:* 1. **to sleep r.,** coucher* sur la dure. 2. **to feel r.,** (a) se sentir malade* (*ou* patraque); (b) se sentir moulu; (c) avoir la gueule de bois. *Voir aussi* **cut up (to),** 3.

rough³ [rʌf] (*noun*). 1. *F:* **to take the r. with the smooth,** prendre le bien avec le mal; à la guerre comme à la guerre. 2. *P:* = **roughneck.** 3. *P:* **to have a bit of r.** = **to have a bit on the side (side,** 2).

rough-house [ˈrʌfhaʊs] (*noun*), *F:* (a) conduite *f* de vaurien*, voyouterie *f;* (b) bagarre* générale, badaboum *m,* barouf(fe) *m,* ramdam(e) *m.*

rough it [ˈrʌfit] (to), *F:* vivre à la dure.

roughneck [ˈrʌfnek] (*noun*), *F:* vaurien*, canaille *f,* voyou *m;* un dur.

rough-up [ˈrʌfʌp] (*noun*), *P:* violente querelle*, cognage *m,* tabassage *m,* dérouillée *f.*

rough up [ˈrʌfˈʌp] (to), *P:* battre*, tabasser, bourrer (qn) de coups.

roundabouts [ˈraʊndəbaʊts] (*pl. noun*), *F:* **what you lose on the r. you gain on the swings,** *c.p.,* à tout prendre on ne gagne ni ne perd.

roundheel(s) [ˈraʊndhiːl(z)] (*noun*) (*U.S.*), *P:* **to be a r.,** être une femme facile, avoir les talons courts; *cf.* **heel,** 2.

round-up [ˈraʊndʌp] (*noun*), *F:* 1. rassemblement *m,* compilation *f,* résumé *m* (des dernières nouvelles, *etc.*). 2. **to be heading for the last r.-u.,** être près de mourir*, sentir le sapin, graisser ses bottes.

rouser [ˈraʊzər] (*noun*), *P:* 1. qch. de sensationnel (*ou* de saisissant), un boum. 2. gros mensonge*, bobard *m* maouss, bourrage *m* de crâne.

roust out [ˈraʊstˈaʊt] (to), *F:* **to r. s.o. o.,** se débarrasser* de qn, flanquer qn à la porte, balancer qn, envoyer balader qn.

roust up [ˈraʊstˈʌp] (to), *F:* aller chercher, dégot(t)er, repérer.

row¹ [raʊ] (*noun*). 1. *F:* querelle*, rififi *m,* badaboum *m.* 2. (a) *F:* chahut *m,* charivari *m* (du diable); (b) *P:* **hold** (*or*

shut) **your r.!** tais-toi! (*se taire**), la ferme! la boucle!

row² [raʊ] (to), *F:* se quereller, s'attraper, pétarder, s'engueuler.

rozzer [ˈrɔzər] (*noun*), *P:* agent* de police, flic *m,* poulet *m.*

rubadub [ˈrʌbəˈdʌb] (*noun*) (*R.S.* = *club*), *P:* club *m.*

rub along [ˈrʌbəˈlɔŋ] (to), *F:* se tirer d'affaire, se débrouiller.

rubber [ˈrʌbər] (*noun*). 1. *P:* capote anglaise, imper *m* à Popaul. 2. (*pl.*) *F:* galoches *f.pl.,* caoutchoucs *m.pl. Voir aussi* **bum-rubber.**

rubberneck¹ [ˈrʌbənek] (*noun*) (*U.S.*), *F:* touriste *mf,* badaud *m,* glaude *f.*

rubberneck² [ˈrʌbənek] (to) (*U.S.*), *F:* excursionner, visiter (monuments, *etc.*).

rubber-stamp [ˈrʌbəˈstæmp] (*noun*), *F:* (a) fonctionnaire *m* qui exécute aveuglément les ordres de ses supérieurs, rond-de-cuir *m;* (b) béni-oui-oui *m.*

rube [ruːb] (*noun*) (*U.S.*), *P:* 1. fermier *m,* cul-terreux *m.* 2. paysan*, pétrousquin *m,* plouc *m.*

rub in [ˈrʌbˈin] (to), *F:* **to r. it i.,** insister, remuer le couteau dans la plaie.

rub off [ˈrʌbˈɔf] (to), *P:* 1. coïter*, caramboler. 2. se masturber*, s'astiquer. 3. **to r. o. on s.o.,** tomber dessus, s'abouler, débouler (*l'argent, la chance, etc.*).

rub-out [ˈrʌbaʊt] (*noun*), *P:* 1. assassinat *m,* tuerie *f,* but(t)age *m,* dessoudage *m.* 2. coït*, baisage *m,* frottage *m,* carambolage *m.*

rub out [ˈrʌbˈaʊt] (to), *P:* 1. tuer*, but(t)er, dessouder, démolir. 2. battre*, bourrer de coups*, dérouiller.

rub-up [ˈrʌbʌp] (*noun*), *P:* acte *m* de masturbation, moussage *m; cf.* **rub up (to),** 2.

rub up [ˈrʌbˈʌp] (to). 1. *F:* **to r. s.o. u. the wrong way,** prendre qn du mauvais côté (*ou* à rebrousse-poil). 2. *P:* se masturber*, s'astiquer. 3. *P:* caresser activement (qn), faire mousser (qn); allumer les gaz.

ruck¹ [rʌk] (*noun*), *P:* querelle*, prise *f* de bec (*ou* de gueule).

ruck² [rʌk] (to), *P:* 1. agacer, énerver, ronchonner. 2. faire beaucoup de bruit*, faire du chahut (*ou* du chambard *ou* du grabuge).

---

* An asterisk indicates that the word so marked is included as a head-word in the Appendix.

ruckus [ˈrʌkəs] (*noun*), *P*: = **ruck**[1].

ructions [ˈrʌkʃənz] (*pl. noun*), *F*: bagarre*, tapage *m*, vacarme *m*; désordre *m*; scène *f*; **if you come home late there'll be r.**, si tu rentres tard, tu te feras incendier (*ou* engueuler).

ruddy [ˈrʌdi] (*adj. & adv.*), *P*: (*euph. pour* **bloody**) **a r. liar**, un sacré menteur; **he's a r. nuisance**, il est vachement enquiquinant; **ain't it grand to be r. well dead**, *c.p.*, on s'en fout quand on est mort et enterré.

rug [rʌg] (*noun*). **1.** *F*: **to cut a r.**, danser*, guincher, gambiller. **2.** *P*: perruque *f*, moumoute *f*. **3.** *F*: **to pull the r. from under s.o.** (*or* **from under s.o.'s feet**), couper l'herbe sous les pieds de qn. *Voir aussi* **dirt**[1], 4.

rugger [ˈrʌgər] (*noun*), *F*: le rugby.

rum [rʌm] (*adj.*), *F*: bizarre; **a r. one**, un drôle de type (*ou* de zèbre), un drôle d'oiseau.

rumble[1] [ˈrʌmbl] (*noun*), *P*: bagarre*; bataille arrangée entre bandes* de voyous.

rumble[2] [ˈrʌmbl] (**to**), *F*: flairer, se douter de (qch.), voir venir (qn).

rumbustical [rʌmˈbʌstikl], **rumbustious** [rʌmˈbʌstiəs] (*adj.*), *F*: tapageur, chachuteur.

rumdum [ˈrʌmdʌm], **rumhound** [ˈrʌmhaund] (*noun*), *P*: ivrogne*, poivrot *m*, saoulot *m*, saoulard *m*.

rummy[1] [ˈrʌmi] (*adj.*), *F*: = **rum**.

rummy[2] [ˈrʌmi] (*noun*), *P*: = **rumdum**.

rump [rʌmp] (**to**), *P*: se droguer à l'héroïne.

rumpot [ˈrʌmpɔt] (*noun*), *P*: = **rumdum**.

rumpus [ˈrʌmpəs] (*noun*), *F*: querelle*, chahut *m*, vacarme *m*; **to kick up a r.**, faire une scène.

run [rʌn] (*noun*), *F*: **1. to have a r. for one's money**, en avoir pour son argent*. **2. the runs**, diarrhée*, courante *f*, chiasse *f*. **3. to be on the r.**, être recherché par la police, être en cavale. **4. dry r.**, essai *m*, répétition *f*.

run-around [ˈrʌnəraund] (*noun*), *F*: **to give s.o. the r.-a.**, donner le change à qn, faire marcher qn.

run-down [ˈrʌndaun] (*noun*), *F*: résumé *m*, récapitulation *f*, topo *m*.

run down[1] [ˈrʌnˈdaun] (*adj.*), *F*: anémié, débile.

run down[2] [ˈrʌnˈdaun] (**to**), *F*: critiquer*, éreinter, débiner.

run-in [ˈrʌnin] (*noun*), *F*: **1.** rôdage *m*. **2.** voie *f* d'accès, abords *m.pl.*

run in [ˈrʌnˈin] (**to**), *F*: arrêter*, embarquer, ramasser.

run-of-the-mill [ˈrʌnəvðəmil] (*adj.*), *F*: ordinaire, quelconque.

run-out [ˈrʌnaut] (*noun*), *P*: **1.** simulacre *m*, de vente aux enchères, lavage truqué. **2. to have a r.-o.**, uriner*, se l'égoutter.

run out [ˈrʌnˈaut] (**to**), *F*: **to r. o. on s.o.**, se défiler, prendre la poudre d'escampette.

runt [rʌnt] (*noun*), *F*: (*a*) nain *m*, nabot *m*; (*b*) avorton *m*, crapoussin *m*, crapaud *m*.

run-through [ˈrʌn-θruː] (*noun*), *F*: (*th., etc.*) lecture *f* rapide, répétition *f*.

runty [ˈrʌnti] (*adj.*), *F*: rabougri, riquiqui.

rush[1] [rʌʃ] (*noun*), *P*: impression *f* de plénitude physique et psychique avec une drogue; flash *m*. *Voir aussi* **bum**[2], 4.

rush[2] [rʌʃ] (**to**), *F*: **to r. s.o. for sth.**, pratiquer le coup de fusil sur qn, écorcher qn.

rush-hour [ˈrʌʃauər] (*noun*), *F*: heure *f* de pointe.

Russky [ˈruski, ˈrʌski] (*noun*), *F*: Russe *m*, Rusco *m*.

rustle up [ˈrʌslˈʌp] (**to**), *F*: dénicher, concocter; **she can always r. u. a meal**, elle sait toujours se débrouiller pour faire de quoi manger.

rusty[1] [ˈrʌsti] (*adj.*), *F*: **to cut up r. = to cut up nasty** (**cut up** (**to**), 3).

rusty[2] [ˈrʌsti] (*noun*), *F*: = **redhead**.

---

* L'astérisque indique que le mot marqué de ce signe figure comme entrée dans le Répertoire.

S

sack¹ [sæk] (noun). I. F: to get the s., être congédié* (ou renvoyé ou sacqué ou flanqué à la porte); to give s.o. the s., se débarrasser* de qn, sacquer, virer, balancer qn. 2. F: to look like a s. of potatoes, avoir l'air de l'as de pique. 3. F: to hit the s., se coucher*, dormir*, pioncer, se pieuter; s. time, (a) temps passé au lit*, temps de pieutage; (b) heure f du coucher (ou du plumard). 4. P: s. game, cour amoureuse, jeux amoureux, fleurette f; voir aussi tiger.

sack² [sæk] (to), F: to s. s.o. = to give s.o. the sack (sack¹, I).

sack out (or up) ['sæk'aut, 'sæk'ʌp] (to), P: se coucher*, se pieuter.

saddle ['sædl] (to), F: to be saddled with s.o., sth., avoir qn, qch., sur le dos.

safe¹ [seif] (adj.), F: to be s., to be on the s. side, (a) être du bon côté; (b) agir pour plus de sûreté; I'll take an extra £1 (just) to be on the s. side, je prendrai une livre en supplément pour plus de sûreté.

safe² [seif] (adv.), F: to play (it) s., agir à coup sûr, jouer serré.

safety ['seifti] (noun), P: capote anglaise, doigt m de sécurité.

sail [seil] (noun), F: to take the wind out of s.o.'s sails, couper l'herbe sous les pieds de qn.

sailing ['seiliŋ] (noun), F: to be (all) plain s., aller tout seul, ne pas faire un pli.

sail into ['seil'intu:] (to), F: (a) attaquer*, assaillir, agrafer (qn); (b) entamer (un travail) avec élan.

sail through ['seil'θru:] (to), F: terminer (un travail, etc.) en moins de deux, faire (qch.) presto, liquider (qch.) comme sur des roulettes; to s. t. an exam, passer un examen haut la main.

sale [seil] (noun), P: no s.! pas mèche! rien à faire!

salt¹ [sɔ:lt] (noun), F: (old) s., marin*, vieux loup de mer. Voir aussi dose, 2.

salt² [sɔ:lt] (to), F: I. to s. a mine, saler une mine (d'or, etc.), tapisser le front d'une mine. 2. truquer, cuisiner (les bénéfices, les comptes, etc.). 3. to s. the bill, saler l'addition.

salt-cellars ['sɔ:lt-seləz] (pl. noun), F: salières f.pl. (derrière les clavicules).

salty ['sɔ:lti] (adj.), F: I. hardi, audacieux, casse-cou, intrépide. 2. un peu fort, difficile à digérer. 3. obscène, scabreux, osé, salé, épicé. 4. désagréable, horrible, difficile à avaler. 5. fringant, pimpant.

sam, Sam [sæm] (noun), P: I. to stand s., payer la tournée, liquider l'ardoise. 2. (U.S.) agent m de la Brigade fédérale des Stupéfiants. Voir aussi Uncle, 6.

sambo, Sambo ['sæmbou] (noun), P: (péj.) nègre*, bamboula m.

sample ['sɑ:mpl] (to), F: to s. the goods, mettre la main au panier (avec une fille).

sand [sænd] (noun) (U.S.), F: courage m, cran m, estome m, vigueur f; cf. grit.

sandboy ['sæn(d)bɔi] (noun), F: (as) happy as a s., gai comme un pinson, heureux comme un poisson dans l'eau.

sandman ['sæn(d)mæn, 'sæn(d)mən] (noun), F: the s. is coming, le marchand de sable passe; cf. dustman.

sap(head) ['sæp(hed)] (noun), P: individu bête*, niguedouille mf.

sappiness ['sæpinis] (noun), F: inexpérience f, nigauderie f.

sappy ['sæpi] (adj.), F: I. bête*, ballot, baluchard. 2. sans expérience, nigaud.

sarge [sɑ:dʒ] (noun), F: (=sergeant) (mil.) sergent m, sergot m.

sarky ['sɑ:ki] (adj.), F: sarcastique, mordant, ironique, caustique, persifleur.

sass¹ [sæs] (noun) (U.S.), F: = sauce¹, I.

sass² [sæs] (to) (U.S.), F: = sauce² (to).

sassy ['sæsi] (adj.) (U.S.), F: = saucy, I.

---

* An asterisk indicates that the word so marked is included as a head-word in the Appendix.

satch [sætʃ], **satchelmouth** [ˈsætʃəl-mauθ] (noun), F: qn qui a une grande bouche*, grande gueule.

sauce[1] [sɔːs] (noun), F: 1. effronterie f, toupet m, culot m. 2. (U.S.) alcool*, goutte f; **to hit the s.**, boire* beaucoup, tomber sur la bouteille; **to be off the s.**, ne plus prendre d'alcool*, suivre la croix bleue, être au régime sec. Voir aussi **apple-sauce**.

sauce[2] [sɔːs] (to), F: = **cheek**[2] (to).

saucebox [ˈsɔːsbɒks] (noun), F: effronté(e) m(f), mufle m, butor m, malotru m.

saucy [ˈsɔːsi] (adj.), F: 1. impertinent, audacieux, gonflé, affronté, culotté. 2. aguichant, coquet, chic. 3. (livre, pièce de théâtre, etc.) scabreux, osé, risqué, épicé.

sausage [ˈsɔsidʒ] (noun). 1. F: **not a s.**, rien* du tout, que dalle. 2. F: (you) **silly s.!** gros bête! gros ballot! 3. F: **s. dog**, chien m dachshund. 4. P: cigarette* de marijuana, stick m (drogues*). 5. P: **s. and mash** (R.S. = cash), argent*, fric m, pognon m.

savage [ˈsævidʒ] (adj.), P: excellent*, sensas(s), du tonnerre. Voir aussi **cut up** (to), 3.

saver [ˈseivər] (noun), F: (turf) pari m de protection. Voir aussi **lifesaver**.

savvy[1] [ˈsævi] (noun), F: bon sens, jugeot(t)e f.

savvy[2] [ˈsævi] (to), F: savoir, connaître, piger, con(n)obler.

sawbones [ˈsɔːbounz] (noun) (now mainly U.S.), F: chirurgien m, charcuteur m, coupe-toujours m.

sawder [ˈsɔːdər] (noun) (U.S.), F: **soft s.** = **soft soap** (soap[1], 1).

sawney [ˈsɔːni] (noun). 1. F: Écossais m, kiltie m. 2. P: individu bête*, baluchard m.

sawn-off [ˈsɔːnɒf] (adj.), F: petit* (individu), demi-portion, inachevé.

sax [sæks] (noun) (abbr. = saxophone), F: saxo(phone) m.

say [sei] (to). 1. F: **I'll s.!** vous avez raison! et comment donc! 2. F: **you don't s.!** ça par exemple! 3. P: **says you!** que tu dis!; cf. **sez you!** 4. P: **says who?** chiche?

say-so [ˈseisou] (noun), F: 1. **to have the s.-s.**, avoir voix au chapitre. 2. parole f, mot m, dire m.

scab[1] [skæb] (noun), F: briseur m de grève, jaune m.

scab[2] [skæb] (to), F: briser la grève.

scabby [ˈskæbi] (adj.), P: minable, mesquin.

scalper [ˈskælpər] (noun), F: qn qui pratique le coup de fusil, empileur m.

scamp[1] [skæmp] (noun), F: **you young** (or **little**) **s.!** petit galopin! petit polisson!

scamp[2] [skæmp] (to), F: 1. = **skive** (to). 2. bâcler, saboter (un travail); faire (un travail) au galop.

scamper [ˈskæmpər] (noun), F: bâcleur m (de travail).

scamping [ˈskæmpiŋ] (noun), F: 1. oisiveté f, flânerie f, traînaillerie f. 2. bâclage m, sabotage m (d'un travail).

scanties [ˈskæntiz], **scants** [skænts] (pl. noun), F: cache-truc m, vignette f, minislip m.

scarce [skɛəs] (adj.), F: **to make oneself s.**, partir*, prendre le large (ou la tangente).

scare-baby [ˈskɛə-beibi], **scaredy-cat** [ˈskɛədi-kæt] (noun), F: poltron*, lâche m, couard m, poule mouillée, vessard m.

scare up [ˈskɛərˈʌp] (to), F: chercher et trouver (qch.).

scarper [ˈskɑːpər] (to), P: s'enfuir*, déguerpir.

scary [ˈskɛəri] (adj.), F: qui fait peur*, effroyable, redoutable.

scat![1] [skæt] (excl.), P: décampe! détale! file! barre-toi!

scat[2] [skæt] (noun), P: 1. (a) chantonnement m, fredonnage m; (b) baragouin m, charabia m. 2. héroïne f (drogues*), jus m.

scatterbrain [ˈskætə-brein] (noun), F: Jean-de-la-lune m, étourdi m, écervelé m.

scatterbrained [ˈskætə-breind] (adj.), F: étourdi, écervelé, évaporé, à tête de linotte.

scatty [ˈskæti] (adj.), F: 1. un peu fou*, toqué, maboul(e). 2. farfelu.

scene [siːn] (noun). 1. F: **behind the scenes**, dans la coulisse, dessous les cartes. 2. F: action f, pratique f; **it's all part of today's s.**, cela fait partie des activités du jour. 3. P: (a) endroit m où les drogués se réunissent, le lieu; **okay s.**, partouze réussie (de drogués); (b) groupement m de drogués. 4. F: **to make a s.**, faire une scène, faire de

---

* L'astérisque indique que le mot marqué de ce signe figure comme entrée dans le Répertoire.

l'esclandre *m*. 5. *F:* to make the s., (*a*) arriver*, s'abouler, se pointer; faire acte de présence; (*b*) réussir, arriver, y avoir la main (*ou* l'oignon *ou* l'os). 6. *F:* bad s., mauvaise posture. 7. *F:* it's not my s., ce n'est pas mon genre, ce n'est pas mon train-train.

schiz(o) [ˈskits(ou)] (*adj. & noun*), *F:* schizo(phrène) (*mf*).

schlemiel, schlemihl [ʃləˈmiːl, ʃleˈmiːl] (*noun*), *P:* nullité *f*, zéro *m*; ballot *m*, gourde *f*.

schlenter [ˈʃlentər] (*adj.*), *P:* toc, camelote.

schlep [ʃlep] (to), *P:* tirer, hâler, remorquer.

schlimazel [ʃliˈmɑːzl] (*noun*) (*U.S.*), *P:* qn qui a de la malchance*, poissard *m*.

schliver [ˈʃlivər] (*noun*), *P:* = chiv[1], 1.

schlong [ʃlɔŋ] (*noun*) (*U.S.*), *P:* pénis*, trique *f*.

schmal(t)z [ʃmælts, ʃmɔːlts, ʃmɔlts] (*noun*), *F:* (*a*) (musique, *etc.*) très sentimental(e); (*b*) sensiblerie *f*.

schmal(t)zy [ˈʃmæltsi, ˈʃmɔːltsi, ˈʃmɔltsi] (*adj.*), *F:* à l'eau de rose.

schmeck [ʃmek], schmee [ʃmiː] (*noun*), *P:* = shmeck.

schmeer [ˈʃmiər] (*noun*), *P:* 1. = dope[1], 1. 2. pot-de-vin *m*. 3. calomnie *f*, bêche *f*.

schmier [ʃmiər] (*noun*), *P:* ristourne *f*, commission *f*, dessous-de-table *m*.

schmo [ʃmou], schmock [ʃmɔk], schmoe [ʃmou] (*noun*), *P:* 1. individu bête*, nigaud *m*, baluchard *m*. 2. individu ennuyeux*, raseur *m*, cassepieds *m*.

schmoose, schmooze [ʃmuːz] (to), *P:* bavarder*, papoter, ragoter.

schmuck [ʃmʌk] (*noun*), *P:* = prick, 1, 2.

schnide [ʃnaid] (*noun*), *P:* = snide[2], 1, 2.

schnook [ʃnʊk, ʃnuːk] (*noun*), *P:* = schmo, 1, 2.

schnorrer [ˈʃnɔːrər] (*noun*) (*U.S.*), *P:* mendiant*, mangav(eur) *m*.

schnozz [ʃnɔz], schnozzle [ˈʃnɔzl], schnozzola [ʃnɔˈzoulə] (*noun*), *P:* nez*, pif *m*.

schnuk [ʃnʌk] (*noun*), *P:* = schnook.

school [skuːl] (*noun*), *F:* personnes réunies pour jouer de l'argent*.

schoolmarm [ˈskuːl-mɑːm] (*noun*), *F:*

(*a*) maîtresse *f* d'école, pionne *f*; (*b*) she's a real s., (i) c'est une pédante; (ii) c'est une vraie prude.

schoolmarmish [ˈskuːl-mɑːmiʃ] (*adj.*), *F:* pédantique, cuistre.

schooner [ˈskuːnər] (*noun*), *F:* grand verre* (d'apéritif, *etc.*).

schpieler [ˈʃpiːlər] (*noun*), *P:* = spieler.

schwar(t)z [ʃwɔːts] (*noun*) (*U.S.*), *P:* (*péj.*) nègre*, bamboula *m*, bougnoul(e) *m*.

scoff[1] [skɔf] (*noun*), *P:* nourriture*, boustifaille *f*.

scoff[2] [skɔf] (to), *P:* (*a*) se goinfrer, s'en foutre plein la lampe; (*b*) manger*, bouffer, bouloter.

scone [skoun] (*noun*) (*Austr.*), *P:* tête*, cassis *m*; to duck the s. = to bow the crumpet (crumpet, 3).

scoop[1] [skuːp] (*noun*), *F:* 1. coup *m* de chance*. 2. (*journal*) nouvelle sensationnelle (que l'on est seul à publier), rafle *f*, scoop *m*.

scoop[2] [skuːp] (to), *F:* 1. avoir un droit exclusif de publication, faire un scoop. 2. rafler, ratiboiser (qn). 3. déjouer les intentions de (qn), dépasser (qn) en finesse.

scoot [skuːt] (to), *F:* 1. s'enfuir*, déguerpir (en quatrième vitesse); s.! détale! file! 2. filer à toute vitesse.

scorch[1] [skɔːtʃ] (*noun*), *F:* allure effrénée, bride abattue.

scorch[2] (along) [ˈskɔːtʃ(əˈlɔŋ)] (to), *F:* conduire comme un fou, aller à un train d'enfer, aller à fond de train.

scorcher [ˈskɔːtʃər] (*noun*), *F:* 1. journée *f* torride; vague *f* de chaleur; it's a s., on se croirait dans un four. 2. amateur *m* de vitesse, avaleur *m* de kilomètres. 3. remarque (*ou* réplique) coupante (*ou* sarcastique), riposte cinglante.

score[1] [skɔːr, skɔər] (*noun*). 1. *F:* to know the s., être au courant (*ou* à la page *ou* dans le coup). 2. *P:* vingt livres sterling. 3. *P:* to make a s. = score[2] (to), 1, 2. 4. *P:* butin*, affure *f*, 5. *P:* affaire réussie (*ou* bien enlevée).

score[2] [skɔːr, skɔər] (to), *P:* 1. obtenir de la drogue. 2. faire une touche; (*prostituée*) faire un levage. 3. être au mieux avec qn, être dans les petits papiers de qn. 4. réussir, se tailler un succès, épater la galerie.

---

* An asterisk indicates that the word so marked is included as a head-word in the Appendix.

Scotch [skɔtʃ] (*adj.*), *F:* **to see through S. mist,** avoir des visions.

Scouse [skaʊs] (*noun*), *F:* 1. habitant *m* de Liverpool. 2. patois *m* de Liverpool.

scout [skaʊt] (*noun*), *F:* un brave homme*, un chic type.

scrag[1] [skræg] (*noun*). 1. *F:* cou décharné, cou de grue, mince collier. 2. *P:* femme* efflanquée (*ou* décharnée).

scrag[2] [skræg] (**to**). 1. *P:* pendre*, garrotter (qn). 2. *F:* (*a*) tuer*, tordre le cou à (qn); (*b*) saisir (un adversaire) au collet.

scram [skræm] (**to**), *P:* partir*, ficher le camp, détaler; **s.!** fous le camp!

scramble! [ˈskræmbl] (*excl.*), *F:* (*R.A.F.*) décollage! (pour intercepter l'ennemi).

scran [skræn] (*noun*), *F:* restes *m.pl.* (de nourriture*), rogatons *m.pl.*

scrap[1] [skræp] (*noun*), *F:* (*a*) querelle*, rixe *f;* (*b*) bagarre*, batterie *f;* (*c*) (*boxe*) match *m;* **to have a s.** = **scrap**[2] (**to**), 2 (*a*), (*b*).

scrap[2] [skræp] (**to**), *F:* 1. mettre (qch.) au rancart. 2. (*a*) se quereller*; (*b*) se battre*, se bagarrer.

scrape[1] [skreip] (*noun*). 1. *F:* **to get into a s.,** se mettre dans un mauvais pas (*ou* dans le pétrin); **to get out of a s.,** se tirer d'affaire. 2. *F:* mince couche *f* de beurre sur une tartine, raclage *m.* 3. *P:* **to have a s.,** se raser*, se racler, se gratter la couenne.

scrape[2] [skreip] (**to**), *F:* 1. **to s. the (bottom of the) barrel,** gratter le fond du panier. 2. **to s. a car,** érafler une voiture. 3. **to s. clear of prison,** friser la prison*.

scrape along [ˈskreipəˈlɔŋ] (**to**), *F:* s'en tirer péniblement, vivoter, à peine joindre les deux bouts.

scrap-heap [ˈskræphiːp] (*noun*), *F:* **to be thrown on the s.-h.,** (*d'une personne*) être mis au rebut; *cf.* **wind up** (**to**).

scratch[1] [skrætʃ] (*noun*). 1. *P:* argent*, pognon *m,* fric *m.* 2. *F:* **to come up to s.,** être à la hauteur. 3. *V:* vagin*, craque(tte) *f,* cicatrice *f.*

scratch[2] [skrætʃ] (**to**), *P:* chasser la drogue. *Voir aussi* **back**[2], 4.

scratcher [ˈskrætʃər] (*noun*), *P:* 1. faussaire *m,* «homme de lettres». 2. allumette *f,* bûche *f,* soufrante *f.* *Voir aussi* **backscratcher.**

scream[1] [skriːm] (*noun*). 1. *F:* (*a*) **she's**

a s., elle est rigolotte, elle est désopilante; (*b*) **it's a s.,** c'est à se tordre, c'est à mourir de rire. 2. *P:* **to put in a s.,** loger un appel en cours de justice.

scream[2] [skriːm] (**to**). 1. *F:* rire* aux éclats (*ou* à ventre déboutonné *ou* à gorge déployée); **he made us s.,** il nous a fait tordre. 2. *P:* = **to put in a scream** (**scream**[1], 2).

screamer [ˈskriːmər] (*noun*), *P:* 1. client jamais satisfait, rouspéteur *m.* 2. grosse en-tête, grande manchette.

screaming [ˈskriːmiŋ] (*adj.*) (*Austr.*), *F:* **s. on s.o., sth.,** monté contre qn, qch. *Voir aussi* **abdabs; meemies.**

screamingly [ˈskriːmiŋli] (*adv.*), *F:* **s. funny,** tordant, crevant.

screaming-match [ˈskriːmiŋmætʃ] (*noun*), *F:* coups *m.pl.* de gueule, engueulade *f* maison.

screw[1] [skruː] (*noun*). 1. *P:* gardien* de prison, gaffe *m,* gâfe *m,* matuche *m.* 2. *V:* (*a*) coït*, baisage *m;* (*b*) femme*, fendue *f;* **a good s.,** une rude baiseuse. 3. *P:* gages *m.pl.,* salaire *m;* **to get a good s.,** être bien payé. 4. *F:* **to have a s. loose,** être un peu fou*, être déboulonné. 5. *F:* **to put the s.** (*or* **screws**) **on s.o.,** forcer (*ou* pressurer) qn, serrer la vis à qn. 6. *F:* cheval*, bidet *m,* canasson *m.* 7. *P:* (*a*) clef*; (*b*) passe-partout *m,* carouble *f.* 8. *P:* coup *m* d'œil*, coup *m* de sabord; **take a s. at this!** zyeute ça!

screw[2] [skruː] (**to**). 1. *V:* coïter* avec (une femme), baiser. 2. *V:* enculer, encaldosser. 3. *P:* **to s. a gaff** (*or* **a drum**), casser une crèche, caroubler une baraque; **to go screwing,** cambrioler*, faire un casse; **to do a screwing job,** faire un fric-frac, caroubler; *cf.* **screwing,** 3. 4. *F:* **to s. money out of s.o.,** extorquer (*ou* soutirer) de l'argent* à qn, taper qn. 5. (*Austr.*) *P:* regarder*, lorgner, gaffer. 6. *F:* **to have one's head (well) screwed on** (*or* **screwed on the right way**), avoir la tête* solide (*ou* sur les épaules). 7. (*U.S.*) *P:* s'enfuir*, décamper, se barrer, se débiner. 8. *P:* duper*, tromper, empiler. 9. *V:* **s. you! get screwed!** va te faire foutre! 10. *P:* gâcher, cafouiller.

screwball[1] [ˈskruːbɔːl] (*adj.*) (*U.S.*), *F:* fou*, tapé, dingue.

screwball[2] [ˈskruːbɔːl] (*noun*) (*U.S.*),

---

* L'astérisque indique que le mot marqué de ce signe figure comme entrée dans le Répertoire.

F: personne étrange, bizarre, excentrique, cinglée; personne excessivement capricieuse.

screwed [skru:d] (*adj.*), *P:* ivre*, rétamé, rondibé; *cf.* **half-screwed.**

screwing [ˈskru:iŋ] (*noun*). 1. *V:* coït*, carambolage *m*, dérouillage *m*. 2. *V:* enculage *m*, encaldossage *m*. 3. *P:* cambriolage *m*, cambriole *f*, fric-frac *m*; *cf.* **screw**² **(to),** 3.

screw off [ˈskru:ˈɔf] **(to),** *V:* se masturber*, se branler, s'astiquer.

screwsman [ˈskru:zmən] (*noun*), *P:* cambrioleur*, casseur *m*, fracasseur *m*.

screw up [ˈskru:ˈʌp] **(to).** 1. *P:* fermer, boucler, brider. 2. *P:* bousiller, rater (qch.). 3. *F:* **to be all screwed up,** (*a*) se tromper, se ficher dedans, se mettre le doigt dans l'œil; (*b*) avoir des idées confuses, être embarbouillé, être dans le brouillard.

screwy [ˈskru:i] (*adj.*). 1. *F:* fou*, cinglé, dingue. 2. *P:* louche, suspect.

scrip(t) [skrip(t)] (*noun*), *P:* ordonnance *f* (de docteur) pour obtenir des drogues.

scrounge¹ [skraundʒ] (*noun*), *F:* 1. = **scrounger,** 1, 2. 2. **he's always on the s.,** c'est un vrai pique-assiette; il ne cherche qu'à vivre aux crochets des autres.

scrounge² [skraundʒ] **(to),** *F:* 1. écornifler. 2. voler*, chiper, chaparder, barboter.

scrounge around [ˈskraundʒəˈraund] **(to),** *F:* (*a*) rabioter à la ronde; (*b*) **to s. a. for sth.,** aller à la recherche de qch, fouiner.

scrounger [ˈskraundʒər] (*noun*), *F:* 1. pique-assiette *m*, écornifleur *m*. 2. voleur*, chapardeur *m*, barboteur *m*.

scrub [skrʌb] **(to),** *F:* (*a*) passer l'éponge sur (qch.); **let's s. it,** passons l'éponge là-dessus; (*b*) effacer, démagnétiser (une bande).

scrubber [ˈskrʌbər] (*noun*), *P:* (*péj.*) femme* *ou* fille* laide* *ou* peu appétissante, mocheté *f*.

scrub round [ˈskrʌbˈraund] **(to),** *F:* = **scrub (to)** (*a*).

scruff [skrʌf] (*noun*), *F:* (*a*) individu* mal soigné (*ou* mal fichu), débraillé *m*.; (*b*) clodo(t) *m*.

scrum [skrʌm] (*noun*), *F:* mêlée *f*, bousculade *f*.

scrumptious [ˈskrʌmpʃəs] (*adj.*), *F:* (*a*) excellent*, épatant, fameux, remarquable; (*b*) délicieux.

scrumpy [ˈskrʌmpi] (*noun*), *F:* cidre *m*, gaulé *m*.

scuffer [ˈskʌfər] (*noun*), *P:* prostituée*, greluche *f*.

scumbag [ˈskʌmbæg] (*noun*), *P:* = **ratbag.**

scummy [ˈskʌmi] (*adj.*), *P:* méprisable, sans valeur.

scunner [ˈskʌnər] (*noun*), *F:* **to take a s. to s.o.,** prendre qn en grippe, avoir qn dans le nez.

scupper [ˈskʌpər] **(to),** *F:* couler, abîmer, massacrer.

sea [si:] (*noun*), *F:* **to be all at s.,** être dérouté (*ou* désorienté); perdre le nord. *Voir aussi* **half-seas-over.**

search [sə:tʃ] **(to),** *F:* **s. me!** je n'en ai pas la moindre idée; je n'en ai pas la queue d'une; mystère et boule de gomme!

sec [sek] (*noun*) (*abbr.* = *second*), *F:* **just a s.! half a s.!** un moment!; *cf.* **jiff(y); mo; shake**¹, 1, 2; **tick**¹, 3.

secko [ˈsekou] (*adj.*) (*Austr.*), *P:* perverti.

seconds [ˈsekəndz] (*pl. noun*), *F:* 1. articles défectueux (*ou* démarqués). 2. portion *f* (de nourriture*) supplémentaire; rab(iot) *m*.

see [si:] **(to),** *F:* **s. you!** au revoir! ciao! *Voir aussi* **dog**¹, 20; **thing,** 7.

seed [si:d] (*noun*). 1. *F:* **to go to s.,** (*d'une personne*) se décatir, s'avachir. 2. *P:* = **roach.** *Voir aussi* **hayseed.**

seedy [ˈsi:di] (*adj.*), *F:* 1. pauvre*, minable, râpé, usé, élimé. 2. malade*, patraque, pas dans son assiette.

see off [ˈsi:ˈɔf] **(to),** *F:* (*a*) **to s. s.o. o.,** régler le compte à qn; (*b*) **to s. sth. o.,** régler, liquider, conclure qch.

see out [ˈsi:ˈaut] **(to),** *F:* survivre à (qn).

see-through [ˈsi-θru:] (*adj.*), *F:* transparent.

sell¹ [sel] (*noun*), *F:* 1. attrape *f*, carotte *f*, blague *f*, fumisterie *f*. 2. déception *f*, désappointement *m*. *Voir aussi* **hard**¹, 5; **soft**¹, 5.

sell² [sel] **(to),** *F:* 1. duper* (qn), amener (qn) à la balançoire, monter le cou à (qn). 2. **to s. s.o. short,** sous-estimer qn. 3. **to be sold on s.o., sth.,** être amené vers qn, qch. 4. **to s. oneself,** se faire accepter, se faire valoir. 5. convaincre, persuader. *Voir aussi* **river,** 1.

sell-out [ˈselaut] (*noun*), *F:* 1. trahison

---

* An asterisk indicates that the word so marked is included as a head-word in the Appendix.

f, judasserie *f*, macaronage *m*. **2.** vente *f* de tous les billets pour un spectacle; séance *f* à guichet fermé. **3.** vente *f* de liquidation.

sell out [ˈselˈaʊt] **(to)**, *F:* **1.** (*a*) dénoncer*, vendre (qn); (*b*) trahir, judasser, lessiver, macaroner (qn). **2.** (*d'une personne*) se vendre. *Voir aussi* **sold out.**

semi [ˈsemi] (*noun*) (*=semi-detached house*), *F:* maison jumelée.

send [send] **(to)**, *F:* **1. she sends me!** elle me transporte! **2.** (*drogues*) faire partir, faire voyager (qn).

send-off [ˈsendɔf] (*noun*), *F:* **1.** fête *f* d'adieu, souhaits *m.pl.* de bon voyage. **2.** inauguration réussie. **3.** enterrement *m*.

send-up [ˈsendʌp] (*noun*), *F:* satire *f*, parodie *f*, éreintage *m*, éreintement *m*.

send up [ˈsendˈʌp] **(to). 1.** *F:* satiriser, parodier, se moquer de, ridiculiser, éreinter. **2.** *P:* **to s. s.o. u.,** emprisonner*, boucler, coffrer qn, mettre qn en taule (*ou* au bloc).

septic [ˈseptik] (*adj.*), *P:* **1.** désagréable, puant. **2. s. tank** (*R.S. = Yank*), Américain *m*, Amerlo *m*, Yankee *m*.

serve [sɔːv] **(to)**, *F:* (**it) serves you right!** c'est bien fait!

session [ˈseʃ(ə)n] (*noun*), *F:* **1. jam s.,** réunion *f* de musiciens qui improvisent collectivement; concert *m* de jazz, jam session *f*. **2.** longue séance. *Voir aussi* **petting.**

set[1] [set] (*adj. & p.p.*), *F:* **to be all s.,** être fin prêt.

set[2] [set] (*noun*), *F:* **1. to make a dead s. at s.o.,** (*a*) attaquer furieusement qn (à la tribune); (*b*) se jeter à la tête de qn, relancer qn, poursuivre qn de ses avances. **2.** (*Navy*) **full s.,** barbe et moustache.

set about [ˈsetəˈbaʊt] **(to)**, *F:* **1. to s. a. s.o.,** attaquer* qn, tomber sur qn. **2. to s. a. (doing)** sth., entreprendre qch., se mettre à qch.

set back [ˈsetˈbæk] **(to)**, *F:* coûter, peser; **the round of drinks s. him b. a pound,** la tournée lui a pesé un faf(f)iot.

set-to [ˈsetˈtuː] (*noun*), *F:* bagarre*, lutte *f*, torchage *m*.

set-up [ˈsetʌp] (*noun*). **1.** *F:* structure *f*, organisation *f*, fonctionnement *m*. **2.** *F:* édifice *m*, installation *f*; **a nice s.-u.**

you have here, vous êtes bien installé ici. **3.** *P:* **= frame-up.**

set up [ˈsetˈʌp] **(to)**, *F:* **1. to s. 'em u. again,** remplir les verres de nouveau, remettre ça, faire une autre tournée, rhabiller les gamins. **2. to s. s.o. u. for the kill,** conditionner qn pour le coup de massue.

sew up [ˈsouˈʌp] **(to)**, *F:* **it's all sewn up,** c'est tout fixé, c'est tout arrangé.

sex [seks] (*noun*), *F:* **1. to have s. with s.o.,** coïter* avec qn, faire l'amour avec qn. **2. the third s.,** homosexuels *m.pl.*, le troisième sexe.

sex-bomb [ˈseksbɔm] (*noun*), *F:* allumeuse *f*, blonde incendiaire.

sexcited [ˈsekˈsaitid] (*adj.*), *F:* =**sexed up.**

sex-crazy [ˈseksˈkreizi] (*adj.*), *F:* = **sex-mad.**

sexed up [ˈsekstˈʌp] (*adj.*), *F:* excité, allumé, aguiché.

sex-kitten [ˈseks-kitn] (*noun*), *F:* fille* aguichante, jeune pin-up alléchante, nénette ronronnante.

sex-mad [ˈseksˈmæd] (*adj.*), *F:* **he's s.-m.,** c'est un obsédé sexuel.

sexo [ˈseksou] (*adj.*) (*Austr.*), *P:* = **secko.**

sex-pot [ˈseks-pɔt] (*noun*), *P:* femme* qui a du sex-appeal, aguicheuse *f*, allumeuse *f*.

sex-ridden [ˈseksridn] (*adj.*), *F:* porté sur la bagatelle, farci de sexe.

sex-starved [ˈsekstɑːvd] (*adj.*), *F:* souffrant du manque d'activité sexuelle, victime de diète sexuelle.

sexy [ˈseksi] (*adj.*), *F:* sensuel, chaud, sexy.

sez you! [ˈsezˈjuː] (*excl.*), *P:* = **says you!** (**say (to),** 3).

shack [ʃæk] (*noun*), *F:* (*a*) taudis *m*, cambuse *f*, bouge *m*; (*b*) guitoune *f*, cabane *f*.

shack-up [ˈʃækʌp] (*attrib. adj.*), *P:* **a s.-u. job,** (*a*) nuit passée avec n'importe quelle femme*; (*b*) femme* d'un soir.

shack up [ˈʃækˈʌp] **(to)**, *P:* **to s. u. with s.o.,** vivre ensemble, se coller avec qn, s'antifler.

shade [ʃeid] (*noun*). **1.** *F:* **to put s.o. in the s.,** laisser qn dans l'ombre, éclipser qn. **2.** (*pl.*) *P:* lunettes* de soleil, vitraux *m.pl.*

shadow[1] [ˈʃædou] (*noun*), *F:* **1. to put a s. on s.o. = to put a tail on s.o.** (**tail**[1], 5). **2. five-o'clock s.,** la barbe du soir, le foin de la journée.

---

* L'astérisque indique que le mot marqué de ce signe figure comme entrée dans le Répertoire.

shadow[2] ['ʃædou] (**to**), F: = **tail**[2] (**to**).

shady ['ʃeidi] (*adj.*), F: louche, équivoque, trouble, véreux.

shaft[1] [ʃɑ:ft] (*noun*), V: pénis*, colonne f.

shaft[2] [ʃɑ:ft] (**to**). **1.** V: coïter* avec (une femme), pinocher. **2.** (U.S.) P: escroquer*, carotter (qn). **3.** (U.S.) P: congédier*, sacquer, dégommer (qn).

shag[1] [ʃæg] (*noun*). **1.** V: coït*, dérouillage m. **2.** V: she's a good s., c'est une rude baiseuse, c'est une Marie-jambe(s)-en-l'air. **3.** P: it's a (bit of a) s., c'est ennuyeux*, c'est pénible (*ou* lassant).

shag[2] [ʃæg] (**to**). **1.** V: (*a*) coïter* avec (une femme), dérouiller, égoïner; (*b*) coïter*, se dérouiller; *cf.* **arse**, 9. **2.** P: fatiguer*, vider, pomper; **to feel shagged**, être vanné.

shag-ass ['ʃægæs] (**to**) (U.S.), V: s'enfuir*, se carapater, prendre ses cliques et ses claques.

shagbag ['ʃægbæg] (*noun*), V: vieille rombière-patte-en-l'air.

shaggable ['ʃægəbl] (*adj.*), V: = **fuckable**.

shagged (out) ['ʃægd('aut)] (*adj.*), P: très fatigué*, éreinté.

shagger ['ʃægər] (*noun*), V: habitué(e) du baisage (*coït**).

shaggy-dog ['ʃægi'dɔg] (*attrib. adj.*), F: **s.-d. story**, histoire f de fous, histoire farfelue (*ou* loufoque), loufoquerie f.

shag-happy ['ʃæg'hæpi] (*adj.*), V: qui pratique avec entrain le baisage (*coït**).

shag-nasty ['ʃæg'nɑ:sti] (*adj.*), P: très désagréable, emmerdant.

shag off ['ʃæg'ɔf] (**to**), V: partir*, décamper; **s. o.!** déguerpis! file!

shake[1] [ʃeik] (*noun*). **1.** F: **half a s.!** un moment! une seconde! **2.** F: **in two shakes (of a cat's** (*or* **lamb's) tail,)** en moins de deux, en deux temps trois mouvements. **3.** F: **to give s.o. a fair s.**, agir loyalement envers qn, être régulier avec qn; **to get a fair s.**, être traité comme il faut, être traité régulier (*ou* régló). **4.** F: **to have the shakes**, (*a*) avoir peur*, avoir les foies; (*b*) avoir le delirium tremens. **5.** F: **no great shakes**, médiocre, rien d'extraordinaire, quelconque. **6.** P: **to put the s. on s.o.** = **to shake s.o. down (shake down (to),** 4). *Voir aussi* **handshake**.

shake[2] [ʃeik] (**to**), F: **1.** **that'll s. him!** cela le fera tiquer! **2.** **s. on it!** tope là!

3. (*Austr.*) **shook on s.o.**, entiché de qn. *Voir aussi* **leg**[1], 3.

shakedown ['ʃeikdaun] (*noun*). **1.** F: lit* de fortune; hébergement m d'une nuit. **2.** P: chantage m, rançon f.

shake down ['ʃeik'daun] (**to**). **1.** P: = **strong-arm**[2] (**to**). **2.** P: fouiller (un prisonnier), fourober. **3.** F: se coucher*, se pieuter. **4.** P: faire casquer (qn), faire cracher (qn).

shakers ['ʃeikəz] (*pl. noun*), P: seins*, flotteurs m.pl.

shake-up ['ʃeikʌp] (*noun*), F: **1.** remaniement m (du personnel). **2.** commotion f, bouleversement m. **3.** mélange m d'alcool* et de whisky.

shaky ['ʃeiki] (*adj.*), F: **a s. do**, une affaire mal menée (*ou* branlante).

shamateur ['ʃæmə'tə:r] (*noun*), F: (athlète) professionnel qui prétend être amateur.

shambles ['ʃæmblz] (*noun*), F: **a s.**, une pagaille.

shambolic [ʃæm'bɔlik] (*adj.*), P: en pleine pagaille.

shammy ['ʃæmi] (*noun*), F: peau f (de chamois).

shampers ['ʃæmpəz] (*noun*), F: = **champers**.

shanghai [ʃæŋ'hai] (**to**), F: forcer (qn) à un travail désagréable; **I was shanghaied into doing it**, on m'a forcé à le faire.

shanks [ʃæŋks] (*pl. noun*), F: **1.** jambes*, gambilles f.pl. **2.** **to ride S.'s pony** (*or* **mare** *or* **nag**), voyager à pied, prendre le train onze, prendre la voiture de Saint-Crépin.

shapes [ʃeips] (*pl. noun*) (U.S.), P: dés* truqués, balourds m.pl.

shark [ʃɑ:k] (*noun*), F: **1.** escroc*, arnaqueur m, dragueur m, requin m. **2.** (U.S.) **as m**, champion m, crack m.

sharp[1] [ʃɑ:p] (*adj.*) (U.S.), F: élégant*, coquet, chic, jojo.

sharp[2] [ʃɑ:p] (*noun*), F: = **shark**, 1.

sharp[3] [ʃɑ:p] (**to**), P: escroquer*, arnaquer, roustir.

sharper ['ʃɑ:pər] (*noun*), F: tricheur* (aux cartes), entôleur m.

sharpie ['ʃɑ:pi] (*noun*), P: **1.** = **shark**, 1. **2.** (U.S.) gandin m, minet m. **3.** malin m, dégourdi m, débrouillard m.

sharpish ['ʃɑ:piʃ] (*adv.*), F: (**a bit) s.**, vite*, presto, rapidos.

---

* An asterisk indicates that the word so marked is included as a head-word in the Appendix.

shave [ʃeiv] (*noun*), *F:* **to have a close (*or* narrow) s.**, l'échapper belle, échapper à un cheveu près; **it was a close (*or* narrow) s.**, il était moins une.

shaved [ʃeivd] (*adj.*) (*U.S.*), *F:* ivre*, bourré, rétamé; *cf.* **half-shaved.**

shaver [ˈʃeivər] (*noun*), *F:* gamin *m*, gosse *m*, môme *m*.

shebang [ʃiˈbæŋ] (*noun*). **1.** *F:* **the whole s.**, tout le bataclan, tout le tremblement; *cf.* **boiling; caboodle; shoot¹, 1; shooting-match. 2.** *P:* cabane *f*, cambuse *f*; boutanche *f*. **3.** *P:* bordel*, clandé *m*, volière *f*.

she-cat [ˈʃiːˈkæt] (*noun*), *F:* chipie *f*, souris *f*, bique *f*.

shee [ʃiː] (*noun*), *P:* = **yen-shee.**

sheenie, sheeny [ˈʃiːni] (*noun*), *P:* (*péj.*) Juif *m*, Youpin *m*.

sheepdog [ˈʃiːpdɔg] (*noun*), *F:* chaperon *m*, chien *m* de garde.

sheer off [ˈʃiərˈɔf] (**to**), *F:* s'écarter; partir*, prendre le large.

sheet [ʃiːt] (*noun*). **1.** *F:* **to be three (*or* four) sheets in (*or* to) the wind**, être ivre*, avoir du vent dans les voiles, en rouler une. **2.** *P:* une livre sterling; **half a s.**, 50 pence. **3.** *P:* journal*, feuille *f* (de chou). **4.** *P:* casier *m* judiciaire (d'un criminel), faffes *m.pl. Voir aussi* **swindle-sheet.**

sheila [ˈʃiːlə] (*noun*) (*Austr.*), *F:* jeune fille*, jeune femme*, nénette *f*.

shekels [ˈʃekəlz] (*pl. noun*), *P:* argent*, fric *m*, pognon *m*.

shelf [ʃelf] (*noun*), *F:* **on the s.**, (*a*) célibataire, laissé(e) pour compte; (*b*) mis(e) de côté, resté(e) dans les cartons.

shelf-kit [ˈʃelfkit] (*noun*), *P:* seins*, avant-scène *f*.

shellac(k) [ʃeˈlæk] (**to**), *F:* **1.** battre*, rosser (qn), passer (qn) à tabac. **2.** vaincre, écraser, griller (qn).

shellacked [ʃeˈlækt] (*adj.*) (*U.S.*), *P:* ivre*, rétamé, culbuté.

shellacking [ʃeˈlækiŋ] (*noun*), *P:* **1.** rossée *f*, flo(p)pée *f*. **2.** (*sports*) défaite *f*, raclée *f*.

shellback [ʃel-bæk] (*noun*), *F:* vieux marin*, vieux loup de mer.

shell out [ˈʃelˈaʊt] (**to**), *P:* payer*, (les) abouler, casquer.

shemozzle¹ [ʃiˈmɔzl] (*noun*), *P:* (*a*) bruit*, boucan *m*, chahut *m*, chambard

m; (*b*) difficultés *f.pl.*, ennuis *m.pl.*, emmerdement *m*.

shemozzle² [ʃiˈmɔzl] (**to**), *P:* = **skedaddle** (**to**).

shenanagin(s) [ʃəˈnænəgin(z)] ((*pl.*) *noun*), *F:* fumisterie *f*, truquage *m*, mystification *f*.

shice [ʃais] (**to**), *P:* **1.** trahir, plaquer, planter. **2.** = **welsh** (**to**).

shickered [ˈʃikəd] (*adj.*), *P:* ivre*, paf, éméché.

shift¹ [ʃift] (*noun*), *F:* **1.** échappatoire *f*, faux-fuyant *m*, biaisement *m*. **2. to get a s. on**, se dépêcher*, se magner le train.

shift² [ʃift] (**to**). **1.** *P:* **s.! file!** bouge-toi!; **he didn't half s.!** il s'est calté en moins de deux! **2.** *F:* **to s. a pint**, écluser un verre, en étrangler un, s'en jeter un derrière la cravate. **3.** *F:* **to s. for oneself**, se débrouiller, se dépatouiller.

shiksa [ˈʃiksə] (*noun*), *P:* (*péj.*) fille* non-juive, goyette *f*.

shill(aber) [ˈʃil(əbər)] (*noun*), *P:* compère *m* dans un tripot de jeux, jockey *m*; compère d'un camelot qui simule un achat pour encourager les clients, baron *m*, appeau *m*.

shimmy¹ [ˈʃimi] (*noun*), *F:* chemise*, liquette *f*.

shimmy² [ˈʃimi] (**to**), *F:* osciller, vaciller, brimbaler.

shindig [ˈʃindig] (*noun*), *F:* **1.** querelle*, chambard *m*, raffut *m*, ramdam *m*; *voir aussi* **kick up** (**to**), **2. 2.** réunion bruyante, boum *f*, partouze *f*.

shindy [ˈʃindi] (*noun*), *P:* = **shindig, 1.**

shine [ʃain] (*noun*). **1.** *F:* **to take a s. to s.o.**, s'éprendre de qn, s'amouracher de qn, prendre qn en affection, s'enticher de qn. **2.** (*U.S.*) *P:* (*péj.*) nègre*, bougnoul(l)e *m*, cireur *m*. **3.** (*U.S.*) *P:* pièce *f* d'or. **4.** (*U.S.*) *P:* = **moonshine, 1. 5.** *P:* = **shindig, 1, 2. 6.** *F:* **to take the s. out of s.o.**, éclipser, dépasser qn. *Voir aussi* **bullshine.**

shiner [ˈʃainər] (*noun*). **1.** *F:* œil* poché (*ou* au beurre noir), coquard *m*. **2.** (*U.S.*) *P:* (*péj.*) = **shine, 2. 3.** *F:* voiture neuve. **4.** *F:* diamant*, brillant *m*. **5.** *F:* pièce (d'argent*) neuve.

shine up to [ˈʃainˈʌptuː] (**to**), *F:* **s. u. t. s.o.**, chercher à se faire bien voir de qn, faire de la lèche auprès de qn.

shin(ny) up ['ʃin(i)'ʌp] (to), F: grimper,
escalader.
ship [ʃip] (noun), F: when my s. comes
home, quand il m'arrivera de l'argent*,
quand mes galions seront arrivés,
quand j'aurai décroché le gros lot.
ship out ['ʃip'aʊt] (to), P: s'enfuir*, se
calter, décamper.
shirash [ʃi'ræʃ] (noun), P: = charas(h).
shirt [ʃə:t] (noun), F: 1. to put one's s.
on sth., miser le tout pour le tout,
parier sa chemise. 2. to lose one's s., (a)
tout perdre, être lessivé; (b) (U.S.)
s'emporter, prendre la chèvre. 3. keep
your s. on! ne t'énerve pas! ne t'emballe
pas! 4. to have one's s. out, être de
mauvais poil, être à rebrousse-poil. 5.
stuffed (or boiled) s., crâneur m,
plastronneur m, collet monté.
shirt-lifter ['ʃə:tliftər] (noun), P: pédéraste*, enculé m.
shirty ['ʃə:ti] (adj.), F: to be s., être de
mauvaise humeur, faire la gueule; to get
s., se mettre en colère* (ou en rogne).
shit¹ [ʃit] (adv.), VV: extrêmement,
complètement, tout à fait; to be s.
poor, être vachement pauvre*; to be s.
out of luck, avoir une poisse noire,
être dans la merde; to be s. hot at sth.,
être vachement calé sur qch.
shit!² [ʃit] (excl.), VV: merde alors!
shit³ [ʃit] (noun), VV: 1. merde*, caca
m, chiasse f. 2. to land (or drop) s.o. in
the s., mettre (ou foutre) qn dans la
merde. 3. to be (right) in the s., être
emmerdé jusqu'au cou. 4. to scare the
s. out of s.o., rendre qn foireux, donner
la chiasse (ou les chocottes f.pl.) à qn;
cf. shit-scared. 5. to eat s., traîner dans
la merde. 6. don't talk s.! ne dis pas
de conneries! 7. I don't give a s., je
m'en fous et contrefous. 8. full of s.,
mal renseigné, chiasseux. 9. (it's) no s.,
c'est la vérité, c'est pas de la merde.
10. =shitbag. 11. emmerdeur m. 12.
camelote f, de la merde. 13. (a) (a)
héroïne f (drogues*), shit m; (b) hachisch
m (drogues*), merde f; (c) drogues* en
général, came f. 14. the shits, diarrhée*,
chiasse f. Voir aussi bullshit¹; creek;
crock¹, 5; horseshit; s.o.b.
shit⁴ [ʃit] (to), VV: 1. déféquer*, chier.
2. exagérer*, chier dans la colle; don't
s. me! ne me bourre pas le crâne!
3. s. or bust, tout ou rien, marche ou

crève, pisse ou fais-toi éclater la vessie.
Voir aussi bullshit² (to).
shit-ass ['ʃitæs] (noun) (U.S.), VV: =
shitbag.
shitbag ['ʃitbæg] (noun), VV: merdaillon
m, merdeux m.
shitcan ['ʃitkæn] (to), V: 1. (Austr.)
casser, enfoncer (qn). 2. (U.S.) se
défaire de (qch.), balancer, larguer
(qch.).
shite¹ [ʃait] (noun), VV: = shit³, 1.
shite² [ʃait] (to), VV: = shit⁴ (to), 1.
shithead ['ʃithed], shitheel ['ʃithi:l]
(noun), VV: = shitbag.
shit-hole ['ʃithoʊl] (noun), VV: anus*,
trou m du cul, rondibé m.
shit-house ['ʃithaʊs] (noun), VV: W.C.*,
chiottes f.pl., débourre f.
shitkicker ['ʃitkikər] (noun) (U.S.),
VV: 1. traîne-la-merde m. 2. paysan*,
rustaud m. 3. but(t)eur m, katangais m.
shitless ['ʃitlis] (adj.), VV: to be scared
s. = to be shit-scared.
shit-list ['ʃitlist] (noun), V: tableau m
des mal-vus, liste f des hors-petits-
papiers, groupe m des abominations;
cf. stink-list.
shit off ['ʃit'ɔf] (to), VV: s'enfuir*,
mettre les bouts; s. o.! calte-toi!
shitpot ['ʃitpɔt] (noun), VV: = shitbag.
shit-scared['ʃit'skəəd] (adj.), VV:chias-
seux, foireux; cf. shit³, 4.
shitstick ['ʃit-stik] (noun) (U.S.), VV:
= shitbag.
shitters ['ʃitəz] (pl. noun), V: the s.,
diarrhée*, la chiasse.
shitty ['ʃiti] (adj.), VV: 1. méprisable,
débectant, dégueulasse. 2. (U.S.) douteux, plein de gourance.
shiv [ʃiv] (noun), P: = chiv¹, 1, 2.
shive [ʃaiv] (to), P: = chiv² (to), 1, 2.
shivers ['ʃivəz] (pl. noun), F: to give
s.o. the s., donner la tremblote (ou le
frisson) à qn.
shivoo ['ʃai'vu:] (noun) (Austr.),
réjouissances*, bamboula f, raout m.
shliver ['ʃlivər] (noun), P: = chiv¹, 1, 2.
shlonger ['ʃlɔŋər] (noun) (U.S.), P: =
schlong.
shmeck [ʃmek], shmee [ʃmi:] (noun),
P: héroïne f (drogues*), schmeck m.
shmo(e) [ʃmoʊ] (noun), P: = schmo,
1, 2.
shnockered ['ʃnɔkəd] (adj.), P: hébété
par un narcotique, bourré à bloc.

* An asterisk indicates that the word so marked is included as a head-word in the Appendix.

shocker [ˈʃɔkər] (*noun*), *F:* horreur *f*, affreux *m* (*personne ou chose*); **you're a s.!** tu es impossible!

shoes [ʃuːz] (*pl. noun*), *F:* **that's another pair of s.**, c'est une autre paire de manches. *Voir aussi* **dead**[1], **9**; **ice**[1], **7**.

shoestring [ˈʃuː-strin] (*noun*), *F:* **to do business on a s.**, faire des affaires avec des moyens financiers très limités; tirer sur la corde.

shonk [ʃɔnk] (*noun*), *P:* (*péj.*) Juif *m*, Youpin *m*.

shook [ʃuk] (*p.p.*): *voir* **shake**[2] (to), **3**.

shook up [ˈʃukˈʌp] (*adj.*), *P:* (all) **s. u.**, secoué, émotionné, remué.

shoot[1] [ʃuːt] (*noun*). **1.** *F:* **the whole (bang) s.**, tout le bataclan, tout le tremblement; *cf.* **boiling**; **caboodle**; **shebang**[1], **1**; **shooting-match**. **2.** *P:* piqûre *f*, piquouse *f* (*drogues*).

shoot[2] [ʃuːt] (to). **1.** *P:* **s.!** vas-y! rentre dedans! **2.** *P:* éjaculer*, arroser; *voir aussi* **load**, **8**. **3.** *F:* filmer, photographier. **4.** *F:* **to get short of s.o.**, sth., se débarrasser* de qn, de qch., défarguer, larguer qn, qch. **5.** *F:* **to s. a line**, exagérer*, blouser, se vanter, en installer, esbrouf(f)er; **to s. s.o. a line**, lancer de la poudre aux yeux de qn; *cf.* **line-shooter**; **line-shooting**. **6.** *P:* **to s. the cat**, vomir*, évacuer le couloir. **7.** (*U.S.*) *P:* **to s. the bull** (*or* **the crap** *or* **the breeze**), bavarder*, dire des banalités *f.pl.*, tailler une bavette. **8.** *F:* **to s. the works**, (*a*) dilapider son argent*, lessiver son pognon; (*b*) avouer*, manger le morceau, faire des aveux *m.pl.*; (*c*) jouer (*ou* miser *ou* risquer) le tout pour le tout, jouer sa chemise; (*d*) y aller de tout son saoul, donner un coup de collier. **9.** *P:* **to s. the moon**, déménager à la cloche de bois. **10.** *F:* **he has shot his bolt**, il a vidé son carquois, il a jeté tout son feu. **11.** *P:* (*à table*) passer (la nourriture); **s. the gravy!** passe la sauce! **12.** *P:* se shooter (*drogues*). *Voir aussi* **lingo**, **2**; **wad**, **4**.

shoot down [ˈʃuːtˈdaun] (to), *F:* **to s. s.o. d.** (**in flames**), rabattre le caquet à qn, torcher le bec à qn, ramener qn à ses justes proportions; **to get shot down in flames**, l'avoir dans l'os.

shooter [ˈʃuːtər] (*noun*), *P:* arme *f* à feu, flingue *m*. *Voir aussi* **line-shooter**; **pea-shooter**; **six-shooter**.

shooting-gallery [ˈʃuːtingæləri] (*noun*), *P:* endroit où on se pique à la drogue, shooterie *f*.

shooting-iron [ˈʃuːtinaiən] (*noun*), *F:* revolver*, flingot *m*, pétard *m*.

shooting-match [ˈʃuːtinmætʃ] (*noun*), *F:* **the whole s.-m.** = **the whole (bang) shoot** (**shoot**[1], **1**).

shoot off [ˈʃuːtˈɔf] (to). *P:* **1.** = **shoot**[2] (to), **2.** **2. to s. one's mouth** (*or* **face**) **o.**, (*a*) révéler un secret, vendre la mèche; (*b*) bavasser, être atteint de diarrhée verbale.

shoot up [ˈʃuːtˈʌp] (to). **1.** *P:* se piquer, se shooter, avoir la piquouse. **2.** *F:* terroriser (une ville, *etc.*).

shop[1] [ʃɔp] (*noun*). **1.** *F:* **all over the s.**, (*a*) en vrac, comme dans un bordel; (*b*) partout, dans tous les coins. **2.** *P:* **you've come to the wrong s.**, vous n'êtes pas au bon guichet, il y a erreur d'aiguillage. **3.** *F:* **to talk s.**, parler affaires, parler boutique; *cf.* **shop-talk**. **4.** *F:* **to shut up s.**, (*sports*) fermer le jeu. **5.** *P:* prison*, boîte *f*. **6.** *F:* **top of the s.:** *voir* **bingo** (**90**). *Voir aussi* **cop-shop**; **dolly-shop**; **fish-shop**; **hock-shop**; **hook-shop**; **kip-shop**; **milk-shop**; **molly-shop**; **porn-shop**; **slopshop**; **sweat-shop**; **whore-shop**.

shop[2] [ʃɔp] (to), *P:* **1.** dénoncer*, trahir, moutonner. **2.** traduire (qn) en justice. **3.** emprisonner*, mettre en boîte.

shop-talk [ˈʃɔp-tɔːk] (*noun*), *F:* jargon *m* de métier, d'un groupe professionnel, d'une (soi-disant) science, *etc.*; *cf.* **shop**[1], **3**.

short[1] [ʃɔːt] (*adj.*), **1.** *F:* **to be a bit s.**, être à court (d'argent*). **2.** *P:* **s. time**, courte séance (*prostituée*). **3.** *P:* **s. arm**, pénis*, la troisième jambe. *Voir aussi* **curly**, **2**; **hair**, **6**.

short[2] [ʃɔːt] (*adv.*), *F:* **to be caught s.**, (*a*) être pris d'un besoin pressant; (*b*) être pris de court. *Voir aussi* **sell**[2] (to), **2**.

short[3] [ʃɔːt] (*noun*), *F:* **1.** un petit verre d'alcool* (*ou* de goutte *f*). **2.** (*U.S.*) petite voiture de sport, petit bolide.

short-arse [ˈʃɔːtɑːs] (*noun*), *V:* bas-du-cul *m*, basduc *m*; *cf.* **shorty**.

shortchange[1] [ˈʃɔːt-tʃeindʒ] (*attrib. adj.*), *F:* **s. artist**, escroc* filou *m*, estampeur *m*.

* L'astérisque indique que le mot marqué de ce signe figure comme entrée dans le Répertoire.

shortchan'ge[2] [ˈʃɔːtˈtʃeindʒ] (**to**), *F:* **to s. s.o.**, voler* qn en lui rendant la monnaie (lui rendre moins qu'il ne lui revient).

short-sheet [ˈʃɔːtˈʃiːt] (**to**), *F:* **to s.-s. a bed**, mettre un lit en portefeuille.

shortweight [ˈʃɔːtˈweit] (**to**), *F:* estamper sur le poids de qch.

shorty [ˈʃɔːti] (*noun*), *F:* homme de petite* taille, courte-botte *m*.

shot[1] [ʃɔt] (*adj.*), *F:* **1**. ivre*, bituré, rétamé, rond; *cf.* **half-shot**. **2**. très fatigué*, vanné.

shot[2] [ʃɔt] (*noun*), *F:* **1**. piqûre *f*, piquouse *f* (*drogues*); *voir aussi* **hot, 24** (*b*). **2**. une mesure d'alcool*, un dé, une rincette. **3. a s. in the arm**, un remontant, un stimulant, un coup de fouet. **4. to have a s. at sth.**, essayer qch., tenter le coup. **5**. (*a*) **a long s.**, (i) un gros risque; (ii) un gros risque (*cheval de course, etc.*); une chance sur mille; (iii) (*cinéma*) une scène filmée à distance; (*b*) **not by a long s.** = **not by a long chalk** (**chalk, 1**). **6. like a s.**, (*a*) très vite* comme l'éclair; (*b*) volontiers, de bon cœur. **7. to make a s. in the dark**, deviner au hasard. **8**. dada *m*, habitude *f*, manie *f*. *Voir aussi* **big**[1], **1**; **pot-shot**.

shotgun [ˈʃɔtɡʌn] (*attrib. adj.*), *F:* **1. s. agreement**, convention signée sous la contrainte. **2. s. wedding**, mariage forcé, régularisation *f*.

shoulder [ˈʃouldər] (*noun*), *F:* **1. to rub shoulders with s.o.**, frayer avec qn, se frotter à qn. **2. straight from the s.**, carrément, sans mettre de gants; **he let me have it straight from the s.**, il ne me l'a pas envoyé dire. *Voir aussi* **cold**[1], **1**; **cold-shoulder** (**to**).

shout [ʃaut] (*noun*), *F:* **1. it's my s.**, c'est ma tournée. **2. give me a s. when you're ready**, fais signe quand tu es prêt.

shouting [ˈʃautiŋ] (*noun*), *F:* **it's all over bar the s.**, c'est dans le sac, les applaudissements suivront.

shove [ʃʌv] (**to**), (*a*) *P:* **you know where you can s. that!** tu sais où tu peux te le mettre!; (*b*) *V:* **you can s. that (right) up your arse!** tu peux te le mettre au cul!

shove around [ˈʃʌvəˈraund] (**to**), *F:* bousculer, ballotter (qn), faire marcher (qn).

shove off [ˈʃʌvˈɔf] (**to**), (*a*) *F:* partir*, décamper; (*b*) *P:* **s. o.!** fiche le camp!

shovel it down [ˈʃʌvəlitˈdaun] (**to**), *F:* se goinfrer, se gaver.

show[1] [ʃou] (*noun*), *F:* **1. a s. of leg**, un étalage de cuisses; **free s.**, striptease *m* à l'œil; **it's a free s.**, elle a soulevé son capot, on voit le moteur. **2. good s.!** bravo! c'est au poil! c'est épatant! **3. to give the s. away**, vendre (*ou* éventer) la mèche, débiner le truc. **4. to stop the s.**, (*th.*) être applaudi avec enthousiasme par les spectateurs, casser la baraque. **5. to steal the s.**, capter l'attention, magnétiser l'assemblée, tirer à soi la couverture. *Voir aussi* **boss**[3] (**to**), **1**; **leg**[1], **2**; **meat-show**.

show[2] [ʃou] (**to**), *F:* = **show up** (**to**), **1**. *Voir aussi* **leg**[1], **1**.

showbiz [ˈʃoubiz] (*noun*). **1**. *F:* l'industrie *f* du spectacle. **2**. *P:* demi-monde *m*, entourage *m* de demi-mondains, le monde où l'on s'amuse.

showdown [ˈʃoudaun] (*noun*), *F:* **1**. confrontation *f*, déballage *m* (de ses intentions). **2**. révélation *f* d'adversité, mise *f* au point; mise *f* à jour.

shower [ˈʃauər] (*noun*), *P:* (*a*) nullité *f*, nouille *f*; **he's a right s.!** quelle andouille! (*b*) **what a s.!** quelle bande* (*ou* quel tas) de crétins!

showman [ˈʃoumən] (*noun*), *F:* (*jazz*) musicien *m* spectaculaire, showman *m*.

show-off [ˈʃouɔf] (*noun*), *F:* individu qui fait du flafla (*ou* de l'épate *f*), esbrouf(f)eur *m*, poseur *m*, m'as-tu-vu *m*, plastronneur *m*.

show off [ˈʃouˈɔf] (**to**), *F:* parader, plastronner, se donner des airs, chercher à épater.

show up [ˈʃouˈʌp] (**to**), *F:* **1**. faire une apparition, faire acte de présence, se pointer. **2**. (*a*) révéler, dévoiler, démasquer; (*b*) attirer l'attention sur (qn); **he's been shown up**, il est grillé.

shrimp [ʃrimp] (*noun*), *F:* individu de petite* taille, crapoussin *m*.

shrink [ʃriŋk] (*noun*), *P:* = **head-shrinker**.

shtup [ʃtʌp] (**to**) (*U.S.*), *P:* = **tup** (**to**).

shuck[1] [ʃʌk] (*noun*), *F:* **1**. (*U.S.*) mystification *f*, supercherie *f*. **2. it's not worth shucks**, ça ne vaut pas chipette.

shuck[2] [ʃʌk] (**to**) (*U.S.*), *F:* **1**. faire

marcher (qn), mystifier (qn). 2. dire des bêtises*, déconner.

shucks! [ʃʌks] (*excl.*), *F:* mince! zut alors! zut alors!

shudders [ˈʃʌdəz] (*pl. noun*), *F:* to give s.o. the s. = to give s.o. the shivers.

shuffles [ˈʃʌflz] (*pl. noun*), *P:* cartes* à jouer, brèmes *f.pl.*

shufty [ˈʃʊfti] (*noun*), *F:* regard *m*, coup *m* de châsse, clinc *m*.

shush [ʃʊʃ] (**to**), *F:* faire taire* (qn), river le clou à (qn); **s.!** tais-toi! un peu de silence!

shut [ʃʌt] (**to**), *P:* to s. it, se taire*, fermer sa boîte (*ou* son clapet), la fermer; *voir aussi* face[1], 1; gob[1], 1; trap, 1.

shuteye [ˈʃʌtai] (*noun*), *F:* sommeil *m*, somme *m*; to get (*or* grab) some s., dormir*, piquer un roupillon, roupillonner.

shutters [ˈʃʌtəz] (*pl. noun*), *F:* to put the s. up, se retirer en soi-même, baisser la vitrine, faire le hibou.

shut up [ˈʃʌtˈʌp] (**to**), (*a*) *F:* faire taire* (qn), clouer le bec à (qn); (*b*) *P:* s. u.! la ferme! ferme ça!

shy[1] [ʃai] (*noun*), *F:* 1. jet *m*, lancement *m*. 2. tentative *f*, essai *m*.

shy[2] [ʃai] (**to**), *F:* jeter*, lancer, balancer.

shyster [ˈʃaistər] (*noun*), *F:* homme d'affaires, *etc.* véreux; marron *m*.

sick [sik] (*adj.*). 1. *F:* furieux, furibard. 2. *F:* déçu, chocolat. 3. *F:* s. joke, plaisanterie *f* macabre. 4. *F:* I'm s. (and tired) of it, j'en ai plein le dos, j'en ai marre. 5. *P:* en manque de drogues.

sickener [ˈsikənər] (*noun*), *F:* 1. aventure écœurante. 2. spectacle écœurant.

sick-making [ˈsikmeikiŋ] (*adj.*), *F:* écœurant, navrant.

sick up [ˈsikˈʌp] (**to**), *F:* vomir* (qch.), dégobiller.

side [said] (*noun*). 1. *F:* to make sth. (*or* a bit) on the s., se faire des petits à-côtés. 2. *P:* to have a bit on the s., dérouiller sa crampette hors du ménage, prendre un petit à-côté. 3. *F:* to split one's sides (with) laughing, se tordre de rire*; *cf.* side-splitting. 4. *F:* crânerie *f*, esbrouf(f)e *f*; to put on s., faire sa poire (anglaise). *Voir aussi* bed[1], 2; right, 1; safe[1].

sideboards [ˈsaidbɔːdz], **sideburns** [ˈsaidbəːnz] (*pl. noun*), *F:* favoris *m.pl.*, pattes *f.pl.* de lapin.

sidekick [ˈsaidkik] (*noun*), *F:* 1. ami*, copain *m*. 2. associé *m*, assistant *m*, sous-fifre *m*.

sideman [ˈsaidmæn] (*noun*), *P:* (*jazz*) musicien *m* de pupitre.

side-splitting [ˈsaid-splitiŋ] (*adj.*), *F:* tordant, désopilant, marrant, crevant; *cf.* side, 3.

sideways [ˈsaid-weiz] (*adv.*), *F:* to knock s.o. s., époustoufler, ébahir, ébaubir qn.

siff [sif] (*noun*), *P:* = syph.

sight [sait] (*noun*), *F:* 1. I can't bear (*or* stand) the s. of him, je ne peux pas le voir en peinture. 2. (*a*) you do look a s.! te voilà bien arrangé! tu es fichu comme l'as de pique!; (*b*) his face was a s., si vous aviez vu son visage*! 3. a s. of..., énormément de...; he's a (damn(ed)) s. too clever for you, il est beaucoup trop malin* pour vous. *Voir aussi* damned[1], 5; out[1], 3.

sign off [ˈsainˈɔf] (**to**), *F:* conclure, terminer, finocher.

silly [ˈsili] (*noun*), *F:* individu bête*, ballot *m*, baluchard *m*.

sim [sim] (*noun*) (*Austr.*), *P:* = alec, 2.

simmer down [ˈsiməˈdaun] (**to**), *F:* se calmer, ne pas s'emballer.

simp [simp] (*noun*), *P:* nigaud *m*, niguedouille *mf*.

simply [ˈsimpli] (*adv.*), *F:* absolument, complètement; you look s. lovely! vous êtes absolument ravissante!; it's s. ghastly weather, il fait un temps de chien.

sing [siŋ] (**to**). 1. *P:* = squeal[2] (**to**), 1, 2. 2. *F:* payer du chantage. 3. *F:* to s. small, se conduire avec humilité, baisser pavillon.

sing out [ˈsiŋˈaut] (**to**), *F:* s. o. if you need me, appelez si vous avez besoin de moi.

sink [siŋk] (**to**), *F:* 1. s. or swim! au petit bonheur! 2. to s. a pint, s'envoyer un demi.

sinker [ˈsiŋkər] (*noun*) (*U.S.*), *F:* mauvaise pièce (d'argent).

sink in [ˈsiŋkˈin] (**to**), *F:* se l'enfoncer dans la tête, pénétrer la comprenette.

sin-shifter [ˈsin-ʃiftər] (*noun*) (*Austr.*), *P:* aumônier *m* militaire, radis-noir *m*.

sirree [səˈriː] (*noun*), *F:* no s.! (*négation facétieuse mais catégorique*) non, monsieur! non, mon cher!

sissy [ˈsisi] (*noun*), *F:* = cissy.

---

* L'astérisque indique que le mot marqué de ce signe figure comme entrée dans le Répertoire.

sit [sit] **(to),** *F:* **to be sitting pretty,**
(*a*) tenir le bon bout (*ou* le filon),
avoir la vie belle, être bidard, être
dans les eaux grasses, se la couler
douce; (*b*) rouler sur l'or. *Voir aussi*
behind; duck[1], 3; **fence**[1], 2; **tight**[2].

sit-in [ˈsitin] (*noun*), *F:* occupation *f*
(des locaux), sit-in *m*.

sit-me-down [ˈsitmi-daun] (*noun*), *F:*
fesses*, arrière-train *m*.

sit on [ˈsitɔn] **(to),** *F:* **1. to s. o. sth.,**
ne pas s'occuper de qch., laisser dormir
qch., faire des conserves avec qch.
2. to get sat on, être réprimandé*,
recevoir un abattage. **3. to s. o. s.o.,**
rabrouer qn, rabaisser le caquet à qn;
he won't be sat on, il ne se laisse pas
marcher sur les pieds.

sitter [ˈsitər] (*noun*), *F:* **1 = sitting
duck** (**duck**[1], 3). **2.** une certitude, du
tout cuit, la loi et les prophètes.

sit up [ˈsitˈʌp] **(to),** *F:* **to s. u. and take
notice,** se réveiller, se secouer; **I'll make
you s. u.!** tu auras de mes nouvelles!

sit-upon [ˈsitəpɔn] (*noun*), *F:* **= sit-
me-down.**

six [siks] (*numeral adj. & noun*), *F:*
1. to be s. feet (*or* **foot**) **under,** être
enterré, être dans le royaume des
taupes. **2. at sixes and sevens,** sens
dessus dessous, en pagaille. **3. it's s.
of one and half a dozen of the other,**
c'est bonnet blanc et blanc bonnet,
c'est kif-kif. *Voir aussi* **knock**[2] **(to), 8.**

six-footer [ˈsiksˈfutər] (*noun*), *F:*
homme* (haut) de six pieds, homme
très grand, double-mètre *m*.

six-shooter [ˈsiksˈʃuːtər] (*noun*), *F:*
revolver* (à six coups), flingue *m*,
pétard *m*.

sixty-four [ˈsikstiˈfɔːr] (*numeral adj. &
noun*), *F:* **the s.-f. (thousand) dollar
question,** (*a*) la question du gros lot,
la question super-banco; (*b*) la question
vitale (*ou* cruciale *ou* qui compte le plus).

sixty-nine [ˈsikstiˈnain] (*numeral adj.
& noun*), *P:* six-à-neuf *m* (coït*
buccal respectif et simultané).

size [saiz] (*noun*), *F:* **1. to cut s.o. down
to s.,** rabaisser qn, rabattre le caquet
à qn, rogner les ailes à qn. **2. that's
about the s. of it,** (*a*) c'est à peu près
cela; (*b*) c'est ainsi (et pas autrement).
Voir aussi **king-size(d); man-size(d);
pint-size(d).**

size up [ˈsaizˈʌp] **(to),** *F:* évaluer,
classer, juger.

sizzler [ˈsizlər] (*noun*), *F:* **= scorcher, 1.**

skag [skæg] (*noun*), *P:* héroïne *f*
(*drogues**), shmeck *m*.

skate [skeit] (*noun*). **1.** (*U.S.*) *P:* **=
cheapskate, 2. 2.** (*U.S.*) *P:* canasson *m*,
bidet *m*. **3.** *F:* **to put** (*or* **get**) **one's
skates on,** se dépêcher*, se grouiller,
se magner le train.

skating-rink [ˈskeitiŋriŋk] (*noun*), *F:*
tête chauve*, mouchodrome *m*, boule *f*
de billard.

skedaddle [skiˈdædl] **(to),** *F:* s'enfuir*,
ficher le camp, filer, s'esquiver.

skelp [skelp] **(to),** *F:* battre* (qn),
talocher.

skerrick [ˈskerik] (*noun*) (*Austr.*), *F:* un
peu* (de...), un chouia.

skewer [ˈskjuːər] (*noun*), *F:* (*a*) épée *f*;
(*b*) baïonnette *f*.

skew-eyed [ˈskjuːaid] (*adj.*), *F:* **to be
s.-e.,** loucher*, avoir un œil qui dit
merde (*ou* zut) à l'autre.

skew-whiff[1] [skjuːˈwif] (*adj.*), *F:* tordu,
biscornu.

skew-whiff[2] [ˈskjuːˈwif] (*adv.*), *F:* en
biais, de traviole.

skid-lid [ˈskid-lid] (*noun*), *F:* casque *m*
de moto.

skid-row [ˈskidˈrou] (*noun*) (*mainly
U.S.*), *F:* quartier mal famé; bas-fonds
m.pl., zone *f*; **a s.-r. joint,** un boui-boui
de la plus basse catégorie.

skids [skidz] (*pl. noun*), *F:* **1.** (*U.S.*)
on the s., sur la pente savonneuse, en
train de perdre prestige, richesse, *etc.*;
en perte de vitesse. **2.** (*a*) **to put the s.
under s.o., sth.,** faire échouer* qn,
qch., huiler la pente; (*b*) **to put the s.
under s.o.,** congédier* qn, flanquer qn à
la porte.

skin[1] [skin] (*noun*). **1.** *F:* **to get under
s.o.'s s.,** ennuyer*, barber, raser qn.
2. *F:* **it's no s. off my nose,** ce n'est
pas mon affaire, ça ne me touche pas,
c'est pas mes oignons. **3.** *F:* **s. off
your nose!** (*toast*) à la bonne vôtre!
4. *F:* **to have s.o. under one's s.,** être
entiché de qn, avoir qn dans la peau.
5. *P:* (*a*) **s. game,** escroquerie*, arnaquage *m*; (*b*) **s. artist,** escroc*, arnaqueur
m. **6.** (*U.S.*) *P:* billet *m* de un dollar.
7. *P:* capote anglaise. **8.** (*pl.*) *P:* (*jazz*)
ensemble *m* de tambours, batterie *f*.

---

* An asterisk indicates that the word so marked is included as a head-word in the Appendix.

9. *P:* pneu *m* de voiture (usé), boudin *m*.
10. *P:* **gimme some s.!** touche là! tope
là! 11. *P:* **s. and blister** (*R.S.* = *sister*),
sœur *f*. *Voir aussi* **popping; thick**[1], 4.

skin[2] [skin] (**to**), *F:* 1. carotter (de
l'argent), dépouiller, écorcher, plumer
(qn). 2. anéantir, écraser. *Voir aussi*
eye, 8.

skin-flick [ˈskinflik] (*noun*), *F:* film *m*
porno(graphique).

skinful [ˈskinful] (*noun*), *P:* 1. **to have
(had) a s.**, être ivre*, avoir une cuite.
2. = **bellyful**.

skinhead [ˈskinhed] (*noun*), *F:* 1. homme
chauve* (*ou* à la tête rasée), individu
qui a une perruque en peau de fesses.
2. jeune voyou *m*, skinhead *m*.

skin-pop [ˈskinpɔp] (**to**), *P:* (*drogues*)
se faire une injection intramusculaire;
voir aussi **popping**.

skin-popper [ˈskinpɔpər] (*noun*), *P:*
qn qui se fait lui-même des piqûres
f.pl. de drogues, piquouseur *m* maison.

skint [skint] (*adj.*), *P:* très pauvre*,
fauché, raide.

skip [skip] (**to**). 1. *P:* coïter* avec (une
femme), envoyer en l'air. 2. *F:* **to s.
the country**, fuir le pays; **to s. school**,
faire l'école buissonnière. 3. **s. it!**
(*a*) *F:* laisse courir!; (*b*) *P:* file! décampe!

skipper [ˈskipər] (*noun*), *F:* (*sports*)
chef *m* d'équipe.

skip off [ˈskipˈɔf] (**to**), *F:* s'enfuir*,
décamper, filer.

skippy [ˈskipi] (*noun*), *P:* (*a*) pédéraste*,
lopette *f*; (*b*) homme efféminé.

skirt [skə:t] (*noun*), *P:* femme*, jeune
fille*, poupée *f*; **a nice bit of s.**, une
jolie pépée; **to go out looking for s.**,
courir les femmes, cavaler; *cf.* **stuff**[1], 3.
Voir aussi **hot**, 1.

skirt-chaser, skirt-hunter [ˈskə:t-
tʃeisər, ˈskə:thʌntər] (*noun*), *P:* cavaleur *m*, coureur *m* de jupons.

skite[1] [skait] (*noun*) (*Austr.*), *F:* vantard*, bluffeur *m*.

skite[2] [skait] (**to**) (*Austr.*), *F:* se vanter,
esbrouf(f)er.

skive [skaiv] (**to**), *F:* s'esquiver, tirer au
flanc.

skiver [ˈskaivər] (*noun*), *F:* tire-au-
flanc *m*.

skiving [ˈskaiviŋ] (*noun*), *F:* tirage-au-
flanc *m*.

skivvy [ˈskivi] (*noun*), *F:* 1. bonne *f* à
tout faire, bonniche *f*. 2. (*U.S.*) (*a*) sous-
vêtement *m* d'homme, sweat-shirt *f*,
tee-shirt *f*; (*b*) caleçon *m*, calcif *m*,
short *m* (en coton).

skivy [ˈskaivi] (*adj.*), *P:* (*a*) malhonnête,
filou; (*b*) renâcleur, tire-au-flanc.

skull [skʌl] (*noun*), *P:* = **egghead**.

skull-job [ˈskʌl-dʒɔb] (*noun*), *V:* = **blow-
job**.

skunk [skʌŋk] (*noun*), *F:* chameau *m*,
mufle *m*, rossard *m*.

sky [skai] (*noun*), *P:* **to see the s. through
the trees**, (*d'une femme*) coïter*, voir
les feuilles (*ou* la feuille) à l'envers.
Voir aussi **limit**, 3.

skyjack [ˈskai-dʒæk] (**to**), *F:* pirater (un
avion).

skyjacker [ˈskai-dʒækər] (*noun*), *F:*
pirate *m* de l'air.

skylark [ˈskai-lɑ:k] (**to**), *P:* batifoler,
chahuter, plaisanter.

sky-piece [ˈskai-pi:s] (*noun*), *P:*
chapeau*, capet *m*.

sky-pilot [ˈskai-pailət] (*noun*), *P:* prêtre*,
pasteur *m*, chapelain *m*.

sky-rocket [ˈskai-rɔkit] (*noun*) (*R.S.* =
pocket), *P:* poche*, fouille *f*.

slab [slæb] (*noun*), *F:* 1. table *f* d'opération, billard *m*. 2. dalle *f* funéraire,
pierre *f* de macchab(e).

slag [slæg] (*noun*), *P:* vieille prostituée*,
tarderie *f*.

slam [slæm] (**to**), *F:* 1. battre avec
conviction. 2. frapper avec violence,
flanquer par terre. 3. critiquer* sévèrement, éreinter, débiner.

slams [slæmz] (*pl. noun*) (*U.S.*), *P:*
the s., prison*, taule *f*.

slanging-match [ˈslæŋiŋmætʃ] (*noun*),
F: prise *f* de bec, engueulade *f* maison.

slanguage [ˈslæŋgwidʒ] (*noun*), *F:*
argot*, jar(s) *m*.

slant[1] [slɑ:nt] (*noun*). 1. *F:* (*a*) point *m*
de vue, manière *f* de voir; (*b*) préjugé
m, biais *m*, point de vue détourné.
2. *P:* coup d'œil*; **take a s. at that!**
jette un coup de châsse!

slant[2] [slɑ:nt] (**to**), *F:* donner un biais
(*ou* un tournant) à (une question, *etc.*).

slanter [ˈslɑ:ntər] (*noun*) (*Austr.*), *P:*
tour *m*, ruse *f*, astuce *f*.

slap[1] [slæp] (*adv.*), *F:* (*a*) directement,
tout droit; **s. in the middle**, en plein
(dans le) milieu, en plein mitan; (*b*)

---

* L'astérisque indique que le mot marqué de ce signe figure comme entrée dans le Répertoire.

brusquement, brutalement, rudement; she put it s. on the table, elle l'a flanqué sur la table; *cf.* slap-bang(-wallop); smack[1]; wallop[1].

slap[2] [slæp] (*noun*), *F:* 1. s. in the eye (*or* face), affront *m*, camouflet *m*, rebuffade *f*; *cf.* eye, 23. 2. s. and tickle, partie *f* de pelotage *m*; we were having a bit of (the old) s. and tickle, on était en train de se peloter (*ou* de se faire des mamours).

slap[3] [slæp] (to), *F:* s. it on the bill! flanque-le sur l'addition!

slap-bang(-wallop) [ˈslæpˈbæŋ(ˈwɔləp)] (*adv.*), *F:* (*a*) tout à coup, de but en blanc, hâtivement; (*b*) brusquement. *Voir aussi* wallop[1], 3.

slap down [ˈslæpˈdaun] (to), *F:* réprimander*, rabrouer rudement.

slap-happy [ˈslæpˈhæpi] (*adj.*), *F:* 1. plein d'entrain (*ou* d'allant), d'humeur joyeuse. 2. farfelu, téméraire, insouciant. 3. (*boxe*) ivre de coups.

slap together [ˈslæptəˈgeðər] (to), *F:* préparer hâtivement, bâcler.

slap-up [ˈslæpʌp] (*adj.*), *F:* chic, dernier cri, prodigue; *cf.* bang-up.

slash [slæʃ] (*noun*), *P:* to have a s., uriner*, jeter de la lance; to go for a s., aller aux W.C.*

slashing [ˈslæʃiŋ] (*adj.*), *F:* excellent*, terrible, du tonnerre.

slate[1] [sleit] (*noun*), *F:* 1. on the s., sur la note, sur le compte. 2. to have a s. loose, être un peu fou*, onduler de la toiture.

slate[2] [sleit] (to), *F:* (*a*) réprimander* (qn) vertement, passer un savon à (qn); (*b*) critiquer*, éreinter (un livre, *etc.*).

slater [ˈsleitər] (*noun*), *F:* critique *m* sévère, abatteur *m*, éreinteur *m*.

slating [ˈsleitiŋ] (*noun*), *F:* (*a*) verte réprimande, savon *m*; (*b*) éreintement *m*.

slats [slæts] (*pl. noun*) (*U.S.*), *P:* côtes *f.pl.*, côtelettes *f.pl.*

slaughter[1] [ˈslɔːtər] (*noun*), *F:* victoire décisive, coup *m* de Trafalgar, hécatombe *f*.

slaughter[2] [ˈslɔːtər] (to), *F:* battre à plate(s) couture(s), mettre à bas.

slave (away) [ˈsleiv(əˈwei)] (to), *F:* travailler* dur, se crever, s'échiner.

slave-driver [ˈsleivdraivər] (*noun*), *F:* garde-chiourme *m*.

slavey [ˈsleivi] (*noun*), *F:* = skivvy, 1.

slay [slei] (to), *F:* you s. me! tu me fais rigoler! tu me fais tordre!

sleazy [ˈsliːzi] (*adj.*), *F:* sordide, répugnant, dégueulasse, débectant; mal soigné.

sleep [sliːp] (to), *F:* this room sleeps four, on peut coucher à quatre dans cette chambre.

sleep around [ˈsliːpəˈraund] (to), *F:* coucher avec n'importe qui; fréquenter les lits.

sleeper [ˈsliːpər] (*noun*), *F:* 1. somnifère *m*, barbiturique *m* (*drogues**), barbitos *m.pl.* 2. (*lutte, judo*) prise *f* qui abasourdit l'adversaire. 3. film *m* qui rapporte beaucoup plus qu'on n'escomptait. 4. livre *m* qui se vend couramment pendant une longue période sans publicité spéciale. 5. (*commerce*) article auquel on découvre soudainement une plus-value jusque-là ignorée. 6. wagon-lit *m*.

sleep off [ˈsliːpˈɔf] (to), *F:* to s. it o., cuver son vin.

sleepy-byes [ˈsliːpibaiz] (*pl. noun*), *F:* = bye-byes.

sleepyhead [ˈsliːpihed] (*noun*), *F:* individu (*surtout* enfant) à moitié endormi, (bon) client du marchand de sable.

slewed [sluːd] (*adj.*), *P:* ivre*, blindé, bourré; *cf.* half-slewed.

slice [slais] (*noun*), *P:* to knock a s. off (a woman), coïter* avec une femme, filer un coup d'arbalète. *Voir aussi* tongue-pie.

slick [slik] (*adj.*), *F:* 1. (*a*) malin*, rusé, marle, roublard; (*b*) habile, adroit. 2. beau parleur. 3. séduisant, aguichant, désirable.

slicker [ˈslikər] (*noun*), *F:* escroc* adroit, combinard *m*; city s., roustisseur *m* de ville, affranchi *m*, mec *m* du milieu.

slide off [ˈslaidˈɔf] (to), *F:* partir* (sans bruit), se défiler, se débiner.

slim [slim] (*adj.*), *F:* = slick 1 (*a*).

slime[1] [slaim] (*noun*), *P:* 1. flatterie *f*, lèche *f*, pommade *f*. 2. grossier personnage, rustaud *m*, valetaille *f*. 3. calomnie *f*, diffamation *f*, débinage *m*, médisance *f*, bêche *f*.

slime[2] [slaim] (to), *P:* flatter*, cirer, pommader.

slim(e)y [ˈslaimi] (*noun*), *P:* lèche-cul *m*, lèche-bottes *m*.

---

* An asterisk indicates that the word so marked is included as a head-word in the Appendix.

slimy [ˈslaimi] (*adj.*), *F:* servile, obsé-
quieux, mielleux, sirupeux.
sling [sliŋ] (**to**) (*U.S.*), *P:* **to s. it** (*or*
the bull) = **to shoot the bull** (**shoot**[2]
(**to**), 7). *Voir aussi* **hook**[1], 5; **lingo**, 2;
mud, 7.
slinger [ˈsliŋər] (*noun*), *P:* individu* qui
écoule la fausse monnaie, fournaise *f*.
Voir aussi **gunslinger; hash-slinger;**
ink-slinger; mudslinger.
sling in [ˈsliŋˈin] (**to**), *P:* **to s. i.** one's job,
lâcher son travail, rendre son tablier.
sling off [ˈsliŋˈɔf] (**to**) (*Austr.*), *P:* =
smoke[2] (**off**) (**to**).
sling out [ˈsliŋˈaut] (**to**), *P:* faire déguerpir, flanquer dehors.
slinky [ˈsliŋki] (*adj.*), *F:* **1.** élégant*,
mince. **2.** qui se meut avec élégance,
gandin. **3.** (vêtement) collant, ajusté.
slinter [ˈslintər] (*noun*) (*Austr.*), *P:*
= **slanter.**
slip[1] [slip] (*noun*), *F:* **to give s.o. the s.**,
fausser compagnie à qn.
slip[2] [slip] (**to**), *F:* **1.** glisser, faufiler (qch.
à qn). **2.** **you're slipping**, tu perds les
pédales. **3. to s. one over on s.o.**,
duper* qn, tirer une carotte à qn.
Voir aussi **cut**[2], 4.
slip-on [ˈslipɔn] (*noun*), *F:* vêtement *m*
(*ou* gaine *f*) facilement enfilé(e).
slipover [ˈslipouvər] (*noun*), *F:* pull-
over *m* sans manches, débardeur *m*.
slippy [ˈslipi] (*adj.*), *F:* (*a*) glissant;
(*b*) rapide, presto.
slipslop [ˈslip-slɔp] (*noun*), *F:* **1.** aliments
m.pl. liquides, bouillie *f*, jaffe *f*. **2.**
sensiblerie *f*, fadeur sentimentale.
slip-up [ˈslipʌp] (*noun*), *F:* erreur *f*,
gaffe *f*, accident *m*.
slip up [ˈslipˈʌp] (**to**), *F:* faire une erreur,
gaffer.
slit [slit] (*noun*), *V:* vagin*, fente *f*;
cf. **pee-slit.**
slob [slɔb] (*noun*), *P:* **1. a big** (**fat**) **s.**, un
gros (sac à) lard, un gros patapouf.
2. = **slouch.**
slobber [ˈslɔbər] (**to**), *F:* **1.** faire du
sentimentalisme, larmoyer, s'attendrir.
2. baver, avoir la bouche* souillée de
nourriture*.
slobberchops [ˈslɔbə-tʃɔps] (*noun*), *F:*
individu *m* aux bajoues baveuses.
slobbery [ˈslɔbəri] (*adj.*), *F:* **1.** sentimental, larmoyant. **2.** baveux de
nourriture.

slog[1] [slɔg] (*noun*), *F:* **1.** coup* violent,
ramponneau *m*, gnon *m*. **2.** travail* dur,
turbin *m*, boulot *m*. **3.** marche *f* pénible.
slog[2] [slɔg] (**to**), *F:* **1.** battre* violem-
ment, tabasser (qn). **2.** (*au jeu de
cricket*) marquer des points en frappant
fort sur la balle. **3.** travailler* dur,
turbiner, bosser. **4.** = **foot-slog** (**to**).
slogger [ˈslɔgər] (*noun*), *F:* **1.** (*boxe*)
cogneur *m*. **2.** travailleur* acharné,
turbineur *m*, bosseur *m*, bûcheur *m*.
Voir aussi **foot-slogger.**
slop [slɔp] (*noun*), *P:* **1.** agent* de police,
flic *m*. **2.** sensiblerie *f*. *Voir aussi*
slipslop; slops.
slop about (*or* **around**) [ˈslɔpəˈbaut,
ˈslɔpəˈraund] (**to**), *F:* patauger, barboter.
slope [sloup] (*noun*), *P:* **to do a s.** =
slope off (**to**).
slope off [ˈsloupˈɔf] (**to**), *P:* s'enfuir*,
se barrer, déguerpir.
sloppy [ˈslɔpi] (*adj.*). **1.** *F:* sale*, souillon,
désordonné, cradingue. **2.** *F:* **s. joe**,
paletot *m* de laine vague. **3.** (*U.S.*) *P:*
ivre*, éméché. **4.** *F:* mièvre, sirupeux;
s. sentimentality, sensiblerie *f*. **5.** *F:*
avec du laisser-aller, sans soin; **s.
English**, anglais mal parlé, anglais
débraillé.
slops [slɔps] (*pl. noun*), *F:* (*argot de
la Marine*) vêtements*, uniforme *m*,
harnais *m*. *Voir aussi* **slop.**
slopshop [ˈslɔpʃɔp] (*noun*), *P:* **1.** braderie
f, décrochez-moi-ça *m*. **2.** (*argot de la
Marine*) boutique *f* à bord d'un bateau
de guerre, bouterne *f*, cambuse *f*.
slosh[1] [slɔʃ] (*noun*), *P:* **1.** sensiblerie *f*,
sentimentalité *f* fadasse. **2.** coup*,
gnon *m*, marron *m*. **3.** (*a*) (le) boire;
(*b*) boisson *f*, pictance *f*.
slosh[2] [slɔʃ] (**to**). **1.** *P:* flanquer un coup*
à (qn), tabasser. **2.** *F:* **to s. paint on**,
flanquer de la peinture partout.
sloshed [slɔʃt] (*adj.*), *P:* ivre*, gris,
pompette.
slot [slɔt] (*noun*). **1.** *P:* (*a*) emploi *m*,
situation *f*, job *m*; (*b*) place *f*; **to finish
in third s.**, finir en troisième place.
2. (*Austr.*) *P:* cellule *f* de prison*, cellotte
f. **3.** *V:* = **slit.**
slouch [slautʃ] (*noun*), *F:* bousilleur *m*,
gâte-métier *m*; **he's no s.**, il est malin*,
il n'est pas empoté.
slow [slou] (*adv.*), *F:* **1. to go s.**, marcher

(*ou* fonctionner) au ralenti; *cf.* **go-slow. 2. to take it s.**, aller doucement, y aller mollo, ne pas agir à la hâte.

slowcoach ['slou-koutʃ] (*noun*), *F:* flâneur *m*, traînard *m*, lambin *m*.

slowpoke ['sloupouk] (*noun*) (*U.S.*), *F:* = **slowcoach**.

slug[1] [slʌg] (*noun*), *P:* **1.** balle* de revolver, pastille *f*. **2.** pièce fausse, mornifle *f*. **3.** coup*, triquée *f*, taloche *f*. **4. to have a s.**, boire* un coup. **5.** (*U.S.*) un dollar.

slug[2] [slʌg] (**to**), *P:* **1.** battre*, frapper, tabasser. **2.** boire*, avaler, ingurgiter. **3.** tirer un coup de fusil (*ou* de revolver*) à qn, fusiller qn.

slugfest['slʌgfest] (*noun*), *P:* match *m* de boxe (entre boxeurs qui frappent dur).

slugger ['slʌgər] (*noun*), *F:* boxeur *m* (qui frappe dur), cogneur *m*.

slug it out ['slʌgit'aut] (**to**), *F:* se battre* en frappant de grands coups*, se rentrer dedans.

slug-up ['slʌgʌp] (*noun*) (*Austr.*), *P:* = **frame-up**.

sluice[1] [sluːs] (*noun*), *P:* trempette *f*, débarbouillage *m*.

sluice[2] [sluːs] (**to**), *P:* **to s. one's ivories** = **to w(h)et one's whistle** (**whistle**[1], **1**).

slum [slʌm] (**to**). **1.** *F:* **to go slumming**, fréquenter les bars des bas quartiers, faire la zone. **2.** *P:* **to s. it** = **to pig it** (**pig**[2], **2**).

slurp [sləːp] (**to**), *F:* boire* *ou* siroter bruyamment, laper.

slush [slʌʃ] (*noun*). **1.** *F:* sensiblerie *f*. **2.** *P:* fausse monnaie, mornifle *f*.

slushy ['slʌʃi] (*adj.*), *F:* sentimental, fadasse.

sly [slai] (*noun*), *F:* **on the s.**, à la dérobée, en cachette, en sourdine.

slyboots ['slaibuːts] (*noun*), *F:* **1.** cachotteur *m*, sournois *m*. **2.** malin *m*, finaud *m*. **3.** vaurien*, coquin *m*.

smack[1] [smæk] (*adv.*), *F:* **1. to hit s.o. s. between the eyes**, frapper qn en plein entre les deux yeux. **2. s. in the middle**, au beau milieu; *cf.* **slap**[1].

smack[2] [smæk] (*noun*). **1.** *F:* **s. in the eye** (*or* **face**) = **slap in the eye** (*or* **face**) (**slap**[2], **1**). **2.** *F:* **to have a s. at sth.**, essayer de faire qch., tenter le coup. **3.** *F:* **to have a s. at s.o.**, donner un coup de patte à qn. **4.** *F:* = **smacker**, **1. 5.** *P:* = **schmeck**.

smack[3] [smæk] (**to**), *P:* donner un coup de poing (*ou* des coups de poing) à (qn), cogner.

smack-bang(-wallop) ['smæk'bæŋ-(-'wɔləp)] (*adv.*), *F:* = **slap-bang(-wallop)**.

smack-botty ['smæk'bɔti] (*noun*), *F:* tutu-panpan *m*; **to give a child a s.-b.**, administrer une fessée à un enfant; *cf.* **bottom**[2], **1**; **botty**.

smack down ['smæk'daun] (**to**), *F:* = **slap down** (**to**).

smacker ['smækər] (*noun*). **1.** *F:* gros baiser, bizou(t) *m*. **2.** *P:* (*a*) une livre sterling; (*b*) (*U.S.*) un dollar. **3.** *P:* **to rub smackers**, se sucer le caillou. **4.** *P:* = **kisser**, **1,2**. **5.**.*P:* coup* retentissant.

small [smɔːl] (*adj.*), *F:* **the s. print**, les petits caractères, l'important du bas de la page. *Voir aussi* **potato**, **2**; **room**.

smalls [smɔːlz] (*pl. noun*), *F:* sous-vêtements *m.pl.*, lingerie *f*.

small-time ['smɔːl-taim] (*adj.*), *F:* insignifiant, médiocre, tocard; **a s.-t. crook**, un petit escroc*; *cf.* **big-time**.

small-timer ['smɔːl-taimər] (*noun*), *F:* individu* insignifiant, minus *m*; *cf.* **big-timer**.

smarm [smɑːm] (**to**), *F:* **1. to s. (all) over s.o.**, flatter* qn, passer la main dans le dos de qn. **2. to s. one's hair down**, s'aplatir (*ou* se pommader) les cheveux*.

smarmer ['smɑːmər] (*noun*), *F:* flagorneur *m*, lèche-bottes *m*.

smarmy ['smɑːmi] (*adj.*), *F:* patelin, mielleux, flagorneur.

smart [smɑːt] (*adj.*), *F:* **1. don't get s. with me!** ne fais pas le malin avec moi! ne la ramène pas! **2. s. guy**, malin *m*, fortiche *m*, roublard *m*. *Voir aussi* **Alec**, **1**.

smart-arsed ['smɑːt-ɑːst] (*adj.*), *P:* malin*, fortiche, démerdard.

smarty(-pants)['smɑːti(pænts)] (*noun*), *F:* cuistre *m*, savantas(se) *m*, Je-sais-tout *m*.

smash[1] [smæʃ] (*adv.*), *F:* **to go s.**, (*a*) se briser; (*b*) faire faillite, mettre la clef sous la porte.

smash[2] [smæʃ] (*noun*). **1.** *F:* = **smash-hit**. **2.** *P:* petite monnaie*, ferraille *f*, mitraille *f*.

---

* An asterisk indicates that the word so marked is included as a head-word in the Appendix.

smashed [smæʃt] (adj.), P: (a) ivre*, bit(t)uré, blindé; (b) défoncé par la drogue*.

smasher ['smæʃər] (noun), F: 1. she's a s., c'est une jolie pépée; what a s.! ce qu'elle est belle* (ou bath ou bien roulée)! 2. qch. d'excellent* (ou d'époustouflant ou de foutral). 3. coup* violent, châtaigne f, marron m. 4. to come a s., tomber*, ramasser un gadin, prendre une pelle.

smash-hit ['smæʃ'hit] (noun), F: réussite f, grand boum.

smash in ['smæʃ'in] (to), P: to s. s.o.'s face i., casser la gueule à qn.

smashing ['smæʃiŋ] (adj.), F: excellent*, formid(able), du tonnerre.

smash up ['smæʃ'ʌp] (to), P: 1. = bash up (to). 2. to be all smashed up, être écrasé (ou assommé ou fracassé).

smell [smel] (to), F: sembler louche, ne pas avoir l'air catholique. Voir aussi rat¹, 4.

smelly ['smeli] (adj.), F: suspect, louche.

smice [smais] (to) (Austr.), P: partir*, déguerpir, lever le pied.

smidgen ['smidʒən] (noun) (U.S.), F: un peu*, un chouia, une miette.

smithereens ['smiðə'ri:nz] (pl. noun), F: morceaux m.pl., miettes f.pl.; to smash sth. to s., briser qch. en mille morceaux, mettre qch. en capilotade.

smizz [smiz] (noun) (U.S.), P: = shmeck.

smoke¹ [smouk] (noun). 1. F: to go up in s., ne servir à rien, partir en fumée. 2. F: the S., une grande métropole; the (Big) S., Londres. 3. F: a s., (a) cigarette*, cibiche f; (b) cigarette* de marijuana (drogues*), stick m; voir aussi giggle, 4. 4. (Austr.) P: in s., en cachette, planqué. 5. (U.S.) P: (péj.) nègre*, noyama m. Voir aussi holy, 1; joy-smoke.

smoke² (off) ['smouk('ɔf)] (to) (Austr.), P: = smice (to).

smoke-o(h) ['smoukou] (noun) (Austr.), F: pause-café f, pause-thé f.

smoker ['smoukər] (noun). 1. F: compartiment m de fumeur. 2. P: voiture f à haut kilométrage. 3. P: pot m de chambre.

smoky ['smouki] (adj.), P: en colère*, en rogne, à cran.

smooch [smu:tʃ] (to). 1. F: s'embrasser*, se bécoter, se baisoter, se faire des mam-

ours m.pl. 2. P: voler*, chiper, garder ce qu'on a emprunté.

smoocher ['smu:tʃər] (noun). 1. F: embrasseur m, peloteur m. 2. P: voleur*, chipeur m, chapardeur m.

smooching ['smu:tʃiŋ] (noun). 1. F: caressage m, pelotage m, fricassée f de museaux. 2. P: vol m, chapardage m.

smoodge [smu:dʒ] (to), smoodger ['smu:dʒər] (noun), smoodging ['smu:dʒiŋ] (noun) (Austr.), F: = smooch (to), 1, smoocher 1, smooching 1.

smooth [smu:ð] (adj.), F: 1. (a) agréable, chouette, badour; (b) doucereux. 2. s. operator, individu malin*, démerdard m.

smoothie, smoothy ['smu:ði] (noun), F: 1. homme* doucereux (ou papelard). 2. homme* qui se prend pour un don Juan.

smother ['smʌðər] (noun), P: (a) pardessus*; (b) imperméable m, imper m.

smother-love ['smʌðəlʌv] (noun), F: amour étouffant (ou accaparant) (d'une mère).

snaffle ['snæfl] (to), P: voler*, barbot(t)er, chiper.

snafu, S.N.A.F.U. ['snæ'fu:] (adj.) (abbr. = situation normal, all fucked (or fouled) up), P: en désordre, en pagaille, confus; amoché, bousillé.

snags [snægz] (pl. noun) (Austr.), F: saucisses f.pl., bifteck m de pan(n)é.

snake-eyes ['sneik-aiz] (pl. noun), F: double un (jeu de dés).

snake-hips ['sneikhips] (noun), F: qn de souple et flexible, danseur m (-euse f) de corde.

snake off ['sneik'ɔf] (to), F: s'esquiver, jouer rip.

snap¹ [snæp] (noun), F: 1. vigueur f, entrain m, allant m, dynamisme m. 2. = cinch.

snap² [snæp] (to), F: 1. s'exprimer avec aigreur, parler* d'un ton sec. 2. (d'une personne) avoir une maladie mentale, perdre la raison. 3. to s. into it, agir avec énergie et rapidité. 4. to s. out of it, se secouer, se remettre d'aplomb, reprendre du poil de la bête.

snaped [sneipt] (adj.) (mainly U.S.), F: ivre*, bourré, saoul; cf. half-snaped.

snap off ['snæp'ɔf] (to), F: to s. s.o.'s head o., manger le nez à qn, avaler qn.

---

snapper [ˈsnæpər] (*noun*). **1.** *V:* vagin*, étau *m*. **2.** *P:* = **amy. 3.** *P:* contrôleur *m* d'autobus. **4.** (*pl.*) *P:* (*a*) = **falsies, 1**; (*b*) dents*, croquantes *f.pl. Voir aussi* **whipper-snapper.**

snappy [ˈsnæpi] (*adj.*), *F:* **1.** acariâtre, hargneux, bourru. **2. look s.! make it s.!** dépêchez*-vous! remuez-vous! grouille-toi! **3.** élégant*, flambard, badour. **4.** sarcastique, mordant, spiri-tuel. *Voir aussi* **catch**[1], **2.**

snap up [ˈsnæpˈʌp] (**to**), *F:* **1. to s. u. a bargain,** enlever une affaire, saisir une occasion. **2. to s. it u.,** activer le mouve-ment; **s. it u.!** grouille-toi!

snarky [ˈsnɑːki] (*adj.*), *F:* désagréable, de mauvais poil, râleur.

snarl [snɑːl] (*noun*), *F:* = **snarl-up.**

snarled up [ˈsnɑːldˈʌp] (*adj.*), *F:* embou-teillé, encombré, coincé.

snarl-up [ˈsnɑːlˈʌp] (*noun*), *F:* embou-teillage *m*, embarras *m* de voitures.

snarly [ˈsnɑːli] (*adj.*), *F:* = **snarky.**

snatch[1] [snætʃ] (*noun*). **1.** *V:* (*a*) vagin*, cramouille *f*; (*b*) coït*. **2.** *P:* (*a*) arresta-tion, accrochage *m*, agrafage *m*; (*b*) enlèvement *m*; **to put the s. on s.o.,** (*a*) arrêter* qn; (*b*) enlever qn. **3.** *F:* vol *m*, cambriolage *m*, casse *m*; **wages s.,** ratissage *m* de la paye.

snatch[2] [snætʃ] (**to**). **1.** *P:* arrêter*, accrocher, agrafer. **2.** *P:* enlever, kidnapper. **3.** *P:* voler*, barbot(t)er. **4. to s. a quick one,** (*a*) *F:* boire *un coup; (*b*) *P:* coïter*, s'envoyer un petit coup.

snazzy [ˈsnæzi] (*adj.*), *F:* (*a*) élégant*, chic; (*b*) criard, voyant, clinquant.

sneak[1] [sniːk] (*adj.*), *F:* **s. attack,** attaque sournoise (*ou* en dessous); **s. preview,** banc *m* d'essai (*film, pièce de théâtre, etc.*); **s. thief,** chapardeur *m*, chipeur *m*, barbot(t)eur *m*.

sneak[2] [sniːk] (*noun*), *F:* indicateur*, mouchard *m*, rapporteur *m*.

sneak[3] [sniːk] (**to**), *F:* **1.** voler* furtive-ment, barbot(t)er, chaparder. **2.** dé-noncer*, moucharder, cafarder. **3.** se conduire en pleutre, caner.

sneakers [ˈsniːkəz] (*pl. noun*), *F:* chaus-sures* souples à semelle en caoutchouc, sneakers *m.pl.*

sneak in [ˈsniːkˈin] (**to**), *F:* **1.** inclure (*ou* glisser) furtivement. **2.** se glisser furtivement, se faufiler, entrer à la dérobée.

sneak on [ˈsniːkˈɔn] (**to**), *F:* dénoncer*, cafarder, moutonner.

sneak out [ˈsniːkˈaut] (**to**), *F:* partir* furtivement, s'éclipser, se défiler.

sneaky [ˈsniːki] (*adj.*), *F:* **1.** sournois, dissimulé. **2.** rampant, servile.

sneeze at [ˈsniːzˈæt] (**to**), *F:* **it's not to be sneezed at,** ce n'est pas de la petite bière, ce n'est pas à cracher dessus.

sneezer [ˈsniːzər] (*noun*), *P:* **1.** nez*, tarin *m*. **2.** prison*, bloc *m*.

snide[1] [snaid] (*adj.*), *F:* **1.** faux, tocard, à la manque. **2.** roublard, ficelle. **3.** sarcastique, persifleur.

snide[2] [snaid] (*noun*), *P:* **1.** voleur*, filou *m*, truqueur *m*. **2.** fausse monnaie, bijouterie *f* factice, toc *m*.

snidy [ˈsnaidi] (*adj.*), *P:* malin*, astu-cieux.

sniff [snif] (**to**). **1.** *P:* inhaler une poudre narcotique, prendre une reni-flette. **2.** *F:* **it's not to be sniffed at = it's not to be sneezed at.**

sniffer [ˈsnifər] (*noun*), *P:* **1.** nez*, reniflant *m*. **2.** mouchoir*, blave *m*.

sniffles [ˈsniflz] (*pl. noun*), *F:* **to have the s.,** être enchifrené.

sniffy [ˈsnifi] (*adj.*). **1.** *F:* arrogant, hautain, pimbêche. **2.** *P:* = **niffy.**

snifter [ˈsniftər] (*noun*). *P:* **1.** vent cara-biné. **2.** petit verre d'alcool*, goutte *f*.

snip [snip] (*noun*), *F:* **1.** affaire* avanta-geuse, trouvaille *f*, occasion *f*. **2.** certitude *f*, affaire* certaine; (*courses aux chevaux*) gagnant sûr., une grosse cote. **3.** tailleur *m*, fringueur *m*. **4.** gamin *m*, gavroche *m*.

snipe[1] [snaip] (*noun*), *P:* (*a*) mégot*, clope *m*; (*b*) mégot* de cigarette de marijuana.

snipe[2] [snaip] (**to**), *P:* voler*, faucher.

sniper [ˈsnaipər] (*noun*), *P:* mégot(t)ier *m*, mégot(t)eur *m*; *cf.* **snipe**[1].

snippy [ˈsnipi] (*adj.*), *P:* insolent, impu-dent, effronté, culotté.

snitch[1] [snitʃ] (*noun*), *P:* **1.** vol *m*, filouterie *f*. **2.** indicateur* de police, mouchard *m*. **3.** un tout petit peu* (de qch.), un chouia. **4.** nez*, tarin *m*, pif *m*. **5.** (*Austr.*) aversion *f*, dégoût *m*.

snitch[2] [snitʃ] (**to**), *P:* = **sneak**[3] (**to**), **1, 2.**

snitcher [ˈsnitʃər] (*noun*), *P:* **1.** indi-cateur*, rapporteur *m*, cafeteur *m*. **2.** (*pl.*) menottes*, cadènes *f.pl.*

---

* An asterisk indicates that the word so marked is included as a head-word in the Appendix.

snitch-rag [ˈsnitʃræg] (*noun*), *P:* mouchoir*, tire-jus *m*, tire-moelle *m*.

snob [snɔb] (*noun*), *P:* cordonnier *m*, bouif *m*, ribouis *m*.

snoddy [ˈsnɔdi] (*noun*), *P:* soldat*, bidasse *m*.

snodger [ˈsnɔdʒər] (*noun*) (*Austr.*), *P:* délectation *f*, agrément *m*.

snog¹ [snɔg] (*noun*), *P:* = **petting session** (*voir* **petting**).

snog² [snɔg] (to), *P:* = **pet** (to).

snogger [ˈsnɔgər] (*noun*), *P:* peloteur *m*; flirteur *m*, juponneur *m*.

snook [snuːk] (*noun*), *F:* **to cock a s. at s.o.**, faire un pied de nez à qn.

snooker [ˈsnuːkər] (to), *F:* **to s. s.o.**, mettre qn dans une impasse; **to be snookered**, se trouver en mauvaise posture, être réduit à l'impuissance.

snooks [snuːks], **snookums** [ˈsnuːkəmz] (*noun*) (*U.S.*), *F:* chéri(e), cocotte *f*.

snoop¹ [snuːp] (*noun*), *F:* **1.** fureteur *m*, fouineur *m*. **2.** (*a*) investigateur *ou* inspecteur officiel; (*b*) détective privé, limier *m*.

snoop² [snuːp] (to), *F:* fureter, fouiner, fourrer le nez* partout.

snooper [ˈsnuːpər] (*noun*), *F:* = **snoop¹**, **1, 2.**

snoopy [ˈsnuːpi] (*adj.*), *F:* curieux, fouineur, fureteur.

snoot¹ [snuːt] (*noun*), *P:* **1.** nez*, pif *m*. **2.** grimace *f*, grigne *f*.

snoot² [snuːt] (to), *P:* dédaigner, mépriser, traiter de haut en bas.

snootful [ˈsnuːtful] (*noun*) (*U.S.*), *P:* **to have (had) a s.**, être ivre*, avoir une cuite.

snootiness [ˈsnuːtinis] (*noun*), *F:* morgue *f*, crânage *m*, pose *f*.

snooty [ˈsnuːti] (*adj.*), *F:* hautain, orgueilleux, dédaigneux; gommeux.

snooze¹ [snuːz] (*noun*), *F:* petit somme; **to have a s.**, piquer un roupillon.

snooze² [snuːz] (to), *F:* dormir*, roupiller, pioncer, dormasser.

snoozer [ˈsnuːzər] (*noun*), *F:* roupilleur *m*, pionceur *m*.

snort¹ [snɔːt] (*noun*), *P:* **1.** = **snorter, 1. 2.** dose *f* d'une drogue.

snort² [snɔːt] (to), *P:* = **sniff** (to), **1.**

snorter [ˈsnɔːtər] (*noun*). **1.** *P:* = **snifter, 2. 2.** *F:* qch. qui donne du fil à retordre. **3.** *F:* réponse *f* ou lettre *f* qui assoit; lettre carabinée. *Voir aussi* **ripsnorter.**

snorty [ˈsnɔːti] (*adj.*), *F:* fâché, contrarié, ronchonneur.

snot [snɔt] (*noun*), *P:* **1.** morve *f*, chandelle *f*. **2.** morveux *m*, merdeux *m*.

snot-rag [ˈsnɔt-ræg] (*noun*), *P:* = **snitch-rag.**

snottie [ˈsnɔti] (*noun*), *F:* = **snotty².**

snotty¹ [ˈsnɔti] (*adj.*), *P:* **1.** qui a le nez* enchifrené. **2.** prétentieux*, culotté, gonflé. **3.** sale*, salingue. **4.** avare*, radin.

snotty² [ˈsnɔti] (*noun*), *F:* aspirant *m* de Marine, aspi *m*.

snotty-nosed [ˈsnɔti-nouzd] (*adj.*), *P:* **1.** morveux. **2.** = **snooty.**

snout [snaut] (*noun*), *P:* **1.** nez*, blaireau *m*. **2.** (*a*) tabac*, perlot *m*; (*b*) cigarette*, sèche *f*; **s. baron**, prisonnier *m* qui vend du tabac aux autres détenus.

snow¹ [snou] (*noun*). **1.** *P:* cocaïne *f* en poudre (*drogues**), neige *f*. **2.** *P:* (*quelquefois*) morphine *f* ou autre narcotique (*drogues**). **3.** *P:* pièce *f* ou article *m* en argent; blanc *m*, blanquette *f*. **4.** *F:* points blancs mobiles sur écran de télévision, neige *f*.

snow² [snou] (to). **1.** *P:* duper*, berner, mystifier. **2.** *F:* **it's snowing down south**, ta combinaison passe; tu cherches une belle-mère?; *cf.* **Charl(e)y², 2.**

snowball¹ [ˈsnoubɔːl] (*noun*), *P:* **1.** (*U.S.*) (*péj.*) nègre*, bougnoul(l)e *m*. **2.** **he doesn't stand a s.'s chance in hell**, il n'a pas l'ombre d'une chance. **3.** = **snowbird.**

snowball² [ˈsnoubɔːl] (to), *F:* faire boule *f* de neige (*dettes, foule, etc.*).

snowbird [ˈsnoubəːd] (*noun*), *P:* drogué*, cocaïnomane *mf*.

snow-dropping [ˈsnou-drɔpiŋ] (*noun*), *P:* vol *m* de linge séchant dans les jardins.

snowed [snoud] (*adj.*). **1.** *P:* drogué* à la cocaïne, enneigé. **2.** *F:* **s. under**, accablé de travail*, abruti.

snow-job [ˈsnou-dʒɔb] (*noun*) (*U.S.*), *F:* flatterie intéressée, pommade *f*; **to give s.o. a s.-j.** = **to shoot s.o. a line** (**shoot²** (to), **5**).

snowman [ˈsnoumən] (*noun*), *F:* **the Abominable S.**, grand animal inconnu de l'Himalaya, yéti *m*.

snow-white [ˈsnouˈwait] (*adj.*), *F:* innocent, blanc (comme la neige); *cf.* **lily-white.**

---

* L'astérisque indique que le mot marqué de ce signe figure comme entrée dans le Répertoire.

snuff [snʌf] (*noun*), *F:* **up to s.**, (*a*) à la hauteur, à la coule; (*b*) malin*, dessalé, dégourdi.

snuff it [ˈsnʌfit] (**to**), *P:* mourir*, éteindre sa lampe, avaler sa chique.

snuffles [ˈsnʌflz] (*pl. noun*), *F:* **to have the s.** = **to have the sniffles**.

snuff out [ˈsnʌfˈaut] (**to**), *P:* **1.** = **snuff it** (**to**). **2.** tuer*, zigouiller.

so [sou] (*adv. & conj.*), *F:* **1. s. long!** à bientôt! à tout à l'heure! **2. s. what?** et après?

soak[1] [souk] (*noun*), *P:* **1.** ivrogne*, pionnard *m*, poivrot *m*. **2.** ivrognerie *f*, saoulerie *f*, ribote *f*, cuite *f*.

soak[2] [souk] (**to**). **1.** *P:* boire* beaucoup, pomper, s'ivrogner; **to get soaked,** s'enivrer, avoir une cuite. **2.** *F:* (*a*) faire payer* trop cher, écorcher; (*b*) taxer à haute dose, assaisonner.

soaker [ˈsoukər] (*noun*), *F:* **1.** = **soak**[1], **1**. **2.** pluie* forte, averse *f*, bouillon *m*.

so-and-so [ˈsouənsou] (*noun*), *F:* **1. Mr. S.-a.-s., Mrs. S.-a.-s.,** Monsieur un tel, Madame une telle; Monsieur (Madame) Machin(-truc). **2.** (*péj.*) sale mec *m*, peau *f* de vache; **she's a right old s.-a.-s.,** c'est une vraie salope.

soap[1] [soup] (*noun*). **1.** *F:* (**soft**) **s.,** flatterie *f*, eau bénite. **2.** *P:* argent* de subornation, fric *m* de chantage. **3.** *F:* **no s.!** = **no dice!** (**dice**[1], **1**). **4.** *F:* **s. opera,** feuilleton *m* (*radio ou T.V.*) à l'eau de rose.

soap[2] [soup] (**to**), *P:* = **soft-soap** (**to**).

soapbox [ˈsoupbɔks] (*noun*), *F:* estrade *f* (en plein air pour orateur); **s. orator,** orateur *m* s'adressant au public en plein air; orateur de carrefour.

soapy [ˈsoupi] (*adj.*), *F:* doucereux, mielleux, patelin.

s.o.b. [ˈesouˈbiː] (*abbr.*), *P:* **1.** = **shit or bust** (**shit**[4] (**to**), **3**.) **2.**) = **son-of-a-bitch**.

sob-act [ˈsɔbækt] (*noun*, *P:* **to put on a.** (*or* **the**) **s.-a.,** pleurer des larmes *f.pl.* de crocodile.

sobs [sɔbz] (*pl. noun*), *P:* livres *f.pl.* sterling.

sob-sister [ˈsɔb-sistər] (*noun*) (*mainly U.S.*), *F:* **1.** journaliste spécialisée dans le mélodrame. **2.** actrice *f* qui joue le mélo(drame), chialeuse *f*.

sob-story [ˈsɔb-stɔːri] (*noun*), *F:* histoire larmoyante. (*ou* au jus de mirettes).

sob-stuff [ˈsɔb-stʌf] (*noun*), *F:* sensiblerie *f*, eau *f* de guimauve.

soccer [ˈsɔkər] (*noun*), *F:* foot(ball) *m*.

sock[1] [sɔk] (*noun*). **1.** *P:* **put a s. in it!** passe la main! la ferme! **2.** *P:* coup* de poing, gifle *f*, taloche *f*. **3.** *F:* **to pull one's socks up,** se remuer, remonter la pente, faire mieux que ça. *Voir aussi* **bobbysock; wet**[1], **6**.

sock[2] [sɔk] (**to**), *P:* **1.** donner un coup* à (qn), flanquer une raclée à (qn). **2. s. it to me!** (*a*) passe-moi ça! flanquemoi ça!; (*b*) fais-moi la cour! fais-moi du plat!; (*c*) continue, tu te débrouilles bien!

sod[1] [sɔd] (*noun*), *V:* **1.** pédéraste*, pédé *m*. **2. poor s.!** pauvre con! pauvre enculé!; **silly s.!** espèce d'andouille!; **rotten s.!** peau *f* de vache! **3. I don't give** (*or* **care**) **a s.,** je m'en fous (comme de l'an quarante *ou* de ma première chemise). *Voir aussi* **odds, 1**.

sod[2] [sɔd] (**to**), *V:* **1.** enculer, empaffer (*coït* anal, **1**.). **2. s. you!** va te faire foutre!; **s. it!** merde alors! bordel de Dieu!

sod about (*or* **around**) [ˈsɔdəˈbaut, ˈsɔdəˈraund] (**to**), *V:* = **bugger about** (**to**).

sod-all [ˈsɔdˈɔːl] (*noun*), *V:* = **bugger-all**.

sod off [ˈsɔdˈɔf] (**to**), *V:* = **bugger off** (**to**).

sod up [ˈsɔdˈʌp] (**to**), *V:* = **bugger up** (**to**).

soft[1] [sɔft] (*adj.*), *F:* **1.** (*a*) crédule, sentimental; (*b*) bête*, niais, nigaud; **s. in the head,** faible d'esprit; (*c*) poltron*, lâche, caneur. **2. a s. job,** un filon, un bon fromage, une planque; **to have a s. time** (**of it**), se la couler douce; *cf.* **berth, 2; cushy. 3. to be s. on s.o.,** être épris (*ou* entiché) de qn. **4. s. drugs,** drogues (toxiques) mineures; *cf.* **hard**[1], **2. 5. s. sell,** publicité discrète; *cf.* **hard**[1], **5**. *Voir aussi* **sawder; soap**[1], **1; spot, 4; touch**[1], **3**.

soft[2] [sɔft] (*adv.*), *F:* **1. don't talk s.!** ne dis pas de bêtises*! **2. to have it s.** = **to have a soft time** (**of it**) (**soft**[1], **2**).

soft-pedal [ˈsɔftˈpedl] (**to**), *F:* y aller doucement, ne pas trop insister, garder le secret, pédaler doux.

soft-soap [ˈsɔftˈsoup] (**to**), *F:* flatter*, passer de la pommade à (qn), pommader, flagorner.

softy [ˈsɔfti] (*noun*), *F:* (*a*) homme mou (*ou* efféminé), hommelette *f*; (*b*) couard

---

* An asterisk indicates that the word so marked is included as a head-word in the Appendix.

m, lavette *f*; (*c*) personne *f* frêle, mauviette *f*; (*d*) individu sentimental à l'excès.

sold [sould] (*p.p.*): *voir* **sell**[2] (**to**); *voir aussi* **sold out.**

soldier[1] [ˈsouldʒər] (*noun*). **1.** *P:* = **Billingsgate pheasant** (Billingsgate, 2). **2.** *F:* (*a*) cigare* entier (*ou* cigare qu'on fume); (*b*) bouteille *f* de bière *ou* de whisky; **dead s.**, (*a*) mégot* froid; (*b*) = **dead man** (dead[1], 2). **3.** *F:* **old s.**, soudard *m*, brisquard *m*; **to come the old s.**, la faire au vieux sergent, poser au vieux brisquard.

soldier[2] [ˈsouldʒər] (**to**), *P:* **to s. on the job**, renâcler à la besogne, flémarder.

soldier on [ˈsouldʒəˈɔn] (**to**), *F:* continuer à se maintenir (*ou* se défendre *ou* se débattre).

sold out [ˈsouldˈaut] (*adj.*), *P:* très fatigué*, vanné, crevé.

solid[1] [ˈsɔlid] (*adj.*). **1.** *F:* **five s. hours**, cinq heures pleines; **six s. weeks**, six bonnes semaines. **2.** *P:* (*a*) excellent*, foutral, épatant; (*b*) emballant, époustouflant.

solid[2] [ˈsɔlid] (*adv.*), *F:* **to be in s. with s.o.**, être dans les petits papiers de qn.

solitary [ˈsɔlitəri] (*noun*), *F:* **in s.**, en réclusion *f*, dans les bondes *f.pl.*

some[1] [sʌm] (*adj.*), *F:* **1.** excellent*, formid(able); **she's a s. girl!** elle est sensas(s)!; c'est une fille* formidable! **2. s. hope!** quelle illusion!

some[2] [sʌm] (*adv.*), *F:* (*a*) dans une certaine mesure; (*b*) considérablement; **to go s.**, y aller en plein, gazer.

some[3] [sʌm] (*pron.*), *F:* ...**and then s.**, ...et le reste, ...et encore plus.

somebody [ˈsʌmbɔdi, ˈsʌmbədi] (*noun*), *F:* **he's a s.**, c'est vraiment quelqu'un, c'est un personnage; *cf.* **nobody.**

something[1] [ˈsʌmθiŋ] (*adv.*), *P:* très, beaucoup*; **she went off at him s. awful**, elle lui a passé un bon savon; *voir aussi* **chronic**[2].

something[2] [ˈsʌmθiŋ] (*noun*), *F:* **1. that's s. like it!** voilà qui est bien! voilà qui est mieux! **2. isn't that s.!** **that really is s.!** n'est-ce pas super!

song [sɔŋ] (*noun*). **1.** *F:* **to make a s. (and dance) about sth.**, faire des histoires (*ou* des tas d'histoires) au sujet de qch. **2.** *F:* **to buy sth. for a s.**, acheter qch. pour un morceau (*ou* une

bouchée) de pain. **3.** *P:* aveu *m*, déboutonnage *m*, accouchage *m*. *Voir aussi* **torch-song.**

sonk [sɔŋk] (*noun*) (*Austr.*), *P:* pédéraste*, lope *f*.

sonny (Jim) [ˈsʌni(ˈdʒim)] (*noun*), *F:* (mon) petit, (mon) fiston.

son-of-a-bitch [ˈsʌnəvəˈbitʃ] (*noun*), *P:* **1.** vaurien*, gredin *m*, fils *m* de pute. **2.** embêtation *f*, emmerdement *m*.

soppiness [ˈsɔpinis] (*noun*), *F:* mollesse *f*, fadasserie *f*.

soppy [ˈsɔpi] (*adj.*), *F:* (*a*) bête*, baluchard; **s. ha'porth!** gros bêta!; *cf.* **date**[1], **1**; (*b*) mou, fadasse.

sore [sɔr] (*adj.*), *F:* **1.** en colère*, fâché, à cran; **to get s. with s.o.**, en vouloir à qn. **2. to be like a bear with a s. head**, être d'une humeur massacrante. *Voir aussi* **eye**, **15**; **thumb**, **4.**

sorehead [ˈsɔːhed] (*noun*), *P:* rancunier *m*, qn plein de ressentiment.

sort [sɔːt] (*noun*). **1.** *F:* **a good s.**, un brave homme*, un chic type. **2.** *F:* **out of sorts**, patraque, pas dans son assiette. **3.** *P:* (*a*) fille*, môme *f*; (*b*) petite amie, nénette *f*.

sort of [ˈsɔːtəv] (*adv.*), *F:* = **kind of.**

sort out [ˈsɔːtˈaut] (**to**), *F:* **to s. s.o. o.**, remettre qn à sa place.

so-so [ˈsousou] (*adv.*), *F:* couci-couça, entre les deux.

soul [soul] (*noun*), *F:* **poor s.!** pauvre créature! pauvre bonhomme! pauvre bonne femme!; **she's a good s.**, c'est une bien brave femme, c'est une bonne pâte.

soul-brother [ˈsoul-brʌðər] (*noun*), *F:* nègre* (parlant d'un autre nègre).

soulful [ˈsoulful] (*adj.*), *F:* (*jazz*) = **funky**, **3.**

sound off [ˈsaundˈɔf] (**to**), *F:* **to s. o. at s.o.**, réprimander* qn, engueuler qn.

soup [su:p] (*noun*). **1.** *F:* **in the s.**, dans le pétrin (*ou* la panade). **2.** *P:* (*a*) nitroglycérine *f* (pour faire sauter les coffres-forts), jus *m*; (*b*) dynamite *f*. **3.** *F:* puissance *f* d'un moteur, jus *m*; *cf.* **soup up** (to), (*a*). *Voir aussi* **duck**[1], **13.**

soup up [ˈsuːpˈʌp] (**to**), *F:* (*a*) augmenter considérablement la puissance du moteur d'une auto (en vue d'une course), gonfler; **a souped-up job**, une affaire survoltée; (*b*) exagérer*, épicer (une publicité, *etc.*).

---

* L'astérisque indique que le mot marqué de ce signe figure comme entrée dans le Répertoire.

soupy [ˈsuːpi] (*adj.*), *F:* (*a*) sentimental, à l'eau de rose; (*b*) (voix) larmoyante.

sourpuss [ˈsauəpus] (*noun*), *F:* individu* morose (*ou* revêche *ou* renfrogné), bonnet *m* de nuit.

souse[1] [saus] (*noun*), *P:* 1. = **sozzler**. 2. ivresse*, cuite *f*, saoulerie *f*.

souse[2] [saus] (**to**), *P:* = **sozzle** (**to**).

soused [saust] (*adj.*), *P:* = **sozzled**.

southpaw [ˈsauθpɔː] (*noun*), *F:* gaucher *m*.

sozzle [ˈsɔzl] (**to**), *P:* 1. boire* beaucoup, picoler. 2. s'enivrer, se charger.

sozzled [ˈsɔzld] (*adj.*), *P:* ivre*, saoul.

sozzler [ˈsɔzlər] (*noun*), *P:* ivrogne*, pionnard *m*, saoulard *m*.

sozzling [ˈsɔzliŋ] (*noun*), *P:* ivresse*, poivrade *f*.

spade [speid] (*noun*). 1. *P:* (*péj.*) nègre*, bougnoul(l)e *m*. 2. *F:* **to call a s. a s.**, appeler les choses par leur nom, appeler un chat un chat.

spank along [ˈspæŋkəˈlɔŋ] (**to**), *F:* aller vite*, filer, foncer, gazer.

spanker [ˈspæŋkər] (*noun*), *F:* 1. beau spécimen, qch. d'épatant (*ou* de super). 2. cheval* rapide, crack *m*.

spanking[1] [ˈspæŋkiŋ] (*adj.*), *F:* 1. rapide, à pleins tubes. 2. grand, énorme, maousse. 3. excellent*, épatant.

spanking[2] [ˈspæŋkiŋ] (*adv.*), *F:* **s. new**, flambant neuf.

spanner [ˈspænər] (*noun*), *F:* **to put** (*or* **throw**) **a s. in the works**, mettre des bâtons dans les roues.

spare[1] [spɛər] (*adj.*), *F:* 1. (*a*) **to go s.**, être furieux, fulminer, pétarder; (*b*) **to drive s.o. s.**, rendre qn furieux, faire marronner qn; (*c*) **there's a glass going s. here**, il y a un verre qui traîne par ici. 2. **s. tyre** (*U.S.:* **tire**), bourrelet *m* de graisse, pneu *m* Michelin.

spare[2] [spɛər] (*noun*), *P:* **to have a bit of s.** = **to have a bit on the side** (**side**, 2).

spare-part [ˈspɛəˈpɑːt] (*attrib. adj.*), *F:* **s.-p. surgery**, chirurgie *f* de greffage.

spark [spɑːk] (**to**) (*Austr.*), *P:* = **screw**[2] (**to**), 5.

sparkle plenty [ˈspɑːklˈplenti] (*noun*), *P:* amphétamine *f* (*drogues**).

sparklers [ˈspɑːkləz] (*pl. noun*), *F:* diamants*, diames *m.pl.*

sparks [spɑːks] (*noun*), *F:* opérateur *m* de TSF, radio *m* (*bateaux, avions*).

sparring-partner [ˈspɑːriŋpɑːtnər] (*noun*), *F:* épouse*, ma (chère) moitié.

sparrow-fart [ˈspærou-fɑːt] (*noun*), *P:* **at s.-f.**, aux aurores, dès potron-ja(c)quet, dès potron-minet.

spat [spæt] (*noun*), *F:* 1. bout filtré (d'une cigarette). 2. (*U.S.*) petite querelle*, bisbille *f*.

speakeasy [ˈspiːk-iːzi] (*noun*) (*U.S.*), *F:* bar clandestin.

spec [spek] (*noun*) (*abbr.* = *speculation*), *F:* **on s.**, à tout hasard. *Voir aussi* **specs**.

specimen [ˈspesimən, ˈspesimin] (*noun*), *F:* individu*, type *m*; **an odd** (*or* **a queer**) **s.**, un drôle de numéro (*ou* de client *ou* d'oiseau).

specs [speks] (*pl. noun*) (*abbr.* = *spectacles*), *F:* lunettes*, berniches *f.pl.*

speed [spiːd] (*noun*). 1. *P:* amphétamine *f* (*drogues**), speed *m*. 2. (*U.S.*) *P:* hédoniste *mf*. 3. *F:* **it's not my s.** = **it's not my scene** (**scene**, 7).

speedball [ˈspiːdbɔːl] (*noun*), *P:* = **goofball**, 3, 4, 5.

speed-cop [ˈspiːdkɔp] (*noun*), *F:* motard *m*.

speed-hog [ˈspiːdhɔg] (*noun*), *F:* chauffard *m*.

speed-merchant [ˈspiːdməːtʃənt] (*noun*), *F:* passionné *m* de la vitesse, fou *m* du volant.

speed-up [ˈspiːdʌp] (*noun*), *F:* allure accélérée.

spellbinder [ˈspel-baindər] (*noun*), *F:* orateur entraînant (*ou* fascinant).

spell out [ˈspelˈaut] (**to**), *F:* expliquer dans le langage le plus simple, comme a, b, c.

spiderman [ˈspaidəmæn] (*noun*), *F:* ouvrier *m* qui travaille au sommet des édifices, homme-mouche *m*.

spiel[1] [spiːl, ʃpiːl] (*noun*), *F:* boniment *m*, baratin *m*.

spiel[2] [spiːl, ʃpiːl] (**to**), *F:* avoir du bagou(t); baratiner, pérorer.

spieler [ˈspiːlər, ˈʃpiːlər] (*noun*). 1. *P:* tricheur* (aux cartes), bonneteur *m*. 2. *P:* escroc*, arnaqueur *m*. 3. *P:* tripot *m* de jeux. 4. *P:* embobineur *m*. 5. *P:* beau parleur, baratineur *m*, bonimenteur *m*.

spiel off [ˈspiːlˈɔf, ˈʃpiːlˈɔf] (**to**), *F:* **to s. o. a whole list of names**, débiter (*ou* dégoiser) toute une liste de noms.

spiffing [ˈspifiŋ] (*adj.*), *F:* ravissant, charmant, délicieux.

---

* An asterisk indicates that the word so marked is included as a head-word in the Appendix.

spifflicate [ˈspiflikeit] (to), F: écraser, aplatir, fracasser, démolir, écrabouiller (un adversaire).

spifflicated [ˈspiflikeitid] (adj.), P: ivre*, rétamé.

spike[1] [spaik] (noun), P: 1. aiguille f hypodermique (pour piqûre de drogues). 2. to get (or cop) the s., se mettre en colère*, prendre la mouche.

spike[2] [spaik] (to). 1. P: injecter (des drogues), piquouser, shooter. 2. F: to s. a drink, ajouter de l'alcool* à une boisson non alcoolisée; to s. coffee with cognac, corser du café avec du cognac. 3. F: to s. s.o.'s guns, contrarier, contrecarrer qn; I spiked his guns for him, je lui ai damé le pion.

spiked [spaikt] (adj.), P: drogué*, défoncé, high.

spiky [ˈspaiki] (adj.), F: susceptible, chatouilleux.

spin [spin] (noun), F: 1. to be in a flat s., être paniqué (ou affolé). 2. to go for a s., aller se balader (en auto), aller faire une randonnée. 3. station f de taxis. 4. to give sth. a s., prendre qch. à l'essai. Voir aussi tail-spin.

spin-off [ˈspinɔf] (noun), F: produit(s) m.(pl.) secondaire(s); dérivé(s) m.(pl.).

spit [spit] (noun). 1. F: s. and polish, astiquage m, fourbissage m; to give sth. a s. and polish, faire reluire qch., astiquer qch. 2. P: s. and drag (R.S. = fag), cigarette*. Voir aussi dead[1], 6.

spit-curl [ˈspitkə:l] (noun), F: accroche-cœur m.

spit out [ˈspitˈaut] (to), F: to s. it o., dire, accoucher, vider son sac.

spiv [spiv] (noun), F: trafiquant m, chevalier m d'industrie. Voir aussi metal-spiv.

spivvy [ˈspivi] (adj.), F: louche, parasite.

splash[1] [splæʃ] (noun), F: 1. to make a (big) s., (a) faire sensation, jeter du jus; (b) = splash out (to). 2. étalage m, déploiement m. 3. jet m de siphon; a whisky and s., un whisky-soda.

splash[2] [splæʃ] (to), F: 1. annoncer en grande manchette. 2. to s. one's money about = splash out (to). Voir aussi boot, 7.

splash out [ˈsplæʃˈaut] (to), F: dépenser* sans compter, claquer du fric.

splay [splei] (noun), P: marijuana f (drogues*).

splendiferous [splenˈdifərəs] (adj.), F: splendide, rutilant.

spliced [splaist] (p.p. & adj.), F: to get s., se marier, s'antifler.

spliff [splif] (noun), P: cigarette* de marijuana (drogues*), stick m.

split[1] [split] (noun). 1. F: = splitter, 1. 2. P: détective m, condé m. 3. P: part f (de butin), gratte f. 4. P: allumette f, bûche f. 5. F: (a) demi-bouteille f d'eau gazeuse; (b) demi-verre m de liqueur.

split[2] [split] (to). 1. F: (a) vendre la mèche; (b) to s. on s.o., dénoncer*, cafarder, vendre, donner qn. 2. P: partager (bénéfices, butin, etc.), faire le fade. 3. P: = split out (to), (a), (b). 4. F: my head is splitting, j'ai un mal de tête fou. Voir aussi side, 3.

split-arse [ˈsplitɑ:s] (adv.), P: to run s.-a., courir avec le feu au derrière.

split out [ˈsplitˈaut] (to), P: (a) partir*, ficher le camp; (b) s'enfuir*, se carapater, mettre les bouts.

splitter [ˈsplitər] (noun), F: 1. dénonciateur*, cafard m, donneur m. 2. mal m de tête fou.

split-up [ˈsplitʌp] (noun), F: 1. querelle*, brisure f. 2. divorce m, séparation légale.

split up [ˈsplitˈʌp] (to), F: 1. rompre avec qn. 2. divorcer, se démaquer.

splodge[1] [splɔdʒ] (noun), F: tache f (de couleur, etc.).

splodge[2] [splɔdʒ] (to), F: flanquer, asperger.

sploff [splɔf] (noun), P: = spliff.

sploshed [splɔʃt] (adj.), P: = sloshed.

splurge[1] [splə:dʒ] (noun), F: esbrouf(f)e f; démonstration bruyante; to make a s. = splurge[2] (to).

splurge[2] [splə:dʒ] (to), F: faire de l'esbrouf(f)e f (ou de l'épate f ou de la chique).

spon [spɔn] (noun), P: = spondulic(k)s.

spondulic(k)s [spɔnˈdju:liks] (pl. noun), P: argent*, fric m, oseille f.

sponge[1] [spʌndʒ] (noun), F: = sponger. Voir aussi throw in (to).

sponge[2] [spʌndʒ] (to), F: (a) écornifler, écumer les marmites; (b) to s. a drink, se faire offrir une tournée; to s. on s.o., vivre aux dépens de qn.

sponger [ˈspʌndʒər] (noun), F: écornifleur m, tapeur m, torpille f.

* L'astérisque indique que le mot marqué de ce signe figure comme entrée dans le Répertoire.

sponging [ˈspʌndʒiŋ] (*noun*), *F:* écorniflage *m*.

spoof[1] [spuːf] (*noun*), *F:* plaisanterie *f*, blague *f*.

spoof[2] [spuːf] (**to**). 1. (*U.S.*) *F:* dire des bêtises*, sortir des sornettes *f.pl.* 2. *P:* flatter*, pommader. 3. *F:* tromper*, filouter, empiler; **you've been spoofed**, on vous a eu. 4. *F:* duper*, faire marcher; mettre en boîte.

spook[1] [spuːk] (*noun*), *F:* fantôme *m*, revenant *m*, apparition *f*.

spook[2] [spuːk] (**to**), *F:* faire peur* à (qn), ficher la frousse à (qn).

spooky [ˈspuːki] (*adj.*), *F:* (*a*) hanté; (*b*) sinistre, étrange, surnaturel.

spoon [spuːn] (**to**), *F:* se faire des mamours *m.pl.* (*ou* des cajoleries *f.pl.*).

spooner [ˈspuːnər] (*noun*), *F:* = **spoon(e)y**[2].

spoon(e)y[1] [ˈspuːni] (*adj.*), *F:* qui fait des mamours *m.pl.*, cajoleur, caressant.

spoon(e)y[2] [ˈspuːni] (*noun*), *F:* cajoleur *m*, peloteur *m*.

sport [spɔːt] (*noun*). 1. *F:* **a** (**good**) **s.**, individu* sympathique, bon type, bonne nature; **be a s.!** sois chic! 2. *P:* fille*, petite amie. 3. **hello, (old) s.!** salut, mon pote!

sporting [ˈspɔːtiŋ] (*adj.*). 1. *F:* qui a bon caractère, d'un bon naturel. 2. *P:* **s. woman**, femme facile, Marie-couche-toi-là.

sporty [ˈspɔːti] (*adj.*), *F:* 1. sportif. 2. **the s. set**, les (bons) viveurs. 3. (*vêtement, etc.*) de couleurs criardes.

spot [spɔt] (*noun*). 1. *F:* **to be in a** (**bit of a**) **s.**, être dans une situation difficile, être dans le pétrin. 2. *F:* **to get into a s. of bother**, avoir des ennuis *m.pl.*, être dans de mauvais draps. 3. *F:* **to knock spots off s.o.**, exceller sur qn, rendre des points à qn, battre qn à plate(s) couture(s). 4. *F:* **to have a soft s. for s.o., sth.**, avoir un faible pour qn, qch. 5. *F:* projecteur *m* (de lumière). 6. *P:* cinq ans *f.pl.* de prison*, gerbement *m* de cinq longes *f.pl.* 7. *F:* **a s.**, un (petit) peu*; **a s. of whisky**, un petit coup de whisky; **how about a s. of lunch?** si nous allions déjeuner? 8. *F:* **on the s.**, (*a*) en danger, sur la corde raide; (*b*) mis à tâche; (*c*) alerte, vif, éveillé, actif; (*d*) immédiatement, sur-le-champ;

to put s.o. on the s., (*a*) *P:* assassiner* qn, descendre qn; (*b*) *F:* mettre qn dans une situation difficile, handicaper qn. 9. *F:* (*T.V.*) message *m* publicitaire. 10. *F:* **s. below:** *voir* **bingo** (89). *Voir aussi* **five-spot; highspots; hot, 23; Johnny-on-the-spot; night-spot; tenspot.**

spotlight [ˈspɔtlait] (**to**), *F:* mettre en vedette (*ou* en relief), souligner.

spot-on [ˈspɔtˈɔn] (*adj.*), *F:* dans le mille, qui fait mouche.

spout[1] [spaut] (*noun*), *P:* 1. **up the s.**, en gage, chez ma tante. 2. **down the s.**, perdu, fichu, foutu. 3. **to put a girl up the s.**, rendre une fille enceinte*, mettre une fille en cloque.

spout[2] [spaut] (**to**), *F:* dégoiser, déblatérer, débiter.

spread [spred] (*noun*), *F:* 1. repas copieux, gueuleton *m*. 2. **middle-age(d) s.**, l'embonpoint *m* de la maturité, pneu *m* Michelin de la quarantaine.

spring [spriŋ] (**to**). 1. (*U.S.*) *P:* faire libérer (qn) de prison*, cautionner. 2. *P:* faire échapper (qn) de prison*, faire larguer (qn). 3. *F:* annoncer à l'improviste, révéler à brûle-pourpoint. 4. *F:* **where did you s. from?** d'où sortez-vous? *Voir aussi* **leak**[1], 1.

sprog [sprɔg] (*noun*), *P:* 1. recrue *f*, conscrit *m*, bleu *m*. 2. enfant*, mioche *mf*, moutard *m*.

sprout [spraut] (**to**), *F:* **to s. wings**, (*a*) faire une bonne action, se faire pousser des ailes; (*b*) mourir*, aller au paradis.

sprung [sprʌŋ] (*adj.*) (*mainly U.S.*), *F:* ivre*, raide, rondibé; *cf.* **half-sprung.**

spud [spʌd] (*noun*), *F:* **s.** (**Murphy**), pomme *f* de terre, patate *f*.

spud-basher [ˈspʌdbæʃər] (*noun*), *F:* (*mil.*) éplucheur *m* de pommes de terre.

spud-bashing [ˈspʌdbæʃiŋ] (*noun*), *F:* (*mil.*) corvée *f* de patates, pluches *f.pl.*

spug [spʌg], **spuggy** [ˈspʌgi] (*noun*), *F:* moineau *m*, piaf *m*.

spunk [spʌŋk] (*noun*). 1. *V:* sperme*, jus *m*. 2. *P:* courage *m*, cran *m*, estomac *m*. 3. *P:* **to put fresh s. into sth.**, ravigoter qch. 4. (*U.S.*) *P:* colère *f*, emportement *m*, soupe *f* au lait.

spunkless [ˈspʌŋklis] (*adj.*), *P:* 1. amorphe, larveux. 2. poltron, froussard.

---

* An asterisk indicates that the word so marked is included as a head-word in the Appendix.

spunky [ˈspʌŋki] (*adj.*), *F:* courageux*, qui en a dans le bide.

spur [spəːr] (to) (*Austr.*), *F:* contre-carrer, mettre des bâtons dans les roues de (qn).

spurge [spəːdʒ] (*noun*) (*Austr.*), *P:* pédéraste*, pédalo *m*.

squad-car [ˈskwɔdkaːr] (*noun*), *F:* car* de police, porte-poulaille *m*.

squaddie, squaddy [ˈskwɔdi] (*noun*), *F:* (*mil.*) (*a*) recrue *f*, conscrit *m* de l'escouade, bleu *m*, blaireau *m*; (*b*) soldat*, bidasse *m*.

square[1] [skwɛər] (*adj.*). 1. *F:* a s. deal, une affaire* honnête, un coup régulier. 2. *F:* a s. meal, un bon repas. 3. *F:* to be all s., être quitte, être à égalité, être réglo. 4. *F:* (*a*) vieux jeu, croulant, périmé; (*b*) honnête, régulier, réglo. 5. *P:* sexuellement normal; *cf.* straight[1], 2. 6. *F:* to get s. with s.o., (*a*) se venger de qn; (*b*) être quitte envers qn. 7. *F:* to be a s. peg in a round hole, être inapte à qch. *Voir aussi* fair[1], 2.

square[2] [skwɛər] (*noun*), *F:* 1. to be back to s. one, repartir à zéro. 2. (*a*) bourgeois démodé croulant *m*; he's a s., il est tout à fait vieux jeu; (*b*) individu* honnête (*ou* réglo). 3. on the s., droit, honnête, comme il faut.

square[3] [skwɛər] (to), *F:* (*a*) suborner, soudoyer, acheter; (*b*) obtenir la complicité de (qn). *Voir aussi* rap[1], 2.

square-bash [ˈskwɛə-bæʃ] (to), *F:* faire l'exercice *m* (militaire).

square-basher [ˈskwɛə-bæʃər] (*noun*), *F:* soldat* à l'exercice.

square-bashing [ˈskwɛə-bæʃiŋ] (*noun*), *F:* exercices *m.pl.* (*ou* manœuvres *f.pl.*) militaires; l'exercice *m*.

squarehead [ˈskwɛəhed] (*noun*), *P:* 1. Allemand*, boche *m*. 2. (*Austr.*) criminel *m* en liberté.

square off [ˈskwɛərˈɔf] (to) (*Austr.*), *P:* se tirer d'un mauvais pas.

squaresville [ˈskwɛəzvil] (*noun*), *P:* société conformiste et bourgeoise.

square up [ˈskwɛərˈʌp] (to), *F:* 1. être prêt à se battre, se mettre en quarante. 2. to s. u. to the facts, faire face à la réalité. 3. régler une affaire avec qn.

square-wheeler   [ˈskwɛəˈ(h)wiːlər] (*noun*), *P:* = palm-tree; *cf.* bottler.

squarie [ˈskwɛəri] (*noun*) (*Austr.*), *P:* = squarehead, 2. *Voir aussi* half-squarie.

squash[1] [skwɔʃ] (*noun*), *F:* réunion pleine de monde, cohue *f*.

squash[2] [skwɔʃ] (to), *F:* 1. faire taire*, la faire boucler, rembarrer. 2. vaincre, battre à plate(s) couture(s), tailler en pièces.

squawk[1] [skwɔːk] (*noun*), *P:* 1. pétition *f* (à un directeur de prison, *etc.*). 2. appel *m* d'une condamnation, rappel *m*. 3. plainte *f*, réclamation *f*.

squawk[2] [skwɔːk] (to), *P:* 1. faire des aveux *m.pl.*, confesser (à la police). 2. se plaindre, rouspéter, ronchonner, rouscailler.

squawker [ˈskwɔːkər] (*noun*), *P:* rouspéteur *m*, ronchonneur *m*.

squeak[1] [skwiːk] (*noun*). 1. *P:* = squeal[1]. 2. *P:* = squealer, 1, 3. 3. *F:* to have a narrow s., l'échapper belle, revenir de loin. 4. *F:* I don't want to hear another s. out of you, je ne veux pas entendre le moindre murmure. *Voir aussi* bubble-and-squeak; pip-squeak[2].

squeak[2] [skwiːk] (to), *P:* = squeal[2] (to), 1, 2.

squeaker [ˈskwiːkər] (*noun*), *P:* 1. = grasser. 2. résultat serré, aboutissement *m* à un fil.

squeal[1] [skwiːl] (*noun*), *P:* plainte *f* (à la police); to put the s. in, moutonner, cafarder.

squeal[2] [skwiːl] (to), *P:* 1. avouer*, manger le morceau, accoucher, vider son sac. 2. moucharder, vendre (*ou* éventer) la mèche; to s. on s.o., dénoncer* qn, balancer, cafarder, donner qn.

squealer [ˈskwiːlər] (*noun*), *P:* 1. = grasser. 2. = holler-wag(g)on. 3. rouspéteur *m*, ronchonneur *m*.

squeeze[1] [skwiːz] (*noun*). 1. *F:* to put the s. on s.o., forcer la main à qn. 2. *F:* a tight s., (*a*) presse *f*, cohue *f*; (*b*) it was a tight s., on tenait tout juste. 3. *P:* empreinte *f* d'une clef*, douce *f*. 4. *P:* main s., épouse*. 5. *P:* soie *f*.

squeeze[2] [skwiːz] (to), *F:* to s. s.o. = to put the squeeze on s.o. (squeeze[1], 1). *Voir aussi* lemon, 5.

squeezebox [ˈskwiːzbɔks] (*noun*), *F:* 1. concértina *f*. 2. accordéon *m*.

---

* L'astérisque indique que le mot marqué de ce signe figure comme entrée dans le Répertoire.

squelch[1] [skweltʃ] (*noun*), *F:* = **squel-cher.**

squelch[2] [skweltʃ] (to), *F:* faire taire* (qn), river le clou à (qn).

squelcher [ˈskweltʃər] (*noun*), *F:* réplique cinglante, riposte *f* qui vous rive le clou.

squiffy [ˈskwifi] (*adj.*), *F:* 1. légèrement ivre*, paf. 2. de travers, biscornu, tordu. 3. bête*, nigaud.

squint[1] [skwint] (*noun*), *P:* coup *m* d'œil*, coup de châsse; **let's have a s. at it!** fais voir!; **take a s. at that!** zyeute-moi ça!

squint[2] [skwint] (to), *P:* (*a*) regarder*, jeter un coup d'œil*, bigler; (*b*) **to s. at sth.**, regarder* qch. de côté (*ou* furtivement); bigler, zyeuter qch.

squirt [skwəːt] (*noun*), *P:* 1. (*a*) freluquet *m*, merdaillon *m*; (*b*) rapiat *m*, rat *m*. 2. rafale *f* de mitraillette. 3. **to have a s.**, uriner, jeter de la lance.

squish [skwiʃ] (*noun*). 1. *F:* boue *f*, bouillabaisse *f*, pulpe *f*. 2. *P:* marmelade *f* d'orange.

squishy [ˈskwiʃi] (*adj.*), *F:* détrempé, pulpeux, bourbeux.

squit [skwit] (*noun*), *P:* 1. = **squirt**, 1, (*a*), (*b*). 2. (*a*) camelote *f*, saleté *f*; (*b*) bêtises*, conneries *f.pl.*, balivernes *f.pl.* 3. (*pl.*) diarrhée*, foirade *f*.

squitters [ˈskwitəz] (*pl. noun*), *P:* 1. = **squit**, 3. 2. **to have the s.**, avoir peur*, avoir les foies *m.pl.*

squitty [skwiti] (*adj.*), *P:* connard, loquedu.

stab [stæb] (*noun*), *F:* **to have a s. (at sth.)**, faire un essai, tenter le coup.

stable-companion [ˈsteiblkəmˈpænjən] (*noun*), *F:* membre *m* d'une même société, bande*, *etc.*

stack [stæk] (*noun*). 1. *F:* (*a*) **to have a s. (or stacks) of money**, être très riche*, être cousu d'or, avoir le sac; (*b*) **to have a s. (or stacks) of work**, avoir beaucoup de travail*, avoir du pain sur la planche. 2. *P:* **to blow one's s.** = **to blow one's top** (**top**[1], 2). 3. *F:* **twin stacks**, double tuyau *m* d'échappement (*auto*). 4. *P:* quantité *f* de cigarettes de marijuana.

stacked [stækt] (*adj.*) = **well-stacked**, 1, 2.

stag[1] [stæg] (*noun*), *F:* 1. célibataire *m*, vieux garçon; **s. party**, réunion *f ou*

dîner *m* d'hommes seuls. 2. (*Bourse*) loup *m*.

stag[2] [stæg] (to). 1. *P:* coïter* avec (une femme), piner. 2. *F:* **to s. it**, se rendre seul à une réunion d'hommes (sans être accompagné de sa femme), sortir en garçon.

stager [ˈsteidʒər] (*noun*), *F:* **an old s.**, un vieux routier, un vieux de la vieille.

staggers [ˈstægəz] (*pl. noun*), *F:* **to have the s.**, chanceler, tituber, être zigzag.

stalk [stɔːk] (*noun*), *P:* pénis*, queue *f*. *Voir aussi* **corn-stalk.**

stamping-ground [ˈstæmpiŋgraund] (*noun*), *F:* lieu *m* que l'on fréquente, coin favori.

stand[1] [stænd] (*noun*). 1. *F:* **(one-night) s.**, représentation *f* d'un soir (*troupe théâtrale, jazz-band, etc.*). 2. *P:* **to have a s.**, être en érection*, avoir le bambou; *cf.* **cock-stand.** 3. (*U.S.*) *F:* barre *f* (de témoins).

stand[2] [stænd] (to), *F:* 1. **to s. s.o. a drink**, offrir un verre (*ou* une tournée) à qn; **I'm standing this one**, c'est ma tournée; *cf.* **sam**, 1. 2. = **stick**[2] (to), 8. *Voir aussi* **gaff**, 4; **racket**[1], 3.

stand for [ˈstændfɔːr] (to), *F:* tolérer, supporter.

stand-in [ˈstændin] (*noun*), *F:* délégué *m*, remplaçant *m*.

stand in [ˈstændˈin] (to), *F:* 1. **to s. i. for s.o.**, être délégué à la place de qn, remplacer qn. 2. **to s. i. (well) with s.o.**, être dans les bonnes grâces (*ou* les petits papiers) de qn.

stand off [ˈstændˈɔf] (to), *F:* faire chômer (qn), licencier (qn).

stand-offish [ˈstændˈɔfiʃ] (*adj.*), *F:* distant, raide, réservé.

stand-offishness [ˈstændˈɔfiʃnis] (*noun*), *F:* raideur *f*, réserve *f*, morgue *f*.

stand-out [ˈstændaut] (*noun*), *F:* (*personnes*) éminence *f*, sommité *f*; (*choses*) hors-ligne *m*, perle *f*.

stand over [ˈstændˈouvər] (to) (*Austr.*), *F:* = **strong-arm**[2] (to).

stand up [ˈstændˈʌp] (to), *F:* 1. faire attendre* (qn), faire poireauter (qn). 2. lâcher (qn), planter là. 3. tromper*, posséder, refaire (qn). 4. **to take it standing up**, ne pas broncher, encaisser le coup.

---

* An asterisk indicates that the word so marked is included as a head-word in the Appendix.

star [stɑːr] (*noun*), *F:* **1. to see stars,** voir trente-six chandelles. **2. there's a s. in the east,** votre braguette est déboutonnée; on voit le moteur. *Voir aussi* **superstar.**

stardust ['stɑːdʌst] (*noun*). **1.** *F:* illusion *f,* vision *f.* **2.** *P:* = **snow**[1], **1.**

stare [stɛər] (to), *F:* **it's staring you in the face,** ça vous saute aux yeux.

starkers ['stɑːkəz] (*adj.*), *P:* (**Harry**) **s.,** tout nu*, à poil.

starry-eyed ['stɑːriˈaid] (*adj.*), *F:* idéaliste, inexpérimenté, ingénu, songe-creux.

stash[1] [stæʃ] (*noun*), *P:* cachette *f,* lieu sûr; **s. man,** homme de carre, carreur *m* (pour des marchandises volées, drogues, *etc.*).

stash[2] [stæʃ] (to), *P:* **1.** cacher*, planquer, planquouser. **2.** arrêter, finir, finocher; **s. it!** arrête!

stashed [stæʃt] (*adj.*), *F:* (**well**) **s.,** riche*, plein aux as, galetteux, rupin.

stash away ['stæʃəˈwei] (to), *P:* **1.** = **stash**[2] (to), **1. 2.** accumuler, amasser, entasser (argent, *etc.*).

state [steit] (*noun*), *F:* **to be in a** (**bit of a**) **s.,** être dans tous ses états; **to get into a terrible s.,** (*a*) se mettre dans tous ses états; (*b*) se trouver dans un état lamentable.

statistics [stəˈtistiks] (*pl. noun*), *F:* **vital s.,** les trois mesures essentielles de la femme (poitrine, taille, hanches).

steady[1] ['stedi] (*adv.*), *F:* **to go s.,** se fréquenter, sortir ensemble (*fille et garçon*).

steady[2] ['stedi] (*noun*), *F:* petit(e) ami(e), l'attitré(e).

steam [stiːm] (*noun*), *F:* **1. to let** (*or* **blow**) **off s.,** (*a*) dépenser son superflu d'énergie; (*b*) épancher sa bile. **2. to get up s.,** (*a*) rassembler son énergie; se mettre sous pression; (*b*) s'exciter, s'emballer, péter le feu. **3. s. radio,** la TSF des familles, la vieille radio.

steamed up ['stiːmdˈʌp] (*p.p. & adj.*), *F:* **to get** (**all**) **s. u.,** (*a*) = **to get up steam** (**steam, 2** (*b*)); (*b*) se mettre en colère*, mousser.

steamer ['stiːmər] (*noun*), *P:* individu bête*, con *m,* couillon *m; cf.* **nit, 1.**

steep [stiːp] (*adj.*), *F:* **1.** trop cher*, exorbitant, excessif, salé. **2.** outrageux, abusif, incroyable; **that's a bit s.!** c'est un peu fort!

steer[1] [stiər] (*noun*) (*U.S.*). **1.** *F:* renseignement*, tuyau *m; voir aussi* **bum**[1]. **2.** *P:* = **steerer.**

steer[2] [stiər] (to), *P:* amorcer les clients (pour tripot, casino, *etc.*).

steerer ['stiərər] (*noun*), *P:* rabatteur *m,* racoleur *m* de clients (*bordels, etc.*).

stem [stem] (*noun*), *P:* pipe *f* à opium, chilom *m.*

step[1] [step] (*noun*). **1.** *P:* **up the steps,** renvoyé aux Assises, devant le comptoir. **2.** *F:* **all the steps:** *voir* **bingo** (39). *Voir aussi* **doorstep.**

step[2] [step] (to), *F:* **to s. outside,** sortir pour se battre*. *Voir aussi* **gas**[2], **2.**

step in ['stepˈin] (to), *F:* intervenir; s'interposer.

step-up ['stepʌp] (*noun*), *F:* promotion *f,* avancement *m.*

step up ['stepˈʌp] (to), *F:* **1. to s. u. the pace,** accélérer le pas, allonger la sauce. **2.** avoir une promotion, monter d'un échelon.

stern [stəːn] (*noun*), *F:* fesses*, postérieur *m.*

stew[1] [stjuː] (*noun*). **1.** *F:* **in a s.,** (*a*) sur des charbons ardents, sur le gril, dans tous ses états; (*b*) (*U.S.*) en colère*, à cran. **2.** *F:* **to work oneself** (**up**) **into a s.** = **to work oneself** (**up**) **into a lather** (**lather**[1], (*a*), (*b*)). **3.** (*Austr.*) *P:* = **jacky.**

stew[2] [stjuː] (to), *F:* **to s. in one's own juice,** cuire (*ou* mijoter) dans son jus.

stewed [stjuːd] (*adj.*), *P:* ivre*, rétamé; *voir aussi* **gills; half-stewed.**

stick[1] [stik] (*noun*). **1.** *F:* **to give s.o. s.,** réprimander* qn, engueuler qn; **to take a lot of s.,** être pilonné, recevoir une dégelée. **2.** *F:* **to wave the big s.,** faire les gros yeux. **3.** *F:* **over the sticks,** steeplechases *m.pl.,* course *f* d'obstacles. **4.** *F:* **the sticks,** (*a*) la campagne*, le bled, la cambrousse; (*b*) la banlieue. **5.** *P:* **s.** (**of tea**), cigarette* de marijuana (*drogues*), stick *m; cf.* **cancer-stick. 6.** *P:* pince-monseigneur*, rossignol *m.* **7.** *V:* pénis* en érection*, canne *f.* **8.** (*Austr.*) *F:* = **stickybeak. 9.** *F:* (*a*) **a queer s.,** un drôle de type, un drôle de zigoto; (*b*) **old s.,** père tartempion; **he's a good old s.,** c'est un brave zigue. *Voir aussi* **bean-stick; drumstick; end, 11; fiddlestick; hype-stick; joystick; kick-stick;**

---

* L'astérisque indique que le mot marqué de ce signe figure comme entrée dans le Répertoire.

knobstick; shitstick; up[5] (to), 1; walking-sticks.

stick[2] [stik] (to). 1. *F:* mettre, placer, coller; **s. it in your pocket,** fourrez-le dans votre poche*. 2. *F:* **to s. at sth.,** persévérer (*ou* s'accrocher) à qch. 3. *P:* **you know where you can s. that,** tu sais où tu peux te le mettre!; *cf.* arse, 6; flue, 2; gonga; jacksie, 1; jumper, 1; Khyber; shove (to). 4. *F:* **to get stuck with s.o.,** avoir qn de coller à soi, avoir qn sur le dos. 5. *F:* **to be stuck on s.o.,** être amoureux de qn, être pincé (*ou* entiché) de qn. 6. *F:* **to s. with s.o.,** se cramponner à qn, soutenir qn. 7. *F:* **to make sth. s.,** faire obéir (un ordre, *etc.*). 8. *F:* supporter, endurer, tenir; **I can't s. him (at any price),** je ne peux pas le sentir (*ou* le blairer). 9. *F:* rester; **to s. to one's room,** ne pas sortir de sa chambre. 10. *F:* **to s. to sth.,** garder qch. pour soi. 11. *P:* **to s. one on s.o.,** battre* qn, rosser qn, passer une peignée à qn. *Voir aussi* bill, 3; gun[1], 5.

stick around [ˈstikəˈraund] (to), *F:* attendre* sur place, poireauter; **to s. a. the house all day,** traîner dans la maison toute la journée; **s. a.! I'll be back in five minutes,** bouge pas! je reviens dans cinq minutes.

stick down [ˈstikˈdaun] (to), *F:* 1. **s. it d. anywhere,** collez-le n'importe où; *cf.* stick[2] (to), 1. 2. **to s. sth. d. in a notebook,** inscrire qch. sur un carnet.

sticker [ˈstikər] (noun), *F:* 1. article *m* invendable, rossignol *m.* 2. travailleur* appliqué, bûcheur *m.* 3. problème *m* difficile, colle *f,* casse-tête *m.* 4. (*d'une personne*) crampon *m.*

stick in [ˈstikˈin] (to). 1. *F:* **to get stuck in,** se cramponner, se maintenir. 2. *V:* **to s. it i.,** coïter*, mettre la cheville dans le trou.

stick-in-the-mud[1]   [ˈstikinðəmʌd] (*adj.*), *F:* conservateur, immobiliste, casanier.

stick-in-the-mud[2]   [ˈstikinðəmʌd] (*noun*), *F:* vieux croûton, vieille perruque.

stickjaw [ˈstikdʒɔ:] (*noun*), *F:* colle-mâchoires *m* (*caramel, chewing-gum, etc.*).

stick out [ˈstikˈaut] (to), *F:* 1. **to s.o. for higher wages,** demander avec insis-

tance une augmentation de salaire. 2. **to s. it o.,** tenir jusqu'au bout. 3. **she sticks out in all the right places,** elle est bien carrossée. *Voir aussi* neck[1], 3; thumb, 4.

stick-up [ˈstikʌp] (*noun*), *F:* = hold-up, 2.

stick up [ˈstikˈʌp] (to), *F:* 1. attaquer* *ou* voler à main armée, braquer. 2. **s. 'em u.!** haut les mains! 3. **to s. u. for s.o.,** prendre la défense de qn.

sticky [ˈstiki] (*adj.*), *F:* 1. peu accommodant, difficile. 2. mauvais*, tocard, désagréable. 3. **to have s. fingers,** voler* avec facilité, chiper, avoir de la poix aux mains, ne rien laisser traîner; *cf.* sticky-fingered. 4. **to bat** (*or* be) **on a s. wicket,** agir lorsqu'il y a peu de chance de réussite, marcher sur un terrain glissant; être dans le pétrin, être dans de mauvais draps.

stickybeak [ˈstikibi:k] (*noun*) (*Austr.*), *F:* curieux *m,* fouinard *m,* fouineur *m.*

sticky-fingered [ˈstikiˈfiŋgəd] (*adj.*), *F:* qui a les doigts crochus; *cf.* sticky, 3.

stiff[1] [stif] (*adj.*). 1. *P:* mort, raide. 2. *P:* ivre*, raide. 3. *F:* **that's a bit s.!** c'est un peu raide! *Voir aussi* bill, 2; lip, 2.

stiff[2] [stif] (*adv.*), *F:* 1. **to bore s.o. s.,** scier (le dos à) qn. 2. **to be scared s.,** avoir une peur* bleue.

stiff[3] [stif] (*noun*), *P:* 1. cadavre*, macchabé(e) *m.* 2. ivrogne*, poivrot *m.* 3. **working stiffs,** travailleurs*, ouvriers*, salariés *m.pl.* 4. lettre *f* de prisonnier passée en fraude. 5. cheval* certain de perdre, fer à repasser. 6. (*U.S.*) clochard*, clodot *m. Voir aussi* big[1], 9; bindle, 3.

stiff[4] [stif] (to) (*U.S.*), *P:* voler*, barbot(t)er, carotter.

stiffener [ˈstif(ə)nər] (*noun*), *F:* boisson alcoolisée, apéritif *m,* remontant *m.*

stiffneck [ˈstifnek] (*noun*), *F:* pharisien *m,* individu entiché de sa personne.

sting [stiŋ] (to), *F:* **to s. s.o. for sth.,** faire payer qch. à qn à un prix exorbitant; **to be** (*or* get) **stung,** attraper (*ou* essuyer) le coup de fusil, se faire écorcher; **he stung me for a quid,** il m'a tapé d'une livre.

stinger [ˈstiŋər] (*noun*), *F:* 1. coup* cinglant, coup raide, torgnole *f.* 2. (*poisson*) (*a*) méduse *f;* (*b*) torpille *f.*

---

* An asterisk indicates that the word so marked is included as a head-word in the Appendix.

stink[1] [stiŋk] (*noun*). **1.** *P:* **to raise** (*or* **kick up**) **a s.**, faire de l'esclandre *m*, rouspéter; **there's going to be a hell of a s.**, il va y avoir du grabuge; **a big s.**, (*a*) chahut *m*, ramdam *m*; (*b*) scandale *m*. **2.** (*pl.*) *F:* la chimie. **3.** *P:* **to work like s.**, travailler* dur, bûcher, se fouler la rate.

stink[2] [stiŋk] (**to**). **1.** *P:* être un vrai salaud; **he (positively) stinks!** c'est un type infect! **2.** *F:* être puant (*ou* infect). **3.** *F:* = **smell** (**to**).

stinkador [ˈstiŋkədɔːr], **stinkaduro** [ˈstiŋkəˈd(j)uːrou] (*noun*), *P:* crapulos *m*.

stinkaroo [ˈstiŋkəˈruː] (*noun*), *P:* article *m* de mauvaise qualité, peau *f* de zèbre.

stink-bomb [ˈstiŋkbɔm] (*noun*), *F:* boule puante.

stinker [ˈstiŋkər] (*noun*), *F:* **1.** individu* méprisable, sale type *m*. **2.** individu* qui sent* mauvais (*ou* qui pue). **3.** **to write s.o. a s.**, (*a*) écrire une verte réprimande à qn; (*b*) écrire une lettre carabinée à qn. **4.** rhume carabiné. **5.** **the algebra paper was a s.**, on a eu une sale (*ou* rosse) composition d'algèbre. **6.** cigare* *ou* cigarette* bon marché. **7.** **to play a s.**, (*sports*) jouer comme un pied. **8.** camelote *f*, navet *m*, toc *m*.

stinking [ˈstiŋkiŋ] (*adj.*). **1.** *F:* **s. (rich)**, **s. with money**, très riche*, plein aux as. **2.** *P:* ivre*, blindé. **3.** *F:* puant, nauséabond, infect. **4.** *F:* **s. weather**, temps *m* de cochon; **a s. cold**, un sale rhume. *Voir aussi* **fish**[1], **1**.

stink-list [ˈstiŋk-list] (*noun*), *P:* **to have s.o. on one's s.-l.**, avoir qn dans le nez, ne pas pouvoir encadrer qn; *cf.* **shit-list**.

stinko [ˈstiŋkou] (*adj.*), *P:* = **stinking, 2**.

stinkpot [ˈstiŋkpɔt] (*noun*), *P:* saligaud *m*, salopard *m*.

stir[1] [stəːr] (*noun*), *P:* prison*, bloc *m*, taule *f*; **in s.**, en prison, à l'ombre.

stir[2] [stəːr] (**to**), *F:* **to s. it** = **to stir it up**. *Voir aussi* **stumps**.

stirrer [ˈstəːrər] (*noun*), *F:* agitateur *m*, fomenteur *m* de difficultés.

stir up [ˈstəːˈrʌp] (**to**), *F:* **to s. it u.**, fomenter la dissension, remuer les eaux *f.pl.* troubles.

stodge[1] [stɔdʒ] (*noun*), *F:* **1.** aliment bourratif, étouffe-chrétien *m*. **2.** qch.

de difficile à retenir (*ou* de dur à digérer).

stodge[2] [stɔdʒ] (**to**), *F:* se goinfrer, se caler les joues *f.pl.*, s'empiffrer.

stoke up [ˈstoukˈʌp] (**to**), *F:* manger* de bon cœur, bouffer.

stomach [ˈstʌmək] (**to**), *F:* endurer, supporter, tolérer, digérer.

stomp[1] [stɔmp] (*noun*), *F:* (*jazz*) tempo assez vif.

stomp[2] [stɔmp] (**to**). **1.** *F:* (*jazz*) jouer d'un tempo assez vif. **2.** *P:* battre*, passer une raclée à (qn).

stone-cold [ˈstounˈkould] (*adv.*), *F:* **I've got him s.-c.**, je le tiens (à ma merci). *Voir aussi* **cold**[1], **1**.

stoned [stound] (*adj.*), *P:* (*a*) ivre*, raide; (*b*) drogué*, camé, chargé.

stone-ginger [ˈstounˈdʒindʒər] (*noun*), *P:* certitude *f*, du tout cuit.

stones [stounz] (*pl. noun*), *P:* testicules*, burettes *f.pl.*

stonewall [ˈstounˈwɔːl] (**to**), *F:* donner des réponses évasives; faire de l'obstruction *f*.

stonkered [ˈstɔŋkəd] (*adj.*), *P:* = **stinking, 2**.

stony [ˈstouni] (*adj.*), *F:* **s. (broke)**, archi-pauvre*, à sec, dans la dèche.

stooge[1] [stuːdʒ] (*noun*) (*often péj.*). **1.** *F:* délégué *m*, remplaçant *m*, nègre *m*. **2.** *F:* individu* trop serviable, ramasse-boulot *m*. **3.** *F:* (*th.*) comparse *m*, faire-valoir *m*. **4.** *P:* indicateur*, bourdille *m*.

stooge[2] [stuːdʒ] (**to**), *F:* **1.** faire le nègre. **2.** servir de comparse *m* (*ou* de faire-valoir *m*) (à un acteur).

stooge about (*or* **around**) [ˈstuːdʒəˈbaut, ˈstuːdʒəˈraund] (**to**), *F:* **1.** faire un tour, flâner. **2.** bricoler.

stoolie [ˈstuːli], **stool-pigeon** [ˈstuːlpidʒin] (*noun*), *F:* (*a*) indicateur*, mouchard *m*; (*b*) compère *m* (d'un escroc).

stop [stɔp] (*noun*), *P:* receleur *m*, fargue *m*. *Voir aussi* **pull out** (**to**), **3**.

stop by [ˈstɔpˈbai] (**to**), *F:* rendre visite (à qn), entrer en passant, passer chez qn.

stop-off [ˈstɔpɔf] (*noun*), *F:* étape *f*, (point *m* d')arrêt *m*, halte *f*.

stop off [ˈstɔpˈɔf] (**to**), *F:* faire une halte (*ou* un arrêt); **to s. o. in London**, faire étape à Londres.

---

* L'astérisque indique que le mot marqué de ce signe figure comme entrée dans le Répertoire.

stopover [ˈstɔpouvər] (noun), F: arrêt m (au cours d'un voyage).

stop over [ˈstɔpˈouvər] (to), F: interrompre son voyage, s'arrêter.

stopper [ˈstɔpər] (noun), F: 1. to put the s. on sth., mettre fin à qch. 2. (boxe) coup* knock-out.

stork [stɔːk] (noun), F: a visit from the s., l'arrivée f d'un bébé.

story [ˈstɔːri] (noun), F: mensonge*, conte m; to tell stories, mentir*, raconter des blagues f.pl.; voir aussi sob-story; tall[1], 2.

storyteller [ˈstɔːri-telər] (noun), F: menteur m, batteur m, chiqueur m.

stove [stouv] (noun), P: chauffage m (auto).

stove-pipe [ˈstouvpaip] (noun). 1. P: crapouillot m. 2. F: chapeau* haut de forme, tuyau m de poêle, huit-reflets m. 3. (U.S.) P: avion m de chasse à réaction.

stow [stou] (to), P: s. it! c'est marre!; ferme ça!

ʾtrafe [strɑːf] (to), F: réprimander*, passer un savon à (qn), engueuler (qn).

strafing [ˈstrɑːfiŋ] (noun), F: réprimande f, verte semonce, engueulade f.

straight[1] [streit] (adj.). 1. F: (a) (cigarettes, tabac) ordinaire (sans narcotiques); (b) (d'une boisson) sec. 2. P: (sexuellement) normal. 3. P: qui ne se drogue pas. 4. F: s. man = stooge[1], 3. Voir aussi strait; ticket, 3.

straight[2] [streit] (adv.): to go s., (a) F: marcher droit, suivre le droit chemin; (b) P: se désintoxiquer (de drogues), se décamer; (c) P: abandonner la pédérastie. Voir aussi horse[1], 2; shoulder, 2; straight up.

straight[3] [streit] (noun), F: to act on the s., agir loyalement.

straighten out [ˈstreit(ə)nˈaut] (to). 1. P: to s. s.o. o. = to put s.o. wise (wise, 2). 2. F: I expect that things will s. o., je pense que ça s'arrangera.

straight up [ˈstreitˈʌp] (adj.), F: honnête, régulier, réglo; s. u.! c'est du vrai! sans blague!

strain [strein] (noun), P: to have a s., uriner*, lancequiner; to go for a s., aller aux W.C.*.

strait [streit] (adj.), F: to follow the s. (faussement straight) and narrow, se

conduire honnêtement, cheminer (ou marcher) droit.

stranger [ˈstreindʒər] (noun), F: 1. (U.S.) say, s.! pardon, monsieur! 2. (dans une tasse à thé) chinois m.

strap[1] [stræp] (noun), P: on the s. = on the drop (drop[1], 8). Voir aussi jock-strap.

strap[2] [stræp] (to), P: coïter* avec (une femme), calecer.

strap-hanger [ˈstræphæŋər] (noun), F: voyageur m debout (dans le métro, le train, etc.).

strapper [ˈstræpər] (noun), F: grand gaillard, escogriffe m.

straw [strɔː] (noun), F: 1. that's the last s., c'est le coup de grâce! c'est le comble! c'est la fin des haricots! il ne manquait plus que cela! 2. it's the last s. that breaks the camel's back, c.p., c'est la dernière goutte (d'eau) qui fait déborder le vase.

stray [strei] (noun), P: to have a bit (or piece) of s. = to have a bit on the side (side, 2).

streak[1] [striːk] (noun), F: a losing s., une série de malchance* (série noire) aux jeux; a winning s., une série de chance*. Voir aussi piss[1], 3; yellow, 1.

streak[2] (along) [ˈstriːk(əˈlɔŋ)] (to), F: aller à toute vitesse, gazer.

streaker [ˈstriːkər] (noun), F: nudiste galopant(e).

street [striːt] (noun), F: 1. to be streets ahead of s.o., dépasser qn par des mille et des cents. 2. it's right up your s., cela te connaît; cf. alley, 1. 3. the horse won by a s., le cheval a gagné dans un fauteuil. 4. it's not in the same s., ce n'est pas du même acabit (ou de la même catégorie). 5. to be on the streets, racoler*, faire le trottoir. Voir aussi easy[1], 1; sunny.

stretch[1] [stretʃ] (noun), P: to do a s., faire de la prison*, faire une longe; he was given a s., on l'a mis au trou. Voir aussi homestretch.

stretch[2] [stretʃ] (to). 1. F: that's stretching it a bit, c'est le tirer par les cheveux. 2. P: être pendu* (ou béquillé ou gruppé).

strewth! [struːθ] (excl.), P: sacrebleu! sapristi! mince (alors)!

strides [straidz] (pl. noun), P: pantalon*, falzar m.

* An asterisk indicates that the word so marked is included as a head-word in the Appendix.

strike [straik] (to), F: 1. s. a light! morbleu! saperlipopette!; s. me pink! tu m'assois! bigre de bougre! scarabombe! 2. to get struck on s.o., s'enticher de qn. Voir aussi cunt-struck; gobstruck; heap, 1; rich[2].

Strine [strain] (noun), F: la langue australienne.

string [striŋ] (noun). F: 1. to have s.o. on a (piece of) s., mener qn par le bout du nez. 2. no strings attached, sans obligations, sans à-côtés, sans os. 3. to pull (the) strings, faire jouer le piston. Voir aussi apron-strings; G-string; shoestring.

string along [ˈstriŋəˈlɔŋ] (to), F: 1. tenir (qn) en suspens, mener (qn) en bateau. 2. to s. a. (with s.o.), filer le train à qn.

string-bean [ˈstriŋˈbiːn] (noun) (U.S.), F: = bean-pole.

string out [ˈstriŋˈaut] (to). 1. F: faire durer (qch.). 2. P: être drogué*, être camé (ou chargé); to be strung out, être défoncé.

string up [ˈstriŋˈʌp] (to), F: pendre* (un condamné). Voir aussi strung up.

strip[1] [strip] (noun), F: 1. to tear s.o. off a s., réprimander* qn, passer un rude savon à qn, sonner les cloches à qn. 2. s. show, spectacle m de nus, striptease m; s. poker, poker m de déshabillage, striptease-poker m.

strip[2] [strip] (to), F: (mil.) faire perdre ses galons m.pl., dégrader, faire passer chez le dernier tailleur.

strip off [ˈstripˈɔf] (to), F: se déshabiller*, se mettre à poil.

stripper [ˈstripər] (noun), F: stripteaseuse f, effeuilleuse f.

strong-arm[1] [ˈstrɔŋɑːm] (attrib. adj.), F: s.-a. man, (a) homme fort, fortiche m, balèze m; (b) battant m, un dur; s.-a. tactics, manœuvres f.pl. de poids (ou à la matraque).

strong-arm[2] [ˈstrɔŋɑːm] (to), F: manier rudement, mener à la baguette.

stroppy [ˈstrɔpi] (adj.), P: de mauvaise humeur, à cran, de mauvais poil.

struck [strʌk] (p.p.): voir strike (to).

strung up [ˈstrʌŋˈʌp] (p.p. & adj.). 1. F: to be s. u., être pendu* (ou béquillé); cf. string up (to). 2. F: to be (all) s. u., être tendu (ou énervé). 3. P: malade par le manque de drogues; en manque.

struth! [struːθ] (excl.), P: = strewth!

stuck[1] [stʌk] (adj.), F: en panne, en rade. Voir aussi stick[2] (to), 4, 5; stick in (to), 1.

stuck[2] [ʃtuk] (noun), P: to be in s., être dans une mauvaise posture (ou dans de mauvais draps).

stuck-up [ˈstʌkˈʌp] (adj.), F: prétentieux*, crâneur, plastronneur.

stud [stʌd] (noun) (U.S.), F: 1. un mâle. 2. un malin, un roué. 3. un homme dans le vent, un minet.

stuff[1] [stʌf] (noun). 1. F: to know one's s., être capable, s'y connaître, être à la hauteur. 2. F: that's the s. (to give the troops)! voilà ce qu'il faut (pour remonter la République)! 3. P: a nice bit of s., une belle pépée, une môme bath; cf. skirt. 4. P: (a) héroïne f (drogues*); (b) drogues*, stups m.pl. 5. P: butin*, contrebande f, pluc m. 6. F: to do one's s., faire ce qu'on doit, faire son boulot. Voir aussi heavy[1], 5; rough[1], 6; sob-stuff; white[1], 1.

stuff[2] [stʌf] (to). 1. V: coïter* avec (une femme), bourrer, égoïner. 2. P: get stuffed! va te faire voir! va te faire foutre! 3. F: manger* abondamment, se goinfrer, s'empiffrer. Voir aussi shirt, 5.

stuffing [ˈstʌfiŋ] (noun), F: to knock the s. out of s.o., (a) battre qn à plate(s) couture(s), flanquer une tripotée à qn, étriper qn; (b) désarçonner, démonter, dégonfler qn, mettre qn à plat.

stuffy [ˈstʌfi] (adj.), F: collet monté, constipé.

stum [stʌm] (noun), P: 1. marijuana f (drogues*), kif m. 2. = stumbler.

stumbler [ˈstʌmblər] (noun), P: somnifère m, barbiturique m, barbitos m.pl.

stumer [ˈstuːmər] (noun), P: 1. chose f qui ne vaut rien. 2. chèque m sans provision, billet m à découvert. 3. bévue*, boulette f, bourde f; to drop a s., faire une gaffe. 4. perdant m, paumé m (cheval, etc.). 5. raté m, paumé m. 6. faillite f, banqueroute f, binelle f.

stump [stʌmp] (to), F: coller (qn), réduire (qn) à quia; to s. s.o. on a subject, faire sécher qn sur un sujet; this stumped me, sur le coup je n'ai su que répondre, ça m'a cloué le bec.

stumps [stʌmps] (pl. noun), F: jambes*,

---

* L'astérisque indique que le mot marqué de ce signe figure comme entrée dans le Répertoire.

guibolles *f.pl.*; **to stir one's s.**, (*a*) se
dépêcher*, se décarcasser; (*b*) se remuer.
stump up [ˈstʌmpˈʌp] (**to**), *F:* payer*,
les abouler.
stun [stʌn] (**to**), *F:* **1.** emballer, combler.
2. abasourdir, abrutir. *Voir aussi*
stunned.
stung [stʌŋ] (*p.p.*): *voir* **sting** (**to**).
stunned [stʌnd] (*adj.*) (*U.S.*), *P:* ivre*,
fadé. *Voir aussi* **stun** (**to**).
stunner [ˈstʌnər] (*noun*), *F:* (*a*) qn
d'irrésistible *ou* de formidable, prix *m*
de Diane, Apollon *m*; (*b*) chose épatante.
stunning [ˈstʌniŋ] (*adj.*), *F:* (*a*) excellent*, formid(able), épatant; (*b*) très
beau*, ravissant, irrésistible.
stupe [stuːp] (*noun*) (*U.S.*), *P:* individu
bête*, cruche *f*, cruchon *m*.
stymie [ˈstaimi] (**to**), *F:* entraver, gêner,
contrecarrer; **I'm completely stymied**,
je suis dans une impasse.
sub[1] [sʌb] (*noun abbr.*), *F:* **1.** (=*subscription*) abonnement *m*, cotisation *f*.
2. (=*sub-editor*) secrétaire *mf.* de
rédaction (*journal*). **3.** (=*subaltern*)
subalterne *mf.* **4.** (=*substitute*) substitut
m, remplaçant *m*. **5.** (=*submarine*)
sous-marin *m*. **6. to get a s. from s.o.**,
emprunter* à qn, faire un emprunt.
sub[2] [sʌb] (**to**) (*verb abbr.*), *F:* **1.** (=*sub-
edit*) corriger, mettre au point (un
article, *etc.*). **2.** (=*substitute*) **to s. for
s.o.**, remplacer qn. **3. to s. s.o.**, preter de
l'argent* a qn, financer qn.
suck [sʌk] (**to**). **1.** *F:* **s. it and see**,
c.p., essaie et tu verras; suce et tu
goûteras. **2.** *F:* **to s. s.o. dry** = **to
drain s.o. dry** (**drain**[2] (**to**)). **3.** *V:* **to
s. s.o.** = **to go down on s.o.** (**go down**
(**to**), **5**). **4.** *F:* **to s. s.o.'s brains**, exploiter
l'intelligence *f* de qn.
suck around [ˈsʌkəˈraund] (**to**) (*U.S.*),
P: **to s. a. s.o.** = **to suck up to s.o.**
suckass [ˈsʌkæs] (*noun*) (*U.S.*), *P:*
lèche-cul *m*, lèche-bottes *m*.
sucker[1] [ˈsʌkər] (*attrib. adj.*), *F:* **s.
punch**, (*boxe*) coup* de pré-attaque.
sucker[2] [ˈsʌkər] (*noun*), *F:* **1.** dupe *f*,
poire *f*, dindon *m*; **there's a s. born
every minute**, *c.p.*, les poires se cueillent
tous les jours; *cf.* **one**, **7**; **to make a
(right) s. out of s.o.**, faire tourner qn
en bourrique; **to be played for a s.**,
être escroqué* (*ou* entubé); **he made a
right s. out of you!** il t'a eu jusqu'à la

gauche! **2.** admirateur *m*, fana *m*, mordu
m; **I'm a s. for a beautiful blonde**, je suis
mordu pour une belle blonde, je suis
porté vers les belles blondes. *Voir aussi*
bum-sucker; cock-sucker.
suck in [ˈsʌkˈin] (**to**), *P:* escroquer*,
carotter, empiler.
suck off [ˈsʌkˈɔf] (**to**), *V:* faire un
coït* buccal à (qn), pomper (qn).
suck up [ˈsʌkˈʌp] (**to**), *F:* **to s. u. to
s.o.**, flatter* qn, faire de la lèche à qn.
sudden [ˈsʌdn] (*adj.*), *F:* **s. death**, match
(*golf*, *etc.*) terminé par élimination.
sugar[1] [ˈʃugər] (*noun*). **1.** *P:* (*a*) argent*,
galette *f*; (*b*) bénéfices*, affure *f*,
gâteau *m*. **2.** *F:* (*a*) une belle* fille*,
une môme bath; (*b*) petite amie,
fiancée. **3.** *P:* (*a*) héroïne *f*, cocaïne *f*,
ou morphine *f* (*drogues**); came blanche,
sucre *m*; (*b*) **s. (lump)**, LSD 25, acide
m lysergique; *cf.* **acid**, **2**. **4.** *F:* flatterie
f, pommade *f*. **5.** *P:* pot-de-vin *m*,
dessous-de-table *m*.
sugar[2] [ˈʃugər] (**to**). **1.** *F:* flatter*,
pommader. **2.** *P:* soudoyer, acheter.
sugar-daddy [ˈʃugə-dædi] (*noun*), *F:*
vieux protecteur (envers une maîtresse),
papa-gâteau *m*; **she's got a s.-d.**, elle
s'est trouvé un vieux.
sugar-hill [ˈʃugəˈhil] (*noun*) (*U.S.*), *P:*
quartier *m* des bordels* dans une région
habitée par les noirs.
summat [ˈsʌmət, ˈsumət] (*adv. & noun*),
P: = **something**, *q.v.*
Sunday [ˈsʌndi] (*attrib. adj.*), *F:* **1. S.
driver**, chauffeur peu expérimenté,
chauffard *m* du dimanche. **2. S. punch**,
(*boxe*) coup* meurtrier.
sundowner [ˈsʌn-daunər] (*noun*), *F:* **1.**
boisson alcoolisée (prise le soir). **2.**
(*Austr.*) clochard*, cloche *m*. **3.** (*U.S.*)
pète-sec *m*, garde-chiourme *m*, gendarme *m*.
sunk [sʌŋk] (*adj.*), *F:* ruiné*, perdu, fichu.
sunny [ˈsʌni] (*adj.*), *F:* **1. the s. side of
the street**, la vie en rose. **2. s. side up**,
(un œuf) sur le plat.
sunset strip [ˈsʌnsetˈstrip] (*noun*), *F:*
voir **bingo** (**77**).
super[1] [ˈs(j)uːpər] (*adj.*), *F:* excellent*,
super, épatant.
super[2] [ˈs(j)uːpər] (*noun*) (*abbr.*), *F:* **1.**
(=*Superintendent* (*of Police*)) com-
missaire *m* de police, quart (d'œil) *m*.
2. (=*supernumerary*) (*th.*) doublure *f*.

---

* An asterisk indicates that the word so marked is included as a head-word in the Appendix.

super-duper [ˈs(j)uːpəˈd(j)uːpər] (adj.), F: excellent*, formid(able), bœuf.

superstar [ˈs(j)uːpə-stɑːr] (noun), F: superstar m.

sup up[ˈsʌpˈʌp] (to), F: lamper son verre.

sure[1] [ʃuər, ʃɔər, ʃɔːr] (adj.), F: (it's a) s. thing, c'est une certitude, c'est sûr et certain; **s. thing!** = sure![2]. Voir aussi egg, 5.

sure![2] [ʃuər, ʃɔər, ʃɔːr] (excl.), F: naturellement! bien sûr!

sure-fire [ˈʃuəˈfaiər, ˈʃɔəˈfaiər, ˈʃɔːˈfaiər] (adj.), F: sûr et certain.

surfie [ˈsəːfi] (noun) (Austr.), F: 1. aquaplaniste mf, fana mf du surfing. 2. habitué(e) de la plage.

suss [sʌs] (to), P: soupçonner, avoir à l'œil.

suss out [ˈsʌsˈaut] (to), P: (a) to s. s.o. o., cataloguer qn, mettre qn en fiche; (b) to s. sth. o., classifier qch., éclairer sa lanterne.

swab [swɔb] (noun), P: lourdaud m, andouille f, propre à rien m.

swacked [swækt] (adj.), P: ivre*, blindé.

swaddie, swaddy [ˈswɔdi] (noun), F: = squaddie, squaddy.

swag [swæg] (noun), F: butin*, fade m, taf m.

swagger [ˈswægər] (adj.), F: élégant*, chic, riflo.

swagman [ˈswægmæn] (noun) (Austr.), F: (a) clochard*, vagabond m; (b) excursionniste m, randonneur m (à pied).

swallow[1] [ˈswɔlou] (noun), F: to have a big s., avoir un bon avaloir, avoir la dalle en pente.

swallow[2] [ˈswɔlou] (to), F: 1. I can't s. that, je ne peux pas l'avaler, je ne peux pas le gober; hard to s., difficile à avaler. 2. he won't s. that, il ne le croira* pas, il ne donnera pas dans le panneau.

swank[1] [swæŋk] (adj.), F: = swanky (b).

swank[2] [swæŋk] (noun), F: 1. élégance f, chic m, coquetterie f. 2. to put on (the) s., prendre des airs m.pl., faire de l'esbrouf(f)e f. 3. prétention f, gloriole f, épate f. 4. épateur m, poseur m, crâneur m.

swank[3] [swæŋk] (to), F: se donner des airs m.pl., crâner, faire de l'épate f.

swanker [ˈswæŋkər] (noun), F: = swank[2], 4.

swanky [ˈswæŋki] (adj.), F: (a) prétentieux*, poseur; (b) élégant*, flambard, ridère.

Swan(n)ee [ˈswɔni] (noun), P: up the S. = up the creek.

swan off [ˈswɔnˈɔf] (to), F: faire l'école buissonnière, jouer rip.

swap[1] [swɔp] (noun), F: (a) échange m, troquage m; (b) article m que l'on échange, troc m; (pl.) doubles m.pl.

swap[2] [swɔp] (to), F: échanger, troquer.

swear [swɛər] (noun), F: to have a good s., lâcher une bordée de jurons.

swear off [ˈswɛərˈɔf] (to), F: abandonner*, balanstiquer.

sweat[1] [swet] (noun), F: 1. travail* pénible, corvée f, turbin m; it's no s., c'est du tout cuit, c'est pas du durillon. 2. (mil.) an old s., un vieux troupier, un vétéran. 3. to work oneself (up) into a s. = to work oneself (up) into a lather (lather[1], (a), (b)). 4. to be in a cold s., s'inquiéter, avoir le trac.

sweat[2] [swet] (to), F: to be sweating on the top line, être agité (ou excité ou emballé), être sur les charbons ardents. Voir aussi blood, 6.

sweater-girl [ˈswetə-gəːl] (noun), F: fille* qui porte des vêtements collants, femme* bien roulée.

sweat out [ˈswetˈaut] (to), F: to s. it o., attendre* patiemment, compter les pavés. Voir aussi guts, 6.

sweat-shop [ˈswetʃɔp] (noun), F: vieille usine où les ouvriers sont exploités, vrai bagne.

Sweeney [ˈswiːni] (noun), P: 1. S. Todd (R.S. = Flying Squad), la brigade mobile (de la police). 2. = holler-wag(g)on.

sweep[1] [swiːp] (noun), F: 1. sweepstake m. 2. vaurien*, voyou m, fripouille f. 3. to make a clean s., faire table rase, faire rafle, rafler le tout, tout ramasser.

sweep[2] [swiːp] (to), F: 1. to be swept off one's feet, (a) être emballé, s'emballer pour qn; (b) être débordé de travail*. 2. to s. the board, emporter tout, nettoyer le tapis. Voir aussi dirt[1], 4.

sweeper [ˈswiːpər] (noun), F: 1. (football) arrière m de défense. 2. leave it for the s., ne ramassez rien, laissez pousser.

sweep up [ˈswiːpˈʌp] (to), F: (football) jouer en arrière de défense.

sweet[1] [swiːt] (adj.). 1. F: to be s. on

s.o., être amoureux de qn, avoir le
béguin pour qn. 2. F: **you can bet
your s. life!** tu peux en mettre la main
au feu. 3. F: **to hand s.o. a s. line**,
faire marcher qn, faire de la lèche à
qn. 4. P: **s. Fanny Adams** (*or* P: **s.
F.A.** *or* V: **s. fuck-all**), rien*, moins
que rien, peau de balle (et balai de
crin), que dalle, des prunes. 5. F: **to
whisper s. nothings**, murmurer des
mots d'amour, conter fleurette. 6. F:
s. talk, flatterie f, lèche f, pommade f.
7. F: facile, lucratif; **a s. job**, une
planque. 8. F: aimable, accueillant,
gentil. 9. P: homosexuel, chouquette.
Voir aussi **tooth**, 1.

sweet[2] [swiːt] (*noun*): *voir* **sweets**.

sweeten [ˈswiːtn] (**to**), F: (*a*) soudoyer,
· acheter (qn), graisser la patte à (qn);
(*b*) flatter*, cajoler, pommader (qn).

sweetener [ˈswiːtnər] (*noun*), F: (*a*) pot-
de-vin, m; (*b*) pourboire*, pourliche m;
I had to give him a s., j'ai dû lui
graisser la patte.

sweeten up [ˈswiːtnˈʌp] (**to**), F: =
sweeten (**to**).

sweetie [ˈswiːti] (*noun*). 1. F: bonbon
m. 2. F: chéri(e) m(f), cocotte f.
3. P: Préludine f (*marque déposée*)
(*drogues*).

sweetie-pie [ˈswiːtipai] (*noun*), F: =
sweetie, 2.

sweets [swiːts] (*pl. noun*), P: amphétamines f.pl. (*drogues**), bonbons m.pl.

sweet-talk [ˈswiːttɔːk] (**to**), F: cajoler,
enjôler (qn).

sweet-talker [ˈswiːttɔːkər] (*noun*), F:
cajoleur m, enjôleur m.

sweety [ˈswiːti], **sweety-pie** [ˈswiːtipai]
(*noun*), F: = **sweetie**, **sweetie-pie**.

swell[1] [swel] (*adj.*). 1. F: élégant*,
flambard. 2. excellent*, chouettos,
épatant. 3. P: **s. mob**, pickpockets
bien fringués.

swell[2] [swel] (*noun*), F: 1. élégant m,
faraud m, suiffard m; **the swells**, les
gens chics, le grand monde. 2. grand
personnage, grosse légume.

swellhead [ˈswelhed] (*noun*) (*U.S.*), F:
prétentieux m, crâneur m, esbrouf(f)eur
m.

swig[1] [swig] (*noun*), F: grand trait,
lampée f (de bière, *etc.*); **to take a s. at**
(*or* **from**) **the bottle**, boire à même la
bouteille.

swig[2] [swig] (**to**), F: boire (un verre) à
grands traits (*ou* à grands coups),
lamper.

swill[1] [swil] (*noun*), P: 1. nourriture*,
bouftance f. 2. (*a*) alcool* de mauvaise
qualité, gn(i)ole f; (*b*) lampée f, rasade
f. 3. bêtises*, foutaises f.pl.; **a prize
load of s.**, un vrai tissu d'âneries.

swill[2] [swil] (**to**). 1. P: **to s. one's food**,
s'empiffrer de la nourriture*. 2. F:
to s. beer, s'entonner de la bière.

swiller [ˈswilər], **swillpot** [ˈswilpɔt]
(*noun*), P: ivrogne*, vide-bouteille m.

swim [swim] (*noun*), F: **in the s.**, dans
le bain, dans le vent, à la coule; **to get
back in the s.** (*or* **into the s. of things**),
se remettre dans le bain; **out of the s.**,
hors du coup, pas à la page.

swimmingly [ˈswimiŋli] (*adv.*), F: à
merveille, comme sur des roulettes.

swindle-sheet [ˈswindlʃiːt] (*noun*), P:
indemnité f pour frais professionnels,
frais de la princesse.

swine [swain] (*noun*), F: salopard m,
salaud m, saligaud m.

swing[1] [swiŋ] (*noun*), F: 1. **to get into
the s. of it** (*or* **of things**), se mettre dans
le mouvement. 2. **everything went
with a s.**, tout a très bien marché.
3. **in full s.**, en pleine activité, en plein
boum. 4. **to take a s. at s.o.**, lancer
un coup de poing à qn. *Voir aussi*
one, 1; **roundabouts**.

swing[2] [swiŋ] (**to**). 1. F: bien marcher,
gazer, ronfler. 2. P: **to s. it** (*or* **a fast
one**) **on s.o.**, duper* qn, (re)faire qn,
tirer une carotte à qn, jouer un tour
de cochon à qn. 3. F: être pendu* (*ou*
béquillé); **I'll s. for him**, je me vengerai
quitte à y aller du caillou. 4. F:
prendre du plaisir à (qch.). 5. F: faire
balancer (qch.) en sa faveur. 6. P:
to s. both ways, être ambivalent,
marcher à voiles et à vapeur. *Voir
aussi* **lead**[1], 2.

swinger [ˈswiŋər] (*noun*). 1. F: qn *ou*
qch. de formid(able) (*ou* d'épatant *ou*
de super). 2. (*pl.*) P: seins*, flotteurs
m.pl. *Voir aussi* **lead-swinger**.

swinging [ˈswiŋiŋ] (*adj.*), F: (*a*) plein
d'allant (*ou* de ressort); (*b*) dans le
vent, avant-garde, flambard.

swipe[1] [swaip] (*noun*), F: 1. (*a*) coup*,
taloche f; **to take a s. at s.o.**, flanquer
une raclée (*ou* une torgnole) à qn;

---

* An asterisk indicates that the word so marked is included as a head-word in the Appendix.

(b) **to have** (or **take**) **a s. at sth.**, se lancer à faire qch. **2.** (pl.) la petite bière.

swipe² [swaip] (**to**), F: **1.** = **to take a swipe at** (**swipe¹**, **1**). **2.** voler*, chiper, chaparder (qch. à qn).

swish¹ [swiʃ] (adj.), F: élégant*, chic.

swish² [swiʃ] (noun), P: pédéraste*, lopaille f.

swish³ [swiʃ] (**to**), P: être efféminé, agir en pédé.

switch¹ [switʃ] (noun), F: **to do a s.**, échanger, troquer, chanstiquer.

switch² [switʃ] (**to**), F: **to s. horses** (**in midstream**), changer son fusil d'épaule (au milieu du combat), changer de cheval de bataille.

switched on [ˈswitʃtˈɔn] (p.p. & adj.), F: **1.** faux*, forcé, artificiel. **2.** euphorique, chargé (par les drogues, etc.). **3.** à la mode, dernier cri, dans le vent. Cf. **switch on** (**to**).

switcheroo [ˈswitʃəˈruː] (noun) (U.S.) P: = **switch¹**.

switch-hitter [ˈswitʃhitər] (noun), P: un ambivalent, qn qui marche à voiles et à vapeur.

switch off [ˈswitʃˈɔf] (**to**), F: se détacher (de qch.), couper l'allumage m.

switch on [ˈswitʃˈɔn] (**to**). **1.** F: **to s. s.o. o.**, (a) éveiller l'intérêt m ou la curiosité de qn; (b) exciter, émoustiller

qn (sexuellement). **2.** P: fumer de la marijuana. **3.** P: initier (par une première piqûre) à la drogue. Cf. **switched on**.

swiz(z) [swiz] (noun), F: = **swizzle¹**, **1, 2**.

swizzle¹ [ˈswizl] (noun), F: **1.** escroquerie*, filoutage m, doublage m. **2.** déception f, déboire m. **3.** (U.S.) cocktail m.

swizzle² [ˈswizl] (**to**), F: escroquer*, filouter, doubler.

swop [swɔp] (noun & verb), F: = **swap**.

swordsman [ˈsɔːdzmən] (noun), P: **1.** receleur*, fourgue m. **2.** (U.S.) libertin m, cavaleur m.

swot¹ [swɔt] (noun), F: (a) bûcheur m, potasseur m; (b) fort m en thème.

swot² [swɔt] (**to**), F: étudier, bûcher, potasser.

swot up [ˈswɔtˈʌp] (**to**), F: rabâcher par cœur, potasser.

syph [sif] (noun), P: (a) syphilis*, syphilo f, syphlotte f; (b) syphilitique mf, naze mf, nazebroque mf.

syrupy [ˈsirəpi] (adj.), F: sirupeux, sentimental.

system [ˈsistəm, ˈsistim] (noun), F: **1. the s.**, le Système, la République. **2. it's all systems go!** tout gaze: on démarre.

T

T [ti:]. **1.** *F:* **that suits me to a T**, cela me va parfaitement, cela me botte. **2.** *P:* = **tea**.

ta [tɑ:] (*excl.*), *F:* merci.

tab [tæb] (*noun*). **1.** *P:* cigarette*, cibiche *f*. **2.** *P:* oreille*, étiquette *f*. **3.** (*U.S.*) *F:* note *f*, facture *f*, addition *f*. **4.** *F:* **to keep tabs on s.o.**, surveiller qn, avoir l'œil sur qn. **5.** (*Austr.*) *F:* **to keep t.** = **to keep nit (nit, 2)**. **6.** *P:* (*abbr.* = *tablet*) comprimé *m*.

tab-end [ˈtæbˈend] (*noun*), *F:* mégot*, clope *f*.

table [ˈteibl] (*noun*), *F:* **to be under the t.**, être ivre*, rouler sous la table.

tack [tæk] (*noun*), *F:* **1.** (*a*) **soft t.**, pain*, bricheton *m*; (*b*) **hard t.**, biscuits *m.pl.* de marin. **2.** nourriture*, fricot *m*. *Voir aussi* **brass**[1].

tacky [ˈtæki] (*adj.*), *F:* minable.

Taffy [ˈtæfi] (*noun*), *F:* habitant *m* du pays de Galles, Gallois *m*.

tag[1] [tæg] (*noun*), *F:* **1.** nom* *ou* surnom *m*, blaze *m*. **2.** (*automobile*) plaque *f* (d'immatriculation). **3.** = **ticket, 2. 4.** (*th.*) **t. line**, mot *m* de la fin. *Voir aussi* **dog-tag**.

tag[2] [tæg] (*to*). **1.** *P:* **to be tagged**, être coincé, être pris (dans une bande*, *etc.*). **2.** *F:* être sur les talons de (qn), filer le train à (qn). **3.** *P:* arrêter*, choper, ceinturer. **4.** *F:* (*boxe*) mettre knock-out, knockouter (qn).

tag along [ˈtægəˈlɔŋ] (*to*), *F:* suivre, être à la traîne de qn.

tag around [ˈtægəˈraund] (*to*), *F:* **to t. a. with s.o.**, être accroché à qn, rouler sa bosse avec qn.

tag on [ˈtægˈɔn] (*to*), *F:* **1.** se joindre à qn, s'accrocher à qn. **2.** apposer, fixer.

tail[1] [teil] (*noun*). **1.** *P:* fesses*, pont-arrière *m*. **2.** *P:* pénis*, queue *f*. **3.** *P:* vagin*, cramouille *f*, conasse *f*. **4.** *P:* **a piece of t.**, un bout de fesses (*ou* de cuisse), conasserie *f*. **5.** *F:* policier*, détective *m* (suivant, épiant qn), limier *m*; **to be on s.o.'s t.**, (*a*) filer le train à qn;

(*b*) être sur le dos de qn; **to put a t. on s.o.**, faire suivre qn, faire filer qn, faire la filoche à qn. **6.** *F:* **to go top over t.**, faire une culbute. **7.** (*pl.*) *F:* habit *m* à queue, queue-de-pie *f*; **to wear tails**, porter l'habit. **8.** *F:* **to turn t.**, s'enfuir*, tourner le dos. **9.** *F:* **to have one's t. up**, (*a*) se sentir très heureux, se sentir pousser des ailes; (*b*) être très optimiste, être en pleine forme. **10.** *F:* **to keep one's t. up**, ne pas se laisser abattre. *Voir aussi* **ringtail**.

tail[2] [teil] (*to*), *F:* suivre, épier (qn). *Voir aussi* **hightail (to)**.

tail-end [ˈteilˈend] (*noun*), *F:* **the t.-e.**, la fin, le bout.

tail-ender [ˈteilˈendər] (*noun*), *F:* dernier *m*, lanterne *f* rouge, der *m* (des ders).

tailgate [ˈteilgeit] (*to*) (*U.S.*), *F:* coller (une voiture, *etc.*).

tail-man [ˈteilmæn] (*noun*), *P:* coureur *m* (de jupons), cavaleur *m*, juponneur *m*.

tail-spin [ˈteil-spin] (*noun*), *F:* **to go into a t.-s.**, être saisi de panique, paniquer.

take[1] [teik] (*noun*), *F:* **the t.**, la recette, les revenus *m.pl.*, le beurre.

take[2] [teik] (*to*). **1.** *F:* **to have what it takes**, (*a*) avoir du courage* (*ou* du battant); (*b*) être capable, être à la hauteur. **2.** *F:* endurer, encaisser. **3.** *P:* tirer sur une cigarette de marijuana *ou* hachisch. **4.** *F:* **I'm not taking any of that!** je ne gobe rien de tout cela! *Voir aussi* **lamb, 4; plunge**[1].

take apart [ˈteikəˈpɑːt] (*to*), *F:* réprimander* fortement, passer un bon savon à (qn).

take in [ˈteikˈin] (*to*), *F:* **1.** comprendre, piger. **2.** **he takes it all in**, il prend tout ça pour argent comptant. **3.** tromper*, ficher dedans.

take-off [ˈteikɔf] (*noun*), *F:* **1.** départ *m*, décollage *m*. **2.** imitation *f*, mimique *f*, pastiche *m*.

take off [ˈteikˈɔf] (*to*). **1.** *F:* s'enfuir*, s'en aller, se barrer; **t. o.!** fiche le camp! déguerpis! **2.** *F:* imiter, copier, singer,

---

* An asterisk indicates that the word so marked is included as a head-word in the Appendix.

mimer. 3. *F:* s'octroyer (une petite vacance, un congé, *etc.*). 4. *P:* (*a*) se faire une piqûre de drogues, se shooter; (*b*) être high, être défoncé par la drogue. 5. *P:* voler*, chiper; to get taken off, être empilé. 6. *P:* mourir*, lâcher la rampe.

take-on [ˈteikɔn] (*noun*), *F:* mystification *f*, farce *f*, canular(d) *m*.

take on [ˈteikˈɔn] (to), *F:* 1. s'émotionner, se retourner. 2. devenir populaire, prendre.

talc [tælk] (*noun*), *P:* cocaïne *f* (*drogues**), talc *m*.

tale [teil] (*noun*). 1. *F:* to tell the t., raconter des boniments *m.pl.*, faire du baratin. 2. *F:* to live to tell the t., survivre, être là pour en parler. 3. *P:* T. of Two Cities (*R.S.* = *titties*): *voir* titty; *cf.* Bristols; fit², 4; threepenny-bits; trey-bits. 4. *P:* sorrowful t. (*R.S.* = *jail*), prison*. *Voir aussi* tall¹, 2.

talent [ˈtælənt] (*noun*), *P:* les filles* (*sexuellement parlant*).

talk [tɔ:k] (to), *F:* 1. now you're talking! maintenant tu y es (*ou* tu y viens)! 2. money talks, l'argent* veut tout dire. 3. t. about luck! tu parles d'une veine! *Voir aussi* Dutch¹, 5; hat, 2; head, 10; sweet-talk (to).

talkie [ˈtɔ:ki] (*noun*), *F:* (*cinéma*) film parlant, talkie *m*.

talking-to [ˈtɔ:kiŋtu:] (*noun*), *F:* réprimande *f*, attrapade *f*, savon *m*.

tall¹ [tɔ:l] (*adj.*), *F:* 1. a t. order, un travail* dur, un sacré boulot. 2. a t. story (*U.S.:* tale), un mensonge*, un bateau, un bidon.

tall² [tɔ:l] (*adv.*), *F:* avec jactance *f*, avec fanfaronnade *f*.

tammy [ˈtæmi] (*noun*), *F:* (=*tam-o'-shanter*) béret écossais.

tampi [ˈtæmpi] (*noun*), *P:* marijuana *f* (*drogues**), tampi *m*.

tangle [ˈtæŋgl] (to), *F:* to t. with s.o., (*a*) se brouiller avec qn; (*b*) embrasser* qn, étreindre qn, serrer qn dans ses bras.

tanglefoot [ˈtæŋglfut] (*noun*) (*U.S.*), *F:* whisky *m* (de mauvaise qualité), casse-pattes *m*.

tank [tæŋk] (*noun*), *P:* 1. coffre-fort *m*, coffio(t) *m*; to blow a t., faire sauter un coffiot. 2. (*U.S.*) (*a*) prison*, coffre *m*; (*b*) cellule *f*, cage *f* à poules; *cf.* fish-tank. 3. ivrogne*, sac *m* à vin. 4. to go

in the t. = to throw a fight (throw (to), 4). *Voir aussi* piss-tank; septic, 2; think-tank.

tanked up [ˈtæŋktˈʌp] (*adj.*), *P:* ivre*, bourré, chargé, blindé.

tank up [ˈtæŋkˈʌp] (to), *P:* boire* beaucoup d'alcool, picoler, pinter.

tanner [ˈtænər] (*noun*), *F:* pièce *f* de six pennies d'autrefois ou 2½ nouveaux pennies.

tanning [ˈtæniŋ] (*noun*), *F:* volée *f* de coups*, raclée *f*, peignée *f*; *cf.* hide, 1; hiding.

tap¹ [tæp] (*noun*), *F:* 1. to be on t., être disponible, être à la disposition. 2. to be on the t., quémander.

tap² [tæp] (to), *F:* demander de l'argent* à (qn), taper. *Voir aussi* claret.

tape¹ [teip] (*noun*), *F:* red t., paperasserie *f*, chinoiseries administratives, bureaucratie *f*.

tape² [teip] (to), *F:* to have s.o., sth., taped, avoir qn, qch., bien cataloguer (*ou* étiqueté *ou* pointé).

tapped out [ˈtæptˈaut] (*p.p. & adj.*) (*U.S.*), *P:* ruiné*, paumé.

tapper [ˈtæpər] (*noun*), *P:* mendiant*, frappeur *m*, tapeur *m*.

tar¹ [tɑ:r] (*noun*), *P:* opium *m* (*drogues**), noir *m*. *Voir aussi* Jack, 7.

tar² [tɑ:r] (to), *F:* to be tarred with the same brush, être du pareil au même, être dans le même panier, faire la paire.

tar-brush [ˈtɑ:-brʌʃ] (*noun*), *F:* to have a touch of the t.-b., avoir du négrillon dans les veines.

tarnation! [tɑ:ˈneiʃən] (*excl.*) (*U.S.*), *F:* euph. pour damnation, *q.v.*

tart [tɑ:t] (*noun*), *P:* 1. prostituée*, fille *f*, cocotte *f*, grue *f*, poule *f*. 2. jeune fille* *ou* femme*, donzelle *f*, gonzesse *f*; *voir aussi* ritzy, 1.

tart up [ˈtɑ:tˈʌp] (to), *P:* (*a*) décorer (qch.) avec du tape-à-l'œil; (*b*) to t. oneself u., s'affubler, s'attifer de clinquant, faire le carnaval.

tarty [ˈtɑ:ti] (*adj.*), *P:* qui a l'air d'une prostituée*, à la pute.

tash [tæʃ] (*noun*), *F:* moustache*, bacchante *f*.

tassel [ˈtæs(ə)l] (*noun*), *P:* 1. pénis*, goupillon *m*. 2. don't get your t. in a twist, ne te mets pas dans tous tes états.

taste [teist] (*noun*). 1. *P:* bénéfice* *ou* partie *f* d'un bénéfice, rabe *m*. 2. *F:*

---

* L'astérisque indique que le mot marqué de ce signe figure comme entrée dans le Répertoire.

boisson *f* alcoolique; **would you like a t.?** tu veux boire* un coup? **3.** *P:* **to have a t.**, coïter*, s'en payer un petit coup.

tasty ['teisti] (*adj.*), *P:* élégant*, chic.

ta-ta ['tæ'ta:, tæ'ta:] (*excl.*), *F:* au revoir, r'voir.

tater ['teitər], **tatie** ['teiti] (*noun*), *P:* pomme *f* de terre, patate *f*.

taters ['teitəz] (*adj.*), *P:* **to be t.**, avoir froid, être frisco, cailler.

Tattersalls ['tætəsɔ:lz, 'tætəsəlz] (*noun*), *F:* (*courses de chevaux*) la pelouse.

tatty-bye ['tæti'bai] (*excl.*), *P:* = **ta-ta**.

tea [ti:] (*noun*), *P:* marijuana *f* (*drogues**); thé *m*; **bush t.**, concoction *f* d'herbes et de marijuana. *Voir aussi* **cup, 1, 2; stick**[1]**, 5; weed-tea.**

teach [ti:tʃ] (to), *F:* **that'll t. you!** ça t'apprendra!; **that'll t. him a thing or two!** ça va (bigrement) le dégourdir; *cf.* **learn (to).**

teach-in ['ti:tʃin] (*noun*), *F:* colloque *m*, teach-in *m*, table ronde.

tead-up ['ti:d'ʌp] (*p.p. & adj.*), *P:* drogué* à la marijuana.

teahead ['ti:hed] (*noun*), *P:* habitué(e) de la marijuana.

tea-leaf ['ti:li:f] (*noun*), *P:* (*R.S. = thief*) voleur*; *cf.* **corned beef.**

team-up ['ti:mʌp] (*noun*), *F:* (*vêtements*) coordonnés *m.pl.*

team up ['ti:m'ʌp] (to), *F:* **to t. u. with s.o.**, collaborer (*ou* coéquiper) avec qn.

tea-pad ['ti:-pæd] (*noun*), *P:* fumerie *f* de marijuana.

tea-party ['ti:-pɑ:ti] (*noun*), *P:* réunion *f* pour fumer la marijuana.

tear[1] [tiər] (*noun*). **1.** *P:* perle *f*, perlouse *f*. **2.** *F:* **to shed a t. for Nelson,** uriner*, changer son poisson d'eau.

tear[2] [tɛər] (to), *F:* **that's torn it!** ça a tout gâché, ça a tout bousillé. *Voir aussi* **pants, 5; tearing.**

tear along ['tɛərə'lɔŋ] (to), *F:* aller très vite*, foncer, brûler le pavé.

tear apart ['tɛərə'pɑ:t] (to), *F:* **to t. s.o. a.**, écharper qn, engueuler qn.

tear-arse ['tɛərɑ:s], **tearaway** ['tɛərəwei] (*noun*), *P:* braillard *m*, grande-gueule *f*.

tearing ['tɛəriŋ] (*pres. part. & adj.*), *F:* **to be in a t. hurry,** avoir le feu au derrière, filer dare-dare.

tear-jerker ['tiədʒə:kər] (*noun*), *F:* mélo-(drame) *m*, (histoire, *etc.*) larmoyant(e).

tear off ['tɛər'ɔf] (to). **1.** *F:* s'enfuir*, se carapater, se cavaler. **2.** *P:* **to t. it o.** (**together**), coïter*, arracher un copeau (*ou* un pavé). *Voir aussi* **strip**[1]**, 1.**

tease [ti:z] (*noun*), *P:* = **prick-tease.**

teaser ['ti:zər] (*noun*). **1.** *F:* casse-tête (chinois). **2.** *P:* = **prick-teaser.**

tea-stick ['ti:-stik] (*noun*), *P:* = **stick of tea (stick**[1]**, 5).**

tec [tek] (*noun*) (*abbr. = detective*), *F:* détective *m*, condé *m*.

tech [tek] (*noun*) (*abbr. = technical college*), *F:* collège *m* technique.

Ted, ted [ted], **Teddy-boy, teddy-boy** ['tedibɔi] (*noun*), *F:* zazou *m*, zaz *m*.

teed off ['ti:d'ɔf] (*p.p. & adj.*), *P:* **to be t. o.**, en avoir par-dessus la tête, en avoir ras le bol.

teed up ['ti:d'ʌp] (*p.p. & adj.*), *P:* ivre*, rétamé.

teeny ['ti:ni] (*adj.*), *F:* = **teeny-weeny.**

teeny-bopper ['ti:nibɔpər] (*noun*), *F:* jeune yé-yé *mf* (*ou* hippie *mf*) en bordée.

teeny-weeny ['ti:ni'wi:ni] (*adj.*), *F:* minuscule, archi-petit, rikiki.

teeth [ti:θ] (*pl. noun*); *voir* **tooth.**

telegraph ['teligrɑ:f] (to), *F:* **to t. a punch,** (*boxe*) annoncer un direct.

tell [tel] (to), *F:* **you're telling me!** tu l'as dit bouffi! et comment! *Voir aussi* **another; marine; tale, 1, 2.**

telling-off ['teliŋ'ɔf] (*noun*), *F:* réprimande *f*, engueulade *f*.

tell off ['tel'ɔf] (to), *F:* réprimander*, enguirlander.

tell on ['telɔn] (to), *F:* dénoncer*, cafarder, bourdiller; **I'll t. Mum o. you!** je (m'en) vais le dire à maman!

telly ['teli] (*noun*), *F:* (*a*) la télé(vision); (*b*) poste *m* de télé; *cf.* **box**[1]**, 2.**

ten [ten] (*numeral noun*), *F:* **1. the upper t.**, l'aristocratie *f*, les aristos *m.pl.*, les cent familles. **2. the top t.**, palmarès *m* des dix; **in the top t.**, (disque, livre, *etc.*) sélectionné parmi les dix meilleurs.

tenderloin ['tendəlɔin] (*noun*) (*U.S.*), *F:* quartier *m* louche, bas-fonds *m.pl.*

tenner ['tenər] (*noun*), *F:* **1.** dix livres *f.pl.* sterling. **2.** billet* de dix livres *ou* de dix dollars.

ten-spot ['ten-spɔt] (*noun*) (*U.S.*), *F:* **1.** billet* de dix dollars. **2.** emprisonnement *m* de dix années, dix longes *f.pl.* (*ou* berges *f.pl.*).

---

* An asterisk indicates that the word so marked is included as a head-word in the Appendix.

terrible [ˈteribl] (*adj.*), *F:* excessif, formidable; **t. prices,** des prix exorbitants (*ou* formidables); **a t. talker,** un bavard du diable.

terribly [ˈteribli, ˈterəbli] (*adv.*), *F:* extrêmement, vachement; **t. rich,** excessivement riche.

terrific [təˈrifik] (*adj.*), *F:* **1.** excellent*, sensas(s), du tonnerre. **2. a t. bore,** un sacré casse-pieds.

terrifically [təˈrifik(ə)li] (*adv.*), *F:* terriblement, énormément; **I'm t. impressed,** cela m'a fait une énorme impression; **it's t. nice of you,** c'est extrêmement gentil de votre part.

terror [ˈterər] (*noun*), *F:* fléau *m*, cauchemar *m*, peste *f*. *Voir aussi* **holy, 3.**

test-tube [ˈtesttjuːb] (*attrib. adj.*), *F:* **t.-t. baby,** bébé-éprouvette *m*.

Thames [temz] (*pr. noun*), *F:* **he'll never set the T. on fire,** il n'a pas inventé la poudre (*ou* le fil à couper le beurre); on ne lui élèvera pas une statue; il est passé à côté de la distribution; il n'a jamais cassé trois pattes à un canard.

that¹ [ðæt] (*adv.*), *F:* jusque-là, si; **he's not t. clever** [ˈðætklevər], il n'est pas si malin*.

that² [ðæt] (*pron.*), *F:* . . . **and t.'s t.!** un point, c'est tout!; **et voilà!; and t. was t.,** plus rien à dire; **Will you help me? – T. I will!** Allez-vous m'aider ? – Mais bien sûr!

thatch [θætʃ] (*noun*), *F:* **to lose one's t.,** devenir chauve*, être dégazonné, perdre ses plumes.

them¹ [ðem] (*used as adj.* = *those*), *P:* **get up t. stairs!** grimpe cet escalier!; **give me t. pencils!** donne-moi ces crayons!; **I know t. people,** je connais ces gens-là. *Voir aussi* **there, 5.**

them² [ðem] (*used as pron.* = *those*), *P:* **t.'s my sentiments,** voilà ce que je pense, moi.

there [ˈðɛər] (*adv.*), *F:* **1.** . . . **so t.!** ...et voilà! **2. all t.,** malin*, débrouillard; **not all t.,** bête*, un peu fou*, loufoque, demeuré; *voir aussi* **all¹, 5. 3. t. you are!** je te l'avais bien dit! **4. t. you go (again)!** te voilà reparti! tu recommences! tu remets ça! **5. them t. sheep,** ces moutons-là. **6. t. you have me,** ça me dépasse. **7. his name was – let me think – t., I've forgotten!** il s'appelait –

voyons – allons, bon! j'ai oublié! **8. nearly t.:** *voir* **bingo (89).**

thick¹ [θik] (*adj.*), *F:* **1.** bête*, ballot, gourde; **he's as t. as a plank,** il est bête* comme ses pieds; **to have a t. head,** (*a*) être bête*, être bouché à l'émeri; (*b*) avoir la gueule de bois. **2. that's a bit t.,** (*a*) cela coûte les yeux de la tête; (*b*) cela dépasse les bornes; c'est un peu raide. **3.** amical, bon copain; **they're as t. as thieves,** ils s'entendent comme des larrons en foire. **4. to have a t. skin,** avoir une peau d'hippopotame (*ou* de rhinocéros). *Voir aussi* **ear, 5.**

thick² [θik] (*noun*), *F:* **through t. and thin,** contre vents et marées.

thickhead [ˈθikhed] (*noun*), *F:* individu bête*, andouille *f*, bas-de-plafond *m*; *cf.* **thick¹**

thickheaded [ˈθikˈhedid] (*adj.*), *F:* bête*, bas de plafond, lourdingue.

thick-skinned [ˈθikˈskind] (*adj.*), *F:* **to be t.-s.,** n'avoir pas l'épiderme *m* sensible, avoir une peau de rhinocéros; *cf.* **hide, 2; thick¹, 4.**

thick-skulled [ˈθikˈskʌld] (*adj.*), *F:* = **thickheaded.**

thin [θin] (*adj.*), *F:* **1. t. on top,** presque chauve*, sans mousse sur le caillou. **2. to have a t. time (of it),** s'ennuyer*, s'embêter, se morfondre. **3. that's a bit t.!** c'est peu convaincant! *Voir aussi* **ice¹, 5; thin-skinned.**

thing [θiŋ] (*noun*). **1.** *F:* **to have a t. about s.o., sth.,** avoir qn, qch., qui trotte sur le ciboulot. **2.** *F:* **it's not the (done) t.,** ça ne se fait pas, c'est peu conforme aux règles, ce n'est pas canonique. **3.** *F:* **the t. is . . .,** le fait est... **4.** *F:* **just the t.,** exactement ce qu'il faut. **5.** *F:* **it's just one of those things,** on ne peut rien y faire. **6.** *F:* (*a*) **to know a t. or two,** être malin*, avoir plus d'un tour dans son sac; (*b*) **I could tell you a t. or two,** je pourrais vous en conter, je pourrais vous en dire des vertes et des pas mûres. **7.** *F:* **to see things,** avoir des visions *f.pl.* **8.** *F:* (*a*) **hello, old t.!** bonjour mon vieux! salut mon pote!; (*b*) **he's a nice old t.,** c'est un bien brave homme*. **9.** *F:* (*a*) **to be on (to) a good t.,** avoir le filon, être sur un bon filon; (*b*) **he makes a good t. out of it,** ça lui rapporte pas mal; il en fait ses choux gras. **10.** *F:* **do your (own) t.!**

exécutetoi! fais ton boulot! **11.** *P:*
pénis*, outil *m.* **12.** *F:* **how's things?**
comment ça va? *Voir aussi* **first.**

thingamy [ˈθiŋəmi], **thingamybob**
[ˈθiŋəmibɔb], **thingamyjig** [ˈθiŋəmi-
dʒig], **thingum(e)bob** [ˈθiŋəm(ə)bɔb],
thingummy [ˈθiŋəmi] (*noun*), *F:* chose
m, machin *m*, machin-chose *m*, machinchouette *m*, truc *m*, bidule *m*.

think¹ [θiŋk] (*noun*), *F:* **you've got
another t. coming!** tu peux toujours
courir! tu te mets le doigt dans l'œil!

think² [θiŋk] (**to**), *F:* **1. I don't t.!**
sûrement pas! et mon œil! **2. just t. of
that!** ça, c'est pas banal! qui l'eût cru!

think-box [ˈθiŋkbɔks], **thinker** [ˈθiŋkər]
(*noun*), *F:* cerveau *m*, ciboulot *m*; **to use
one's t.**, faire travailler ses méninges *f.pl.*

think-in [ˈθiŋkin] (*noun*), *F:* colloque *m*,
séminaire *m*, groupe *m* d'études.

thinking-cap [ˈθiŋkiŋkæp] (*noun*), *F:* **to
put one's t.-c. on**, aviser à ce qu'on doit
faire, réfléchir, méditer sur qch.

think-piece [ˈθiŋkpiːs] (*noun*), *F:* **1.** =
think-box. 2. qch. qui fait réfléchir,
remue-méninges *m*.

think-tank [ˈθiŋktæŋk] (*noun*), *F:* (*a*)
réunion *f* d'une société savante; (*b*) des
réservoirs *m.pl.* d'idées.

thin-skinned [ˈθinˈskind] (*adj.*), *F:* **to be
t.-s.**, avoir l'épiderme *m* sensible, être
susceptible (*ou* chatouilleux).

thrash¹ [θræʃ] (*noun*), *P:* **1.** coït*,
dérouillage *m.* **2.** réjouissances *f*, boum
f, noce *f*, nouba *f*.

thrash² [θræʃ] (**to**), *F:* = **plaster** (**to**),
1, 2.

thrashing [ˈθræʃiŋ] (*noun*), *F:* = **plastering, 1, 2.**

thread [θred] (**to**), *P:* coïter* avec (une
femme), enfiler.

threads [θredz] (*pl. noun*), *P:* = **vines**
(**vine, 2**).

threepenny-bits [ˈθrupniˈbits] (*pl. noun*)
(*R.S.* = **tits**), *P:* voir **tit, 1**; *cf.* **Bristols;
fit², 4; tale, 3; trey-bits.**

thrill [θril] (*noun*), *P:* spasme provoqué
par l'héroïne.

throat [θrout] (*noun*), *F:* **1. to ram sth.
down s.o.'s t.**, rabattre les oreilles à qn
de qch.; **we're always having it rammed
down our throats that we've never had
it so good**, on nous rabat les oreilles en
répétant que tout est au mieux. **2. he's
cutting his own t.**, il travaille à sa

propre ruine; il creuse sa tombe. *Voir
aussi* **cut-throat; jump²** (**to**), **11.**

throne [θroun] (*noun*), *P:* siège *m* de
W.C.*, trône *m*.

throne-room [ˈθrounruːm] (*noun*), *P:*
W.C.*, cabinets *m.pl.*

through¹ [θruː] (*adv.*), *F:* **1. to get t. to
s.o.**, faire comprendre qch. à qn, faire
piger. **2. to be t.**, (*a*) en avoir vu la fin; (*b*) être fichu (*ou*
foutu). **3. to be t. with s.o.**, rompre avec
qn, couper les ponts.

through² [θruː] (*prep.*), *F:* **he's been t. it**,
il en a vu de dures, il en a vu des vertes
et des pas mûres, il en a bavé, il en a vu
de toutes les couleurs.

throw [θrou] (**to**), *F:* **1. I trust him as far
as I can t. him**, je n'ai pas la moindre
confiance en lui. **2. to t. a party**, donner
une réception. **3.** étonner, estomaquer.
4. to t. a fight, se laisser battre volon-
tairement, se coucher. *Voir aussi*
bathwater; book¹, 1; mud, 7.

throw about (*or* **around**) [ˈθrouəˈbaut,
ˈθrouəˈraund] (**to**), *F:* **to t.** (**one's**)
money a., dépenser* sans compter,
faire valser le fric; **he doesn't t. his
money a.**, il n'attache pas son chien
avec des saucisses.

throwaway¹ [ˈθrouəwei] (*adj.*), *F:* **a t.
line, remark**, un aparté.

throwaway² [ˈθrouəwei] (*noun*), *F:* prospectus *m*.

thrower-out [ˈθrouəˈraut] (*noun*), *F:* =
chucker-out.

throw in [ˈθrouin] (**to**), *F:* **to t. i. the
towel** (*or* **the sponge**), (*a*) (*sports*)
abandonner la lutte (*ou* la partie); (*b*)
s'avouer vaincu, quitter le dé. *Voir
aussi* **end, 13.**

throw-out [ˈθrouaut] (*noun*), *F:* un
laissé pour compte, rebut *m*.

throw up [ˈθrouˈʌp] (**to**), *F:* vomir*,
dégobiller.

thrush [θrʌʃ] (*noun*), *P:* réjouissances*,
bamboche *f*, nouba *f*.

thrust [θrʌst] (*noun*), *P:* amphétamine *f*
(*drogues**).

thumb [θʌm] (*noun*), *F:* **1. to be all
thumbs**, être lourdaud (*ou* pataud); **his
fingers are all thumbs**, il a la main
malheureuse, il est gauche, c'est un
brise-tout. **2. thumbs up!** bravo!
victoire! **3. to twiddle one's thumbs
(and do nothing)**, se tourner les pouces.

---

* An asterisk indicates that the word so marked is included as a head-word in the Appendix.

4. it stands (or sticks) out like a sore t.,
ça saute aux yeux, ça crève les yeux.
Voir aussi green[1], 5; Tom, 4.

thump [θʌmp] (to), *F:* battre*, tabasser,
rouster (qn).

thumping ['θʌmpiŋ] (adj.), *F:* (a) gros*
et grand, excellent*, maousse, bœuf;
(b) = thundering.

thunderbox ['θʌndəbɔks] (noun), *P:*
cuvette *f* (de cabinets).

thundering ['θʌndəriŋ] (adj.), *F:* du
tonnerre; to win with a t. majority,
l'emporter avec une majorité écrasante;
he's a t. nuisance, il est assommant au
possible.

thunder-mug ['θʌndəmʌg] (noun), *P:*
pot *m* de chambre.

tich [titʃ] (noun), *P:* = titch.

tichy ['titʃi] (adj.), *P:* = titchy.

tick[1] [tik] (noun). 1. *P:* individu*
méprisable, salaud *m*, saligaud *m*. 2. *F:*
crédit *m*, croum(e) *m*; on t., à crédit, à
croum(e). 3. *F:* moment *m*, instant *m*;
hang on a t.! (attends) une seconde!;
cf. jiff(y); mo; sec; shake[1], 1, 2.

tick[2] [tik] (to), *F:* I'd like to know what
makes him t., je voudrais bien savoir ce
qui le pousse.

ticker ['tikər] (noun), *F:* 1. cœur*,
palpitant *m*; to have a dicky t., avoir le
cœur branlant. 2. montre*, pendule *f*,
tocante *f*.

ticket ['tikit] (noun), *F:* that's (just) the
t.! exactement ce qui colle! 2. contra-
vention *f*, papillon *m*; to get a parking
t., se faire coller un biscuit. 3. (U.S.)
liste électorale; to vote a straight t.,
voter pour toute la liste; to vote a split
t., faire du panachage; the Republican t.,
le programme du parti républicain. 4. to
give s.o. a round t., donner carte blanche
à qn. *Voir aussi* meal-ticket.

tickety-boo ['tikiti'bu:] (adj.), *F:*
excellent*, parfait, bœuf, au poil, aux
pommes.

ticking-off ['tikiŋ'ɔf] (noun), *F:* réprimande *f*, savon *m*, engueulade *f*; *cf.*
tick off (to).

tickle[1] ['tikl] (noun), *F:* de la chance*,
coup *m* de pot; to make a t., faire une
touche. *Voir aussi* slap[2], 2.

tickle[2] ['tikl] (to), *F:* 1. to t. s.o., to t.
s.o.'s fancy, amuser qn. 2. to be tickled
pink, être ravi, être aux anges. 3. to be
tickled to death, se tordre de rire*, se

boyauter. *Voir aussi* ivories, 4.

tickler ['tiklər] (noun), *F:* 1. moustache*,
charmeuses *f.pl.* 2. martinet *m*, fouet *m*.
Voir aussi rib-tickler.

tick off ['tik'ɔf] (to), *F:* réprimander*,
attraper, enguirlander; to get ticked off,
être réprimandé*, écoper, recevoir un
savon; *cf.* ticking-off.

tick over ['tik'ouvər] (to), *F:* 1. (commerce, etc.) suivre son petit bonhomme
de chemin. 2. (auto, machines, etc.) bien
marcher, tourner rond.

tidderly push ['tid(ə)li'puʃ] (adv.), *F:*
... and t. p., et patati et patata.

tiddle[1] ['tidl] (noun), *F:* (langage
enfantin) urine *f*, pipi *m*; to have a t. =
tiddle[2] (to).

tiddle[2] ['tidl] (to), *F:* (langage enfantin)
uriner*, faire pipi.

tiddler ['tidlər] (noun), *F:* 1. petit
poisson, friture *f*. 2. petit garçon,
môme *m*, moutard *m*. 3. pièce *f* d'un
demi-penny.

tiddl(e)y[1] ['tidli] (adj.), *F:* 1. légèrement
ivre*, pompette, éméché. 2. très petit,
minuscule.

tiddl(e)y[2] ['tidli] (noun), *F:* a drop of t.,
un petit coup d'alcool*, une goutte de
gnôle.

tiddl(e)y push ['tidli'puʃ] (adv.), *F:* =
tidderly push.

tide-mark ['taidmɑ:k] (noun), *F:* ligne *f*
de crasse autour du cou *ou* sur la
baignoire.

tide over ['taid'ouvər] (to), *F:* I borrowed a pound to t. me o., j'ai emprunté
une livre pour pouvoir tenir le coup (ou
pour me dépanner).

tidy ['taidi] (adj.), *F:* a t. sum, une somme
rondelette; a t. fortune, une jolie
fortune.

tie on ['tai'ɔn] (to), *P:* to t. one o., to t. o.
a load, s'enivrer, se biturer, prendre une
cuite, se piquer le nez.

tie up ['tai'ʌp] (to), *F:* 1. I'm rather tied
up at the moment, pour le moment je
suis pas mal occupé, j'ai pas mal à
faire. 2. that ties up with what I've just
said, cela correspond à ce que je
viens de dire. 3. our firm is tied up with
yours, notre entreprise a des accords
avec la vôtre.

tiger ['taigər] (noun), *P:* t. in the sack,
amoureux déchaîné, chaud *m* de la pince.

tight[1] [tait] (adj.), *F:* 1. ivre*, saoul,

---

* L'astérisque indique que le mot marqué de ce signe figure comme entrée dans le Répertoire.

rétamé, raide; **to get t.,** prendre une cuite; *voir aussi* **newt. 2.** avare*, serré, ladre, dur à la détente. **3.** *(en parlant d'argent)* à court. *Voir aussi* **squeeze**[1], **2.**

tight[2] [tait] *(adv.)*, *F:* **to sit t.,** *(a)* voir venir, serrer les fesses; *(b)* ne pas bouger, ne pas se laisser ébranler.

tight-fisted [ˈtaitˈfistid] *(adj.)*, *F:* = **tight**[1], **2.**

tightwad [ˈtait-wɔd] *(noun)*, *F:* avare *m*, radin *m*, grigou *m*.

tike [taik] *(noun)*, *P:* = **tyke.**

tile [tail] *(noun)*, *F:* **1.** chapeau*, bitos *m*; haut-de-forme *m*, gibus *m*. **2. to have a t. loose,** être un peu fou*, onduler de la toiture. **3. he spends his nights on the tiles,** il traîne dehors toute la nuit.

time [taim] *(noun)*, *F:* **to do t.,** être en prison*, purger sa peine. *Voir aussi* **all-time; big-time; day, 3; good-time; short**[1], **2; small-time.**

timothy [ˈtiməθi] *(noun)* *(Austr.)*, *P:* bordel*, boxon *m*.

tin[1] [tin] *(adj.)*, *F:* **1. t. hat** *(or* **lid),** casque *m* (de soldat). **2. that puts the t. lid on it,** c'est le comble, c'est la fin des haricots. **3. little t. god,** individu* qui se croit sorti de la cuisse de Jupiter, esbrouf(f)eur *m*, poseur *m*. **4. t. fish,** torpille *f*.

tin[2] [tin] *(noun)*, *P:* argent*, galette *f*, pognon *m*, fric *m*.

tinker [ˈtiŋkər] *(noun)*. **1.** *F:* petit diable, vilain *m*. **2.** *P:* **I don't care** *(or* **give) a t.'s** *(or* **a t.'s cuss** *or* **a t.'s toss),** je m'en fiche, je m'en bats l'œil, je m'en soucie comme de l'an quarante *(ou* de ma première chemise).

tinkle[1] [ˈtiŋkl] *(noun)*, *F:* **to give s.o. a t.,** téléphoner *(ou* passer un coup de fil) à qn.

tinkle[2] [ˈtiŋkl] (to), *F:* *(langage enfantin)* uriner*, faire pipi.

tinkler [ˈtiŋklər] *(noun)*, *P:* pot *m* de chambre, Jules, Thomas.

tinned [tind] *(adj.)*, *F:* **t. music = canned music (canned, 2).**

tin-pan alley [ˈtinˈpænˈæli] *(noun)*, *F:* **1.** quartier *m* des éditeurs de musique populaire. **2.** les compositeurs *m.pl.* de musique populaire.

tinpot [ˈtinˈpɔt] *(adj.)*, *F:* inférieur, de second ordre, camelote.

tiny [ˈtaini] *(adj.)*, *F:* **you must be out of your t. mind,** tu es en train de perdre le peu de raison que tu avais.

tip [tip] (to). **1.** *F:* donner*, passer, lancer (qch. à qn). **2.** *P:* coïter* avec (une femme), envoyer en l'air. *Voir aussi* **fin, 1; flipper; wink.**

tip-off [ˈtipɔf] *(noun)*, *F:* renseignement*, avertissement *m*, tuyau *m*.

tip off [ˈtipˈɔf] (to), *F:* avertir, affranchir, mettre (qn) dans le coup.

tipple [ˈtipl] *(noun)*, *P:* boisson corsée, très alcoolisée.

tip-top [ˈtipˈtɔp] *(adj.)*, *F:* excellent*, extra, super.

tit [tit] *(noun)*. **1.** *V:* sein*, nichon *m*, téton *m*. **2.** *V:* **to get on s.o.'s tits,** taper sur le système à qn. **3.** *P:* individu bête*, idiot *m*, crétin *m*; **you big t.!** grand imbécile! sacré crétin! *Voir aussi* **arse, 4; Tom, 3.**

titch [titʃ] *(noun)*, *F:* petit* individu, bas-du-cul *m*, astèque *m*.

titchy [ˈtitʃi] *(adj.)*, *P:* petit, crapoussin.

titfer [ˈtitfər] *(noun)* *(R.S. = tit-for-tat = hat)*, *P:* chapeau*

titty [ˈtiti] *(noun)* *(pl. titties)*, *V:* = **tit, 1.**

titty-bottle [ˈtiti-bɔtl] *(noun)*, *P:* biberon *m*.

tizwas [ˈtizwɔz] *(noun)*, *F:* **to be all of a t.,** être aux cent coups, être démonté, être affolé; *cf.* **doodah; tizzy.**

tizzy [ˈtizi] *(noun)*, *F:* *(a)* affolement *m*, remue-ménage *m*, débandade *f*; *(b)* panique *f*, bile *f*, mauvais sang; **to be in a t.,** être affolé.

toast [toust] *(noun)*, *F:* **to have s.o. on t.,** avoir qn à sa merci, tenir qn.

toby [ˈtoubi] *(noun)*, *P:* **the t.,** la grande route*, le grand trimard.

tod, Tod [tɔd] *(noun)* *(R.S. = Tod Sloan = alone)*, *P:* **to be on one's t.,** être tout seul, être seulabre.

toddle[1] [ˈtɔdl] *(noun)*, *F:* petite promenade, balade *f*.

toddle[2] [ˈtɔdl] (to), *F:* **1.** se balader, se baguenauder, déambuler. **2.** = **toddle off (to).**

toddle along *(or* **off)** [ˈtɔdl-əˈlɔŋ, ˈtɔdl-ˈɔf] (to), *F:* partir*, se trotter, se carapater.

to-do [təˈduː] *(noun)*, *F:* remue-ménage *m*; **what a t.-d.!** quelle affaire! quelle histoire!

toe [tou] *(noun)*, *F:* **1. to tread on s.o.'s toes,** marcher sur les pieds de qn, offenser qn, froisser qn. **2. to be on one's toes,** être alerté, être sur le qui-vive, ouvrir

---

* An asterisk indicates that the word so marked is included as a head-word in the Appendix.

l'œil. **3. to turn up one's toes,** mourir*, casser sa pipe, avaler sa chique.

toehold [ˈtouhould] *(noun), F:* **to get a t.,** avoir une prise précaire.

toe-ragger [ˈtou-rægər] *(noun) (Austr.), P:* prisonnier *m* de courte durée, enschibé *m* d'une courte.

toey [ˈtoui] *(adj.) (Austr.), P:* inquiet, anxieux, bileux.

toff [tɔf] *(noun), F:* rupin(os) *m*, cossu *m*, milord *m*; **the toffs,** le grand monde, le gratin.

toffee [ˈtɔfi] *(noun), F:* **he can't play for t.** (*or* **for t. apples** *or* **for t. nuts**), il joue comme un pied.

toffee-nose [ˈtɔfi-nouz] *(noun), F:* snob *m*, crâneur *m*, poseur *m*.

toffee-nosed [ˈtɔfi-nouzd] *(adj.), F:* prétentieux*, bêcheur, pincé.

together [təˈgeðər] *(adv.), F:* sans mousse, pénard.

tog out [ˈtɔgˈaut] *(to), F:* **to t. (oneself) o.,** se mettre sur son trente et un.

togs [tɔgz] *(pl. noun), F:* vêtements*, nippes *f.pl.*, frusques *f.pl.*

tog up [ˈtɔgˈʌp] *(to), F:* **to t. (oneself) u.** = **to tog (oneself) out.**

toke[1] [touk] *(noun), P:* **1.** pain*, bricheton *m*, larton *m*. **2.** bouffée *f*.

toke[2] [touk] *(to), P:* tirer, traîner, remorquer.

toke up [ˈtoukˈʌp] *(to), P:* allumer (une cigarette*).

tokus [ˈtoukəs] *(noun), P:* **1.** fesses*, pétrus *m*, pétrousquin *m*. **2.** anus*, troufignon *m*.

Tom, tom [tɔm] *(noun).* **1.** *F:* **any T., Dick, or Harry,** Pierre et Paul, n'importe qui, le premier venu. **2.** *P:* **Tom Mix,** (*a*) *(R.S. = fix)* piqûre *f* de narcotique; (*b*) *voir* **bingo** (6). **3.** *P:* **T. Tit, t. tit** *(R.S. = shit):* **to go for a t. tit,** aller déféquer*, aller faire caca. **4.** *P:* **T. Thumb** *(R.S. = rum),* rhum *m; cf.* **kingdom-come, 3; touch-your-bum. 5.** *F:* (=*tom cat*) matou *m. Voir aussi* **Uncle, 9.**

tomato [təˈmeitou] *(noun) (U.S.).* **1.** *F:* jolie fille*, fleur *f*, pépée *f*, poulette *f*. **2.** *P:* prostituée*.

tommy[1] [ˈtɔmi] *(noun).* **1.** *P:* pain*, provisions *f.pl.;* nourriture*. **2.** *F:* **t., T.** (**Atkins**), soldat* anglais, Tommy *m*.

tommy[2] [ˈtɔmi] *(to) (Austr.), P:* s'enfuir*, décamper, filer.

tommy-rot [ˈtɔmiˈrɔt] *(noun), F:* bêtises*, tissu *m* d'âneries.

ton [tʌn] *(noun), F:* **1.** = **ton-up. 2. tons of . . .,** une abondance* de..., une tripotée de...; **to have tons of money,** avoir beaucoup d'argent*, avoir des masses d'argent*, avoir de l'argent* à gogo; **to have tons of time,** avoir largement le temps. **3.** cent livres *f.pl.* sterling. **4. to weigh a t.,** peser lourd, peser des mille et des cents. *Voir aussi* **come down (to), 3.**

tongue [tʌŋ] *(to):* **to t. a woman,** (*a*) *P:* filer une langouse à une femme; (*b*) *V:* sucer une femme (*coït* buccal).

tongue-kiss [ˈtʌŋkis] *(noun), F:* = **French kiss (French**[1], **1).**

tongue-pie [ˈtʌŋˈpai] *(noun), F:* **to get a slice of t.-p.,** se faire dire ses (quatre) vérités *f.pl.,* en prendre pour son grade.

tonk [tɔŋk] *(noun), P:* pénis*, tringle *f. Voir aussi* **honky-tonk.**

ton-up [ˈtʌnʌp] *(noun), F:* **to do a t.-u.,** faire cent milles (160 km) à l'heure (en moto); **the t.-u. boys,** les motards *m.pl.* bolides.

toodle-oo [ˈtuːdlˈuː] *(excl.), F:* **1.** au revoir, ciao. **2.** *voir* **bingo** (22).

toodle-pip [ˈtuːdlˈpip] *(excl.), F:* = **toodle-oo, 1.**

tool [tuːl] *(noun), P:* **1.** pénis*, outil *m*. **2.** pickpocket *m*, tire *m*, tireur *m*, fourche *f*, fourchette *f*. **3.** (*pl.*) attirail *m* de camé.

tool along [ˈtuːləˈlɔŋ] *(to), F:* se balader, se baguenauder.

tool off [ˈtuːlˈɔf] *(to), P:* partir*, se barrer.

tooth [tuːθ] *(noun) (pl. teeth), F:* **1. to have a sweet t.,** aimer les sucreries *f.pl.* **2. to be long in the t.,** n'être plus jeune, avoir de la bouteille. **3.** (*Austr.*) **on the t.,** (*a*) affamé; (*b*) de bon goût, savoureux, succulent. **4. to get one's teeth into sth.,** se mettre pour de bon à qch., s'acharner à faire qch. **5. to knock s.o.'s teeth in,** battre* qn, rentrer dans le chou à qn, amocher le portrait à qn. **6. to go at it t. and nail,** travailler* d'achar. *Voir aussi* **dress up (to), 2; fed up, (a).**

toothy-peg [ˈtuːθi-peg] *(noun), F: (langage enfantin)* petite dent* d'enfant, quenotte *f*.

tootle [ˈtuːtl] *(to), F:* corner, klaxonner.

---

* L'astérisque indique que le mot marqué de ce signe figure comme entrée dans le Répertoire.

tootle along [ˈtuːtl-əˈlɒŋ] (**to**), *F:* suivre son petit bonhomme de chemin.

toots [tuts] (*noun*), *F:* chéri(e), mon petit, ma petite; **hello, t.**! bonjour (*ou* salut) coco, cocotte!

tootsie [ˈtutsi] (*noun*). **1.** *F:* = **toots**. **2.** *P:* lesbienne*, gouchotte *f.* **3.** (*pl.*) *F:* = **tootsie-wootsies**.

tootsie-wootsies [ˈtutsiˈwutsiz] (*pl. noun*), *F:* (*langage enfantin*) pieds*, petons *m.pl.*, paturons *m.pl.*

tootsy [ˈtutsi] (*noun*), *F:* = **toots**; **tootsie**.

tootsy-footsy [ˈtutsiˈfutsi] (*noun*), *F:* = **footsy**.

top[1] [tɒp] (*noun*), *F:* **1.** to go over the t., exagérer*, y aller fort. **2.** to blow one's t., se mettre en colère*, éclater, sortir de ses gonds; *cf.* **flip**[3] (**to**), **2.** **3.** the t. of the morning to you! je vous souhaite le meilleur des bonjours! **4.** off the t., la première réaction, (le mouvement) d'instinct. **5.** t. of the shop: *voir* **bingo** (**90**). *Voir aussi* **copper-top**; **heap, 2** (*a*); **rag-top**; **tail**[1], **6**; **thin, 1**.

top[2] [tɒp] (**to**), *P:* pendre*, exécuter, agrafer; **topped** (**and chopped**), pendu, exécuté.

top-flight [ˈtɒpˈflait], **top-hole** [ˈtɒpˈhoul] (*adj.*), *F:* excellent*, foutral, le dessus du panier, le bouquet.

top-knot [ˈtɒpnɒt] (*noun*), *P:* tête*, bobèche *f,* plafond *m.*

topless [ˈtɒplis] (*adj.*), *F:* torse nu, seins* nus.

top-line [ˈtɒpˈlain], **top-notch** [ˈtɒpˈnɒtʃ] (*adj.*), *F:* = **top-flight**.

top-liner [ˈtɒpˈlainər], **top-notcher** [ˈtɒpˈnɒtʃər] (*noun*), *F:* as *m,* expert *m* (dans sa profession), crack *m.*

top off [ˈtɒpˈɒf] (**to**) (*Austr.*), *P:* **1.** to t. s.o. o., rabrouer qn, remettre qn à sa place. **2.** dénoncer*, servir d'indicateur* de police.

topper [ˈtɒpər] (*noun*), *F:* **1.** le dessus du panier, le bouquet, la crème, la fleur des petits pois. **2.** chapeau* haut de forme, gibus *m.*

topping [ˈtɒpiŋ] (*adj.*), *F:* excellent*, formid(able), épatant.

topping-out [ˈtɒpiŋˈaut] (*noun*), *F:* cérémonie qui marque la terminaison de la construction de la grosse œuvre d'un bâtiment.

tops [tɒps] (*noun*), *F:* the t., le dessus du panier, la crème.

torch [tɔːtʃ] (*noun*) (*U.S.*), *F:* **1.** to carry the t. for s.o., aimer* qn qui ne vous aime pas, soupirer en vain. **2.** pyromane *m,* incendiaire *m,* pétroleur *m.*

torch-song [ˈtɔːtʃsɒŋ] (*noun*) (*U.S.*), *F:* chanson *f* d'amour déçu, lamentation *f* d'amour.

torch up [ˈtɔːtʃˈʌp] (**to**), *P:* = **toke up** (**to**).

torn [tɔːn] (*p.p.*): *voir* **tear**[2] (**to**).

torpedo [tɔːˈpiːdou] (*noun*) (*U.S.*), *P:* but(t)eur *m* de louage.

tosh [tɒʃ] (*noun*). **1.** *P:* individu*, mec *m,* type *m.* **2.** *F:* bêtises*, sornettes *f.pl.*, blague *f.*

tosher [ˈtɒʃər] (*noun*), *P:* = **tosh, 1**.

tosh-light [ˈtɒʃlait] (*noun*), *P:* feu pris à une autre cigarette.

toss-off [ˈtɒsɔf] (*noun*), *V:* acte *m* de masturbation, moussage *m* maison.

toss off [ˈtɒsˈɔf] (**to**). **1.** *V:* to t. (**oneself**) **off**, se masturber*, se faire mousser. **2.** *F:* to t. o. a pint, boire*, s'enfiler un verre, écluser un godet.

toss-pot [ˈtɒs-pɒt] (*noun*), *F:* ivrogne*, vide-bouteilles *m.*

toss-up [ˈtɒsʌp] (*noun*), *F:* (*a*) une chance sur deux, chance égale, pile ou face; (*b*) affaire* à issue douteuse.

tote[1] [tout] (*noun*), *F:* (*turf*) totaliseur *m,* totalisateur *m* (des paris), le pari mutuel, le P.M.U.

tote[2] [tout] (**to**), *F:* **1.** porter, trimballer, transbahuter; to t. a gun, être armé (*ou* flingué). **2.** to t. for business, chercher à faire des affaires, quémander du travail.

tote-bag [ˈtoutbæg] (*noun*), *F:* (sac) fourre-tout *m.*

tother, t'other [ˈtʌðər] (*adj. & pron.*) (=*the other*), *F:* l'autre; you can't tell one from t., you can't tell t. from which, ils sont du pareil au même, on ne peut les distinguer l'un de l'autre, ils se ressemblent comme deux gouttes d'eau.

touch[1] [tʌtʃ] (*noun*). **1.** *P:* to make a t., to put the t. on s.o., emprunter* de l'argent à qn, taper qn. **2.** *F:* it was t. and go, it was a near t., cela ne tenait qu'à un fil; *voir aussi* **touch-and-go. 3.** *F:* soft t. = easy mark (**easy**[1], **3**).

touch[2] [tʌtʃ] (**to**). **1.** *P:* to t. s.o. for money = to make a touch (**touch**[1], **1**). **2.** *F:* to t. lucky, avoir de la chance*, être veinard. **3.** *P:* arrêter*, épingler, alpaguer. *Voir aussi* **rock**[1], **4**; **wood, 1**.

---

* An asterisk indicates that the word so marked is included as a head-word in the Appendix.

touch-and-go [ˈtʌtʃənˈgou] (adj.), F:
(a) très incertain, douteux, dans la
balance; (b) hasardeux, chanceux, aléa-
toire; voir aussi touch¹, 2.
touched [tʌtʃt] (adj.), F: t. (in the head),
fou*, toqué, timbré.
touch up [ˈtʌtʃˈʌp] (to), P: to t. u. a girl,
peloter une fille.
touch-your-bum [ˈtʌtʃjəˈbʌm] (noun)
(R.S. = rum), P: rhum m; cf. kingdom-
come, 3; Tom, 4.
tough¹ [tʌf] (adj.), F: 1. a t. nut (or guy),
un dur (à cuire), un coriace. 2. he's a t.
customer, il est peu commode. 3.
difficile*. 4. t. luck, a t. break,
malchance*, déveine f, guigne f.
tough² [tʌf] (noun), F: 1. vaurien*,
voyou m. 2. brute f, crapule f, fripouille
f, sale type m. 3. gangster m, criminel m,
saigneur m.
toughie [ˈtʌfi] (noun), F: 1. = tough², 1,
2, 3. 2. problème m difficile à résoudre,
casse-tête m.
tousing [ˈtauziŋ] (noun), F: = roasting.
towel [taul, ˈtauəl] (to), P: battre*,
rosser, dérouiller.
towelling [ˈtau(ə)liŋ] (noun), P: raclée f,
peignée f, dérouillée f.
town [taun] (noun), F: 1. to go to t., (a)
faire la bombe (ou la foire ou la noce);
(b) réussir, arriver, percer; (c) dépenser*
sans compter, mettre le paquet. 2. to go
on the t. = to go to town (a). 3. to go to
t. on s.o., réprimander* qn, engueuler
qn. Voir aussi red¹, 3.
townified [ˈtaunifaid], towny [ˈtauni]
(adj.), F: urbain, citadin.
track¹ [træk] (noun). 1. F: (=sound
track) piste f sonore (d'un film). 2. F:
disque m. 3. F: to have the inside of the
t. with s.o., l'emporter sur qn, avoir le
dessus, tenir le bon bout. 4. F: to hit
the t., to make tracks, partir*, se
mettre en route, plier bagage, mettre les
bouts, se tailler; to make tracks for
home, rentrer chez soi, regagner le
bercail. 5. (pl.) P: trous m.pl. (de
piqûres hypodermiques). Voir aussi
dirt-track.
track² [træk] (to) (Austr.), F: to t. with a
girl, faire la cour à une fille. Voir aussi
backtrack (to).
trad¹ [træd] (adj.), F: (=traditional)
traditionnel; t. jazz, jazz m Nouvelle-
Orléans et ses dérivés.

trad² [træd] (noun), F: (=traditional jazz),
jazz traditionnel.
trade¹ [treid] (noun). 1. F: to take it out
in t., se faire payer en nature plutôt
qu'en argent. 2. P: clientèle f (d'une
prostituée ou d'un pédéraste); miché m,
micheton m. 3. F: he knows all the
tricks of the t., il la connaît dans les
coins.
trade² [treid] (to). 1. F: to t. punches,
échanger des coups*, se crêper le
chignon. 2. P: chercher des rapports
sexuels, faire le trottoir.
trade-in [ˈtreidin] (noun), F: (article m
de) reprise f.
trade in [ˈtreidˈin] (to), F: to t. i. a car,
acheter une voiture avec reprise, donner
une auto en reprise.
trading-in [ˈtreidiŋˈin] (noun), F: vente
f en reprise.
trail [treil] (noun), F: to hit the t. = to
hit the track (track¹, 4).
train [trein] (noun), P: fille* qui suit les
bandes de garçons, les groupes de pop,
etc.; groupette f; to pull a t., (pour une
fille) coïter* avec une succession de
garçons, caramboler à la file. Voir aussi
gravy, 1; milk-train; puffer(-train).
tramp [træmp] (noun), P: femme* facile,
chaude lapine, baiseuse f.
trap [træp] (noun). 1. P: bouche*,
gueule f; shut your t.! tais-toi! (se
taire*), ferme-la! ferme ton clapet!; to
keep one's t. shut, taire sa gueule, la
fermer; cf. rat-trap. 2. P: agent* de
police, flic m. 3. (pl.) F: vêtements*,
fringues f.pl. 4. (pl.) F: possessions
f.pl., affaires f.pl., effets m.pl., armes et
bagages; to pack up one's traps, plier
bagage. Voir aussi bug-trap; flea-
trap.
trash [træʃ] (noun) (U.S.), P: mendiant*,
clodot m, mangav m.
travel-agent [ˈtrævəlˈeidʒənt] (noun),
P: fournisseur m de LSD (drogues*),
agent m de voyage.
traveller [ˈtræv(ə)lər] (noun), F:
romanichel m, manouche mf.
trawler [ˈtrɔːlər] (noun) (Austr.), P: car*
de police, panier m à salade, fourgon m.
treacle [ˈtriːkl] (noun), P: opium m
(drogues*), noir m.
tread [tred] (noun), P: to do (or chuck) a
t., coïter*, faire l'amour, faire un
carton.

---

* L'astérisque indique que le mot marqué de ce signe figure comme entrée dans le Répertoire.

treat¹ [tri:t] (a) (adv.), F: agréablement, extrêmement bien; **that whisky went down a t.**, ce whisky a fait du bien par où il a passé.

treat² [tri:t] (noun), F: **to stand t.**, offrir la tournée; **I'm standing t.**, c'est moi qui régale.

tree [tri:] (noun), F: **1. up a t. = up a gum-tree. 2. they don't grow on trees,** on n'en trouve pas à la douzaine. Voir aussi **apple-tree; Christmas-tree; palm-tree.**

tremble [ˈtrembl] (noun), F: **to be all of a t.,** avoir la tremblote.

tremendous [triˈmendəs, trəˈmendəs] (adj.), F: **1.** énorme, immense; **a t. decision,** une décision très importante. **2.** passionnant, palpitant; **a t. game of tennis,** une partie de tennis formidable.

tremendously [triˈmendəsli, trəˈmendəsli] (adv.), F: énormément, démesurément; **he is t. popular,** il jouit d'une immense popularité.

trendiness [ˈtrendinis] (noun), F: nouvelle mode, dernier cri.

trendy¹ [ˈtrendi] (adj.), F: à la mode, dans le vent.

trendy² [ˈtrendi] (noun), F: qn à la mode, dandy m, gandin m.

trey [trei] (noun), P: colis m ou paquet m ou sachet m de stupéfiants.

trey-bits [ˈtreibits] (pl. noun) (Austr.), P: **= threepenny-bits.**

tribe [traib] (noun), F: énfants mf.pl. d'une même famille, rejetons m.pl., smala(h) f; (toute) une kyrielle (d'enfants).

trick¹ [trik] (noun). **1.** F: **how's tricks?** quoi de neuf? **2.** F: **he doesn't miss a t.,** rien ne lui échappe; il est roublard. **3.** F: **that should do the t.,** ça fera l'affaire. **4.** P: **to turn a t.,** (d'une prostituée) trouver un client, faire une passe. **5.** F: **to be up to all sorts of tricks,** faire les cent coups. Voir aussi **bag**¹, **6, 7; funny**¹, **2; trade**¹, **3.**

trick² [trik] (to), P: coïter* avec (une femme), godiller, pinocher.

trick-cyclist [ˈtrikˈsaiklist] (noun), P: psychiatre mf.

trig [trig] (noun) (abbr. = trigonometry), F: la trigo(nométrie).

trigger-happy [ˈtrigəhæpi] (adj.), F: **to be t.-h.,** être rapide à la gâchette, avoir la gâchette facile.

trigger-man [ˈtrigəmæn] (noun), P: (a)

assassin*, professionnel m de la gâchette; (b) but(t)eur m, flingueur m; (c) garde f du corps, gorille m.

trilbies [ˈtrilbiz] (pl. noun) (Austr.), P: jambes*, gambettes f.pl.

trim [trim] (to), P: coïter* avec (une femme), fourailler.

trip¹ [trip] (noun), P: **1.** mesure f de LSD (drogues*). **2. to take** (or **make** or **go on**) **a t.,** (a) être sous l'effet du LSD, être du voyage; (b) purger sa peine en prison*, faire sa taule.

trip² [trip] (to), P: **= to take a trip** (**trip**¹, **2** (a)).

tripe [traip] (noun), F: **1.** bêtises*, sornettes f.pl., fichaises f.pl. **2.** camelote f, quincaillerie f.

tripehound [ˈtraiphaund] (noun), P: vaurien*, charogne f.

tripperish [ˈtripəriʃ], **trippery** [ˈtripəri] (adj.), F: envahi de touristes, popu(lo), populmiche.

tripy [ˈtraipi] (adj.), F: camelote, gnognot(t)e; **a t. novel,** roman m sans valeur, navet m.

trizzer [ˈtrizər] (noun) (Austr.), P: W.C.*, chiottes f.pl.

trog [trɔg] (noun), P: **1.** spéléologue m, troglodyte m. **2.** individu vieux jeu, collet monté, vieux tableau, vieille baderne.

trolley [ˈtrɔli] (noun) (U.S.), F: **off one's t. = off one's rocker** (**rocker, 2**).

trot [trɔt] (noun). **1.** F: **on the t.,** (a) à la suite, coup sur coup; **to win four times on the t.,** gagner quatre fois de suite; (b) (après s'être échappé de prison) en fuite, en cavale. **2.** F: **to keep s.o. on the t.,** faire trotter qn, actionner qn. **3.** P: prostituée*, marcheuse f, roulure f. **4.** P: **the trots,** diarrhée*, courante f.

trotter [ˈtrɔtər] (noun), P: **1.** déserteur m, franc-fileur m. **2.** individu recherché par la police, décarreur m. **3.** (pl.) pieds*, trottinets m.pl.

trouble [ˈtrʌbl] (noun). **1.** F: **to get a girl into t.,** rendre une fille enceinte*. **2.** P: **t. and strife** (R.S. = wife), épouse*.

trousers [ˈtrauzəz] (pl. noun), F: **to wear the t.,** (d'une épouse) porter la culotte; cf. **pants, 7.**

trouser-snake [ˈtrauzə-sneik] (noun) (Austr.), P: **one-eyed t.-s.,** pénis*, anguille f de calecif.

trout [traut] (noun), P: vieille femme*,

---

* An asterisk indicates that the word so marked is included as a head-word in the Appendix.

vieille savate, vieux trumeau, vieille guenon, vieille rombière, charogne *f*.

truck-driver [ˈtrʌkdraivər] (*noun*), *P*: = **driver, 2**.

trump [trʌmp] (*noun*), *F*: **1**. brave homme*, chic type *m*. **2**. **to turn up trumps**, (*a*) réussir mieux que l'on espérait, avoir de la chance*; (*b*) rendre service donner un bon coup de main. *Voir aussi* **card, 7**.

trusty [ˈtrʌsti] (*noun*), *F*: prisonnier *m* à qui l'on donne certains privilèges, un sûr, un prévot.

try [trai] (*noun*), *F*: **just (you) have a t.!** = **just (you) try it on!** (*voir* **try on (to)**).

tryanthewontigong [ˈtrai-ænθiˈwɔntigɔŋ] (*noun*) (*Austr.*), *F*: = **thingamy**.

try-on [ˈtraiɔn] (*noun*), *F*: **1**. ballon *m* d'essai. **2**. (coup *m* de) bluff *m*.

try on [ˈtraiˈɔn] (**to**), *F*: **don't (you) t. it o. with me!** ne cherche pas à me bluffer (*ou* à me mettre dedans)! il ne faut pas me la refaire!; **just (you) t. it o.! chiche!** vas-y qu'on voit!

try-out [ˈtrai-aut] (*noun*), *F*: premier essai, essai préliminaire (*ou* préalable).

tub [tʌb] (*noun*), *F*: **1**. gros ventre*, bedaine *f*. **2**. **old t. (of a boat)**, raf(f)iot *m*.

tube [tjuːb] (*noun*), *F*: **1**. **it's my tubes** [miˈtjuːbz], c'est mes bronches. **2**. **the T.**, le Métro; **we came by T.**, nous avons pris le Métro. *Voir aussi* **test-tube**.

tub-thumper [ˈtʌbθʌmpər] (*noun*), *F*: = **soapbox orator**.

tuck [tʌk] (*noun*), *F*: (*école*) friandises *f.pl.*, sucreries *f.pl.*; *cf.* **tuckshop**.

tuck away [ˈtʌkəˈwei] (**to**), *F*: **1**. mettre à gauche. **2**. **to t. it a.**, boire* et/ou manger*, s'en mettre derrière la cravate, s'en mettre jusque-là, se caler les côtes.

tucker [ˈtʌkər] (*noun*) (*Austr.*), *F*: nourriture*, mangeaille *f*. *Voir aussi* **bib**.

tuckered [ˈtʌkəd] (*adj.*), *P*: fatigué*, éreinté, vanné.

tuck-in [ˈtʌkˈin] (*noun*), *F*: repas faramineux, gueuleton *m*, bombance *f*; **to have a good t.-i.** = **tuck in (to)**.

tuck in [ˈtʌkˈin] (**to**), *F*: manger* de bon cœur, s'en mettre jusqu'au menton, s'en mettre plein la lampe; **t. i.!** vas-y, mange!

tuck into [ˈtʌkˈintuː] (**to**), *F*: **to t. i. a meal**, manger* un repas à belles dents, faire bonne chère.

tucks [tʌks] (*pl. noun*), *F*: **to be in t.**, se tordre de rire*, se fendre la bouille, être plié en deux.

tuckshop [ˈtʌkʃɔp] (*noun*), *F*: (*école*) annexe *f* de la cantine où se vendent les friandises *f.pl.*; *cf.* **tuck**.

tumble[1] [ˈtʌmbl] (*noun*), *F*: **to have a t. with** = **tumble**[2] (**to**), **1**.

tumble[2] [ˈtʌmbl] (**to**), *F*: **1**. **to t. (a woman)**, culbuter (une femme). **2**. **to t. to sth.**, comprendre qch. tout à coup, entraver qch.

tummy [ˈtʌmi] (*noun*), *F*: (*a*) ventre*, bide *m*, bidon *m*; (*b*) bedaine *f*.

tummy-ache [ˈtʌmi-eik] (*noun*), *F*: mal *m* au ventre.

tune [tjuːn] (*noun*), *F*: **1**. **to the t. of . . .**, pour la somme (pas mal salée) de... **2**. **to change one's t.**, changer de ton (*ou* de langage), chanter sur une autre note. *Voir aussi* **old, 5**.

tune in [ˈtjuːnˈin] (**to**), *F*: **1**. se mettre au diapason. **2**. être pris dans l'engrenage *m*.

tune up [ˈtjuːnˈʌp] (**to**), *F*: se conditionner, s'entraîner.

tup [tʌp] (**to**), *P*: coïter* avec (une femme), calecer, caramboler, sch(e)-nailler.

tuppence [ˈtʌp(ə)ns] (*noun*) (=*twopence*), *F*: **I don't care t.**, ça m'est bien égal, je m'en fiche pas mal; **it's not worth t.**, ça ne vaut pas deux sous, ça ne vaut pas chipette.

tuppenny [ˈtʌp(ə)ni] (*adj.*) (=*twopenny*), *F*: **I don't give (**or** care) a t. damn (**or** V: fuck)**, je m'en contre-fiche, *V*: je m'en fous pas mal; *cf.* **damn**[3].

tuppenny-ha'penny [ˈtʌp(ə)niˈheip(ə)ni] (*adj.*) (=*twopenny-halfpenny*), *F*: insignifiant, piètre, de quatre sous.

tupp'ny [ˈtʌpni] (*adj.*) = **tuppenny**.

turd [təːd] (*noun*), *P*: **1**. étron*, colombin *m*. **2**. saligaud *m*, salaud *m*, fumier *m*. **3**. **to skin a t.**, être avare*, être constipé du morlingue.

turd-burglar [ˈtəːdbəːglər], **turd-snipper** [ˈtəːd-snipər], *V*: pédéraste*, qui est de la bague (*ou* du rond).

turf [təːf] (*noun*) (*U.S.*), *P*: **to be on the t.**, racoler*, faire le bitume (*ou* le trottoir *ou* le pavé).

---

* L'astérisque indique que le mot marqué de ce signe figure comme entrée dans le Répertoire.

turf out [ˈtəːˈfaut] **(to),** *F:* flanquer dehors, balancer, envoyer dinguer.

turk, Turk [təːk] *(noun),* *F:* (little) t., petit démon, sale gosse *m*, vermine *f*.

turkey [ˈtəːki] *(noun).* **1.** *P:* **cold t.,** sevrage *m* de drogues. **2.** *F:* **to talk t.,** parler* sérieusement, en venir au fait.

turn [təːn] *(noun), F:* **1.** *(a)* **it gave me quite a (nasty) t.,** (tout) mon sang n'a fait qu'un tour; *(b)* **you gave me such a t.!** vous m'avez fait une belle peur*! vous m'avez retourné le sang! **2. she had one of her turns yesterday,** hier elle a eu une de ses crises (*ou* attaques).

turn-about-face [ˈtəːnəbautˈfeis] *(noun), F:* volte-face *f*.

turned on [ˈtəːndˈɔn] *(p.p. & adj.), F:* = **switched on, 1, 2, 3.**

turn in [ˈtəːnˈin] **(to),** *F:* **1.** se coucher*, se pieuter. **2.** rendre, rapporter (qch.); **to t. oneself i. (to the police),** se constituer prisonnier, se faire coffrer.

turniphead [ˈtəːniphed] *(noun), P:* individu bête*, cruche *f*, ballot *m*.

turn-on [ˈtəːnɔn] *(noun), P:* une séance particulière de drogues.

turn on [ˈtəːnˈɔn] **(to)** = **switch on (to), 1, 2, 3.**

turnout [ˈtəːnaut] *(noun).* **1.** *F:* assemblée *f*, foule *f*, assistance *f*, auditoire *m*, public *m*. **2.** *F:* vêtements*, tenue *f*, uniforme *m*. **3.** *P:* coït* d'un groupe avec une seule fille ou femme; dérouillage *m* à la une.

turnover [ˈtəːnouvər] *(noun), P:* perquisition *f*, fouille *f*.

turn over [ˈtəːnˈouvər] **(to),** *P:* **1. to t. s.o. o.,** voler*, refaire qn, rouler qn. **2. to t. o. a cell,** fouiller une cellule.

turn-up [ˈtəːnʌp] *(noun), P:* **1. that's a t.-u. (for the book),** c'est une sacrée surprise. **2.** chahut *m*, tapage *m*, boucan *m*, chambard *m*.

turn up [ˈtəːnˈʌp] **(to),** *F:* **1.** arriver* (à l'improviste), débarquer, faire une apparition. **2.** arriver, se passer, se produire. **3.** découvrir*, trouver, dégot(t)er. **4. that turns me up,** ça m'écœure, ça me soulève le cœur. **5. t. it u.!** arrête (les frais)! c'est marre! *Voir aussi* **nose, 6; toe, 3.**

turps [təːps] *(noun)* (=*turpentine*), *F:* (essence *f* de) térébenthine *f*.

turtles [ˈtəːtlz] *(pl. noun), P:* (*R.S.* = *turtle-doves* = *gloves*) gants *m.pl.*

twack [twæk], **twam(my)** [ˈtwæm(i)] *(noun), P:* = **twat, 1.**

twang [twæŋ] *(noun)* (*Austr.*), *P:* opium *m* (*drogues**), touffiane *f*.

twat [twɔt] *(noun).* **1.** *V:* vagin*, con *m*, con(n)asse *f*. **2.** *P:* individu bête*, idiot *m*, con *m*, connard *m*.

twee [twiː] *(adj.), F: (a)* gentil, mignon; *(b)* (*péj.*) maniéré, mignard.

tweetie(-pie) [ˈtwiːti(ˈpai)] *(noun), F:* = **sweetie(-pie).**

twenty-five [ˈtwentiˈfaiv] *(noun), P:* LSD *m* (*drogues**), vingt-cinq *m*.

twerp [twəːp] *(noun), F:* individu bête*, ballot *m*, crétin *m*.

twiddly [ˈtwidli] *(adj.), F:* **t. bits,** *(a)* (*musique*) enjolivure *f*; *(b)* fanfreluche *f*, colifichet *m*.

twig [twig] **(to),** *P:* comprendre, saisir, piger; **now I t. it!** j'y suis maintenant!

twink [twiŋk] *(noun), P:* pédéraste*, homme efféminé, chochotte *f*, chouquette *f*.

twinkle [ˈtwiŋkl] *(noun), P:* **1.** pénis* (d'enfant), zizi *m*. **2. to have a t.,** uriner*, pisser.

twirl [twəːl] *(noun), P:* **1.** gardien* de prison, maton *m*, matuche *m*. **2.** clef*, passe-partout *m*, carouble *f*. **3.** cigarette*, cibiche *f*.

twirp [twəːp] *(noun), F:* = **twerp.**

twist[1] [twist] *(noun), P:* **1. to go round the t.** = **to go round the bend** (**bend**[1], **1**). **2.** cigarette* de marijuana (*drogues**), stick *m. Voir aussi* **knickers; tassel, 2.**

twist[2] [twist] **(to),** *F:* **1.** escroquer*, frauder, filouter. **2. he likes to have his arm twisted,** il aime se faire prier. *Voir aussi* **burn**[1], **1** *(a)*; **finger**[1], **8.**

twisted [ˈtwistid] *(adj.), P:* chargé, défoncé (par les drogues).

twister [ˈtwistər] *(noun), F:* **1.** faux bonhomme, faux jeton, fripouille *f*, filou *m*. **2.** casse-tête (chinois).

twisty [ˈtwisti] *(adj.), P:* malhonnête, fripouille, filon.

twit [twit] *(noun), P:* individu bête*, ballot *m*, con(n)ard *m*; **he's a hopeless t.,** il en a une couche.

twitter [ˈtwitər] *(noun), F:* **1. to be all of a t.** (*or* **in a t.**), être sens dessus dessous, être dans tous ses états. **2. to have the twitters,** avoir la tremblote (*ou* la trouille). *Voir aussi* **ring**[1], **1.**

---

* An asterisk indicates that the word so marked is included as a head-word in the Appendix.

twitty [ˈtwiti] (*adj.*), *P:* bête*, stupide, con(n)ard.

two [tuː] (*numeral adj. & noun*), *F:* **1.** to put t. and t.together, tirer (*ou* en déduire) ses conclusions. **2.** all the twos: *voir* **bingo** (22). *Voir aussi* **one-two; thing, 6.**

two-bit [ˈtuːˈbit] (*adj.*) (*U.S.*), *F:* insignifiant, à la manque, à la gomme.

two-fisted [ˈtuːˈfistid] (*adj.*), *F:* = **ham-fisted.**

twopenny-halfpenny [ˈtʌp(ə)niˈheip(ə)ni] (*adj.*) = **tuppenny-ha'penny.**

two-piece [ˈtuːpiːs] (*noun*), *P:* testi-cules*, paire *f.*

twot [twɔt] (*noun*) = **twat, 1, 2.**

two-time [ˈtuːˈtaim] (to), *F:* **1.** tromper (qn) (en amour), être infidèle. **2.** duper*, tromper.

two-timer [ˈtuːˈtaimər] (*noun*), *F:* **1.** mari qui trompe sa femme *ou* femme infidèle. **2.** dupeur *m*, roustisseur *m.*

tycoon [taiˈkuːn] (*noun*), *F:* grosse huile, ponte *m*, grand manitou.

tyke [taik] (*noun*), *P:* **1.** natif *m* du comté du Yorkshire. **2.** malotru *m*, rustre *m*, rustaud *m.* **3.** vilain chien*, sale cabot *m.*

U

ugly [ˈʌgli] (adj.) (U.S.), F: abject*, dégueulasse, salingue. Voir aussi cut up (to), 3; plug-ugly.

umpit(t)y [ˈʌmpiti] (adj.), F: en colère*, de mauvaise humeur, en rogne, à cran.

umpteen [ˈʌmptiːn, ʌmpˈtiːn] (adj.), F: je ne sais combien; he has u. children, il a je ne sais combien d'enfants; to have u. reasons for doing sth., avoir trente-six raisons de faire qch.

umpteenth [ˈʌmptiːnθ, ʌmpˈtiːnθ] (adj.), F: trente-sixième, ennième.

umpty [ˈʌm(p)ti] (adj.), P: un peu malade*, mal fichu, pas dans son assiette.

'un [ən] (pron.) (=one), F: individu*, quelqu'un, type m, mec m; a little 'un, un petiot; a wrong 'un, un fripon, un coquin, un chenapan.

unchubb [ˈʌnˈtʃʌb] (to), P: ouvrir*, faire jouer la serrure, débloquer, débrider; cf. chubb in (to); unmiln (to).

Uncle, uncle [ˈʌŋkl] (noun). 1. P: agent* de police, flic m. 2. P: indicateur* (de police), ma tante. 3. P: U. Dick (R.S.), (a) (=prick) pénis*; cf. dick[1]; (b) (=sick) malade*. 4. P: U. Ned (R.S.), (a) (=bed) lit*; (b) (=head) tête*. 5. F: prêteur m (sur gages), tante f; at (my) u.'s, chez ma tante, au clou. 6. F: U. Sam, l'oncle Sam, les États-Unis d'Amérique. 7. P: receleur*, fourgueur m. 8. (U.S.) P: = Sam, 2. 9. (U.S.) F: U. Tom, noir m qui s'insinue dans les bonnes grâces des blancs, Oncle Tom. Voir aussi Bob[2]; Dutch[1], 5.

uncool [ˈʌnˈkuːl] (adj.), P: = cool[1], 5.

under [ˈʌndər] (prep.), F: to be u. the doctor, être en traitement, être sous surveillance médicale.

undergrad [ˈʌndəgræd] (noun) (=undergraduate), F: étudiant(e) (qui n'a pas encore ses diplômes).

underground [ˈʌndəgraund] (adj.), F: révolutionnaire, contestataire.

under-the-counter [ˈʌndəðəˈkauntər]

(adj.), F: au marché noir. Voir aussi counter.

undies [ˈʌndiz] (pl. noun), F: sous-vêtements feminins, lingerie f, dessous m. pl.

unflappable [ˈʌnˈflæpəbl] (adj.), F: flegmatique, calme, qui ne s'affole pas.

un-get-at-able [ˈʌngetˈætəbl] (adj.), F: inaccessible.

unglued [ˈʌnˈgluːd] (adj.) (U.S.), P: 1. frénétique, fᵒrcené, affolé. 2. fou*, loufoque, piqué.

unhitched [ˈʌnˈhitʃt] (adj. & p.p.), F: to get u., divorcer, se séparer, se démaquer; cf. hitch[2] (to), 2.

unlucky [ˈʌnˈlʌki] (adj.), F: u. for some: voir bingo (13).

unmiln [ˈʌnˈmiln] (to), P: = unchubb (to).

unscramble [ˈʌnˈskræmbl] (to), F: (a) débrouiller (un message); (b) I'll try and u. my appointments, j'essaierais de remanier mes rendez-vous*.

unscrewed [ˈʌnˈskruːd] (adj.) (U.S.), P: = unglued, 1, 2.

unstuck [ˈʌnˈstʌk] (adj. & p.p.), F: to come u., (a) (d'un projet, etc.) s'effondrer, s'écrouler, se disloquer; (b) (d'une personne) (i) tomber sur un bec, faire un bide; (ii) s'effondrer, faire la culbute.

unwashed [ˈʌnˈwɔʃt] (adj. & p.p.), F: the Great U., les prolétaires m.pl., les prolos m.pl., les pouilleux m.pl.

up[1] [ʌp] (adj.), F: 1. euphorique dû à la drogue, high, défoncé, planant. 2. u. drugs, drogues stimulantes psychiques; cf. down[1]. 3. heureux, en pleine forme.

up[2] [ʌp] (adv.). 1. F: to be u. against it, avoir la malchance* (ou la guigne ou la déveine). 2. F: to be u. to sth., fabriquer qch., mijoter qch. 3. F: it's all u., the game's u., c'est fichu (ou flambé); voir aussi all[2], 1. 4. F: what's u.? que se passe-t-il? qu'y a-t-il? 5. P: en coït* (avec une femme), en mise. Voir aussi move[1], 2.

up[3] [ʌp] (noun). 1. F: to be on the u. and

---

* An asterisk indicates that the word so marked is included as a head-word in the Appendix.

u., (a) être en bonne voie, prospérer, faire son beurre; (b) être honnête (ou correct ou impec). **2.** P: = **upper**[2]. **3.** F: **to give s.o. a quick u. and down,** jauger qn, faire le tour de qn. Voir aussi **high-ups.**

up[4] [ʌp] (prep.), P: **1. u. yours!** colle (ou fous) ça dans la poche (et ton mouchoir par-dessus)!; tu peux te le mettre (ou te le fourrer) quelque part! cf. **arse, 6; flue, 2; gonga; jacksie, 1; jumper, 1; Khyber. 2.** en coït* avec (une femme). Voir aussi **creek; spout**[1], **1, 3.**

up[5] [ʌp] (to). **1.** F: **to u. sticks,** déménager, décaniller, bouger ses bois m.pl. **2.** P: (a) se lever d'un bond; **then he upped and left the room,** puis d'un bond il se mit debout et quitta la pièce; (b) agir avec élan; **so I ups and tells him what I think,** et je me suis lancé et lui ai dit exactement ce que je pensais.

up-and-downer [ˈʌpənˈdaʊnər] (noun), F: querelle*, prise f de bec, engueulade f, attrapage m.

upbeat [ˈʌpbiːt] (adj.), F: pétillant, fringant, pimpant, euphorique; cf. **downbeat.**

upholstery [ʌpˈhoʊlstəri] (noun), P: = **shelf-kit;** cf. **well-upholstered.**

upper[1] [ˈʌpər] (adj.), F: **1. u. storey,** tête*, cerveau m, ciboulot m; **to be weak in the u. storey,** avoir une araignée dans le plafond. **2. u. bracket,** tête f de liste. **3. u. crust,** les huiles f.pl., la crème, le gratin, le dessus du panier. Voir aussi **lip, 2; ten, 1.**

upper[2] [ˈʌpər], **uppie** [ˈʌpi] (noun), P: amphétamine f (drogues*); cf. **downer, 1; downie.** Voir aussi **uppers.**

uppers [ˈʌpəz] (pl. noun), F: **to be down on one's u.,** être très pauvre*, être dans la purée noire, marcher à côté de ses pompes. Voir aussi **upper**[2].

uppish [ˈʌpiʃ] (adj.), F: = **uppity, 1.**

uppity [ˈʌpiti] (adj.), F: **1.** prétentieux*, arrogant, rogne, crâneur, hautain. **2.** (U.S.) (nègre américain) qui réclame ses droits. **3.** féroce, brutal, sauvage.

ups-a-daisy! [ˈʌpsəˈdeizi] (excl.), F: hoop-là!

upset [ˈʌpset] (noun), F: querelle*, remue-ménage m.

upsides [ˈʌpsaidz] (adv.), F: **to be u. with s.o.,** être quitte avec qn, rendre la pareille à qn.

upstage[1] [ˈʌpˈsteidʒ] (adj.), F: prétentieux*, snob, bêcheur, plastronneur.

upstage[2] [ˈʌpˈsteidʒ] (to), F: **1.** (th.) mettre (un autre acteur) à l'ombre du public, retirer le haut des planches à (un autre acteur). **2.** remettre (qn) à sa place, faire semblant de ne pas voir (qn).

upstairs [ˈʌpˈstɛəz] (adv.), F: **to have sth. u.,** avoir le ciboulot bien rempli, être intelligent. Voir aussi **kick upstairs (to).**

upsy-daisy! [ˈʌpsiˈdeizi] (excl.), F: = **ups-a-daisy!**

uptake [ˈʌpteik] (noun), F: (a) **to be quick on the u.,** comprendre (ou savoir) vite, avoir l'esprit vif (ou éveillé), avoir la comprenette facile; (b) **to be slow on the u.,** avoir la comprenette difficile.

uptight [ˈʌpˈtait] (adj.), F: **1.** tendu, ému, agité. **2.** survolté. **3.** (U.S.) connu à fond, su sur le bout du doigt, notoire. **4.** complexé, inhibé. **5.** fielleux, rancunier.

urger [ˈəːdʒər] (noun) (Austr.), P: = **shill(aber).**

us [ʌs, əs] (pron.) (=me), F: moi; **give u. a kiss!** alors on m'embrasse!; **let's have a look!** laisse-moi regarder!

use [juːz] (to). **1.** F: exploiter, tirer parti de (qn), abuser de (qn). **2.** F: prendre plaisir à, profiter de (qch.); **I could u. a cup of tea,** une tasse de thé me ferait plaisir. **3.** P: se droguer*, se camer.

used up [ˈjuːzdˈʌp] (adj. & p.p.), P: très fatigué*, crevé, claqué.

useful [ˈjuːsful] (adj.), F: efficace, habile; **he's pretty u. with his fists,** il sait bien jouer des poings.

user [ˈjuːzər] (noun), P: drogué*, camé m, toxico m.

usual [ˈjuːʒʊ(ə)l] (noun), F: **the u.,** ce que l'on a (ou prend) d'habitude, l'ordinaire.

---

* L'astérisque indique que le mot marqué de ce signe figure comme entrée dans le Répertoire.

V

vac [væk] (*noun*) (*abbr.* = *vacation*), *F:* vacances *f.pl.*; **the Long V.**, les grandes vacances.

vamoose [vəˈmuːs] (**to**), *P:* s'enfuir*, décamper, filer.

varieties [vəˈraiətiz] (*pl. noun*), *F:* **all the v.**: *voir* **bingo (57)**.

varmint [ˈvɑːmint] (*noun*), *F:* (*a*) vermine *f*; (*b*) **young v.**, verminard *m*, petit polisson.

varnish[1] [ˈvɑːniʃ] (*noun*), *P:* mauvais alcool*, camphre *m*, cogne *f*.

varnish[2] [ˈvɑːniʃ] (**to**), *P:* **to v. the cane**, se masturber*, s'astiquer la colonne.

varsity, Varsity [ˈvɑːsiti] (*noun*), *F:* l'Université *f*, la Faculté, la Fac.

veep [viːp] (*noun*) (*U.S.*), *F:* vice-président *m*.

velvet [ˈvelvit] (*noun*). **1.** *P:* **blue v.**, drogues* (parégorique et antihistamine). **2. black v.**, (*a*) *F:* mélange *m* de champagne et de stout; (*b*) *P:* négresse *f*, bougnoul(l)e *f*. **3.** *F:* **to be on v.**, (*a*) jouer sur le velours; (*b*) vivre comme un prince, mener la vie de château. **4.** *F:* (*a*) bénéfice*, velours *m*, gâteau *m*; (*b*) argent*, galette *f*, galtouze *f*.

verbal [ˈvɑːbəl] (*noun*), *P:* **the v.**, bavardage *m*, bavette *f*.

vet[1] [vet] (*abbr.*), *F:* **1.** (=*veterinary surgeon*) vétérinaire *mf*. **2.** (*U.S.*) (=*veteran*) ancien combattant.

vet[2] [vet] (**to**), *F:* **1.** examiner, soigner, traiter (une bête, qn) (médicalement). **2.** revoir, corriger, mettre au point.

vibes [vaibz] (*pl. noun*) (*abbr.*), *F:* **1.** (*jazz*) vibraphone *m*, vibraharpe *f*, *etc.* **2.** (=*vibrations*) vibrations *f.pl.*

vice [vais] (*noun*) (*abbr.*), *F:* **1.** (=*vice-president, vice-chairman*) vice-président

m, sous-Mec *m*. **2.** (=*vice-chancellor*) recteur *m* (d'une université), recto *m*. **3.** (=*deputy*) substitut *m*, délégué *m*, sous-Mec *m*.

villain [ˈvilən] (*noun*), *F:* **1.** bandit *m*, scélérat *m*. **2.** coquin *m*, garnement *m*; **you little v.!** petit polisson!

villainy [ˈviləni] (*noun*), *F:* **to do a v.**, (*a*) cambrioler*, faire un fric-frac; (*b*) commettre un crime, faire un acte criminel.

vim [vim] (*noun*), *F:* vigueur *f*, force *f*, énergie *f*, vitalité *f*.

vine [vain] (*noun*). **1.** *P:* **the v.** = **the grapevine. 2.** (*pl.*) *P:* vêtements*, fringues *f.pl.*, frusques *f.pl.* **3.** *F:* **clinging v.**, femme* possessive, pot *m* de colle.

vino [ˈviːnou] (*noun*), *P:* vin*, gros rouge, pinard *m*.

V.I.P. [ˈviːaiˈpiː] (*abbr.* = *very important person*), *F:* personnage important, grosse légume, huile *f*; **to give s.o. V.I.P. treatment**, recevoir qn avec la croix et la bannière.

viper [ˈvaipər] (*noun*) (*U.S.*), *P:* (*a*) drogué* à la marijuana; (*b*) fourgueur *m* de marijuana.

visit [ˈvizit] (*noun*), *F:* **to pay a v.**, aller faire pipi, aller faire sa petite commission.

vocab [ˈvoukæb, vəˈkæb] (*noun*) (*abbr.* = *vocabulary*), *F:* vocabulaire *m*.

vocals [ˈvoukəlz] (*pl. noun*), *P:* **to give with the v.**, chanter*, pousser une goualante, y aller de sa goualante.

voyager [ˈvɔiədʒər] (*noun*), *P:* drogué(e)* au LSD, voyageur *m*; *cf.* **trip**[1], **2** (*a*).

---

* An asterisk indicates that the word so marked is included as a head-word in the Appendix.

W

wack [wæk] (noun), P: 1. fou m, fêlé m, cinglé m, détraqué m. 2. excentrique m, original m, farfelu m. 3. = wacker.

wacker ['wækər] (noun), P: ami*, copain m, pote m.

wacky ['wæki] (adj.), P: 1. fou*, fêlé, cinglé, détraqué. 2. excentrique, original, farfelu. 3. de qualité inférieure, camelote.

wad [wɔd] (noun), F: 1. (a) petit pain; (b) sandwich m; tea and a w., casse-croûte m. 2. liasse f de billets* de banque, matelas m de faf(f)iots. 3. abondance*, une bardée (de…), un tas (de…). 4. to shoot one's w., risquer le tout pour le tout, parier sa chemise. Voir aussi tightwad.

wade in ['weid'in] (to), F: s'attaquer à qch., intervenir, s'interposer.

wade into ['weid'intu:] (to), F: 1. to w. i. s.o., (a) attaquer* qn; agrafer qn; (b) critiquer* qn sévèrement, cafarder, éreinter qn. 2. to w. i. sth., entamer un travail, s'y mettre.

waffle¹ ['wɔfl] (noun), F: verbosité f, verbiage m, fariboles f.pl.

waffle² ['wɔfl] (to), F: 1. épiloguer, écrire (ou parler) dans le vague. 2. dire des bêtises*, sortir des niaiseries f.pl. 3. bavarder*, dégoiser, jaboter.

waffle on ['wɔfl'ɔn] (to), F: = waffle² (to), 3.

waffler ['wɔflər] (noun), F: 1. baratineur m. 2. épilogueur m, individu verbeux.

wag¹ [wæg] (noun), F: to hop the w., vagabonder, faire l'école buissonnière.

wag² [wæg] (to), F: to w. it = to hop the wag (wag¹).

wag(g)on ['wægən] (noun), F: 1. to be on the (water) w., s'abstenir de boissons alcooliques, être buveur d'eau, être au régime sec; to be off the w., s'adonner à la boisson. 2. (U.S.) to fix s.o.'s w., se venger sur qn, avoir qn au tournant. Voir aussi bandwagon; cop-wagon; holler-wag(g)on; meat-wag(g)on; milk-wag(g)on; paddy-wag(g)on.

wag out ['wæg'aut] (to), P: devenir

défoncé par la drogue, glisser dans le high.

wake-up ['weikʌp] (noun), P: 1. première piqûre de drogues du matin. 2. amphétamine f (drogues*). 3. dernier jour de prison*.

wakey(-wakey)! ['weiki('weiki)] (excl.), F: 1. réveille-toi! debout! au jus! 2. secoue-toi! secoue tes puces!

walk [wɔːk] (to), F: 1. (sports) to w. it, arriver dans un fauteuil. 2. (d'un article) disparaître, passer à l'as. Voir aussi jaywalk (to).

walk-about ['wɔːkəbaut] (noun), F: bain m de foule.

walk-away ['wɔːkəwei] (noun), F: = walkover.

walk away ['wɔːkəˈwei] (to), F: 1. to w. a. with sth. = to walk off with sth. 2. to w. a. from a competitor, semer un concurrent.

walkie-talkie ['wɔːkiˈtɔːki] (noun), F: walkie-talkie m, talkie-walkie m.

walking-sticks ['wɔːkiŋ-stiks] (pl. noun), F: voir bingo (77).

walk into ['wɔːkˈintu:] (to), F: attaquer* (qn), enguirlander (qn).

walk off ['wɔːkˈɔf] (to), F: to w. o. with sth., voler* qch., faucher qch., ratiboiser qch.

walk-out ['wɔːkaut] (noun), F: grève f, mise f à bas.

walk out ['wɔːkˈaut] (to), F: 1. se mettre en grève. 2. to w. o. on s.o., abandonner* qn, lâcher qn, plaquer qn.

walkover ['wɔːkouvər] (noun), F: victoire f facile (ou dans un fauteuil ou les doigts dans le nez), promenade f.

walk over ['wɔːkˈouvər] (to), F: to w. all o. s.o., agir abominablement envers qn, traiter qn par-dessus la jambe (ou comme du poisson pourri).

wall [wɔːl] (noun), F: 1. to be up the w., (a) (d'une personne) être fou*, être cinglé; (b) (d'une chose) être trompeur. 2. to drive s.o. up the w., rendre qn fou*, taper sur les nerfs (ou le système) à qn.

---

* L'astérisque indique que le mot marqué de ce signe figure comme entrée dans le Répertoire.

3. to go to the w., (a) succomber; (b) perdre la partie; (c) faire faillite. **4. to go over the w.**, s'échapper de prison*, faire le mur. **5. to hit** (or **knock** or **run**) **one's head against a** (**brick**) **w.**, **to come up against a blank w.**, ne rien tirer de qn; se heurter contre une porte de prison, se buter à l'impossible. **6. he can see through a brick w.**, il a le nez fin. **7. you might just as well talk to a brick w.**, autant vaut parler à un sourd. Voir aussi back², 7.

walla [ˈwɔlə] (noun), F: = **wallah**.

wallaby [ˈwɔləbi] (noun), F: Australien m.

wallah [ˈwɔlə] (noun), F: **1.** individu*, homme*. **2.** (av.) **ground w.**, rampant m; **ground wallahs**, personnel m de terre.

wall-eyed [ˈwɔːlˈaid] (adj.), P: ivre*, raide, rétamé.

wallflower [ˈwɔːl-flauər] (noun). **1.** F: fille qui, à un bal, n'est pas invitée à danser; **to be a w.**, faire tapisserie. **2.** (U.S.) P: = **bar-fly**, 2.

wallop¹ [ˈwɔləp] (adv.), F: **smack** (or **slap**), **bang**, **w.!** pan, vlan, boum!; voir aussi **slap-bang(-wallop)**.

wallop² [ˈwɔləp] (noun). **1.** F: gros coup*, torgn(i)ole f. **2.** F: **and down he went with a w.!** et patatras, le voilà par terre! **3.** P: bière f; cf. **codswallop**, 2.

wallop³ [ˈwɔləp] (to), F: **1.** battre* (qn), rosser (qn), flanquer une tournée à (qn). **2.** vaincre, écraser, griller (qn).

walloping¹ [ˈwɔləpiŋ] (adj.), F: énorme, fantastique, phénoménal.

walloping² [ˈwɔləpiŋ] (noun), F: **to give s.o. a w.**, (a) donner une volée de coups* à qn, donner une roulée (ou une raclée) à qn; (b) battre qn à plate(s) couture(s).

wally [ˈwɔli] (noun), P: pénis*, frétillard m.

waltz into [ˈwɔlsˈintuː] (to), F: **1.** se taper dans (qn ou qch.). **2.** = **wade into** (to), **1** (a).

waltz off [ˈwɔːlsˈɔf] (to), F: partir*, déhotter, jouer rip.

wampum [ˈwɔmpəm] (noun) (U.S.), P: argent*, fric m.

wangle¹ [ˈwæŋgl] (noun), F: moyen détourné, truc m malhonnête, manigance f.

wangle² [ˈwæŋgl] (to), F: **1.** cuisiner, resquiller. **2.** obtenir par subterfuge, manigancer, carotter. **3.** pratiquer le

système D, se débrouiller.

wangle-dangle [ˈwæŋglˈdæŋgl] (noun), P: = **dingle-dangle**.

wangler [ˈwæŋglər] (noun), F: fricoteur m, carotteur m, resquilleur m.

wangling [ˈwæŋgliŋ] (noun), F: fricotage m, resquille f.

wank¹ [wæŋk] (noun), V: **to have a w.**, se masturber*, tirer son coup, se l'astiquer, se branler.

wank² [wæŋk] (to), V: **to w.** (**oneself off**) = **to have a wank** (**wank¹**).

wanker [ˈwæŋkər] (noun), V: **1.** masturbateur m, branleur m. **2. w.'s doom**, masturbation excessive.

wanna [ˈwɔnə] (to) (=**want to**), F: vouloir.

want [wɔnt] (to), F: **1. you don't w. much, do you!** (iron.), tu ne doutes de rien! **2.** (a) **to w. in**, vouloir participer à qch., vouloir être dans le coup; (b) **to w. out**, vouloir se retirer, retirer ses marrons du feu.

war [wɔː] (noun), F: **to be in the wars**, être malmené, être tarabusté.

warb [wɔːb] (noun) (Austr.), P: **1.** ouvrier m, prolétaire m, prolo m. **2.** personne sale* ou désordonnée, souillon m, salope f, cochon m.

warby [ˈwɔːbi] (adj.) (Austr.), P: sale*, désordonné, salingue, crado, craspignol.

war-horse [ˈwɔːhɔːs] (noun), F: **an old w.-h.**, (a) un vieux soldat*; (b) un vétéran de la politique.

warm [wɔːm] (adj.), F: **1. to be** (**getting**) **w.**, être sur le point de trouver qch., brûler. **2. to make things** (or **it**) **w. for s.o.**, punir qn, en faire baver à qn. **3.** riche*, flambant, galetteux.

war-paint [ˈwɔːpeint] (noun), F: maquillage m, badigeon(nage) m; **to put on the w.-p.**, se maquiller*, faire le (ou son) ravalement.

war-path [ˈwɔːpɑːθ] (noun), F: **to be on the w.-p.**, être sur le sentier de la guerre, chercher noise; **the boss is on the w.-p.**, le patron* est d'une humeur massacrante.

wash¹ [wɔʃ] (noun), F: **1. to hold up in the w.**, tenir à l'usage. **2. to come out in the w.**, (a) être révélé un jour ou l'autre; (b) se tasser. Voir aussi **bellywash**; **eyewash**; **hogwash**; **pigwash**; **whitewash¹**.

wash² [wɔʃ] (to), F: **it won't w. with me**,

---

cela ne prend pas, cela ne passe pas. *Voir aussi,* **linen; whitewash**[2] **(to).**

washed out [ˈwɔʃtˈaʊt] *(adj.)*, *F:* **1.** = **washed up, 1. 2.** annulé, supprimé.

washed up [ˈwɔʃtˈʌp] *(adj.)*, *F:* **1.** fatigué*, exténué, vanné, lessivé. **2.** mis au rancart, fichu en l'air.

washer-upper [ˈwɔʃəˈrʌpər] *(noun)*, *F:* qn qui fait la vaisselle, plongeur *m*.

washing [ˈwɔʃiŋ] *(noun)*, *F:* **to take in one another's w.,** se rendre mutuellement service.

washout [ˈwɔʃaʊt] *(noun)*, *F:* **1.** échec*, fiasco *m*. **2.** raté *m*, propre à rien, fruit sec.

wash out [ˈwɔʃˈaʊt] **(to),** *F:* **you can w. that right o.,** il ne faut pas compter là-dessus, barre cela de tes tablettes; **the best thing is to w. o. the whole business,** mieux vaut passer l'éponge là-dessus.

wasp [wɔsp] *(noun)* *(U.S.)*, *P:* (=*white Anglo-Saxon Protestant*) parpaillot *m*.

watch [wɔtʃ] **(to),** *F:* **w. it!** attention! fais gaffe! acré! gare!

water [ˈwɔːtər] *(noun)*, *F:* **1. to pour cold w. on sth.,** jeter une douche froide sur qch. **2. to keep one's head above w.,** réussir tant bien que mal, surnager, se maintenir sur l'eau. **3. to hold w.,** avoir du sens, tenir debout. **4. to be in low w.,** *(a)* être sans le sou, être dans les eaux basses; *(b)* être déprimé, être dans le troisième dessous. *Voir aussi* **bathwater; bilge-water; bridgewater; dishwater; ditchwater; duck**[1], **8; fire-water; hell, 17; hot, 14; jerkwater; wag(g)on, 1.**

waterworks [ˈwɔːtəwəːks] *(pl. noun)*, *F:* **to turn on the w.,** *(a)* se mettre à pleurer*, ouvrir les écluses *f.pl.*, gicler des mirettes *f.pl.*; *(b)* uriner*, faire pipi.

wavelength [ˈweivleŋθ] *(noun)*, *F:* **on the same w.,** sur la même longueur d'ondes; *cf.* **beam, 1.**

wavy [ˈweivi] *(adj.)*, *F:* **the W. Navy** (*W.W.II* = *Royal Naval Volunteer Reserve*), réservistes *m.pl.* de la Marine.

wax [wæks] *(noun)*, *F:* accès *m* de colère, crise *f*, rage *f*.

waxy [ˈwæksi] *(adj.)*, *F:* en colère, en rogne.

way[1] [wei] *(adv.)* (=*away*), *F:* **it was w. back in 1900,** cela remonte à 1900.

way[2] [wei] *(noun)*, *F:* **1. all the w.,** *(a)* complètement, sans réserve, à bloc; **I'll**

go all the w. with you on that, là-dessus, je te soutiendrai jusqu'à la gauche; *(b)* jusqu'à une complète satisfaction sexuelle; **to go all the w.,** casser la canne jusqu'au bout. **2.** *(a)* **to go for s.o., sth., in a big w.,** s'emballer follement pour qn, qch.; *(b)* **to do sth. in a big w.,** mettre les petits plats dans les grands. **3. to know one's w. about** (*or* **around**), être malin*, être roublard (*ou* démerdard). **4. to put s.o. out of the w.,** se débarrasser* de qn, virer qn, vider qn. **5. down our w.,** chez nous. **6. no w.,** balpeau, des clous, que dalle, que pouic. **7. any w. round:** *voir* **bingo (69).** *Voir aussi* **family, 1.**

way out [ˈweiˈaʊt] *(adj.)*, *F:* **1.** anticonformiste, outré. **2.** original, excentrique. **3.** dans l'erreur, gour(r)é, fichu dedans.

weapon [ˈwepən] *(noun)*, *P:* pénis*, carabine *f*, arbalète *f*.

wear[1] [wɛər] *(noun)*, *F:* **to feel the worse for w.,** avoir la gueule de bois.

wear[2] [wɛər] **(to),** *F:* admettre, tolérer, fermer les yeux sur; **he won't w. it.,** ne consentira pas, il ne marchera pas.

weasel out [ˈwiːzlˈaʊt] **(to),** *F:* se défiler, se rétracter.

weather [ˈweðər] *(noun)*, *F:* **under the w.,** *(a)* malade*, patraque; *(b)* déprimé, qui n'a pas le moral. *Voir aussi* **fairweather; heavy**[1], **3.**

weave [wiːv] **(to),** *F:* **to get weaving,** s'y mettre, se lancer; **get weaving!** vas-y!

wedge [wedʒ] *(noun)*, *P:* LSD *m* (*drogues**).

wee [wiː] *(noun & verb)*, *F:* = **wee-wee**[1,2].

weed [wiːd] *(noun)*, *F:* **1.** *(a)* cigare*; *(b)* cigarette*; *(c)* tabac*, perlot *m*. **2.** marijuana *f* (*drogues**), chiendent *m*, herbe *f*; **to be on the w.,** être esclave des cigarettes* de marijuana, marcher au chiendent; *voir aussi* **giggle, 4; loveweed. 3.** personne étique (*ou* malingre *ou* chétive); chiffe *f*.

weedhead [ˈwiːdhed] *(noun)*, *P:* habitué(e) de la marijuana.

weed-tea [ˈwiːdˈtiː] *(noun)*, *P:* marijuana *f* (*drogues**), thé (vert).

week [wiːk] *(noun)*, *F:* **to knock s.o. into the middle of next w.,** donner à qn un fameux coup*, envoyer valdinguer qn.

weener [ˈwiːnər] *(noun)*, *P:* = **weeny**[2].

---

* L'astérisque indique que le mot marqué de ce signe figure comme entrée dans le Répertoire.

weeny¹ [ˈwiːni] (adj.), F: minuscule, menu; cf. teeny-weeny.

weeny² [ˈwiːni] (noun), P: pénis*, petit frère.

weepers [ˈwiːpəz] (pl. noun), F: favoris m.pl. (barbe*), côtelettes f.pl., pattes f.pl. de lapin.

weeping [ˈwiːpiŋ] (adj.), P: w. willow (R.S. = pillow), oreiller m.

weepy [ˈwiːpi] (noun), F: film (livre, etc.) larmoyant.

wee-wee¹ [ˈwiːwiː] (noun), (langage enfantin) F: pipi m; to do w.-w. = (go) wee-wee² (to).

wee-wee² [ˈwiːwiː] (to), (langage enfantin) F: to (go) w.-w., uriner*, faire pipi.

weigh in [ˈweiˈin] (to), F: arriver*, s'amener.

weigh off [ˈweiˈof] (to), P: juger, condamner, gerber, saper; cf. Follies.

weight [weit] (noun), F: to take the w. off (one's feet), s'asseoir, poser ses fesses*. Voir aussi chuck about (to), 2; lightweight.

weirdie [ˈwiədi], weirdo [ˈwiədou], weirdy [ˈwiədi] (noun), F: individu étrange, excentrique m, olibrius m, drôle m de coco.

welcome-mat [ˈwelkəmˈmæt] (noun), F: to put out the w.-m. for s.o., accueillir qn à bras ouverts.

well-endowed [ˈwelenˈdaud], well-equipped [ˈweliˈkwipt] (adj.), F: 1. (homme) riche en géniteurs m.pl. (ou en bijoux de famille). 2. (femme) aux seins* développés, à la belle devanture; cf. well-stacked; well-upholstered, 1.

well-fixed [ˈwelˈfikst], well-heeled [ˈwelˈhiːld] (adj.), F: riche*, plein aux as, rupin, galetteux.

wellies [ˈweliz] (pl. noun), F: bottes f.pl. en caoutchouc.

well-lined [ˈwelˈlaind] (adj.), F: = well-fixed.

well-off [ˈwelˈof] (adj.), F: 1. to be w.-o., être riche*, avoir de quoi. 2. you don't know when you're w.-o., vous ne connaissez pas votre bonheur. 3. to be w.-o. for sth., être bien pourvu de qch.

well-stacked [ˈwelˈstækt] (adj.), F: 1. = well-fixed. 2. = well-endowed, 2.

well-upholstered [ˈwelʌpˈhoulstəd] (adj.), F: 1. = well-endowed, 2; cf. upholstery. 2. grassouillet, bien rembourré.

welsh [welʃ] (to), F: partir* sans payer, se refuser à payer une dette, poser une ardoise, planter un drapeau; to w. on s.o., manquer à une obligation, chier dans les doigts à qn.

welsher [ˈwelʃər] (noun), F: tire-au-cul m, tire-au-flanc m.

welt [welt] (to), P: battre*, rosser, flanquer une raclée à (qn).

wench [wentʃ] (noun), F: 1. fille*, gaillarde f. 2. prostituée*, traînée f.

wencher [ˈwentʃər] (noun), F: = wolf¹, 1.

west [west] (adv.), F: to go w., (a) mourir*, casser sa pipe; (b) (vêtements) s'user, être fichus; (c) (d'une affaire) faire faillite, passer en lunette; (d) that's another fiver gone w., encore un billet (ou un faf(f)iot) de claqué.

wet¹ [wet] (adj.). 1. F: he's a bit w., il est plutôt bête*, c'est une vraie nouille. 2. F: w. blanket, rabat-joie m. 3. F: à l'eau de rose. 4. (U.S.) F: qui a la permission de vendre de l'alcool. 5. F: to be w. behind the ears, être né d'hier, être né de la dernière pluie; cf. dry, 2. 6. F: w. sock, main* molle et flasque. 7. F: to be all w., se fourrer le doigt dans l'œil. 8. P: the w. season, menstrues*. Voir aussi dream², 2; rag¹, 11.

wet² [wet] (noun), F: 1. individu bête*, nouille f, andouille f. 2. to have a w., boire* un coup, se rincer la dalle.

wet³ [wet] (to), F: to w. the baby's head, arroser la naissance d'un bébé; boire* un coup, prendre un pot. Voir aussi whistle¹, 1.

wet-head [ˈwethed] (noun), F: = wet², 1.

whack¹ [(h)wæk] (noun). 1. F: coup*, taloche f, torgnole f. 2. F: to have a w., tenter, faire un essai. 3. F: to get a good w., avoir un bon salaire, toucher un bon paquet. 4. P: = wack, 1, 2. 5. F: part f, portion f.

whack² [(h)wæk] (to). 1. F: battre*, rosser, bourrer de coups*. 2. F: battre, rouler (une équipe, etc.); vaincre, défaire. 3. P: partager, répartir.

whacked [(h)wækt] (adj.), F: fatigué*, éreinté, vanné.

whacker [ˈ(h)wækər] (noun), F: 1. qch. de colossal; énormité f, mastodonte m. 2. gros mensonge*, sacré bourrage de crâne; what a w.! en voilà une (d'un peu) forte! Voir aussi bush-whacker.

---

whacking[1] [ˈ(h)wækiŋ] (*adj.*), *F:* énorme, maousse, bœuf. '

whacking[2] [ˈ(h)wækiŋ] (*noun*), *F:* rossée *f*, raclée *f*, volée *f* de coups*.

whacko! [ˈ(h)wækou] (*excl.*), *F:* magnifique! épatant! formid!

whack up [ˈ(h)wækˈʌp] (to). **1.** *F:* to w. u. the pace, aller plus vite*, forcer (*ou* allonger) le pas. **2.** *F:* augmenter (prix, etc.). **3.** *P:* diviser et partager en parts égales. **4.** *P:* distribuer un butin* *ou* un gain, fader le barbotin.

whacky [ˈ(h)wæki] (*adj.*), *P:* = wacky, **1, 2, 3.**

whale [(h)weil] (*noun*), *F:* **1.** we had a w. of a time, on s'est follement amusé. **2.** to be a w. at sth., être un as (*ou* un crack) à qch. **3.** to have a w. for sth., être engoué (*ou* enthousiasmé) par qch.

wham [(h)wæm] (to). **1.** *F:* battre*, frapper fort, botter, assaisonner. **2.** *P:* coïter* avec (une femme), envoyer en l'air.

wham-bam [ˈ(h)wæmˈbæm] (*noun*) (*U.S.*), *P:* coït* rapide et sans tendresse; bourre *f*.

whammy [ˈ(h)wæmi] (*noun*), *F:* **1.** a w. of a smile, un large sourire, un sourire éclatant. **2.** (*U.S.*) to put the w. on, mettre des bâtons dans les roues.

whang[1] [(h)wæŋ] (*noun*), *P:* pénis*, berdouillette *f*.

whang[2] [(h)wæŋ] (to), *P:* **1.** frapper fortement, mettre en pièces. **2.** = bung[2] (to), **1, 2.**

whank [(h)wæŋk] (*noun & verb*), *V:* = wank[1,2].

what-all [ˈ(h)wɔtɔːl] (*noun*), *F:* . . . and I don't know w.-a., . . . et je ne sais quoi encore.

whatcha(ma)callit [ˈ(h)wɔtʃə(mə)ˈkɔːlit], **what-do-you-call-it** [ˈ(h)wɔtdjuːˈkɔːlit], **what-d'ye-call-it** [ˈ(h)wɔtdjəˈkɔːlit] (*noun*), *F:* machin *m*, chose *m*, machin-chose *m*.

what-for [ˈ(h)wɔtˈfɔːr] (*noun*), *F:* to give s.o. w.-f., réprimander* qn, laver la tête à qn, flanquer une bonne raclée à qn.

what-ho! [ˈ(h)wɔtˈhou] (*excl.*), *F:* **1.** eh bien! eh alors! **2.** salut!

whatnot [ˈ(h)wɔtnɔt] (*noun*), *F:* = whatcha(ma)callit.

what's-(h)er-name [ˈ(h)wɔtsəneim] (*noun*), *F:* Madame Machin-Truc.

what's-(h)is-name [ˈ(h)wɔtsizneim] (*noun*), *F:* Monsieur Machin-Truc.

whatsit [ˈ(h)wɔtsit] (*noun*). **1.** *F:* = whatcha(ma)callit. **2.** *P:* Willie's w.: *voir* bingo (**1**).

what-you-may-call-it [ˈ(h)wɔtʃəməˈkɔːlit] (*noun*), *F:* = whatcha(ma)callit.

wheel[1] [(h)wiːl] (*noun*), *F:* **1.** there are wheels within wheels, les rouages (de la chose) sont très compliqués. **2.** big w. = big shot (big[1], **1**). **3.** to take (over) the w., prendre la barre, prendre les commandes. **4.** it greases the wheels, cela fait marcher les affaires, cela graisse les roues. *Voir aussi* cartwheel.

wheel[2] [(h)wiːl] (to), *F:* to w. and deal, brasser des affaires plus ou moins louches.

wheeler-dealer [ˈ(h)wiːləˈdiːlər] (*noun*), *F:* brasseur *m* d'affaires louches, arrangeman *m*.

wheeze [(h)wiːz] (*noun*), *F:* ruse *f*, artifice *m*, truc *m*.

wheezy [ˈ(h)wiːzi] (*adj.*), *F:* poussif.

whelk [wilk, welk] (*noun*), *P:* crachat*, glaviot *m*.

wherewithal [ˈ(h)wɛəwiðɑːl] (*noun*), *F:* the w., argent*, le Saint-Fric.

whet [(h)wet] (*noun*), *F:* to have a w. = to have a wet (wet[2], **2**).

whiffy [ˈ(h)wifi] (*adj.*), *P:* = nifty, **3**; *cf.* niffy.

whing-ding [ˈ(h)wiŋdiŋ] (*noun*) (*U.S.*), *P:* = wing-ding.

whinge [(h)windʒ] (to) (*Austr.*), *F:* grogner*, bougonner, râler.

whingy [ˈ(h)windʒi] (*adj.*), *F:* geignard, grincheux, grognon.

whip[1] [(h)wip] (*noun*), *F:* **1.** to get a fair crack of the w., avoir sa (bonne) part, en tirer un bon parti; *cf.* shake[1], **3**. **2.** to hold the w. hand (*U.S.:* handle), avoir le dessus. **3.** (*Austr.*) whips of . . . = tons of . . . (ton, **2**). **4.** to crack the w., montrer le fouet, faire preuve d'autorité.

whip[2] [(h)wip] (to). **1.** *F:* battre*, rosser, dérouiller, passer à tabac. **2.** *P:* voler*, faucher, piquer. **3.** *F:* vaincre, battre à plate(s) couture(s), tailler en pièces. **4.** *P:* w. it to me! = sock it to me! (sock[2] (to), **2**).

whipcracker [ˈ(h)wipkrækər] (*noun*), *F:* individu* à po(i)gne pète-sec *mf*.

whipped [(h)wipt] (*adj.*), *F:* très fatigué*, vanné, occis.

---

* L'astérisque indique que le mot marqué de ce signe figure comme entrée dans le Répertoire.

whipper-snapper [ˈ(h)wipə-snæpər] (*noun*), *F:* freluquet *m*, paltoquet *m*.

whippy [ˈ(h)wipi] (*adj.*), *F:* agile, leste, preste.

whip-round [ˈ(h)wipˈraund] (*noun*), *F:* to have a w.-r. for s.o., faire une collecte (*ou* un appel) en faveur de qn, faire la (*ou* une) manche à qn.

whip through [ˈ(h)wipˈθruː] (to), *F:* faire (qch.) rapidement, bâcler, liquider.

whip up [ˈ(h)wipˈʌp] (to), *F:* 1. to w. u. a meal, préparer (*ou* fricoter) un repas rapidement, faire un repas à la va-vite. 2. to w. u. one's friends, rallier ses amis.

whirl [(h)wəːl] (*noun*), *F:* to give sth. a w., essayer qch., faire l'essai de qch.

whirly-bird [ˈ(h)wəːlibəːd] (*noun*) (*U.S.*), *F:* hélicoptère *m*, battoir *m* (à œufs).

whirly-boy, -girl [ˈ(h)wəːlibɔi, -gəːl] (*noun*), *F:* pilote d'hélicoptère.

whisker [ˈ(h)wiskər] (*noun*), *F:* 1. to win (a race) by a w., gagner dans un mouchoir. 2. to have whiskers, être vieux jeu, être vieux comme Hérode. *Voir aussi* **cat, 8.**

whistle[1] [ˈ(h)wisl] (*noun*). 1. *F:* gorge*, avaloir *m*, gargoulette *f*; to wet (*or* whet) one's w., boire*, s'humecter le gosier, se rincer la dalle. 2. *P:* w. (and flute) (*R.S.* = *suit*), complet *m* (pour homme). 3. *P:* to blow the w. on s.o., dénoncer* qn, vendre la mèche. *Voir aussi* **clean, 1; wolf-whistle.**

whistle[2] [ˈ(h)wisl] (to). 1. *F:* you can w. for it! tu peux te fouiller (*ou* te brosser)! 2. *V:* to w. in the dark = **muff**[2] (to), 3.

whistle-stop [ˈ(h)wislstɔp] (*noun*) (*U.S.*), *F:* (a) halte *f* de chemin de fer; (b) patelin *m*, trou *m*, bled *m*; w.-s. tour, campagne électorale menée du wagon d'un train.

white[1] [(h)wait] (*adj.*). 1. *P:* w. cross (*or* stuff), (a) cocaïne *f* (*drogues**), coco *f*, (fée) blanche *f*, neige *f*; (b) héroïne *f* (*drogues**); (c) morphine *f* (*drogues**); *voir aussi* **white**[2], 4. 2. *F:* honnête, intègre, estimable; to play the w. man, se bien conduire, agir en «honnête homme». *Voir aussi* **angel, 4; lily-white; snow-white.**

white[2] [(h)wait] (*noun*), *P:* 1. cinq livres *f.pl.* sterling et au-dessus. 2. platine *m* (*bijouterie*), blanc *m*, blanquette *f*. 3. pièces *f.pl.* d'argent*, blanchettes *f.pl.*; *voir aussi* **phon(e)y**[1], 2 (b). 4. (old lady)

w., (a) = **white cross** (b) (**white**[1], 1); (b) amphétamine *f* (*drogues**); (c) Benzédrine *f* (*marque déposée*).

white-collar [ˈ(h)waitˈkɔlər] (*attrib. adj.*), *F:* w.-c. worker, employé de bureau, gratte-papier *m*.

white-headed [ˈ(h)waitˈhedid] (*adj.*), *F:* the w.-h. boy, le chouchou de la famille.

white-livered [ˈ(h)waitˈlivəd] (*adj.*), *F:* = **yellow-bellied;** *cf.* **lily-livered.**

white-slaver [ˈ(h)waitˈsleivər] (*noun*), *F:* souteneur*, mangeur *m* de blanc (*ou* de brioche), marchand *m* de barbaque (*ou* de bidoche *ou* de viande).

whitewash[1] [ˈ(h)waitwɔʃ] (*noun*), *F:* (*sports*) défaite *f* à zéro.

whitewash[2] [ˈ(h)waitwɔʃ] (to), *F:* 1. blanchir, disculper, réhabiliter. 2. (*sports*) to w. one's opponents, battre ses adversaires sans qu'ils aient marqué un point.

whitey, whitie [ˈ(h)waiti] (*noun*), *P:* 1. homme blanc. 2. amphétamine *f* (*drogues**).

whittled [ˈ(h)waitld] (*adj.*) (*Austr.*), *P:* ivre*, rétamé.

whiz(z)[1] [(h)wiz] (*attrib. adj.*). 1. *P:* w. gang, bande* de pickpockets, flèche *f* de fourchettes. 2. *F:* w. kid, jeune cadre *m* qui monte en flèche, jeune coq *m*.

whiz(z)[2] [(h)wiz] (*noun*), *F:* 1. to be a w. at sth., être un as (*ou* un crack) à qch. 2. dynamisme *m*, entrain *m*, vitalité *f*.

whiz(z)[3] [(h)wiz] (to). 1. *F:* aller très vite*, bomber, gazer, filer à plein tube. 2. *P:* voler* à la fourchette (*ou* à la tire).

whizz-bang [ˈ(h)wizˈbæŋ] (*noun*), *P:* 1. (a) obus *m* à vitesse accélérée; (b) feu *m* d'artifice. 2. mélange *m* de morphine et de cocaïne; un bang; piquouse-bang *f*.

whizzer [ˈ(h)wizər] (*noun*), *P:* = **dip**[1], 1.

whizzing [ˈ(h)wiziŋ] (*noun*), *P:* vol *m* par une bande de pickpockets.

who [huː] (*pron.*), *F:* you know w., qui-vous-savez.

whodunit [huːˈdʌnit] (*noun*), *F:* roman policier, série noire, polar *m*.

whole [houl] (*adj.*), *F:* there's not a w. lot you can do about it, tu ne peux pas y faire grand-chose.

whole-hogger [ˈhoulˈhɔgər] (*noun*), *F:* (a) qn qui s'engage à fond, qn qui fonce tête baissée; (b) partisan *m*, supporte(u)r acharné; *cf.* **hog**[1], 2.

---

* An asterisk indicates that the word so marked is included as a head-word in the Appendix.

whole-hoggism [ˈhoʊlˈhɔgizm] (*noun*), *F:* jusqu'au-boutisme *m.*

whoopee![1] [ˈwuˈpi:] (*excl.*), *F:* youpi! youp!

whoopee[2] [ˈwupi:] (*noun*), *F:* **to make w.**, (*a*) fêter bruyamment, faire du chahut, faire la noce; (*b*) bien s'amuser.

whoops-a-daisy! [ˈ(h)wupsəˈdeizi] (*excl.*), *F:* oup-là (boum)! debout!

whoosh [(h)wuʃ] (**to**), *F:* conduire très vite*, rouler *ou* voler à plein gaz.

whop [(h)wɔp] (**to**), *P:* = **whack**[2] (**to**), 1, 2.

whopper [ˈ(h)wɔ:pər] (*noun*), *F:* = **whacker**, 1, 2.

whopping[1] [ˈ(h)wɔpiŋ] (*adj.*), *F:* 1. = **whacking**[1]. 2. **w. lie** = **whacker**, 2.

whopping[2] [ˈ(h)wɔpiŋ] (*noun*), *P:* volée *f* de coups*, rossée *f*, raclée *f*, dérouillée *f*, trempe *f.*

whore[1] [hɔər, hɔ:r] (*noun*), *P:* **dirty w.**: *voir* **bingo** (34). *Voir aussi* **forty-four.**

whore[2] [hɔər, hɔ:r] (**to**), *P:* putasser, courir la gueuse.

whore-house [ˈhɔ:(ə)haus] (*noun*), *P:* bordel*, baisodrome *m.*

whoring [ˈhɔ:(ə)riŋ] (*noun*), *P:* putasserie *f*, dragage *m.*

whore-shop [ˈhɔ:(ə)ʃɔp] (*noun*), *P:* = **whore-house.**

wibbly-wobbly [ˈwibliˈwɔbli] (*adj.*), *F:* branlant, chancelant.

wick [wik] (*noun*), *P:* 1. **to get on s.o.'s w.**, taper sur les nerfs (*ou* le système) à qn. 2. **to dip** (*or* **bury**) **one's w.**, coïter*, mouiller le goupillon; *cf.* **Hampton.**

wicked [ˈwikid] (*adj.*), *P:* = **groovy.**

widdle [ˈwidl] (*noun & verb*), *F:* = **piddle**[1,2].

wide [waid] (*adj.*). 1. *F:* malin*, roublard, marloupin, retors; a **w. boy**, un affranchi, un débrouillard, un fortiche. 2. *P:* **w. world**, (*courses hippiques*) la pelouse. *Voir aussi* **berth**, 1.

wide-awake [ˈwaidəˈweik] (*noun*), *F:* chapeau* de feutre à larges bords, capeline *f.*

wife [waif], **wifey** [ˈwaifi] (*noun*), *F:* **the w.**, l'épouse*, la bourgeoise, la ménagère.

wig [wig] (*noun*), *P:* **to blow** (*or* **flip** *or* **lose**) **one's w.**, être très en colère*, fulminer, sortir de ses gonds, piquer une crise. *Voir aussi* **bigwig.**

wigging [ˈwigiŋ] (*noun*), *F:* réprimande *f*, engueulade *f*, verte semonce, savon

m; **to get a good w.**, se faire réprimander*, se faire laver la tête.

wiggle [ˈwigl] (*noun*), *F:* **to get a w. on**, se dépêcher*, se dégrouiller, faire vinaigre.

wiggy [ˈwigi] (*noun*), *F:* (*langage enfantin*) pénis*, zizi *m.*

wig out [ˈwigˈaut] (**to**), *P:* = **freak out** (**to**).

wild [waild] (*adj.*), *F:* 1. en colère*, furibard. 2. **to be w. about s.o.**, être emballé pour qn. 3. = **fun**[1]. 4. passionnant, palpitant, captivant. *Voir aussi* **woolly.**

wildcat [ˈwaildkæt] (*adj.*), *F:* 1. téméraire, risqué, douteux. 2. **a w. venture**, une entreprise risquée (*surtout* au point de vue financier). 3. **a w. strike**, une grève non-officielle, grève sur le tas.

Willie [ˈwili] (*pr. noun*), *P:* 1. pénis*, petit frère. 2. **W.'s whatsit**: *voir* **bingo** (1).

willies [ˈwiliz] (*pl. noun*), *F:* **to give s.o. the w.**, donner la chair de poule (*ou* la tremblote) à qn; **to have the w.**, avoir peur*, avoir la trouille.

win [win] (**to**). 1. *F:* **you can't w.** (**can you**)! *c.p.*, tu auras toujours tort! 2. *F:* **you can't w. them all**, *c.p.*, on ne peut pas plaire à tout le monde. 3. *P:* voler*, rouler, soulever.

wind [wind] (*noun*), *F:* 1. **to raise the w.**, se procurer de l'argent*, battre monnaie. 2. (*a*) **to get the w. up**, avoir peur*, avoir les foies *m.pl.*; (*b*) **to put the w. up s.o.**, faire peur* à qn, ficher la frousse à qn. 3. **to be all w.** (**and water**), être comme une bulle de savon. 4. **to be full of w.**, mentir*, mener en barque. 5. **to sail close to the w.**, (*a*) friser l'illégalité, l'insolence, l'indécence, *etc.*; (*b*) faire des affaires* douteuses. 6. **there's something in the w.**, il y a anguille sous roche, il se manigance quelque chose. *Voir aussi* **bag**[1], 3; **load**, 7; **sail**; **sheet**, 1.

wind up [ˈwaindˈʌp] (**to**), *F:* **to w. u. on the scrap-heap**, finir sur la paille (*ou* en décrépitude); **to w. u. in prison**, finir en prison*.

windy [ˈwindi] (*adj.*), *F:* **to be w.**, avoir peur*, avoir le trac (*ou* la frousse).

wing [wiŋ] (*noun*), *P:* bras*, aile *f*, aileron *m. Voir aussi* **ping; sprout** (**to**).

---

* L'astérisque indique que le mot marqué de ce signe figure comme entrée dans le Répertoire.

wing-ding [ˈwiŋdiŋ] (*noun*) (*U.S.*), *P:* **1.** attaque *f*, crise *f* d'épilepsie, digue-digue *f*. **2.** accès *m* de folie dû aux drogues, le flip. **3.** prétendue crise (pour s'attirer la sympathie). **4.** coup *m* de colère*, rage *f*. **5.** réjouissances* bruyantes, réunion pleine de bruit*, chahut *m*, ramdam(e) *m*, boum déchaînée.

wing(e)y [ˈwindʒi] (*adj.*) =**whingy**.

wink [wiŋk] (*noun*), *F:* **to tip s.o. the w.**, avertir qn, faire signe de l'œil à qn, lancer une œillade à qn, faire le châsse à qn. *Voir aussi* **forty.**

winkers [ˈwiŋkəz] (*pl. noun*), *F:* clignotants *m.pl.*

winking [ˈwiŋkiŋ] (*noun & pres. part.*), *F:* **1.** (**as**) **easy as w.**, simple comme bonjour. **2. like w.**, en un clin d'œil, en rien de temps.

winkle [ˈwiŋkl] (*noun*), *P:* pénis*, frétillard *m*, frétillante *f*.

winkle-pickers [ˈwiŋkl-pikəz] (*pl. noun*), *F:* chaussures *f.pl.* à bout pointu.

winner [ˈwinər] (*noun*), *F:* (*a*) réussite certaine, succès assuré; (*b*) roman (pièce, *etc.*) à grand succès.

wino [ˈwainou] (*noun*), *P:* ivrogne*, sac *m* à vin.

win out [ˈwinˈaut] (**to**), *F:* surmonter les difficultés *f.pl.*, arriver au but.

wipe[1] [waip] (*noun*), *P:* **1.** mouchoir*, tire-jus *m*. **2.** = **swipe**[1], **1.**

wipe[2] [waip] (**to**), *P:* **1. to w. the floor with s.o.**, (*a*) fermer le bec à qn; (*b*) battre qn à plate(s) couture(s), n'en faire qu'une bouchée; (*c*) réprimander* qn, agonir qn de sottises *f.pl.*, incendier qn. **2.** battre*, flanquer une raclée à (qn).

wipe out [ˈwaipˈaut] (**to**), *F:* **1.** liquider, passer l'éponge sur (qch.). **2.** tuer*, nettoyer, ratatiner, lessiver (qn); **the whole lot were wiped out**, toute la bande a été zigouillée.

wire [waiər] (*noun*). **1.** *F:* **to give s.o. the w.**, donner un tuyau à qn, mettre qn dans le coup. **2.** *P:* **to pull one's w.**, se masturber*, se l'allonger; *cf.* **wire-puller; wire-pulling, 2. 3.** *F:* **a live w.**, un malin, un dégourdi, un débrouillard. **4.** *F:* télégramme *m*, petit bleu. **5.** *F:* **to get in under the w.**, arriver* au dernier moment, s'abouler pile. **6.** *F:* **to get one's wires crossed**, se tromper, se

gour(r)er, s'embrouiller, se mettre le doigt dans l'œil. **7.** *P:* pickpocket *m*, fourlineur *m*, fourchette *f*. **8.** *F:* **to pull (the) wires**, tirer les ficelles *f.pl.*, faire jouer le piston.

wired [ˈwaiəd] (*adj.*), *P:* (*a*) adonné à une drogue; (*b*) (*drogues*) défoncé, high.

wire into [ˈwaiəˈrintuː] (**to**), *P:* = **wade into** (**to**), **1** (*a*).

wire-puller [ˈwaiə-pulər] (*noun*). **1.** *F:* intrigant *m*, manœuvrier *m*. **2.** *P:* masturbateur *m*, branleur *m*; *cf.* **wire, 2.**

wire-pulling [ˈwaiə-puliŋ] (*noun*). **1.** *F:* l'art *m* de tirer les ficelles *f.pl.*, intrigues *f.pl.* de couloir *m*, manigances *f.pl.* **2.** *P:* masturbation *f*, allongement *m*, astiquage *m.*; *cf.* **wire, 2.**

wise [waiz] (*adj.*), *F:* **to get w.**, se mettre à la coule, se dessaler; se dégourdir; **to get w. to sth.**, s'apercevoir de la vérité; saisir qch.; **to put s.o. w.**, affranchir qn, mettre qn à la page; **put me w. about it**, expliquez-moi ça. *Voir aussi* **guy**[1], **1.**

wisecrack[1] [ˈwaizkræk] (*noun*), *F:* **1.** bon mot, mot spirituel, boutade *f*. **2.** riposte impertinente, coup *m* de langue, pointe *f*, rosserie *f*.

wisecrack[2] [ˈwaizkræk] (**to**), *F:* faire de l'esprit, aiguiser un trait.

wise up [ˈwaizˈʌp] (**to**), *F:* (*a*) = **to get wise**; (*b*) **to w. s.o. u.** = **to put s.o. wise.**

wish [wiʃ] (**to**), *F:* **it's been wished on me**, c'est une chose que je n'ai pas pu refuser.

wisher [ˈwiʃər] (*noun*) (*U.S.*), *P:* = **fed**[2], **2.**

wishy-washy [ˈwiʃiwɔʃi] (*adj.*), *F:* fade, insipide, lavasse.

with [wið] (*prep.*), *F:* **1.** (*a*) **to be w. it**, être dans le vent (*ou* dans le mouvement *ou* à la page); (*b*) **to get w. it**, se mettre dans le bain, se mettre au diapason. **2. I'm not w. you**, je ne comprends pas, je ne pige pas, je n'y suis pas.

with-it [ˈwiðit] (*attrib. adj.*), *F:* **w.-i. gear**, des vêtements* dernier cri.

without [wiˈðaut] (*prep.*), *F:* **w. any**, sans alcool*, au régime sec.

wizard [ˈwizəd] (*adj.*), *F:* excellent*, épatant, au poil.

wodge [wɔdʒ] (*noun*), *F:* (*a*) gros morceau, bloc *m*, quartier *m*; (*b*) liasse *f* (de papiers).

wog [wɔg] (*noun*), *P:* (*péj.*) **1.** Levantin *m*, Égyptien *m*, Arabe *m*, bico(t) *m*, bougnoul(l)e *m*. **2.** un étranger.

---

* An asterisk indicates that the word so marked is included as a head-word in the Appendix.

wolf[1] [wulf] (*noun*). **1.** *F:* séducteur *m*, coureur *m* de cotillons (*ou* de jupons *ou* de gueuses), juponneur *m*, homme *m* à femmes. **2.** *F:* **to keep the w. from the door**, se mettre à l'abri du besoin (de nourriture). **3.** *P:* pédéraste* actif, loup *m* de Sibérie, chien *m* jaune. **4.** *F:* **lone w.**, (*a*) = **loner**; (*b*) célibataire endurci, vieux bouc.

wolf[2] [wulf] (to). **1.** *F:* manger* abondamment, s'empiffrer, dévorer, se goinfrer. **2.** *P:* séduire la femme d'un autre, griller.

wolfish [ˈwulfiʃ] (*adj.*), *P:* plein de convoitise, allumé.

wolf-whistle [ˈwulf(h)wisl] (*noun*), *F:* sifflement admiratif à l'adresse d'une femme.

woman-chaser [ˈwumən-tʃeisər] (*noun*), *F:* coureur *m* de jupons, dénicheur *m* de fauvettes.

woman-crazy [ˈwumənˈkreizi], **woman-mad** [ˈwumənˈmæd] (*adj.*), *F:* qui a les femmes dans la peau; *cf.* **man-crazy; man-mad.**

wonder[1] [ˈwʌndər] (*noun*), *F:* **1. wonders will never cease!** *c.p.*, il y a toujours des miracles! c'est un prodige! **2. no w.!** pas étonnant!

wonder[2] [ˈwʌndər] (to), *F:* **1. I shouldn't w.**, cela ne me surprendrait pas. **2. I w.**, j'en doute, j'ai des réserves *f.pl.*, que tu dis.

wonk [wɔŋk] (*noun*) (*Austr.*), *P:* pédéraste*, empapaouté *m*.

wonky [ˈwɔŋki] (*adj.*), *P:* **1.** titubant, chancelant, branlant, zigzaguant. **2.** hésitant, vacillant, oscillant. **3.** mal fichu, patraque. **4.** (*Austr.*) homosexuel.

wood [wud] (*noun*), *F:* **1. touch** (*U.S.* **knock on**) **w.!** touche du bois! **2. you can't see the w. for the trees**, *c.p.*, on se perd dans les détails *m.pl.*; les arbres empêchent de voir la forêt. **3. he's w. from the neck up**, il est bouché à l'émeri, il a une tête de bûche. *Voir aussi* **bird-wood.**

woodbine [ˈwudbain] (*noun*), *P:* **African w.**, cigarette* de marijuana (*drogues*).

wooden [ˈwudn], *F:* **to win the w. spoon**, arriver le dernier (*ou* à la queue), faire la lanterne rouge; **the w. spoon goes to X**, X fermait la marche. *Voir aussi* **overcoat.**

woodshed [ˈwudʃed] (*noun*), *F:* **there's**

something nasty in the w.**, on nous cache quelque chose, il y a un cadavre dans la grange.

wool [wul] (*noun*). **1. to lose one's w.**, (*a*) *P:* se mettre en colère*; **keep your w. on!** ne te frappe pas! calme-toi!; (*b*) *F:* = **to lose one's thatch. 2.** *F:* **to pull the w. over s.o.'s eyes**, jeter de la poudre aux yeux de qn. *Voir aussi* **cotton-wool.**

woolie, wooll(e)y, woollie [ˈwuli] (*noun*), *F:* (*a*) tricot *m*; lainage *m*, paletot *m* de laine; **put your w. on**, mets ta laine; (*b*) **winter woollies**, sous-vêtements chauds.

woolly [ˈwuli] (*adj.*), *F:* (**wild and**) **w.**, (*a*) ignare, inculte, mal léché; (*b*) hirsute, hérissé.

woozy [ˈwuːzi] (*adj.*). **1.** *F:* étourdi, qui a le vertige, dont la tête tourne. **2.** *P:* ivre*, blindé, chargé.

wop [wɔp] (*noun*), *P:* (*péj.*) Italien *m*, macaroni *m*.

work[1] [wəːk] (*noun*), *F:* **a nasty piece of w.**, un sale type, une peau de vache. *Voir aussi* **bodywork; cut out (to), 3, 4; homework; legwork; works.**

work[2] [wəːk] (to). **1.** *F:* arranger, manigancer, machiner, trafiquer; **to w. a fiddle**, manigancer une combine. **2.** *P:* coïter* avec (une femme), bourrer.

working over [ˈwəːkiŋˈouvər] (*noun*), *P:* **to give s.o. a w. o.** = **to work s.o. over.**

workout [ˈwəːkaut] (*noun*). **1.** *F:* essai *m*, tentative *f*, ébauche *f*. **2.** *P:* volée *f* de coups*, raclée *f*, tabassée *f*.

work over [ˈwəːkˈouvər] (to), *P:* **to w. s.o. o.**, battre* qn, passer une peignée à qn.

works [wəːks] (*pl. noun*). **1.** *P:* **to give s.o. the w.**, (*a*) battre* qn, tabasser qn, passer qn à tabac; (*b*) tuer* qn, zigouiller qn, faire son affaire à qn. **2.** *P:* **the w.** = **the business** (**business, 4** (*a*), (*d*), (*e*)). **3.** *F:* **the whole w.**, tout le bataclan, tout le bazar; *cf.* **boiling; caboodle; shebang, 1; shoot**[1], **1.** *Voir aussi* **foul up (to); gum up (to); shoot**[2] **(to), 8; spanner; waterworks.**

work up [ˈwəːkˈʌp] (to). **1.** *P:* exciter sexuellement, émoustiller. **2.** *F:* mettre (qn) en colère, échauffer, affoler; **don't get worked up** (**about it**), ne t'emballe pas, ne te monte pas le bourrichon. *Voir aussi* **lather**[1]; **sweat**[1], **3.**

---

* L'astérisque indique que le mot marqué de ce signe figure comme entrée dans le Répertoire.

world [wə:ld] (*noun*), *F:* **1. to feel on top of the w.**, être en pleine forme, être au septième ciel. **2. out of this w.**, mirifique, transcendant, sensas(s). **3. to think the w. of s.o.**, estimer hautement qn, porter qn aux nues. *Voir aussi* **come down (to)**, 4; **dead**[1], 7; **wide**, 2.

worry [ˈwʌri] (to), *F:* **1. not to w.!** faut pas s'en faire! **2. I should w.!** ce n'est pas mon affaire! c'est le cadet de mes soucis!

worryguts [ˈwʌrigʌts] (*U.S.:* **worry wart** [ˈwʌriwɔːt]) (*noun*), *P:* bileux *m*, qn qui se met martel en tête (*ou* qui se fait des cheveux).

worth [wə:θ] (*adj.*), *F:* **1. for all one is w.**, de toutes ses forces. **2. was she w. it?**: *voir* **bingo** (76).

wotcher! [ˈwɔtʃə] (*excl.*), *P:* **w., mate! w., cock!** comment ça gaze, mon vieux?

wow![1] [wau] (*excl.*), *F:* oh la la! héhé!

wow[2] [wau] (*noun*), *F:* succès *m* formidable (*ou* du tonnerre *ou* à casser la baraque). *Voir aussi* **pow-wow**.

wow[3] [wau] (to), *F:* stupéfier, époustoufler, en mettre plein la vue.

wowser [ˈwauzər] (*noun*) (*Austr.*), *F:* rabat-joie *m*, trouble-fête *m*.

W.P.B., w.p.b. [ˈdʌbljuːˈpiːˈbiː] (*abbr.* = *waste paper basket*), *F:* corbeille *f* à papier.

wrap[1] [ræp] (*noun*) **to be under wraps**, être à la zyeute du flic.

wrap[2] [ræp] (to), *F:* **1. w. yourself round that!** mange* (*ou* bois*) cela! tape-toi cela! mets-toi ça derrière la cravate! **2. he wrapped his car round a tree**, il a encadré un arbre.

wrap-up [ˈræpʌp] (*noun*), *P:* **1.** résumé *m*, topo *m*. **2.** colis *m* contenant des drogues.

wrap up [ˈræpˈʌp] (to). **1.** *P:* se taire*, la fermer, la boucler; **w. u.!** ta gueule! la ferme! **2.** *F:* terminer, achever, boucler; **it's all wrapped up**, tout est arrangé (*ou* bouclé).

wringer [ˈriŋər] (*noun*), *P:* **to put s.o. through the w.**, en faire voir des vertes et des pas mûres à qn, passer qn à la casserole.

wrinkle [ˈriŋkl] (*noun*), *F:* **1.** tuyau *m*, truc *m*, combine *f*; **to know all the wrinkles**, la connaître dans les coins, connaître les ficelles. **2.** nouveauté *f*, idée originale, novation *f*; **that's a new w.**, c'est du neuf.

wrist [rist] (*noun*), *V:* **1. limp w.**, pédéraste*, chouquette *f*, chochotte *f*. **2. one off the w.**, masturbation *f*, un astiquage maison, un branlage maison.

write [rait] (to), *F:* **it's nothing to w. home about**, cela n'a rien d'extraordinaire, cela ne casse rien.

write-off [ˈraitɔf] (*noun*), *F:* individu désemparé, épave *f*.

wrong[1] [rɔŋ] (*adj.*), *F:* **to get on the w. side of s.o.** = **to be in w. with s.o.** (**wrong**[2], 2). *Voir aussi* **bed**[1], 2; **end**, 11.

wrong[2] [rɔŋ] (*adv.*), *F:* **1. to get s.o. in w. with s.o.**, disgracier qn aux yeux de qn d'autre. **2. to be in w. with s.o.**, ne pas être dans les bonnes grâces (*ou* les petits papiers) de qn, être mal vu.

wrongheaded [ˈrɔŋˈhedid] (*adj.*), *F:* bête*, demeuré.

Y

yabber[1] [ˈjæbər] (*noun*), *F:* bavardage *m*, bavasse *f*, jactage *m*.

yabber[2] [ˈjæbər] (**to**), *F:* bavarder*, bavasser, jacter.

yack[1] [jæk] (*noun*), *F:* = yackety-yack.

yack[2] [jæk] (**to**), *F:* (*a*) bavarder*, jacasser; (*b*) ragoter, papoter; (*c*) caqueter, dévider.

yackety-yack [ˈjækətiˈjæk] (*noun*), *F:* caquetage *m*, jacasserie *f*, bla-bla *m*; *cf.* clackety-clack.

yahoo [jɑːˈhuː, jəˈhuː] (*noun*), *F:* 1. homme* bestial, brute *f*, sauvage *m*. 2. (*U.S.*) (*a*) paysan*, petzouille *m*, croquant *m*, cul-terreux *m*; (*b*) buse *f*, niguedouille *mf*.

yak[1] [jæk] (*noun*), *F:* = yackety-yack.

yak[2] [jæk] (**to**), *F:* = yack[2] (**to**).

yammer [ˈjæmər] (**to**), *F:* bavarder*, bavasser, dégoiser.

yancy [ˈjænsi] (*adj.*) (*U.S.*), *F:* = antsy; *cf.* yantsy.

yang [jæŋ] (*noun*) (*U.S.*), *P:* pénis*, zobi *m*.

yank[1] [jæŋk] (*noun*), *F:* secousse *f*, saccade *f*, coup sec.

yank[2] [jæŋk] (**to**). 1. *F:* tirer d'un coup sec; to y. the bedclothes off s.o., découvrir qn brusquement 2. (*U.S.*) *P:* arrêter*, agrafer.

Yank[3] [jæŋk], Yankee[1] [ˈjæŋki] (*adj.*), *F:* américain, amerlo(que), yankee, ricain.

Yank[4] [jæŋk], Yankee[2] [ˈjæŋki] (*noun*), *F:* 1. habitant *m* de la Nouvelle Angleterre ou d'un des états du nord des États-Unis. 2. Américain *m*, Amerlo *m*, Amerloque *m*, Yankee *m*, Ricain *m*.

yankeeism [ˈjæŋkiːiz(ə)m] (*noun*), *F:* (*a*) mot américain; (*b*) américanisme *m*, amerloche *m*.

yantsy [ˈjæntsi] (*adj.*) (*U.S.*), *F:* = antsy; *cf.* yancy.

yap[1] [jæp] (*noun*), *P:* 1. (*a*) bavardage bruyant, caquetage *m*; (*b*) bouche*, goule *f*. 2. (*U.S.*) individu bête*, gourde *f*, crétin *m*, navet *m*.

yap[2] [jæp] (**to**), *P:* 1. grogner*, bougonner, rouspéter. 2. parler* beaucoup, déblatérer, en dégoiser, japper.

yapper [ˈjæpər] (*noun*), *P:* bavard*, jacasseur *m*.

yapping [ˈjæpiŋ] (*noun*), *P:* bavardage *m*, dévidage *m*, jactage *m*.

yard[1] [jɑːd] (*noun*), *F:* words a y. long, mots longs d'une toise; statistics by the y., statistiques *f.pl.* à gogo; a face a y. long, visage* long d'une au(l)ne. *Voir aussi* bone-yard; churchyard.

yard[2] [jɑːd] (**to**), *P:* to y. s.o., coïter* avec qn de tout à fait étranger.

yardbird [ˈjɑːdbəːd] (*noun*) (*U.S.*), *F:* = jailbird.

yard-dog [ˈjɑːddɔg] (*noun*) (*U.S.*), *P:* malappris *m*, chien galeux.

yarn[1] [jɑːn] (*noun*), *F:* (*a*) histoire *f* (*ou* conte *m*) de matelot; (*b*) longue histoire; to spin (*or* pitch *or* pull) a y., (*a*) raconter (*ou* débiter) une histoire; (*b*) mentir*, raconter des histoires *f.pl.*, bourrer le crâne à qn.

yarn[2] [jɑːn] (**to**), *F:* débiter des histoires *f.pl.*

yarra [ˈjærə] (*adj.*) (*Austr.*), *F:* (stone) y., fou*, loufoque.

yatter[1] [ˈjætər] (*noun*), *P:* bavardage *m*, baratin *m*, déblatérage *m*.

yatter[2] [ˈjætər] (**to**), *P:* bavarder*, baratiner, déblatérer, tenir le crachoir.

yawny [ˈjɔːni] (*adj.*), *F:* ennuyeux*, rasoir, qui fait bâiller (à s'en décrocher la mâchoire).

yawp [jɔːp] (**to**) (*U.S.*), *F:* = yap[2] (**to**), 1.

yeah [ˈjeə, ˈjeəː] (*adv. & excl.*), *F:* (*a*) oui*, gy, gygo; (*b*) oh y.? et alors? et après?

year [jiər, jəːr] (*noun*), *F:* to put years on s.o., donner du mal à qn, donner des cheveux blancs à qn. *Voir aussi* donkey, 3.

yegg [jeg] (*noun*) (*U.S.*), *P:* 1. coffioteur *m*, déboucleur *m* (*ou* casseur *m*) de coffiot. 2. voleur*, caroubleur *m*.

---

* L'astérisque indique que le mot marqué de ce signe figure comme entrée dans le Répertoire.

yell [jel] (*noun*), *F:* it's a y. = it's a scream (**scream**[1], **2**).

yellow ['jelou, 'jelə] (*adj.*), *F:* **1.** lâche, couard; **to have a y. streak**, être poltron* (*ou* froussard), avoir les foies *m.pl.* (*ou* les grolles *f.pl.*), ne rien avoir dans le ventre. **2. the Y. Press**, presse *f* qui vise à la sensation, journaux* à scandales. *Voir aussi* **dirt**[1], **7; jack**[1], **13**.

yellow-bellied ['jelou-belid, 'jelə-belid] (*adj.*), *F:* qui a peur*, déballonné, flubard; **to be y.-b.**, avoir les foies (blancs).

yellow-belly ['jelou-beli, 'jelə-beli] (*noun*), *F:* froussard *m*, trouillard *m*, foie blanc (*ou* bleu).

yellow-jacket ['jelou-dʒækit, 'jelə-dʒækit] (*noun*), *P:* pilule *f* à base de barbital, barbiturique *m* (*drogues**).

yellow-livered ['jelou-livəd, 'jelə-livəd] (*adj.*), *F:* = **yellow-bellied**.

yen[1] [jen] (*noun*). **1.** *F:* désir ardent et obsédant, appétit *m*. **2.** *P:* = **yen-yen**. *Voir aussi* **pen-yen**.

yen[2] [jen] (**to**), *F:* désirer ardemment, en vouloir.

yen-shee ['jen'ʃi:] (*noun*), *P:* = **pen-yen**.

yen-yen ['jenjen] (*noun*), *P:* besoin *m* de la drogue, guêpe *f*, guenon *f*.

yep [jep] (*excl.*), *P:* = **yeah** (*a*).

yer [jɔːr] (*pron.* = *you*), *P:* tu, vous; **will y. or won't y.?** veux-tu ou veux-tu pas?

yesca ['jeskə] (*noun*), *P:* marijuana *f* (*drogues**).

yes-girl ['jesgəːl] (*noun*), *P:* fille facile, Marie-couche-toi-là, fille qui se couche quand on lui dit de s'asseoir.

yes-man ['jesmæn] (*noun*), *F:* individu* qui dit oui à tout, béni-oui-oui *m*.

Yid [jid] (*noun*), *P:* (*péj.*) Juif *m*, Youpin *m*.

ying-yang ['jiŋjæŋ] (*noun*) (*U.S.*), *P:* = **yang**.

yippee! ['ji'pi:] (*excl.*), *F:* bravo! hourrah!

yippie ['jipi] (*noun*), *F:* hippie turbulent et tapageur.

yob [jɔb] (*noun*), *P:* **1.** (*péj.*) gars *m*, fiston *m*. **2.** rustre *m*, lourdaud *m*, paltoquet *m*.

yobbo ['jɔbou] (*noun*), *P:* = **yob, 2**.

yogs [jɔgz] (*pl. noun*), *F:* longtemps, des années*, des berges.

Yorkshire ['jɔːkʃə] (*pr. noun*), *P:* **to come** (*or* **put**) **Y. on** (*or* **over**) **s.o.**, escroquer*, posséder, rouler qn.

you-and-me ['juən'mi:] (*noun*) (*R.S.* = *tea*), *P:* thé *m* (*boisson*).

yours [jɔːz, jɔəz] (*pron.*), *F:* **1. what's y.?** qu'est-ce que tu prends? **2. y. truly**, moi-même, mézigue, bibi. *Voir aussi* **up**[4], **1**.

yow [jau] (*noun*) (*Austr.*), *F:* **to keep y.** = **to keep nit** (**nit, 2**).

yowly ['jauli] (*adj.*), *F:* pleurnicheur, geignard.

yuck! [jʌk] (*excl.*), *F:* pouah!

yucky ['jʌki] (*adj.*), *F:* **1.** odieux, dégueulasse. **2.** à l'eau de rose, mauviette.

yummy ['jʌmi] (*adj.*), *F:* très bon, délicieux, du nanan, de derrière les fagots.

yum-yum! ['jʌm'jʌm] (*excl.*), *F:* du nanan!

Z

zany [ˈzeini] (*adj.*), *F:* bouffon, gugusse, gourdiflot.

zap [zæp] (to) (*U.S.*), *P:* 1. tuer* d'un coup de feu, zigouiller. 2. battre à plate(s) couture(s), anéantir. 3. se dépêcher*, se décarcasser.

zazzle [ˈzæzl] (*noun*), *P:* désir sexuel, tracassin *m*.

zazzy [ˈzæzi] (*adj.*), *F:* appétissante, bien roulée, qui a du chien.

Z car [ˈzedkɑːr] (*noun*), *F:* voiture *f* de police, voiture pie.

Zen [zen] (*noun*), *P:* instant Z., LSD *m* (*drogues**).

zing [ziŋ] (*noun*), *F:* vitalité *f*, vigueur *f*, énergie *f*, dynamisme *m*.

zingy [ˈziŋi] (*adj.*), *F:* plein de vitalité *f* (*ou* d'entrain *m*), qui pète le feu.

zip [zip] (*noun*), *F:* 1. énergie *f*, entrain *m*; **put some z. into it!** mets-y du nerf! secoue-toi! 2. = **zipper**.

zip along [ˈzipəˈlɔŋ] (to), *F:* aller très vite*, aller à toute pompe.

zipper [ˈzipər] (*noun*) (=*zip-fastener*), *F:* Fermeture *f* Éclair (*marque déposée*), fermeture *f* à curseur.

zippy [ˈzipi] (*adj.*), *F:* vif, plein d'allant, dynamique; **look z.!** grouille-toi! magne-toi (le train)!

zip up [ˈzipˈʌp] (to), *F:* **will you z. me u.?** veux-tu fermer ma Fermeture Éclair?

zit [zit] (*noun*) (*U.S.*), *P:* bouton *m* (de l'épiderme), bourgeon *m*.

zizz[1] [ziz] (*noun*), *F:* petit somme *m*, roupillon *m*.

zizz[2] [ziz] (to), *F:* dormir*, faire dodo, piquer un roupillon (*ou* une ronflette).

zombi(e), zomby [ˈzɔmbi] (*noun*), *F:* 1. individu* sans force de caractère, lavette *f*, chiffe *f*, avachi *m*. 2. individu bête*, duschnock *m*.

zonk [zɔŋk] (to), *P:* = **zap** (to), 1, 2, 3.

zonked (out) [ˈzɔŋkt(ˈaut)] (*adj.*), *P:* (*a*) ivre* mort, cuit, rétamé; (*b*) (*drogues*) défoncé à zéro, complètement ivre.

zoom [zuːm] (*noun*), *P:* amphétamine *f* (*drogues**), speed *m*.

zoom up [ˈzuːmˈʌp] (to), *F:* **to z. u., to come zooming up,** arriver en trombe.

zoot [zuːt] (*adj.*), *F:* (*a*) voyant, criard; (*b*) à la mode, (au) dernier cri; **z. suit,** complet *m* d'homme avec veston long et pantalon étroit; costume *m* zazou.

zosh [zɔʃ] (*noun*) (*U.S.*), *P:* femme* (*péj.*), tarderie *f*, rombière *f*.

---

* L'astérisque indique que le mot marqué de ce signe figure comme entrée dans le Répertoire.

Répertoire alphabétique de synonymes argotiques et populaires

(N.B.—Ce répertoire offre un choix de synonymes et de termes analogiques pour tous les mots suivis d'un astérisque dans le Dictionnaire.)

abandonner: balancer, balanstiquer, bouler, débarquer, déposer, foutre à la cour, lâcher, laisser choir (*ou* courir *ou* glisser *ou* tomber), laisser en carafe (*ou* frime *ou* panne *ou* plan *ou* rade), larguer, plaquer, quimper, scier, semer, virer.
Voir aussi **débarrasser de, se.**

abîmer: amocher, bousiller, esquinter, fusiller, rangemaner, saboter.

abject (*adj.*): cradingue, crado, débectant, dégueulasse, dégueulbif, salingue.

abondance *f*: aboulage *m*, bardée *f*, bottée *f*, des bottes *f.pl.*, charibotée *f*, chiée *f*, flanquée *f*, flopée *f*, flottes *f.pl.*, foul(e)titude *f*, des mille et des cents, potée *f*, ribambelle *f*, secouée *f*, séquelle *f*, suée *f*, tapée *f*, tas *m*, tassée *f*, tinée *f*, tirée *f*, trimbalée *f*, tripotée *f*.

accord, d' (*excl.*): banco, ça biche, ça boume, ça colle, ça gaze, ça marche, dac, d'acc, gy, O.K.

accoucher: abouler, chier (*ou* faire) un lard (*ou* un lardon *ou* un môme *ou* un salé), débouler, larder, pisser sa (*ou* une) côtelette (*ou* son os), pondre.

adultère *m*: carambolage *m* en douce, char *m*, coup *m* de canif (dans le contrat), découchage *m*, doublage *m*, galoup *m*, impair *m*, mise *f* en double, paille *f*, paillons *m.pl.*, queues *f.pl.*

adversité *f*: bouillasse *f*, bouillie *f*, cerise *f*, confiture *f*, choux *m.pl.*, emmerdement *m*, emmouscaillement *m*, guigne *f*, limonade *f*, marmelade *f*, mélasse *f*, merde *f*, mouise *f*, mouscaille *f*, panade *f*, purée *f*, schkoumoun *m*.

affaire *f*: balle *f*, blot *m*, boulot *m*, combine *f*, coup *m*, filon *m*, flanche *m*, fric(-)frac *m*, parcours *m*, travail *m*, truc *m*, turbin *m*.

agent *m* **de police:** bourrin *m*, cogne *m*, condé *m*, fachiste *m*, flic *m*, flicard *m*, gardien *m* (de la paix), mannequin *m*,

maton *m*, matuche *m*, pélerin *m*, raper *m*, sergot *m*, tige *f*.

agent cycliste: cyclo *m*, hirondelle *f*, raper *m*, roulette *f*.
Voir aussi **policier.**

agent *m* **en moto:** mobilard *m*, motard *m*.

agression *f*: accrochage *m*, braquage *m*, colletage *m*, cravate *f*, mise *f* en l'air, serrage *m*.

aimer: s'amouracher de, avoir à la bonne (*ou* à la chouette), avoir dans les globules (*ou* dans la peau), avoir un (*ou* le) béguin pour, avoir un pépin pour, se casquer de, se chiper de, se coiffer de, en croquer pour, s'enticher de, être chipé pour, être entiché (*ou* pincé *ou* toqué) de, gober, être mordu pour, en pincer pour, raffoler de.

alcool *m*: blanche *f*, camphre *m*, casse-gueule *m*, casse-pattes *m*, cogne *f*, cric *m*, élixir *m* de hussard, fil *m* en quatre, ginglard *m*, gn(i)ole *f*, gnôle *f*, goutte *f*, pousse-au-crime *m*, raide *f*, schnap *m*, schnick *m*, tafiat *m*, tord-boyau(x) *m*, vitriol *m*.

alibi *m*: berlanche *f*, berlue *f*, chauffeuse *f*, couverte *f*, couverture *f*, couvrante *f*, parapluie *m*, pébroc *m*, pébroque *m*.

Allemand *m*: alboche *m*, boche *m*, chleu(h) *m*, doryphore *m*, fridolin *m*, friscou *m*, frisé *m*, fritz *m*, frizou *m*, prusco(t) *m*.

amant *m*: coquin *m*, dessous *m*, doublard *m*, gigolo *m*, gigolpince *m*, Jules *m*, matou *m*, matz *m*, mec *m*, miché *m*, micheton *m*.

ami *m*: aminche *m*, amunche *m*, camerluche *m*, cop(a)in *m*, fiston *m*, frangin *m*, frelot *m*, gonze *m*, gonzier *m*, pote *m*, poteau *m*, vieille branche, zig(ue) *m*.

(très) amusant (*adj.*): à se crever de rire, astap(e), bidonnant, bolant, boyautant, cocasse, crevant, désopilant, drôlichon, fendant, gondolant, impayable, marrant, pilant, pissant, poilant, rigolard, rigolboche, rigouillard, roulant, tirebouchonnant, tordant.

an *m*, **année** *f* : berge *f*, carat *m*, gerbe *f*, longe *f*, pige *f*.

anus *m* : anneau *m*, bagouse *f*, bague *f*, boîte *f* à pâté, chevalière *f*, chouette *m*, croupion *m*, échalote *f*, entrée *f* des artistes, fias *m*, fion(ard) *m*, foiron *m*, motte *f*, œil *m* de bronze, oignon *m*, pastille *f*, pot *m*, petit guichet, rond *m*, rondelle *f*, rondibé *m*, trou *m* (de balle *ou* du cul), troufignard *m*, troufignon *m*, troufion *m*.

argent *m* (*monnaie*) : ardèche *f*, artiche *m*, aspine *f*, auber *m*, aubère *m*, avoine *f*, beurre *m*, blanc *m*, blé *m*, boules *f.pl.*, braise *f*, bulle *m*, caire *m*, carbi *m*, carbure *m*, carme *m*, carmet *m*, dolluche *m*, douille *f*, ferraille *f*, fifrelin *m*, flouse *m*, flouze *m*, fric *m*, galette *f*, galtouze *f*, grisbi *m*, kope(c)ks *m.pl.*, lovés *m.pl.*, mitraille *f*, mornifle *f*, oseille *f*, osier *m*, pécune *f*, pépètes *f.pl.*, pépettes *f.pl.*, pèse *m*, pésètes *f.pl.*, pésettes *f.pl.*, pèze *m*, picaillons *m.pl.*, po(i)gnon *m*, quibus *m*, radis *m.pl.*, rond *m*, rotin *m*, Saint-Fric *m*, soudure *f*.

billet(s) : biffeton *m*, faf *m*, faf(f)iot *m*, la grosse artillerie, image *f*, papier *m*, taffetas *m*, talbin *m*.

argot *m* : arguemuche *m*, jar(s) *m*, largongi *m*.

arrêter (*procéder à une arrestation*) : accrocher, agrafer, agricher, agriffer, alpaguer, arquepincer, baiser, bicher, ceinturer, cercler, chauffer, chiper, choper, coffrer, coincer, cravater, croquer, cueillir, emballer, embarquer, embastiller, embourmaner, engerber, entoiler, épingler, fabriquer, faire (marron), friser, gauf(f)rer, gauler, grouper, harponner, lever, mettre (*ou* jeter *ou* poser) le grappin sur, mettre la main sur l'alpague de, paumer, pincer, pingler, piper, piquer, poisser, poivrer, quimper, rafler, ramasser, ratisser, sauter, secouer, serrer, servietter, sucrer.

être arrêté : être baisé (*ou* bon *ou* fabriqué *ou* fait *ou* marron *ou* propre *ou* têtard), se faire bondir, se faire faire, se faire piger.

Voir aussi **emprisonner.**

arriver : s'abouler, amener sa graisse, s'amener, s'annoncer, débarquer, débouler, rabattre, radiner, rappliquer.

assassin *m* : but(t)eur *m*, flingueur *m*, metteur *m* en l'air, repasseur *m*, saigneur *m*, scionneur *m*, surineur *m*, tueur *m*.

assassiner : arranger, bousiller, but(t)er, crever, dégommer, démolir, descendre, dessouder, dézinguer, escoffier, effacer, estourbir, expédier, faire avaler son bulletin de naissance à, faire la peau à, ficher (*ou* flanquer *ou* foutre) en l'air, flinguer, gommer, lessiver, liquider, mettre en l'air, nettoyer, ratatiner, rectifier, refroidir, repasser, saigner, suriner, zigouiller.

assez (en avoir) : arrêter les frais, en avoir sa claque, en avoir par-dessus la tête, en avoir plein les bottes (*ou* le derche *ou* le dos), en avoir (plus que) marre, en avoir quine, en avoir ras (le bol), en avoir soupé.

assez! (*excl.*) : arrête les frais! barca! basta! ça va comme ça! c'est class(e)! c'est marre! écrase! flac! passe la main! quine! rideau!

attaquer : agrafer, chabler dans, harponner, râbler, rentrer dans le lard (*ou* le mou) à, rentrer dedans, sauter dessus, serrer, tomber dessus, tomber sur l'alpague (*ou* le paletot *ou* le poil) de.

attendre : compter les pavés, draguer, faire le pied de grue, faire le poireau, se faire poser un lapin, moisir, poireauter, poser, prendre racine.

avare (être) : avoir un cactus dans la poche, avoir un oursin dans la fouille, coucher dessus, être chien (*ou* dur à la desserre *ou* dur à la détente), être grigou (*ou* grippe-sou *ou* pignouf *ou* pingre *ou* radin *ou* rapiat *ou* rat), être constipé du crapaud (*ou* du morlingue), les lâcher avec un lance-pierre, les planquer, ne pas les lâcher (avec des saucisses), ne pas les sortir.

avocat *m* : bavard *m*, baveux *m*, cravateur *m*, débarbot *m*, débarbotteur *m*, menteur *m*, perroquet *m*.

avouer : accoucher, s'affaler, s'allonger, blutiner, casser (le morceau), cracher (dans le bassin), déballer ses outils, déballonner, se déboutonner, dégorger, dégueuler, lâcher le paquet, manger le morceau, se mettre à table, ouvrir les vannes, vider son sac.

bagarre *f* : badaboum *m*, baroud *m*, bigorne *f*, castagne *f*, chambard *m*, chambardement *m*, cognage *m*, cogne *f*, coup *m* de chien, crêpage *m* de chignon(s) (*ou* de tignasse(s)), grabuge *m*, razzia *f*, rififi *m*, serrage *m*, torchage *m*, torchée *f*.

balle *f* (*armes à feu*): bastos *f*, bonbon *m*, dragée *f*, pastille *f*, praline *f*, prune *f*, pruneau *m*, valda *f*.

bande *f* (*groupe d'individus*): action *f*, brigade *f*, équipe *f*, flèche *f*, gang *m*, soce *f*, tierce *f*, tribu *f*.

barbe *f*: artichaut *m*, bacchante *f*, barbouze *f*, foin *m*, piège *m*.

battre: abîmer le portrait à, amocher, aplatir, aquiger, arranger, assaisonner, astiquer, attiger, avoiner, battre comme plâtre, bigorner, botter (le cul à), bourrer de coups, brosser, carder le cuir à, casser la gueule à, cogner, crêper (le chignon *ou* la tignasse à), décrasser, démolir, dérouiller, encadrer, étriller, filer (*ou* foutre) une avoine (*ou* une danse *ou* une pâtée) à, se frotter, moucher, passer à tabac, passer une peignée (*ou* une raclée *ou* une trempe) à, ramponner, rentrer dans le chou (*ou* le lard) à, rentrer dedans, rosser, rouster, sataner, scionner, sonner, tabasser, talmouser, tamponner, tarter, tatouiller, tisaner.

battre, se: s'amocher (le citron *ou* la gueule *ou* le portrait), se bagarrer, se bigorner, se bouffer le blair, se bûcher, se châtaigner, se colleter, se coltiner, se crêper le chignon (*ou* la tignasse), se crocheter, se filer des toises, se flanquer (*ou* se foutre) sur la gueule, se flanquer (*ou* se foutre) une peignée, se frotter, se peigner, se riffer, se torcher.

bavard *m*: baratineur *m*, bavasseur *m*, jacasse *f*, jacasseur *m*, jacteur *m*, jaspineur *m*, mitraillette *f*, pie *f*, tapette *f*, vacciné *m* à l'aiguille de phono.

bavarder: avoir une platine, baratiner, bavacher, bavasser, baver, blablater, caqueter, dégoiser, dévider, jaboter, jacasser, jacter, jasper, jaspiner, musiquer, palasser, papoter, pomper de l'air, potiner, rouler, tailler une bavette, en tailler une, tenir le crachoir, user sa salive.

Voir aussi **parler**.

beau, belle (*adj.*): badour, bath, baveau, bavelle, bœuf, choucard, chouctose, chouettard, chouette, chouettos, girofle, girond(e), impec, jojo, juteux, lobé, mirobolant, nickel, au poil, ridère,

riflo, roulé(e) au moule, schbeb, soinsoin, soua-soua, du tonnerre, urf.

beaucoup (*adv.*): bézef, bigrement, bougrement, lerche, vachement.

bébé *m*: criard *m*, gluant *m*, ourson *m*, petit salé.

bénéfice *m*: affure *f*, bénef *m*, beurre *m*, gants *m.pl.*, gâteau *m*, gras *m*, gratouille *f*, gratte *f*, rab(e) *m*, rabiot *m*, velours *m*.

bête (*adj.*): andouille, ballot, baluchard, baluche, bas de plafond, bébête, bec d'ombrelle, bêta, bidon, bille, bouché (à l'émeri), bourrique, branque, buse, carafon, cave, cavé, con, con(n)ard, con(n)asse, con(n)eau, cornichon, couillon, crétin, cruche, cruchon, cul, culcul, déphosphaté, déplafonné, duschnock, empaillé, empaqueté, emplâtré, empoté, enflé, fada, gourde, gourdiflot, lavedu, lourdingue, moule, navet, niguedouille, noix, nouille, oie, panard, patate, pied, plat de nouilles, pocheté, pomme, saucisse, schnock, serin, à tête de linotte, tourte, truffe, veau.

bêtise *f*: de la balançoire, des balançoires *f.pl.*, bidon *m*, blague *f*, bourdes *f.pl.*, connerie *f*, eau bénite de cour, eau *f* de bidet, fadaise *f*, faribole *f*, fichaise *f*, focard(e) *f*, focardise *f*, focardité *f*, foutaise *f*, pommade *f*, salades *f.pl.*, sornettes *f.pl.*, sottise *f*.

bévue *f*: boulette *f*, bourde *f*, cagade *f*, caraco *m*, char *m*, connerie *f*, gaffe *f*, galoup(e) *f*, impair *m*.

billets: *voir* **argent**.

blennorragie *f*: castapiane *f*, chaudelance *f*, chaude-pince *f*, chaude-pisse *f*, chtouille *f*, coulante *f*, schtouille *f*.

blesser: abîmer, allumer, amocher, aquiger, arranger, attiger, jambonner, maquiller, moucher, servir.

 blesser au couteau: faire des boutonnières à, mettre les tripes à l'air à, piquer, poser un portemanteau dans le dos de, rallonger.

bluffer: *voir* **exagérer**.

boire: s'arroser l'avaloir (*ou* la dalle), biberonner, chopiner, écluser (un godet), s'enfiler un verre, s'envoyer un coup, en étouffer un, en étrangler un, se gargariser, se graisser le toboggan, s'humecter les amygdales, se jeter une jatte, s'en jeter un (derrière la cravate), lamper, se laver les dents, lever le coude, lécher, lichailler, licher, se mouiller la dalle (*ou* la meule), picoler, picter, pinter, se piquer la ruche, pitancher, pomper, se rincer la dalle (*ou* le fusil *ou* le plomb), siffler, siroter, soiffer, sucer, téter.

bordel *m*: baisodrome *m*, bobinard *m*, bocard *m*, bocsif *m*, boxon *m*, bric *m*, cabane *f*, clac *m*, clandé *m*, claque *m*, foutoir *m*, lupanard *m*, maison d'abattage (*ou* bancale *ou* de passe), taule *f*, tringlodrome *m*, volière *f*.

bouche *f*: accroche-pipe *m*, bec *m*, boîte *f*, claque-merde *m*, dalle *f*, égout *m*, gargoulette *f*, gargue *f*, goule *f*, goulot *m*, gueule *f*, malle *f*, margoulette *f*, marmouse *f*, micro *m*, museau *m*, porte-pipe *m*, saladier *m*, terrine *f*, tirelire *f*, trappe *f*.

bourreau *m*: arrangeur *m*, correcteur *m*, faucheur *m*, grand coiffeur, rectifieur *m*.

bouteille *f*: boutanche *f*, pot *m*, rouillarde *f*, rouille *f*.

bouteille de champagne: roteuse *f*.

bouteille de vin rouge: kilbus *m*, kilo *m*, légionnaire *m*, litron *m*, négresse *f*, pieu *m*.

bouteille vide: cadavre *m*.

boutique *f*: boucard *m*, bouclard *m*, boutanche *f*, boutoche *f*, clapier *m*, estanco *m*, piaule *f*.

boutique de receleur: moulin *m*.

bras *m*: aile *f*, aileron *m*, anse *f*, aviron *m*, balancier *m*, ballant *m*, bradillon *m*, brandille *f*, brandillon *m*, nageoire *f*.

brave (être): avoir du battant (*ou* des couilles *ou* du cran *ou* de l'estomac *ou* du poil), avoir quelque chose dans le slip, en avoir au cul (*ou* dans le bide *ou* dans le moulin *ou* dans le ventre), n'avoir pas froid aux yeux, être accroché, être d'attaque, être gonflé, être un peu là.

briquet *m*: briquetoque *m*, chalumeau *m*, flamme *f*, lance-flamme *m*.

bruit *m*: bacchanal *m*, barouf *m*, bastringue *f*, boucan *m*, bousin *m*, boxon *m*, brouhaha *m*, cacophonie *f*, casse-oreilles *m*, casse-vitres *m*, chabanais *m*, chahut *m*, chambard *m*, foin *m*, grabuge *m*, musique *f*, pétard *m*, potin *m*, raffut *m*, rafût *m*, ramdam(e) *m*, zin-zin *m*.

butin *m*: barbotin *m*, bouquet *m*, fade *m*, rafle *f*, taf *m*, taffe *m*:

cacher: camoufler, car(r)er, étouffer, mettre à l'ombre (*ou* en planque *ou* en veilleuse *ou* au vert), planquer, planquouser.

cacher, se: se carrer, se nicher, se placarder, se planquer, se planquouser.

cachette *f*: placarde *f*, plan *m*, planque *f*, planquouse *f*, trou *m*.

cadavre *m*: allongé *m*, can(n)é *m*, croni *m*, macchab *m*, macchabé(e) *m*, refroidi *m*, saumon *m*, viande froide.

café *m* (*boisson*): cafeton *m*, cao *m*, caoua(h) *m*, cahoua *m*, chaud *m*, jus *m* de chaussette (*ou* de chique *ou* de shako), maza *m*, noir *m*.

café *m* (*débit*): abreuvoir *m*, bar *m*, bistre *m*, bistro *m*, bistroquet *m*, bistrot *m*, caboulot *m*, estanco(t) *m*, tapis *m*, troquet *m*.

cambrioler: caroubler, casser, faire un baluchonnage (*ou* une cambriole *ou* un casse *ou* un fric-frac), faire du bois, fracasser, frapper, fricfraquer, mettre (*ou* monter) en l'air, travailler au bec de canne.

cambrioleur *m*: baluchonneur *m*, cambrio *m*, caroubleur *m*, casseur *m*, chevalier *m* de la lune, fracasseur *m*, lourdeur *m*.

Voir aussi **voleur**.

campagne *f*: bled *m*, bouse *f*, brousse *f*, cambrousse *f*, parpagne *f*, patelin *m*, savane *f* au vert.

caprice *m*: béguin *m*, dada *m*, foucade *f*, pépin *m*, toquade *f*.

car *m* **de police**: car *m*, familiale *f*, fourgon *m*, panier *m* à salade, portepoulaille *m*, poulailler ambulant, voiture *f* de mariée, voiturin *m*.

caresses *f.pl.*: chatouilles *f.pl.*, chouteries *f.pl.*, mamours *m.pl.*, pattes *f.pl.* d'araignées (*ou* de velours), papouilles *f.pl.*, patouilles *f.pl.*, pelotes *f.pl.*

cartes *f.pl.* **à jouer**: bauches *f.pl.*, biftons *m.pl.*, brèmes *f.pl.*, cartons *m.pl.*, papiers *m.pl.*, poisseuses *f.pl.*

casquette *f*: bâche *f*, deffe *f*, gapette *f*, gaufre *f*, grivelle *f*, guimpe(tte) *f*.

cercueil *m*: boîte *f* à dominos, caisse *f*, paletot *m* (*ou* redingote *f*) de sapin, pardessus *m* sans manches.

chambre *f*: cabine *f*, cambuse *f*, carrée *f*, case *f*, crèche *f*, garno *m*, gourbi *m*, guitoune *f*, niche *f*, piaule *f*, planque *f*, quatre murs *m.pl.*, strasse *f*, taule *f*, turne *f*.

chance (avoir de la): avoir du baraka (*ou* du bol *ou* du cul *ou* du fion *ou* du gluck *ou* du pot *ou* du proze *ou* du vase *ou* de la veine), être beurré (*ou* bidard *ou* chançard *ou* cocu *ou* doré *ou* veinard *ou* verni).

chanter: dégosiller, l'envoyer, gargouiller, goualer, la pousser, pousser la goualante, y aller de sa goualante.

chapeau *m*: bada *m*, bibi *m*, bitos *m*, bloum *m*, capet *m*, doul(e) *m*, doulos *m*, galurin *m*, papeau *m*, pétase *m*, toiture *f*.

   chapeau haut de forme: cylindre *m*, décalitre *m*, gibus *m*, huit-reflets *m*, lampion *m*, tube *m*, tuyau *m* de poêle.

chaussures *f.pl.*: bateaux *m.pl.*, boîtes *f.pl.* à violon, crocos *m.pl.*, croquenots *m.pl.*, écrase-merde *m.pl.*, flacons *m.pl.*, godasses *f.pl.*, godilles *f.pl.*, godillots *m.pl.*, grôles *f.pl.*, lattes *f.pl.*, pompes *f.pl.*, ribouis *m.pl.*, rigadins *m.pl.*, savates *f.pl.*, sorlots *m.pl.*, targettes *f.pl.*, tartines *f.pl.*, tatanes *f.pl.*, tiges *f.pl.*

chauve (être): avoir une boule de billard (*ou* le caillou dégarni *ou* un crâne de limace *ou* un mouchodrome *ou* le melon déplumé *ou* la tête comme un genou *ou* une tête de veau), n'avoir une perruque en peau de fesse, n'avoir plus de chapelure (*ou* de cresson *ou* de mousse) sur le caillou, n'avoir plus de cresson sur la fontaine, être dégazonné (*ou* déplumé *ou* jambonneau *ou* zigué).

chemise *f*: bannière *f*, drapeau *m*, limace *f*, lime *f*, limouse *f*, liquette *f*, sac *m* à lard (*ou* à puces).

cher, chère (*adj.*) (*coûteux*): chaud, chérot, grisole, lerche, lerchem, salé.

cheval *m*: bidet *m*, bique *f*, bourdon *m*, bourrin *m*, bousin *m*, canard *m*, canasson *m*, carcan *m*, carne *m*, dada *m*, gail(le) *m*, hareng *m*, rossard *m*, rosse *f*, tréteau *m*.

cheveux *m.pl.*: cresson *m*, crins *m.pl.*, douilles *f.pl.*, gazon *m*, plumes *f.pl.*, tiffes *m.pl.*, tifs *m.pl.*, tignasse *f*.

   couper les cheveux à quelqu'un: épiler la pêche à quelqu'un, tiffer quelqu'un, varloper la toiture à quelqu'un.

chien *m*: azor *m*, bougnoul(e) *m*, cabot *m*, cador *m*, chien-chien *m*, clébard *m*, clebs *m*, oua(h)-oua(h) *m*, toutou *m*.

cigare *m*: churchill *m*, long *m*.

   gros cigare: barreau *m* de chaise.

   petit cigare: clou *m* de cercueil, crapulos *m*.

cigarette *f*: baluche *f*, cibiche *f*, cousue *f*, grillante *f*, pipe *f*, pipette *f*, sèche *f*, taf *f*, taffe *f*, tige *f*.

cigarette à filtre: périodique *f*, tampax *f*.

cigarette papier maïs: chinois *m*.

Voir aussi **drogues: cigarette de marijuana.**

cimetière *m*: boulevard *m* (*ou* jardin *m*) des allongés, champ *m* des refroidis, chez les têtes en os, jardin *m* des claqués, parc *m* des cronis.

clef *f*: carouble *f*, gerbière *f*, tournan..e *f*.

clitoris *m*: berlingot *m*, berlingue *f*, bouton *m* (de rose), clicli *m*, clito(n) *m*, flageolet *m*, framboise *f*, grain *m* de café, haricot *m*, noisette *f*, praline *f*, soissonnais *m* (rose).

clochard *m*: cloche *m*, clodo(t) *m*, traîne-lattes *m*, traîne-patins *m*, traîne-sabots *m*, traîne-savates *m*, trimardeur *m*, zonard *m*.

Voir aussi **vagabond.**

cœur *m*: battant *m*, horloge *f*, palpitant *m*, grand ressort, toquant *m*.

coït *m*: baisade *f*, baisage *m*, bourre *f*, carambolage *m*, chique *f*, coup *m* d'arbalète, crampe *f*, crampette *f*, criquon-criquette *m*, dérouillade *f*, dérouillage *m*, fouraillage *m*, frottage *m*, giclée *f*, mise *f*, partie *f* de balayette (*ou* d'écarté *ou* de jambes en l'air *ou* de piquet), passe *f*, pelée *f*, politesse *f*, soupe *f* à la quéquette, torpillage *m*, tringlage *m*, tronchage *m*, tronche *f*, truc *m*, yensage *m*, zizi-panpan *m*.

   coït anal: 1. **pratiquer la pédérastie active (sur)**: (*a*) (*intransitif*) baiser à la riche, casser coco, casser le pot, prendre de l'oignon, tourner la page, tremper la soupe; (*b*) (*transitif*) caser, dauffer, emmancher, empaffer, empaler, empapaouter, empétarder, emproser, encaldosser, enculer, enfifrer, enfigner, miser, planter.

   2. **pratiquer la pédérastie passive**: (*intransitif*) filer de la jaquette, lâcher de l'anneau, *etc.* (*voir* **anus**), ramasser des épingles, se faire taper dedans.

   faire un coït buccal: (*a*) (*intransitif*) bouffer la chatte (*femme*), brouter (le cresson) (*femme*), se faire allonger, se faire croquer, faire mimi (*femme*), faire minette (*femme*), faire un pompier, se laver les dents, prendre la pipe, rogner l'os, souffler dans la canne (*ou* le mirliton *ou* le tube), tailler une plume; (*b*) (*transitif*) dévorer, manger, pomper, prendre en poire, sucer.

coïter : 1. (*intransitif*) aller à la bourre (*ou* aux cuisses *ou* au cul *ou* au taponard), aller au mâle (*femme*), amener le petit au cirque, arracher un copeau (*ou* un pavé), asperger le persil, besogner, casser la canne, cracher dans le bénitier, cramper, décrasser les oreilles à Médor, se dégraisser, dérouiller (son petit frère *ou* Totor), effeuiller la marguerite, s'envoyer (en l'air), s'envoyer une femme, le faire, faire l'amour, faire la bête à deux dos, faire ça, faire un carton, faire criquoncriquette, faire une partie de jambes en l'air, faire zizi-panpan, se farcir du mâle (*femme*), se farcir une femme, filer un coup d'arbalète (*ou* de brosse *ou* de patte *ou* de sabre *ou* de tromblon), fourailler, foutre un coup de brosse (*ou* de manche de plumeau *ou* de rouleau), godailler, godiller, se mélanger, le mettre, mettre la cheville dans le trou, nettoyer son verre de lampe, niquer, planter le mai, pousser sa pointe, prendre du mâle (*femme*), tirer sa chique (*ou* son coup *ou* sa crampe *ou* sa crampette), tirer son (*ou* un) coup, voir la feuille à l'envers.
    coïter avec... : 2. (*transitif*) aiguiller, baiser, biquer, bit(t)er, bourrer, bourriner, bourriquer, brosser, calecer, caramboler, caser, chevaucher, coller, coucher avec, égoïner, enfiler, enjamber, envoyer en l'air, fourailler, fourrer, foutre, frotter, goupillonner, grimper, guiser, limer, mettre au bout (*ou* au chaud), miser, niquer, piner, pinocher, piquer, planter, pointer, ramer, ramoner, sabrer, sauter, sch(e)nailler, tomber, torcher, torpiller, tringler, trombiner, troncher, verger, yenser.

colère *f* (**être en**) : attraper le coup de sang, l'avoir à la caille, crosser, éclater, s'emballer, être à cran (*ou* en fumasse *ou* furibard *ou* en rogne *ou* en suif), exploser, fulminer, fumer, marronner, monter à l'échelle (*ou* sur ses grands chevaux), mousser, pétarder, piquer une crise, râler, renauder, roter, rouspéter, sortir de ses gonds, voir rouge.

complice *m* : baron *m*, cheville *f*, équipier *m*, gaffeur *m*.

concierge *mf* : bignole *mf*, cloporte *mf*, lourdier *m*, pibloque *mf*, pipelet *m*, pipelette *f*. tortue *f*.

condamnation *f* : gerbage *m*, sape *m*, sapement *m*, sucrage *m*.

condamné (être) : cascader, écoper, être bon(nard), être sucré, gerber, morfler, payer, saper, trinquer.

congédier : balancer, balayer, bouler, débarquer, dégommer, déposer, envoyer dinguer (*ou* paître), flanquer (*ou* mettre) à la porte, sa(c)quer, scier, sortir, vider, virer.
    Voir aussi **débarrasser de, se.**

corbillard *m* : balai *m*, corbi *m*, dernier autobus, roulotte *f* à refroidis, trottinette *f* (à macchab).

cou *m* : col *m*, colbaque *m*, kiki *m*, sifflet *m*, vis *f*.

coucher, se : aller au dodo (*ou* à la dorme *ou* au paddock *ou* au page *ou* au pageot *ou* au pieu *ou* au plumard *ou* à la ronflette *ou* au schloff), se bâcher, se borgnot(t)er, se crécher, faire banette, se filer dans les toiles, se glisser dans les bannes, se grabater, mettre sa viande dans le torchon, se paddocker, se pager, se pagnoter, se pajoter, se pieuter, se plumarder, se plumer, se sacquer, se zoner.

coup(s) *m* (*pl.*) : atout *m*, avoine *f*, baffe *f*, baffre *f*, beigne *f*, brossée *f*, cabachon *m*, calotte *f*, châtaigne *f*, danse *f*, décoction *f*, dégelée *f*, dérouillée *f*, fricassée *f*, frictionnée *f*, frottée *f*, gnon *m*, jeton *m*, marron *m*, passage *m* à tabac, pâtée *f*, pêche *f*, peignée *f*, pile *f*, pipe *f*, purge *f*, raclée *f*, ramponneau *m*, ratatouille *f*, rincée *f*, rossée *f*, roulée *f*, tabassée *f*, talmouse *f*, taloche *f*, tannée *f*, tarte *f*, tartine *f*, tatouille *f*, tisane *f*, torchée *f*, torgn(i)ole *f*, tournée *f*, trempe *f*, trempée *f*, trifouillée *f*, tripotée *f*, triquée *f*, valse *f*.
    Voir aussi **recevoir (des coups).**

courageux : *voir* **brave.**

courir : affûter ses gambettes (*ou* ses pincettes), se carapater, cavaler, crapahuter, drop(p)er, jouer des flûtes (*ou* des guibolles), tricoter des bâtons, des gambettes, *etc.* (*voir* **jambe**).

couteau *m* : coupe-lard *m*, cure-dent *m*, lame *f*, lardoir *m*, ouvre-saucisses *m*, pointe *f*, rallonge *f*, rapière *f*, saccagne *f*, sorlingue *m*, surin *m*.

couverture *f* : *voir* **alibi.**

crachat *m* : glaviot *m*, gluau *m*, graillon *m*, huître *f*, mol(l)ard *m*, postillon *m*.

cracher : glavioter, graillonner, mollarder.

crâne *m* : caillou *m*, mansarde *f*, plafond *m*, toiture *f*.

crier: beugler, brailler, braire, donner des coups de gueule, goualer, gueuler (au charron), péter, piailler, piauler, pousser des gueulements.

critiquer: abîmer, aquijer, assassiner, bêcher, carboniser, charrier, chiner, débiner, déchirer (à belles dents), dégrainer, démolir, déshabiller, éreinter, esquinter, faire un abattage de, griller, jardiner, jeter la pierre à, vanner.

croire: couper dedans, donner dedans (*ou* dans le panneau), encaisser, gober, marcher, rendre.

danser: gambiller, gigoter, guincher, en suer une, (faire) tourner.

débarrasser de, se: balancer, balanstiquer, se décramponner de, se défarguer de, dégommer, envoyer (*ou* faire) dinguer, laisser choir, larguer, lessiver, sa(c)quer, scier, vider, virer.
Voir aussi **abandonner; congédier.**

débrouiller, se: avoir la combine (*ou* le système D), la connaître (dans les coins), se défendre, se démerder, se démouscailler, se dépatouiller, savoir s'expliquer (*ou* nager *ou* se retourner).

découvrir: dégot(t)er, dénicher, dépiauter, frimer, piger, repérer.

déféquer: aller où le Roi va à pied, caguer, chier, couler un bronze, déballer, débloquer, déboucher son orchestre, débourrer (sa pipe), déflaquer, faire caca, faire sa grande commission, faire ses affaires, faire ses grands besoins, flasquer, foirer, lâcher (*ou* poser) un colombin (*ou* une prune *ou* une sentinelle), planter une borne, tartir.

dénoncer: balancer, balanstiquer, balloter, bourdiller, bourriquer, brûler, cafarder, donner, filer, griller, moucharder, moutonner, retapisser.

dénonciateur *m*: bordille *m*, bourdille *m*, bourricot *m*, bourrique *f*, cafard *m*, cafardeur *m*, casserole *f*, chacal *m*, chevreuil *m*, croqueur *m*, donneur *m*, fileur *m*, grilleur *m*, indic *m*, mouchard *m*, mouche *f*, mouton *m*, tante *f*.
Voir aussi **indicateur.**

dents *f.pl.*: castagnettes *f.pl.*, chocottes *f.pl.*, crochets *m.pl.*, crocs *m.pl.*, croquantes *f.pl.*, dominos *m.pl.*, pavés *m.pl.*, piloches *f.pl.*, quenottes *f.pl.*, râteaux *m.pl.*, ratiches *f.pl.*, ratoches *f.pl.*, touches *f.pl.* de piano.

dépêcher, se: s'activer, allonger le pas (*ou* la sauce), se décarcasser, se dégrouiller, se déhotter, se démancher, se démerder, se dérouiller, faire fissa (*ou* vinaigre), se grouiller (les puces), se magner (le cul *ou* le derrière *ou* le popotin *ou* le train), en mettre (*ou* filer) un rayon.

dépenser: balancer (*ou* bouffer *ou* claquer *ou* croquer) de l'argent, carmer, casquer, cigler, décher, les écosser, les faire valser, les lâcher, larguer son fric.

dépensier *m*: claque-fric *mf*, décheur *m*.

dés *m.pl.*: bobs *m.pl.*, doches *m.pl.*
      dés truqués: artillerie *f*, balourds *m.pl.*, bouts *m.pl.* de sucre, matuches *m.pl.*, pipés *m.pl.*, plateaux *m.pl.*, plats *m.pl.*

déshabiller: décarpiller, défagoter, défringuer, défrusquer, déloquer, dénipper, désaper, désharnacher, foutre (*ou* mettre) à l'air (*ou* à poil), trousser la cotte.

dessous *m.pl.* (*féminins*): falbalas *m.pl.*, fringues *f.pl.* de coulisses, linges *m.pl.*, mouillettes *f.pl.*, soies *f.pl.*

détester: avoir à la caille, avoir dans le blair (*ou* dans le cul *ou* dans le nez *ou* dans le tube), ne pas pouvoir blairer (*ou* encadrer *ou* encaisser), ne pas pouvoir voir en peinture.

diamant *m*: bauche *m*, bouchon *m* de carafe, caillou *m*, diam(e) *m*, éclair *m*, pierre *f*, speech *m*.

diarrhée *f*: chiasse *f*, cliche *f*, courante *f*, foirade *f*, foire *f*, foireuse *f*, riquette *f*.

difficile (*adj.*): coton, duraille, duraillon, duringue, glandilleux, turbin.

discours *m*: baratin *m*, boniment *m*, palas(s) *m*, parlotte *f*, postiche *m*, salade *f*, speech *m*.

doigt *m*: (*main*) apôtre *m*, fourchette *f*, phalangette *f*, piloir *m*; (*pied*) racine *f*, radis *m*.

donner: abouler, allonger, balancer, balanstiquer, coller, ficher, filer, flanquer, foutre, lâcher, refiler.

dormir: baisser la vitrine, dormailler, dormasser, en écraser, faire dodo (*ou* schloff), pioncer, piquer une ronflette (*ou* un roupillon), ronfler, roupiller, roupillonner, tomber dans les bras de Morphée, zoner.

      dormir dehors: coucher à la belle étoile (*ou* sur la dure), être de la zone, refiler la comète.

drap m: bâche f, banne f, lingerie f, toile f, torchon m.

drogué (adj.): bourré, camé, chargé, défoncé, dynamité, envapé, high, junké.

drogué m: camard m, camé m, camelinque m, dynamité m, enschnouffé m, junkie m, toxico m.

droguer, se: se camer, se charger, se chnouffer, se doper, s'envaper, se piquer, se piquouser, prendre une reniflette (ou une respirette) (cocaïne), se schnouffer, tirer sur le bambou (opium).

drogues f.pl.: came f, chnouff m, narcs m.pl., schnouff(e) m, stups m.pl.

   amphétamines f.pl.: bleues f.pl., bonbons m.pl., rouquine f, serpent vert, speed m, topette f.

   barbituriques m.pl.: barbitos m.pl., balles f.pl. de copaille.

   Benzédrine f (marque déposée): b f, bennie f, benz m.

   cannabis m: voir **marijuana**.

   cocaïne f: bigornette f, blanche f, la c, cécile m, coco f, dynamite f, fée blanche, fillette f, métro m (1 gr.), neige f, poison blanc, poudrette f, talc m, topette f.

   drinamyl m: arbre m de Noël, bleuet m, bleue f, bleuette f.

   éphédrine f: Freddie m.

   ha(s)chisch m: fée verte, griffs m.pl., merde f.

   héroïne f: boy m, cheval m, H f, héro f, horse m, jus m, naph(taline) f, niflette f, poudre f, shit m, shmeck m.

   LSD m: acide m, D m, sucre m, vingt-cinq m.

   marijuana f: bambalouche f, canapa f, chanvre m, chiendent m, dagga m, douce f, foin m, gania m, gold m, herbe (douce), juana f, juju f, kif m, Maria f, Marie(-Jeanne) f, pot m, thé m (des familles ou vert).

   cigarette f **de marijuana**: bouffée f, drag m, fume f, joint m, juju f, pipe f, reefer m, stick m.

   morphine f: lili-pioncette f, morph f.

   opium m: bénarès m, boue (verte), chandoo m, dross m, fée brune, lourd m, noir m, op m, pavot m, touffiane f.

duper: voir **escroquer**.

eau f: bouillon m, Château-la-Pompe m, flotte f, jus m (de parapluie), lance f, lancequine f, sirop m de canard (ou de grenouille ou de parapluie).

échec m: bec m de gaz, bide m, black-boulage m, bouchon m, bûche f, cassage m de nez, chou blanc, fiasco m, foirage m, four m, gamelle f, loupage m, marron m, pelle f, pipe f, vert m, veste f.

échouer: se casser le nez, claquer, faire chou blanc, faire la culbute, faire un four, finir dans les choux (ou en eau de boudin ou en queue de poisson), foirer, louper, péter dans la main, ramasser une veste, récolter un bide, remporter une pelle, tomber dans le lac.

économiser: carrer, faire son beurre (ou sa pelote), garer, en mettre à gauche, planquer, planquouser.

éjaculer: voir **orgasme (avoir un)**.

élégant (adj.): badour, (super-)chic, eulpif, flambard, tout flambe, gandin, en grand tralala, hiche-life, en jetant (un jus), jojo, juteux, minet, régence, rider, ridère, riflo, sur son trente et un, tiré à quatre épingles, urf(e).

embrasser: bécoter, biser, coquer un bécot à, faire un bec (ou un bécot) à, faire une langue (fourrée) à, lécher (ou se sucer) le caillou (ou le citron ou le museau ou la poire ou la pomme) à, rouler une galoche (ou un patin ou des saucisses) à.

emploi m: voir **travail**.

emprisonner: bloquer, boucler, coffrer, encager, enchetarder, enchrister, ench(e)tiber, ficher (ou flanquer ou fourrer) dedans, mettre au bloc (ou au clou ou au gnouf ou à l'ombre ou au trou), mettre derrière les barreaux, mettre en taule, remiser, serrer.

emprunter (de l'argent) à: bottiner, latter, relancer, sonner, taper, tartiner, torpiller.

enceinte (être): s'arrondir, attraper le ballon, avoir avalé le pépin, avoir du ballon, avoir sa butte, avoir un pain dans le four, avoir un polichinelle (ou un moufflet ou un petit salé) dans le tiroir (ou sous le tablier), avoir sucé son crayon, être cloquée (ou en cloque), être engrossée, être tombée sur un clou rouillé, gondoler de la devanture, travailler pour Marianne.

enfant m: bout m de zan, chiard m, chiot m, crapaud m, gamin m, gniard m, gosse mf, graine f de bois de lit, lardon m, loupiot m, merdeux m, mioche mf, môme mf, momichon m, momignard m, morbac m, morpion m, moucheron m, moufflet *m*, moujingue *m*, moussé *m*, moutard *m*, niston *m*, pitchoun *m*, salé *m*, tchiot *m*, têtard *m*.

enfuir, s' : *voir* **partir.**

ennuyer : assassiner, assommer, barber, bassiner, canuler, casser le bonbon (*ou* les couilles *ou* les pieds) à, cavaler, courir (*ou* taper) sur le système à, cramponner, emmerder, emmieller, emmouscailler, empoisonner, enquiquiner, faire chier (*ou* suer), raser, scier, tanner.

ennuyeux (*adj.*) : accrocheur, assommant, assommoir, barbant, barbe, bassin, canulant, canule, casse-burettes, casse-burnes, casse-couilles, casse-pieds, colique, crampon, emmerdant, gluant, pot de colle, raseur, rasoir, sciant, scie, tannant.

épouse *f* : baronne *f*, bergère *f*, bobonne *f*, boulet *m*, bourgeoise *f*, gouvernement *m*, légitime *f*, ma (chère) moitié, particulière *f*, vieille *f*.

érection *f* (**être en**) : avoir le bambou (*ou* le bâton *ou* la canne *ou* la gaule *ou* le gourdin *ou* le manche *ou* le mandrin *ou* l'os *ou* le tracassin *ou* la trique), avoir des coliques cornues, l'avoir dur (*ou* en l'air), bander, bandocher, être en l'air, être triqué, goder, lever, marquer midi, présenter les armes (*ou* son offrande), redresser, répondre du starter, triquer.

escroc *m* : arnaqueur *m*, arrangeur *m*, carambouilleur *m*, carotteur *m*, dragueur *m*, empileur *m*, entôleur *m*, estampeur *m*, faisan *m*, faisandier *m*, faiseur *m*, filou *m*, floueur *m*, musicien *m*, pipeur *m*, rangemane *m*, rangeur *m*, repasseur *m*, roustisseur *m*, turbineur *m*.

escroquer : arnaquer, arranger, avoir, baiser, carotter, caver, doubler, écailler, écorcher, empaumer, empiler, endormir, enfiler, englander, engourdir, entuber, estamper, fabriquer, faisander, farcir, filouter, flouer, mener au double, monter le coup à, posséder, pigeonner, rangemaner, refaire, rouler, roustir, tirer une carotte à.

escroquerie *f* : arnac *f*, arnaquage *m*, arnaque *f*, bourrage *m*, carambouillage *m*, carottage *m*, carotte *f*, coup *m* d'arnac, doublage *m*, doublure *f*, entôlage *m*, entubage *m*, filouterie *f*, repassage *m*, resquille *f*.

estomac *m* : bocal *m*, boîte *f* à ragoût, buffet *m*, burlingue *m*, cornet *m*, estom(e) *m*, fanal *m*, fusil *m*, garde-manger *m*, gésier *m*, jabot *m*, lampe *f*, lampion *m*, tube *m*.

Voir aussi **ventre.**

étonner : abasourdir, aplatir, asseoir, en boucher un coin (*ou* une surface) à, clouer, couper la chique à, épater, époustoufler, estomaquer, occire.

étrangler : dévisser le coco à, donner le coup de pouce à, nouer la cravate à, serrer le kiki (*ou* la vis) à.

étron *m* : bronze *m*, caca *m*, colombin *m*, déflaque *f*, factionnaire *m*, orphelin *m*, pêche *f*, prune *f*, rondin *m*.

évader, s' : les agiter, se barrer, (se) calter, se carapater, se casser, se cavaler, chier du poivre, décarrer, se donner de l'air, en jouer un air, jouer rip (*ou* la fille de l'air), (se) faire la malle (*ou* la valise), filer, larguer les amarres, mettre les bouts (*ou* les voiles), se mettre en cavale, riper, se tirer, se trotter.

évanouir, s' : tomber dans le cirage (*ou* les frites *ou* les pommes *ou* le sirop *ou* les vapes), tomber en digue-digue, tourner de l'œil.

exagérer : attiger (la cabane), bêcher, blouser, broder, charrier, cherrer (dans les bégonias), chier dans la colle, chiquer, cravater, se donner des coups de pied, enfler des chevilles, envoyer le bouchon, esbrouf(f)er, faire de l'esbrouf(f)e (*ou* de la musique *ou* du pallas), en faire une tartine, forcer la dose, se gonfler, gonfler le mou, graisser, en installer, jardiner, majorer, se monter le job, pousser, se pousser du col, en rajouter, vanner, y aller fort.

excellent (*adj.*) : à tout casser, baisant, bath, bœuf, bolide, chouette, chouettos, de première, doré sur tranche, du tonnerre, épatant, époustouflant, faramineux, formid(able), foutral, impec, meu-meu, nickel, au poil, sensas(s), soin-soin, super, terrible, wif.

faim (avoir) : avoir un creux, avoir les crochets (*ou* les crocs *ou* la dalle *ou* la dent), avoir l'estomac dans les talons, bouffer des briques, se brosser, claquer du bec, la crever, danser devant le buffet, se mettre la ceinture, la péter, la sauter, la serrer, (se) serrer la ceinture, se taper.

faire : s'appuyer, fabriquer, ficher, foutre, fricoter, goupiller.

fatigué (être): avoir le coup de bambou (*ou* de barre *ou* de pompe), avoir son compte, être à bout (*ou* à plat), être affûté (*ou* avachi *ou* brisé *ou* claqué *ou* crevé *ou* crevetant *ou* éreinté *ou* esquinté *ou* flagada *ou* flapi *ou* fourbu *ou* foutu *ou* lessivé *ou* pompé *ou* raplapla *ou* rendu *ou* rincé *ou* rompu *ou* sur le flanc *ou* vanné *ou* vaseux *ou* vasouillard *ou* vidé), être sur les dents (*ou* les genoux *ou* les rotules).

faux (*adj.*): bidon, chinetoque, toc, tocard.

femme *f* (*péj.*): baronne *f*, bougresse *f*, chipie *f*, créature *f*, donzelle *f*, dragon *m*, fatma *f*, femelle *f*, fendue *f*, fumelle *f*, garce *f*, gisquette *f*, gonzesse *f*, greluche *f*, grognasse *f*, harpie *f*, hotu *f*, houri *f*, lamdé *f*, lamfé *f*, largue *f*, limace *f*, mémé *f*, ménesse *f*, mistonne *f*, moukère *f*, mousmé(e) *f*, nana *f*, nénette *f*, pépée *f*, pétasse *f*, polka *f*, poule *f*, poulette *f*, pouliche *f*, rombière *f*, souris *f*, tarderie *f*, tartavelle *f*, toupie *f*, typesse *f*.

jeune femme: bergère *f*, garce *f*, gisquette *f*, gonzesse *f*, greluche *f*, grimbiche *f*, Julie, lamdé *f*, lamfé *f*, mistonne *f*, môme *f*, mousmé(e) *f*, nana *f*, nénette *f*, palombe *f*, pépée *f*, poule *f*, poulette *f*, pouliche *f*.

(vieille) femme laide: bique *f*, carabosse *f*, carcan *f*, guenon *f*, guimbarde *f*, hotu *m*, mémée *f*, mocheté *f*, prix *m* à réclamer, remède *m* d'amour, rombière *f*, tarderie *f*, tartignol(l)e *f*, tardingue *f*, tartavelle *f*, vieille chèvre (*ou* galoche *ou* mocheté *ou* noix *ou* savate), vieux trumeau.

fesses *f.pl.*: arrière-boutique *f*, as *m*, baba *m*, bernard *m*, cadran *m* (solaire), dédé *m*, der *m*, derche *m*, derge *m*, dossière *f*, faubourg *m*, fessier *m*, fouettard *m*, griottes *f.pl.*, joufflu *m*, lune *f*, miches *m.pl.*, montre *f*, mouilles *f.pl.*, moutardier *m*, noix *f.pl.*, panier *m* à crottes, père-fouettard *m*, pétard *m*, pétoulet *m*, pétrousquin *m*, pétrus *m*, pont-arrière *m*, popotin *m*, postère *m*, potard *m*, prose *m*, prosinard *m*, proze *m*, prozinard *m*, radada *m*, sonore *m*, tal *m*, tapanard *m*, trafanard *m*, train *m*, valseur *m*, vase *m*, verre *m* de montre.

fête *f*: *voir* **réjouissances**.

figure *f*: *voir* **visage**.

(jeune) fille *f*: benette *f*, caille *f*, frou-frou *f*, gamine *f*, gisquette *f*, gosse *f*, gosseline *f*, loulou *f*, minette *f*,

mômaque *f*, môme *f*, nistonne *f*, pisseuse *f*, quille *f*, tendron *m*.

flatter: baratiner, bonimenter, bourrer la caisse (*ou* le crâne *ou* le mou) à, casser le nez à coups d'encensoir à, cirer, enduire, faire de la lèche à, faire du boniment (*ou* du flan *ou* du plat) à, lécher les bottes (*ou* le cul) à, passer la main dans le dos à, passer (de) la pommade (dans les cheveux) à, peloter, pommader.

fort (être): en avoir, être d'attaque (*ou* balèze *ou* bien balancé *ou* bien baraqué *ou* costaud *ou* fortiche *ou* mailloche *ou* malabar *ou* maousse), être un peu là, se poser là.

fou (*adj.*): azimuté, branque, braque, chabraque, cinglé, cinoque, cintré, déboussolé, déplafonné, dérangé, détraqué, dévissé, dingo, dingue, fada, fêlé, focard, follingue, fondu, frappé, givré, locdu, louf, louffe, loufoque, louftingue, maboul(e), marteau, percuté, piqué, sinoc, sinoque, siphonné, sonné, tapé, timbré, tocbombe, toctoc, toqué, tordu, touché.

devenir fou: déménager, dérailler, partir du ciboulot, perdre la boule (*ou* la boussole *ou* la carte *ou* le nord), piquer le coup de bambou.

être fou: avoir une araignée au plafond (*ou* une chauve-souris dans le beffroi), avoir reçu un coup de bambou, avoir une fissure (*ou* un grain), battre la breloque, bouillir de la cafetière, se décarcasser le boisseau, être cucu (la praline), onduler de la toiture, travailler du chapeau (*ou* du cigare), yoyoter de la mansarde.

foule *f*: populo *m*, trèfle *m*, trèpe *m*, trèple *m*.

frère *m*: frangibus *m*, frangin *m*, frelot *m*, frérot *m*, moré *m*.

fromage *m*: coulant *m*, frome *m*, frometon *m*, fromgi *m*, fromtogomme *m*, puant *m*, rampant *m*, tapant *m*.

fumer: bombarder, bouffarder, en griller une, piper, sécher, tiger, tirer (sa touche *ou* sa taf *ou* sa taffe).

gagner (de l'argent): affurer, arrondir (*ou* faire) sa pelote, en amasser, en ramasser, faire du pèse, faire son beurre, prendre le paquet, se remplir (les poches), se sucrer (tant et plus).

gain *m*: affure *f*, bénef *m*, beurre *m*, bonus *m*, velours *m*.

gardien m (de prison): gâfe m, gaffe m, maton m, matuche m.

gardien-chef m: double m.

gendarme m: bédi m, pandore m, sansonnet m, sauret m, schmit m.

goinfre m & adj.: bâfreur (m), bec m à tout grain, (béni-)bouftou(t) (m), bouffe-la-balle (m), bouffe-tout (m), crevard (m), goulu (m), gueulard (m), morfal (m), morfalou (m), piffre (m), porc m.

gonorrhée f: voir **blennorragie**.

gorge f: avaloir m, cornet m, couloir m, courgnole f, dalle f, fanal m, gargane f, gargoulette f, goulot m, tube m.

gras (adj.): voir **gros**.

gratuit (adj.): au béguin, au châsse, gratis (pro Deo), à l'œil, pour la peau, pour que dalle.

grogner: bougonner, être en boule (ou à cran ou comme un crin ou en rogne), groumer, marronner, râler, la ramener, renâcler, renauder, ronchonner, rouscailler, rouspéter, tousser.

gros (adj.): bibendum, bouboule, boulot(te), dondon, gravos, mailloche, malabar, maousse (poil-poil), patapouf, pépère, plein de soupe, rondouillard, soua-soua.

guetter: avoir à l'œil, broquer, faire le gaffe (ou le pet ou la planque), gaffer, mater, zyeuter.

guillotine f: abbaye f de Monte-à-regret, bascule f, bécane f, coupante f, coupe-cigare m, faucheuse f, hachoir m, machine f à raccourcir, Veuve f.

être guillotiné: y aller du caillou, basculer du chou (ou du gadin), cracher dans le panier, épouser la Veuve, éternuer dans le son, se faire décoller le cigare, se faire raccourcir, mettre la tête à la fenêtre, tirer sa crampe avec la Veuve.

habile (être): avoir le coup (ou le truc), la connaître dans les coins, en connaître un rayon, se démerder, être ferré (ou marle), savoir y faire.

habiller: fagoter, fringuer, friper, frusquer, harnacher, linger, loquer, nipper, sabouler, saper.

mal habillé: mal fagoté, mal ficelé, fringué comme l'as de pique.

habiter: crécher, nicher, percher.

habits m.pl.: voir **vêtements**.

homme m: artiste m, asticot m, birbe m, bougre m, client m, coco m, escogriffe

m, fias m, frangin m, frelot m, gars m, gazier m, gniasse m, gnière m, goncier m, gonze m, Jules m, Julot m, lascar m, loulou m, loustic m, matz m, mec m, mecton m, mironton m, moineau m, numéro m, oiseau m, paroissien m, piaf m, pierrot m, pistolet m, sujet m, tartempion m, type m, zèbre m, zigomard m, zigoto m, zigue m.

hôpital m: castre m, host(e)au m, hosto m, planque f aux attigés.

ignorant (adj.): bûche, crétin, croûte, croûton, cruche, en retard d'une rame, pas affranchi, pas à la page, pas au parfum, pas dans le coup.

imaginer, s': avoir la berlue (ou des visions), se berlurer, croire que c'est arrivé, entendre des voix, se faire du cinoche, se fourrer le doigt dans l'œil, se monter le bourrichon (ou le cou).

indicateur m (police): balanceur m, bordille m, bourdille m, cafeteur m, casserole f, chacal m, chevreuil m, coqueur m, donneur m, gamelle f, indic m, mouchard m, mouche f, mouton m.

Voir aussi **dénonciateur**.

individu m: voir **homme**.

initier: affranchir, dessaler, éclairer (sur la couleur), mettre à la page (ou au parfum ou dans le coup).

injurier: agoniser, baptiser, engueuler, enguirlander, incendier, rembarrer.

insouciant (adj.): je-m'en-fichiste, je-m'en-foutiste, pas bileux, qui ne s'en fait pas, qui se les chauffe, qui se la coule (douce), qui se laisse vivre.

interdiction f de séjour: badine f, bambou m, bâton m, trique f.

interrogatoire m: baratin m, blutinage m, cuisinage m, cuisine f, musique f, saignement m de nez.

ivre (être): s'arrondir, avoir du vent dans les voiles, avoir pris la bit(t)ure (ou la cuite), avoir sa cuite (ou son plumet), avoir un coup dans l'aile, avoir un verre dans le nez, se bit(t)urer, être asphyxié (ou beurré ou bit(t)uré ou blindé ou blindezingue ou bourré (à bloc) ou brindezingué ou chargé ou chicoré ou cuit ou dans le cirage ou dans les vapes ou éteint ou fabriqué ou fadé ou fait ou fara ou gazé ou givré ou mâchuré ou mûr ou murdingue ou noir ou noiricot ou paf ou parti ou pion ou pionnard ou plein (comme une bourrique) *ou* raide *ou* rétamé *ou* rond *ou* rondibé *ou* saoul (comme un Polonais) *ou* schlass *ou* soûl *ou* teinté), se pionner, se piquer le nez, ramasser une beurrée, en rouler une, en tenir une bit(t)ure (*ou* une cuite).

être légèrement ivre : avoir chaud aux plumes, avoir son aigrette (*ou* sa pointe), être allumé (*ou* attendri *ou* ébréché *ou* éméché *ou* émoustillé *ou* ému *ou* entre deux vins *ou* gris *ou* parti *ou* pompette).

ivresse *f* : beuverie *f*, bit(t)ure *f*, caisse *f*, cuite *f*, cuvée *f*, pionnardise *f*, poivrade *f*, saoulerie *f*, saoulographie *f*, soûlerie *f*.

ivrogne *m* : bibard *m*, licheur *m*, picoleur *m*, pion *m*, pionnard *m*, pochard *m*, poivrier *m*, poivrot *m*, riboteur *m*, sac *m* à vin, saoulard *m*, saouloir *m*, saoulot *m*, soiffard *m*, soiffeur *m*, soûlard *m*, soûlographe *m*, soûloir *m*, soûlot *m*, vide-bouteille(s) *m*.

jambes *f.pl.* : baguettes *f.pl.*, bâtons *m.pl.* (de chaise), bégonias *m.pl.*, béquilles *f.pl.*, brancards *m.pl.*, cannes *f.pl.*, compas *m.pl.*, flubards *m.pl.*, fusains *m.pl.*, fuseaux *m.pl.*, gambettes *f.pl.*, gambilles *f.pl.*, gigots *m.pl.*, gigues *f.pl.*, guibolles *f.pl.*, pattes *f.pl.*, pivots *m.pl.*, quenelles *f.pl.*, quilles *f.pl.*

jambes faibles : crayons mal attachés, genoux *m.pl.* en pâté de foie.

grosses jambes : colonnes *f.pl.*, poteaux *m.pl.*

jambes maigres : allumettes *f.pl.*, crayons *m.pl.*, échalas *m.pl.*, échasses *f.pl.*, fils *m.pl.* de fer, flûtes *f.pl.*, fumerons *m.pl.*, pinceaux *m.pl.*, pincettes *f.pl.*

avoir les jambes torses : avoir les jambes Louis XV (*ou* en manches de veste), faire du cheval sur un tonneau, pisser entre parenthèses.

jeter : balancer, balanstiquer, envoyer dinguer, ficher (*ou* foutre) en l'air, virer.

jeu *m* : attrape-pognon *m*, flambe *m*, flanche *m*.

jouer : flamber, flancher.

jouer aux cartes : taper le carton, taquiner les bauches (*ou* les brèmes).

journal *m* : babillard *m*, canard *m*, cancan *m*, feuille *f* de chou, menteur *m*, torchon *m*.

là (*adv.*) : ladé, laga, lago, laguche.

laid (*adj.*) : bléchard, blèche, blèque,

miteux, mochard, moche, mocheton, pas jojo, roupie, tarde, tartavelle, tarte, tartouille, tartouse, toc, tocard.

Voir aussi **(vieille) femme laide.**

personne laide : caricature *f*, carnaval *m*, gueule *f* en coin de rue (*ou* à coucher dehors *ou* d'empeigne *ou* en fer de cheval *ou* à la manque *ou* de raie), roupie *f*.

laisser : *voir* **abandonner.**

langue *f* : battant *m*, bavarde *f*, bavette *f*, baveuse *f*, chiffe *f*, chiffon *m*, clapette *f*, langouse *f*, lavette *f*, membrineuse *f*, menteuse *f*, mouillette *f*, patin *m*, platine *m*, râpeuse *f*, tapette *f*, torche *f*, torchette *f*.

lent (*adj.*) : à la bourre, à la traîne, en retard d'une rame, longin.

lesbienne *f* : éplucheuse *f* de lentilles, gavousse *f*, gouchotte *f*, goudou *f*, gougne *f*, gougnette *f*, gougnot(t)e *f*, gouine *f*, gousse *f*, marchande *f* d'ail, qui aime (*ou* tape) l'ail, vrille *f*.

lettre *f* (*missive*) : babillarde *f*, bafouille *f*, biffeton *m*, lazagne *f*, lazane *f*.

lèvre *f* : babine *f*, babouine *f*, badigoince *f*, bagougnasse *f*, baiseuse *f*, baveuse *f*, limace *f*, pompeuse *f*.

lit *m* : bâche *f*, banette *f*, dodo *m*, nid *m*, paddock *m*, page *m*, pageot *m*, panier *m*, pieu *m*, plumard *m*, plume *f*, pucier *m*, sac *m* à puces.

litre *m* (*de vin*) : kil *m*, kilbus *m*, kilo *m*, litron *m*, rouillarde *f*, rouille *f*.

Voir aussi **bouteille.**

logement *m* : bahut *m*, baraque *f*, bercail *m*, bocal *m*, cabane *f*, cagna *f*, cambuse *f*, carrée *f*, casba(h) *f*, case *f*, crèche *f*, gourbi *m*, guitoune *f*, niche *f*, piaule *f*, planque *f*, poulailler *m*, strasse *f*, taule *f*, tôle *f*, turne *f*.

loucher : avoir les châsses qui font du billard (*ou* qui se surveillent), avoir les mirettes qui se croisent les bras, avoir un œil qui dit merde (*ou* zut) à l'autre, bigler (en biais), boiter des calots.

lunettes *f.pl.* : berniches *f.pl.*, binocle *m*, carreaux *m.pl.*, faux quinquets, pare-brise *m.pl.*, quat-zyeux *m.pl.*, vitraux *m.pl.*

maigre (*adj.*) : désossé, gras comme un cent de clous, maigrichon, maigrot, sec comme une trique (*ou* un coup de trique), sécot.

personne maigre : asperge *f*, échalas *m*, fil *m* de fer, gringalet *m*, planche *f* à pain.

main *f*: agrafe *f*, battoir *m*, croche *f*, cuiller *f*, grappin *m*, grattante *f*, louche *f*, mimine *f*, palette *f*, paluche *f*, papogne *f*, patte *f*, pat(t)oche *f*, pince *f*, pogne *f*, quintuplée *f*, toucheuse *f*.

maître-chanteur *m*: goualeur *m*, musicien *m*, musico *m*, serinette *f*.

malade (*adj*.): affûté, amoché, ayant un pet de travers, mal fichu (*ou* foutu *ou* vissé), pas dans son assiette, patraque, plombé, vaseux.

atteint de maladie vénérienne: assaisonné, attigé, ayant le panaris chinois, fadé, faisandé, lazziloffe, mangé aux vers, nase, nasebroque, naze, nazeloque, nazicoté, plombé, poivré, pourri.

Voir aussi **blennorragie; syphilis.**

très malade: cuit, fichu, flambé, foutu, fricassé, frit, paumé, qui a un pied dans la tombe, qui bat de l'aile, qui file un mauvais coton, qui marche à côté de ses pompes, qui sent le sapin, rétamé.

malchance *f*: bouillabaisse *f*, bouscaille *f*, cerise *f*, confiture *f*, guigne *f*, guignon *m*, marmelade *f*, masque *m*, moutarde *f*, pestouille *f*, pétrin *m*, poisse *f*, pommade *f*, scoumoune *f*, sirop *m*, vape *f*.

avoir de la malchance: être dans de beaux (*ou* mauvais *ou* vilains) draps.

malin (*adj*.): affranchi, à la coule, à la page, dans le train, débrouillard, dégourdi, démerdard, fortiche, mariole, marle, marloupin, roublard, sondeur.

manger: aller à la graille, becqueter, bouffer, boulotter, boustifailler, brichetonner, briffer, buffer, se caler les côtes (*ou* les joues), casser la croûte (*ou* la graine), claper, cléber, croquer, croustiller, croûter, se dérouiller les crochets, s'en donner par les babines, grailler, grainer, jaffer, lipper, mastéguer, mastiquer, morfiler, morganer, muffler, recharger les accus, se remplir le bocal (*ou* le cornet *ou* le garde-manger *ou* la lampe), se taper la cloche (*ou* la tête), tortorer.

manger abondamment: bâfrer, bouffer (à crever), s'empiffrer, se faire péter la sous-ventrière, s'en foutre plein la lampe, s'en jeter (*ou* s'en mettre) derrière la cravate, s'en mettre jusque-là (*ou* plein le fusil), se goinfrer, se graisser la gueule, morphaler, prendre une bonne ventrée, se tasser une plâtrée.

manières prétentieuses: chichis *m.pl.*, épates *f.pl.*, esbrouf(f)es *f.pl.*, magnes *f.pl.*, pal(l)as *m*, singeries *f.pl.*

maquiller, se: se badigeonner, se faire une façade (*ou* un raccord *ou* un ravalement), se plâtrer, se sucrer la gaufre (*ou* la gaufre).

marchandise *f*: came *f*, camelote *f*, lamedu *m*.

marcher: affûter des pinceaux, aller à pattes, les allonger, arpenter, arquer, bagoter, battre le bitume, charrier sa viande, giguer, prendre le train onze (*ou* la voiture de Saint-Crépin), ripatonner, tricoter (des guibolles), trimarder.

mariage *m*: conjungo *m*, entiflage *m* de sec, maquage *m*, marida(t) *m*.

marin *m*: cachalot *m*, col bleu, loup *m* de mer, marsouin *m*, mataf *m*, matave *m*, mathurin *m*, pompon *m* rouge.

masturber, se: se l'agiter, se l'allonger, s'astiquer (la colonne *ou* le manche), s'astiquer le boilton (*femme*), s'en battre une, se branler (la colonne). épouser (*ou* fréquenter) la veuve poignet, étrangler Popaul (*ou* Popol), faire cinq contre un, faire glouglouter le poireau, se faire malice tout seul, se faire mousser, se fréquenter, se griffer, jouer de la mandoline (*femme*), se palucher, se pogner, se secouer le bonhomme, se taper (sur) la colonne, se taper un rassis, se tirer son (*ou* un) coup, tomber sur le (*ou* un) manche.

mauvais (*adj*.): à la noix, bidon, blèche, creux, locdu, loquedu, moche, raté, tarte, tartouse, toc, tocard.

méchant *m*: carne *f*, chameau *m*, charogne *f*, gale *f*, peste *f*, pou *m*, salaud *m*, salope *f*, salopard *m*, teigne *f*, vache *f*.

médire: bêcher, casser du sucre sur le dos (*ou* sur la tête) de, débiner, dégraisser, habiller.

mégot *m*: clope *m*, meg *m*, orphelin *m*, sequin *m*.

mendiant *m*: clodo(t) *m*, frappeur *m*, manchard *m*, mangav(eur) *m*, mendiche *m*, mendigot *m*, pied *m* de biche, pilon *m*, pilonneur *m*, quelqu'un de la cloche, tapeur *m*, torpille *f*, torpilleur *m*, tubard *m* (*mendiant du métro*).

mendicité *f*: frappe *f*, manche *f*, mangave *f*, mendiche *f*, mendigoterie *f*, pilon *m*, pilonnage *m*, tape *f*, torpille *f*.

mendier: aller à la mangave, faire la manche (*ou* le tube), frapper, mangaver, marcher à la torpille, mendigoter, pilonner, taper, torpiller.

menottes *f.pl.*: bracelets *m.pl.*, brides *f.pl.*, cabriolets *m.pl.*, cadènes *f.pl.*, cadenettes *f.pl.*, chapelet *m*, ficelles *f.pl.*, fichets *m.pl.*, manchettes *f.pl.*, pinces *f.pl.*, poucettes *f.pl.*

mensonge *m*: balançoire *f*, bateau *m*, bidon *m*, blague *f*, bobard *m*, boniment *m*, bourde *f*, bourrage *m* (de crâne), du bourre-mou, contes *m.pl.* à dormir debout, couleuvre *f*, craque *f*, doublage *m*, frime *f*, pilule *f*, van(n)e *m*.

menstrues *f.pl.*: anglais *m.pl.*, argagnasses *f.pl.*, cardinales *f.pl.*, carlets *m.pl.*, doches *f.pl.*, histoires *f.pl.*, ours *m.pl.*, rue barrée, sauce *f* tomate, trucs *m.pl.*

avoir ses menstrues: avoir ses affaires, être confiture, faire relâche, jouer à cache-tampon, marquer, pavoiser, repeindre sa grille (en rouge).

mentir: bourrer la caisse (*ou* le crâne *ou* le mou), en conter, envoyer du vent, mener en barque (*ou* en bateau), monter le cou.

mère *f*: dabe *f*, dabesse *f*, dabuche *f*, daronne *f*, doche *f*, mam(an) *f*, mater *f*, matouse *f*, vieille *f*.

mitraillette *f*: arroseuse *f*, arrosoir *m*, distributeur *m*, lampe *f* à souder, machine *f* à coudre (*ou* à percer *ou* à secouer) le paletot, mandoline *f*, moulin *m* à café, moulinette *f*, sulfateuse *f*, tititine *f*, vaporisateur *m*.

mollet *m*: jacquot *m*, molleton *m*, moltegomme *m*.

monnaie *f*: carmouille *f*, ferraille *f*, mitraille *f*, monouye *f*, mornifle *m*, vaisselle *f* de fouille.

montre *f*: bob *m*, broquante *f*, dégoulinante *f*, montrouze *f*, tocante *f*, toquante *f*, trotteuse *f*.

moquer de, se: acheter, bêcher, blaguer, chambrer, charrier, chiner, se ficher de, se foutre de, mettre en boîte, se payer la gueule (*ou* la tête) de.

mouchoir *m*: blave *m*, tire-jus *m*, tire-moelle *m*.

mourir: avaler son acte de naissance (*ou* sa chique), boucler sa malle, bouffer (*ou* manger) les pissenlits (par la racine), cadancher, calancher, caner,

cascader, casser sa pipe, clamser, clapoter, clapser, claquer, cramser, crever, cronir, la déchirer, déposer le bilan, dépoter son géranium, déramer, (la) dessouder, dévisser son billard, éteindre sa lampe, faire couic, graisser ses bottes, lâcher la rampe, se laisser glisser, oublier de respirer, partir les pieds devant (*ou* en avant), passer l'arme à gauche, perdre le goût du pain, plier bagage, quimper, remercier son boulanger, sauter le pas, souffler la veilleuse, tourner le coin.

moustaches *f.pl.*: bacchantes *f.pl.*, baffes *m.pl.*, balai *m* (à chiottes), charmeuses *f.pl.*, ramasse-miettes *m*.

nègre *m*: bamboula *m*, bougnoul(l)e *m*, canaque *m*, gobi *m*, moricaud *m*, négrillot *m*, négro *m*, noyama *m*.

nez *m*: baigneur *m*, blair *m*, blaireau *m*, blaze *m*, boîte *f* à morve, cep *m*, naze *m*, pif *m*, piffard *m*, piton *m*, pivase *m*, priseur *m*, reniflant *m*, step *m*, tarin *m*, trompette *f*.

nez épaté: patate *f*, pied *m* de marmite, truffe *f*.

grand nez: éteignoir *m*, fer *m* à souder, quart *m* de brie, step *m* à trier, tasseau *m*, tassot *m*.

nez rouge: aubergine *f*, betterave *f*, pif communard, piment *m*, tomate *f*.

nom *m*: blaze *m*, centre *m*, chouette *m*.

non (*excl.*): bernique, des bigorneaux, des clopes, des clopinettes, des clous, des daches, macache (et midi sonné), mon œil, mon zob, nib, nibe, de la peau, peau de balle (et balai de crin), que dalle.

nourriture *f*: avoine *f*, becquetance *f*, bectance *f*, bouffe *f*, bouftance *f*, boustifaille *f*, briffe *f*, croustance *f*, croustille *f*, croûte *f*, frichti *m*, fricot *m*, frip(p)e *f*, graille *f*, graine *f*, grinque *f*, jaffe *f*, mangeaille *f*, mastègue *f*, tambouille *f*, tortore *f*.

mauvaise nourriture: graillon *m*, ragougnasse *f*, rata *m*, ratatouille *f*.

nu (*adj.*): à loilpé, à loilpuche, comme un savon, (le) cul à l'air, en Jésus.

nuit *f*: borgne *f*, borgniot *m*, borgnon *m*, brune *f*, neuille *f*, sorgue *f*.

œil *m*: bille *f*, calot *m*, carreau *m*, châsse *m*, clignotant *m*, coquillard *m*, lampion *m*, lanterne *f*, lentille *f*, loupe *f*, lucarne *f*, mire *f*, mirette *f*, mironton *m*, œillet *m*, quinquet *m*, yakas *m*.

coup d'œil : coup *m* de sabord.

œil poché : coquard *m*, coquelicot *m*, œil au beurre noir, œil pavoisé, poche-œil *m*.

œillade (faire une) : lancer un appel (*ou* un coup de châsse *ou* un coup de sabord *ou* son prospectus), jouer des châsses, reluquer, renoucher.

or *m* : jonc *m*, joncaille *f*.

lingot *m* **d'or :** lingue *m*, quart *m* de beurre.

oreille *f* : ance *f*, anse *f*, cliquette *f*, écoute *f*, écoutille *f*, esgourde *f*, esgourdille *f*, étagère *f* à mégot, étiquette *f*, feuille *f* (de chou), pavillon *m*, portugaise *f*, soucoupe *f*, voile *f*, zozore *f*.

grande oreille : escalope *f*, grande feuille, plat *m* à barbe.

orgasme (avoir un) : y aller du voyage, balancer le jus (*ou* la purée), se balancer, briller, cracher son venin, décharger, dégorger, envoyer la came, s'envoyer en l'air, faire pleurer le cyclope, jouir, juter, lâcher sa came (*ou* une giclée *ou* le jus), mouiller le goupillon, prendre son fade (*ou* son panard), rayonner, se régaler, reluire, vider ses burettes.

Voir aussi **coïter.**

orgueilleux *m* : bêcheur *m*, cracheur *m*, faiseur *m* de magnes, frérot *m*, gommeux *m*, plastronneur *m*, poseur *m*.

oui (*excl.*) : banco, ça botte, ça colle, c'est bon, dac, d'acc, gy, gygo, jave, lygodu, O.K., positif.

ouvrier *m* : bosseur *m*, boulonneur *m*, boulot *m*, bûcheur *m*, piocheur *m*, prolo *m*, pue-la-sueur *m*, turbineur *m*.

ouvrir : débâcler, déboucher, débrider, mettre en dedans.

pain *m* : bricheton *m*, briffeton *m*, brignole *f*, brignolet *m*, brignoluche *m*, larton *m*.

pain bis : brutal *m*.

pain blanc : larton savonné.

pantalon *m* : bénard *m*, cotte *f*, culbutant *m*, falzar(d) *m*, fendard *m*, flosse *m*, froc *m*, futal *m*, grimpant *m*, montant *m*, valseur *m*.

pantalon étroit : fourreau *m*, fuseau *m*, tuyau *m* de poêle.

papier *m* : faf(f)e *m*, faf(f)elard *m*, faf(f)iot *m*, papelard *m*, pelure *f*.

paquet *m* : lacson *m*, pacsif *m*, pacson *m*.

parapluie *m* : pare-flotte *m*, pare-lance *m*, pébroc *m*, pébroque *m*, pépin *m*, riflard *m*.

pardessus *m* : lardeusse *m*, lardingue *m*, lardosse *m*, pardaf *m*, pardingue *m*, pardosse *m*, pelure *f*.

parents *m.pl.* : dabs *m.pl.*, darons *m.pl.*, vieux *m.pl.*, viocards *m.pl.*, vioques *m.pl.*

paresse *f* : cosse *f*, flemme *f*, poils *m.pl.* dans la main, rame *f*.

paresser : avoir la râme, les avoir palmés (*ou* à la retourne *ou* retournés), s'endormir sur le mastic, enfiler des perles, feignasser, ne pas en ficher (*ou* foutre) un coup (*ou* une rame), flânocher, flémarder, flemmarder, ne pas se fouler (la rate), ne rien se casser, tirer sa cosse (*ou* sa flemme), tirer au cul (*ou* au flanc), se tourner les pouces, traîner les patins (*ou* la savate).

paresseux *m* : cagnard *m*, cossard *m*, feignant *m*, feignasse *m*, flânocheur *m*, flemmard *m*, ramier *m*, tire(ur)-au-cul *m*, tire(ur)-au-flanc *m*, vachard *m*.

parler : bagouler, baratiner, bonnir, déblatérer, dégoiser, dévider, jacasser, jacter, jaspiner, l'ouvrir, tailler une bavette, tenir le crachoir.

Voir aussi **bavarder.**

partir : se barrer, (se) calter, se carapater, se cavaler, débarrasser les lieux (*ou* le plancher), se débiner, déblayer le terrain, décambuter, décamper, décaniller, décarrer, déguerpir, se déhotter, démarrer, détaler, se donner de l'air, s'éclipser, s'évaporer, ficher (*ou* foutre) le (*ou* son) camp, foncer dans le brouillard, jouer (à) rip, en jouer un air, les jouer, lever l'ancre, lever le pied, mettre les adjas (*ou* les baguettes *ou* les bouts *ou* les cannes *ou* les voiles), les mettre, plaquouser, plier bagage, prendre la clef des champs (*ou* le large *ou* la poudre d'escampette *ou* la tangente), prendre ses cliques et ses claques, riper, se tailler, se tirer, se tracer, se trisser, se trissoter, se trotter.

partir sans payer : faire jambe de bois, faire une queue, laisser une feuille de chou, planter un drapeau, poser une ardoise.

patron *m* : boss *m*, chef *m*, dab(e) *m*, daron *m*, direlot *m*, dirlingue *m*, dirlot *m*, le grand manitou, latron *m*, singe *m*, taulier *m*, tôlier *m*.

patron de café: bistranche *m*, bistre *m*, bistrotier *m*, mastroquet *m*, troquet *m*.

patronne *f* **(de maison de tolérance)**: bordelière *f*, daronne *f*, maquerelle *f*, maquesée *f*, marquise *f*, mère-maca *f*, mère-maquerelle *f*, rombière *f*, taulière *f*, tôlière *f*.

pauvre (*adj.*): à la côte, cisaillé, crève-la-faim, dans la dèche (*ou* la mélasse *ou* la purée *ou* le ruisseau), décavé, déchard, fauché (comme l'as de pique *ou* comme les blés), fauchemane, grand schlem, lavé, lessivé, miséreux, miteux, mouisard, nettoyé, pané, panné, paumé, purotin, qui traîne les patins (*ou* la savate), raide, raqué, rincé, rôti, sec, sur la paille (*ou* le pavé), tondu, vacant, vidé, de la zone.

pauvreté *f*: bouillabaisse *f*, débine *f*, dèche *f*, mélasse *f*, mistoufle *f*, mouise *f*, mouscaille *f*, panade *f*, purée *f*.

payer: les abouler, les aligner, aller au refil (*ou* au rembour), les allonger, allumer, arroser, banquer, carburer, carmer, casquer, cigler, cracher (dans le bassin), décher, douiller, éclairer, envoyer la valse, s'exécuter, se fendre, les lâcher, mouiller, raquer, régaler, les sortir, valser.

paysan *m*: boueux *m*, bouseux *m*, cambroussard *m*, croquant *m*, culterreux *m*, glaiseux *m*, pécore *m*, péd(e)zouille *m*, peigne-cul *m*, péquenaud *m*, péquenot *m*, pétrousquin *m*, petzouillard *m*, petzouille *m*, plouc *m*.

pédéraste *m*: chochotte *f*, chouquette *f*, coquine *f*, emmanché *m*, empaffé *m*, empapaouté *m*, emprosé *m*, encaldossé *m*, enculé *m*, enfifré *m*, enfoiré *m*, enviandé *m*, fagot *m*, fiotte *f*, gazier *m*, girond *m*, joconde *f*, lopaille *f*, lopart *m*, lope *f*, lopette *f*, Madame Arthur, papaout *m*, P.D. *m*, pédale *f*, pédalo *m*, pédé *m*, pédéro *m*, pédoque *m*, qui en est, qui est de la bague (*ou* du rond *ou* du zéro), qui est de la famille tuyau de poêle, qui est de la joyeuse, rivette *f*, sœur *f*, tante *f*, tantouse *f*, tapette *f*, tata *f*, travesti *m*.

pendre: agrafer, anguer, béquiller, grupper.

pendu *m*: duc *m*, qui bénit avec ses pieds, qui garde des moutons à la lune.

pénis *m*: andouille *f* à col roulé, anguille *f* de calecif, arbalète *f*, asperge *f*, baigneur *m*, baïonnette *f*, baisette *f*, balayette *f*, baveuse *f*, berdouillette *f*, berloque *f*, biroute *f*, bit(t)e *f*, (gros) bout *m*, bra(c)quemard *m*, canne *f*, carabine *f*, Charles-le-Chauve, chibre *m*, chinois *m*, cigare *m* à moustache, clarinette *f*, colonne *f*, cyclope *m*, dard *m*, dardillon *m*, défonceuse *f*, fifre *m* à grelots, flageolet *m*, frétillante *f*, frétillard *m*, gaule *f*, gland *m*, goupillon *m*, gourde *f* à poils, gourdin *m*, guignol *m*, guise *m*, instrument *m*, jambe *f* du milieu, macaroni *m*, mandrin *m*, marsouin *m*, mohican *m*, nœud *m*, os *m* à moelle, outil *m*, paf *m*, panais *m*, le père frappart, petit frère, pine *f*, pointe *f*, poireau *m*, polard *m*, Popaul *m*, Popol *m*, quéquette *f*, queue *f*, quique *f*, quiquette *f*, sabre *m*, Totor, tracassin *m*, tringle *f*, trique *f*, verge *f*, zeb *m*, zigouigoui *m*, zizi *m*, zob(i) *m*.

perdre (au jeu): être enfoncé (*ou* entubé *ou* lessivé *ou* plumé), se faire enfiler, manger la ferme, paumer.

père *m*: dabm, daron *m*, papa *m*, papy *m*, pater *m*, paternel *m*, pépère *m*, vieux *m*.

pet *m*: boule *f*, cloque *m*, loffe *f*, louffe *f*, pastille *f*, pastoche *f*, perle *f*, perlouse *f*, perlouze *f*, vesse *f*.

péter: annoncer son matricule, cloquer, déchirer son froc (*ou* la toile), en écraser un, fuser, en lâcher un, lâcher les gaz (*ou* une perle *ou* une perlouse), louffer, vesser.

petit individu: astèque *m*, avorton *m*, basduc *m*, bas-du-cul *m*, bout-de-cul *m*, courte-botte *m*, crapaud *m*, crapoussin *m*, demi-portion *f*, échappé *m* de bidet, fabriqué *m* au compte-gouttes, fond-de-bain *m*, inachevé *m*, merdaillon *m*, microbe *m*, mignard *m*, nabot *m*, pot *m* à tabac, puce *f*, qui est haut comme trois pommes, ras-de-bitume *m*, ras-de-mottes *m*, rasduc *m*, ras-du-cul *m*, rikiki *m*, riquiqui *m*, tom-pouce *m*.

peu (un): un (petit) bout, un chouia, pas bésef(f), pas bézef(f), pas gras, pas lerche, pas lourdingue, une larme, une miette.

peur *f*: chiasse *f*, chocottes *f.pl.*, colombins *m.pl.*, flubes *m.pl.*, frousse *f*, fuchsias *m.pl.*, grelots *m.pl.*, pétasse *f*, pétoche *f*, pétouille *f*, taf *m*, taffe *m*, trac *m*, tracsir *m*, traquette *f*, traquouse *f*, trouille *f*.

avoir peur : avoir chaud aux fesses, avoir les baguettes (*ou* les blancs *ou* la colique *ou* les copeaux *ou* les foies *ou* les jetons), avoir les miches qui font bravo, avoir le trouillomètre à zéro, les avoir à zéro, caler, caner, chier dans son froc, se déballonner, se dégonfler, fluber, foirer, les mouiller, serrer les fesses (*ou* les miches), trouilloter.

pieds *m.pl.* : argasses *m.pl.*, arpions *m.pl.*, artous *m.pl.*, nougats *m.pl.*, panards *m.pl.*, patins *m.pl.*, pattes *f.pl.*, paturons *m.pl.*, péniches *f.pl.*, petons *m.pl.*, pinceaux *m.pl.*, pingets *m.pl.*, pingouins *m.pl.*, raquettes *f.pl.*, ribouis *m.pl.*, ripatons *m.pl.*, trottinants *m.pl.*, trottinets *m.pl.*

pince-monseigneur *f* : clarinette *f*, dauphin *m*, dingue *f*, dombeur *m*, dur *m*, jacques *m*, jacquot *m*, plume *f*, sucre *m* de pomme.

pipe *f* : bouffarde *f*, brûle-gueule *m*, chiffarde *f*, gnaupe *f*, quenaude *f*.

pleurer : baver des clignotants, chialer, gicler des mirettes (*ou* des œillets), miter, ouvrir les écluses, pisser des châsses, viauper.

pluie *f* : bouillon *m*, flotte *f*, lancequine *f*, rincée *f*, saucée *f*.

poche *f* : bacreuse *f*, ballade *f*, farfouillette *f*, fouille *f*, fouillette *f*, fouillouse *f*, glande *f*, pocket *m*, profonde *f*, vague *f*, valde *f*.

poing *m* : *voir* **main.**

poitrine *f* : armoire *f*, caisse *f*, caisson *m*, coffre *m*, plastron *m*.

police *f* : arnaque *f*, bigorne *f*, bourrique *f*, condaille *f*, flicaille *f*, maison arrangemane (*ou* bourremane *ou* cognedur *ou* parapluie *ou* pébroc *ou* poulaga *ou* poulardin *ou* poulemane), ces Messieurs, poulaille *f*, poule *f*, raclette *f*, renâcle *f*, renifle *f*, rousse *f*, volaille *f*.

policier *m* : argousin *m*, bourre *m*, chaussette *f*, cogne *m*, condé *m*, drauper *m*, flic *m*, flicaillon *m*, flicard *m*, guignol *m*, ham *m*, hambourgeois *m*, lardu *m*, matou *m*, perdreau *m*, pied-plat *m*, plancton *m*, poulaga *m*, poulard *m*, pouleminche *m*, poulet *m*, raper *m*, roussi *m*, roussin *m*.

poltron *m* : baisse-froc *m*, caneur *m*, capon *m*, chiasseur *m*, déballonné *m*, dégonflard *m*, dégonflé *m*, dégonfleur *m*, flubard *m*, foireux *m*, froussard *m*, grelotteur *m*, péteux *m*, pétochard *m*,

poule mouillée, taffeur *m*, traqueur *m*, trouillard *m*, vessard *m*.

portefeuille *m* : lasagne *m*, lazingue *m*.

portefeuille plein : matelas *m*, mateluche *m*.

porte-monnaie *m* : artichaut *m*, artiche *m*, crapaud *m*, lasagne *m*, lazingue *m*, morlingue *m*, morniflard *m*, portebiffeton *m*, porte-faf(f)iots *m*, portemorfic *m*, morpion *m*, piocre *m*, toto *m*.

pou *m* : crabe *m*, galopard *m*, gau *m*, grain *m* de blé, guêpe *f*, mie *f* de pain (mécanique *ou* à ressort), morbac *m*, morfic *m*, morpion *m*, piocre *m*, toto *m*.

pourboire *m* : bouquet *m*, gants *m.pl.*, pièce *f*, pourliche *m*, poursoif *m*.

prétentieux (être) : bêcher, crâner, se croire sorti de la cuisse de Jupiter, s'en croire, épater, esbrouf(f)er, faire des chichis (*ou* de l'épate *ou* de l'esbrouf(f)e *ou* des magnes), faire du vent (*ou* du zeph), se gober, se gonfler, s'en installer, se monter le job, plastronner, pontifier.

prêtre *m* : calotin *m*, coin-coin *m*, corbeau *m*, cureton *m*, radis noir, rase *m*, ratiche *m*, ratichon *m*, sac *m* à carbi, sanglier *m*.

prison *f* : ballon *m*, bigne *f*, bing *m*, bloc *m*, boîte *f*, cabane *f*, carluche *f*, centrouse *f*, chétard *m*, clou *m*, coffre *m*, coquille *f*, gn(i)ouf *m*, grande marmite, grosse *f*, jettard *m*, lazaro *m*, malle *f*, mitard *m*, ombre *f*, ours *m*, petit château, placard *m*, ratière *f*, schib *m*, schtard *m*, schtib *m*, schtilibem *m*, séchoir *m*, taule *f*, tôle *f*, trou *m*, violon *m*.

prostituée *f* : béguineuse *f*, bisenesseuse *f*, boudin *m*, bourrin *m*, catin *f*, chamelle *f*, chèvre *f*, essoreuse *f*, fille *f*, frangine *f*, frangipane *f*, gagneuse *f*, garce *f*, gerce *f*, girelle *f*, gisquette *f*, gonzesse *f*, goton *f*, greluche *f*, grue *f*, langouste *f*, marcheuse *f*, mistonne *f*, morue *f*, moukère *f*, mousmé(e) *f*, nana *f*, pépée *f*, péripatéticienne *f*, persilleuse *f*, ponette *f*, pouffiasse *f*, poule *f*, putain *f*, pute *f*, raccrocheuse *f*, racoleuse *f*, radeuse *f*, respectueuse *f*, rouchie *f*, roulure *f*, souris *f*, tapin *f*, tapineuse *f*, traînée *f*, truqueuse *f*, turfeuse *f*, volaille *f*, zigouince *f*.

prostituer, se : *voir* **racoler.**

provoquer : chercher la cogne (*ou* des crosses *ou* des patins *ou* du rif *ou* des rognes *ou* du suif) à, crosser.

querelle *f*: accrochage *m*, asticotage *m*, attrapade *f*, attrapage *m*, badaboum *m*, barabille *f*, baroud *m*, barouf *m*, barouffe *m*, baroufle *m*, bigorne *f*, bisbille *f*, châtaigne *f*, corrida *f*, crosse *f*, engueulade *f*, pétard *m*, prise *f* de bec (*ou* de gueule), rif *m*, rififi *m*, rogne *f*, salade *f*, savon *m*, suif *m*, tabac *m*, tapage *m*, torchée *f*.

querelleur (*adj.*): asticoteur, crosseur, crosson, mauvais coucheur, pétardier, péteur, râleur, renaudeur, saladier, suiffeur.

racoler (*prostituée*): aller aux asperges, chasser le mâle, se défendre, draguer, emballer, s'expliquer, faire le business (*ou* le bitume *ou* les boules *ou* la grue *ou* un levage *ou* le macadam *ou* le pavé *ou* le quart *ou* le raccroc *ou* le rade *ou* la retape *ou* le ruban *ou* le tapin *ou* le tas *ou* le trottoir *ou* le truc *ou* le turbin *ou* le turf), faire son persil, lever un client, michetonner, en moudre, persiller, raccrocher, en retourner, tapiner, truquer, turbiner, turfer.

rafle *f*: coup *m* de filet (*ou* de serviette *ou* de torchon), cueille *f*, descente *f*, dragage *m*, drague *f*, piquage *m*, (coup *m* de) raclette *f*.

raser, se: se gratter, se gratter (*ou* se peler) la couenne, se racler.

rasoir *m*: coupe-chou *m*, grattoir *m*, racloir *m*, rasibe *m*, rasife *m*, razif *m*.

receleur *m*: fourgat *m*, fourgue *m*, fourgueur *m*, franquiste *m*, laveur *m*, lessiveur *m*.

recevoir (*des coups ou des insultes*): déguster, dérouiller, écoper, effacer, encaisser, étrenner, palper, en prendre pour son grade.

recommencer: rebiffer, remaquiller, remettre ça, remmancher, (y) remordre, repiquer (au truc).

reconnaître: reconnobler, reconnobrer, redresser, retapisser.

regarder: allumer, bigler, borgnoter, châsser, frimer, gaffer, lorgner, loucher sur, mater, matouser, mirer, mordre, rechâsser, reluquer, remoucher, tapisser, viser, zyeuter.

réjouissances *f.pl.*: bamboche *f*, bamboula *f*, bombe *f*, bordée *f*, bosse *f*, boum *f*, bringue *f*, faridon *f*, fiesta *f*, foire *f*, foiridon *f*, java *f*, noce *f*, nouba *f*, renversée *f*, ribote *f*, ribouldingue *f*,

riboule *f*, surboum *f*, vadrouille *f*, virée *f*.

rendez-vous *m*: rambour *m*, rancart *m*, rembo *m*, rencart *m*, rendève *m*.

renseignement *m*: duce *m*, rancard *m*, rencard *m*, rencart *m*, tubard *m*, tube *m*, tuyau *m*.

renseigner: affranchir, éclairer la lanterne à, embrayer sur, mettre à la page (*ou* dans le coup), parfumer, rancarder, rembiner.

réprimander: agonir, agrafer, assaisonner, attraper, casser, donner le bal à, doucher, engueuler, enguirlander, filer (*ou* flanquer *ou* passer) un savon à, habiller, incendier, laver la tête à, lessiver, mettre sur le tapis, moucher, passer une bonne engueulade (*ou* quelque chose) à, ramasser, ramoner, sabouler, secouer (les puces à), sonner les cloches à.

être réprimandé: écoper, en prendre pour son grade, recevoir une saucée (*ou* une savonnée).

revolver *m*: azor *m*, bagaf *m*, basset *m*, boukala *m*, boum-boum *m*, brelica *m*, brûle-parfum(s) *m*, calibre *m*, feu *m*, flingot *m*, flingue *m*, pétard *m*, pétoire *m*, pistolache *m*, remède *m*, ribarbère *m*, riboustin *m*, rifle *f*, riflette *f*, rigolo *m*, rigoustin *m*, soufflant *m*, tic-tac *m*.

riche (*adj.*): bourré (à bloc), calé, cousu d'or, flambant, au fric, galetteux, gonflé, gros, oseillé, péseux, plein aux as, qui a du foin dans ses bottes, qui a le sac, qui roule dans le fric (*ou* sur l'or), rempli, rupin, rupinos, tombé sur un champ d'oseille.

rien (*adv.*): balpeau, des clopinettes, des clous, des prunes, macache, de la merde, négatif, nib, niente, nix, la peau, peau de balle (*ou* de zébi(e)), que dalle, que pouic, que t'chi, du vent, zéro.

rire: se bidonner, se boler, se boyauter, se crever, se fendre le bol (*ou* la bouille *ou* la gueule *ou* la pipe), se gondoler, se marrer, s'en payer une tranche, se poiler, se pouffer, se rouler, se tenir les côtes, se tirebouchonner, se tordre (comme une baleine).

route *f*: antif(fe) *f*, bitume *m*, ruban *m*, tire *f*, trimard *m*, trime *f*.

ruiné (*adj.*): *voir* pauvre.

rupture *f*: lâchage *m*, largage *m*, malle *f*, mallouse *f*, plaquage *m*, valise *f*, valoche *f*.

sale (*adj.*): cochon, cracra, cradingue, crado, crapoteux, crasp, craspec, craspèque, craspet, craspignol, craspouette, craspouillard, débectant, dégueulasse, dégueulbif, merdeux, miteux, pouilleux, saligaud, salingue.

saleté *f*: crotaille *f*, crotte *f*, merdoie *f*, merdouille *f*, saloperie *f*.

séduire: chauffer, emballer, embobiner, faire des boniments (*ou* du pal(l)as(s) *ou* du plat *ou* du rentre-dedans) à, frotter, gringuer, musiquer, pal(l)asser, quimper, rambiner, tomber.

seins *m.pl.*: amortisseurs *m.pl.*, avantages *m.pl.*, avant-postes *m.pl.*, avant-scène *f*, balcon(s) *m* (*pl.*), ballons *m.pl.*, boîtes *f.pl.* à lait (*ou* à lolo), devanture *f*, doudounes *f.pl.*, flotteurs *m.pl.*, globes *m.pl.*, hémisphères *m.pl.*, loloches *m.pl.*, lolos *m.pl.*, mappemondes *f.pl.*, du monde au balcon, montgolfières *f.pl.*, nénés *m.pl.*, nichons *m.pl.*, pelotes *f.pl.*, roberts *m.pl.*, rondins *m.pl.*, ropoplots *m.pl.*, rotoplots *m.pl.*, rototos *m.pl.*, tétasses *f.pl.*, tétés *m.pl.*, tétons *m.pl.*

sentir: blairer, renifler.

    sentir mauvais: boucaner, cocot-(t)er, cogner, comancher, corner, foisonner, fouetter, plomber, polker, puer, refouler, renifler, rougnotter, (s)chlinguer, taper, troufigner, trouilloter.

    sentir mauvais de la bouche: plomber du goulot, puer du bec, refouler, repousser (du goulot), taper du saladier, tuer les mouches à quinze pas.

sœur *f*: fraline *f*, frangine *f*, frangipane *f*, frelotte *f*, sister *f*, sistère *f*.

soif (avoir): avoir la dalle en pente, avoir le gosier sec, avoir la pépie, cracher blanc, la sécher.

soldat *m*: bidasse *m*, biffin *m*, chti *m*, déguisé *m*, deuxième pompe *f*, gribier *m*, grif(e)ton *m*, griveton *m*, grivier *m*, pioupiou *m*, tourlourou *m*, troubade *m*, trouf(f)ion *m*.

sou *m*: bourgue *m*, croque *m*, fléchard *m*, jacques *m*, kope(c)k *m*, pelot *m*, radis *m*, rond *m*, rotin *m*.

sourd (*adj.*): constipé (*ou* dur) de la feuille, ensablé des portugaises, sourdingue (comme un pot).

sous-maîtresse *f* (**d'un bordel**): retirée *f* des banquettes, sous-baloche *f*, sous-maque *f*, sous-maquerelle *f*, sous-maquesée *f*.

souteneur *m*: Alphonse *m*, barbe *f*, barbeau *m*, broche *f*, brochet *m*, croc *m*, dauphin *m*, dos *m* (vert), estaf(f)ier *m*, hareng *m*, Jules *m*, Julot *m*, mac *m*, mangeur *m* de blanc (*ou* de brioche), maquereau *m*, marchand *m* de barbaque (*ou* de bidoche *ou* de viande), marle *m*, marlou *m*, marloupin *m*, mec *m*, mecton *m*, merlan *m*, poiscaille *m*, poiscal *m*, poisse *f*, poisson *m*, rabat *m*, rabatteur *m*, sauré *m*, sauret *m*.

sperme *m*: blanc *m*, came *f*, foutre *m*, jus *m* (de corps *ou* de cyclope), purée *f*, venin *m*.

stupéfait (*adj.*): asphyxié, assis, baba, bleu, comme deux ronds de flan (*ou* de frites *ou* de tarte), époustouflé, estomaqué, occis, sidéré, soufflé, suffoqué.

suicider, se: se but(t)er, se déramer, s'envoyer (*ou* se filer) en l'air, se faire sauter la caisse (*ou* le caisson), s'occire (la cervelle).

syphilis *f*: chtouille *f*, daube *f*, lazziloffe *f*, naze *m*, nazebroque *m*, schtouille *f*, sigma *m*, syphilo *f*, syphlotte *f*.

tabac *m*: fume *f*, gris *m*, herbe *f*, percale *m*, perle *m*, perlot *m*, pétun *m*, tref *m*, trèfle *m*.

taire, se: avoir la bouche cousue, la boucler, écraser, s'éteindre, s'étouffer, fermer sa boîte (*ou* son clapet *ou* sa gueule), la fermer, y mettre un cadenas, ne pas moufter, ne pas piper, poser sa chique, rengracier, taire sa gueule, tirer sa fermeture éclair.

    faire taire: boucler la trappe à, brider, clouer (le bec à), museler, rabattre le caquet à, rembarrer, river le clou à.

tatouer: bouziller, brider, marquouser, piquer.

taxi *m*: bahut *m*, brutal *m*, fiacre *m*, hotte *f*, loche *f*, rongeur *m*, sapin *m*, taquemard *m*.

téléphone *m*: bigophone *m*, bigorneau *m*, biniou *m*, cornichon *m*, grelot *m*, phonard *m*, ronfleur *m*, télémuche *m*, tube *m*.

testicules *f.pl.*: balloches *f.pl.*, ballustrines *f.pl.*, bijoux *m.pl.* de famille, billes *f.pl.*, blosses *f.pl.*, bonbons *m.pl.*, burettes *f.pl.*, burnes *f.pl.*, claoui(e)s *m.pl.*, clopinettes *f.pl.*, couilles *f.pl.*, couillons *m.pl.*, croquignoles *f.pl.*, génitoires *f.pl.*, joyeuses *f.pl.*, montgolfières *f.pl.*, noisettes *f.pl.*, noix *f.pl.*, olives *f.pl.*, paire *f*, parties *f.pl.* (nobles), pendeloques *f.pl.*, précieuses *f.pl.*, rognons *m.pl.*, roubignolles *f.pl.*, rouleaux *m.pl.*, roupes *f.pl.*, roupettes *f.pl.*, roupignolles *f.pl.*, roustons *m.pl.*, valseuses *f.pl.*

tête *f*: baigneur *m*, balle *f*, bille *f*, binette *f*, bobèche *f*, bobéchon *m*, bobine *f*, bougie *f*, bouille *f*, bouillotte *f*, boule *f*, bourrichon *m*, boussole *f*, burette *f*, caberlot *m*, caboche *f*, cabochon *m*, cafetière *f*, caillou *m*, carafe *f*, carafon *m*, cassis *m*, chou *m*, ciboulot *m*, cigare *m*, citron *m*, citrouille *f*, coco *m*, coloquinte *f*, fiole *f*, gadin *m*, gourde *f*, nénette *f*, patate *f*, plafond *m*, poire *f*, pomme *f*, sinoquet *m*, siphon *m*, terrine *f*, tétère *f*, téterre *f*, théière *f*, tirelire *f*, tomate *f*, toupie *f*, tranche *f*, trogne *f*, trognon *m*, trombine *f*, tronc *m*, tronche *f*.

tirer (*une arme à feu*): défourailler, envoyer (*ou* lâcher) la fumée (*ou* la purée *ou* la sauce), flingot(t)er, flinguer.

tomber: aller à dame, aller valser dans les décors, se casser la figure, chuter, faire une valdingue, se ficher (*ou* se foutre) la gueule en l'air (*ou* par terre), partir à dame, prendre (*ou* ramasser) un billet de parterre (*ou* une bûche *ou* un gadin *ou* une pelle *ou* un traînard *ou* une valdingue), quimper.

tracasser, se: se biler, se cailler, se casser la tête, être aux cent coups, s'en faire, se faire de la bile (*ou* des cheveux (blancs) *ou* des crins *ou* du mauvais sang *ou* du mouron *ou* de la mousse), se monter le bourrichon, se turlupiner.

travail *m*: bibelotage *m*, bis(e)ness *m*, boulot *m*, bricolage *m*, charbon *m*, coltin *m*, coltinage *m*, flambeau *m*, flanche *f*, gâche *f*, gratin *m*, groupin *m*, job *m*, placarde *f*, truc *m*, turbin *m*.

travailler dur: bosser, boulonner, bûcher, buriner, se cailler, se casser (le cul), se décarcasser, en donner (une secousse), s'échiner, s'éreinter, s'esquinter, s'expliquer, en ficher (*ou* en foutre) un coup (*ou* une secousse), se fouler la rate, gratter, marner, pinocher, piocher, pisser du sang, suer (sang et eau), taper dans la butte, trimer, turbiner, usiner.

travailleur *m*: *voir* **ouvrier**.

tricher: arnaquer, arrangemaner, biseauter, doubler, échauder, empalmer, escan(n)er, étriller, faisander, maquiller, quiller, rangemaner.

tricheur *m*: arnaqueur *m*, arrangeman *m*, biseauteur *m*, empalmeur *m*, entôleur *m*, faisandier *m*, faiseur *m*, graisseur *m*, maquilleur *m*.

triste (*adj.*): bourdon, cafardeux, dépon(n)é, fouille-merde, tout chose.

tromper: arnaquer, arranger, avoir, bidonner, blouser, carotter, charrier, doubler, empiler, endormir, enfiler, enfler, enfoncer, entôler, entuber, faire (à l'oseille), ficher (*ou* foutre) dedans, gour(r)er, jobarder, maquiller, mettre dedans, posséder, quiller, ranger, refaire, rouler, roustir.

trottoir *m*: bitume *m*, pavé *m*, ruban *m*, turf *m*.

trouver: *voir* **découvrir**.

tuer: *voir* **assassiner**.

uriner: aller faire sa petite commission, faire pipi, faire son petit besoin, lâcher l'eau (*ou* l'écluse *ou* un fil), lancecailler, lancequiner, lansquiner, lisbroquer, lispoquer, ouvrir les écluses, pisser, renverser la vapeur; (*homme*) changer son poisson d'eau, égoutter son colosse (*ou* son cyclope *ou* sa sardine), se l'égoutter, faire pleurer le colosse, jeter de la lance, prendre une ardoise à l'eau, tenir l'âne par la queue, verser de l'eau; (*femme*) arroser le persil, humecter sa fourrure, mouiller son gazon.

urinoir *m*: ardoises *f.pl.*, lavabe *m*, pissoir(e) *m*, pissotière *f*, pissotoire *f*, tasse *f*, théière *f*.

vagabond *m*: cloche *f*, clodo *m*, clodomir *m*, clodot *m*, grelotteux *m*, mouisard *m*, refileur *m* de comète, traîne-lattes *m*, traîne-patins *m*, traîne-pattes *m*, traîne-sabots *m*, traîne-savates *m*, trimard *m*, vacant *m*.
Voir aussi **clochard**.

vagin *m*: *voir* **vulve**.

vantard *m*: baratineur *m*, blagueur *m*, bluffeur *m*, bourreur *m* de crâne, chiqueur *m*, cracheur *m*, cravateur *m*, esbrouf(f)eur *m*, fort *m* en gueule, fumiste *m*, grande gueule, gueulard *m*, musicien *m*, rambineur *m*.

vaurien *m*: affreux *m*, apache *m*, bon-à-rien *m*, bordille *f*, (sale) bougre *m*, bourdille *f*, canaille *f*, charognard *m*, charogne *f*, copaille *f*, couillon *m*, crapule *f*, dur *m*, fan *m* de pute, fias *m*, fils *m* de pute, fripouillard *m*, fripouille *f*, fumier *m*, gale *f*, gouape *f*, locdu *m*, loquedu *m*, malfrappe *m*, mange-punaise *m*, mauvaise graine, muf(f)e *m*, mufle *m*, ordure *f*, peau *f* de vache, poisse *f*, pourriture *f*, pute *f*, raclure *f*, rien-du-tout *m*, salaud *m*, sale coco *m*, saligaud *m*, salopard *m*, salope *f*, varlot *m*, (sale) vicelard *m*.

ventre *m*: ballon *m*, balourd *m*, baquet *m*, battant *m*, bedaine *f*, bedon *m*, bide *m*, bidon *m*, bocal *m*, boîte *f* à ragoût, brioche *f*, buffedingue *m*, buffet *m*, bureau *m*, burlingue *m*, caisse *f*, fusil *m*, gras-double *m*, panse *f*, sac *m* à tripes, tiroir *m*.
Voir aussi **estomac**.

verre *m* **à boire**: auge *f*, baquet *m*, canon *m*, chope *f*, godot *m*, guindal *m*, pot *m*.

veste *f*: alezingue *f*, alpague *f*, alpingue *f*, pelure *f*, vestouse *f*.

vêtements *m.pl.*: fringues *f.pl.*, frip(p)es *f.pl.*, frusques *f.pl.*, harnais *m.pl.*, linges *m.pl.*, loques *f.pl.*, nippes *f.pl.*, pelure *f*, sapes *f.pl.*, vêtures *f.pl.*

viande *f*: barbaque *f*, bidoche *f*, carne *f*, charogne *f*, crigne *f*, crignolle *f*, criolle *f*.

vieillir: avoir (*ou* prendre) de la bouteille (*ou* du flacon), être bon pour la casse (*ou* la refonte), faire d'occasion, se fossiliser, prendre un coup de vieux, sentir la fin de saison, vioquer.

vieux (*adj.*): bibard, bléchard, blèche, croulant, périmé, schnocke, viocard, vioque.

vieux *m*: bonze *m*, croulant *m*, fossile *m*, mironton *m*, périmé *m*, son-et-lumière *m*, vestige *m*, vieille baderne (*ou* noix), vieux birbe (*ou* croûton *ou* jeton *ou* rococo), vioc *m*, viocard *m*, vioquard *m*, vioque *m*.

vin *m*: jaja *m*, pinard *m*, pive *m*, piveton *m*, pivois *m*, tutu *m*; (*blanc*) blanquette *f*, savonné *m*; (*rouge*) anti-dérapant *m*, aramon *m*, brutal *m*, décapant *m*, gobette *f*, gorgeon *m*, du gros (qui tache), gros bleu, gros *m* rouge, petit velours *m*, pichetegorne *m*, pichtogorme *m*, pichtogorne *m*, picolo *m*, picrate *m*, picton *m*, reginglard *m*, reguinglet *m*, rouquemoute *mf*, rouquin *m*, rouquinos *m*, sens *m* unique, tumec *m*, vinasse *f*, tutu *m*.

visage *m*: balle *f*, bille *f*, binette *f*, bobine *f*, bougie *f*, bouille *f*, bouillotte *f*, boule *f*, burette *f*, cerise *f*, fiole *f*, fraise *f*,

frime *f*, frimousse *f*, frite *f*, gaufre *f*, gueule *f*, hure *f*, margoulette *f*, museau *m*, poire *f*, pomme *f*, portrait *m*, terrine *f*, tirelire *f*, trogne *f*, trognon *m*, trombine *f*, trompette *f*, tronche *f*.

vite (*adv.*): à bride abattue, à fond de train, à plein(s) tube(s), à tout bersingue (*ou* berzingue), à toute blinde, à toute barre, à toute bombe, à toute(s) pompe(s), comme un zèbre, dare-dare, en cinq secs, en moins de deux, en quatrième vitesse, fissa, presto, quatre à quatre, rapidos, rapio, à tombeau ouvert.

aller vite: bomber, bousculer les bornes, brûler le pavé (*ou* la route), foncer, gazer, se magner le train, rouler à plein(s) gaz (*ou* à plein(s) tube(s) *ou* à toute pompe).

(vieille) voiture *f* (*auto*): bagnole *f*, bahut *m*, berlingot *m*, bouzine *f*, charrette *f*, chignole *f*, chiotte *f*, guimbarde *f*, guinde *f*, hotte *f*, tacot *m*, tape-cul *m*, tarare *f*, tine *f*, tinette *f*, tire *f*, tombereau *m*.

voler: accrocher, acheter à la foire d'empoigne, aller (en) chercher, arranger, asphyxier, barbot(t)er, bichotter, calotter, chaparder, chauffer, chiper, choper, chouraver, dégraisser, doubler, écorcher, empiler, emplafonner, emplâtrer, engourdir, enquiller, escan(n)er, estamper, étouffer, étourdir, fabriquer, faire, faire sauter, faucher, gauler, grapper, grappiner, griffer, grincher, lever, pégrer, piquer, plumer, poirer, poisser, raboter, ratiboiser, ratisser, refaire, rincer, roustir, secouer, soulever, sucrer, tirer.
Voir aussi **cambrioler**.

voleur *m*: barbot(t)eur *m*, carotteur *m*, chapardeur *m*, chipeur *m*, chopeur *m*, doubleur *m*, encanneur *m*, faucheur *m*, filou *m*, gauleur *m*, grinche *m*, leveur *m*, pégriot *m*, piqueur *m*, roustisseur *m*.
Voir aussi **cambrioleur**.

vomir: aller au refil(e) (*ou* au renard), bader, débagouler, dégobiller, dégoupillonner, dégueuler, évacuer le couloir, gerber, lâcher une fusée, refiler, remesurer, renarder.

vulve *f*: abricot *m*, baba *m*, barbu *m*, baveux *m*, bénitier *m*, bijou *m* de famille, boîte *f* à ouvrage, bonbonnière *f*, bréviaire *m* d'amour, chagatte *f*, chat *m*, chatte *f*, cheminée *f*, cicatrice *f*, con *m*, con(n)asse *f*, crac *m*, cramouille *f*, craque *f*, craquette *f*, crevasse *f*, didi *m*, didine *f*, étau *m*, fente *f*, figue *f*, fri-fri *m*, grippette *f*, millefeuille(s) *m*, mimi *m*, minet *m*, minou *m*, motte *f*, moule *f*, nénuphar *m*, pâquerette *f*, pince *f*, portail *m*, tabernacle *m*, tirelire *f*.

W.C. *m.pl.*: azor *m*, cabinces *f.pl.*, chiards *m.pl.*, chiottes *f.pl.*, débourre *f*, débourroir *m*, garde-manger *m*, gogs *m.pl.*, goguenots *m.pl.*, gogues *m.pl.*, lieux *m.pl.*, ouatères *m.pl.*, petit coin, tartiss(es) *m.pl.*, tartissoires *m.pl.*, téléphone *m*, tinettes *f.pl.*, vécés *m.pl.*

yeux *m.pl.*: *voir* œil.

PART TWO

FRENCH—ENGLISH

FOREWORD

The present work is not intended only for the specialist. An ever-increasing number of English-speaking people travel in France, and are interested in French novels, plays and films. Our purpose is to enable them to cope with the familiar and slangy elements of the French language they are likely to come across.

It is not claimed that this dictionary is exhaustive. It contains what is hoped to be a far-reaching and, at the same time, a judicious selection of popular words and phrases with appropriate English renderings. Some inclusions are admittedly rarely to be met with outside certain *milieux* and contexts, but they are nevertheless of sufficient frequency to justify their admission.

Popular expression is something shifting and uncertain. The changes it undergoes from one period to another make it difficult to assign categories. The distinction between what is colloquial and familiar and what is popular and vulgar is not easy to establish, as can readily be seen by reference to one's own language. No attempt has therefore been made to tackle this delicate, even thorny problem. It is evident that the frontiers of slang, in particular, are difficult to draw. There comes a moment when a slang word or phrase attains a wide enough currency to pass into common speech and, in some cases, into literature. It then ceases to be slang, but it usually carries with it some association with its origin or former use to give it a flavour or a colouring which is not quite that of the medium into which it has moved. Such terms and forms have, of course, their place in these pages, apart from the historical justification of their presence.

It is a commonplace to recall that, at the outset, slang was linked with the language of the underworld. The vocabulary of thieving and deception, of prostitution and sexual intercourse still figures among its richest elements. In this domain, it is hardly possible to be squeamish, for the coarse, the violent and the obscene are part and parcel of popular expression. To call a spade a spade presents no problem nowadays. It is precisely when a spade is no longer a spade that the lexicographer's interest awakens. It may be added that the popular mentality was never greatly concerned with spades as such. It has moved in other fields, as has been noted above, with vigour and inventiveness, but without any regard for social or moral conventions. We have not deemed it necessary to avoid printing in full English or French words that are often considered taboo. Nor have we thought it useful to indicate such entries as "vulgar" or "obscene". Apart from the fact that labels of this sort are subject to varying standards of appreciation, the translation itself usually affords a clear enough clue to the nature of the term.

The student of French generally finds himself attracted by argot and is often tempted to use it, feeling that it gives the impression of a greater familiarity with the spoken language. But it suffices to think of the many pitfalls slang offers in English—and not merely to foreigners—for one to be very cautious before letting out some of the expressions found in this dictionary. Argot, it should be remembered, is linked not only with a particular *milieu* but often with specific circumstances. Used "out of situation" and so away from its normal context it can appear ludicrous if not offensive.

Argot is also characterized by a special intonation, elision and vocal modifications which we could not attempt to indicate—**je m'en fous** will be heard more often as **j'm'en fous** or even **m'en fous.** Strongly expressive terms are often pronounced with a change of stress: f̄ormidable! s̄ensass! and in the ignoble drawl of the Paris *voyou* with lengthened and opened vowels **il s'est barré le salaud!** will become **i's'est b̄arré l'sal̄aud.** The negative particle *ne*, usually disappears in popular speech *e.g.* **t'as rien à dire, j'suis pas maboule.** It is therefore very treacherous to embark upon the forms and turns of argot or slang without some preliminary initiation.

In the English equivalents we have tried to strike a balance between, on the one hand, expressions of long standing which may strike younger users of the dictionary as old fashioned but which are frequent in plays and novels of the first half of this century, and, on the other, very recent slang which may well turn out to be ephemeral.

Popular language, both French and English, is so rich in synonyms that, in order to save space and avoid repetition, it has been decided to give the generic term followed by an asterisk (*e.g.* **galette,** *f.* money*), the asterisk indicating that under that word in the *Table of English Slang Synonyms* will be found a selection of familiar and popular synonyms or near-synonyms from which a choice can be made. Occasionally the generic term has been followed by one of these synonyms whenever there seemed to be a close correspondence between the French and English expressions (*e.g.* **effacer,** to kill*, to wipe out). In the case of (*drugs**) and (*expletives**) the reader is being referred to a wider group than the synonyms for a specific word.

To facilitate reference, nouns have normally been taken as key-words, and the first noun serves this purpose if a phrase contains two or more nouns (*e.g.* **perdre le goût du pain** will be found under **goût**). Cross-references are also sometimes given in cases where it was thought useful to do so.

The death of Mr. Joseph Marks before his work was completely ready for the press has necessitated one or two changes in the original preface. This made grateful acknowledgment to his numerous and various sources of information, both printed and oral, and, in particular, to the author's wife and son for their invaluable suggestions concerning French and English colloquial usage.

Mrs Marks and Professor Farmer who have carried the work to completion desire to reiterate their thanks to those who have helped to make the publication of this dictionary possible: to Mr R.P.L. Ledésert, Modern Languages editor of Messrs Harrap, for his encouragement and help, and to various members of the firm for their advice, especially Mr F.G.S. Parker, sub-editor of this work, for his invaluable and friendly assistance at all stages; also to Monsieur Jean Ruer of the University of Strasbourg for timely aid in the correction of the first proofs.

AVANT-PROPOS

Cet ouvrage ne s'adresse pas seulement au spécialiste. Un nombre toujours croissant de touristes de langue anglaise voyagent en France, veulent comprendre l'homme de la rue, s'intéressent aux romans français, aux pièces de théâtre, aux films. Notre but est de leur permettre d'assimiler les éléments populaires et argotiques de la langue française et aussi d'aider le francophone curieux de la transposition en anglais des expressions courantes et vivantes du français non-académique.

Aucun dictionnaire ne peut prétendre être complet. Celui-ci veut présenter une sélection — personnelle peut-être — mais aussi étendue et judicieuse que possible de mots et de phrases populaires et de leur équivalent en anglais. Certaines expressions sont rares et ne se rencontrent que dans certains contextes et certains milieux, mais semblent cependant assez fréquentes pour justifier leur inclusion.

La langue du peuple est fluide, changeante et incertaine. Son évolution, d'une époque à une autre, rend très difficile de la déterminer. La distinction entre ce qui est courant et familier, populaire et vulgaire n'est pas facile à établir et pour en juger, l'étranger doit se rapporter à l'expression correspondante dans sa propre langue. Nous n'avons donc pas essayé de résoudre ce problème délicat, voire insoluble; nous n'avons pas essayé de tracer les frontières de ce qu'on appelle *l'argot*. Il vient un moment où un mot, une phrase deviennent assez usuels pour passer dans la langue de tous les jours et même dans la littérature. Ils cessent alors d'être argot mais portent avec eux une association avec leur sens primitif qui leur donne une saveur et une tournure bien particulières. De tels mots et expressions ont évidemment leur place dans cet ouvrage.

On sait qu'à son origine l'argot était la langue de la pègre, et du « milieu ». Le vocabulaire des truands et des larrons, celui de la prostitution et des rapports sexuels lui procure encore ses éléments les plus riches. Dans ce domaine il est impossible de se montrer pudibond: le grossier, le violent et l'obscène font partie intégrante de l'expression populaire. On est habitué aujourd'hui à appeler les choses par leur nom: *un chat, un chat et Rolet un fripon* mais c'est précisément quand un chat n'est plus un chat que l'intérêt du lexicographe s'éveille. La mentalité populaire a tendance à broder sur le côté *fripon* de *Rolet* et cela avec vigueur et pittoresque sans se soucier des conventions sociales et morales. Il ne nous a donc pas semblé nécessaire d'éviter d'écrire en toutes lettres des mots français et anglais que certains déclarent tabous. Il ne nous a pas semblé nécessaire d'indiquer si certains mots et expressions pouvaient être considérés comme « vulgaires » ou « obscènes ». De tels qualificatifs sont difficiles à définir et à délimiter, et la traduction donnée suffit en elle-même pour faire comprendre au lecteur la nature du terme.

Quiconque étudie une langue moderne semble attiré par le parler populaire et essaie de s'en servir, ayant ainsi l'impression qu'il se familiarise avec le langage courant du pays. Mais il suffit de penser à tous les traquenards que rencontre même le francophone s'il veut parler argot, pour ne l'employer qu'avec beaucoup de précautions. L'argot comme le *slang* appartient non seulement à un milieu déterminé mais aussi dépend de circonstances précises; si on le sort hors de son cadre et de son contexte normal, il devient choquant et grotesque.

La langue populaire de chaque pays est aussi caractérisée par des intonations et des modifications vocaliques qu'un dictionnaire ne peut indiquer. Ainsi l'expression argotique **je m'en fous** devient **j'm'en fous** et même plus souvent **m'en fous**. Dans des exclamations comme **formidable! sensass!** l'accent tonique est déplacé sur la première syllabe. Si le voyou de Paris veut dire **il s'est barré le salaud**, ses voyelles ouvertes et traînantes en font **i's'est barré l'salaud**. Remarquons aussi que le plus souvent dans la langue populaire l'adverbe de négation *ne* est omis; *ex.* **t'as rien à dire, j'suis pas maboule.**

On comprend donc les risques et les dangers de jouer avec le *slang* ou l'argot sans une initiation préalable.

En donnant les équivalents anglais nous avons essayé de tenir la balance entre des expressions populaires que la jeune génération pourrait qualifier de vieux jeu, mais qui se trouvent fréquemment dans les pièces et les romans de la première moitié du siècle, et, d'autre part, des termes argotiques récents qui, peut-être, n'auront qu'une vie éphémère.

La langue populaire en français et en anglais est si riche en synonymes que pour éviter les répétitions, il a été décidé de donner le terme générique suivi d'un astérisque (*ex.* **galette,** *f.* money*). L'astérisque indique que ce mot figure dans *Table of English Slang Synonyms* à la fin du Dictionnaire où l'on peut trouver une liste de synonymes et de termes apparentés. Dans certains cas le terme générique est suivi de l'un de ces synonymes lorsqu'il semble plus proche de l'expression française (*ex.* **effacer,** to kill*, to wipe out). Dans le cas des drogues (*drugs**) et des explétifs (*expletives**) le lecteur trouvera plus que des synonymes, une liste plus complète de termes affiliés.

Pour faciliter l'emploi du dictionnaire, les noms sont pris comme mots-clefs dans une phrase. Si la phrase contient plus d'un nom, le premier nom sert de repère (e.g. **perdre le goût du pain** se trouvera sous le mot **goût**). Certains renvois peuvent aussi aider le lecteur à relier plusieurs expressions similaires.

Monsieur Joseph Marks est décédé avant que son ouvrage ne soit complètement achevé. Dans la préface qu'il avait ébauchée, il exprimait sa reconnaissance envers ceux qui l'avaient aidé dans sa tâche, mentionnant surtout sa femme et son fils.

Madame Marks et le Professeur Farmer espèrent avoir mené à bonne fin cette présente publication et désirent réitérer leurs remerciements à tous ceux qui l'ont rendue possible. A Monsieur R.P.L. Ledésert et à ses collaborateurs de la maison Harrap pour leurs encouragements et leur aide, surtout à Monsieur F.G.S. Parker dont l'amical dévouement et les conseils furent inestimables; enfin à Monsieur Jean Ruer, de l'Université de Strasbourg, qui a bien voulu revoir les premières épreuves.

ABBREVIATIONS

abbrev.	abbreviation		*nav.*	naval
adj.	adjective		*neut.*	neuter
adv.	adverb, adverbial		*num.*	numerical
Am.	American			
approx.	approximately		*pej.*	pejorative(ly)
art.	article		*pl.*	plural
av.	aviation		*pop.*	popular(ly)
			poss.	possessive
cf.	refer to		*p.p.*	past participle
conj.	conjunction		*prep.*	preposition
c.p.	catch phrase		*pr.n.*	proper name
			pron.	pronoun
dem.	demonstrative		*qch.*	quelque chose
dial.	dialect(al)		*qn(e)*	quelqu'un(e)
f., fem.	feminine		*rad.*	radio
fig.	figurative(ly)		*rel.*	relative
			R.S.	rhyming slang
i.e.	that is		*r.t.m.*	registered trade mark
indef.	indefinite			
int.	interjection		*sch.*	schools and universities
interr.	interrogative		*sg., sing.*	singular
iron.	ironic(ally)		*sl.*	slang
			s.o.	someone
jest.	jesting(ly)		*sth.*	something
joc.	jocular(ly)			
journ.	journalism		*th.*	theatre
			t.v.	television
lit.	literal(ly)			
liter.	literary use		*W.W.I.*	World War I
			W.W.II.	World War II
m., masc.	masculine			
mil.	military		=	equivalent in meaning to
motor.	motoring			

A

---

abat-faim, *m.* stodge, damper (*substantial dish of food*).

abat(t)age, *m.* **1.** reprimand*. **2.** (*of actor, etc.*) brio, dash, gusto, attack. **3.** (*of book, etc.*) pot-boiler. **4.** severe criticism*.

abattis, *m.pl.* hands and feet, fins and stumps; **numérote** (*or* **tu peux numéroter) tes a.!** (*threat before physical attack*) I'll break every bone in your body!

abattre: en a., to get through a lot of work, to be a glutton (*or* a beggar) for work; (*of distance*) to cover a lot of ground.

abbaye, *f.* **l'a. de Monte-à-regret**, the scaffold, the guillotine.

abîmer. **1.** to criticize* severely. **2.** to exaggerate*. **3.** = **amocher 2.**

ablette, *f.* **taquiner l'a.**, to be a bit of an angler, to do a bit of fishing.

abondance, *f.* weak wine-and-water.

abouler, to give, to hand over, (*of money*) to pay* up

(s') abouler, to arrive*, to come along.

aboyeur, *m.* **1.** barker (*tout at fairground, side-show, etc.*), spieler. **2.** revolver*, barker.

abreuvoir, *m.* bar, pub.

abricot, *m.* vagina*.

abruti, *m.* **1.** beast, pig, sot. **2.** fool*.

abus, *m.* **(il) y a de l'a.!** that's the limit!* it's a bit thick! that's too much of a good thing! that's going too far!

acabit, *m.* **du même a.** = **du même bateau (bateau 2).**

accord, *m.* **d'a.!** agreed!* O.K.!

accoucher, to confess*; **accouche(z)!** out with it! cough it up! spit it out! come clean! trot it out! shoot! fire away!

accrochage, *m.* **1.** quarrel*. **2.** hitch, snag. **3.** (*mil.*) skirmish, brush. **4.**

(*boxing*) clinch. **5.** (*cycling*) recovery.

accroché, *p.p.* **1.** in debt. **2.** detained (after police-raid). **3.** brave, plucky. **4.** infatuated, hooked.

accroche-cœur, *m.* kiss-curl, lovelock, spit-curl.

accroche-pipe, *m.* mouth*.

accrocher. **1.** to steal*. **2.** to pawn*. **3.** to buttonhole (s.o.). **4.** to hook (*e.g.* a husband). **5. a. avec qn**, to get off (*or* to click) with s.o. **6.** to get into debt.

accrocher, s'. **1. s'a. avec qn**, to quarrel (*or* to come to blows) with s.o.; (*sport*) to hang on. **2. s'a. à qn**, to importune (*or* to buttonhole *or* to stick to *or* to hang on to) s.o. **3. se l'a.**, to have to do without, to go without food, to tighten one's belt; **tu peux (toujours) te l'a.** (*or* **te les a.**)! you can whistle for it!

accrocheur, -euse, *m.f.* tenacious bore*.

achar, *m.* **d'a.**, relentlessly, tooth and nail, like billy-o(h). *See* **autor.**

acheter. **1.** to bribe, to square, to get at (s.o.). **2.** to hoax*; **on vous a acheté!** you've been had (*or* sold)!

à-côtés, *m.pl.* extra profits, extras, perquisites, perks.

acrais! *or* **acré!** *int.* look out! careful! nix!

acrobate, *m.* queer*, odd person.

acte, *m.* **avaler son a. de naissance**, to die*.

acteuse, *f.* (*pej.*) actress devoid of talent.

activer: active(z)! hurry* up!

adieu, *int.* (*in South of France often* = **bonjour!**) good morning!

adja, *m.* **se faire l'a.** *or* **mettre les adjas**, to decamp*.

adji, *m.* **à ses adjis**, on his track.

adjupète, *m.* (*mil.*) warrant officer, (company) sergeant-major.

adresse, *f.* **vous vous êtes trompé d'a.!** you've come to the wrong person (*or* shop)!

afanaf, *adv.* half-and-half; **marcher** (*or* **faire**) **a.,** to go halves, to go fifty-fifty.

affaire, *f.* **1. a. de . . .,** in order to . . ., just for . . ., by way of . . . **2. c'est une a.),** it's a (real) bargain; it's a certainty; it's a snip. **3. être à son a.,** to be in one's element; to be on the job. **4. l'a. est dans le sac,** it's as good as settled, it's a certainty*, it's in the bag. **5. faire son a. à qn.,** to kill* (s.o.). **6. la belle a.!** (*a*) is that all? what does that matter? (*b*) a nice thing, I must say! **7. montrer son a.,** (*e.g. of child*) to show one's 'private property'.

affaires, *f.pl.* **1.** menses* (*e.g.* **elle a ses a.**). **2. faire** (*or* **aller à**) **ses a.,** to defecate*.

affaler, s', to confess*.

affiche, *f.* showing-off, swank*.

affiché, *p.p.* **c'est a.!** it's a certainty!*

affligé, *m.* cripple.

afflure, *f.,* **afflurer**=**affure** *f.,* **affurer.**

affranchi, *m.* **1.** totally unscrupulous person. **2.** wide-awake* person.

affranchir. 1. to put (s.o.) wise, to put (s.o.) in the picture, to let (s.o.) in the know, to teach (s.o.) the game. **2.** to corrupt.

affreux, *m.* **1.** objectionable* person. **2.** mercenary soldier.

affure, *f.* profit, gain, bunce; **faire** (*or* **avoir**) **de l'a.,** to find it profitable.

affurer, to earn, to win, to receive, to get, to keep, to cop; **en a. une,** (*cycle racing*) to win a lap.

affûter, (*of thieves, etc.*) to entice (an accomplice) by offering a share of the booty.

affûtoir, *m.* **a. à fromage,** French long loaf of bread.

afnaf, *adv.* =**afanaf.**

agiter. 1. les a., to decamp*. **2. se l'a.,** to masturbate*.

agoniser (**de sottises**), to heap abuse on, to slang, to give it (s.o.) hot.

agrafer. 1. to buttonhole (s.o.). **2.** to arrest*. **3.** to steal*. **4.** to reprimand*.

agrég, *f.* (=*agrégation*) highest state competitive examination for teaching posts in *lycées* and universities.

agricher *or* **agriffer. 1.** to arrest*. **2.** to seize, to grab.

agro, *m.* (=*Institut national agronomique*) agricultural college; student at this college.

aguicher, to allure, to lead (s.o.) on, to give the glad eye to, to set (s.o.) all agog.

aguicheuse, *f.* vamp, (prick- *or* cock-) teaser, P.T.

aigle, *m.* **ce n'est pas un a.,** he's no genius.

aigre, *m.* **tourner à l'a.,** to become acrimonious, to take a nasty turn, to get sticky.

aigrette, *f.* **avoir son a.,** to be slightly drunk*.

aiguille, *f.* **être vacciné avec une a. de phono,** to talk* volubly.

aiguiller, to have coition* with.

ail, *m.* **aimer** (**sentir, taper**) **l'a., manger** *or* **vendre de l'a..** to be a lesbian*; **marchandes d'a.,** lesbians.

aile, *f.* **1.** arm (*limb of person*); **passe ton a. sous mon abattis,** take my arm. **2. avoir un coup dans l'a.,** to be drunk*. **3. prendre un virage sur l'a.,** (*of car*) to take a corner on two wheels.

aileron, *m.* =**aile 1.**

aimer. 1. j'aime mieux pas! I'd rather not! **2. va te faire a.!** go to blazes!*

air, *m.* **1. autant cracher en l'a.,** it's a waste of breath, it's like water off a duck's back, it's like pouring water on a duck's back, it's a sheer waste of time, it's like talking to a brick wall. **2. cracher en l'a. pour que cela retombe sur le nez,** (*fig.*) to spit into the wind. **3. de l'a.!** go to blazes!* buzz off! **4. envoyer en l'a.,** (*a*) to kill*; (*b*) to floor (an adversary). **5. s'envoyer en l'a.,** (*a*) to have coition*; (b) to be high on drugs. **6. flanquer** (*or* **fiche(r)** *or* **foutre**) **en l'a.,** (*a*) to chuck

away, to chuck up; (b) to kill*.
7. se flanquer (or se foutre) en l'a., to commit suicide, to do oneself in. 8. l'avoir en l'a., =bander. 9. mettre en l'a., (a) to kill*; (b) to steal*; (c) to wreck (a place). 10. ne pas avoir l'a. d'y toucher, to look as if butter would not melt in one's mouth. 11. ne pas manquer d'a., to be plucky, to have guts, to have nerve. 12. n'avoir l'a. de rien=faire mine de rien*. 13. ne plus tenir en l'a., (of person) to be ready to drop (with fatigue). 14. en jouer un a., to decamp*. 15. pomper de l'a., to talk* volubly.

ajisme, m. (from Auberges de la jeunesse) youth hostel movement; youth hostelling.

ajiste, m.f. youth hosteller.

alevin, m. young pimp.

al(l)ezingue, m. jacket.

aligner: a. le fric, les a., to pay* up.

aligner, s', to toe the line; **tu peux (toujours) t'a.!** just you try it on! you can whistle for it! **tu t'alignes?** are you willing to bet? is it a bet? **s'a. avec qn,** to take s.o. on, to have a set-to with s.o.

allant, m. **avoir de l'a.,** to have plenty of drive (or dash or go or pep or punch or spunk or zip), to have what it takes.

aller. 1. (=a. à la selle) to evacuate, to go to stool. **2. a. avec une femme,** to have coition*. **3. ça n'a pas l'air d'a.,** you look as if there's something the matter; you don't look up to the mark. **4. faire a. qn,** (a) to order s.o. about; (b) to lead s.o. on; (c) to take s.o. in (=faire marcher qn). **5. se laisser a.,** (a) to become discouraged; (b) to neglect oneself. **6. y a. de** (sum of money, speech, song, etc.), to contribute, to put up, to pay up*. **7. y a. fort:** see **fort,** adv.

allongé, m. corpse*; **le boulevard des allongés,** the cemetery, boneyard, bone-orchard.

allonger. 1. to aim, to land, to hand out (blow, slap, etc.). **2. (les) a.,** to

pay* up. **3. se l'a.,** to masturbate*. **4. se faire a.,** (sch.) to be ploughed, plucked, failed.

allonger, s'. 1. =s'affaler. **2. s'a.** (qch.), (a) to treat (or to stand) oneself (sth. good); (b) to have to do (sth. unpleasant).

alloques, f.pl. **1.** allowance (mil., family). **2.** unemployment benefit, dole.

allouf, f. match (allumette).

allumé, adj. **1.** amative, excited (sexually), randy, rorty, horny. **2.** slightly drunk*, lit up, squiffy.

allumer. 1. to excite (sexually). **2.** to look at, to watch. **3.** to kill*. **4.** to wound (with a fire-arm). **5.** to pay* up. **6.** to hurry* up. **7.** to booze. **8.** (at gambling) to put one's stakes down, to show the colour of one's money. **9. se faire a.,** to attract attention, to make oneself conspicuous; (mil.) to fall into an ambush.

allumettes, f.pl. legs*.

allumeur, m. confederate (of gambler, swindler, etc.), decoy.

allumeuse, f. =aguicheuse.

alors, adv. **1. et a.?** or **a. quoi?** so what? **2. et puis a.?** what then? **3. ça, a.!** or **non, mais a.!** well, I never! well, I'll be hanged! you don't say! well, I like that! can you beat that?

aloufs, f.pl. matches (allumettes).

alpague, m. **1.** jacket; coat. **2.** back (of human body); **avoir sur l'a.,** to be saddled with (a crime, etc.); **mettre sur l'a. à qn,** to saddle s.o. with sth., to pass the buck; **les avoir sur l'a.,** to be sought after by (rival gang or police).

alpaguer, to arrest*.

alphonse, m. procurer, pimp, ponce, bully.

alpingue, m. =alpague 1.

amant, m. **a. de cœur,** fancy man.

amarrer, to get hold of, to collar, to nab.

amazone, f. high class prostitute*.

amen, int. **dire toujours a.** or **dire a. à tout,** to be a yes-man.

amende, *f.* **mettre qn à l'a.,** to exact racket-money (*or* protection-money) from s.o.

amener, s'. 1. to arrive*, to come along. **2. il peut toujours s'a.,** let him try it on!

amère, *adj. f.* **l'avoir a.** *or* **la trouver a.** =l'avoir mauvaise.

Amerloc(k), Amerlo(t), Amerloque, *m.* American, Yank.

amie, *f.* **petite a.,** lady-friend.

aminche, *m.* friend*.

amocher. 1. to make a mess of. **2.** to knock (s.o.) about, to beat (s.o.) up, to bash (s.o.) up, to spoil s.o.'s beauty.

amocher, s' *or* **amochir, s',** (*of person*) to be much the worse for wear.

amortis, *m.pl.* **les a.,** (*teenagers' term for*) the thirty-to-forty-year-olds.

amortisseurs, *m.pl.* breasts* (of female).

amour, *m.* **1. un a. de . . .,** (*of person or thing*) a darling (*or* a lovely *or* a sweet) . . .; **vous êtes un a.!** you're a dear (*or* a darling *or* an angel)! **2. faire l'a.** (**avec**), to have sexual intercourse* (with). **3. vivre d'a. et d'eau fraîche,** to live on bread and cheese and kisses.

amphi, *m.* **1.** lecture-room. **2.** lecture; a paper (on a subject).

amuse-gueule, *m.* cocktail snack, cocktail canapé.

amusement, *m.* **je vous souhaite bien de l'a.,** I hope you'll have a jolly good time (*usually ironical*).

amusette, *f.* child's play, kid stuff, small-time racket.

amygdales, *f.pl.* **1. se caler les a.:** *sec* **se caler 2. 2. s'humecter les a.**=**se rincer la dalle.**

an, *m.* **s'en ficher** (*or* **s'en moquer** *or* **s'en soucier**) **comme de l'a. quarante,** not to care a rap*.

anar *or* **anarcho,** *m.* **anarchote,** *f.* anarchist.

Anastasie, *f.* (*W.W.I.*) 'Dora' (*the censorship*).

Anatole, *pr.n.* (*rhyming c.p. used as exclamation or query*) **ça colle, A.!**

right-o, old cock! **ça colle, A.?** how's tricks, old chap?

ance, *f.* ear*.

ancêtres, *m.pl.* parents, old folks.

andosses, *f.pl.* shoulders; back; **en avoir plein les a.,** (*a*) to be exhausted*; (*b*) to be depressed*.

andouille, *f.* **1.** simpleton, fool*; **faire l'a.,** to act the (giddy) goat; **bougre** (*or* **espèce**) **d'a.!** you silly ass! you B.F.! **2. a. à col roulé,** penis*.

âne, *m.* **tenir l'â. par la queue,** to urinate*.

anéanti, *adj.* exhausted*.

ange, *m.* **1. faire l'a.,** to procure an abortion; **faiseur (faiseuse) d'anges,** abortionist, 'angel-maker'. **2. un a. passe** *or* **il passe un a.!** (*c.p. said during an uncomfortable lull or an embarrassed silence in a conversation*) an angel passes! **3. voir les anges**=**jouir. 4. mettre aux anges,** to give sexual pleasure. **5. les anges** (*long-distance drivers' slang*), motor-cycle cops.

anglais, *m.pl.* **elle a ses a.** *or* **les a. sont débarqués** (*or* **ont débarqué**)=**elle a ses affaires.**

Angliche, *m.,* *adj.* English.

anguille, *f.* **a. de calcif,** penis*.

animal, *m.* fellow*, brute.

anis, *m.* **de l'anis!**=**des clous!** (**clou 7**).

anneau, *m.* anus*.

anse, *f.* **1.** =**ance. 2.** arm (*limb of person*).

antif(fe), *f.* road, **battre l'a.,** to loaf about.

antiffer, to enter, to come in.

antifle, *f.* **1.** =**antiffe. 2.** church.

antifler, s': s'a. (**de sec**), to get married*.

antisèche, *f.* (*sch.*) crib (at an examination).

apache, *m.* hooligan, tough, thug.

apaiser, to kill*, to put to sleep.

apé *or* **apéro,** *m.* appetizer, cocktail.

aplatir. 1. to dumbfound*. **2.** to beat* hollow.

apôtre, *m.* finger.

appareil, *m.* **dans le plus simple a.,** stark naked*.

appel, *m.* faire des appels à, to make a pass at; faire des appels de (*or* du) pied = faire du pied.

apporter, s' = s'amener.

appuyer, s': s'a. qch. = s'allonger qch.

aprèm', *m.* (= *après-midi*) cet a., this afternoon.

après, *adv.* et (puis) a.? what of (*or* what about) it? so what? what then? want to make something of it?

aquijer *or* **aquiger**. 1. to criticize*. 2. to injure = amocher.

arabe, *adj. see* combine, fourbi.

araignée, *f.* avoir une a. au (*or* dans le) plafond, to have bats in the belfry, to be mad*; to have a bee in one's bonnet.

aramon, *m.* (inferior red) wine.

arbalète, *f.* 1. fire-arm, rifle. 2. penis*; filer un coup d'a. = aiguiller.

arbi *or* **arbico(t)**, *m.* Arab, wog.

arbre, *m.* 1. human body. 2. faire monter qn à l'a., to hoax* s.o.

arcan, *m.* hooligan.

archer, *m.* police officer of the Sûreté.

archi, *prefix added to nouns, adjectives and past participles to express a superlative degree*—e.g. **archicon**, too bloody silly; **archifou**, stark mad; **archifauché**, broke to the wide.

archicube, *m.* former student of the *École Normale Supérieure.*

archipointu, *m.* archbishop.

arcpincer *or* **ar(c)quepincer**, to arrest*; (ces messieurs de) la Maison J't'ar(c)quepince, the police.

ardoise, *f.* 1. credit (*score chalked up—e.g. at a pub on slate or wall*). avoir une a. chez . . ., to have credit with . . ., to be able to chalk it up at . . .; inscrire à (*or* porter sur) l'a., to chalk it up, to put it on the slate; laisser une a., to leave behind unpaid debts; liquider une vieille a., to pay off an old score; poser une a., to depart without paying. 2. prendre une a. (à l'eau), to urinate* (in a street urinal).

argagnasses, *f.pl.* elle a ses a. = elle a ses affaires.

argasses, *f.pl.* feet*.

argomuche, *m.* slang*; jaspiner l'a., to talk slang.

argougner *or* **argouiner**, to get hold of, to collar, to nab, to grab.

argousin, *m.* policeman*.

aria, *m.* fuss, bother; faire des arias, to kick up a fuss, to make a song (and dance) about sth.; quel a.! *or* que d'arias! what a how-d'ye-do!

aristo *or* **aristoche**, *m.* toff, swell, nob.

arlequin, *m.* resurrection-pie; arlequins, shackles (*i.e.* scraps of meat left over in a butcher's shop).

arme, *f.* passer l'a. à gauche, to die*.

armé, *p.p.* être a. = bander.

Arménouche, *m.* Armenian.

armoire, *f.* 1. a. à glace, (*mil.*) haversack, knapsack, pack. 2. a. (normande) *or* a. à glace, hefty fellow, hulking brute. 3. a. à sous, (*a*) piano, 'joanna'; (*b*) barrel-organ, hurdy-gurdy.

arnac *or* **arnaque**, *f.* fraud, swindle; un coup d'a., a treacherous blow; monter une a., faire de l'a., to practise fraud, to go in for swindling.

arnaquer, to cheat*, to swindle, to defraud.

arnaqueur, *m.* cheat*, swindler*, sharper, crook.

arnau, *adj.* in a vile temper*.

arpenteuse, *f.* prostitute*, streetwalker.

arpète *or* **arpette**, *f.* milliner's apprentice *or* errand-girl.

arpion, *m.* foot*; taper des arpions, to have smelly feet.

arquepincer = arcpincer.

arquer, to foot it, to hoof it, to pad the hoof.

arquin, *m.* safe-cracker.

arquinche, *adj.* tight, close-fisted.

arracher. 1. on se l'arrache, he (she, it) is all the rage (*or* is in great demand); on s'arrache ce livre, there is a rush for this book. 2. s'a., to escape; to decamp*.

arrangemaner. 1. = arranger 1. 2. = amocher 2.

arranger. 1. to swindle*. **2.** to cook, to doctor (accounts, figures, etc.). **3.** to kill*. **4.** to steal*. **5.** = amocher 2. **6. je t'arrangerai!** I'll fix you! **7. se faire a.,** (a) to be swindled (or diddled or victimized or overcharged); (b) to get hurt (or wounded), to cop a packet; (c) to get ticked off; (d) to catch a venereal disease, to cop a dose (i.e. of V.D.). **8. ça s'arrangera!** it'll turn out all right! it will sort itself out! it'll all come out in the wash!

arrangeur, m. = arnaqueur.

arrimer, to corner (s.o.), to grab.

arrivé, p.p. **croire que c'est a.,** (a) to be extremely gullible, to take it all for gospel truth; (b) to have a high opinion of oneself, to be full of self-confidence, to fancy oneself.

arriviste, m.f. careerist, go-getter, pusher.

arrondir, s'. 1. to get drunk*. **2.** to be pregnant*. **3. tu peux te l'a.!** = tu peux te l'accrocher! **4. se l'a.,** to go without food.

arroser. 1. to celebrate with a drink; **a. ses galons,** to wet (or to christen) one's stripes; to stand drinks, to stand (a) shout, to stand treat, to stand Sam; **c'est moi qui arrose,** it's my call (or my round or my shout) this time, the drinks are on me; **ça s'arrose,** this calls for a drink. **2.** to bribe, to square (s.o.). **3.** to pay (s.o.) sth. on account. **4.** (mil.) to strafe, to paste. **5. se faire a.,** to get a thorough wetting, to get soaked to the skin.

arroseuse, f., **arrosoir,** m. (mil.) machine-gun, sten-gun.

arsouille, m. blackguard*.

arti, f. artillery.

artichaut, m. purse, pocket-book. See also **cœur** 2.

artiche, f. **1.** money*. **2.** purse, pocket-book.

article, m. **1. faire l'a.,** to puff (or to boost or to plug) one's goods. **2. être porté sur l'a.** = être porté sur la bagatelle. **3.** = surin. **4.** weapon in general (revolver*, etc.).

artiflot, m. artilleryman.

artiller = aiguiller.

artillerie, f. **1.** loaded dice. **2.** firearms. **3.** stodgy food. **4. la grosse a.,** paper money, notes, 'big stuff'. **5. sortir la grosse a.** (= employer les grands moyens), to take strong measures.

artiste, m. fellow*.

artou, m. foot*.

Arverne, m. = Auverpin.

as, m. **1.** (sport, etc.) expert, top-notcher, first-rater*, wizard, star (performer, player), crack (player, driver), ace (pilot). **2.** (in restaurant, etc.) (table) no. 1. **3. a. de carreau,** knapsack, haversack, pack. **4. a. de pique,** (a) (of fowl) rump, parson's nose; (of person) buttocks*; (b) nonentity; (c) **fichu comme l'a. de pique,** botched, bungled; dressed like a guy. **5. aller à l'a.,** to come a cropper*. **6. bouffer à l'a.,** to go without food. **7. être (plein) à l'a.** (or aux a.), to be rich*. **8. passer à l'a.,** to vanish into thin air. **9. passer qch. à l'a.,** to juggle sth. away. **10. veiller à l'a.,** to keep a sharp look-out, to keep one's eyes peeled (or skinned).

ascenseur, m. **renvoyer l'a.,** to return a favour.

asperge, f. **1.** penis*. **2. aller aux asperges,** to be a prostitute*. **3. une a. montée (en graine), une grande a.,** a tall*, thin person.

asphyxier. 1. to steal*. **2.** to dumbfound*. **3.** to have a foul breath.

aspi, m. (from 'aspirant') (nav.) midshipman.

aspine, f. money*.

assaisonner. 1. to thrash* soundly. **2.** to reprimand* soundly. **3.** to affect venereally, to give s.o. a dose (i.e. of V.D.). **4. se faire a.** = se faire assassiner.

assassiner. 1. to make a mess of, to ruin, to smash up. **2.** to bore* (s.o.) to death. **3.** to charge a shocking price. **4. se faire a.,** (a) to catch (or to get) a severe thrashing*; (b) to get a stiff (or heavy) sentence, to get the book thrown at one.

asseoir. 1. to snub, to crush. **2.** to nonplus, to bowl over, to floor.
asseoir, s' : je m'assieds (or je m'assois) dessus! I don't care a rap* about it! I couldn't care less about it! **2. va t'a.!** go to blazes!* See also **assis.**
assez, adv. en avoir a., to be fed up, to be depressed*.
assiette, f. **1. l'a.** au beurre, fat government jobs, cushy jobs, jobs for the boys, gravy train, gravy boat, pork-barrel; **taper dans l'a. au beurre,** to ride the gravy train. **2. les Assiettes,** the Assize Court.
assis, p.p. en être (or en rester) a., to be dumbfounded*; **ça m'a a.,** that floored (or shook) me, that knocked me all of a heap, that took my breath away.
assommant, adj. wearisome, boring.
assommer, to bore*.
assommer, s', to be bored.
assommeur, m. (of person) bore*.
assommoir, m. **1.** low pub, low dive. **2.** (of person) bore*.
Assottes, les, f.pl. Assize Court.
astap(e), adj. (abbrev. of à se taper le derrière) (or le cul or les fesses) par terre (or sur le bord du trottoir); **c'est a.!** (a) it's a scream! (i.e. very funny); (b) it's frightful!
astec or **astèque,** m. = **aztèque.**
asteure, adv. (= à cette heure) at that moment, then; now.
astibloc or **astibloche,** m. maggot.
astic, m. = **astique.**
asticot, m. **1.** miser*. **2.** fellow*; **un drôle d'a.,** a queer* person; **engraisser les asticots,** to be dead.
asticotage, m. teasing, ragging, plaguing, nagging.
asticoter, to tease, to rag, to plague, to nag.
asticoter, s', to quarrel, to squabble, to bicker.
astique, f. (mil.) **passer à l'a.,** to polish, to furbish. See **frotte.**
astiquer. 1. = **asticoter. 2.** to thrash*.
astiquer, s'. 1. to smarten* oneself up, to dress up*. **2.** = **s'asticoter.**

astuce, f. **1.** joke, witticism, wheeze. **2.** gadget*.
atmosphère, f. être dans l'a., to disappear.
atout, m. blow*.
attaque, f. **1.** être (or se sentir) d'a., to be (or to feel) fit. **2.** travailler d'a., to work with a will. **3.** ... d'a., (of things) first-rate*, (of persons) resolute, game.
atteler: (of pimp) a. à deux or être **attelé à deux,** to live on two women.
atteler, s' : s'a. à, to tackle, to buckle to.
attendri, adj. slightly drunk*, maudlin.
attigé, adj. syphilitic.
a(t)tiger. 1. to hit, to wound; to get hit, to get wounded, to cop a packet. **2.** = **assaisonner 3. 3. a.** (la cabane), to exaggerate*; **n'attige pas!** come off it! come off the grass! don't come it! draw it mild! **sans a.** = **sans blague.**
attrapade, f. **attrapage,** m. **1.** quarrel*. **2.** reprimand*.
attrape, f. hoax*.
attrape-couillons, attrape-cons, attrape-gogos, attrape-nigauds, m. hoax*.
attrape-pèze, swindle*.
attrape-pognon, m. gambling.
attraper. 1. to reprimand*. **2.** to cheat*. **3. en a. pour X ans,** to get (a sentence of) X years. **4. attrape!** take that! put that in your pipe and smoke it! **5. se faire a.,** (a) to be reprimanded*; (b) to be diddled, to be taken in.
attriquer, to get, to buy stolen goods; **s'a.,** to treat oneself to.
auber or **aubère,** m. money*.
auberge, f. **1.** prison*. **2. on n'est pas sorti de l'a.,** we are not out of the wood yet.
aubergine, f. = **betterave 1.**
aubert, m. = **auber.**
auge, f. plate.
Auguste, pr. n. comme de juste (or tout juste), A.! (rhyming c.p.) you've said it, chum!

autiche, *f.* **faire de l'a.**=**rouspéter.**

auticher, to excite sensually; **s'a.,** to become randy.

auto(r), d', *adv.* off one's own bat; on the spur of the moment; unhesitatingly; **travailler d'a. et d'achar,** to work with a will; **d'a. et de rif** (*or* **de rif et d'a.**), without further ado.

Auverpin *or* **Auverploum,** *m.* **1.** native of Auvergne, Auvergnat. **2.** =**bougna(t) 2.**

auxi, auxigo, *m.* **1.** (*mil.*) non-combatant. **2.** (*in prison*) prisoner performing menial jobs.

avachi, *adj.* flabby, sloppy.

avachir, s'., to become flabby (*or* sloppy); to go to seed.

avaler. 1. to bite (*or* to snap) s.o.'s head off. **2. l'a.,** to die*. *See also* **langue 2.**

avaloir, *m.,* **avaloire,** *f.* throat, gullet; **s'arroser l'a.,** to wet one's whistle*.

avantage, *m.* **faire un a. à qn,** to do s.o. a favour, to be nice to s.o.; to pleasure (a woman).

avantages, *m.pl.* breasts* (of female).

avant-scène, *f.* **il y a du monde à l'a.-s.**=**il y a du monde au balcon.**

avant-scènes, *f.pl.* =**avantages.**

avarié, *adj., m.* syphilitic (person).

avaro, *m.* accident, bad luck, trouble.

avec, *prep. See* **ça 1** *and* **2.**

aveux, *m.pl.,* **passer à la chambre des a. spontanés,** to be put through the third degree.

avocat, *m.* **1. a. bêcheur,** (*approx.*) Public Prosecutor. **2. faire l'a.**= **baronner.**

avoine, *f.* **1.** food*. **2. filer** (*or* **refiler) une a. à**=**avoiner.**

avoiner, to thrash*.

avoir. 1. to fool* (s.o.), to get the better of (s.o.), to lick (s.o.); **se faire** (*or* **se laisser) a.,** to be taken in, to be had; **on vous a eu!** you've been had! **on les aura!** we'll beat them yet! **2. en a.,** to have guts, to have spunk. **3. j'en ai jusque-là!** I'm fed up to the teeth! **4. a. qn à la pitié, à la sympathie, etc.,** to play on s.o.'s pity, sympathy, etc.

avorton, *m.* runt, half-pint, undersized person*.

azimut, *m.* **dans tous (les) azimuts,** all directions; right, left and centre; **entourloupe dans l'a.,** trouble ahead.

azimuté, *adj.* mad*.

azor, *m.* **1.** dog*. **2.** revolver*. **3.** (*mil.*) haversack, knapsack, pack. **4.** servant; **appeler a.,** to whistle to (*or* up) s.o.

aztèque, *m.* (*pej.*) undersized* person.

B

b . . ., *abbrev.* = bougre.
B.A. ba, *m.* **le B.A. ba,** the first rule, the A.B.C.
baba, *adj.* en être (*or* en **rester** *or* en **demeurer**) b., to be dumbfounded*.
baba, *m.* 1. buttocks*; **le mettre dans le b. à qn,** to dupe* s.o.; **l'avoir** (*or* **se le faire mettre** *or* **se laisser taper**) **dans le b.,** to be duped*. 2. vagina*.
babafier, to dumbfound*.
babillard, *m.* 1. newspaper. 2. letter (*missive*), brief.
babillarde *or* **babille,** *f.* = babillard 2.
babines *or* **babouines,** *f.pl.* (*of person*) lips, chops; **se caler** (*or* **s'en mettre plein** *or* **s'en donner par**) **les b.,** to eat* heartily; **s'en (pour)lécher les b.,** to smack (*or* to lick) one's lips (*or* one's chops) (over it).
bac, *m.* (i) baccarat (*card game*); **tailler un b.,** to have a game of baccarat.
bac, *m.* (ii) (= *baccalauréat*). French school-leaving examination.
baccara, *m.* 1. **avoir b.** = l'avoir dans le **baba.** 2. **être en plein b.,** (*a*) to have a run of bad luck; (*b*) to be lifeless, not to react.
bacchanal, *m.* uproar*.
bacchanale, *f.* noisy, drunken revel, orgy.
bac(ch)antes, *f.pl.* moustache, tash, face-fungus, tickler; **avoir les b. en guidon (de course),** to have a handle-bar moustache.
bâche, *f.* 1. cap*. 2. sheet (of bed); **se mettre dans les bâches** = se bâcher.
bâcher, se, to go to bed*.
bâcheuse, *f.* lodging-house keeper, landlady.
bachot, *m.* = bac (ii); **un four** (*or* **une boîte** *or* **une usine**) **à b.,** a cramming-shop, a crammer's (establishment).
bachotage, *m.* cramming.
bachoter. 1. to cram (for an examination). 2. to talk like a ninny.

bachoteur *or* **bachotier,** *m.* 1. crammer. 2. swot.
bâclé, *p.p.* scamped, botched.
bâcler, to scamp, to botch, to bungle.
bâcleur, *m.* botcher, bungler.
bacreuse, *f.* pocket*.
bada, *m.* 1. hat*. 2. **porter le** (*or* **un**) **b.,** (*a*) to be (*or* to be made) the scapegoat, to get the blame*; (*b*) to be a police-informer*.
badaboum, *m.* scuffle, brawl, shindy, free-for-all, rough-house.
badaf, *m.* = bat' d'Af'.
baderne, *f.* **une vieille b.,** an old fog(e)y*, (*mil.*) a Colonel Blimp.
badigeon, *m.* make-up, face-paint, war-paint.
badigeonner, to make up, to paint (one's face).
badigeonneur, *m.* dauber.
badigoinces, *f.pl.* = babines; **jouer des b.** = se caler les babines.
Badingue *or* **Badinguet,** *pr.n.* nickname for Napoléon III.
les Badingues, Batignolles (*district in Paris*).
badour, *adj.* 1. good-looking, pretty. 2. pleasant.
baffe, *f.* (i) *or* **baffre,** *f.* blow* (in the face).
baffe, *f.* (ii) **baffis,** *m.* = bac(ch)antes.
baffrer = bâfrer.
bafouille, *f.* = babillard 2.
bafouillette, *f.* short letter
bâfre, *f.* 1. feasting. 2. = baffe (i).
bâfrée, *f.* feasting.
bâfrer, to feast, to guzzle.
bâfrer, se, to stuff oneself.
bâfrerie, *f.* gluttony, guzzling.
bâfreur, -euse, *m.f.* glutton*.
bagaf, *m.* revolver*.
bagage, *m.* **plier b.,** (*a*) to pack up; (*b*) to decamp*; (*c*) to die*.
bagali, *m.* mud.

bagarrer, se, to fight, to scuffle, to scrap, to brawl, to have a punch-up.

bagarreur, m. scrapper, battler, bruiser, brawler.

bagatelle, f. 1. être porté sur la b., to be fond of sexual intercourse*, to be hot stuff, to be randy, to like one's greens. 2. les bagatelles de la porte, preliminaries to sexual intercourse, heavy petting, heavy necking.

bagnard, m. convict.

bagne, m. penal servitude.

bagnole, f. 1. (old, ramshackle) motor-car*. 2. taxi.

bagot(t)er, to tramp (or to knock or to gad or to loaf) about; to trot off, to toddle off.

bagots, m.pl. luggage, traps.

bagougnasses, f.pl. lips.

bagouler, to talk, to jabber away.

bagouse, f. 1. ring (jewellery). 2. luck. 3. anus*; l'avoir dans la b.=l'avoir dans la baba; filer (or prendre) de la b., to be a homo(sexual)*.

bagou(t), m. avoir du b., to have the gift of the gab.

bagouze, f. =bagouse.

bague, f. =bagouse.

baguenaude, f. pocket*.

baguenauder, (se), to mooch about, to loaf around, to fool around, to tootle about, to arse around.

baguette, f. 1=bagouse 2. 2. filer un coup de b. à=aiguiller.

baguettes, f.pl. 1. legs*; mettre les b., to decamp*. 2. avoir les b.=avoir les foies.

bahut, m. 1. school, lycée. 2. motor-car;* taxi. 3. motor lorry.

bahutien, bahutier, bahuteur, m. (sch.) pupil, school-mate.

baigneur, m. 1. face*. 2. head*; se casser le b., to rack one's brains. 3. nose*.

bail, m. 1. il y a un b. (or ça fait un b.) qu'on ne s'est pas vus! it's ages (or it's an age) since we met! we haven't met for ages (or for donkey's years)! 2. casser le b., to get a divorce.

baille, f. 1. water (of sea, river, etc.); boire à la (grande) b., to go to Davy Jones's locker. 2. rain. 3. old tub (ship). 4. La B., the École navale in Lanvéoc-Poulmic.

bain, m. 1. b. de pieds, coffee etc. over-flowing into the saucer, (jest.) 'half and half' coffee (etc.) (i.e. half in the cup, half in the saucer). 2. c'est un b. qui chauffe, there's a storm brewing. 3. envoyer qn au b., to send s.o. packing*. 4. être dans le b., (a) to be in a fix*; (b) to be implicated (or involved or mixed up) in an affair, to be up to the neck in it; (c) to be in the know; (d) to have got one's hand in. 5. flanquer qn dans le b., to accuse s.o., to put s.o. on the spot. 6. mettre qn dans le b., (a) to implicate s.o.; (b) to let s.o. in on a deal. 7. prendre un b. de pieds, to be sent to a penal colony. 8. se mettre dans le b., (a) to get the feel of things; (b) to get down to it. 9. sortir qn du b., to get s.o. out of a fix*. 10. tremper dans le b., to be up to the neck in it. 11. un bain sulfureux, aniseed drink.

bain-marie, m. bidet.

baïonnette, f. penis*.

baisant, adj. first-rate*; peu b., lousy.

baise-en-ville, m. 1. vaginal douche. 2. small overnight bag, night-stop bag.

baiser. 1. to have coition* with. 2. to arrest*; se faire b., to get nabbed. 3. to steal*. 4. to deceive*, to fool*; faire b., to be taken in, to be fooled, to be done brown. 5. to catch, to cop (illness, etc.).

baisette, f. penis*.

baiseur, -euse, m.f. fornicator, fuckster, fuckstress.

baiseuses, f.pl. lips.

baisodrome, m. 1. brothel*. 2. bedroom.

baisoter, to peck at (i.e. to kiss s.o. perfunctorily), to keep pecking at (s.o.).

baisse-froc, m. coward*.

bak(h)chich, m. gratuity, tip.

bal, *m.* **1. donner le b. à,** to reprimand*.
2. (*mil.*) **faire le b.,** to do punishment
drill, to be on jankers.
balade, *f.* outing: stroll, ramble; joy-
ride, run, drive; spin.
balader. 1. to take (s.o.) for an outing
(*see* **balade**), to trot s.o. round, to tote.
2. envoyer b. qn, to send s.o. packing*.
3. envoyer b. qch., to chuck sth. up (*or*
away).
balader, se, to go for a stroll, an outing (*see* **balade**); to trapes (*or* traipse).
balai, *m.* **1.** last bus, train (at night).
2. coup de b., clean sweep (of staff),
clean-out, brush-off. **3. du b.!** hop* it!
4. il fait b. neuf, new brooms sweep
clean. **5. rôtir le b.,** to go the pace, to
lead a fast life. **6. sacré b.!** you bally
idiot!
balaise, *m. & adj.* hefty (fellow).
balançage, *m.* denouncing, informing.
balance, *f.* dismissal, sacking.
balancé, *adj.* **1. bien b.,** well-built, well
set-up, shapely. **2. ça, c'est b.!** = ça,
c'est envoyé!
balancement, *m.* conviction, sentence
(of thief, etc.).
balancer. 1. to throw (*or* to chuck) up
(*or* away). **2.** to land (a blow, etc.), to
let fly (at s.o.), to let s.o. have it.
3. to dismiss*. **4.** to sell off. **5.** to
swindle*. **6.** to denounce*. **7.** to say.
8. en b. une = en pousser une. **9. je
m'en balance!** I don't care a rap*!
balanceur, -euse, *m.f.* denouncer, informer.
balancier, *m.* arm (*limb*).
balançoire, *f.* **1. de la b.** *or* **des
balançoires,** nonsense*; **je ne coupe
pas dans tes balançoires,** you can't kid
me, I'm not falling for that. **2. envoyer qn à la b.,** to send s.o. packing*.
3. b. à Mickey, sanitary towel.
balanstiquer, = balancer 1, 3, 6.
balayer, to dismiss*.
balayette, *f.* penis*.
balcon, *m.* (**il**) **y a du monde au b.!** (*said
of a woman with well-shaped breasts*)
she's well-stacked.
baleine, *f.* **1. rire** (*or* **se tordre**) **comme**

une b., to laugh* uproariously. **2.
gueuler comme une b.** = gueuler
comme un putois. **3. grosse b.,** big
top, fun fair.
balès(te), balèz(e), *m. & adj.*
= balaise.
ballade, *f.* pocket*; **faire les ballades à
qn,** to go through s.o.'s pockets.
balle, *f.* **1.** head*. **2.** face*. **3.** franc
(*from ten onwards*). **4. c'est ma b.,**
that's my business; **ça fait ma b.,** that
suits* me down to the ground. **5.
raide comme b.,** like lightning, like a
shot; with assurance, straight out.
6. b. de copaille, barbiturates, goof
balls (*drugs*). *See also* **peau, trou.**
baller: envoyer b. qn, to send s.o.
packing*.
ballerines, *f.pl.* dancing-shoes.
balleste, *m. & adj.* = balaise.
balloches, *f.pl.* = baloches.
ballon, *m.* **1.** buttocks*. **enlever le b.
à qn,** to give s.o. a kick in the pants,
to toe s.o.'s behind; to thrash* s.o.
2. prison*; **faire du b.,** to do time.
3. stomach*. **4. faire b.,** to go without
food; to meet with a disappointment,
to be done out of sth. **5. avoir** (*or*
attraper) **le b.,** to be pregnant*. **6.** *pl.*
= avantages.
ballot, *m. & adj.* fool*; **tu parles d'un
b.!** he's a prize idiot! **t'es pas b.?** are
you crazy? **les bons ballots,** the mugs.
See also **bout 2.**
balloter = abouler.
balluchon, *m.* = baluchon.
ballustrines, *f.pl.* = baloches.
balmuche, *m.* = balpeau 1.
balochard, *m.* = balocheur.
balocher, to mooch about.
baloches, *f.pl.* testicles*.
balocheur, *m.* idler, moocher.
balourd, *adj.* false, imitation (jewels,
etc.); *m.pl.* **1.** false bank-notes. **2.**
false identity papers. **3.** loaded dice.
balpeau, *m.* **1.** = peau de balle (peau
2). **2. faire b.** = ballon 4 (*b*).
balthasar *or* **balthazar,** *m.* sump-
tuous feast.

baluchard, baluche, *m.* = baluchon 2.

baluchon, *m.* 1. bundle, pack; swag; faire son b., to pack up (bag and baggage) and go. 2. fool*.

baluchonner. 1. to rob. 2. to pack away the swag.

baluchonneur, *m.* swag(s)man.

bamban, *m., f.* lame person.

bambochade, *f.* bit of a spree*.

bambochard, *m.* = bambocheur.

bamboche, *f.* 1. feast, spree*; faire (une) b., être en b., to go (to be) on the spree*. 2. = aztèque.

bambocher, to go on the spree*.

bambocheur, *m.* reveller*.

bambou, *m.* 1. opium pipe; tirer sur le bambou, to smoke opium. 2. coup de b., (a) sunstroke; (b) sudden attack of madness; il a reçu un (*or* le) coup de b., he's gone mad*. 3. donner un coup de b. à qn, to stun s.o. (with bad news). 4. = bâton (i) 4.

bamboula, *m.* negro, darkie (*or* dark(e)y), snowball, Sambo.

bamboula, *f.* = bamboche 1.

bambouter = donner un coup de bambou.

banal, *adj.* ce n'est pas b., ça! well, that's the limit!*

banane, *f.* 1. (*mil.*) decoration (*medal, cross, etc.*), 'gong'. 2. (*motor*) overrider. 3. avoir la b. = bander. 4. porter la b., to wear the yellow sweater of the leader of the Tour de France.

banban, *m., f.* = bamban.

banc, *m.* avoir commencé (*or* débuté) sur le b., (*of the 'madam' of a brothel*), to have begun as a practitioner.

bancal, *m.* (*mil.*) sword, sabre.

banco! *int.* O.K.! I'm game! I'm on!

bancuche, *f.* 1. bank. 2. cash-desk.

bandaison, *f.* erection, horn-colic.

bandante, *adj.f.* sexually exciting.

bander, to have an erection, to have (*or* to get) the horn, to feel horny, to be randy, to have a bone on; b. pour, to have a yen for; ne b. que d'une, to be in a tight corner, to be in a spot, to feel far from happy.

bandeur, *m.* sexually obsessed person, horny customer.

bandit, *m.* scoundrel; swindler*, shark.

banette, *f.* bed*; faire b., to go to bed*.

banlieusard, *m.* suburbanite.

bannes, *f.pl.* bed-sheets.

bannette, *f.* apron.

bannière, *f.* être en b., to be in one's shirt(-tails).

banque, *f.* (i) aller (*or* passer) à la b., to draw one's wages; tailler une b., to bet at cards.

banque, *f.* (ii) (*of mountebank, etc.*) patter, spiel; faire de la b., to puff one's goods.

banquer, to pay* up; to pay for.

banquettes, *f.pl.* (*th.*) jouer devant les b., to play to an empty house.

banquezingue, *m.* banker.

banquiste, *m.* showman, circus performer.

baptiser, to water down, to christen (wine, milk).

Baptiste, *pr.n.* être tranquille comme B., to be as cool as a cucumber; to feel quite confident; (*of child*) to be as quiet as a mouse.

baquer, se, to take a bath.

baquet, *m.* 1. stomach*. 2. en avoir dans le b., to have guts. 3. plate. 4. = baba 2.

barabille : mettre la b., to sow discord.

baragouinette, *f.* third degree.

baraka, *m.* luck.

baraque, *f.* 1. ramshackle house, hovel, hole, shanty, dump. 2. toute la b., (a) the whole bag* of tricks; (b) the whole gang. 3. genitals, 'private property'. 4. faire b., to fail; to have nothing to say.

baraqué, *adj.* bien b. = bien balancé.

baratin, *m.* 1. glib talk, smooth (*or* sweet) talk, blah, blarney, spiel, patter; faire du b. = baratiner. 2. questioning, cross-examining (of prisoner).

baratiner, to spin the (*or* a) yarn to (s.o.), to tell (s.o.) the tale, to hand (s.o.) a sweet line, to sweet-talk (s.o.), to chat (s.o.) up, to sweeten (s.o.) up.

baratineur, *m.* **1.** glib talker, yarn-spinner, tale-pitcher, line-shooter, spieler. **2.** (*turf*) tipster.

barbacque, *f.* =barbaque.

barbant, *adj.* boring.

barbaque, *f.* **1.** meat (of poor quality). **2.** skin, body (*of person*). **3.** **marchand de b.**=marchand de viande.

barbe, *f.* **1.** bore* (*of thing or person*); **c'est la b. et les cheveux!** it's no end of a bore! it's a perfect curse! **2.** (oh,) **la b.!** (*a*) shut* up! (*b*) I'm fed up! **3.** **vieille b.**=vieille baderne. **4.** **b. à papa**, candy-floss. **5.** **prendre une b.**, to get drunk*. **6.** **faire la b.**, to win at cards. **7.** **faire une b. à qn**, to fool s.o. **8.** *adj.* =barbant.

barbeau, *m.* procurer, pimp, ponce, bully.

barbelouzes, *f.pl.* barbed wire (round concentration camp, etc.).

barber, to bore*; **se b. à cent sous** (*or* **francs) de l'heure**, to be (to get) bored* stiff.

barbichonner=faire la barbe (barbe 6).

barbifiant, *adj.* =barbant.

barbifier, (se). **1.** to shave. **2.** =se barber.

barbiflard, barbillon, barbiquet, barbiset, *m.* young (*or* small-time) barbeau.

barbiquet, barbot, *m.* =barbeau.

barboter. **1.** to steal*, to scrounge. **2.** to be muddled.

barboteur, *m.* pilferer.

barbotin, *m.* proceeds of theft, swag, loot, booty.

barbotte, *f.* **1.** frisking (of prisoner in jail). **2.** medical inspection (of prostitutes).

barbouille, *f.* **être dans la b.**=être dans le pétrin.

barbouiller. **1.** **avoir le cœur** (*or* **se sentir) tout barbouillé**, to feel sick (*or* squeamish); **ça me barbouille le cœur**, that turns my stomach, that makes me feel sick. **2.** **se b.**, to make up (one's face). **3.** **s'en b.**=s'en balancer.

barbouse, barbouze, *f.* **1.** beard.

2. unofficial secret agent, clandestine counter-terrorist.

barbu, *m.* vulva, 'puss'.

barca! *int.* nothing doing! that's enough! cut it out!

barda, *m.* **1.** (*mil.*) kit, pack. **2.** things, belongings, traps, paraphernalia. **3.** thousand francs.

bardane, *f.* bed-bug.

barder: ça barde! things are humming! things are warming (*or* hotting) up! **ça va b.!** things are going to hum! now for it! there's trouble brewing! breakers ahead! **ça va b. pour toi!** you're in for it! you're in for a hot time! **ça a dû b.!** I'll bet the fur was flying! **il faut que ça barde!**=il faut que ça saute! (sauter 4). *See also* matricule.

barguigner, to haggle, to shilly-shally, to hum and haw.

barjo, *m.* mug, sucker.

barka! *int.* =barca!

barnum, *m.* **1.** uproar*. **2.** **montrer tout son b.**=montrer son affaire (affaire 7).

baron, *m.* accomplice, confederate.

baronne, *f.* the missis, the ball and chain (*i.e. wife*).

baronner, to act as a baron.

baroud, *m.* **1.** fight(ing), scrap(ping). **2.** =bordel 2 *and* 3. **3.** **b. d'honneur**, brawling; a face-saving last stand.

barouder, to fight, to scrap.

baroudeur, *m.* fighter, scrapper, bruiser.

barouf(fe), baroufle, *m.* uproar*; **un b. du diable**, a hell of a row.

bar-presto, *m.* quick-service restaurant, snack-bar.

barque, *f.* **mener qn en b.**=mener qn en bateau.

barrabille, *f.* brawl, disturbance.

barraqué, *adj.* =baraqué.

barre, *f.* **1.** **avoir le coup de b.**, to be exhausted*. **2.** **homme de b.**, staunch friend, crony, henchman. **3.** **à toute b.**=à toute(s) pompe(s). **4.** **avoir b. sur qn**, to have a pull over s.o. **5.** **se rincer les barres**, to drink.

barreau, *m.* b. de chaise, cigar.
barrer, (se), to decamp*.
basane, *f.* 1. la b., the cavalry. 2. skin, hide. 3. tailler une b. à qn, to insult s.o. (by making an obscene gesture of contempt).
bascule, *f.* la b. (à Charlot), the guillotine. *cf.* Charlot 1.
bas-de-plafond, *m.* fool*.
basduc, *m.* =bas-du-cul.
bas-du-cul, basduc, *m.* (*of undersized* *person*) shrimp, short-arse, duck's disease, (*Am. sl.*) dusty butt.
basoche, *f.* the legal fraternity, the Bar.
basset, *m.* revolver*.
bassin, *m.* 1. (*of person*) bore. 2. cracher dans le (*or* au) b., (*a*) to pay* up; (*b*) to confess*. 3. *adj.* =bassinant.
bassinant, *adj.* boring.
bassiner, to bore*.
bassinet, *m.* cracher dans le (*or* au) b. =cracher dans le bassin.
bassinoire, *f.* 1. (*of thing or person*) bore. 2. large old-fashioned watch, turnip, 'frying-pan', 'warming-pan'.
basta! *int.* =barca!
Bastoche, la, *pr.n.* the Bastille district (in Paris).
baston, *m.* scuffle, brawl, free-for-all.
bastonner, to fight.
bastos, *f.* bullet.
bastringue, *m.* 1. low dance-hall, honky-tonk (joint). 2. uproar*. 3. =barda 2.; tout le b., the whole bag* of tricks.
bastringuet, *m.* cheap eating-house.
bataclan, *m.* (et) tout le b., (and) the whole bag* of tricks.
bataillon, *m.* inconnu au b., (*c.p.*) we don't know him from Adam; he's not one of us.
bat' d'Af', *m.* (=*bataillon d'Afrique*) disciplinary unit (formerly stationed in North Africa); soldier serving in this unit.
bateau, *m.* 1. hoax*; monter un b. à qn, mener (*or* emmener) qn en b., to fool* s.o.; se laisser mener en b., to let oneself be taken in. 2. du même b., of the same kidney (*or* stamp), tarred

with the same brush; des gens du même b., birds of a feather. 3. être du dernier b., to be in the latest fashion, to be bang up-to-date. 4. bateaux (-mouches), big boots*; big feet*.
bath, *adj.* first-rate*; b. aux pommes, tip-top.
bath(e)ment, *adv.* in a first-rate* manner.
batifoler. 1. to frolic, to skylark. 2. to cuddle, to neck, to smooch.
batifouiller, to get muddled, to be all at sea.
bâtiment, *m.* être du b., (*a*) to belong to the same trade *or* profession, to be in the same line (of business); (*b*) to know all the tricks of the trade.
bat-la-dèche, *m.* down-and-out.
bâton, *m.* (i) 1. tours de b., illicit gains, pickings, perks, graft. 2. mener une vie de b. de chaise, to go the pace, to live it up, to have a 'ball'. 3. un b. merdeux, a contemptible fellow, a real stinker, a regular (*or* an awful) shit. 4. (*of convicted person*) prohibition from entering certain specified areas.
bâton, *m.* (ii) (=*bataillon*) battalion.
bâtonné, *adj.* être b., to be prohibited from entering certain specified areas (*cf.* bâton (i) 4).
bâtons, *m.pl.* legs*; mettre les b., to decamp*.
batousard, *m.* =batouseur.
batouse, *f.* faire la b., to work the markets.
batouseur, batouzard, batouzeur, *m.* cheap-jack, travelling hawker.
battage, *m.* boosting, bluff, ballyhoo, plugging; faire du b., to boost, to puff, to boom.
battant, *m.* 1. heart, ticker. 2. tongue, clapper. 3. fighter, scrapper; avoir du b., to be full of fight. 4. stomach*; se remplir le b., to feast, to have a tuck-in. 5. money put by for a rainy day, nest-egg. 6. *pl.* hours.
batterie, *f.* b. de cuisine, array of medals and ribbons (*on uniform*), gongs, 'fruit salad'.
batteur, *m.* 1. liar. 2. pander.

battoir, *m.* **b. à œufs,** (*av.*) helicopter.

battoirs, *m.pl.* big or clumsy hands*, hands like hams.

battre, to pretend, to tell lies. *See* Niort.

bauches, *f.pl.* playing-cards.

bavacher, to talk* volubly.

bavacheur, *m.* talkative person, gasbag; *adj.* talkative.

bavard, *m.* 1. defending counsel, mouthpiece. 2. revolver*. 3. backside.

bavarde, *f.* 1. tongue, clapper. 2. mouth*. 3. =**babillard** 2.

bavasser, to talk at random, to gas.

baveau (*f.* **bavelle**), *adj.* beautiful.

baver. 1. to talk, to talk drivel. 2. (**en**) **b.,** (*a*) to be furious*; **faire b. qn,** to get s.o.'s goat; (*b*) to have to suffer* a lot; **en faire b. à qn,** to put s.o. through it, to make it warm (*or* hot) for s.o.; (*c*) to work* hard. 3. **en b.** (**des ronds de chapeau** *or* **des ronds de citron**), to be dumbfounded*.

bavette, *f.* tongue; **tailler une b.,** to (have a little) chat*.

baveux, *m.* 1. =**bavacheur,** *m.* 2. =**bavard.** 3. soap. 4. (*W.W.I.*) newspaper.

bavocher =**baver** 1.

bavocheux, *m.* =**bavard.**

baz(e), bazar, *m.* 1. place of work (*school, office, etc.*). 2. **tout le b.,** the whole bag* of tricks. 3. =**baraque** 3. 4. **l'avoir dans le b.**=**l'avoir dans le baba.**

bazarder, to sell off, to flog; to get rid of, to chuck up, to brush off.

beau, *adj.* 1. **être b.,** to be in a fix*; **nous voilà beaux!** here's a fine mess! 2. **se faire b.,** to dress* up. 3. simpleminded, green.

beau-dab(e), *m.* father-in-law.

beauf(fe), *m.* (=*beau-frère*) brother-in-law.

beaujolpif, *m.* Beaujolais (wine).

beauté, *f.* **se faire une b.**=**se faire beau.**

bébête, *adj.* silly, simple, childish.

bébé-trott, *m.* go-cart (*for child*).

bec, *m.* 1. mouth*. 2. nose*. 3. **avoir le b. salé,** to be a thirsty customer, to be always ready for a drink; **un b.-salé,** a thirsty mortal. 4. **boucler** (*or* **clore** *or* **clouer** *or* **river**) **le b. à qn,** to silence* s.o. 5. **claquer du b.,** to be hungry*. 6. **faire un b. à qn,** to kiss s.o. 7. **ferme** (*or* **tais**) **ton b.!** shut* up! 8. **laisser qn le b. dans l'eau,** to leave s.o. in the lurch, to leave s.o. stranded, to run out on s.o.; **rester le b. dans l'eau,** to be left stranded (*or* in the lurch), to be stymied; **tenir qn le b. dans l'eau,** to keep s.o. on a string. 9. **c'est comme si je pissais sur un b.** (**de gaz**), I might as well keep my breath to cool my porridge. *See also renderings for* **autant cracher en l'air** (**air** 1). 10. **se prendre de b. avec,** to quarrel with; **une prise de b.,** a (violent) quarrel*. 11. **se rincer le b.,** to wet one's whistle*; **rincer le b. à qn,** to stand s.o. a drink. 12. **tenir son b.,** to shut up*, to keep quiet. 13. **tomber sur un b.** (**de gaz**), to come up against a snag, to catch a Tartar, to come a cropper* (*fig.*), to get what's coming to one. 14. **vesser du b.,** to have a foul breath.

béca, *m.* bacillus, germ.

bécamel, *m.* (*bec à mélasse*) grocer (*W.W.II*).

bécane, *f.* 1. bicycle, bike. 2. locomotive. 3. typewriter. 4. (*prison slang*) guillotine.

bécasse, *f.* silly girl or woman, goose.

bécassine, *f.* silly little girl, silly little goose.

because, *prep.* 1. on account of, because of, '(all) down to'. 2. (*interr. use*) why?

bec-de-cane, *m.* **travailler au b.-de-c.,** to burgle.

bêchage, *m.* disparagement*.

béchamelle, *f.* **être dans la b.,** to be in a fix.

bêche, *f.* **jeter de la b. à,** to adopt a haughty attitude towards, to scorn, to look down on.

bêcher, to disparage*.

bêcheur, *m.* 1. hard worker, plodder, slogger. 2. supercilious person, conceited puppy, swank(er)*, snob. 3.

backbiter. *See also* **avocat 1. 4.** *adj.*
supercilious, snobbish, conceited*.

bécif, *adv.* quickly and forcibly.

bécot, *m.* peck (*perfunctory kiss*); **gros
b.,** big kiss, smack(er), slobber;
coquer un b. à qn, to give s.o. a kiss.

bécotage, *m.* billing and cooing,
spooning, necking, smooching.

bécoter, to kiss, to peck; to neck.

bécoter, se, to bill and coo; to spoon,
to canoodle, to smooch.

bec(que)tance, *f.* food*.

bec(que)ter. 1. to eat*. **2. en b.=en
croquer** (**croquer 4** (*a*) *and* (*b*)).

bec-salé, *m. See* **bec 3.**

bedaine, *f.* paunch*; **grosse b.,** pot-
belly.

bédi, *m.* gendarme.

bedon, *m.* = **bedaine.**

bedonnant, *adj.* paunchy*.

bedonner, 1. to grow paunchy*. **2. b.
qn,** to dupe* s.o., to betray s.o.

bégaler, se, 1. to enjoy food, drink,
etc. **2.** to deceive oneself.

bégonias, *m.pl.* **1. charrier** (*or* **cherrer**)
dans les b., to exaggerate*. **2. piétiner
les b.,** to drop a brick, to put one's
foot in it; to barge in. **3.** legs*.

béguin, *m.* **1.** sweetheart, boy-friend,
girl-friend, flame. **2.** infatuation;
avoir un (*or* **le**) **b. pour qn, avoir qn au
b.,** to be infatuated* with s.o., to have
an infatuation for s.o.

béguineuse, *f.* prostitute*.

beigne, *f.* blow*.

beignet, *m.* face*; **claquer** (*or* **tarter**)
le b. a qn, to sock s.o. on the jaw.

bêlant, *m.* sheep.

Belgico, *m.* Belgian.

Belgique, *f.* **filer en B.,** (*of embezzler,
etc.*) to abscond, to bolt.

belle, *f.* **1. (se) faire la b.,** to escape
(from prison). **2. mener** (*or* **emmener**)
qn en b., (*of gangsters, etc.*) to take
s.o. for a ride. **3. l'avoir b.,** to find
it easy going. **4. se la faire b.,** (*a*) to
have a cushy time; (*b*) to go on the
spree*.

belle-dabe(sse) *or* **belle-doche,** *f.*
mother-in-law.

bellot, -otte, *adj.* pretty, dainty.

bellure, bêlure, *f.* simpleton, fool*.

belote, *f.* belote (*card game*); **taper une
b.,** to have a game of belote.

ben, *adv.* (=*bien*) eh ben! well! why!
ben oui! why, yes! **ben quoi?** so what?

bénard, *m.* trousers*.

bénarès, *m.* opium.

bénédiction, *f.* **il pleut que c'est une
b.!** it isn't half raining! it's coming
down in bucketfuls! it's raining like
hell!

bénef, *m.* profit, gain, bunce; **les petits
bénefs,** pickings, perquisites, perks.

benette, *f.* girl*.

béni-bouftou(t), *m.* glutton*.

béni-mouff-mouff, *m.* Parisian.

béni-oui-oui, *m.* yes-man, rubber-
stamp.

bénisseur, *adj.* unctuous and glib,
soapy, oily.

bénouse, *m.* = **bénard.**

béquillard, *m.* man with a wooden leg,
peg-leg; cripple (on crutches).

béquilles, *f.pl.* legs*.

berdouillette, *f.* penis*.

bérésina, *f.* disaster, catastrophe.

berge, *f.* (*usually in the plural*) year;
tirer dix berges en prison, to do a ten
(year) stretch.

bergère, *f.* **1.** woman*, girl*; tart; wife,
missis. **2.** last card dealt (by a card-
sharper).

berlanche, *f.* blanket.

berlingot, *m.* **1.** rickety vehicle, old
crock. **2.** pimple, boil. **3.** = **berlingue.**

berlingue, *m.* virginity, maidenhead.

berloque, *f.* **1.** penis*. **2. battre la b.=
battre la breloque.**

berlue, *f.* **1. avoir la b.,** to be blind
(*fig.*), not to see things as they are;
je n'ai pas la b.! my eyes don't deceive me! *or* do my eyes deceive me?
se faire des berlues, to labour under a
delusion, to kid oneself. **2.** blanket.
3. = **couverte 3.**

berlurer, se = **se faire des berlues**
(**berlue 1**).

bernard, *m.* buttocks*.

bernicles, *f.pl.* spectacles.

bernique! *int.* nothing doing! it's no go! no sale! no soap!

bersillée, *f.* drunkenness.

bersingue, *m.* =berzingue.

Bertha, *pr.n.* la grosse B. 1. Big Bertha (*the German heavy gun that shelled Paris in W.W.I*), Long Tom. 2. big guns (*metaphorically*).

berzingue, *m.* à tout b., at full speed; donner à tout b., to go all out.

bésef, béseff, *adv.* much, a lot, many.

bésiclard, *m.* bespectacled person, 'four-eyes'.

besoins, *m.pl.* faire ses petits b. = faire ses affaires (affaires 2).

bêta (*f.* bêtasse), *adj.* silly, stupid, soft, wet; gros b.! you big silly (*or* ninny)!

bête, *f.* 1. une bonne b., a good-natured simpleton, a good sort. 2. b. noire, pet aversion. 3. b. à concours, examination fiend. 4. chercher la petite b., to be hypercritical, to be pernickety, to pick holes. 5. faire la b. à deux dos, to have coition*.

bête, *adj.* 1. b. comme chou, (*a*) very easy*; (*b*) very silly; b. comme une oie, b. à manger du foin, b. à pleurer, as silly as can be. *See also* couteau, pot. 2. pas si b.! not likely!

betterave, *f.* 1. red nose*. 2. bottle of red wine. 3. fool*.

beuglant, *m.* low *café-concert*, gaff.

beurre, *m.* 1. money*; profit. 2. au prix où est le b., as things go nowadays; at the present cost of living. 3. ça fait mon b., that's the very thing for me; that just suits my book. 4. ça mettra du b. dans les épinards (*or* sur mon pain), that will make life easier (*or* more comfortable), that will oil (*or* that will help to grease) the wheels of life, that will help to keep the pot boiling. 5. c'est du b.! it's an easy* job! 6. comme dans du b., quite easily, without the slightest difficulty. 7. compter pour du b., not to count for anything. 8. faire son b., to feather one's nest, to make one's pile. 9. pas plus de . . . que de b. en broche (*or* que

de b. aux fesses *or* que de b. au cul), damn all (*or* sweet Fanny Adams *or* sweet F.A. *or* bugger all) in the way of. . . . *See also* assiette, œil 5.

beurré, *adj.* b. comme une huître (*or* comme un coing), dead drunk*.

beurrée, *f.* ramasser (*or* en avoir) une b., to be dead drunk*, to have a skinful.

beurrer, se =faire son beurre (beurre 8).

beuverie, *f.* drinking bout, binge, soak.

bézef(f), *adv.* =bésef.

bi, *m.* =bise.

bibard *or* **bibart,** *m.* 1. old drunkard*. 2. old fog(e)y*.

bibendum, *m.* fat man, fatty.

biber, to cheat.

biberon, *m.* drunkard*.

biberonner, to tipple*.

bibi, *m.* 1. (*woman's*) hat. 2. mon b., my darling*. 3. un simple b., a private (soldier). 4. I, me, myself, this child, yours truly, my nibs, number one; pas pour b.! I'm not having (*or* taking) any! not for me! not for this child! not for Joe! pour b. ça! that's mine! bags! bags I (that)! 5. (*to a child*) fais b. à pépère! kiss daddy!

bibiche, *f.* =biche.

bibine, *f.* 1. inferior (*or* tasteless) drink, gnat's piss. 2. low-class pub(lic-house).

bibli *or* **biblio,** *f.* library.

bic, *m.* =arbico(t).

bica, bicarré, *m.* fourth-year student of advanced mathematics.

bicause=because.

biche, *f.* ma biche, my darling*.

bicher. 1. ça biche! (*a*) it's going swimmingly! it's going fine! things are going well! (*b*) agreed! I'm on! ça biche avec . . ., he (etc.) gets on well with . . . ça biche? everything O.K.? how goes it? all going well? how's things? how's tricks? are you game? 2. ça me fait b., that does my heart good.

bichof, *m.* =bischof.

bichonner, se, to dress* up.

bichonnet, *m.* chin

bichot(t)er, 1. to cuddle, to hug. **2.** to steal*.

biclo, *m.* =**bécane.**

bicoque, *f.* shanty, shack.

bico(t), *m.* **1.** arbico(t). **2.** kid (*animal*).

biçoteaux, *m.pl.* biceps.

bidard, *m., adj.* lucky (blighter).

bidasse, *m.* private (soldier).

bide, *m.* **1.** stomach*; **avoir du b.,** to be paunchy*; **prendre du b.,** to get paunchy*; **ça ne tient pas au b.,** (*of food*) it's not very substantial; **en avoir dans le b.,** to be plucky, to be tough, to have guts; **n'avoir rien dans le b.,** to lack guts, to lack spunk; **s'en mettre plein le b.,** **se remplir le b.,** to feast, to have a good tuck-in; **pantalon à la mal au b.;** trousers with sloping front pockets. **2.** (*play, record, etc.*) flop.

bidet, *m.* **1.** jade, hack, nag; **2. ne pas se prendre pour de l'eau de b.,** to swank*, to think no small beer of oneself.

bidoche, *f.* **1.** =**barbaque 1. 2. sac à b.,** sleeping-bag. **3. vider son sac à b.** = **vider son sac (sac 15).**

bidocher, (*sch.*) to crib.

bidon, *m.* **1.** stomach*. **2. du b.,** rubbish, lies, bunkum, baloney, tommy-rot; trickery, swindling, monkey business, jiggery-pokery; **c'est pas du b.!** it's gospel truth! **3.** *adj.* false, not genuine, self-styled, fake, phoney, bogus.

bidonnant, *adj.* very funny*; **c'est b.!** it's a scream!

bidonner. 1. to tipple*. **2.** to deceive, to trick, to take in.

bidonner, se, to laugh* uproariously.

bidonville, *m.* shanty-town.

bidou, *m.* dice gambling game.

bidul(e), *m.* **1.** gadget*. **2.** =**machin.**

biduleur=**bricoleur.**

bielle, *f.* (*cycling*) **appuyer sur les bielles,** to pedal hard.

bière, *f.* **1.** ce n'est pas de la petite b., (*of person*) (*a*) he's an important* person, he's somebody; (*b*) he's not a bad sort; (*of thing*) it's not to be sneezed at, it's not so dusty. **2. ne pas se prendre pour de la petite b.,** to think a lot of oneself, to have a good opinion of oneself, to think no small beer (*or* no small potatoes) of oneself.

bif, *m.* **1.** =**biffeton 1. 2.** beefsteak.

biffe, *f.* **1.** rag-picker's trade, junk business. **2.** infantry, the P.B.I.

bif(f)eton, *m.* **1.** bank note. **2.** short letter. **3.** ticket (*rail, boat, plane, theatre, etc.*). **4.** *pl.* playing cards.

biffin, *m.* **1.** rag-picker, rag-and-bone man, tatter, dustman, junkman. **2.** infantry-soldier, foot-slogger.

bifteck, biftèque, *m.* **1. gagner son b.,** to earn one's daily bread (*or* one's living). **2. faire du b.,** to get saddlesore. **3.** =**gagneuse. 4.** *See* **course.**

bifton, *m.* =**biffeton.**

bigarrée, *adj. f.* **elle n'est pas mal b.,** she's not so dusty.

bigler, to look (at), to see, to notice, to eye, to (have a) squint at; **b. en biais,** (*a*) to squint; (*b*) to give (s.o.) the glad eye.

bigne, *m.* prison*.

bignol(l)e, *m.f.* **1.** concierge. **2. casser les bignoles à qn**=**casser les pieds à qn (pied 8).**

bignolon, *m.* prison guard, warder, screw.

bigophone, *m.* telephone, 'phone, blower; **donner (***or* **filer** *or* **passer) un coup de b. à qn** to 'phone s.o., to give s.o. a ring (*or* a buzz *or* a tinkle).

bigophoner, to telephone, to 'phone.

bigorne, *f.* **1.** fight, battle. **2.** slang; **rouscailler b.,** to speak slang. **3.** police.

bigorneau, *m.* **1.** =**bigophone. 2. se taper des bigorneaux,** (*a*) to be on one's beam-ends; (*b*) to live on thin air. **3.** small change; **sors tes bigorneaux,** fork out your pennies. **4.** fool*.

bigorner, to thrash.

bigorner, se, to fight, to scrap.

bigornette, *f.* cocaine (*drugs*).

bigoudi, *m.* **travailler du b.**=**travailler du chapeau.**

bigre! *int.* gosh! (*expletives*)

bijou, *m.* **1. mon b.,** my darling*. **2. b. de famille,** vagina*. **3. bijoux de famille,** testicles*, 'family jewels'.

bilan, *m.* **déposer son b.,** to die*.

bilboque, *f.* concierge.

bile, *f.* **se faire de la b.,** to worry, to fret, to 'worrit', to get stomach ulcers.

biler, se =se faire de la bile; il ne se bile pas, he takes it (*or* he takes things) easy, he's a cool hand (*or* a cool customer *or* a cool one).

bileux, -euse, **1.** *adj.* (addicted to) worrying (*or* fretting); **pas b.,** easy-going, happy-go-lucky. **2.** *m.* 'worrit', worryguts.

billard, *m.* **1.** bald head, 'billiard ball'. **2.** operating-table; **monter** (*or* **passer**) **sur le b.,** to be operated on. **3. dévisser son b.,** to die*. **4. monter sur le b.,** (*W.W.I.*) to go over the top. **5. du b.,** (*said of sth. that is*) very easy*.

bille, *f.* **1.** face*. **2.** head*. **3. b. de billard**=**billard 1. 4. b.** (**de clown**), fool*. **5. trop d'effet sur la b.,** (*cycling*) a header. **6.** *pl.* testicles*.

biller, (*W.W.II.*) to bomb.

billet, *m.* **1.** ten franc note. **2. je vous en** (**je t'en**) **donne** (**fiche, flanque, fous**) **mon b.** (**que . . .**), I take my davy that . . .; you can take it from me that . . .; you can bet your boots (*or* your bottom dollar *or* your life) that . . .; I'll bet you what you like that . . .; I'll eat my hat if (*plus negative*). **3. prendre un b. de parterre,** to come (*or* to go) a cropper*.

billoquet, *m.* =**billet 1.**

billot, *m.* =**ballot.**

binaise, *f.* =**combine.**

binette, *f.* **1.** head*. **2.** face*.

bing, *m.* prison*; **descendre au b.,** to go to jail; **b. à perpète,** life-sentence, lifer.

bingre, *m.* executioner.

binoclard, *m.* person wearing eyeglasses, 'four-eyes'.

binze, *m.* bean.

bique, *f.* **1.** old horse, nag, jade, screw. **2. une vieille b.,** an old hag, an old bitch.

bique, *m.* **biquette,** *f.* =**bico(t) 1.**

biquet, *m.* kid (*animal*); **mon biquet, ma biquette,** my pet.

birbasse, *f.* old hag.

birbe, birbon, *m.* **vieux b.,** old fog(e)y*.

biribi, *m.* (*mil.*) =**bat' d'Af'.**

biroute, *f.* penis*.

bisbille, *f.* petty quarrel*; **être en b.** (**avec**), to be at loggerheads (*or* at odds *or* on bad terms) (with).

bischof, *m.* bishop, mulled wine.

biscotteaux, biscot(t)os, *m.pl.* biceps; **rouler les** (*or* **des**) **b.,** to adopt a swaggering attitude (*in speech or action*).

biscuit, *m.* **1. coller un b. à qn,** (*of police*) to take s.o.'s name and address, to book s.o.; **choper un b.,** to be booked. **2. tremper son b.,** to have coition*.

bise, *f.* kiss; (*to child*) **fais b. à . . .!** kiss . . .! **grosse bise,** smacker.

biser, to kiss.

bis(e)ness, *m.* **1.** (shady) business, job, bag, racket. **2. faire son** (*or* **le**) **b.,** to be a streetwalker, to be on the game.

bis(e)nesseuse, *f.* prostitute*.

bisquant, *adj.* vexing, annoying, riling.

bisque, *f.* bad temper, wax, pet.

bisquer, to be vexed*; **faire b. qn,** to rile s.o.; **bisque! bisque! rage!** (*schoolchildren's term of derision*) (boo) sucks to you!

bistouille, *f.* **1.** poor quality spirits. **2.** coffee laced with brandy.

bistre, bistroquet, bistro(t), *m.* **1.** bar-keeper. **2.** bar, pub; **le bistrot du coin,** the 'local'.

bistrouille, *f.* =**bistouille.**

bisut(h), *m.* first-year student (at most of the *grandes écoles*), fresher, freshman.

bitard, bitau, *m.* =**bitos.**

bite, *f.* penis*.

biter, to have coition* with; **se laisser b.,** to be diddled.

bitonner, to be undecided, to be in two minds.

bitos, *m.* hat*; **b. à la reculette,** hat on the back of the head.

bitte, *f.* =**bite.**

bitume, *m.* **faire** (**arpenter, fouler**) **le b.,** to be a prostitute*.

bit(t)ure, *f.* booze, binge; **prendre une b.,** to get drunk*; **se donner (se flanquer) une b. de . . .,** to have one's fill of . . .; **qu'est-ce qu'il tient comme b.!** he's had a skinful!

biturer, se, to get drunk*.

bizet, *m.* = barbiflard.

biz(e)ness, *m.* = bis(e)ness.

bizut(h), bizut(h), *m.* = bisut(h).

bla-bla(-bla), *m.* silly or useless talk, blah.

blablater, to blether.

blackbouler, to fail* (s.o. at an examination); **se faire b.,** to be ploughed.

blafarde, *f.* 1. death. 2. moon.

blague, *f.* 1. practical joke, trick, hoax*; lie*; blunder; **une sale b.,** a dirty trick, a bad do; **faire une b.,** to make a blunder; **faire une b. à qn.,** to fool s.o.; **c'est de la b.,** it's all rot! it's phoney! **prendre qch. en b.** (*or* à la b.), to take sth. as a joke; **raconter des blagues à qn,** to pull s.o.'s leg; **sans b.?** no kidding? honest Injun? straight up? **sans b.! b. à part! b. dans le coin!** (*a*) joking apart! no kidding! straight up! without a word of a lie! honestly! (*b*) you don't say so! 2. **blagues à tabac,** (woman's) flabby breasts.

blaguer. 1. to fool about, to talk nonsense; to joke; **b. avec,** to make light of, not to take seriously. 2. to chaff*, to make fun of.

blagueur, -euse, *m.f.* humbug, joker, leg-puller, spoofer; *adj.* bantering, ironical.

blair, *m.* nose*; **bouffer (jambonner) le b. à qn,** to bash s.o.'s face in, to biff s.o. on the nose, to knock s.o.'s head off; **se bouffer le b.,** to fight, to have a scrap, to pitch into one another; **avoir qn dans le b.** = **ne (pas) pouvoir blairer qn.**

blaireau, *m.* = blair.

blairer: ne (pas) pouvoir b. qn (*or* qch.), not to be able to stand (*or* to stomach *or* to bear *or* to stick) s.o. (*or* sth.); **je le blaire bien,** I don't dislike him.

blanc, *m.* 1. money*, silver. 2. cocaine, coke, (*drugs**). 3. **s'en jeter un coup de b.** (*or* **un petit b.**), to toss off (*or* to knock back) a glass of white wine. 4. **se saigner à b.** = **se saigner aux quatre veines,** to bleed oneself white (in an effort to pay).

blanc, *adj.* 1. **être b.,** to have a clean (police) record. 2. **ne pas être b.,** to be in a (bit of a) spot. 3. **je ne te vois pas b.,** you're (in) for it; you're not out of the wood yet; you'll not get off scot-free.

blanc-bleu, *m.* dependable, trustworthy fellow, white man.

blanche, *f.* 1. = blanc 2. 2. glass of brandy

blanchecaille, *f.* laundress.

blanchi, *m.* **un mal(-)b.** = bamboula, *m.*

blanchir, 1. to clear (*s.o. of a charge*). 2. to cure of V.D.

blanchisseur, *m.* = bavard.

blanchisseuse, *f.* term for a customer who doesn't buy and says 'I'll come again' (*je repasserai*).

blanchouillard, *adj.* = blanc, *adj.*

blanco, *m.* glass of white wine; *adj.* pale.

blanquette, *f.* = blanchecaille.

blanquignol, *m.* white man, whitey.

blanquiste, *m.* = blanco.

blase, *m.* = blaze.

blaser, se, to be named, to call oneself.

blave, blavec, *m.* handkerchief.

blavin, *m.* 1. scarf. 2. = blave.

blaze, *m.* 1. name, mon(n)iker; nickname. 2. nose*.

blé, *m.* money*.

bléchard, blèche, *adj.* 1. = moche. 2. old.

bled, *m.* 1. open, rolling country. 2. God-forsaken place; **en plein b.,** at the back of beyond, in the blue. 3. underworld, gangsterdom. 4. (*W.W.I.*) no-man's land; **monter sur le b.** = **monter sur le billard (billard 4).**

blédard, *m.* colonist, settler (living up-country).

bleu, *m.* **1.** greenhorn, (*mil.*) raw recruit, rookie; (*R.A.F. slang*) sprog; **me prends-tu pour un b.?** do you see any green in my eye? **2.** bruise (as result of blow); **n'être qu'un b., être couvert de bleus,** to be a mass of bruises, to be black and blue all over. **3. gros b.,** coarse, very dark red wine. **4. petit b.,** (*a*) light red wine; (*b*) express letter sent in Paris by pneumatic tube. **5. n'y voir que du b.,** to be hoodwinked, to be none the wiser. **6. passer au b.,** to pass unnoticed, not to come to light; to vanish into thin air; **passer qch. au b.,** to hush sth. up; to juggle sth. away.

bleubite, *m.* = **bleu,** *m.* **1.**

bleu, *adj.* **1. en être, en rester, b.,** to be dumbfounded. **2. colère bleue,** towering rage; **envie bleue,** overpowering desire; **peur bleue,** blue funk. **3. les hommes bleus,** tattooed gang.

bleue, *f.* **1.** absinthe. **2. un paquet de bleues,** a packet of Gauloises (cigarettes). **3. la Grande B.,** the sea, the ocean, the briny.

bleus, *m.pl.* (worker's) overalls, dungarees, boiler-suit; **b. de chauffe,** boiler-suit worn by engine driver or stoker (on ship, etc.).

bleusaille, *f.* **1.** (*mil.*) raw recruit, rookie. **2.** (*mil.*) young rookies, the awkward squad.

blindé, *adj.* **1.** immune, impervious, proof, hardened. **2. b. (à zéro),** dead drunk*. **3.** stoned, under influence of drugs.

blinder, se, to get drunk*.

bloblotte, *f.* **avoir la b.** = **avoir la tremblote.**

bloc, *m.* **1.** prison*; **mettre (flanquer) qn au b.,** to imprison* s.o. (*mil.*); **flanquer X jours de b. à qn,** to give s.o. X days C.B. **2. bourré à b.,** very rich*. **3. gonflé à b.,** keyed up; trained to the last ounce (*or* to the minute); very confident. **4. ça gaze à b.,** things are going like a house on fire.

bloche, *f.* maggot.

blond, *m.* **le beau b.,** the sun.

blonde, *f.* **1.** (bottle of) white wine. **2.** pale ale.

bloquer. 1. to imprison*. **2.** = **coller 1.**

blosses, *f.pl.* testicles*.

blot, *m.* **1.** price; **faire un b. à qn,** to knock sth. off the price for s.o. **2.** job lot. **3.** personal business, concern; job, work; **c'est mon b.,** it's my business; it's in my line; **ce n'est pas ton b.,** it's none of your business; **ça fait mon b.,** that'll just do for me; that just suits me; **c'est le même b.** = **c'est kif-kif.**

bloum, *m.* hat*.

blouser, to deceive, to fool*.

blouser, se, to make a mistake*.

blouson, *m.* **b. noir,** Teddy-boy, teenage hooligan.

blutinage, *m.* questioning (of prisoner), third degree.

blutiner, to confess*.

bob, *m.* **1.** watch*. **2.** = **bobinard.**

bobard, *m.* tall story, humbug, nonsense*, bosh; **des bobards (à la noix** *or* **à la gomme),** tommy-rot; **bobards dans le coin** = **blague dans le coin; envoyer des bobards à qn,** to make a dirty crack about s.o.; **couper dans les bobards à qn,** to fall for s.o.'s yarn; **monter un b.,** to shoot a line; **monter un b. à qn,** to pull s.o.'s leg.

bobèche, *f.* head*; **se payer la b. de qn,** to fool* s.o.

bobéchon, *m.* head*; **monter le b. à qn.** = **monter la tête à qn; se monter le b.** = **se monter la tête; perdre le b.** = **perdre la tête.**

bobinard, *m.* brothel*.

bobine, *f.* **1.** head*. **2.** face*. **3.** ninny, simpleton*. **4.** gambling-game with three dice (*kind of three-card trick*). **5. se payer une b.,** to go to the cinema, to see a film.

bobinette, *f.* = **bobine 4.**

bobo, *m.* (*child's word*) sore, sore spot, pain; **avoir (du) b.,** to have a pain; **ça fait b.,** it hurts, it aches.

bobonne, *f.* **1.** nurse, nanny; housemaid, skivvy. **2. (ma) b.,** (*term of endearment to wife*) wifey, sweetie-pie.

bobosse, *m.* = **fantabosse.**

bobs, *m.pl.* **1.** dice, 'bones'; **manier les b.**, to play at dice. **2. lâcher les b.**, to cry off, to throw up the sponge, to quit, to throw in one's cards, to drop out.

bocal, *m.* **1.** stomach*. **2.** room; house. **3. un échappé de b.**, (*of person*) f(o)etus, stunted person, little squirt, little runt.

boc(c)ard, *m.* **1.** =bobinard. **2.** anger.

boche, *m. and adj.* German, Jerry, Hun, Fritz, Kraut, Heinie.

Bochie, *f.* Germany.

bocson, *m.* =boxon.

bœuf, *m.* **1. avoir (se mettre) un b. sur la langue**, to keep one's own counsel, to keep mum. **2. faire du b. à la mode=faire du bifteck. 3. gagner son b.=gagner son bifteck. 4. travailler comme un b.**, to work like a Trojan. **5.** *adj.* tremendous, colossal, stunning, bully, a hell of a . . . (with words like *effet, succès, toupet*).

B.O.F., bof, *m.* spiv, black marketeer (*originally the French profiteers in Beurre, Œufs, Fromages during W.W.II.*).

boire: il y a à b. et à manger (là-dedans), (*a*) (*of muddy wine, etc.*) it's food as well as drink; (*b*) (*fig.*) there's both good and bad in it, it has advantages as well as drawbacks; (*c*) there are things in it to suit all tastes, there's a bit of everything in it.

bois, *m.* **1. casser du b.**, (*aviat.*) to make a crash-landing, to crash-land. **2. être dans ses b.**, not to live in lodgings, to have one's own sticks; **se mettre dans ses b.**, to buy one's own furniture. **3. faire du b.**, to burgle, to break in. **4. il lui pousse du b.**, he's a cuckold, his horns are sprouting. **5. mettre les b.=mettre les bouts (de b.). 6. on n'est pas de b.**, (*as excuse for sexual indulgence*) one's only human, the flesh is weak. **7. touche(z) du b.!** touch wood! keep your fingers crossed. **8. tirer sur le b. mort**, to row. *See also* **gueule.**

boisseau, *m.* **1. se remuer comme un b.**

du puces, to fidget. **2. se décarcasser le b. = travailler du chapeau.**

boîte, *f.* **1.** place where one works, etc. (*e.g. school, office, shop, factory, café, restaurant, firm, concern, etc.*); (*pej.*) hole, joint, dump; **une sale b.**, a rotten hole; **quelle b.!** what a hole! what a beastly place! **2. b.** (**de nuit**), night-club, cabaret, nightspot. **3.** prison*, (*mil.*) guard-room. **4.** mouth*; **ferme ta b.!** shut* up! **5. mettre qn en b.**, to make a fool of s.o.; **mise en b.**, leg-pull, spoof(ing). **6. avoir l'air de sortir d'une b.**, to look as if one had just stepped out of a band-box. **7.** *various uses of* **boîte: b. à bachot**, cram-shop, crammer's; **b. à cancans**, gossip-shop; **b. aux claqués** (*or* **aux dégelés** *or* **aux refroidis**), mortuary, morgue; **b. à** (*or* **aux**) **dominos**, coffin; **b. à fressures**, stomach; **boîtes à lait** (*or* **à lolo**), (*of woman*) breasts,* milk-shop, milk-bottles; **b. à morve**, nose*; **b. à ouvrage**, pudenda; **b. à pâté**, anus*; **b. à ragoût**, stomach*; **b. à sel**, (*of theatre*) control office; **b. à vice**, sly dog, cute one; **b. à violon**, coffin; **boîtes à violon**, big boots*.

boit-sans-soif, boit-tout, *m.* tippler, drunkard*.

bol, *m.* **1.** luck; **un coup de b.**, a bit of luck; **avoir du b.=avoir du pot**; **manque de b.=manque de pot. 2. cheveux coupés au b.**, pudding-basin haircut, basin crop. **3. en avoir ras le b.**, to be fed to the teeth, to have a basinful. **4. il en fait un drôle de b.**, it's devilishly hot. **5. ne pas se casser le b. =ne pas s'en faire. 6. prendre un bon b. d'air**, to have one's fill of fresh air. **7. se fendre le b.**, to laugh*.

bolant, *adj.* very funny*.

boler, se, to have no end of fun, to laugh* uproariously.

bombarder. 1. to pitchfork (*or* to foist) (s.o. into a job) (*influence or unexpectedness is implied*); **être bombardé . . .**, to be pitchforked into . . ., to be jumped up to . . .; **se faire b.**, to

get oneself pitchforked (into a post).
2. to smoke excessively.

bombe, *f.* **1.** feast, spree*; **faire la b., être en b.,** to go (*or* to be) on the spree*; **une b. carabinée, une b. à tout casser,** a rare old beano, a blind; **passer la nuit en b.,** to make a night of it; **lendemain de b.,** the morning after (the night before). **2. gare la b.!** look out for squalls!

bombé, *m.* hunchback.

bomber, se. 1. to go without food. **2. se b. de . . .,** to do without . . .; **tu peux (toujours) te b.!** you can whistle for it! wouldn't you like to get it! nothing doing!

bon, *adj.* **1. être b.,** (*a*) to be a victim (*or* a dupe *or* a sucker), to be done, to be had; (*b*) to be a goner, to be done for; (*c*) to be arrested (*see* arrest*). *See also* **romaine. 2. ne pas être b.,** to refuse, not to agree; **je ne suis pas b.!** I'm not having any! I'm not on! **3. être b. pour . . .,** to be due for (sth. unpleasant), to be in for . . ., to be booked for . . ., to be sure to cop it. **4. être b. à rien, être b. à tuer,** (*of person*) to be a dead loss, to be a hopeless case. **5. y a b.!** O.K.! **6. avec X minutes de b.,** with X minutes to spare (*or* in hand). *See also* **bonne.**

bonbon, *m.* **1. b. anglais,** acid drop. **2.** *pl.* testicles*. **3.** sweets (*drugs*).

bondieu, *int.* **quel b. de . . .,** what vile . . ., what a blithering . . .

bondieusard, *m.* **1.** sanctimonious (*or* churchy) person. **2.** dealer in **bondieuseries.**

bondieuseries, *f.pl.* church ornaments, religious frippery.

bondir: se faire b., to be arrested*.

bonheur, *m.* **au petit b. la chance!** (*a*) here's chancing it! (*b*) at random, haphazard.

bonhomme, *m.* **1.** fellow*. **2.** (*mil.*) soldier, man. **3. connaître son b.,** to have s.o. weighed (*or* sized) up, to have s.o.'s number (*or* wave-length). **4. faire** (*or* **aller**) **son petit b. de chemin,**

to jog along, to go one's own little way. **5. nom d'un petit b.!** good heavens! by jiminy! ye gods! **6. petit b. vit encore,** (*said of s.o. who is*) still alive and kicking, still going strong. **7. salut, b.!** greetings, old cock!

boni, *m.* sheer profit, bunce.

boniche, bonichonne, *f.* =**bonniche.**

boniment, *m.* **1.** patter, sales-talk, claptrap, spiel (*of showman, street-vendor, quack, etc.*). **2. du b.** (*or* **des boniments**) (**à la graisse (d'oie)** *or* **à la graisse de bigorneau** *or* **à la noix** *or* **à la peau de toutou** *or* **à la graisse de chevaux de bois** *or* **à la graisse de hareng saur**), tommy-rot, nonsense*. **3. avoir qn au b.,** to get round s.o., to talk s.o. into it. **4. faire du b. à,** to try to get round (s.o.), to tell (a woman, a girl) the tale, to hand (s.o.) a sweet line, to make up to (s.o.).

bonimenter. 1. to fool*. **2.** =**faire du boniment à.**

bonimenteur, *m.* **1.** barker, ballyhooer, spieler. **2.** kidder, spoofer, legpuller.

bonir, to speak, to talk*, to tell, to say, to gas; **personne n'en bonit une,** no one uttered a word.

bonisseur, *m.* glib cheap-jack.

bonjour, *m.* **1. c'est simple comme b.,** it's very easy*. **2. avoir le b.,** to come too late, to arrive when it's all over.

bonnard, *m.* victim, dupe, sucker, simpleton*; *adj.* =**bon 1** *and* **3. être (fait) b., se faire faire b.** =**être bon 1.**

bonne, *adj., f.* **1. une bien b.,** a good story (*or* yarn *or* joke), a good 'un; **elle est (bien) b., celle-là!** that's a good one, that is! that's rich, that is! I like that! **en voilà une b.!** that's a good joke! **vous en avez (tu en as) de bonnes!** you've got queer ideas (*or* a queer sense of humour); it's all very well for you to talk. **2. avoir qn à la b.,** to have a soft spot (*or* a liking) for s.o.; to take a liking to s.o.; **ne pas avoir qn à la b.,** to have a down on s.o. **3. prendre qch. à la b.,** to take sth. in good part.

bonnet, *m.* **1. gros b.**, important* person. **2. b. d'évêque**, parson's nose (of fowl). **3. triste comme un b. de nuit**, as dull as ditchwater; as glum as a funeral. **4.** = **bonneteau**.

bonneteau, *m.* **taper le** (*or* **tâter du**) **b.**, to play the three-card trick.

bonneteur, *m.* three-card trickster, spieler.

bonniche, *f.* domestic servant, slavey, skivvy.

bonnir = **bonir**.

bono! *int.* **b.** (**bézef**)! O.K.! goodo(h)! whacko!

bonze, *m.* **1.** (*sch.*) supervisor. **2. vieux b.**, old fog(e)y*.

book, *m.* bookmaker, bookie.

boquillonner, to limp.

bord, *m.* **sur les bords**, slightly, a bit of a . . .

Borda, le, *pr.n.* name of a former training-ship at Brest for cadets of the *École navale*.

bordache, *m.* naval cadet.

bordée, *f.* **être en b.**, **faire** (**courir, tirer**) **une b.**, to be (to go) on the spree*.

bordel, *m.* **1.** brothel*. **2.** regular beargarden, bedlam. **3.** the very devil (of a row, of a mix-up, of a job, of a difficulty). **4. tout le b.** = **tout le bataclan**. **5.** *often used as* (*part of*) *an oath*—*e.g.* **b.** (**de Dieu**)! damn and blast it!

bordelier, -iere, *m.f.* brothel keeper.

bordille, *f.* (*of person*) **1.** dirty dog, bastard. **2.** police informer*.

bordurer: se faire b., **être borduré**, to be prohibited (by the underworld or by the police) from frequenting certain specified places; (*of doctor*) to be struck off the register.

borgne, *f.* **borgnio(t)**, **borgnon**, *m.*, night.

borgnot(t)er, **1.** to keep a sharp lookout; to gaze at. **2.** to go to bed.

borne, *f.* **1.** kilometre; **bousculer les bornes**, to speed along. **2.** clod, dolt. **3. planter une b.**, to evacuate, to defecate*.

bosco, *m.* (*nav.*) boatswain, bo'sun.

boscot, -otte, *adj.* hunchbacked; *m.f.* **1.** hunchback, hump(e)y. **2. rire** (**rigoler, se tordre**) **comme un b.**, to laugh uproariously.

bosse, *f.* **1. avoir la b. de . . .**, to have a gift (*or* a bent) for . . . **2.** (*sch.*) **coller sa b.**, to make a back (at leap-frog). **3. s'en donner** (**s'en flanquer, s'en payer**) **une b.**, (*a*) to have lots of fun, to have a spree*; (*b*) to have a jolly good tuck-in. **4. rouler sa b.** (**un peu partout**), to knock about (the world), to be a rolling stone, to rough it.

bosseler, to thrash*; **la machine à b.**, the fist, bunch of fives; **passer à la machine à b.** = **passer à tabac**.

bosser, to work hard.

bosser, se = **s'en donner une bosse** (*a*).

bosseur, *m.* hard worker.

bossoirs, *m.pl.* = **avant-scènes**.

bossu, *m.* **petit b.**, coffee with brandy.

botte, *f.* (i) **des bottes**, **à la b.**, a great quantity*.

botte, *f.* (ii) **1. avoir les bottes à bascule** (*or* **à rouleaux**), to be drunk*. **2. ça fait sa b.**, that suits* him perfectly. **3. coup de b.** = **coup de bottine**. **4. en avoir plein les** (*or* **ses**) **bottes**, (*a*) to be exhausted; (*b*) to be fed up*. **5. graisser** (*or* **cirer**) **ses bottes**, to prepare for the other world (*or* for kingdom come), to die*. **6. lécher** (*or* **cirer**) **les bottes de qn**, to toady to s.o., to flatter* s.o. **7. proposer la b. à**, (*a*) to make direct amorous overtures to; to make a pass at; (*b*) to challenge (s.o.) to a fight. **8. sortir dans la b.**, to graduate brilliantly at the *École polytechnique* (*one who does so is called a* **bottier**, *m.*). **9. y laisser ses bottes**, to die* there. **10. chier dans les bottes de qn**, to play a dirty trick on s.o., do the dirty on s.o.

botter. 1. to suit*; **ça lui botte** = **ça fait sa botte** (**botte** (ii) **2**). **2. b.** (**le derrière** *or* **les fesses à**) **qn**, to kick s.o.'s backside, to kick s.o. in the pants, to boot (*or* to root) s.o.

bottier, *m. See* **sortir dans la botte** (**botte** (ii) **8**).

bottine, *f.* **1.** the world of lesbians*. **2. filer un coup de b. à qn** = bottiner.
bottiner, to tap (s.o.) (for money, etc.).
bouboule, *m.* fat* person.
bouc, *m.* **1.** = bouic. **2. planquer son b.**, to take shelter.
boucan, *m.* uproar*; **faire un b. infernal** (*or* **du tonnerre** *or* **de tous les diables**), to kick up an infernal racket (*or* a hell of a row).
boucaner, to stink*.
boucarnier, *m.* shop breaker.
bouche, *f.* **1. à b. que veux-tu**, to one's heart's content, any amount of, profusely. **2. avoir la** (*or* **faire la** *or* **faire sa**) **b. en cul de poule**, to prim up one's mouth, to purse one's lips. **3. être sur sa b.**, être porté sur la b., to be fond of good food. **4. ta b.** (**bébé, t'auras une frite**)! shut* up! **5. b. cousue!** mum's the word! **6. faire la b. en cœur**, to give oneself airs. *See also* **palissandre**.
bouché, *adj.* être b. (à l'émeri), to be extremely stupid*.
bouchée, *f.* **1. ne faire qu'une b. de . . .**, to make short work of (s.o., sth.), to make mincemeat of (s.o.), to wipe the floor with (s.o.). **2. mettre les bouchées doubles**, to wolf one's food, (*fig.*) to work at double speed. **3. pour une b. de pain** = pour un morceau de pain.
boucher: *See* **coin, surface**.
bouchon, *m.* **1.** low pub. **2.** the baby (*youngest child*) of a family. **3.** traffic jam. **4.** (*nav.*) **bouchons gras**, engine-room artificers. **5. un petit b.**, a little (*or* a mere) wisp of a man. **6. b. de carafe**, large diamond, sparkler. **7. c'est plus fort que de jouer au b.** (avec des queues de radis)! that's the limit*. **8. envoyer le b.**, to exaggerate*; to go too far. **9. mets-y un b.!** shut* up! put a sock in it! **10. ramasser un b.**, to come a cropper* (*fig.*). **11. être torché comme un b.**, to be got up like a guy.
bouclage, *m.* imprisonment; prison*.
bouclard, *m.* shop.

bouclarès, *adj.* closed.
boucle, *f.* **1. se serrer la b.** = se serrer la ceinture. **2.** = bouclage. **3. la grande B.**, the Tour de France (*cycle racing*).
boucler. **1.** to imprison*. **2.** to close, to shut; **la b.**, to keep quiet; **boucle-la!** shut* up! **3. b. la boucle** (*or* **son budget**), to make (both) ends meet. **4. ça vous la boucle!** that's a clincher (*or* choker) for you! **5. se la b.** = se b. la ceinture.
bouder. **1.** (*at dominoes*) to pass. **2. b. à la besogne**, to be afraid of work. **3. cet article boude**, this article doesn't sell well.
boudin, *m.* **1.** tyre (of a car). **2.** bludgeon. **3.** prostitute*. **4.** *m.pl.* podgy fingers. **5. avoir du b.**, to have the master cards (at a card game). **6. être plein comme un b.**, to be drunk*, to have a skinful. **7. faire du b.**, (*a*) to spill blood; (*b*) to have the sulks. *See also* **eau**.
boudiné, *adj.* **1.** dressed in tight-fitting clothes. **2.** (*of fingers*) podgy.
boueur, boueux, *m.* scavenger, dustman, garbage-man.
bouffarde, *f.* stubby pipe, cutty.
bouffe, *f.* food*; **faire la b.**, to do the cooking.
bouffe-la-balle, bouftou(t), *m.* glutton*.
bouffée, *f.* drag (*drugs**).
bouffer. **1.** to eat; **b. à en crever**, to blow one's hide out. **2.** to spend, to squander, to blue, to run (*or* to get) through, to do in (money). *See also* **blair**.
bouffetance, *f.* food*.
bouffi, *m.* **tu l'as dit, b.!** (*R.S.*) you('ve) said a mouthful (*or* a bibful)! you said it!
bougeotte, *f.* **avoir la b.**, to have the fidgets*.
bougie, *f.* **1.** face*. **2.** head*. **3.** five-franc piece.
bougna(t), *m.* **1.** native of Auvergne, Auvergnat. **2.** coalman (*retailer*). **3.** keeper of small **bistrot**.

bougne, *f.* **la b.,** (*collective term*) coalmen.

bougnoul(l)e, *m.* **1.** negro. **2.** Arab, North-African, wog. **3.** dog, mongrel. **4.** half-breed.

bougnouliser, to mate with a **bougnoul.**

bougonner, to grumble*.

bougre, *m.* (*f.* **bougresse**). fellow*; **un bon b.,** a good sort, a brick; **un pauvre b.,** a poor devil, a poor sod; **un sale b.,** a rotter*; **b. de temps,** filthy weather; **b. d'idiot!** you blinking idiot! *int.* crikey! hell!

bougrement, *adv.* damnably, devilishly, darned, bloody*, hellishly.

boui-boui, *m.* low* dive (for eating or entertainment), honky-tonk joint.

bouic, *m.* brothel*.

bouif, *m.* **1.** cobbler, 'snob'. **2. faire du b.,** to swank*.

bouillasse, *f.* **1.** mud, slush, **2. être dans la b.,** to be in a fix*.

bouille, *f.* **1.** face*. **2.** head*. **3.** victim, mug, sucker. **4. une bonne b.,** a good chap, a good sort. **5. taper une b.** = **taper une belote.**

bouillon, *m.* **1.** water; **boire le b.,** to be nearly drowned; **boire le grand b.,** to go to Davy Jones's locker; **tomber dans le b.,** to get a ducking. **2.** heavy downpour. **3.** cheap, popular restaurant. **4. un b. de onze** (*or* **d'onze**) **heures,** (a dose of) poison, a poison(ed) draught. **5. un b. pointu,** a clyster. **6.** *m.pl.* unsold copies (of newspaper, book), returns. **7. boire** (*or* **prendre**) **un b.,** to sustain a heavy financial loss, to drop a pot of money.

bouillotte, *f.* **1.** head*. **2.** face*.

bouisbouis, *m.* = **boui-boui.**

boukala, *m.* revolver*.

boulange, *f.* **la b. aux faffes, la Grande B.,** the Bank of France.

boulanger, *m.* **remercier son b.,** to die*.

boulangère, *f.* prostitute supporting a fancy-man, 'meal-ticket'.

boule, *f.* **1.** head*; **perdre la b.,** to lose one's presence of mind; to go mad*; **avoir la b. détraquée,** to be off one's

head, to be mad*; **un coup de b.,** a butt; **b. de billard** = **bille de billard.** **2.** face*; **b. de son,** freckled face. **3.** fist. **4.** frog, lump (in one's throat). **5.** (*mil., prison*) bread; **b. de son,** ration loaf. **6.** money*; **rentrer dans ses boules,** to recover one's outlay; **remonter les** (*or* **ses**) **boules, faire remonter les boules,** to raise the wind (*i.e. to get money*). **7.** (**yeux en**) **boules de loto,** goggle-eyes, eyes as big as saucers. **8. b. de feu, b. de fer** = **croix de bois, croix de fer. 9. b. de suif,** (*of person*) dumpling, podge, fatty. **10. avoir des boules de gomme dans les zozos** (*or* **dans les portugaises**), to be deaf. **11. être rond comme une b.,** (*a*) to be podgy; (*b*) to be dead drunk*. **12. se mettre en b.,** to take offence*; **être en b. contre qn,** to be annoyed with s.o.; **ça me met (les nerfs) en b.,** that gets my monkey up. **13. se serrer la b.** = **se serrer la ceinture.** *See also* **mystère. 14. avoir la b. à zéro,** to be cropped like a coot, bald-headed.

boul(1)é, *adj.* hooked (on drugs).

bouler. 1. to make a mess of; (*th.*) to fluff (one's lines, an entrance). **2. envoyer b.,** to send (s.o.) packing*.

boulet, *m.* **1.** ball and chain (*i.e. wife*). **2. mettre qn sur les boulets,** to wear s.o. out.

boulette, *f.* blunder, mistake*; **grosse b.,** howler, boner; **faire une b.,** to boob (it), to drop a clanger.

boulevard, *m.* **le b. des allongés:** *see* **allongé.**

Boul' Mich', le, *pr.n.* Boulevard Saint-Michel (*in the Latin quarter of Paris*).

bouliner, to steal* (by making hole in wall or ceiling).

boulonner, to work* hard.

boulot, *m.* **1.** work, job; drudgery, grind, slog, swot; **quel b.!** what a sweat! **s'atteler au b.,** to pitch in, to get down to it; **faire son b.,** to get on with one's job; **au b.!** get cracking! **du b. tout cuit,** an easy* job.

2. workman. 3. business; **c'est ton b.**, that's your business! that's your look-out. 4. burglary, job, crack. 5. food*. 6. *adj.* être b., to be fond of work, to be a grafter (*Australian sl.*).
boulot, -otte, *adj. and m.f.* podgy, dumpy, plump, (person); a podge, a roly-poly.
boulotter. 1. =bouffer 1. 2. =bouffer 2. 3. to jog along; **ça boulotte! ça boulotte?=ça biche! ça biche?** (bicher).
boum, *m.* 1. success; prosperity; **faire un b.**, to be a success, to be a hit. 2. **être en plein b.**, to be up to the neck in work. 3. teen-agers' party. 4. hat*. 5. **faire b.**, to have coition*.
boum-boum, *m.* 1. war. 2. fire arm, revolver*.
boumer. 1. to succeed, to go swimming-ly; **ça boume! ça boume?=ça biche! ça biche?** (bicher). 2. **être bien** (*or* **mal**) **boumé**, to be in a good (*or* bad) temper*.
boumiane, *m.f.* gipsy.
bouniol, *m.* =bougnol(l)e.
bouquet, *m.* 1. **(ça,) c'est le b.! v'là le b.!** that's the limit!* 2. gift, present, tip. 3. share of the swag, cut, whack.
bouquin, *m.* book.
bourbier, *m.* **être dans le b.**, to be in a fix*.
bourde, *f.* 1. lie*. 2. =boulette. 3. *pl.* humbug, nonsense*.
bourdille, *m.* =bordille.
bourdon, *m.* 1. old horse, old nag. 2. **avoir le b.**, to be depressed*.
bourgeois, *m.* 1. boss, governor. 2. **en b.**, in mufti, in plain (*or* civilian) clothes, in civvies. 3. **les en b.**, police-men of the vice squad.
bourgeoise, *f.* **la b.**, one's wife*, the missis.
bourgue, *m.* (i) 1. sou (*coin*). 2. minute.
bourgue, *m.* (ii) **bourguignon,** *m.* sun.
bourin, *m.* =bourrin.
bourjouille, *f.* (*pej. for bourgeoisie*) middle-classes.
bourlinguer =rouler sa bosse.

bourotter =boulotter 3.
bourrage, *m.* **b. de crâne** (*or* **de mou**), (*a*) eyewash*, ballyhoo; (*b*) cramming, swotting.
bourratif, *adj.* (*of food*) very filling, stodgy; **un plat b.**, a damper.
bourre, *m.* policeman*.
bourre, *f.* 1. struggle, rivalry; **tirer la b. à**, to compete with; **se tirer la b.**, to compete with one another. 2. copula-tion, stuffing. 3. **de première b.**, first-rate*. 4. **être à la b.**, to be late, un-punctual, behindhand; **être à la bourre de . . .**, to be the loser by . . . 5. police. 6. *pl.* lies*.
bourré, *adj.* 1. drunk*; **b. à zéro, b. comme un cochon**, dead drunk*. 2. rich*. 3. loaded, drugged.
bourrée, *f.* thrashing*.
bourreman(e), *m.* police inspector, **la Maison B.**, the police, the cops.
bourre-mou, *m.* **du b.=bourrage de crâne** (*a*).
bourrepif, *m.* biff on the nose, conker.
bourrer. 1. to cram (a student). 2. to thrash*; **b. qn de coups**, to slug s.o.; **b. les côtes à qn**, to thrash* s.o.; **b. la gueule à qn**, to bash s.o.'s face in. 3. **b. le crâne** (*or* **le mou**) **à qn**: *see* **crâne**. 4. to have coition* with, to stuff. 5. (*motor*) to speed (along).
bourrer, se. (*a*) to stuff oneself, to stodge (*with food*), to stoke up; (*b*) to make a pile (of money).
bourre-toujours, *m.* scorcher, road hog, speed-merchant.
bourreur, *m.* **b. de crâne(s)**, hum-bug(ger), sweet-talker.
bourriche, *f.* =bourrichon.
bourrichon, *m.* head*; **monter le b. à qn, se monter le b.=monter la tête à qn, se monter la tête.**
bourricot, *m.* donkey, moke, neddy, cuddy.
bourrin, *m.* 1. horse, screw, nag, (*turf*) stumer. 2. =bourricot. 3. policeman*. 4. long-distance lorry-driver, trunker, trucker. 5. prostitute*. 6. *adj.* **être b.=être porté sur la bagatelle.**
bourriner, to wench.

bourrique, *f.* **1.** =bourricot. **2.** dunce, donkey. **3.** pig-headed person. **4.** policeman*. **5.** police-informer*. **6.** **faire tourner qn en b.,** to drive s.o. crazy. **7.** **plein** (*or* **soûl**) **comme une b.,** dead drunk*.

bourriquer, 1. to fornicate. **2.** to inform.

bourru, *adj.* **1.** **être b.,** to be arrested*; to be victimized. **2.** **faire qn b.,** to catch s.o. in the act.

bourses, *f.pl.* testicles*.

bouscaille, *f.* =bouillasse.

bousculade, *f.* **vol à la b.,** hustling (by pickpocket).

bousculé, *adj.* **bien b.**=**bien balancé.**

bousculer, to exaggerate*. *See* **pot.**

bousculette, *f.* rush-hour crowd.

bouseux, *m.* peasant*.

boursicoter, to gamble on the Stock Exchange, to dabble in stocks and shares.

bousillage, *m.* **1.** bungling, botching, scamping. **2.** bungled (*or* scamped) work. **3.** smashing up. **4.** killing, murdering; **b. en série,** war(fare). **5.** tattooing.

bousiller. 1. to bungle*, to spoil, to goof, adulterate drugs. **2.** to smash up; to prang (a 'plane). **3.** to kill*; **se faire b.,** to get done in, to be wiped out. **4.** to tattoo.

bousilles, *f.pl.* tattooing.

bousilleur, *m.* **1.** bungler, botcher. **2.** tattooist.

bousin, *m.* **1.** low boozing den. **2.** =bordel **1** *and* **2. 3.** uproar*.

bousingot, *m.* =bousin **1.**

boussole, *f.* **perdre la b.,** to lose one's bearings, to be all abroad, to be all at sea; to lose one's head, to go mad*.

boustifaille, *f.* food*, feast*.

boustifailler, to eat* voraciously.

boustiffe, *f.* =boustifaille.

bout, *m.* **1.** **au b. le b.,** we'll see the end in due course, all in good time. **2.** **au b. du quai les ballots!** (*c.p. of contempt*) get lost! **3.** **c'est (tout) le b. du monde,** at the utmost, at the outside. **4.** **connaître le b. de gras, en connaître un**

b., to know a thing or two, to know the score. **5.** **discuter le b.** (**de gras**), to argue endlessly, to argue the toss, to chew the rag (*or* the fat), to argle-bargle, to have a session on sth., to have a natter. **6.** **faire un b. de conduite à qn,** to set s.o. on his way. **7.** **mettre les bouts** (**de bois**), to decamp*. **8.** **pousser qn un b.** (**de chemin**), to give s.o. a lift (in a car); to walk part of the way with s.o. **9.** **prendre le b. de bois,** to take the wheel (of a car). **10.** **b.-de-zan, b. d'chou,** (*terms of affection for a*) tiny tot. **11.** **bouts de sucre,** loaded dice. **12.** **tenir le bon b.,** to have the whip hand, to hold the right end of the stick. **13.** **le gros b.,** penis*.

boutanche, *f.* **1.** bottle. **2.** shop.

bouteille, *f.* **1.** **avoir de la b.,** (*of person*) to be getting on (in years), to be an old-timer, to be long in the tooth; (*of joke*) to be hoary, to be stale, to be a chestnut. **2.** **prendre de la b.,** to be getting on (in years). **c'est la b. à l'encre,** it's a hopeless mess (*or* muddle), it's as clear as mud.

bouterolle, *f.* church.

bout(h)éon, botéhon, *m.* (*mil.*) **1.** dixie. **2.** (*W.W.II*) cookhouse rumour.

boutique, *f.* **1.** =boîte **1. 2.** **toute la b.,** the whole bag* of tricks. **3.** **montrer** (**toute**) **sa b.,** to expose one's genitals (*or* one's private parts *or* one's 'private property').

bouton, *m.* **1.** clitoris. **2.** **s'en jeter un** (*or* **un coup**) **derrière le b. de col,** to toss off (*or* to down) a drink. **3.** **cirer toujours le même b.,** to be always harping on the same string.

boutonnière, *f.* **faire une b. à qn,** to slash s.o. (with a knife, razor, etc.), to give s.o. a stripe, to stripe s.o.

boutoque, *f.* shop.

bouzillage, *m.* =bousillage.

bouziller =bousiller.

bouzilles, *f.pl.* =bousilles.

bouzin, *m.* =bousin.

bouzine, *f.* ramshackle motor-car*.

boxer, to strike, to knock about.

boxon, *m.* brothel*.

boy, *m.* heroin (*drugs**).

boyau, *m.* **1.** (*mil.*) communication trench. **2. avoir le b. de la rigolade,** to want to burst out laughing.

boyautant, *adj.* =bidonnant.

boyauter, se =se bidonner.

bracelets, *m.pl.* handcuffs*.

braco, *m.* poacher.

bracquemart, *m.* penis*; **dérouiller son b.,** to have coition*.

bradillon, *m.* arm (*of body*).

braise, *f.* money*. *See also* **chaud 5.**

bramer, to weep*, to bawl.

bran, *m.* excrement, shit.

brancards, *m.pl.* **1.** legs*. **2. ruer dans les** (*or* **sortir des**) **b.,** to protest, to kick, to get out of hand; to kick over the traces; to leave one's wife.

branche, *f.* **1.** (**ma**) **vieille b.,** old chap*, old cock, old bean. **2. avoir de la b.,** to have an aristocratic air, to have breeding.

brancher, to get into contact with (s.o.).

brancher, se, 1. to get turned on (*drugs, jazz, etc.*). **2.** to get mated with.

branco, *m.* stretcher-bearer.

brandillon, *m.* =bradillon.

branlage, branlée, branlette, branlure, *f.* act of masturbation, toss-off.

branler. 1. qu'est-ce qu'il branle? what's he up to? **2. ne pas en b. une** = s'en b.

branler, se. 1. to masturbate*. **2. se les b.** =se les rouler. **3. s'en b., se b. de qch.,** not to care a rap*.

branleur, *m.* **1.** masturbator. **2.** (*mil.*) batman. **3.** lazybones.

branlocher =branler.

branlotin, *m.* (*École des Beaux-Arts slang*) idler, slacker.

branque, *m.* **1.** simpleton*, mug, sucker. **2.** *adj.* crazy, mad*.

branquignol(le), *adj.* =branque, *adj.*

braquage, *m.* armed attack, hold-up, stick-up.

braque, *adj.* mad*.

braquemart, *m.* =bracquemart.

braquer. 1. to hold up, to stick up. **2.** to get s.o.'s back up.

braquet, *m.* (*cycling*) gear; **pousser un grand b.,** to use maximum gear.

braqueur, *m.* stick-up man.

bras, *m.* **1. avoir les b. cassés** (*or* **retournés**), to be lazy*; **des b. cassés,** loafers, weary Willies. **2. avoir les b. en pâté de foie, avoir des b. de saindoux,** to have arms like matchsticks. **3. faire le gros b.,** to play the bully; to strike with all one's might.

brelica, *m.* revolver*.

breloque, *f.* **battre la b.,** (*of clock, watch*) to go badly, not to keep time; (*of heart*) to miss a beat, to go pit-a-pat; (*of person*) to be off one's head, to rave, to have a screw loose.

brêmard, *m.* telegraph boy.

brème (*or* **brême**), *f.* **1.** playing-card; **manier** (*or* **taquiner** *or* **taper**) **les brèmes,** to play cards; **maquiller les brèmes,** to mark (*or* to fake) the cards, to be a (card-)sharper, to fake the broads. **2.** identity card. **3.** policeman's card. **4.** prostitute's card; **en b.** =en carte. **5.** telegram.

bric, *m.* (licensed) brothel*.

brich(e)ton, *m.* bread.

brich(e)tonner, to eat.

bricolage, *m.* pottering about, tinkering, doing odd jobs, do-it-yourself.

bricole, *f.* trifle, odd job; *pl.* odds and ends.

bricoler, to potter* about; to wangle, to fiddle.

bricoleur, *m.* handy-man, Jack-of-all-trades, tinkerer, potterer.

bride, *f.* **1.** chain lock. **2. se mettre la b.** =se mettre la ceinture. **3.** *pl.* handcuffs*.

brider. 1. to close (a door). **2. se faire b.,** to be tattooed.

briffe, *f.* food*.

briffer, to eat*.

briffeton, *m.* bread.

brigadier, *m.* (*th.*) the stick with which one gives the three blows (to indicate that the performance is about to begin).

brignol(et), brignoluche, *m.* bread.

brillant, *adj.* **pas b.,** ça! that's not too good! that's not so hot!

briller. 1. to swank*. **2.** to be in clover. **3.** =jouir.

brindes, brindezingues, *f.pl.* être dans les b., to be drunk*.

brindezingu , *adj.* drunk*.

bringue, *adj.* mad*.

bringue, *f.* (i) faire la b., to go on the spree*.

bringue, *f.* (ii) (*of female*) une grande b., a big gawk.

bringuer =faire la bringue.

brioche, *f.* **1.** mistake*. **2.** panic, scare. **3.** paunch*; **avoir (prendre) de la b.,** to be (to get) pot-bellied. **4. partir en b.,** to go all to pieces. **5. tortiller (de) la b.,** to dance. **6.** *pl.* buttocks*.

brique, *f.* **1.** one million old francs. **2. bouffer des briques,** to go without food, to live on air. *See also* **poil.**

briquer. 1. to polish, to furbish. **2. se b.,** to wash oneself. **3.** to work hard.

briquet, *m.* **battre le b.,** to knock one's ankles together in walking.

brisant, *m.* wind.

briscard, *m.* old soldier, old campaigner, veteran.

brisé, *adj.* exhausted*.

briser. 1. les b. à qn=casser les pieds à qn; **ça me les brise,** it gets on my tits. **2. se la b.,** to decamp*.

brisquard, *m.* =briscard.

bristol, *m.* visiting-card.

briveton, *m.* =briffeton.

broc, *m.* (i) **ne pas valoir un b.,** to be worthless*.

broc, *m.* (ii) (=*brocanteur*) second-hand dealer.

broche, *m.* =brochet.

broches, *f.pl.* **se gratter les b.,** to clean one's teeth.

brochet, *m.* =alphonse.

brocheton, *m.* young **brochet.**

bromure, bromuré (-maison), *m.* soldier's wine ration.

bronze, *m.* **couler un b.,** to defecate*.

broque, *f.* **de la b.,** worthless (*or* dud) stuff.

broquette, *f.* **ça ne vaut pas une b.,** it's absolutely worthless*.

broquille, *f.* minute; *pl.* mince.

brosse, *f.* **1. une coupe de cheveux en b.,** a crew-cut. **2. manier (passer) la b. à reluire,** to flatter*, to fawn upon.

brossée, *f.* **1.** thrashing*. **2.** quarrel*, brush.

brosser. 1. to thrash*. **2.** to possess (a woman).

brosser, se: se b. (le ventre), to have to go without (food, etc.), to tighten (*or* to pull in) one's belt; **tu peux te b.!** you can whistle for it! you've had it!

brouillard, *m.* **1.** (*av.*) 'soup' (*bad weather*). **2. être dans le b.,** to be in a fog, to be a little fogged (*or* hazy *or* muzzy). **3. être dans les brouillards,** to be drunk*. **4. s'évanouir (*or* foncer) dans le b.,** (*a*) to decamp*; (*b*) to take a leap in the dark.

brouillé, *adj.* **être b. avec les dates,** to be unable to remember dates, to be hazy about dates; **être b. avec la musique,** etc., not to take to music, etc.

brouille-ménage, *m.* ordinary red wine.

brousse, *f.* countryside; backwoods, bush; **au fin fond de la b.,** at the back of beyond.

brouter, se: elles se broutent, they're a couple of lesbians.

broutille, *f.* trifling matter, trifle, (mere) flea-bite; chicken-feed.

brûlé, *adj.* **être b.,** (*a*) to be done for, ruined, to have lost one's reputation (*or* credit *or* influence); (*b*) to have been betrayed, to have been given away.

brûle-gueule, *m.* short clay pipe, cutty(-pipe), nose-warmer.

brûle-parfum(s), *m.* rifle; gun, revolver*, firearm.

brûler. 1. to spot, to nose out (a spy, etc.). **2. se laisser b.,** to give oneself away. **3.** to kill*.

brutal, *m.* **1.** strong wine; raw spirits. **2.** black bread.

brution, *m.* cadet at the military college of la Flèche.

bûchante, *f.* **faire une grosse b.,** to swot* hard.

bûche, *f.* (i) **1.** fool*. **2.** match (*allumette*). **3.** bad card in gambling games. **4.** **ramasser une b.,** to come a cropper* (*lit. and fig.*).

bûche, *f.* (ii) swotting.

bûcher. 1. to work* hard (at), to swot* (at). **2.** to thrash*.

bûcher, se, to fight, to have a scrap, to exchange blows, to slog one another.

bûcheur, *m.* swot, swotter, sap, slogger, plodder.

budgétivores, *m.pl.* (*pej.*) officials paid out of government funds.

buffe, *f.* = **baff(r)e.**

buffecaille, *m.* = **buffet 1.**

buffet, *m.* **1.** stomach*; **piquer qn au b.,** to knife s.o. in the guts; **se remplir le b.** = **se remplir le bide; en avoir dans le b.,** to be plucky, to have guts. **2. danser devant le b.,** to go without food, to go hungry, to have nothing to eat. **3.** large lorry on the road (making passing impossible). **4. rémouleur de b.,** organ-grinder.

buis, *m.* **1. avoir reçu un coup de b.,** to be exhausted*. **2. recevoir** (*or* **prendre**) **un coup de b.,** to be the victim of circumstances; **une patte de b.,** wooden leg.

buissonner: b. l'école (*or* **faire l'école buissonnière**), to play truant.

bulle, *m.* money*.

bulle, *f.* **1. coincer la** (*or* **sa**) **b.,** to laze about, to be idle, to hit the hay; to skive. **2. attraper une b.** (*sch.*) to get naught in examinations, etc.

bulletin, *m.* **avaler son b.** (**de naissance**) = **avaler son acte de naissance.**

bureau, *m.* **1.** stomach*; **en avoir dans le b.** = **en avoir dans le buffet. 2.** un vrai **b. de renseignements,** (*of person*) a mine of information, a walking encyclopedia. **3. b. des pleurs,** complaints department. **4.** (*th.*) **jouer à bureaux fermés,** to play to capacity.

burette, *f.* **1.** face*. **2.** head*. **3.** *pl.* testicles*.

buriner. 1. = **bûcher 1. 2. faire b. qn,** to make s.o. snap out of it, to make s.o. sit up.

bur(e)lingue, *m.* **1.** office. **2.** = **buffet 1.**

burnes, *f.pl.* testicles*; **casser** (*or* **râper**) **les b. à qn** = **casser les pieds à qn.**

burnous, *m.* **faire suer le b.,** to slavedrive, to sweat (cheap labour).

buse, *f.* fool*.

buté, *adj.* stubborn, pig-headed, dead set.

but(t)er, to kill*; **se faire b.,** to get bumped off.

but(t)er, se, to commit suicide, to knock oneself off.

but(t)eur, *m.* **1.** killer. **2.** goal-scorer.

butte, *f.* **1.** guillotine; **monter à la b.,** to be guillotined. **2.** killing, bumping off. **3. la B.,** Montmartre. **4. les Buttes,** les Buttes-Chaumont (*district in Paris*).

buvable, *adj.* bearable, acceptable, tolerable, passable, fairly good; **une personne pas b.,** an impossible type, a bounder.

buvarder, to blot.

buverie, *f.* = **beuverie.**

buveur, *m.* **b. d'encre** (*of author, journalist, clerk*) ink-slinger, penpusher.

C

C, la, *f.* cocaine (*drugs**).

ça, *dem. pron. neut.* **1. avec ç.!** nonsense! rubbish! get away with you! tell that to the marines! tell me another! **2. avec ç. que . . .,** (just) as if . . .; don't tell me that . . . **3. avoir de ç.,** (*a*) to have plenty of money, to be rich*; (*b*) (*of female*) to have sex-appeal, to be sexy, to have 'it', to have oomph. **4. ç. alors!** *see* **alors. 5. ce n'est (c'est) pas tout ç.,** that's all very well, that won't do at all, you can't get away with it like that, let's get down to brass tacks. **6. faire ç. = faire l'amour.**

cabane, *f.* **1.** prison*. **2.** brothel*. **3.** poor dwelling-house, shanty. **4. attiger la c.,** to exaggerate*. **5. c. bambou,** strip-tease side-show.

cabe, *m.* = **cabot.**

cabèche, cabêche, *f.,* **caberlot,** *m.* = **caboche 1.**

cabinces, *f.pl.* W.C.*

cabochard, *m., adj.* stubborn (*or* pig-headed *or* mulish) (*person or animal*), a bullhead.

caboche, *f.* **1.** head*. **2.** intelligence*. **3. avoir la c. dure,** (*a*) to be thick-headed, to be slow on the uptake; (*b*) to be obstinate.

cabochon, *m.* **1.** blow*. **2.** = **caboche 1. and 2.**

cabombe, *f.* glim (*i.e. a light, lamp, candle, torch, etc.*).

cabosse, *f.* bruise, bump.

cabosser, to bruise, to bump; to batter, to dent, to bash in.

cabot, *m.* **1.** dog*. **2.** = **cabotin. 3.** (*mil.*) corporal, lance-jack.

cabotin, -e, *m.f.* inferior actor (actress), ham-actor, stagey person.

cabotinage, *m.* **1.** inferior acting, hamming. **2.** = **battage.**

cabotiner, to overact, to ham (it), to play to the gallery, to rant.

cabotinisme, *m.* = **cabotinage.**

caboulot, *m.* dive (*low-class bar, dance-hall, night-club, etc.*).

cabri, *m.* **1.** kid (*animal*). **2.** = **cabriolet.**

cabriole, *f.* **faire la c.,** to swing, go, with the tide.

cabriolet, *m.* handcuffs*.

caca, *m.* (*nursery word*) excrement, cack; **faire c.,** to do one's duty, to do one's jobs; **c'est (du) c.,** it's dirty (*or* nasty *or* cacky).

cacafouiller = **cafouiller.**

cache-fri-fri, *m. See* **fri-fri.**

cachemire, *m.* duster, dishcloth, clout.

cache-pot, *m.* knickers.

cacheton, *m.* fee (*of teacher, performer, etc.*); **palper son c.,** to receive (*or* to pocket) one's fee.

cachot, *m.* prison*.

cachottier, -ière, *adj., m.f.* secretive (*or* close *or* cagey) (person); **quel c. vous faites!** well, you are a sly one!

cacique, *m.* **1.** first on list of successful candidates for the *École normale supérieure, agrég. etc.* **2.** headmaster. **3.** land-owner.

cactus, *m.* **1.** nuisance, hitch. **2. avoir un c. dans la poche** (*or* **portefeuille**), to be a miser.

cadancher, to die*.

cadavre, *m.* **1.** empty wine-bottle, dead man, dead 'un, dead soldier, dead marine. **2.** unlucky gambler.

caddie, *m.* truck, (supermarket) trolley.

cadeau, *m.* prostitute's fee.

cadenassé, *adj.* close-tongued, buttoned-up.

cadenasser, se, to keep a secret, to button up one's lip.

cadènes, cadenettes, cadennes, *f.pl.* handcuffs*.

cador, *m.* **1.** dog*. **2.** = **caïd.**

cadran, *m.* **1.** buttocks*. **2. faire le tour du c.,** to sleep round the clock.

cafard, *m.* (i) **1.** tale-bearer*. **2.** spy. **3.** smug, sanctimonious person, humbug.

cafard, *m.* (ii) **avoir le c.**, to be depressed*; **donner le c. à qn**, to give s.o. the hump.

cafardage, *m.* tale-bearing, sneaking.

cafarder, to sneak on, to inform* on.

cafardeur, *m.* tale-bearer*.

cafardeux, -euse, *adj.* **être c. = avoir le cafard** (ii).

caf'-conc', caf'-conce, *m.* (*= café-concert*) kind of old-time music-hall.

café, *m.* **c'est un peu fort de c.! = c'est un peu fort!**

cafeter = cafarder.

cafeteux, *m.* **= cafardeur**.

cafetière, *f.* **1.** head*; **travailler** (*or* **bouillir**) **de la c. = travailler du chapeau; se payer la c. de qn = se payer la tête de qn. 2. = cafardeur.**

cafeton, *m.* café.

cafouillage, *m.* (*motor*) misfiring, missing; (*sports, etc.*) bungling, floundering.

cafouiller, (*motor*) to misfire, to miss; (*sports*) to bungle, to flounder, to be all adrift; (*rowing*) to be all abroad, to pull out of time; (*of speech*) to splutter; (*in general*) to make a mess of things.

cafouilleur, cafouilleux, *m.* blunderer, bungler, muddler.

cafouine, *f.* excrement, dung, manure.

cafter = cafeter.

cafteur, *m.* **= cafard** (i) **1.**

cagade, *f.* blunder; **faire une c.**, to slip up, to make a mess of things.

cage, *f.* **1.** prison*; **mettre en c.**, to imprison*. **2. c. à poules**, (*a*) doll's house (*iron., i.e. very small room, flat, etc.*), (*b*) since the law now forbids prostitutes to stand on the pavement the hotels in certain well-known Paris streets have replaced the front door by a large glass door behind which the women can stand and be seen. Behind them is another door and the space between the two doors is referred to as 'la cage à poules'. **3.** ribs (*human body*).

cagibi, *m.* lumber-room, cubby-hole, glory-hole.

cagna, *f.* room, shanty, hut, den; (*mil.*) dug-out.

cagnard(e), *m.f.* good-for-nothing.

cagne, *f.* class (*section lettres*) preparing for the entrance examination to the *École normale supérieure*; *also written* **khâgne**.

cagner = caner 1.

cagneux, *m.* student in a **cagne**.

caguer, to defecate*.

cahier, *m.* police record.

cahoua, *m.* coffee (*drink*), java; **c. au lard**, coffee and absinthe.

caïd, *m.* leader (of gang, etc.), big shot, boss, baron, topman.

caille, *f.* **1.** girl*. **2.** (*to child or female*) **ma (petite) c.**, my darling*. **3. avoir qn à la c.**, to hate the sight of s.o., to hate s.o.'s guts. **4. l'avoir à la c.**, to be put out, to be furious*. **5. être à la c.**, to grouse, to be awkward, to show fight. **6. se retourner la c. = se cailler.**

cailler. 1. on caille (*or* **ça caille**), it's cold enough to freeze the balls off a brass monkey. **2. = avoir qn à la caille.**

cailler, se. 1. to work hard. **2.** to worry. **3.** to get in a rage.

caillou, *m.* **1.** head*; **c. déplumé**, bald* head; **n'avoir plus de mousse** (*or* **n'avoir plus un poil**) **sur le c.**, to be bald. **2. se sucer le c.**, to kiss one another, to rub smackers. **3. battre le c.**, to loaf about the streets, to tramp the streets; to pound the pavement (in search of work). **4. envoyer casser des cailloux**, to send to a penal colony; **casser les cailloux**, to be in prison; to do time. **5.** *pl.* jewels, precious stones, diamonds, sparklers, 'rocks'.

caïman, *m.* **= surgé** (*at the École Normale Supérieure*).

caire, *m.* money*.

caisse, *f.* **1.** head*; **bourrer la c. à qn = bourrer le crâne à qn; se faire**

sauter la c. = se faire sauter le caisson. 2. stomach*; n'avoir rien au fond de la c., to be starving, to feel very empty, to have nothing in one's bread-basket. 3. (mil.) (grosse) c., prison*; faire de la grosse (c.), to be in clink. 4. chest; être malade (or souffrir) de la c., to be consumptive; partir (or s'en aller) de la c., to be dying of consumption. 5. coffin. 6. battre la grosse c., to talk big, to bang the big drum. 7. mettre qn en c. = mettre qn en boîte; mise en c. = mise en boîte. 8. passer à la c., to be paid off. 9. la c. noire, boodle (money stolen from public funds); graft, 'soap' (money used for bribery). 10. (cycling) rouler la c., to go all out. 11. la c. d'épargne, mouth.

caisse, m. c'est du c. = c'est du quès.

caiss(e)mar, m. cashier.

caisson, m. 1. head*; se faire sauter le c., to blow one's brains out. 2. stomach*.

calamar(d), m. tall* person.

calamiteux, adj. dilapidated, broken-down, wretched, rotten.

calanche, f. death; c. vépé (v.p. = voie publique), sudden death on a public highway.

calancher, to die*.

calbard, m. (pair of men's) drawers.

calbombe, f. = cabombe.

calcer, to have coition* with.

calcif, m. = calbard.

caldard, m. = calbard.

cale, f. 1. à fond de c., penniless*. 2. être de la c., to be a pederast*.

calé, adj. 1. well-informed, proficient, well up, a dab (hand). 2. well off, well-to-do, rich*. 3. sated, full up. 4. difficult, stiff, dodgy.

calebasse, f. 1. head*. 2. face*.

calebombe, f. = cabombe.

calecer = calcer.

calecif, m. = calcif.

cale-dent, m. snack.

calencher = calancher.

calendo(sse), m. Camembert cheese.

caler. 1. to back out, to back down, to climb down, to cave in; to be afraid, to get cold feet. 2. (motor) to stall.

caler. se. 1. to ensconce oneself, to settle comfortably. 2. se c. les côtes (or les amygdales or les badigoinces or les joues), se les c., se la c., to eat* heartily.

caleter = calter.

caleur, m. = caneur.

calfouette, m. = calbard.

calibre, m. pistol, revolver*.

calicot, m. counter-jumper, shop assistant.

calot, m. 1. eye*; rouler (or ribouler) des calots, to roll one's eyes, to goggle; boiter des calots, to squint. 2. (mil.) forage-cap.

calotin, m. 1. priest. 2. over-zealous church-goer. 3. adj. churchy.

calotte, f. 1. box on the ear, clout, cuff. 2. clergy, priesthood; the clerical party; à bas la c.! down with clericalism!

calotter. 1. to box s.o.'s ears, to clout, to cuff. 2. to steal*. 3. to arrest*.

calpette, f. tongue.

calsif, m. = calcif.

calter, to decamp*.

calva, m. glass of calvados (apple-brandy).

Camarde, f. la C., death.

camaro, m. friend*.

cambouis, m. the Army Service Corps; soldier in this corps.

cambrio, m. burglar, cracksman, crib-cracker, screwsman.

cambriole, f. 1. room, crib. 2. burgling, crib-cracking, screwing.

Cambronne, pr. n. le mot de C. = merde.

cambrousard, m. peasant*.

cambrous(s)e, f. (pej.) country (as opposed to town); au fin fond de la c., at the back of beyond.

cambuse, f. 1. (pej.) house, room, hovel, hole. 2. = boui-boui.

cambut, m. faire un c., to ring the changes (i.e. to substitute imitation for real jewels, bad money for good, one coin for another, etc.).

cambuter. 1. to (ex)change. **2. c. un coffre,** to crack a safe. **3.** to turn topsy-turvy.

came, *f.* **1.** cocaine; narcotics, dope, junk. **2.** money*. **3.** =camelote.

cam(e), *m.* =camelot 1.

camé, *adj.* **1.** drunk*. **2.** drugged. **3.** *m.* drug addict, junkie, junky, dosser.

camelot, *m.* **1.** street-hawker, cheap-jack. **2. les camelots du roi,** (young) supporters of *l'Action Française,* a royalist party and its newspaper (1899–1944).

camelote, *f.* **1.** inferior (*or* shoddy) goods, rubbish, trash, junk; . . . **de c.,** trashy (*or* rubbishy *or* catchpenny) . . . **2.** goods (*generally*), stuff.

cameloter, to bungle*.

camembert, *m.* traffic beacon; traffic policeman's raised platform.

camer, se, to take drugs, to be a drug-addict, to get high. *See* **camé,** *m.*

camisard, *m.* =bat' d'Af'.

camouf(l)e, *f.* =cabombe; **souffle la c.!** dowse (*or* douse) the glim!

camoufler, se, to hide, to go into hiding.

camouflet, *m.* snub, insult.

camoufleur, *m.* faker.

camp, *m.* **ficher** (*or* **foutre**) **le c.,** to decamp*; **fiche(z)** (*or* **fous** *or* **foutez**) **(-moi) le c.!** hop* it!

camp', *f.* **la c'.**=cambrous(s)e.

campagne, *f.* **1. aller à la c.,** to go to prison (*of women prisoners*). **2. emmener qn à la c.**=emmerder qn.

campêche, *m.* **bois de c.,** inferior champagne.

camphre, *m.* **1.** alcohol. **2.** =casse-pattes.

camplouse, campluche, *f.* =cambrous(s)e.

campo(s), *m.* holiday, day off.

canadienne, *f.* **1.** sheepskin jacket; lumber-jacket. **2. une c. en sapin,** coffin, wooden (*or* pine) (over-)coat.

canaque, *m.* nigger, (*Am. sl.*) boogie.

canard, *m.* **1.** false report, hoax, rumour. **2.** inferior newspaper, rag. **3.** (*pej.*) horse, nag, screw, broken-down hack. **4.** lump of sugar dipped in brandy or coffee. **5.** (*music*) false note, quack, squawk. **6. marcher comme un c.,** to waddle. **7. trempé** (*or* **mouillé**) **comme un c.,** drenched to the skin, as wet as a drowned rat. **8. froid de c.,** beastly cold.

canarder. 1. (*mil.*) to take pot-shots at, to snipe at, to pepper. **2.** (*music*) to make a **canard 5.**

canasson, *m.* =canard 3.

cancre, *m.* dunce, duffer, dud, wash-out, blockhead.

cané, *m.* =canné, *m.*

caner. 1. to be a coward*; **ne pas c.,** to keep one's pecker up. **2.** =caler 1. **3.** =canner. **4.** to stay away from (school, work, etc.); to cut (lectures, etc.).

caneur, *m.* coward*.

canevas, *m.* (*boxing*) floor (of the ring); **envoyer qn au c.,** to floor s.o.

caniche, *m.* **ce n'est** (*or* **c'est**) **pas fait pour les caniches,** (*joc. variant*) =**ce n'est** (*or* **c'est**) **pas fait pour les chiens** (chien 10).

canif, *m.* **donner un coup de c. dans le contrat (de mariage),** to be unfaithful (*of husband or wife*), to step out on, to two-time.

canne, *f.* **1.** death. **2.** prohibition from entering certain towns or areas. **3. avoir l'air d'avoir avalé sa** (*or* **une**) **c.,** to be as stiff as a poker. **4. avoir** (*or* **tenir**) **la c.**=bander. **5. casser la c.,** to have coition*. **6. casser sa c.,** to die*. **7.** *pl.* legs*; **mettre les cannes,** to decamp*; **être sur les cannes,** to be exhausted*, to be out on one's feet.

canné, *m.* corpse*; *adj.* exhausted*.

canner, to die*.

canon, *m.* **1.** glass of wine. **2.** stomach*. **n'avoir rien à se mettre dans le c.**= n'avoir rien au fond de la caisse (caisse 2).

canotier, *m.* **travailler du c.**=travailler du chapeau.

cantaloup, *m.* =Auverpin.

canter, *m.* **un vrai c.,** an easy* job.

cantoche, *f.* canteen.

canulant, *adj.* boring.

canular(d), *m.* practical joke, hoax, leg-pull, (student's) rag; tall story; **monter un c. à qn,** to hoax s.o.

canulard, *m.* **1.** informer*. **2.** male nurse.

canule, *f.* bore* (*person or thing*).

canuler. 1. to bore*. **2.** to hoax* (s.o.).

caoua(h), *m.* **1.** = cahoua. **2.** breakfast.

capet, *m.* hat.

capilotade, *f.* **mettre en c.,** (*of things*) to smash to smithereens, to crush to a pulp (*or* to a jelly); (*of persons*) to beat to a jelly, to make mincemeat of, to beat black and blue.

capiston, *m.* captain.

capital, *m.* virginity, maidenhead; **entamer le (petit) c. de,** to seduce (a virgin).

capitonnée, *adj. f.* **être bien c.,** to be nice and plump, to be well covered (*or* well upholstered *or* well padded), to come out in all the right places.

capon, -onne, *m.f.* **1.** coward*. **2.** (*sch.*) tale-bearer. **3.** *adj.* cowardly*.

caponner. 1. to be a coward*. **2.** (*sch.*) to sneak, to tell tales, to peach.

caporal, *m.* coarse tobacco, shag.

capote, *f.* **c. anglaise,** contraceptive (*or* safety) sheath, condom, French letter, frenchie, rubber.

capout, *adj.* dead, killed, done for; **faire c.,** to kill*.

capsule, *f.* head*.

caquer, to defecate.

cara, *m.* character.

carabin, *m.* **1.** doctor, medic(o); surgeon, sawbones; medical student. **2. c. de la comète,** swindler, sharper.

carabine, *f.* penis*.

carabiné, *adj.* very strong, intense, a whale of a . . ., the father and mother of a . . ., violent (headache, cold), raging (toothache, fever), stiff (wind, grog, story, bill, etc.); **une bombe** (*or* **une noce**) **carabinée,** a rare old binge; **un toupet c.,** a hell of a nerve.

carabinier, *m.* **arriver comme les carabiniers (d'Offenbach),** to come a day after the fair.

caraco, *m.* **1.** Spaniard. **2.** blunder.

carafe, *f.* **1.** head*. **2. rester** (*or* **demeurer** *or* **tomber**) **en c.,** to be left in the lurch; to be unable to continue, to be (*or* to get) stuck; to have a breakdown; **laisser qn en c.,** to leave s.o. in the lurch, to leave s.o. out of it, to run out on s.o. **3.** = **cruche**

carafon, *m.* head*; **avoir du c.,** to have a good memory.

carambolage, *m.* **1.** collision. **2.** coition*.

caramboler. 1. to collide with, to run into. **2.** to have coition* with.

carambouillage, *m.*, **carambouille,** *f.* fraudulent conversion (for cash, of goods bought on credit).

carambouilleur, *m.* swindler* guilty of **carambouillage.**

carante, *f.* **1.** table (*of cheap-jack*). **2. se mettre en c.,** to cut up rough (*or* rusty), to turn nasty.

carapatage, *m.* hurried departure.

carapater, (se), to decamp*.

caraque, *f.* dirty slut.

carat, *m.* **1.** age. **2.** year (*of age or of prison sentence*). **3. un sot à vingt-quatre** (*or* **à trente-six**) **carats,** an utter idiot, a prize fool. **4. jusqu'au dernier c.,** up to the nines.

carbi, *m.* **1.** coal. **2.** coal-man. **3.** money*. **4.** work, job.

carbo, *adj.* discredited.

carbonade, *f.* washing soda.

carboniser, to discredit, to malign, to run down; **c. un coup,** to dish attempt, plans, etc.

carbure, *m.* **1.** money*. **2.** petrol, 'gas'.

carburer. 1. to pay* up. **2. ça carbure** = ça gaze (**gazer 3**). **3.** to drink.

carcan, *m.* **1.** = canard **3**. **2.** tall, gawky woman, big gawk. **3.** shrew, old hag, battle-axe. **4.** high stiff collar, choker.

cardinales, *f.pl.*, **carlets,** *m.pl.*: **avoir ses c.** = avoir ses affaires.

caricature, *f.* (*of grotesque-looking person*) fright.

Carlingue, *f.* Gestapo.
carluche, *f.* prison.
carme, *m.* money*.
carmer, to pay* up.
carmouille, *f.* payment, settling up.
carnaval, *m.* (*of person*) guy, scare-crow.
carne, *f.* **1.** tough, inferior meat. **2.** =canard **3. 3.** objectionable person; **vieille c.,** old hag, bitch.
carogne, *f.* =carne.
carottage, *m.* cadging, wangling, diddling.
carotte, *f.* **1.** hoax, swindle, take-in; **tirer une c. à qn,** (*a*) to lie*, (*b*) to diddle s.o. (out of sth.). **2.** tobacconist's sign. **3.** (*tennis*) drop-shot. **4.** plug (of tobacco). **5. les carottes sont cuites,** it's as good as in the bag; **ses carottes sont cuites,** he's done for, he's 'had' it.
carotter, to diddle (s.o.), to wangle (a leave), to shirk (a task); **c. qch. à qn** (*or* **qn de qch.**), to swindle s.o. out of sth., to con sth. off s.o., to con s.o. out of sth.
carotteur, carottier, *m.* **1.** diddler, wangler, artful dodger, chiseller. **2.** shirker, malingerer*.
carouble, *f.* **1.** (*of burglar*) skeleton key, screw, twirl. **2.** lock.
caroubler. 1. to burgle (a house), to screw a gaff (*or* a drum), to crack a crib. **2.** to drub, to beat up.
caroubleur, *m.* **1.** burglar, screwsman. **2.** bruiser, scrapper.
carpette, *f.* funk, quitter.
carrante, *f.* =carante **1.**
carre, *f.* **1.** rooms, digs. **2.** hiding place. **3.** total stakes (at poker, etc.).
carré, *m.* **1.** second-year student. **2.** four of a kind (at poker).
carreau, *m.* **1.** eye*; **avoir un c. à la manque,** to be blind in one eye. **2.** monocle, 'window-pane'. **3.** *pl.* large spectacles, goggles, gig-lamps. **4. le Petit C.,** court of summary jurisdiction; **le Grand C.,** Assize Court. **5. en avoir un coup dans les carreaux,** to be drunk*. **6. rester sur le c.,** (*a*) not

to survive, not to come back (from battle, duel); (*b*) to be dangerously wounded; (*c*) to be left on the shelf, to be left out of the running; (*d*) (*at examination*) to be ploughed. **7. se garder** (*or* **se tenir**) **à c.,** to be on one's guard, to keep on the safe side, to keep one's eyes skinned (*or* peeled). **8. être sur le c.,** to be out of work, on the dole, on the street.
carrée, *f.* **1.** room. **2.** head*.
carrer. 1. to put, to place; to plank down (money etc.). **2.** to hide. **3.** to steal*.
carrer, se, to decamp*.
carreur, *m.* stake-holder (at poker, etc.).
carreuse, *f.* shop-lifter.
Carrière, *f.* (**être de**) **la C.,** (to be in) the Diplomatic Service.
carriole, *f.* ramshackle motor-car*.
carrosse, *m.* police bus.
carrossée, *adj. f.* **bien c.**=bien balancée
carrosserie, *f.* (*of person*) build.
carte, *f.* **1.** wet dream. **2. la c. forcée,** (a case of) Hobson's choice. **3. femme** (*or* **fille**) **en c.,** registered prostitute; **faire mettre une femme en c.,** to have a woman listed as a common prostitute. **4. piquer une c.,** to cheat (at cards).
carton, *m.* **1.** playing card; **taper du** (*or* **le**) **c., manier le c.,** to play at cards. **2. faire un c.,** to fire at s.o. **3. faire** (*or* **tirer**) **un c.,** to have coition*.
cartonner, to play cards.
cartonnier, *m.* card-sharper.
cartouse, *f.* card.
cas, *m.* **c'est bien le c. de le dire!** and no mistake! and how!
casaque, *f.* **tourner c.,** to be a turn-coat, to rat.
casaquin, *m.* jumper; **tomber sur le c. à qn,** to give s.o. a sound thrashing*.
casba(h), *f.* house, shanty, den, hut.
cascader. 1. to lead a fast life, to go the pace. **2.** (*th.*) to gag one's part. **3.** to serve a prison sentence, to do time, to do bird.

cascadeur, *m.* **1.** roisterer, rip, rake. **2.** (*th.*) gagger. **3.** (*cinema*) stunt man.

case, *f.* **1.** house. **2.** prison*; **bouffer de la c.**, to do time, to do bird. **3. il a une c. de moins** (*or* **une c. (de) vide** *or* **une c. qui manque**) (**dans la tête**), he's barmy on the crumpet, he's not all there, he has a slate loose.

caser. 1. to have coition* with, to go case with, to case. **2. va te faire c.!** fuck off! **3. se c.**, to get married.

cash, *adv.* **payer** (*or* **casquer**) **c.**, to pay cash down.

casingue, casino, *m.* **1.** room, bar, pub, restaurant, etc. **2.** hand-bag.

casque, *m.* **1. avoir** (*or* **prendre**) **son** (*or* **le**) **c.**, to be (*or* to get) drunk*. **2. avoir le c.**, to have a head (after a drinking-bout).

casque, *f.* pay; **donner le coup de c.=casquer 1.**

casquer. 1. to pay* up; to pay (s.o.). **2. =cascader 3.**

casquette, *f.* **1. prendre une c.**, être **c.**, to be (*or* to get) drunk*. **2.** money lost at gambling.

casqueur, *m.* cashier.

cassage, *m.* burglary, house-breaking, screwing.

cassantes, *f.pl.* teeth, 'ivories'.

casse, *m.* **=cassage; monter** (*or* **grimper**) **sur un c.**, **faire un c.**, to burgle, to crack a crib, to screw a drum (*or* a gaff), to do a screwing job.

casse, *f.* **1. il y aura de la c.**, there'll be trouble(*or* ructions *or* a row); **faire de la c.**, to kick up a row; **gare la c.!** look out for squalls! **2. être bon pour la c.**, to be old, to be ready for the dump.

cassé, *adj.* **qu'est-ce qu'il y a de c.?** what's all the trouble (*or* row *or* hoo-ha) about? **il y a quelque chose de c.**, something's gone wrong, there's a spot of bother.

casse-burnes, *m.*, **casse-couilles**, *m.* **=casse-pieds.**

casse-croûte, *m.* **1.** snack; snack-bar. **2. se mettre au c.-c.=casser le morceau** (**morceau 4**). **3. c.-c. de cheval**, straw hat.

casse-cul, *m.* **=casse-pieds.**

casse-dalle, *m.*, **casse-graine**, *m.* **= casse-croûte 1.**

casse-gueule, *m.* **1.** low dive. **2. =casse-pattes.**

cassement, *m.* **=casse**, *m.*

casse-noisette, *m.* être **c.-n.=être casse-pieds.**

casse-olives, *m.* **=casse-pieds.**

casse-pattes, *m.* strong spirits* (*drink*).

casse-pieds, *m.* (*of person*) crashing bore*, bloody nuisance; (*of thing*) **c'est rudement c.-p.**, it's a hell of a bore (*or* of a bind); it's enough to give you a pain in the neck. *See* **casser les pieds à qn** (**pied 8**).

casse-pipe(s), *m.* war; **le c.-p. garanti**, certain death (in the front-line). *See* **casser sa pipe.**

casse-poitrine, *m.* **=casse-pattes.**

casser. 1. =c. le morceau (**morceau 4**). **2. c. qch.** (*or* **c. ça**) **à qn**, to reprimand* s.o. severely; **qu'est-ce qu'il va te c. quand il le saura!** you won't half cop it when he finds out! **3.** ... **à tout c.**, a hell of a ..., a helluva ..., a smashing ..., no end of a ..., the devil of a ..., a slap-up ..., the father and mother of a ... **4. ça ne casse rien**, it's no great shakes, it's not up to much, it's not so hot, that cuts no ice, it's nothing to write home about. **5. je t'en casse!** don't you wish you may get it! **6. la c.=c. sa pipe. 7. les** (*or* **la**) **c. à qn=c. les pieds à qn** (**pied 8**); **tu me les casses!** you give me a pain in the neck! **8. vouloir tout c.**, to go all out. **9. =faire un casse. 10. ne pas en c. une**, not to say a word, to keep mum.

casser, se. 1. il ne se casse rien, he takes it easy, he doesn't kill himself (with work); **se c. le cul**, to work like hell. **2.** to decamp*.

casserole, *f.* **1.** informer*. **2.** old piano, 'tin-kettle'. **3.** ramshackle old motor-car*. **4.** big, old-fashioned, silver watch*. **5.** (*of person*) failure, wash-

out. 6. low-class prostitute*. 7. **passer
à la c.**, to be raped.
casseur, *m.* 1. burglar, screwsman.
2. **c. d'assiettes,** swaggerer, blusterer.
cassine, *f.* hovel.
cassis, *m.* 1. head*; **en avoir gros sur le
c.**, to be badly disappointed. 2. **c. de
lutteur,** heavy, rough wine.
castagne, *f.* 1. brawl, free fight. 2.
blow*.
castagner, se = **se bagarrer.**
castapiane, *f.* gonorrhoea, clap.
castel, *m.* prison*.
casuel : faire le c., to hire a room for a
brief assignation.
catalogué, *adj.* = **affiché.**
cataloguer, to size up.
catastrophe, *f. av.* 1. **atterrir en c.**, to
make a crash landing. 2. **en c.**, all in a
flurry.
cateau, *f.* = **catiche.**
catholique, *adj.* sound, genuine, ship-
shape; **ce n'est pas (très) c.**, it's a bit
fishy, it's not altogether above-board;
c'est un peu plus c., that's more like it.
catiche, catin, cato, *f.* prostitute*.
causant, *adj.* **n'être guère c.**, not to be
very talkative.
cause, *f.* **et pour c.**, and for a (*or* and
with) good reason.
causette, *f.* little chat, chit-chat.
cautère, *m.* **c'est un c. sur une jambe
de bois**, it's no earthly use, it will do
no good, you might as well put a
poultice on a wooden leg.
cavalant, *adj.* boring.
cavale, *f.* 1. escape (from prison),
flight; **être en c.**, to be in flight (from
the police), to be on the run, to be on
the lam. 2. (*of woman*) big gawk.
cavalendour, *m.* = **cave 1.**
cavaler. 1. to bore*. *See* **ciboulot.** 2. to
run, to leg it. 3. to decamp*. 4. to
chase girls (*or* skirts).
cavaler, (se), to decamp*.
cavalerie, *f.* 1. loaded (*or* crooked)
dice; **envoyer la c.**, to substitute
loaded dice. 2. **de la grosse c.**, stodgy,
unappetizing food, stodge. 3. **la c. de
Saint Georges,** British gold (for

subsidizing troops, for bribing enemy,
etc.). 4. false cheques etc.
cavaleur, *m.* = **coureur.**
cave, *m.* 1. anybody not belonging to
the **milieu.** 2. simpleton, mug, sucker,
juggins, twerp, clot. 3. prostitute's
paying customer. 4. *adj.* = **décati.**
cavé, *m.* = **cave 2, 3.**
caver, to diddle; **être cavé, se faire c.**,
to be diddled.
cavette, *f.* stupid girl, dumb-bell.
caviar, *m.* **passer au c.** = **caviarder.**
caviardage, *m.* censored passage (in
newspaper).
caviarder, to suppress, to censor, to
block out (passage in newspaper).
cavillon, -onne, *m.f. diminutive forms*
of **cave** and **cavette.**
cavouze, *f.* cellar.
cavu, *m.* = **cul 1.**
ceinture, *f.* 1. **se boucler** (*or* **se serrer** *or*
se mettre) **la c.** (**d'un cran**), **serrer sa
c.** (**d'un cran**), **faire un cran de plus à
sa c., faire c.**, (*a*) to tighten one's belt
(another notch), to go without food;
(*b*) to (have to) do without, to have to
whistle for it, to say good-bye to it.
2. **c.!** you can whistle for it! nothing
doing! you've had it! 3. **s'en donner**
(*or* **s'en mettre**) **plein la c.**, to eat*
heartily.
ceinturer, to arrest*.
cellot(t)e, *f.* 1. cell (in prison). 2. **faire
de la c.** = **faire de la cellule.**
cellule, *f.* **faire de la c.**, to go into hiding
(from the police), to go under cover.
cencul, *m.* (*sch.*) vice-principal (of
lycée).
cent, *num. adj.* 1. **le numéro c.**, the
W.C.* 2. **je vous le donne en c.**, I bet
you'll never guess it. 3. **c. sept ans**, the
year dot.
Centrale, *f.* (= *École centrale*) State
School of Civil Engineering.
centre, *m.* name, mon(n)iker.
centriot, *m.* nickname.
centrouse, centrouze, *f.* (= *Maison
centrale*) prison*.
cep, *m.* nose*.
ce que, how—*e.g.* **ce qu'il joue bien!**

how well he plays! doesn't he play well! **ce que je m'en fiche!** I couldn't care less!

cerbère, *m.* concierge.

cerceaux, *m.pl.* ribs (*human body*).

cercleux, *m.* club-man, man about town; *adj.* clubbish.

cerise, *f.* **1.** head*. **2.** face*; **se taper la c.,** to eat* heartily, to feed one's face. **3.** bad luck; **avoir la c.,** to be out of luck, to be down on one's luck; **ficher** (*or* **foutre** *or* **porter**) **la c. à qn,** to bring s.o. bad luck, to put a jinx on s.o. **4. se (re)faire la c.,** (*a*) to pick up after illness or setback; (*b*) to do oneself proud. **5. cela lui fera la c. = cela lui fera les pieds (pied 7). 6.** ramener **sa c. = ramener sa fraise. 7. le temps des cerises,** happy bygone days.

certals, *m.pl.* (=*certificats de licence*) diploma, degree.

certif, *m.* certificate, certif.

césarienne, *f.* **faire une c.,** to steal* a pocket-book (*or* a purse), to relieve s.o. of (his purse, etc.).

ceusses, *dem. pron.* **les c. qui = ceux qui.**

cézig(ue), *pron.* he, him(self), his nibs.

cézigos, *pron.* they, themselves.

chabanais, *m.* uproar*.

chabler. 1. to attack* (s.o.). **2. = amocher.**

chabraque, *adj.* mad*.

chagatte, *f.* vagina*.

chahut, *m.* **1.** uproar*; **faire du c., en faire un c.,** to kick up a row. **2.** rowdyism, horse-play, rough-house. **3.** rag, ragging. **4.** noisy, vulgar, high-kicking dance.

chahutage, *m.* rowdyism; booing, ragging, barracking.

chahuter. 1. to kick up a row. **2.** to indulge in horse-play. **3.** to rag, to boo, to barrack. **4.** to dance the **chahut 4. 5.** to upset and break (sth.).

chahuteur, *m.* **1.** ragger, a rowdy. **2. c. de macchabées,** undertaker's assistant. **3.** *adj.* rowdy.

Chaillot, *pr. n.* **envoyer qn à C.,** to send s.o. packing*.

chaillotte, *f.* tooth.

chair, *f.* **un(e) marchand(e) de c. fraîche,** a white-slaver.

chaise, *f.* **rester le derrière entre deux chaises,** to fall between two stools (*fig.*).

chaleur, *f.* **avoir les chaleurs,** to be afraid*; **être en c.,** to be sexually excited.

chaleureux, *adj.* cowardly*.

chambard, *m.* **= chahut 1.**

chambardement, *m.* upheaval, upset; **le grand c. (social),** the great socialist revolution.

chambarder. 1. to turn upside down, to turn topsy-turvy. **2.** to sell.

chamberlain, *m.* umbrella*.

chambouler. 1. = chambarder. 2. to give (s.o.) quite a turn, to give (s.o.) a nasty turn, to bowl (s.o.) over.

chambrer, to chaff*; **c. qn à froid,** to chaff s.o. while keeping a straight face.

chameau, *m.* **1.** rotter*, (*of woman*) bitch; **un vieux c.,** an old so-and-so; **petit c.,** (*jest.*) you little devil! you little blighter! **2.** doctor's inspection table.

chamelle, *f.* **1.** (*of woman*) bitch. **2.** prostitute*.

champ', champe, *m.* champagne*.

champ des refroidis, *m.* cemetery.

champignard, *m.* mushroom.

champignon, *m.* (*motor.*) accelerator (pedal); **appuyer sur** (*or* **écraser**) **le c.,** to step on the gas, to step on it, to let her rip; **c. au plancher** (*or* **aux planches**), **filer le paquet sur le c.,** to put one's foot on the floor, with one's foot on the floor, to give it the gun, to gun it.

champoreau, *m.* coffee laced with brandy or rum.

champs, *m.pl.* **aller aux c.,** to go to the races, to go racing.

chançard, *adj.* lucky; *m.* lucky person, lucky dog, lucky blighter.

chance, *f.* **ça c'est pas de c.!** that's hard luck! **(il) y a des chances!** most likely!

you bet! **joue ta c.!** risk it! have a go! back your luck! **(une) c. (que),** ..., luckily, ...

chancetiquer. 1. to wobble, to reel. **2.** to change, alter.

'chand, *m.* (=*marchand*). **'chand de vin,** publican, keeper of a *bistro*(*t*). **'chand d'habits,** old-clothes man; (*as a street-cry*) 'old clo!'

chandelle, *f.* **1.** drop (at end of the nose), dewdrop. **2. faire des chandelles,** (*at tennis*) to lob. **3. souffler sa c.,** to die*. **4. voir (danser) trente-six chandelles,** to see stars (*as a result of a blow, etc.*). **5. tenir la c.,** to be a compliant third (for a couple).

chandoo, *m.* opium.

chanson, *f.* **1. chansons que tout cela!** nonsense!* that's all tommy-rot (*or* all baloney)! **2. c'est toujours la même c.,** it's always the same old story; **c'est une autre c.,** that's another story; **on connaît la c.!** we've heard that yarn before! we know what's what!

chansonnette, *f.* **1.** third degree. **2. avoir qn à la c., le faire à la c.,** to lead s.o. up the garden(-path), to lead s.o. on (by seemingly innocuous interrogation).

chanstique, *m.* **faire un c.,** (*a*) =**faire un cambut;** (*b*) to substitute loaded dice.

chanstiquer =**cambuter.**

chanter. 1. c. à qn, to please s.o., to suit s.o.—*e.g.* **si ça vous chante,** if you feel like it, if you like the idea of it. **2. c'est comme si je chantais** (*or* **tu chantais** *or* **on chantait**), it's a waste of breath, one might as well save one's breath, one might as well talk to oneself, it's like pouring water on a duck's back, it's like water off a duck's back, it's like talking to a brick wall. **3.** to turn informer*. **4.** to kick up a row. **5. qu'est-ce que vous (me) chantez là?** what fairy-tale are you trying to tell me? what yarn are you spinning? what on earth are you talking about? **6. tu vas c.,** you are going to yell (blue murder).

chanterelle, *f.* **appuyer sur la c. 1.** to stress a point, to hammer it home, to rub it in. **2.** to step on the gas. (*See* **champignon**).

chanvre indien, *m.* Indian hemp (*drugs**).

chapardage, *m.* pilfering; scrounging.

chaparder, to pilfer*; to scrounge.

chapardeur, *m.* pilferer; scrounger.

chapeau, *m.* **1. c.!** (*abbrev. for* **je vous (lui, etc.) tire mon c.!**) hats off! I raise (*or* lift *or* take off) my hat to you (to him, etc.)! congratulations! one has to hand it to you (to him, etc.)! **2. avoir le** (*or* **aller au**) **c. de paille,** to be sentenced to transportation with hard labour. **3. (ne) t'occupe pas du c. de la gamine!** (*c.p.*) mind your own business! **4. porter le c.,** to be a police-informer*. **5. travailler du c.,** to be mad*. **6. faire c.,** to overturn (of *boat, etc.*).

chapeautée, *adj., f.* **bien c.,** wearing a pretty (*or* smart) hat.

chapelet, *m.* handcuffs*; **défiler son c.,** to spill one's guts.

chapelle, *f.* **faire c.,** (*of woman*) to lift one's dress in order to warm one's legs by the fire.

Chapelouse, la, *pr.n.* la Chapelle (*district in Paris*).

chapiteau, *m.* **1.** circus tent, (big) top. **2.** head*.

char, *m.* **1. sans c.!** (**sans c.?**), no kidding! (no kidding?); **c'est pas du c.!** I'm not kidding! **arrête ton c.!** stop your kidding! **un sale c.,** a dirty trick. **2. faire du c. à qn**=**baratiner qn. 3. faire des chars à qn**=**faire des paillons à qn.**

charabia, *m.* gibberish.

charbon, *m.* **(aller) bosser au c.,** to do irksome manual work (*instead of being 'on the crook', i.e. leading a life of crime*).

charcutage, *m.* bungled surgical operation, butchering.

charcutaille, *f.* =**cochonaille.**

charcuter, (*of clumsy surgeon*) to butcher, to hack (s.o.) about.

charcutier, *m.* (*of clumsy surgeon*) butcher, sawbones.

Charenton, *pr. n.* lunatic asylum, madhouse, loony-bin; **un échappé de C.,** a crazy* person.

chargé, *adj.* être c. **1.** to be armed, to be heeled, to pack a gun. **2.** to be drunk*. **3.** to have a criminal record. **4.** to be hooked on drugs.

charger, se. 1. to arm oneself, to carry a fire arm, to pack a gun. **2.** to inject a drug.

charibotage, *m.* criticism.

charibotée, *f.* large quantity*.

chariboter=charrier.

charivari, *m.* uproar*.

Charlemagne, *pr. n.* **faire C.,** to stop gambling when one is winning, to quit while the going is good.

charlemagner =faire Charlemagne.

Charles, *pr. n.* **tu parles, C.!** (*R.S.*) now you're talking! *cf.* **tu l'as dit, bouffi!**

Charlot, *pr. n.* **1.** public executioner; **embrasser C.,** to be guillotined. **2.** Charlie Chaplin.

charme, *m.* **1. faire du c.,** to turn on (*or* to lay on) the charm. **2. chanteur de c.,** crooner.

charmeuses, *f.pl.* moustache, facefungus, tickler, tash.

charnelle, *f.* girl*, bird.

charnière, *f.* **nom à c.,** a name containing the nobiliary particle (*i.e. de*).

charognard, *m.* rotter*.

charogne, *f.* =carne.

charre, *m.* =char.

charrette, *f.* motor-car*.

charriage, *m.* chaffing, leg-pulling.

charrier. 1. to chaff*; **se faire c.,** to have one's leg pulled. **2.** to joke; **sans c. =sans char. 3.** to exaggerate*; to pile it on. *See* **bégonias 1.**

charrieur, *m.* =**blagueur.**

charron, *m.* **gueuler** (*or* **aller** *or* **crier**) **au c.,** to cause a disturbance, to raise Cain (*or* hell), to holler. to yell blue murder.

charronner. 1. to hit out. **2.** =**gueuler au charron.**

chass d'Af, *m.* soldier serving in the *chasseurs d'Afrique*, light cavalry formerly serving in Africa.

châsse, *m.* eye*; **cligner du c. vers qn, filer** (*or* **jeter** *or* **lancer**) **un coup de châsse(s) à qn,** to look at s.o., to give s.o. the glad eye; **avoir les châsses en portefeuille,** to have bags under one's eyes; **un(e) n'a qu'un c.,** a one-eyed man (woman); **pisser des châsses,** to weep; **au c.=à l'œil.**

chasser, to flirt.

châsser, to look at*.

châssis, *m.* **1. c'est un beau c.,** she's got a shapely figure. **2.** *pl.* eyes*; **fermer les c.,** to sleep*.

chat, *m.* **1.** clerk of the court. **2.** examining magistrate, beak. **3.** vagina*. **4. arriver dès les chats,** to arrive home with the milk. **5. avoir un c. dans la gorge** (*or* **le gosier**), **avoir avalé un c. par la queue,** to be hoarse, to have a frog in one's throat. **6. avoir d'autres chats à fouetter,** to have other fish to fry. **7. ce n'est** (*or* **c'est**) **pas fait pour les chats=ce n'est** (*or* **c'est**) **pas fait pour les chiens** (**chien 10**). **8. écrire comme un c., avoir une écriture de c.,** to write a dreadful scrawl. **9. il n'y a pas de quoi fouetter un c.,** it's nothing to make a fuss about, it's a (very) trifling offence. **10. mon** (**petit**) **c., ma** (**petite**) **chatte,** my darling*. **11.** (**non,**) **c'est le c.!** (*ironical c.p. in reply to s.o. who denies having done sth.*) it was Mr. Nobody, I suppose! **12. pas un c.,** not a (living) soul.

châtaigne, *f.* **1.** blow*; **passer à la c.,** to get a good hammering. **2.** fisticuffs, scrap.

châtaigner, (se), to pinch, to belabour, to pummel.

château, *m.* **1.** prison*. **2. mener la vie de c.,** to live like a lord, to live on the fat of the land. **3.** hospital.

Château-la-Pompe, *m.* water (for drinking), Adam's ale, (*children's joc. term*) corporation pop.

chat-fourré, *m.* judge.

chatouille, *f.* =**chtouille.**

chatouiller: **c. une serrure,** to pick a lock.

chatte, *f.* = chat 3.

chaud, *adj.* **1. avoir eu c.**—*e.g.* **on a eu c.,** we didn't half get a fright; we had a narrow escape. **2. ça va vous coûter c.,** (*a*) it'll cost you a pretty penny, you'll pay through the nose for it; (*b*) you'll smart for it. **3.** keen, enthusiastic, game. **4.** difficult, risky, tricky, dodgy, dicey. **5. être c. comme (la) braise, être c. de la pince** (*or* **de la pointe**), to be hot stuff (*sexually*). *See also* **lapin** 4. **6. cela ne lui fait ni c. ni froid,** it's all the same (*or* it's all one) to him, he doesn't care a rap. **7. il fera c.!** never! nonsense! **il fera c. quand . . .,** it'll be the age of miracles when . . ., that'll be the day!

chaude-lance, chaude-pince, chaude-pisse, *f.* clap.

chaudron, *m.* **1.** old tinkling piano, 'tin-kettle'. **2. écurer son c.,** to confess*.

chauffage, *m.* cramming (for an examination).

chauffard, *m.* reckless driver, road-hog, scorcher, speed-merchant, hit-and-run driver.

chauffer. 1. to coach, to cram (s.o. for an examination). **2.** to arrest*; **se faire c.,** to get pinched. **3. c. une place,** to canvas for a post. **4. ça va c.!** = ça va barder!; ça chauffe! = ça barde!

chauffeur, *m.* coach, crammer (for an examination).

chauffoir, *m.* cramming establishment, cramming-shop, crammer's.

chaumière, *f.* **une c. et un cœur,** love in a cottage.

chaussette, *f.* **1.** (*long-distance drivers' slang*) tyre. **2.** plain-clothes policeman. **3. mettre les chaussettes à la fenêtre,** to be sexually disappointed (*of woman*).

chaussons, *m.pl.* **tresser** (*or* **fabriquer**) **des c. (de lisière),** to be in jail, to do time, to 'pick oakum'.

chaussure, *f.* **trouver c. à son pied,** to find exactly what one is looking for (*or* what one wants); to find one's match; to make a good match.

chaux, *f.* **être bâti à c. et à sable,** to be as strong as a horse, to have an iron constitution.

chéchia, *f.* **travailler de la c.** = travailler du chapeau.

chelem, *adj.* **être grand c.,** to be absolutely penniless*.

chelinguer, to stink*; **c. du bec,** to have a foul breath.

chemin, *m.* **1. le c. des écoliers,** the longest way round. **2. ne pas y aller par quatre** (*or* **trente-six**) **chemins,** not to beat about the bush, to make no bones about it.

cheminée, *f.* half-bottle of red wine.

chemise, *f.* **1. s'en moquer** (*or* **s'en ficher**) **comme de sa première c.,** not to care a rap*. **2. changer d'idée comme de c.,** to chop and change. **3. compter ses chemises,** to vomit*.

chêne, *m.* man; **faire suer un c.,** to kill* a man. *See* **sueur.**

chenoque, *m.* = schnock.

chenu, *adj.* **c'est du c.!** that's first-rate!*

cher, *adv.* **1. je ne vaux pas c.,** I feel unwell*. **2. cavaler c.,** to run hard.

chercher. 1. to blame (s.o.), to pick on (s.o.). **2. il l'a cherché,** he's been asking for it (*i.e. trouble*), he stuck his neck out. **3. aller en c.,** to earn money. **4. aller les c.,** to get money, to raise the wind (feloniously). **5. où vas-tu c. ça? qu'est-ce que tu vas c.?** what (*or* who) put that idea in your head? **que vas-tu c. là?** where did you get that idea from? where did you dig that one up? **6. ça va c. dans les trois mille francs,** that fetches about three thousand francs; **ça va c. (dans les) combien?** what'll that come to? **elle va sûrement c. dans les quarante berges,** she must surely be about forty (years of age). **7. ça va chercher loin,** that can have serious consequences. **8. il me cherche,** he is trying to pick a quarrel with me.

chéro(t), *adj.* rather dear, somewhat

expensive, on the dear side, pric(e)y; *adv.* ça vaut c., it's pretty expensive.

cherrer, to exaggerate*; **ne cherre pas!** come off it! *See also* **bégonias** *and* **tas 6.**

cherreur, *m.* (*of boxer, cyclist, etc.*) all-outer.

chetar(d), *m.* =**chtar(d).**

chetouille, *f.* =**chtouille.**

cheval, *m.* **1.** masculine woman, Amazon. **2.** (vieux) **c. de retour,** (*a*) old jail-bird, old offender, old lag; (*b*) old has-been. **3. un c. pour le travail** (*or* à l'ouvrage), a glutton for work. **4. manger** (*or* **becqueter** *or* **dîner**) **avec les chevaux de bois,** to go without food, to go dinnerless. **5.** heroin (*drugs**).

chevalier, *m.* **1. c. de la guirlande,** convict. **2. c. de la lune,** burglar. **3. c. de la rosette, c. du prépuce-cul,** pederast*. **4. c. de la piquouse,** drug-addict, junky.

chevalière, *f.* anus*.

cheveu, *m.* **1. avoir mal aux cheveux, avoir le c. triste,** to have a hangover*. **2. avoir un c. sur la langue,** to be thick in one's speech. **3. il y a un c.,** there's a fly in the ointment, there's a hitch somewhere. **4. passer la main dans les cheveux à qn,** to flatter* s.o. **5. se faire des cheveux (blancs),** to worry oneself grey, to go grey with worry. **6. se prendre aux cheveux,** to come to blows, to scrap. **7. tiré par les cheveux,** (*of argument, etc.*) far-fetched. **8. travailler du c.**=**travailler du chapeau. 9. venir comme un c.** (*or* **des cheveux**) **sur la soupe,** to be most inappropriate, to be quite uncalled for, to be quite out of place, to have nothing to do with the matter under discussion. **10. trouver un c. dans le potage,** to find something amiss. **11. y trouver un c.,** to find a difference (for the worse).

cheville, *f.* **1. être en c. avec,** to be in collusion with, to be in cahoots with, to play ball with. **2. vivre en c. avec,** to cohabit with, to shack up with. **3. ne pas monter** (*or* **venir**) **à la c. de**

qn, not to be a patch on s.o., not to be named (*or* mentioned) in the same breath with s.o.

cheviller, se =être en cheville avec (**cheville 1**).

chevilleur, (**-euse**), *m.f.* go-between, stooge.

chèvre, *f.* **1.** fast girl. **2. prendre la c.,** to get angry*.

chevreuil, *m.* **1.** peasant*. **2.** informer*.

chez, *prep.* non, mais c. qui? (*expression indicating strong denial or refusal*) no damn fear! not bloody likely! not if I know it! what next!

chiader =bûcher **1.**

chiadeur, *m.* =bûcheur.

chialer, to weep*.

chiale-toujours, *m.,* **chialeur,** *m.* cry-baby, sniveller, grizzler.

chiant, *adj.* perfectly sickening.

chiard, *m.* (*péj.*) child*.

chiasse, *f.* **avoir la c.,** (*a*) to have diarrhoea*; (*b*) to be afraid*.

chiasser =avoir la chiasse (*b*).

chiasseur, chiasseux, *m.* coward*.

chibre, *m.* penis*.

chibrer, to have coition* with.

chic, *m.* **1.** knack, skill, dexterity, trick; **avoir** (*or* **attraper**) **le c. pour faire qch.,** to get the hang of sth., to have the knack of doing sth. **2.** style, elegance, smartness; **du dernier c.,** in the latest style. **3. peindre de c.,** to paint a picture from memory, without a model; **écrire de c.,** to dash sth. off. **4. un c. à** (*or* **pour**) . . .**,** three cheers for . . .

chic, *adj.* **1.** stylish, smart, elegant, fashionable; **ça fait c.,** it looks smart. **2.** first-rate*. **3.** decent, nice, fine; **c'est très c. de votre part,** it's awfully (*or* jolly) decent of you; **ce n'est pas c. de sa part,** it's mean of him; **un c. type,** a brick, a (good) sport, a decent chap.

chic, *int.* c. (**alors**)! great! fine! grand! good show!

chicandier, -ière, *m.f.* **1.** quarrelsome person, awkward customer. **2.** swank(er)*.

chiche, *adj.* stingy, close(-fisted).

chiche, *int.* **c.!** *or* **c. que . . !,** I dare you! try it on! (I) bet you I will! (*or* I bet you you can't! *or* I bet you don't! *or* I bet you won't!); *adj.* **(ne pas) être c. de le faire,** (not) to have the guts to do it.

chichi, *m.* **1.** fuss, to-do; affected manners; **en voilà du c.!** what a fuss! **faire des chichis,** to make (*or* to kick up) a fuss; to give oneself airs, to put on airs, to put on side, to put on frills; **des gens à chichis,** affected people, snobs; **toutes sortes de chichis,** all kinds of complications. **2.** false curl, false hair.

chichite, *f.* vague illness.

chichiteur, chichiteux, *m.* **chichiteuse,** *f.* very fussy person, fuss-pot.

chicore, chicor, *adj.* drunk*, shickered.

chicorée, *f.* **1.** reprimand*. **2.** **être c.,** to be drunk*. **3. défriser la c.,** to make up to a woman.

chiée, *f.* great quantity*.

chien, *m.* **1.** brandy. **2. mon c.,** my darling*. **3. le c. du commissaire,** the police-station clerk. **4.** (*mil.*) **le c. de quartier = adjupète. 5. avoir du c.,** (*a*) = **avoir de ça** (**ça 3** (*a*)); (*b*) to have plenty of go, to have plenty of pluck; **un peu de c.!** put some guts into it! **6. avoir un c. pour = avoir un béguin pour. 7. un coup de c.,** a sudden violent riot (*or* dust-up *or* clash). **8. . . . de c.,** beastly, awful—*e.g.* **quel temps de c.** (*or* **quel c. de temps**)! what beastly (*or* filthy) weather! **9. faire les** (*or* **faire la chronique des** *or* **tenir la rubrique des) chiens écrasés** (*or* **chiens crevés** *or* **chiens perdus**), to be a hack reporter, to be in charge of the accident column. **10. ce n'est** (*or* **c'est**) **pas fait pour les chiens,** it's meant to be used, it's not there as an ornament. **11. garder à qn un c. de sa chienne,** (*a*) to have a rod in pickle for s.o.; (*b*) to have a grudge against s.o. **12. il n'attache pas ses chiens** (*or* **son c.) avec des saucisses,** he's a skinflint.

13. piquer un c., to take a nap. **14. porter des chiens, se coiffer** (*or* **être coiffé) à la c.,** to wear a straight fringe. **15. se donner un mal de c.,** to be at no end of pains, to kill oneself. **16. les chiens aboient, la caravane passe,** (*c.p.*)—I don't care what Mrs. Grundy says. **17.** *adj.* (*a*) mean, stingy, close(-fisted); **être c. comme tout,** to be as mean as they make 'em; (*b*) **avoir l'air c.,** to have a disagreeable look, to look a (bit of a) swine.

chienchien, *m.* **1.** doggie. **2.** darling*.

chiendent, *m.* **1.** difficulty, rub, snag. **2.** marihuana (*drugs*). **3. arracher du c.,** to be stood up.

chie-en-lit, chienlit, *f.* **1.** bed-shitter. **2.** masquerade, rowdy disorder. **3. crier à la c.,** to boo.

chiennerie, *f.* beastliness, mean (*or* shameless) action.

chier. 1. to shit, to shite, to crap. **2. faire c. qn = emmerder qn; tu me fais c.!** *or* **(ne) me fais pas c.!** you make me sick! you get on my bloody nerves! you give me the pip! **va te faire c.!** go to hell! piss off! **envoyer qn c.,** to send s.o. to hell, to tell s.o. to piss off; **y a pas à c.,** you can say what you like, you can't get away from it; **se faire c.** to be bored stiff, to be fed to the teeth; **ça (ne) chie pas!** it doesn't matter a tupp'ny damn! **ça va c. (dur)!** now the squit's going to fly! (*see also* **matricule**); **ça, c'est chié! = ça, c'est envoyé** (*or* **tapé**).

chierie, *f.* bloody nuisance; **quelle c. de temps!** what stinking weather!

chie-tout-debout, *m. f.* tall*, thin person.

chieur, *m.* **1.** (*of person*) shit-pot. **2. c. d'encre = buveur d'encre.**

chiffe, *f.* **1.** person with no backbone (*or* no grit), wash-out. **2. mou comme une c.,** as limp as a rag, like a (wet) rag. flabby. **3. = biffe 1.**

chiffe, *m.* **= biffin 1.**

chiffon, *m.* **1. parler** (*or* **causer) chiffons,** to talk dress, to talk fashion. **2.** handkerchief.

chiffonner, to worry, to vex, to rile, to bother, to irritate, to needle.

chiffortin, m. = biffin 1.

chiftir(e), m. 1. rag. 2. = biffin 1.

chigner. 1. to weep*. 2. to grumble*.

chignol(l)e, f. = bagnole.

chignon, m. 1. head*. 2. brain, intelligence. 3. un c. véreux, (of woman) a bitch. 4. se crêper le c., (of women) to have a scrap (c a set-to), to tear each other's hair; un crêpage de chignon(s), a scrap, a set-to.

chinago, adj. = chinetoc.

chine, f. cadging. . . . de c., cadged . . .; aller à la c., to beg from door to door, to be a door-to-door hawker.

chiner. 1. to beg, to cadge. 2. to chaff*. 3. to be a rag-picker. 4. to work* hard.

chinetoc, chinetok, chinetoque, m.f., adj. Chinese, Chinee, Chink.

chineur, m. 1. cadger. 2. carping critic. 3. second-hand dealer.

chinois, m. 1. 'stranger' (i.e. floating tea-leaf in cup). 2. fellow*. 3. penis*. 4. tremper ses c., to get involved (or implicated). 5. ça ne fait pas mes c., that doesn't suit my book. 6. c'est du c. pour moi, it's double Dutch to me. 7. adj. (of person) awkward, difficult; crafty, twisty; (of things) complicated, involved.

chinoiser, to raise footling objections.

chinoiseries, f.pl. fuss, complicated formalities, red-tape.

chiot, m. pup, puppy.

chiots, m.pl. = chiottes.

chiotte, f. 1. motor-car*. 2. c'est la c., it's a beastly bore.

chiottes, f.pl. W.C.*; (mil.) la corvée des c., latrine fatigue.

chipé, adj. 1. être c. pour, to be infatuated* with. 2. elle n'est pas mal chipée, she's not a bad-looker.

chiper, 1. to steal*. 2. to catch (a cold, a disease), to cop.

chipette, f. ne pas valoir c., to be worthless*.

chipeur, m. 1. pilferer. 2. man who steals another man's girl.

chipie, f. 1. ill-natured and disagree-

able woman, stinker, sourpuss; une vieille c., an old cat; une petite c., a spiteful little minx. 2. adj. catty.

chipolata, m. penis*.

chipotage, m. haggling, quibbling.

chipoter. 1. to haggle, to quibble. 2. to nibble (or to peck or to pick) at one's food, to toy with (one's food). 3. to waste time. 4. = chiffonner.

chipoterie, f. = chipotage.

chipoteur, -euse, m.f. 1. fastidious person. 2. haggler, quibbler. 3. adj. fastidious, choosy.

chiquage, m. = chiqué, m.

chique, f. 1. avaler (or poser) sa c., to die*. 2. avoir la c., (a) to chew a quid of tobacco; (b) to have a gumboil. 3. couper la c. à qn, to cut s.o. short, to stump s.o., to cramp s.o.'s style; cf. ça te la coupe! (couper 2). 4. couper la c. à quinze pas, to have a foul breath. 5. mou comme une chique = mou comme une chiffe. 6. poser sa c., (a) to die*; (b) to fart; poser sa c. et faire le mort, to keep mum. 7. tirer sa c., to have coition*.

chiqué, m. 1. sham, fake, make-believe, eye-wash; tout ça, c'est du c., that's all eye-wash, that's all phoney; c'est pas du c., it's straight from the horse's mouth; le (or la) faire au c., to sham, to make believe. 2. fuss, to-do; faire du c., to swank; un faiseur de c., a swank(er).

chiquement, adv. (from chic, adj.) stylishly, smartly; nicely, decently; in first-rate* style.

chiquer. 1. to pretend, to sham, to make believe. 2. c. à . . ., to pretend to be . . ., to put on an act of . . .; rien à c.! nothing doing! no soap! 3. y a pas à c.! there are no two ways about it! there's no getting away from it! 4. to eat*. 5. to fake, to cook (accounts).

chiqueur, -euse, m.f. swanker.

chiure, f. chiures de mouche, fly-blow.

chlaff(e), m. = chlof(e).

chlass(e), adj. = schlass.

Chleu(h), m. (W.W.II) German, Jerry.

chlinguer = chelinguer.
chlof(e), *m.* = schloff(e).
chloroforme-en-barre, *m.* bludgeon.
chnaps, *m.* = schnaps.
chnoc, chnoque, *m.* = duch(e)nock, schnock.
chnouf, *f.* cocaine, heroin (*drugs**).
chnoufer, se, to be a drug addict, to be a junkie (*or* junky), a dosser.
chochoter, to put on airs.
chochoteuse, *adj., f.* affected, finical, genteel.
chochotte, *f.* 1. **ma c.**, my darling*. 2. **une vieille c.**, (*of woman*) an old has-been. 3. **faire sa c.** = faire sa sainte-nitouche. 4. **de la c.**, something nice. 5. affected effeminate person. 6. pederast*.
choco, *m.* chocolate, choc.
chocolat, *adj.* **être c.**, to be duped*, to be done brown; (*of boxer*) to be knocked out, to be K.O.; **demeurer** (*or* **rester**) **c.**, to be left stranded (*or* in the lurch).
chocottes, *f.pl.* 1. teeth. 2. **avoir** (*or* **prendre**) **les c.**, to be afraid*; **filer les c. à qn**, to put the wind up s.o.
choléra, *m.* (*of person*) sickener, nasty piece of work, blight; (*of thing*) nasty business, nasty affair.
chôme, *f.* unemployment.
chômedu, chôm'du, *m.* unemployment; man out of work; Labour Exchange.
chômeur, *m.* glass of mineral water.
choper. 1. = chiper 1 *and* 2. 2. to arrest*; **se faire c.**, to be nabbed.
chopeur, *m.* = chipeur 1.
chopin, *m.* 1. bit of luck, windfall, godsend. 2. love-conquest, catch; **faire un (beau) c.**, to make a good catch, to find a wealthy lover.
chopine, *f.* 1. bottle (*half-litre of wine, etc.*). 2. penis*.
chopiner, to tipple*.
chopot(t)e, *f.* 1. bottle. 2. penis*.
chose, *f.* 1. (**Monsieur** *or* **Madame**) **C.**, (Mr. *or* Mrs.) what's-his (her) name, (Mr. *or* Mrs.) what-d'you-call him (her). *cf.* **machin.** 2. **un(e) pas grand-c.**,

a worthless person, a rotter*. 3. **de deux choses l'une . . .**, it's either this or that . . ., it's one thing or the other . . . 4. **être porté sur la c.** = être porté sur la bagatelle. 5. *adj.* **se sentir** (*or* **être**) **tout** (*or* **un peu**) **c.**, to feel unwell*.
chosette, *f.* love-making.
chottes, *f.pl.* = chiottes.
chou, *m.* 1. head*; intelligence, brains; **avoir le c. farci**, to have a headache. **se casser** (*or* **se creuser**) **le c.**, to rack one's brains; **travailler du c.** = travailler du chapeau; **avoir le c. pourri**, to have queer ideas; **se monter le c.** = se monter la tête. 2. **mon (petit) c., ma choute**, my darling*; **mon petit c. en sucre** (*or* **en susucre**), sweetie-pie; **c'est un vrai c.!** he's a real pet! he's a perfect darling! 3. **être dans les choux**, (*a*) to be in a fix*; (*b*) (*a scheme*) to come to grief; (*of horse in a race*) to come nowhere, to be an also ran; **laisser dans les choux**, (*in a race*) to leave standing. 4. **faire c. blanc**, to fail completely, to draw a blank. 5. **faire ses choux gras**, to make plenty of profit, to feather one's nest, to make a good thing of it. 6. **faites-en** (*or* **vous en ferez**) **des choux, des raves**, do just what you like with it. 7. **rentrer dans le c. à qn**, to attack* s.o. 8. **se taper le c.**, to eat. 9. **sauter sur le c.**, to jump on s.o., to arrest*. 10. *adj.* **ce que tu es c.!** you're a perfect darling! **c'est c.!** it's just divine!
chouaga, *adj.* = chouette 1.
chouaye, *adv.* = chouïa.
choubiner, to heat; **ça choubine** = gazer 3.
choubinette, small stove.
choucard, *adj.* = chouette 1.
choucarde, *f.* electric torch, flash-light.
chouchou, *m.* (*f.* **chouchoute**), darling, favourite, blue-eyed (*or* white-headed *or* white-haired) boy, teacher's pet.
chouchouter, to pet, to coddle; **se c.**, to coddle oneself, to have a cushy time.

choucroûte, *adj.* first-rate*.

chouette, *adj.* **1.** first-rate*. **2. avoir qn à la c.**=avoir qn à la bonne. **3.** *int.* fine! swell! goody-goody! **c. alors!** good show! whizzo! fine! thumbs up!

chouette, *m.* buttocks*; **prendre** (*or* **filer**) **du c.,** to be a pederast*.

chouettement, *adv.* in first-rate* style, fabulously.

chouettes, *f.pl.* **marcher sous ses c.,** to have one's identification papers in order.

chouettos(e), *adj.* =chouette, *adj.* **1.**

chou-fleur, *m.* **1. avoir les oreilles en c.-f.,** to have cauliflower ears (*boxer*). **2.** *pl.* piles, hemorrhoids.

chouflique(ur), *m.* shoemaker, cobbler, 'snob'.

chouïa, chouilla, *adv.* **1. un c. de . . .,** a little . . ., a small quantity of . . .; **pas c.,** not much. **2. vas-y c.!** go easy! steady on!

choumaque, *m.* =chouflique(ur).

choupiner* =chouchouter.

chouquette, *f.* **1.** affected young woman. **2.** *m.* pederast*.

chourave, *f.* thieving.

chouravé, *adj.* mad*.

chouraver, to steal*.

chouraveur, *m.* thief.

chourin, *m.,* **chouriner, chourineur,** *m.* =surin, suriner, surineur.

choute, *f. See* chou 2.

chouter =chouchouter.

chouterie, *f.* caress(ing), fondling.

chouya, *adv.* =chouïa.

chpile, *m.* =schpile.

chtar(d), ch'tar, *m.* prison*; disciplinary cell.

chtib(e), *m.* prison*.

ch'timi, *m.* native of Northern France, northerner.

chtouille, *f.* venereal disease, clap; **ramasser la c.,** to cop a dose.

chtourbe, *f.* trouble, spot of bother; **dans la c.,** in a fix*.

chut-chut, *int.* **à la c.-c.,** on the (strict) Q.T.

chuter, to fall, to come to grief, to come a cropper; (*of play*) to be a flop; (*of female*) to (make a) slip, to go wrong; (*at cards*) to lose, go down.

ciao, *int.* =tchaô.

cibiche, *f.* cigarette*.

ciblot, *m.* =civelot.

ciboule, *f.* **1.** head*. **2. entrer en c.,** to come in first.

ciboulot, *m.* **1.** head*. **2.** intelligence, brains, brain-pan; **se creuser le c.,** to rack one's brains. **3. tu me cours** (*or* **tu me cavales**) **sur le c.,** you get on my nerves (*or* on my wick), you send me up the wall.

cicatrice, *f.* clitoris; vulva.

cidre, *m.* **1.** water. **2. ne pas valoir un coup de c.,** to be absolutely worthless*.

ciel, *m.* **approcher du c. à reculons,** to be guillotined.

cigare, *m.* **1.** head*; **couper le c. à qn,** to guillotine s.o.; **se faire décoller le c.,** to be guillotined, to get topped; **y aller du c.,** to risk one's neck; **en filer un coup de c. à qn,** to bludgeon (*or* to club) s.o.; **se remettre le c. à l'endroit,** to pull oneself together. **2.** intelligence, brains; **avoir du c.,** to be brainy. **3. c. à moustaches,** penis*.

cigler, to pay* up, to settle.

cigotin, *m.* =cique.

cigue, *m.* **1. avoir un c.,** to be twenty years of age; **avoir deux cigues et un peu de mornifle,** to be forty two or forty three years old. **2.** a gold louis.

cil, *m.* **avoir les cils cassés,** to feel very sleepy; **plier les cils,** to sleep*.

cimetière, *m.* **rendre le c. bossu,** to be buried.

ciné, *m.* cinema, pictures, movies, flicks.

cinéac, *m.* news theatre.

cinecroque, *m.* =ciné.

cinéma, *m.* **1. faire du c.,** to feign madness. **2. se faire du c., s'emmener au c.,** to have delusions, to imagine things.

cinetoche, *m.* =ciné.

cinglé, *adj., m.* mad* (person); **raide c.,** raving mad.

cingler, to arrest*.

cinochard, cinoche, *m.*=ciné.

cinoque, *adj., m.* =cinglé.

cinq, *num. adj.* **1.** il était moins c., it was a narrow escape*. **2.** en c. secs, immediately*. **3.** faire c. et trois font huit, to limp, to be lame. **4.** les c. lettres, *euphemism for* merde; répondre en c. lettres à qn, dire c. lettres à qn (*i.e. to say 'merde' to s.o.*), to tell s.o. to go to hell. **5.** y aller de c., to shake hands; un vigoureux c.-en-c., a hearty (hand)shake. *See also* écraser 5. **6.** faire c. contre un, to masturbate*. **7.** les c. à sept, clandestine lovers. **8.** c. à sept=maison 1.

cinq-cinq: c'est c.-c., it's fab.

cinquante-pour-cent, *m.* (*joc.*) wife*.

cintrant, *adj.* = bidonnant.

cintré, *adj.* être c., (*a*) to be mad*; (*b*) = avoir du toupet.

cipal, *m.* (*pl.* **cipaux**) (= *garde municipal*) member of the military police (in Paris).

cirage, *m.* **1.** être dans le c., (*a*) to be in a fix*; (*b*) to be in a kind of stupor, to be absolutely in the dark, to be all at sea, to be utterly confused; (*c*) to be depressed*; (*d*) (*av.*) to be flying blind. **2.** être en plein c., to be dead-drunk*.

circuit, *m.* être dans le c., to be in the thick of it.

circulation, *f.* disparaître de la c., to vanish into thin air.

cirer, (*sch.*) to bump (a boy's behind on the ground).

cirque, *m.* **1.** (*jest.*) Chamber of Deputies. **2.** domestic brawl. **3.** mener le petit au c., to have coition*.

cisaillé, *adj.* penniless*; c. à zéro, stony broke.

cisailler, to fleece (s.o. at gambling), to clean out.

ciseaux, *m.pl.* à coups de c., with scissors and paste.

citoyen, *m.* fellow*.

citron, *m.* = ciboulot 1 *and* 2.

citron, *f.* Citroën car.

citrouille, *f.* **1.** head*. **2.** fool*, juggins; avoir l'air c., to look like a ninny.

civ(e)lot, *m.* civilian, civvy; en c.=en civil.

civil, *m.* **1.** dans le c., in civil life. **2.** en c., in plain clothes, in civvies, in mufti.

claboter, to die*.

clac, *m.* = claque, *m.*

clam(e)cer, to die*.

clampin, *m.* slacker, loafer, lazybones, sluggard, slow-coach, lay-about, (*mil.*) straggler.

clampiner, to slack, to mooch about.

clam(p)ser, to die*.

clandé, *m.* clandestine (*or* illicit) gambling joint, opium-den, brothel, speak-easy, clip-joint.

clandès, *m.* black market (*W.W.II*).

claoui(e)s, *m.pl.* testicles*; casser les c. à qn=casser les pieds à qn.

claper, to eat.

clapet, *m.* mouth*; fermer (*or* boucler son c., to shut* up.

clapette, *f.* tongue, clapper.

clapper = claper.

clapser = clam(p)ser.

claque, claquedent, *m.* brothel*.

claque, *f.* **1.** une tête à claques, a cheeky-looking blighter (*i.e. with the sort of face one would like to clout*). **2.** en avoir sa c., (*a*) = en avoir marre; (*b*) to be exhausted*.

claqué, *adj.* exhausted*; *adj. and noun* corpsed; dead('un); le jardin des claqués, the cemetery; la boîte aux claqués, the mortuary.

claque-fric, *m.* spendthrift.

claque-merde, *f.* mouth*; ferme ta c.-m.! shut* up!

claque-patins, *m.f.* sloven.

claquer. **1.** to die*. **2.** to fail, to fall through. **3.** il m'a claqué dans la main, he has let me down at the last moment. **4.** = bouffer 2. *See also* bec 5.

claquer, se, to tire oneself out, to knock oneself up; to work oneself to death; (*sports*) to crock up.

claquette, *f.* = clapette.

clarinette, *f.* **1.** rifle. **2.** jemmy. **3.** becqueter (*or* bouffer) des clarinettes = bouffer des briques.

classe, *f.* (*mil.*) age-group; être de la c., to be due for demob(ilization); vive la c.! (*mil. and fig.*) it won't be long now (before we're out of it)!

class(e), *adv.* enough; en avoir c. (et reclass(e)) = en avoir assez; c'est c.! that'll do! attends que ça soit c.! wait till it's over!

classique, *adj.* le coup c., the same old trick, the usual stunt.

claveter, se = claquer, se.

clavier, *m.* set of false teeth*.

clébard, *m.* = cleb(s) 1.

cléber, to eat.

clèb(s), clèps, *m.* 1. dog*. 2. corporal, lance-jack.

clef, clé, *f.* 1. mettre la c. sous la porte (*or* sous le paillasson), to do a moonlight flit(ting), to shoot the moon, to skip, to abscond. 2. prendre la c. des champs, to decamp*. 3. ... à la c., ... into the bargain, ... with something tacked on to it. 4. nager comme une c., to swim like a brick. 5. essayer la c. dans le portail, to rape.

cliche, *f.* diarrhoea*, colic.

clicli, *m.* clitoris.

client, *m.* fellow*; un sale c., an ugly customer; un drôle de c., a queer chap, a queer customer.

clignotants, *m.pl.* eyes*; baver des c., to weep.

clille, *m.* customer (of prostitute).

clinoche, *f.* clinic, nursing-home.

clique, *f.* (*pej.*) gang, crowd, crew, 'shower'.

cliques, *f.pl.* prendre ses c. et ses claques, to clear out (*or* off) (with bag and baggage), to pack up bag and baggage, to pack up and clear out, to pick up one's sticks and cut.

cliquettes, *f.pl.* ears*.

clochard, *m.* tramp, bum, hobo, down-and-outer.

cloche, *f.* 1. poor wretch, clot; (*sometimes used more or less affectionately— e.g.*) quelle c.! poor devil! sacrée c.! you poor dope! vieille c.! poor old chap! 2. = clochard; être de la c., (*a*) to be a tramp; (*b*) to have nowhere to sleep. 3. *adj.* ce que tu es c.! what a dope (*or* a poor mutt) you are!

4. déménager à la c. (de bois) = mettre la clef sous la porte. 5. qui n'entend qu'une c. n'entend qu'un son, there are two sides to every question, one should hear both sides of a question; un (tout) autre son de c., a (quite) different account (*or* version). 6. sonner les cloches à qn, to reprimand* s.o. severely; se faire sonner (les cloches), to get severely reprimanded*. 7. se (bien) taper la c., to eat* heartily.

clocher. 1. to go wrong; qu'est-ce qui cloche? what's the trouble? il y a quelque chose qui cloche, there's something wrong (*or* amiss), there's a hitch somewhere, there's something not quite right. 2. to hear.

clodo, clodomir, *m.* = clochard.

clop(e), *m.* cigarette-end*; ramasseur (*or* piqueur) de clop(e)s, man who picks up cigarette-ends.

clopinettes, *f.pl.* des c., nothing, damn all; des c.! nothing doing! no sale!

cloporte, *m.* concierge.

cloque, *f.* 1. hour. 2. fart. 3. être en c., to be pregnant*; mettre en c., to make pregnant*.

cloquer. 1. to put, to bung, to land, to give, to hand over. 2. to fart.

cloquer, se. 1. to plank oneself, to take up one's stand. 2. se c. un godet, to knock back a drink.

clos, *adj.* maison close, brothel*.

clou, *m.* 1. chief attraction, star-turn, climax, high spot, highlight, sensation. 2. pawnshop, uncle's; mettre au c., to pawn*. 3. boil (carbuncle). 4. old, worn-out machine *or* instrument; un vieux c., an old crock (*car, bicycle, etc.*). 5. (*mil.*) prison*; ficher qn au c., to run s.o. in. 6. jemmy; *pl.* burglar's tools. 7. des clous! *or* des clous et du vent! not bloody likely! no blooming fear! you be blowed! not for me! not for Joe! don't you wish you may get it! nothing doing! nuts (to you)! the answer's a lemon! 8. bouffer des clous = bouffer des briques. 9. maigre comme un c. (*or* comme un cent de clous), as thin as a lath (or as a rake), all skin and bone. 10. poser ses clous, to down tools, to go on strike. 11. pour des clous, for nothing at all, for sweet Fanny Adams. 12. river son c. à qn, to silence* s.o.; ça lui a rivé son c., that was a clincher for him. 13. ne pas (en) ficher un c., not to do a stroke (of work), not to do a hand's turn, to do damn all. 14. traverser dans les clous, to cross at a pedestrian crossing (un passage clouté). 15. ne pas valoir un c., to be worthless*. 16. arriver sur le c., to be dead on time. 17. c. de cercueil, small cigar.

clouant, adj. amazing, staggering, stunning.

clouer, to silence* (s.o.). See also bec 4.

coaltar, m. cheap red wine; être dans le c., to be in a mess.

cocard, m. = coquard.

cocarde, f. avoir sa c., to be drunk*.

cocarder, se, to get drunk*.

coche, m. manquer (or rater) le c., to miss one's chance, to miss the boat (or the bus).

cochon, m. 1. (of person) rotter*; lewd person, dirty pig, dirty beast. 2. adroit comme un c. de sa queue, clumsy-fisted, fingers all thumbs. 3. amis (or copains) comme cochons, as thick as thieves, to be buddy buddy. 4. bouffer de la tête de c., to be butted in the stomach. 5. (et) c. qui s'en dédit, (and) to the devil with him who says otherwise. 6. c. de payant, (a) the income-tax payer; (b) the poor mug (or sucker or mutt) (who pays for his seat at the theatre, etc., as opposed to those who have free tickets, who travel free, have expense accounts, etc.). 7. jouer un tour de c. à qn, to play s.o. a dirty (or lousy) trick. 8. jouer un pied de c. à qn, to leave s.o. in the lurch. 9. nous n'avons pas gardé les cochons ensemble! or est-ce que nous avons gardé les cochons ensemble? don't be so familiar! je n'ai pas gardé les cochons avec lui! he's no right to be so familiar with me! 10. plein comme un c., dead drunk*. 11. quel c. de temps! = quel chien de temps! (chien 8). 12. adj. dirty, disgusting, filthy, swinish; lustful; (of joke or story) smutty, hot, obscene, blue. 13. ce n'est pas c., it's first-rate*.

cochonnaille(s), f. (pl.) pork butcher's cooked meats.

cochonceté, f. smutty joke.

cochonner, to bungle*.

cochonnerie, f. filth; rubbish, trash; dirty trick; vile food; (of talk or action) smut, dirt, obscenity.

cocktail, m. speed ball (drugs*).

coco, m. 1. (child's vocabulary) (a) = cocotte 1; (b) egg; (c) pl. shoes. 2. head*; avoir le c. fêlé (or détraqué), to be mad*. 3. stomach*. 4. throat, gullet; dévisser le c. à qn, to strangle s.o. 5. (mil.) horse. 6. liquorice water; c. en poudre, sherbet. 7. fellow*; un drôle de c., a queer* person; un vilain (or un sale) c., a bad 'un, a sweep, a rotter*; un joli (or un beau) c., (pej. and iron.), a nice 'un (i.e. a dirty dog). 8. mon c., my darling*. 9. adj. old-fashioned.

coco, f. cocaine, coke, snow (drugs*).

coco-bel-œil, m. (of person) conceited puppy, coxcomb.

cocodès, m. dandy, masher.

cocotier, m. 1. gagner le c., to win the big prize, to hit the jackpot. 2. il descend de son c., he is a bit of a fool*. 3. buttocks*.

cocotte, f. 1. (child's word) hen, chicken, chuck-chuck, chucky, (chicka)biddy. 2. paper (folded in the shape of a) hen. 3. gee-gee. 4. tart, floozie (floosie, floozy). 5. ma (petite) c., my darling*.

cocot(t)er, to stink*.

cocu, m. 1. cuckold. 2. avoir une veine (or une chance) de c., to have the devil's own luck; c.! you lucky devil! 3. et bien c. qui s'en dédit = et cochon qui s'en dédit (cochon 5).

cocufier, to cuckold, to two-time (one's husband).

cœur, *m*. **1. avoir du c. au ventre**, to be game, to have plenty of guts (*or* plenty of spunk); **donner du c. au ventre à qn**, to put some stomach into s.o.; **remettre du c. au ventre à qn**, to put fresh spunk into s.o., to buck s.o. up. **2. avoir un c. d'artichaut** (*une feuille pour tout le monde*), to be a flirt, to be a fickle lover. **3. dîner** (*or* **déjeuner**) **par c.**, to go without food. **4. un joli(-)c.**, an effeminate man, a sissy; **faire le joli(-)c.**, to put on airs and graces. **5. mettre c. sur carreau**, to vomit*. **6. si le c. vous en dit**, if you feel like it, if it appeals to you.

coffio(t), *m*. safe, peter.

coffioteur, *m*. safe-breaker, peterman.

coffre, *m*. **1.** chest, lungs, wind; constitution; **avoir bon c.**, to be sound in wind and limb. **2.** motor-car*. **3.** prison*.

coffrer. 1. to arrest*. **2.** to imprison*; **se faire c.**, to get run in.

cognard, cogne, *m*. policeman*.

cogner. 1. to strike, to hit, to knock (s.o.) about; **la Maison Cogne-dur**, the police; **se faire c. par la police**, to get beaten up by the police. **2.** to stink*. **3. se c. qch.**, to treat (*or* to help) oneself to sth. **4. se c. de qch.**, to do without sth.

cogner, se. 1. to come to blows, to have a fight (*or* a scrap *or* a punch-up). **2.** to have coition*.

cogner, s'en, not to care a rap*.

cognerie, *f*. police-station.

cogneur, *m*. hard hitter, bruiser, slogger.

cognon, *m*. fight, scrap, punch-up.

coiffé, *adj*. **1. être né c.**, to be born lucky (*or* under a lucky star *or* with a silver spoon in one's mouth). **2. être c. de**, to be infatuated* with.

coiffer. 1. to cuckold, to two-time (one's husband). **2.** (*in a race*) to beat, to defeat, to pip.

coiffer, se : se c. de=être coiffé de.

coiffeur, *m*. **le Grand C.**, executioner.

coin, *m*. **1. en boucher un c. à qn**, to dumbfound s.o.; **ça vous en bouche un c.!** that's a clincher (*or* a choker *or* a corker) for you! that licks you hollow! that knocks you! that makes you sit up! **2. la connaître dans les coins**, to be very wide-awake*. **3. le petit c.**, the W.C.*; **aller au petit c.**, to go to the loo; **montrer le petit c. à qn**, to show s.o. the geography of the house. **4. blague dans le c.!** See **blague 1.**

coincé, *adj*. cornered, up a gum-tree, bunkered, stymied.

coincer, to arrest*.

coinceteau, coinsteau, coinsto(t), *m*. (little) corner; quarter, district, 'manor'; **dans le c.**, in these parts.

coincoin, *m*. =**palmé**, holder of the *palmes académiques*.

coing, *m*. **beurré comme un c.**, dead drunk*.

col, *m*. **1. c. bleu**, sailor*. **2. faux c.**, head (of froth on glass of beer). **3. c. à manger de la tarte**, old-fashioned stand-up collar. **4. se pousser** (*or* **se hausser**) **du** (*or* **le**) **c.**, to swank*.

colbac, colbaque, *m*. neck.

colbasse, *f*. room.

colère, *f*. **une c. bleue**, a towering (*or* tearing *or* white) rage, a raging temper; **piquer** (*or* **se mettre dans**) **une c. bleue**, to flare up.

coletin, *m*. =**coltin.**

colibard, *m*. (*prison slang*) (food-) parcel.

colibri, *m*. a bad friend, a rat.

colignon, *m*. =**collignon.**

colique, *f*. **1.** (*of person*) bore*. **2. avoir la c.**, to be afraid*. **3. avoir des coliques cornues=bander.**

colis, *m*. **1.** clumsy (*or* incompetent) person, duffer, dolt. **2.** prisoner. **3.** prostitute (sent by a *placier* to a brothel-keeper).

collabo, *m*. (*W.W.II*) collaborator.

collage, *m*. cohabitation, unmarried couple 'living in sin'; **avoir un c.**, to live with a lover or mistress.

collant, *m*. thief.

collant, *adj.* **ce qu'il est c.!** what a tenacious bore* he is!

collante, *f.* (*sch.*) notification by letter of date and place of an examination.

colle, *f.* **1.** poser (*difficult question*); **pousser** (*or* **poser**) **des colles à qn**, to quiz s.o., to stump s.o. **2.** (*sch.*) detention, keeping-in; **ficher une c. à qn**, to keep s.o. in; **attraper une c.**, to be kept in. **3.** (*of person*) tenacious bore*. **4. faites chauffer la c.!** (*joc. c.p. to s.o. who has broken sth.*) that's right (*or* go on), break up the happy home! **5. ménage** (*or* **mariage**) **à la c.** = collage. **6. c'est de la c.!** it's all bunkum! **7. chier dans la c.** = charrier dans les bégonias. **8.** (*sch.*) prep. test.

collé, *adj.* **1.** ploughed (at an examination). **2.** completely baffled, stumped, gravelled, floored. **3.** (*sch.*) in detention, kept in. **4. être c. avec** = se coller avec.

coller. **1.** to give, to land (a blow, etc.); to put, to place, to stick, to shove, to plank, to bung (sth. somewhere); to palm off (*or* to foist) (sth. on s.o.). **2. se c. qch.**, to treat oneself to sth. **3.** (*sch.*) to give detention to, to keep in. **4.** to puzzle, to stump, to floor. **5.** to fail* (s.o. at an examination); **se faire c.**, to fail* (at an examination). **6. ça colle!** agreed! O.K.! right-o! that's the ticket! **ça colle?** how goes it? how's tricks? **ça ne colle pas**, there's something wrong, it doesn't come right! it doesn't work out; **ça ne colle pas avec lui**, I can't get on (*or* hit it off) with him, I can't cotton on to him, we don't click. **7.** (*of person*) to stick like a leech. **8.** to have coition*. **9.** (*cycling, motoring*) to follow closely.

coller, se. 1. se c. avec, to cohabit with, to set up house with, to shack up with. **2. s'y c.**, to pitch in.

colletar = **coaltar**.

colleter, se = **se coltiner**.

colletin, *m.* = **coltin**.

colleur, *m.* (*sch.*) examiner.

collier, *m.* **1. donner un coup de c.**, to put one's back into it, to put on a spurt, to get down to it, to pull one's weight. **2. reprendre le c.** (**de misère** *or* **du travail**), to resume work, to get back into harness, to get back to drudgery. **3. c. de corail**, piles, hemorrhoids.

collignon, *m.* cab-driver, cabby, cabbie.

colloquer = **coller 1**.

colombin, *m.* **1.** turd; **poser un c.**, to defecate*; **être de c.**, (*mil.*) to be on latrine fatigue. **2. avoir les colombins** = **avoir les foies**. **3. des colombins!** = **des clous!** (**clou 7**).

colon, *m.* **1.** colonel. **2. eh bien, mon c.!** well, old cock! **mon pauvre c.!** poor old chap!

colonel, *m.* ten franc banknote.

colonne, *f.* **1. ne pas avoir chié la c.** (**Vendôme**), not to have set the Thames on fire; **il croit qu'il a chié la c.** (**Vendôme**), he thinks he's absolutely it, he thinks he's the cat's pyjamas (*or* the cat's whiskers). **2. se taper** (**sur**) **la c.**, to masturbate*.

coloquinte, *f.* head*; **ça lui a tapé sur la c.**, it drove him barmy.

coltin, *m.* work, graft (*Australian sl.*).

coltiner, to lug (about).

coltiner, se 1. to fight, to (have a) scrap, to come to blows, to have a punch-up (*or* a bundle) (with s.o.). **2.** = **s'allonger 2(b)**.

coma, *m.* **être dans le c.**, to be dead drunk*.

comac, comaco, comaque, *adj.* **1.** very big, huge, whopping. **2.** hefty, broad-shouldered, beefy.

combinaise, *f.* = **combine**.

combinard, *m.* racketeer, grafter, spiv, wide boy, smart guy.

combine, *f.* **1.** racket, shady scheme, fiddle, fiddling, trick, knack; **connaître les combines**, to be wide-awake*; **jouer une c. sûre**, to be on a sure thing, to be on velvet; **des combines arabes** = **un fourbi arabe**; **une c. à la gomme**, one of your fancy tricks, a hopeless fiddle. 2. woman's slip (*i.e. combinaison*).

combiner, to arrange, to cook up; **ça ne se combine pas bien,** it does not look good.

comble, *m.* ça, c'est le (*or* un) c.! that's the limit!*

comédie, *f.* 1. c'est une vraie c., it's as good as a play. 2. faire une (*or* la) c., faire une de ces comédies, to make a scene, to kick up a shindy. 3. jouer la c., to sham, to play-act, to put on an act. 4. être à la c., to be out of work; envoyer à la c., to stand (a workman) off.

comète, *f.* refiler la c., to sleep in the open. *See also* vin.

comm', *f.* =commission.

commande, *f.* 1. police protection. 2. (*of thieves, etc.*) job. 3. une drôle de c., a queer business, a queer affair. 4. connaître la c., to be in the know. 5. louper la c.=manquer le coche.

comme, *adv.* 1. c. ci, c. ça, (fair to) middling, so-so. 2. c'est tout c., it comes to (much) the same thing; it's as good as done. 3. c'est c. fait! it's all but done. 4. et c. ça ..., alors c. ça ..., and so ..., and then ...

comment, *adv.* 1. et c.! and how! not half! you bet! rather! you said it! 2. (mais) c. donc! by all means! to be sure! (why, yes) of course! only too pleased (to oblige)!

commission, *f.* 1. faire une (*or* sa) petite c., to urinate*. 2. faire une (*or* sa) grosse c., to defecate*.

commode, *adj.* il n'est pas c., he's an awkward customer, he's pig-headed (*or* bloody-minded), he's a hard nut to crack; il n'est pas c. à vivre, he's not easy to live with (*or* to get along with *or* to get on with).

commode, *f.* faire la c., to be a furniture remover; se taper la c., to do one's own furniture removing.

compas, *m.* 1. avoir le c. dans l'œil, to have a good (*or* an accurate) eye (for measurements or distances). 2. al-

longer le (*or* son) c., to step out. 3. *pl.* legs*; jouer des c., to decamp*.

compère, *m.* (=c.-*loriot*) un c. à l'œil, a stye.

compisser, to piss on.

complet, *adj.* ça, c'est c. alors! well, that's the limit!*

compliment, *m.* rengainer son c., to keep back what one was going to say, to say no more about it, to drop the matter.

compo, *f.* (*sch.*) composition, essay; test paper, revision test.

compote, *f.* 1. mettre en c.=mettre en capilotade. 2. être tout en c., to feel like nothing on earth. 3. avoir la tête en c., to have a splitting headache.

compotier, *m.* head*.

comprendre. 1. je comprends (, oui)! I should jolly well think so! yes, sure enough! rather! 2. je me comprends, I know what I'm talking about. 3. je le comprends! I don't blame him!

comprenette, *f.* avoir la c. dure (*or* difficile *or* lente), ne pas avoir la c. facile (*or* vive), to be slow (*or* not to be quick) on the uptake.

comprenoire, *f.* =comprenette.

compte, *m.* 1. avoir son c., (*a*) to be done for, to have 'had' it; (*b*) to get what was coming to one; (*c*) to have had enough; (*d*) to be dead drunk*. 2. en avoir son c., to get hauled over the coals. 3. un c. d'apothicaire, an exorbitant bill. 4. (*boxing*) aller à terre (*or* être étendu) pour le c., to be counted (*or* knocked) out, to be (*or* to be put) out for the count. 5. être laissée pour c., (*of woman*) to be left on the shelf. 6. rendre des comptes, to vomit*.

comptée, *f.* earnings (of prostitute).

compte-gouttes, *m.* 1. au c.-g., in driblets. 2. fabriqué au c.-g., (*of person*) =aztèque.

compteur, *m.* relever le c., (*of pimp*) to collect a prostitute's earnings; (*of racketeer*) to collect one's dues.

con, *m.* 1. vagina*. 2. (*of person*) silly bastard, silly bugger, silly clot(-face), silly cunt; **espèce de c.! tête de c.!** you silly sod! you silly bugger! you bloody fool! **faire le c., jouer au c.**, (*a*) to play the bloody fool, to arse about; (*b*) to pretend to be crazy; ... **à la c.**, bloody silly ..., damn silly ..., cock-eyed ... **3.** *adj.* **être c. comme la lune** (*or* **comme un balai** *or* **comme un brêl(e)**), to be a bloody fool, to be an absolute twerp; **elle est rien c., ton histoire!** your story is all balls! **c'est trop c.!** it's too bloody silly! **c'est drôlement c.!** it's a lot of crap! **pas c.!** a bloody good idea!

con(n)ard, *m.*, *adj.* =con 2. *and* 3.

conasse, *f.* =connasse.

concal, *m.* examination, exam.

concepige, *m.f.* concierge.

conchiage, *m.* excrement, shit, crap, turd.

conchier, to shit (*or* to crap) on.

condé, *m.* **1.** plain clothes detective. **2.** police permit or protection; **avoir le** (*or* **du**) **c.**, to be authorized to carry on a more or less illicit activity. **3.** scheme (for making easy money with minimum risk), fiddle. **4.** favour, kindness.

condisse, *f.* condition; circumstance.

conduite, *f.* **1.** (**s'**)**acheter une c.**, to turn over a new leaf, to settle down (after a fast life), to (a)mend one's ways. **2.** **faire à qn une c. de Grenoble**, to run s.o. out of town, to give s.o. a rough handling.

confiture, *f.* **1.** flattery*. **2.** **de la c. aux chiens**, caviar for the general. **3.** **chier dans la c.**, to exaggerate*. **4.** opium.

conjungo, *m.* marriage, married life, holy wedlock.

connaissance, *f.* boy (*or* girl) friend.

connaître. 1. la c. =**la c. dans les coins** (coin 2). **2. ça me connaît!** I know all about that! you can't teach me anything about that! I'm an old hand (*or* a dab) at that! that's just my line! **3. je ne connais que lui!** don't I (just) know him! **je ne connais que ça!** I

know that (only too) well! **4. il s'y connaît**, he's wide-awake*.

connasse, *f.* **1.** (*pej.*) woman*. **2.** prostitute*. **3.** =con 1 *and* 2.

conne, *f.* prostitute*; *adj.*, *f.* =con 3.

conneau, *m.* =con 2.

connement, *adv.* like a bloody fool.

connerie, *f.* (*of action or speech*) bloody nonsense, boloney, balls, crap; **dire des conneries** =déconner.

con(n)obler, con(n)obrer. to know.

connu! *p.p.* =**ça me connaît!** (**connaître** 2).

conscience, *f.* (*jest.*) **ça m'est resté sur la c.**, it's lying on my stomach (*said after a hearty meal*).

conscrard, *m.* (*slang of the École polytechnique*) conscript.

conscrit, *m.* (*slang of the École normale supérieure*) first-year student.

conséquent, *adj.* big, important.

consigne, *f.* **avaler** (*or* **manger**) **la c.**, to forget one's orders *or* instructions, to disregard orders.

consolation, *f.* brandy.

consomme, *f.* drink (in a café, etc.); **faire les consommes**, to play at cards, etc., to decide who pays for the drinks.

conspuer: conspuez X! down with X!

constipé, *adj.* **1.** miserly*. **2.** uneasy, ramroddy, stuffed-shirt.

contact, *m.* connection for drugs.

content, *m.* **avoir son petit c.**, to have coition*.

continuation, *f.* **bonne c.!** I hope things will continue to go well with you! all the best!

contrebande, *f.* =contredanse.

contrecarre, *f.* **1. faire une c. à qn**, to put obstacles in the way of s.o., to thwart s.o. **2.** rivalry.

contrecoup, *m.* foreman, boss, gaffer.

contredanse, *f.* summons, police ticket; **flanquer une c. à qn**, to take s.o.'s name and address, to book s.o.

contreficher, se, (*strong form of* **se ficher**): **je m'en fiche et je m'en contrefiche!** I don't care a damn! (*an even stronger form is* **je m'en fous et je m'en contrefous!**).

contremarque, *f.* une c. pour **Bagneux** ou **Pantin**, a doctor's prescription. (*A 'contremarque' is a pass-out ticket (at a theatre); there are cemeteries at Bagneux and Pantin, near Paris*).

contremouche, *f.* smuggling.

contrer, to thwart, to cross (s.o.).

convalo, *f.* convalescence, sick-leave.

converse, *f.* conversation, chatter.

convoi, *m.* être du même c., to be in the same boat (*fig.*).

convoque, *f.* summons.

coopé, *f.* =copé.

cop, *m.* =copain.

copaille, *f.* despicable person, good-for-nothing.

copain, *m.* friend*; être bons copains, to be pally (*or* chummy).

copé, *f.* la c., the Co-operative Society, the co-op.

copeaux, *m.pl.* avoir les c., (*a*) to have little or nothing; des c., nothing at all, damn all; (*b*) to be afraid*; **foutre les c. à qn**, to put the wind up s.o.

copie, *f.* pisser de la c., to write an article.

copier. 1. celle-là, tu me la copieras! you'll not catch me out again! I'll know better next time! I'll pay you back for that! **2.** je la ferai c., celle-là, well, I like that! that's a good one, that is!

copine, *f.* girl chum.

copiner, to chum up, to pal up.

copinerie, *f.* the gang.

copurchic, *adj.* ultra-smart.

coquard, *m.* black eye*.

coque, *f.* à la c., tip-top, first-rate*.

coquelicot, *m.* **1.** =coquard. **2.** elle a ses coquelicots=elle a ses affaires.

coqueluche, *f.* idol, great favourite, darling*.

coquer, to give.

coquetier, *m.* gagner le c.=gagner le cocotier.

coquetterie, *f.* **1.** être en c. avec, to have fallen out with, not to be on good terms with. **2.** avoir une c. dans l'œil, to squint.

coqueur, *m.* informer*.

coquillard, *m.* eye*; s'en battre (*or* s'en tamponner) le c.=s'en battre l'œil (œil 7).

coquille, *f.* **1.** prison*. **2.** virginity, cherry.

coquin, *m.* **1.** (*jest.*) (*a*) husband; (*b*) fancy man. **2.** c. de sort! *int.* (*used in the Midi*) hang it! blow it! by Jove!

coquinas, *adj.* être c., to be a rascal, a scamp.

cor, *m.* **1.** a he-man. **2.** emmaillotté dans un c. de chasse, bandy-legged.

corbaque, *m.* crow, raven.

corbeau, *m.* **1.** priest, clergyman. **2.** anonymous letter writer, poison pen.

corbi, *m.* hearse.

corbillard, *m.* monter dans le c., to die*, to step into one's last bus.

corde, *f.* **1.** être à la c., (*a*) to be at the end of one's tether; (*b*) to be penniless*. **2.** être sur la c. raide, to be out on a limb. **3.** sauter à la c.=se mettre la ceinture. **4.** se mettre la c. au cou, to get married*. **5.** se mettre la c. pour . . ., to give up all hope of . . . **6.** il pleut (*or* il tombe) des cordes, it's raining cats and dogs, it's coming down in bucketfuls. **7.** ça n'est pas (*or* ça ne rentre pas) dans mes cordes, that's not (in) my line, that's not up my street; c'est tout à fait dans mes cordes, that just suits* me. **8.** (*motor.*) prendre un virage (*or* un tournant) à la c., to cut a corner close.

corder. 1. to die*. **2.** c. avec qn, to hit it off with s.o., to get on swimmingly with s.o.

cormoran, *m.* Jew.

cornac, *m.* a guide.

cornanche, *f.* marked (playing-) card.

cornancher. 1. to cheat at cards, to play with marked cards. **2.** to kill*. **3.** to stink*.

cornaquer, to shepherd (tourists).

cornard, *m.* cuckold.

corne, *f.* **1.** faire les cornes à, to jeer (*or* to mock) at. **2.** porter des cornes, to be a cuckold, to wear horns; faire pousser (*or* faire porter) des cornes à qn, to cuckold s.o.

corner. 1. **les oreilles ont dû lui c.**, his ears must have been burning. 2. to stink*.

cornet, *m.* throat, gullet; stomach*; **se rincer le c.**, to have a good swig; **se coller** (*or* **s'enfiler**) **qch. dans le c.**, **se remplir le c.**, to have a good tuck-in.

cornette, *f.* (female) cuckold.

corniaud, *m., adj.* 1. =**con** 2. 2. =**cornichon** 1.

corniche, *f.* 1. class preparing for Saint-Cyr military school. 2. top-hat.

corniches, *m.pl.* first-year students at Saint-Cyr.

cornichon, *m.* 1. fool*. 2. telephone. 3. student preparing for Saint-Cyr. 4. penis*.

Cornouaille, *f.* **aller en C.** =**porter des cornes.**

corps, *m.* 1. **un drôle de c.**, a queer*, odd, person. 2. **aller au c.**, to go to stool.

correct, *adj.* quite good; decent.

correctance, *f.* **maison de c.**, reformatory, (*approx.*) Borstal (institution).

corrida, *f.* violent free fight, free-for-all (fight).

corridor, *m.* **refiler** (*or* **trouilloter**) **du c.**, to have a foul breath.

corser: c. une note, to charge extortionately, to stick it on (the bill).

corser, se: ça (*or* **l'affaire**) **se corse**, things are getting serious, the plot thickens.

Corsic(o), *m.* Corsican.

corsif, *m.* corset.

cortausse, *f.* severe thrashing*.

corvée, *f.* irksome task, drudgery; **quelle c.!** what a fag (*or* a bind *or* a sweat)!

cossard, *m.* lazybones, sluggard, slacker, slug-abed, lazy bum; *adj.* lazy; sluggish.

cosse, *f.* **avoir la c.**, to feel (*or* to be) lazy; **tirer sa c.** =**tirer sa flemme.**

cossu, *adj.* rich*.

costar(d), *m.* costume, suit, dress, rigout, jacket, coat.

costaud, costeau, costo (*f.* **cos-**

taude, costote), *adj.* (*of persons*) (*a*) hefty*; (*b*) clever; (*of things*) difficult, tough. *m.* hefty person, tough guy, muscle-man; **ne pas se sentir c.**, not to feel so good, to feel a bit out of sorts.

costume, *m.* 1. **dans le** (*or* **en**) **c. d'Adam**, stark naked*. 2. **se faire faire un c. de bois**, to die*.

cote, *f.* 1. reputation; **avoir une grosse c.**, to be highly thought of; **faire monter la c. de qn**, to send up s.o.'s stock. 2. favouritism; **avoir la c.** (**d'amour**), **avoir la** (*or* **une**) **bonne c.**, **avoir une drôle de c.**, to be in great favour, to be persona grata.

côte, *f.* (i) (*lit.* ='rib') 1. **avoir les côtes en long**, to be lazy*. 2. **se tenir les côtes (de rire)**, to laugh* uproariously. 3. **se caler les côtes**, to eat* heartily. 4. **chatouiller** (*or* **tanner**) **les côtes à qn**, to give s.o. a good thrashing*.

côte, *f.* (ii) (*lit.* ='hill-slope') **arracher les côtes**, (*cycle racing*) to keep speed up-hill.

côte, *f.* (iii) (*lit.* ='coast') **être à la c.**, to be penniless*.

côté, *m.* **n'avoir rien du c. gauche**, to be heartless.

cotelard, *adj.* =**cottard.**

côtelette, *f.* 1. **pisser sa** (*or* **une**) **c.**, to give birth to a baby, 'to piss bones'. 2. **sauver ses côtelettes**, to save one's skin. 3. *pl.* side-whiskers, side-boards, side-burns, burnsides, mutton-chops. 4. *pl.* ribs (*human body*).

coton, *m.* 1. trouble, difficulty, danger; **il y a eu du c.**, it wasn't an easy job, it wasn't all plain sailing; **avoir un sacré c. pour . . .**, to have a devil of a job to . . . 2. fog, mist, (*aviation*) clouds. 3. **élevé dans le** (*or* **dans du**) **c.**, brought up in cotton-wool, molly-coddled. 4. **filer un mauvais** (*or* **un sale** *or* **un vilain**) **c.**, to be in a very bad way, to be going downhill, to be going to the bad. *See also* **jambe.** 5. *adj.* **c'est c.!** it's a tough job!

cottard, *adj.* 1. hefty, 2. (*of things*) difficult, tough.

cotte, *f.* trousers.

cou, *m.* se monter le c. = se monter la tête.

couac, *m.* et puis c.! and then he (etc.) snuffed it! *cf.* couic.

couchage, *m.* = coucherie.

couche, *f.* 1. en avoir une c., en tenir une c. (*i.e.* de bêtise), to be an absolute fool, to be hopelessly dumb, to be as stupid (*or* as thick) as they make 'em, to be wood from the neck up; quelle c.! what a chump! 2. une fausse c., a misbegotten person, an abortion. 3. faire une fausse c., to have a wet dream.

couché!, *p.p.* (*to dog*) down!

couché, coucher, *m.* avoir (*or* faire) un c., (*of prostitutes*) to have an all-night client, an all-nighter.

coucher, 1. c. avec une femme, to have sexual intercourse (*or* to go to bed *or* to go case) with a woman, to case a woman. 2. c. dessus, to be miserly*.

coucher, se: envoyer c. qn, to send s.o. packing*; va te c.! go to blazes!

coucherie, *f.* sexual intercourse.

coucheur, *m.* un mauvais c., a cantankerous (*or* bloody-minded) fellow, an awkward customer.

couci-couça, *adv.* = comme ci comme ça.

coucou, *m.* 1. aeroplane, kite, crate, 'bus'. 2. (*jest. for* cocu) cuckold. 3. (*nav.*) chronometer.

coude, *m.* 1. avoir mal au c. = avoir la cosse. 2. huile de c., elbow-grease. 3. 'lâche-moi le c.! don't bother me! 4. lever (*or* hausser *or* plier) le c., to tipple*; to lift one's elbow. 5. ne pas se moucher du c. = ne pas se moucher du pied. *See also* doigt 8.

couenne, *f.* 1. skin; gratter la c. à qn, to shave s.o.; se faire racler (*or* se peler) la c., to have a shave. 2. fool* 3. *adj.* stupid; ce qu'il est c.! what a blinking idiot he is!

couic, *m.* 1. faire c., to die*; il n'a pas fait c., he just popped off, he never cheeped: *cf.* couac. 2. n'y comprendre

que c. = n'y entraver que pouic. 3. *int.* look sharp!

couille, *f.* 1. testicle*. 2. c'est de la c. (*or* des couilles) (en barre), it's all balls; une c. molle, a milksop; avoir des couilles au cul, to have guts (*or* spunk); en avoir plein les couilles = en avoir plein le dos; casser les couilles à qn. = casser les pieds à qn; tomber (*or* partir) en c., to go to pot, to flag; ça, c'est c.! that's a bugger (*or* a bastard)!

couillon, *m., adj.* 1. = con 2 *and* 3; faire le c. = faire le con; être c. comme la lune = être con comme la lune; être c. comme devant, to be as big a twerp as ever; et c. qui s'en dédit! = et cochon qui s'en dédit! 2. coward, funk.

couillonnade, couillonnerie, *f.* = connerie; faire une couillonnade, to make a balls of it; dire des couillonnades = déconner.

couillonner. 1. to make a fool of s.o., to take s.o. in, to make a sucker of (s.o.); to make a balls of (sth.), to balls-up (sth.); être couillonné, se laisser c., to have been a sucker, to have been 'had', to be buggered. 2. to muck about, to arse around.

couiner. 1. to weep*, to whine. 2. to manipulate a radio-set.

coulage, *m.* waste, leakage, pilfering.

coulant, *m.* milk.

coulante, *f.* 1. colic, diarrhoea*. 2. blennorrhoea, gonorrhoea, clap.

coule, *f.* être à la c., (*a*) to be wide-awake*; (*b*) to be easy-going; mettre qn à la c., to show s.o. the ropes, to wise s.o. up; se mettre à la c. (de), to get wise (to), to get hep (to), to get with it.

coulé, *p.p.* done* for.

couler, to ruin, to discredit, to do for, to dish; se c., to do for oneself, to dish oneself; se la c. douce (*or* bonne), to take it easy*.

couleur, *f.* 1. lie*, fib. 2. affranchir (*or* annoncer) la c., (*a*) to show one's hand; (*b*) to name one's poison (*i.e.* one's *choice of drink*); faut pas changer de c., don't mix your drinks. **3. affranchir** (*or* **éclairer**) **qn sur la c.,** to inform s.o., to put s.o. in the know, to put s.o. wise, to keep s.o. posted. **4. défendre ses couleurs,** to defend one's interests, to stand up for oneself, to know how to look after oneself. **5. en dire de toutes les couleurs à qn,** to give s.o. the rough side of one's tongue, to slang s.o. right and left. **6. en voir de toutes les couleurs,** to have a rough time of it; **en faire voir de toutes les couleurs à qn,** to lead s.o. a pretty dance; **en avoir vu de toutes les couleurs,** to have been through the mill, to have had a rough time of it. **7. être à la c.,** to be wide-awake*.

couloir, *m.* **1. c. à** (*or* **aux**) **lentilles,** anus, arse. **2. évacuer le c.,** to vomit.*

coup, *m. N.B. For entries containing a noun additional to* coup (*e.g.* coup de torchon, avoir un coup dans le nez), *see under the other noun.* **1. avoir le c. de faire qch.,** to have the knack of doing sth. **2. boire un c.,** (*a*) to have a drink, to have a wet; (*b*) = **boire une tasse. 3. ça, c'est un sale c.** (**pour la fanfare**), that's a bad job, that's a bit of bad luck, that's a bad show. **4. discuter le c.** (**de gras**) = **discuter le bout** (**de gras**). **5. écraser le c.,** to forget old scores, to let bygones be bygones, to say no more about it. **6. en avoir un c.,** to be insane, to be mad*. **7. être au c.,** to be in the know, to be on the ball; **mettre qn au c.,** to put s.o. wise. **8. être aux cent coups,** to be off one's head with worry, to be worried stiff. **9. être dans le c.,** to be in on the racket, to be involved, to be in on sth.; to know what's going on; **être dans tous les coups,** to be in on everything, to have a finger in every pie. **10. être là pour un c.,** to be on hand (to help s.o.), to stand by (s.o.), to be there when wanted. **11. expliquer le c.,** to explain the situation, to explain how matters stand. **12. faire le c.**—*e.g.* **il a fait le c.,** he's (been and) gone and done it. **13. faire le**

c. à qn, to play a trick on s.o. **14. faire les cent** (*or* **les quatre cents** *or* **les cinq cents** *or* **les cent mille** *or* **les cent dix-neuf**) **coups,** (*a*) to lead a fast life, to have a riotous time, to paint the town red; (*b*) to be capable of anything, to be up to all sorts of tricks (*or* pranks), to run amok; (*c*) to kick up a hell of a row. **15. ne pas en faire** (*or* **ficher** *or* **foutre**) **un c.,** not to do a stroke (of work), to be a lazy dog, to sit on one's behind, to do damn all. **16. en jeter** (*or* **en mettre**) **un c.,** to put a jerk (*or* some vim *or* one's back) into it, to buckle to, to go all out, to wire into it, to get busy. **17. monter un c.,** to do a job; **monter un c. contre qn,** to frame s.o.; **un c. monté,** a frame-up, a put-up job, a carve-up, a plant. **18. monter le c. à qn,** to take s.o. in, to spoof s.o., to humbug s.o. **19. monter sur un c.** = **monter sur un casse. 20. se monter le c.,** to kid oneself. **21. tenir le c.,** to stick it (out), to be able to take it, to keep a stiff upper lip. **22. tenter le c.,** to chance it, to chance one's arm, to have a bash (*or* a whack *or* a shot *or* a shy *or* a stab), to take a crack (at). **23. tirer un** (*or* **son**) **c.,** to have coition*. **24. valoir le c.**—*e.g.* **ça ne vaut pas le c.,** it's not worth while; **ça vaut le c.,** it's worth trying. **25. prendre un c. de vieux,** to start to look old, to put on years.

coupante, *f.* guillotine.

couparès, *adj.* = **coupé,** *adj.*

coup-de-poing, *m.* **c.-de-p. américain,** knuckleduster.

coupe, *f.* **1. avoir la bonne c. pour . . .,** to be cut out for . . . **2. avoir une vilaine** (*or* **sale**) **c.,** to have an ugly jib (*i.e. face*). **3. faire sauter la c.,** (*card-sharper's trick*) to slip the cut.

coupé, *adj.* **être c.** (**à blanc**), to be penniless*.

coupe-choux, *m.* cut-throat (razor).

coupe-cigare, *m.* guillotine.

coupe-lard, *m.* knife.

couper. 1. c. qn, to interrupt s.o., to cut s.o. short. **2. la c. à qn,** to silence s.o. **ça te la coupe!** that's a clincher for you! that stumps you! that stimies you! beat that if you can! **3. c. à qch.,** to avoid (*or* to dodge *or* to shuffle out of) sth., to get away with it, to cut (a class, etc.). **4. ne pas c. dans qch.,** not to be deceived (*or* not to be taken in) by sth., not to fall for sth; **je n'y coupe pas!** I'm not to be taken in by that! **c. dedans,** to fall into the trap.

couper, se, to contradict oneself, to give oneself away.

couperet, *m.* **passer au c.,** to get the axe (*i.e. to be discharged as redundant*).

coupe-tif(f)es, *m.* barber.

Coupolard, *m.* member of the French Academy.

coupure, *f.* **1.** excuse, loop-hole; **trouver une c.,** to produce an alibi, to find a way out. **2. faire la c.,** to make a sudden change of conversation. **3. la c.!**=je n'y coupe pas! (couper 4).

cour, *f.* **la c. est pleine,** that's enough!

courailler, to gad about, to gallivant, to run after women (*or* the girls).

courailleur, *m.* =coureur.

courant, *m.* **1.** leak(age), denunciation. **2. se déguiser** (*or* **se transformer**) **en c. d'air,** to decamp*. **3. tortiller** (*or* **se taper**) **des courants d'air,** to have nothing to eat.

courante, *f.* diarrhoea*.

courette, *f.* =courrette, *f.*

coureur, *m.* gadabout, gallivanter, philanderer; **c. de cotillons** (*or* **de jupes** *or* **de jupons** *or* **de femmes** *or* **de filles**), skirt-hunter, petticoat-chaser, woman-chaser, wolf, fastie, bird-watcher, organ-grinder.

coureuse, *f.* **1.** gadabout, fast girl (*or* woman). **2.** prostitute*.

courgnole, *f.* throat.

courir. 1. to gallivant, to run after women (*or* the girls); **c. les filles,** to chase the girls; **c. la gueuse,** to wench, to go with prostitutes. **2. tu me cours (sur l'haricot)!** you get on my nerves! **3. tu peux (toujours) c.!** there's nothing doing! it's no go! you

won't get it! you can whistle for it! what a hope! you've 'had' it! you've (got) another think coming! not on your Nelly! **4. laisser c.,** to give it up, to let the matter drop.

courrette, *f.* **1.** little journey, little trip. **2.** flight; **être en c.,** to be on the run (from justice), to be on the lam. **3.** pursuit; **faire une c. à qn** to pursue s.o.; **se faire faire la c. par,** to be pursued by.

course, *f.* **1. être dans la c.,** to be in on the game; **2. c. au bifteck,** rat-race.

courser: c. qn, to chase s.o., to run after s.o.

coursette, *f.* **1. faire la c.,** to run about (in vain). **2. piquer une c.,** to break into a run.

court, *adj.* **la faire** (*or* **l'avoir**) **courte et bonne,** to have a short life and a gay one.

court-bouillon, *m.* =bouillon 1.

court-jus, *m.* short circuit, electric breakdown.

courtille, *f.* **1. de la c.,** on the short side. **2. être un peu de la c.,** to be short of cash, to be hard up.

courtines, *f.pl.* (*turf*) races, race-track; **flamber dur aux c.,** to be a heavy backer.

couru, *p.p.* **c'est c. (d'avance),** it's a certainty*.

cousette, *f.* **1.** dressmaker's assistant *or* apprentice. **2.** pocket sewing-outfit, housewife, hussy.

cousin, *m.* **1. ils ne sont pas cousins,** they don't hit it off, they don't get on together; **je ne suis pas son c.,** I don't get on well with him. **2. le roi n'est pas son c.,** he's as proud as a peacock, he's as pleased as Punch, he wouldn't call the king his cousin. **3. recevoir ses cousins**=avoir ses affaires.

cousue, *f.* **une (toute) c.,** a cigarette (*machine-made as opposed to*) **une c.-main,** a hand-made cigarette.

cousu-main, *m.* **c'est du** (*or* **un travail** *or* **un boulot**) **c.-m.,** it's a certainty*.

couteau, *m.* bête à couper au c., as silly as can be.

coûter: pour ce que ça vous coûte! as if it made any difference to you!

couture, *f.* 1. battre à plate(s) couture(s), to beat* (s.o.) hollow. 2. sur toutes les coutures, through and through, from every angle. 3. gêné aux coutures=gêné aux entournures.

couvercle, *m.* fermenter (frissonner, bouillonner) du c.=travailler du chapeau.

couvert, *m.* 1. mettre le c., to prepare for a game of poker. 2. remettre le c., to begin again, to start all over again.

couverte, *f.* 1. blanket; passer (passage) à la c.=passer (passage) à la couverture. 2. tirer (toute) la c. à soi=tirer (toute) la couverture à soi. 3. front (for some illegal activity), blind.

couverture, *f.* 1. passer (passage) à la c., to toss (tossing) in a blanket. 2. tirer (toute) la c. à soi, to grab the lion's share, to look after number one. 3. =couverte 3.

couvrante, *f.* 1. blanket. 2. =couverte 3.

couyonner =couillonner.

coxer, to arrest*.

crabe, *m.* 1. old-timer. 2. old tank (*W.W.II*). 3. crab louse.

crachat, *m.* 1. decoration, medal, ribbon, star. 2. se noyer dans un (*or* dans son) c., to be drowned in a puddle (*or* in a tea-cup), to make a mountain out of a molehill.

craché, *adj.* c'est son père tout c., he's the (dead) spit (*or* the spit and image *or* the spitting image) of his father.

cracher. 1. to pay* up. 2. to confess*, to spit it out; crache-le!=accouche! 3. to drop (s.o.), to give s.o. a lift (in a car). 4. ne pas c. sur qch., not to turn one's nose up at sth., not to sniff at sth.; il ne faut pas c. dessus, it's not to be sneezed at. 5. c. blanc, to be very thirsty, to be parched, not to be able to spit sixpence. *See also* air, bassinet feu, sac, son.

cracheur, *m.* show-off.

crachoir, *m.* tenir le c., to do all the talking, to monopolize the conversation, to spout.

crachouiller, to splutter.

crack, *m.* crack player; crack horse.

cracra, cradeau, cradingue, crado(s), *adj.* dirty, lousy, filthy, crummy.

craindre =être en cavale.

crais! crais! *int.* =acrais!

cramer. 1. to burn (out). 2. to die*.

cramouille, *f.* =chagatte.

crampe, crampette, *f.* 1. tirer sa c., to have coition*. 2. tirer sa crampe avec la Veuve, to be guillotined.

crampon, *m.* tenacious bore*; *adj.* ce qu'il est c.!=ce qu'il est collant!

cramponner, to bore*.

cram(p)ser =clam(p)ser.

cran, *m.* 1. avoir du c., to have plenty of pluck (*or* grit *or* guts), to be plucky. 2. baisser d'un c., to come down a peg. 3. être à c., to be in a very bad temper*; cela le foutait à c., that made him see red. 4. ne pas lâcher qn d'un c., not to leave s.o. for a moment, to dog s.o.'s footsteps. 5. (*mil.*) dix jours de c., ten days C.B. *See also* ceinture.

crâne, *m.* bourrer le c. à qn, to stuff s.o. (up) (with lies *or* empty talk), to gee s.o. up. *See also* bourrage de crâne.

crâner, to swank*; to bluster, to brazen it out.

crâneur, -euse, *m.f.* swanker*; faire le c.=crâner.

crapaud, *m.* 1. child*. 2. purse.

crapautard, *m.* small purse; constipé du c., miserly*.

crap(ette), *f.* dice game.

crapoteux, *adj.* =cracra.

crapouillot, *m.* (*W.W.I*) trench mortar, trench-mortar shell, 'stove-pipe'.

crapoussin, *m.* undersized person, shrimp.

crapser =clam(p)ser.

crapulados, *m.* =crapulos.

crapule, *f.* rotter*; (*collective use*) scum; *adj.* foul, filthy, scoundrelly, treacherous.

crapuleuse, *adj.* **se la faire c.,** to go on the razzle, to paint the town red.

crapulos, *m.* very cheap cigar, stinka-duro.

craquante, *f.* match, lucifer.

craque, *f.* trifling lie, fib, cram, tara-diddle.

craquer. 1. to strike (a match). **2. plein à c.,** (*a*) chock-full; (*b*) rich*, flush. **3. faire c.,** to burgle, to break in.

craquette, *f.* =chagatte.

craqueur, -euse, *m.f.* fibber.

crasp', craspec, craspèque, craspet, craspignol, craspouillard, *adj.* =cracra.

crasse, *f.* **1. faire une c. à qn,** to play a dirty trick on s.o., to do the dirty on s.o. **2.** (*nav.*) thick weather.

crasseux, *adj.* mean, stingy; *m.* **1.** mean (*or* stingy) person. **2.** comb.

cravacher, to speed along.

cravacheuse, *f.* flagellator.

cravate, *f.* **1.** =faux col. **2.** aggression. **3. c'est de la c.!** it's all bluff! **4. c. de chanvre,** (death by) hanging. **5. s'en jeter** (*or* **s'en mettre** *or* **s'en envoyer** *or* **se verser**) **un coup derrière la c.,** to knock back a drink, to sink a drink down one's hatch. **6.** (*wrestling*) neck-hold.

cravater, 1. to arrest*. **2.** to attack. **3.** (*sports*) to collar, to scrag.

cravateur, *m.* **1.** counsel, barrister. **2.** bluffer, boaster.

cravetouse, *f.* tie.

crayon, *m.* credit.

crayons, *m.pl.* **1.** legs*. **2.** hair.

crébleu! *int.* =sacrebleu!

crèche, *f.* **1.** room. **2.** house.

crécher. 1. to live, to dwell, to hang out. **2.** to go to bed*.

crédié! crédieu! cré bon Dieu! *int.* =sacré nom de Dieu!

crédo, *m.* credit.

crémaillère, *f.* **pendre la c.,** to have (*or* to give) a house-warming (party); **une pendaison de c.,** a house-warming (party).

crème, *f.* **1. la c.,** the upper crust, the upper classes, the (whipped-) cream. **2. la c. de . . .,** the pick of . . . **3. c'est**

pas de la c.! it's no easy matter! it's no walk-over! it's not all milk and honey!

crémerie, *f.* **changer de c.,** to make a change (of surroundings, of quarters, of activities, etc.).

crénom! *int.* =sacré nom de Dieu!

crêpage, *m. See* **chignon 4.**

crêpe, *f.* **1. une c.,** a perfect rabbit (at games). **2. plaquer qn comme une c.,** to leave s.o. flat. **3. se retourner comme une c.,** to turn one's coat, to change sides. **4. faire la c.,** (*of motor-car*) to turn turtle.

crêper: se c. le chignon (*or* **la tignasse**), *see* **chignon 4.**

cresson, *m.* **1.** hair, thatch, moss; **n'avoir plus de c. sur la fontaine** (*or* **sur la cafetière** *or* **sur le caillou** *or* **sur la truffe**), to be bald*. **2. idem au c.,** ditto. **3. arroser le c.,** to have coition*. **4. brouter le c.,** to eat hair pie. **5.** *pl.* bluff, humbug, ballyhoo.

crétin, *m.* hopeless fool, wash-out, dead loss; **quelle bande** (*or* **quel tas**) **de crétins!** what a shower!

creuser. 1. ça vous creuse (l'estomac), ça vous la creuse, it gives you an appetite (*or* a twist *or* a hollow (*or* an empty) feeling), it makes you feel empty (*or* peckish). **2. se c. la tête** (*or* **le cerveau** *or* **la cervelle** *or* **le citron** *or* **le ciboulot** *or* **le navet**), to cudgel (*or* to rack) one's brains.

creux, *m.* **avoir un c.,** to be hungry*.

crevaille, *f.* feast*.

crevaison, *f.* **1.** exhausting work; ex-haustion. **2.** death.

crevant, *adj.* **1.** boring, **2.** exhausting*. **3.** very funny*; **une histoire crevante,** a scream.

crevard, *m.* **1.** glutton*, starveling. **2.** person seriously ill, almost a goner.

crève, *f.* **1.** death. **2. attraper** (*or* **paumer**) **la c.,** to catch one's death, to catch a fatal cold.

crevé, *adj.* **1.** exhausted*. **2.** dead. **3.** arrested.

crève-la-faim, *m.* starveling.

crever. 1. to work (s.o.) to death, to knock (s.o.) up. **2.** to arrest*. **3.** to wound. **4.** to kill*. **5. la c.**, to starve, to be starving, to be famished. **6. ça (vous) crève les yeux,** it stares (it's staring) you in the face, it's under your very nose, it stands out a mile, it's as plain as the nose on your face. **7.** to die*. **8. c. de** (*or* **c. la**) **faim**=**la c. 9.** to have a puncture. **10. c. de rire,** to laugh* uproariously. **11. tu peux (toujours) c.!**=**tu peux (toujours) courir! 12. qu'il crève!** to hell with him! **13. marche ou crève!** do or die!

crever, se. 1. se c. (**de travail**), to work oneself to death, to kill oneself with work; **se faire c.,** to get killed. **2. se c.** (**de rire**)=**c. de rire. 3.** to stuff oneself; **se faire c.,** to have a real blowout, to blow one's hide out. **4. tu t'en ferais c.!**=**tu peux toujours courir!**

crevettant, *adj.* feeling seedy, out of sorts.

crevette, *f.* **la môme c.,** a dwarfish, undersized* person, a little shrimp.

cri, *m.* **1. le** (**tout**) **dernier c.,** the latest fashion, the latest thing out, the latest fad, all the go, all the rage. **2.** uproar; **faire du c., aller au(x) cri(s),** to kick up a row, to make a big fuss; **du c. sec, du drôle de c.,** a hell of a row.

criard, *m.* baby, squaller, howler.

cric, *m.* brandy, spirits, hard liquor.

cricri, *m.* **1.** cricket (*insect*). **2. c.** (**ravageur**), skinny, wizened little female.

crigne, crignolle, *f.* =**barbaque 1.**

crin, *m.* **1. être comme un c., être c.,** to be in a bad temper*; **un vieux c.,** (*of person*) an old crab; **être de mauvais c.**=**être de mauvais poil. 2. à tout c., à tous crins,** out-and-out, thoroughgoing. **3. avoir qn dans le c.**=**avoir qn dans la peau. 4.** *pl.* hair, thatch.

crincrin, *m.* **1.** screechy fiddle; **racler le c.,** to scrape on the fiddle. **2.** poor fiddler, scraper. **3.** telephone.

criolle, *f.* =**barbaque 1.**

criquer, se, to decamp*.

criquet, *m.* (*of a man*) little shrimp.

crise, *f.* **piquer une c., attraper une c. de nerfs,** (*a*) to throw a fit, to become hysterical; (*b*) to fly into a passion, to get angry*.

crispant, *adj.* irritating, annoying, aggravating; **ce que tu es c.!** what a pest you are!

crispation, *f.* **donner des crispations à qn,** to exasperate s.o., to get on s.o.'s nerves.

cristaux, *m.pl.* washing-soda.

cristi, *int.* curse it! blast it!

crob(e), *adj.* (*from 'microbe'*) tiny, small.

crocher. 1. to arrest*. **2.** to grab. **3.** to pick (a lock).

crocher, se: se c. avec, to have a set-to (*or* a scrap) with.

croche, *f.* lock; *pl.* hands*.

crochet, *m.* **1.** =**carouble. 2.** (*boxing*) hook. **3.** (*th., radio, T.V.*) **coup du c.,** amateur night; **faire le coup du c. à qn,** to give s.o. the bird. **4.** *pl.* teeth; **avoir les crochets**=**avoir les crocs. 5. vivre aux crochets de qn,** to live at s.o.'s expense, to sponge (*or* to scrounge) on s.o.

crocheter, (*boxing*) to hook.

crocheter, se: se c. avec=**se crocher avec.**

crochu, *adj.* **avoir les doigts crochus** (*or* **les mains crochues**), (*a*) to be light-fingered; (*b*) to be grasping, to be close-fisted.

croco, *m.* **1.** crocodile (leather). **2.** (*sport*) tough player.

crocs, *m.pl.* teeth; **avoir mal aux c.,** to have the toothache; **se faire virer les c.,** to have one's teeth extracted; **avoir les c.,** to be hungry*; **n'avoir plus mal aux c.,** to die*.

croire. 1. je vous crois! (**j'te crois!**) you bet! sure! rather! I should jolly well think so! **2. croyez-vous! (crois-tu!)**— *e.g.* **quel temps, crois-tu!** did you ever see such weather! (*of good or bad weather*), what awful (*or* what wonderful) weather! **3. j'aime mieux le c. que d'y aller voir!** I have my doubts! I'll take your word for it!

croire, se: se c. (*or* **s'en c.**) (**un peu**), to be self-conceited*.

croître: cela ne fait que c. et embellir,

it keeps going from bad to worse, it's getting worse and worse.

croix, *f.* **1.** mug, juggins, mutt. **2.** c'est (*or* il faut) la c. et la bannière pour . . ., it's the very devil to . . ., it's a devil of a job to . . . **3.** faire la c. des vaches à qn, to mark s.o. (with a knife-scar or a razor-cut). **4.** il faut faire une c. à la cheminée, we must mark that in red letters, we must chalk it up. **5.** c. de bois, c. de fer, cross my heart (*said by children to imply* 'I swear that I'm telling the truth'). **6.** mettre une c. dessus, to consider it over and done with.

croni, *m.* **1.** corpse*; le parc des cronis, the cemetery, the boneyard. **2.** *adj.* dead.

cronir. 1. to kill*. **2.** to die*.

cropinettes, *f.pl.* tu peux en faire des c.! you can do what you damn well like with it!

croquaillon, *m.* little sketch (*drawing*).

croquant, *m.* peasant*; boor.

croquante, *f.* mouth.

croque, *m.* **1.** =croquant. **2.** pas un c., not a brass farthing, not a cent.

croque, *f.* food*.

croque-monsieur, *m.* kind of Welsh-rarebit with ham.

croquemuche, *m.* undertaker's assistant.

croquenots, *m.pl.* big boots*.

croquer. 1. =bouffer 1 *and* 2. **2.** to arrest*. **3.** être gentil(le) (*or* joli(e)) à c., (*of person*) to be perfectly sweet. **4.** en c., (*a*) to be a police-informer*; (*b*) to take part in, to share in; (*c*) to be a pederast*; (*d*) =faire le voyeur. **5.** en c. pour qn, to be infatuated* with s.o.

croqueuse, *f.* c. de diamants, (*of female*) gold-digger.

croquignoles, *f.pl.* testicles*.

croquignole(t), *adj.* small and pretty, dainty.

crosse, *f.* **1.** chercher des crosses à qn, to pick a quarrel with s.o. **2.** se mettre (*or* se foutre) en c., to get angry*. **3.** prendre les crosses, to espouse s.o.'s quarrel, to stick up for s.o.

crosseur, crosson, *m.* quarrelsome, overbearing fellow.

crotte, *f.* **1.** ma c., my darling*. **2.** crotte(s) de bique, rubbish, tripe. **3.** *int.* c.! (*euphemism for* merde!) blast (it)! oui ou c.?=oui ou merde? **4.** être à la c., to be depressed*, to feel mouldy.

crougnat, crouilla(t), crouille, crouilledouche, *m.* Algerian, North-African, Arab.

croulant, *m.* (*teen-agers' contemptuous term for a fifty-to-sixty year old person*) old fossil, old dodderer, back-number, square.

croum(e), *m.* credit.

crouni, *m., adj.* =croni.

crounir =cronir.

croupanche, *m.* croupier.

croupe, *f.* buttocks*.

croupière, *f.* tailler des croupières à qn, to make things difficult for s.o., to give s.o. a tough job.

croupion, *m.* **1.** parson's nose (of fowl). **2.** buttocks*; tortiller du c.=croupionner.

croupionner, to waggle one's bottom (while walking).

croustance, *f.* food*.

croustillant, *adj.* spicy (*of story, song*); attractive, glamorous, sexy (*of female*).

croustille, *f.* food*.

croustiller, to eat.

croustilleux, *adj.* spicy (*of story, song*).

croûte, *f.* **1.** food*; casser une (*or* la) c., to have a snack (*or* a bite of something), to snatch a bite; la c. et la dorme, food and lodgings. **2.** gagner sa c., to earn one's living (*or* one's daily bread *or* one's bread-and-butter), to make a living, to bring home the bacon. **3.** badly painted picture, daub. **4.** old fog(e)y*. **5.** s'ennuyer (*iron.* s'amuser) comme une c. derrière une malle, to be bored* stiff.

croûter, to eat; de quoi c., something to eat, a bite.

croûton, *m.* **1.** un vieux croûton, an old fog(e)y. **2.** s'ennuyer (*iron.* s'amuser) comme un vieux croûton derrière une malle: *see* croûte 5.

croûtonner, se : se c. (à mort), to be bored* to death.

cruche, *f.*, **cruchon**, *m.* fool*.

cube, *m.* third-year student (at the *École normale supérieure*).

cuber, (*sch.*) to stay a third year in a class.

cubillot, *m.* stove.

cucu(l), *m.* **le (p'tit) c.**, the bottom, backside, botty.

cucu(l) **(la praline)**, *adj.* silly*, stupid, 'wet'.

cueille, *f.* round-up, raid, comb-out (by police).

cueillir. 1. to arrest*; to round up (suspects); **se faire c.**, to get nabbed, to be picked up (by police). 2. to collect, to pick up (*i.e. to call for and accompany s.o.*). 3. **où as-tu cueilli ça?** where did you fish that out? where did you dig that up?

cuiller, cuillère, *f.* 1. hand*; **serrer la c. à qn**, to shake hands with s.o.; **serre-moi la c.!** tip us your fin! 2. **argenté comme une c. de bois**, penniless*. 3. **en trois (*or* en deux) coups de c. à pot**, immediately, very quickly*. 4. **être à ramasser à la (petite) c.**, to be exhausted*. 5. (*tennis*) **servir à la c.**, to serve underhand. *See also* **dos.**

cuir, *m.* skin, hide; **tanner (*or* carder) le c. à qn**, to give s.o. a good thrashing*; **se rôtir le c.**, to sunbathe, to take a sun-bath; **se racler le c.**, to shave.

cuirasse, *f.* chest.

cuirassé, *adj.* = blindé 1 *and* 2.

cuire. 1. **il vous en cuira**, you'll smart for it, you'll be sorry for it. 2. **on cuit ici**, it's broiling hot here, it's stifling here. *See also* **dur**, *m.* 2.

cuisinage, *m.* interrogation (by police), grilling, third degree.

cuisine, *f.* 1. underhand scheming, wangling, dirty work. 2. faking, cooking (of accounts, etc.). 3. = **cuisinage.**

cuisiner. 1. to cook up (scheme, manœuvre, etc.). 2. to cook (accounts), to fake, to tamper with.

3. to interrogate (prisoner), to grill, to pump.

cuisse, *f.* 1. **se croire (*or* s'imaginer *or* croire qu'on est) sorti de la c. de Jupiter**, to have a big opinion of oneself, to think one is the Lord God Almighty. 2. **aller aux cuisses**, to have coition*. 3. **avoir la c. hospitalière (*or* gaie *or* légère), (*of female*)** to be of easy virtue, to be an easy conquest.

cuistance, *f.* 1. (*mil.*) cookery, cooking. 2. kitchen.

cuistancier, cuisteau, cuistot, *m.* (*mil.*) cook.

cuit, *adj.* 1. drunk*. 2. done* for; down and out. 3. **c'est du tout c.!** it's a certainty*! **ce n'est pas du tout c.!** it's not all plain sailing!

cuite, *f.* drunkenness, drunken bout; **avoir sa (*or* tenir une) c.**, to be dead drunk*; **cuver sa c.**, to sleep oneself sober, to sleep it off; **prendre la (*or* sa *or* une) c.**, to get drunk*; **tenir une bonne c.**, to have a skinful, to be gloriously drunk.

cuiter, se, to get drunk*; to be a boozer.

cuivre, *m.* **nous n'avons pas fait les cuivres ensemble!** = nous n'avons pas gardé les cochons ensemble! (cochon 8).

cul, *m.* 1. buttocks*. 2. very silly and uncouth person; **un sale petit c.**, a dirty little sod; **un vieux c.**, a silly old bugger. 3. **un c.-de-plomb**, a clot; a lazy swine; a blimp; a petty bureaucrat, a pen-pusher. 4. **un c.-terreux**, a peasant*. 5. **un gros c.**, (a) a long-distance lorry; a driver of a long-distance lorry, a trunker; (b) a large ship. 6. **du gros c.**, ordinary coarse tobacco, shag, (*mil.*) coarse army tobacco. 7. **avoir qn au (*or* dans le) c.** = avoir qn quelque part. 8. **en avoir plein le c.** = en avoir plein le dos. 9. **avoir chaud au c.**, (a) to be in a blue funk; (b) to be hot stuff (sexually) (*of female*). 10. **bas de c.** *or* **bout de c.**, short, stumpy person. 11. **c. par-dessus tête**, head over heels, arse over tip.

12. être à c., to be penniless*, to be cleaned out; mettre qn à c.; to clean s.o. out. **13.** être (comme) c. et chemise, être copains comme c. et chemise, (of persons) to be inseparable, to be as thick as thieves. **14.** faire c. sec, to drink up, to leave no heel-taps; c. sec! cheerio*!. **15.** faire le c. de poule = faire la bouche en c. de poule. **16.** lécher le c. à qn, to flatter* s.o. Cf. lèche-c. **17.** tu peux te le (or la) mettre au c.! you can shove (or stick) it up your arse! **18.** cela (or ça) lui pend au c. comme un sifflet de deux ronds = cela lui pend au nez. **19.** je lui pisse au c.! = je l'ai quelque part. **20.** rire comme un c., to laugh without opening one's mouth. **21.** se crever le c., to work like hell. **22.** tirer au c. = tirer au flanc. **23.** péter plus haut que son (or le) c., to swank*, to put on airs, to be snooty. **24.** se taper le c. par terre, to be overjoyed; il n'y a pas de quoi se taper le c. par terre, there's nothing to be jubilant about. Cf. astap(e). **25.** il chante comme mon c., he can't sing for nuts. **26.** adj. = cucu(l), adj.

culbutant, m., **culbute,** f. (i) trousers*.

culbute, f. (ii) faire la c., (a) to fall, to come a cropper*; (b) to make a hundred per cent profit, to make a scoop; (c) to double one's stakes.

culbuté, adj. **1.** c. (à zéro), (dead) drunk*. **2.** bien c. = bien fichu 5.

culbuter. 1. to tumble (a woman). **2.** = faire la culbute. **3.** to convince.

culbuteur, m. c. de femmes = tombeur de femmes.

culot, m. impudence*; avoir du c., to be impudent*; avoir un c. monstre (or un fier c. or un c. infernal), to have a hell of a cheek, to have the cheek of the devil; vous en avez du c.! well, you have got a nerve! I like your nerve! ne pas manquer de c., to be a cool hand (or a cool one), not to be lacking in cheek.

culotté, adj. **1.** impudent*; vous n'êtes pas c., vous! (iron.) you don't want much, do you? être c. comme tout, to have a hell of a nerve. **2.** brave, game, tough, spunky.

culotte, f. **1.** avoir sa c., to be drunk*. **2.** prendre une c., (a) to get drunk*; (b) to lose heavily (at cards, etc.), to be hard hit, to take a knock. **3.** faire dans sa c., to be scared stiff, to have the wind up. **4.** dans cette maison, c'est la femme qui porte la c., in that house it's the wife who wears the breeches (or the trousers). **5.** s'en moquer comme de sa première c. = s'en moquer comme de sa première chemise. **6.** une c. de gendarme, a little patch of blue sky (after rain), enough (blue sky) to patch a sailor's trousers (or a Dutchman's breeches). **7.** une vieille c. de peau, an old dug-out, an old sweat, a regular Colonel Blimp.

culotter, se, to get drunk*.

culott'man, adj. = culotté 1.

cumulard, m. pluralist.

cunuter, to count (numerically).

curé, m. manger (or bouffer) du c., to be a rabid anti-clericalist, to be a priest-hater.

cure-dents, m. **1.** (mil.) bayonet, 'toothpick', **2.** knife. **3.** venir en c.-d., to turn up at the end of a dinner, to gate-crash (an evening-party).

cureton, curetot, curetosse, m. (pej.) curé, parish priest.

curieux, m. **1.** examining magistrate, beak. **2.** police superintendent.

cuti, f. (= cuti-réaction) skin-test (for T.B., etc.); penser à virer sa c., to grow up, to change one's tune.

cuver. 1. c. son vin = c. sa cuite. **2.** to laze about.

cyclard, m. cyclist.

cyclo, m. policeman on a bicycle, cop on wheels (= hirondelle 1.).

cyclope, m. penis*; faire pleurer le c. = jouir.

cynoque, adj. = sinoc.

Cyrard, m. cadet training at the Saint-Cyr military school.

D

D. le système D: *see* **système.**

dab(e), dabuche, *m.* **1.** father*. **2.** the boss, the gov.

dabe, dabesse, dabuche, *f.* mother, the old woman, the old-lady.

dab(e)s, *m.pl.* parents, the old folk; **les beaux-dab(e)s,** parents-in-law; **le beau-d.,** father-in-law; **la belle-dabesse,** mother-in-law.

d'acc! dac! *int.* =d'accord, *See* **accord.**

Dache, *pr.n.* va le dire à (*or* va-t'en chez) D., (le perruquier des zouaves)! go to blazes!*

dada, *m.* **1.** horse, gee-gee. **2.** aller à d., (*a*) to ride a-cock-horse; (*b*) to have coition* with (a woman), to ride (a woman). **3.** hobby, fad, pet subject; **chevaucher** (*or* **enfourcher**) **son d.,** to ride one's pet hobby. **4.** **les dadas,** (*turf*) racehorses, the gee-gees.

dadais, *m.* ninny, boob, gawk.

daf, d'Af, *m.* =badaf.

dahlia, *m.* symbol of the lesbians.

daim, *m.* simpleton*, booby, mug.

dal, dalle, *adv.* **que dal(le),** nothing at all, not a thing, damn all, (sweet) Fanny Adams; **n'y entraver** (*or* **n'y piger**) **que d.,** to be unable to make head or tail of it, not to understand a damn thing. *Similarly with verbs like comprendre, entendre, foutre, valoir, voir.*

dalle, *f.* throat, mouth*; **arroser la d. à qn,** to stand s.o. a drink, to wet s.o.'s whistle*; **avoir la d. en pente,** to be a thirsty mortal, to be a boozer, to be a tippler; **crever la d.,** to starve; to die of thirst; **se rincer** (*or* **s'arroser** *or* **se mouiller**) **la d.,** to wet one's whistle.

dame, *f.* **1.** d. blanche, bottle of white wine. **2.** d. de pique, pack of cards; **chatouiller** (*or* **peloter** *or* **taquiner** *or* **faire valser**) **la d. de pique,** to play (to be fond of playing) cards. **3.** aller à d., to fall, to come a cropper*; **envoyer qn à d.,** to fell s.o. with a blow, to send s.o. sprawling. **4.** faire la d., to set up for a lady, to queen it. **5.** entrer en d. avec, to strike up a conversation with. **6.** vot' d., your missis, your good lady.

dame-pipi, *f.* lavatory-attendant.

damer. 1. =aller à dame. **2.** d. le pion, to outwit.

damner: faire d. qn, to drive s.o. crazy.

dandillante, *f.* little bell.

danse, *f.* thrashing*; **filer une d. à qn,** to give s.o. a good thrashing*; **ramasser une d.,** to get a good thrashing*.

danser: la d. =ramasser une danse.

danseuse, *f.* (*cycling*) **pédaler** (**aller, piler, rouler, monter une côte**) **en d.,** to cycle uphill standing up on one's pedals.

dard, *m.* penis*; **avoir du d.** =être porté sur la bagatelle.

dardillon, *m.* =dard; **avoir le d.** = bander.

dare-dare, *adv.* post-haste, like a shot, in less than no time.

dariole, *f.* slap in the face, clout.

daron, *m.* father; husband, old man; *pl.* parents.

daronne, *f.* mother.

darracq, *m.* hammer.

datte, *f.* **1.** ne pas en fiche(r) une d. =ne pas en fiche(r) un coup (coup 14). **2.** des dattes! =des clous! (clou 7). **3.** comme des dattes, impossible, non-existent.

daube, *f.* **1.** rotten meat. **2.** syphilis.

dauffer, to commit sodomy with, to bugger.

dauphin, *m.* **1.** pimp, ponce, bully. **2.** (burglar's) jemmy.

dé, *m. See* **dés,** *m.pl.*

débagouler. 1. to vomit*. **2.** to pour forth (insults, abuse, one's feelings, etc.); to spout, talk volubly.

déballage, *m.* **1.** venting, pouring forth (of feelings, etc.). **2.** (*of woman*) display of one's personal (*or* artificial) charms.

déballé, *adj.* disheartened.

déballer: **déballe!** = **accouche! d. ce qu'on a sur le cœur,** to get it off one's chest; **d. ses connaissances,** to tell all one knows, to do one's stuff; **d. ses outils,** to confess*, to come clean; **d. le jars,** to talk in slang.

déballonné, *m.* coward, funk, quitter.

déballonner, se. **1.** to confess*. **2.** to back out.

débarbe, débarbot, débarboteur, *m.* counsel for the defence.

débarboter, se = se débrouiller.

débarbouiller, se. **1.** = se débrouiller. **2.** (*of weather*) to clear up.

débarcade, *f.* release (from prison), discharge.

débarouler, to tumble down.

débarqué, -e, *m.f.* **un nouveau (une nouvelle) d.,** a country cousin.

débarquer. **1.** to dismiss*; to get rid (*or* to get shot *or* shut) of. **2.** to arrive fresh from the country. **3. ça débarque,** her monthlies have come (*menses**).

débauchée, *f.* knocking-off time.

débaucher. **1.** to knock off (after a day's work). **2.** to lay off (a workman).

débectage, *m.* disgust, revulsion.

débectant, *adj.* disgusting. sickening.

débec(que)ter. **1.** to disgust, to make sick; **ça me débecte,** I can't stomach that; **je les débecte,** they make me spew, **je me débecte,** I am bored stiff. **2.** to vomit*.

débinage, *m.* disparagement*.

débine, *f.* **être dans la d.,** to be penniless*.

débiner. **1.** to disparage*. **2. d. le truc,** (*a*) to confess*; (*b*) (*mil.*) to be killed, to die*.

débiner, se. **1.** to decamp*. **2.** to come down in the world. **3.** to crack up, to break down, to go to pieces.

débineur, *m.* disparager, backbiter.

déblayer: **d. le terrain,** to run away, to decamp*; **déblaie!** hop it*!

débloquer. **1.** to vomit*. **2.** = débourrer. **3. d. (à pleins tubes)** = déconner.

débonder, se, to pour out one's heart, to unburden oneself.

déboucler. **1.** to break open (door, safe, till, etc.); to 'crack'. **2.** to release (prisoner).

déboucleur, *m.* burglar.

débouler. **1.** to tumble down, to roll down. **2.** to be off, to set out. **3.** = déboulonner.

déboulonnage, déboulonnement, *m.* **1.** debunking. **2.** dismissal.

déboulonner. **1.** to debunk. **2.** to dismiss*.

débourrer: **d. (sa pipe),** to defecate*.

débourroir, *m.* (*sing.* or *pl.*) W.C.*

déboussolé, *adj.* mad*.

debout, *adv.* **cela ne tient pas d.,** that doesn't make sense, that doesn't hold water.

déboutonner, se, to unbosom oneself, to get sth. off one's chest.

débrayage, *m.* going on strike, work stoppage.

débrayer, to go on strike, to come out on strike, to down tools.

débridage, *m.* breaking open, 'cracking' (*of door, safe, etc.*).

débrider. **1.** = déboucler. **2. sans d.,** without stopping, at a stretch.

débringué, *adj.* slovenly.

débrouillard, *adj.*, *m.* resourceful* (person).

débrouillardise, débrouille, *f.* resourcefulness.

débrouiller, se. **1.** to shift for oneself, to get by; **savoir se d.,** to know one's way about; **se d. tant bien que mal,** to muddle through; **se d. pour avoir qch.,** to wangle sth.; **débrouillez-vous!** that's your look-out! **se d. sur le voisin,** to pass the buck (*or* the baby) to s.o., to come the acid. **2.** (*of weather, of difficulty*) to clear up.

décade, *f.* (*W.W.I and II*) tobacco ration.

décalitre, *m.* top hat.
décalqué, *adj.* c'est son père tout d.,
(*a*) =c'est son père tout craché;
(*b*) he's a chip of the old block.
décambuter, to come (*or* to go) out,
to emerge.
décamper, to decamp*.
décanillage, *m.* hurried departure,
flight.
décaniller. 1. to decamp*. 2. d. (du
page), to get out of bed, to show a leg.
décapant, *m.* bad liquor, rot-gut, rat
poison.
décapitonnage, *m.* undressing.
décarcasser, se : se d. (le trou de balle),
to wear oneself out, to wear oneself to
a shadow, to put oneself out, to lean
over backwards.
décarpiller. 1. to sort out, to share out
(proceeds of a robbery). 2. to undress.
décarrade, *f.* escape, flight, exit (from
prison, etc.).
décarrer. 1. to go out. 2. to decamp*;
to escape. 3. to take out. 4. d. de belle,
to be acquitted.
décartonner, se, to grow old, to be
getting on in years.
décati, *adj.* (*of person*) old and worn,
decrepit, the worse for wear; un
vieux d., an old crock, an old dodderer,
a back-number, a has-been; elle n'est
pas trop décatie, she's not so dusty.
décatir, se, to show the effects of age,
to be the worse for wear.
décavé, *adj.* 1. penniless*. 2. =décati.
3. *m.* le d., police dossier (of criminal).
décaver, to clean (s.o.) out (at gambling).
décesser: ne (pas) d. de=*the normal*
ne (pas) cesser de—*e.g.* il ne décesse
pas de se plaindre, he has never done
complaining, he keeps on complaining.
déchanter: (en) d., to sing a different
(*or* another) tune, to sing small, to
come down a peg (or two).
déchard, *m.* penniless* person.
décharger =jouir.
lèche, *f.* 1. poverty, distress, straits;
être dans la d., être dans une d. noire,

tomber dans la d., battre la d., to be
penniless*, to be (down) on one's
uppers. 2. expense(s). 3. sans d., scot-
free.
décher. 1. to pay up. 2. to spend. 3. to
pay for.
déchet, *m.* (*of person*) failure, wash-out;
un vieux d., a back-number.
décheur, décheux, *m.* spendthrift.
déchirée, *adj., f.* elle n'est pas trop
d.=elle n'est pas trop décatie.
déchirer: la d., to die*.
décoconner=déconner.
décocter=débourrer.
décoction, *f.* thrashing*.
décoffrer, to give birth to a child.
décolérer: ne pas d., not to cool (*or*
not to calm) down.
décoller. 1. to die*. 2. (*of person,
physically*) to go to pieces, to be in a
bad way. 3. ne pas d., (*of person*) not
to budge, to stick like a leech, to stay
for ever. 4. sans d., at a stretch.
décoller, se. 1. =décoller. 2. (*sport*) to
draw (*or* to forge) ahead.
déconnage, *m.* rot*, tripe, cock, balls,
crap.
déconner: d. (à pleins tubes), to talk
rot*.
décoqueter =décocter.
décor, *m.* 1. (*of a motor-car*) entrer
(rentrer, passer, aller) dans les décors
(*or* le d.), to collide with (*or* to run
into) a wall (tree, lamp-post, house,
etc.), to skid off to one side. 2. envoyer (*or* expédier) dans le(s) décor(s),
to send flying. 3. ça fait bien dans le
d.=ça fait bien dans le tableau.
découronner, to debunk (a person).
décramponner, se, to shake off s.o.
décrasser. 1. to polish (*or* to smarten)
up (a person), to improve (s.o.'s) manners, to lick (s.o.) into shape. 2.
=barder.
décrasser, se, to polish up one's
manners, to take on polish, to smarten
up.
décrassing-room, *m.* bath-room.
décrocher. 1. to manage (ultimately)
to get, to wangle, to hook, to land, to

pull down (a good job), to win. 2. to redeem (from pawn). 3. se faire d., to get shot. 4. to eat.

décrochez-moi-ça, *m.* 1. garment bought off the peg, reach- (or hand-) me-downs, garment bought ready-made. 2. wardrobe dealer's.

décrotter = décrasser.

décuiter, (se), to sober up, to get over one's drink.

déculottée, *f.* **prendre la d.,** to get a thrashing*.

déculotter, se = se déboutonner.

dedans, *adv.* 1. mettre (fiche(r), fourrer, foutre, flanquer) qn d., (*a*) to humbug* s.o., to bamboozle s.o., to take s.o. in; (*b*) *mil.* to confine to barracks. **être mis d.,** (*a*) to be fooled, to be taken in, to be 'had'; (*b*) to be imprisoned, to be put in clink. 2. **être d.,** (*a*) to be in prison*; (*b*) to be drunk*. 3. **rentrer d. à qn,** to pitch into s.o., to go for s.o. 4. **mettre les pieds d.,** to put one's foot in it. 5. **mettre une porte en d.,** (*of burglar*) to break open a door, to break in. *See also* **donner 8.**

dédé, *m.* buttocks*, botty.

dédouaner. 1. to give (s.o.) a clean bill of health. 2. to clear (s.o.) of a charge.

dédouaner, se, to get out of trouble, to get out of a scrape (*or* out of a jam).

def, dèfe, deffe, deffouse, *f.* cap.

défarguer, to exonerate, to clear (s.o. of a charge).

défarguer, se. 1. to get rid of (sth. incriminating). 2. se d. sur le dos de qn, to lay the blame on s.o., to pass the buck (*or* the baby).

défargueur, *m.* witness for the defence.

défausser, se = se défarguer 1.

défendre, se. 1. to get along (fairly well), to know how to look after oneself, to manage one's affairs, to hold one's own, to stand up for oneself. 2. (*of prostitute*) to solicit. 3. **elle se défend bien,** she wears (her age) well.

défense, *f.* 1. swindle, ramp, racket. 2. **avoir de la d.** = se défendre 1. 3. = bâton 4.

défiler, se. 1. to decamp*. 2. to shirk, to dodge the column, to get out of the rain. 3. to back out (of sth. unpleasant), to duck out.

déflaque, *f.* excrement, shit(e).

déflaquer. 1. to defecate*. 2. = jouir.

défoncé, *adj.* 'blocked' (= *under influence of drugs*).

défonceuse, *f.* penis*; **être amputé de la d.,** to lack virility.

déforme, *f.* **être (un peu) en d.,** to be (temporarily) out of luck (*especially at gambling*).

défourailler, to draw (a revolver); **d. dedans,** to fire (a revolver), to let s.o. have it.

défrimer, to stare at, to look at*.

défringuer, to undress (s.o.).

défringuer, se, to undress.

défrisé, *adj.* avoir l'air d., to look down in the mouth, to look crushed.

défrisement, *m.* disappointment.

défriser, to disappoint, to put (s.o.) out, to put a damper on (s.o.).

défriser, se, to lose heart, to feel crushed.

défrusquer, se défrusquer = défringuer, se défringuer.

défunter, to die*.

dégaine, *f.* ungainly appearance (*or* gait *or* bearing).

dégauchir. 1. = décrasser. 2. to find, to obtain.

dégelée, *f.* good thrashing*, shower (of blows, etc.).

dégeler, se, (*of person*) to become less reserved, to thaw, to unbend.

déglingué, *adj.* dislocated, out of order; slovenly, decrepit.

déglinguer, to dislocate, to put out of order, to smash up, to make a mess of.

déglinguer, se, to become dislocated.

dégobillage, *m.* vomiting, spew(ing).

dégobiller, to vomit*.

dégobillis, *m.* vomit, spew.

dégoiser: (en) d., to talk* volubly (*or* aimlessly); **d. tout,** to shoot (off) one's mouth.

dégommage, *m.* dismissal, sacking.

dégommer. 1. to dismiss*, to remove

from office; **se faire d.**, to be dismissed. **2.** to oust. **3.** to beat, to lick. **4.** to kill*.

dégonflade, *f.*, **dégonflage**, *m.*, **dégonflement**, *m.* backing down, backing out, climbing down, getting cold feet.

dégonflard, *m.* one who backs out, one who is chicken, quitter.

dégonflé, *m.* (*of person*) funk, quitter.

dégonfler, to take the wind out of s.o.'s sails; to debunk.

dégonfler, se. 1. to climb down, to back out (of it); to have cold feet, to sing small, to funk it, to chicken out, to cave in, to buckle up. **2.** to confess*. **3.** = se déboutonner.

dégonfleur, *m.* = dégonflé, *m.*

dégot(t)er. 1. to get, to find, to pick up, to dig out, to spot. **2.** to beat, to lick, to get the better of, to scare off. **3.** to oust, to supplant. **4. elle dégot(t)e bien** (*or* **mal**) = elle marque bien (*or* mal). **5. ça dégot(t)e,** it's first-rate*.

dégoulinante, *f.* **1.** time-piece, clock, watch*, ticker. **2.** run of bad luck.

dégouliner, to trickle (down), to drip (slowly, drop by drop).

dégoupillonner, to vomit*.

dégourdi, *adj.* wide-awake*; **il est mal d.** *or* **il n'est pas d. pour deux sous,** he's a bit slow on the uptake.

dégourdir, to sharpen s.o.'s wits, to liven (*or* to ginger) (s.o.) up, to wise (s.o.) up, to put (s.o.) wise.

dégourdir, se, to smarten up, to wise up, to get wise, to get hep.

dégourrer. 1. to disgust; to dishearten. **2.** to slander, to malign.

dégoûtance, *f.*, **dégoûtation**, *f.* disgusting person *or* thing.

dégoûté, *adj.* **1. faire le (la) dégoûté(e),** to pick at one's food, to be finicky (about one's food); to turn up one's nose (at sth.); to be squeamish. **2. vous n'êtes pas dégoûté(e)!** (*iron.*) you don't want much, do you?

dégrafer, to decamp*.

dégrainer. 1. to disparage*. **2.** to seduce. **3.** to get round (s.o.).

dégraisser. 1. to steal*. **2.** to empty (one's purse).

dégraisser, se. 1. to be ruined. **2.** to have coition*.

dégraisseur, *m.* tax-collector.

dégrener = dégrainer.

dégringolade, *f.* fall, tumble, cropper, purler; come-down; collapse, slump.

dégringoler. 1. to tumble down; to fall, to come a cropper*; to come down in the world; to slump. **2.** to kill*. **3.** to debunk. **4.** to lend (money). **5.** to steal and hide quickly.

dégrossi, *adj.* licked into shape; **un (individu) mal d.,** a boor, a lout.

dégrossir, se dégrossir = décrasser, se décrasser.

dégrouillard, *adj.*, *m.* = débrouillard.

dégrouiller, se. 1. = se débrouiller. **2.** = se grouiller.

déguerpir, to decamp*.

déguerpissement, *m.* clearing off (*or* out), skedaddling.

dégueulade, *f.* vomit, spew.

dégueulasse, *adj.* disgusting, repulsive, sickening, lousy; *m.f.* (*of persons*) disgusting creature, filthy beast, louse.

dégueulasserie, *f.* repulsiveness, vileness.

dégueulbif, *adj.* = dégueulasse, *adj.*

dégueulée, *f.* **1.** vomit, spew. **2.** volley (of abuse).

dégueulement, *m.* = dégueulade.

dégueuler. 1. to vomit*. **2.** to utter a volley of abuse; **d. sur le compte de qn,** to disparage s.o., to run s.o. down.

dégueulis, *m.* vomiting.

déguster. 1. to receive (blows); **d. des coups,** to get a good hiding; **qu'est-ce qu'on a dégusté!** we didn't half catch (*or* cop) it!

dehors, *m.* **faire le d.** = faire le trottoir.

déhotter, to eject, to turn (s.o.) out.

déhotter, se, to get going (*or* cracking), to get a move on, to make a hurried exit.

déjeté, *adj.* = décati; **ne pas être déjeté(e),** to be well-preserved; **être bien déjeté(e),** to look older than one's years.

D.K.V. = décavé.

délicatesse, *f.* être en d. (avec), to be on somewhat strained relations (with).

délinger, se délinger, déloquer, se déloquer = défringuer, se défringuer.

délourder, to break open (a door).

démanché, *adj.* (*of person*) hulking, ungainly.

démancher, se = se décarcasser.

demander. je vous demande un peu! I ask you! just think of it! did you ever hear of such a thing?

démantibuler, to put out of order (*or* out of gear *or* out of joint); to smash up, to make a mess of.

démaquer, se, to separate, break up house when unmarried.

déménager. 1. to be mad*; **faire d. qn,** to send s.o. off his head. **2.** to decamp*; **faire d. qn,** to chuck s.o. out; **allez, déménagez!** hop* it! **3.** (*of burglars*) **d. la maison,** to strip the house bare.

démerdard, *adj., m.* = débrouillard; **un d. à rebours,** a clumsy blighter, a muff, a gawk.

démerde, démerdeur, *adj., m.* = démerdard.

démerder, se. 1. = se grouiller. **2.** = se débrouiller. **3. se d. de,** to get rid of.

demeuré, -e, *m.f.* mentally deficient, mentally retarded person.

demi, *m.* (= d.-litre), glass of beer.

demi-: d.-cercle, *m.* pincer (repincer) qn au d.-cercle, to catch s.o. napping (*or* off his guard *or* on the hop *or* bending); to get even with s.o., to fix s.o.; to arrest* s.o.; **d.-cigue,** *m.* ten francs; **d.-jambe, d.-jetée, d.-livre, d.-pile,** *f.* fifty francs; être en d.-molle, not to be keen; **d.-plombe,** *f.* half an hour; **d.-pomme,** *f.* dayboarder (*sch.*), **d.-porkesse, d.-portion,** *f.* under-sized* person, sawn-off (*or* sawed-off) person, 'half-pint'; **d.-sac,** *m.* five hundred francs; **d.sel,** *m.* small-time crook; petty pimp; **d.-sigue,** *m.* = d.-cigue; **d.-tour!** *int.* hop* it!

démieller (*euphemistic form of* démerder), to get (s.o.) out of a jam.

démieller, se = se démerder.

démoduler, to silence* s.o.

demoiselle, *f.* half a bottle of red wine.

démolir. 1. to thrash* soundly; **2.** to kill*.

démolissage, *m.* severe criticism*.

démonté, *adj.* (*of a pimp*), temporarily without a woman to live on.

démonter, to flummox; se (laisser) d., to be flummoxed, to lose countenance, to be put out.

démouscailler, se = se débrouiller.

démurger, se démurger = déhotter, se déhotter.

dénipper, se, to undress.

dent, *f.* **1. avoir la d.,** avoir les dents comme des baïonnettes, to be hungry*; j'ai une de ces dents! I've got such a twist! I could eat the hind leg off a donkey! **2. avoir les dents (trop) longues,** (*a*) to be very hungry; (*b*) to be over-ambitious; (*c*) to be greedy (*or* grasping), to have an itching palm. **3. avoir (conserver, garder) une d. contre qn,** to have a grudge against s.o., to have a bone to pick with s.o., to have it in for s.o. **4. avoir mal aux dents,** (*turf, of a horse in a race*) to be pulled (*i.e. to be prevented from winning*). **5. être guéri du mal de dents,** to be dead, to be out of all one's troubles. **6. il n'y en a pas pour ma d. creuse** *or* **il y a juste de quoi remplir une d. creuse,** (*of very tiny portion of food or drink*), there's hardly a toothful *or* there's not enough to fill a bad tooth. **7. n'avoir rien à se mettre sous la d.,** to have nothing to eat. **8. être sur les dents,** (*a*) to be exhausted*; (*b*) to be hard pressed by work *or* business, to be in a flap. **9. mettre qn sur les dents,** to work s.o. to death, to knock s.o. up. **10. avoir la d. dure,** to be biting, sarcastic.

dentiste, *m.* **aller au d.,** to look for food.

dépager, se, dépagnoter, se, to get out of bed, to show a leg.

dépanner, to get (s.o.) out of a hole, to help (s.o.) out, to tide (s.o.) over.

départ, *m.* **piquer un d.,** to decamp*.

dépassé, *adj.* out-of-date.

dépasser: cela me dépasse, that's beyond me! (*i.e. beyond my comprehension*), that beats me! that licks me!

dépatouiller, se, to get out of a mess (*or* a scrape), to wriggle out of a fix*, to shift for oneself.

déphasé, *adj.* confused, out of joint, out of touch.

dépiauter, to pull (a book, a play, a writer) to pieces.

dépiauter, se, to undress, to strip, to peel.

dépieuter, se = se dépager.

déplanquer. 1. to take out (of hiding-place, of pocket). **2.** to come out of hiding, to come out of prison.

déplumé, *adj.* **1.** bald*. **2.** penniless*, cleaned out. **3.** *m.* bald-head, bald-pate.

déplumer, to clean out, to pluck (at gambling).

déplumer, se. 1. to become bald*. **2. = se dépager.**

dépoivrer, to lay off the booze.

dépon(n)er. 1. to discourage. **2.** to disgust.

dépoter, to unload, to drop, a baby.

dépuceler. 1. to deflower (a virgin). **2.** to open for the first time (*e.g. bottle of wine, packet of cigarettes, uncut pages of a book, etc.*). **3. d. sa gueule,** to be sea-sick.

der, *adj.* last. **1. le d. des ders,** the last of all; **viens boire le d. des ders,** let's have a last drink (*or* one for the road). **2. la d. des ders,** the war to end all wars.

dérailler, to talk rubbish (*or* rot), to talk out of (*or* through) one's hat, to go off the rails, to be off the beam.

déramer, to die*.

déramer, se, to commit suicide, to do oneself in.

dérater, (se), to run like mad.

derche, derge, *m.* buttocks*; **papier à d.,** toilet-paper, bum-fodder, bumf;

se magner le d., to get a move on; **un faux(-)d.,** a shifty (*or* sly) customer.

dergeot, *prep., adv.* behind.

dériper, to decamp*.

derjo, *prep., adv.* **= dergeot.**

dernier, *m.* **le d. des salauds,** an utter swine.

dernière, *f.* (*turf*) **toucher la d.,** to back the winner of the last race.

dérober. 1. to decamp*; **je dérobe en douce,** I slip off on the Q.T. **2.** to back out of sth.

dérober, se, 1. to deviate, to leave the straight and narrow. **2.** to go on the loose.

dérondir, se dérondir = décuiter, se décuiter.

dérouille, dérouillade, dérouillée, *f.* good thrashing*; **passer qn à la dérouille,** to give s.o. a good thrashing*; **prendre la d.,** to get a good thrashing*.

dérouiller, to thrash*. **1. (en) d.,** to get punishment, to take the rap; **qu'est-ce qu'il va d.!** he won't half cop it! **se faire d.,** (*a*) **= en d.;** (*b*) to get killed. **2.** (*of prostitute*) to pick up the first client of the day.

dérouiller, se, to hurry* up.

dérouler, to go pub-crawling, to do a P.C. (*i.e. pub crawl*), to gallivant.

derrière, *m.* **1. se lever le d. le premier,** to get out of bed on the wrong side. **2. péter plus haut que son d. = péter plus haut que son cul. 3. se taper le d. par terre** (*or* **sur le coin d'un meuble**) **= se taper le cul par terre. 4. tomber le d. à terre entre deux selles,** to fall between two stools. *See also* **botter 2.**

des, *partitive art.* **d. qui ... = ceux qui ...**

dés, *m.pl.* **lâcher** (*or* **passer**) **les d.,** to throw in one's hand, to throw (*or* to chuck) up the sponge.

désaper, se désaper = défringuer, se défringuer.

désargenté, *adj.* penniless*.

descendre. 1. to kill*; **se faire d.,** to get bumped off. **2.** to debunk (s.o.). **3.** to down, to knock back (a drink).

4. **ça ne descend pas,** it won't go down, it lies heavy on the stomach.

descente, *f.* 1. capacity for downing drinks. 2. police raid.

desentiffer, se, =**sortir des brancards.**

désert, *m.* deserter.

déshabillage, *m.* 1. severe criticism* (of play, etc.), dressing-down. 2. strip-tease.

déshabiller, to criticize* severely (a play, etc.), to give a dressing-down.

désordre, *adj.* untidy.

désossé, *m.* tall* lanky person.

dessalé, *adj.* wide-awake*.

dessaler, se dessaler =**dégourdir, se dégourdir.**

desserre, *f.* **dur à la d.,** close-fisted, stingy, miserly*.

dessin, *m.* **je vais te faire un d.** *or* **veux-tu que je te fasse un d.?** I'll explain it to you in words of one syllable; do I have to draw you a picture? do you want a diagram? want me to do you a drawing?

dessouder. 1. to kill*. 2. **(la) d.,** to die*.

dessous, *m.* 1. **un d. de table,** a bribe, underhand commission, palm-grease, kickback, back-hander. 2. **être tombé dans le trente-sixième** (*or* **le troisième** *or* **le sixième**) **d.,** to be penniless* and without prospects, to be down-and-out, to be in a hell of a mess, to be in the dog-house. 3. pimp's second woman. 4. prostitute's fancy man.

dessus, *adv.* **tomber d.,** (*a*) to attack* (s.o.), to go for (s.o.); (*b*) to reprimand* severely; (*c*) to come on s.o. unexpectedly.

détaler, to decamp*.

dételer. 1. to take it easy, to go slow, to ease off. 2. to settle down (after a merry life). 3. =**sortir des brancards.** 4. **sans d.,** without stopping, at a stretch.

détente, *f.* **dur à la d.=dur à la desserre.**

déterré, *m.* **avoir une mine** (*or* **une figure** *or* **une tête**) **de d., avoir l'air d'un d.,** to look ghastly, to look like a living corpse.

détrancher. 1. to distract s.o.'s attention. 2. **se faire d.,** to be spotted.

détrancher, se, to turn round; to turn aside.

détraqué, *adj.* mad*; **être un peu d.,** to have a screw loose.

détroncher, se détroncher =**détrancher, se détrancher.**

deuil, *m.* 1. **en faire son d.,** to resign oneself to (the loss of) sth., to kiss sth. good-bye. 2. **aller au d.,** to be in touch with the police. 3. **il y a du d.,** it's dangerous (*i.e. risk of being arrested*). 4. **porter le d.,** to lodge a complaint. *See also* **ongles.**

deusio, *adv.* =**deuxio.**

deux, *num. adj., m.* 1. **en moins de d.,** very quickly*. 2. **entre les d.,** neither one thing nor the other, so-so, betwixt and between. 3. **X et Y, ça fait d.** (*or* **c'est d.**), X and Y are two different matters. 4. **d. s'amusent, trois s'embêtent,** two's company, three's none. 5. **se casser en d.,** to double up (after a blow *or* with laughter). 6. **faire le coup de d., atteler à d.,** (*of pimp*), to live off two women. 7. **il était moins d.=il était moins une.** 8. **mes d.** (*i.e. mes d. couilles*): **tiens, mes d.!** not bloody likely! ... **de mes d.**—*e.g.* **sacré bavard de mes d.!** you bloody balls-aching gas-bag!

deuxio, deuzio, *adv.* secondly.

deux soutados, *m.* =**crapulos.**

devant, *prep.* **avoir de l'argent** (*or* **du temps**) **d. soi,** to have money (*or* time) to spare (*or* in hand).

devant, *m.* 1. **se faire arrondir le d.,** to be pregnant*. 2. **bâtir sur le d.,** to get pot-bellied, to get a corporation, to have a bow-window.

devanture, *f.* 1. breasts* (of woman). 2. **faire la d.,** to carry out a smash-and-grab raid. 3. **lécher les devantures,** to go window-shopping. 4. **gondoler de la d.,** to be pregnant.

déveinard, *m.* person who is always unlucky.

déveine, *f.* run of bad luck; **avoir la d., être en** (*or* **dans la**) **d.,** to be out of (*or* down on one's) luck, to strike a bad patch.

dévider, to talk. *See* **jars.**

dévisser, se. 1. to decamp*. **2. un nom qui se dévisse,** a double-barrelled name.

dévoreuse, *f.* red-hot mamma, hot baby, hot number, hot stuff.

dézinguer, to kill*, to demolish.

diabolo, *m.* drink of lemonade and *menthe* (peppermint syrup). (*Similarly* **d.-fraise, d.-cassis, d.-grenadine, d.-menthe,** *etc.*).

diam(e), *m.* diamond (*in pl.* sparklers, rocks, ice).

Diane, *pr.n.* **prix de D.:** *see* **prix 2.**

diapason, *m.* **monter le d.,** to yell at the top of one's voice.

diche, *f.* headmistress of a school.

dico, *m.* dictionary, dicker, dic.

didine, *f.* vagina*.

didis, *m.pl.* fingers, digits.

digérer, to stomach; **je ne digère pas ça,** that sticks in my gizzard.

dig(ue)-dig(ue), *f.* **tomber en d.-d.,** (*a*) to faint; (*b*) to have an epileptic fit.

dimanche, *m.* **être venu au monde** (*or* **être né) un d.,** to be born tired.

dinde, *f.* **1. petite d.,** (*of girl*) little softy, little goose. **2. vieille d.,** (*of woman*) old hen.

dindon, *m.* **être le d. de la farce,** to be duped (*or* gulled), to be the mug.

dindonner, to fool* s.o.

dingo, dingue, *adj.* mad*; **être dingue de,** to be infatuated* with, to be crazy about; *m.f.* crackpot, nut-case, screwball; **la baraque aux dingues,** the mad-house, the loony-bin; **battre** (*or* **taper) le dingue,** to pretend to be mad.

dingue, *f.* jemmy.

dinguer: envoyer d., to send (s.o.) packing, to send (s.o.) spinning; to chuck (sth.) up, to fling (sth.) away.

dire. 1. à qui le dites-vous? you're telling me! as if I didn't know! don't I just know it! **2. cela ne me dit rien,** that doesn't appeal to me. **3. ce n'est (c'est) pas pour d., mais . . .,** I hate to say so, but . . ., if you don't mind my saying so, . . ., you can say what you like, but . . ., there's no getting away from it . . ., though I says it as shouldn't . . . **4. ce n'est (c'est) pas dit,** it's not so certain. **5. ce n'est rien de le d.,** and no mistake! you bet! **6. c'est tout d.,** I need say no more, there's nothing to add. **7. il n'y a pas à d., y a pas (à d.),** there's no denying it (*or* no getting away from it), there are no two ways about it, . . . and no mistake. **8. je ne croyais pas si bien d.,** I didn't realize how right I was. **9. je ne le lui ai pas envoyé d.,** I told him so straight (*or* straight to his face), I let him have it straight from the shoulder. **10. je ne vous le fais pas d.,** I'm not putting the words into your mouth, you don't have to tell me, you said it yourself. **11. je (ne) vous dis que ça!** you can take my word for it! need I say more? **12. on se l'est dit,** they passed it (*or* the word) round. **13. qu'il dit,** says he; **que tu dis!** sez you! that's what you say. **14.** (*at auction*) **qui dit mieux?** any advance? **15. qu'est-ce à d.?** what does it mean? what's it all about? **16. si on peut d.!** what an idea!

dirigeoir, *m.* handlebars (of bicycle).

dirlingue, dirlo(t), 1. headmaster. **2.** director.

discagogo, *m.* juke-box.

discutailler, to argufy.

disciplote, *f.* **compagnies de d.,** disciplinary companies (stationed formerly in North Africa).

disposer: vous pouvez d., (*after an interview, etc.*) you may go, that will be all, thank you!

disque, *m.* **1. change(z) de d.!** put another record on! (*said to s.o. who keeps on harping on the same old theme*). **2. siffler au d.,** (*a*) to whistle for a thing; (*b*) to ask for s.t. in vain. **3.** anus*; **casser le d. = casser le pot.**

disserte, *f.* (=*dissertation*) essay.

distribe, *f.* (=*distribution*) issue (of army rations).

distribution, *f.* thrashing*.

dix, *num. adj., m.* **1.** ça vaut d.! *or* d. sur d.! that's something to write home about! that's a good 'un, that is! that's rich! ten out of ten and excellent! **2. je vous le donne en d.,** I'll give you ten guesses. **3.** (*of prisoner in his cell*) **piquer le d.,** to pace up and down (in order to tire oneself out and so capture sleep).

doc, *m.* doctor.

doche, *m.* father, *f.* mother.

doches, *m.pl.* **1.** dice, 'bones'. **2.** *f.pl.* menses*.

dodo, *m.* (*nursery word*) sleep; bed; **faire d.,** to (go to) sleep; **aller à** (*or* **au**) **d., aller faire d.,** to go to bed, to go to bye-bye(s), to go to roost; *int.* hushaby!

doigt, *m.* **1. être comme les (deux) doigts de la main,** to be hand in glove. **2. gagner** (*or* **arriver**) **les doigts dans le nez,** to win* easily. **3. mon petit d. me l'a dit,** a little bird told me so. **4. ne rien faire de ses dix doigts,** not to do a hand's turn. **5. obéir à qn au d. et à l'œil,** to be at s.o.'s beck and call, to obey s.o. at the lift of a finger. **6. recevoir sur les doigts,** to be reprimanded*. **7. se mettre** (*or* **se fourrer** *or* **se ficher** *or* **se foutre**) **le d. dans l'œil** (**jusqu'au coude**), to be (very) wide of the mark, to bark up the wrong tree, to be all wet (*i.e. all wrong*). *See also* **crochu.**

dolluche, *m.* dollar, money*.

dombeur, *m.* jemmy.

dominos, *m.pl.* **1.** teeth, ivories, choppers; **jeu de d.,** teeth; **avoir mal aux d. = avoir mal aux crocs. 2. boîte à** (*or* **aux**) **d.,** coffin. **3. durophet capsules** (*drugs**).

dondon, *f.* **grosse** (*or* **forte**) **d.,** big lump of a girl (*or* woman), big fat wench, whopper.

donne, *f.* **1.** alms. **2.** generosity. **3. être de la d.,** to lose money, to be a loser. **4. ne pas être de la d.,** to be a miser*.

donné, *m.* **un d.,** an easy* job.

donner. 1. d. qn, to denounce s.o., to

inform* on s.o. **2. c'est donné!** (*a*) it's dirt cheap!; (*b*) it's a gift! it's a piece of cake! **3. ça doit se d.,** it must be catching. **4. je vous le donne en mille:** *see* **mille. 5. on vous en donnera!** (*iron.*) you don't want much, do you? **6. s'en d.,** to have a good time. **7. se la d. de qn,** to mistrust s.o., to suspect s.o., to have one's suspicions about s.o. **8. d. dedans,** to walk right into the trap, to fall for it.

donneur, -euse, *m.f.* **1.** informer*. **2. il n'est pas d.,** he doesn't like parting with his money.

donzelle, *f.* hussy, fast girl*.

dorancher, to gild.

doré, *adj.* lucky.

dormailler, dormasser, to drowse.

dorme, *f.* **1.** sleep. **2.** doss house.

dorto, *m.* (*sch.*) dormitory.

dorure, *f.* **une vraie d.,** an easy* job.

doryphore, *m.* (*W.W.II*) German soldier, Jerry, Kraut.

dos, *m.* **1. un dos (-vert), un d. fin,** a pimp, ponce, bully. **2. avoir bon d.,** (*fig.*) to have broad shoulders, to have a broad back. **3. en avoir plein le d.,** to be fed up (with it), to be sick (and tired) of it, to have had a bellyful. **4. être toujours sur le d. de qn,** to be always nagging at s.o., to be always finding fault with s.o.; to keep one's eye on s.o. **5. faire le gros d.,** (*of person*) (*a*) to put on important airs; (*b*) to bristle up. **6. filer** (**donner, prendre**) **du d.,** to be a pederast*. **7. l'avoir dans le d.,** to be duped*. **8. les avoir dans le d.,** to have the police on one's track. **9. mettre qch. sur le d. de qn,** to saddle s.o. with sth., to let s.o. else shoulder sth. **10. n'avoir rien à se mettre sur le d.,** not to have a rag to one's back, not to have a stitch to put on. **11. ne pas y aller avec le d. de la cuiller,** to lay it on thick, to lay it on with a trowel, to make no bones about it, to go at it hammer and tongs, to go at it bald-headed. **12. pas large du d.,** miserly*. **13. passer la main dans le d. à qn,** to flatter* s.o.; **se passer la main dans le d.**, to pat oneself on the back. **14. scier le d. à qn**, to bore* s.o. **15. se mettre qn à d.**, to make an enemy of s.o. **16. tomber sur le d. à qn**, to jump down s.o.'s throat, to come down heavily on s.o., to crack down on s.o.

dose, *f.* **1. en avoir une d., avoir sa bonne d. de qch.**, to have had more than one's share of sth. **2. en tenir une d. = en tenir une couche. 3. forcer la d.**, to go a bit too far. **4. en prendre une bonne d.**, to enjoy oneself immensely.

dossière, *f.* **1.** buttocks*; **jouer de la d.**, to waggle one's backside. **2. avoir de la d.**, to have astonishing luck. **3. prendre (*or* refiler) de la d. = prendre du dos (dos 6).**

douanier, *m.* glass of absinthe.

doublage, *m.* double-crossing, lie.

doublard, *m.* **1.** head-warder (in a prison). **2.** sergeant-major. **3.** pimp's second woman.

double, *m.* **1. mener (*or* mettre) qn en d. = mener qn en bateau. 2. = doublard 3.**

double-mètre, *m.* very tall* man, a regular lamp-post.

doubler. 1. to double-cross, to diddle, to two-time. **2.** to steal*.

double-six, *m.* **1. rendre le d.-s. à qn**, to be more than a match for s.o. **2.** *pl.* molars, grinders. **3.** *pl.* faked dice.

doubleur, *m.* thief.

doublure, *f.* **1. les doublures se touchent**, I'm penniless*, I'm broke. **2. numérote les doublures de tes poches! = numérote tes abattis! 3. = doublard 3.**

douce, *adj.* **1. se la couler d.:** *see* **couler 2. 2. se porter à la d.**, to be so-so (in health), to be fair to middling. **3. en d. (poil-poil)**, discreetly, quietly, on the quiet, on the Q.T., between you and me and the gate-post (*or* lamp-post); **vas-y en d.!** easy does it! **glisser qch. en d.**, to tell sth. in confidence. **4.** marihuana (drugs*).

douceur, *f.* **en d. = en douce.**

douché, *p.p.* **être d.**, (*a*) to be drenched, to be soused; (*b*) to be seriously shaken; (*c*) to be fleeced; (*d*) to have suffered a loss; (*e*) (*fig.*) to have burnt one's fingers.

doucher, to cool (s.o.) off.

doudounes, *f.pl.* (*of woman*) breasts*; well-rounded charms.

douillard, *adj.* **1.** rich*. **2.** with a good thatch of hair.

douille, *f.* **1.** money*. **2.** forking-out.

douiller, to pay*; to pay for; to finance; to spend.

douilles, *f.pl.* hair, thatch, crop (of hair).

doul(e), *m.* **1.** hat*. **2. porter le d. = porter le bada.**

douleurs, *f.pl.* rheumatism, 'rheumatics'.

doulos, *m.* = bada 1 *and* 2.

douloureuse, *f.* **la d.**, the bill, the reckoning, the check (*in hotel, restaurant, etc.*), the damage.

douter: il ne doute de rien, he is full of self-confidence.

doux, *adv.* **filer d.**, to sing small, to knuckle under, to draw in one's horns.

douzaine, *f.* **il s'en trouve à la d.**, they are as common as blackberries; **on n'en trouve pas à la d.**, you don't come across them every day, they don't grow on every tree (*or* on trees), they're not to be had for the asking.

douze, *m.* **faire le (*or* un) d.**, to make a blunder.

drag, *f.* marihuana cigarette (*drugs**).

dragage, *m.* **1.** police raid. **2.** whoring.

drage, *f.* **faire la d.**, to sell quack remedies.

dragée, *f.* **1.** bullet*; **envoyer une d.**, to fire a bullet (at s.o.). **2. avaler la d.**, to swallow the pill.

draguer. 1. to prowl about. **2.** to look for (s.o.), to be on s.o.'s track. **3.** to be on the look-out for pick-ups.

dragueur, *m.* = coureur de jupes.

drap, *m.* **1. dans de beaux draps**, (*a*) in a nice fix*; (*b*) in a bad way, critically ill. **2. se mettre dans** (*or* **entre**) **les draps,** to go to bed*.

drapeau, *m.* **1. planter un d.,** to run up a debt and to decamp without paying it. **2.** shirt*.

drauper, draupère, draupière, *m.* policeman*.

dresser: d. qn, to make s.o. toe the line, to make s.o. come to heel, to put the screw on s.o.

driver. 1. to drive (motor-car). **2.** to conduct (a business, etc.).

droguer, to cool one's heels, to hang about, to dance attendance, to be kept waiting; **faire d. qn,** to keep s.o. waiting.

droguer, se, to be a drug addict, to be a junkie, a dosser, to take dope, to go on the charge.

drogué, *m.* drug addict, dope fiend, junky.

drôle, *adj.* **se sentir tout d.,** to feel quite queer; **un d. de mec** (**coco, type paroissien**), a queer cuss.

drôlement, *adv.* excessively, terribly, jolly, devilish(ly); **et d.!** and how!

drôlichon, *adj.* funny.

droper, to act (*or* to run *or* to walk) quickly.

droper, se, to decamp*.

dross, *m.* residue in opium pipe, 'green mud'.

drouille, *f.* unusable goods, left-overs.

duc, *m. See* **tournée.**

duce, *m.* **balancer** (*or* **envoyer** *or* **expédier** *or* **faire**) **le d. à qn,** to give s.o. the tip-off (*or* the wire), to tip s.o. off.

duch(e)nock, duchenoque, ducon, duconneau, duconnard, *m.* = **schnock.**

dudule, *m.* = **machin** (*of person*).

dur, *adj.* **1. avoir été élevé à la dure,** to have had a hard bringing-up. **2. croire d. comme fer,** to pin one's faith in, to believe firmly in. **3. en avoir vu de dures,** to have had a bad (*or* rough *or* hard *or* thin) time (of it), to have been (*or* gone) through the mill; **en faire voir de dures à qn,** to give s.o. a bad time, to put s.o. through it, to give s.o. beans, to give s.o. a raw deal, to play old Harry with s.o. **4. être d. à cuire,** to be a tough nut (*or* customer). **5. il n'est pas d.!** he doesn't want much! he's got a nerve! **6. l'avoir dure pour qne, en avoir d. pour qne,** to have a sexual yen for s.o. **7. ne pas être d. à piger,** to be quick on the uptake, to be quick to twig. **8. sur la dure,** on the cold hard ground, on bare boards. *See also* **desserre, feuille 2, lâcher 2.**

dur, *m.* **1.** train; railway; **prendre le d.,** to go by train; **brûler le d.,** to travel without paying, *hence:* **un brûleur de d. 2. un d.** (**à cuire**), **un d. de d.,** a tough guy, a tough 'un, a hard nut to crack, a roughneck; **jouer au d., jouer les durs, jouer les durs de durs,** to play the tough guy. **3.** gold coins (*hard cash as opposed to notes*). **4.** jemmy. **5. les durs,** penal servitude, hard labour; **monter aux durs,** to do hard labour.

duraille, *adj.* **1.** difficult, tough. **2.** miserly*, stingy.

dure, *f.* **1.** ground; **coucher sur la d.,** to sleep on the floor. **2. à la d.,** violently, the hard way.

durillon, durillot, *adj.* difficult, tough.

duschnock, *m.* = **schnock.**

dynamite, *f.* cocaine (*drugs**).

dynamité, *adj.* drugged, high; *m.* junky.

E

eau, *f.* **1.** **e. de bidet,** something worthless, cheap, contemptible. **2.** . . . **à l'e. de rose,** inoffensive, harmless, milk-and-water . . . **3.** **comptez là-dessus** (*or* **croyez ça**) **et buvez de l'e.!** swallow that if you can! don't you believe it! **4.** **être (tout) en e.,** to be dripping with perspiration, to be in a sweat, to be in profuse perspiration. **5.** **il y a de l'e. dans le gaz,** there's trouble brewing, things are beginning to look dirty. **6.** **mettre de l'e. dans son vin,** to draw in one's horns, to come down a peg (or two). **7.** **tomber à l'e.,** (*of plan, etc.*) to fall through, to peter (*or* to fizzle) out, to come to nothing, to end in smoke. **8.** **tomber** (*or* **lâcher**) **de l'e.,** to urinate*. **9.** **tourner** (*or* **s'en aller** *or* **finir**) **en e. de boudin** = **tomber à l'e. 10.** **e. à ressort,** à pédale, soda water. **11.** **avoir les eaux basses,** to be penniless*.

ébouser *or* **ébouzer,** to overwhelm, to crush, to nonplus, to floor; to kill*.

ébréché, *adj.* slightly drunk*.

écailler, to swindle, to fleece, to clean out.

échalas, *m.* tall*, thin person; *pl.* long, skinny legs.

échalote, *f.* **1.** anus*. **pratiquer la course à l'é.,** to dog s.o.'s footsteps. **2.** *pl.* ovaries.

échasses, *f.pl.* = **échalas,** *pl.*

échassier, *m.* = **échalas.**

échassière, *f.* prostitute* (who sits on high stool at the bar).

échauder, to cheat*; **se faire é.,** to get fleeced.

échelle, *f.* **1.** **monter à l'é.,** (*a*) to be hoaxed*; (*b*) to get angry*; **faire monter qn à l'é.,** (*a*) to fool* s.o.; (*b*) to make s.o. angry*, to get s.o.'s monkey up. **2.** **après cela** (*or* **ça**), **il faut** (*or* **il n'y a plus qu'à**) **tirer l'é.,** that's the limit!* you can't beat that!

Also said of persons—e.g. **après lui, il faut tirer l'é.,** he takes the cake!

échelon, *m.* = **berge.**

échiner, to exhaust (s.o.).

échiner, s', to work oneself to death.

éclairer. 1. to pay* up; (*at gambling*) to stake one's money. **2.** **les é.,** to show the colour of one's money. **3.** **é. la dépense,** to pay what's owing.

éclipser, s', to decamp*.

écluse, *f.* **1.** **lâcher** (*or* **ouvrir**) **les écluses,** to start weeping, to weep*. **2.** **lâcher l'é.,** to urinate*.

écluser, to drink, to swig, to knock back, to sink (a drink).

éconocroques, *f.pl.* savings.

écoper. 1. to catch it, to cop (it), to get it in the neck, to take the rap; **é. de six mois de prison,** to cop six months in jail; **il va é.,** he's (in) for it, he's got it coming to him, he'll cop it (hot), he's for the high jump; **il a salement écopé,** he got the book thrown at him (*i.e. he got a heavy sentence*). **2.** to be hit, to be wounded.

écorcher. 1. to murder (a language). **2.** to fleece, to overcharge, to make (s.o.) pay through the nose; **se faire é.,** to be overcharged. **3.** to exaggerate*.

écosser. 1. to pay* up, to shell out. **2.** to get through (work). **3.** to spend (lavishly); **elle m'en a fait é.,** she cost me a pretty penny. **4.** **en é.,** to be a prostitute*.

écouter: j' t'écoute! sez you!

écouter, s', to coddle oneself.

écoutes, écoutilles, *f.pl.* ears*.

écrabouiller, to crush, to squash, to spifflicate.

écrase-merde, *m.pl.* big boots*.

écraser. 1. **écrase!** shut* up! **2.** **en é.** = **en écosser. 3.** **en é.** (**dur**), to sleep like a log, to hog. **4.** **en é. une** (**en lousdoc**), to let a silent fart. **5.** **je t'en**

89

écrase cinq, I shake your hand.
6. é. l'affaire, to hush the matter up.
7. se faire é., to get run over (by a vehicle).
écraser, s', to keep silent, to lie low.
écraseur, m. road-hog.
écrémer, to give sexual satisfaction to, to cream off.
écrevisses, f.pl. (boiled) lobsters (old nickname for British soldiers).
écu, m. 1. avoir des écus, to be rich*. 2. faire valser les écus, to make the money fly, to spend money like water.
écumeur, m. é. de marmite, sponger, hanger-on.
écureuil (à roulettes), m. cyclist circling round a cycle-racing track.
écurie, f. 1. a regular pigsty. 2. sentir l'é., to be in a hurry to get back home, to hurry back home.
édicule, m. street urinal, public convenience.
effacer, 1. to kill*, to wipe out. 2. to receive, to cop (a blow). 3. to polish off (food, drink).
effaroucher, to steal*.
effet, m. 1. il (ça) m'a coupé mes effets, he (it) took the wind out of my sails. 2. cela m'a fait de l'e., cela m'a fait un drôle d'e., it gave me (quite) a turn. 3. si c'est ça (tout) l'e. que ça te fait! if that's the way you feel about it! 4. si c'était un e. de votre bonté (or gentillesse) de . . ., if you would only be so kind as to . . .
effeuillage, m. striptease.
effeuilleuse, f. stripteaser, stripper.
église, f. être marié derrière l'é., to be married but not churched.
égoïner = balancer 3.
égorger, to fleece (customer); to ruin (creditor).
égoutter: é. son colosse (or cyclope or sa sardine), to urinate*.
égratigner, to exaggerate*.
élastique, m. les lâcher avec un é., to be close-fisted, stingy, mean.
élixir de hussard, m. hard liquor.
emballage, m. 1. reprimand*. 2. round-up, raid (by police). 3. (sport)

faire (or piquer) un e., to put on a spurt.
emballé, adj. enthusiastic; être e. pour (or sur), to be keen on; m.f. un(e) emballé(e), an enthusiast, a 'fan'.
emballement, m. 1. (transitory) enthusiasm; burst of energy. 2. passing (or sudden) fancy.
emballer. 1. to excite, to thrill, to fire with enthusiasm; ça ne m'emballe pas, I am not keen on (or impressed by) it, I don't go for it. 2. to arrest*; se faire e., to get run in. 3. to reprimand*; se faire e., to get ticked off. 4. to make a pick-up, to get off with (man or woman). 5. (sports) to (put on a) spurt.
emballer, s'. 1. to flare up, to fly into a temper, to get worked up (or excited), to go off the deep end, to fly off the handle; ne vous emballez pas! keep cool! keep your hair on! keep your shirt on! 2. s'e. pour, to be very keen on, to take a fancy to, to become a 'fan' of.
emballes, f.pl. faire des e. = faire des épates.
embaquer, s', to be a loser.
embarber, to insert, put in.
embarbouiller, to mix up, to confuse.
embarquer. 1. to arrest*. 2. to take away. 3. e. de l'eau, to ship a sea.
embarras, m. faire de l'e. (or des e.), (a) to be fussy, to make a fuss, to 'create', to 'perform'; (b) to put on airs (or side), to swank*; un faiseur d'e., a fuss-pot.
embastiller: se faire e., to be arrested, to be run in.
embellemerdé, adj. saddled with a troublesome mother-in-law.
embellie, f. stroke of luck; profiter de l'e., to take advantage of favourable circumstances, to make hay while the sun shines.
emberlificoter. 1. to entangle, to ball(s) up. 2. to wheedle, to get round (s.o.).
embêtant, adj. tiresome, irksome, boring; c'est diablement e.! c'est e.

comme la pluie! it's a confounded nuisance!

embêté, adj. bored*, fed up; worried, narked.

embêtement, m. **1.** nuisance; bore*, bother. **2. chercher** (or **se préparer**) **des embêtements,** to look for trouble, to stick one's neck out; **s'attirer des embêtements,** to get into hot water; **avoir des embêtements,** to be in a fix*.

embêter. 1. to bore*. **2.** to bother, to pester, to worry, to be a nuisance to, to make (s.o.) sick.

embêter, s'. 1. to be bored*. **2.** to be worried. *Intensive forms:* **s'e. comme une carpe, s'e. ferme** (or **un bon coup** or **à crever** or **à mourir** or **à cent sous** (or **à cent francs**) **de l'heure**), to be bored stiff, to be bored to death; **tu ne t'embêtes pas!** you do yourself well!

embistrouiller =**emberlificoter.**

embobeliner, embobichonner, embobiner, to cajole, to wheedle, to get round (s.o.), to bamboozle, to come the old soldier over (s.o.); **se laisser e.,** to let oneself be hoodwinked, to let oneself be roped in.

emboiser, to make (a woman) pregnant*.

emboîtage, m. (th.) hooting, booing, giving the bird, razzing.

emboîter. 1. (th.) to hoot, to boo, to hiss, to give the bird to, to razz. **2.** to arrest*; to imprison*. **3.** =**mettre en boîte.**

emboucané, adj. =**embêté.**

emboucaner. 1. =**embêter. 2.** to stink, to stink out.

emboucaner, s'. 1. =**s'embêter. 2.** to be poisoned.

embourrer, s'. 1. to swill down (wine, etc.). **2.** to possess (a woman). **3.** to do sth. unpleasant.

embouser: je l'embouse=**je l'emmerde.**

emboutir, s', to crash (into), to collide (with).

emboutissage, m. (motor.) collision.

embrayer. 1. to start work, to get cracking. **2.** to explain oneself, to say what one means. **3.** to win a woman's favour.

embringuer, s'. 1. to get involved, to get mixed up with. **2. s'e. mal,** to get off to a bad start.

embrouille, f. **1.** confusion, muddle, hell of a mess. **2. faire une e. à qn,** to play a dirty trick on s.o.

embrouiller: ni vu, ni connu, j't'embrouille (c.p. *with reference to a clever trick of substitution*) the more you watch, the less you see!

embusqué, m. shirker, slacker, (column-)dodger, Cuthbert.

embusquer, to arrest*; **se faire e.,** to get nabbed.

embusquer, s', to shirk (active service), to get a safe billet, to dig oneself in, to dodge the column.

éméché, adj. slightly drunk*.

émeraudes, f.pl. (i.e. *hémorroïdes*) piles.

émeri, m. See **bouché.**

emmanché, m. pederast*.

emmancher: se faire e., to indulge in sodomy.

emmancher, s', to commit sodomy with one another.

emmener: être emmené en belle, to be taken for a ride (by gangsters, etc.).

emmerdant, adj. (vulgar for) **embêtant; ça, c'est e.!** that's a bugger (or a bastard)!

emmerdation, f., **emmerdement,** m. (vulgar for) **embêtement; quel emmerdement!** what a bloody mess!

emmerdé, adj. (vulgar for) **embêté; être e.,** to be in the shit.

emmerder. 1. to shit on, to crap on. **2.** =**embêter; je l'emmerde!** he can go to hell! he can go and bugger himself! bugger him!

emmerder, s' =**s'embêter.**

emmerdeur, -euse, m.f. bloody nuisance, a regular shit, an awful shit, shit-house, shit-pot, shit-bag, bastard.

emmieller, *euphemism for* **emmerder.**

emmistoufler =**embêter.**

emmouscaillement, *m.*, emmous-cailler, *euphemisms for* emmerdement, emmerder.

emmoutarder, *euphemism for* emmerder.

émos, *f.* emotion, excitement, shock, 'turn'.

émoustiller. 1. to ginger up. 2. to kindle the senses of s.o.

empaffé, *m.* pederast*.

empaffer, to engage in sodomy.

empaffer, s', to get drunk.

empaillé, *m.* dim-wit, dope, stick-in-the-mud, stuffed owl, mutt, noodle.

empalmer, to palm (card, coin).

empalmeur, *m.* card-sharper.

empapaouté, *m.*, empapaouter =empaffé, *m.*, empaffer.

empaqueté, *m.* fool*

empaqueter. 1. to arrest*. 2. to imprison*. 3. to fool s.o.

empaumer. 1. to dupe*. 2. to arrest*.

empégaler, to pawn*.

empéguer, to dupe*.

empeigne, *f. See* gueule (B 11).

empétardé, *m.*, empétarder =empaffé, *m.*, empaffer.

empiffrer, s', to eat* greedily.

empiler, to cheat*, to swindle, to 'do', to rook; se faire e., to be diddled.

empiler, s' =s'empiffrer.

empileur, *m.* cheat, swindler, fraud, trickster.

emplacarder, to imprison*.

emplafonner. 1. to pummel; to butt. 2. to steal*.

emplâtre, *m.* 1. boob, sap, dud, noodle. 2. blow*. 3. c'est mettre un e. sur une jambe de bois, you might as well put a poultice on a wooden leg, it's not the slightest use. *Cf.* cautère. 4. petty pilfering.

emplâtrer. 1. =emplafonner 1 *and* 2. 2. (*motor.*) to crash (*or* to cannon) into another car.

empoignade, *f.* set-to, row, shindy.

empoigne, *f. See* foire (i) 3.

empoigner, to arrest*.

empoigner, s', to have a set-to.

empoisonnant, *adj.* irritating, noying, sickening; putrid; c'est e., it's a bally nuisance.

empoisonné, *adj.* =embêté.

empoisonnement, *m.* =embêtement.

empoisonner (s') =embêter, (s').

empoivrer, s', to get drunk*.

emporter: se faire e., to get run in (by the police).

empoté, *adj.* clumsy, awkward; être e. comme un casse-pot, to be as clumsy as they make 'em, to be all thumbs.

emprosé, *m.*, emproser=empaffé, *m.*, empaffer.

encadrer. 1. ne (pas) pouvoir e. qn=ne (pas) pouvoir blairer qn. 2. to attack* (s.o.). 3. tu peux le faire e.! (*c.p.*) you can shove it (up your arse)!

encager, to imprison*.

encaisse, *f.* (*boxing*) punishment.

encaisser. 1. to receive (blows), to take (punishment), to swallow (insults); savoir e., to be a glutton for punishment, to be able to take it. 2. encaisse!=attrape! 3. ne pas pouvoir e.=ne (pas) pouvoir blairer. 4. e. des salades, to swallow the guff.

encalbécher, to butt (with the head).

encaldosser, to commit sodomy with, to bugger.

encanner, to steal.

encanneur, *m.* crook, thief.

encarrade, *f.* entry, entering.

encarrer, to enter.

encarter, to register (a prostitute).

enceintrer, to make pregnant*.

enchariboter =embêter.

enchaudelancer, to give s.o. the chaude-lance.

enchetarder, enchetiber. 1. to arrest*. 2. to imprison*.

enchoser. 1. to make pregnant*. 2. =emmerder.

enchrister, ench(e)tiber =enchetarder 2.

encloquer, to make pregnant*.

encoinstas(s), *m.*, door-wedge (used by burglars).

encorner, to cuckold.

encotillonné, *adj.* under a woman's thumb, under petticoat government.

encroumé, *adj.* in debt.

encroumer, s', to get into debt.

encroûté, *m.* old fog(e)y*.

encroûter, s', to get into a rut, to vegetate, to become an old fog(e)y*.

enculage, *m.* **e. de mouches,** quibbling, hair-splitting.

enculé, *m.* **1.** pederast*. **2.** twerp, clot, B.F.

enculer. 1. to commit sodomy with; **va te faire e.!** bugger off! you be buggered! **2.** to be a pederast. **3.** =embêter.

enculeur, *m.* **1.** pederast*. **2. e. de mouches,** quibbler, hair-splitter.

endêver, to be furious, to be in a wax, to get angry*; **faire e. qn,** to drive s.o. wild, to put s.o. in a paddy, to get s.o.'s goat.

endoffer = encaldosser.

endormant, *adj.* dull, boring, soporific.

endormeur, *m.* **1.** bore*. **2.** thief. **3.** =bourreur de crâne(s).

endormi, *m.* magistrate, judge, beak.

endormir. 1. to bore*. **2.** to humbug*. **3.** to kill*, to put to sleep. **4.** (*boxing*) to knock (s.o.) out. *See also* rôti.

endosses, *f.pl.* =andosses.

endroit, *m.* **1. le petit e.,** the W.C.* **2. le bon e.,** the buttocks*.

enduire, to flatter*.

enfance, *f.* **c'est l'e. de l'art,** it's very easy*.

enfant, *m.* **1. les enfants s'amusent, (les nourrices auront (du) bon (*or* beau) temps),** (*c.p.*) (*used ironically of adults*) babies will play. **2. il n'y a plus d'enfants!** (*c.p.*) all children are grown up nowadays! children know everything nowadays!

enfariné, *adj.* **1. la langue (*or* la bouche *or* la gueule) enfarinée, le bec e.,** mealy-mouthed. **2. être e. = être dans le pétrin.**

enfifré, *m.*, **enfifrer** = empaffé, *m.*, empaffer.

enfilade, *f.* run of bad luck.

enfilé, *m.* =empaffé, *m.*

enfiler. 1. to swindle*, to cheat, to dupe*. **2.** to swallow, to drain, to knock back (a drink). **3.** to have coition* with; **va te faire e.!** = va te faire enculer!

enfiler, s' =s'envoyer 1 *and* 2.

enfileur, *m.* swindler*, cheat.

enflaquer =emmerder 1.

enflé, *m.* **espèce d'e.!** you blinking idiot! you dope!

enfler. 1. to cheat*, to double-cross. **2.** =enceintrer.

enflure, *f.* =enflé, *m.*

enfoiré, *m.* **1.** =empaffé, *m.* **2. espèce d'e.!** you silly bugger (*or* sod)! **3.** *adj.* =emmerdé.

enfoirer =enculer 1.

enfoncé, *p.p.* bested, beaten, licked, outdone.

enfoncer. 1. to best, to beat, to lick, to dish, to have the edge on (s.o.); **e. qn dans les grandes largeurs,** to beat* s.o. hollow; **ça enfonce tout!** that beats all! **2.** to accuse, to betray.

enfoncer, s' =s'envoyer.

enfonceur, *m.* **e. de portes ouvertes,** braggart, man of big words and little deeds.

enfouiller, to pocket; to cash in.

enfouraillé, *adj.* armed (with (*or* carrying) a gun), well-heeled.

enfourailler =empaffer.

enfourailler, s', to carry a 'rod', to pack a gun.

enfourner. 1. to gobble (food). **2. e. un enfant à,** to make (a woman) pregnant*.

enfourner, s', to crowd (into), to pile (into).

engailler, to deceive, to take in.

engerber, to arrest*.

englandé, *m.* =empaffé.

englander: se faire (*or* se laisser) e., to be diddled, to be taken in.

Engliche, *adj. and m.f.* English.

engourdir, to steal*.

engrainer, to inveigle.

engraisser: c'est elle qui l'engraisse,

(*of prostitute and pimp*) she's his meal-ticket; **se faire e.**, to be kept.

engrosser, to make pregnant*.

engueulade, *f.* reprimand*; **e.-maison**, good telling off.

engueuler, to reprimand*; **se faire e.**, to get a bawling-out, to get told off.

engueuler, s', to have a row (with); **s'e. (ferme)**, to slang one another. *See also* **poisson.**

enguirlander = engueuler.

enjamber, to have coition* with (a woman), to mount.

enjambeur, *m.* womanizer.

enkroumé, *adj.*, **s'enkroumer = encroumé, s'encroumer.**

enlever, to reprimand*.

énormité, *f.* 1. howler, bunkum. 2. outrageous statement *or* action; **dire des énormités**, to say shocking things.

enquiller, (s'), to enter; **se faire e.**, to get involved.

enquilleuse, *f.* woman thief, shoplifter, who hides her booty between her legs.

enquiquinant, *adj.* **il est e.**, he gives me a pain in the neck (*or* in the arse), he gets in my hair.

enquiquinement, *m.* **= embêtement.**

enquiquiner, (s') = embêter, (s').

enquiquineur, -euse, *m.f.* **= emmerdeur, -euse.**

enroupiller, s', to fall asleep.

ensuqué, *adj.* dazed.

ensuquer, to tire out, to get on s.o.'s nerves, to besot.

entendre, s': je m'entends! I know what I mean!

entendu! *int.* right-o! O.K.! **comme de bien e.**, as a matter of course, naturally.

enterrement, *m.* 1. **avoir une figure** (*or* **un air** *or* **une mine** *or* **une tête) d'e.**, to have a face as long as a fiddle, to look down in the mouth. 2. **faire un e. de 1ère classe**, to damn with faint praise.

enterrer. 1. **e. sa vie de garçon**, to give a bachelor's farewell party. 2. **il nous enterrera tous**, he'll outlive the lot of us.

entiché, *adj.* infatuated*.

enticher, s', to be infatuated*.

entifler, (s') = (s')enquiller.

entoiler, to arrest*.

entôlage, *m.* inveigling and robbing (by prostitute); diddling; swindling; fleecing.

entôler, to inveigle and rob; to diddle, to swindle*; to fleece, to rook.

entôleur, *m.* thief, sharper, trickster.

entôleuse, *f.* prostitute who inveigles and robs a client.

entonner. 1. to swill, to swig, to toss off (a drink). 2. to booze, to tipple, to drink like a fish.

entonnoir, *m.* 1. throat, gullet. 2. stomach*. 3. hard drinker, drunkard*.

entortiller, to wheedle, to get round s.o.

entourer, to dupe*.

entourloupe, *f.* **= entourloupette.**

entourlouper, to play a trick on (s.o.).

entourloupette, *f.* trick, ruse, trouble; **une e.-maison**, a dirty trick.

entournures, *f.pl.* **gêné** (*or* **bridé) aux e.**, (*a*) stiff, awkward, ill at ease; (*b*) short of cash, in financial difficulties.

entraîneur, *m.* decoy, shill.

entraîneuse, *f.* dance hostess, B-girl, bar-girl.

entraver, to understand, to twig; **n'e.** (*or* **n'y e.) que dalle** (*or* **que pouic**), not to have the foggiest idea about it, not to dig sth., not to get it at all.

entre-cogner, s', to fight, to have a scrap.

entrée, *f.* **e. des artistes**, anus*, backside.

entre-sort, *m.* huckster's stall.

entripaillé, *adj.* fat*.

entrouducuter, = empaffer.

entubage, *m.* swindle.

entuber. 1. to dupe*. 2. to swallow (food).

envapé, *adj.* dop(e)y, muzzy, woozy, goofed up (by drugs).

envelopper. 1. to dupe*, to victimize. 2. to arrest*; **se faire e.**, to get nabbed. 3. to steal*.

envers, *m.* **les avoir à l'e.**=**avoir les bras retournés.**
enviandé, *m.* =**empaffé.**
envie, *f.* **1. avoir une e. malade** (*or* **folle) de,** to be just dying to. **2. avoir e.,** (*child's expression*) to want to wee-wee.
envoyé, *p.p.* **ça, c'est e.,** that's a clincher! **that's the stuff to give him** (her, them, 'em).
envoyer. 1. les e., to pay* up. **2. en e. une,** to sing a song, to tell a story (*each person in turn*). See also **dire** 9 *and* **promener.**
envoyer, s'. 1. to treat oneself to, to stand oneself (sth.), to down (*or* to knock back) (a drink), to get outside (a meal); to have it off with (a woman). **2.** to have to put up with (sth. unpleasant). **3.** to get through (work). **4.** to decamp*.
épahules, *f.pl.* shoulders; **rouler des é.**=**rouler des biscotteaux.**
épais, *adj.* **en avoir é.**=**en avoir class(e).**
épaisseur, *f.* **se tirer d'é.,** to manage to get out of a scrape.
éparpiller: en é. de première=**en écraser dur.**
épastouiller, épater, to astound, to bowl (s.o.) over.
épatamment, *adv.* staggeringly, fabulously.
épatant, *adj.* first-rate*.
épate, *f.* swank; **faire de l'é.,** to swank*; **faire des épates,** to make (*or* to kick up) a fuss, to be fussy; **un faiseur d'é.,** a swank(er)*.
épateur, *m.* swank(er)*.
épaule, *f.* **1. faire qch. par-dessus l'é.,** to do sth in a perfunctory manner. **2. en avoir par-dessus les épaules**=**en avoir par-dessus la tête (tête** 3). **3. rouler des épaules**=**rouler des biscotteaux.**
épée, *f.* =**caïd.**
éperdument, *adv.* **s'en ficher (s'en foutre) é.,** not to care a damn.
épicemar, *m.* grocer.
épicerie, *f.* **changer d'é.**=**changer de crémerie.**

épinard, *m.* **1.** See **beurre** 4. **2. aller aux épinards,** to be kept by a prostitute. **3. plat d'épinards,** a highly painted landscape.
épingle, *f.* **1. monter qch. en é.,** to make much of sth., to spotlight sth., to make a song and dance about sth. **2. ramasser des épingles,** to practise sodomy. **3. tiré à quatre épingles,** dressed* up to the nines.
épingler, to arrest*; **é. un truc,** to crack a crib.
épique, *adj.* fantastic, sensational, a scream, as good as a play.
éplucheuse, *f.* **e. de lentilles,** lesbian.*
épluchures, *f.pl.* **attention aux é.!** watch your step!
éponges, *f.pl.* lungs, 'bellows'; **avoir les é. mitées (à zéro), avoir les é. bouffées aux mites,** to have consumption, to be T.B.
éponger. 1. to clean (s.o.) out (at gambling, etc.). **2.** to clean up (a large profit, etc.). **3.** (*of prostitute*) to give sexual satisfaction to; **se faire é.,** to have coition*.
époques, *f.pl.* **avoir ses é.**=**avoir ses affaires.**
époustouflant, *adj.* amazing, staggering, stunning, terrific.
époustoufler, to dumbfound*.
équiper, s', to gang up (with).
équipier, *m.* accomplice.
éreintant, *adj.* exhausting*.
éreinté, *adj.* exhausted*.
éreintement, *m.* severe criticism*.
éreinter. 1. to exhaust*. **2.** to thrash*. **3.** to criticize* severely. **4.** to spoil, to make a mess of.
éreinter, s', to work hard*.
éreinteur, *m.* slashing critic, scalp-hunter, knocker.
ergots, *m.pl.* **monter** (*or* **se dresser) sur ses e.,** to get on (*or* to mount) one's high horse.
erreur, *f.* **(y a) pas d'e.!** and no mistake!
esballonner, s', to escape from prison.
esbigner, s', to decamp*.
esbloquer, to dumbfound*.
esbloquer, s', to be dumbfounded.

esbrouf(f)ant, adj. =époustouflant.
esbrouf(f)e, f. =épate; faire de l'e.
(or des esbrouf(f)es)=faire de l'épate;
faire à l'e., to bluff, to come the old
soldier; vol à l'e., snatch-and-grab
robbery, 'blagg'.
esbrouf(f)er, to swank*.
esbrouf(f)eur, m. 1. swank(er)*. 2.
snatch-and-grab thief.
esbrousser, s', to decamp*.
escagasser, 1. to kill*. 2. to dumbfound.
escalope, f. 1. rouler une e. à qn=
rouler une saucisse à qn. 2. pl. ears*.
escaner, to steal*; to cheat.
escargot, m. 1. telephone. 2. escalier
en e., spiral staircase.
escarpe, m. ruffian, tough, thug,
hoodlum, cut-throat.
escarpins, m.pl. e. en cuir de brouette,
galoshes.
esclaffer, s', to laugh* uproariously.
escobar, m. staircase.
escoffier, to murder, to kill*.
escogriffe, m. un grand e., a tall* thin
fellow.
escopette, f. rifle, gun.
esgourde, esgourne, f. ear*; écar-
quillez vos esgourdes! pin back your
lug-holes!
esgourder, to hear, to listen to.
espadoches, f.pl., espagas, m.pl.
(=espadrilles) canvas, cord-soled
shoes.
espèce, f. e. de ... (stresses the term of
abuse which follows—e.g.) e. d'idiot (or
d'imbécile or d'andouille or d'animal
or de con, etc.), you blithering idiot!
you bloody fool (or B.F.)! e. de
salaud! you bloody swine!
espérer. 1. (provincial use) to expect,
to wait for. 2. j'espère que c'est une
belle robe que vous portez! I must say
you've got a nice frock on! 3. j'espère!
I should say!
Espingo, Espingouin, m., adj.
Spaniard, Spanish, Spanish language.
espion, m. 1. concealed microphone,
'bug'. 2. snooper.
espion(n)ite, f. spy-fever.

esquimau, m. 1. choc-ice, ice-brick.
2. woolly (or siren) suit (for child).
esquintant, adj. =éreintant.
esquinté, adj. =éreinté.
esquintement, m. 1. exhaustion. 2.
thrashing*.
esquinter=éreinter; s'e. les yeux, to
ruin one's eyes.
esquinter, s'. 1. to get spoiled. 2.
=s'éreinter.
essayer: tu peux toujours e.! (iron.) just
(you) have a try! just (you) have a
shot at it!
essence, f. e. de panards, sweat on feet.
essorer, to clean (s.o.) out (of money),
to squeeze (s.o.) dry.
essoreuse, f. prostitute*.
estaf(f)ier, m. pimp.
estaminet, m. bar of a brothel.
estampage, m., estampe, f. fleecing;
swindling.
estamper, to fleece, to overcharge, to
rush, to rook, to soak; to swindle*.
estampeur, m. fleecer; swindler*.
estanco(t), m. 1. shop. 2. furnished
rooms. 3. pub.
estom', estome, m. 1. stomach*.
2. faire à l'e.=faire à l'estomac. 3.
avoir de l'e.=avoir de l'estomac.
estomac, m. 1. avoir (or se sentir) l'e.
dans les talons, (a) to be famished;
(b) to be in a blue funk. 2. avoir de
l'e., avoir bon e., to have guts; (lit.
and fig.) to be able to stand a lot; (c) to
have plenty of impudence*; avoir un
certain e.=ne pas manquer de culot.
3. faire à l'e., to bluff.
estomacs, m.pl. breasts* (of woman).
estomaquer, to dumbfound*.
estomme, m. =estome.
estourbir, to kill*.
établi, m. aller à l'é., to go to work.
étagère, f. é. à mégot, ear*.
étal, m. sortir de l'é., to steal from shop-
fronts.
étaler: en é., to swank*.
étaler, s'. 1. to go sprawling, to
measure one's length on the ground.
2. to swank*. 3. to confess*.
état, m. être dans tous ses états, to be

in a great state* (of anger, excitement, etc.).

état-major, *m.* wine and lemon.

étau, *m.* vagina*.

éteignoir, *m.* **1.** wet blanket (*fig.*), kill-joy. **2.** big nose*. **3.** top-hat. **4. é. de concupiscence,** passion-killer, cockfreezer.

étendre. 1. to kill*; **se faire é.,** to get killed, to be done in. **2.** to fail (s.o. at an examination); **se faire é.,** to fail (in an examination).

étendu, *p.p.* ploughed (at an examination).

éterniser, s': s'é. (chez qn), to stay for ages, to outstay one's welcome (*of guest or visitor*).

éternité, *f.* **il y a une é. que je ne vous ai vu,** it's ages since I saw you, I haven't seen you for ages (*or* for donkey's years *or* for a month of Sundays).

Étienne, *pr.n.* **à la tienne, É.!** (*stock rhyming c.p. for a toast*) cheerio!*

étiquette, *f.* =**esgourde.**

étoffe, *f.* **avoir de l'é.,** to have what it takes.

étoile, *f.* **voir les étoiles en plein midi =** **voir trente-six chandelles.**

étouffer. 1. to steal*. **2. é. le coup,** to forget old scores, to let bygones be bygones, to hush matters up, to stop proceedings. *Cf.* **écraser le coup (coup 5). 3.** (*turf*) **é. un cheval,** to 'pull' a horse. **4. en é. un,** to knock back a drink. **5. ce n'est pas la charité qui t'étouffe,** charity is not exactly your strong point.

étouffoir, *m.* stuffy (*or* sweltering) room, an 'oven'.

étourdir, to steal*.

étrangler: en é. X, to toss off X glasses in succession.

étrangleuse, *f.* neck-tie.

être. 1. en ê. (comme un phoque), to be a pederast*, to be one of 'them', to be like that. **2. en ê.,** to belong to the police, to be a police-informer*. **3. l'ê. = ê. cocu. 4. y ê.,** to understand*.

étrenne, *f.* **avoir l'é. de qch.,** to be the first to use sth.; **donne-moi l'é. de ta barbe,** let me be the first to kiss you since you shaved.

étrenner, to be reprimanded*; to get a thrashing*.

étrier, *m.* **ne pas perdre les étriers,** to keep one's wits about one.

étriller. 1. to thrash*. **2.** to cheat*, to fleece. **3.** to give s.o. a dressing down, to reprimand*.

étron, *m.* turd; **poser un é.,** to defecate*.

étuve, *f.* =**étouffoir.**

eulpif, *adj.* smart, stylish, natty, nobby, nifty.

eustache, *m.* clasp-knife, pig-sticker, jack-knife.

euzig(ue)s, *pron.* them, themselves.

évaporée, *f.* **une petite é.,** (*of girl*) a flighty little piece, a featherbrain.

évaporer, s'. 1. to decamp*. **2.** to fade away.

Ève, *pr.n.* **je ne le connais ni d'È. ni d'Adam,** I don't know him from Adam.

exécuter, s', (*a***)** to pay* up; (*b*) to toe the line.

exister: ça n'existe pas! (*to express strong denial or contempt or refusal to believe*) (*a*) it's beneath contempt, it's absolute tripe; (*b*) I don't believe it!

expédier. 1. to kill*. **2.** to ruin (s.o.).

expliquance, *f.* explanation.

expliquer, s'. 1. to have it out (man to man) (with s.o.). **2.** (*slang of the* **milieu**) to practise prostitution.

expo, *m.* (=*exposé*) (*sch.*) **faire un e. (sur),** to give a talk (on).

exprès, *adj.* **c'est comme un fait e.!** you could almost believe that it was done on purpose to annoy me!

expression, *f.* **réduit à sa plus simple e.,** (*of attire*) reduced to a minimum, practically in one's birthday-suit.

extra, *m.* **1. faire un e.,** (*a*) to take on a temporary job; (*b*) to give oneself a treat. **2.** *adj.* first-rate*.

extrait, *m.* **avaler son e. de naissance,** to die*.

F

fabriquer. 1. to do, to be up to, to cook up. 2. to steal*. 3. to cheat, to fool*; **se faire f.,** to be diddled. 4. to arrest*; *see* **tas 4.**

Fac, *f.* **la F.** (=*la Faculté*), the University.

façade, *f.* 1. blind, pretence, cover. 2. **(re)faire sa f.,** to make up (one's face).

façon, *f.* 1. **faire des façons=faire des chichis.** 2. **en voilà des façons!** that's a nice way to behave! where are your manners?

façonnier, -ière, *adj.* fussy; *m.f.* fussy person, fusspot.

fada, *adj.* (*Southern dial.*) foolish, crazy, dopey; *m.* fool, ninny, dope.

fade, *m.* 1. share of booty, cut, whack, split; **aller au f.,** to share out the spoils *or* the swag; to go whacks; **toucher son f.,** to get one's cut; **doubler qn au f.,** to do s.o. out of his share. 2. **avoir son f.,** (*a*) to have one's full share (of illness, suffering, bad luck, etc.); (*b*) to be drunk*. 3. **prendre son f.=jouir.** 4. =**piquouse.**

fadé, *adj.* 1. **être f.,** (*a*) to have had one's whack, to have had (more than) one's share; (*b*) to be in a bad way, to be in a nice mess; (*c*) to have copped a dose of V.D.; (*d*) to be drunk*, to be well away. 2. (*of bill, prison sentence, etc.*) excessive, steep, stiff.

fader. 1. to give (s.o.) his share (*or* whack *or* cut). 2. to punish severely, to give it hot to s.o.; **être fadé,** to get the book thrown at one (*i.e. to get a heavy prison sentence*). 3. to kill*. 4. to ruin, to spoil, to make a mess of.

faf(fe)s, *m.pl.* 1. identity papers; **maquiller les f.,** to fake identity papers; **taper aux f.,** to check identity papers. 2. banknotes, flimsies.

fafiot, *m.* 1. guy, scarecrow. 2. convict. 3. *pl.* banknotes. 4. identity papers.

fagot, *m.* 1. **un f. d'épines,** a cross-patch, a regular bear. 2. **une bouteille de vin de derrière les fagots,** a bottle of wine kept for the best, a bottle of the best. 3. (*turf*) **un cheval de derrière les fagots,** a rank outsider, a dark horse.

fagoté, *adj.* dressed like a guy, dowdy, frumpish; **femme mal fagotée,** frump.

fagoter, to dress (s.o.) like a guy, to tog up.

fagoter, se, to dress like a guy (*or* a scarecrow).

faiblard, *adj.* weakish, rather feeble, sissified.

faible, *adj.* **tomber f.,** to faint*.

faignant, *adj.* (*a*) idle; (*b*) cowardly; *m.* (*a*) lazy-bones, sluggard; (*b*) coward*.

faillot, *m.* =**fayot.**

faim, *f.* 1. **j'ai une de ces faims=j'ai une de ces dents (dent 1).** 2. **il fait f.,** I feel peckish, I feel empty.

fainéasse, *adj.* idle, lazy*.

faire. 1. to steal*; **on m'a fait ma montre,** somebody has pinched my watch; **f. les poches à qn,** to pick s.o.'s pockets. 2. to bamboozle, to have s.o. on; **tu es fait!** you've been 'had'! you've had it! **se laisser f.,** to let oneself be taken in; **on ne me la fait pas!** *or* (**il ne) faut pas me la f.!** you can't fool me! don't try it on with me! 3. to kill*. 4. to pick up (one of the opposite sex). 5. **la f. à qn à la vertu, à l'innocence, aux larmes, etc.,** to assume a virtuous, an innocent, a tearful, etc. air for s.o.'s benefit. (*Cf. in English* 'to do the grand', 'to put on an act'). 6. (*of shopkeeper*) to keep, to stock, to sell (certain articles). 7. (*of child*) to evacuate, to forget oneself (*e.g.* **un gosse qui fait dans ses draps** *or* **dans ses culottes** *or* **sa culotte**). 8. (*of age*) to look; **il faisait dans les vingt-cinq ans,** he looked about twenty-five; **il**

fait plus vieux que sa femme, he looks older than his wife. **9. savoir y f.,** to be very wide-awake*. **10. faites donc!** don't mention it! do so by all means! **11. ça fait chic!** that looks smart! **12. j'ai de quoi f.!** I've my work cut out. **13. ça commence à bien f.!** that's enough of that! that's too much of a good thing!

faire, s'en: ne pas s'en f., not to worry; **faut pas s'en f., (ne) t'en fais pas!** don't worry! not to worry! don't let it get you down! take it easy! don't get het up!

faisan(t), *m.* =**faisandier.**

faisander, to cheat*.

faisandier, *m.* unscrupulous person, swindler*, twister.

faiseur, *m.* swindler*, fraud, bluffer. *See also* **ange, embarras.**

fait, *p.p.* **1. être f.,** to be arrested, caught, nabbed, copped. **2. bien f.!: c'est bien f. pour vous (pour lui, etc.)!** (it) serves you (him, etc.) right! **3. comme te voilà f.!** what a sight you are!

fait, *m.* **le f. est!** (*as a reply—e.g.*) **vous devez vous croire dans une maison de fous!—le f. est!** you must think that you're in a lunatic asylum!—you've said it!

falot, *m.* (*mil.*) court-martial; **passer le** (*or* **au**) **f.,** to be court-martialled.

faloter; =**passer au falot.**

false, falzar(d), *m.* trousers*.

fameux, *adj.* first-rate*; **ce n'est pas f.,** it's not up to much, it's no great shakes.

fana, *m.* (=*fanatique*) enthusiast, 'fan'.

fanal, *m.* stomach*.

fandard, *m.* =**falzar(d).**

fanfan, *m.* (*deformation of* '*enfant*') *pet name for* little boy or girl.

fanfare, *f.* **en avant la f.,** off we go (again)!

fantabosse, *m.* infantryman, foot-soldier, foot-slogger.

faramineux, *adj.* colossal, knock-out.

farce, *adj.* very funny, very comical; *f.* **faire ses farces,** to lead a gay life, **to sow one's wild oats.**

farcir. 1. to deceive*, to trick, to do the dirty on (s.o.) **2.** to fill s.o. with lead. **3.** to have coition* with, to stuff.

farcir, se. 1. to serve (years in prison). **2.** =**s'envoyer 1** *and* **2.**

fard, *m.* **piquer un** (*or* **son**) **f.,** to blush, to colour up. (*Also spelt* **phare.**)

farfelu, *adj.* odd, queer, crazy, hare-brained; *m.* whipper-snapper, young puppy.

farfouiller, to rummage.

farfouillette, *adj.* **les galeries F.,** (*jest.*) popular nickname for *les Galeries Lafayette* in Paris.

fargue, *m.* accusation, charge, indictment.

farguer, to accuse, to charge, to indict.

farguer, se =**s'enfourailler.**

faridon, *f.* **1. faire la f.,** to go on the spree*. **2. être de la f.,** to be penniless*.

farine, *f.* **1. de (la) même f.,** of the same kidney, of the same sort. **2. rouler qn dans la f.,** to make a complete fool of s.o. **3. se les rouler dans la f.,** to laze, to shirk one's duty.

faro, *m.* kind of three-card trick.

fatma, fatmuche, *f.* (*pej*) woman*.

fauche, *f.* **1.** theft. **2.** stolen goods.

fauché, *adj.* penniless*; **f. comme les blés,** stony-broke, broke to the wide.

faucher. 1. to steal*. **2.** to clean out (at gambling). **3.** to guillotine.

faucheur, *m.* **1.** thief. **2.** executioner.

faucheuse, *f.* guillotine.

Fauchman, *m.* **la Maison F. et Cie**= **fauché.**

fausse-couche, *f. See* **couche 2** *and* **3.**

faute, *f.* **la f. à pas de chance,** nobody's fault.

fauter, (*of female*) to go wrong, to (make a) slip.

fauteuil, *m.* (*turf, etc.*) **arriver** (*or* **gagner**) **(comme) dans un f.,** to win* easily.

faux-col, *m. See* **col 2.**

faux-poids, *m.* prostitute under age.

favouille, *f.* =**fouille.**

fayot, *m.* **1.** kidney-bean. **2.** (*sch.*) swot.

3. (*mil.*) re-enlisted man. 4. (*mil.*) =**sous-off.** 5. **aller becqueter des fayots,** to go to jail, to do time.
fayoter, (*mil.*) to re-enlist.
fée, *f.* **la f. blanche,** cocaine; morphine; **la f. brune,** opium, poppy, pop; **la f. verte,** hashish (*drugs**).
feignant, *m.* =**faignant.**
feignasse, *m.* lazy* bum.
feignasser, to laze, to idle away one's time.
feignasson, *m.* =**feignasse.**
feinter, to fool* (s.o.).
fêlant, *adj.* very funny*.
fêlé, *adj.* mad*, cracked.
félouse, *m.* North African soldier.
fêlure, *f.* **avoir une f.,** to be mad*, to be cracked.
femelle, *f.* (*pej.*) female, woman*, creature.
femme. 1. **une petite f.,** lady friend, little bit of fluff (*or* of skirt). 2. **f. à passions,** sexual pervert. 3. (*at cards*) Queen.
femmelette, *f.* effeminate man, womanish man, mollycoddle, sissy.
fendard, fendart, *m.* =**falzar(d).**
fendre, se, to be generous, to put one's hand down, to do the handsome (thing); **il s'est fendu de mille francs,** he forked out (*or* stumped up *or* coughed up *or* came down with *or* parted with) a thousand francs; **il ne s'est pas fendu,** he wasn't over-generous. *See also* **se fendre la pipe.**
fendue, *f.* (*pej.*) woman*.
fenêtre, *f.* 1. a hundred francs. 2. **il faut passer par là ou par la f.,** it's a case of Hobson's choice. 3. **jeter l'argent par la f.** (*or* **les fenêtres**), to be a spendthrift, to throw money down the drain. 4. **mettre la tête** (*or* **le nez**) **à la f.,** to be guillotined.
fente, *f.* vagina*, crack.
féo, féodal, *adj.* =**formidable.**
fer, *m.* **un mauvais f.,** a dangerous fellow, an ugly customer.
fer-blanc, *m.* **en f.-b.,** worthless, shoddy, tinpot.
ferblanterie, *f.* decorations, medals.

fermer: ferme ta boîte (*or* **ta gueule** *or* **ta malle**)! **ferme ça! ferme-la! la ferme!** shut* up!
fermeture, *f.* **f.! tu me cours!** shut* up! you get on my nerves!
ferraille, *f.* small coins; small change, chicken-feed.
ferré, *adj.* =**calé 1.**
ferrer: f. dur, to make a start in earnest, to get down to it.
ferte, *f.* **la bonne f.,** fortune-telling; **diseuse de bonne f.,** fortune-teller; **taper** *or* **tirer la bonne f.,** to tell fortunes.
fesse, *f.* 1. **avoir chaud aux fesses,** (*a*) to be afraid*, to have the jitters; (*b*) to have the police hot on one's track. 2. **magasin de fesses,** brothel*. 3. **n'y aller que d'une f.,** to do sth. only half-heartedly. 4. **occupe-toi de tes fesses!** mind your own business! 5. **poli comme mes fesses,** unmannerly, rude. 6. **prendre ses fesses à poignée,** to run like hell, to run split-arse. 7. **serrer les fesses,** to resist in spite of intense fear, to be jittery. 8. **il y a de la f.** (*or* **des fesses**), there are girls*, women, about. 9. **poser ses fesses,** to sit down.
fessier, *m.* buttocks*.
feston, *m.* **faire des festons en marchant**=**festonner.**
festonner, to zigzag (*or* to lurch) along, to reel about.
fête, *f.* 1. **être à la f.,** to be overjoyed. 2. (*iron.*) **ça va être** (*or* **ce sera**) **ta f.!** you're going to cop it! 3. **il n'a jamais été** (*or* **il ne s'est jamais trouvé** *or* **il ne s'est jamais vu**) **à pareille f.,** he never had such a good time, he never enjoyed himself as much. 4. **faire la f.,** to lead a gay life, to go on the spree*. 5. **ce n'est pas tous les jours f.!** this calls for a celebration! Christmas comes but once a year! 6. **souhaiter la** (*or* **sa**) **f. à qn,** (*a*) to give s.o. a sound thrashing*; (*b*) to kill* s.o.
feu, *m.* 1. revolver*, pistol. 2. **avoir le f. quelque part** (*or* **au derrière** *or* **au cul** *or* **aux fesses** *or* **aux miches**), to be in a

devil of a hurry, to run split-arse; to have hot pants, to have ants in one's pants; **il courait comme s'il avait le f. au derrière,** you couldn't see him for dust. 3. **cracher le f.,** péter le (or du) f., to be full of beans (or of pep), to be a live wire, to be on one's toes. 4. **être dans son coup de f., être en plein coup de f.,** to be at one's busiest. 5. **jeter f. et flamme,** to flare up, to fume and rage, to be in a towering rage. 6. **le f. n'est pas à la maison!** or **il n'y a pas le f.!** there's no great (or no special) hurry; there's tons of time! where's the fire? 7. **n'y voir que du f.,** not to see through it, not to make head or tail of sth., to be none the wiser for it, to be quite taken in by sth.

feuille, f. 1. purse. 2. ear*; **être dur de la f., ne pas être synchro de la f., être constipé des feuilles,** to be hard of hearing; **feuilles de chou,** big ears; **avoir les feuilles de chou ensablées** = **avoir les portugaises ensablées,** to be hard of hearing. 3. newspaper; **f. de chou,** gutter-rag, gutter-sheet, (local) rag. 4. **voir les feuilles** (or **la feuille**) **à l'envers,** (of woman) to have coition*, to see the sky through the trees, to see the stars lying on one's back.

feuillées, f.pl. (mil.) latrines.

fias, fiaz(e), m. 1. (péj.) fellow*, blighter, bloke. 2. anus*.

fiasse, f. (péj.) girl*; pl. people.

ficelard, m. = **ficelle 1.**

ficelé, adj. = **fagoté; être f. comme quat' sous,** to look a guy, to be dressed like a guy.

ficeler, to tog (s.o.) up, to dress (s.o.) like a guy.

ficelle, f. 1. trickster, twister, artful dodger; **une vieille f.,** a wily (old) bird, an old hand, a deep one. 2. **connaître les ficelles,** to be wide-awake*, to know the ropes. 3. (mil.) stripe, (approx.) pip; pl. tapes. 4. (of bread) small baguette. 5. **casser la f.,** to get a divorce. 6. **faire f.** = **faire fissa.** 7. **après ça il faut tirer la**

f. = **après ça il faut tirer l'échelle.** 8. (long-distance drivers' slang) **se faire prendre en f.,** to be taken in tow. 9. pl. (a) handcuffs*; (b) (boxing turf, etc.) **les ficelles,** the ropes. 10. adj. cunning, knowing, cute, up to snuff, wily.

fichaises, f.pl. rubbish*, rot.

fichant, adj. annoying, bothersome, aggravating.

fiche, ficher. 1. to do, to be up to; **ne rien fiche(r), ne pas en ficher un coup** (or **une secousse**), **ne pas en ficher lourd:** see **coup 15.** 2. to matter. **qu'est-ce que ça fiche?** what does that matter? who the hell cares? **ça ne fiche rien,** it doesn't matter, I don't care a rap*. 3. to put, to place, to stick, to shove, to bung, to sling, to chuck, to pitch, to land (s.o. a kick or a blow). See also **air 6, billet, camp, clou 5, dedans, frousse, paix, porte, trouille.** 4. **va te faire fiche!** go to blazes! get to hell out of here! **envoyer faire fiche,** to send (s.o.) packing*; to chuck (sth.) up. 5. **j' t'en fiche!** or **va te faire fiche!** nothing of the sort (or of the kind)! not at all! not on your Nellie! not a bit of it! it was no go! 6. **à la va-te-faire-fiche** = **à la va-comme-je-te-pousse.** 7. **ça la fiche** (or **ça la fout**) **mal,** that makes a bad impression, it looks lousy.

ficher, se. 1. **se f. de,** (a) to make fun of, to laugh at, to have (s.o.) on, to pull s.o.'s leg, to chip s.o.; (b) not to care a rap* about; **c'est se f. du monde!** they (he, she, etc.) couldn't care less! **je m'en fiche (pas mal)!** or **ce que je m'en fiche!** I don't care a damn! I couldn't care less! A fat lot I care! **s'en f. et s'en contreficher, s'en f. comme de l'an neuf** (or **de l'an quarante**), **s'en f. éperdument** (or **totalement**), not to care a damn. 2. **se f. dedans,** to make a bad blunder (or a bad break). 3. **se f. par terre,** to go sprawling, to come a cropper.

fichets, m.pl. handcuffs*.

fichtre, int. 1. (surprise, admiration)

by Jove! by gad! by gum! gosh!
crikey! cripes! crumbs! **2.** (*annoy-
ance*) hang it! dash it all! blow it! **3.**
(*intensive*) **f. oui!** rather! I should say
so! **f. non!** no fear! **je le sais f. bien!**
I know it jolly well! don't I just know
it! **je n'en sais f. rien!** I'll be hanged
if I know! **ça n'est f. pas agréable
de . . .**, it's no bally joke to . . .

fichtrement, *adv.* (*intensive*) extremely, awfully, terribly, jolly,
deucedly, confoundedly, infernally;
c'est f. loin! its' a hell of a way!

fichu, *adj. and p.p.* (*of* **fiche** *or* **ficher**).
1. beastly, rotten, awful, wretched,
blooming, bally, blessed, confounded,
god-forsaken, blankety-blank. **2.**
done* for. **3. f. de,** likely to, capable
of; **il est f. de partir avant que j'arrive,**
it's quite on the cards that he'll leave
before I get there; **il n'est pas f. de
faire son lit,** he isn't even up to making
his bed. **4. être mal f.,** (*a*) to feel unwell*; (*b*) to be badly dressed, to be
badly turned out. *See as* **4**(*c*) *and*
sou 1. (*c*) to be ugly, ill-favoured; to
be ill-shaped. **5. être bien f.,** (*a*) to be
well-dressed; (*b*) to be good-looking,
(*of woman*) to have a million-dollar
figure; (*of man*) to be well-built, to be
hefty. **6.** (*with the force of* **fiche**(r) **3**).
**qui est-ce qui m'a f. un imbécile
pareil?** what have I done to be landed
with such an idiot?

fiérot, *adj.* uppish, snobbish, stuck-up.
fiesta, *f.* feast, jollification, spree*.
fieu, *m.* son(ny); lad; fellow*; **un bon
f.,** a good sort, a good chap.
fifi, *m.* **fifille,** *f.* darling*; teacher's
pet (*or* favourite).
fifine, *f.* sanitary towel.
fiflot, *m.* =**fantabosse.**
fifre, *indef. pron.* ne . . . que **f.,** nothing
at all, not a damn thing, sweet Fanny
Adams.
fifre, *m.* **un grand f.,** a tall* thin
person.
fifrelin, *m.* **ne pas avoir un f.,** to be
penniless*; **cela ne vaut pas un f.,**
that's not worth a brass farthing (*or*

a red cent); **mon dernier f.,** my last
farthing.
fifti, fifty, *m.* half; **fifti-fifti,** half and
half; **trois balles fifti,** three francs
fifty; **à deux plombes fifti,** at half past
two; **faire fifti,** to go halves.
figaro, *m.* **1.** barber. **2.** (*waiter's slang*)
faire f., not to get a tip.
fignard, figne, fignedé, *m.* buttocks*.
figue, *f.* **1.** mi-f., **mi-raisin,** neither one
thing nor the other. **2. faire la f. à
qn,** to make a gesture of contempt
at s.o. **3.** clitoris.
figure, *f.* **1. casser la f. à qn,** to punch
s.o.'s head. **2. se payer la f. de qn** = se
payer la tête de qn.
fil, *m.* **1. avoir le f.,** to be very wide-
awake*. **2. avoir un f. à la patte,** to
have an entanglement (*e.g. a mistress*),
not to be a free agent, to be tied down,
to be lumbered; to be married*; **se
nouer le f. à la patte, se mettre un f. à
la patte, se laisser attacher un f. à la
patte,** to get married*. **3. donner du
f. à retordre à qn,** to give s.o. a lot
of trouble, to give s.o. a headache, to
lead s.o. a pretty dance; **avoir du f. à
retordre,** to have one's work cut out,
to get more than one bargained for.
**4. il n'a pas inventé le f. à couper le
beurre,** he'll never set the Thames (*or*
the world) on fire. **5. baver dans les
fils de fer,** to exaggerate*. **6. f. de
fer** = **échalas. 7. un vrai f.,** (*of female*)
a mere slip (*i.e. slim*). **8. être au bout
du f.,** to be on the phone (*or* on the
line), to be speaking (on the phone);
donner un coup de f. à qn, to give s.o.
a ring (*or* a tinkle *or* a buzz). **9.
sécher sur le f.,** to be stood up.
filasse, *adj.* (*of hair*) tow-coloured, of a
washed-out colour.
filature, *f.* shadowing (*e.g. by detective*),
dogging; **prendre qn en f.,** to shadow
s.o., to tail s.o.
filaturer = **prendre en filature.**
fil-en-quatre, *m.* strong spirits*.
filer. 1. to shadow, to dog, to trail, to
tail. **2.** to denounce*. **3.** to hand over,
to give, to pass, to bung over; to palm

off (sth. on s.o.); **file-moi une pipe,** slip me a fag; **en f. une bonne à qn,** to land s.o. a clout (*or* a fourpenny one). **4.** to decamp*. **5. f. doux,** to back down, to knuckle under, to sing small, to eat humble pie, to pull in one's horns. **6. en f.,** to practise sodomy.

filer, se: se f. (dans), to get involved (in).

filet, *m.* **avoir le f.,** to be tongue-tied; **avoir le f. (bien) coupé, ne pas avoir le f.,** to have a glib tongue, to have the gift of the gab, to be a chatterbox.

filetouze, *m.* (= *filet*) string bag, net bag.

filière, *f.* **passer par** (*or* **suivre**) **la f.,** to go through the regular (official) channels; to go through the (whole) mill, to work one's way up.

fille, *f.* **1. f. (publique), f. de joie,** (*in a brothel*) **f. de maison,** prostitute*; **courir les filles,** to wench. **2. f.-mère,** unmarried mother. **3.** bottle of wine. **4. jouer la f. de l'air,** to decamp*. **5. la plus belle f. du monde ne peut donner que ce qu'elle a,** (*c.p.*) no one can be expected to do more than his utmost.

fillette, *f.* half-bottle (of wine).

filoche, *f.* **prendre qn en f., prendre la f., prendre la f. de qn** = **filer 1; être pris en f.,** to be shadowed, to be tailed.

filocher. 1. = **filer 1. 2. f. devant une corvée,** to shirk a fatigue duty.

filon, *m.* **1.** cushy (*or* soft *or* fat) job; **les meilleurs filons,** the plums; **ça n'est pas le f.!** (*or* **ça c'est pas le f.!** that's a rotten job! **2. avoir le f.,** to be sitting pretty. **3. trouver le f., trouver un bon f., dénicher le bon f.,** to strike oil, to strike it rich, to strike a bonanza.

filonner. 1. to shirk, to be a shirker. **2.** (*sch.*) to cheat, to crib.

filonneur, *m.* **1.** shirker. **2.** cheat, cribber.

fils, *m.* **1.** fellow*, lad, sonny, chap. **2. f. à papa,** rich man's son, young man with an influential father, play-

boy, papa's boy. **3. f. de pute!** son of a bitch!

fin, *f.* **1. à la f. des fins,** when all is said and done. **2. c'est la f. des haricots,** that's the limit*. **3. faire une f.,** (*of young man*) to turn over a new leaf, to get married and settle down.

fin, *m.* **c'est le f. du f.,** its first-rate*, it's the last word.

fin, *adv.* **1. être f. prêt,** to be absolutely ready*, to be fully prepared; (*of athlete, race-horse, etc.*) to be trained to the minute; **tout est f. prêt,** everything is under control. **2. f. soûl,** dead drunk*.

fin, *adj.* **j'avais l'air f.,** I looked a proper Charlie.

finasser, to outsmart; **f. avec qn,** to play hanky-panky with s.o.

fine, *f.* **une f.,** a glass of liqueur-brandy; **une f. à l'eau,** a brandy and soda.

fini, *adj.* **n.i.ni; (c'est) f.!** and that's an end of it!; it's all over between us!; and that's all you'll get!

finocher, to finick (over).

fiole, *f.* **1.** head*; **se payer la f. de qn** = **se payer la tête de qn; il se paye ma f.,** he's pulling my leg. **2.** face*; **j'en ai soupé de ta f.!** I'm fed up with you! you make me tired! **ici il faut secouer sa f.,** here you've got to get a move on. **3.** person; own self.

fion, *m.* **1.** anus*. **2.** luck; **un f. du tonnerre,** the devil's own luck. **3. donner le (coup de) f. à qch.** to clean up, to give sth. the finishing touch(es). **4. avoir le f. pour faire qch.,** to have the knack of sth., to be a dab (hand) at sth. **5. l'avoir dans le f.** = **l'avoir dans le baba.**

fiot(t)e, *m.* **1.** fellow*, blighter; **bon f.,** a good sort. **2.** *f.* pederast*.

first-bourre, *adj.* = **de première bourre.**

fissa, *adv.* **faire f.,** to be quick about it, to get a move on, to lose no time.

fissure, *f.* **1. avoir une f.,** to be crazy, to be slightly cracked. **2. mastiquer une f.,** to dumbfound*.

fiston, *m.* **(mon) f.,** my lad, sonny boy.

fistot, *m*. first-year naval cadet.
fixe, *adj*. je ne te vois pas f. = je ne te vois pas blanc (blanc *adj*. 3).
fixe, *m*. regular pay.
fixé, *adj*. être f., to know where you stand.
flacdalle, flaquedalle, *adj*. spineless.
flacon, *m*. 1. (avoir (prendre) du f. = avoir (prendre) de la bouteille. 2. *pl*. boots*, shoes.
flafla, *m*. faire du f. (*or* des flaflas), to make a fuss; to swank*.
flag(r)(e), *m*. être pris en f., se faire piquer en f., to be caught red-handed, to be caught in the (very) act, to be caught bang (*or* dead) to rights, to be done to rights, to be caught high (*drugged*).
flagada, *adj*. = flapi.
flagdas, *m.pl*. = fayots 1; la fin des f. = la fin des haricots (fin, *f*. 2).
flageolet, *m*. penis*; *pl*. thin legs.
flague, *m*. = flag.
flahutes, *m.pl*. (*cycling slang*) Belgian racers.
flamb', *adj*. stupendous.
flambante, *f*. match (*allumette*), lucifer.
flambard, *m*. gay dog; faire le f., to swank*.
flambard, *adj*. all dressed up*.
flambe, *m*. gambling, gambling game.
flambé, *adj*. done* for.
flambeau, *m*. avoir du f., to be lucky (*especially at gambling*).
flamber. 1. to gamble; f. dur, to be a heavy gambler (*or* plunger), to put one's shirt on (a horse in a race). 2. to lead a life of ostentation. 3. f. une allumette, to strike a match.
flambeur, *m*. gambler, heavy better, plunger.
flamme, *f*. 1. ça va chier des flammes, there'll be a hell of a row. 2. péter la f. = péter le feu (feu 3).
flan, *m*. 1. put-up job, frame-up. 2. à la f., free-and-easy, happy-go-lucky; (*of work*) bungled, botched; un truc à la f., a trivial matter. 3. du f.! = des clous! (clou 7). 4. c'est du f.! it's all bunkum!

it's all claptrap! it doesn't mean a thing! you're pulling my leg! 5. faire du f., to tell lies, to deceive. 6. en rester (en être) comme du f. = en rester (en être) comme deux ronds de f. 7. au f., at random; venir au f., to come on the off-chance, to chance it. 8. travail au f., pilfering.
flanc, *m*. 1. être sur le f., (*a*) to be laid up, to be on the sick list; (*b*) to be exhausted*; mettre qn sur le f., to knock s.o. up. 2. se battre les flancs, to rack one's brains. 3. tirer au f., to malinger*.
flanchard, *m*. shirker, quitter; *adj*. slightly unwell, weakish, dicky.
flanche, *m*. 1. job, business; c'est pas ton f.! it's none of your business! monter un f., to do a job (*i.e. robbery, etc.*). 2. aller au f., to go gambling.
flancher. 1. = se dégonfler. 2. to rat. 3. (*turf, of horse*) to crack up, to compound. 4. (*sch.*) to be ploughed, to come a cropper.
flancheur, *m*. = bonneteur.
flandrin, *m*. un grand f., a tall,* lanky (*or* gawky) fellow, a big lout.
flanelle, *f*. faire f., to be a platonic (*or* unprofitable) customer (in brothel, café, etc.).
flânocher, to loaf; to mooch around, to potter about, to arse around.
flânocheur, *m*. loafer, moocher, bum.
flanquer. 1. = fiche(r) 3. 2. se flanquer par terre = se ficher par terre. See air 6.
flanquette, *f*. à la bonne f. (= à la bonne franquette), simply, without ceremony; venez dîner chez nous à la bonne f., come and take pot-luck with us.
flapi, *adj*. exhausted*.
flash, *m*. bang (*drugs*).
flasquer. 1. = chier 1. 2. faire f. qn = faire chier qn.
flaupée, *f*. = flop(p)ée.
flauper = flop(p)er.
flèche, *m*. 1. pas un f., not a cent (*or* a brass farthing); sans un f., penniless*. 2. trick, wangle.

flèche, *f.* **1.** meat. **2.** gang. **3.** =truc 1.

flécher: f. ensemble *or* **se f.,** to join up, to go cahoots, to gang up.

flémard, flemmard, *adj.* lazy*, idle, work-shy; *m.* lazy-bones, idler, slacker, weary Willie, slug-a-bed.

flème, flemme, *f.* laziness; **avoir la f.,** to feel lazy*, not to feel up to (*or* not to feel like) work; **j'ai la f. de lire,** I don't feel like reading; **ça me donne la f.,** I can't be bothered to do it; **battre** (*or* **tirer**) **sa f.,** to do nothing.

fleur, *f.* **1.** favour, gift, present; **faire une f. à qn,** to do s.o. a favour; to give s.o. sth. gratis; to let s.o. off lightly. **2.** =bouquet 2. **3.** être f., to be penniless*. **4.** s'envoyer des fleurs, to give oneself a pat on the back, to blow one's own trumpet. **5.** arriver (*or* s'amener) comme une f., to drop in on s.o. unceremoniously, without turning a hair. **6.** perdre sa f., to lose one's maidenhead. **7.** f. de nave: *see* nave 2. **8.** f. bleue, sentimentally amorous, spoony, gooey. **9.** f. des pois, pederast*.

flibuster, to steal*.

flic, *m.* policeman*; **à bas les flics!** down with the cops!

flicaille, *f.* police, cops.

flicard, *m.* =flic.

flingot, *m.* rifle, revolver*, fire-arm.

flingot(t)er =flinguer 1, 2, 3.

flingue, *m.* =flingot.

flinguer. 1. to kill*, to shoot dead; to wound. **2.** to fire at. **3.** to steal*. **4.** to guillotine. **5.** être flingué, to be penniless*, to be hard up.

flingueur, *m.* killer.

fliquaille, *f.* =flicaille.

flique, *m.* =flic.

flop(p)ée, *f.* **1.** thrashing*. **2.** shower (of blows). **3.** great quantity*.

flop(p)er, to thrash*.

flot, *m.* être à f., to be prosperous, to be flush (*i.e.* rich*).

flottant, *m.* (*sch.*) track-suit, gym-clothes.

flottard, *m.* naval cadet.

flotte, *f.* **1.** rain, 'juice'; **il tombe de la f.,** it's raining. **2.** water, Adam's ale. **3.** la F., Naval Academy. **4.** intégrer à F.,** to be admitted at the Naval Academy.

flottes, *f.pl.* **des f.,** great quantity*; crowds, swarms.

flotter: il flotte =il tombe de la flotte.

flotteurs, *m.pl.* **1.** breasts (of female). **2.** falsies.

flouer, to swindle*.

floueur, *m.* swindler*.

flouse, flouss, flouze, *m.* money*.

flouzer =flouer.

flub(b)es, *m.pl.* **avoir les f.,** to be a coward*, to be afraid; **filer (ficher, flanquer, foutre) les f. à qn,** to put the wind up s.o.; *m. sing.* tip (*gambling*).

flûtant, *adj.* **c'est f.,** it's a bally nuisance.

flûte! *int.* **1.** bother! dash! blow! darnation! (*expletives**). **2.** **oui ou f.?** *euphemistic form of* **oui ou merde?**

flûter. 1. to drink hard, to tipple*. **2.** **envoyer qn f.,** to send s.o. packing*. **3.** **c'est comme si je flûtais** =c'est comme si je chantais (chanter 2).

flûtes, *f.pl.* legs*; **jouer** (*or* **se tirer**) **des f., mettre les f., arpigner ses f.,** to decamp*.

Fluviale, *f.* **la F.,** the River Police.

focard(e), focardise, focardité, *f.* stupidity, rubbish*.

fofolle, *adj. f.* silly, foolish, flighty.

foies, *m.pl.* **1.** **avoir les f. (blancs)** = avoir les flub(b)es. **2.** **manger** (*or* **bouffer**) **les f. à qn,** to make mince meat of s.o., to knock s.o.'s head off.

foin, *m.* **1.** uproar*; **faire du f.,** to kick up a row, to protest vehemently; **faire un f. de tous les diables,** to raise Cain, to raise a hell of a stink, to make a great song and dance (*about* sth.), **2.** **faire ses foins,** to make money, to make big profits. **3.** **mettre du f. dans ses bottes** (*or* **dans ses sabots**), to feather one's nest; **avoir du f. dans ses bottes,** to have feathered one's nest. **4.** **être bête à manger du f.:** *see* **bête,** *adj.* **1.** **5.** tobacco, baccy. **6.** marihuana (*drugs**). **7.** beard.

foirage, *m*. fiasco, failure, flop, wash-out.

foirailleur, *m*. small-time reveller.

foire, *f*. (i) 1. crowd, crush, bedlam, bear-garden. 2. **faire la f.**, to go on the spree*. 3. **la f. d'empoigne**, the game of grab, rat-race; **acheter (acquérir, gagner) qch. à la f. d'empoigne**, to get sth. on the crook. 4. **la f. est sur le pont! we've got to get a move on! il n'y a pas la f. sur le pont** *or* **la f. n'est pas sur le pont**, there's no great hurry.

foire (ii), **foirade**, *f*. **avoir la f.**, (*a*) to have diarrhoea*; (*b*) to be funky, to be in a blue funk.

foirer. 1. to misfire, to (be a) flop, to fizzle out, to fall through, to come unstuck, to go phut. 2. =**avoir la foire** (ii) (*a*) *and* (*b*). 3. to defecate*.

foireur, *m*. reveller, gay dog, gay spark.

foireux, *adj*. 1. suffering from diarrhoea. 2. funky, jittery. 3. *m*. person suffering from diarrhoea. 4. *m*. coward, funk.

foiridon, *f*. spree*.

foirinette, *f*. **faire la f.**=**faire la foire** (i) 2.

foiron, *m*. buttocks*.

fois, *f*. 1. **des f.**, sometimes. 2. **des f. que vous le verriez** *or* **si des f. vous le voyez**, if by any chance you (should) happen to see him, just in case you happen to see him. 3. **non mais des f.! not likely! don't make me laugh!** well, I like that! what do you take me for?

foisonner, to stink*.

folichon, *adj*. **ce n'est pas f.**, it's not exactly funny, it's far from being wildly hilarious.

folichonner, to lark, to frolic, to play the (giddy) goat; to carry on (with women).

folie, *f*. **faire des folies**, (*a*) to be extravagant, to squander one's money, to throw one's money about; (*b*) to do sth. silly.

follement, *adv*. **f. drôle**, extremely (*or* screamingly) funny; **je me suis f. amusé**, I had a rare old time, I enjoyed myself immensely.

follette, *adj*. **faire la f.**, to act silly (*oj* women).

fol(l)ingue, *adj*. mad*.

foncer. 1. to make tracks, to get a move on, to get one's skates on, to speed along, to get cracking, to go full steam ahead. 2. **f. dans le brouillard**, to decamp*, to go blindly ahead. 3. to pay* up.

fonceur, *m*. smuggler.

fondu, *adj*., *m*. (*Marseilles slang*) mad*, madman.

fondu, *m*. **faire un f.**, to drop out (of circulation), to fade away.

fontaine, *f*. **ouvrir la f.**=**ouvrir les écluses**.

forçat, *m*. **les forçats de la route**, competitors in the *Tour de France* race.

forcir, to put on flesh, (*of child*) to grow (strong *or* stronger).

format, *m*. **un grand f.**, a hundred franc note.

forme, *f*. **être en (pleine) f.** (*or* **avoir** *or* **tenir la f.**), to be up to the mark, to be up to scratch, to be in fine form.

formid, formidable, *adj*. stupendous*, super, smashing; **c'est formidable! well, I never! did you ever! elle est formidable!** (*a*) she's a caution! she's the limit! (*b*) she's a smasher (*or* a clinker)!

fort, *adj*. 1. clever. 2. **c'est un peu trop f.!** *or* **c'est plus f. que tout!** *or* **c'est un peu f.** (de café *or* de chicorée)! that's too thick (*or* a bit thick *or* too bad *or* too stiff *or* too steep)! that's coming it a bit strong! that's putting it on a bit thick! that's the limit!* 3. **c'est plus f. que moi!** I just can't help it! 4. **en voilà une forte!** *or* **celle-là est forte!** (*a*) well, I never! (*b*) that's a whopper (*or* a thumper)! (*i.e. a lie*). *See also* **bouchon, gueule, thème**.

fort, *adv*. **y aller f.**, to lay it on thick, to go hard at it; to exaggerate*; **ne pas aller f.**, (*of health*) not to be very well.

fortiche, *adj.*, *m.f.* **1.** crafty, smart, clever. **2. ne pas être f. sur,** not to be keen on. **3. être f.,** to be wide-awake*. **4. faire le f.,** to talk big. **5.** strong, hefty, burly.

fortif(e)s, *f.pl.* (=*fortifications*) the old defence works around Paris.

fortune, *f.* **1. dîner** (*or* **manger**) **à la f. du pot,** to take pot-luck. **2. être en (quête de) bonnes fortunes,** to try to click with a girl, to be on the prowl.

fossiliser, se, to become an old fossil, to become stupid.

fou, *adj.* **1.** tremendous (*of its kind*) *e.g.* howling (success), tons *or* pots of (money), splitting (headache), breakneck (speed), fearful (crowd, price); **un succès f.,** a smash hit. **2. f. à lier,** mad as a hatter, raving mad. **3. tu n'es pas** (*or* **t'es (pas)**) **f.?,** you must be barmy! **4. c'est f. ce que...,** it's amazing (*or* extraordinary) how ...—*e.g.* **c'est f. ce qu'il est drôle!** he's a perfect scream!

fouaron, *m.* =foiron.

foucade, *f.* passing craze.

fouchtra, *m.* **1.** native (*or* inhabitant) of Auvergne (=Auverpin). **2.** *int.* =fichtre!

foudre, *f.* **le coup de f.,** love at first sight.

fouettard, *m.* **1. le Père F.,** (*a*) bogy man; (*b*) passive flagellant. **2. un père f.,** a father who doesn't spare the rod. **3.** buttocks*; **l'avoir dans le f.,** to be taken in, to be diddled; **se le faire mettre dans le f.,** to get the worst of it; **botter le f. à qn**=**botter qn.; il y a de quoi botter le père f. par terre**=**c'est astap(e).**

fouetter, to stink*.

fou-fou, *adj.* silly, foolish, idiotic.

fou(i)gnedé, *m.* =fignard.

fouille, *f.* **1.** pocket*; **en avoir plein les fouilles,** to be flush, to be rich*. **2. c'est dans la f., l'avoir dans la f.**= **c'est dans la poche. 3.** frisking, rubbing down.

fouille-merde, *m.* **1.** scavenger (of cesspools). **2.** (*fig.*) muck-raker.

fouiller. 1. to rub down, to frisk (a prisoner by running one's hands over his body). **2.** to have coition* with, to poke.

fouiller, se. 1. to rummage in one's pockets. **2. tu peux te f.** (**si tu as des poches**)!=**tu peux toujours courir!**

fouillouse, *f.* =fouille.

Fouilly-les-Oies, Fouilly-les-Chaussettes, Fouilly-les-Coucous, etc. *pr.n.* (*jest.*) nickname for an unimportant little town, a one-horse town; Much Binding in the Marsh.

fouinard, *adj.* inquisitive, nosey; *m.* Nosey Parker, snooper, big ears.

fouinasser=**fouiner.**

fouine, *f.* **à figure de f.,** weasel-faced; **des yeux de f.,** ferrety eyes.

fouiner, to ferret (about), to nose about, to pry (into), to poke one's nose (into), to snoop (around).

fouineur, *adj.*, *m.* =fouinard.

foulant, *adj.* tiring, fagging; **ce n'est pas f.,** it's not a back-breaking job.

fouler: ne pas se f. la rate (*or* **le poignet**), **ne pas se la f.,** to take it easy, to kill not oneself, not to get into a sweat. *See also* **méninges.**

foul(e)titude, *f.* crowd, heaps, lots, piles, pots, bags.

four, *m.* **1.** (*of play*, *etc.*) failure*; **faire f.,** to flop, to fall flat, to be a frost (*or* a flop), to fold up; **un f. noir, un f. complet, un vrai f.,** a fearful frost; a dismal failure, a hopeless frost, a proper wash-out. **2. chauffer le f.,** to get drunk*.

fourailler=**fouiller 2.**

fourbi, *m.* **1.** (*mil.*) kit, equipment. **2.** belongings, goods and chattels, luggage. **3.** gadget*. **4. un (vrai) f. arabe,** a most complicated business, the very devil of a job, a hell of a business, a tricky business; **un sale f.,** a rotten job; **c'est tout un f.,** it's quite a business. **5. connaître le f.,** to be wide-awake*. **6. (et) tout le f.,** (and) the whole bag* of tricks.

fourbu, *adj.* exhausted*.

fourchette, f. **1.** avoir un bon (or joli) coup de f., être une bonne f., jouer bien de la f., to be a good trencherman, to ply a good knife and fork, to be a hearty eater. **2.** la f. du père Adam, fingers. **3.** donner le coup de f. à qn, (at catch-as-catch-can wrestling) to gouge out s.o.'s eyes. **4.** pickpocket. **5.** bayonet.

fourgat, m. =fourgue.

fourgonner. 1. to rummage (or to poke) about. **2.** =fabriquer 1.

fourgue, fourgueur, m. receiver of stolen goods, fence; vendor of drugs, pusher.

fourguer, to sell (illicitly), to flog.

fourlineur, m. pickpocket.

fourmi, f. avoir des fourmis dans les jambes, to have pins and needles in one's legs; j'ai des fourmis dans les jambes, my legs have gone to sleep.

fourneau, m. fool*.

fourniquer, to keep a watch over s.o.

fourré, adj. être toujours f. chez qn, to be always on (or never off) s.o.'s doorstep; être toujours f. avec qn, to hobnob with s.o.

fourreau, m. trousers*.

fourrer. 1. =fiche(r) 3. **2.** f. qn dedans, (a) to cheat* s.o.; (b) to imprison* s.o. **3.** f. son nez (or le nez) partout, to poke (or to stick) one's nose (or to pry) into everything. **4.** =fouiller 2.

fourrer, se. 1. ne savoir où se f., not to know where to hide oneself. **2.** se f. dans un trou de souris, to want to go through the floor. **3.** s'en f. jusque-là,** (a) to have a regular tuck-in; (b) to get an eyeful.

foutaise, fouterie, f. rot, rubbish*, hog-wash.

foutoir, m. **1.** house (or room) in disorder. **2.** brothel*.

foutre, vulgar form of fiche(r); int. vulgar form of fichtre!; m. sperm, semen, spunk.

foutre, se. 1. vulgar form of se ficher. **2.** se f. à, to begin to.

foutrement, adv. vulgar forms of fichtrement.

foutrer =jouir.

foutriquet, m. little squi(r)t, little whipper-snapper.

foutu, p.p. (of foutre), vulgar form of fichu.

foutument, adv. vulgar form of fichtrement.

fracas, m. faire du f., to kick up a row, to make an uproar*.

fracasseur, m. burglar, cracksman.

fraîche, f. money*.

frais, adj. **1.** me voilà f.! or je suis f. (comme un porc)! I'm in a pretty (or nice) fix*! I've 'had' it! je ne me vois pas f.! I can see I'm (in) for it! **2.** f. comme l'œil, f. comme une rose, as fresh as a daisy (or as a rose or as paint).

frais, m.pl. **1.** aux f. de la princesse, at the expense of the State (or of the Government or of the Company or of the firm, etc.), buckshee, on the expense account, on the cuff, on the house. **2.** faire ses f. = se défendre 1. **3.** arrête les f.! that's enough!

fraise, f. **1.** face*; se sucrer la f., se refaire la f., to powder one's face. **2.** ramener sa f., (a) to put on side; to shoot a line; (b) =rouspéter; (c) =s'amener 1. **3.** sucrer les fraises, to be doddering, to have the shakes. **4.** envoyer sur les fraises, to send s.o. packing*. **5.** tit (breast).

fraline, f. =frangine.

framboise, f. clitoris.

franc, adj. without risk, safe; ce n'est pas très f., it's dangerous (or tricky or risky or dodgy or dicey).

Francaoui, m. term used by the Europeans of Algeria to denote the metropolitan French.

Franchecaille, la, pr. n. France.

franco, adj. =franc.

François, pr.n. faire le coup du père F. à qn, to throttle s.o., to garrotte s.o.

frangibus, m. =frangin.

frangin, m. **1.** brother. **2.** friend*. **3.** monk, friar. **4.** petit f., penis*.

frangine, f. **1.** sister. **2.** (pej.) woman*, girl. **3.** prostitute*, tart. **4.** nun.

franquiste, *m.* =fourgue.

fransquillon, *adj.* French.

frappada, **frappa(dingue)**, *adj.* mad*.

frappe, *f.* blackguard*.

frappe-dingue, *m.* prisoner.

frapper, se, to panic, to get into a state*, to get flurried; **(ne) vous frappez pas!** keep cool! keep your hair (*or* your shirt *or* your wool) on!

frelot, *m.* brother.

frelotte, *f.* sister, nun.

fréquenter, se, to masturbate*.

frère, *m.* **1.** friend*; real pal, a brick. **2.** fellow*. **3.** **faux f.**, traitor. **4. f. Trois Points**, Freemason. **5. petit f.**=petit frangin; **dérouiller son petit f.**, to have coition*.

frérot, *m.* little brother.

frétillante, *f.* tail.

frétillard, *m.* penis*.

frétillon, *m.* restless fellow, fidget.

fretin, *m.* =frottin.

fric, *m.* money*; **être au f.**, to be rich*; **aboule ton f.!** stump up! fork out!

fricandeau, *m.* =fric.

fricassée, *f.* thrashing*.

fricasser, to squander, to blue (one's money). *See also* **museau**.

fric-frac, **fricfrac**, *m.* **1.** burglary, house-breaking; **faire un f.-f.**, to crack a crib, to screw a gaff (*or* a drum), to go screwing. **2.** burglar, cracksman.

fricfraquer =faire un fric-frac.

frichti, *m.* food*; meal; stew.

fricot, *m.* **1.** stew; cooking; cooked dish. **2.** soft (*or* cushy) job.

fricotage, *m.* **1.** cooking. **2.** feasting. **3.** wangling, wire-pulling; underhand practice. **4.** shirking, skrimshanking.

fricoter. **1.** to cook. **2.** to feast. **3.** to wangle, to fiddle. **4.** to shirk, to skrimshank. **5.** to make one's pile, to make one's little bit on the sly, to be a grafter. **6.** to squander, to run through (*money*). **7.** to have coition* with. **8. je me demande ce qu'il fricote!** I wonder what's his little game!

fricoteur, *m.* **1.** wangler, fiddler, embezzler. **2.** shirker, skrimshanker.

frictionnée, *f.* thrashing*.

Fridolin, *m.* German, Fritz, Jerry, Kraut.

fri-fri, *m.* vagina*; **cache-fri-fri**, *m.* briefs, panties.

frigo, *m.* **1.** refrigerator, fridge. **2.** frozen meat. **3.** *adj.* **il fait f.**, it's cold (*or* nippy).

frigorifié, *adj.* (*of person*) chilled to the bone, frozen to death.

frigousse, *f.* **1.** cooking. **2.** feast(ing). **3.** graft.

frimage, *m.* confrontation.

frimand, **frimant**, *m.* **1.** gaper, rubber-neck. **2.** (*th.*) walker-on, super (numerary), extra, bit-player.

frime, *f.* **1.** sham, pretence, make-believe, bunk(um), eye-wash; **c'est de la f.**, it's all bunkum; **pour la f.**, for appearance's sake, for show. **2.** appearance, aspect, looks; head, face. **3.** (*th.*) **faire une f.**, **faire de la f.**, to be a super, to walk on. **4. laisser (rester) en f.**=laisser (rester) en panne. **5. en f.**, on one's own.

frimer. **1.** to pretend. **2.** to look; **f. bien**, to look well, to cut a dash. **3.** to look at, to stare at, to spot.

frimousse, *f.* face*.

fringale, *f.* **avoir la f.**, to be ravenously hungry, to have a twist.

fringuer, (se), to dress, to rig (oneself) out, to tog (oneself) up.

fringues, *f.pl.* clothes*; **f. de coulisses**, woman's underwear.

fringueur, *m.* second-hand clothes dealer.

frio, *adj.* cold.

fripe, *f.* food*, grub.

fripes, *f.pl.* rags, old clothes*.

fripouillard, *m.*, **fripouille**, *f.* blackguard*.

fripouillerie, *f.* blackguardism.

friquet, *m.* **1.** whipper-snapper. **2.** informer (in prison).

Friquets, *m.pl.* =Frisés.

frire: **rien à f.!** nothing doing! not on your Nellie!

frisco, *adj.* = frisquet.

Frisés, Frisous, *m.pl.* German soldiers, Jerries.

frisquet, *adj.* chilly, nippy, parky; **il fait f.,** there's a nip in the air.

frit, *adj.* done* for.

frite, *f.* 1. face*. 2. a blow*.

frites, *f.pl.* 1. chip potatoes, chips, French fries. 2. **tomber dans les f.** = **tomber dans les pommes.** *See also* bouche 4, rond, *m.* 3.

Fritz, *m.* = Fridolin.

Frizous, *m.pl.* = Frisous.

froc, *m.* 1. trousers*. 2. faire (chier, foirer, lâcher tout) dans son f., to be in a frightful funk. *Cf.* culotte 3. 3. *pl.* clothes*.

frocard, *m.* = froc 1.

fromage, *m.* 1. soft (*or* cushy) job, plum, (*mil.*) cushy billet. 2. **faire de ça un f.,** to kick up a fuss about it.

from(e), fromegi(e), fromgi(s), from(e)ton, frometegomme, fromogomme, *m.* cheese, bung, bunghole.

frotin, *m.* = frottin.

frotte, *f.* 1. scabies, itch. 2. **la f. et l'astique,** (*mil.*) spit and polish, bull, bulsh(it).

frotté, *adj.* être f. de, to have a smattering of.

frottée, *f.* thrashing*.

frotter. 1. to thrash*; f. les oreilles à qn, to box (*or* to warm), s.o.'s ears. 2. **en f. une,** to have a dance.

frotter, se. 1. to fight, to (have a) scrap. 2. to have coition*.

frotteuse, *f.* match (*allumette*), lucifer, striker.

frottin, *m.* faire une partie de f., faire un f., to have a game of billiards.

frotting, *m.* low dance hall.

frou-frou, *m.* (*burglar's*) skeleton-key.

froussard, *adj.* cowardly; *m.* coward*.

frousse, *f.* cowardice; **avoir la f.,** to be afraid*; **ficher (flanquer, foutre) la f. à qn,** to put the wind up s.o.; **une sainte f.,** a blue funk.

fruit, *m.* un f. sec, (*of person*) failure, dud, wash-out.

frusquer = fringuer.

frusques, *f.pl.* = fringues.

frusquin, *m.* tout le f., the whole bag of tricks*.

fuite, *f.* vive la f.! (*sch.*) hurrah for the hols (*i.e. the holidays*)! (*mil.*) roll on, demob. day!

fuiter, se fuiter, to decamp*.

fumant, *adj.* 1. fuming, furious. 2. wonderful, smashing.

fumasse, *f.* anger; être en f., to be angry*.

fumée, *f.* balancer (*or* envoyer) la f., (*a*) to fire (revolver, etc.); (*b*) to have coition*.

fumelle, *f.* (*pej.*) female, woman*.

fumer. 1. to fume, to rage, to be furious. 2. **ça fume, ça va f.** = ça barde, ça va barder. 3. to blow (*i.e. smoke marihuana*).

fumeron, *m.* 1. chain-smoker. 2. *pl.* legs* (*thin and skinny*).

fumier, *m.* f. (de lapin), rotter*.

fumiste, *m.* practical joker, hoaxer, fraud, leg-puller.

fumisterie, *f.* hoax*; tout ça, c'est de la f.! that's all my eye!

funérailles! *int.* (*in S. of France*) blimey! crikey! (*expletives*).

furax, *adj.* = furibard.

furet, fureteur, *m.* Nosey Parker.

furibard, *adj.* furious, mad with rage, livid.

furieusement, *adv.* (*intensive use*) awfully, tremendously, terribly.

furieux, *adj.* (*intensive use*) awful, tremendous, terrible.

fusains, *m.pl.* legs*.

fuseaux, *m.pl.* 1. legs*, spindle-shanks. 2. skiing trousers. 3. drain-pipe trousers.

fusée, *f.* lâcher une f., lancer des fusées, to vomit*.

fuser, to fart.

fusil, *m.* 1. stomach*, belly; se bourrer le f., to stuff oneself; n'avoir rien dans le f., to have an empty stomach, to have nothing in one's breadbasket. 2. coup de f., exorbitant

charge, overcharging, fleecing; **essuyer le** (*or* **recevoir un**) **coup de f.**, to be fleeced (*or* rooked *or* rushed *or* stung). **3. f. à deux coups,** trousers*.
fusiller. 1. to smash (up), to make a mess of. **2.** to fritter away (one's money). **3.** to sell off. **4. se faire f.** = essuyer le coup de fusil.
futal, *m.* trousers*.
futur, -e, *m.f.* intended, fiancé(e).

G

gabarit, m. =acabit.
gabegie, f. 1. muddle, mess, disorder, waste (due to fraud or mismanagement). 2. intrigue, trickery, foul play, dirty work, graft.
gabelou, m. custom-house officer; tax-collector.
gâche, f. une bonne g. = fromage 1.
gadiche, f. = gadin 1.
gadin, m. 1. fall; ramasser (prendre) un g., to come a cropper*. 2. head*; il y va du g., it's a hanging job.
gadzart, m. student at the École des Arts et Métiers.
gaffe, f. 1. mistake*; faire une g., to make a mistake*. 2. avaler sa g., to die*. 3. (mil.) faire la g., to be on sentry duty.
gaffe, gâfe, m. 1. (slang of the 'milieu') 'crow' (confederate on the watch). 2. faire g., to be careful, to take care, to be on one's guard; fais g.! look out! watch it! 3. prison warder, 'screw'.
gaffer (i). = faire une gaffe.
gaffer (ii). to look (at), to observe, to keep an eye on, to 'crow'.
gaffeur, m. 1. blunderer. 2. look-out man, 'crow'.
gafouiller = gaffer (ii).
gaga, adj. doddering, (in a state of) senile (decay); m. dodderer, dotard.
gagneuse, f. prostitute (one profitable to a pimp), a good earner, a good meal-ticket.
gai, adj. un peu g., slightly drunk*, elevated, high, merry, jolly.
gail(le), m. horse, nag, gee(-gee).
galapiat, m. loafer, layabout, good-for-nothing.
gale, f. (of person) pest.
galéjer, to tell tall stories, to shoot a line.
galerie, f. poser devant (or pour) la g., amuser la g., to show off.

galetouse, galetouze, f. 1. = galette 1. 2. mess-tin.
galettard, adj. = galetteux.
galette, f. 1. money*; aboule la g.!= aboule le fric! 2. épouser la grosse g., to marry a rich girl. 3. hard, thin mattress. 4. (mil.) (dog-)biscuit, (nav.) hard-tack. 5. duffer, nonentity. 6. plat comme une g., as flat as a pancake (or as porridge-plates). 7. pl. pancake breasts.
galetteux, adj. rich*.
galipette, f. 1. somersault, caper, gambol. 2. faire des galipettes, to sky-lark, to be up to one's tricks.
galoche, f. 1. vieille g., old fog(e)y*. 2. French kiss.
galon, m. quand on prend du g. on n'en saurait trop prendre, never do things by halves, you can't have too much of a good thing, as well be hanged for a sheep as for a lamb.
galonnard, galonné, m. (mil.) officer, brass-hat; les galonnards, the (top) brass.
galop, m. reprimand*.
galopard, m. louse.
galoup(e), m. faire un g. à qn, to do the dirty on s.o.
galtouse, galtouze, f. = galetouse, galetouze.
galuche, f. 1. Gauloise cigarette. 2. pl. (mil.) stripes.
galure, galurin, galurot, m. = bada.
gamahuche, f. fellatio, gamaroosh, gamaruche, gam.
gamberge, f. thought, reflection; à la g., on second thoughts.
gamberger, to think, to reflect (on), to meditate, to imagine things, to understand.
gamberger, se, to think hard; to worry.
gambettes, f.pl. legs*; jouer des g., to decamp*; tricoter des g., (a) to decamp*; (b) to dance, to shake a leg.

gambille, f. dance; pl. =gambettes.
gambiller. 1. to dance, to shake a leg.
2. to skip about, to fidget. 3. to be
lame, to limp.
gambilleur, m. dancer.
gamelle, f. ramasser une g., to come a
cropper*.
gamine, f. t'occupe pas de la g., mind
your own business!
gamme, f. changer de g., to change
one's tune; chanter sa g. à qn, to tell
some home truths.
gano(t), m. treasure, booty.
gapette, f. cap, hat*.
garce, f. 1. (of woman) bitch. 2.
prostitute*. 3. fils de g.! son of a gun!
quelle g. de vie! what a hell of a life!
4. adj. bitchy.
garçon, m. See enterrer.
gare, f. à la g. (au bout du quai les
ballots)! go to blazes!*
garer, to store away, to salt away, to
salt down, to stash away, tuck away;
gare-toi! get out of the way!
garga, gargane, gargarousse, f.
throat, gullet.
gargariser, se. 1. to tipple*, to (have
a) gargle. 2. to delight (in), to relish,
to be tickled to death, to revel (in).
gargot(t)e, f. 1. cheap eating-house,
hash-house, cheap cook-shop. 2.
food*.
gargotier, m. 1. keeper of a gargot(t)e.
2. bad cook, hash-slinger.
gargouillades, f.pl. vocal gurglings
(of bad singer).
gargoulette, gargue, f. mouth*;
throat, gullet.
garni, adj. elle est bien garnie, she's
well upholstered.
garni, garno, m. furnished apartments, lodgings, digs; 'drum',
'gaff'.
garouse, f. (railway) station.
garrot, m. throat, gullet.
gars, m. fellow*, lad, chap; les g. de la
marine, sailors, tars; mon g., my son
(or my young man or my hubby).
garse, f. =garce.
gas, m. =gars.

gaspard, m. 1. rat. 2. avaler le g., to
receive Holy Communion.
gâteau, m. 1. profits; partager le g., to
share (or to split) the profits, to share
the swag. 2. c'est du g.! it's very
easy*, it's a piece of cake! 3. papa-g.,
over-indulgent father; sugar-daddy;
similarly oncle-g., maman-g., grand-
papa-g., etc.
gau, m. louse.
gauche, f. jusqu'à la g., (right) up to
the hilt, (up) to the last, to the bitter
end, to the finish; aller jusqu'à la g.,
to go the whole hog; ton copain
jusqu'à la g., yours to a cinder, yours
till the cows come home, Y.T.H.F.
(i.e. yours till Hell freezes).
gauche, adj. 1. (en) mettre à g.=garer;
avoir un peu d'argent à g., to have a
bit of cash tucked away. 2. passer à
g., to be done out of one's share. See
also arme, main, pied.
gauf(f)rer, to arrest*; se faire g., to be
caught in the act.
gaufre, f. 1. face*; se sucrer la g., to
powder one's face. 2. food*. 3. cap*.
4. ramasser une g., to come a cropper*.
gaule, f. avoir la g.=bander.
gaulé(e), adj. =bien balancé.
gauler. 1. to arrest*; se laisser g., to
get nabbed. 2. to steal*.
gaupe, f. slut, trollop.
gavion, gaviot, m. throat, gullet.
gavousse, f. lesbian*.
gaye, f. =gail(le).
gaz, m. 1. à pleins g., pleins g., at full
speed (or at full lick), full out, flat
(or all) out, a hell of a lick; (motor.)
with the throttle full open; ouvrir
(mettre, envoyer) les g., (motor.) to
open the throttle, to step on it, to
step (or to tread) on the gas; marcher
à plein(s) g., y aller (or donner or
filer) plein(s) g., to rip (or to whizz)
along, to give it the gun. 2. éteindre
(or fermer) son g., to die*. 3. avoir des
g., to suffer from flatulence (or from
wind). 4. lâcher un g., to break wind.
gaz, adj. terrific, gas.
gazé, adj. drunk*.

gazer. 1. =marcher à plein(s) gaz. **2.** to get a move on. **3.** to go smoothly (or swimmingly); ça gaze? how goes it? how're (or how's) tricks? ça gaze! things are humming! things are fine! everything is going swimmingly! things are going like a house on fire! **g. au poil, g. à bloc,** to go without a hitch; **ça va g.!=ça va barder! 4.** (sch.) to get on fine (at an examination). **5.** to stink*.

gazier, m. 1. fellow*. **2.** pederast*.

gazon, m. 1. hair, thatch; **n'avoir plus de g.** sur la plate-bande, to be quite bald*, to have a bladder of lard; **son g. est mité,** he's lost his thatch; **se faire tondre le g.,** to get one's hair cut; **se ratisser le g.,** to comb one's hair. **2.** mouiller son g., to urinate (of women).

gazouiller. 1. ça gazouille!=ça gaze! (gazer 3). **2.** =gazer 5.

G.D.B., avoir la : see **gueule 4.**

géant, m. les géants de la route, (of cyclists) the giants of the open road.

gelé, adj. g. (à zéro), (dead) drunk*.

gelée, f. g. de coing, mess, fix, hot water.

gendarme, m. 1. virago, termagant, amazon. **2.** red herring, 'Billingsgate pheasant', 'soldier'. **3.** dormir en g., to sleep with one eye open. **4.** =étron.

gêner, se. 1. ne vous gênez pas! (iron.) don't mind me! make yourself quite at home! **2.** je me gênerai(s)! or (si) je vais me g.! or avec ça que je vais me g.! you bet I will! you see if I don't!

genou, m. 1. bald head; **chauve comme un g.,** as bald as a coot (or as a bladder or as a billiard ball). **2.** être sur les **genoux,** to be exhausted*. **3.** faire du g., to play footsie (or kneesies) (under the table).

genre, m. faire (or se donner) du g., to put on (or to give oneself) airs, to put it on.

géo, f. (sch.) geography.

géranium, m. dépoter son g., to die.

gerbage, m. =gerbement.

gerbe, f. 1. year in jail. **2.** masturbation, finger fuck.

gerbement, m. conviction, sentence.

gerber. 1. to convict, to sentence. **2.** to be convicted, to be sentenced, to serve a prison sentence. **3.** to vomit*.

gerbier, m. judge, magistrate, beak.

gerbière, f. key.

gerce, f. prostitute*.

gi, adv. =gy.

giboulée, f. thrashing*; shower of blows.

giclée, f. 1. burst (of a machine-gun). **2.** envoyer une g. à, filer une g. de sulfateuse à, to fire at. **3.** tirer une g.=tirer un coup (coup 23).

gifle, f. une tête à gifles=une tête à claques.

gigal, m. 1, slater. **2.** plumber.

gigo, adv. =gy.

gigolette, f. fast girl, floosie, floozy.

gigolo, gigolpince, m. fancy-man, lounge-lizard, gigolo.

gigoter, to dance, to shake a leg.

gigoteur, m. dancer.

gigots, m.pl., gigues, f.pl. legs*.

gigue, f. 1. tall girl, bean pole. **2.** pl. legs.

gilet, m. 1. stomach*; **se remplir le g.,** to stuff oneself. **2.** pleurer dans le g. de qn, to pour out one's troubles to s.o.

gileton, gilogue, m. waistcoat.

gingin, m. common sense, gumption, nous.

ginglard, m. brandy, spirits.

girafe, f. peigner la g., to laze, to shirk, to malinger*.

girelle, f. prostitute.

giries, f.pl. faire des g., (a) to make no end of a fuss; (b) to put on airs.

giroflée, f. une g. à cinq feuilles (or à cinq branches), a slap in the face.

giron(d), m. pederast*; adj. good looking.

gironde, adj. f. sexually cuddlesome, hugsome, bonny, buxom.

gisquette, f. =gonzesse.

gîter, to lodge, to live, to hang out.

giton, m. pederast*.

givré, adj. 1. drunk*. **2.** mad*.

givrer, se, to get drunk*.

glace, f. passer (or se bomber) devant la

g., to be done out of (*or* not to get) one's share.

glace, *m.* = glass(e).

glagla, *m.* je les ai à g. = ça caille (cailler 1).

glaise, *f.* ground; il couche sur la g., he sleeps on the bare ground.

glaiseux, *m.* 1. catamite. 2. peasant*.

glaive, *m.* guillotine.

gland, *m.* penis*; se taper sur le g., to masturbate*; effacer le g., to have coition*.

gland, *adj.* silly*, foolish.

glande, *f.* se tirer sur la g., to masturbate*.

glander, to idle, to moon about, to fritter away one's time.

glandilleux, *adj.* difficult, dangerous, risky, dicey = glander.

glandocher = glander.

glandouiller. 1. = glander. 2. to wait.

glaner. 1. to pilfer. 2. laisser g. = laisser courir.

glass(e), *m.* drink, glass(ful); sécher (siffler, vider) un g., to toss off a glass (of wine, etc.).

glaude, *f.* pocket*.

glaviot, *m.* 1. gob (*clot of spittle*). 2. se noyer dans un g. = se noyer dans un crachat.

glavioter, to gob.

glisse, *f.* faire de la g. à, to do (an accomplice) out of his share of the spoils.

glisser. 1. g. qch. en douce à qn. to tell s.o. sth. confidentially. 2. se laisser g., la g., to die*. 3. laisser g. = laisser courir. 4. to possess (a woman).

globe, *m.* 1. stomach*. 2. se faire arrondir le g., to become pregnant*. 3. globes arrondis, plump breasts.

gloire, *f.* 1. être prêt à partir pour la g., être parti pour la g., to be slightly drunk*. 2. faire qch. pour la g., to do sth. for nothing (at all), to do sth. for love.

gloria, *m.* coffee laced with brandy or rum, gloria.

glouglou, *m.* faire g., to pour out a drink.

glousser, to chuckle.

glu, *adj.* = collant.

glu, *f.* comme la g. = barbant; avoir la g. aux doigts, to be acquisitive, to have money stick to one's fingers.

gluant, *m.* 1. baby. 2. soap.

gluau, *m.* = glaviot 1.

gluck, *m.* luck.

gnaf, *m.* = gniaf.

gnangnan, *adj.* namby-pamby, soppy; *m.* 1. milksop*, mollycoddle. 2. dawdler, slow-coach.

gnard, *m.* = gniard.

gnaupe, *f.* pipe, cutty.

gniaf, *m.* 1. cobbler, 'snob'. 2. bungler, botcher. 3. rotter*. 4. vice-principal (in charge of *pions* in *lycée*) = surveillant général.

gniangnian, *adj. m.* = gnangnan.

gniard, *m.* 1. child, brat. 2. fellow*.

gniasse, *m.* 1. = gniard. 2. mon g., I, me; ton g., you; son g., he, him.

gniaule, *f.* = gnôle.

gnière, *m.* = gniard 2.

gniol(l)e, *f.* = gnôle.

gnion, *m.* = gnon.

gniouf, *m.* = gnouf.

gnognot(t)e, *f.* (*of persons or things*) trash, rubbish, junk, tripe; de la g., peanuts, small fry, small beer; ça, ce n'est pas de la g.! that's something like! that's a little bit of all right!

gnôle, gnole, *f.* hard liquor, hard stuff, hootch, fire-water; un coup de g., a 'wee drappy'.

gnol(l)e, *adj.* silly*, foolish.

gnon, *m.* blow*; flanquer un g. à qn, to dot s.o. one, to take a swipe at s.o.

gnouf, *m.* cell (in police-station), lock-up; (*mil.*) prison*.

gnoufard, *m.* (*sch.*) taupin preparing for the *École normale supérieure.*

go, *m.* = gau.

gobe-la-lune, *m.* credulous person, gull, simpleton*, sucker, juggins, easy mark.

gobelot(t)er, to tipple*.

gobe-mouches, *m.* = gobe-la-lune.

gober. 1. to swallow (a story, all that one is told), to be a sucker for, to lap up; **faire g. une blague à qn,** to kid s.o., to pull s.o.'s leg. *See also* **morceau. 2.** to be keen on.

gober, se, to fancy oneself, to think no small beer of oneself, to have a swelled head, to grow too big for one's boots.

goberger, se, to do oneself well, to live in clover; to guzzle.

gobette, *f.* **1.** drink, booze. **2.** wine ration in prison.

gobeur, *m.* = **gobe-la-lune.**

gobi, *m.* coloured man, negro, black(ie).

gobichonner, to swill and guzzle.

godaille, *f.* tippling, swilling; guzzle, guzzling.

godailler. 1. to tipple, to swill; to guzzle. **2.** to go pub-crawling. **3.** to go wenching, to have coition*, to have one's oats. **4.** to rejoice. **5.** = **bander.**

godailleur, *m.* tippler; guzzler.

godailleux, *adj.* randy.

godasse, *f.* (big) boot*.

goddam, *m.* Englishman.

gode(miché), *m.* false penis, dildo.

gode, *f.* . . . **à la g.** = . . . **à la godille.**

goder, to be sexually excited, to be on heat; **g. pour,** to have a sexual yen for; **faire g. qn,** to give s.o. a thrill (*sexually*).

godet, *m.* = **glass(e); s'envoyer (se cloquer, se taper, écluser) un g.,** to down a drink, to treat oneself to a drink, to knock back a drink.

godiche, godichon, *adj.* simple, foolish, silly, dumb; awkward, gawky; **je ne suis pas g. autant que j'en ai l'air,** I'm not such a fool as I look; *m.* fool*, simpleton; gawk.

godiche, *f.* fever.

godille, *f.* . . . **à la g.,** of no account, bogus, lousy, phoney, trashy, cock-eyed, worthless*.

godiller = **godailler** 3.

godillot, *m.* army boot, hobnailed boot, big boot*.

godmiché, *m.* = **gode(miché).**

gogaille, *f.* **en g.** = **en goguette.**

gogo, *m.* = **gobe-la-lune.**

gogo, à, *adv. phrase.* in abundance,

galore, no end of, plenty and to spare, tons of, lashings of.

gogs, gogues, goguenots, *m.pl.* W.C.,* latrines. **aller aux g.,** (*sch.*) to do a dike.

goguette, *f.* **être en g.,** to be on the spree*.

goinfre, *m.* guzzler.

goinfrer, se. 1. to guzzle. **2.** to make lots of money.

gomme, *f.* **1. la (haute) g.,** the smart set, the upper crust. **2. à toute g.** = **à plein(s) gaz; mettre (toute) la g.,** (*a*) = **ouvrir les gaz;** (*b*) to exaggerate*. **3.** . . . **à la g.** = . . . **à la godille. 4. g. à effacer le(s) sourire(s)** (*or* **les risettes),** bludgeon, truncheon (of police).

gommeux, *m.* swell, toff, dandy, masher.

gonce, *m.* = **gonze.**

goncesse, *f.* = **gonzesse.**

goncier, *m.* = **gonze.**

gondolant, *adj.* very funny*.

gondoler, se, to laugh* uproariously.

gonds, *m.pl.* **sortir de ses g.,** to be angry*.

gone, gonesse, *m.f.* (*dial.,* *Lyons region*) **1.** child*, brat, kid. **2.** fellow*.

gonflant, *adj.* very funny*.

gonflé, *adj.* **1. être g. à bloc,** to be full of pep (*or* of beans), to be thoroughly keyed-up, to have one's tail up, to feel like a million, to be trained to the minute; (*of motor-car*) to be hotted up (*or* souped up). **2.** rich*, flush.

gonfler, to make (a woman) pregnant*.

gonse, gonze, gonzier, *m.* fellow*.

gonsesse, gonzesse, gonzière, *f.* (*pej.*) woman*, dame, girl*, tart, floosy.

gorgeon, *m.* **1.** glass (*for drinking*). **2.** money for drink. **3.** copious round of drinks. **4. se taper un g.,** to knock back a drink. **5.** coarse red wine.

gorille, *m.* **1.** thug. **2.** bodyguard of any V.I.P.

gosier, *m.* throat, gullet; **avoir le g. en pente** = **avoir la dalle en pente; avoir le g. pavé** (*or* **blindé),** to have a cast-iron throat; **avoir le g. sec,** to be parched, to be thirsting for a drink; **s'humecter le g.** = se **rincer la dalle.**

gosse, *m.f.* **1.** youngster, child*, kid. **2.** young man, young girl; **ma g.** **d'amour,** my girl friend. **3. être beau** (*or* **belle**) **g.,** to be a good-looking chap (*or* girl). **4. g. de riche** = **fils 2. 5. g. de g.,** ninny.

gosselin, -e, *m.f.* little boy (*or* girl).

got, *m.* = **gau.**

goton, *f.* trollop, prostitute*.

gouaille, *f.* banter(ing), jeering.

gouailler, to banter, to chaff, to jeer (at).

gouaillerie, *f.* banter, chaff.

gouailleur, *adj.* bantering, jeering; *m.* banterer, chaffer, jeerer.

goualante, *f.* song; **pousser une g., envoyer la g.,** y **aller de sa g.,** to sing a song.

gouale, *m.* **1.** blackmail. **2.** swindle, racket. **3. faire du g., aller au g.** = **faire du cri.**

goualer. 1. to sing; to shout, to bawl (out). **2.** to confess*.

goualeur, *m.* (*pej.*) singer, bawler.

gouape, *f.* blackguard*.

gouaper. 1. to loaf, to be a layabout. **2.** to lead the life of a **gouape.**

gouapeur, *m.* layabout.

goudou, *f.* lesbian*.

gouge, *f.* coin (5 *old francs*).

gougnaf(f)ier, gougn(i)afier, *m.* fool*, clot.

gougnot(t)e, *f.*, se **gougnot(t)er,** = **gouine, se gouiner.**

gouine, *f.* lesbian*, les, dyke.

gouiner, se, to practise lesbianism.

goujon, *m.* **1.** young pimp. **2. avaler le g.,** to die. **3. taquiner le g.** = **taquiner l'ablette.**

goulaffe, *adj.* greedy, guzzling.

goule, *f.* **1.** big mouth*. **2.** throat.

goulée, *f.* **1.** (big) mouthful, gulp. **2. tirer une g.,** to have a puff (of a cigarette), to have a drag.

goulette, *f.* = **goulot.**

gouliafre, *m.* glutton, guzzler.

goulot, *m.* throat, mouth, gullet; **repousser** (*or* **taper** *or* **trouilloter**) **du**

g., to have a foul breath, to have strong halitosis; se **rincer le g.** = se **rincer la dalle.**

goumi, *m.* rubber bludgeon, cosh.

goupiller, to manage, to contrive, to wangle, to cook up; **g. un truc,** to wangle sth.

goupiller, se, to work, to work (out), to happen, to take place; se **g. bien,** to go off all right, to shape well.

goupillon, *m.* penis*.

goupillonner, to have coition*.

gourance, *f.* **1.** mistake*. **2.** mistrust, doubt; **avoir des gourances** = se **gourer.**

gourbi, *m.* **1.** funk-hole, fox-hole, dug-out. **2.** house, cabin, shack, hut; room. **3. faire g.,** (*in prison cell*) to club together.

gourde, *f.* **1.** fool*. **2.** head*. **3. g. à poils,** penis*. **4.** *adj.* silly*, dumb, dense, thick, gormless.

gourderie, *f.* nonsense*, boloney.

gourdichon, gourdiflot, *m.* = **gourde 1.**

gourdin, *m.* **1.** penis*. **2. avoir le g.** = **bander. 3. avoir du g.,** to be a womanizer; **avoir du g. pour** = **goder pour.**

gour(r)er, to trick, to cheat*, to deceive, to take in.

gour(r)er, se. 1. to make a mistake*. **2. se g.** (de), to suspect, to have an idea, to imagine; **je m'en gourais,** I thought as much.

gourgandine, *f.* prostitute*.

gourme, *f.* **jeter sa g.,** to sow one's wild oats, to have one's fling.

gourrance, gourrer, se gourrer = **gourance, gourer, se gourer.**

gouspin, *m.* young rascal, young scamp.

gousse (d'ail), *f.* = **gouine.**

goussepain, *m.* = **gouspin.**

gousser, se = se **gouiner.**

goût, *m.* **1.** perdre le **g. du pain,** to die*. **2. faire perdre** (*or* **faire passer** *or* **ôter**) **le g. du pain à qn,** to kill* s.o.

goutte, *f.* **1.** nip* (of brandy, etc.); **boire la g.,** to tipple*; **un verre de g.,** a glass of brandy *or* hard liquor. 2. se noyer dans une g. d'eau = se noyer dans un crachat.

gouvernement, *m.* (*joc.*) mon g., my wife*.

goyau, *f.* low prostitute*.

goy(e), *m.* 1. non-Jewish man. 2. dupe, sucker.

grabater, se, to go to bed*.

grabuge, *m.* row, uproar*, ructions, bit of a breeze.

gradaille, *f.* officers and N.C.O.s.

grade, *m.* en prendre pour son g., to be severely reprimanded*; il en a pris pour son g.! he got what was coming to him! prendre qch. pour son g. = prendre qch. pour son rhume.

graille, *f.* food*; aller à la g., to eat*.

grailler, to eat*.

graillon, *m.* 1. thick phlegm, gob. 2. greasy food*.

graillonner, to bring up, cough up phlegm; to hawk.

grain, *m.* (i) 1. avoir un g., to be slightly mad*. 2. avoir son g., to be slightly drunk*. 3. lancer (*or* mettre) son g. de sel, to make an uncalled-for remark, to butt (*or* to chime *or* to chip *or* to horn) in. 4. le g. de café, clitoris.

grain, *m.* (ii) 1. veiller au g., to watch out for danger, to look out for squalls, to keep a sharp look-out, to keep one's weather eye open. 2. voir venir le g., to foresee danger.

graine, *f.* 1. food*; casser la g., to eat*; casser une (petite) g., to have a bite (to eat). 2. en prendre de la g., to profit by (*or* from) an example, to take a leaf from s.o.'s book, to follow s.o.'s example. 3. monter (*or* pousser) en g., to go (*or* to run) to seed; (*of girl*) to grow into an old maid, to be left on the shelf; (*of child*) to grow long and thin. 4. (*mil.*) g. d'épinards, bullion-fringe (*i.e. gold braid on senior officers' epaulets, etc.*), 'scrambled eggs'. 5. *used in various expressions implying* 'breed', 'strain', 'stock'— (*e.g.* mauvaise g., (*of person*) bad lot;

de la g. de bois de lit, child*; de la g. de con, ninny, clot; de la g. de bagne, jail-bird).

grainer, to eat*.

graisse, *f.* 1. money*. 2. faire de la g., to exaggerate*. 3. prendre la g., to put on (*or* to go to) fat. 4. traîner sa g., to hump one's fat. 5. ils auront la g. mais ils n'auront pas la peau! (*c.p.*) they'll put me (*or* us) through it but they won't get me (*or* us) down! *See also* boniment.

graisser, to exaggerate. *See also* botte (ii) 5. patte 5.

grand-chose, grand'chose, *m.f.* un(e) pas g.-c., a good-for-nothing, a ne'er-do-well, a rotter*.

grand-dab, *m.* grand-father.

grappin, *m.* mettre (*or* jeter *or* poser) le g. sur, (*a*) to lay (*or* to get) one's hands on, to bag, to get hold of, to get one's hooks on to; to set one's cap at; (*b*) to arrest*.

grappiner = mettre le grapin.

gras, *adj.* 1. il n'y (en) a pas g., ça n'est pas g., c'est pas g., there's not much (of it), that's not much, that's not a lot. 2. *m.* benefit, profit, bunce. *See also* bout 4 *and* 5.

gras-double, *m.* paunch*.

grasse, *adj.* se la faire g., to live like a lord, to live on the fat of the land; to spend money like water.

grassouillette, *adj.* se la faire g. = se la faire grasse.

gratin, *m.* 1. smart set, swells, upper ten, top-notchers. 2. the pick of the basket.

gratiné, *adj.* swell*, tip-top.

gratouille, *f.* 1. itch; scratch. 2. = gratte 1.

gratouiller, to itch; to scratch.

grattante, *f.* match (*allumette*), lucifer.

gratte, *f.* 1. illicit profits*; faire de la g., to get pickings, to graft. 2. = frotte 1.

grattée, *f.* thrashing*.

gratter. 1. to overtake, to pass, to show a clean pair of heels to. 2. to get the better of, to lick, to wipe the floor with. 3. to scrape together (a sum

of money). **4. g. du papier,** to be a pen-
pusher. **5.** to scrape on (a musical
string instrument) **6.** to work* hard.
7. to get pickings, to graft. **8.** (of
d*rink*) to have a biting taste; **un verre
de qch. qui gratte,** a glass of sth.
strong. **9. en g. pour,** to be infatuated*
with.

gratter, se. 1. to hesitate, to feel ill at
ease, to think it over. **2. tu peux te
g.!=tu peux toujours courir! (courir
3). 3. se faire g.,** to get a shave, to get
shaved.

grattiche, *f.* itch.

grattin, *m.* **1.** =gratin. **2. aller au g.,**
to go to work.

grattoir, *m.* razor.

grattouse, *f.* =grattiche.

grattouiller, =gratouiller.

gravos(se), *adj.* big.

grec, *m.* card-sharper, swindler*; **faire
le g.,** to work the broads; **vol à la
grecque,** confidence-trick.

greffer, to fast (in prison).

greffier, *m.* **1.** cat, mog(gy). **2.** =chat 3.

grègues, *f.pl.* **tirer ses grègues,** to decamp*.

grelot, *m.* **1. avoir les grelots,** to be
afraid*; **flanquer (foutre) les grelots à
qn,** to put the wind up s.o. **2. passer
un coup de g. à qn,** to (tele)phone s.o.,
to give s.o. a ring (*or* a buzz *or* a
tinkle).

grelotte, *f.* **avoir la g.=avoir les
grelots.**

grelotteur, *m.* coward*.

greluche, *f.* **1.** woman, girl, tart. **2.**
telephone bell, tinkle.

greluchon, *m.* fancy man.

grenouillage, *m.* scandalous gossip.

grenouillard, *m.* teetotaller.

grenouille, *f.* **1. g. de bénitier,** (of
woman) bigoted church-goer, church
hen. **2.** prostitute*. **3. manger** (*or*
faire sauter) la g., to embezzle, to
make off with the cash-box (*or* with
the kitty *or* with the funds *or* with
the club-money), to scoop the till.

grenouiller, to plot; to go into a
huddle.

grenu, *m.* corn.

gribelle, *f.* =grivelle.

gribier, *m.* =griveton.

grif(e)ton, *m.* =griveton.

griffard, *m.* cat, mog(gy).

griffe, *f.* **1.** hand*. **2.** foot*; **à griffes,** on
foot; **taper des griffes,** to have smelly
feet. **3. la G.,** the army; the infantry;
military service.

griffer.· 1. to seize, to catch, to nab.
2. to steal*.

griffer, se, to masturbate*.

grif(fe)ton, *m.* =griveton.

grignolet, *m.* =brignolet.

grigou, *m.* miser*.

grillante, *f.* cigarette*, fag.

grille, *f.* **repeindre sa g.** (**en rouge**)=
avoir ses affaires.

grillé, *adj.* **être g.,** (*a*) to be spotted, to
be detected, to be found out, to be
shown up; (*b*) to be forestalled;
(*c*) =être brûlé (*a*).

griller. 1. to denounce (s.o.), to unmask
(s.o.), to show (s.o.) up. **2.** to race past,
to leave (s.o.) standing. **3.** to supplant
(s.o.), to do (s.o.) out of sth. **4.** to do
harm to (s.o.). **5. g. les feux rouges,** to
overshoot the traffic lights, to run
through a red light. **6. g. une cigarette,
en g. une,** to smoke a cigarette, to
have a gasper.

griller, se, to lose one's reputation
(one's credit, etc.).

grillot, *m,* unscrupulous opportunist.

grimbiche, *f.* young woman*.

grimoire, *m.* police-record.

grimpant, *m.* trousers*.

grimper. 1. to have coition* with, to
mount; to rape. **2. faire g. qn (à
l'arbre)**=faire monter qn à l'arbre.

grimpouzer =grimper 1.

grinche, *m.* thief, burglar.

grincher, to be a burglar, to steal*.

gringue, *m.* **faire du g. à**=faire du
plat à (plat 1 (*b*)).

gringuer =faire du gringue à.

griottes, *f.pl.* buttocks*.

grippe-sou, *m.* miser*.

grippette, *f.* **1.** influenza, flu. **2.**
vagina*.

gris, *adj.* slightly drunk*.

gris, *m.* 1. shag (*tobacco*). 2. wine (of a very light red colour).

grisbi, *m.* money*; **(ne) touchez pas au g.,** lay off the lolly!

grisbinette, *f.* hundred franc coin (*old francs*).

grisol(l)e, *adj.* dear, expensive, costly, pricey.

grive, *f.* 1. **la g.=la griffe (griffe 3).** 2. **faire sa g.,** to do one's military service.

grivelle, *f.* cap*.

griveton, grivier, *m.* soldier, infantryman, foot-slogger.

grognasse, *f.* (*pej.*) woman*; prostitute*, bitch.

grognasser, to grouse.

grogne, *f.* grumbling, grousing.

grogner, grognoter=corner 2.

groin, *m.* ugly mug.

grôle, *m.* louse.

grolle, *f.* boot*.

grolles, *f.pl.* **avoir les g.=avoir les grelots; flanquer (foutre) les g. à qn =flanquer les grelots à qn.**

gros, *m.* 1. **les g.,** the nobs. 2. **du g. qui tache, du g.** (**rouge**), ordinary red wine. 3. **faire son g.,** to defecate*, to do number two.

groseille de cocher, *f.* wine.

grosse, *f.* prison*; **faire de la g.,** to be (put) in clink, to do time; **deux ans de g.,** a two year stretch (*i.e. two years' imprisonment*).

grossium, *m.* important* rich* person.

grouille, *f.* **les balancer à la g.=se la faire grasse; à la g.** *adv.,* all over the place.

grouiller, (se), to hurry* up; **grouille (-toi)!** get a move on! get cracking!

grouillot, *m.* 1. child, kid, brat. 2. errand-boy, page-boy, messenger boy, bell-boy, bell-hop. 3. peanut politician.

groumer, to grumble*.

groumeur, *adj.* grumpy.

grouper. 1. to arrest*; **se faire g.,** to get nabbed. 2. to scrounge, to collar, to grab. 3. **g. le dur,** to catch a train.

grue, *f.* prostitute*. *See also* **pied 14.**

guenon, guenuche, *f.* 1. ugly woman*, hag, bag, fright. 2. **avoir la g.,** to feel the need for drugs.

guêpe, *f.* shrew, bitch.

guêtres, *f.pl.* 1. **tirer ses g.,** to decamp*. 2. **traîner ses g.,** to loaf about, to knock about.

guette-au-trou, *f.* **=vise-au-trou.**

gueugueule, *f.* **=gueule.**

gueulante, *f.* **=goualante.**

gueulard, *adj.* loud-mouthed, loud-voiced; *m.* 1. bawler, brawler, bellower, loud-mouth, big-mouth. 2. glutton*.

gueularde, *f.* loudspeaker.

gueulardise, *f.* greediness, gluttony.

gueule, *f.* (A) mouth*. 1. **ta g.! ferme** (*or* **tais) ta g.!** shut* up! 2. **aller de la g.,** to spout. 3. **avoir de la g.,** to have the gift of the gab. 4. **avoir la g. de bois,** to have a hangover*. 5. **avoir la g. pavée=avoir le gosier pavé.** 6. **des coups de g.,** shouting, bawling, slanging match. 7. **être fort en g.,** (*a*) to be loud-mouthed, to be foul-mouthed; (*b*) to have too much to say for oneself. 8. **être porté sur la g.,** to be fussy about (*or* fond of) one's food; **une fine g.,** an epicure, a gourmet. 9. **s'en mettre plein la g.,** se taper la **g.,** to stuff, to gorge. 10. **se soûler la g.,** to get drunk*.

(B) face*. 1. **avoir de la g.,** to have an air, to have sth. about one, to look posh. 2. **avoir une sale g.,** (*a*) to have an ugly mug; (*b*) to look rotten, to look down in the mouth; (*c*) to look a nasty customer. 3. **casser** (*or* **bourrer) la g. à qn,** to bash s.o.'s face in, to beat s.o. up, to pitch into s.o., to break s.o.'s neck, to knock s.o.'s block off, to knock the stuffing out of s.o.; **se (faire) casser la g.,** to get smashed up, to get one's face smashed in. 4. **en faire une (sale) g.,** to pull a long face, to look down in the mouth. 5. **faire la** (*or* **sa) g.,** to sulk, to pull a long face, to look down in the mouth.

6. se fendre la g. = se fendre la pipe.
7. se ficher (se foutre) la g. par terre, to fall flat on one's face, to take a spill, to come a cropper*. **8. foutre qn sur la g.**, foutre sur la g. à qn, to slug s.o., to beat s.o. up; **se foutre sur la g.**, to (have a) scrap, to beat up one another. **6. Gueules Cassées,** ex-servicemen whose faces were disfigured in the 1914–1918 War. **10. gueules noires,** (a) miners; (b) engine-drivers. **11. g. de raie,** sale (or vilaine) g., g. d'empeigne, g. à caler les roues de corbillard, g. à coucher dehors avec un billet de logement, ugly (or repulsive) face, face that would stop a clock, 'clock-stopper'. **12. se payer (se foutre de) la g. de qn.** = se payer la tête de qn. **13. petite g.** = petite tête.

gueulements, m.pl. bawling.
gueuler, to bawl (out), to bellow, to holler (out); **g. au charron,** to kick up a row.
gueulerie, f. brawl(ing).
gueuleton, m. feast*; **un g. à chier partout,** a hell of a spread.
gueuletonner, to feast, to have a good tuck-in.
gueuloir, m. mouth*.
gueusaille, f. rabble, riff-raff, scum.
gueuse, f. **1.** prostitute*; **courir la g.,** to go wenching. **2. la G.,** the republic.
gugusse, m. clown, B.F.
guibolles, f.pl. legs*; **jouer des g.,** to leg it, to hook it; **tricoter des g.,** to hare along; **ne pas tenir sur ses g.,** to be shaky on one's pins.
guiche, f. **1.** = accroche-cœur. **2.** company of pimps.
guichet, m. **1. il est trop tard, les guichets sont fermés!** (c.p.) = c'est macache et midi sonné! **2. le petit g.,** anus.
guignard, adj. unlucky; m. unlucky person.
guigne, f. bad luck, tough break; **porter (ficher, flanquer, fourrer) la g. à qn,** to bring s.o. bad luck, to jinx s.o., to hex s.o., to hoodoo s.o.; **avoir**

la g., to have a run of bad luck, to be dead out of luck, to be down on one's luck; **il porte (la) g.** = c'est un porte-guigne.
guignol, m. **1.** tribunal. **2.** judge, 'beak'. **3. faire le g.,** to play the fool, to play the (giddy) goat. **4.** pl. police*.
guignon, m. bad luck; **c'est un abonné au g.,** he's got a hoodoo on him, he's a regular Jonah.
guili-guili, m. **faire g.-g. à,** to tickle (a child) under the chin.
guilledou, m. **courir le g.,** to gad about, to lead a fast life (or gay life).
guimauve, f. **1.** sloppy poem, sugary song, etc. **2.** penis*.
guimbarde, f. **vieille g.,** ramshackle old motor-car*.
guimpe(tte), f. cap*.
guinche, f. low dance-hall; dance, hop.
guincher, to dance, to shake a leg, to hoof it.
guincheur, -euse, m.f. dancer, hoofer.
guindal, m. = godet.
guinde, f. motor-car*.
guise, m. penis*.
guiseau, m. = guise; **filer le coup de g.** = guiser.
guiser, to have coition*.
guisot, m. **1.** leg*. **2.** penis*.
guitare, f. **1. c'est toujours la même g.,** it's the same old story again; **ne jouez** (or ne pincez) **pas de cette g.-là!** don't keep on harping on that old string! **2. avoir une belle g.,** (of female) to have shapely buttocks*. **3.** bidet.
guitoune, f. **1.** = gourbi 1 and 2. **2.** restaurant.
guizot, m. = guisot.
gun, m. syringe for drug injection.
gus(s), m, = mec.
gy, adv. **1.** yes; **faire g. de la tête,** to nod assent. **2. faire g.** = faire gaffe (gaffe, m. 2).
gym', gymn, gymbour, gymbourique, f. **1.** gymnastics. **2. au pas (de) g.,** at the double.

H

H. *m.* heroin (*drugs**).
habillés, *m.pl.* uniformed police*.
habitants, *m.pl.* lice, greybacks, grey-backed 'uns.
hambourgeois, *m.* policeman* in plain clothes.
hanneton, *m.* **1.** avoir un h. dans le plafond (*or* dans la boîte à sel) = avoir une araignée dans le plafond. **2.** pas piqué des hannetons = pas piqué des vers.
haquenée, *f.* tall*, gawky woman.
hareng, *m.* **1.** pimp, ponce, bully. **2.** la mare aux harengs, (*a*) the Herring-Pond (*i.e. the Atlantic Ocean*); (*b*) the sea. **3.** h. saur, German, Fritz (*W.W. II*). **4.** skinny horse.
haricot, *m.* **1.** courir (*or* cavaler *or* taper) sur le h. (*or* l'h.) à qn, to bore* s.o. **2.** des haricots! = des clous! **3.** (jambes en) haricots verts, skinny legs. **4.** aller manger des haricots, to go to jail. **5.** haricots verts, Germans, Boches. **6.** clitoris. **7.** *pl.* feet. **8.** défilocher les haricots verts, to make a fool of s.o. *See also* **fin,** *f.* **2.**
haridelle, *f.* bicycle.
harnacher, to rig out.
harnacher, se, to rig oneself out, to put one's togs on.
harnais, *m.pl.* clothes*; **mettre les h.,** to put one's glad rags on.
harnaquer = harnacher.
harnaqueur, *m.* swindler*.
harpe, *f.* **jouer de la h.,** to be in jail.
harpigner, to take.
harpigner, se, to come to blows.
harpion, *m.* = arpion.
harponner. 1. to grab; to buttonhole (s.o.). **2.** to arrest*; **se faire h.,** to get nabbed.
haute, *f.* **la h.,** the smart set, the upper ten, the nobs, the swells; the upper crust; **un filou de la h.,** a swell-mobs-man.

hauteur, *f.* **1.** être à la h., to be up to the job, to be wide-awake*. **2.** ça, c'est à la h.! that's the stuff to give 'em! that's the cheese!
Havre, le Grand, God.
hebdo (= *hebdomadaire*), *m.* weekly (paper *or* magazine).
hé bé, *int.* (= *eh bien!*) well! why!
herbe, *f.* **1.** manger l'h. par la racine, to be dead and buried, to be pushing up the daisies. **2.** grass, cannabis (*drugs**).
héro, *m.* heroin (*drugs**).
heure, *f.* je ne te (*or* vous) demande pas l'h. (qu'il est)! *or* dis donc, je t'ai demandé l'h. (qu'il est)? I wasn't talking to you! mind your own business! speak when you're spoken to! **faire l'h.,** to be on time.
hic, *m.* **voilà le h.!** there's the rub! that's the snag!
hiche-life, *adj.* (= *high-life*) elegant, swell, dressed up*.
hier, *adv.* je ne suis pas né d'h.! I wasn't born yesterday! d'you see any green in my eye? you don't catch me that way! do you take me for a mug?
high, *adj.* in a state of euphoria after drugs, high.
hirondelle, *f.* **1.** policeman* on bicycle. **2.** h. d'hiver, (*a*) hot chestnut seller; (*b*) chimney-sweep. **3.** avoir une h. dans le soliveau = avoir une araignée dans le plafond. **4.** les hirondelles volent bas, there's trouble (*or* a storm) brewing. **5.** h. de cimetière, bomb (*W.W.II*).
histoire, *f.* **1.** (*of thing*) = machin. **2.** c'est toute une h., it's a long story, it's no end of a job. **3.** la belle h.! is that all (there is to it)? what does that matter? so what? **4.** h. de rire (*or* de s'amuser *or* de se marrer *or* de rigoler), just for a joke, just for fun, just for the fun of it, just for the fun

of the thing, just for laughs. **5.** pudenda, privates. **6. faire des histoires, faire un tas d'histoires,** to make (no end of) a fuss, to kick up a fuss; **pas d'histoires!** no fuss! no monkeytricks! come off it! **7. avoir des histoires avec,** to fall foul of, to come to loggerheads with. **8. chercher** (*or* **faire**) **des histoires à qn,** to make trouble for s.o. **9. avoir ses histoires** = **avoir ses affaires** (**affaires,** *f.pl.* **1**). **10. tout ça, c'est des histoires!** that's all bunkum (*or* all boloney *or* all my eye (and Betty Martin) *or* all stuff and nonsense)!

hiviau, hivio(t), *m.* winter.

holpif, *adj.* = **eulpif.**

homme, *m.* **1. mon h.,** my hubby, my bloke. **2. dépouiller ie vieil h.,** to turn over a new leaf. **3. h.-orchestre** oneman band (*expert lover*), Pooh-bah.

hommelette, *f.* (*of man*) weakling, little weed.

honte, *f.* **il n'a pas chié la h.,** he's got nerve enough for anything.

horizontale, *f.* prostitute*; **elle fait l'h.,** she earns her money on her back.

Horloge, *f.* **la Grosse H.,** the Conciergerie (*prison in Paris*).

horripilant, *adj.* exasperating, provoking, maddening.

horripilation, *f.* exasperation, provocation.

horripiler, to exasperate, to provoke, to aggravate.

host(e)au, hosto, *m.* **1.** hospital, gaff, ozzy. **2.** prison*.

hotte, *f.* **1.** motor-car*; taxi. **2.** = **gueule 1. 3.** paunch*.

hotu, *m.* rotter*, layabout; bitch (*of woman*).

houp-là! *int.* ups-a-daisy!

houri, *f.* woman*, bitch.

houst(e)! *int.* = **oust(e)!**

hublots, *m.pl.* eyes*.

huile, *f.* **1.** money*. **2. h. de bras** *or* **h. de coude,** elbow-grease. **3. tête à l'h,** (*th.*) badly made-up super. **4. une h.,** an important* person.

huître, *f.* **1.** fool*. **2.** clot of phlegm, gob. **3. plein** (*or* **beurré**) **comme une h.,** as drunk* as a lord.

huit-reflets, *m.* silk hat, topper, shiner, stove-pipe.

humecter, s', to have a drink.

humeur, *f.* **être d'une h. massacrante** (*or* **d'une h. de chien** *or* **d'une h. de dogue**), to be in a very bad temper*.

huppé, *adj.* smart, swell; **les gens huppés,** the toffs, the nobs, the swells.

hure, *f.* **1.** head*. **2.** face*; **se gratter** (*or* **se ratisser**) **la h.,** to shave.

hurf(e), *adj.* = **urf(e).**

I

ici, *adv.* **je vois ça d'i.,** (*a*) I can just picture it; (*b*) I can see it coming.

icigo, *adv.* here.

idée, *f.* **1.** very small quantity, a suspicion, a touch, a drop. **2.** cela **vous changera les idées,** a change will do you good. **3. a-t-on i. de . . .,** who ever heard of . . . **4. se faire des idées,** to imagine things.

idiot, *m.* **faire l'i.,** to act dumb.

idole, *f.* pop idol; **déboulonner les idoles,** to debunk the great.

illico, *adv.* **i.** (presto), at once, straight (*or* right) away (*or* off), instanter, immediately*.

image, *f.* bank note.

imbuvable, *adj.* (*of person*) insufferable, unsociable, socially unacceptable, impossible.

Immortels, les, *m.pl.* members of the French Academy.

impair, *m.* **1.** mistake*; **faire un i.,** to make a mistake*. **2. faire un i. à qn,** to play a dirty trick on s.o., to do the dirty on s.o.

impayable, *adj.* very funny*, priceless; **il est i.!** he's the limit! he's a corker!

impec, *adj.* (=*impeccable*) impeccable, faultless, perfect.

imper, imperme, *m.* (=*imperméable*) mac(kintosh), waterproof, raincoat.

incendié, *adj.* **être i.**=**être brûlé.**

incendier, to reprimand*; **se faire i.,** to catch it hot; **s'incendier,** to wrangle, to go for each other.

incollable, *adj.* unbeatable.

inconnobré, *adj.* unknown.

incruster, s', to outstay (*or* to wear out) one's welcome, to stick on, to take root, to dig oneself in.

indécrottable, *adj.* incorrigible, hopeless, past praying for; boorish, loutish; *m.* boor, oaf, lout.

indérouillable, *adj.* **1.** stuck. **2.** sexually repulsive.

index, *m.* **mis à l'i.,** black listed.

indic(ateur), *m.* police-spy, informer*.

indigestion, *f.* **en avoir une i.,** to be fed to the teeth.

infectados, *m.* =**crapulos.**

influence, *f.* **le faire à l' i.,** to give oneself airs, to be bumptious, to put it on.

infourgable, *adj.* unsaleable.

innocent, *m.* **aux innocents les mains pleines,** beginners have all the luck; mugs for luck!

insoumise, *f.* **une (fille) i.,** an unregistered prostitute.

installer: (en) i., to swank, to put on a bold front.

intégrer. 1. to enter. **2.** to be admitted to a *Grande École.*

inter, *m.* **1.** tout (for brothels, etc.), hustler, steerer. **2.** (*telephone*) **l'i.,** trunks.

introduire: l'i. à qn, to take s.o. in, to cod (*or* to kid) s.o.; **se la laisser i.,** to let oneself be taken in.

Invatloches, les, *pr.n.* les Invalides (*in Paris*).

invite, *f.* invitation; **des invites,** advances.

invitation, *f.* **i. à la valse,** unwelcome invitation (to do sth. unpleasant— *e.g. to pay up, etc.*).

ioutre, *m.* =**youtre.**

Italboche, Italo, Italgo, *pr.n.* Italian.

itou, *adv.* too, also, likewise; **et puis moi i.,** and me too.

ivoire, *m.* **taquiner l'i.,** to play the piano, to tickle the ivories.

Ivans, *m.pl.* **les I.,** the Russians, the Russkies.

ix(e), *m.* =**x.**

J

J3, *m.f.pl.* les **J3**, teen-agers (*term origi-nally applied to adolescents during the rationing days of W.W.II*).

jabot, *m.* **1.** stomach*; **se remplir le j.**, to have a good blow-out (*or* a good tuck-in), to fill one's belly. **2. enfler le (*or* se pousser du) j.**, to put on airs, to strut.

jaboter, to jabber, to chatter, to clack, to jaw, to yak, to yackety-yak.

jacasse, *f.* chatterbox*.

jacasser =**jaboter.**

jack, *m.* **1.** meter (of taxi). **2. Master J.**, penis*, John Thomas.

jacot, *m.* jemmy.

jacots, *m.pl.* calves (of leg).

Jacques, *pr. n.* **faire le J.**, to play the fool (*or* the ape *or* the (giddy) goat); to try to be funny, to pull funny stuff.

jacques, *m.* **1.** jemmy, 'buster'. **2.** safe, crib, peter. **3.** chamber-pot*. **4.** =**gode(miché).**

jacquot, *m.* =**jacot.**

jacquots, *m.pl.* =**jacots.**

jactance, *f.* gift of the gab, yackety-yak.

jacter, to talk* (volubly).

jaffe, *f.* **1.** soup. **2.** food*.

jaffer, to eat*.

jag, *f.* Jaguar (*motor-car*).

jaja, *m.* **1.** wine; **écluser un j.**, to down a glass of wine. **2. jouer du j. au patatrot**, to decamp*.

jalmince, *adj.* jealous; *f.* jealousy, jealous person.

jalmincerie, *f.* jealousy, jealous per-son.

jambard, *m.* (*of person*) bore*.

jambe, *f.* **1.** avoir les jambes en coton (*or* en laine *or* en osier *or* en papier mâché *or* en italiques), to feel weak (*or* wobbly) on one's legs. **2.** avoir les jambes en manches de veste, to be bow-legged (*or* bandy-legged). **3.** avoir les jambes en pâté de foie, to feel funky, to have the wind up. **4.** ça vaut mieux que de se casser la j., ça vaut mieux qu'une j. cassée, (*c.p.*) that's better than a kick in the pants. **5.** ça vous fera une belle j.! a (fat) lot of good that will do you! that won't get you very far! **6.** en aurai-je la j. mieux faite? shall I be any the better for it? **7.** faire une partie de jambes en l'air *or* lever la j., to have coition*. **8.** la j.! what a bore (*or* a bind)! you make (*or* that makes) me sick! nuts! **9.** s'en aller sur une j., to have one round of drinks only. **10.** tenir la j. à qn, (*a*) to bore* s.o.; (*b*) to keep s.o. talking. **11.** tricoter des jambes, to hare along. **12.** faire j. de bois, to depart without paying.

jamber=tenir la jambe à qn.

jambon(neau), *m.* **1.** gratter du j., to play the banjo (*or* the mandoline). **2.** *pl.* legs*.

jambonner =tenir la jambe à qn. See also **blair.**

jambons, *m.pl.* legs*.

jantes, *f.pl.* se trouver sur les j., to be penniless*, to be on one's uppers.

japonais, *m.pl.* money*.

jaquette, *f.* **1.** tirer qn par la j., to buttonhole s.o., to stick to s.o. like a limpet. **2.** être de la j. (flottante), (re)-filer (*or* travailler) de la j.=en filer (filer 6).

jardin, *m.* j. des refroidis, cemetery.

jardiner. **1.** =bêcher. **2.** to exagger-ate*.

jarret, *m.* avoir du j., to be strong in the leg.

jar(s), *m.* slang*. dévider (bagouler, dé-baller, jaspiner, rouler) le j., to talk slang, to sling the lingo; entendre (entraver) le j., (*a*) to understand slang; (*b*) to be very wide-awake*.

jasante, *f.* prayer.

jaser. 1. to divulge* a secret, to blab. **2.** to pray.

jasper. 1. to talk*, to chatter. **2.** =jaser 1.

jaspiller =jasper 1.

jaspiner =jasper 1.

jaune, *m.* **1.** (*of workman*) blackleg, scab, rat, knobstick. **2. être peint en j.,** to be a cuckold.

jaunet, *m.* twenty-franc coin, gold coin, yellow-boy.

jaunisse, *f.* **en faire une j.,** to be green with envy, to be mad with jealousy.

java, *f.* **1.** spree*; **partir en j.,** to go on the razzle. **2.** thrashing*. **3. emmener qn en j.,** to take s.o. for a ride.

javanais, *m.* special conventional cant language of the Second Empire (about 1860) (*certain syllables* (*e.g.* '*va*', '*av*', '*pi*') *were introduced into words*—*e.g.* '*jardin*' *became* '*javardavin*', '*jeudi*' *became* '*javeudavi*', *etc.; often used by children*).

javotte, *f.* (*of woman*) chatterbox*, gasbag.

Jean-fesse, Jean-foutre, *m.* rotter*, washout, good-for-nothing.

jeanjean, *m.* simpleton*, ninny.

jecte, *f.* a tear drop.

je-m'en-fichisme (*or* **-foutisme**), *m.* don't-care-a-hang (*or* I-couldn't-care-less *or* I should-worry) attitude.

Je-sais-tout, *m.* **Monsieur J.-s.-t.,** Mr. Knowall, a know-it-all.

Jésus : être en J., to be stark naked.

jetée, *f.* **1.** hundred francs. *Cf.* **demi-j. 2.** successful robbery.

jeter. 1. ça, c'est jeté! that's the stuff to give 'em! **2. en j.**=j. du jus; **elle en jette!** she's the goods! **en j. à qn,** to impress s.o. **3. j. qn dedans,** to imprison* s.o., to run s.o. in. **4. la j. mal,** to give (*or* to make) a bad impression, to be of unprepossessing appearance, to look lousy. **5. n'en jetez plus (la cour est pleine)!** that'll do! that's (more than) enough! come off it! draw it mild! (*usually said to s.o. bestowing lavish praise or compliments*). **6. s'en j. un,** to have a drink,

to have one; **s'en j. un dernier,** to have one for the road. *See also* **coup 16.**

jeton, *m.* **1.** blow*. **2. un vieux j.,** an old man (*or* woman), an old has-been, a back number. **3. un faux j.,** a double-dealer, a two-timer, a shifty customer. **4. avoir les jetons,** to be afraid*; **donner (flanquer, foutre) les jetons à qn,** to put the wind up s.o., to give s.o. the jitters. **5. prendre le** (*or* **un**) **j.** (**de mat(e)** *or* **de voyeur**)=*faire le voyeur.*

jet(t)ard, *m.* prison*, prison cell.

jetouille, *f.* =jetons 4.

jeu, *m.* **vieux j.,** old-fashioned, old hat, square; **être vieux j.,** to be a back number.

jeudi, *m.* **dans la semaine des quatre jeudis,** in a month of Sundays, when (the) pigs begin to fly, once in a blue moon, when Hell freezes.

jeunabre, *adj.* youngish.

jeune, *adj.* **1. trop j.!** young and immature! wet (*or* not dry) behind the ears! **2. c'est un peu j.,** it's a bit on the short (*or* small) side.

jeunesse, *f.* girl*, flapper, mere chit of a girl.

jeunet, jeunot, *adj.* young and inexperienced; *m.* youngster, greenhorn, Johnny Raw.

Jèze, *m.* Jesuit.

ji, *adv.* =gy.

jinjin, *m.* red wine.

job, *m.* (i) **1.** job, position, employment. **2.** soft (*or* safe) job.

job, *m.* (ii) **1.** =jobard 1. **2. monter le j. à qn,** (*a*) =monter un bateau à qn; (*b*) =monter la tête à qn; (se) **monter le j.**=se monter la tête.

jobard, *m.* **1.** simpleton*, mug, gull*. **2.** madman.

jobarder, to dupe*.

jockey, *m.* **1.** shill (*i.e. confederate or decoy in gambling joint, etc.*). **2. faire j.,** to diet.

joice, *adj.* merry, joyful, cheerful, gay, pleased.

joie, *f.* **fille de j. :** *see* **fille 1.**

joint, *m.* **1. trouver le j.,** to hit upon the

right plan (*or* the right dodge), to get the knack of it. 2. **aller au j.**, to have coition*. 3. marihuana cigarette.

joisse, *adj.* =joice.

jojo, *adj.* 1. nice. 2. pretty, good-looking; (*by antithesis*) ugly, hideous.

joli, *adj.* (*iron.*) fine, nice; **un j. coco**, a fine rotter*; **je serais j.**! a nice mess I'd be in! *m.* **c'est du j.**! a nice (*or* pretty) mess (*or* pickle)! it's shameful (*or* disgraceful)! **il a encore fait du j.**! he's made a nice (*or* fine) mess of it again!

joliment, *adv.* (*intensive use*) extremely, awfully, frightfully; **je me suis j.** amusé, I had a ripping time; **il a j.** raison! he's jolly well right! how right he is! **je suis j. content**, I'm awfully glad.

jonc, *m.* 1. money*; **avoir du j.**, to be rich*. 2. gold. 3. **se peler le j.**, to be chilled to the bone. 4. penis. 5. **foutre un coup de jonc**, to steal*.

joncaille, *f.* 1. money*. 2. gold. 3. jewels.

jongler: **faire j. qn de qch.**, to do s.o. out of what is due to him.

jornaille, *f.* =journaille.

jorne, *m.* day.

Joseph, *pr.n.* **faire son** (*or* **le**) **J.**, to affect chaste, virtuous airs.

Joséphine, *pr.n.* 1. (*mil.*) bayonet. 2. **faire sa J.**, (*a*) to play the prude; (*b*) to put on airs.

jouailler, to play a musical instrument badly.

jouasse, *f.* kick, thrill after drugs.

joue, *f.* **se caler les joues**: *see* **se caler**.

jouer. 1. **j. qn**, to fool* s.o. 2. **les j.**, to decamp*.

jouge, *m.* **en moins de j.** = **en deux temps trois mouvements**.

jouir, to experience the sexual spasm, to have an orgasm, to 'come'.

jouissance, *f.* orgasm.

joujou, *m.* 1. toy, plaything. 2. **faire j. avec**, (*a*) to play with; (*b*) to have coition* with.

jour, *m.* 1. **long comme un j. sans pain**, (*of person*) a regular lamp-post (*see* **tall***), thin person. 2. **tous les jours que** (**le bon**) **Dieu fait**, every blessed day; every day that God sends; day in, day out. 3. **ne pas voir le j.** (*of stolen goods that cannot be shown or sold without risk*) 'hot stuff'; clandestine.

jourdé, *m.* day.

journaille, journanche, journe, *f.* day.

journaleux, *m.* (*pej.*) journalist.

journanche, *f.*, **journe,** *m.* day.

joyeuses, *f.pl.* testicles*.

joyeux, *m.* soldier serving in the **bat' d'Af'**.

J't'arquepince: **la Maison J't'arquepince**, the (Prefecture of) Police.

jugeot(t)e, *f.* 1. common sense, gumption, nous, savvy, nonce (*or* nunce). 2. **passer en j.**, to be brought up for trial, to stand one's trial.

juif, *m.* **le petit j.**, the funny-bone (*in the elbow*).

juivoler, to overcharge.

Jules, *pr.n.* 1. chamber-pot*. 2. latrine-pail. 3. fancy man. 4. pimp, ponce. 5. German, Jerry (*W.W.II*). 6. heroin (*drugs**).

Julie, *pr.n.* 1. prostitute*. 2. woman*. 3. **faire sa J.**, to play the prude.

Julot, *pr.n.* 1. =**Jules** 3 *and* 4. 2. reliable man.

jumelles, *f.pl.* buttocks*.

jupé, *adj.* =**juponné**.

jupon, *m.* **courir le j.**, to run after women, to chase the girls, to womanize.

juponnard, *m.* **être j.** = **courir le jupon**.

juponné, *adj.* drunk*.

jus, *m.* 1. water; **c'est clair comme du j. de boudin** *or* **de chique**, it's as clear as mud; **j. de boudin** (*or* **de chaussette** *or* **de serpillière**), dish-water, cat-lap. 2. coffee, (*mil.*) thick; **j. de chapeau,** watery coffee; (*mil.*) **aller au j.**, (*a*) to go for the coffee; **c'est du 10 au j.**, it's 10 days to demob. day; (*b*) to go over the top (*W.W.I.*) 3. current (*electricity*), **donner le j.**, to switch on. 4. petrol, juice, gas; **donner du j.**, to step on the gas, to open the throttle; **à**

plein j., full throttle. 5. blurb (on book). 6. long speech; faire un j., to spout at length. 7. elegance, smartness; avoir du j., to look swell; jeter du (or un) j., to look classy; elle en jette (un j.)! she's the goods! 8. sperm, spunk. 9. ça vaut le j., it's worth while. 10. j. de coude=huile de coude. 11. mariner (or mijoter) dans son j., to stew in one's own juice. 12. y mettre du j., to put some vim into it. 13. heroin (drugs*). 14. j. de parapluie, water.

jusqu'auboutiste, m.f. die-hard, last-ditcher, all-outer, whole-hogger.
juste, adj. ça a (or ç'a) été j.! it was a narrow escape*; être j., to have barely enough.
juter. 1. to swank*. 2. to speechify*. 3. =jouir.
juteux, adj. elegant, smart (cf. jus 7); m. (mil.) =adjupète.
J.V. (police slang for 'jeune voyou') young hoodlum, juvenile delinquent.
jy, adv. =gy.

K

kapo, *m.* = capo(ral) (*used mostly in concentration camps in W.W.II for the 'surveillant'*).
kasba(h), *f.* = casba(h).
kébour(g), *m.* kepi, peaked cap*.
khâgne, *f.* = cagne.
khâgneux, *m.* = cagneux.
kick, *m.* thrill (from drugs).
kif, kif-kif, *adj.* c'est k.-k. (bourricot), c'est du k., c'est toujours du k. au même, it's all one, it comes to the same (thing), it's six of one and half a dozen of the other, it's as broad as it's long, it makes no odds, it's much of a muchness, it's tweedledum and tweedledee; **c'est pas du k.,** it's quite another matter, it's not the same thing at all.

kif, *m.* cannabis (*drugs**).
kiki, *m.* = quiqui.
kil(e), *m.*, **kilbus,** *m.*, **kilo,** *m.* (i) litre (of wine); **payer un k. a qn,** (*approx.*) to stand s.o. a 'pint'.
kilo, *m.* (ii) **poser un k.** = poser un colombin.
kir, *m.* white wine and blackcurrant liqueur or syrup.
klébard, klèb(s), *m.* = clèb(s) 1.
knokout(e), K.O., *adj.* knocked out, tired out.
kopeks, *m.pl.* money*.
kroum(e), *m.* = croum(e).
krounir = crounir.
kyrielle, *f.* long string (of names, words, insults, 'tribe' of children, etc.).

L

là, *adv.* 1. être un peu l., (*of person*) to be all there, to be reliable; (*of thing*) to be the real Mackay. 2. **ils ne sont pas l.**, I'm penniless*. 3. **avoir qn l.=avoir qn quelque part.** 4. **tout est l.**, that's the whole point.

labago, labadé, *adv.* (over) yonder.

labo, *m.* laboratory, lab.

lac, *m.* **être dans le l.**, (*of person or undertaking*) to be done for*.

lacet, *m.* **marchand de lacets**, gendarme.

lâcher. 1. **l. qn**, to drop (*or* to chuck *or* to jilt) s.o., to throw s.o. over, to leave s.o. in the lurch, to give s.o. the cold shoulder, to walk out on s.o., to give s.o. the mitten. 2. **les l.**, to pay* up; **être dur à les l.=les l. avec un élastique.**

lâcheur, *m.* unreliable person, one who lets you down, quitter.

lacsatif, lacsé, *m.* 1. handbag. 2. thousand franc note: see **sac** 1.

lacson, *m.* package; **l. de pipes**, cigarette packet.

ladé, *adv.* there.

laf(fe)s, *f.pl.* =**fortif(e)s.**

laga, lago, *adv.* =**ladé.**

laidasse, *f.*, **laideron**, *m.* ugly woman (*or* girl), ugly duckling, fright, plain Jane.

lait, *m.* 1. **boire du (petit) l.**, to lap it up, to take it all in eagerly; **avaler qch. comme du petit l.**, to purr with delight over sth.; **ça se boit comme du petit l.**, (*of a drink*) it slips down your throat like mother's milk. 2. **l. de chameau** (*or* **de panthère** *or* **de tigre**), pernod. 3. **l. de poule**, egg-flip.

laitue, *f.* novice in prostitution.

laïus, *m.* speech, lecture, jaw; **piquer** (*or* **faire**) **un l.**, to speechify*.

laïusser=piquer un laïus.

laïusseur, *m.* speechifier, spouter, waffler.

lambda, *adj.* ordinary, commonplace.

lame, *f.* 1. knife. 2. **pisser des lames de rasoir (en travers)**, to piss pins and needles (*i.e. to suffer from gonorrhoea*).

lamedu, *m.* goods.

lamer, to knife.

laminer, to suppress, to wipe out.

lampe, *f.* 1. stomach*; **s'en mettre** (*or* **s'en coller** *or* **s'en foutre**) **plein la l.**, **s'en mettre à travers la l.**, **se garnir la l.**, to have one's fill, to (have a) good tuck-in, to guzzle. 2. **l. à souder**, machine-gun, tommy-gun.

lampion, *m.* 1. eye*. 2. **un coup dans le l.**, a drink, a swig. 3. =**lampe** 1. 4. **l'air des lampions**, rhythmical stamping of feet to indicate impatience.

lampiste, *m.* scapegoat.

lance, *f.* 1. rain. 2. water. 3. urine; **jeter de la l.**, to urinate*. 4. V.D. 5. syringe for drugs.

lancé, *adj.* slightly drunk*.

lancecailler, to urinate*.

lance-parfum, *m.* =**lampe à souder** (**lampe** 2).

lance-pierres, *m.* 1. rifle. 2. **les envoyer** (*or* **envoyer le fric**) **avec un l.-p.=les lâcher avec un élastique.** 3. **être nourri avec un l.-p.**, to be on a strict diet.

lancequinade, *f.* steady downpour (of rain).

lancequine, *f.* 1. rain. 2. water.

lancequiner. 1. to rain; **l. à pleins tubes**, to rain cats and dogs. 2. to weep*. 3. to urinate*.

lancer: **ça me lance**, it gives me a stabbing pain.

langouse, *f.* tongue; **filer une l.=faire une langue fourrée (langue** 5).

langouste, *f.* prostitute*.

langue, *f.* 1. **l. verte**, slang*. 2. **avaler sa l.**, (*a*) to die*; (*b*) to hold one's tongue, to keep mum; (*c*) to yawn one's head off. 3. **avoir la l. bien pendue**, to have the gift of the gab. **4. donner** (*or* **jeter**) **sa l. au(x) chat(s)** (*or* **aux chiens**), (*of question or riddle*) to give it up, to give up guessing; **je donne ma l. au chat!** go on, I'll buy it! **5. faire une l. fourrée,** to give a French kiss (*or* a tongue-kiss). **6. ne pas avoir sa** (*or* **la**) **l. dans sa poche,** not to be at a loss for a reply, to have a ready tongue, to be quick on the come-back, to have plenty to say for oneself. **7. tirer la l.,** (*fig.*) to show signs of exhaustion, to be near the end of one's tether. **8. faire tirer la l. à qn,** to keep s.o. waiting indefinitely, to string s.o. along.

languette, *f.* tongue.

lanlaire : envoyer qn se faire l., to send s.o. packing*; **va te faire l.!** go to blazes!*

lansquine, *f.* =**lancequine.**

lansquiner =**lancequiner.**

lanterne, *f.* **1.** window. **2.** eye*. **3.** stomach*. **4. l. rouge,** (*a*) (*approx.*) 'wooden spoon' (*formerly awarded to the competitor last in a race*); (*b*) brothel*. **5. éclairer la l. de qn,** to give s.o. the necessary information (*in order that he may understand what is being discussed*), to put s.o. wise. **6. à la l.!** string him (etc.) up! lynch him (etc.)!

lanterner, lantiponner, to dilly-dally.

lap(e), nothing; **un bon à l.,** a good-for-nothing; **que l. =que dal(le).**

lape-verres, *m.* tippler, boozer.

lapin, *m.* **1. un rude** (*or* **fameux** *or* **fier**) **l.,** a fine fellow, a brick; a tough nut; an artful dodger, a knowing one; **un drôle de l.,** a queer customer; **un sacré l.,** a hell of a tit; **mon vieux l.,** old chap*, old cock. **2. mon petit l.,** my darling*. **3. l. de gouttière,** cat, mog(gy). **4. chaud comme un l., un chaud l.,** a hot customer (*sexually*), hot stuff. **5. faire** (*or* **donner**) **le coup du l. à qn,** to kill* s.o. (by a treacherous blow); to give s.o. the finishing stroke. **6. poser un l. à qn,** not to keep an appointment, to fail to turn up, to

let s.o. down, to stand s.o. up, to slip (a girl) up; **becqueter du l.,** to be let down, to be stood up. **7. sentir le l.,** to smell fuggy. *See also* **pet 6.**

lapine, *f.* **une mère l.,** a woman with many children.

lapinoche, lapinski, lapinskoff, *m.* rabbit, bunny.

lapp(e), lapuche =**lap(e).**

laquépem, *m.* packet.

larbin, *m.* flunkey.

lard, *m.* **1.** =**lardon. 2. être gras à l.,** to be as fat as a pig, to be porky. **3. faire** (*or* **se faire**) **du l.,** to get fat (*with idleness*), to put on weight, to put on flesh; **reprendre du l.,** to get one's weight back. **4. un gros l.,** a big slob. **5. rentrer dans** (*or* **sauter sur**) **le l. à qn,** to attack* s.o. **6. ne savoir si c'est du l. ou du cochon,** to be unable to tell one thing from t'other, to be unable to tell butter from margarine. **7. se racler le l.,** to have a shave. **8.** = **lardon.** *See also* **tête 20.**

larder: l. qn, to get on s.o.'s nerves.

lardeus(se), lardingue, *m.* (over)-coat.

lardoir, *m.,* **lardoire,** *f.* **1.** sword. **2.** knife.

lardon, *m.* baby, brat, child*; **faire un l.,** to conceive, to have a brat.

lardoss(e), *m.* (over)coat.

lardu, *m.* superintendent of police.

large, *m.* **prendre le l., pousser** (*or* **tirer**) **au l.,** to decamp*; *adj. see* **mener.**

largement, *m.* **avoir l. le temps,** to have tons of time.

largeot, *adj.* wide, broad.

largeur, *f.* **dans les grandes largeurs,** thoroughly, in a big way, in fine style, with a vengeance.

largonji, *m.* butcher's slang (*in which 'l' is substituted for the first consonant of a word, with or without the addition of a suffix such as 'em', 'oc', 'ique', 'uche', etc.*).

largue, *f.* prostitute*; thief's wife.

larguer. 1. to release. **2.** to repudiate (a woman). **3.** =**abouler.**

larme, *f.* **1.** une l. de . . ., just a drop of (a drink), a wee drappy. **2.** **y aller de sa (petite) l.,** to shed a tear, to turn on the waterworks.

larméleauté, larteaumic, *m.* hammer.

larmichette, *f.* extra drop (of drink).

larron, *m.* **s'entendre comme larrons en foire,** to be as thick as thieves.

larton, *m.* bread; **l. savonné,** white bread.

lasane, *f.* letter (*missive*).

lascar, *m.* fellow*, blighter; smart fellow; **un rude l.,** a tough customer, a tough guy; **quel l.!** what a lad!

latte, *f.* **1.** boot*, shoe. **2.** donner (*or* filer) **un coup de l. à qn=latter qn,** **1** *and* **2.** **3.** traîner ses lattes, to pad the hoof. **4.** marcher à côté de ses **lattes,** to be penniless*, to be on one's uppers.

latter. 1. to boot (s.o.). **2.** to tap (s.o. for money).

lattoche, *f.* =latte **1.**

laubé, laubiche, *adj.* beautiful.

lavabe, *m.* lavatory, lav, toilet, W.C.*

lavage, *m.* **1.** pawning. **2.** selling-off (at any price).

lavasse, *f.* tasteless stuff (*of wine, soup, drink*).

lavé, *adj.* penniless*, cleaned out.

lav(e)du, *m.* =cave **2;** *adj.* =moche.

lavement, *m.* (*of thing or person*) bore*.

laver, to sell (cheap *or* at a loss), to sell off, to turn into cash. *See also* **tête 8.**

lavette, *f.* **1.** tongue. **2.** (*of person*) wash-out, sissy, dud, softie.

laveur, *m.* receiver (of stolen goods).

lavure, *f.* =lavasse.

laxé, *m.* **1.** =lacsé **2.** **2.** =laxon.

laxon, *m.* linen.

laza(g)ne, *f.* **1.**=lasane. **2.** purse, wallet.

lazaro, *m.* prison*, prison cell, (*mil.*) clink.

lazingue, *m.* purse, wallet.

lazziloffe, *adj.* syphilitic.

lèche, *f.* **faire de la l. à qn,** to flatter* s.o., to suck up to s.o.

lèche-bottes, *m.* flatterer*

lèche-carreaux, *m.* **faire du l.-c.,** to go window-shopping.

lèche-cul, *m.* flatterer*.

lèche-motte, lèche-train, *m.* =lèche-bottes.

lécheur, *m.* **l.** (de bottes)=lèche-bottes.

lèche-vitrines, *m.* =lèche-carreaux.

lecture, *f.* être en l.=être sous presse.

légionnaire, *m.* bottle of red wine.

légitime, *f.* ma l., my wife*.

légume, *f.* **1.** les grosses légumes, the important* persons. **2.** perdre ses légumes=avoir ses affaires.

légumier, *m.* V.I.P.'s car.

lentilles, *f.pl.* eyes*; éplucheuses de l., lesbians*.

lerche, lerchem, lerchot, *adj.* dear, costly; *adv.* much, many; **c'est pas l.** *or* **y a pas l.,** there isn't much (of it).

lesbombe, *f.* prostitute*.

lessivage, *m.* **1.** selling-off. **2.** l. de crâne, brain-washing.

lessive, *f.* **1.** selling-off. **2.** heavy loss (at cards, etc.), clean-out.

lessivé, *adj.* **1.** ruined (financially), cleaned-out. **2.** exhausted*, completely washed out.

lessiver. 1. to sell out, to flog. **2.** to blue (one's money). **3.** to polish off (opponent); **se faire l.,** to get licked. **4.** to ruin, to clean (s.o.) out.

lessiveur, *m.* =laveur.

lettre, *f.* **1.** passer comme une l. à la poste, to go through easily (*or* smoothly *or* without any difficulty), to go without a hitch. **2.** les cinq **lettres,** *euphemism for* merde. (*Cf. the English 'a four-letter word'*).

leur(s)zig(ue)s, *pron.* they, them.

levage, *m.* faire un l.=lever **3.**

lever. 1. to arrest*. **2.** to steal*. **3.** to make a pick-up, to pick up (a woman, a mug, a tart, etc.). *See also* **pied 18.**

leveur, *m.* thief.

leveuse, *f.* prostitute*.

lézard, *m.* **faire le** (*or* **son**) **l.,** to bask in the sun, to sun-bathe.

lézarder. 1. =**faire le lézard. 2.** to idle, to laze, to loaf.

liant, *adj.* **être l., avoir du l.,** to be a good mixer.

liasse, *f.* wad (of banknotes), roll.

lichade, *f.* swig, booze.

lichailler, licher, to tipple, to booze.

liche, *f.* nip, wee drappy.

lichedu, ligedu, *m.* **1.** stinker. **2.** =**tige,** *m.*

licheur, *m.* tippler, boozer.

lichoter =**licher.**

lignard, *m.* infantryman, foot-slogger.

ligne, *f.* **1. avoir de la l.,** to have a good figure. **2. tirer à la l.,** (*of writer*) to pad (*or* to spin) out an article. **3. c'est dans ma l.!** that's right up my street!

ligoter, to read.

lili-pioncette, *f.* morphia (*drugs**).

limace, *f.* **1.** shirt*. **2.** (*pej.*) woman*, a bit of skirt.

limande, *f.* slap in the face.

limasse, lime, *f.* =**limace 1.**

limer, to have coition* with, to (do a) grind.

limogeage, *m.* (*mil.*) superseding, shelving, bowler-hatting.

limoger, (*mil.*) to supersede, to shelve, to bowler-hat (s.o.).

limonade, *f.* **1. être dans la l.,** (*a*) to be in a fix*; (*b*) to keep a bar, to be one of the 'Trade' (*i.e. retail drink trade*). **2. piquer dans la l.,** to dive, to take a header (into the briny).

limonadier, *m.* bar-keeper, publican.

limouse, limouze, *f.* =**limace.**

linge, *m.* **1. avoir du l.,** (*a*) to be well dressed*; (*b*) to be well off. **2. du beau l.** (*of female*) a good-looker.

lingé, *adj.* **être bien l.**=**avoir du linge 1** (*a*).

linger, to dress, to rig out, to tog up; **se l.,** to dress, to tog up,

lingre, lingue, *m.* knife, chiv, chive, chivey.

linguer, to stab, to chiv (*i.e. to stab with knife or razor*).

lion, *m.* **avoir mangé** (*or* **avoir bouffé**) **du l.,** to be on the rampage.

lipper, to eat, to drink*.

liquette, *f.* =**limace 1.**

liquider, to kill*, to liquidate (s.o.).

lisbroquer, lispoquer, to urinate*.

Lisette, *pr.n.* **pas de ça, L.!** (*c.p.*) none of that! come off it! nothing doing!

lisotter, to be a cursory reader, to glance through.

lisse, *adj.* **être l.,** to be a fool*.

lisses, *f.pl.* stockings.

lit, *m.* **l. en portefeuille,** apple-pie bed.

litron, *m.* **1.** litre (of wine). **2. ne pas tenir le l.,** not to be able to carry one's wine.

lixdré, *adj.* ten.

locdu, *m.* =**loquedu.**

loche, *m.* taxi-driver.

loche, *f.* =**loque.**

locomotive, *f.* **fumer comme une l.,** to be a heavy smoker, to smoke like a chimney.

loffe, *adj.* =**louf.**

loffiat, *m.* blackguard*.

loge, *f.* **être aux premières loges,** (*fig.*) to have a front (*or* a ringside) seat, to have a grandstand view.

loger. 1. to dwell, to stay, to live. **2.** (*of police*) to track (s.o.) down.

loi, *f.* **avoir la l.,** (*a*) to have the upper hand, to be the boss; (*b*) to get the best of it, to be the winner.

loilpé, loilpuche, *adj.* **à l.**=**à poil** (**poil 1**).

loinqué, *m.* corner; *adv.* far off.

lolo, *m.* **1.** (*child's word*) milk, moo. **2. c'est du l.!** it's nice! **3. lolos, boîtes à l.,** breasts* (of female).

long, *adj.* **1. les avoir longues,** to be ravenously hungry, to be greedily ambitious. **2. de longue,** uninterruptedly, on end. **3.** *m.* cigar. **4. y aller de tout son l.,** to go at it hammer and tongs, to wire in.

longe, *f.* year (of prison sentence).

lopaille, *f.*, **lopart,** *m.*, **lope,** *f.*, **lopette,** *f.* **1.** rotter*; **sale petite lope,** dirty little bugger. **2.** pederast*.

loque, *f.* **être comme une l.,** to be as

limp as a rag, to feel like a (wet) rag, to have no fight left in one.

loqué, *adj.* togged-up.

loquedu, *adj.* =**moche; m.** (*a*) worthless fellow, good-for-nothing; (*b*) dangerous fellow, bastard.

loquer, to dress.

loques, *f.pl.* clothes*.

lorgne, *f.* ace (*playing-card*).

lot, *m.* **1. gagner le gros l.**, to win the first prize, to strike it lucky, to hit the jackpot. **2. un beau petit l.**, (*of girl*) a bit of all right, a nice bit of goods (*or* of homework).

loti, *adj.* **bien** (*or* **mal**) **l.**, well (*or* poorly) off.

loto, *m.* **ribouler des lotos**, to goggle. *See also* **boule 7.**

louba, *f.* =**nouba.**

loubac, *adj.* mad.

loubarde, *f.* light.

loubé, *m.* a wee bit.

loubiats, *m.pl.* beans.

loucedé, loucedoc(k), *adj.* **en l.** =**en douce.**

louche, *f.* hand*; **serrer la l. à qn**, to shake hands with s.o., to tip s.o. a fin; **filer la l. à qn**, to give s.o. a helping hand.

louchébem, loucherbem, loucherbème, *m.* **1.** butcher. **2.** more complex form of **largonji.**

loucher: l. vers (*or* **sur**) **qch.**, to covet sth., to cast longing eyes at sth., to squint at sth.

louf, louf(e)tingue, *adj.* =**loufoque.**

louffe, *f.* fart; **lâcher une l.** =**louffer.**

louffer, to fart.

louf(f)iat, *m.* **1.** waiter (in café, restaurant). **2.** =**loffiat. 3.** (*nav.*) lieutenant.

loufoque, *adj.* mad*; *m.* madman, crackpot. **histoire l.**, shaggy dog tale.

loufoquerie, *f.* craziness, daftness, barminess.

louftingue, *adj.* =**loufoque.**

loulotte, *f.* =**loulout(t)e.**

loulou, *m.f.* **1.** darling*. **2.** *m.* pom (*dog*)

loulout(t)e, *f.* darling*.

loup, *m.* **1. mon (petit** *or* **gros) l.**, my

darling*. **2.** (*th.*) fluffed entrance, fluff. **3. elle a vu le l.**, she has lost her innocence (*or* her virginity *or* her maidenhead), she's had it, she has lost her cherry, she's seen the elephant. **4. un vieux l. de mer**, an old salt, an old tar, an old sea-dog.

loupague, loupel, loupenne, *m.* louse.

loupe, *f.* laziness.

louper. 1. to miss (one's turn, train, opportunity). **2.** to bungle. **3.** to misfire, to go haywire. **4.** (*th.*) to fluff (one's lines, entry).

loupiot, *m.* child*, kid, brat.

loupiotte, *f.* **1.** little girl, **2.** light, torch, flash-lamp.

lourd, *adj.* =**lourdingue; adv. il n'en reste pas l.**, there's not much left; **je ne donnerais pas l. de . . .**, I wouldn't give much for . . .; **il n'en fait pas l.**, he doesn't overwork; **gagner l.**, to earn good money.

lourd, *m.* **1.** peasant*. **2.** opium.

lourde, *f.* door, jigger; **boucler la l.**, to close (*or* to shut) the door; **boucle la l.!** put a bit of wood in it! (*i.e. shut the door*); **casser la l., mettre la l. en dedans**, to burgle, to break in.

lourder, to close (a door); to close down; to lock in.

lourdeur, *m.* burglar, house-breaker.

lourdier, -ière, *m.f.* doorkeeper, concierge.

lourdingue, *adj.* stupid, dull-witted, dense, thick; **en avoir l. sur la conscience**, to have a load on one's conscience.

lousdé, lousdoc, *adj.* **en l.** =**en douce** (**douce 3**).

loustic, *m.* **1.** joker, wag. **2.** fellow*; **un drôle de l.**, a funny guy.

loute, *f.* =**loulout(t)e.**

lovés, *m.pl.* money.

Lucal, Luco, *pr.n.* Luxembourg gardens in Paris.

lucarne, *f.* **1.** eye*. **2.** monocle.

luette, *f.* **se rincer la l.** =**se rincer la dalle.**

luisant, *m.* daylight; *m.pl.* patent-leather shoes.

luisante, *f.* moon.

lundi, *m.* **faire** (*or* **fêter**) **le l., fêter la Saint-L.,** not to work on Mondays, to take Monday off.

lune, *f.* 1. buttocks*. 2. whim, mood. 3. fool*. 4. **pleine l.,** moonface. 5. **être dans la l.,** to be wool-gathering. 6. **faire voir la l. à qn en plein midi,** to gull s.o., to hoax* s.o. 7. **tomber de la l.,** to be struck all of a heap, to look blank. 8. **elle a vu la l.** = **elle a vu le loup** (loup 3). 9. **... à riper la l.,** worthless* ... 10. **je vous parie la l.**

que ..., you can bet your boots that ... *See also* **con, trou** 7.

luné, *adj.* **être bien** (*or* **mal**) **l.,** to be in a good (*or* bad) humour (*or* mood *or* temper).

lunette, *f.* **mettre la tête à la l.,** to be guillotined.

lupanar, *m.* brothel*.

lurelure, à, *adv. phrase.* at random, without knowing what one is doing.

lustucru, *m.* simpleton, fool*.

lyre, *f.* **toute la l.,** the whole bag* of tricks.

M

maboul(e), *adj.* mad*.
mac, *m.* 1. =maquereau. 2. =mec.
3. boss, gov'nor.
macab, *m.* =macchab(e).
macache, *int.* (c'est) m. (et midi
sonné)! not likely! nothing doing! no
fear! it can't be done! not on your
Nellie!
macadam, *m.* 1. faire le m.=faire le
trottoir. 2. faire (*or* piquer) un m.,
to feign an accident (in order to get
compensation).
macaron, *m.* 1. steering-wheel (of
motor car); manier le m., to drive
(car), to take the wheel; as du m.,
crack driver. 2. *pl.* (*hairdressing*)
tight coils, 'ear-phones'.
macaroni, *m.* 1. Italian*. 2. penis*;
s'allonger le m., to masturbate*.
macchab(e), mac(c)habée, *m.*
corpse*.
machin, *m.* (*of thing*) what's-its-name*,
(*of person*) what's-his (her)-name,
what-d'ye-call-him (her).
machin-chose, machinchouette,
m. =machin.
machine, *f.* 1. =machin. 2. (*of book,
play, film, etc.*) production, show,
publication. 3. m. à raccourcir,
guillotine. 4. passer qn à la m. à
bosseler=passer qn à tabac. 5. *pl.*
testicles*. 6. m. à coudre (à percer, à
secouer) le paletot, machine-gun.
machinette, *f.* pickpocket.
machin-truc, *m.* =machin.
mâchoire, *f.* 1. bâiller à se décrocher
la m., to yawn one's head off. 2. nom
(*or* phrase) à décrocher la m., tongue-
twister.
mâchon, *m.* feast*.
mâchuré, *adj.* drunk*.
macque, macquesée, *f.* =maquerelle.
macreuse, *f.* avoir du sang de m., to be
a cold fish.
macrotin, *m.* young mec.

madame, *f.* madam (*female manager
or hostess of a brothel*).
Madeleine, *pr.n.* pleurer comme une
M., to weep bitterly, to shed bitter tears.
magaze, *m.* shop.
magner, se: se m. (le train *or* le mou
or le derche *or* le popotin *or* la
rondelle), to hurry up*.
magnes, *f.pl.* faire des m.=faire des
manières.
mago=magaze.
magot, *m.* treasure, pile (of money),
hoard, savings; avoir un joli m., to
have a nice little bit put by; épouser
un gros m., to marry a rich girl.
mahousse, *adj.* =maous(se).
mailloche, *f.* brutality; *adj.* big,
hefty*.
main, *f.* 1. faire sa m., to feather one's
nest. 2. ne pas y aller de m. morte,
to make no bones about it, to go at it
bald-headed, to let s.o. have it. 3. ne
pas se moucher de la m. gauche=ne
pas se moucher du pied. 4. passer la
m., to throw up the sponge, to chuck
it, to chuck (*or* to throw) one's hand
in; je vous passe la m., I'll hand over
to you, you can carry on now. 5.
passer la m. dans le dos (*or* les
cheveux) à qn, to flatter* s.o.; se
passer la m. dans le dos, to give oneself a pat on the back. 6. péter dans
la m. à qn, (*of person*) to let s.o. down,
not to keep one's promise to s.o.;
(*of thing*) to fall through, to fail, to
come to nothing. 7. se faire la m.
(sur), to practise (on), to try one's
hand (on). 8. se marier de la m.
gauche, to marry over the broomstick, to jump the besom; mariage de
la m. gauche, broomstick wedding.
9. m. armée, armed attack. 10. avoir
les mains palmées (*or* à la retourne),
to be lazy*. 11. homme de m., hired
killer. *See also* sac.

maintenir, se: ça va?—ça se maintient, how goes it?—so-so (or I'm holding my own).

mairie, f. se marier à la m. du 21e (arrondissement) or se marier derrière la m. = se marier de la main gauche.

mais, adv. non, m.! no, really though! I ask you! I say! See also chez and fois.

maison, f. 1. m. close, m. à gros numéro, m. de tolérance, m. publique, brothel*; être en m., (of prostitute) to be in a licensed brothel; m. de passe, (prostitutes') house of call; m. d'abattage, cheap brothel*, cat-house. 2. m. tire-bouchon (or tire-bouton), liaison between two lesbians. 3. un(e) ...m.: originally applied to items on a menu (e.g. pâté, tarte, etc. maison, i.e. special, home-made), this use of maison in the sense of huge, first-rate of its kind, etc., has been extended—e.g. une châtaigne m., a hell of a clout, a fourpenny one; une engueulade m., a first-class ticking-off, etc. 4. la (Grande) M., the Police.

mal, adv. 1. pas m., not at all bad, not half bad, quite tolerable, not so dusty, quite good-looking; je m'en fiche pas m.! a fat lot I care! I couldn't care less! 2. pas m. de ..., quite a lot (or quite a bit) of ..., a good (or a great) deal of ..., a good many (or a good few) of ..., quite a few ... 3. tu vas m., toi! you're exaggerating*, that's a bit stiff! 4. se trouver m. dessus, to appropriate sth. 5. tu me fais m.! you give me the pip!

mal, m. 1. il n'y a pas de m. (or y a pas d'mal)! don't mention it! 2. il n'y a que demi-m.! it's not half so bad as it might have been! 3. se donner un m. de chien, to go to endless trouble 4. m. caduc, epilepsy.

malabar, adj. 1. first-rate*. 2. hefty*. 3. m. hefty* fellow.

malade, adj. 1. (of thing) in a very bad condition, in a wretched state, very shaky. 2. tu es m.! or non, mais tu n'es (or t'es) pas m.? you must be crazy! you must be out of your mind! are you off your rocker? 3. (mil.) se faire porter m., to report sick. See also envie 1.

maladie, f. 1. il en fera une m., he'll be frightfully upset, he'll have a fit. 2. m. de neuf mois, pregnancy.

malaga, m. un m. de boueux, a glass of red wine.

malagauche, malapatte, adj. clumsy, awkward, butterfingers, all thumbs, ham-fisted (or ham-handed); m. clumsy oaf.

malchançard, m. unlucky person.

maldonne, f. il y a m., there's been a mistake.

mâle, m. 1. un beau m., a real he-man, a glamour boy. 2. aller au m., prendre (or se farcir) du m., (of woman) to have coition*.

malfrappe, malfrat, malfrin, m. = frappe.

malheur, m. 1. faire un m., to do sth. desperate; to commit murder (or suicide). 2. jouer de m., to be out of luck. 3. le beau (or le grand) m.! there's no harm in that! what are you complaining about? what of it? 4. (ne) parle pas de m.! God forbid! have a heart!

malheureux, adj. 1. beggarly, paltry, wretched, trivial, pitiful. 2. te voilà, ce n'est pas m.! here you are at last, and about time too! (or and a good job too)! 3. si c'est pas m.! c'est-y pas m.! isn't it a shame? it's a wicked shame! isn't it too bad! See also pierre.

malice, f. se faire m. tout seul, to masturbate*.

malin, adj., m. 1. faire le (or son) m., to try to be clever (or smart or funny), to show off. 2. ce n'était pas très m.! (iron.) c'était m.! that was clever (of you)! 3. ce n'est (or c'est) pas m.! that's easy enough! that's not very difficult! there's nothing clever in that! 4. un (gros) m., a smart guy, a smart Alec(k).

malle, f. 1. mouth*; ferme ta m.! shut* up! 2. (mil.) prison*. 3. boucler sa m., to die*. **4.** (se) **faire la m.**, to de-camp*. **5. faire la malle à qn**=**lâcher qn. 6. m. à quatre nœuds**, handker-chief (containing one's savings, etc.).

maller, mallouser, mallouzer= faire la malle.

mallette, *f.* **1. m. et paquette**, walking-out on, jilting, breaking-off, bust-up. **2. m. à quatre nœuds**=**malle à quatre nœuds.**

maltouze, *f.* **pastiquer la m.**. to smuggle.

malva, *(back slang* ('code verlen') *for* '*va mal*') it's going badly.

mamelu, *adj.* full-breasted.

mamie, *f.* =mémé **1.**

manchard, *m.* beggar.

manche, *m.* **1.** fool*; ... **comme un m.,** ... like a perfect fool, ... in a cock-eyed fashion (*e.g.* **il conduit comme un m.**, he's a hopeless driver, he can't drive for nuts (*or* for toffee). **2. m. à balai,** (*a*) tall*, thin person; (*b*) (*of* '*plane*) joy-stick. **3. avoir le m.** =**bander. 4. branler dans le m.**, to be in a parlous state, to be in jeopardy. **5. tomber sur le** (*or* **un**) **m.**=**tomber sur un bec (de gaz). s'astiquer le m.**, to masturbate.

manche, *f.* **1. faire la m.**, to beg (for alms). **2. faire la** (*or* **une**) **m. à qn**, to open a subscription for s.o., to go round with the hat for s.o., to make a whip-round for s.o. *See also* **jambe 2** *and* **paire.**

manchettes, *f.pl.* handcuffs*.

manchot, *adj.* **il n'est pas m.,** (*a*) he's clever with his hands; (*b*) he's no fool, he's all there, there are no flies on him.

manchouillard, *adj.* one-armed.

mandal(l)e, *f.* slap in the face, clout.

mandarin, *m.* intellectual, egghead.

mandarines, *f.* tiny breasts* (of woman).

mandibules, *f.pl.* jaws; **claquer des m.,** (*a*) to chatter (*teeth*); (*b*) =**la crever.**

mandoline, *f.* **1.** machine-gun. **2.** round bed-pan; bidet.

mandrin, *m.* penis*; **avoir le m.**= **bander.**

manettes, *f.pl.* **1.** perdre (*or* **lâcher) les m.**=perdre (*or* lâcher) les pédales. **2.** appuyer (*or* pousser) **sur les m.,** to pedal away.

mangav, *m.* =manchard.

mangeaille, *f.* food*.

mange-merde, *m.* miser, muck-worm.

manger. 1. on en mangerait, it looks appetizing. **2.** on mangerait par terre, (*of clean, well-kept room*) you could eat off the floor. **3.** en m. = en croquer (croquer 4 (*a*)).

mange-tout, *m.pl.* Germans (*during occupation of France (W.W.II)*).

mangeur, *m.* **m. de blanc,** pimp, ponce, white-slaver.

manier, se =se magner.

manière, *f.* **1. faire des manières**= faire des chichis; pas tant de manières! don't make such a fuss! none of your airs! come off it! **2. en voilà des manières!** *or* **voyez manières!** fine manners you have, I must say! that's a nice way to behave!

manieur, *m.* **m. de fonte,** dumb-bell wielder.

manigance, *f.* underhand trick (*or* dealing *or* work), hanky-panky, jiggery-pokery, fiddle, fiddling, dodge, goings-on; *pl.* underhand practices, wire-pulling, fishy business, hole-and-corner work.

manigancer, to plot, to scheme, to wangle; **qu'est-ce qu'il manigance?** what's he up to? what little game is he up to?

manigancer, se : comment est-ce que ça se manigance? how does that work? **je me demande ce qui se manigance,** I wonder what's going on, I wonder what's in the wind, I wonder what's cooking.

manitou, *m.* important* person; **être le grand m.,** to be the boss (of the show), to boss the show, to be the head cook and bottle-washer.

mannezingue, *m.* bar-keeper, publi-can.

manoche, *f.* manille (*card game*); se

tailler la (*or* **une**) **m.**, to have a game of manille.

manouche, *m.f.* gipsy, Romany; *m.* gipsy lingo.

manque, *m.* **1.** (*of drug addict*) être dans le m., souffrir du m., to be depressed (through lack of drug). **2.** m. de pot, no luck.

manque, *f.* **1.** un(e) ... à la m., (*of thing or person*) worthless, dud, sham, useless, twopenny-ha'penny. **2.** avoir une chose à la m., to be without a . thing.

manquer: il ne manquerait plus que ça (*or* cela)! that would be (*or* that is) the limit* (*or* the last straw)! that would be the finishing touch! that beats (*or* caps *or* crowns) all! that would put (*or* puts) the lid on it!

mansarde, *f.* yoyoter de la m. = travailler du chapeau.

maous(s), maousse, *adj.* (*of sth. very large, fine, good*) whacking, whopping, corking, slap-up, tip-top, pukka. (*To intensify* pépère *or* poil-poil *or* soua-soua *is sometimes added*).

mappemondes, *f.pl.* breasts* (of woman).

maq(ue), *m.* = mac.

maqué, *adj.* être m. avec = être collé avec.

maquer, se = se coller **1.**

maquereau, *m.* pimp, procurer, ponce, bully.

maquereautage, *m.* pimping.

maquerelle, maquesée, *f.* procuress, bawd, 'madam' (of brothel).

maquillage, *m.* faking.

maquille, *f.* **1.** marking (of playing-cards). **2.** car-faking; faire de la m., to hustle 'hot' cars.

maquiller, to fake (up); to fiddle (accounts). *See also* brème. **1.**

maquiller, se. 1. to malinger, to fake an illness, to inflict a wound on oneself. **2.** = se manigancer.

maquilleur, *m.* cheat, swindler*.

marant, *adj.* = marrant.

maravédis, *m.* sans un m., penniless*.

marca(t), *m.* market.

marchand, *m.* **1.** m. de barbaque (*or* de bidoche *or* de viande), white-slaver. **2.** m. de lacets, gendarme. **3.** m. de participes, teacher, schoolmaster, pedant. **4.** m. de puces, old-clothes man. **5.** m. de quat', costermonger, barrow-boy. **6.** m. de sommeil, hotel-keeper. **7.** m. de soupe, headmaster of a boarding-school, a regular Squeers.

marchandise, *f.* = merde **1.**

marché, *m.* m. aux puces, rag-fair, flea-market.

marcher, to be fooled, to be taken in, to fall for it, (*of female*) to take it (*i.e. to be willing to bestow her favours*); je marche (avec vous)! I'm on! agreed! count me in! je ne marche pas! nothing doing! don't count me in! count me out! I'm not having (*or* taking) any! not for me! not for Joe! I'm not playing! ça ne marche pas pour moi! that doesn't suit my book! ça n'a pas marché! it didn't work! il marchera! he'll do as he's told! il a marché! he fell for it! faire m. qn, (*a*) to fool* s.o., to order s.o. about, to be bossy with s.o.; (*b*) on vous a fait m.! you've been 'had'! on ne me fait pas m.! I'm not a starter!

marcheur, *m.* **1.** housebreaker, burglar, cracksman. **2.** vieux m., old rake, old rip, dirty old man.

marchis, *m.* = margis.

marcot(t)in, *m.* month.

marder, to look at, to stare at.

mardoche, *m.* Tuesday.

mare, *f.* (i) *See* hareng.

mare, *f.* (ii) en avoir m. = en avoir marre.

marer, se = se marrer.

margis, *m.* (*mil.*) sergeant (in cavalry *or* artillery).

margotin, *f.* trollop.

margoulette, *f.* **1.** face*; casser la m. à qn, to break s.o.'s jaw, to spoil s.o.'s beauty for him. **2.** mouth*; emporter la m. à qn, (*of highly-spiced food or drink*) to burn one's mouth out.

margoulin, *m.* black marketeer, crook, spiv.

marguerite, *f.* 1. effeuiller la m., (*a*) to play 'she loves me, she loves me not'; (*b*) to have coition*. 2. French letter.

Marianne, *pr.n.* (nickname for) the French Republic.

marida(t), *m.* marriage, holy wedlock, marriage bells; **aller au m.**, to get married*; *adj.* married, churched.

Marie-Chantal, *pr.n.* affected young lady, 'Miss de Vere'.

Marie-couche-toi-là, *f.* = **Marie-salope.**

mariée, *f.* 1. se plaindre que la m. est trop belle, trouver la m. trop belle, to complain about a good bargain, not to know how lucky one is. 2. pint of beer.

Marie-graillon, Marie-salope, *f.* slut, trollop, slattern.

marie-jeanne, *f.* marihuana cigarette (*drugs**).

mariner, to wait.

marinette, *f.* W.R.E.N.

mariol(e), *adj.* clever, knowing, shrewd, cute; **faire** (*or* **jouer**) **le m.** = faire le malin.

marle, *adj.* = **mariole.**

marle, marlou, marloupatte, marloupin, *m.* 1. procurer, pimp, ponce, bully. 2. = **mariole.**

marloupinerie, marlouserie, *f.* sly (*or* cunning) trick.

marmaille, *f.* (crowd of) kids, brats.

marmelade, *f.* 1. en m., in a frightful mess; **mettre en m.**, to smash up, to make mincemeat of, to beat to a jelly. 2. être dans la m., to be in a fix*.

marmitage, *m.* bombardment with heavy shells, strafe, strafing.

marmite, *f.* 1. (*mil.*) heavy shell, 'coalbox'. 2. (*mil.*) dixie. 3. = **boulangère.** 4. faire bouillir (*or* faire aller) la m., (*fig.*) to keep the pot boiling. 5. la grande m. = **centrouse.**

marmiter. 1. (*mil.*) to strafe. 2. se faire m., (*in prison*) to get caught infringing regulations.

marmot, *m.* 1. brat, nipper. 2. croquer le m., to be kept cooling one's heels, to kick (*or* to cool) one's heels.

marmouset, *m.* urchin, kid, nipper.

marner, to work* hard.

marneur, *m.* hard worker, grafter (*Australian sl.*).

maronner = **marronner.**

maroquin, *m.* minister's portfolio.

marotte, *f.* fad, hobby; **avoir une m. pour qn.**, to be infatuated* with s.o.

marqua(s), *m.* = **marca(t).**

marqué, *m.* one month's imprisonment, 'moon'; **tirer six marqués de ballon**, to do a six-month stretch.

marqué, *adj.* 1. être m., to be well-known to the police, to be a marked man. 2. elle est un peu marquée, she looks the worse for wear.

marque-mal, *m.* shady customer.

marquer: m. mal (*or* **bien**), to make a bad (*or* a good) impression, to have a bad (*or* good) appearance.

marquet, *m.* = **marqué**, *m.*

marquise, *f.* la m. = **madame.**

marquotin, *m.* = **marcottin.**

marquouser. 1. to mark (playing-cards). 2. to tattoo.

marquouses, *f.pl.* 1. marks (*on playing cards*). 2. scars, tattoo marks.

marrant, *adj.*, *m.* very funny*; **il est m.!** *or* **quel m.!** he's a perfect scream! what a card!

marre, *f.* 1. en avoir m., to be fed up (with it); **il y en a m.** *or* **y en a m.**, I've had a bellyful (*or* basinful) of it. 2. (et puis) c'est m.! *or* un point, c'est m.! *or* en v'là m.! and that's all there is to it! nuff said! and that's that!

marrer, se: se m. (**un bon coup**), to have a good time, to laugh* uproariously; **tu me fais m.** = tu me fais rire.

marron, *m.* 1. blow*; **coller** (**flanquer, foutre**) **un m. à qn**, to fetch (*or* to land) s.o. a clout; **fous-lui un m.!** fetch him one! 2. secouer la poêle à marrons, to thrash*.

marron, *adj.* 1. unlicensed, clandestine; sham, shady. 2. être (fait) m., (*a*) to be arrested*; (*b*) to be duped, to be taken in, to be 'had', to be done brown; être m. de qch., to be done out of sth. 3. faire m., to arrest*; se faire

faire m., to get nabbed. *See also* paumer 2, tas.

marronnant, *adj.* =embêtant.

marronner, to grumble*.

marsiale, *f.* un de la m., a native of Marseilles.

marsouin, *m.* 1. marine, sailor*. 2. penis*.

marteau, *m.* 1. avoir un coup de m., to be mad*. 2. l'homme au coup de m., mythical figure who knocks out the géants de la route. 3. m. à boules, penis*.

marteau, *adj.* mad*.

Martigue, *m.* native of Marseilles.

masquard, *adj.* unlucky.

masque, *f.* 1. petite m., little minx. 2. bad luck.

massacrant, *adj. See* humeur.

massacre, *m.* une tête à m.=une tête à claques.

masse, *f.* 1. (*artist's slang*) money*. 2. coup de m.=coup de massue. 3. des masses de, heaps of, lots of, a great quantity* of.

masser. 1. =marner. 2. to exaggerate*.

massue, *f.* coup de m., (*a*) staggering blow, knock-out blow, floorer, crusher; (*b*) heavy bill, overcharging, fleecing (at hotel, restaurant, etc.).

mastard, *adj.* =maous(se).

mastègue, *f.* food*.

mastéguer, to eat*.

mastic, *m.* 1. mess, muddle, mix-up. 2. cherrer dans le m.=cherrer dans les bégonias. 3. s'endormir sur le m.= s'endormir sur le rôti. 4. péter dans le m., to drop one's work. 5. bouder le m., to pick at one's food.

masticotte, *f.* avoir une bonne m., to have the gift of the gab.

mastiquer, to eat*.

mastoc, *adj.* heavy, loutish, lumpish.

mastodonte, *m.* (*of big vehicle*) (road-) monster; (*of person*) hulk, whacker; (*of object*) whopper.

mastroquet, *m.* bar-keeper, publican.

m'as-tu-vu, *m.* (*pej.*) conceited actor, ham-actor; show-off, smart Alec(k).

mat', **mate**, *m.* morning; à quatre plombes du m., at four a.m.

matador, *m.* =caïd.

mataf, **matave**, *m.* sailor*.

mate, *f.* door.

matelas, *m.* 1. well-filled wallet, wad (of banknotes), roll; avoir le m., to be rich*. 2. =magot.

mater, to watch closely, to observe.

matère, *f.* =maternelle.

matérielle, *f.* necessities of life; gagner (assurer, faire) sa m., to make a living, to earn a livelihood.

maternelle, *f.* mother, mater.

mateur, *m.* =voyeur.

matheux, *m.* (*sch.*) clever mathematician.

maths, *m.pl.* mathematics, maths.

mathurin, *m.* sailor*.

matière, *f.* avoir de la m. grise, to be intelligent, to be brainy.

matin, *m.* un de ces quatre matins, one of these fine days.

mâtin! *int.* my word! by Jove! crikey! (*expletives*).

maton, *m.* 1. policeman*. 2. prison warder, 'screw'.

matou, *m.* 1. tom-cat, tom. 2. lover.

matouser, matouzer =mater.

matraque, *f.* 1. coup de m.=coup de massue; pratiquer la m., to overcharge, to sting. 2. mettre la m., to take drastic measures. 3. avoir la m., (*at poker*) to have a strong hand.

matraquer, to cosh.

matricule, *m.* ça va barder (*or* ça va chier) pour ton m.! you're (in) for it! you're going to cop it!

matuche, *m.* 1. policeman*. 2. *pl.* loaded dice.

matz, *m.* fellow*.

Maub', Maub(e), la, *pr.n.*, la Place Maubert (*on left bank of the Seine in Paris*).

mauresque, *m.* pastis drink with orgeat.

mauvais, *adj.* l'avoir (*or* la trouver) mauvaise, not to find it at all funny, to find it no joke, to take it amiss, to be

pretty wild about it, to take a poor (or dim) view of it.
mauviette, f. 1. milksop*. 2. **manger comme une m.,** to eat like a sparrow.
maxée, f. =macquesée.
maxi, m. 1. maximum. 2. **donner** (or **taper**) **le m.,** (motor.) to go all out, to step on it. 3. **je suis bon pour le m.,** I'm sure to get the maximum sentence; **récolter le m.,** to get the maximum sentence, to get the book thrown at one. 4. long skirt.
mazagran, m. 1. coffee served (cold) in a glass. 2. coffee mug.
mazette, f. (sport) duffer, (perfect) rabbit.
mazette, int. good heavens! my word! my! crikey! (expletives*).
mec, m. 1. fellow*; **un drôle de m.,** (a) a queer cuss; (b) a brick; **le pauvre** (or **pauv'**) **m.!** poor sod! **le m. des mecs, le grand M.,** God. 2. =maquereau.
mécanique, f. 1. gadget*. 2. **rouler les mécaniques**=rouler les biscotteaux.
mécano, m. mechanic, grease-monkey.
méchamment, adv. =vachement 1.
mèche, f. 1. **être de m.** (avec), to be in league (with), to be hand in glove (with), to be in cahoots (with). 2. **et m.!**=et le pouce! 3. (il n'y a) **pas m.!** it's quite impossible! it's no go! (there's) nothing doing! there's not the ghost of a chance! no soap! no sale! 4. **vendre la m.,** to divulge* a secret. 5. **éventer la mèche,** (a) to get wind of a secret; (b) (from confusion with 4) to divulge a secret.
méchoui, m. lambkin.
mécol(le), pron. =mézigue.
mecqueton, mecton, m. =mec.
médaille, f. **porter la m.,** to be framed.
médicale, f. **sortir en m.,** to be released (from prison) on medical grounds.
médoche, méduche, f. medal.
méduser, to petrify, to dumbfound*.
mégot, m. cigarette-end*, dimp; cigar-stump.
mégotage, m. small-time activities; chicken-feed.

mégot(t)er. 1. to collect cigarette-ends. 2. to live meanly. 3. to be a small-time operator. 4. **ne pas m. sur,** not to be stingy with.
mégot(t)ier, mégot(t)eur, mégot(t)eux, m. 1. picker-up of cigarette-ends, sniper. 2. small-time operator; poor fish.
mélasse, f. **être dans la m.,** to be in a fix*.
mêlécasse, mêlé-cass(e), m. mixture of vermouth and cassis (black-currant liqueur); **voix de m.,** raucous voice.
mêler, se: **de quoi je me mêle** (or **tu te mêles**)? what's it got to do with you? what business is it of yours? what do you know about it? who asked you to interfere?
méli-mélo, m. jumble, hotch-potch, mishmash, mess(-up).
mélo, m. melodrama, blood-and-thunder drama.
melon, m. 1. (chapeau) m., bowler (hat), billycock. 2. simpleton*. 3. head*; **avoir le m. déplumé,** to be bald*. 4. Arab.
membre, m. **se saigner aux quatre membres,** to work oneself to the bone.
membrer =marner.
membrineuse, f. tongue, clapper.
même, adv. 1. **mais tout de m.!** but dash it all! 2. **ah! tout de m., vous voilà!** so you've turned up at last!
mémé(e), f. 1. granny. 2. old woman*.
mémère, f. 1. =mémé(e). 2. mother, mammy. 3. **une grosse m.,** a fat, elderly woman.
mémoire, f. **il a une m. de lièvre,** he's got a memory (or a head) like a sieve, he'd forget his head if it wasn't screwed on (properly).
ménage, m. 1. **m. à trois,** matrimonial triangle. 2. **se mettre en m.,** (of unmarried couple) to cohabit, to live together, to shack up. 3. homosexual liaison (between two males or two females).
mendigo(t), m. beggar, bum.
mendigoter, to beg, to bum.
mener: ne pas en m. large, to be in a

tight spot, to feel (very) small, to feel pretty cheap, to cut a sorry figure, to have one's heart in one's boots.

ménesse, *f.* =gonzesse.

mengave, *f.* begging.

Ménilmuche, *pr.n.* Ménilmontant (*district of Paris*).

méninges, *f.pl.* se casser (*or* se creuser *or* se fatiguer *or* se retourner *or* se torturer) les m., to rack one's brains; il ne s'abîme (*or* il ne se fatigue *or* il ne se foule) pas les m., he doesn't overtax his brain; cela lui a tourneboulé les m., that unhinged his mind; casse-toi les m.! *or* fais (un peu) travailler tes m.! use your loaf! it's up there you want it! that's where you want it!

méningite, *f.* il ne s'est pas donné une m., he didn't overtax his brain.

menotte, *f.* tiny hand; *pl.* handcuffs*.

menouille, *f.* money*.

mental(e), *f.* avoir une bonne (*or* mauvaise) m., to be reliable (*or* unreliable).

menteuse, *f.* 1. tongue. 2. la Grande M., the Press.

méquer, to order s.o. about.

mequeton, *m.* =mecton.

mer, *f.* 1. ce n'est pas la m. à boire, that's easy enough, that's no great matter, there's nothing much to that. 2. j'avalerais la m. et les poissons, I could drink the sea dry.

mer, *adj.* marvellous, super, 'boss'.

mercanti, *m.* profiteer, shark.

mercenaire, *m.* travailler comme un m., to work like a horse.

merdailleux, merdaillon, *m.* dirty dog, dirty skunk, dirty beast.

merde, *f.* 1. excrement, shit. 2. (*of thing*) crap. 3. (*of person*) une (grosse) m., une grossière m., a turd. 4. faire sa m., ne pas se croire (*or* se prendre pour) une m., to think no end of oneself. 5. l'avoir à la m., to be in a foul humour. 6. c'est-il oui ou m.? is it yes or no? 7. être dans la m., to be in a hell of a fix*. 8. m. pour . . ., to hell with . . . 9. *int.* m. (alors)! *or* m. et contre-m.! *or* et puis m.! *or* m. de m.!

damn and blast it! bloody hell! bugger it! (*expletives**) ah! m., ce qu'elle est bath! Christ! but she's a corker!

merdeux, *adj.* filthy, nasty, shitty; *m.* 1. (*of person*) =merde 3. 2. un petit (*or* p'tit) m., a little squirt, a little stinker, a dirty little bugger. 3. faire le m. =faire sa merde.

merdouille, *f.* =merde, 1.

merdouiller, merdoyer, to flounder, to be all at sea (*in answer, in speech*).

mère-maca, *f.* madam of a brothel.

mère-pipi, *f.* =dame-pipi.

mère-poule, *f.* over-indulgent mother.

mérinos, *m.* laisser pisser le m., to bide one's time, to wait till the moment is ripe.

merlan, *m.* 1. hairdresser, barber. 2. pimp.

merle, *m.* un vilain m., a nasty fellow, a nasty piece of work.

merlifiche, *m.* showman, mountebank.

mérovingien, *adj.* =mer, *adj.*

mésigue, *pron.* =mézigue.

messe, *f.* 1. dire (*or* tenir *or* faire) des messes basses, to carry on a conversation in an undertone; je n'aime pas les messes basses, (*c.p.*) I don't like people whispering to each other. 2. je ne répète pas la m. pour les sourds, *or* je n'aime pas chanter la m. pour les sourds, (*c.p.*) I don't boil my cabbage twice.

m(es)sieurs-dames, stock popular greeting (to one or more persons) when coming or going.

métallo, *m.* metal-worker, steel-worker.

météo, *m.* meteorologist; *f.* weather report.

métèque, *m.* (*pej.*) dago, wop, wog.

métier, *m.* être du m. = être du bâtiment.

mètre, *m.* 1. piquer un cent mètres, to take to one's heels, to decamp*. 2. one franc.

métro, *m.* one gram of cocaine (*drugs**).

metteur en l'air, *m.* killer, murderer.

mettre. 1. les m. (en vitesse *or* en cinq

secs), to decamp*. **2. m. qn dedans,** (*a*) to fool* s.o.; **être mis dedans,** to be taken in; (*b*) to imprison* s.o. **3. en m.** (**un coup**): *see* **coup 16. 4. le m. à qn,** (*a*) to fool* s.o.; **se le faire m.,** to be taken in; **il vous l'a bien mis!** he made a right sucker out of you! (*b*) to have coition* with s.o. **5. qu'est-ce qu'elle lui met!** she isn't half giving it him hot! **qu'est-ce qu'on se ferait m.!** we wouldn't half cop it! **6. se m. avec qn = se m. en ménage avec qn. 7. s'en m. jusque-là, s'en m. plein la lampe,** to guzzle, to tuck in. **8. il se met bien,** he does himself proud.

meubles, *m.pl.* **1. être dans ses m.,** to have one's own furniture (*or* home), not to be in lodgings. **2. faire partie des m.,** (*of person*) to be a fixture. **3. sauver les m.,** to save sth. out of the wreckage.

meules, *f.pl.* buttocks*.

meumeu, *adj.* first-rate*.

meurtre, *m.* crime, crying shame, sheer vandalism.

mézigo, mézig(ue), *pron.* I, me, myself, this child, my nibs, yours truly. (*Similarly:* **tézig(ue) cézig(ue)** *or* **sézig(ue)** (= *celui-là*), **no(s)zig(ue)(s), vo(s)zig(ue)(s), euzig(ue)s** *or* **leur(s)-zig(ue)s.** (= '*toi*', '*soi*' *or* '*lui*', '*nous*', '*vous*', '*eux*'.).

miam! miam! *int.* yum-yum!

miauler, to weep*, to grouse.

miché, michet, micheton, *m.* **1.** man who pays a prostitute. **2.** mug, flat.

micher, se, to disguise oneself.

miches, *f.pl.* **1.** buttocks*; **avoir les m. à zéro, avoir les m. qui font bravo,** to be in a blue funk; **serrer les m. = serrer les fesses; occupe-toi de tes m.!** mind your own business! **2.** breasts*.

michetonner, (*of prostitute*) to solicit.

mich(e)tonneuse, *f.* female of easy virtue, dolly-girl.

michto, *adj.* **c'est m.,** it's fine.

mickey, *m.* adulterated drink.

micmac, *m.* **1.** = **manigance. 2.** jumble, mess, complication.

micro, *m.* **1.** mike. **2.** = **gueule (A).**

midi, *m.* **1. chacun voit m. à sa porte,** there's no accounting for tastes. **2. ne pas voir clair en plein m.,** to be blind to the obvious. **3. c'est m.** (**sonné**)! = **macache! 4. marquer m. = bander.**

midinette, *f.* milliner's (*or* dressmaker's) apprentice (*or* work-girl).

mie, *f.* **1. . . . à la m.** de pain, worthless, flashy, dud, small-time. **2. m. de pain mécanique, m. de pain à ressorts,** louse, flea.

miel, *m.* **du (pur) m.,** easy* job.

miette, *f.* **ne pas s'en faire une m.,** not to worry in the slightest, not to care a rap*.

mieux, *adv.* **qui dit m.?** (*said by auctioneer*) any advance?

mignard, *m.* little child, nipper, kid.

mignon, -ne, *m.f.* = **giton.**

mignoter, se, to coddle oneself, to have a cushy time.

mijaurée, *f.* **faire la m.,** (*of woman*) to be a stuck-up thing, to be toffee-nosed.

mijoter, se: qu'est-ce qui se mijote? what's brewing? what's cooking? what's buzzing? what's in the wind?

milieu, *m.* **le m.,** the underworld.

militaire, *adj.* **à deux heures, heure m.,** at two o'clock sharp.

mille, *num. adj.* **1. des m. et des cents,** tons (*or* pots) of money. **2. je vous le donne en m. = je vous le donne en cent. 3. m. mettre** (*or* **taper**) **dans le m.,** to hit the mark (*or* the target *or* the jackpot), to hit the nail on the head.

mille-feuille(s), *m.* **1. c'est du m.-f.,** it's an easy* job. **2.** vagina*.

millimètre, *m.* **faire du m.,** to economize, to skimp.

milord, *m.* very rich man.

mimi, *m.* **1.** pussy cat. **2.** darling* (*fem.* **mimine**). **3.** vagina*. **4.** *adj.* sweet, a darling*, a real pet.

mimines, *f.pl.* hands*.

mince! *int.* (*mild form of* **merde!**—*expresses surprise, admiration, incredulity*). (**ah!** *or* **oh!**) **m. alors!** gosh! my hat! my (giddy) aunt! Lord love a duck! lorlumme! well, I'll be blowed!

golly! my eye! my word! by Jove!
you don't say (so)! **m. de . . .!** what
a . . .! some . . .!—*e.g.* **m. de rigolade!**
what a lark! what a giggle! **m. de
souris!** some girl! what a dish!
mine, *f.* **faire m. de rien, avec des
mines de rien, faire m.** de peler des
œufs, to look (*or* looking) as if nothing
had happened, to look (*or* looking)
like the cat that has just eaten the
canary; **m. de rien et bouche cousue!**
mum's the word!

miner =marner.

minet, *m.* **1.** =mimi **1, 2** (*fem.*
minette), *and* **3. 2.** natty individual.

minot, *m.* youngster, child*.

minou, *m.* pussy cat.

minouche, *f.* darling*.

minoye, *f.* midnight.

minus (habens), *m.* mental defective,
nitwit, one who is not quite all there.

minute, *f.* **1. se poser là cinq minutes,**
to be hefty, to be beefy. **2.** *int.* **m.
(, papillon)!** half-a-mo'! not so fast!
hold on! hold hard! hold your horses!
half a tick!

mioche, *m.* **1.** child*, baby. **2. faire
descendre le m.,** to bring about an
abortion.

mirand, *adj.* short-sighted, half-blind.

mirante, *f.* mirror.

mirer, to look at.

mirettes, *f.pl.* eyes*; **gicler des m.,** to
weep*.

mirifique, *adj.* =mirobolant.

miro, *adj.* =mirand.

mirobolant, *adj.* stupendous, astound-
ing, staggering.

mironton, *m.* **1.** fellow*; **un drôle de
m.,** a queer* cuss. **2.** eye*.

mise, *f.* **1. faire une m. en scène à qn,**
to hoax* s.o. **2. m. à pied,** dismissing,
sacking, firing. **3. m. en l'air,** house-
breaking, burglary; hold-up; taking
(s.o.) for a ride. **4. m. en boîte** (*or* **en
caisse**), spoofing, hooting, razzing.

miser. 1. m. (sur), to count (on), to
bank (on). *See also* **tableau 2.** to have
coition*.

misérables, *m.pl.* **1. jouer les m.,** to

have a run of bad luck. **2.** five franc
notes.

misère, *f.* **1. une m.!** a mere trifle! a
mere nothing! **2. quelle m.!** what a
life! **3.** ça vous tombe dessus comme
la m. sur le pauvre monde!** (*c.p.*) it
happens to you before you can say
Jack Robinson! it's like a bolt from
the blue! **4. faire des misères à qn,** to
torment s.o., to give s.o. a bad time,
to put s.o. through it, to be a dreadful
worry to s.o. **5.** pleurer (*or* crier) m.,**
to whine about one's poverty.

mistenflûte, *m.* (*of person*) =machin.

mistigri(s), *m.* cat, kitty cat, puss(y),
mog(gy).

miston, *m.* **1.** child*. **2.** =miché,
michet, micheton.

mistonne, *f.* (*pej.*) woman*, girl*.

mistouflard, *m.* down-and-out(er).

mistoufle, *f.* **1. être dans la m.,** to be
down-and-out. **2. faire des mistoufles
à qn,** to play dirty tricks on s.o.

mitaines, *f.pl.* **1.** boxing-gloves,
mittens; **mettre les m.,** to box, to put
the gloves on; **croiser les m.,** to box,
to have a punch-up. **2. enlève tes m.!**
(*c.p. to clumsy dealer at cards*) take
your gloves off!

mitan, *m.* **1.** middle; **en plein m.,** right
in the middle, a bull's eye. **2.** =le
milieu.

mitard, *m.* **1.** disciplinary cell (in
prison), cooler. **2. faire du m.,** to lie
low.

mitarder: se faire m., to be put in a
mitard 1.

mite, *f.* **bouffé aux mites,** mad*.

mite, *m.* =mitard **1.**

miter, to weep*.

miteux, *adj.* **1.** shabby*, seedy-looking,
out at the elbows, lousy. **2.** *m.* child*.

mitonnard, *m.* =mitan.

mitraille, *f.* =ferraille.

mitrailleuse, *f.* **1.** chatterbox*. **2.**
stamping machine.

mobilard, *m.* policeman (of special
mobile squad).

mobylette, *f.* *r.t.m.* moped, pop-
bottle.

moche, *adj.* ugly, rotten*; **pas si m.**, not so dusty; **ce qu'il est m.!** what a mess he is! **un article m.**, a dud; **elle est m. à pleurer**, she's as ugly as sin.

mocheté, *f.* ugly woman, a mess.

Moco, **Moko**, *m.* native of Marseilles or Provence.

Mocobo, la, =**la Maub.**

mœurs, *f.pl.* **les m.**, **la brigade (de la police) des m.**, *(in Paris)* the vice-squad.

moineau, *m.* **1.** *(pej.)* fellow*; **un drôle de m.**, a queer* bird *(or* customer); **un sale** *(or* **vilain) m.**, a bad egg, a heel. **2. avoir une cervelle de m.**, to be feather-brained, to be empty-headed.

moins, *adv.* **1. au m.**, I hope *(e.g.* **tu n'es pas malade, au m.?**). **2. c'est bien le m.!** it's the least he (etc.) can do! *See also* **deux**. **3.** *prep.* **il était m. une** *(or* **m. deux** *or* **m. cinq)**, it was a narrow escape*.

mois, *m.* **1.** *(of person's age)* ... **plus les m. de nourrice** *or* ... **sans compter les m. de nourrice**, ... plus a bit; ... and a little bit more; **oublier les m. de nourrice**, to pretend to be younger than one really is. **2. avoir ses m.**, to have the monthlies. *See also* **trente-six**.

moisi, *adj.* **pas m.**, strong, robust.

moisir, to stay too long, to hang about, to be kept hanging about; **m. en prison**, to rot in prison.

moite, *adj.* **les avoir moites**, to be in a funk.

moitié, *f.* **ma (chère) m.**, my wife*.

mol(l)ard, *m.* expectoration, gob.

mollarder, to expectorate, to spit, to gob.

mollasse, *adj.* flabby, spineless, gutless.

mollasson, *m.* flabby person, milksop*.

mollet, *m.* **des mollets de coq**, spindle-shanks.

molletogommes, **molletons**, *m.pl.* calves (of leg).

mollo(-mollo), *adv. and int.* easy (does it)! **vas-y mollo!** easy now! go easy!

mollusque, *m.* **c'est un m.**, he has no go in him, he's got no backbone.

moltegommes, **moltogommes**, *m.pl.* =**molletogommes**.

môme, *m. & f.* **1.** child*. **2.** young boy, young girl*; **un beau m.**, a fine-looking lad; **une belle m.**, a good-looking girl, a good-looker. **3. faire descendre le m.** =**faire descendre le mioche. 4. pisser un m.** =**pisser une côtelette. 5. une m.**, *(of pimp or gangster)* a moll.

mômerie, *f.* **1.** kids, youngsters. **2.** kid stuff.

momichon, *m.* child*.

momie, *f.* **1.** sluggard. **2.** old fog(e)y*.

momignard, *m.* child*.

momi(nette), *f.* small glass of absinthe.

monacos, *m.pl.* money*.

Mondaine, *f.* **la M.**, *(of police)* vice-squad.

monde, *m.* **1. en faire un m.**, to make a lot of fuss, to make a song and dance about it. **2. se faire un m.** *(or* **des mondes) de qch.**, to make a mountain out of a molehill. **3. ça (alors), c'est un m.!** well, that beats everything! well, that beats the band! **4. c'est le m. renversé!** I've never seen the like of it! it's topsy-turvydom! **5. il se moque du m.!** he's got a confounded cheek! **6. il faut de tout pour faire un m.**, it takes all kinds to make a world. *See also* **balcon**.

monnaie, *f.* **1. rendre la m.**, *(of woman)* to be old and ugly. **2. payer qn en m. de singe**, to bilk s.o.

monome, *m.* students' rag (consisting of a march in single file through the streets).

monseigneur, *m.* jemmy.

monsieur, *m.* **1. faire le (gros) m.**, to do the heavy (swell). **2. un joli** *(or* **vilain) m.**, a bad lot, a bad 'un, a bad hat.

monstre, *adj.* huge, enormous, whopping, whacking, no end of a ...; *m.* **se**

faire un m. (*or* **des monstres**) **de tout,** to make mountains out of molehills.
montagne, *f.* **se faire une m. de rien, se faire des montagnes,** to make mountains out of molehills; **se faire une m. de qch., s'en faire une m.,** to make heavy weather of sth.
montant, *m.* ladder.
montants, *m.pl.* trousers*.
monte, *f.* =passe 2.
monté, *adj.* 1. slightly drunk*. 2. **être bien m.,** (*a*) to be well-equipped; (*b*) (*iron. use*) to be in a pretty fix. 3. **être m. contre qn,** to be very angry* with s.o., to have a down on s.o. 4. **un coup m.:** *see* **coup 17.**
monte-en-l'air, *m.* cat-burglar.
monter. 1. **m. qn contre,** to set s.o. (*or* to egg s.o. on) against. 2. **faire m. qn,** (*a*) to take a rise out of s.o.; (*b*) to make s.o.'s blood boil. 3. =**grimper 1.** 4. **m. un client**=**faire une monte.**
monter, se: se m. (**pour un rien** *or* **pour des riens**), to get worked up (*or* to get excited *or* to do one's nut *or* to blow one's top) (over a trifle *or* trifles). *See also* **bateau 1, bourrichon, coup 17, échelle 1, tête 9.**
montgolfières, *f.pl.* 1. testicles*. 2. breasts* (of female).
Montparno, *pr.n.* Montparnasse (*in Paris*).
montrouze, *f.* watch*.
Mont Valo, *pr.n.* Mont Valérien (*near Paris*).
moral, *m.* **avoir le m.,** to be in high spirits, to feel on top of the world.
morbac, morbaque, *m.* 1. crab-louse. 2. (*of person*) little squi(r)t.
morceau, *m.* 1. **ne faire qu'un m. de,** to make one mouthful of, to swallow it all at one gulp. 2. **pour un m. de pain,** (*of purchase or sale*) for a (mere) song, for next to nothing, for an old song. 3. **casser le m.** (*or* **en casser un m.**) **à qn,** to give it s.o. straight, to give s.o. a piece of one's mind, to let s.o. have it. 4. **manger** (**casser, bouffer, lâcher, cracher**) **le m.,** to confess*, to turn informer. 5. **manger un m.** (**sur le**

pouce): *see* **pouce 7. 6. emporter le m.,** to win out. **7. gober le m.,** to swallow the bait, to fall for it. **8. un m. de roi,** a dainty titbit. **9. un beau m.,** (*of girl*) a bit of all right, a nice bit of stuff.
morcif, *m.* =**morceau.**
mordante, *f.* file (*tool*).
mordants, *m.pl.* scissors.
mordicus, *adv.* stubbornly, doggedly, tenaciously.
mordre. 1. (**ne pas**) **m. à.,** (not) to take to (*a subject of study*), (not) to be able to do. 2. **ça ne mord pas!**=**je ne marche pas!** 3. **m. dans le truc,** to fall into the trap, to fall for it. 4. **c'est à se les** (*or* **la**) **m.!** it's very funny*, it's a scream! **5. ... à la mords-moi le doigt,** worthless; tricky, dodgy. **6. mords** (*or* **mordez**) (**-moi ça**)! just have a look (*or* a dekko) at that!
mordu, *adj.* mad (on, about), madly in love (with), infatuated*; **m. un mordu du cinéma,** a film fan.
moré, *m.* brother.
morfaler, morfil(l)er, to eat*, to guzzle.
morfal(ou), *m.* =**morphalou.**
morfic, *m.* =**morpion 1.**
morfler, to get*, to cop (*punishment, a sentence*), to cop it; **m. le maxi,** to get the maximum sentence; **faire m. qn,** to put s.o. through it, to give it s.o. hot and strong.
morganer, to eat*; to bite.
morlingue, *m.* purse, wallet; **être constipé** (*or* **dur**) **du m., avoir un hérisson** (*or* **des oursins** *or* **un piège à loups**) **dans le m.,** to be miserly*.
mornifle, *f.* 1. money*. 2. blow* (in the face), slap; **flanquer** (**refiler**) **une m. à qn,** to give s.o. a warmer, to land s.o. one on the jaw.
mornifleur, *m.* coiner, counterfeiter.
morphaler, to guzzle.
morphalou, *m.* 1. guzzler, glutton*. 2. grasping person, grabber.
morphiller =**morfiler.**
morphino, *m.* junky.
morpion, *m.* 1. crab-louse. 2. brat, child*.

mort, *adj.* **1. c'est m.!** *or* **elle est morte!** it's all over and done with! **2. encore une de morte!** *or* **elle est morte!** that's another day's work done!

mort, *m.* **faire le m.,** to lie low, to keep mum, to play possum; (*at cards*) to play dummy.

morticole, *m.* doctor, medico, sawbones.

morue, *f.* prostitute*.

morveux, *m.* **1. brat. 2. un petit m.,** a snotty-nose, a young puppy, a whipper-snapper.

moscoutaire, *m.* communist, commy (*or* commie), bolshie.

mot, *m.* **pas un m. à la reine mère!** (*c.p.*) mum's the word!

motard, *m.* road cop, speed cop.

motif, *m.* **pour le bon m.,** with a view to matrimony, with honourable intentions.

moto, *f.* mo(tor)-bike.

motobécane, *f.* light motor-cycle.

motocyclard, *m.* =**motard.**

motorisé, *adj.;* être m., to have a car.

motte, *f.* **1. half; faire la m.,** to go halves. **2. anus*. 3. vagina.**

mou, *m.* **1. human flesh, body; rentrer dans le m. à qn,** to attack* s.o. **3. bourrer le m. à qn**=**bourrer le crâne à qn.** *See also* **bourre-mou. 4. c'est du m.!**=**c'est du bourre-mou. 5. gonfler le m.,** to exaggerate*. **6. bout de m.,** penis*. **7. les mous,** the lungs. **8. paper money.**

mou, *adj.* spineless.

mou, *adv.* **vas-y m.!**=**vas-y mollo!**

mouchard, *m.* **1. sneak, tell-tale. 2. police-informer*, police-spy. 3. spy-hole (in prison cell).**

mouche, *f.* **1. =mouchard 1** *and* **2; faire la m.,** to turn informer. **2. quelle m. vous pique?** what's biting you? **3. tuer les mouches à quinze pas,** to have strong halitosis. **4. c'est à cause des mouches!** (*c.p. used to avoid answering a question*) ask me another!

moucher. 1. to snub, to tell (*or* to tick) off; **se faire m.,** to get ticked off, to get sat on. **2.** to thrash* severely; **se**

faire m., to get a licking; to get wounded, to get crocked up.

moucher, se: je m'en mouche!=je m'en fiche! *See also* **coude 5, pied 23.**

moucheron, *m.* child*.

mouchodrome, *m.* **avoir un m.,** to be bald headed*, to have a flies' skating rink.

mouchoir, *m.* (*turf, of a race*) **finir dans un m.,** to make a close finish.

moudre: en m., to be a prostitute*.

Mouffe, la, *pr.n.* rue Mouffetard (*in Paris*).

mouffeter =**mouf(f)ter.**

mouf(f)let, *m.* child*.

mouf(f)lette, *f.* young girl, baby doll, chick.

mouf(f)ter, to blab, to blow the gaff; **ne pas m., ne m. rien,** to keep mum.

mouillé, *adj.* **1. il fait m.,** it's raining, it's wet. **2. être m.,** to be involved, to be implicated.

mouiller. 1. to compromise, to implicate. **2.** to make the pass (at cards). **3. il mouille, ça mouille,** (*of rain*) it's pelting down. **4. m. pour qn,** to have a yen for s.o. **5.** to pay up*.

mouiller, se, 1. to compromise (*or* to implicate) oneself, to run serious risks, **2.** to let oneself in for sth., to commit oneself. **3.** to bet heavily.

mouillette, *f.* **1.** sippet (of bread dunked in soft boiled egg, in milk, etc.). **2.** tongue. **3. aller à la m.**=**se mouiller 1.**

mouisant, *m.* (*sch.*) poverty-stricken student.

mouisard, *m.* poverty-stricken person, down-and-out(er).

mouise, *f.* **être dans la m.,** to be penniless*.

moujingue, *m.* **1. child*. 2. tricoter le m.,** to bring about an abortion.

moukala, *m.* revolver*.

moukère, *f.* **1. (*pej.*) woman. 2. wife. 3. prostitute*.**

moule, *f.* **1. fool*. 2. vagina*; avoir la m. qui bâille,** to be on heat.

moule, *m.* **m. à gaufre,** fool.

mouler: en m.=**en moudre.**

moulin, *m.* 1. engine (of motor-car, 'plane). 2. (*mil.*) m. à café, machine-gun. 3. m. à paroles, chatterbox*. 4. on y entre (*or* on entre ici) comme dans un m., the place is open to anybody (*or* to all comers). 5. pimp's moll. 6. avoir un m. qui tourne (*or* des moulins qui tournent), to have a profitable source of income.

mouliner, (*cyclist's slang*) to pedal along at a steady, easy pace.

moulinette, *f.* tommy-gun, submachine-gun.

moulu, *adj.* exhausted*; aching all over.

moumoute, *f.* 1. darling*; tu es une belle m.! you're a perfect darling! 2. pussy, kitty. 3. false hair.

mouquère, *f.* =moukère.

mourant, *adj.* 1. very funny*. 2. exasperating.

mourir. 1. c'est à m. de rire, it's very funny*, it's absolutely killing. 2. tu t'en ferais m.!=des clous! (clou 7).

mouron, *m.* 1. se faire du m., to worry; te fais pas de m. pour moi! don't worry about me! 2. n'avoir plus de m. sur la cage, to be bald*. 3. hair (on woman's pubis); c'est pas du m. pour ton serin, this chickweed is not for your birdie. 4. =cafard.

mouronner =se faire du mouron.

mouscaille, *f.* 1. mud, dirt, gunge. 2. =merde 1. 3. être dans la m., to be in a mess*. 4. avoir qn à la m., to have it in for s.o.

mousmé(e), *f.* woman*.

moussante, *f.* beer.

mousse, *f.* 1. se faire de la m., to worry, to fret. 2. n'avoir plus de m. sur le caillou, to be bald*.

mousser. 1. to foam with rage, to get angry*; faire m. qn, to rile s.o., to make s.o. fly off the handle. 2. faire m., to praise highly, to crack up, to boost, to puff (up); se faire m., to show off, to blow one's own trumpet.

mousseux, *m.* champagne*.

moussu, *adj.* hairy.

moutard, *m.* child*.

moutarde, *f.* 1. la m. lui monte au nez, he's flaring up, his monkey is up, he's getting riled (*or* huffy). 2. c'est (comme) de la m. après dîner, it comes too late, it comes a day after the fair.

moutardier, *m.* se croire (*or* se prendre pour) le premier m. du pape, to be too big for one's boots, to think oneself a little tin god.

moutatchou, *m.* =moutard.

moute, *f. adj.* (*of female*) nice, sweet.

mouton, *m.* 1. police-informer*, counter-spy. 2. laisser pisser le m.= laisser pisser le mérinos. 3. un m. à cinq pattes, something very rare or impossible. 4. fluff (under bed, furniture).

moutonner. 1. to spy on, to inform against (a prisoner). 2. to pump (s.o.), to sound (s.o.).

mouvement, *m.* 1. être dans le m., to be in the swim, to be up-to-date. 2. un bon m., voyons! come on, be a sport!

moyen, *m.* 1. ôter ses moyens à qn, to cramp s.o.'s style. 2. tâcher m. de, to try to find a way to.

moyenner: il n'y a pas moyen (de m.), it's no good (*or* no use), it can't be done, there's nothing doing.

mucher, to hide.

mud, *m.* opium.

muette, *f.* la Grande M., the Army.

muf(f)e, *m.* =mufle.

muffée, *f.* 1. prendre une m., to get drunk*; avoir la (*or* une) m., to be dead drunk*; to have a skinful. 2. y en a une m., there's tons of it.

mufle, *m.* 1. (*pej.*) face*. 2. rotter*.

muflerie, *f.* caddish (*or* dirty) trick.

mur, *m.* 1. (*mil.*) faire le m., to climb (*or* to jump *or* to hop) over the wall (*of barracks, of camp*). 2. être logé entre quatre murs, to be in prison*. 3. coller qn au m., to stand s.o. up against a wall and shoot him.

mûr, *adj.* drunk*. See also vert, *adj.*

murdinguer, se =se mûrir.

mûre, *f.* blow*.

mûrir, se, to get drunk*.

museau, *m.* 1. face*. 2. mouth*. 3.

nose*. 4. se fricasser le m., to smooch; fricassée de museaux, smooching.

musée, *m*. m. des refroidis, mortuary.

musette, *f*. 1. bal m., popular (*or* low) dance-hall. 2. un(e) ... qui n'est (n'était, ne sera, ne serait) pas dans une m., a rare old ..., a ... that one won't forget for a long time. 3. c'est dans la m. =sac 4.

musicaux, *m.pl.* musicians, orchestra.

musicien, *m*. 1. flatterer*. 2. crook. 3. *pl.* beans; lentils.

musico(t), *m*. musician.

musique, *f*. 1. flattery*. 2. blackmail. 3. cross-examination. 4. connaître (un peu) la m., to be wide-awake*. 5. faire de la m., en faire une m., to kick up a row*. 6. réglé comme du papier à m., as regular as clockwork. 7. baisse un peu ta m.! pipe down, will you!

mystère, *m*. m. et boule de gomme! (*c.p.*) heaven knows what it's all about! search me!

N

na! *int.* (so) there! and that's that! I don't care!

nageoire, *f.* arm (*of person*).

nager. 1. to be quite out of one's depth, to be all at sea, to flounder, not to have a clue. 2. savoir n., to be resourceful, to be wide-awake*. *See also* clef.

nana, *f.* 1. woman*, girl*, 'bird'; moll; la vraie n., the goods. 2. prostitute*.

nanan, *m.* c'est du n.! (*of things nice to eat or things generally*) (*a*) yum-yum! it's yummy!; (*b*) it's a piece of cake! it's money for jam (*or* for old rope)!

nanard, *adj.* silly, foolish, soft; *m.* simpleton*.

Nantoche, *pr.n.* Nanterre (*suburb of Paris*).

nap, *m.* (=*napoléon*) twenty-franc gold coin.

naphtalinard, *m.* re-enlisted retired officer, old dug-out.

naphtaline, naphte, *f.* heroin (*drugs**).

napo, *m.* Neapolitan.

nappe, *f.* 1. mettre la main sur la bonne n., to strike oil (*fig.*). 2. trouver la n. mise, to marry a fortune. 3. être dans la n., to be hazy, to imagine things.

narc, *m.* narcotics.

nardu, *m.* police superintendent.

nase, *m.* nose*, *adj.* broken.

nasi, *adj.*=nazi.

natchaver, (se), to decamp*.

nature, *f.* 1. disparaître (*or* sauter *or* s'évanouir *or* se perdre) dans la n., to vanish, to disappear; être dans la n., to have vanished from sight. 2. une petite n., (*of person*) a weakling, a person without guts, a delicate nature (*iron.*). 3. *adj.* (*of person*) (*a*) unaffected, open, frank; blunt; (*b*) gullible*, simple-minded; (*c*) (*of drink*) neat, 4. *adv.* naturally! of course! natch!

naturellement, *adv.* n. et comme de bien entendu! absoballylutely!

naturlich(e), *adv.* of course.

navaler=cavaler 2 *and* 3 (*largonji de cavaler*).

nave, *m.* 1. =cave 1 *and* 2. 2. fleur de n., essence de n., chump, dumb-bell. 3. (*of film*) =navet 2.

nav(e)du, *m.* =cave 1 *and* 2 (*largonji de cave*).

navet, *m.* 1. =cave 2. 2. (*of book*) dud, (*of picture*) daub, (*of film, etc.*) tripe, (*of play*) pure ham. 3. des navets!= des clous! (clou 7). 4. se creuser le n.=se creuser la tête. 5. le champ de navets, cemetery. *See also* sang 3.

naveton, navetot, *m.* chump, idiot.

navette, *f.* 1. head*. 2. stupid woman.

naze, *m.* 1. syphilis. 2. nose*. 3. *adj.* (*a*) syphilitic; (*b*) worthless, rotten, sham, inferior.

nazebroque, *adj.* =naze, *adj.*

nazi, nazicoté, *adj.* syphilitic.

naziquer =plomber 1.

n. d. D., *abbrev.* =nom de Dieu!

nécro, nécrops, *f.* post-mortem.

nèfles, *f.pl.* 1. des n.!=des clous! (clou 7). 2. avoir qch. pour des n., to get sth. dirt-cheap.

nègre, *m.* 1. hack-writer, ghost(-writer), devil, stooge; faire le n., to stooge. 2. parler petit n., to talk 'pidgin French'. 3. travailler comme un n., to work like a Trojan; fais comme le n; continue! carry on, sailor! 4. first on the list of successful candidates at the military academy of St. Cyr.

négresse, *f.* 1. flea. 2. bottle of red wine; étouffer (*or* éventrer) une n., to down a bottle of red wine.

neige, *f.* cocaine (*drugs**).

nénés, *m.pl.* breasts* (of female).

nénette, *f.* 1. head*; travailler de la n.=travailler du chapeau; se casser la n., (*a*) =se casser la tête; (*b*) =se casser le nez. 2. =nana.

nerf, *m.* 1. avoir les nerfs en pelote, to be

all on edge, to be jumpy (or jittery);
mettre les nerfs en pelote à qn, to set
s.o.'s nerves on edge. 2. porter (or
taper or donner) sur les nerfs à qn, to
get (or to jar) on s.o.'s nerves, to get
in s.o.'s hair, to get on s.o.'s wick, to
get s.o. down, to get s.o.'s goat, to
give s.o. a pain in the neck. 3. mets-y
du n.! put some vim (or some go) into
it! put your back into it! 4. pas un n.,
not a cent.
nervi, m. hooligan, gangster, gunman.
nespa(s)sien, m. (joc.) person who
makes excessive use of n'est-ce pas? in
speaking.
nettoyé, adj. 1. n. (à sec), cleaned out
(financially). 2. dead, wiped out.
nettoyer. 1. (mil.) to mop up. 2. to
clean out (financially), to strip bare.
3. to kill*, to wipe out.
neuf, adj. 1. quoi de n.? what's the
news? 2. être tout n., to be quite inexperienced, to be a greenhorn.
neuil(le), f. night.
Neuneu, Neuneuille, pr.n. Neuilly-
sur-Seine (suburb of Paris); aller à la
fête à N., to dress up*.
neveu, m. un peu, mon n.! (R.S.) =un
peu!
nez, m. 1. face*; (en) faire un n., faire
un drôle de n., faire un sale n., to make
(or to pull) a long face, to look sick,
to look down one's nose; voyez le n.
qu'il fait! or voyez quel n. il fait! just
look at the face he's pulling! 2. avoir
le n. creux (or fin), avoir du n., avoir
bon n., to be well inspired, to be cute,
to smell trouble; to have a flair for a
bargain. 3. avoir qn dans le n., to take
a scunner to s.o., to have a down on
s.o., not to be able to stand (or to
stick) s.o. 4. avoir un (petit) coup dans
le n., avoir un coup de trop dans le n.,
avoir le n. sale, avoir le n. piqué, to
be drunk*, to have a drop in one's
eye. See also verre 2. 5. cela (or ça) lui
pend au n., he's got it coming to him,
he's in for it. 6. cela (or ça) va nous
retomber sur le n.—comme un sifflet
de deux ronds (or de deux sous), we're

sure to get the blame for it. 7. fourrer
(or mettre) le n. partout: see fourrer 3.
8. mener qn par le bout du n., to lead
s.o. by the nose, (of wife) to henpeck.
9. mouche ton n.! mind your own
business! 10. saigner du n., to be in a
funk, to have the wind up. 11. se
casser (or se cogner) le n., (a) to find
nobody at home (when calling at a
house); (b) to be frustrated; (c) to fail
(in business), to come a cropper. 12.
se manger (or se bouffer) le n., to
quarrel, to be always wrangling; to
fight, to scrap. 13. se salir (or se
piquer) le n., to be a boozer, to hit the
bottle, to liquor up. 14. si on lui
pressait (or pinçait or tordait) le n., il
en sortirait du lait, he hasn't cut his
eye-teeth yet, he's still damp (or wet
or not dry) behind the ears. 15. ton n.
branle! you're fibbing! 16. un n. en
pied de marmite, un n. dans lequel il
pleut (or un n. où il pleut dedans), a
turned-up nose, a pug-nose. 17. à vue
de n., at a rough estimate. See also
ver, verre.
niagué, adj. Chinese.
niard, m. =gniard.
niasse, m. =gniasse.
nib, adv. nothing; bon à n.=bon à
lap(e); n. de . . ., no . . . at all; n. de n.,
n. de rien, nothing whatever, damn
all, not a sausage, sweet Fanny
Adams.
nibe! int. silence! quiet!
nibé, m. 1. trifling matter. 2. small-
time robbery.
nicher, to live, to dwell, to hang out.
nichons, m.pl. breasts* (of female).
nickel, adj. c'est n.(-n.)! (a) it's first-
rate*! (or bang on!) it's the goods! (b)
spick and span.
nickelé, adj. See pied.
nicodème, m. =niguedouille.
niçois, adj. être n., (at poker, etc.) not
to increase one's stake, to stand pat.
nième, adj. pour la n. fois, for the
umpteenth time.
nienne, f., **nien,** m. yearning for drugs.
niente, f. nonentity.

nière, *m.* **1.** =gniard **2. 2.** accomplice, confederate; **un n. à la manque,** an unreliable accomplice.

niflette, *f.* cocaine, heroin (*drugs**).

nigaudinos, niguedouille, *m.* fool*, simpleton, booby, noodle.

ninas, *m.* cheap small cigar, whiff.

nini, *m.* fool*.

niôle, *f.* =gnôle.

Niort, *m.* **aller à N., battre à N.,** to deny, to swear blind that one is innocent.

nippe, *f.* **n'avoir plus une n. à se mettre,** not to have a rag to one's back; *pl.* clothes*.

nippé, *adj.* dressed, rigged out, togged up.

nipper, to dress (up), to rig out, to tog up.

nipper, se, to dress, to rig oneself out, to tog oneself up.

niquedouille, *m.* =niguedouille.

niquer, to have coition* with.

nisco! *int.* nix! nothing doing!

niston, -onne, *m.f.* child*, boy, girl.

niston, *adj.* =niçois.

nobler, to know.

nobler, se, to be called, to be named.

noblesse, *f.* =milieu.

nocdu, *adj.* ugly.

noce, *f.* **1.** spree*; **faire la n.,** to go on the spree*. **2. ne pas être à la n.,** to feel far from comfortable, to feel un-easy, not to feel very happy, to be on thorns, to have the wind up. **3.** il n'avait jamais été à pareille(s) noce(s), he had never had such a good time, he had the time of his life; (*iron.*) he had never seen such a shambles.

nocer =faire la noce.

noceur, -euse, *m.f.* rake, gay dog; fast woman.

nœud, *m.* **1.** penis*. **2. mon n.!**=mon œil! **3. filer son n.,** (*a*) to die*; (*b*) to decamp*. **4. ... de mon n.**=... de mes deux.

noie, noille, *f.* =neuille.

noir, *m.* **1. avoir le n.**=avoir le cafard. **2.** black market; **faire du n.,** to be a black marketeer. **3.** opium. **4.** petit

n., cup of black coffee, small black. **5.** (*mil.*, *W.W.I.*) heavy shell, 'Jack Johnson'.

noir, *adj.* (soûl) *n.*, (dead) drunk*. **2.** with a black police record. *See also* œil.

noircicot, *adj.* slightly drunk*, tipsy.

noircif, *m.* black market (*W.W.II*).

noircir, se, to get drunk*.

noire, *f.* **1.** night. **2.** opium.

noisettes, *f.pl.* testicles.

noite, *f.* night.

noitée, *adj.*, *f.* être bien n., to have a shapely posterior.

noix, *f.* **1.** fool*, silly chump; (*as adj.*) avoir l'air n., to look an utter fool; ce que tu es n.! what an ass you are! **2.** vieille n., old fog(e)y*; (*joc. term of address*) old thing. **3.** face*. **4.** head*. **5. ... à la n.** (de coco *or* de veau)= ... à la godille; des bobards (*or* des boniments) à la n., empty talk, eye-wash, bosh. **6. faire qch. à la n. de coco,** to bungle* sth. **7.** *pl.* testicles*; **te me fais mal aux n.!** you get on my tits! **8.** buttocks*; **serrer les n.**= serrer les fesses.

nom, *m.* **1. n. de n.! n. d'un n.! n. d'un chien! n. d'un (petit) bonhomme! n. d'une pipe! n. de deux! n. d'un tonnerre! tonnerre, de n.!** *etc.* (*mild variations for the oath 'n. de Dieu!'*) by jove! by jingo! good heavens! heavens above! hang it! confound it! (*expletives**). **2. un n. à coucher dehors** (avec un billet de logement), **un n. à coucher à la porte, un n. du tonnerre de Dieu,** a long name (*or* word), a mouthful, a jaw-breaker, a jaw-twister, a nice name to go to bed with. **3. ça n'a pas de n.!** it's incredible! it's beyond words! *See also* **charnière, rallonge, tiroir.**

nonnette, *f.* bandaged finger, dolly.

nono, *adj.* **zone n.,** unoccupied zone (*W.W.II*).

nord, *m.* **perdre le n.**=perdre la boussole.

Nordaf(e)s, *m.pl.* natives of former French North Africa.

Normale, *f.: see* **Norm' Sup'**.

Normand, *m.* **répondre en N.**, to give an evasive answer; **réponse de N.**, evasive reply.

Norm' Sup' =l'École normale supérieure, (*the highest educational institution for the intellectual élite of France*).

no(s)zig(ue)s, *pron.* we, us, ourselves. *Cf.* **mézig(ue)**.

note, *f.* **piquer une bonne** (*or* **mauvaise**) **n.**, to get a good (*or* bad) mark. *See* **saler** 1.

nouba, *f.* **faire la n.** = **faire la noce.**

nougat, *m.* 1. **du n.**, **un** (*or* **du**) **vrai n.**, an easy* job. 2. **toucher son n.**, to get one's share (*or* one's whack *or* one's cut). 3. *pl.* feet*.

nougatine, *f.* **de la** (**vraie**) **n.** = **du nougat** (**nougat** 1).

nouille, *f.* fool*; *adj.* **ce qu'il est n.!** what a drip (*or* a wet) he is!

nounou, *f.* (*nursery word*) nurse, nursie, nursey, nanny.

nounours, *m.* (*nursery word*) teddy (-bear).

nourrice, *f. See* **mois.**

nourrisson, *m.* any dependant (*used ironically*).

nouvaille, *f.* New Year.

nouvelles, *f.pl.* 1. **vous m'en direz** (*or* donnerez) **des n.**, you'll tell me what you think of it, I'm sure you'll be delighted with it, I'm sure you'll find it first-rate, you'll see how nice it is. 2. **vous aurez de mes n.**, (*as threat*) you shall hear from me! I'll give you something to think about! I'll make you sit up for that! I'll get my own back on you! I'll fix you for that!

nouzailles, *pron.* =no(s)zig(ue)s.

noyau, *m.* (*of bed*) **rembourré avec des noyaux de pêche**, hard and lumpy.

noye, *f.* night.

noyé, *adj.* out of one's depth, hopelessly at sea.

noyer: *see* **poisson.**

noyer, se: *see* **crachat, goutte, verre.**

numéro, *m.* 1. queer*, odd, person, card. 2. **un vieux n.**, (*of person*) a back number, an old stick-in-the-mud. 3. ... **n. un**, best ...; ... **n. deux**, second-best ... 4. (**maison à**) **gros n.**, brothel*. 5. **n. cent**, W.C.* 6. **je retiens votre n.!** (*threat*) =vous aurez de mes nouvelles. 7. **un bon n.**, a valuable piece of information, a good tip. 8. **tirer le bon n.**, to draw the lucky number. 9. **faire son n.**, to put on one's act.

nunu, *m.* nudist.

O

obitus, *m.* death.

obligado, *adv.*, faire qch. o., to do sth. under compulsion.

occase, *f.* 1. opportunity. 2. bargain; d'o., second-hand.

occasion,*f.* faire d'o., to look old, shop-worn.

occup, l', *f.* (*W.W.II*) German occupation.

occuper, s' : (ne) t'occupe pas (du pot de chambre)! don't worry! not to worry! carry on! leave it to me! forget it!

œil, *m.* 1. à l'o., gratis*; avoir l'o., to be given credit. 2. o. de bronze, anus*. 3. avoir l'o. (américain), to be wide-awake, to have a sharp eye (*or* sharp eyes), to keep one's eyes skinned (*or* peeled). 4. avoir (*or* tenir) qn à l'o., avoir l'o. sur qn, to keep a close watch on s.o. 5. avoir un o. au beurre noir, avoir un o. à la coque, to have a black eye*. *See also* poché. 6. avoir un o. qui dit zut (*or* merde) à l'autre, to be cross-eyed (*or* swivel-eyed), to (have a) squint. 7. s'en battre l'o., not to care a rap*. 8. cela a de l'o., it looks good (*or* smart); cela manque d'o., it lacks style. 9. être très sur l'o., to be very strict. 10. faire de l'o. à qn, to give s.o. the glad (eye), to make a pass at s.o., to tip s.o. the wink. 11. faire un o. de crapaud mort d'amour, to look like a dying duck in a thunderstorm. 12. l'avoir dans l'o., to be duped, to be done in the eye. 13. mon o.! *or* et mon o.! (*to express strong disbelief or contradiction*) my foot! nuts! baloney! my Aunt Fanny! 14. ne dormir que d'un o., to cat-nap. 15. ouvrir l'o. (et le bon), to keep one's weather eye open, to keep one's (best) eye skinned (*or* peeled). 16. pisser de l'o., to weep*. 17. se rincer l'o., to have (*or* to get) an eyeful (of a woman's charms), to feast one's eyes on, to be all eyes. 18. risquer un o., to have a peep, to have a look-see. 19. taper de l'o., to be drowsy. 20. taper (*or* donner) dans l'o. à qn, to take s.o.'s fancy, to click with s.o., to get off with s.o. 21. tourner de l'o., (*a*) to die*; (*b*) to faint*. *N.B. see also* yeux. 22. l'o. du cul, anus*.

œillade, *f.* lancer (*or* faire) une o. en lousdoc, to give s.o. the glad (eye).

œillets, *m.pl.* eyes*; gicler des o., to weep*.

œuf, *m.* 1. fool*; espèce d'o.! you silly ass! fais pas l'o.! don't act the (giddy) goat! 2. aux œufs = aux petits oignons. 3. avoir l'o. colonial, to be pot-bellied. 4. casser son o. (*or* ses œufs), to have a miscarriage. 5. des œufs sur le plat, (*of woman*) flat breasts. 6. donner un o. pour avoir un bœuf, to throw out a sprat to catch a mackerel (*or* a herring). 7. l'avoir dans l'o., (*a*) to be duped; (*b*) to fail, to come a cropper. 8. marcher (comme) sur des œufs, to walk warily, to walk on very thin ice. 9. plein comme un o., (*a*) chock-full; (*b*) dead drunk*. 10. rond comme un o., as drunk as a lord. 11. tondre (sur) un o., to be a skinflint, to skin a flint. 12. va te faire cuire un o.! (*c.p.*) go to blazes*! 13. *pl.* testicles*.

offense, *f.* y a pas d'o.! don't mention it! it's quite all right! excuse my saying so! don't mind me!

officemar, *m.* officer.

officiel, *adj.* de l'o., genuine, authentic, the real Mackay. o.! no kid! straight up! offish! (*i.e.* = '*official*') it's a certainty*.

oie, *f.* envoyer qn ferrer des oies, to send s.o. on a fool's errand.

oignards, *m.pl.* = oignon 3.

oignes, *m.pl.* aux o. = aux petits oignons.

oignon, *m.* 1. large watch*. 2. en rang d'oignons, in a row. 3. *pl.* buttocks*. 4. luck; avoir l'o. qui décalotte, to have all the luck. 5. ce n'est (*or* ce ne sont *or* c'est) pas mes oignons, it's none of my business, it's not my funeral; it's not my pigeon; occupe-toi de tes oignons! mind your own business! 6. aux petits oignons, first-rate*, in first-class style.

oiseau, *m.* 1. (*pej.*) fellow*; un drôle d'o., a queer*, odd, person. 2. aux oiseaux = aux petits oignons.

olive, *f.* 1. bullet, slug, lead. 2. *pl.* testicles*. 3. changer ses olives d'eau, to urinate*.

ollé-ollé, *adj.* fast, flighty, 'oo-la-la'.

olpette, olpiche, olpif, *adj.* = eulpif.

ombre, *f.* 1. être à l'o., to be in prison*; mettre qn à l'o., to imprison* s.o. 2. avoir peur de son o., to be afraid to say boo to a goose.

ongles, *m.pl.* avoir les o. en deuil, to have dirty (finger) nails, to have one's nails in mourning.

onze, *num. adj.* See bouillon 4 *and* train 8.

opérer: o. qn (de), to swindle s.o. (out of sth.), to tap s.o. (for money).

or, *m.* 1. c'est en o., it's an easy* job. 2. un caractère d'o. (*or* en o.), a lovely nature. 3. l'avoir en o., to be lucky.

orange, *f.* 1. payer une o. à qn, to give s.o. a blow. 2. avoir des oranges sur l'étagère (*or* sur son étagère *or* à l'étalage), (*of woman*) to have small, hard breasts.

orchestre, *m.* déboucher son o., to defecate*.

ordure, *f.* (*of person*) une belle o., an awful (*or* a regular) shit.

oreille, *f.* 1. se faire un peu tirer l'o., to need a bit of persuading. 2. dormir sur les deux oreilles, (*a*) to sleep soundly; (*b*) (*fig.*) to feel quite safe about sth. See also frotter 1.

original, *m.* = numéro 1.

orphelin, *m.* = mégot.

orties, *f.pl.* n'poussez pas mémé(re) dans les o., don't flog it to death.

os, *m.* 1. difficulty, snag. 2. dangerous customer (to have to deal with). 3. ça vaut l'o.! it's worth while! 4. c'est le même o. = c'est kif-kif. 5. gagner son o., to earn one's living. 6. jusqu'à l'o., thoroughly, completely. 7. l'avoir dans l'o., to be diddled, to be taken in, to be 'had'. 8. ne pas faire de vieux o., not to make old bones, not to be long for this world. 9. refiler un o. à qn, to sell s.o. a pup. 10. sauver ses o., to save one's skin. 11. se casser les o., to fail, to come a cropper. 12. tourner en o. de boudin = tourner en eau de boudin. 13. o. à moelle, (*a*) nose*; (*b*) penis*; faire juter l'o. à moelle, (*a*) to use one's fingers instead of a handkerchief; (*b*) to masturbate*.

oseille, *f.* 1. money*; faire son o., to get rich*. 2. la faire à l'o à qn, to (try to) gull s.o., to make a sucker of s.o. 3. un(e) ... à l'o = ... à la godille. 4. faire à l'o., to dissimulate, to make-believe, to put on an act. 5. avoir mangé de l'o., to be angry*.

oseillé, *adj.* rich*.

osier, *m.* = oseille 1; avoir un champ d'o., to be very rich*.

osselets, *m.pl.* 1. courir sur les o. à qn, to keep a close watch on s.o., to keep tabs on s.o. 2. ne me cours pas sur les o., don't bother me.

ost(e)au, osto, *m.* hospital.

ostrogoth, *m.* rough, uncouth fellow.

ôter, s': ôte-toi de là que je m'y mette! you get out and let me in! make room for your betters!

ôticher, to seduce.

oua(h)-oua(h), *m.* dog*, bow-wow.

ouallou! ouat! ouatt(e)! *int.* ah! o.! *or* mais o.! not a bit of it! don't you believe it! oh, no! nothing of the kind!

ouatères, *m.pl.* W.C.*

oubli, *m.* marcher à l'o., to pretend one doesn't know, to feign ignorance.

oublier, s', to have an 'accident' (*i.e. to be taken short*).

ouf! *int.* avant de pouvoir (*or* d'avoir pu) dire o., ne pas avoir (*or* avoir eu) le

ouiche! 157 ovale

temps de dire o., before you could say
Jack Robinson (or knife).
ouiche! int. = ouat!
ouistiti, m. bloke, blighter, fellow*.
ourdé, adj. drunk*; o. à zéro, dead
drunk*.
ourdée, f. tenir une bonne o., to be
dead drunk*, to have a skinful.
ours, m. 1. manuscript (frequently rejected). 2. white elephant. 3. (mil.)
prison*. 4. avoir ses o. = avoir ses
affaires, 5. prison*.
oursin, m. See morlingue.
ourson, m. baby.
ousque, pop. for où est-ce que ...
oust(e)! int. hop it! get along with you!
be off with you, get a move on!

outil, m. 1. clumsy person, silly duffer.
2. penis*. 3. knife. 4. pl. weapons.
5. déballer ses outils, (a) to confess*;
(b) to expose one's genitals, to take
one's trousers off; remballer ses
outils, to put one's trousers on
again.
outiller, to knife (s.o.).
ouverture, f. avoir l'o. retardée, to be
slow on the uptake.
ouvrage, m. (of burglar, etc.) job.
ouvrier, m. burglar, house-breaker.
ouvrir, 1. l'o., to speak, to confess*.
2. l'o. sur qn, to disparage *s.o., to
'knock' s.o.
ovale, m. avoir un bel o. = être bien
noitée.

P

pac(k)son, pacq(ue)son, pacsif, m.
1. parcel, package. 2. (turf) toucher le pacson, to make a packet (i.e. a large sum of money).

padoc, pad(d)ock, m. bed*.

paddocker, padoquer, se, to go to bed*.

paf, adj. drunk*; p. à rouler, dead drunk.

paf, m. 1. penis*. 2. tomber sur un p. = tomber sur un bec (bec 13).

paffer, se, to get drunk*, to booze.

pagaie, pagaille, pagaye, f. muddle, jumble, confusion, mess; en p., in disorder*; une belle p., an absolute muddle, a real shambles.

page, f. 1. être à la p., to be up-to-date, posted up, in the swim, abreast of the times; to be in the know, to be in the picture, to know what's what, to be hep, to be with it. 2. tourner la p. = filer du dos (dos 6).

page, pageot, m. bed*; se mettre (aller, se filer) au p., to go to bed*, to get into bed.

pageoter, se, pager, se, to go to bed*.

pagnot, m. bed*.

pagnoter, se, to go to bed*.

paie, f. = paye.

paillasse, f. 1. belly; crever (or trouer) la p. à qn, to knife s.o. in the guts. 2. low prostitute*.

paillasson, m. = paillasse 1. 2. See also clef 1. 3. old tennis racket.

paille, f. 1. une p.! a mere trifle! a mere flea-bite! 2. faire des pailles à = faire des paillons à. 3. être sur la p., to be down and out.

paillon, m. faire des paillons à, to be unfaithful to (husband or wife), to step out on, to let (s.o.) down, to two-time (s.o.).

pain, m. 1. blow*; coller (flanquer, foutre) un p. (sur la gueule) à qn, to

land (or to dot or to sock) s.o. one (on the mug), to give s.o. a plug (in the ear-hole). 2. avoir du p. sur la planche, to have plenty of work on hand, to have one's work cut out, to have enough on one's plate. 3. bon comme du bon p., good-hearted. 4. c'est p. bénit! it serves him (you, her, etc.) right! 5. je ne mange pas de ce p.-là! I don't go in for that sort of thing! it's not in my line! it's not my cup of tea! I'd rather starve! 6. se vendre (or s'enlever) comme des petits pains, to sell (or to go) like hot cakes. 7. il n'a pas inventé les pains à cacheter = il n'a pas inventé le fil à couper le beurre (fil 4). 8. p. au lait, penis*. 9. p. de fesse (of prostitute), earnings, money earned on one's back. See also goût, morceau.

paire, f. 1. c'est une autre p. de manches! that's quite another matter (or story)! that's another (or a very different) kettle of fish! that's another cup of tea! that's a horse of another colour! that alters matters (or the case)! 2. se faire la p., to decamp*. 3. avoir une p. de lunettes contre le soleil, to have two lovely black eyes. 4. avoir une belle p., en avoir une p., to have guts, to have spunk.

paître: envoyer p. qn, to send s.o. packing*.

paix, f. ficher (or foutre) la p. à qn, to leave s.o. alone; fiche (or fous)-moi la p.! leave me alone! don't bother me! shut* up! hop* it!

pajot, m. = pageot.

pakson, m. = pac(k)son.

palace, adj. first-rate*.

palas(s), m. palaver, patter, gas; du p. (en tartine), idle talk, baloney, eye-wash; faire du p., (a) to swank*; (b) = faire du boniment à (boniment 4) or faire du plat à (plat 1).

palasser, to palaver, to gas.

pâle, *m.* corpse*.

pâle, *adj.* (*mil.*) **se faire porter p.,** (*a*) to go (*or* to report) sick; (*b*) to malinger*.

paletot, *m.* 1. **le dernier p.** *or* **le p. de sapin,** coffin, 'wooden overcoat'. 2. **se faire un p. sans manches** *or* **prendre mesure d'un p. de sapin,** to die*, to put on a 'wooden overcoat'. 3. **une machine à secouer le p.,** a Tommy-gun. 4. **tomber** (*or* **bondir** *or* **sauter) sur le p. à qn,** to pitch (*or* to sail) into s.o. 5. **prendre tout sur le p.,** to assume full responsibility. 6. **avoir qn sur le p.,** to be saddled with s.o.; **le mettre sur le p. à qn,** to saddle s.o. with sth.

palette, *f.* hand*.

palissandre, *m.* **avoir la bouche** (*or* **la gueule) en p.,** to have a hangover*.

pallas, *m.* =**palas(s); adj.** beautiful.

palmé, *adj.* **les avoir palmées,** to be workshy.

palombe, *f.* woman*, bird.

palper, to touch, to receive, to pocket (money); **p. son mois,** to receive one's month's screw; **aller les p.,** to draw one's pay.

palper, se: tu peux te p.!=**tu peux toujours courir!** (**courir** 3).

palpitant, *m.* heart, ticker, pump.

palpouser=**palper.**

paluche, *f.* hand*; **écraser les paluches,** to shake hands.

palucher, se. 1. to masturbate*. 2. to imagine, to kid oneself.

panache, *m.* 1. **avoir son p.,** to be drunk*. 2. **faire p.,** to overturn; **le cycliste a fait p.,** the cyclist pitched over the handlebars.

panaché, *m.* shandy(gaff) (*drink*).

panade, *f.* **être dans la p.,** to be penniless*, to be in a fix*.

panais, *m.* 1. fool*, ninny. 2. **des p.!**= **des clous!** (**clou** 7). 3. penis*; **dérouiller** (*or* **dégraisser** *or* **planter** *or* **tremper) son p.,** to have coition*.

Panam(e), *pr.n.* Paris.

panard, *m.* 1. foot*. 2. =**fade** 1. **prendre son p.**=**prendre son fade.**

pandore, *m.* policeman*.

pane, *f.* =**panne** 6.

panet, *m.* =**panais** 1.

paneton, *m.* basket.

panier, *m.* 1. **p. à salade,** prison-van, Black Maria, meat-waggon, the hurry-up cart. 2. **p. de** (*or* **aux) crabes,** rat-race; all at each other's throats. 3. **p.** (**à crottes), buttocks*; remuer** (*or* se **secouer) le** (*or* **son) p. à crottes,** to dance, to wiggle. 4. **mettre la main au p.,** to have one's fingers in the fruit basket, to feel a woman.

paniquard, *m.* panic-monger, scaremonger, jitterbug.

paniqué, *adj.* mad*.

panne, *f.* 1. shortage (of petrol); **avoir une p. d'essence, avoir une p. sèche,** to run out of petrol. 2. black-out (of electricity). 3. **être** (*or* **rester** *or* **tomber) en p.,** to be (*or* to get) stuck, to be at (*or* to be brought to) a stand-still, to have a breakdown, to conk out; **laisser qn en p.,** to leave s.o. in the lurch, up in the air; to let s.o. down. 4. (*th.*) small part (in play). 5. (*of picture*) daub. 6. poverty; **dans une p. noire,** terribly hard-up, stony-broke.

pan(n)é, *adj.* penniless*.

panosse, panouillard, *m.*, **panouille,** *f.* 1. fool*, stick-in-the-mud. 2. mug, sucker, easy mark.

pan-pan, *int.* biff-baff, biff-bang; **faire p.-p. à,** to smack a child's bottom, to give (a child) a 'smack-botty'.

panse, *f.* 1. **grosse p.,** paunch*. 2. **ne pas faire une p. d'a,** not to do a stroke of work, to do damn all. 3. **se faire péter la p.,** to blow one's hide out.

pansement, *m.* **p. à brioche,** corset.

pante, *m.* 1. fellow*. 2. mug, sucker, easy mark, jay.

panthère, *f.* 1. **ma p.,** my wife*. 2. **faire sa p.,** to laze.

pantouflard, *m.* stay-at-home person, home-bird.

pantoufle, *f.* 1. (*of person*) dud, wash-out. 2. **jouer comme une p.**=**jouer comme un pied** (**pied** 15). 3. **raisonner comme une p.,** to talk through one's hat. **4. et caetera p.**=et patati et patata.

pantoufler, to put one's feet up.

pantre, *m.* =pante.

Pantruchard, *m.* Parisian.

Pantruche, *pr.n.* Paris.

panuche, *f.* =panade.

papa, *m.* **1. un bon gros p.,** a nice, old stout party. **2. à la p.,** in a simple (*or* quiet *or* leisurely *or* homely) way. **3. un gros p.,** a bank-note of big denomination (*a hundred or fifty francs*). **4. le Paris** (*or* **le football,** etc.) **de p.,** old time Paris, football, etc. *See also* **gâteau.**

papaout, *m.* pederast*.

papeau, *m.* hat*.

papelard, *m.* **1.** (piece of) paper; letter; official document; bill, handbill, notice. **2.** reputation, record. **3.** *pl.* identity papers; business papers; newspapers.

papier, *m.* **1.** article, copy (*of journalist*). **2. avoir un bon p.,** to have a good record (*or* a good reputation). **3. connaître le p.** (**de**), to be well informed (about). **4.** (*turf*) forecast, form; **faire le p.,** to study form; **jouer le p.,** to bet upon form; **faire son p.,** to make out one's bet. **5. p. à douleur,** protested unpaid note; rent bill (presented by the landlord). **6. un p.,** a thousand-franc note. **7. réglé comme du p. à musique,** as regular as clockwork. **8. une partie de petits papiers,** a game of consequences. **9.** *pl.* playing cards. **10. figure** (*or* **mine**) **de p. mâché,** washed-out face. **11. être dans les petits papiers de qn.,** to be in s.o.'s good books.

papillon, *m.* **p. d'amour,** crab-louse.

papognes, *f.pl.* hands*.

papouille, *f.* caress, cuddle, squeeze; **faire des papouilles à qn,** to paw s.o.

papouiller, to caress, to cuddle, to hug.

paquerettes, *f.pl.* **cueillir les p.,** to moon about. **2. tiges de p.,** thin legs*.

paques(s)on, paquelin, *m.* =pac(k)-son.

paquet, *m.* **1. avoir son p.,** (*a*) to get one's deserts, to get a good thrashing*;

(*b*) to get reprimanded*; (*c*) to be dead drunk*, to have all one can carry. **2. faire ses paquets,** (*a*) to pack up (and go); (*b*) to be dismissed*. **3. faire descendre** (*or* **faire dégringoler**) **le p.**=faire descendre le mioche. **4. lâcher le p.,** sortir tout le p., to confess*. **5. lâcher** (*or* **dire**) **son p. à qn,** to let fly at s.o., to let s.o. have it, to give s.o. a piece of one's mind. **6. mettre le p.,** (*cycle race*) to go all out. **7. recevoir son p.,** (*a*) to get a thrashing*; (*b*) to be reprimanded*; (*c*) to be dismissed*. **8. risquer le p.,** to chance it, to go the whole hog (*or* the whole shoot), to chance the lot, (*turf*) to put one's shirt on (a horse), to go a bundle, to go nap. **9. un p. de nerfs,** a bundle of nerves. **10. fichu comme un p. de linge sale,** got up like a guy. **11. un p. d'os,** (*of person*) a bag of bones. **12.** =baraque 3. **13.** load, stock, of illegal drugs. **14.** *adj.* (*a*) frumpish, dowdy; (*b*) clumsy, loutish.

para, *m.* (*mil.*) paratrooper.

parade, *f.* **1. c'est pour la p.,** it's just for show. **2. défiler la p.,** to die*.

paradis, *m.* **1.** upper gallery (*in theatre*), the gods, chicken-roost, pigeon-roost. **2. vous ne l'emporterez pas en p.!** you won't get away with it! I'll be (*or* I'll get) even with you yet! you'll pay for this!

paradouze, *m.* paradise.

paralance, *m.* umbrella*.

parallèle, *m.* currency black-market.

parapluie, *m.* **1.** alibi. **2. la Maison P.,** the police. **3. fermer son p.,** to die*. **4. avoir l'air d'avoir avalé un p.,** to be stiff and starchy. **5. envoyer qn chercher le p. de l'escouade,** to send s.o. on a fool's errand.

parc, *m.* **p. des refroidis,** cemetery, bone-park, bone-orchard.

parcours, *m.* undertaking, venture.

pardaf, pardess, pardeuss(e), *m.* overcoat.

pardessus, *m.* **1. se faire faire un p. en sapin,** to die* (*cf.* paletot). **2. p. sans manche,** coffin.

pardingue, pardoss(e), *m.* overcoat.
pardon! *int.* 1. p.! t'y vas fort! steady on!
2. (*expletive of admiration*) p! c'est pas de
la camelote! it's far from being trash!
paré, *adj.* 1. rich*; être p., to have a fat
banking account. 2. un boulot p., a
cushy job.
pare-brises, *m.pl.* spectacles, specs.
pare-chocs, *m.pl.* breasts* (of female).
pareil, *adv.* in the same way; *adj.* c'est
du p. au même = c'est kif-kif.
parfait, *adj.* p.! capital! fine! splendid!
good show!
parfaitement, *adv.* p.! of course!
quite so! exactly!
parfum, *m.* être au p. (de), to know all
about it, to be well informed, to be
tipped off; mettre qn au p., to inform
s.o., to warn s.o., to tip s.o. off.
parfumer = mettre au parfum.
Parigot, *m.* Parisian.
Paris, *pr.n.* Monsieur de P., the public
executioner (*who operates the guillotine*).
parler. 1. tu parles! (*a*) rather! not
half! you bet! you're telling me! I
should jolly well think so! (*b*) what a
hope! what do you take me for? oh
yeah! 2. tu parles d'une rigolade! talk
about a lark! it was a right giggle! 3.
trouver à qui p., to find one's master,
to catch a Tartar; se p., (*dial.*) to be
courting, to keep company.
parlot(t)e, *f.* palaver, empty chatter,
talkativeness*.
paroissien, *m.* un drôle de p., a queer*
fellow.
parole! *int.* 1. (*at cards*) pass! no bid!
2. upon my word!
parpaillot, -e, *m.f.* protestant, prot.
parrains, *m.pl.* witnesses.
part, *f.* See quelque part.
partant, *m.* je suis p.! I'm game! I'm
on! count me in!
parterre, *m.* See billet.
parti, *adj.* (un peu) p., slightly drunk*,
tipsy, muzzy, woozy.
particule, *f.* avoir la p., to belong to
the nobility, to have a handle to one's
name.

particulier, *m.* un drôle de p., a
queer* fellow (*or* party).
particulière, *f.* sa p., his sweetheart,
his best girl, his steady.
partie, *f.* 1. une p. de traversin, a nap, a
snooze. 2. une p. carrée, double-two
party, double date. 3. *pl.* les parties
nobles, testicles*. See also jambe 7.
partouse, partouze, *f.* a collective
necking (*or* petting) party, sex orgy,
(*Amer. slang*) daisy chain.
pas, *m.* mettre qn au p., to make s.o. toe
the line; sauter le p., to take the
plunge.
pas, *adv.* 1. p.? = *n'est-ce pas?* 2. y a p. =
il n'y a pas à dire (dire 7).
pasque, *conj. pop. for 'parce que,'* because, 'cos.
passade, *f.* short-lived love affair, brief
liaison. *Cf.* toquade.
passage, *m.* See tabac.
passe, *f.* 1. maison de p., hôtel de p., (*of
prostitutes*) house of call, assignation
hotel (*or* joint); chambre de p., bedroom let by the hour. 2. une p., (*of
prostitutes*) short-time, 'quickie'. 3. p.
anglaise, gambling game with dice;
rouler la p., to shake the bones.
passe-lacet, *m.* raide comme un p.-l.,
penniless.*
passer. 1. cela me passe! that quite
beats me! 2. qu'est-ce que je lui ai
passé! I didn't half tick him off!
qu'est-ce qu'il va se faire p.! I
won't half tick him off! I won't half
let him have it! he won't half cop it
(from me)! 3. il faut p. par là ou par
la porte (*or* la fenêtre), it's a case of
Hobson's choice, there's no alternative. 4. y p., (*a*) to be done for, to be a
goner; (*b*) to die*; (*c*) to go through
it; (*d*) (*of female*) to be screwed;
tout le monde y passe, it's the
common lot, it's the lot of everyone,
we've all got to go through it;
j'y ai passé, I've been through it,
I've had some. 5. le faire p., to bring
on a miscarriage. 6. to faint*.
passe-sirop, *m.* telephone, mouth-
piece, spittle-strainer.

passion, *f.* un homme (une femme) à passions, a sexual pervert, hot-stuff.

passoire, *f.* 1. memory like a sieve. 2. spendthrift.

pastag(u)a, *m.* =pastis.

pastèque, *f.* 1. envoyer une p., to fire (a gun, revolver, etc.). 2. vagina*. 3. buttocks.

pastille, *f.* 1. bullet. 2. venir en pastilles de Vichy=venir en cure-dents. 3. blow*.

pastiquer, to smuggle.

pastiquette, *f.* =passe.

pastiqueur, *m.* smuggler.

pastis, *m.* 1. aniseed apéritif. 2. muddle, mess; être dans le p., to be in a fix*; être dans un drôle de p., to be in a hell of a mess.

pasto, *m.* blind alley, by-street.

patachon, *m.* mener une vie de p., to lead a fast life, to go the pace, to beat it up a lot.

patapouf, *m.* 1. un gros p., a big fat* man, a big slob, a podge. 2. faire p., to come a cropper, to fall down flop.

patate, *f.* 1. potato, spud; tater, Murphy (*pl.* taties, Murphies). 2. head*; avoir qch. sur la p., to have sth. on one's mind; en avoir gros sur la p., to have plenty to be sad (*or* to worry) about. 3. peasant*. 4. fool*, chump, clumsy clot. 5. large nose*. 6. des patates!=des clous! (clou 7). 7. sentir la p., to sound fishy *or* suspicious.

patati, *int.* et p. et patata! (*of endless gossiping*) and so on (and so forth)!and all the rest of it! and tidderly push!

patatrot, *m.* 1. hurried flight, speedy escape. 2. (horse-)races.

pataud, *m.* =Francaoui.

pâtée, *f.* thrashing*.

patelin, *m.* (*a*) birth-place, hometown; (*b*) small town, small village, one-horse town.

pater, paternel, *m.* father*; *pl.* parents.

pâteux, *adj.* =vaseux.

patin, *m.* 1. tongue. 2. (*long-distance drivers' slang*) brake. 3. rouler un p.,

to give s.o. a French kiss. 4. *pl.* feet*. 5. traîner ses patins, to loaf around. 6. chercher des patins, to pick a quarrel. 7. prendre (*or* porter) les patins, to espouse a friend's quarrel, to take up the cudgels on s.o.'s behalf.

patiner, to paw (a female), to mess about with, to muck (s.o.) about, to monkey with.

patoche, *f.* hand*.

patouille, *f.* 1. mud. 2. gentle caress. 3. *nav.* sea.

patouiller =patiner.

patraque, *adj.* (*of person*) unwell*; (*of machine, etc.*) out of order, wornout; avoir le cœur p., to have a wonky, dicky, heart.

patro, *m.* (=*patronage*) church club.

patron, -onne, *m.f.* 1. boss; the master, the missis. 2. superintendent of police.

patte, *f.* 1. leg; à quatre pattes, on all fours; aller à pattes, to foot (*or* to leg *or* to pad *or* to hoof) it, to pad the hoof; tirer la p., to limp; traîner la p., to limp along; to lag behind; jouer des pattes, se tirer des (*or* les) pattes, tricoter des pattes, to decamp*. 2. casser les pattes à qn, to put a spoke in s.o.'s wheel, to bring s.o. a cropper. 3. être fait aux pattes, to be fairly caught, to be nabbed. 4. faire qch. aux pattes, to pinch (*or* to bone) sth. 5. graisser la p. à qn, to bribe s.o., to grease (*or* to oil) s.o.'s palm, to tip s.o.; graissage de p., palm-oiling. 6. faire des pattes d'araignée à qn, to caress s.o.'s body delicately with the tips of one's fingers, to 'goose'. 7. pattes de lapin, short side-whiskers, side-boards. 8. (à) bas les pattes! (*a*) hands* (*or* paws) off! keep your hands to yourself! (*b*) no fighting! no fisticuffs here! 9. il n'a jamais cassé trois pattes à un canard, he'll never set the Thames on fire.

patuche, *f.* licence (for a pedlar, market-trader, etc.).

paturons, *m.pl.* feet*; jouer des p., to decamp*.

paumaquer = paumer.

paumard, loser.

paumé, *adj.* **1.** penniless*. **2.** exhausted*. **3.** *m.* down-and-out(er); wash-out; moral and physical wreck.

paumer. 1. to lose (at gambling). **2.** to arrest*; **p. qn marron**, to catch s.o. red-handed; **se faire p.**, (*a*) to get nabbed; (*b*) to be diddled. **3.** to catch (illness, disease). **4.** to steal*. **5.** to waste (one's time). **6.** to smack (s.o.'s face). **7.** (*motor.*) to do (so many miles an hour).

paumer, se. 1. to get lost. **2.** to go down in the world.

pauvreté, *f.* **se jeter là-dessus comme la p. sur le monde**, to jump unhesitatingly at sth.

pavé, *m.* **1. fusiller le p.**, to blow one's nose in the street with one's fingers. **2. malheureux comme le p. de bois** = **malheureux comme les pierres (pierre 3). 3. battre le p.**, to tramp the street for work. **4. n'avoir plus de p. dans la cour**, to be toothless.

pav(e)ton, *m.* paving-stone; pavement.

pavillons, *m.pl.* ears*.

pavoiser. 1. to have a black eye*; (*boxing*) to have one's claret tapped. **2.** to display. **3.** to blush, to colour. **4.** = **avoir ses affaires.**

pavot, *m.* buttocks*.

pavoule, *f.* = **poule 1.**

pavute, *f.* prostitute*.

paye, *f.* (ça fait) **une p.!** that's quite an age! that's a goodish while! **il y a une p. que . . .**, it's ages since . . .; **il y en a pour une p.**, it'll take ages.

payer. 1. tu me le paieras *or* **tu vas me p. ça!** you'll pay (*or* you'll smart) for that! I'll get my own back for that! I'll pay you out! **2. je suis payé** (*or* **j'ai payé**) **pour le savoir**, I've learnt (*or* I know) it to my cost. **3. se p. qch.**, (*a*) to treat oneself to sth.; (*b*) to have to stand (*or* to suffer) sth., to have to put up with sth. **4.** to be sentenced. **5. s'en p.**, to have a good time, to have the time of one's life. *See also* **figure, place, tête.**

pays, (*m.*) **payse**, *f.* **1.** fellow-countryman, -countrywoman; **être p.**, to come from the same parts (*same village, same town*). **2.** *f.* sweetheart (*used by countryfolk*).

paysage, *m.* **cela fait (fera, ferait) bien dans le p.**, it looks (will look, would look) well in the picture; that just suits me (will just suit, would just suit) my (his, etc.) book, that just fills (will just fill, would just fill) the bill.

P.B.I. (= *pas de bouches inutiles*), (we will have) no unwelcome guests!

P.D., *m.* (= *pédé*), pederast.

peau, *f.* **1. la p.!** = **des clous! (clou 7). 2. p. de balle (et balai de crin)!** *or* **p. de balle et variété!** *or* **p. de nœud!** *or* **p. de zébi(e)!** nothing doing! damn all! sweet Fanny Adams! **3. . . . à la p. de toutou** = . . . **à la godille. 4.** prostitute*; **une vieille p.**, an old trollop, an old bag, an old trout. **5. une p. de vache**, (*of person*) a dog's body, a stinker, a lousy bum. **6. avoir la p. (trop) courte**, to be lazy*. **7. avoir la p. de qn**, to kill* s.o. **8. avoir qn dans la p.**, to have s.o. under one's skin, to be infatuated* with s.o. **9. bouffer à s'en faire crever la p. du ventre**, to eat heavily, to blow one's hide out. **10. faire la p. à qn**, to kill* s.o.; **se faire (crever) la p.**, to kill* oneself. **11. faire p. neuve**, to turn over a new leaf. **12. manger la p. sur le dos à qn**, to starve s.o. **13. péter dans sa p.**, to be too big for one's boots (*or* for one's breeches). **14. porter à la p. à qn**, to excite s.o. sensually, to work s.o. up. **15. quitter sa p.**, to cast off the old Adam. **16. se sentir bien dans sa p.**, to feel wonderfully at ease. **17. tanner la p. à qn**, to thrash* s.o. **18. traîner sa p.**, to loaf about. **19. y laisser sa p.**, to die*, to be killed. **20. p. de couille**, (*nav.*) oilskin.

peaux-rouges, *m.pl.* blackguards*.

pébroc, pébroque, *m.* **1.** umbrella*. **2. la Maison P.** = **la Maison Parapluie. 3.** = **couverte 3.**

pécaïre, int. (South of France) alas!

pêche, f. 1. blow*; filer (balancer, foutre, tasser) une p. à qn (en pleine poire), to biff s.o. in the jaw. 2. face*; head*; sucer la p. à qn, to kiss s.o.; se fendre la p. = se fendre la pipe. 3. aller à la p., to be out of work; to be dismissed*, to be sacked. 4. turd; poser (or déposer) une (or sa) p., to defecate*. 5. avoir la p. = avoir le moral.

pêchecaille, f. fishing; m. fisherman, angler.

péchère, int. = pécaïre.

pecnaud, m. = péquenaud.

pécore, m. peasant*; f. (pej.), goose.

pécul, m. old paper(s); faire un p. sur . . ., to read a paper on . . .

pécune, f. money*.

pédalard, m. (cycling) scorcher.

pédale, f. 1. perdre (or lâcher) les pédales, (a) to lose all self-control, to get flustered (or flurried); (b) to be at death's door; (c) to throw up the sponge. 2. la p., the world of male homosexuals, pansyland; être de la p., to be a pederast*; une p., a pederast*.

pédaleur, m. cyclist.

pédalo, m. pedal-craft, pedal-boat.

pédard, m. clumsy (or reckless) cyclist.

pédé, pédéro, m. pederast*.

pédezouille, m. = pedzouille.

pedibus, adv. p. (cum jambis), on Shanks' mare (or pony).

pédigree, m. (of criminal) police record, charge sheet, 'form'.

pédoc, pédoque, m. pederast*.

pedzouille, m. peasant*.

pégal(e), m. pawnshop, uncle's.

pègre, f. underworld, riff-raff.

pégrer: se faire p., to get nabbed.

pégriot, m. petty thief, pilferer.

peigne, m. (of burglar) crow-bar, jemmy.

peigne-cul, peigne-derche, m. 1. miser*. 2. rotter*.

peignée, f. 1. thrashing*; ficher une p. à qn, to give s.o. a thrashing. 2. fight, scrap.

peigner, se, to (have a) fight, to have a set-to, to scrap.

peinard, adj. quiet, sly; en (père) p., quietly, slyly, on the sly, on the Q.T.; être (or rester or se tenir) p., to take things easy, to lie doggo.

peinardement, adv. = en (père) peinard.

peintre, m. avoir les peintres = avoir ses affaires.

peinture, f. je ne peux (or puis) pas le voir en p.! I can't bear (or stand or stick) the sight of him! I hate the (mere) sight of him!

pékin, m. civilian; en (tenue de) p., in civvies, in mufti.

pelé, m. quatre pelés et un tondu or trois pelés et quatre tondus, ragtag and bobtail, a scratch lot, a few nonentities, a few odd bods, a few odds and sods.

pelé, adj. 1. bald*. 2. cleaned out, fleeced.

peler. 1. to fleece s.o. 2. p. de froid, to freeze, to be shrammed.

pèlerin, m. 1. policeman*. 2. (railwaymen's slang) traveller.

pelle, f. ramasser une p., to come a cropper (lit. and fig.).

pello(t), m. = pelo(t).

pelops! int. nothing doing! not likely!

pelo(t), pélo(t), m. pas un p., not a cent, not a bean.

pelotage, m. 1. cuddling, heavy petting (or necking), pawing, feeling; pas de p. avant le mariage, (c.p.) no sampling the goods! 2. y a du p.! (of a female) she's cuddlesome!

pelote, f. 1. pile (of money); faire (or arrondir) sa (petite) p., to make one's pile, to feather one's nest. 2. une p. d'épingles, (of person) a cross-patch. 3. (mil.) defaulter's squad; faire la p., to do punishment drill. 4. envoyer qn aux pelotes, to send s.o. packing*. See also nerf.

peloter. 1. to cuddle, to pet, to neck, to paw, to feel, to maul about, to have a feel. 2. to flatter*.

peloteur, m. 1. cuddler, petter, pawer. 2. flatterer*.

pelousard, *m.* race-goer, horse-racing fan, one who 'follows' the horses.

pelure, *f.* **1.** overcoat; fur-coat; outer garments; **enlever sa p.,** to peel. **2. une vraie p.,** a stupid* person, a bone-head. **3.** hand-out (*of speech*), flimsy. **4.** *pl.* (*of racing cycle*) tyres.

pénard, *adj.* =**peinard.**

penco, *m.* (*sch.*) boarder.

pendantes, *f.pl.* earrings.

pendard, *m.* rascal, rogue.

pendule, *f.* **remonter la p. à qn contre qn d'autre,** to work s.o. up against s.o. else.

péniche, *f.* **1.** big boot*. **2.** *pl.* feet*.

penscu, *m.* =**penco.**

pense-bête, *m.* memory jogger, memory tickler.

penser. 1. penses-tu (*or* **pensez-vous**)! **tu penses** (*or* **vous pensez**)! what an idea! you bet not! not likely! no fear! not on your life! don't you believe it! **2. vous n'y pensez pas!** surely you don't mean it! you're not serious! you're joking! **3. p.** *is sometimes used to avoid a more precise term—e.g.* **bande de ce que je pense!** (*roughly equivalent to* **bande de salauds!**), you shower of so-and-sos! **il peut le mettre où je pense,** he can stuff it (up his arse). *Cf.* **savoir 5** *and English* 'you know what', 'you know where', 'you know whom I mean', etc.

pensio, *m.* =**penco.**

pente, *f.* **1. avoir une p. dans le gosier**=**avoir le gosier en p. 2.** glisser **sur une mauvaise p.,** to go downhill.

pépé, *m.* grandpa.

pépée, *f.* **1.** (*child's word*) doll(y). **2.** prostitute*; **courir les pépées,** to go wenching. **3.** (*pej.*) girl*.

pépère, *m.* **1.** father*, daddy. **2.** grandfather. **3.** easy-going old codger (*or* buffer). **4.** *adj.* **p.**(**-maous**), cushy (*job*); easy-going (*person*); first-rate*; huge, whopping. **5.** *adv.* **jouer p.,** to play nicely; **rouler p.,** (*motor.*) to dodder along.

pépètes, pépettes, *f.pl.* money*.

pépie, *f.* **1. avoir la p.,** to be a thirsty

mortal; **to be fond of wetting one's whistle. 2. ne pas avoir la p.,** to talk* incessantly *or* volubly, not to be short of words.

pépin, *m.* **1.** umbrella*. **2.** hitch, snag, facer; **avoir un p.,** to have a spot of bother, to strike a snag. **3. avoir un** (*or* **le**) **p. pour qn,** to be infatuated* with s.o. **4. avoir avalé le p.,** to be pregnant*. **5.** (*av.*) parachute.

pépite, *f.* **ne pas avoir une p.,** to be penniless*.

péquenaud, péquenot, *m.* peasant*.

péquin, *m.* =**pékin.**

percale, *m.* tobacco, baccy.

percer. 1. to kill*. **2.** (*cycling*) to have a puncture. **3. va te faire p.!** go and get stuffed!

perche, *f.* **1. tendre la p. à qn,** to give s.o. a helping hand. **2. une grande p.,** a tall*, thin person.

percher, to live, to dwell, to hang out.

perchoir, *m.* **p. à moineaux,** butterfly bow.

percuté, *adj.* mad*.

perdre. 1. elle l'a perdu, she's lost her maidenhead. **2. ne pas en p. une,** to see everything, not to miss a thing.

perdreau, *m.* plain-clothes policeman*.

père, *m.* **1. le p. presseur,** the tax-collector. **2. l'avoir dans le p. fouettard,** to be diddled, to be taken in. **3. le p. frappart,** penis*. **4. repartir avec son p. frappart sous le bras,** to return empty-handed. *See also* **François** *and* **peinard.**

périmé, *m.* (*of person 50 to 60 years old*) back number.

péripatéticienne, *f.* prostitute*.

perle, *f.* **1.** (*of person*) jewel, gem, pearl, treasure. **2.** (*sch.*) howler, gem, peach. **3. passer son temps à enfiler des perles,** to idle one's time away. **4. lâcher la p.,** to die*. **5. lâcher une p.,** to let out a fart; **écraser une p.,** to fart silently.

perlot, *m.* tobacco, baccy, 'snout'.

perloter, (*of boxer*) to pack a punch.

perlouse, perlouze, *f.* **1.** pearl. **2.** fart.

perm(e), f. (mil.) leave, furlough; pass.
pernaga, perniflard, m. Pernod (apéritif).
Pérou, pr.n. ce n'est pas le P., (a) it's not exactly a fortune, it's not so very much (i.e. money); (b) it's nothing to write home about, it's not such a wonderful catch.
perpète, f. à p., for ever (and ever), world without end; être condamné à p., to get a life sentence, to get a lifer.
perquise, f. house search (by police).
perroquet, m. 1. counsel, barrister. 2. (mil.) sniper. 3. mixture of pastis and peppermint syrup; étrangler (or avaler) un p., to drink a glass of perroquet or absinthe.
perruque, f. 1. hair. 2. une vieille p., an old fog(e)y*. 3. faire de la p., to do sth. on the side.
persil, m. 1. faire son p., to get above oneself, to be cocky. 2. faire son (or aller au) p., (of prostitute) to solicit. 3. hairs under armpits and on pubis.
persilleuse, f. prostitute*.
pescal(e), m. = poiscal.
pèse, m. = pèze.
pésetas, pésettes, pésètes, f.pl. money*.
péseux, adj. rich*.
peste, f. (of person) plague, pest, nuisance; petite p., little horror, little demon.
pestouille, f. bad luck.
pet, m. 1. danger, peril, trouble; il n'y a pas de p., it's all serene; pas de p. que ..., there's no danger that ... 2. fart; lâcher (or faire) un p., to fart. 3. accomplice, 'crow' (confederate on the look-out); faire le p., to keep a lookout, to be on the watch, to keep nix. 4. p.! p.! look out! 5. avoir un p. de travers, to feel unwell*. 6. ça ne vaut pas un p. de lapin, it's absolutely worthless*. 7. faire du p., to kick up a row. 8. fleurer le p. à, to pick a quarrel* with. 9. porter le (or aller au) p., (a) to denounce*; (b) to lay a charge (against s.o.).
pétant, adj. (of time) = tapant.

Pétaouchnock, pr.n. imaginary faraway place.
pétarader, to be mad with anger*, to make the fur fly.
pétard, m. 1. row, uproar*; faire du p., to kick up a row; un coup de p., a rumpus. 2. = pet 1. 3. buttocks*; se manier (or se magner) le p., to hurry up, to get a move on. 4. fire arm, revolver*. 5. être en p., to be angry*; se mettre (or se filer or se foutre) en p., to get angry*; mettre qn en p., to make s.o. angry. 6. aller au p. = porter le pet (pet 9). 7. = pelot.
pétarder = faire du pétard (pétard 1).
pétarder, se, to quarrel; to fight, to scrap.
pétardier, adj., m. irascible (person); rowdy (person).
pétase, m. hat*.
pétasse, f. 1. fear, fright, funk; avoir la p., to be afraid*. 2. mess, fix, predicament. 3. buttocks*. 4. prostitute*.
pet-de-nonne, m. fritter, doughnut.
pète, m. = pétard 3.
pétée, f. tirer une p. = tirer un coup (coup 23); filer une p. = jouir.
pet-en-l'air, m. short jacket, bumfreezer.
péter. 1. to break wind, to fart. 2. to protest violently, to kick up a row. 3. ça va p. (sec)! things are going to hum! there's going to be a hell of a row (or of a stink or of a bust-up)! il faut que ça pète! things have got to hum! 4. envoyer p. qn, to send s.o. packing*. 5. arriver (or gagner) en pétant, to win* easily. 6. la p., to go hungry. See also cul 23, derrière 2, feu 3, flamme 2, mastic 4, soie.
pète-sec, m. martinet, sneezer.
péteur, m. 1. farter. 2. lout, oaf. 3. coward.
péteuse, f. motor-bike.
péteux, m. 1. coward, funk. 2. snob. 3. wretch, stinker.
pètezouille, m. = pedzouille.
petiot, adj. tiny, wee.
petit, m. 1. mon p., my pet, my darling*

(*masc. form can be used also in speaking to a woman*). 2. buttocks*. 3. s'en jeter un p. (blanc), to down a glass of white wine.

petite, *f.* 1. mettre en p., (*a*) to pilfer, to do a bit of shop-lifting; (*b*) to put (money) away (for a rainy day). 2. prendre une p., to be a drug addict, to be a junky, to have a 'fix'.

petit-nègre, *m.* parler p.-n., to talk pidgin French.

pétochard, *m.* coward*; *adj.* funky.

pétoche, *f.* fear, funk; avoir la p., to be afraid*; avoir une p. de tous les diables, to be in a hell of a funk.

pétoir, *m.*, **pétoire,** *f.* 1. =pétard 4. 2. =pétrolette. 3. child's pop-gun.

peton, *m.* (*child's word*) tiny foot, tootsie (*or* tootsy), tootsie-wootsie.

pétouille, *f.* 1. =pétoche. 2. =pétrin.

pétoulet, *m.* buttocks*; avoir le p. à zéro, to be in a blue funk.

pétouze, *f.*, **petzingue,** *m.* =pétard.

pétrin, *m.* être (se mettre) dans le p., to be (to get) in a nasty fix*; mettre qn dans le p., to put s.o. in the cart; un beau (*or* joli) p., a nice fix*.

pétrole, *m.* hard liquor, liquid fire, strong spirits*.

pétrolette, *f.* light motor-bike.

pétrousquin, *m.* 1. =pédzouille. 2. buttocks*. 3. civilian. 4. (*pej.*) fellow*, blighter.

pétrus, *m.* buttocks*.

pétun, *m.* tobacco, baccy.

pétuner, to smoke.

petzouillard, petzouille, *m.* =pedzouille.

peu, *adv.* 1. un p. (mon neveu)! (*R.S.*) not half! you bet! I should jolly well think so! 2. ah! non, très p. (pour moi *or* de ce genre)! not for me! not blooming likely! I'm not having any! 3. un p. beaucoup, far too much. 4. excusez du p.! is that all? how modest!

peur, *f.* 1. avoir une p. bleue, to be in a blue funk, to be scared stiff. 2. vous n'avez pas p.! you *have* got a nerve! you don't want much, do you?

peut-être, *adv.* j'en sais autant que

vous, p.-ê.! I know as much as you, I suppose!

pèze, *m.* money*. être au p., to be very rich*.

pfui! *int.* pooh! bah! phooey!

P.G. (*abbrev. for 'prisonnier de guerre'*), prisoner of war, P.O.W.

phalanges, *f.pl.* hands*.

phalangettes, *f.pl.* fingers.

phalzar, *m.* =falzar.

phare, *m.* piquer un p.=piquer un fard.

pharmaco, *m.* chemist.

pharo, *m.* (=*pharaon*) faro (*card game*).

phéno, *adj.* phenomenal.

phénomène, *m.* queer* fellow.

philo, *f.* (*sch.*) form preparing for the second part of the bachot.

phonard, *m.* 1. telephone. 2. telephonist.

phonarde, *f.* switchboard-girl, switch-board-operator.

phono, *m.* gramophone.

phoque, *m.* les avoir à la p.=les avoir à la retourne.

photographier: se faire p., to be spotted.

photo-stoppeur, *m.* street-photographer.

phrasicoter, to talk* volubly, to speechify.

phrasicoteur, *m.* speechifier, windbag, gasbag.

physionomiste, *m.* je ne suis pas (bon) p., I've no memory for faces.

piaf, *m.* 1. bird. 2. sparrow, spug, spuggy. 3. un drôle de p., a queer* person.

piaffer. 1. to swank*, to swagger. 2. to fidget.

piano, *m.* 1. p. à bretelles, p. des pauvres, accordeon. 2. passer au p., jouer du p., to have one's fingerprints (*or* one's dabs) taken. 3. vendre des pianos, to talk tommy rot.

piaule, *f.* room, house, diggings (*or* digs).

piauler, se, to go home, to turn in.

pic, à, *adv. phrase.* arriver (tomber) à p., to come (to happen) in the (very) nick of time (*or* just at the right time); **répondre à p.**, to answer pat.

picaillons, *m.pl.* **1.** small coins, coppers. **2.** money*; **avoir des p.**, to be rich*.

pichet, *m.* wine.

pichpin, *m.* **c'est du (vrai) p.**, it's very easy* work.

pichtegorne, pichtogorne, pichtogorme, *m.* ordinary red wine.

pick-up, *m.* **travailler du p.-u.**, to talk rot*.

picoler, to tipple*.

picoleur, *m.* tippler, boozer, elbowbender.

picolo, *m.* wine.

picoter, to tease.

picoterie, *f.* teasing, pin-pricks.

picotin, *m.* **pas un p.**, not a cent, not a bean.

picouse, *f.* = piquouse.

picrate, *m.* wine.

pictance, *f.* alcoholic drink, liquor.

pictancher, picter, to tipple*.

picton, *m.* ordinary red wine.

pictonner, to tipple*.

pie, *f.* **1.** (**voiture**) **p.**, police car, squad car (with radio transmitter), Z car. **2.** chatterbox*.

pièce, *f.* **1. cracher des pièces de dix sous**, to be very thirsty, not to be able to spit sixpence. **2. donner la p. à qn**, to give s.o. a gratuity (*or* a tip). **3. jouer une p. à qn, faire p. à qn**, to take a rise out of s.o. **4. mettre en pièces détachées**, to smash to smithereens, to spifflicate. **5. p. de dix ronds**, buttocks*; **avoir perdu sa p. de dix ronds**, to be a pederast*. **6. p. humide**, syringe; **artilleur de la p. humide**, male nurse.

pied, *m.* **1.** fool*. **2. avoir** (*or* **toucher**) **son p.** = **toucher son fade; aller au p.** = **aller au fade. 3. avoir les pieds chauds**, to be well-off, to be in clover. **4. avoir les pieds nickelés**, to sit tight, to refuse to budge (*or* to work). **5. avoir les pieds en dentelle** = **avoir les pieds nickelés. 6. avoir les pieds dans les reins** (*or* **dans le dos**), to have the police on one's track. **7. ça lui fera les pieds!** that will serve him right! that will teach him a good lesson! that'll 'larn' him! **8. casser les pieds à qn**, to bore* s.o. **9. c'est bien fait pour ton p.!** it serves you right. **10. en avoir p. de . . .**, **en avoir son p.**, to be fed up with it. **11. être bête comme ses pieds**, to be very stupid*, to be a perfect ass, to be thick. **12. faire un p. de nez à qn**, to thumb one's nose at s.o., to make a long nose at s.o., to pull bacon at s.o., to cut (*or* to cock) a snook at s.o. **13. faire du p. à qn**, to play footsie (*or* footsie-wootsie *or* footums *or* footy-footy *or* tootsy-footsy) with s.o. *Cf.* **faire du genou. 14. faire le p. de grue**, to kick (*or* to cool) one's heels, to dance attendance, to be kept waiting (about). **15. jouer comme un p.**, to play very badly; **il joue comme un p.**, he can't play for nuts (*or* for toffee *or* for toffee-apples); **conduire comme un p.**, to be a hopeless driver. **16. il y a du p. (dans la chaussette)!** we'll manage it! we'll get by! we've tons of time! **17. jouer un p. de cochon à qn**, to play a dirty trick on s.o., to let s.o. down. **18. lever le p.**, to decamp*, to abscond, to bolt; **un financier qui lève le p.**, a fly-by-night. **19. mettre qn à p.**, to dismiss* s.o. **20. mettre les pieds dans le plat**, to put one's foot in it, to drop a brick. **21. ne pas se donner des coups de p.**, to blow one's own trumpet, to give oneself a pat on the back. **22. ne pas savoir sur quel p. danser**, not to know what to do, not to know which way to turn, to be in a quandary, to be flummoxed. **23. ne pas se moucher du p.**, to do things in great style, to do oneself well, to cut a dash. **24. prendre son p.**, (*a*) = **tirer un coup** (coup 23); (*b*) = **jouir. 25. se laver (aller se laver) les pieds**, to be sentenced to hard labour, to get a stiff sentence. **26. se lever du p. gauche**, to get out of bed on the wrong side; **partir du p. gauche**, to start off on the wrong foot.

27. **se tirer des pieds,** (*a*) to decamp*; (*b*) to get out of a scrape. 28. **sortir** (*or* **s'en aller**) **les pieds devant** (*or* **en avant**), to die*, to go off feet foremost. 29. **p. de biche,** (*of burglar*) jemmy; **faire le p. de biche,** to canvass from house to house; **tirer le p. de biche,** to beg from house to house. 30. **p. de banc,** (*mil.*) sergeant. 31. **p.-de-figuier**=arbicot. 32. **p.-noir,** Algerian-born French person. 33. **coup de p. de Vénus,** dose of venereal disease. 34. kick, thrill (after drugs); **j'ai pris le p.,** it was a gas.

piège, *m.* 1. beard. 2. bookmaker, bookie. 3. (*long-distance drivers' slang*) motor lorry. 4. prison*. 5. **p. à poux,** comb.

piéger, to be a bookmaker, to take bets.

pie-grièche, *f.* (*of woman*) shrew.

Pierre, *pr.n.* **P. et Paul** (*or* **P., Paul et Jacques**), Tom, Dick, and Harry.

pierre, *f.* 1. **c'est une p. dans mon jardin,** that's a sly dig at me, that's one for me. 2. **jeter la p. à qn,** to accuse s.o., to blame s.o. 3. **malheureux comme les pierres,** (*a*) as unhappy as can be; (*b*) utterly penniless*. 4. **p. de taille,** miser*. 5. *pl.* jewels, sparklers, 'rocks'.

pierreuse, *f.* common prostitute*, street-walker.

pierrot, *m.* 1. =piaf 2. 2. country-bumpkin. 3. **un drôle de p.,** a queer* fellow. 4. **étrangler un p.,** to drink a glass of white wine.

piétaille, *f.* infantry, foot-sloggers.

piétard, *m.* pedestrian.

piéton, *m.* traffic cop.

pieu, *m.* 1. bed*; **se mettre au p.**=se pieuter. 2. bottle of red wine.

pieuter, to sleep*.

pieuter, se, to go to bed*.

pif, *m.* 1. nose*. 2. **avoir qn dans le p.**=avoir qn dans le nez. 3. **se manger le p.**=se manger le nez. 4. **avoir** (*or* **en avoir**) **un coup dans le p., avoir un coup de p.**=avoir un coup dans le nez (nez 4). 5. **cela lui pend au p.**=cela lui pend au nez. 6. **se casser le p.**=se casser le nez.

piffard, *m.* 1. =pif. 2. man with a big nose.

piffeur, *m.* man with a flair for nosing out things.

piffer: ne (pas) pouvoir p. qn=ne (pas) pouvoir blairer qn.

pif(f)omètre, *m.* **au p.,** at a rough estimate, at a rough guess.

piffrer, se, to eat* greedily.

pige, *f.* 1. year (*of age, of prison sentence*). 2. **faire la p. à qn,** to go one better than s.o., to leave s.o. standing, to lick s.o. 3. freelance journalism; **être payé à la p.,** to be a penny-a-liner.

pigeon, *m.* 1. dupe, gull, sucker; **plumer un p.,** to gull s.o., to pluck a pigeon. 2. **il fait un croquis comme un p. avec sa queue!** he can't draw for nuts!

pigeonner, to gull, to victimize, to take in.

piger. 1. to steal*. 2. to understand*; **il n'a pas pigé,** it hasn't registered with him, he hasn't got it, he's fogged, he's off the beam, he hasn't a clue; **je n'ai rien pigé,** I couldn't make head or tail of it; **il a pigé,** the penny's dropped; **avez-vous pigé? compree?** get me? get the drift? **p. rapidement,** to be quick on the uptake. 3. to catch, to cop (s.o., a cold, a prison sentence); **se faire p.,** to spot (the winner of a race); to get nabbed. 4. to look at*.

pigette, *f.* =pige 1.

pigiste, *m.* freelance journalist.

pignocher, to pick (*or* to nibble) (at one's food).

pignocher, se, to come to blows, to have a scrap.

pignole, *f.* masturbation.

pignoter, to pinch and scrape.

pignouf, *m.* 1. blackguard*, cad, bounder. 2. miser*.

pilant, *adj.* very funny*.

pile, *f.* 1. thrashing*; **donner (flanquer, foutre) une** (*or* **la**) **p. à qn,** (*a*) to thrash* s.o.; (*b*) to get the better of s.o., to beat* s.o., to lick s.o. 2. one hundred francs.

pile, *adv.* in the very nick of time, bang on time; **s'arrêter p.,** to stop dead, to stop short, to come to a dead stop; **arriver p.,** to arrive on the dot; **vous tombez p.,** you've come just at the right moment; **à six heures p.,** on the dot of six.

piler. 1. to toil away, to slog. **2.** (*cycling*) **p. une montée,** to toil up a hill. **3. la p.,** to be famished. **4. en p.,** to have a bad time of it. **5. être à p.,** to be objectionable. *See also* **poivre.**

piloches, *f.pl.* teeth*, ivories, grinders.

piloirs, *m.pl.* fingers.

pilon, *m.* **1.** beggar. **2.** thumb.

pilonner. 1. to shell, to bomb, to prang. **2.** to work* hard. **3.** to beg.

pilule, *f.* **1.** failure*. **2. prendre la p.,** to come a cropper (*fig.*). **3.** thrashing*. **4. dorer la p.,** to gild the pill.

piment, *m.* nose*.

pinard, *m.* wine.

pinarium, *m.* brothel*.

pince, *f.* **1.** hand*; **serrer la p. à qn,** to shake s.o.'s hand; **serre-moi la p.!** tip us your fin (*or* your flipper)! **2.** foot*; **à pince(s),** on foot; **se taper la route à pinces,** to foot (*or* to hoof) it, to pad the hoof. **3.** jemmy. **4.** (*of man*) **être (un) chaud de la p.,** (*of woman*) **être chaude de la p.,** to be hot stuff (sexually). **5. gare la p.!** mind you're not nabbed! **6.** *int.* **bonne p.!** well done! **7. pinces d'Adam,** fingers. **8.** *pl.* handcuffs*.

pinceau, *m.* **1.** foot, leg*; **affûter des pinceaux,** to walk. **2. se laver les pinceaux=se laver les pieds. 3. s'emmêler les pinceaux,** to be in a muddle. **4.** penis*. **5.** sweeping-brush, broom.

pince-cul, pince-fesses, *m.* low-class dance-hall.

pincer. 1. to arrest*; **se faire p.,** to get nabbed. **2.** to catch (a cold). **3. en p. pour, être pincé pour,** to be infatuated* with.

pincettes, *f.pl.* **1. il n'est pas à prendre avec des p.,** (*a*) he's like a bear with a

sore head; (*b*) I wouldn't touch him with (the end of) a barge-pole (*or* with a pair of tongs). **2. tricoter des p., se tirer les p.,** to decamp*. **3. embrasser qn à p.,** to kiss s.o. and pinch his (*or* her) cheeks at the same time.

pine, *f.* penis*.

piné, *adj.* first-rate*.

piner, to have coition*.

pingler, =épingler.

pingots, *m.pl.* feet*.

pingouins, *m.pl.* **1.** feet*. **2.** =espingo(uin)s.

pingre, *adj.* miserly*; *m.* miser*.

pingrerie, *f.* miserliness, stinginess.

pinoche, *adj.* first-rate*.

pinocher=pignocher.

pinte, *f.* **se payer** (*or* **se faire** *or* **s'offrir**) **une p. de bon sang,** to have a good laugh, to have a high old time.

pinter, to tipple*.

pinter, se, to get drunk*.

piochage, *m.* swotting.

pioche, *f.* **1.** hard work, slogging. **2. tête de p.,** pig-headed person.

piocher, to study* hard (at).

piocheur, *m.* hard worker, swot(ter), sap, plugger.

piocre, *m.* louse.

piole, *f.* =piaule.

pion, *m.* **1. pas un p.,** not a cent, not a bean; **pas un p. de . . .,** not a ha'porth of . . . **2.** (*pej.*) assistant-master.

pion, *adj.* drunk*.

pioncer, to sleep*; **p. un bon coup,** to have a good snooze.

pionceur, *m.* sleeper, snoozer.

pionnard, *m.* boozer.

pionnarder, se, to get drunk*.

pionne, *f.* assistant-mistress in school.

pionner, se, to get drunk*.

pionneur, *m.* (*sch.*) tell-tale, sneak.

pioteur, *m.* rag-picker.

pioupiou, *m.* soldier, private.

pipard, *m.* pipe smoker.

pipe, *f.* **1.** cigarette*. **2. casser sa p.,** to die*. **3. se fendre la p.,** to laugh* uproariously. **4. prendre la p., remporter une p.,** to come to grief, to come a cropper (*fig.*). **5. tailler** (*or* faire) **une p. (à qn)=tailler une plume.** See also **tête de p.**

pipé, adj. **cartes pipées,** marked cards; **dés pipés,** cogged dice.

pipelet, pipelette, m.f. 1. concierge, janitor. 2. nosey and gossipy person.

piper. 1. to arrest*; **se faire p.,** to get nabbed. 2. =blairer. 3. to be a pipesmoker. 4. **ne pas p., ne p. mot,** not to utter a word, to keep mum, to take it lying down.

pipette, f. 1. cigarette*. 2. **ne pas valoir p.=ne pas valoir chipette.** 3. **vol à la p.,** (motor.) stealing petrol by siphoning it off.

pipeur, m. cheat, swindler*.

pipi, m. 1. **faire p., faire un** (or **son**) **petit p.,** to urinate*. 2. **c'est comme si je faisais p. dans un violon=c'est comme si je chantais** (chanter 2). 3. **c'est du p. de chat,** it's absolute rubbish (or tripe).

Pipo, f. the École polytechnique in Paris; m. student at the École polytechnique.

piqué, adj. mad*. See also **hanneton** and **ver.**

pique-gâteau, pique-gaufrette, m. nose*.

pique-lard, m. flick knife.

pique-pouces, pique-prunes, m. tailor.

piquer. 1. to arrest*; **se faire p.,** to get nabbed. 2. to steal*. 3. to give an injection to. 4. **faire p. son chien,** to have one's dog put away, put down. 5. to knife. N.B. This verb is used with various nouns with the force of to get, to have, to take—e.g. **p. un seize sur vingt,** (sch.) to get (a mark of) sixteen out of twenty. Such uses of 'piquer' will be found listed under the noun.

piquer, se, to be a drug-addict, to be a junkie, a dosser. See also **nez 13.**

piqueton, m., **piquette,** f. =**picton.**

piqueur, m. 1. pickpocket; thief. 2. **p. de troncs,** one who steals from a poor-box (in church).

piquouse, piquouze, f. narcotic injection, hypo, 'shot', jab.

piquouser=piquer 3.

piscine, f. **en pleine p.,** in a fearful mess.

pissant, adj. very funny*.

pisse, f. piss.

pisse-copie, m. (pej.) penny-a-liner.

pisse-froid, m. (of person) cold fish.

pissement, m. pissing.

pissenlit, m. **manger des** (or **les**) **pissenlits** (or **bouffer du p.**) **par la racine,** to be dead and buried, to be pushing up the daisies.

pisser. 1. (aller) **p.,** to urinate*. 2. **envoyer p. qn,** to send s.o. packing*, to tell s.o. to piss off. 3. **faire p. qn,** to make s.o. laugh fit to split, to make s.o. piss (or pee) himself laughing. 4. **ne se sentir plus p.,** to feel like a million. 5. **en faire p. à qn,** to put s.o. through it, to give s.o. beans. 6. **c'est comme si je pissais dans un violon= c'est comme si je chantais** (chanter 2). 7. **p. de l'œil,** to weep*. 8. **p. entre parenthèses,** to have bandy legs. See also **côtelette 1, cul 19, lame 2, môme 4, sang 8.**

pisser, se, to laugh fit to split, to piss (or to pee) oneself laughing.

pisseuse, f. 1. (pej.) brat. 2. prostitute*, slut.

pisseux, m. (of person) dirty dog.

pissoir(e), m., **pissotière, pissotoire,** f. urinal, pisshouse.

pistache, f. **avoir sa p.,** to be dead drunk*; **prendre une p.,** to get drunk*.

pistard, m. (cycle racing) track-racer.

pister, se, to decamp*, to make tracks.

pisteur, m. tout (for hotels, nightclubs, etc.).

pistoche, f. (sch.) swimming-pool, the baths.

pistolache, m. revolver*.

pistole, f. cell (in prison).

pistolet, m. 1. **un drôle de pistolet,** an odd, queer* person. 2. bed-urinal.

piston, m. 1. backstairs influence, pull, string-pulling, wire-pulling, backing; **un coup de p.,** backstairs influence; **avoir du p.=être pistonné.** 2. candidate for (or student of) the École centrale. 3. =**capiston.**

pistonnage, *m.* =piston 1.
pistonner, to use one's influence for, to push, to back, to pull strings for; se faire p., être pistonné, to have friends at court, to get s.o. to pull the wires (*or* the strings) on one's behalf, to get s.o. to use his influence (*or* his pull) on one's behalf, to be given a lift.
pistonneur, *m.* backer, friend at court.
pitaine, *m.* (*mil.*) captain, cap'n.
pitancher, to drink*.
pi(t)choun, *adj.* tiny, wee.
piton, *m.* (big) nose*.
pitou, *m.* soldier, private, raw recruit.
pivase, *m.* nose*.
pive(ton), pivois, *m.* wine.
pivoine, *f.* piquer sa p., to blush.
pivoiner=piquer sa pivoine.
pivoter : faire p. qn, to boss s.o. about.
pivots, *m.pl.* legs*.
pivre, *m.* =pive(ton).
P.J. (*abbrev.*) la P.J., la Police Judiciaire (*approx.*) Criminal Investigation Department, C.I.D.
placard, *m.* prison*; cell (in prison).
placarde, *f.* 1. public square. 2. job, situation. 3. une bonne p., (*of street hawker*) a good pitch. 4. louer des placardes, to book seats.
placarder, to place; to find a job for.
placarder, se, to get a job, to get a situation, to go into service.
placardier, *m.* =inter 1.
place, *f.* 1. p. d'armes, stomach*. 2. c'était à payer sa p., I wouldn't have missed it for a fortune.
placeur, *m.* =inter 1.
plafond, *m.* 1. head*. 2. être bas de p., to be stupid, to be thick, to be lowbrow. 3. sauter au p., (*a*) to jump for joy; (*b*) to flare up, to blow one's top, to hit the roof.
plafonnard, *m.* =plafond 1.
plaga, à, *adv.* =à plat.
plaie, *f.* (*of person*) pest, plague.
plan, *m.* (i) laisser en p., (*a*) to leave (s.o.) in the lurch, to give (s.o.) the slip, to walk out on (s.o.), to ditch (s.o.); (*b*) to leave (sth.) unfinished;

rester en p., to be left in the lurch, to be left stranded, to be left out in the cold, to be ditched.
plan, *m.* (ii) il n'y a pas p.! y a pas p.! there's nothing doing! it's no go! no sale! no soap!
plan, *m.* (iii) metal tube containing precious objects hidden in the anus.
planche, *f.* 1. (*sch.*) blackboard; passer à la p., to go up to the blackboard (to do a sum, etc.). 2. monter sur les planches, to go on the stage, to tread the boards; brûler les planches, to act with fire; balayer les planches, to act in the curtain-raiser. 3. il y a du travail sur la p., there's plenty of work to be done, there's lots to do. *Cf.* pain 2. 4. une vraie p. à pain, (*of woman*) a flat-breasted woman, a woman as flat as a board. 5. s'habiller de quatre planches, être entre quatre planches, to die*, to be dead.
plancher, *m.* 1. le p. des vaches, terra firma, dry land. 2. débarrassez(-moi) (*or* videz(-moi)) le p.! hop*it! clear out!
plancher, (*sch.*) to be sent to the blackboard; faire p. un élève, to send a pupil to the blackboard.
planer, to buzz (*i.e. have feeling of exhilaration after drugs*).
planète, *f.* écraser la p., (*av.*) to crash.
planque, *f.* 1. place, spot. 2. hiding-place, hide-out, stash, plant; funkhole. 3. soft (*or* cushy) job, safe berth. 4. savings, pile, nest-egg. 5. en p., under observation by the police.
planqué, *m.* =embusqué.
planquer. 1. to hide. 2. =garer. 3. to plant (*stolen goods*). 4. to place, to put, to stick, to shove. 5. avoir envie de tout p. = avoir envie de tout plaquer.
planquer, se. 1. to hide (oneself), to go into hiding, to go to ground. 2. to park oneself. 3. to get a cushy job.
planquouse, *f.* =planque 2.
planquouser, (se) = (se) planquer.
planter. 1. =planquer 4. 2. to knife, to kill*. 3. to have coition* with (a woman). 4. p. qn là, to leave s.o. flat, to let s.o. down, to jilt s.o., to give

s.o. the chuck (*or* the mitten); to give s.o. the slip. **5.** to default and disappear.

plaquage, *m.* throwing over, jilting, chucking.

plaqué, *m.* de p., faked, false, sham.

plaquer. 1. to jilt, to give the chuck to, to walk out on, to get rid of, to ditch, to leave in the lurch; **avoir envie de tout p.,** to feel like chucking everything up. **2.** to give up, to chuck up (*or* to throw up) the sponge.

plaquouser=plaquer.

plastron, *m.* chest (*of human body*).

plastronner, to show off.

plat, *m.* **1.** faire du p. à, (*a*) to flatter*; (*b*) to make up to, to try to get off with, to sweeten (s.o.) up, to make advances to, to spin (s.o.) the yarn, to tell (s.o.) the tale, to sweet-talk (s.o.). **2. en faire (tout) un p.,** to kick up a fuss about sth., to make a great song about it, to make a song (and dance) about it, to pile on the agony; **ne pas faire un p. de,** to make no bones about. **3. il en fait un p.** (*or* **un de ces plats)!** it's broiling hot! it's a regular scorcher! **4. prendre un p.,** (*in diving*) to come a belly-flopper. **5. envoyer du p. à,** to tip s.o. the wink. **6. repiquer au p.,** to have a second helping. **7. p. de nouilles**=nouille. **8.** *pl.* faked dice.

plat, à, *adv. phrase.* **1. être complètement à p.,** to be completely run down, to feel quite washed out. **2. mettre qn à p.,** (*e.g. of illness*) to take it out of s.o. **3. mettre à p.,** (*of money*) to save, to put by, to stash it away.

plateaux, *m.pl.* loaded dice.

plate-bande, *f.* **1. marcher sur** (*or* **piétiner) les plates-bandes de qn,** to poach on s.o.'s preserves, to poke one's nose into s.o.'s business. **2. marcher** (*or* **piétiner) sur les plates-bandes,** to exaggerate*.

platée, *f.* dishful (of food).

platine, *f.* **avoir une p.,** to talk* volubly; **quelle p.!** what a gas-bag (*or* wind-bag)!

plato, *m.* platonic love.

plâtre, *m.* money*; être (plein) au p., to be rich*.

plâtrer, se, (*of woman*) se p. (le visage), to paint one's face, to make up.

plat-ventre, *m.* **1.** belly-flop. **2.** =billet de parterre.

plein, *adj.* **1.** drunk*; p. comme un boudin (*or* une bourrique *or* un fût *or* une huître *or* un œuf), dead drunk*. **2.** rich*. *See* as **7. 3.** faire le p., faire son p. d'essence, to fill up (*with petrol*). **4.** faire le p., to eat, to stoke up, to coal up.

plein, *adv.* **tout p.,** very much, a lot; être gentil(le) tout p., être tout p. gentil(le), to be awfully nice (*or* pretty), to be as nice as can be, to be ever so nice.

pleurer: je veux ça ou je pleure! give it me or I'll scream! *See also* **vache 7, veau 6.**

pleuvoir. 1. il pleut tant qu'il peut, it's chucking it down. **2.** il pleut! (*a*) not likely! not on your life! not on your Nellie! (*b*) =vingt-deux!

pleuvoter, to drizzle.

pli, *m.* **1.** ça ne fait pas un p., it's a certainty*. **2.** cela ne fera pas un p., it'll be all plain sailing. **3.** mettre au p. = mettre au pas.

plié, *p.p.* p. en deux, doubled up with laughter, in tucks.

plomb, *m.* **1.** ça te mettra du p. dans la tête, that will steady you down a bit! **2.** avoir du p. dans l'aile, (*a*) to be ill; (*b*) to be on the way out, in difficulties.

plombard, *m.* plumber.

plombe, *f.* hour; à cinq plombes pile! on the dot of five!

plombé, *adj.* infected with syphilis.

plomber. 1. to infect with syphilis, to give (s.o.) a dose; se faire p., to cop a dose. **2.** to fill (s.o.) with lead. **3.** to stink*; p. du goulot, to have a foul breath.

plonge, *f.* dish-washing, washing-up; faire la p., être à la p., to be a washer-up.

plongeur, *m.* dish-washer, washer-up (*jest.*) 'washer-upper'.

plouc, plouk, plouque, *m.* 1. peasant*. 2. simpleton*, mug, pie-can.

ploum, *m.* 1. =Auverploum. 2. =plouc. 1.

pluches, *f.pl.* (*mil.*) cook-house fatigue, spud-bashing.

pluie, *f.* 1. il n'est pas né (*or* tombé) de la dernière p., he wasn't born yester-day, there are no flies on him. *Cf.* hier. 2. en mettre un à l'abri de la p., to down a drink, to put one down the hatch.

plumard, *m.* bed*; aller (rappliquer) au p., se fourrer au p., to go to bed*.

plumarder, se=aller au plumard.

plume, *f.* 1. jemmy. 2. passer à la p.,to get a thrashing*; passer qn à la p., to thrash* s.o. 3. tailler une p., to gamaroosh (*or* gamaruche). 4. voler dans les plumes à qn, to attack* s.o. 5. y laisser des plumes, to lose one's money (at gambling, in some under-taking), to lose a packet; to be fleeced; not to get off scot-free. 6. *pl.* hair, 'wool'; perdre ses plumes, to lose one's thatch.

plume, *m.* =plumard.

Plumeau, *pr.n.* va chez P.! go to blazes*!

plumer, to fleece* (s.o.), to trim (s.o.), to clean (s.o.) out; se faire p., to get cleaned out.

plumer, se=aller au plumard.

plumet, *m.* avoir (*or* tenir) son p., to be slightly drunk*.

P.L.V. (=*pour la vie*), for ever.

P.M.U., (*abbrev.*) le P.M.U. (=*le pari mutuel*), the totalizator, the tote.

pneu, *m.* 1. tyre. 2. =petit bleu (bleu, *m.* 4(*b*)).

pochard, *m.* drunkard*.

pocharder, se, to tipple*, to get drunk.

pochardise, *f.* boozing.

poche, *f.* 1. c'est dans la p., it's a certainty*. 2. connaître comme (le fond de) sa p., to know through and through, to know like the palm (*or* the back) of one's hand, to be able to read (s.o.) like a book. 3. faire les poches à qn, to go through s.o.'s

pockets. 4. mettez cela (*or* ça) dans votre p. et votre mouchoir dessus (*or* par-dessus)! put that in your pipe and smoke it! 5. en être (largement) de sa p., to be (well) out of pocket by it. 6. j'y ai été de ma p.! I had to fork out (*or* stump up)! 7. mettre qn dans sa p., to be more than a match for s.o., to wipe the floor with s.o., to make mincemeat of s.o. 8. tousser des deux poches, to fire (revolvers) from both holsters. *See also* fouiller, se, 2, langue 6, yeux 11.

poché, *adj.* un œil p.=un œil au beurre noir (œil 5).

pocher: p. (l'œil à) qn, to give s.o. a black eye*.

poche-revolver, *f.* hip-pocket.

pochetée, *f.* 1. fool*. 2. en avoir (*or* en tenir) une p.=en avoir une couche.

pochon, *m.* black eye*.

poème, *m.* c'est un p.! it's a beauty! it's simply priceless!

pogne, *f.* 1. hand*. 2. grip; à ma p., in my power; homme à p., strong (*or* masterful) man, muscle man. 3. prendre la p., to take the initiative. 4. avoir les pognes retournées=avoir les bras retournés (bras 1). 5. passe la p.! let's shake (hands) and make peace! 6. se faire une p., (*a*) to crow over (s.o.'s downfall); (*b*) to mastur-bate*. 7. =pognon.

pogner, se, to masturbate*.

pognon, *m.* money*; être au p., to be rich*.

poids, *m.* 1. avoir du p., (*a*) to be getting on in years; (*b*) to be a man of weight, of influence (*or* of importance). 2. prendre du p., to age, to grow old. 3. avoir deux p. et deux mesures, to have two standards (*or* two laws). 4. il ne fait pas le p., he isn't up to the job.

poigne, *m.* =pogne.

poignet, *m.* 1. ne pas se fouler le p.= ne pas se fouler la rate. 2. se casser les poignets (*or* le p.) sur qch., to steal* sth.

poil, *m.* 1. à p., stark naked*; se mettre (se foutre) à p., to strip (to the

skin) (*or* to the buff). 2. **au p.**! super!
wizard! bang on! on the nose! on the
button! smashing! a rave! 3. **avoir un**
(**fameux**) **p.** (dans la main), to have
no liking for work, to be work-shy, to
have a bone in one's leg. 4. **avoir du p.**
(**aux yeux** *or* **au cul**), to be plucky, to
have spunk. 5. **chercher des poils sur**
l'œuf, to split hairs. 6. **de tout p.,** of
every shade and hue, of all sorts and
conditions. 7. **être de mauvais p.,** to
be in a bad (*or* ugly) mood*; **être de**
bon p., to be in a good mood. 8. **faire**
le p. à qn, to best s.o., to lick s.o. 9. **p.**
de carotte, p. de brique, redhead,
carrots, carrot-top, copper-nob, copper-top, ginger, rusty, Rufus. 10.
reprendre du p. (de la bête), to pick up
(after serious illness or set-back), to
be one's own self again; not to lose
heart, to have another go (*or* try).
11. **tomber sur le p. à qn, dresser le p.**
à qn, ficher (**flanquer, foutre**) **un p. à**
qn, to give s.o. a thrashing, to 'go' for
s.o., to give s.o. beans. 12. **un homme**
(**un bougre**) **à poil(s),** an energetic
man, a man full of go. 13. **ça ne tient**
qu'à un p., it hangs by a hair. 14. **j'ai**
eu mon train, mais au p.! I caught my
train, but only just! 15. **p. au nez,**
pointless rhyming c.p. to conclude
any remark which ends with a similar
sound—*e.g.* **et en fin de compte je n'ai**
pas dîné,—p. au nez.
poilant, *adj.* very funny*.
poiler, se, to laugh* uproariously, to
enjoy oneself no end.
poil-poil, *adv.* **en douce p.-p.:** *see*
douce 3.
poilpuche, à, *adv. phrase* =à poil 1.
poilu, *m.* 1. French soldier (*of W.W.I*).
2. he-man.
poing, *m.* **dormir à poings fermés,** to
sleep like a log (*or* like a top).
point, *m.* 1. franc. 2. **un p., c'est tout!**
and that's that! and that's all there
is to it! and there's an end of it!
period! 3. **p. noir,** anus*. 4. **être mal**
en p., to be in a bad way.
point-de-côté, *m.* creditor.

pointe, *f.* 1. knife. 2. **avoir sa p.,**
to be slightly drunk*. 3. **être chaud**
(*or* **dur**) **de la p.**=être chaud de la
pince.
pointé, *adj.* arrested, detained,
rounded-up (by the police).
pointer=planter 3.
pointer, se, to appear on the scene,
to pop up, to show up.
pointeur, *m.* great womanizer, hot-
pants.
poire, *f.* 1. head*; **se payer la p. de**
qn=se payer la tête de qn. 2. face*;
sucer la p. à qn, to kiss s.o.; **une**
pêche en pleine p., one (*i.e. a blow*)
right in the kisser. 3. gull, mug,
sucker, easy mark; **l'impôt des**
poires, the mugs' tax (*i.e. income-tax*).
4. **couper la p. en deux,** to split the
difference. 5. **faire sa p.** (**anglaise**), to
put on side, to give oneself airs. 6.
garder une p. pour la soif, to put sth.
away for a rainy day. 7. **la p.** est
mûre, the opportunity is ripe to be
seized. 8. **ma p.**=ma pomme. 9. *adj.*
être p., to be a mug.
poireau, *m.* 1. =poire 3. 2. penis*;
faire glouglouter le p., to masturbate.
3. **le P.,** decoration (*le Mérite agricole*)
awarded to farmers, etc. 4. **faire le**
p.=poireauter.
poireauter, to be kept waiting, to
kick (*or* to cool) one's heels, to hang
about, to be kept hanging about; **faire**
(*or* **laisser**) **p. qn,** to keep s.o. waiting
(*or* hanging about).
poirer, to catch, to lay hold of; **se faire**
p., to get nabbed.
poiscaille, poiscal, *m.* 1. fish. 2.
pimp.
poison, *m.f.* (*of person*) pest; *m.* (*of*
thing) damn nuisance.
poissant, *adj.* 1. bothersome. 2. bring-
ing bad luck.
poissard, *m.* unlucky guy.
poissarde, *f.* fish-wife.
poisse, *f.* 1. bad (*or* tough) luck; **avoir**
la p., to have tough luck; **porter (la)**
p. à qn, to bring s.o. bad luck; 2. **être**
dans la p., to be in a fix*. 3. bore*, fag;

quelle p.! what a bind! 4. (*of person*) =
crampon.
poisse, *m.* 1. pimp. 2. hooligan, layabout, corner-boy.
poisser. 1. to steal*. 2. to arrest*; être
poissé, se faire p., to get nabbed. 3. to
bore* (s.o.) to death. 4. poissez-en
d'autres (*or* un autre), moi je ne
marche pas! tell that tale to s.o.
else!
poisson, *m.* 1. pimp. 2. attraper
(engueuler, enguirlander) qn comme
du p. pourri (*or* comme du p. pas
frais), to give s.o. a first-class bawling
out. 3. changer son p. (d'eau), to
urinate*. 4. donner à manger aux
poissons, to be sea-sick, to feed the
fishes. 5. faire des yeux de p. frit =
faire des yeux de merlan frit. 6. noyer
le p., to practise obstruction, deliber-
ately to confuse the issue, to employ
delaying tactics.
poisson-lune, *m.* avoir une figure de
p.-l., to be moon-faced.
poitringle, *adj.* = tubard (ii) *adj.*
poivrade, *f.* en avoir une p., to be
drunk*.
poivre, *m.* 1. jeter (*or* chier) du p., to
decamp*. 2. piler du p., to talk
maliciously of s.o., to backbite s.o.
poivré, *adj.* 1. drunk*. 2. = plombé.
poivrer. 1. to make drunk*. 2.
= plomber 1.
poivrer, se. 1. se p. (la gueule), to get
drunk*. 2. se faire p., (*a*) to get
drunk*; (*b*) = se faire plomber
(plomber 1).
poivrier, *m.* thief who robs drunken
men.
poivrot, *m.* drunkard*.
Pola(c)k, *m.* Pole.
polar, *m. and adj.* swot, 'gnome'.
polard, *m.* penis*.
poli, *adj. See* fesse 5.
Police, *f.* 1. Équipe Police Secours, riot
squad. 2. faire ses polices, (*of registered
prostitute*) to report weekly.
polichinelle, *m.* 1. avoir un p. dans le
tiroir, to be pregnant*. 2. mener une
vie de p., to go the pace, to lead a

loose life. 3. un secret de p., an open
secret, everybody's secret.
politesse, *f.* faire une p. à, to pleasure
(a woman).
polka, *f.* 1. woman*. 2. pimp's woman.
3. buttocks*.
polker, to stink.
polochon, *m.* 1. bolster. 2. une partie
(*or* un coup) de p., a nap, a snooze.
pol(l)op(e)! *int.* look out! watch out!
careful!
pomaquer, to lose.
pommade, *f.* 1. flattery*; passer (de)
la p. (dans les cheveux) à qn, to
flatter* s.o.; couper dans la p., to fall
for flattery. 2. être dans la p., to be
in a fix*.
pommadin, *m.* 1. dandy, toff. 2.
barber.
pomme, *f.* 1. head*. 2. face*; sucer la
p. à qn, to kiss s.o. 3. simpleton*, mug,
sucker. 4. aux pommes = aux petits
oignons. 5. des pommes! = des clous!
(clou 7). 6. haut comme trois pommes,
(*usually of child*) a little mite, a little
nipper, about as high as three
pennyworth of coppers, (*Amer. sl.*)
knee-high to a mosquito. 7. ma p., I,
me, myself, this child. (*Similarly* ta
p., sa p., votre p., nos pommes, vos
pommes, leurs pommes). 8. pour des
pommes = pour des prunes. 9. pour
nous (etc.) les pommes sont cuites,
we've (etc.) 'had' it. 10. recevoir des
pommes cuites, (*of actor*) to get the
bird. 11. tomber dans les pommes, to
faint*. 12. c'est aux pommes! it looks
good! 13. *adj.* simple, silly, green.
pommé, *adj.* = aux petits oignons.
pompard, pomplard, *m.* fireman.
pompe, *f.* 1. boot*, shoe. un coup de p.,
a kick. 2. à toute(s) pompe(s), at full
speed, pretty damn quick. 3. avoir
(reçu) le (*or* un) coup de p. = être
pompé. 4. balancer (*or* filer) un coup
de p. à qn, to borrow (money) from
s.o. 5. marcher à côté de ses pompes,
to be (down) on one's uppers.
pompé, *adj.* exhausted*.
pompelard, *m.* fireman, fire-bobby.

pomper. I. to borrow (money), to tap (s.o. for money). 2. to exhaust* (s.o.). 3. to drink*. 4. to tipple*; **p. dur,** to be a soak. 5. (*sch.*) to swot, to grind.

pompette, *adj.* slightly drunk*.

pompeuses, *f.pl.* lips.

pompier, *m.* I. **fumer comme un p.** = **fumer comme une locomotive.** 2. **faire un p.** = **plume** 3. 3. *adj.* square, traditional, uninspiring.

pompon, *m.* I. **avoir son p.** = **avoir son plumet.** 2. **avoir le p.,** to take the biscuit (*or* the bun *or* the cake); **à lui le p.!** he takes the cake! he's the tops! he's easily first! **ça, c'est le p.!** that's the limit!*

pomponnette, *f.* **boire à la p.,** to drink a glass of wine (etc.) at a draught (*or* in one gulp).

pondeuse, *f.* **une bonne p.,** a very prolific woman, a woman with many children.

ponette, *f.* pimp's moll.

pont, *m.* I. **couper dans le p.** = **couper dedans (couper 4).** 2. **faire le p.,** to keep holiday on a working day between two days (*e.g. between a Sunday and a legal holiday or vice versa*), to make a long week-end of it.

ponte, *f.* gambling.

ponte, *m.* I. (*at gambling*) punter; **un gros p.,** a heavy gambler, a plunger. 2. important* person, pundit. 3. trafficker in drugs, pusher.

ponter, to be a heavy gambler, to plunge; to place one's bets.

pontife, *m.* pundit (*literature etc.*).

pontifier, to lay down the law.

Pont-Neuf, *pr.n.* **se porter comme le P.-N.,** to be as fit as a fiddle, to be hale and hearty.

Pontoise, *pr.n.* **avoir l'air de revenir de P.,** to seem to be out of touch.

Popofs, *m.pl.* **les P.,** Russians, Ruskies.

popote, *f.* I. (*mil.*) mess; **faire p. (ensemble),** to mess together. 2. messmate. 3. canteen. 4. cooking; **faire la p.,** to do the cooking. 5. *adj.* (*of person*) stay-at-home, homely. 6. implements for drug addicts.

popotier, *m.* (*mil.*) messing-officer.

popotin, *m.* I. buttocks*; **se trémousser** (*or* **se remuer**) **le p.,** to dance, to shake a leg; **magne-toi le p.!** hurry* up! 2. luck.

popu, populo, *m.* riff-raff, rabble; mob, crowd.

popu, *adj.* popular; vulgar, common.

porcelaine, *f.* bidet.

porcif, porsiffe, *f.* portion (of food), dish for one person.

portail, *m.* vagina*. *See also* **clef** 5.

porte, *f.* I. **mettre (ficher, flanquer) qn à la p.,** to turn s.o. out; to dismiss* s.o.; **à la p.!** throw him (her, etc.) out! out with him (her, etc.)! 2. **vous vous êtes trompé de p.!** = **vous vous êtes trompé d'adresse!** 3. **trouver (la) p. de bois** = **trouver visage de bois.** 4. **aimable comme une p. de prison,** as surly as a bear. 5. **enfoncer des portes ouvertes,** to labour the obvious.

porte-: **p.-biffetons, p.-fafiots,** *m.* pocket-book, wallet; **p.-feuille,** *m.* **mettre un lit en p.-feuille,** to make an apple-pie bed; **p.-flingue,** *m.* bodyguard, henchman; **p.-griffard,** *m.* penholder; **p.-guigne,** *m.* (*of person*) hoodoo, jinx, jonah, flivver; **p.-manteau,** *m.* shoulders; **p.-pipe,** *m.* face*; mouth*; **p.-viande,** *m.* stretcher.

porté, *adj.* I. **c'est bien p.,** it's the right thing to do; **c'est mal p.,** it's bad style. 2. **être p. sur,** to have a liking for. *See* **article, bagatelle, chose** 4, **truc** 9.

porter: en p. = **p. des cornes.**

porter, se: **un(e) . . . qui se porte bien,** a rare old . . .—*e.g.* **recevoir un savon qui se porte bien,** to get a telling-off one won't forget in a hurry.

porteur, *m.* accomplice.

portillon, *m.* **ça se bouscule au p.,** (*of person's speech*) he's spluttering.

portrait, *m.* I. face*. 2. **le p. tout craché,** the dead spit, the spitting image, the spit and image. 3. **s'adorner le p.** = **se faire beau (beau** 2). 4. **rentrer dans le p. à qn,** to pitch into s.o., to give s.o. a sock⁻ on the jaw. 5. **abîmer le p. à qn,** to spoil s.o.'s beauty (for him); **se faire abîmer le p.**, to get one's face bashed in; **rectifier le p. à qn**, to bash s.o.'s face.

portugaises, *f.pl.* ears*; **avoir les p. ensablées,** (*a*) to be deaf; (*b*) to fail to understand; **embouteiller les p. à qn**, to pierce (*or* to split) s.o.'s ears.

pose, *f.* le (*or* la) **faire à la p.**, to swank*.

poser. 1. ça vous pose, it gives you standing. **2. p. ça là**, to chuck up one's work, to down tools. **3.** to be kept waiting, to kick (*or* to cool) one's heels; **faire p. qn**, to keep s.o. waiting, to keep s.o. cooling his heels. **4. p. un porte-manteau,** to knife s.o. in the back.

poser, se. 1. il se pose là, (**comme gaffeur**), for putting one's foot in it, he takes the cake. **2. il se pose (un peu) là**, he's a hefty* bloke.

poseur, *m.* swank(er)*.

position, *f.* **être dans une p. intéressante**, to be pregnant*.

posséder, to dupe* (s.o.); **se faire p.**, to be taken in, to be 'had'.

possible, *adj.* **1. p.!** it's quite possible! very likely! maybe! **2. pas p.!** *or* **ce n'est pas Dieu p.!** you don't say so! not really! well, I never! **3. si c'est p.!** (*a*) = **pas possible!**; (*b*) how could you?

poste, *m.* **toujours solide** (*or* **fidèle**) **au p.**, still going strong, still alive and kicking.

poste, *f.* **courir la p.**, to make a fast getaway.

postère, *m.* buttocks*.

postiche, *f.* **1.** street-vendor's (*or* barker's) sales talk, spiel. **2. faire une p. à qn**, to pick a quarrel with s.o., to row with s.o.

posticheur, *m.* **1.** barker, spieler. **2.** = **batouseur.**

postillon, *m.* spluttering; **envoyer** (*or* **lancer**) **des postillons,** to splutter.

postillonner, to splutter.

postillonneur, *m.* splutterer.

pot, *m.* **1.** anus*; **se manier le p.** = **se magner; casser le p.**, (*a*) to deflower; (*b*) to commit sodomy. **2.** luck; **coup de p.**, lucky break, fluke; **manque de p.!** *or* **pas de p.!** bad

luck! hard luck (*or* hard lines *or* hard cheese)! **avoir du** (*or* **le**) **p.**, to be in luck; **un p. du tonnerre** *or* **un p. d'enfer**, the devil's own luck. **3.** drink, a wet, a short, a shot; **prendre un p.**, to treat oneself to a drink, to stand oneself a drink. **4. p. de colle** = **crampon. 5.** (*at gambling*) kitty. **6. p.-à-tabac**, tubby man, pot-bellied man. **7. découvrir le p. aux roses**, to find out the secret. **8. être à p. et à rôt**, to be bosom friends. **9. faire son p.**, to make one's fortune (*or* one's pile). **10. payer les pots cassés**, to pay the piper, to stand the racket, to hold the baby, to take the can back, to carry the can (back), to be left holding the bag (*or* the baby). **11. sourd comme un p.**, as deaf as a post. **12. tourner autour du p.**, to beat about the bush, to shilly-shally. **13. bête comme un p.**, as silly as can be. **14. bousculer le p. de fleurs**, to exaggerate*. **15.** marihuana (*drugs**). *See also* **cuiller 3, s'occuper, yaourt.**

potable, *adj.* = **buvable.**

potache, *m.* schoolboy (at a *lycée* or a *collège*).

potage, *m.* **1. pour tout p.**, all told, all in all. **2. envoyer** (*or* **expédier**) **le p. à qn**, (*a*) to kill* s.o.; (*b*) to let s.o. have the works. **3. être dans le p.** = **être dans le cirage** (**cirage 1** (*b*)). **4. servir le p. à la seringue**, to live parsimoniously.

potard, *m.* **1.** chemist, chemist's assistant. **2.** pharmacy student.

potasser = **piocher.**

potasseur, *m.* = **piocheur.**

potauf', *m.* = **pot-au-feu.**

pot-au-feu, *m.* = **boulangère;** *adj.* plain, homely.

pot-au-rif, *m.* boiled beef with vegetables out of the pot.

pot-de-vin, *m.* bribe, hush-money, palm oil, sweetener, fix, rake-off, baksheesh.

pote, *m.f.* friend*.

poteau, *m.* **1.** = **pote. 2. X au p.!** down with X! **3. avoir son p.**, to be drunk*. **4.** (*sch.*) **mettre au p.**, to put (s.o.) against the wall. **5.** *pl.* fat legs, 'bed-posts'.

potée, *f.* great quantity*.
poteuf, *m.* = pot-au-feu, *m.*
potin, *m.* 1. row, uproar*; **un p. d'enfer** *or* **un p. de tous les diables,** a devil (*or* a hell) of a row; **faire du p.,** to kick up a row (*or* a shindy). 2. (piece of) gossip, scandal, tittle-tattle, chit-chat; **ça a fait du p.,** it caused quite a scandal. 3. **prendre les potins de qn,** to get news about s.o.
potiner, to gossip, to talk scandal, to tittle-tattle.
potinière, *f.* centre of gossip, gossip-shop.
potiron, *m.* 1. horse carriage. 2. *pl.* members of the jury.
pou, *m.* 1. **chercher des poux à qn** (*or* **sur la tête de qn**), to pick a quarrel with s.o. 2. **écorcher un p. pour en avoir la peau,** to be a miser*, to skin (*or* to flay) a flint. 3. *in comparisons:* **laid comme un p.,** as ugly as sin; **orgueilleux** (*or* **fier**) **comme un p.,** as proud (*or* as vain) as a peacock. 4. (*W.W.II*) member of the maquis.
pouacre, *adj.* filthy, lousy.
pouce, *m.* 1. **et le p.** (avec)! *or* **et puis le p.!** and a bit over! and a bit more! and the rest! plus a bit! 2. (je demande un) **p.!** pax! **faire p.,** to cry pax (*or* barley). 3. **donner le coup de p. à,** (*a*) to give the finishing touch to, to finish off; (*b*) to strangle; (*c*) to cook (accounts). 4. **faire** (**donner, filer**) **le coup de p.,** (*of shopkeeper*) to give short weight, to weigh the thumb in. 5. **avoir un coup de p.** = être pistonné. 6. **ne pas se fouler le p.** = ne pas se fouler la rate. 7. **manger** (**un morceau**) **sur le p.** = casser la croûte; **un morceau sur le p.,** a snack. 8. **mettre les pouces,** to give (*or* to cave) in, to knuckle under, to eat humble pie, to throw up the sponge. 9. **lire un livre du p.,** to skim through a book. 10. **tourner ses pouces, se tourner les pouces,** to (sit and) twiddle one's thumbs, to be idle. 11. **sur le p.,** (*a*) gratis*; (*b*) extempore. 12. **s'en mordre les pouces,** to be sorry for it, to smart for it.

13. **être malade du p.,** to be miserly*.
14. **trois pouces et le cul tout de suite,** (*of very small person*) all body and no legs, (*Amer. sl.*) dusty butt.
poucettes, *f.pl.* handcuffs*.
poudre, *f.* **il n'a pas inventé la p.,** he won't set the Thames on fire.
poudrée, *f.* road, highway.
poudrette, *f.* cocaine (*drugs*).
pouet(te)-pouet(te), faire, to make up (to s.o.).
pouf, *m.* **faire un p.,** to go bankrupt, to abscond, to do a bunk (without paying one's debts).
pouffant, *adj.* very funny*.
pouffer: p. (**de rire**), to burst out laughing.
pouffer, se, to burst out laughing, to chortle, to guffaw.
pouffiasse, *f.* 1. (*pej.*) woman*, bird. 2. common prostitute*.
pouic, *adv. See* **entraver.**
pouilladin, pouillasson, *adj.* = pouilleux, *adj.*
pouillerie, *f.* 1. squalor. 2. lousy hole.
pouilles, *f.pl.* **chanter p. à qn,** to abuse s.o.
pouilleux, *adj.* 1. lousy, crummy, chatty, bummy; *m.* lousy person; down-and-out(er). 2. jack of spades (*cards*).
poulaga, *m.* policeman* **la Maison P.,** the police.
poulaille, *f.* police, cops, the 'law'.
poulailler, *m.* = paradis 1.
poulain, *m.* (*sport*) promising youngster, colt.
poulardin, poulardos, *m.* = poulaga.
poulasse, *f.* = poule 1.
poulbot, *m.* street-urchin (*of Paris*), guttersnipe, mudlark.
poule, *f.* 1. prostitute*; **sa p.,** his little bit of stuff (*or* fluff); his mistress; **p. de luxe,** high-class tart. 2. **ma petite p.!** my darling*! 3. **la P.,** the police. 4. **une p. mouillée,** a milksop*. 5. **habiter au-delà des poules,** to live at the back of beyond. 6. **quand les poules auront des dents,** when pigs

(begin to) fly, when the cows come home, once in a blue moon. **7. ce n'est pas à la p.** à chanter devant le coq, a wife should not tell her husband what to do.

pouleman(n), *m.* **la Maison P.** (*or* **Poulemince** *or* **Pouleminche** *or* **Pouleminse**), the Police, Police headquarters.

poulet, *m.* **1.** policeman*, detective. **2.** (*to a child*) ducky. **3.** love-letter (*to a female*); letter (*especially an unpleasant one*). **4. c'est du p.!** it's jammy! easy!

poulette, pouliche, *f.* (i) **1.** girl, lass(ie). **2.** pretty young thing. **3. ma poulette,** my darling*.

pouliche, *f.* (ii) **pouliche faux-poids** = **faux-poids.**

poulo, *m.* = **paradis 1.**

pouloper, to gallop along, to run hard.

poulton, *m.* = **paradis 1.**

poupée, *f.* **1.** (*pej.*) girl*. **2.** bandaged finger, dolly.

poupoule, *f.* **ma p.,** my darling*.

pouponner. 1. to dandle (a baby). **2.** to mother, to coddle.

pour, *prep.* **1. c'est du p.!** it's a pack of lies! **c'est pas du p.!** it's gospel truth! **2. p. . . ., c'est . . .**—*e.g.* **p. de la pluie, c'est de la pluie!** it's raining and no mistake!

pourliche, *m.* gratuity, tip.

pourri, *adj.* **1.** (*of child*) thoroughly spoilt. **2.** (*of weather*) dank, muggy. **3. être p. d'argent,** to be simply rolling in it (*i.e. money*), to stink of money. **4. il n'est pas p.,** he's hale and hearty. **5.** *m.* rotter*.

pourriture, *f.* (*of person*) rotter*.

poursoif, *m.* = **pourliche.**

pourvoyeur, *m.* pusher (of drugs).

poussah, *m.* paunchy*, tubby man.

pousse-au-crime, *m.* strong spirits*.

pousse-ballon, *m.* poor football player.

pousse-café, *m.* small glass of spirits or liqueur (*after coffee*), chaser.

pousse-cailloux, *m.* infantryman, footslogger.

pousse-canule, *m.* male nurse; medical orderly.

pousse-dehors, *m.* early morning nip (*i.e. drink*).

pousser. 1. to exaggerate. **2. en p. une** = **p. une goualante.** *See also* **à la va-comme-j'-te-pousse.**

poussette, *f.* syringe for drugs.

poussières, *f.pl.* (*of sums of money, etc.*—*e.g.*) **cela m'a coûté cent mille balles et des** (*or* **quelques**) **p.,** it cost me a hundred thousand francs and a few francs more (*or* a hundred thousand francs odd).

p.p.p.d.c., au, (= *au plus petit poil du cul*) = **au poil** (**poil 2**).

praline, *f.* **1.** blow*. **2.** bullet, slug. **3.** clitoris.

pravise, pravouse, *f.* dose of cocaine (*drugs*).

prêchi-prêcha, *m.* preachifying.

Préfectance, *f.* police headquarters.

première, *f.* **de p.,** first-rate*; in first-rate style.

prendre. 1. to catch it, to get it hot and strong; **qu'est-ce que j'ai pris!** I didn't half catch (or cop) it! **qu'est-ce que tu vas p.!** you're for it! **2. qu'est-ce qui vous prend?** what's the matter with you? what's up with you? **3. ça ne prend pas (avec moi)!** that (trick) won't work with me! nothing doing! it's no go (with me)! **4. j'en prends et j'en laisse,** (*a*) I take it easy, I don't kill myself, I do as much as I feel like; (*b*) I take it all with a pinch of salt; **il faut en p. et en laisser,** you can't believe all he (she, etc.) says. **5. je sors** (*or* **je viens**) **d'en p.!** I've had some, thanks! **6. en p.,** to get rich*, to amass a fortune. **7. où prends-tu ça?** how do you make that out?

presse, *f.* **être sous p.,** (*of a prostitute*) to be with a client.

presto, *adv.* = **illico.**

prêt, *adj.* **fin p.:** *see* **fin,** *adv.*

preu, *adj.* (*sch.*) first.

prévence, *f.* remand in custody, confinement pending trial.

prévent, *m.* observation sanatorium.

prévette, *f.* = **prévence**.
prévôt, *m.* (*in prison*) privileged prisoner.
priante, *f.* prayer, church service.
primeur, *f.* virginity, maidenhead.
princesse, *f.* See **frais**, *m.pl.*
prise, *f.* **1.** See **bec**. **2.** cocaine (*drugs**).
prise, *p.p.* **être p.**, to be pregnant*.
priseur, *m.* **p. de came** = **camé**, *m.*
pristo, *m.* prisoner.
prix, *m.* **1. dans les grands p.** = **dans les grands largeurs. 2. un p. de Diane**, a very pretty girl (*or* woman). **3. un p. à réclamer**, an ugly woman. **4. ce n'est pas un p. de vertu**, she's (he's) no angel. See **beurre 4**.
pro, *m.* professional, pro.
probloc, probloque, *m.* = **proprio**.
probzi, *m.* (*sch.*) problem in math(ematic)s.
proc(u), *m.* public prosecutor.
prof, *m.* teacher (school)master; lecturer, prof(essor).
profonde, *f.* pocket*.
prolo, *m.* proletarian.
promenade, *f.* easy victory (*or* undertaking), walk-over.
promener, se. 1. envoyer p. qn, to send s.o. packing*. **2.** (*of things*) to be lying about, to be kicking about, to be lying all over the shop.
promis, promise, *m.f.* **mon promis, ma promise**, my intended.
propé, *f.* (= *propédeutique*) year of study before beginning a degree course. (*It no longer exists*).
propre, *adj.* **1. me voilà p.!** I'm in a fine (*or* nice) fix*! here's a pretty go! **2.** *m.* **c'est du p.!** *or* **en voilà du p.!** it's a fine (old) mess!
proprio, *m.* **1.** proprietor, owner, landlord. **2. venez faire le tour du p.**, come on, I'll show you round the place.
prose, *m.* = **proze**.
prosinard, *m.* buttocks*.
proto, *m.* (*sch.*) headmaster (of *lycée*).
prout, *m.* fart.
prove, provise, *f.* **chèque sans p.**, dud cheque, stumer, bouncer.
provo, *m.* = **proto**.

proxémac, *m.* pimp.
proze, prozinard, *m.* **1.** buttocks*. **2.** luck.
prune, *f.* **1.** bullet, slug. **2.** blow*; **avoir de la p.**, (*of boxer*) to pack a punch. **3. des prunes!** = **des clous!** (clou 7). **4. aux prunes**, never. **5. pour des prunes**, for nothing, without profit, for shucks. **6. compter pour des prunes**, not to count for anything. **7. se faire coller une p.**, (*motor.*) to be booked. **8. se fendre la p.** = **se fendre la pipe** (pipe 3). **9. poser une p.** = **poser une pêche. 10. avoir sa p.**, to be drunk. **11.** *pl.* testicles*.
pruneau, *m.* **1.** = **prune. 1.** *and* **2. 2. des pruneaux!** = **des prunes! 3. pour des pruneaux** = **pour des prunes. 4.** *pl.* = **prunes 9. 5.** quid of tobacco.
prunelle, *f.* **jouer de la p.**, to ogle, to make sheep's eyes.
prusco(t), *m.* Prussian.
pschtt, *m.* (*sch.*) **faire un p.**, to show one's admiration and approval.
pschutteux, *adj.* smart, stylish; *m.* swell.
puant, *adj.* (*of person*) objectionably conceited.
puce, *f.* **1.** undersized person*. **2. boisseau de puces**, fidgety child. **3. charmer ses puces**, to get drunk before going to bed, to take a night-cap. **4. chercher des puces à qn**, to provoke s.o. **5. marché aux puces**, flea-market (*in Paris*), junk-market. **6. marchand de puces**, junkman, old-clothes man. **7. mettre la p. à l'oreille à qn**, to make s.o. smell a rat, to make s.o. feel uneasy, to make s.o. see the red light. **8. secouer ses puces**, to stretch oneself (out). **9. secouer les puces à qn**, (*a*) to reprimand* s.o.; (*b*) to thrash* s.o.
pucelage, *m.* virginity, maidenhead.
pucier, *m.* bed*.
pue-la-sueur, *m.* (*pej.*) workman, worker.
puits, *m.* **p. de science**, walking encyclopaedia.
pullupper = **pouloper**.

punaise, *f.* **1.** female of easy virtue. **2.** shrew. **3.** p. de sacristie (*or* de confessionnal), bigoted church-woman. **4.** punaises vertes, (*W.W.II*) German soldiers, Jerries.

punich, puniss, *f.* (*sch.*) punishment.

pur, *m.* un (vrai) pur, a dependable fellow.

purée, *f.* **1.** hail of bullets. **2.** balancer la p., (*a*) to fire (*bullet*); (*b*) =jouir. **3.** être dans la p., to be penniless*; être dans la p. noire, to be on the rocks. **4.** p. de pois, peasouper (fog). **5.** drink of absinthe. **6.** (*contemptuous form of address*) you twerp!

purge, *f.* thrashing*; **coller (donner, filer) une p. à qn,** to thrash* s.o.; **prendre la p.,** to get a thrashing*, to be put through it.

purotin, *m.* penniless* person, down-at-heel fellow.

purpurines, *f.pl.* avoir les p. en bagarre, to be on heat.

pus, *adv.* (=*plus*) y a p.! (=*il n'y en a plus*) it's no go!

putain, *f.* **1.** prostitute*. **2.** *intensive use—e.g.* cette p. de guerre, ce p. de pays, p. de sort! p. de métier! un p. de boulot. **3.** *occasionally as a grudgingly affectionate form of address to a young man—e.g.* petite p.! you little tyke! **4.** *expletive in the Midi:* golly! dammit! blast! (*expletives*).

putasse, *f.* =putain.

putassier, *m.* woman-chaser, whoremonger.

pute, *f.* =putain; fils (*or* fan) de p.! son of a bitch!

putois, *m.* crier (*or* gueuler) comme un p., to kick up a hell of a row, to squeal like a pig.

pyjama, *m.* faire du p., to stay at home (in order to save money).

Q

quai, *m. See* bout 2.
quarante, *f.* = carante.
quarante, *num. adj.* 1. se mettre en q.,
(*a*) to fly into a rage; (*b*) to square up
(to s.o.). 2. dites q.-quatre! (*said by
doctor to patient*) say ninety-nine! *Cf.*
trente-trois. 3. un q.-quatre maison,
a good kick in the pants. *See also* an.
quart, *m.* 1. police station. 2. q.(-d'œil),
superintendent of police. 3. (*mil.*) tin
drinking-mug (*holding a quarter of a
litre*). 4. faire le (*or* battre son) q., (*of
prostitute*) to walk one's beat. 5.
partir au q. de tour, to move at the
double. 6. passer un mauvais (*or*
fichu) q. d'heure, to have a hard (*or*
bad) time of it, to have a hell of a
time. 7. pour le q. d'heure, for the
time being, for the present. 8. q.-de-
brie, q.-de-rire, big nose*.
Quartier, *m.* le Q., the Latin Quarter
(*in Paris*).
quatre, *num. adj.* 1. manger comme q.,
to eat ravenously. *See also* épingle,
sou, yeux. 2. un de ces q. = un de ces
q. matins.
quat'crans, *m.* (*mil.*) very strict
N.C.O.
Quat'z-Arts, *m.pl.* le bal des Q.-A.,
ball given by the students of the *École
des Beaux-Arts* (in Paris).
quat'zyeux: *See* yeux.
que, *interr. pron.* what?; *int.* why!
quelque chose, *indef. pron.* prendre
q. c., to get a bashing, to cop it. *See*
grade.
quelque part, *adv.* 1. aller q. p., to go
to the W.C.* 2. donner à qn un coup
de pied q. p., to kick s.o.'s bottom (for
him). *Similarly:* je lui mettrai mon
pied q. p. 3. avoir qn q. p., not to care
a rap* for s.o.; je les ai q. p.! you know
where you can put 'em! 4. il peut se le
(*or* la) mettre q. p.! he can stuff it (up
his arse)!

quelqu'un, *indef. pron.* se croire (*or* se
prendre pour) q., to be self-conceited*.
quenaupe, *f.* pipe.
qu'en-dira-t-on, *m.* se moquer du q.,
not to care about what people say,
not to care about Mrs. Grundy.
quenotte, *f.* tooth, peg(gy).
quenottier, *m.* dentist.
quéquette, *f.* penis*.
quès, *m.* c'est du q. = c'est du kif; c'est
jamais du q., it's never the same.
qu'es-aco? *adv. phrase.* (*dial. South of
France*) what's that (*or* this)? what's
the matter? what's the (big) idea?
what's this in aid of?
question, *f.* cette (*or* c'te *or* c't') q.!
what a thing to ask!
que t'chi, *adv.* (*gipsy slang*) = que
dal(le).
queue, *f.* 1. penis*. 2. q. de cervelas,
(*prison slang*) daily walk in the
prison-yard. 3. q. de cheval, (*of hair-
style*) pony-tail. 4. q.-de-morue, q.-de-
pie, swallow-tail coat, tails. 5. faire
une q. de poisson, (*motor.*) to cut in. 6.
q. de vache, (*colour of hair*) off-brown,
mousy-coloured. 7. faire des queues
à = faire des paillons à. 8. faire une
tête-à-q., (*motor.*) to swing right round,
to swing round tail-end first. 9. finir
en q. de poisson, to fizzle out, to peter
out, to end in smoke (*or* in talk), to
come to nothing, to go phut. 10.
laisser une q., to leave without
settling one's debts. 11. n'avoir ni q.
ni tête, to be pointless, to have neither
head nor tail; une histoire sans q. ni
tête, a story that one cannot make
head or tail of. 12. ne pas se prendre
pour une q. de poire, to be self-
conceited*. 13. pas la q. d'un(e), not a
blessed one, absolutely nothing, not
the tail end of one; n'en avoir pas la q.
d'un, to be penniless*. 14. tenir la q.

de la poêle, to run (*or* to boss) the show, to rule the roost.

queutard, *m.* womanizer, hot-pants.

queuter, to fornicate.

quibus, *m.* money*.

quille, *f.* 1. leg*; ne pas tenir sur ses quilles, to be shaky on one's pins; jouer des quilles, to decamp*. 2. girl. 3. (*mil.*) end of one's service, demobilization; *cf.* la classe.

quiller, to trick, to cheat* (s.o.).

quimper. 1. to arrest*. 2. to seduce (a woman). 3. laisser q. qn, to forsake s.o., to drop s.o. 4. to fall into a trap, to be victimized. 5. to be sentenced; q. chéro, to get a stiff sentence, to get the book thrown at one.

quincaille, *f.* 1. money*. 2. jewels.

quincaillerie, *f.* 1. decorations, medals. 2. jewels.

quine, *f.* en avoir q., avoir q. de, to be fed up with (it).

quinquets, *m.pl.* eyes*; allumer ses q., to open one's eyes; faux q.,

spectacles, specs; ribouler des q. = ribouler des calots.

quinquin, *m.* p'tit q. = ch'timi.

quinte, *f.* avoir (*or* attraper) q. et quatorze et le point, to have (*or* to cop) a dose (of V.D.).

quintuplée, *f.* hand*.

quique, *f.* = quéquette.

quiqui, *m.* neck, throat; serrer le q. à qn, to throttle (*or* to strangle) s.o., to wring s.o.'s neck.

quoi, *rel. pron.* 1. avoir de q., to have plenty of money*. 2. comme q., as how. 3. il n'y a pas de q.! don't mention it!

quoi, *int.* 1. enfin, q., c'est la vie! well, well, such is life! il est mort, q.! he's dead, and that's that! 2. de q.? *or* de q. je me mêle? *or* non, mais, de q.? (*to express defiance, aggressive attitude to a person who interferes, etc.*) you and who else? who's going to help you? what's it got to do with you? want to make something of it?

R

rab(e), m. =rabiot.

rabat, rabatteur, m. (a) tout, steerer; (b) pimp.

rabattre, (se), to return, to come back.

rabiau, m. =rabiot.

rabiauter=rabioter.

rabibocher. 1. to tinker up, to patch up. 2. to reconcile (people), to make it up between, to patch up (a quarrel).

rabibocher, se, to become reconciled, to make it up again, to kiss and make up.

rabiot, m. (mil.) anything extra or surplus–(a) pickings, graft; (b) buckshee, gash(ion); (c) extra work, extra ration, extra period of service; en r., buckshee; un petit r.? (of drink) how about a drop more?

rabioter. 1. to get illicit profits, to make a bit extra. 2. to scrounge (something extra). 3. to wangle sth. extra (food, leave, etc.).

râble, m. (of person) back; sauter (tomber, dégringoler) sur le r. à qn, to jump on s.o., to collar s.o.

râbler, to attack*.

raboter, to steal*.

rabouin, m. 1. devil. 2. m.f. gipsy.

raccord, m. (se) faire un r., to touch up (or freshen up) (one's face).

raccourcir, to behead, to guillotine, to 'top'; la machine à r., the guillotine; être raccourci, to be 'topped'.

raccroc, m. 1. faire le r., (a) to tout; (b) (of prostitute) to solicit, to accost (men in the street), to be on the streets, to hook, to be on the game (or on the beat). 2. par r., by a fluke.

raccrocher=faire le raccroc.

raccrocheuse, f. prostitute*.

race, f. 1. il (or bon chien) chasse de r., he's a chip off the old block. 2. sale (or méchante) petite r.! naughty little brats!

racine, f. prendre r., (of boring person) to cling like a limpet; pl. toes.

racketteur, m. racketeer.

raclé, p.p. penniless*.

raclée, f. thrashing*; donner (filer, flanquer, foutre) une (or la) r. à qn, to thrash* s.o.

racler. 1. r. qn, to clean s.o. out (at gambling). 2. r. les fonds de tiroir, to scrape the barrel.

racler, se, to shave; se faire r., to get shaved.

raclette, f. squad-car; coup de r., round-up, raid (by police).

racloir, m. razor.

raclure, f. (a) slut, trollop; (b) (of persons) scum.

racolage, m. touting; (of prostitute) accosting, soliciting.

racoler. to accost, to solicit, to pick up.

racoleur, m. tout, steerer, hustler.

racoleuse, f. prostitute*.

radada, m. buttocks*.

rade, m. 1. =zinc 1. 2. faire le r. =faire le raccroc.

rade, f. en r. =en carafe.

rader =faire le raccroc.

radeuse, f. prostitute*.

radin, adj. miserly*; m. miser*.

radiner (i), to be miserly*.

radiner, (se) (ii), to arrive*.

radis, m. 1. ne pas avoir un r., to be penniless*. 2. ça ne vaut pas un r., it's worthless*. 3. des r.!=des clous! (clou 7). 4. pl. (a) feet*; (b) toes.

radis-noir, m. 1. priest*. 2. negro.

raffut, rafût, m. noise, uproar*; faire du r., to kick up a row; un r. du diable (or de tous les diables), a devil of a row.

rafiau, raf(f)iot, m. vieux r., (of ship) old tub.

rafistoler, to mend, to tinker up.

ragaga, m. faire du r., to waste one's time.

ragoter, to gossip, to tittle-tattle.
ragots, *m.pl.* gossip, tittle-tattle.
ragougnasse, *f.* poor quality food*.
raidard, *adj.* penniless*.
raide, *adj.* 1. drunk*. 2. penniless*; (*intensive comparisons:* **r. comme une barre, r. à blanc, r. comme la justice, r. comme un passe-lacets,** stony broke). 3. **ça c'est (un peu) r.!** *or* **celle-là est r.!** *or* **elle est r., celle-là!** that's too bad! that's a bit thick (*or* a bit stiff *or* a bit steep)! 4. **en raconter de raides,** to tell some tall (*or* some spicy *or* some smutty) stories. 5. **en avoir vu de raides,** to have been in some hot corners, to have been through it. 6. (*mil.*) **se porter** (*or* **se faire porter**) **r.,** to go (*or* to report) sick. 7. **un coup r. comme balle,** (*of a blow*) a stinger. 8. *adv.* **être r. fou,** to be clean off one's head, to be raving mad.
raide, *m.* strong spirits* (*drink*). 2. thousand franc note.
raidillard, *m.* =raide, *m.* 2.
raidillon, *m.* =raide, *m.* 1.
raidir: se faire r., to get cleaned out (at gambling).
raie, *f.* 1. buttocks*. 2. **jeu de la r.,** penny-rolling (*game*). 3. vagina*.
raisin, *m.* blood, 'claret', 'rosy'; **avoir du r.,** to be courageous, spunky; **avoir qn dans le r.,** to be madly in love with, to have a crush on, s.o.; **prendre un coup de r.,** to be angry*.
raisiné, *m.* blood 'claret', 'rosy'; **faire du r.,** to have a nose-bleed.
raison, *f.* 1. **chercher des raisons à qn,** to try to pick a quarrel with s.o. 2. **se faire une r.,** to accept the inevitable, to make the best of a bad job.
rajouter: en r., to exaggerate*.
râlant, *adj.* infuriating.
ral(1)éger, to return, to come back.
râler, to be furious, to grumble*; (*intensive forms:* **r. ferme, r. sec, r. comme un pou**).
râleur, râleux, *adj.* ill-tempered, snarly; *m.* grumbler, grouser.
rallonge, *f.* 1. **un nom à r.,** a double-barrelled name, a handle to one's name. 2. knife (*long-bladed, with stop-catch*). 3. rise in pay, extra money.
rallonger, to knife.
ramarrer, to meet s.o. again.
ramasser. 1. to arrest*. 2. to reprimand*. 3. **se faire r.,** (*a*) to get copped (*or* nabbed *or* pinched *or* picked up) (by the police); (*b*) to be reprimanded*; (*c*) (*sch.*) to fail an exam.
ramastiquer=ramasser.
rambin, *m.* 1. **faire du r.** (*a*) =faire du **plat;** (*b*) to court, to chat up (a woman). 2. **marcher au r.,** to try to make excuses, to wriggle out.
rambiner, 1. to make peace. 2. to put new life into (s.o.).
rambineur, -euse, *m.f.* peace-maker.
rambot, *m.* =rancart.
rambour, *m.* =rancart; *pl.* information.
ramdam(e), *m.* row, uproar*.
rame, *f.* 1. **avoir la r.,** to be lazy*, not to feel up to work. 2. **ne pas (en) faire** (*or* **fiche(r)** *or* **foutre**) **une r.,** not to do a stroke of work.
ramée, *f.* =rame 2.
ramener: la r., (*a*) =rouspéter; (*b*) to swank*.
ramener, se, to arrive*.
ramer, 1. to have coition*. 2. to get tired.
ramier, *m.* 1. lazybones. 2. prostitute*.
ramolli, *adj.* half-witted; *m.* dodderer.
ramollir, se, to go soft in the head.
ramollo(t), *m.* 1. **un vieux r.,** an old fog(e)y*. 2. **se taper un r.**=se taper un rassis.
ramoner. 1. to reprimand*. 2. to clean out (at gambling). 3. to have coition* with.
rampant, *m.* **les rampants,** (*av.*) the ground staff, 'penguins', ground wallahs.
rampe, *f.* 1. **lâcher la r.,** to die*. 2. **tenir bon** (*or* **dur**) **la r.,** to be still going strong; **tiens bon la r.!** (*c.p. to s.o. falling down*) hold tight!
ramponneau, *m.* blow*.

ramponner, to thump, to pummel.
rancard, *m.* **1.** information, tip, gen. **2.** =rancart.
rancarder, **1.** to inform, to give information* to. **2.** to give a rendezvous.
rancarder, se, to make inquiries, to find out.
rancart, *m.* rendezvous, appointment, date, confab, 'bivvy', 'meet'.
rançonner, to fleece (s.o.).
rançonneur, *adj.* extortionate.
rancuneux, *adj.* spiteful.
ranger, se, to settle (*or* to sober) down (*after sowing one's wild oats*); to get married*.
ranquiller=renquiller.
rantanplan, *m.* **faire qch. au r.**, to bluff.
raousser, raouster, to expel.
rapapilloter, se rapapilloter=rabibocher, se rabibocher.
râper. 1. =ramer. **2. les r. à qn**=casser les pieds à qn (pied 8).
raper, *m.* policeman* on bicycle.
râpeuse, *f.* tongue.
rapiat, *adj.* miserly*, grasping; *m.* miser*.
rapido(s), *adv.* very quickly*.
rapière, *f.* knife.
rapiérer, to knife.
rapin, *m.* art student; dauber.
rapio, *adv.* =rapido(s).
raplapla, *adj.* spiritless, exhausted*.
rappliquer, (se), to return, to arrive*; **r. sur qn**, to make a bee-line for s.o.
rapport, *m.* **1. r. à**, on account of, because of, all 'along of'; on the subject of. **2. faire des rapports**, to tell tales out of school. **3. être de bon r.**, (*of prostitute*) =gagneuse.
rapporter. 1. to tell tales, to sneak, to tell on (s.o.), to be a tell-tale. **2. ça rapporte!** it pays!
râpure, *f.* bore.
raquer, 1. to pay* up. **2.** to spit.
raquettes, *f.pl.* feet*.
rare, *adj.* **vous vous faites r.** *or* **vous devenez r** *or* **vous devenez r. comme les beaux jours**, you're quite a stranger.

rarranger : se faire r.=se faire arranger (arranger 7).
ras, *m.* **en avoir r. le bord**=en avoir assez. *See also* **bol 3.**
rasant, *adj.* boring*.
ras-de-bitume, *m.* short, stumpy, undersized* person.
rasduc, ras-du-cul, *m. and adj.* shortie.
rase, *m.* **1.** priest*. **2.** prison chaplain.
rase-pet, *m.* veston r.-p. =pet-en-l'air.
raser, to bore* (s.o.).
raser, se, to be bored* stiff.
raseur, *m.* (of person) bore*.
rasibe, *m.* razor.
rasibus, *adv.* **couper r.**, to cut close, to cut very short; *int.* **r.!** nothing doing! . . . **et puis r.!** . . . and then it was all over!
rasif, *m.* rasibe.
rasoir, *m.* (*of person or thing*) nuisance, bore*; *adj.* boring*.
rassembler : se faire r., to be reprimanded*.
rassis, *m.* **se coller** (*or* **se taper**) **un r.**, to masturbate*.
rasta, rastacaille, rastaquouère, *m.* flashy and fishy adventurer (*generally from South America*).
rat, *m.* **1. mon (petit) r.**, my darling*. **2. r. de bibliothèque**, bookworm; **r. de cave**, exciseman; **r. d'église**, assiduous church-goer; beggar who frequents churches; **r. d'hôtel**, hotel thief; **petit r.**, young female ballet-dancer (*at the Opéra*). **3. être fait** (*or* **fabriqué** *or* **paumé**) **comme un r.**, to be caught out, to be caught like a rat in a trap, to be done for, to be caught bang to rights. **4. s'ennuyer** (*or* **s'embêter**) **comme un r. mort**, to be bored* stiff. **5. il a bouffé du r.**, (*of s.o. running quickly*) you can't see him for dust. **6. voir les rats**, to have persecution mania; **voir les rats bleus**, to have hallucinations, to see pink elephants. **7.** *adj.* miserly*; **il est d'un r.!** he's as mean as they make 'em!
rata, *m.* (*pej.*) =ratatouille **1.**
ratagasse, ratage, *m.* failure*.

ratatiner, to kill*, to destroy, to wipe out.

ratatouille, *f*. 1. (*a*) stew, hash, skilly; (*b*) poor quality food*. 2. thrashing*.

ratatout, *int*. (*at cards*) atout, ratout, et r.! trump, trump and trump again!

rate, *f*. 1. **ne pas se fouler la r.**, to take things easy, not to kill oneself with work. 2. **se désopiler** (*or* **se dilater**) **la r.**, to split one's sides with laughter.

raté, *m*. (*of person*) failure, wash-out, dud, nowhere cat.

râteau, *m*. 1. comb. 2. *pl*. teeth, **être sur les râteaux**, to be exhausted*.

râtelier, *m*. 1. (set of) false teeth, denture. 2. **manger** (*or* **brouter**) **à deux** (*or* **à plusieurs**) **râteliers**, to have two (*or* several) sources of income.

rater: il n'en rate pas une! he always makes a mess of things! he's always putting his foot in it!

ratiboiser. 1. to fleece (s.o.), to clean (s.o.) out. 2. **r. qch. à qn**, to filch sth. from s.o., to do s.o. out of sth., to chisel s.o. out of sth. 3. **r. sur les notes de frais**, to fiddle the expense accounts.

ratiche, *f*. 1. knife. 2. church. 3. *pl*. teeth.

ratichon, *m*. (*pej*.) priest*.

ratichonne, *f*. (*pej*.) nun.

ratière, *f*. prison*.

ratissage, *m*. combing (by police).

ratissé, *adj*. penniless*; **complètement r.**, broke to the wide.

ratisser. 1. =**ratiboiser**. 2. to arrest*. *See also* **hure**.

raton, *m*. 1. **mon petit r.**, my darling*. 2. Arab, North-African native, wog.

Ravachole, la, *f*. song of the anarchists. (*play on words*: *Ravachol, well-known anarchist, and la Carmagnole, French Revolution song.*)

ravagé, *adj*. mad*.

ravalement, *m*. **faire le** (*or* **son**) **r.**, to make up (one's face) again, to put on the war paint.

ravelin, *m*. vintage motor-car*.

ravelure, *f*. ugly old hag.

ravigotant, *m*. pick-me-up.

ravigoter, to buck (s.o.) up, to put new life into (s.o.).

ravigoter, se, to buck up, to pull oneself together.

ravissant, *m*. (*of person*) pansy, sissy.

rayon, *m*. 1. **c'est (de) mon r.**, that's just my cup of tea, that's right up my street; **ce n'est pas (de) mon r.**, that's not my cup of tea, that's not my line (of country), that's off my beat. 2. **en connaître un r.**, to be an old hand at it. 3. **en filer un r. = en mettre un coup (coup 16)**.

rayonner = jouir.

raz de marée, *m*. (*fig.*) (political, etc.) landslide.

razif, *m*. razor.

razis, *m*. =rase.

re-, *prefix*. *N.B. When* **re-** *in the sense of 'again' is prefixed to a verb already given, the verb with its* **re** *form is not normally listed again* (*e.g.* **rechoper, recoller, redécarrer, redouiller, relourder**, *etc.*).

rébecca, *m*. **faire du r.**, (*a*) to grumble*. (*b*) to kick up a shindy.

rebectage, *m*. petition for reprieve.

rebec(que)tant, *adj*. appetizing.

rebec(que)ter. 1. to reconcile. 2. to buck (s.o.) up.

rebec(que)ter, se. 1. to become reconciled, to make it up. 2. to pick up (physically *or* financially).

rebec(que)teur, *m*. doctor.

rebichoter, to identify.

rebiffe, *f*. 1. vengeance. 2. **faire de la r.**, **aller à la r. = se rebiffer**.

rebiffer: r. (au truc), to begin again, to have another shot (*or* another go), to start all over again.

rebiffer, se, to jib, to take offence, to kick, to kick over the traces, to bristle (*or* to bridle) up, to get one's back up.

rebiquer: ça me rebique, it gets on my nerves.

rebondir: envoyer r. qn, to send s.o. packing*.

recal, *adj*. rebellious.

recalé, *p.p.* **être r.,** to fail, to be failed* (at an examination).

recaler. 1. to fail* (s.o. at an examination); **se faire r.,** to be failed*. 2. =**ravigoter.**

recharger, to fill up again (drinks).

réchauffante, *f.* wig.

réchauffé, *m.* **c'est du r.!** that's stale news! Queen Anne's dead!

recluse, *f.* solitary (confinement).

reconnaître: je vous reconnais bien là! that's just like you! that's you all over!

reconnobler, reconnobrer, to recognize.

recta, *adv.* punctually, on the dot, to a T, on the nail.

rectifier. 1. to kill*. 2. to rob, to fleece, to skin (s.o.). 3. *See* **portrait.**

rectifieur, *m.* executioner, killer.

redingote, *f.* **r. de sapin,** 'wooden overcoat' (*i.e. coffin*).

redingue, *f.* frock-coat.

redouiller, to fork out again.

redressage, *m.* confrontation (*of prisoner, etc.*).

redresse, *f.* 1. **être à la r.,** to be wide-awake*; **un mec à la r.,** a hep guy. 2. **mettre qn à la r.,** to give s.o. a telling-off, to blow s.o. up.

redresser. 1. =**mettre qn à la redresse.** 2. to look at*. 3. to recognize, to identify.

refaire. 1. to steal*. 2. to dupe*; **il ne faut pas me la r.!** don't try it on with me!

refaire, se=**se rebec(que)ter.** *See also* **cerise.**

refait, *p.p.* duped*, done brown, taken in, stung; **être refait de qch.,** to be done out of sth.

refil(e), *m.* 1. **aller au r., être au r.,** (*a*) to vomit*; (*b*) to disgorge, to pay back, to pay* up. 2. **faire un r.,** to lend (money).

refiler: r. qch. à qn, (*a*) to give (*or* to give back) sth. to s.o., to pass sth. on to s.o., to hand over sth. to s.o., to slip sth. to s.o.; (*b*) to fob (*or* to

palm) sth. off on s.o.; **se faire r. qch.,** to get fobbed off with sth.

refouler, to stink*.

refourgue, *f.* selling stolen goods to a fourgue.

refrain, *m.* **c'est toujours le même r.!** it's always the same old story!

refroidi, *m.* corpse*. *See also* **boîte 7, jardin, musée, parc.**

refroidir, to kill*, to make cold meat of.

refus, *m.* **ce n'est pas de r.!** I'll not (*or* I won't *or* I wouldn't) say no (to that)! I don't mind if I do!

refuser, se: il ne se refuse rien, he does himself well, he indulges his every wish.

régalant, *adj.* **cela n'est pas r.,** it's no joke, it's far from funny.

régaler. 1. to stand a round of drinks; **c'est moi qui régale,** I'm standing treat, this one's on me, it's my shout. 2. to pleasure (a woman).

régaler, se: il s'en régale, he's thoroughly enjoying it.

regarder: vous ne m'avez pas regardé(e)! *or* **vous m'avez bien regardé(e)?** what do you take me for? do you think I'm a mug?

régime, *m.* **r. jockey,** strict diet.

reginglard, *m.* wine.

règles, *f.pl.* menses*.

reglinguet, *m.* kind of wine.

réglo, *adj., adv.* regular, correct, in order; **il est r., c'est un type r.,** he's a regular fellow*, he's on the level, he's a straight guy; **il s'est conduit réglo avec moi,** he's been straight with me.

regonfler: ça m'a regonflé, that's put me on my feet again.

regriffer, to take back.

régul(e), *adj.* =**réglo.**

régulier, *m.* =**un type réglo.**

régulière, *f.* **ma r.,** my wife*.

reins, *m.pl.* 1. **les avoir dans les r.**=**les avoir dans le dos (dos 8).** 2. **être chaud des r.,** to be hot stuff.

relâche, *f.* **faire r.**=**avoir ses affaires.**

relance, *f.* borrowing.

relancer. 1. **r. qn,** to badger s.o., to

pester s.o., to run after s.o., to be at s.o., to be on s.o.'s track. **2.** (*at poker*) to raise the bid.

relarguer, to release, to set free.

relax, *adj.* relaxed.

relaxe, *m.* reclining chair.

relègue, *f.* preventive detention.

relingé, *adj.* togged up again.

reluire. 1. to enjoy oneself immensely. **2.** =jouir. *See also* **brosse.**

reluquer. 1. to ogle, to eye, to leer at. **2.** to have one's eye on, to covet (sth.).

remâcher, to brood (*or* to ponder) over, to nurse (a grievance).

remballer=**rembarrer.**

rembarrer, to snub*; **se faire r.,** to get sat on.

rembiner. 1. to reconcile. **2.** to put s.o. in his place.

rembo, *m.* rendezvous.

rembour, *m.* **1.** =rancart. **2. aller au r.,** to pay* up.

rembrayer, to start work again.

remède, *m.* **1. un r. de cheval,** a drastic remedy, a kill-or-cure remedy. **2.** (*of woman*) **un r. d'amour** *or* **un r. contre l'amour,** a perfect fright, a woman as ugly as sin. **3.** revolver*.

remercier, to dismiss*.

remesurer, to vomit*.

remettre. 1. to recognize, to remember; **je ne le remets pas,** I can't place him. **2. r. ça,** to have another try (*or* another go), to begin again, to be at it again, to repeat the process; **remettons ça!** let's have another go (*or* another drink)! **remettez-nous ça!** set 'em up again! (*i.e. another drink*). **3. en r.** (**un peu**), to exaggerate*, to overdo it, to go one better.

remiser. 1. r. qn (**à sa place**), to put s.o. in his place, to take s.o. down a peg, to snub* s.o. **2.** to superannuate. **3.** =lâcher **1. 4.** =dételer **1.** *and* **2.**

remmancher, to patch up again, to set going again.

remontant, *m.* tonic, pick-me-up, bracer.

remonte, *f.* procuring girls for brothels.

remonter, to buck (s.o.) up, to set (s.o.) right.

remordre : y r., to have another go (*or* another bash) at it, to have another bite at the cherry.

remoucher. 1. =moucher **1. 2.** to recognize, to spot. **3.** to look* at.

remue-fesses, *m.* any dance.

rempiffer, se, to put on weight (*or* flesh).

rempilé, *m.* (*mil.*) re-enlisted man.

rempiler, (*mil.*) to re-enlist.

rempli, *adj.* rich*.

remplir, se, to get rich, to amass a fortune.

remplumer, se, (*a*) to put on weight (*or* flesh); (*b*) to pick up again (*of health, spirits, financially, etc.*).

renâcler, to grumble*, to jit.

renard, *m.* **1.** =jaune **1. 2. un vieux** (*or* **un fin**) **r.,** (*of person*) a sly old fox, a sly dog. **3. faire** (*or* **cracher** *or* **écorcher** *or* **lâcher** *or* **piquer**) **un r.,** to vomit*. **4. tirer au r.,** to shirk, to jib at one's work, to be work-shy, to malinger*.

renarder, to vomit*.

renaud, *m.* anger; **être en** (*or* **aller au**) **r.,** to get angry*; **mettre** (*or* **filer**) **qn en r.,** to rile s.o.

renaude, *f.* **faire de la r.**=**renauder.**

renauder=**rouspéter.**

renaudeur, *m.* =rouspéteur.

rencard, *m.* information.

rencarder, to inform*.

rencart, *m.* rendezvous.

rencarter, to arrange to meet s.o.

rencontre, *f.* (**le**) **faire à la r.,** to pretend that it is a chance meeting.

rencontrer, se : comme on se rencontre! it's a small world!

rendève, *m.* rendezvous.

rendez-moi, *m.* **vol au r.-m.,** ringing the changes.

rendre. 1. to vomit*. **2. ça rend!** it does the trick! it works!

rendu, *adj.* **r.** (**de fatigue**), exhausted*.

rengaine, *f.* **c'est toujours la même r.!**=**c'est toujours le même refrain!**

rengrâcier, rengrâcir. 1. to cool down. **2.** to come to terms.

reniflant, *m.* nose*.

renifle, *f.* police.

renifler. 1. = blairer. **2.** r. le coup, to sense (*or* to smell) the danger. **3.** r. sur, to sniff at, to turn one's nose up at. **4.** ça renifle, it stinks*.

reniflette, *f.* cocaine (*drugs**).

reniquer = rouspéter.

renquiller. 1. to come back, to return. **2.** to pocket again. **3.** = rempiler.

renseignements, *m.pl.* aller aux r., to court (a girl) with the hands, to sample the goods.

rentes, *f.pl.* tu penses à mes r.? (*said by a prostitute to a client*) how about a little present?

rentoiler, se, to pick up, to put on weight again.

rentre-dedans, *m.* faire du r.-d. à, to make amorous advances to, to make a pass at.

rentrer : *See* chou 7, dedans 3, mou, *m.* 1, portrait 4.

renversant, *adj.* staggering, stunning, amazing.

renverser, 1, to dumbfound*. **2.** to conciliate. **3.** to go on the spree*.

repapilloter, (se) = (se) rapapilloter.

réparouze, *f.* repair, repairing.

repassé, *p.p.* être r., to be done out of one's fair share of the swag.

repasser. 1. to diddle, to cheat*. **2.** to kill*. **3.** pour . . ., tu repasseras! as for . . ., there's nothing doing! (*or* you can call again!).

repaumer. 1. to grab back. **2.** to lose again.

repêcher, to help (s.o.) out of a mess, to give (s.o.) a helping hand.

repérer. 1. to spot, to pick out. **2.** to watch closely, to keep an eye on.

repiquer. 1. r. (au truc) = rebiffer (au truc). **2.** to recuperate, to pick up again (in health). **3.** to recapture, to nab again.

répondant, *m.* avoir du r., to have money behind one.

répondre : je vous en réponds! you bet! take my word for it! and no mistake! I should jolly well think so!

report, *m.* (*turf*) any to come.

repousser, to stink*. *See also* goulot.

requimpe, *f.* full-length coat.

requimpette, *f.* frock-coat.

requinquant, *m.* tonic, pick-me-up, (corpse-) reviver.

requinquer, (*a*) to smarten* (*or* to spruce) (s.o.) up; (*b*) to buck (s.o.) up.

requinquer, se, (*a*) to smarten* (*or* to spruce) oneself up; (*b*) to buck (*or* to pick *or* to perk) up (after an illness).

resco, *m.* = gargote 1.

respectueuse, *f.* prostitute*.

respirante, *f.* **1.** mouth*. **2.** = reniflette.

respirer. 1. dur à r., incredible, hard to swallow. **2.** un dur à r., a tough guy.

respirette, *f.* = reniflette.

resquillage, *m.* gate-crashing; wangling.

resquille, *f.* faire de la r. = resquiller.

resquiller, to gate-crash; to wangle.

resquilleur, *m.* gate-crasher; wangler.

ressaut, *m.* **1.** mettre (*or* foutre) qn à r., to provoke s.o., to drive s.o. mad, to get on s.o.'s nerves. **2.** aller (*or* être) à r., to flare up, to lose one's temper*.

ressauter, to protest, to kick, to show fight; faire r. qn = mettre qn à ressaut.

ressent, *m.* warning; porter le (*or* aller au) r., to alert the police.

ressentir, s'en: (ne pas) s'en r. pour, (not) to have a liking for, (not) to be keen on.

restau, resto, *m.* restaurant.

rester: y r., to be killed on the spot; cette fois, tu vas y r.! this time your number's up!

resucée, *f.* **1.** stale news. **2.** re-hash. **3.** (on en boit) une petite r.? how about another little drink? how about another one?

retailler, to hesitate.

rétamé, *adj.* **1.** penniless*. **2.** dead drunk*.

rétamer, to make drunk; se (faire) r., to get drunk*.

retape, *f.* faire la r. = faire le trottoir; être à la r., to be on the beat.

retaper. 1. to do (or to touch) up, to repair, to mend. **2.** to buck (s.o.) up. **3.** to fail* (s.o. at an examination).

retaper, se = **se requinquer** (b).

retapissage, m. **passer au r.,** to submit to an identification parade.

retapisser, to identify, to recognize.

retenir. 1. je te retiens! I'll pay you back for that! I'll watch it next time! I'll get my own back for that! **2. je la retiens, celle-là!** (a) I'll not forget that! I'll get my own back for that! (b) that's a good one, that is! **3. pour le tact (etc.), je te retiens!** (iron.) I'll come to you when tact (etc.) is wanted!

retoquer, to fail* (s.o. at an examination).

retour de flamme, m. **1.** backfire; back-lash. **2.** return to an old flame.

retourne, f. **les avoir à la r.** = **avoir les bras retournés.**

retourné, p.p. **les avoir retournés** = **avoir les bras retournés.**

retourner. 1. ça m'a retourné(e), that gave me quite a turn (or quite a shock); **être tout(e) retourné(e),** to be all of a dither. See also **sang 10. 2. en r.,** to take to prostitution.

retourner, se: savoir se r. = **savoir se débrouiller.**

rétro, m. (= **rétroviseur**) driving-mirror.

retrousser. 1. to earn (money). **2. elle en retrousse,** she lives on her charms. **3. il en retrousse,** he's seen better days.

retrouver, se. 1. to recover one's expenses. **2. comme on se retrouve!** fancy meeting you again! it's a small world! **3. s'y r.,** to find one's bearings; **je ne puis m'y r.,** I can't make head or tail of this.

réussi, adj. **c'est r., ça!** (iron.) a nice mess you've made of it (or of things)!

réussir. 1. le poisson (etc.) ne me réussit pas, fish (etc.) doesn't agree with me, I'm allergic to fish (etc.). **2. r. le coup,** to bring it off, to do the trick, (iron.) to make a fine mess of it.

rêve, m. **c'est le r.!** it's just perfect! it's everything one could desire! **ce n'est pas le r.!** it's not all one could wish for!

revenant, m. **mais c'est un r.!** or **quel r. vous faites!** you're quite a stranger!

revendre: en r. à qn, to outwit s.o., to take s.o. in; **avoir de qch. à r.,** to have enough and to spare of sth.

revenez-y, m. **1. un r. de jeunesse,** a return to one's youth. **2. avoir un (petit) goût de r.,** (of food) to taste more-ish. **3. attendre qn au r.,** to wait till s.o. tries it on again.

revenir. 1. sa figure (ne) me revient (pas), I (don't) like the look of him (of her). **2. je n'en reviens pas!** I can't get over it! that beats me! well, I never! it's amazing! **3. il revient de loin,** he was at death's door, he's had a narrow escape, it was touch and go with him. **4. il n'en reviendra pas,** he'll never get over it, he won't recover, he won't pull through.

reverdir, to grow young again.

revoici, revoilà, adv. **me revoici!** here I am again! **le revoilà!** there he is again!

revoyure, f. **à la (bonne) r.!** so long!*

revue, f. **1. être de r.,** être (des) gens de r., to meet again (or often), to meet again before long. **2. être encore de la r.,** (a) to be diddled (or done) again; (b) to be in for it again, to be for the high jump again.

rez-de-chaussée, m. (journ.) article, ĩn the lower half of a page.

rhabiller. 1. se faire r., to be swindled*. **2. allez vous r.!** go to blazes!* **3. aller se r.,** to start afresh (in business, etc.).

rhéto, f. (= 'classe de rhétorique', now called 'classe terminale') sixth form.

rhume, m. **prendre qch. pour son r.,** to be severely reprimanded*; **qu'est-ce qu'il a pris pour son r.!** he didn't half cop it!

ribambelle, f. long string (of kids, of names, of insults, etc.).

ribarbère, m. revolver*.

ribote, f. drinking bout, booze (up), binge; **faire (la) r.,** to go on the spree*; **en r.,** on the spree*.

riboter = faire (la) **ribote**.

riboteur, *m.* boozer.

ribouis, *m.* **1.** boot*, shoe. **2.** foot*. **3.** cobbler, 'snob'.

ribouldingue, *f.* spree*; **faire la r.**, to go on the spree*.

ribouldinguer = faire la **ribouldingue**.

riboule, *f.* **partir en r.** = faire la **ribouldingue**.

ribouler : *See* **calot, quinquets**.

riboustin, *m.* revolver*.

ric-rac, ric et rac, ric-à-rac, *adv.* (*a*) punctually, to (*or* at) the last minute; (*b*) on the nail, to the last penny; (*c*) barely, narrowly, only just.

Ricains, *m.pl.* Americans, Yanks.

richard, *m.* rich* person, wealthy person; **un gros r.**, a pluto.

riche, *adj.* (*of idea, etc.*) first-rate*; **comme offre (etc.), ce n'est pas r.,** it's not up to much as an offer (etc.); **ça fait r.!** it looks posh!

richissime, *adj.* extremely rich*.

rideau, *m.* **1. r.!** that'll do! lay off! **2. en r.** = **en panne (panne 3). 3. faire r., passer au r.,** to be done out of sth.

rider, ridère, *adj.* first-rate*, dressed up*; *m.* smart man's suit.

rien, *indef. pron.* **1. de r.!** (*in reply to apology*) (please) don't mention it! (*in reply to thanks*) you're welcome! **2. ce n'est pas r.!** that's quite something! **3. pour trois fois r.,** for next to nothing. **4. r. que cela** (*or* **ça**)! is that all! no less! **5. en un r. de temps** *or* **en moins de r.,** immediately*. **6.** *adv.* (*intensive use*) very, not half—*e.g.* **elle est r. laide!** she's as ugly as sin! **elle est r. bath!** she's a stunner! **il est r. drôle!** he's a real caution! **c'est r. bath!** it's simply terrific! **ce serait r. chouette!** that'd be super (*or* smashing)! **il fait r. froid!** it ain't half cold! **il est r. salaud!** he's a dirty bastard! **tu as r. de la veine!** you've got the devil's own luck!

rien-du-tout, *m.f.* rotter*.

rif(e), riff(e), *m.* **1.** fire; **mettre** (*or* **coller**) **le r. à,** to set fire to. **2. chercher du r. à qn,** to pick a quarrel with s.o.

3. war(fare); **aller** (*or* **monter**) **au r.,** to go to war, to go to the front-line (*or* the firing-line). **4. de rif (et d'autor):** *see* **autor d'. 5. mettre qn en r.,** to make s.o. angry, to get s.o.'s dander up.

riffauder, to set fire to.

riffer, se, to fight, to scrap, to have a set-to.

rififi, *m.* violent brawl, set-to, free-for-all, fireworks, ructions, rough house.

riflard, *m.* umbrella*.

rifle, *m.* = **rif 1**.

rifler. 1. to steal*. **2.** = **chercher du rif à qn**.

rif(f)lette, *f.* **1.** = **rif 3**. **2.** pistol, revolver*.

riflo, *adj.* **1.** first-rate*; dressed up*. **2. avoir des goûts de riflos,** to have expensive tastes.

rigolade, *f.* fun, fun and games, lark; **une partie de r.,** a jollification; **prendre qch. à la r.,** not to take sth. seriously, to laugh sth. off; **tout ça, c'est de la r.,** that's all tommy-rot, it's just tomfoolery; **ce n'est pas de la r.,** it's no laughing matter; **une vraie r.,** (*a*) mere child's play; (*b*) a right giggle.

rigolard, *adj.* (*a*) funny*, comical; (*b*) fond of fun; *m.* joker.

rigolboche, *adj.* = **rigolo**, *adj.*

rigoler, to laugh, to joke, to have fun, to have a good time; **vous voulez r.,** you're not serious (*or* in earnest), are you? you're only joking; **pour rigoler,** for fun; **je ne rigolais pas,** it was no laughing matter.

rigoleur, *adj.* fond of a laugh (*or* a lark *or* a joke); jolly, jovial; *m.* joker.

rigolo (*f.* -**ote**), **1.** *adj.* (*a*) funny*, comical; **c'est r.!** what a lark (*or* a giggle)! **ce n'était pas r.!** it was no joke! **c'était d'un r.!** it was a scream! **il est r.,** he's a card; (*b*) queer, rum. **2.** *m.* (*a*) joker; (*b*) revolver*.

rigouillard, *adj.* = **rigolard**, *adj.*

rigoustin, *m.* revolver*.

rikiki, *m.* = **riquiqui**.

rimer : cela ne rime à rien, there is neither rhyme nor reason in it, there's no sense in it, it doesn't add up; **à quoi cela rime-t-il?** what's this in aid of? what does all that mean?

rimmel, *m.* mascara, eye-black.

rince, *f.* **remettre la r.**, to have another round of drinks.

rincé, *adj.* **1.** penniless*, cleaned out. **2.** exhausted*. **3.** done* for.

rince-cochon, *m.* glass of mineral water drunk after a binge.

rincée, *f.* **1.** drenching, downpour. **2.** thrashing*.

rince-gueule, *m.* = pousse-café.

rincer. **1.** to clean (s.o.) out (at gambling), to skin (s.o.) dry; **se faire r.**, to be skinned. **2.** to thrash*; **se faire r.**, to get a thrashing*. **3.** to drench; **se faire r.**, to get a drenching. **4.** to stand (s.o.) a drink; **se faire r.**, to get s.o. to stand one a drink, to sponge on s.o. for a drink. **5.** **(se) r.**, to drink, to (have a) gargle. *See also* **bec 11, dalle, œil 17.**

rincette, rinçonnette, *f.* = pousse-café.

rinçure, *f.* **de la r.** (de bouteilles *or* de bidet), weak wine, belly-wash, slops.

riné, *m.* cinema; **r. à bicol,** stereoscopic cinema.

ringard, *m.* **1.** opium pipe. **2.** 'square'.

rip(e), *m.* **jouer r.**, to decamp*.

ripaille, *f.* tuck-in, spread.

ripatonner, to walk; to decamp*.

ripatons, *m.pl.* **1.** boots, shoes (*poor or old ones*). **2.** feet*; **se tirer des r.**, to decamp*.

riper. **1.** to decamp*. **2.** to steal*. **3.** to clean out, to skin (s.o.).

ripeur, *m.* dustman's assistant.

ripincelle, *m.* = riz-pain-sel.

ripopée, *f.* **1.** = rinçure. **2.** hash, hotchpotch (*of ideas, etc.*).

ripopo, *adj.* badly played (*sport*).

riquiqui, *m.* **1.** undersized* person. **2.** the little finger, pinky. **3.** poor quality brandy, rotgut.

rire. **1.** **c'est pour r.** *or* **histoire de r.**, (just) for fun, (just) for a joke, for kicks. **2.** **vous me faites r.!** you're kidding! don't try to fool me! that's

a laugh! **3.** **vous voulez r.!** you're joking (*or* kidding)! you're not in earnest! **4.** **laissez-moi r.!** you make me laugh! **5.** **un(e) ... pour r.**, an apology for a ... **6.** (*of garment*) to gape (at the seam).

rire, *m.* (*of play*) **un fou r.**, a screaming farce.

risette, *f.* **faire (la) r. à qn,** (*of child*) to give s.o. a smile.

Rital, *m.* Italian*.

ritournelle, *f.* **c'est toujours la même r.** = c'est toujours le même refrain.

riz-pain-sel, *m.* (*mil.*) soldier or officer in the French Army Service Corps.

roberts, *m.pl.* breasts* (of female).

robinet, *m.* **1.** **ouvrir le r.** = ouvrir les écluses. **2.** **r. d'eau tiède**, a drivelling bore*.

rock, *adj.* tip-top, super, wizard.

rôdeuse, *f.* = pierreuse.

rogne, *f.* **1.** bad temper; **être en r.**, to be in a bad temper*; **se mettre (se foutre) en r.**, to get angry*; **mettre (ficher, foutre) qn en r.**, to exasperate* s.o. **2.** **chercher des rognes à qn,** to pick a quarrel with s.o.

rogner. **1.** to be angry*. **2.** to grumble*.

rognons, *m.pl.* testicles*.

rognure, *f.* trollop, low prostitute*.

rogomme, *m.* spirits, liquor; **voix de r.**, (*of drunkard*) husky (*or* beery) voice, croak.

rogommeux, *adj.* husky, beery.

roi, *m.* **1.** **un morceau de r.**, a dainty bit, a dish fit for a king. **2.** **aller où le r. va à pied** (*or* **en personne**), to go to the toilet. **3.** **le r. n'est pas son cousin** (*or* **son oncle**), he's as proud as Punch, he wouldn't call the king his cousin. **4.** **travailler pour le r. de Prusse,** to work for nothing (at all), to work for love, to get nothing out of it.

romaine, *f.* **être bon comme la r.**, (*a*) to be done* for, to be certain to get it in the neck. (*b*) to be pushed into sth. unpleasant.

romance, *f.* **piquer une r.**, to sleep*.

romanis, romanos, *m.pl.* gipsies.

rombier, *m.* fellow*.

rombière, *f.* 1. (*pej.*) woman*. 2. une vieille r., an old hag, an old bag, an old trout. 3. =sous-mac (*or* maq).

roméo, *m.* rum and water drink.

rompre: ça me les rompt!=ça me les brise (briser 1).

rompu, *p.p.* r. (de fatigue), exhausted*.

ronchon, *adj.* grouchy; *m.* grumbler.

ronchonneau, *m.* =ronchon(n)ot.

ronchonnement, *m.* grumbling.

ronchonner, to grumble*.

ronchon(n)ot, *m.* 1. (*mil.*) le colonel R. griping army officer. 2. old griper.

rond, *adj.* 1. drunk*; fin r., r. comme une boule (*or* une bille *or* un boudin), dead drunk*. 2. *adv.* tourner r., to run smoothly; ne pas tourner r., to go haywire, to go to the dogs, (*of person*) to go potty.

rond, *m.* 1. ne pas (ne plus) avoir un (*or* le) r., to be penniless*. 2. il n'est pas ... pour un r.=il n'est pas ... pour un sou. 3. être (*or* en être *or* en rester) comme deux ronds de flan (*or* de frites *or* de tarte), to be dumbfounded*. 4. anus*; prendre (donner, refiler) du r., to be a pederast*. 5. faire des ronds dans l'eau, to be idle.

rond-de-cuir, *m.* clerk, civil servant, penpusher, Jack-in-office.

rondelle, *f.*, rondibé, *m.* 1. =rond, *m.* 4; être de la r., to be a pederast*. 2. baver sur les rondelles=rouleau 3.

rondin, *m.* =étron; *pl.* breasts* (of woman).

rondir, to make drunk.

rondir, se, to get drunk*.

rondouillard, *adj.* small and fat, chubby, podgy; *m.* tubby, podge.

rondouille, *adj.* =rondouillard, *adj.*

ronflaguer, to snore, to sleep.

ronfler. 1. =barder. 2. r. avec, to sleep with, to go to bed with.

ronflette, *f.* nap, snooze, forty winks; faire (*or* pousser) une r., to have a nap.

ronfleur, *m.* 1. telephone, blower. 2. envoyer le r. =envoyer le duce.

ronflon, *m.* =ronflette.

rongeur, *m.* taximeter, trip-recorder, the 'clock'.

ronibus, *m.* bus.

ropoplots, *m.pl.* breasts* (of woman).

roquet, *m.* pug(-dog), mongrel, cur, pooch, mutt; (*of person*) puppy, whippersnapper.

Rosalie, *f.* (*mil.*, *W.W.I*) bayonet, 'toothpick', 'meat-skewer'.

rosbif, *m.* Englishman.

rose, *f.* 1. envoyer qn sur les roses, to send s.o. packing*. 2. cela ne sent pas la r., that smells nasty. 3. ce n'était pas des roses, it wasn't all plain sailing. 4. bouton de r., clitoris.

rossard, *m.* 1. (*of horse*) old screw, sorry nag. 2. (*of person*) lazybones; wash-out; rotter*.

rosse, *adj.* beastly, nasty, catty, bitchy, smutty, very strict; scurrilous, satirical; *f.* 1. =rossard 1. 2. (*of person*) rotter*.

rossée, *f.* thrashing*.

rosser, to thrash*.

rosserie, *f.* beastly (*or* dirty *or* rotten) trick (*or* talk *or* remark *or* story *or* action); faire une r. à qn, to do the dirty on s.o.

rossignol, *m.* 1. unsaleable article, white elephant, sticker; passer (*or* écouler) un r. à qn, to sell s.o. a pup. 2. skeleton-key, screw, betty, picklock. 3. bung (of barrel). 4. r. à glands, pig. 5. *pl.* old stock. 6. *pl.* (*motor.*) queer noises (in car).

rot, *m.* belch, burp; lâcher (*or* faire) un r.=roter 1.

roter. 1. to belch, to burp, to gurk. 2. en r.=en baver. 3. en r. des ronds de chapeau, to be dumbfounded*.

roteuse, *f.* bottle of champagne*.

rôti, *m.* s'endormir sur le r., to dawdle over one's work, to go to sleep over it, not to get on with the job.

rôti, *adj.* être r.=être brûlé; tout est r., (*of scheme*) it's all U.P., its no go.

rotin, *m.* small money*; ne pas avoir un r., to be penniless*.

rôtissoir, *m.* crematorium.

rotoplo(t)s, *m.pl.* =roberts.

rototos, *m.pl.* **1.** =roberts. **2.** faire des r. =roter 1.

rotules, *f.pl.* être sur les r., to be exhausted*; mettre qn sur les r., to exhaust s.o.

roubignolles, *f.pl.* testicles*; en avoir plein les r. =en avoir plein les couilles.

roublard, *adj.* crafty, cunning; *m.* crafty person, artful dodger.

roublardise, *f.* craftiness, cunning; sly trick.

rouchie, *f.* trollop, low prostitute*.

roudoudou, *m.* **1.** fellow*, blighter; un vieux r., an old fog(e)y*. **2.** liquorice.

roue, *f.* **1.** r. de derrière, five-franc piece, cart-wheel, coach-wheel. **2.** r. de devant, two-franc piece. **3.** sucer la r., (*cycling*) to follow closely preceding competitor. **4.** être dans la r., to be with it. **5.** montrer sa r. arrière, to be a winner.

roué, *adj.* exhausted*.

rouflaquette, *f.* **1.** =accroche-cœur. **2.** *pl.* side-whiskers, side-burns.

rouge, *m.* **1.** red wine; gros r., coarse red wine; un coup de r., a glass of red wine. **2.** red, bolshie, commie. **3.** mettre le r., (*a*) to break off with s.o.; (*b*) to create a disturbance. **4.** envoyer le r., to shoot.

rougnot(t)er, to stink*.

rouillarde, *f.* bottle (of wine, etc.).

rouille, *f.* =rouillarde.

roulant, *adj.* very funny*; il est r.! he's a scream!

roulant, *m.* **1.** commercial traveller. **2.** taxi. **3.** foot-plate man (*railways*).

roulante, *f.* **1.** motor-car. **2.** (*mil.*) field-kitchen. **3.** *pl.* bowls (*game*).

rouleau, *m.* **1.** change(z) de r.! = change(z) de disque! **2.** *pl.* =couilles; avoir mal aux rouleaux, to suffer from V.D. **3.** baver sur les rouleaux (*or* casser les rouleaux) à qn, to get on s.o.'s nerves (*or* on s.o.'s tits *or* on s.o.'s wick), to give s.o. a pain in the neck. **4.** être au bout de son r., to be at one's wits' end, to be at the end of one's tether, to be near the end.

roulée, *f.* **1.** hand-made cigarette. **2.** donner une r. à qn, to beat s.o. up.

roulée, *adj.,* *f.* elle est bien r.! *or* ce qu'elle est bien r.! *or* elle n'est pas mal r.! she's got a marvellous figure! she's certainly curvaceous! she's well-stacked! she's got a shape!

rouler. 1. r. qn, (*a*) to gull* s.o.; (*b*) to beat, to lick s.o.; se faire r., to be diddled, to be done in the eye. **2.** se les r., not to work at all, to twiddle one's thumbs, to have a cushy time, to do damn all. **3.** en r. une, to hand-roll a cigarette. **4.** to lead a fast life. **5.** to throw the dice, to roll the bones. **6.** to talk* a lot, to be a gas-bag, to rattle on. **7.** ça roule! = ça biche! **8.** =r. sa bosse (bosse 4).

rouler, se, to laugh* uproariously.

rouletabille, *m.* (*of person*) rolling stone.

rouletaille, *f.* (game of) roulette.

roulettes, *f.pl.* **1.** ça marche (*or* ça va) comme sur des r., things are going swimmingly (*or* like clockwork *or* like one o'clock *or* like a house on fire). **2.** les r. *or* les vaches (*or* les guignols) à r., policemen on bicycles.

rouleur, *m.* **1.** cheat, diddler. **2.** (*of person*) rolling stone. **3.** (*of person*) gas-bag; diddler.

rouleuse, *f.* trollop, prostitute*.

roulotte, *f.* vol (*or* chourave) à la r., stealing from parked cars; voleur à la r. =roulottier.

roulotter: ça roulotte! =ça roule! (rouler 7).

roulottier, *m.* car-thief (*from parked cars*).

roulure, *f.* =rouleuse.

roupane, *f.* clothing; woman's dress.

roupanner: se les r. =se les rouler (rouler 2).

roupes, roupettes, *f.pl.* testicles*.

roupie, *f.* **1.** snot, dew-drop (at end of nose). **2.** de la r. (de sansonnet *or* de singe), worthless rubbish. **3.** une vieille r., an old hag.

roupignolles, *f.pl.* testicles*.

roupiller, to sleep*.

roupilleur, *m.* sleeper, snoozer.

roupillon, *m.* snooze, nap; **piquer un r.**, to snooze.

roupillonner, roupionner, to sleep*.

rouquemoute, *m.f.* 1. = **rouquin(e)**, *f.* 2. red wine, 'rosy'.

rouquin, -e, 1. *adj.* red-haired, carroty-haired, carroty. 2. *m.f.* red-head, ginger, carrots, carrot-nob. 3. *m.* un **coup de r.**, a glass of red wine. **rouquins**, *m.pl.* = **rousse** 1.

rouscailler, to grumble*. *See also* **bigorne**.

rouscailleur, *m.* grumbler.

rouspétance, *f.* **faire de la r.** = **rouspéter**.

rouspéter, to grumble*; to be obstreperous, to kick, to show fight.

rouspéteur, *m.* grumbler; obstreperous person.

rouspignolles, *f.pl.* = **roubignolles**.

rousqui, *m.* **faire du r.** = **rouspéter**.

Rousqui, *m.* = **Rousski**.

rousse, *f.* 1. police, cops, coppers, the 'law'; **un mec de la r.**, a policeman*. 2. **faire de la r.** = **rouspéter**.

rousser = **rouspéter**.

roussi, *adj.* done* for; *m.* **ça sent le r.**, trouble is brewing, there's danger on the line.

roussin, *m.* (*a*) policeman*; (*b*) police-spy, copper's nark.

Rousski, *m.* Russian, Russki.

roustasse, rouste, *f.* severe thrashing*.

rouster, to thrash*.

rousti, *f.* (*Provençal dial.*) thrashing*.

rousti, *adj.* 1. done* for. 2. diddled, done brown.

roustir. 1. to deceive, to diddle, to do brown. 2. to rob, to steal*.

roustisseur, *m.* crook, sharper.

roustissure, *f.* 1. **de la r.**, des roustissures = de la roupie (roupie 1 *and* 2). 2. double dealing.

roustons, *m.pl.* testicles*; **baver sur les r. à qn** = **baver sur les rouleaux à qn**.

routier, *m.* **vieux r.**, old stager, old hand, old trouper.

royalement, *adv.* **s'en ficher r.**, not to care a rap* about it; **je m'en fiche r.!** I couldn't care less! I don't give a damn!

royaliste, *adj.* **être plus r. que le roi**, to be over-punctilious.

ruban, *m.* 1. road; **se taper** (*or* **s'appuyer**) **un bon bout de r.**, to walk a fair step. 2. pavement; **faire le r.** = **faire le trottoir**. 3. *pl.* (*racing*) starting gate.

rubanner = **faire le trottoir**.

rubrique, *f.* trick, dodge; **il en sait des rubriques!** he knows all the tricks of the trade!

rude, *adj.* first-rate*.

rudement, *adv.* awfully, extremely, like anything, no end of.

rupin, *adj.* 1. elegant, smart, first-rate*. 2. rich*. 3. *m.* swell, toff, nob, nut, filbert.

rupiner. 1. (*sch.*) to do well (at an examination), to get on swimmingly. 2. **ça rupine!** I'm doing fine! I'm quids in! 3. to slog away at.

rupinos, rupinskoff, *adj.* = **rupin**, *adj.*

Ruscoff, Ruskoff, *m.* Russian, Russki.

rustine, *f.* 1. *r.t.m.* 1., rubber patch (*for bicycle puncture*). 2. a sticker, a bore, a button-holer.

S

sable, *m.* 1. avoir du s. dans les yeux, (*of children*) to be sleepy; le marchand de s. a (*or* est) passé, the sandman is coming, the sandman (*or* dustman) has gone by (*said of children showing signs of sleepiness*). 2. être sur le s., (*a*) to be penniless*; (*b*) to be out of work.
sabler. 1. to sing. 2. to toss off (drink).
sabord, *m.* coup de s., searching glance.
sabot, *m.* 1. old crock (*of car, ship, violin, etc.*). 2. bungler, botcher; travailler comme un s., to botch one's work. 3. dormir comme un s., to sleep like a top. 4. raisonner comme un s. = raisonner comme une pantoufle. 5. je vous vois (*or* je vous entends) venir avec vos gros sabots, I can see what you're after, I can see what your little game is. 6. ne pas rester (*or* ne pas avoir) les deux pieds dans le même s., (*a*) not to remain idle*; (*b*) to be wide-awake*. 7. jouer comme un s. = jouer comme un pied (pied 15).
sabouler, to reprimand*.
sabouler, se, to dress*, to tog up.
sabre, *m.* 1. penis*. 2. le s. et le goupillon, the Army and the Church.
sabrer. 1. to bungle, to botch, to make a mess of. 2. to have coition* with. 3. to eliminate, to knock off.
sabreur, *m.* 1. bungler, botcher. 2. fornicator.
sac, *m.* 1. thousand francs. 2. stomach*. 3. en avoir plein son s., avoir son s., to be drunk*, to have a skinful. 4. l'affaire est dans le s. *or* c'est dans le s., it's a certainty*, it's in the bag. 5. avoir le (gros) s., être au s., to be rich*. 6. cracher (*or* éternuer) dans le s., to be guillotined. 7. donner son s. à qn = sacquer qn. 8. épouser un s. (*or* le gros s.), to marry a rich girl, to marry money. 9. faire (*or* gagner) son s., to make one's pile. 10. fichu comme mon

s., (*a*) bungled, botched; (*b*) dressed like a guy. 11. mettre la tête dans le s. à qn, to lead s.o. astray, to hoodwink s.o.; to nonplus s.o. 12. mettez ça dans votre s.! put that in your pipe and smoke it! 13. prendre qn la main dans le s., to catch s.o. red-handed (*or* in the (very) act). 14. travailler le s., (*boxing*) to practise with the punch-bag. 15. vider son s., to get it off one's chest, to say all one knows (*or* all one has to say), to speak one's mind, to make a clean breast of it. 16. un(e) ... qui n'est pas dans un s. = un(e) ... qui n'est pas dans une musette. 17. *miscellaneous uses:* s. à charbon (*or* à carbi), priest*; s. à malices, (*a*) bag of tricks; (*b*) trickster; s. à viande, sleeping-bag; s. à vin, tippler, boozer; s. d'os, person all skin and bones, bag of bones.
saccagne, saccaille, *f.* knife.
saccagner, to knife.
sachets, *m.pl.* socks.
sacouse, *m.* hand-bag.
sacquer, to discharge, to give the sack.
sacquer, se, to go to bed.
sacré, *adj.* damned, confounded; s. nom de Dieu! s. nom d'un chien! (God) damn it (all)! (*expletives**).
sacrer, to curse and swear.
safran, *m.* aller au s., to throw away one's money.
sagouin(e), *m.f.* dirty, slovenly individual.
saïdi, *m.* = sidi 1.
saindoux, *m.* (*mil.*) corporal.
sainfoin, *m.* en faire un s., to kick up a hell of a row.
Saint-Crépin, *m.* 1. shoemaker; shoemaker's trade. 2. prendre la voiture de S.-C., to foot it, to go on Shanks's pony. 3. tout son S.-C. = tout son Saint-Frusquin.
Sainte-Anne, *pr.n.* être bon (*or* fait

or **mûr**) **pour S.-A.**, to be fit for the lunatic asylum (*or* for the loony-bin), to be mad*; **un échappé de S.-A.** = **un échappé de Charenton.**

Sainte-Nitouche, *f.* (*of girl*) demure little hypocrite; **elle fait la** (*or* **elle a l'air d'une** *or* **elle a un air de**) **S.-N.,** she looks as if butter wouldn't melt in her mouth.

Sainte-Touche, *f.* pay-day.

Saint-Frusquin, *m.* **tout le S.-F.,** the whole bag* of tricks; **tout son S.-F.,** all one's worldly goods.

Saint-Glinglin, *f.* **à la S.-G.,** never, when pigs (begin to) fly; **jusqu'à la S.-G.,** until the cows come home, till Hell freezes (over).

Saint-Jean, *f.* **1. en S.-J.,** naked*. **2. c'est de la S.-J.!** it's worthless*! **3. employer toutes les herbes de la S.-J.,** to leave no stone unturned.

Saint-Lago, *pr.n.* prison of Saint-Lazare.

Saint-Lundi, *f.* **faire la S.-L.** = **fêter le lundi.**

saint-truc, *m.* **tout le s.-t.,** the whole bag* of tricks.

salade, *f.* **1. s.** (**russe**), mix-up, brawl, holy mess. **2. vendre sa s.,** to ply one's trade, to make one's living. **3. savoir vendre sa s.,** to have the gift of the gab, to know how to sell oneself; **bon(n)ir sa s. à qn,** to spin s.o. the yarn, to chat s.o. up. **4. passer une s. à qn,** to reprimand* s.o. **5.** *pl.* (*a*) scandal, backbiting; (*b*) lies; (*c*) nonsense*; **tout ça, c'est des salades!** that's a lot of poppycock! **rencaisse** (*or* **avale**) **tes salades!** stow it! **faire un brin de s.,** to depart without paying. *See also* **panier.**

saladier, *m.* **1.** glib talker; line-shooter; fuss-pot; trouble-maker. **2.** mouth*; **taper du s.,** to have halitosis.

salaud, *m.* (*of person*) rotter*, swine, sod; **un beau s.,** a dirty bastard; **petit s.!** you little bastard! **espèce de s.!** you bloody swine!

sale, *adj.* (*of price, of court-sentence*) exorbitant, stiff; (*of joke, talk*) spicy, blue; (*of people, weather, etc.*) beastly.

salé, *m.* (**petit**) **s.,** child*, brat; **avoir un p. s. dans le tiroir,** to be pregnant*.

salement, *adv.* = **rudement.**

saler. 1. to overcharge, to sting, to soak; **s. la note,** to soak s.o. properly, to salt it for s.o., to stick it on. **2.** to be rough (*or* tough) on (s.o.).

saleté, *f.* **1.** dirty trick (*or* talk *or* story). **2.** = **salaud.**

salière, *f.* salt-cellar (*hollow at each side of the base of a woman's neck*).

saligaud, *m.* = **salaud.**

salingue, *adj.* dirty, filthy.

salir : tu la salis! you're laying it on thick!

salivard, *m.* chatterbox*, windbag.

salive, *f.* **1. perdre** (*or* **gaspiller** *or* **user**) **sa s.,** to waste one's breath. **2. dépenser beaucoup de s.,** to talk* volubly.

salle, *f.* (*th.*) **jouer à la s.,** to play to the gallery.

salle à manger, *f.* **s. à m. démontable,** set of false teeth.

saloir, *m.* **mettre la viande au s.,** to go to bed.

salop(ard), *m.* = **salaud.**

salope, *f.* (*of man or woman*) rotter*.

saloper, to botch, to bungle, to make a mess of, to muck up.

saloperie, *f.* **1.** rubbish*; dirty trick; dirty talk, smut. **2.** = **salaud. 3. s. de temps!** filthy weather!

salopiau(d), salopin, *m.* = **salaud.**

salsifs, *m.pl.* fingers; **une poignée de s.,** punch.

salut! salutas! *int.* **1.** greetings! how do! **2.** so long!

sana, *m.* sanatorium.

san(s-)dos, *m.* high stool.

sandwich, *m.* **être pris en s.,** to be caught between two fires.

sang, *m.* **1. attraper le coup de s., en prendre un coup de s.,** (*a*) to burst a blood vessel; (*b*) to fly into a rage. **2. avoir du s. dans les veines,** to be full of pep. **3. avoir du s. de navet,** to have no guts, to be chicken-livered (*or* lily-livered). **4. avoir qn dans le**

s. =avoir qn dans la peau. **5. bon s. (de bon s.)! bon s. de bon Dieu!** damn and blast it! **bon s. d'imbécile!** you bloody fool! **6. se faire du mauvais s.** (*or* **se cailler le s.** *or* **se faire un s.**), to worry, to fret (and fume), to bother one's head; **se manger** (*or* **se dévorer** *or* **se miner** *or* **se ronger** *or* **se tourner) le(s) sang(s),** to worry oneself sick. **7. se payer** (*or* **se faire) du bon s., se faire une pinte de bon s.,** to have a good time, to have a jolly good laugh. **8. pisser du s.,** to sweat one's guts out, to sweat (*or* to piss) blood. **9. suer s. et eau,** to toil and moil, to sweat blood. **10. (tout) mon s. n'a fait qu'un tour** *or* **ça m'a tourné** (*or* **retourné) les sangs,** that gave me quite a turn, that upset me no end.

sanguiner, se, to get drunk*.

sans-châsses, sans-mirettes, *adj.* blind.

sans-le-sou, *m.* penniless* person.

sans-loches, *adj.* deaf.

sansonnet, *m.* gendarme.

Santaga, *pr.n.* =Santoche.

santé, *f.* **1. il en a une s.!** *or* **il a une certaine s.!** he's got a nerve! I like his cheek! **2. avoir une s.,** to be long-suffering. **3. avoir une petite s.,** to be always ailing, to have poor health; **soigner sa petite s.,** to look after one's precious health, to be a molly-coddle.

santoche, *f.* health.

Santoche, *pr.n.* **la S.,** the Santé prison (*in Paris*).

sape, sapement, *m.* sentence, conviction; **s. de gonzesse,** light sentence.

saper. 1. to sentence; **être sapé,** to be sentenced. **2.** to dress.

saper, se, to dress (oneself).

sapes, *f.pl.* clothes*.

sapeur, *m.* **avaler le s.,** to take Holy Communion.

sapin, *m.* **1.** four-wheeler, cab, rumbler, growler. **2.** coffin; **ça sent le s.!** *or* **voilà une toux qui sent le s.!** that's a graveyard (*or* churchyard) cough!

saquer =sacquer.

sarbacane, *f.* rifle.

sarcif, sarcigol, *m.* =sauciflard.

sarco, *m.* coffin.

sardine, *f.* (*mil.*) N.C.O.'s stripe.

satané, *adj.* confounded, cursed, damned, infernal.

sataner, satonner, to pummel.

sataner, se, to fight, to scrap, to have a set-to.

saton, *m.* blow*.

sauce, *f.* **1.** rain; **recevoir une s.,** to be drenched. **2. allonger** (*or* **rallonger) la s.,** (*of book, speech, etc.*) to spin it out. **3. balancer** (*or* **envoyer) la s.,** (*a*) to fire (pistol, gun, etc.); (*b*) =**jouir. 4. être dans la s.,** to be in a fix*. **5.** motor-fuel, diesel-oil.

saucé, *adj.* **être s.** =se faire saucer **1** *and* **2.**

saucée, *f.* **1.** shower, downpour; drenching, soaking; **attraper une s.,** to get drenched. **2.** reprimand*.

saucer. 1. to drench, to soak to the skin; **se faire s.,** to get drenched, to get a soaking. **2.** to reprimand*; **se faire s.,** to get reprimanded.

sauciflard, *m.* sausage, salami.

saucisse, *f.* **1.** (*W.W.I*) (*a*) observation balloon, blimp; (*b*) trench mortar shell. **2. il ne les attache pas avec des saucisses** =il n'attache pas ses chiens avec des saucisses (chien **12**). **3. rouler des saucisses,** to exchange French kisses (*or* tongue-kisses). **4. rouler les saucisses,** to have one's finger-prints (*or* one's dabs) taken. **5.** fool*, duffer, noodle.

saucisson, *m.* **1.** (*pej.*) woman*. **2.** fool*, silly sausage.

saucissonner. 1. to tie (s.o.) up like a sausage. **2.** to arrest*. **3.** to eat.

saumâtre, *adj.* nasty, not to one's liking; **l'avoir s.** =l'avoir mauvaise.

saumure, *f.* sea.

sauré, sauret, *m.* **1.** gendarme. **2.** pimp.

saut, *m.* **faire un s. chez qn,** to pop along to *or* to pop round to *or* to pop over to *or* to slip along to *or* to drop in at *or* to nip round (*or* down *or* over) to s.o.'s house.

sautée, *f*. **grande s.**=échalas.

sauter. **1.** to arrest*; **se faire s.**, to get nabbed. **2.** to mount (a woman). **3.** to flare up, to go through the roof. **4. il faut que ça saute!** *or* **allez, et que ça saute!** make it snappy! look lively about it! put a jerk (*or* some vim) into it! jump to it! **5. la s.**, to go without food, to starve, to be clemmed. **5. se faire s.**, to commit suicide.

sauterelle, *f*. tall girl.

sauteur, *m*. unreliable person, weathercock.

sauteuse, *f*. **1.** bottle of champagne*. **2.** flea.

sauvage, *adj*. unauthorized, escaping control; **grève s.**, wild cat strike; **amour s.**, (hippies') free-love.

sauvette, *f*. **vendre à la s.**, (*of streetvendors*) to sell goods in the street illicitly, without having a licence, to be 'fly-pitching'; **à la s.**, ready to cut and run.

savate, *f*. **1.** bungler, botcher. **2.** tough meat. **3. traîner la s.**, to be down at heel.

savater, to bungle, to botch.

saveur, *f*. **coup de s.** =coup de sabord.

savoir. **1. s.!** (*elliptical for* **c'est à s.** *or* **reste à s.**), that remains to be seen! **2. il n'a rien voulu s.**, he just wouldn't hear of it, he just wouldn't listen, he wasn't having any. **3. je n'ai pas à le s.!** it's no concern of mine! **4.** ... **tout ce qu'il (elle, etc.) savait** (*or* **sait**), ... like the very devil, ... for all he (she, etc.) was worth. **5. qui-vous-savez**, (*said of person one does not wish to name*) you know who.

savon, *m*. **1.** reprimand*; **donner** (*or* **flanquer** *or* **passer**) **un s. à qn**, to reprimand* s.o.; **recevoir un s.**, to be reprimanded*. **2. être comme un s.**, to be stark naked.

savonnage, *m*. =savon.

savonner: s. (la tête à) qn=donner un savon à qn; **se faire s. (la tête)** =recevoir un savon.

sbire, *m*. **1.** policeman*. **2.** prison warder, screw.

scène, *f*. **faire une s.**, to make a scene, to kick up a row (*or* a fuss), to carry on, to 'create'; **faire une s. terrible**, to carry on something awful; **faire une s. à qn**, to have a row with s.o., to go for s.o.

schbeb, *adj*. beautiful.

sch(e)beb, *m*. pederast*.

schib, *m*. **1.** prison*. **2.** policeman*.

schlague, *f*. flogging.

schlass(e), *adj*. drunk*.

schlinguer, **schlingoter**, **schlipoter**=chelinguer.

schlof(f), **schloff(e)**, *m*. bed; **faire s.**, **aller au s.**, to go to bed*.

schloffer, to sleep*.

schmit, *m*. gendarme.

schnaps, **schnick**, *m*. spirits, brandy.

schnock, **schnoque**, *m*. fool*, fathead; **vieux s.**, old dodderer.

schnouff(e), *f*. =chnouf.

schnouper, to be a dipsomaniac.

schpile, *m*. gambling; **avoir beau s.**, (*a*) to have a good chance, to have no difficulty, to find it easy, to find it all plain sailing; (*b*) to have a good hand (*at cards*).

schpiler, to gamble.

schpileur, gambler.

schproom, **schproum(e)**, *m*. **faire du s.**, to kick up a row; **aller au s.**= ressauter.

schtard, **schtilibem**, *m*. prison*.

schtimmi, *m*. =ch'timi.

schtouillard, *m*. person suffering from V.D.

schtouille, *f*. =chtouille.

sciant, *adj*. boring.

scie, *f*. **1.** (*of thing or person*) bore*, bind. **2.** catch-word, wheeze. **3.** popular refrain. **4. monter une s.** (*or* **des scies**) **à qn**, to pull s.o.'s leg, to have s.o. on (*by repetition of same joke or leg-pull*).

Sciences-Po, *f.pl.* =École supérieure des Sciences politiques.

scier, to dismiss*, to get rid of, to throw over, to jilt, to chuck up. *See also* **dos.**

scion, *m.*, scionner=saccagne, saccagner.

sciure, *f.* avoir de la s. dans le tronc, to be a fool*.

score, *m.* prison sentence.

scotch, *m.* 1. *R.t.m.* Sellotape. 2. whisky.

scoubidou, *m.* =machin, truc 2.

scoumoune, *f.* persistent bad luck.

scribouillard, *m.* pen-pusher, quill-driver.

scro(n)gneugneu, *m.* (*mil.*) old sweat; Colonel Blimp.

scroum, *m.* =schproom.

seau, *m.* 1. il pleut (*or* il tombe) à (pleins) seaux, il tombe des seaux, it's coming down in buckets (*or* in bucketfuls), it's raining cats and dogs, it's pelting down, it's chucking it down. 2. être dans le s., to be in a fix*.

Sébasto, *pr.n.* le S., Boulevard Sébastopol (*in Paris*).

sec, *adj.* 1. être à s., (*a*) to be penniless*; mettre qn à s., to clean s.o. out; (*b*) to run out of words (*or* ideas). 2. aussi s., immediately*. 3. (*sch.*) rester s., to be stumped. 4. quatorze (etc.) livres s., a cool fourteen (etc.) nicker (*or*) quid. 5. l'avoir s., (*a*) to be thirsty; (*b*) to be furious, to be simply fuming; (*c*) =l'avoir mauvaise. 6. les envoyer s., to pay* up.

sec (=seconde), *f.* f. en cinq secs, immediately*, in a tick.

seccotine, *f.* (*of person*) tenacious bore*.

sèche, *f.* 1. cigarette*; griller une s., to smoke a fag; piquer une s., to cadge (*or* to bum) a fag. 2. (*sch.*) piquer une s., to be stumped.

séché, *adj.* dead.

sécher. 1. to fail (a candidate); être séché, to be ploughed (*or* plucked). 2. to cut (a lecture, a class, etc.). 3. to kill*. 4. s. un pot, to swig a glass. 5. la s., to be thirsty, to spit feathers. 6. to be stumped, to be floored (at an examination).

séchoir, *m.* prison*.

secor, *adi.*, *m.* Corsican (*code verlen*).

séco(t), *adj.* lean; lanky; *m.* un petit s., a wiry little chap.

secouée, *f.* 1. reprimand*. 2. great quantity*.

secouer. 1. to shake (s.o.) up, to make (s.o.) sit up. 2. to reprimand*. 3. to arrest*. 4. to steal*.

secouer, se, to get a move on, to be up and doing, to snap out of it, to pull oneself together, to stir one's stumps.

secousse, *f.* ne pas en ficher (*or* foutre) une s., not to do a stroke of work, not to do a hand's turn.

seg, *m.* (*sch.*) second master.

seins, *m.pl.* tu me fais mal aux s.! you get on my tits!

selon, *prep.* c'est s., that depends, it all depends.

semer, to shake off, to give the slip to, to get rid of, to shed, to drop (s.o.); (*in race*) to leave (s.o.) behind, to outdistance (s.o.).

semeur, *m.* s. de virgules, teacher, schoolmaster (*cf. Amer. sl.* 'comma-counter' =pedant).

sens, *m.* un coup de s. unique, a glass of red wine.

sensas(s), *adj.* =au poil (poil 2); c'est s.! it's a rave!

senti-bon, sent-bon, *m.* perfume, scent; sentir le s.-b., to smell nice.

sentiment, *m.* avoir qn au s. *or* le faire au s. à qn, to play on s.o.'s (better) feelings.

sentinelle, *f.* turd.

sentir. 1. je ne peux pas le s., I can't bear (*or* stand *or* stick) him (at any price), I hate the very sight of him. *Cf.* blairer. 2. ça sent mauvais, it's a dangerous business, I don't like the look of it, it stinks.

sentir, s'en: ne pas s'en s., not to feel like it, not to be keen on it.

seoir: sieds-toi! sit down!

serbillon, *m.* sign. faire (*or* envoyer) le s. à qn=faire le serre à qn.

sergot, *m.* policeman*.

série, *f.* s. noire, run of bad luck.

sérieux, *m.* large glass of beer.

serin, *m.* fool*, noodle, ninny.
seriner, to hammer sth. into s.o.
serinette, *f.* expressionless singer.
seringue, *f.* 1. rifle. 2. sub-machine-gun. 3. (*of person*) bore*. 4. chanter comme une s., to sing out of tune. 5. coup de s. = coup de pompe 6.
seringuer, to riddle with bullets.
serpent, *m.* 1. un s. à lunettes, four-eyes (*i.e. person wearing spectacles*). 2. = glaviot 1.
serre, *m.* faire (*or* envoyer) le s. à qn, to warn s.o., to give s.o. the tip-off, to tip the wink to s.o., to give (*or* to tip) s.o. the griff(in), to give s.o. the wire.
serré, *adj.* miserly*.
serrer. 1. to arrest*; se faire s., to be nabbed. 2. to rob (s.o.). 3. to strangle. 4. to exaggerate*. 5. se la s., (*a*) to shake hands; (*b*) = se s. la ceinture.
sert, *m.* = serre.
servi, *p.p.* 1. être s., to get all one wants and more. 2. être s., to be sentenced, to be condemned.
service, *m.* 1. être s.(-s.), faire du s., to be over-zealous, to overdo it, to be an eager beaver. 2. s., s.! duty is duty! 3. s. trois pièces, man's genitals, bag of tricks.
serviette, *f.* coup de s., raid (by police).
seug, *m.* = seg.
seul, *adj.* cela n'ira pas tout s., it won't be all plain sailing.
seulabre, *adj.* alone, on one's Tod (Sloan) (*R.S. for* 'on one's own').
seulet, *adj.* alone, lonely.
sexe, *m.* sex organ; *adj.* très s., very sexy.
sézig(ue), *pron.* oneself, himself, her-self, his nibs.
si, *conj.* si que . . ., suppose . . .
sibiche, *f.* = cibiche.
sidéré, *adj.* dumbfounded, thunder-struck, flabbergasted.
sidi, *m.* 1. North African. 2. (*pej.*) fellow*.
siècle, *m.* il y a un s. que je ne vous ai vu, I haven't seen you for ages.
sienne, *f.* 1. faire des siennes, to be up to one's old tricks. 2. y aller de la s.,

to make one's contribution (of stories, songs, etc.).
sifflard, *m.* sausage, banger.
siffler. 1. to swig, to toss off (a drink). 2. siffle-le! = accouche! 3. c'est comme si je sifflais! = c'est comme si je chantais (chanter 2).
sifflet, *m.* 1. throat; couper le s. à qn, (*a*) to strangle s.o.; to throttle s.o.; (*b*) to silence* s.o. 2. se rincer le s. = se rincer la dalle. 3. = queue-de-morue.
sifflote, *f.* syphilis.
sig, sigaillon, *m.* twenty (old) franc piece.
sigma, *m.* syphilis.
sigue, *m.* = cigue.
silencieux, *m.* 1. revolver*. 2. se taper un s., to masturbate*.
simili, *m.* en s., imitation, artificial.
singe, *m.* 1. boss, guv'nor. 2. (*mil.*) bully beef, corned dog.
sinoc, sino(c)que, *adj.* mad*.
sinoquet, *m.* head*.
siouplaît, siouplé = s'il vous plaît.
siphon, *m.* head*.
siphonné, *adj.* mad*.
siphonner = dérailler.
sirop, *m.* 1. alcoholic drink. 2. s. de grenouille (*or* de canard *or* de para-pluie), water, Adam's ale. 3. low dive, gambling-den. 4. avoir un coup de s., to be tipsy. 5. être dans le s., (*a*) to be in a fix*, to be in a very hot spot: (*b*) to be dop(e)y, muzzy, woozy. 6. tomber dans le s., to faint*. 7. s. de rif., speed ball (*drugs**).
siroter, to booze, to tipple*.
situation, *f.* être dans une s. intéres-sante, to be pregnant*.
six-quatre-deux, à la, *adv. phrase.* anyhow, in a slap dash manner; faire qch. à la s.-q.-d., to botch sth.
skating, *m.* un s. à mouches, a bald pate, a 'skating rink'.
skoumoune, *f.* = poisse, *f.* 1.
smala(h), *f.* large family; un père avec toute sa s., a father with all his tribe (*or* brood *or* circus).
smicard, *m.* anyone receiving a

S.M.I.C. (*salaire minimum interprofessionnel de croissance*).

smigard, *m*. anyone receiving a *S.M.I.G.* (*salaire minimum interprofessionnel garanti*).

sniffer, to take drugs nasally, to sniff.

snober: s. qn, to give s.o. the cold shoulder (*or* the brush-off), to cold-shoulder s.o.

soce (=*société*), *f*. gang; **bonsoir la s.!** good evening all!

social, *m*. friend*.

sœur, *f*. 1. =gonzesse. 2. **et ta s.?** (*c.p.*) tell that to the marines! 3. **et ma s., elle en a?** (*c.p.*) a variant of 2.

soie, *f*. 1. **péter dans la s.**, to swank*. 2. back; **avoir qn sur la s.**, to have s.o. on one's track.

soif, *f*. 1. **il fait s.!** it's thirsty weather! it's thirsty work! 2. **jusqu'à plus s.**, endlessly, world without end, till the cows come home.

soiffard, *m*. drunkard*.

soiffer. 1. to booze, to soak. 2. to spend (one's money) on drink.

soiffeur, *m*. =soiffard.

soigné, *adj*. first-rate*, capital, (*of thrashing*) sound; **un rhume s.**, a hell (*or* a stinker) of a cold.

soigner, se, to coddle oneself; to do oneself well.

soin(-)soin, *adj*. tip-top, excellent, first-rate*.

soir, *m*. **le Grand S.**, the day of the great social revolution (*or* upheaval).

soissonnais (rose), *m*. clitoris.

soldat, *m*. **faire s.**, to do (s.o.) out of his share.

soleil, *m*. 1. **piquer un s.**=piquer un **fard**. 2. **avoir un coup de s.**, to be tipsy. 3. **ça craint le s.**, (*of stolen goods*) those goods are 'hot'. *Cf*. **jour** 3. 4. **user le s.**, to laze about. 5. a million francs.

somme, *m*. **piquer un s.**, to have a nap (*or* a snooze), to have (*or* to snatch) forty winks, to have a cat-nap, to drop off.

sommiers, *m.pl*. finger-print records department.

son, *m*. (i) **cracher** (*or* **éternuer**) **dans le s.**, to be guillotined.

son, *m*. (ii) **les s. et lumière**, old people, the over sixties, 'squares'.

sonnage, *m*. borrowing.

sonnanche, *f*. bell.

sonné, *adj*. 1. mad*. 2. (*boxing*) shaky, groggy. 3. sentenced, condemned; **il est s.**, he's had it.

sonner. 1. to kill*. 2. to kill (*or* to stun) by banging s.o.'s head against wall or ground. 3. to beat (s.o.) up. 4. to dumbfound*. 5. **on ne vous a pas sonné(e)!** who asked you to speak (*or* to butt in)? 6. **se faire s. (les cloches), s. les cloches à qn**: *see* **cloche** 6.

sonneur, *m*. 1. **dormir comme un s. de cloche**, to sleep like a log. 2. **ronfler comme un s.**, to snore like a pig.

Sophie, *pr.n*. **faire sa S.**, to put on airs.

sorbonnard, *m*. member of the Sorbonne (*professor, student*).

sorbonne, *f*. head*.

sorcier, *adj*. **ce n'est pas (bien) s.!** there's nothing very difficult about that! that's not very hard to do (*or* to understand)!

sorcière, *f*. **une vieille s.**, an old hag.

sorgue, *f*. evening; night.

sorlots, *m.pl*. boots*, shoes.

sort, *m*. **faire un s. à**, to polish off, to dispose of, to make short work of.

sortie, *f*. 1. **faire une s. à qn**, to pitch into s.o., to give it s.o. hot (and strong). 2. **être de s.**, nowhere to be found.

sortir. 1. to get about, to go places. 2. **d'où sortez-vous?** (*a*) don't you know that? where have you been all this time? (*b*) where are your manners? where were you dragged up? 3. **merci, je sors d'en prendre!** thanks, I'm not having any! I've had some, thank you! 4. **je ne sors pas de là** (*or* **je n'en sors pas**), I stick to that, you can't make me think otherwise; **il n'y a pas à s. de là!** you can't get away

from that! **5.** to say, to come out with, to pitch (a yarn). **6.** to dismiss*, to expel; **se faire s.**, to get thrown (*or* chucked) out. **7. s. avec**, to sleep with.
sortir, s'en, to make ends meet.
sou, *m.* **I. fichu comme quatre sous** = fichu comme l'as de pique (as **4** (*c*)). **2. en être** (*or* **en rester) comme deux sous de frites**, to be dumbfounded*. **3. être près de ses sous**, to be mean, to be tight-fisted. **4. être sans le s.**, to be penniless*. **5. il n'est pas . . . pour un s.** (*or* **pour deux sous**), he's not in the least . . .
soua-soua, *adj.* = soin(-)soin.
souche, *f.* fool*, blockhead.
soucoupes, *f.pl.* ears*.
soudure, *f.* **I.** money*; **envoyer la s.**, to pay* up. **2. faire la s.**, (*of money, supplies, etc., that have run short*) to bridge the gap, tide over.
soufflant, I. *adj.* breath-taking. **2.** *m.* revolver*.
soufflante, *f.* trumpet.
souffle, *m.* impudence*, cheek.
soufflé, *p.p.* **I.** dumbfounded, flabbergasted. **2.** impudent*; **tu es s., toi!** you've got a cheek (*or* nerve).
souffler. I. s. qch. à qn, (*a*) to swindle s.o. out of sth.; (*b*) to suggest sth. to s.o. **2. s. dans la canne** (*or* **le mirliton**), to gamaroosh.
soufflerie, *f.* lungs.
soufflet, *m.* **s. à punaises**, concertina, accordion.
soufrante, *f.* (sulphur-tipped) match.
souhait, *m.* **à vos souhaits!** bless you! (*said to s.o. who has sneezed*).
soulager: s. qn de qch. (*or* **qch. à qn**), to steal* sth. from s.o.
soulager, se, to relieve nature.
soûlard, *m.* drunkard*.
soûlardise, *f.* drunkenness.
soûlaud, *m.* drunkard*.
soûlerie, *f.* drunkenness, binge.
soulever, to steal*.
soulier, *m.* **être dans ses petits souliers**, to be shaking in one's shoes, to be ill at ease.
soûlographe, *m.* drunkard*.

soûlographie, *f.* = soûlerie.
soûlot, *m.* = soûlaud.
soupe, *f.* **I. s'emporter** (*or* **monter**) **comme une s. au lait**, to flare up in a jiffy, to fly off the handle, to be fiery-tempered. **2. une s.-au-lait**, a fiery-tempered person (who flares up easily). **3. trempé comme une s.** = trempé comme un canard. **4. un gros plein de s.**, a fat, pompous ass, a big slob, a big-head. **5.** (*mil.*) **être de s.**, to be on cook-house fatigue; **aller à la s.**, to go home for grub. **6. par ici la bonne s.!** (*c.p.*) come and get it! (*i.e. come and get a good thrashing*) **7. manger de la s. à la grimace**, (*of married couple after a quarrel*) to be in the sulks. **8.** (*skiing*) soft snow. **9. servir la s.**,(*th.*) to have a minor part.
souper: j'en ai soupé, I'm fed up with it (*or* with him, her, etc.). *See also* **fiole.**
sourdine, *f.* secret police.
sourdingue, *adj.* deaf.
souricière, *f.* police-station, lock-up.
souris, *f.* **I.** (*pej.*) woman*, bird. **2. s. d'hôtel**, (female) hotel-thief. **3. s. de sacristie**, bigoted churchwoman.
sous-fifre, *m.* underling, understrapper, second fiddle.
sous-mac, sous-maîtresse, sous-maq(ue), sous-maxe, *f.* brothel hostess, madam.
sous-maque, *m.* (*of prison*) deputy governor.
sous-off, *m.* non-commissioned officer, non-com, N.C.O.
sous-ventrière, *f.* **manger à se faire péter la s.-v.**, to blow one's hide out; **rire à se péter la s.-v.**, to split one's sides with laughter.
souteneur, *m.* pimp.
soutirer: s. qch. à qn, to wheedle sth. out of s.o.
souvent, *adv.* **plus s.!** no (blooming) fear! not on your life! not likely! **plus s. que je le ferai** (*or* **ferais**)! not if I know it!
sous-verge, *m.* = sous-fifre, sous-off.
'spèce, *f.* **'spèce de . . .** = espèce de . . .
spé, spécial, *m.* **filer** (*or* **prendre**) **du s.**,

1. to be a pederast*. 2. 'backside special' (woman).

spéciale, *f.* (*sch.*) advanced mathematics class.

spécialo, *m.* specialist.

sport, *m.* il y aura du s.! *or* nous allons voir du s.! there'll be a hell of a row! we'll see some fun!

steak, *m.* gagner son s. = gagner son **bifteck.**

step, *m.* nose*. s. à trier, big nose.

stick, *m.* marihuana cigarette (*drugs**).

stop, *m.* hitch-hiking; **faire du s.,** to hitch-hike.

store, *m.* eye-lid; **baisser les stores,** to close one's eyes.

strasse, *f.* 1. (*sch.*) administration. 2. room.

stratège, *m.* s. en chambre (*or* s. de café *or* s. du Café du Commerce), armchair strategist.

stropiat, *m.* cripple.

stups, *m.pl.* narcotic, drugs, 'junk'.

suante, *f.* week.

subito, *adv.* s. (presto), all of a sudden, in a jiffy, pronto.

subodorer, to get wind of.

subtiliser, to steal*.

sucer. 1. s. qn, to bleed s.o. white. **2.** to booze, to tipple*. **3.** to gamaroosh.

sucette, *f.* lollipop, lolly.

suçon, *m.* red mark made by a prolonged kiss.

sucrage, *m.* sentence, conviction.

sucre, *m.* 1. **casser du s. sur le dos** (*or* **sur la tête) de qn,** to speak ill of s.o., to run s.o. down. **2.** c'est du (vrai) s., it's an easy* job! **3.** un vrai s., (*of person*) a real pet. **4.** je ne suis pas en s., I won't melt (*i.e. by going out in the rain*). **5.** s. de pomme, jemmy. **6.** L.S.D. (*drugs**).

sucrée, *adj.* **faire la s.,** to put on demure airs.

sucrer. 1. to arrest*; **se faire s.,** to get nabbed. **2.** to steal*. *See also* **fraise.**

sucrer, se, to get rich*; to take the lion's share.

sucrette, *f.* **aller à la s.,** to compromise with one's conscience.

suée, *f.* 1. fright. 2. hard work, fag, grind, sweat. 3. large quantity*.

suer. 1. faire s. qn, to bore* s.o.; **tu me fais s.!** you get on my nerves! 2. **en s. une,** to (have a) dance. 3. **envoyer s. qn,** to send s.o. packing*.

sueur, *m.* s. de chêne, killer.

suffocant, *adj.* startling; stunning.

suffoquer, to dumbfound*, to take s.o.'s breath away.

suif, *m.* 1. reprimand*; **donner** (*or* **flanquer** *or* **passer**) **un s. à qn,** to reprimand* s.o. 2. quarrel*; **chercher du s. à qn,** to pick a quarrel with s.o.; **être en s.,** to be at loggerheads. 3. uproar*. 4. scandal. 5. **se faire du s.** = **se faire du mauvais sang (sang 6).** 6. (*card-sharping fraternity*) **faire en s.,** to cheat (at cards).

suiffard, *m.* 1. toff, dandy, swell, nut. 2. cheat (at cards).

suiffée, *f.* thrashing*.

suiffer. 1. to reprimand* severely. 2. **to** pick a quarrel* with.

suiffer, se, to quarrel.

suiffeur, *m.* quarrelsome person.

suisse, *m.* 1. **faire s., picoler en s.,** to drink all by oneself, not to stand treat. 2. **boire en s.,** to be a secret drinker.

sujet, *m.* **grands sujets, petits sujets,** ballet dancers (*at the Opéra*).

sulfater, to shoot at, to pepper.

sulfateuse, *f.* tommy-gun, submachine-gun.

sulfureux, *m.* absinthe.

sultane, *f.* mistress.

supin, *m.* (*sch.*) = **surgé.**

supposition, *f.* **une s. que . . .,** suppose (*or* supposing) that . . .

suppositoire, *m.* **s. d'autobus,** bubble car.

sûr, *adj.* **c'est s. et certain,** it's absolutely (*or* abso-blooming-lutely) certain, it's as sure as eggs is eggs, it's in the bag.

surbiner, to watch.

surboum, *f.* hectic party, shindig, a 'ball'.

Sûrepige, *f.* (= *Sûreté*) Criminal Investigation Department, C.I.D., (*approx.*) Scotland Yard.

surface, *f.* **en boucher une s. à qn**=en boucher un coin à qn (coin 1).

surgé, surgeot, surgo, *m.* (=*surveillant général*) (*sch.*) vice-principal, chief master on duty.

surin, *m.* knife, chiv, chive, chivey, shiv, shliver.

suriner, to knife, to stab to death, to shive.

surineur, *m.* knifer, chiv(e)-man, chivmerchant.

surnombre, *m.* nickname.

surpatte, *f.* =surboum.

sur(-)place, *m.* **faire du s.(-)p.,** (*of cyclist*) to balance, (*of motorist*) to inch forward, (*of pilot*) to rev up.

surprenante, *f.* **1.** illegal and faked lottery. **2. à la s.,** unawares, by surprise.

surprise-party, *f.* bottle-party.

surrincette, *f.* a second **rincette.**

survolté, *adj.* worked up, all het up.

swing, *adj.* hep, hip; **les gens s.,** hepcats, swingers.

sympa, *adj.* (=*sympathique*) congenial, likeable; **être très s.,** to be a good mixer, to have fetching ways.

syphlotte, *f.* syphilis.

système, *m.* **1.** device, gadget*. **2. le s. D** (*i.e.* **le s. débrouillard**), wangling. **employer** (*or* **pratiquer**) **le s. D,** to wangle (it), to fiddle it. **3. donner** (*or* **porter** *or* **taper**) **sur le s. à qn**=donner (etc.) **sur les nerfs à qn** (nerf 2).

systusse, *m.* =système 1.

T

tabac, *m.* **1.** **passer qn à t.**, to give s.o. a rough handling, to slug s.o., to put s.o. through it, (*of police, etc.*) to give s.o. the third degree, to beat s.o. up, to give s.o. the works (*or* a working-over); **passage à t.**, beating up, third degree. **2.** **c'est le** (*or* **du**) **même t.**, it's much of a muchness, it's the same thing; **ce n'est pas le même t.!** it's quite a different matter. **3.** **faire un t.=en faire tout un plat (plat 2). 4. il y aura du t.**, there'll be hell to pay, we're (in) for it, we're up against it. **5. un coup de t.**, (*a*) a set-to, a scrap; (*b*) (*nav.*) bad weather. **6. un mauvais t.**, a bad business. **7. se donner un t. terrible,** to give oneself no end of trouble. **8. t. de Chine**, O.P. (*=other people's*) tobacco.

tabassage, *m.* third degree.

tabassée, *f.* thrashing*.

tabasser: t. qn=passer qn à tabac.

tabasser, se, to have a scrap.

table, *f.* **se mettre** (*or* **passer**) **à t.**, to turn informer*.

tableau, *m.* **1. au t.**, (*av., hunting*) in the bag. **2. un vieux t.**, an old frump. an old has-been, a painted old hag. **3. décrocher ses tableaux**, to pick one's nose. **4. jouer** (*or* **miser**) **sur les deux tableaux**, to lay odds both ways; to hedge, to play for safety; **jouer** (*or* **miser**) **sur le même t.**, to put all one's eggs in one basket. **5. gagner** (*or* **être gagnant**) **sur tous les tableaux**, to be a winner all round, to win all along the line. **6. cela fera(it) bien** (*or* **cela ne fera(it) pas mal**) **dans le t.=cela fera(it) bien dans le paysage.**

tablier, *m.* **rendre son t.**, to give notice, to leave one's employment, to ask for one's cards.

tabourets, *m.pl.* teeth; **n'avoir plus de t. dans la salle à manger** (*or* **dans la croquante**), to be toothless.

tac, *m.* **1.** taxi. **2. riposter** (*or* **répondre**) **du t. au t.**, to give tit for tat.

tache, *f.* five-franc piece.

tacot, *m.* **1.** ramshackle old motor-car*. **2.** small local train, puffer.

taf(fe), *m.* **1. avoir le t.**, to be afraid*. **2.** share of the swag; **aller au t.=aller au fade (fade 1). 3. prendre son t.=jouir.**

taf(fe), *f.* cigarette.*

taffetas, *m.* money*: banknotes.

taffeur, *m.* coward*.

tafia, *m.* drink, booze.

tafiater, to booze.

tailler: en t. une=t. une bavette.

tailler, se, to decamp*.

tailleur, *m.* croupier (*roulette*).

tal, *m.* buttocks*.

tala, *m.f.* (*slang of the École normale supérieure: from 'celui qui va-t-à la messe'*) person with religious and conservative beliefs; *adj.* pi, sanctimonious.

talbin, *m.* bank-note.

talc, *m.* cocaine (*drugs*).

talentueux, *adj.* talented.

talmouse, *f.* blow*.

talmouser, to thrash*.

taloche, *f.* clout, cuff.

talocher, to clout, to cuff.

talon, *m.* **avoir les talons courts**, (*of female*) to be of easy virtue (*cf. Amer. sl.* 'to be a roundheel(s)').

tambouille, *f.* cooking, cookery; food*.

tambour, *m.* **1. raisonner comme un t.** (**mouillé**) **=raisonner comme une pantoufle. 2. marcher comme un t.**, to fall for it like a mug. **3. il n'y a pas de quoi faire passer le t. de ville**, it's nothing to make a song and dance about, it's nothing to write home about.

tampon, *m.* **1.** (*mil.*) orderly, batman. **2. coup de t.**, collision; violent blow*; brawl. **3.** *pl.* fists.

tamponnement, *m.* drubbing, thumping.

tamponner, to thrash*.

tamponner, se, to have a set-to, to come to blows; **s'en t. (le coquillard)** = **s'en battre l'œil (œil 7).**

tamponnoir, *m.* sanitary towel.

tam-tam, *m.* **faire du t.-t.,** to make a great to-do (*or* a splash *or* a lot of ballyhoo).

tandem, *m.* two associates; couple.

tangent, *m.* **1.** border-line candidate (at an examination); **être t. à un examen,** to fail (*or* to pip) an exam. by a narrow margin. **2. c'était t.,** it was touch and go.

tangente, *f.* **1.** (*sch.*) porter, usher. **2. prendre (s'échapper par, filer par) la t.,** (*a*) to fly off at a tangent; (*b*) to decamp* hurriedly; (*c*) to wriggle out of a difficult situation.

tannant, *adj.* boring*.

tannée, *f.* thrashing*.

tanner. 1. to bore*. **2.** to thrash*. *See also* **côte** (i) **4, cuir, peau 17. 3. t. les oreilles à qn au sujet de qch.,** to din sth. into s.o.'s ears.

tanneur, *m.* =**tapeur. 1.**

tant, *adv.* **1. il y en avait t. et plus,** there was any amount of it; **il a rouspété t. et plus,** he groused for all he was worth; **gagner de l'argent t. et plus,** to earn pots of money. **2. il pleut t. qu'il peut,** it's raining as hard as it can. **3. t. qu'à faire,** while I'm (you're, etc.) at it (*or* about it). **4. pour t. faire que**+*infin.,* **à t. faire que de**+*infin.,* if it comes to ... **5. vous m'en direz t.!** (*a*) you don't say so! (*b*) now I understand.

tante, *f.* **1.** pederast*. **2. chez ma t.,** in the pawnshop, in pawn, up the spout.

tantine, *f.* auntie.

tantinette, tantouse, tantouze, *f.* =**tante 1.**

tantôt, *m.* afternoon; **à t.!** so long! **sur le t.,** towards evening.

tapage, *m.* cadging, tapping (s.o. for money), touching.

tapanard, *m.* buttocks*.

tapant, *adj.* **arriver t.** (*or* **à l'heure tapante**), to arrive dead (*or* bang) on time, on the dot; **à cinq heures t.,** on the stroke of five, at five sharp.

tape, *f.* **1.** failure, setback, knock; (*th.*) flop; **quelle t.!** what a sell! **2. ramasser** (*or* **remporter** *or* **prendre**) **une** (*or* **la**) **t.,** to come a cropper*; to take the rap; (*th.*) to get the bird.

tapé, *adj.* **1.** mad*. **2.** first-rate*; **réponse tapée,** smart answer, an answer straight from the shoulder, crusher; **ça, c'est (bien) t.!** that was a good one! that's the style! that's the stuff (to give the troops)! nice work!

tape-à-l'œil, *adj.* flashy, showy, loud; *m.* **du t.-à-l'o.,** flashy stuff; eye-wash.

tape-cul, *m.* **1.** ramshackle motor-car*, (*of bicycle with solid tyres*) boneshaker. **2. faire du t.-c.,** to trot (on horseback).

tapée, *f.* great quantity* (*of things or people*).

taper. 1. to tap (*or* to touch) (s.o. for a sum of money), to cadge (to bum) (*sth. from s.o.*), to put the bite on (s.o.). **2. t. une belote** *or* **en t. une,** to have a game of **belote. 3.** (*motor.*) **t. le** (*or* **du**) **200,** to clock (*or* to hit) the 200 (kilometres) mark. **4. t. sur,** (*a*) to slang (*or* to slate) (s.o.); (*b*) (*mil.*) to paste (*or* to strafe) (an objective); **t. ferme,** to slog; **on lui a tapé dessus,** they pitched into him; **se t.,** to pitch into one another. **5.** (*of the sun*) to beat down; **ça tape!** it's a scorcher! it's cracking the flags. **6.** to stink*. *See also* **cloche 7, nerf 2, œil 19** *and* **20, tas 6, ventre 5.**

taper, se. 1. tu peux te t.! = **tu peux toujours courir! (courir 3). 2. se t. qch.** (*a*) to treat oneself to (*or* to stand oneself) sth. (nice)—*e.g.* **se t. un bon gueuleton, se t. la cloche,** to stand oneself a slap-up meal (*or* a good tuck-in *or* a good blow-out). *Can also be said of a person*—*e.g.* **se t. une belle fille, je me la taperais bien,** *etc.*; (*b*) to have to do sth. (unpleasant)—*e.g.* **se t. vingt kilomètres (à pied),** to have to trudge twenty kilometres (on foot); **se t. le ménage,** to have to do the housework. **3. se t. de,** not to care a rap* about (*a thing or person*).

tapette, *f.* **1.** pederast*. **2.** tongue, clapper, gift of the gab; **avoir une fière** (*or* **fameuse** *or* **sacrée) t.,** (**en) avoir une t.,** **avoir une de ces tapettes,** to be a great chatterbox*.

tapeur, *m.* **1.** inveterate borrower, cadger, sponger. **2.** piano-strummer.

tapin, *m.* **1.** drummer. **2.** faire le t., **aller** (*or* **descendre) sur le t.,** aller au t. =faire le trottoir. **3.** =tapineuse. **4.** work=**boulot.**

tapiner. 1. to work. **2.** =faire le trottoir.

tapineuse, *f.* prostitute*.

tapir, *m.* (*sch.*) **1.** private pupil. **2.** private lesson (*much used at the École normale supérieure.*)

tapiriser, to coach.

tapis, *m.* **1.** low drinking-den *or* gambling-joint, dive. **2. faire un t.,** to kick up a row*. **3.** *adj.* **être t.,** to be penniless*.

tapissage, *m.*, **tapisser**=retapissage, **retapisser.**

tapisserie, *f.* **faire t.,** to be a wallflower (at a dance).

taquet, *m.* blow*.

taquiner, to worry, to bother, to upset. *See also* **dame** 2, **goujon.**

tarabuster. 1. to pester, to plague, to badger; **se t. l'esprit,** to rack one's brains. **2.** to bully.

taratata, *int.* nonsense! baloney! bunkum!

tarauder. 1. =tarabuster 1. **2.** to thrash*.

tarde, *f.* night.

tarderie, *f.* **une vraie t.,** (*of woman or thing*) a perfect mess, an old hag.

tar(e)bouif, *m.*=tarin.

targette, *f.* **1. coup de t.,** loan. **2.** *pl.* shoes, boots.

tarin, *m.* nose*; **se casser le t.**=se casser le nez (nez 11); **avoir qn dans le t.**=avoir qn dans le nez (nez 3).

tartavelle, tardingue, *f.*, *adj.* ugly (woman).

tarte, *adj.* **1.** ugly, rotten, worthless, lousy, crummy, scruffy. **2.** silly, stupid.*

tarte, *f.* **1.** slap, smack. **2. se fendre la t.**=se fendre la pipe (**pipe 3**). **3. c'est de la (vraie) t.,** it's a very easy* matter, it's a piece of cake; **la vie ce n'est pas de la t.,** life's not all milk and honey.

Tartempion, *pr.n.* (*of person*)=machin. **2.** any Tom, Dick or Harry.

tarter: t. qn, to slap s.o.'s face.

tartignol(le), *adj.*=tarte, *adj.*

tartinage, *m.* borrowing.

tartine, *f.* long, rambling speech (*or* story *or* letter *or* article), long rigmarole; **en faire une t.** (*or* **faire des tartines) sur qch.,** to waffle about sth.

tartiner. 1. to be long-winded, to waffle. **2.** to work fast.

tartiner, se. 1. to look the worse for wear. **2. je m'en tartine!** I don't care a rap*.

tartines, *f.pl.* **1.** boots*, shoes. **2.** feet*.

tartir. 1. =chier 1. **2.** (*fig.*)=embêter.

tartiss(es), tartissoires, *m.pl.* W.C.*

tartouillard, tartouse, tartouze, *adj.*=tarte, *adj.*

tas, *m.* **1. être sur le t.,** to be at work, to be on the job. **2. faire le t.**=faire le trottoir. **3. piquer dans le t.,** to pick at random, to help oneself, to take one's choice, to pick where one likes. **4. prendre qn sur le t.,** to catch s.o. redhanded (*or* bang to rights); **être pris** (*or* **crevé** *or* **fabriqué** *or* **fait** *or* **piqué) sur le t., être marron sur le t.,** to be caught in the act, to be caught redhanded. **5. sécher sur le t.,** to wait in vain. **6. taper** (*or* **cherrer) dans le t.,** to strike out blindly, to take on all comers. **7. la grève sur le t.,** stay-in *or* sit-down strike.

tasse, *f.* **1. la grande t.,** the sea, the brin(e)y, the drink; **boire à la grande t.,** to get drowned at sea, to go to Davy Jones'(s) locker; **boire** (*or* **prendre) une** (*or* **la) t.,** to get a mouthful (when swimming). **2. en**

avoir sa t., to be fed up with it. **3. les tasses,** street urinals; W.C.*
tassé, *adj.* **1.** first-rate*; **un petit whisky bien t.,** a nice double whisky; **un dîner bien t.,** a slap-up dinner; **deux heures bien tassées,** two whole (*or* solid) hours. **2. t. par l'âge,** shrunk with age.
tasseau, *m.* = **tassot.**
tassée, *f.* a great quantity*.
tasser, to give, to dish out, to let s.o. have it; **qu'est-ce que je lui ai tassé!** I gave him what for! I didn't half let him have it! **qu'est-ce qu'il s'est tassé au dîner!** he didn't half put it away at dinner!
tasser, se. 1. to settle down; **(tout) ça se tassera** (*or* **finira par se t.**), it will (all) sort itself out, it'll all come out in the wash; **tout finit par se t.,** everything comes out all right in the end. **2.** (*of person*) to shrink with age.
tassot, *m.* nose*.
tata, tati, *f.* **1.** auntie. **2.** = **tante 1.**
tatanes, *f.pl.* boots*, shoes.
tâter, se. 1. va te faire t.! = **va te promener!** (**promener, se 1**) **2.** to think it over, to weigh the pros and cons.
tatoué, *m.* a tough guy.
tatouille, *f.* thrashing*.
tatouiller. to thrash*.
taulard, *m.* jail-bird, old lag.
taule, *f.* **1.** prison*; **faire de la t.,** to do time, to do a stretch; **la Grande T.,** the Central Police Headquarters. **2.** room; house; (*thieves' slang*) 'drum', 'gaff'; **rappliquer à la t.,** to return home. **3.** brothel*.
taulier, *m.* proprietor, owner, keeper (of pub, cheap lodging-house, brothel).
taulière, *f.* brothel-owner, 'madam'.
taupe, *f.* **1.** (*sch.*) advanced mathematics class (*or* member of the class) preparing for the *Grandes Écoles.* **2. vieille t.,** old hag, old crone. **3.** prostitute*. **4. partir pour le** (*or* **s'en aller au**) **royaume des taupes,** to die*.
taupin, *m.* student of **taupe 1.**
taupinière, *f.* (*student's slang*) room, study.

taxi, *m.* motor-car.
tchao! *int.* **1.** so long! cheerio*! 'see yer!' **2.** = **d'ac(c)!**
tchin-tchin, *int.* good health! chin-chin!
t'chi: que t'chi, nothing.
té, *int.* (*in S. of France*) why! of course!
técolle, *pron.* you.
teigne, *f.* (*of woman*) shrew, (*of child*) pest, plague, handful.
teigneux, *m.* scurvy individual, stinker.
teint, *m.* **bon t.,** authentic.
teinté, *adj.* drunk*.
teintée, *f.* drunkenness, binge.
télé, télévise, téloche, *f.* television, telly, goggle-box, the idiot-box.
télégraphe, *m.* **faire le t.** = **faire le serre.**
télémuche, *m.* telephone, blower.
téléphone, *m.* w.c.*, **aller au t.,** to relieve oneself, to relieve nature, to make a 'call'.
tème: faire t., to watch out.
tempérament, *m.* **1. avoir du t.,** to be highly sexed, to be hot stuff, (*of man*) to have hot pants, (*of woman*) to be a hot skirt. **2. se crever** (*or* **s'escrimer** *or* **s'esquinter**) **le t.,** to knock oneself up. **3. vous en avez un t.!** you've got a nerve!
température, *f.* **prendre la t.,** to make inquiries.
temps, *m.* **1. en deux t.** (**trois mouvements**), immediately*. **2. prendre** (*or* **se payer** *or* **s'en payer** *or* **passer**) **du bon t.,** to have a good time, to have fun and games. **3. tirer son t.,** to do time (in prison), to do a stretch.
tendeur, *m.* highly sexed man, hot-pants.
tendron, *m.* young girl, lassie.
tenir. 1. qu'est-ce qu'il tient (comme cuite *or* **comme muffée)!** what a skinful he's got! he's got all (*or* more) than he can carry! he's as tight as a drum! he's got his load! he's well oiled! **2. en t. pour,** to be infatuated* with. **3. tenez-vous bien!** just listen to this!

tentiaire, *f.* (*in prison*) penitentiary.
tenu, *p.p.* t.! (*with reference to a wager*) done! I take you! you're on!
tenue, *f.* **de la t.!** behave yourself! **en voilà une t.!** that's a nice way to behave! where are your manners?
terminé, *adj.* **se sentir t.**, to feel exhausted.
terre, *f.* **insulter** (*or* **traiter**) **qn plus bas que t.**, to treat s.o. like dirt.
terre-neuve, *m.* **faire le t.-n.**, to help lame ducks.
terreux, *m.* peasant*.
terrible, *adj.* terrific, stupendous*.
terrine, *f.* **1.** face*; **se fendre la t.** = **se fendre la pipe** (**pipe** 3). **2.** head*; **souffrir de la t.**, to have headaches; **t. de gelée d'andouille**, a fool*.
têtard, *m.* **1.** baby, brat. **2.** boozer, tippler, bibber. **3. être t.**, (*a*) to be a victim, to be a sucker; (*b*) to be arrested, to be nabbed. **4. faire qn t.**, to deceive s.o., to kid s.o.
têtarer = **faire têtard** (**têtard** 4).
têtasses, *f.pl.* large breasts* (of female).
tête, *f.* **1. avoir une bonne t.**, (*a*) to look a decent chap; (*b*) to look a bit of a mug; (*c*) to have a brain. **2. avoir une t. à coucher dehors** (**avec un billet de logement dans sa poche**), to have a very ugly dial, to have a face that would stop a clock. **3. casser la t. à qn**, to talk s'o.'s head off, to get on s.o.'s nerves. **4. en avoir par-dessus la t.**, (*a*) to be fed up with it; (*b*) to be up to the eyes in it. **5.** (**en**) **faire une t.**, to look sick, to pull a long face, to look glum; **faire une drôle de t.**, to look pretty queer, to look quite put out. **6. faire la** (**mauvaise**) **t.**, to sulk. **7. faire la t. à qn**, to look black at s.o. **8. laver la t. à qn**, to reprimand* s.o. **9. monter la t. à qn**, to work on s.o., to poison s.o.'s mind; **on lui a monté la t. contre nous**, they've set him against us; **avoir la t. montée**, to have one's blood up; **se monter la t.**, (*a*) to get excited, to work oneself up, to get one's dander up, to go (in) off the deep end; (*b*) to

imagine things, to kid oneself. **10. n'en faire qu'à sa t.**, to go one's own sweet way. **11. où ai-je la t.?** I must be dreaming! I must be wool-gathering! **12. petite t.** (**d'épingle**), (*affectionate term of address—e.g.*) comment ça va, **petite t.?** how goes it, little 'un (*or* young 'un *or* laddie *or* young fellow-me-lad)? **13. piquer une t. dans la flotte** (*or* **dans le bouillon**), to take a header into the water. **14. savonner la t. à qn**, to reprimand* s.o. **15. se casser** (*or* **se creuser**) **la t.**, to rack one's brains. **16. se payer la t. de qn**, to fool* s.o. **17. se taper la t.**, to have a good tuck-in (*or* a good blow-out). **18. tomber sur la t.**, to go mad*; **je ne suis pas tombé sur la t.**, I'm not so daft. **19. t. de pipe**, (*a*) **avoir une t. de pipe**, to have a funny face; to be a chump; (*b*) **tant par t. de pipe**, so much per person, so much per head, so much a nob; (*c*) **compter des têtes de pipes**, to count noses. **20. t. de cochon** (*or* **de lard** *or* **de mule** *or* **de pioche**), stubborn person, pig-headed person, mule. **21. t. à l'huile:** see **huile** 3. **22. t. de Turc**, (*a*) (*at fair*) try-your-strength machine; (*b*) scapegoat, butt. **23. t. de veau**, (*a*) bald head, 'billiard ball'; (*b*) silly-looking blighter. *See also* **claque**, *f.* **1**, **gifle**.
téter, to booze, to tipple*.
têtère, téterre, *f.*, head*.
tétés, tétons, *m.pl.* breasts* (of woman).
tettes, *f.pl.* nipples (of woman).
teuf-teuf, *m.* **1.** (*child's word, for train or car*) puff-puff, puffer. **2.** ramshackle old motor-car*.
tévé, *f.* = **télé**.
texto, textuel, textuo, *adv.* textually, word for word, his (etc.) very words.
tézig(ue), *pron.* you, yourself.
thala, *m.f.* = **tala**.
thé, *m.* **marcher au t.**, (*a*) to be drunkard; (*b*) to smoke marihuana.
théâtreux, -euse, *m.f.* (*pej.*) actc (actress) of sorts.
théière, *f.* **1.** head*. **2.** *pl.* = **tasses** 3.

thème, *m.* **c'est un fort en t.,** he's good at school-work, he's brainy but not very original; **faire t.,** to keep mum.

Thomas, *m.* chamber-pot*; **aller voir la veuve** (*or* **la mère**) **T.,** to pay a visit to Mrs. Jones.

thunard, *m.,* **thune,** *f.,* **thunette,** *f.* five-franc piece.

thunarder, to pinch and scrape.

thurne, *f.* study, room (*at the École normale supérieure*).

tic, *m.* **prendre qn à t.,** to take a dislike to s.o.

ticket, *m.* **1. un drôle de t.,** a queer* person. **2.** nympho(maniac). **3. prendre un t.** = **faire le voyeur. 4.** thousand franc note. **5. faire** (*or* **avoir**) **un t. avec** = **faire** (*or* **avoir**) **une touche avec.**

tickson, *m.* = **ticket 4** *and* **5.**

tic-tac, *m.* revolver*.

tiédasse, *adj.* lukewarmish.

tienne, *poss. pron.* **1. à la** (**bonne**) **t.!** cheerio!* **2. tu as encore fait des tiennes!** you've been up to your old tricks again!

tierce, *f.* **1.** gang (of hoodlums, etc.). **2. avoir t. belote et dix de der,** to be 50 years old.

tiers, *m.* **se moquer du t. comme du quart,** not to care a rap* for anybody or anything.

tif(fe)s, *m.pl.* hair, thatch.

tiffier, *m.* hairdresser, barber.

tige, *f.* **1.** cigarette*. **2. vieille t.,** old chap*. **3. des t. de pâquerettes,** spindle-shanks. **4.** shoe, boot*.

tige, *m.* policeman*.

tignasse, *f.* (*of hair*) shock, mop.

tilleul, *m.* drink of red and white wine mixed.

tilt, *adv.* **faire t.,** to hit the mark.

timbre, *m.* head*; **avoir le t. fêlé, avoir un coup de t.,** to be mad*, to be cracked.

timbré, *adj.* mad*, cracked.

tinche, *f.* **faire la t.** = **faire la manche** (**manche,** *f.* **1** *and* **2**).

tinée, *f.* great quantity*.

tinette, *f.* **1.** vintage car. **2. faire une t. sur,** to disparage.

tinettes, *f.pl.* latrines, W.C*.

tintin, *m.* **1.** (**c'est**) **t.!** nothing doing! not a hope! **2. faire t.,** to have to do without, to get damn all.

tintouin, *m.* worry, trouble, bother, a headache; **avoir du t.,** to be hard put to it; **donner du t. à qn,** to give s.o. a lot of trouble, to give s.o. a headache; **tout le t.,** the whole bag* of tricks.

tiquer, to show signs of surprise (*and* dissatisfaction *or* interest *or* emotion *or* disappointment *or* disapproval), to wince; **ne pas t.,** not to turn a hair; **sans t.,** without batting an eyelid; **t. sur,** to react unfavourably to.

tirage, *m.* **1.** difficulty, trouble; **il y a du t. entre eux,** there's some friction between them, they don't hit it off. **2. le premier t.,** the first time, at the first shot.

tirailleur, *m.* free-lance.

tirants, *m.pl.* stockings.

tire, *f.* **1.** motor-car*, taxi, 'drag'. **2. vol à la t.,** pick-pocketing; **voleur à la t.,** pickpocket, 'dipper', 'whizzer'; **faire la t.,** to be a pickpocket.

tire-au-cul, tire-au-flanc, *m.* malingerer*.

tirebouchonnant, *adj.* very funny*.

tirebouchonner, se, to laugh* uproariously.

tire-fesses, *m.* ski-lift.

tire-jus, *m.* handkerchief*.

tirelire, *f.* **1.** face* and mouth*. **2.** head*. **3.** stomach*. **4.** vagina*.

tire-moelle, *m.* = **tire-jus.**

tirer. 1. to steal*, to pick pockets. **2.** to pass, to spend (*of time*); **six mois à t.,** six months to go (*or* to do *or* to get through); **en voilà encore un(e) de tiré(e)!** that's another year (day, month, etc.) gone! **3.** to serve a prison sentence; **t. de la prison, t. son temps,** to do time; **deux longes à t.,** to do a two-year stretch.

tirer, se. 1. to decamp*; **tirez-vous de**

là! hop* it! *See also* flûtes, patte 1, pied 26, ripatons 2. 2. ça se tire, the end is in sight, it's nearly finished; ça s'est bien tiré? did everything go off all right? did you have a good time?

tireur, *m.* pickpocket.

tire(ur)-au-flanc, tire-au-cul, *m.* malingerer*.

tiroir, *m.* stomach*. *See also* polichinelle 1.; nom à t. = nom à rallonge.

tisane, *f.* 1. wishy-washy drink, catlap. 2. severe thrashing*.

tisaner, to beat up.

tisanier, *m.* male nurse.

titi, *m.* pert street arab, cheeky (Paris) urchin.

toboggan, *m.* se graisser le t., to tipple*.

toc, *adj.* 1. worthless, sham, rubbishy, trashy, dud, 'schlenter'. 2. mad*. 3. ugly. 4. stupid*. 5. (*of person*) dangerous, vicious. 6. *m.* fake (*or* sham *or* snide) jewellery (*or* goods *or* stuff); c'est du t.! it's sham (*or* faked)! 7. marcher (*or* circuler) sous des tocs (*or* un t.), to go about with false identity papers. 8. manquer de t., to lack selfconfidence, to lack nerve.

toc! *int.* (et) t.! so there! put that in your pipe!

tocade, *f.* = toquade.

tocante, *f.* = toquante.

tocard, *adj.* 1. = toc, *adj.* 1. 2. showy. 3. *m.* (*of person*) hopeless case, dead loss, stumer; (*turf*) horse with no chance of winning, rank outsider.

tocasson, *adj.* = toc, *adj.* 3 *and* 4.

tocbombe, toctoc, *adj.* mad*.

toile, *f.* 1. se payer une t., to go to see a film, to go to the flicks. 2. déchirer la t., to fart. 3. se mettre (*or* se filer *or* se glisser) dans (*or* entre) les toiles, to go to bed*.

toise, *f.* 1. thrashing*. 2. se filer des toises, to fight, to scrap.

toison, *f.* = tignasse.

toiture, *f.* head*. onduler de la t., to be mad*; varloper la t., to have a haircut.

tôlard, *m.* 1. = taulard. 2. prisoner.

tôle, *f.* = taule.

tolérance, *f.* 1. maison de t., licensed brothel*. 2. société de t., permissive society.

tôlier, *m.* 1. = taulier. 2. superintendent of police.

tomate, *f.* 1. face*. 2. head*. 3. red nose. 4. mixture of *anis* (*or absinthe*) and *grenadine*. 5. des tomates! = des clous! (clou 7). 6. fool*, juggins. 7. en être (*or* en rester) comme une t. = en être (*or* en rester) comme deux ronds de flan.

tombeau, *m.* 1. à t. ouvert, at breakneck speed. 2. c'est un vrai t., (*of person*) he won't breathe a word about it, a secret is safe with him, he's an absolute oyster (*or* a clam).

tomber. 1. to be arrested (*or* condemned *or* sentenced). 2. laisser t. qn, (*a*) to let s.o. down, to go bent on s.o.; (*b*) to drop s.o. (like a hot potato), to ditch s.o. 3. laisse t.! forget it! cut it out! give it a rest! forget the whole thing! drop it! 4. to floor, to knock down. 5. to tumble (a woman); il les tombe toutes, they all fall for him, he's a regular Romeo. 6. (*of prostitute*) to pick up (a client). 7. qu'estce qu'il (*or* qui) tombe! it's raining cats and dogs! it's pouring down! *See also* bec 13, dessus, eau 7, veste.

tombereau, *m.* motor-car*.

tombeur, *m.* 1. wrestler. 2. (grand) t. (de femmes *or* de filles), sexually aggressive male, seducer, sheik(h), wolf, a Casanova.

tondre, to fleece* (s.o.).

tondu, *adj.* penniless*.

tonneau, *m.* ce sont gens du même t., they are birds of a feather; c'est du même t., it's much of a muchness.

tonnerre, *m.* 1. . . . du t. (de Dieu *or* du t. du diable *or* de tous les tonnerres), something sensational, terrific, a whale of a . . ., a wow of a . . ., a thundering good . . ., a helluva . . .; a stunner, a bang-up . . ., a rattling good . . ., a father and mother of a (row, thrashing, etc.). 2. *int.* t.! t. de chien! t. de Dieu! mille tonnerres!

mille tonnerres de Brest! by thunder! by jingo! (*expletives**).

tonton, *m.* uncle, nunky.

tonus, *m.* **avoir du t.,** to be resilient.

top, *m.* pip (of speaking clock).

topaze, *m.* grafter.

topo, *m.* **1.** (*sch.*) demonstration, essay, lecture, talk, paper; **faire un t. sur,** to spout on, to hold forth on. **2.** (*journ.*) article. **3.** plan, outline, sketch, short description.

Topol, *m.* **Le T.** = **Le Sébasto.**

toquade, *f.* **avoir une t. pour,** to be infatuated* with. *cf.* **béguin 2.**

toquant, *m.* heart, ticker.

toquante, *f.,* watch*.

toquard, *m.* (*turf*) = **tocard 3.**

toqué, *adj.* **1.** mad*. **2. t. de,** infatuated* with.

toquer, se: se t. de, to become infatuated* with.

torché, *adj.* **mal t.,** botched, scamped, knocked-off.

torche-cul, *m.* **1.** toilet-paper, bumfodder, bumf. **2.** rag (*newspaper*).

torchée, *f.* **1.** fight, scrap. **2.** thrashing*.

torcher. 1. to knock off, to dash off (an article, etc.). **2.** to botch, to scamp, to louse up. **3. t. un enfant,** to wipe a child's bottom; **se faire t.,** to get a thrashing*.

torcher, se. 1. to wipe oneself, to wipe one's arse. **2.** to have a scrap. **3. je m'en torche!** I don't care a rap*.

torchon, *m.* **1.** slattern, draggle-tail. **2.** = **torche-cul 1** *and* **2. 3. un coup de t.,** (*a*) a fight, a scrap, a set-to; (*b*) a clean sweep, a clean-up. **4. le t. brûle (chez eux),** (*e.g., of married couple*) they don't hit it off, they're always nagging at each other, they live a cat and dog life. **5. il ne faut pas mélanger les torchons et les serviettes,** we must not compare things of unequal value, we must not get our values mixed.

torchonner = **torcher 1** *and* **2.**

tordant, *adj.* very funny*.

tord-boyaux, *m.* **1.** very strong spirits* *or* brandy, rot-gut. **2.** rat-poison.

tordre, to kill.

tordre, se: se t. (de rire), rire à se t., to split one's sides with laughter, to laugh* uproariously; **c'était à se t.!** it was screamingly funny*! it was a perfect scream! **vous me faites t.!** = **vous me faites rire!**

tordu(e), *adj.* mad*; *m.f.* crackpot, chump, silly bugger.

torgn(i)ole, *f.* **1.** blow*. **2.** thrashing*.

tornif, *m.* handkerchief.

torpille, *m.* professional beggar.

torpiller. 1. to borrow money from (s.o.), to tap (s.o.). **2.** to have coition* with.

torpilleur, *m.* **1.** borrower, cadger, sponger. **2.** beggar.

torsif, *adj.* = **tordant.**

tortillard, *m.* **1.** slow, local stopping train, 'crawler'. **2.** deformed cripple. **3.** expresso coffee.

tortiller. 1. il n'y a pas à t., it's got to be done, there's no getting out of it; there's no denying it. **2. il tortille bien,** he's got a good appetite. **3.** *See* **croupion 2.**

tortore, *f.* food*.

tortorer, to eat*.

tôt, *adv.* **ce n'est pas trop t.!** and about time too! and not before time!

total, *m.* in short, to sum up, when all is said and done.

toto, *m.* **1.** darling*. **2.** (head) louse.

totoche, totote, *f.* darling*.

toubib, *m.* **1.** (*mil.*) medical officer, M.O. **2.** doctor, doc, medico.

toubibaille, *f.* medical fraternity.

touche, *f.* **1.** (*pej.*) appearance, look(s); **je n'aime pas sa t.!** I don't like the cut of his jib! **quelle (drôle de) t.! il en a une t.!** what a queer-looking guy! **2. t. de piano,** tooth. **3.** (*prison slang*) drag (*i.e puff at cigarette passed round*). **4. faire une** (*or* avoir une *or* la) **t. avec,** to make a hit with (s.o. of the opposite sex), to get off with, to click with; **essayer de faire une t. avec,** to make a pass at. **5.** = **piquouse.**

touché, *adj.* =tordu.

toucher. I. ne pas avoir l'air d'y t., to look as if butter wouldn't melt in one's mouth; sans avoir l'air d'y t., as if quite unconsciously. 2. (*to child*) pas touche! mustn't touch! 3. t. beau, to touch lucky.

toucher, se, to masturbate*; s'en t., not to care a rap* about.

touffiane, *f.* I. opium. 2. opium pipe.

touillage, *m.* stirring (up).

touiller, to stir(up), to shuffle (cards).

toupet, *m.* impudence*; payer de t., to brazen it out; il a du t.! he's got a nerve!

toupie, *f.* I. head*. 2. vieille t., old frump, old trout. 3. weak-willed (*or* flighty) person.

tour, *m.* I. faire le t. du cadran, to sleep the clock round. 2. jouer un sale t. (*or* un t. de cochon) à qn, to play a dirty trick upon s.o. 3. t. de bête, promotion by seniority. *See also* bâton 1, proprio 2, sang 10.

tour, *f.* la T. Pointue, la T. de l'Horloge, I. the Conciergerie (*prison in Paris*). 2. Criminal Investigation Dept.

tourlourou, *m.* foot-soldier, foot-slogger.

tourlousine, tourlouzine, *f.* thrashing*.

tournanche, *f.* I.=tournée 1 *and* 3. 2. thrashing*.

tournanché, *adj.* être bien t., (*of person*) to be shapely, to be well set up.

tournant, *m.* I. avoir (*or* choper *or* pincer *or* rattraper) qn au t., (*a*) to arrest* s.o.; (*b*) to get one's own back on s.o., to serve s.o. out, to catch s.o. by the short hairs. 2. faire un (drôle de) t. à qn, to play a dirty trick (*or* the dirty) on s.o. 3. être dans un sale t., to be in a nice fix*.

tournebouler, to upset.

tournée, *f.* I. round of drinks; c'est ma t.! it's my round (*or* call *or* treat *or* shout)! the drinks are on me! payer (*or* offrir) une t., to stand a round (of drinks), (*nav. sl.*) to push out the boat. 2. thrashing*. 3. =balade. 4. faire la t. des grands ducs, to paint the town red.

tourner. *See* bourrique 6, œil 21, rond, *adv.*, sang 6 *and* 10.

tournicoter, tourniquer, to wander round and round; to hang round (s.o.)

tourniquet, *m.* (*mil.*) passer au t., to be court-martialled.

tourte, *f.* I. fool*. 2. en rester comme une t.=en rester comme deux ronds de flan. 3. =tarte, *f.* I.

tousser. I. to grumble*. 2. non, c'est que je tousse! (*c.p.*)—*e.g.* il n'est pas poivré, non, c'est que je tousse! (*iron.*) he isn't drunk, oh no, I don't think! (*iron.*) he isn't drunk, oh dear no! tu ne connais pas la rue X?—non, c'est que je tousse! j'y demeure, do you happen to know X Street?—don't I just! (*or* you bet I do!) I live there!

tout, *indef.pron.* I. ce n'est pas t. ça, that's not the point at all, that won't do at all. 2. et t. et t., and all the rest of it. 3. pardon, madame.—du t. monsieur, I beg your pardon.—don't mention it.

toutiche, toutim(e), totu, *m.* (tout le t.), all the rest of it, the whole bag* of tricks; (le) t. et la mèche, and so on and so forth.

tout-le-monde, *m.* Monsieur T.-le-m., the man-in-the-street, the average man.

toutou, *m.* (*child's word*) dog*, doggy, doggie, bow-wow. *See also* peau 3.

Tout-Paris, *m.* fashionable Paris, Parisian smart set, the Paris-that-matters.

tout-va, à, *adv.* abundantly, copiously.

toxico, *m.* junkie.

trac, *m.* fear, funk; stage-fright; examination nerves; avoir le t., se prendre de t., to be afraid*; filer le t. à qn, to put the wind up s.o.

tracassin, *m.* avoir le t., (*a*) to be worried; (*b*) to have the fidgets; (*c*)=bander.

tracer, (se,) to decamp*, to run.

tracsir, traczir, *m.*=trac.

Trafalgar, *pr.n.* un (coup de) **T.**, a sudden catastrophe (*or* calamity *or* disaster).

train, *m.* 1. buttocks*. *See also* magner, se, manier, se. 2. avoir le feu au t. = avoir le feu quelque part (feu 2). 3. être dans le t., to be up-to-date, to be in the swim. 4. être en t., to be tipsy. 5. faire du t., to kick up a dust. 6. filer le t. à qn, coller qn au t., coller au t. à qn, to follow s.o. closely, to dog s.o.'s footsteps. 7. ne pas être en t., not to be up to the mark. 8. prendre (*or* aller par) le t. onze (*or* le t. d'onze heures), to go on foot, to go by Shanks's pony, to foot it, to hoof it, to pad the hoof. 9. se crever (*or* se casser) le t., to work oneself to death. 10. remettre au t., to compel s.o., to twist s.o.'s arm.

traînard, *m.* ramasser (*or* faire) un t., to come a cropper*.

traîne, *f.* arriver à la t., to turn up late; être à la t., to be late, to lag behind.

traînée, *f.* common prostitute*.

traîne-lattes, -patins, -pattes, -sabots, -savates, *m.* tramp, hobo, bum.

trainglot, *m.* = tringlot.

train-train, *m.* le t.-t. de la vie, the daily round (*or* routine *or* grind).

trait, *m.* faire des traits à, to be unfaithful to (*one's wife or husband*), to be a two-timer, to two-time.

tralala, *m.* 1. en grand t., sur șon t., dressed* up to the nines. 2. faire du t., to make a big fuss, to make a great show. 3. et tout le t., and the whole bag* of tricks.

tranche, *f.* (i) 1. fool*; faire la t., to act the goat. 2. en avoir une t. = en avoir une couche. 3. s'en payer une t., to have the time of one's life, to have one's fling, to have no end of fun; s'en payer une (bonne) t., to let oneself go.

tranche, *f.* (ii), **trancher** = tronche, troncher.

tranchouillard, *m.* = tranche (i) 1.

trans, *adj.* = sensas(s).

transat, *m.* 1. deck-chair. 2. ocean liner.

transbahuter, to transport, to convey, to carry, to cart, to lug about.

transparent, *adj.* vous n'êtes pas t. = votre père n'était pas vitrier.

transpiration, *f.* passer à la t. = en suer une.

trantran, *m.* = train-train; aller son petit t., to jog along.

trapanelle, *f.* (*av.*) glider.

trappe, *f.* mouth*; boucle la t., shut* up!

traquette, traquouse, *f.* = trac.

traqueur, *m.* coward*.

travail, *m.* 1. faire un petit t., (*of burglar*) to crack a crib. 2. aller au t., (*of prostitute*) to go on the beat.

travailler: aller t., (*of prostitute*) = aller au travail.

travailleuse, *f.* une bonne t. = gagneuse.

travelo, *m.* 1. drag (*men's transvestite female apparel*). 2. transvestite, 'drag queen'.

travers, *m.* 1. être en plein t., to be dead out of luck. 2. passer au t., (*a*) to escape trouble (*or* danger), to slip through the net, to beat the rap; (*b*) to draw a blank.

traversin, *m.* faire un coup de t., to have a nap (*or* a snooze).

traviole, travioc, de, *adv. phrase.* awry, askew, crooked, cock-eyed, skew-whiff; au t. = travers 2.

travs, *m.pl.* les t. (à perpète), penal servitude (for life).

tref, trèfle, *m.* 1. tobacco, baccy. 2. = trèpe. 3. money*. 4. passer au t., to beat up. 5. crowd.

tremblement, *m.* tout le t. (et son train), the whole bag* of tricks.

tremblote, *f.* avoir la t., to be all of a tremble (*or* all of a dither *or* all of a twitter), to have the shivers (*or* the shakes *or* the jitters).

trempe, *f.,* **trempée,** *f.* thrashing*.

trente, *num. adj.* 1. se mettre (*or* être) sur son t.-et-un, to dress (*or* to be dressed*) up to the nines. 2. t.-six,

umpteen; **le t.-six,** C.I.D. (*police*);
t.-sixième, umpteenth; **tous les t.-
six du mois,** once in a blue moon;
faire les t.-six volontés de qn, to
dance attendance on s.o., to be
s.o.'s slave, to be at s.o.'s beck and
call. *See also* **chandelle 4, chemin 2,
dessous 2. 3. dites t.-trois! = dites
quarante-quatre!**
trèpe, trêple, *m.* crowd, throng, mob.
trésor, *m.* **mon (petit) t.,** my darling*.
tréteau, *m.* horse, nag.
tri, *m.* (=*triporteur*), carrier-tricycle,
tri-car.
triage, *m.* **plusieurs triages,** several
times; **à chaque t.,** each time.
tricard, *m.* 1. ex-convict prohibited
from entering specified areas. 2. *adj.*
sent to Coventry.
triche, *f.* cheating.
tricoter. t. des bâtons, (des gambettes,
etc.). 1. to dance. 2. to decamp*. 3.
to leg it.
trictrac, *m.* shady deal.
trifouillée, *f.* severe thrashing*.
trifouiller. 1. to rummage about. 2. to
meddle (*or* mess about *or* fiddle)
with.
trimard, *m.* (high) road, highway;
battre le t., to be a tramp, to be on the
tramp (*or* on the pad), to pad the
hoof.
trimarder. 1. =**battre le trimard.** 2.
=**trimer.**
trimardeur, *m.* tramp, hobo, bum.
trimbalée, *f.* crowd, swarm (of kids,
brats, etc.).
trimbaler, to cart (*or* to lug) about, to
tote; **se faire t.,** to get a lift.
trimbaler, se, to drag oneself along.
trimer: t. (**dur** *or* **comme un mercenaire**), to work* hard; **t. la galère du
matin au soir,** to toil like a galley-
slave from morning till night.
trimeur, *m.* hard worker, toiler,
drudge.
tringle, *f.* 1. **se mettre la t.,** to be de-
prived of, to go without. 2. **travailler
pour la t.,** to work for nothing at all.
3. **être de la t. = être porté sur la baga-**

telle; **coup de t.,** copulation. 4. **en
avoir t. = en avoir marre.**
tringle, *adj.* silly.
tringler, to have coition* with.
tringleur, *m.* fornicator.
tringlomane, *m.* =**tringleur.**
tringlot, *m.* soldier in the French
Army Service Corps.
trinquer, to get the worst of it, to pay
the piper, to receive punishment (*or* a
thrashing* *or* a prison sentence, etc.),
to cop it, to get the rap, to get it in
the neck.
tripaille, *f.* 1. offal. 2. flabby breasts
(of woman).
Tripatouille (*or* **Tripatouillis)-les-
Oies,** *pr.n.* =**Fouilly-les-Oies.**
tripatouiller. 1. to tamper with. 2.
=**patiner.** 3. to rummage.
tripes, *f.pl.* tripes, guts, bowels; **rendre**
(*or* **dégueuler) t. et boyaux,** to be as
sick as a dog, to bring up one's inside;
mettre les t. au soleil (*or* **à l'air) à qn,**
to kill* s.o., to rip s.o. open.
tripette, *f.* **ne pas valoir t. = ne pas
valoir chipette.**
tripotage, *m.* crooked deal; **t. de
comptes,** cooking of accounts.
tripotée, *f.* 1. thrashing*. 2. great
quantity*.
tripoter = patiner.
**tripoter, se: il se tripote quelque
chose,** there's something brewing (*or*
afoot) (*implying something fishy*).
triquard, *m.* =**tricard.**
trique, *f.* (i) prohibition from entering
specified areas.
trique, *f.* (ii) 1. **mener qn à la t.,** to rule
s.o. with a rod of iron. 2. **sec** (*or*
maigre) comme une t. (*or* **comme un
coup de t.**), as thin as a rake. 3. **avoir
la t. = bander.** 4. *pl.* **mettre les triques,**
to decamp*.
triquée, *f.* thrashing*.
triquer, = bander.
trisser, se trisser, se trissoter,
to decamp*.
trogne, *f.* bloated face.
trognon, *m.* 1. head*; **se casser le t.,** to
rack one's brains; **y aller du t.,** to risk

one's neck; **dévisser le t. à qn,** to
strangle s.o. **2.** face*. **3. jusqu'au t.,**
thoroughly, up to the neck; **avoir qn
jusqu'au t.,** to take s.o. in completely.
4. darling*. **5. un petit t.,** a little slip
of a girl.

trois-six, *m.* proof spirit.

trombine, *f.* face*.

trombiner, to have coition* with.

tromblon, *m.* **1.** broad-topped high hat.
2. filer un coup de t., to have coition*.

tromblonard, *m.* face*; **se casser le t.,**
to come a cropper*, to fall flat on one's
face.

trompe, *f.* **1.** face*. **2.** head*.

trompe-la-mort, *m.* death-dodger.

trompette, *f.* **1.** face*. **2.** mouth*. **3.**
nose*. **4. avoir le** (*or* **un**) **nez en t.,** to
have a turned-up nose. **5. la t. du
quartier,** (*of person*) the local gossip
(*or* chronicle).

tronc, *m.* **1.** head*; **se casser le t.,** to
worry. **2. se taper le t.,** to have a good
tuck-in. **3.** kitty (*tips received and
shared out by a staff*). **4. t. (de figuier),**
Arab, North African, wog.

tronche, *f.* **1.** head*; **filer un coup de t.
à qn,** to butt s.o.; **se faire décoller la t.,**
to be guillotined, to be topped; **ne pas
se casser la t.,** not to rack one's
brains. **2.** face*. **3.** twerp, clot. **4.
entrer en t.,** to come in first.

troncher=**tringler.**

troncheur, *m.*=**tringleur.**

trône, *m.* W.C.*, 'throne'.

troquet, *m.* **1.** =**mastroquet. 2.** bar,
pub; **une tournée de troquets,** a pub-
crawl.

trot, *m.* **au t.!** be quick about it! hurry*
up!

trotte, *f.* **une bonne t.,** a good distance,
a good walk, a good step; **ça fait une
bonne t.!** that's a tidy step from here!

trotter, se, to decamp*.

trottin, *m.* errand-girl (of milliner or
dressmaker).

trottinant, trottinet, *m.* foot*, trotter.

trottinette, *f.* **1.** (*motor.*) runabout. **2.
t. à macchabs,** hearse, meat-wagon.

trottoir, *m.* **faire le t.,** (*of prostitute*) to
go on (*or* to walk) the streets, to be a
street-walker.

trou, *m.* **1.** (dead-and-alive) hole,
dump, backwater; **un petit t. pas
cher,** a quiet, inexpensive little holiday resort. **2.** prison*. **3. boire comme
un t.,** to drink like a fish. **4. boucher
un t.,** to pay off a debt. **5. descendre
qn dans le t.,** to bury s.o.; **être dans le
t.,** to be dead and buried. **6. faire son
t.,** to make one's name, to get on (in
the world). **7. faire un t. à la lune,** to
abscond, to shoot the moon. **8. ne pas
avoir les yeux en face des trous,** not to
see things as they are, not to see
straight, to be 'blind'. **9. ne rien voir
que par le t. d'une bouteille,** to know
nothing of the world. **10. t. normand,**
glass of *calvados* (apple-brandy)
drunk in the course of a meal. **11. t.
de balle, t. du cul,** arse(-hole); **un
vieux t. de balle,** an old dodderer;
jusqu'à la saint-t.-du-cul=**jusqu'à la
Saint-Glinglin; avoir le t. du cul qui
fait bravo**=**avoir le trouillomètre à
zéro; se démancher** (*or* **se décarcasser**
or **se dévisser**) **le t. du cul,** to make
every effort, to go all out.

troubade, *m.* private, foot-soldier,
swad(dy).

trouble-ménage, *m.* ordinary red
wine.

trouduc, *m.* (*abbrev. of* **trou du cul**). **1.**
fool*. **2.** arse(-hole).

trouer: t. qn, to fill s.o. with lead, to
riddle s.o. with bullets.

troufignard, *m.* arse.

troufigner, to stink*.

troufignon, *m.*=**troufignard.**

trouf(f)ion, *m.*=**troubade.**

trouillard, *m.* coward*, funk.

trouille, *f.* =**frousse; avoir la t.**=**avoir
la frousse; ficher** (*or* **flanquer** *or* **foutre**)
la t. à qn=**ficher la frousse à qn;
une t. verte** (*or* **noire**), a blue funk. **ne
pas avoir la t.,** (*a*) to be plucky; (*b*) to
be impudent*.

trouillomètre, *m.* **avoir le t. à zéro,**
to be in a blue funk.

trouilloter. 1. to stink*. **2.** to be afraid*. *See also* **corridor, goulot.**

troupe, *f.* **en route, mauvaise t!** (*to children*) come along (*or* get a move on), you young rascals!

troupier, *m.* = **troubade.**

trousses, *f.pl.* **troussequin,** *m.* buttocks*.

truand, *m.* hobo, gangster.

truc, *m.* **1.** trick, dodge, wheeze, caper, fiddle, wrinkle; **les trucs du métier,** the tricks of the trade. **2.** thing, what's-its-name*. **3.** knack, hang (of it), know-how, the savvy; **prendre le t. pour faire qch.,** to get the hang of it. **4.** **couper** (*or* **mordre**) **dans le t.,** to fall into the trap, to fall for it. **5. faire le t.** *or* **aller au t.** = **faire le trottoir. 6.** (*mil.*) **faire son t.,** to furbish one's kit. **7.** **lâcher** (*or* **débiner**) **le t.,** to let the cat out of the bag, to spill the beans. **8. piquer au t.,** to have a go; **repiquer au t., refaire le t.,** (*a*) to have another go (*or* another try *or* another shot); (*b*) to re-enlist. **9. être porté sur le t.** = **être porté sur la bagatelle.**

trucmuche, *m.* = **truc 1, 2** *and* **3.**

truffe, *f.* **1.** bulbous nose*, bottle-nose, snout. **2.** fool*, mug. **3.** bumpkin, lout, clot. **4. se piquer la t.** = **se piquer le nez (nez 13).** *See also* **cresson 1.**

truffer : t. qn = **trouer qn.**

trumeau, *m.* **un vieux t.,** an old hag, an old bag, mutton dressed as lamb.

truquage, *m.* faking.

truquer. 1. to fake, to 'rig'. **2.** = **faire le trottoir.**

truqueur, *m.* faker.

truqueuse, *f.* low-class prostitute*, trollop.

tsoin-tsoin, *adj.* = **soin-soin.**

tuant, *adj.* (*of work*); killing, backbreaking; (*of person*) exasperating, boring.

tubard, *m.* (i) tip (*at races, etc.*); **refiler un t. à qn,** to give s.o. a tip, to tip s.o. off, to give s.o. a tip-off.

tubard, *m.* (ii) consumptive, a T.B. case, a 'lunger'; *adj.* tubercular.

tubardise, *f.* consumption, T.B.

tube, *m.* **1.** top-hat, topper. **2.** stomach*. **3.** telephone, blower; **filer** (*or* **passer**) **un coup de t. à qn,** to ring s.o. up, to give s.o. a ring (*or* a buzz *or* a tinkle); **avoir qn au t.,** to get s.o. on the phone. **4.** = **tubard** (i). **5.** = **tubard** (ii). **6. à plein(s) tube(s),** at full speed, all out; **donner à plein(s) tube(s),** (*motor.*) to step on the gas. **7.** **débloquer** (*or* **déconner**) **à plein(s) tube(s),** to talk utter nonsense, to talk rot* (*or* bilge), to talk through one's hat, to talk out of the back of one's head. **8.** underground, metro. **9.** 'top of the pops' record.

tuber. 1. to (tele)phone. **2.** to sell tips (*at the races*). **3.** = **refiler un tubard à qn** (**tubard** (i)).

tubeur, *m.* tipster.

tuer, to bore* (*or* to tire) to death.

tuile, *f.* unexpected mishap, nasty blow, bit of bad luck, facer; **il vient de me tomber une t.!** I've just had a nasty knock! **une t. imprévue,** a bolt from the blue.

tumec, *m.* wine.

tunnel, *m.* (*th.*) long speech.

turbin, *m.* **1.** (hard) work, drudgery, graft, grind, slog, (*sch.*) swot(ting). **2. aller au t.** = **aller au turbin (travail 2). 3. faire un petit t.** = **faire un petit travail (travail 1). 4. faire un vache t.** (*or* **un drôle de t.**) **à qn,** to do the dirty on s.o. **5. faire le t. promis,** to deliver the goods.

turbiner, to work* hard.

turbineur, *m.* hard worker, slogger, grinder.

turbineuse, *f.* = **gagneuse.**

turf, *m.* **1.** racing; racecourse; racing world. **2.** job, work. **3.** prostitute's beat; **fille de t.,** prostitute*; **faire le t.** = **faire le trottoir; aller au** (*or* **sur le**) **t.,** to go on the beat.

turfeuse, *f.* prostitute*.

turfiste, *m.* race-goer.

turlupiner, to bother, to worry, to annoy; **qu'est-ce qui vous turlupine?** what's eating you?

turne, *f.* hovel, hole; diggings, digs; (*at*

École normale supérieure) room, study, den.

tutoyer: se faire t., to be severely reprimanded*, to get told off (*or* ticked off).

tutu, *adj.* être t., to be consumptive, to be T.B.

tutu, *m.* **1.** (*child's word*) backside, bottom, botty. **2.** ballet dancer's short 'sticking out' skirt. **3.** flared mini-skirt. **4.** telephone, blower. **5.** wine. **6. faire t. dans la carafe,** to talk into thin air. **7. se remplir le t.,** to eat.

tutu-panpan, *m.* smack-bottom.

tututter. to drink wine, to tipple.

tuyau, *m.* **1.** tip, pointer, helpful hint, wrinkle; **marchand de tuyaux,** (*at races*) tipster; **un t. increvable,** a dead cert, a nap; **un t. de première main,** inside information, a tip straight from the horse's mouth. **2. t. de poêle,** top-hat, topper, stove-pipe, chimney-pot. **3. la famille 't. de poêle',** (*a*) the world of pederasts*; (*b*) extraordinary family. **4. pantalon en t. de poêle,** drain-pipe trousers. **5. à pleins tuyaux = à pleins tubes.**

tuyauter. to give a tip (*or* tips) to, to give s.o. the tip-off, to give s.o. the office, to tip s.o. the wink; **être bien tuyauté,** to have good inside information, to be in the know; **tuyauter qn sur,** to give s.o. the low-down on.

tuyauteur, *m.* tipster.

type, *m.* **1.** fellow*; **un chic t.,** a good chap, a brick, a swell (*or* a regular) guy, a good skin; **un pauvre t.,** a poor kind of blighter; **un sale t.,** a rotter*, a bad egg; **un t. à passions,** a sexual pervert. **2.** queer* person. **quel t.!** what a character (*or* card *or* caution)!

typesse, *f.* woman*, girl*, dame, (bit of) skirt.

typo, *m.* printer, compositor.

U

u, *m.* uniform.

un, une, *num. adj., indef. art., and pron.* 1. être sans un, to be penniless*. 2. le un, the first (*in a charade*), (*th.*) the first act, Act One. 3. il était (*or* c'était) moins une, it was a narrow escape*; s'en tirer à moins une, to have a narrow squeak. 4. ne faire (*or* sans faire) ni une ni deux, not to hesitate, not to think twice about it, to make no bones about it, without more ado. 5. l'un dans l'autre, (taking) one thing with another, on the (*or* on an) average. 6. et d'un(e)! so much for that one! that settles it for that one! 7. de deux choses l'une, it is one thing or the other, it's either this or that, it's one of two things. 8. la une, the first (*or* front) page (of a newspaper); cinq colonnes à la une, banner headline, front page spread. 9. un, une, (*used* (*with* en) *in more or less set expressions with omission of the noun*) en boucher un (*coin*); en coller un (*marron*); en griller une (*cigarette*); n'en pas bonnir une (*parole*); n'en pas rater une (*sottise*); en savoir plus d'une (*chose*); n'en pas avoir un (*poil*) de sec.

unif, *m.* uniform.

unique, *adj.* il est u.! he's priceless! he's the limit!

unité, *f.* one million old francs.

urf(e), *adj.* swell, posh, dressed up*, first-rate*.

urger: ça urge! it's urgent! it can't wait!

usé, *adj.* =fichu 2.

user: u. sa salive, to talk* volubly. *See also* soleil 4.

usine, *f.* aller à l'u., to go to work. *See also* bachot.

usiner. 1. to exploit, to sweat. 2. en u.=aller au travail.

utilité, *f.* (*th.*) utility-man; jouer les utilités, to play small parts.

V

va, à tout, *adv. phrase.* (*a*) right and left, on all hands; (*b*) like a house on fire, like blazes, like one o'clock, like mad (*i.e. quickly and vigorously*).

va, (*intensive use*) you can be sure; **je t'aime bien, va!** of course I love you!

va pour ..., O.K. for ...

vacciné, *adj.* 1. être v. avec une aiguille (*or* une pointe) de phono, to talk* volubly. 2. être v. au salpêtre (*or* avec une queue de morue), to be a thirsty mortal.

vachard, *m.* (*of person*) lazy dog; *adj.* =vache, *adj.*

vachardise, *f.* laziness.

vache, *f.* 1. (*of man*) brute, beast, swine, pig, dirty dog, stinker, (*of woman*) bitch, cow. 2. policeman*; **mort aux vaches!** down with the cops! v. à roulettes = hirondelle. 3. v. à lait, mug, sucker. 4. manger (*or* bouffer *or* se taper) de la v. enragée, to rough it, to have a hard time of it. 5. le plancher des vaches, dry land, terra firma. 6. plein comme une v., dead drunk*. 7. pleurer comme une v., to weep* copiously. 8. il pleut comme v. qui pisse, it's raining cats and dogs, it's pissing down with rain, it's pissing (it) down. 9. un coup de pied en v., an underhand trick. 10. oh! la v.! damn and blast it! vache de ...! the bloody ...! 11. *adj.* (*of person*) nasty, awkward, caddish, (*of problem, question, etc.*) damn difficult, a stinker; allez, (ne) sois pas v.! come on, be a sport! il a été v. comme tout avec moi, he was a perfect pig (*or* a perfect swine *or* an absolute bastard) with me; un coup v., a dirty trick.

vachement, *adv.* 1. damned, fantastically, hellishly, bloody; avoir v. soif, to have a hell of a thirst. 2. exceedingly; c'est v. bien, its dead good!

vacherie, *f.* dirty trick.

va-comme-je-te-pousse, à la, *adv. phrase.* in a slapdash (*or* in a happy-go-lucky) manner, anyhow, any old how; élevé à la v., dragged up.

vachère, *f.* police bus.

va-de-la-gueule, *m.* (*of person*) big-mouth, loud-mouth.

vadrouille, *f.* être en v., to be on the spree*; to be on the prowl.

vadrouiller, (se). 1. to gad (*or* to knock) about, to gallivant. 2. to go on the spree*.

vadrouilleur, *m.* gallivanter, gad-about.

vague, *f.* pocket*.

vaguer: v. qn, to go through s.o.'s pockets, to frisk s.o., to rub s.o. down.

vaguotte, *f.* jacket, coat.

vaillant, *adj.* in good health, fit, up to the mark.

vaisselle, *f.* 1. decorations, medals and stars. 2. v. de fouille, (pocket) money*.

valable, *adj.* perfect.

valade, *f.* =vague.

valda(ga), *f.* 1. bullet. 2. green traffic light.

valdingue, *f.* 1. suit-case; faire la v., to decamp*. 2. la Grande V., death.

valdingue, *m.* ramasser un v., to come a cropper* (*lit. and fig.*).

valise, *f.* faire la v. =valiser.

valiser, to walk out on (s.o.).

valoche, valouse, *f.* suit-case.

valse, *f.* 1. envoyer la v., lâcher les valses lentes, to pay* up. 2. faire la v. à qn, to step out on s.o. 3. filer une v. à qn, to thrash* s.o. 4. inviter qn à la v., to challenge s.o. to (step outside and) fight.

valser. 1. v. de ..., to lose a clear ... (*sum of money*). 2. faire v. qn, (*a*) to lead s.o. a dance; (*b*) to kick (*or* to boot) s.o. out. 3. faire v. l'argent, to

make the money fly, to spend money like water, to play ducks and drakes with one's money.
valseur, *m.* **1.** buttocks*. **2.** trousers*.
valseuses, *f.pl.* testicles*.
van(n)e, *m.* **1.** witty (but sarcastic) remark, unkind reflection, (nasty) crack. **2.** dirty trick. **3.** spot of bother.
vanné, *adj.* exhausted*.
vanneau, *m.* =vannot.
vanner. 1. to exhaust, to tire out. **2.** to make a crack. **3.** to brag, to talk big.
vanneur, *m.* braggart, boaster.
vannot, *m.* **1.** =vanne. **2.** *pl.* bargain goods.
vanterne, *f.* window.
vape, *f.* **1.** être dans les vapes, être en pleine v., (a) to be dop(e)y, to be muzzy, to be woozy; (b) to be dogged by bad luck, to be up against it. **2.** sentir (or renifler or respirer) la v., to smell a rat, to have a hunch. **3.** *pl.* Turkish baths.
vaporisateur, *m.* tommy-gun.
varloper, to window-shop.
vase, *f.* **1.** water. **2.** rain. **3.** être dans la v., to be in a fix*.
vase, *m.* **1.** buttocks*. **2.** luck; avoir du v.=avoir du pot (pot 2).
vaser. 1. to rain. **2.** to do badly (at an examination, etc.).
vaseux, *adj.* **1.** (of person) unwell*. **2.** (of answer, idea, thought, etc.) woolly, muddle-headed.
vasouillard, *adj.*=vaseux 2.
vasouiller, to be stumped, to be floored (at an examination, etc.), to make a mess (or a balls) of it.
vatères, *m.pl.* les v.=les ouatères.
vautour, *m.* landlord.
va-vite, à la, *adv. phrase.* hastily, hurriedly; fait à la v. (of work) rushed.
veau, *m.* **1.** (tête de) v., fool*, lout, clod. **2.** faire le v., to loll, to lounge, to sprawl. **3.** tête de v., bald-head. **4.** prostitute*. **5.** (turf)=tocard 3. **6.** pleurer comme un v., to weep* copiously, to cry like a baby.
vécés, *m.pl.* W.C.*

vécu, *p.p.* avoir beaucoup v., to have seen life.
veilleuse, *f.* **1.** souffler sa v., to die*. **2.** mettre qch. en v., (of an activity of any kind, e.g. a business, a hobby) just to keep it going, keep it ticking over, to all but stop it, to shelve temporarily. **3.** la mettre en v., to keep silent about it, to hold one's tongue, to keep it under one's hat.
veinard, *adj.* lucky; *m.* lucky person, lucky dog; (sacré) v.! you lucky devil.
veine, *f.* luck; coup de v., lucky stroke, lucky strike, lucky break; fluke; avoir de la v., être en v., to be lucky, to touch lucky, to get a break; c'est bien ma v.! just my luck! pas de v.! bad (or hard or rotten) luck! avoir une v. de cocu (or de cornard or de pendu), to have the devil's own luck; une v. que . . ., it was lucky that . . .
veines, *f.pl.* se saigner aux quatre v., see blanc *m.*
Vel' d'Hiv', *m.* (=Vélodrome d'Hiver) Paris cycling-track (also used for mass meetings).
vélo, *m.* bicycle, bike; faire du v., to go in for cycling.
vélodrome, *m.* un v. à mouches=un skating à mouches.
velours, *m.* **1.** profit, winnings. **2.** c'est du v., it's very easy*. **3.** jouer sur le v., to play (or to be) on velvet; rouler sur le v., to be winning.
vendange, *f.* loot, swag.
vendetta, *f.* flick-knife.
vendre. 1. v. qn, to denounce* s.o., to give s.o. away. **2. v. un piano,** to bluff. **3.** (th.) to be on (of play).
vendu, *m.* double-crosser, fink.
venette, *f.* funk; avoir la v.=avoir la frousse.
venin, *m.* cracher (or filer) son.v.=jouir.
venir: je vous vois v. or je vois où vous voulez en v., I see what you're after (or what you're driving at or what you're getting at), I rumble you.
vent, *m.* **1.** empty words; c'est du v.! it's all nonsense*. **2.** du v.!=des clous! (clou 7). **3.** envoyer du v., to

tell lies. **4. jouer du v.**, to decamp*. **5·
lâcher un v.**, to break wind, to fart.
6. perdre son v., to waste one's
breath. **7. avoir du v.** (*or* **un peu de v.**)
dans les voiles, to be drunk*, to be
three sheets in the wind. **8. être dans
le v.**, to be with it.

ventilateur, *m.* (*av.*) helicopter,
chopper.

ventouse, *f.* tenacious bore*.

ventre, *m.* **1. avoir qch.** (*or* **en avoir**)
dans le v., to have vitality and ability,
to have guts; **n'avoir rien dans le v.**,
to be lacking in guts (*or* talent *or* fire,
etc.); **savoir ce que qn a dans le v.**, to
find out what s.o. is made of. **2. se
brosser le v.**: *see* **se brosser**. **3. prendre
du v.**, to get pot-bellied, to put on a
corporation. **4. se serrer le v.**, to
tighten one's belt. **5. taper sur le v. à
qn**, to be too familiar with s.o., to dig
(*or* to poke) s.o. in the ribs. **6. tu me
fais mal au v.!** you make me sick!

ventrée, *f.* bellyful; **s'en mettre** (*or*
s'en flanquer) **une v.**, to have a good
tuck-in (*or* a good blow-out).

Vénus, *pr.n.* **recevoir un coup de pied de
V.**, to cop a dose (*i.e. of V.D.*).

ver, *m.* **1. nu comme un v.**, stark
naked*. **2. pas piqué des vers**, not so
dusty, first-rate*, not half bad; **un(e)
... qui n'est pas piqué des vers** =
**un(e) ... qui n'est pas dans une
musette. 3. tirer les vers du nez à qn**,
to pump s.o., to worm sth. (*or* a
secret) out of s.o. **4. tuer le v.**, to take
(*or* to have) an early morning bracer
(*or* reviver), to have a pick-me-up
before breakfast, to take an eye-
opener, to keep the damp out.

verdâtres, *m.pl.* **les v.** = **les verts-de-
gris.**

verdine, *f.* gipsy's caravan.

véreux, *m.* old offender.

verge, *f.* penis*.

verjo(t), *m.*, *adj.* **avoir du v., être v.**,
to be lucky.

verlan, verlen, *m.* (code) v., backslang.

verni, *adj.* **être v.**, to be lucky, to be a

lucky dog, to bear a charmed life; **ne
pas être v.**, to be out of luck.

verre, *m.* **1. avoir un v. de trop**, to have
had one too many, to have had one
over the eight. **2. avoir un v. dans le
nez**, to be drunk*. **3. boire un petit v.**,
to have a nip (*or* a bracer *or* a short
(one) *or* a snort *or* a snifter *or* a reviver). **4. manier qn comme du v.
cassé**, to handle s.o. with kid gloves.
5. se noyer dans un v. d'eau = **se noyer
dans un crachat. 6. une tempête dans
un v. d'eau**, a storm in a teacup. **7. v.
de montre**, buttocks*; **casser son v.
de montre**, to fall on one's backside.
8. c'est réglé comme du v. pilé, it
never fails, it comes off every time.

verse, *f.* rain.

versé, *m.* (*waiter's slang*) black coffee.

vert, *adj.* **1.** (*of story, joke*) spicy,
smutty, risky, blue. **2. en être v.**, to
be dumbfounded*. **3. langue verte**,
slang. **4. se mettre au v.**, to retire to
the country, to settle down to a quiet
life. **5. ils sont trop verts!** it's a case of
sour grapes! **6. en dire des vertes et
des pas mûres à qn**, (*a*) to tell s.o.
risky stories; (*b*) to tell s.o. tall stories;
(*c*) to give it s.o. straight from the
shoulder, not to mince one's words.
**7. en avoir vu des vertes et des pas
mûres**, to have been through it (*or*
through a lot *or* through the mill); **en
faire voir des vertes et des pas mûres à
qn**, to put s.o. through it, to give s.o.
a bad time of it. **8. en faire avaler des
vertes et des pas mûres à qn**, to make
s.o. believe one's tallest stories.

verte, *f.* **1.** spicy (*or* smutty *or* risky)
story, blue gag. **2.** glass of absinthe.

verts-de-gris, *m.pl.* (*W.W.II*) German soldiers, Jerries.

vertu, *f.* **ce n'est pas une v.!** she's no
saint! (*or* no angel! *or* she's no better
than she should be *or* (*Amer. sl.*) she's
not so lily white!).

vesse, *f.* **1.** noiseless fart. **2.** = **frousse.**

vesser, to fart. *See also* **bec 14.**

veste, *f.* **1.** failure, set-back. **remporter**

(*or* **ramasser**) **une v.**, to fail, to be un-successful. **2. tourner** (*or* **retourner**) **sa v.**, to be a turncoat, to change sides. **3. tomber la v.**, to take (*or* to peel) one's coat off.

vestiaire, *m.* (*at restaurant, etc.*) **son v.**, one's hat and coat.

Vésuve, *pr.n.* **c'est le V. en éruption,** she's a red-hot mamma.

vestige, *m.* (*teenage slang*) person over forty years of age. (*The gradation is* **amorti, vestige, croulant, son et lumière.**)

vétéran, *m.* (*sch.*) pupil repeating a course; **les vétérans,** the seniors.

vétos, *m.pl.* veterinary surgeons, vets.

vêtures, *f.pl.* clothes*.

veuve, *f.* **I. la V.,** the guillotine; **épouser la V.,** to be guillotined. **2. fréquenter la v. poignet,** to masturbate*. **3. la v. sapin,** coffin.

viande, *f.* **I.** human body, carcass; **amène** (*or* **bouge**) **ta v.!** move your carcass! shift! **plaque ta v.!** hide yourself! **2. une v. froide,** a corpse*. **3. de la v. soûle,** drunkards, drunks. **4. marchand de v.,** white-slaver. **5. v. à pneus,** pedestrian.

viander, se, to kill oneself.

viauper = **pleurer comme un veau.**

vibure, *f.* speed.

vice, *m.* **I. avoir du v.,** (*a*) to be sly (*or* cute *or* knowing); (*b*) to be impudent*. **2. avoir du v. pour,** to be infatuated* with (a woman).

vicelard, *adj.* **I.** cute, sly, knowing. **2.** depraved; **un vieux v.,** an old repro-bate, an old rip.

viceloque, *adj.* = **vicelard.**

vicelot, *m.* **I.** sexually depraved person. **2.** cute person.

vidage, *m.* dismissal, sacking, chuck-ing-out.

vidé, *adj.* **I.** exhausted*. **2.** penniless*. **3.** dismissed, sacked.

vider. I. to dismiss*; **se faire v.,** to get thrown out, to get the sack; to be sent out of the room. **2.** to exhaust*. **3.** to ruin, to clean out, to squeeze dry.

videur, *m.* chucker-out.

vie, *f.* **I. faire la v., mener la v.,** to lead a fast (*or* gay *or* wild *or* riotous) life. **2. faire une v.,** to kick up a row (*or* a dust); **il m'a fait une v.!** he led me a dance! **3. enterrer sa v. de garçon,** to give a farewell bachelor party. **4. mener une v. de bâton de chaise** (*or* **une v. de patachon**) = **faire la v. 5. une v. de chien,** a dog's life. **6. une chienne de v.,** a beast of a life.

vieille, *f.* **I. la v.,** mother, the old lady. **2. dis donc, (ma) v.,** I say, old girl; (*can also be said to a man*).

viergot, *m.* **viergotte,** *f.* virgin.

vieux, *m.* **I.** father, the old man, the governor, the gaffer. **2. mes v.,** my parents, the old folk. **3. dis donc, (mon) v.!** I say, old chap* (*or* old bean *or* old thing)! **4. un v. de la vieille,** one of the old brigade, a die-hard, a veteran. **5. se faire v.,** (*a*) to be getting old, to be getting on in years; (*b*) to be kept hanging about. **6. avoir** (*or* **prendre**) **un coup de v.,** to age suddenly.

vif, *m.* **être pris sur le v.,** to be caught in the very act, to be caught red-handed, to be caught bang to rights.

vif-argent, *m.* **avoir du v.-a. dans les veines,** to be always on the go, never to be still for a minute.

vigne, *f.* **I. (bonne) v.,** generous giver. **2. être dans les vignes du Seigneur,** to be drunk.

vilain, *m.* **il y aura** (*or* **il va y avoir**) **du v.,** there's going to be trouble, there's trouble brewing, there'll be dirty work at the cross-roads.

village, *m.* **il est bien de son v.,** he's as green as grass, he's a real bumpkin.

villégiature, *f.* **être en v.,** to be in prison.

vin, *m.* **I. avoir le v. mauvais,** to be quarrelsome when drunk. **2. c'est comme le v. de la comète,** that happens once in a blue moon.

vinaigre, *m.* **I.** (*at rope-skipping*) pepper. **2. faire v.,** to get a move on, to buck up. **3. la situation tourne au v.,** things are taking a turn for the worse (*or* are taking an ugly turn). **4. crier**

au v., (a) to get angry; (b) to call for help.

vinasse, f. weak wine, wishy-washy wine.

vingt, num. adj. **1. v.-deux!** cave! nix! look out! **v.-deux, (v'là) les flics!** beat it! here come the cops! **2. filer la v. et une,** (of juvenile delinquents) to be sent to a penitentiary until one is of age.

vioc(ard), adj. old; m.f., old buffer, old bag.

violent, adj. **ça, c'est un peu v.!** = c'est un peu trop fort (fort, adj. 1).

violette, f. = fleur 1 and 2.

violon, m. **1.** prison*. **2. boîte à v.,** coffin. **3. jouer du v.,** to escape (from prison by filing through the bars of one's cell). **4. c'est comme si tu pissais** (or tu pisses) **dans un v.** = c'est comme si tu chantais (chanter 2). **5. payer les violons,** to pay the piper.

vioquard, vioque, adj., m.f. = viocard.

vioque, f. **à v.,** (of prison sentence) for life, a lifer.

viorner: faire v., to make things hum.

virage, m. **choper qn au v.** = choper qn au tournant. See also **aile 3.**

virée, f. **1.** = balade. **2.** spree*.

virer. 1. to dismiss*; **se faire v.,** to get the order of the boot. **2. tourner et v. qn,** to turn s.o. inside out (by thorough questioning), to put s.o. through it.

vis, f. **serrer la v. à qn,** (a) to put the screw on s.o.; (b) to strangle s.o.

visage, m. **trouver v. de bois,** to find no one at home, to find no one in, to find the door shut.

viscope, f. cap; peak (of cap).

vise-au-trou, f. **madame v.-au-t.,** midwife.

viser, to look* (at), to watch; **vise-moi ça!** just look at that! get a load of that!

visions, f.pl. **avoir des v.,** to labour under delusions, to kid oneself.

vissé, adj. **être mal v.,** to be in a vile temper*.

visselot, m. = vicelot.

visser. 1. v. qn = serrer la vis à qn. **2.** (mil.) to put in clink.

vite-fait, m. **un v.-f.,** (of a drink) a quick 'un.

vitesse, f. **en quatrième v.,** at top (or full) speed.

vitre, f. **casser les vitres,** (a) to kick up a row (or a shindy), to make a scene, to raise hell; (b) not to mince one's words.

vitrier, m. **votre père n'était pas v.,** (joc. c.p. to s.o. standing in the light) you're not made of glass, your father wasn't a glazier, you make a better door than a window.

vitrine, f. **lécher les vitrines** = faire du lèche-vitrines.

vitriol, m. strong spirits* (drink).

vivoter, to rub along, to live from hand to mouth.

vivre. 1. apprendre à v. à qn, to teach s.o. manners. **2. être difficile à v.,** to be difficult to get on with. **3. se laisser v.,** to take it easy*.

vlan, à la, adv. phrase. in a stylish manner.

vocabulaire, m. **être dans le v.,** to be well informed.

voilà, prep. **1. (ne) v.-t-il pas que . . ., (ne) v'là-t-y pas que . . .,** well, I'm hanged (or I'll be blowed) if . . ., bless me (or blow me) if . . ., blest if . . . **2. en v.-t-il!** what a lot! **3. en veux-tu en v.,** as much as you like, lots of, tons of, no end of, . . . galore.

voiles, f. **1. mettre** (or larguer) **les v.,** to decamp*. **2. marcher à v. et à vapeur,** to be A.C.D.C., to be 'ambidextrous' (i.e. to go with women and men).

voir. 1. c'est à v.! that remains to be seen! we shall see about that! **2. en faire v. à qn** = en faire v. de toutes les couleurs à qn (couleur 6). **3. faudrait v.!** = c'est à v.! **4. il ferait beau v.!** what a hope! that'll be the day! **5. il faudrait v. à . . .,** see to it that . . ., I'd like you to understand that . . . **6. ne pas pouvoir v. qn** = ne pas pouvoir v. qn en peinture. **7. se faire v. par le**

médecin, to get examined by the doctor. **8. va-t'en v. si j'y suis!** go to blazes!* **9. va te faire v.!** go and get stuffed! get lost! **10. voyez-vous ça!** did you ever hear of such a thing! well, I never! *See also* **vu.**

voir, *expletive adv. (added to an imperative)* **dites v.!** just tell me! **écoutez v.!** just listen to this! get a load of this! **essayez v.** (un peu)! just try it on! just you have a try! **montrez v.!** let's just have a look! **regardez v.!** just have a dekko! **voyons v.!** let's have a look!

voiture, *f.* **1.** être rangé *(or* barré *or* garé) des voitures, to live a respectable and secure life. **2. v. pie,** Z car.

voiturin, *m.* prison van, Black Maria.

vol, *m.* **v. à la carre,** asking for change and giving false notes in exchange; **v. au kangourou,** shop-lifting (in large stores by putting goods in a large special 'poacher's pocket'; **v. à la pipette,** syphoning petrol from cars; **v. au raton,** theft carried out by young slum thief who hides in a shop and then opens up to the gang; **v. à la roulotte,** stealing from parked cars; **v. à la saccagne,** stealing by slashing pockets.

volaille, *f.* prostitute*.

volant, *m.* trapeze performer.

volante, *f.* **la V.,** *(police)* flying squad.

volée, *f.* thrashing*.

voler: il ne l'a pas volé, it serves him right! serves him right! he asked (*or* he's been asking) for it! **v. dans les plumes,** to go for s.o.

voleur, *m.* **1. rouspéter comme un v.,** to kick up a hell of a row. **2. gueuler comme un v.** = **gueuler comme un putois. 3. v. à l'américaine,** confidence trickster, con-man.

volière, *f.* licensed brothel*.

volo (= *volonté*) *f.* **à v.,** at will, ad lib.

volume, *m.* **faire du v.,** to swagger, to throw (*or* to chuck) one's weight about.

vo(s)zig(ue)s, *pron.* you, yourselves.

vôtre, *poss. pron.* **à la (bonne) v.!** *(said when drinking a toast)* cheerio!*, good health!

voui, *adv. (pop. pronunciation for oui.)* yeah.

vouloir. 1. je veux! *(in answer to a question)* sure! certainly! rather! you bet! and how! **2. comme il veut!** *(said of a horse winning a race easily)* it's romping home! **3. je m'en voudrais! tu ne voudrais (vous ne voudriez) pas!** *(polite but strong denial)* not likely! **4. veux-tu!** *(to a child misbehaving)* stop it at once! **5. il en veut,** he is full of vim. *See also* **voilà 3.**

voyage, *m.* **1. faire le** (*or* partir pour) **le grand v.,** to die*. **2. gens du v.,** circus people. **3. emmener en v.,** to have coition* with s.o. **4. faire le v.,** to take a trip (*i.e. to experience the effects of drugs*).

voyante, *f.* **passer à la v.,** to be guillotined.

voyeur, *m.* voyeur, Peeping Tom.

voyoucratie, *f.* mob rule, mobocracy.

vrai, *adv.* **1. non, v.?** really? **2. pour de v.,** really and truly, in earnest, for good, once and for all. **3. eh bien v. (alors)!** well, really! well, I must say! **4. v. de v.!** really and truly! honest (Injun)! it's true, on my word it is! **5.** *m.* **un v. de v.,** a hoodlum. **6. c'est le v. du v.,** *or* c'est du v. de v., it's the real stuff, it's the real Mackay (*or* McCoy).

vrille, *f.* lesbian*, les, dyke.

vu, *p.p.* **1. c'est tout v.!** *(stock reply to* c'est à voir *or to* nous verrons) it's all settled! there's not the slightest doubt about it! **2. on aura tout v.!** what next, I wonder? wonders will never cease! **3. où avez-vous v. que . . ., a-t-on v. que . . .,** did you ever hear of . . . **4. ni v. ni connu (, je t'embrouille),** *(a)* on the (strict) Q.T.; *(b)* keep it under your hat! *(c)* no one is (was, will be) any the wiser. **5. v.? agreed? c'est v.!** O.K. **6. elle n'a pas

v. (*or* elle n'a rien v.) ce mois-ci, she's not seen anything this month (*i.e. she has not had her monthly courses*). 7. un m'as-tu-vu, braggart, windbag.

vue, *f.* 1. à v. de nez, at a rough guess (*or* estimate). 2. en mettre (*or* en jeter) plein la v. à qn, to bluff s.o., to hoodwink s.o. 3. s'en mettre plein la v. = se rincer l'œil (œil 17).

vurdon, *m.*, (*gipsy slang*) gipsy's caravan.

W

wagonnet, *m.* **recharger les wagonnets,** (*of round of drinks*) to fill (*or* to set) 'em up again.

wallace, *f.* drinking-fountain (*in Paris*).

waterloo, *m.* **1.** rout, defeat. **2. en plein w.,** dead out of luck.

waters, *m.pl.* **les w.,** the W.C.*

watrin, *m.* trousers.

wif, *adj.* first rate*.

X

X, *m.* l'**X**, the *École polytechnique* (in Paris); **un X**, a student of the *École polytechnique*; **un fort en X**, **une tête à X**, a gifted mathematician.

Y

---

y, *pron.* **y a pas = n'y a pas à dire.**

yakas, *m.pl.* eyes*.

yaourt, *m.* **un pot de y.,** (*motor., joc.*) bubble-car.

yearling, *m.* youngster.

yeuter = zyeuter.

yeux, *m.pl.* **1. avoir les y. plus gros que le ventre,** to have eyes bigger than one's stomach, to bite off more than one can chew. **2. coûter** (*or* **payer qch.**) **les y. de la tête,** to cost (*or* to pay) the earth (*or* a packet *or* a pretty penny *or* a mint of money). **3. en mettre plein les y. à qn = en mettre plein la vue à qn. 4. entre quat'zyeux,** between you and me (and the lamp-post). **5. faire les y. en coulisse à qn,** to ogle s.o. **6. faire les y. doux à qn,** to make goo-goo eyes at s.o., to give s.o. the glad eye, to give s.o. the look. **7. faire les gros y. à qn,** to look sternly (*or* severely *or* reprovingly) at s.o. **8. faire** (*or* **tourner**) **des y. de merlan frit** (*or* **de carpe** *or* **de carpe pâmée**), to turn up the whites of one's eyes, to look (*or* to turn up one's eyes) like a dying duck in a thunderstorm. **9. faire qch. pour les beaux y. de qn,** to do sth. entirely for s.o.'s sake, to do sth. for the love of s.o. **10. ne pas avoir froid aux y.** (*a*) to be plucky, not to have cold feet; (*b*) to have plenty of cheek, to be a cool hand (*or* customer), not to be backward in coming forward. **11. ne pas avoir les** (*or* **ses**) **y. dans la** (*or* **sa**) **poche,** to be wide-awake*, to have one's wits about one. **12. ne pas avoir les y. en face des trous,** to be unable to see straight, to be cock-eyed, not to have got eyes in one's head. **13. avoir** (*or* **ouvrir**) **les y. comme des portes-cochères,** to be wide-eyed, flabbergasted. **14. y bordés au jambon** (*or* **aux anchois,** red, inflamed eyes.

yéyé, *m.* and *adj.* teenage, rocker.

youdi, youpin, youtre, youvance, *m.* Jew, Yid, Sheeny, Ikey, Ikey Mo.

yoyoter: y. de la mansarde, to be slightly mad.

Yvans, *m.pl.* Russians, Russkies.

Z

zacharie, *m.* skeleton.

zan, *m.* 1. liquorice. 2. un bout de z., a child, a nipper, a little mite.

zanzi, zanzibar, *m.* gambling game with dice.

zazou, *m.* Teddy-boy; un costume z., a zoot-suit.

zeb, *m.* penis*.

zébie, *f. See* peau 2.

zèbre, *m.* 1. fellow*. 2. faire le z., to play the fool, to play the (giddy) goat.

zéf(f), zéph, zèphe, *m.* wind.

zèle, *m.* faire du z., to be overzealous, to be over-officious, to be an eager beaver.

zéphir(e), zéphyr(e), *m.* soldier of the bat'd'Af'.

zéro, *m.* 1. (*of person*) un vrai z., un z. à gauche, un z. en chiffre, un z. fini, an absolute non-entity, a mere cipher, an absolute wash-out, a dud. 2. (*sch.*) un z. pointé, a nought, a duck, a goose-egg. 3. être à z., to be exhausted*. 4. les avoir à z., to be in a blue funk, to be scared stiff. 5. bander à z., to be (*or* to get) highly excited, to get all worked up, to be all agog. 6. partir de (*or* à) z., to start from scratch. 7. le z., anus*. 8. *int.* nothing doing!

zézette, *f.*, tot of absinthe.

ziber, to frustrate.

zieuter = zyeuter.

zig, *m.* = zigue.

zigomar, zigoteau, zigoto, *m.* 1. queer*, odd person. 2. faire le zigoto, to show off; to play the fool, to act the (giddy) goat.

zigouigoui, *m.* = zob.

zigouiller, to kill*.

zigue, *m.* fellow*. un bon z., a good sort, a good egg, a brick. un drôle de z., a queer, odd* person.

zigué, *adj.* bald-headed*.

ziguer, to clean out (at cards, etc.).

ziguoince, *f.* prostitute*.

zigzag, *adj.* être z., to have the staggers, to be staggering drunk.

zim badaboum, *m.* war, 'boom boom'.

zim boumboum, *m.* concert, noisy music.

zinc, *m.* 1. bar, counter; prendre un verre sur le z., to have a drink at the bar. 2. plane, crate, kite, 'bus'; vider le z., to bale out.

zingue, *m.* 1. = mannezingue. 2. = zinc 1.

zinzin, *m.* 1. noise, row, uproar. 2. = machin.

zizi, *m.* 1. = machin, truc. 2. penis*; faire z. pan-pan, to have coition*.

zizique, *f.* music; se farcir de la z., to go to a concert.

zob, *m.* penis*; mon z. = mon œil.

zobi, *m.* 1. = zob. 2. peau de z. = peau de zébie.

zonard, *m.* one who lives in the Zone.

zone, *f.* la Z., slums, the site of the former fortifications of Paris; être de la Z., to be homeless, penniless.

zoner, se, to go to bed*, to turn in.

zoom, *m.* (*students' slang*) faire un z., to indulge in ill-natured ragging.

zou, *int.* allez z.! hop* it!

zouave, *m.* 1. faire le z., (*a*) to play the fool; (*b*) to brag, to show off. 2. première de z., (old) third-class (on railway).

zouaviller = faire le zouave.

zouzou, *m.* = zouave.

zozo, *m.* gullible* person, mug.

zozor, *m.* du z., money*.

zozores, *m.pl.* ears*.

zozoter, to lisp.

zut, *int.* z. (alors)! z. de z.! dash it! darn it! blow it! et puis z.! oh rats! z. pour vous! you be blowed! rats! (*expletives**); dis-lui z. de ma part! tell him to go to blazes!* *See also* œil 6.

zyeuter, to have a look* at; zyeute-moi ça! just have a dekko at that!

zygue, *m.* = zigue.

Table of English
Slang Synonyms

Table of English Slang Synonyms

(*N.B.—The table offers a choice of popular synonyms or near synonyms for all the terms followed by an asterisk in the dictionary.*)

afraid, to be: *see* **coward, to be a.**

agreed! check! O.K.! it's O.K. by me! okey-doke! fair enough! Roger!

angry, to be: to be as mad as can be; to be as mad as Barney's bull; to be foaming; to be huffy, to be in (*or* to get into) a paddy; to be in a wax; to be needled; to be on edge; to be put out; to be raging; to be shirty; to be waxy; to blow a fuse; to blow one's top; to blow up; to bristle up; to cut up rough; to cut up rusty; to do one's block; to do one's nut; to flare up; to fly off the handle; to get mad; to get one's back up; to get one's dander up; to get one's monkey up; to get one's rag out; to get one's shirt out; to get ratty; to get shirty; to get sore; to get (*or* to cop) the spike (*or* the needle); to get steamed up; to get waxy; to go (in) off the deep end; to go through the roof; to go up in smoke; to go up in the air; to have one's back up; to hit the ceiling; to hit the roof; to lose one's rag (*or* one's shirt *or* one's wool); to make the fur fly; to see red; to work oneself into a lather (*or* a sweat *or* a stew). *See also* **temper.**

anus: arse, arse-hole, hole.

arrest, to: to bag; to collar, to cop; to grab; to haul in; to hook; to lag; to lay by the heels; to lumber; to nab; to nail; to pick up; to pinch; to pull in; to round up; to run in; to send up (the river); to shop; to snaffle; to snag. *See also* **imprison, to.**

arrive, to: to blow along; to blow in; to bob up; to breeze in; to lob in; to pop in, to pop up; to roll along; to roll up; to show up; to turn up; to weigh in.

attack s.o., to: to crack down on; to fall foul of; to go for; to lay into; to pitch (*or* to sail *or* to slip *or* to wade *or* to waltz *or* to wire) into; to set about.

bag of tricks, the whole: (and) all that jazz; all the paraphernalia; all the rest of it; and I don't know what all; and what have you; every blessed thing; the whole bloody (*or* bang *or* blinking *or* jolly) lot; the whole (bally) show; the whole bang shoot; the whole boiling; the whole caboodle; the whole issue; the whole kit (and caboodle); the whole set-up; the whole shebang; the whole shooting match; the whole works.

bald-head(ed person): baldie, baldy; billiard-ball; bladder of lard; skating-rink; as bald as a coot (*or* a badger *or* an egg *or* a mushroom).

beat hollow, to: to beat (in)to fits; to beat (*or* to lick) to a frazzle; to knock into a cocked hat; to knock spots off; to make (*or* to run) rings round; to wipe the floor with.

bed: bug-trap; bug-walk; doss; downy; flea-bag; hay; kip; letty; pit; sack; shake-down.

bed, to go to: to doss (down); to get between the sheets; to get down to it; to go to kip; to go to perch; to go to roost; to hit the hay; to hit the sack; to kip (down); to turn in. *See also* **sleep, to go to.**

betray, to: *see* **divulge a secret, to.**

blackguard: bad lot; cad; corner-boy; hooligan; hoodlum; layabout; rough-(neck); scallywag; thug; tyke; yahoo; yob. *See also* **rotter.**

blame, to get the: to carry the can back; to catch it; to cop it; to cop out; to get it in the neck; to get (*or* to take) the rap; to hold (*or* to be left holding) the baby.

blazes!, go to: beat it! bugger off! buzz off! chase yourself! clear off! clear out! creep away and die! drop dead! fade away! fuck off! get (out)! get going! get lost! get knotted! get weaving! git! go and be hanged! go and eat coke! go and get stripped (*or* stuffed)! go and take a (running) jump at yourself! go to the devil (*or* to the deuce *or* to Halifax *or* to Hell *or* to Jericho)! go to pot! pack off! piss off! push off! run away and play (trains)! scat! scoot! scram! shag off! shift! shit off! shove off! skiddoo! you be blowed! you can lump it!

bloody (*euphemisms for*): bally; blank-etty; blanky; blasted; blazing; bleeding; blessed; blighted; blinking; blithering; blooming; blurry; confounded; cursed; flaming; flipping; perishing; ruddy.

blow, (to give s.o.) a: a back-hander; a bang; a bash; to bash s.o.; to bash the (living) daylights out of s.o.; belt; to belt s.o., to catch (*or* to give) s.o. a belt on the ear *or* on the earhole); to catch s.o. an awful belt; belt him one! a biff; to biff s.o. one on the boko! a bonk; a clinker; to give s.o. a clip on the ear; to clobber s.o.; to clock s.o.; a clout; to fetch (*or* to catch) s.o. a clout; to clump s.o.; to fetch s.o. a crack; to crown s.o.; a cuff; to dot s.o.; to drop s.o. one; to fetch s.o. one; to give s.o. a fourpenny one; to knock s.o.'s block off; to give s.o. a plug in the eye; to slam s.o.; to slosh s.o. on the dial (*or* in the eye); to slug s.o.; to smack s.o. in the chops; to smash s.o.; to sock s.o. on the kisser; to give s.o. a sock on the jaw; to fetch s.o. a stinger; a thump; a wallop; to take a swipe at s.o.; a whack; a whang.

boosting: ballyhoo; blurb; log-rolling; plugging; puff; write-up.

boots, big: beetle-crushers; boats; clod-crushers; clod-hoppers; cobblers; crab-shells; daisy-roots (*R.S.*); dogs; gunboats; puddle-jumpers; treaders; trotter-cases; violin-cases.

bore, to: to badger; to bore s.o. to death (*or* to tears); to bore s.o. stiff, to bug; to buttonhole s.o.; to get in s.o.'s hair; to get on s.o.'s nerves (*or* tits *or* wick); to get s.o. down; to give s.o. a pain in the neck; to give s.o. the bellyache (*or* the balls-ache); to make s.o. sick; to pester (the life out of) s.o.; to plague s.o.; to put years on s.o.

bore, a tenacious (*or* **crashing** *or* **deadly**): barnacle; bind; bromide; burr; buttonholer; clinger; (*of woman*) clinging vine; drip; fixture; hanger-on; leech; limpet; menace; pain in the neck; perfect (*or* bloody) nuisance; pest; pill; sticker; one who sticks like glue (*or* like a leech *or* like a limpet); wet sod.

bored, to be: to be bored stiff (*or* to death *or* to tears); to be cheesed (off); to be chocker; to be fed-up; to be fed to the back teeth. *See also* **depressed**.

breasts (*of female*): bazookas; bristols; bristlers; bubs; bubbies; Charlies; charms; dairies; dairy arrangements; knockers; milk-bottles; milk shop; ninnies; threepenny bits (*R.S. for* 'tits'); tits; titties; top 'uns; t.b. (=two beauties).

brothel: bad (*or* disorderly) house; bawdy house; cat house; cross-crib; dress-house; kip-shop; knocking shop; meat-house; molly-shop; mot-case; nanny-shop; red-lamp; red-light house; whore-house.

bungle, to: to ball(s) up; to bitch (everything up); to boob; to botch; to cock up; to gum up (the works); to jigger up; to louse things up; to make a balls-up *or* a (right) balls *or* a (right) mess *or* a muck of; to mess up; to muck up; to muff; to smash up.

buttocks: arse; arse-hole; backside; behind; breech; bum; can; fanny; hole; jacksie; jacksey; posterior; prat(t); rear-end; rump; sit-me-down.

cap: *see* hat.

certainty, it's a: a (dead) cert; a cinch; a doddle; a good thing; all buttoned up; all cut and dried; all over bar (the) shouting; a moral certainty; a piece of cake (*or* of pie); a sure card (*or* a sure thing *or* sure fire); a sitter; a snip; a stone-ginger; as sure as eggs is eggs; it's in the bag; it's money for jam (*or* for old rope); it's open and shut. *See also* easy, very.

chaff, to: to ballyrag; to cod; to crab; to gee up; to guy; to have s.o. on; to humbug; to jolly; to josh; to kid; to needle; to pull s.o.'s leg; to rag; to rib; to razz; to twit.

chamber-pot: jemima; jerry; jerker; jordan; latrine-bucket; latrine-pail; piss-pot; po; pottie; smoker; thunder-mug; tinkler.

champagne: the boy; (the) bubbly; cham(p); champers; fizz; sham(my); shampers; the widow.

chap, old: old bean; buddy; chammy; chum; old pal; old thing. *See also*: fellow.

chat, to: to chew the fat (*or* the rag); to have a chin-wag; to (have a) confab; to have a crack. *See also* talk volubly, to.

chatterbox: babbling brook; gas-bag; gramophone; jabbering ape; parrot; wind-bag; to be all gas; to have the gift of the gab. *See also* talk volubly, to.

cheat, to: *see* fool, to.

cheated, to be: to be done brown; to be had; to be sold; to be taken in; to get bitten. *See also* fooled, to be.

cheerio!: bottoms up! bung-ho! cheero! cheers! chin chin! down the hatch! happy days! happy landings! here's how! here's to you! here's looking at you! (here's) mud in your eye! skin off your nose! skoal!

child: brat; chick; (mere) chit; kid, kiddy; mite; nipper; toddler; (tiny) tot; little type; little shaver.

cigarette: butt; cig; coffin-nail; another nail in one's coffin; dokka; fag; faggeroo; gasper; nub; pill; reefer (=doped cigarette); snout; spit and drag (*R.S. for* 'fag'); tab; tiggy; weed; wood, Woodbine, Woodie.

cigarette-end: blink; butt-end; dead soldier; dimp; dog, dog-end; fag-end; nicker; nub-end; old soldier; snipe.

clergyman: bible-puncher; black coat; crow; cushion-smiter; devil-dodger; haul-devil; holy Joe; pulpit-thumper; sky-pilot.

clothes: clobber; duds; gear; rig out; toggery; togs.

coition (with), to have: to (have a) bang; to case; to go case with; to (have a) charver; to dig; to do; to ease oneself; to fuck; to get it up; to go to bed with; to grind; to have a bit (of love); to have a bit of crumpet; to have one's crumpet; to have bayonet practice; to have a blow (-through); to get down to it; to have a nibble; to have it off with; to have sex; to have a tumble with; to join the mounties; to jump; to lay; to play put and take; to poke; to ride; to roger; to screw; to shaft; to stag; to stuff; to thread.

conceited: *see* self-conceited.

confess, to: *see* divulge a secret, to.

corpse: cold meat; dead meat; deader; dead 'un; stiff; stiff 'un; stiffy.

coward, to be a; cowardly, to be: to back out (of it); to balk at; to be afraid to say 'boo' to a goose; to be all of a tremble; to be chicken (*or* chicken-hearted *or* chicken-livered); to be a fraidy cat; to be a funk; to be funky; to be in a blue funk; to funk it; to be jittery; to be a scare baby; to be spunkless; to be windy; to be yellow; to be a yellow belly; to have a yellow streak; to chicken out; to give in; to have the breeze up; to have cold feet; to jib at; to have the collywobbles (*or* the dithers *or* the jitters *or* the shakes *or* the squitters *or* the twitters *or* the willies *or* the wind up); not to be game; to shirk; to sing small; to turn milky; to wilt.

crazy: *see* **mad.**

criticism, severe (or scathing *or* **slashing)**: cutting-up; panning; roasting; slashing; slating; a stinker.

criticize, to severely: *see* **disparage, to.**

cropper, to come a: to come a mucker; to come a purler; to come to grief; to have (*or* to take) a spill.

darling: dearie; duck, duckie, ducky, ducks; honey; little chick; lovey; pet; poppet; popsy-wopsy; precious; sweet; sweetie; sweetie-pie.

decamp, to: to beat it; to beetle off; to belt it; to be off; to blow; to bolt; to bugger off; to bunk (off); to buzz off; to check out; to clear off; to clear out; to cut along; to cut and run; to cut one's stick (*or* one's lucky); to do a bunk (*or* a guy *or* a mickey *or* a mike *or* a slope); to fade away; to flit; to fly the coop; to hare off; to hook it; to hop it; to hop off; to leg it; to make a bolt (*or* a break) for it; to make a get-away; to make oneself scarce; to make off; to make tracks; to (do a) mizzle; to nip along; to off it; to pack up and go; to pop off; to push off; to scamper away; to scamper off; to (do a) scarper; to scat; to scoot; to scram; to scurry off; to scuttle off (*or* away); to shemozzle; to shoot off; to shove off (*or* along); to show a clean pair of heels; to ske-daddle; to skiddo; to skip (it); to slide (out); to sling one's hook; to slip away; to slope (off); to streak off (like greased lightning); to take oneself off; to take a powder; to take the air; to toddle off; to tootle off; to vamo(o)se; to walk one's chalks.

deceive, to: *see* **fool, to.**

defecate, to: to (have a) bog; to clear one's bowels; to (do a *or* to have a) crap; to do a dike; to do a job for oneself; to do number two; to do one's business (*or* one's duty); to ease oneself; to rear; to relieve oneself, to relieve nature; to (have a) shit; to do sth. no one else can do for you.

denounce, to: *see* **divulge a secret, to.**

depressed: bored stiff; (proper) brassed off; browned off; cheesed off (up to the eyebrows); chocker; creased; down in the mouth; fed to the (back) teeth; fed-up; in a black mood; (down) in the doldrums (*or* the dumps); hipped; sick (and tired) of it; to feel mouldy; to feel pipped; to have a black dog on one's back; to have (a fit of) the blues; to have the blue devils; to have the dismals; to have the heebie-jeebies; to have the hip (*or* the hump *or* the pip); to have had a basinful (*or* a bellyful).

diarrhoea: Bombay cruds; jerry-go-nimble; the runs; shitters; shits; squitters; summer complaint; trots.

die, to: to be with one's fathers; to cash in; to cash (*or* to hand *or* to pass) in one's checks; to check out; to conk (out); to cop it; to cop out; to corp out; to croak; to fall off the perch; to give one's last gasp; to go for a Burton; to go off the hooks; to go on one's last journey; to go to glory; to go to kingdom come; to go west; to hop the perch; to hop the twig; to join the great majority; to kick the bucket (*or* the beam *or* the tin); to lay down one's knife and fork; to lose the number of one's mess; to off it; to pass out (*or* away *or* over); to peg out; to pike off; to pop off; to shuffle off; to sling one's hook; to slip one's cable; to snuff it; to step into one's last bus; to take a blinder; to take off for eternity; to turn the lights out; to turn it in; to turn one's toes up (*or* to turn up one's toes).

dismiss, to: to axe; to boot (out); to bounce; to cashier; to chuck out; to fire (out); to give s.o. the axe (*or* the air *or* the bird *or* the boot *or* the order of the boot *or* the bullet *or* his cards *or* the chuck *or* his marching (*or* his walking) orders *or* the one-two *or* the push *or* the run *or* the sack *or* the order of the sack *or* the shoot *or* the shove); to show s.o. the door; to sling out; to throw (*or* to pitch) s.o. out (on his ear); to turf out; to turn out. *See also*: **packing, to send s.o.**

dismissed, to be: to be fired; to be thrown out on one's ear; to get the air (*or* the axe *or* the bird *or* the (order of) the boot *or* the bullet *or* one's cards *or* the chopper *or* the kick *or* the push *or* the run *or* the (order of the) sack *or* the shove *or* one's marching-orders *or* one's marching papers *or* one's walking-ticket); to get kicked out (neck and crop).

disorder, in: all anyhow; all balled up; all in a clutter; all over the place; all over the shop; all sixes and sevens; higgledy-piggledy; hugger-mugger; in a hell of a mess.

disparage, to: to backbite; to carp at; to crab; to cut up; to cut to pieces; to jump (up)on; to knock; to pick holes in; to pull to pieces; to run down; to scalp; to slash; to slate; to tomahawk.

disparagement: backbiting; crabbing; knocking; running down; slashing; slating.

divulge a secret, to: to blab (one's mouth); to be a blab(ber)mouth; to blab about sth.; to blow the gaff; to blurt it out; to come clean; to give the show away; to let the cat out of the bag; to sell the pass; to snitch; to spill the beans. *See also* **inform on, to.**

dog: bow-wow; cur; doggie; mutt; pooch; poddle; tyke.

done for; caput (*or* kaput); come undone; come unput; come unstuck; dished; down and out; finished; a gone chicken; a gone coon; a goner; gone to bust; gone to pot; gone under; his goose is cooked; he's had it; he's had his chips; he has bought it; his little game is up; his number is up; it's curtains for him; it's all over with him; it's all up (*or* all U.P.) with him; napoo; shagged (out); sunk; up a tree; wiped out.

dress up, to: to doll up; to posh up; to put on one's best bib and tucker; to put on one's glad rags; to put on one's Sunday best; to spruce (oneself) up; to titivate; to tog oneself up.

dressed up, all: all dolled up; all togged up; dressed (fit) to kill; dressed (*or* got up) like a (*or* the) dog's dinner; dressed up (*or* got up) to the nines (*or* to the teeth *or* to the knocker); got up regardless; got up to kill; in full feather; in full fig; in full rig; in one's best bib and tucker; in one's glad rags; natty; snazzy; in one's Sunday best; in war-paint; looking as if one had just stepped out of a band-box.

drink, inferior: belly-wash, biddy; bilge (-water); cat-lap; dishwater; skilly; slops; swill; swipes; wish-wash; wishy-washy stuff.

drink, to: *see* **whistle, to wet one's.**

drugs: (*Amphetamines and barbiturate combinations*): bennies; red birds; black and tan; black and white; black and white minstrels; black bombers; crystal; crank; red devils; dex, dexie (dexedrine); dominoes; double blue; French blue; downers; green dragons; goof balls; goofers; yellow jackets; nigger minstrels, phenies; purple hearts, sweets, tooies. (*Cannabis (marihuana)*): canapa; chara(sh); charge; Congo mataby; benny; dagga; gage; ganga; gear; grass; hash; (Indian) hemp; herb; India; kif; Mary-Jane; muggles; pot; rope; stuff; tampi; tea; weed. (*Cannabis (marihuana) cigarettes*): African woodbine; bhang; boo; broccoli; drag; joint; rainy-day woman; reefer; sausage; smoke; sploff; stick. (*Cocaine*): Charlie; coke; girl; snow. (*Drinamyl*): bluey, Christmas tree, speed. (*Heroin*): H.; caps; boy; horse; Jack; shmee; shmeck; shit. (*LSD*): D., acid; sugar (lump). (*Morphia*): M. (*Paregoric and histamine*): blue velvet.

drunk: bevvied; blind (drunk); blotto;

boozed (up); canned; dead drunk; dead to the world; elevated; fuddled; full (as a tick *or* to the brim); fuzzy; half-seas over; happy; to have a drop in the eye; to have a jag (*or* a load) on; to have had one over the eight; to have as much as one can carry; to have a skinful; helpless; (a bit) high; jagged; lit up; well lit; loaded; looped to the eye-balls; lubricated; lushed up; merry; muzzy; obfuscated; (well) oiled; paralysed; paralytic; pickled; pinko; pissed (up); pissed to the wide; plastered; well primed, screwed; shickered; shot; skew-whiff; sloshed; well soaked; soused; sozzled; speechless; squiffy; stewed; stinking (drunk); stinko; three sheets in the wind; tiddl(e)y; tight; tipsy; under the influence; well away; woozy; as drunk as a coot (*or* a fiddler *or* a kite *or* a lord *or* a newt *or* an owl).

drunkard: booze-hound; boozer; booze-mopper; drunk; lush(ington); pot-walloper; soak; souse.

dumbfound, to: to beat; to bowl out; to bowl over; to crush; to flabbergast; to knock (all of a heap.*or* cold *or* flat *or* down with a feather *or* over *or* sideways *or* silly); to rock; to spifflicate; to squash; to stagger; to strike all of a heap; to stun; to take aback; to take the wind out of s.o.'s sails.

dupe, to: *see* **fool, to.**

dupe: *see* **fool.**

duped, to be: *see* **fooled, to be.**

ears: ear-holes; flappers; flaps; lug-holes; lug'oles; lugs.

easy, very: easy job: a bit of fat (*or* of jam); a cake-walk; (mere) child's play; cushy job; dead easy; a gift; it's money for jam (*or* for old rope); it's a piece of cake (*or* of pie); a push-over; a soft job; soft snap; a walk-over; as easy as A.B.C. (*or* as damn it *or* as falling off a chair (*or* off a log) *or* as kiss my (*or* your) hand (*or* thumb) *or* as pie *or* as shelling peas *or*

as winking); it's a shame to take the money. *See also* **certainty, it's a.**

easy, to take it: to do oneself grand; to have a good (*or* an easy *or* a cushy *or* a soft) time (of it); to lead a soft life.

eat greedily (*or* heartily *or* voraciously), to: to blow one's hide out; to bolt; to chew up; to cram (oneself); to dig in; to eat till one bursts; to feed one's face; to get outside of; to gobble; to gorge; to gormandize; to gulp; to guzzle; to have a good feed; to have a good (*or* a regular) blow-out (*or* tuck-in); to knock (it) back; to line one's inside (*or* stomach); to nosh; to put (it) away; to put out of sight; to scoff; to shovel one's food; to stodge (oneself); to stoke up; to stow (it) away; to stuff oneself to the gills; to stuff one's face; to swill; to tuck in; to tuck it away; to wolf (it); to yam.

escape, a narrow: a close call; a close (*or* narrow) shave; a close (*or* a near) thing; a narrow squeak; a tight squeeze; it was as near as dammit; it was touch and go.

exaggerate, to: to come it (a bit *or* rather) strong; to come the acid; to draw the long bow; to go a bit too far; to lay it on (thick); to pile it on; to pile on (*or* to pile up) the agony; to pitch it (too) strong; to shoot a line.

exaggerate! don't: come off! come off it! come off the grass! draw it mild!

exasperate, to: to get s.o.'s goat; to get s.o.'s monkey up; to make s.o. see red; to nark s.o.; to get on s.o.'s wick.

excellent: *see* **first-rate.**

exhaust, to: to knock up; to take it out of s.o.; to wear out.

exhausted, to be: to be aching (*or* to ache) all over; all in; all out; beat (to the wide); buggered; busted; chewed up; cooked; to crack up; creased; dead-beat; dead tired; dog-tired; done for; done to the wide; done to the world; done to a frazzle; (fair) done up; to be dropping; fagged (out); to feel like a wet rag; fit to drop; frazzled; to have no go at all; to have shot one's bolt; jaded; jiggered; knocked up; knackered; on one's last legs; played out; pooped (out); pumped (out); ready to drop; shagged (out); sore all over; spun; stiff all over; tired to death; washed-out; washed up; whacked to the wide (world); worked to death; worn out.

exhausting: back-breaking; fagging; gruelling; killing; tiring.

expletives: bugger (me); blast (it); (well) I'm blessed; (well) I'm blowed; (well) I'm damned; (cor *or* gor) blimey; by gum; by Jove; can you beat it; coo; (for) Chrissake; crikey; cripes; crumbs; dammit; damn and blast; dash; dear(y) me; fancy; fuck (a duck); for crying out loud; Gawd (Almighty); gee; God; for God's sake; golly; (good) gracious; go on; great Scott; hang it all; (what the) heck; (what the) hell, hell's bells; (well) I'll be hanged; (Jesus) Christ; jeez; (lor) lummy; my (giddy) aunt; my hat; (my) goodness; my word; shit; stone the crows; strewth; strike a light; strike me pink; sufrin Crise; what the deuce; what the devil; ye gods.

eye, to give s.o. a black: to black s.o.'s eye; to bung s.o.'s eye up; to put s.o. in mourning.

eye, a black: an eye (*or* a peeper) in mourning; a painted peeper; a mouse; a shiner; (*of both eyes*) to have one's eyes in full mourning.

eyes: blinkers; daylights; glims; lamps; lights; mince-pies (*R.S.*); minces; oglers; optics; peepers.

eyewash: *see* **nonsense.**

face: clock; dial; dial-piece; dish; jaw; kisser; map; mug; pan; physog; phiz; puss.

fail s.o., to: (*in an examination*) to flunk; to pip; to plough; to pluck; to spin; to turn down.

fail, to: **to be failed:** (*in an examination*) to be flunked; to muff an exam.; to be (*or* to get) ploughed; to be (*or* to get) plucked; to be spun; to be turned down; to come down.

failure: fiasco; flop; frost; wash-out.

faint, to (throw a): to chuck a dummy; to keel over; to pass out; to do a flop.

fat person: fatty; pot-belly; pudge; roly-poly; tubby; bladder of lard.

father: dad; da(r); the governor, the guv'nor; the old man (*or* the old boy); the ole feller; pa; the pater; pop.

feast: *see* **spree.**

feet: beetle-crushers; dogs; hoofs; puppies; pedal extremities; plates of meat (*R.S.*); tootsies (*nursery word*); trotters.

fellow: artist; beezer; beggar; bleeder; blighter; blinker; blister; bloke; boob; bozo; buckeroo; bucko; bugger; card; case; cat; caution; chap; character; chum; client; coon; cove; cully; cuss; customer; galoot; geezer; gink; guy; jerk; johnny; joker; josser; merchant; old bean; old buffer; old codger; old geezer; perisher; queer (*or* strange) bird; shaver; sod; wallah. *See also* **chap.**

fidgets: *see* **state, in a great.**

first-rate: A.1.; bang-up; bang on; the berries; a (little) bit of all right; bonza; capital; the cat's pyjamas (*or* the cat's whiskers); champion; classy; clinking; clipping; corking; cute; dandy; fab(ulous); fabby; first-class; gear; glorious; gorgeous; great; groovey; hunky-dory; ikey; jammy; natty; nibby; nifty; nobby; nutty; out of this world; plummy; plushy; posh; pukka; rattling; a rave; ripping; scrumptious; slap-up; smashing; snappy; spanking; spiffing; spiffy; spifflicating; splendacious; splendiferous; stunning; super; super-duper; supersonic; swagger; swell; terrific; tip-top; top-hole; top-notch; topping; w(h)izzo! wizard.

first-rater: ace; blinder; clinker; clipper; corker; (a fair) cough-drop;

crack; dab (hand); dabster; knock-out; nailer; oner; phenomenon; pukka sahib; smasher; spanker; star; stunner; top-notcher; topper; the tops; wizard.

fit, to feel: to be as fit as a fiddle; to be fighting fit; to be full of beans; to be game; to be in the pink; to be up to the mark.

fix, to be in a: bunkered; in a hole; in a jam; lumbered; in a fine (*or* holy *or* nice *or* regular) mess; in a (fine *or* nice *or* pretty *or* sorry) pickle; in a pretty (*or* nice) how-d'ye-do; in a spot; in a tight corner; in hot water; in Queer Street; in the barrel; in the cart; in the soup; stymied; up against it; up a tree (*or* a gum-tree); up a pole; up the cove; up the creek; up the drain; up the shute. *For* to be in a financial fix, *see* **penniless, to be.**

flatter, to: to apple-polish; to back-scratch; to be a crawler (*or* a creeper); to blarney; to bootlick; to butter s.o. up; to carn(e)y; to flannel; to give s.o. (a little bit *or* plenty of) the old moody; to give s.o. a load of old moody; to grease s.o. up; to hand out the soft soap; to jolly s.o. about; to lay it on thick; to lay it on with a trowel; to lick s.o.'s boots (*or* shoes); to smarm (on *or* over s.o.); to smoo(d)ge; to soft-sawder; to soft-soap; to suck up to s.o.; to sugar s.o up; to sweeten s.o. up.

flatterer: apple-polisher; arse-crawler; arse-creeper; arse-licker; boot-licker; bum-sucker; creeper; greaser; lickspittle; soft-soap artist.

flattery: apple-polishing; apple-sauce; arse-crawling; blarney; banana-oil; butter; carn(e)y; eyewash; flannel; soft-sawder; soft soap.

fleece, to: to rook; to rush; to soak; to trim; to twist.

fob sth. off on s.o., to: to foist sth. on s.o.; to palm off (*or* to pass off *or* to unload) sth. on s.o.; to work sth. off on s.o.

fog(e)y, old: back number; blimp;

has been; old buffer; old codger; old crock; old dodderer; old dodo; old dotard; old duffer; (*mil.*) old dug-out; old footler; old fossil; old fuddy-duddy; old geezer; old has-been; old moss-back; old stick-in-the-mud.

food: bait; belly-timber; chow(-chow); chuck; (*mil.*) chuff; eats; grub; nosh; prog; scoff; stodge; tack; tuck; tucker; victuals.

fool: berk; burk; B.F. (*i.e.* bloody fool); blister; blithering idiot; blockhead; bonehead; boob(y); bright specimen; chuckle-head; chump; clod-hopper; clot; cretin; cuckoo; daftie; dead from the neck up; dim type; dimwit; d.o.a. (=dead on arrival); dolt; donkey; dope; dozey-arsed bastard; drip; duffer; dumb-bell; dunce; easy mark; fathead; flat; gab(e)y; gink; goon; goof; gowk; greenhorn; gull; jackass; juggins; moron; mug; muggins; mutt; nincompoop; ninny; nit; nit wit; noodle; numskull; palooka; pin-head; prize idiot; proper Charlie; sap(head); sawney; silly Billy; simp; slob; softy; softie; soppy date; stiff; sucker; twerp, twirp; twit; ulcer; wart; wet; zombie.

fool s.o., to: to make a fool of s.o.; to bamboozle; to best; to bilk; to bull-doze; (*mil.*) to cart; to chisel (s.o. out of sth.); to chip; to chouse (sth. out of s.o.); to cod; to diddle; to dirt; to do s.o. out of sth.; to do s.o. brown; to do s.o. down; to do the dirty on s.o.; to double-cross; to gammon; to give s.o. the razz(berry) (*or* the rasp-berry); to gull; to guy; to gyp (*or* to gip); to have s.o. on; to humbug; to kid; to lead s.o. up the garden(-path); to make a monkey (*or* a sucker) out of s.o.; to play s.o. up; to poke fun at; to pull a fast one on s.o.; to pull s.o.'s leg; to put it across s.o.; to razz; to rib; to sell s.o. a pup; to spoof; to string s.o. along (*or* on); to stuff s.o. (up); to suck s.o. in; to take s.o. in; to take s.o. for a ride; to take the mick-(e)y (*or* the mike) out of s.o.; to take a rise out of s.o.; to trick; to two-time.

fooled, to be: to be bamboozled, *etc.* (*see* **fool, to**); to be had; to be left holding the baby; to buy (*or* to be sold) a pup; to fall for it; to have had it.

foot: *see* **feet.**

friend: buddy; chum; crony; cully; mate; old China; pal; side-kick.

funny, very: a (real) crease; killing; priceless; a riot; a (perfect *or* regular) scream; screamingly funny; side-splitting; rollicking; too funny for anything (*or* for words).

furious, to be: *see* **angry, to be.**

gadget: *see* **what's-its-name.**

get, to: to dig up; to ferret out; to hit upon; to land (*e.g.* a job); to pick up; to spot; to unearth.

gibberish: balderdash; gobbledygook; double Dutch.

girl: babe; baby; bint; bird; (boss) chick; bit of crumpet; (nice *or* little) bit of alright (*or* fluff *or* of crackling *or* of skirt *or* of stuff *or* of homework); broad; cutie; cutey; dish; filly; floosie; floozey; flossy; frail; Jane; Judy; a lovely; moll; peach (of a girl); pick-up; piece (of stuff *or* of muslin); skirt; tart; titter; tottie.

glutton: gormandizer; greedy guts; guzzle-guts; guzzler; hog.

gratis: buckshee; free, gratis and for nothing; on credit; on the cuff; on the free list; on the house; on the nod; on tick.

grudge against, to have a: to have a down on s.o.; to have it in for s.o.

grumble, to: to beef; to belly-ache; to bitch; to bleat; to brass off; to chew the fat (*or* the rag); to crab; to create; to crib (at, about); to gripe; to grizzle; to grouch; to grouse; to kick; to moan; to tick (like a clock); to yap.

grumbling: belly-aching; binding; griping; grousing.

gull, gullible person: *see* **fool.**

gull, to: *see* **fool, to.**

hand: daddle; fin; fist; flapper; flipper; handy-pandy (*nursery word*); mitt; paw; dooks *or* dukes (= fists); bunch of fives (= fist); forks; mawlers.

handcuffs: bracelets; darbies; government securities; screws; snips; snitches.

handkerchief: hankie, hanky; nose-wipe(r); sneezer; snot-rag; snotter; snottinger; sweat-rag; wipe(r).

hangover, to have a: to feel like the morning after (the night before); to have the (*or* a) 'morning after the night before' feeling; to have a (bad *or* sore) head; to have a Dutchman's head(ache); to have a shocking head on one; to have hot coppers; to have a mouth (*or* a tongue) like (the bottom of) a parrot's cage.

hat: billy-cock; blocker; boater; cady (= straw-hat); decker; lid; tile; titfer (*short for* 'tit-for-tat'. *R.S. for* 'hat').

head: attic; bean; block; bonce; bun; brain box; brain-pan; chump; cocoa-nut; cokernut; crumpet; dome; filbert; garret; headpiece; knapper; loaf (= 'loaf of bread', *R.S.*; *cf.* use your loaf = think hard); napper; nob; noddle; noggin; nut; onion; pate; sconce; top (*or* upper) storey.

health! good: *see* **cheerio!**

hefty: beefy; brawny; cobby; husky; lusty; stocky; strapping; stubby.

hoax: blarney; booby-trap; bunk(um); catch; clap-trap; cock-and-bull story; eyewash; flummery; gag; guff; hanky-panky; hooey; humbug; jiggery-pokery; leg-pull; plant; sell; spoof; swizz; swizzle; take-in; take-on; yarn.

hoax, to: *see* **fool, to.**

homosexual: dirt-track rider; fag; faggot; fairy; homo; (ship's) Mary; (Miss) Molly; nance; (Miss) Nancy; nancy-boy; one of them; pansy; poof; ponce; quean; queen(ie); queer; third-sexer; turd-burglar; to be on the bottle.

hop it! *see* **blazes! go to.**

humbug, to: *see* **fool, to.**

hungry, to be: to be belly-pinched; to be clemmed; to be famished; to be pinched with hunger; to feel peckish; to have a twist; to live on thin air; my belly thinks my throat's cut.

hurry (up), to: to be nippy (*or* slippy); to buck up; to get a move on; to get busy; to get cracking; to get going; to get mobile; to get one's skates on; to put on one's skates; to get stuck into it; to go like a bookie with the runs; to get weaving; let's hear from you! to hustle a bit; to jump to it; to look alive (*or* sharp *or* slippy); to make it snappy; to press on; to put a jerk in(to) it; to put some guts (*or* some vim) into it; to shake a leg; to snap out of it; to step lively; to step on it; to stir one's stumps.

immediately: *see* **quickly, very.**

important person: big bug; big cheese; big gun; big noise; big pot; big shot; big-time operator; big wheel; bigwig; the boss of the show; (*mil.*) the brass, the top-brass, brass-hat; high-up; kingpin; nob, the nobs; (grand) Panjandrum; Pooh Bah; tycoon; V.I.P.

imprison, to: to cage; to clap in jail; to jug; to lock up; to nick; to put away; to put in the can (*or* in the bag). *See also* **arrest, to.**

impudence: back-chat; bounce; brass; buck; 'none of your old buck!'; cheek; crust; face; gall; lip; mouth; neck; nerve; pluck; sauce; apple-sauce; slack.

impudent, to be: to be brassy; to be as bold as brass; to be brazen-faced; to cheek s.o.; to be cheeky; not to be short of cheek; to be cocky; to be a cool hand (*or* a cool one *or* a cool card *or* a cool customer); to be fresh; to have a neck (*or* a nerve); to have plenty of cheek (*or* of nerve); to sauce s.o.; to be saucy.

infatuated, to be: to be batty over; to be crazy about (*or* for *or* over); to be daft over; to be dippy about; to be (dead) gone on; to be goofy about; to be keen on (*or* about *or* over); to be nutty on (*or* about); to be potty on; to be soft on; to be sold on; to be soppy on; to be spoony on; to be struck on (*or* with); to be stuck on; to be sweet on; to be swept off one's feet by s.o.; to be a sucker for (*or* about); to carry the torch for s.o.; to fall for s.o.; to go for s.o.; to have a crush on; to have a (mad) pash for; to have a G.P. (*i.e. grande passion*) on; to have a rave for; to have a yen for.

inform on (*or* against), to: informer, to turn (*or* to be an): to grass (to the police); to nark; to turn nark; to nose on s.o.; to peach on s.o.; to rat on s.o.; to shop s.o.; to skunk; to sneak on s.o.; to split on s.o.; to squeal on s.o.; to turn snitch, to snitch. *See also* **divulge a secret, to.**

information, to give: dope; gen (duff (*or* phoney) gen = *unreliable* information); to give (*or* to tip) s.o. the griff (*or* the griffin *or* the office); to tip s.o. off; to give s.o. the tip-off; to give s.o. the wire; to put s.o. in the picture.

informer, police: finger; copper's nark; nose; rat; rusty; shamus; shopper; snitch(er); split(ter); stool(-pigeon); squealer.

intelligence: common (*i.e.* common-sense); grey matter; gumption; horse-sense; nous; savvy.

intoxicated: *see* **drunk.**

irritable: crusty; ratty; shirty; snappy; snorty.

Italian: Antonio; dago; Eyetalian; Eyetie; macaroni; spaghetti; Tony; wop.

kill s.o., to: to account for; to blot out; to bump off; to cook s.o.'s goose; to crease; to croak; to dispatch; to do away with; to do for; to do s.o. in;

to erase; to get s.o.; to give s.o. the works; to liquidate; to knock s.o. off; to lay s.o. out; to make away with s.o.; to make cold meat (*or* cold mutton) of s.o.; to out s.o.; to polish off s.o.; to put out s.o.'s lights; to put s.o. to sleep; to run s.o. out; to scrag; to scrub out; to send s.o. to kingdom come; to settle s.o.'s hash; to spif(f)licate; to take s.o. for a ride; to top s.o.; to wipe s.o. out.

laugh uproariously, to: to be in tucks (*or* kinks *or* stitches); to crease oneself; to die (*or* to double up *or* to be doubled up *or* to rock *or* to shake *or* to shriek *or* to split (*or* to burst) one's sides) with laughter; to guffaw; to laugh like anything; to laugh one's head off; to laugh oneself silly.

lazy, to be: to be bone-idle; to be born tired; to be workshy; to be a lazybones; to have no hinge in one's back; to have a bone in the knee (*or* in one's arm); not to feel up to work; to be a weary Willie.

legs: drumsticks (= thin legs); gam(b)s; pegs, pins; shanks; sticks; stumps; toothpicks (= thin legs).

lesbian: dyke, les, lizzy.

lie: blazer; bouncer; bung; clinker; corker; cracker; cram; crammer; fairy-tale; fib; plumper; taradiddle; thumper; whopper.

life, to lead a soft: to ca' canny; to have an easy (*or* a good *or* a cushy) time; to have a soft time of it. *See also*: **easy, to take it.**

limit, that's the: can you beat that (*or* it)? that beats all; that beats the band (*or* cock-fighting *or* the Dutch)! that caps (*or* crowns) all (*or* everything)! that's done (*or* torn) it! that puts the (tin) lid on it! that takes the cake (*or* the biscuit *or* the bun)! that tops the bill! that's too bad! that's the last straw!

long! so: cheerio! cheery-bye! ciao! I'll be seeing you! pip-pip! see you later! 'see yer'! ta-ta (then)! toodle-oo!

look at, to: to clock; to dig; to get a load of; to have (*or* to get) an eyeful; to have a butcher's at (*i.e.* a butcher's hook, *R.S. for* 'look'); to have a look-see; to lamp; to screw; to (take a) squint at; to take (*or* to have) a dekko (*or* a gander) at; to take a mike (*or* a screw *or* a shufti *or* a shufty) at.

mad: barmy; batchy; bats; batty; bonkers; bug-house; cracked; cracky; crackers; crackpot; cuckoo; (plumb) crazy; daft; dippy; doolally (tap); dotty; gaga; (clean) gone; gone (*or* wanting *or* weak) in the upper storey; goofy; haywire; half-baked; to have apartments to let; to have a button (*or* a screw *or* a slate) loose (*or* missing); to have a slate off; loco; loony; loopy; mad as a hatter (*or* as a March hare); mental; not (quite) all there; nutty (as a fruit cake); a nutter; a nut-case; off one's dot (*or* bean *or* head *or* hinges *or* napper *or* nut *or* onion *or* rocker *or* one's trolley *or* the rails); only tenpence to the shilling; queer in the attic; (clean) round the bend; scatty; screwy; soft in the head; there is nobody at home; (a little bit *or* slightly) unhinged *or* touched; up the creek; up the loop; up the stick; up the wall; wacky; wrong in the attic.

malinger, to: to dodge the column; to shirk; to skive; to skrimshank; to skulk; to swing the lead; to swing it.

malingerer: (*mil.*) column-dodger; head-worker; lead-swinger; shirker; skiver; slacker; skrimshanker.

married, to get: to do the double act; to get churched; to get hitched (up); to get spliced; to get tied up; to put a halter round one's neck; to put one's neck in the noose.

masturbate, to: to beat the dummy; to jerk off; to jerk one's jelly (*or* one's juice); to play with oneself; to pull one's wire; to toss off; to w(h)ank off.

menses: the curse; to have the decorators (*or* the painters *or* the printers) in; to have the monthlies; to have the rag(s) (on); to have the reds; her country cousins (*or* her relations) have come.

mess, in a: *see* **fix, in a.**

milksop: drip; mollycoddle; sissy; soppy date; softie, softy; weed; wet.

miser: hunks; lickpenny; mingy-arsed bastard; money-grubber; scrapepenny; screw; cheap (*or* old) screw; skinflint; tight-wad.

miserly: close-fisted; mean; mingy; stingy; tight.

mistake (to make a): bish; to put up a black; blob; bloomer; blunder; to make (*or* to pull) a boner; boob; to be in the wrong box; to drop a brick; to make a bad break; to make a bad shot; bungle; to drop a clanger; floater; to goof; howler; to put one's foot in it; to slip up; to trip up.

money: ackers; bawbees; beans; bees and honey (*R.S.*); berries; blunt; boodle; brass; cabbage; chink; chips; crinkle; dibs; dimmock; dosh; dough; dust; the filthy; filthy lucre; gelt; gilt; jack; lolly; loot; mazuma; moola(h); the necessary; the needful; nuggets; oof; pelf; quids; the ready; rhino; shekels; shiners; splosh; spondulicks; stumpy; stuff; sugar; syrup; tin; the wherewithal.

mood, to be in a bad: *see* **angry, to be.**

motor-car: (*pej. terms for* ramshackle *or* old *or* small and cheap car): boneshaker; (old) crate; old crock; flivver; jalop(p)y; rattletrap; tin-Lizzie; (old) wreck.

mouth: chops; domino-box; box of dominos; gob; jaw; kisser; map; north-and-south (*R.S.*); pan; rattletrap; smacker; trap; yap.

naked, stark: in one's birthday suit; in the altogether; in the buff; in the raw; stripped to the buff; without a stitch on.

nip: (*of brandy, etc.*) bracer; drop; shot (in the arm); sip; snifter; snort; tot; wet; wee drappy.

nonsense: all madam; all my eye (and Betty Martin); balderdash; ballyhoo; baloney; balls; bilge; blah-blah; blarney; blather; blether; bluff; bollocks; bollox; boloney; bosh; (*mil.*) bull, bulsh; bunkum; claptrap; codology; crap; eye-wash; fiddlesticks; flam; flapdoodle; flim-flam; flummery; fudge; gammon (and spinach); gas; gubbins; guff; hokum; hooey; hot air; humbug; malarkey; moonshine; piffle; poppycock; punk; rats! rot; unadulterated shit; spoof; stuff (and nonsense); tommy rot; tosh; trash; tripe (and onions); load of tripe; twaddle; waffle; yackety-yak.

nose: beak; beezer; boko; conk; foghorn; honker; hooter; horn; leading article; neb; nozzle; proboscis; razzo; scent-box; s(ch)nozzle; smeller; snifter; snitch; snot-box; snout.

objectionable person: *see* **rotter.**

offence, to take: *see* **angry, to get.**

packing, to send s.o.: to choke s.o. off; to give s.o. the air; to send s.o. to blazes (*or* to the deuce *or* to the devil or to Halifax *or* to Jericho *or* to the right-about *or* about his business); to send s.o. off with a flea in his ear; to tell s.o. where he gets off; to tell s.o. to piss off (*or* to fuck off). *See also* **blazes! go to.**

paunch: bay-window; belly; bowwindow; bread-basket; corporation; (to acquire (*or* to develop) a corporation); middle-aged spread; (*of person*) pot-belly; spare-tyre. *See also* **stomach.**

paunchy: pot-bellied; portly; pursy; tubby.

pawn, to: in pawn: to dip; to hock,

in hock; to lumber; to put in hock (*or* in lug *or* in pop); to pop up the spout; to put up the spout; at my (his, etc.) uncle's.

pay (up), to: to ante (up); to brass up; to come across (with it); to come down with it; to cough up; to dish out; to down the dust; to foot the bill; to dub up; to fork out; to fork over; to part with; to pay the piper; to plank down; to put one's hand down; to shell out; to stump up; to tip up; to weigh in.

peasant: chawbacon; clodhopper; country bumpkin; hayseed; hick; hodge; joskin; rube; yahoo; yap; yokel.

pederast: *see* **homosexual.**

penis: bone; cock; dick; John Thomas; mutton-dagger; peter; prick; roger; short-arm; tool.

penniless: beanless; bent (=nearly penniless); broke; dead broke; clean broke; flat broke; stoney broke; broke to the wide; broke to the world; bust(ed); button B; cleaned out; down and out; (down) on one's uppers; hard-up; in a tight hole; in low water; in Queer Street; in the soup; mopped out; not to have a bean (*or* a bob *or* a brass farthing *or* a brown *or* a cent *or* a sausage *or* a stiver); to be on one's beam-ends; to be on the floor; to be on one's last legs; to be on the rocks; skint; dead skint; stony; to be up against it; to be up a tree. *See also* **fix, in a.**

pilfer, to: *see* **steal, to.**

pinch, to: *see* **steal, to.**

plucky, to be: to be game; to have (lots of) backbone; to have grit; to have guts; to have plenty of go; to have spunk.

pocket: bin; cly; kick; poke.

policeman: blue-bottle; the blues; bobby; bog(e)y; cop; copper; crusher; dick; duff; flattie; flatty; flick; jack; a law (*collective*, the law); man in blue; peeler; Robert; rozzer; screw; scuffer; slop; (*collective*) the traps.

poser: catch question; 64(000) dollar question; floorer; puzzler; quiz; searcher; sticker; stumper; teaser.

potter about, to: to do odd jobs; to fiddle; to muck about; to stooge around; to tinker.

pregnant, to be (to make): to be big with child; to be expecting; to be in the club; to be (to put) in the family way; to be in pod; to be knocked up; to knock up; to be on the tub; to be up the stick; to be with (*or* to have) a bun in the oven; to have one in the oven; to get a girl into trouble; to join the pudding-club; she let the window-cleaner in; (*father not known*) she got it from the coal-man *or* from behind the hoarding; she made it back of the boozer; she found it in the bulrushes.

prepared, all: *see* **ready, absolutely.**

priest: *see* **clergyman.**

prison: the big house; in bird; to do bird; to be in cold storage, box; can; (*mil.*) C.B.; (*mil.*) booby-hatch; calaboose; (*mil.*) cells; chok(e)y; (*mil.*) clink; (*mil.*) cooler; coop; dark; (*mil.*) digger; (*mil.*) glass-house; (*mil.*) guard-room; hokey; hoosegow; jail; (*mil.*) jankers; (*mil.*) jigger; (*mil.*) (stone) jug; kitty; limbo; lock-up; the nick; pen; pokey; quod; shop; stir; to do time.

proficient, to be: to be a dab hand at; to be good at; to be well up in; to know all the answers.

profits, illicit: cabbage; graft; gravy; perks; pickings; profits on the side; rake-off; side-profits.

prostitute: bag; bat; B-girl; broad; C-girl; call-girl; chippie; cow; doxy; easy Jane; floozey; floozie; free-for-all; hooker; bustler; moll; pavement-pounder; pross(y); screw; street-walker; tart; tottie; trollop; zook.

prostitute (to be a): to be a street-walker; to walk the streets; to be on the beat (*or* on the batter *or* on the bash *or* on the game *or* on the hoist *or* on the streets); to hawk one's mutton;

to hawk it; to solicit; anytime Annie; fore-and-aft Fanny; pole-squatter; endless belt.

protest, to: *see* **grumble, to.**

pudenda: *see* **vagina.**

quantity, a great: bags; heaps; lashings; loads; lots; no end of; oodles; piles; pots; scads; scores; stacks; tons; umpteen.

quarrel, a: barney; bicker(ing); breeze; brush; bust up; dust up; flare-up; hoo-ha; (*nav.*) to part brass rags; rough up; ructions; rumpus; schemozzle, shemozzle; scramble; session; set-to; shindy; slanging match; squabble; squall; tiff; wrangle.

quarrelsome, to be (*or* **to become**): to cut up nasty (*or* rough *or* rusty *or* ugly).

queer person: queer (*or* strange) bird; (queer) card; case; caution; (rum) character; corker; coughdrop; queer (*or* rum) cove; cure; queer cuss; queer (*or* rum) customer; queer fish; freak; funny (*or* odd) guy; queer Johnny; lulu; oner; rum 'un; screwball; queer specimen; queer stick; wacky bird.

quickly, very: as quick (*or* as soon) as dammit; bang-off; before you can say Jack Robinson (*or* before you can say knife); in a couple (*or* a brace) of shakes; in a crack; in a flash; in a jerk; in a jiffy; in a pig's whisper; in half a shake; in two shakes; in double-quick time; in a tick; in two ticks; in half a tick; flat-out; in the shake (*or* in one shake *or* in two shakes) of a (dead) lamb's tail; in the twinkling of an eye; in two ticks of a donkey's tail; in two twos; in less than (*or* in next to) no time; like a shot; like (a streak of) greased lightning; pretty damn quick (*or* p.d.q.); lickety-split; pronto.

rap, not to care a: not to care (*or* to give) a bean (*or* a bit *or* a brass farthing *or* a button *or* a curse *or* a (tupp'ny) damn *or* a fig *or* a hang *or* a hoot *or* two hoots *or* a jot *or* a pin *or* two pins *or* a sausage *or* a sod *or* a straw *or* two straws *or* a tinker's cuss *or* a tinker's damn); I couldn't care less.

rascal: *see* **rotter.**

ready, absolutely: all buttoned up; all laid on; all set; all sewn up; all ship-shape; all taped; all teed up; all tuned up; all wrapped up; at concert pitch.

reprimand: bawling out; blowing-up; calling-down; dressing-down; jawing; raking; roasting; rocket; scolding; slating; slanging; talking-to; telling-off; trimming; wigging. *See also* **thrashing.**

reprimand, to: to abuse right and left; to ball (*or* bawl) out; to blow skyhigh; to burn up; to call down; to call over the coals; to chew s.o.'s ears off; to choke s.o. off; to come down (up)on s.o. like a ton of bricks; to crack down on s.o.; to dress s.o. down; to drop on s.o.; to give s.o. beans (*or* a blowing-up *or* a good dressing-down *or* hell *or* a hot time (of it) *or* a lick with the rough side of (*or* the length of) one's tongue *or* a piece of one's mind *or* a rocket *or* socks *or* a sound raking over the coals *or* a good talking-to *or* a good ticking-off *or* a (good) wigging *or* what for *or* what's what); to give it s.o.; to go for s.o.; to haul s.o. over the coals; to jaw s.o.; to jump on; to let s.o. have it; to let fly at s.o.; to make it hot for s.o.; to roast s.o.; to row s.o.; to see s.o. off; to sit (up)on s.o.; to slang; to slate; to smack down on; to strafe; to talk to; to tear a strip off s.o.; to tear s.o. off a strip; to tell s.o. a thing or two; to tell s.o. off; to tick s.o. off; to walk into s.o. *See also* **thrash, to.**

reprimanded, to be: to be (*or* to get) bawled out; to get a bawling-out; to be on the carpet; to carry the can; to catch it (hot); to catch a rocket; to catch it well and truly; to cop it (hot); to cop out; to get hauled over the coals *or* to get hell *or* to get it in the neck; to get it hot; to get one's gruel; to get a severe panning; to get a raking over the coals; to get into a row; to get a rare talking-to; to get a telling-off (*or* a ticking-off); to get ticked off (*or* told off *or* told off good and proper); to get what for; to get a wigging.

resourceful: *see* **wide-awake.**

reveller: fast (*or* loose) liver; gay dog; spark; hell-bender; hell-raiser; high stepper; rake; rip; roisterer.

revolver: barker; gat; gun; (barking) iron; shooter; shooting-iron; rod.

rich, to be: caked up (*or* lousy *or* stinking) with money; doughy; filth-(il)y rich; filthy with lucre; flush; full of beans; to have bags (*or* pots *or* tons) of money; to have money to burn; to have the dibs; to have wads of dough; to be in the money; to be in the chips; loaded; oofy; rolling in money; rolling in it; wallowing in wealth; well-breeched; well-heeled; well-off; well-to-do; to be worth quite a packet.

ropes, to know the: *see* **wide-awake.**

rot: *see* **nonsense.**

rot, to talk: to shoot off one's mouth; to talk baloney (*or* balls *or* (a lot of) cock *or* crap *or* tripe); to talk out of the back of one's head (*or* of one's neck); to talk through one's hat; to talk through the back of one's neck.

rotten: beastly; blinking (*or* bloody *or* flipping) awful; bum; cheesy; chronic; corny; crappy; crummy; dud; foul; ghastly; lousy; mingy; mouldy; mucky; no bloody good; pesky; poisonous; punk; putrid; rancid; ropey; shocking; shoddy; stinking.

rotter: bad egg; bad hat; bad lot; bad 'un; basket; bastard; beast; (*fem.*) bitch; blackguard; blighter; blister; bounder; bugger; cad; (*fem.*) cat; cheap skate; clot; creep; dirty dog;

dirty rat; dumb lick; four-letter man; erk; get; heel; hog; hoodlum; (*fem.*) jade; jerk; louse; nasty piece of work; old so-and-so; out-and-outer; outsider; perisher; pig; scab; scally-wag; shicer; shit; shocker; shyster; slob; skunk; (*fem.*) slut; sod; sore; son of a bitch; spalpeen; squirt; stinker; sweep; swine; tick; tike; tyke; tripe-hound; (*fem.*) trollop; twerp; twirp; twit; ugly customer; ulcer; wart; wrong 'un.

row (i): *see* **quarrel.**

row (ii): *see* **uproar.**

rubbish: *see* **nonsense.**

sack, to: *see* **dismiss, to.**

sailor: A.B.; blue jacket; (*Amer. sl.*) gob; Jack afloat; Jack-tar; tar; jolly; (*Amer. sl.*) leather-neck; matlow; (*nav.*) pongo; old ship; shell-back (=amateur sailor).

scoundrel: *see* **rotter.**

self-conceited, to be: to be big-headed; to be chesty; to be toffee-nosed; to fancy oneself (a bit); to get a big head; to have a big (*or* no small) opinion of oneself; to suffer from swelled head; to think a great deal (*or* a lot) of oneself; to think oneself somebody; to think no small beer of oneself.

shift for oneself, to: to cope; to get along; to get by; to get out of a mess (*or* a fix); to manage; to muddle through; to rub along; to see it through; to sort it out for oneself.

shirt: Dicky Dirt (*R.S.*); flesh-bag; shift; shimmy.

short-tempered: *see* **irritable.**

shut up!: belt up! button up your face (*or* your lip *or* your gob)! can it! cheese it! chuck it! clam up! cut the cackle! cut it out! cut your clack! don't bother me! drop dead! drop it! dry up! give it a rest! go and chase yourself! hold your jaw! jack it (in)! keep mum! nark it! none of your lip! pack it in! pack it up! pipe down! put a sock (*or* a bung) in it! put the zipper on! shut your face (*or* gab *or* gob *or* rattle *or* trap)! stow it! stow your gab! turn it up! wrap it up! *See also* **blazes, go to** *and* **packing, to send s.o.**

silence s.o., to: to choke s.o. off; to give s.o. a clincher; to put the kibosh on s.o.; to score off s.o.; to settle s.o.'s hash; to shut s.o. up; to sit upon s.o.; to squash s.o.

silly person: *see* **fool.**

simpleton: *see* **fool.**

slang: cant; jive; lingo; flash lingo.

slave, to: *see* **work hard, to.**

sleep, to go to: to (do a) doss; to drop off; to get down to it; to get one's head down; (*nursery talk*) to go to beddy-bye; to go to bye-byes; to go to kip; to go to (*or* to get some) shut-eye; to have a dose of the balmy; to have forty winks; to have (*or* to take) a nap (*or* a cat-nap); to have a snooze; to hog it; to kip (down); to pound one's ear; to zizz.

smarten up, to: *see* **dress up, to.**

snub, to: to bite (*or* to snap) s.o.'s head (*or* nose) off; to jump down s.o.'s throat; to put s.o. in his place; to send s.o. away with a flea in his ear. *See also* **reprimand, to.**

speechify, to: to blather; to gas; to hold forth; to jaw; to spout; to waffle. *See also* **talk volubly, to.**

spend, to: (money) to blue; to blew; to do in; to get through; to run through.

spirits, strong: (drink) hair-curler; hoo(t)ch; reviver; corpse reviver; rotgut; tanglefoot.

spoil, to: *see* **bungle, to.**

spree, a: a ball; a (right) barney; beanfeast; beano; bend(er); binge; blow-out; bust(er); a (proper) do; flutter; jag; jamboree; high jinks; pub-crawl; shindig; shindy; slap-up meal; spread; (good) tuck-in.

spree, to be (*or* to go) on the: to beat it up (a lot); to burn up the town; to do a pub-crawl; to go on the bat (*or* on the batter *or* on a bend(er) *or* on a binge *or* on a (*or* the) bust *or*

on the booze *or* on the hoist *or* on a jag *or* on the loose *or* on a pub-crawl *or* on the racket *or* on the rantan *or* on the razzle *or* on the razzle-dazzle); to go pub-crawling; to go the pace; to go the dizzy round; to have a ball; to have a do (*or* one's fling *or* a high old time *or* the time of one's life); to hit the high spots; to lead a fast (*or* a gay) life; to live it up; to make hell pop loose; to make a night of it; to make whoopee; to make hoopla; to paint the town red; to racket about; to raise Hell; to run wild; to shake a loose leg.

start immediately, to: *see* **hurry (up), to.**

state (of emotion), to be in a great: all of a dither; all of a doodah; all of a flutter; all het-up; all steamed up; all of a tizz(y); all of a tremble; all of a twitter; to get into a flap (*or* a stew *or* a tizzy *or* a flat spin); to have ants in one's pants; to have the jerks (*or* the jim-jams *or* the jimmies *or* the jitters *or* the jumps); to be in a proper tizz (*or* tizzy); to be jittery.

steal, to: to acquire; to bag; to bone; to borrow; to collar; to cop; to dip; to filch; (*mil.*) to find; to gip; to half-inch (*R.S. for* 'to pinch'); to have it away with; to hook; to lift; to knock off; to make away with; to nab; to nail; to nick (sth. off); to pilfer; to pinch; to pocket; to prig; to rifle; to scrounge; to snaffle; to sneak; to snipe; to snitch; to swipe; to walk off with; to whip; to win.

stink, to: to hum; to niff; to be niffy; to pong; to whiff; to be whiffy.

stomach: bread-basket; bread-box; belly; Derby Kell(y) (*R.S. for* 'belly'); little Mary; tummy; tum(-tum); vic-tualling office. *See also:* **paunch.**

study hard (at), to: to bone up on; to cram for (*an exam*); to grind for; to grind away at; to mug (up); to peg away (at); to sap; to slog (away); to smug; to stew; to swot at, to swot up. *See also* **work hard (at), to.**

stupendous: almighty; blistering; something to write home about; tremendous. *See also* **first-rate.**

stupid, extremely: dense; dumb; to be a dumb-bell; obtuse; slow on the uptake; thick; wood from the neck up.

suffer a lot, to: to go through it; to go through the mill; to have a rough passage; to have a rough time of it; to rough it; to sweat blood.

suit, to: that suits me down to the ground; that suits my book; that suits me to a T; that's just what the doctor ordered; that's right up my street; that's just my cup of tea; that's right up my alley.

swagger, to: *see* **swank, to.**

swank, to: to be above oneself; to bounce; to come it (strong); to come the acid; to come the heavy; to cut a dash; to make a splash (*or* a splurge); to put on (the) dog; to put on frills; to put on the ritz; to put on side; to show off; to talk big; to throw (*or* to chuck) one's weight about; to shoot a line.

swank(er): blow-hard; bluffer; bouncer; bounder; braggart; dasher; hot-rock; line-shooter; show-off; splurge; swaggerer; swank-pot; stuffed shirt; toffee-nose; toffee-nosed person.

swell: dandy; dude; fop; Johnny; knut; masher; high-hat; la-di-dah; nob; toff.

swindle, to: *see* **fool, to.**

swindler: chiseler; crook; diddler; fiddler; racketeer; twister; wangler.

swot (at), to: *see* **study hard (at), to.**

tale-bearer: creep; informer; sneak; squealer; tale-teller; tell-tale.

talk volubly, to: to gas; to be a gas-bag; to chinwag; to have the gift of the gab; to jaw; to bunny away nineteen to the dozen; to buzz; to chew the fat (*or* the rag); to chin; to chunter; to gab; to nag; to natter; to palaver; to prattle; to rabbit; to rattle on; to spout; to yap(-yap). *See also* **speechify, to.**

talkativeness: chin-music; chinwag; gab; gas; to have a good old natter; palaver; prattle; yackety-yack; yak-yak.

tall, thin person: bag of bones; bean-pole; big gawk; broomstick; drain pipe; flag-pole; (walking *or* regular *or* giddy) lamp-post; lofty; longshanks; long string of misery; matchstick; maypole; rasher of wind; scaffold-pole; (*fem.*) skinny Lizzie; skin and bone; spindle legs, spindle shanks, spindle-sticks; streak; yard of pump water.

temper, to be in a bad (*or* **a nasty** *or* **an ugly** *or* **a vile**)**:** a crab; cranky; as cross as two sticks; as cross as the devil; in a devil of a temper; in a filthy (*or* an ugly) mood; edgy; in one's tantrums; like a bear with a sore head; like tinder; like touchwood; nervy; ready to blow up; ready to explode; rusty; in a rux ; snappish; touchy. *See also* **angry, to be.**

testicles: balls; ballocks; bollocks; bollexes; Charleys; cobblers; cobbler's (=cobbler's awls, *R.S. for* 'balls'); orchestra stalls (*R.S.*); cods; goolies; jocks; marriage prospects; nuts.

thrash, to: to bash s.o. up; to baste (s.o.'s jacket); to beat up; to beat the hell out of s.o.; to belt; to biff; to clout; to drub; to dust s.o.'s jacket (for him); to give s.o. beans (*or* a dose of strap oil *or* what for *or* what's what *or* gip (gyp, jip) *or* a taste of the leather *or* socks); to give it s.o. hot and strong; to knock s.o. about; to knock s.o. into the middle of next week; to lam (into) s.o.; to lambast(e); to larrup; to lay into; to leather; to let s.o. have it; to lick; to paste; to pitch into; to pummel; to put s.o. through it; to skin s.o. alive; to slosh; to sock; to tan the hide off s.o.; to tan s.o.'s hide; to spif(f)licate; to thump; to trim s.o.'s jacket; to trounce; to walk into s.o.; to wallop; to waltz into s.o.; to warm s.o.; to warm s.o.'s jacket; to welt; to whack; to whop. *See also* **reprimand, to.**

thrashing: bashing; beating (up); belting; biffing; caning; clouting; coshing; dressing-down; drubbing; dose of strap-oil; dusting; to get it in the neck; gruelling; hammering; hiding; lambasting; lamming; larruping; leathering; licking; pasting; pummeling; rough handling; shellacking; sloshing; slugging; spanking; strapping; swishing; tanning; thumping; towelling; trimming; trouncing; walloping; welting; whacking; whipping; wigging. *See also* **reprimand.**

tip: (=*inside information*) dope; the (straight) griffin; office; pointer; tip-off; wire; wrinkle. *See also* **information.**

tip s.o. off, to: to give s.o. the tip (*or* the dope *or* the gen *or* the low-down *or* a pointer *or* a wrinkle); to put s.o. up to all the tips; to tip (*or* to give) s.o. the griffin (*or* the office); to wise s.o. up.

tipple, to: to booze; to hit the bottle; to lift (*or* to bend *or* to crook *or* to raise) cne's (*or* the) elbow; to have a crooked elbow; to be fond of the bottle; to liquor up; to shicker; to soak; to swig; to swill; to swizzle.

trousers: bags; breeks; drumstick-cases; pair of bins; pants; slacks; strides.

umbrella: brolly; gamp; gingham.

undersized person: bum-droop; half-pint; runt; shorty; little squit (*or* squirt); shrimp; stumpy; weed.

understand, to: to be on the beam; to catch on; to cotton on; to dig; to get the hang of; to rumble; to savvy; to tumble to; to twig; to undercomestumble, to underconstumble, to undercumstumble.

unwell, to feel (or to be): all anyhow; all no-how; all-overish; badly; (a bit) below par; bleary; cheap; chippy; dick(e)y; to feel like death warmed up; to feel like nothing on earth; funny; groggy; in poor shape; knocked up; mouldy; not quite the thing; not too clever; not up to much; not up to the mark; off colour; off form; off one's oats (*or* one's feed); out of sorts; poorly; queer(ish); rotten; seedy; shaky; (a bit) under the weather; washed out; wanky; wonky.

uproar, to make an: (a right) barney; to be rowdy; a breeze; to create; to cry blue murder; dust-up; hubbub; hullabaloo; to kick up a dust (*or* (a deuce of) a row *or* a racket *or* a shindy *or* (a hell of) a stink *or* a shine); to make the fur fly; to play old Harry; to raise Cain; to raise (merry) Hell; to raise the roof; to raise (a hell of) a rumpus; to raise a (hell of a) stink; rough-house; shindy.

urinate, to: to disappear for a moment; to do number one; to do sth. no one else can do for you; to drain one's tatters; to go to see one's Aunt(ie); to go plumbing; to have a Jimmy Riddle (*R.S. for* 'piddle'); to make water; to pay a call (*or* a visit); to be excused; to (have a) pee; to piddle; to (do a) piss; to pump ship; to pump one's bilges; to see a man about a dog; to shed a tear for Nelson; to have (*or* to go for) a slash; to spend a penny; to (do) wee-wee.

vagina: crumpet; cunt; hole; twat; puss; pussy(-cat); quim.

vexed: in a pet; ratty; riled; waxy; in a wax.

vomit, to: to be as sick as a cat; to bring up; to cat; to heave; to honk; to puke; to shoot (*or* to whip) the cat; to spew; to throw up.

watch: clock; jerry; kettle; ticker; turnip (*or* frying-pan *or* warming-pan) (=big silver watch).

W.C.: Aunt Jane; bog; the bogs; bog-house; can; crapper; crappus; dubs; hoosegow; jacks; jakes; the John; Johnny; (*mil.*) karzey; lat; lat-house; the lats; lav; the loo; little boy's room; petty house; privy; rear; shit-house; shittus; shooting-gallery; the smallest room.

weep, to: to bawl; to be a cry-baby; to blub; to blubber; to grizzle; to pipe one's (*or* an) eye; to snivel; to turn the tap on; to turn on the water-works; to whimper.

what's-its-name: contraption; the doings; do-da; doodah; gadget; gim-mick; the gubbins; ooja(-ka-piv); ooja(-ka-pivvy); jigger; thingamy; thingum(a)bob; thingumajig; thing-umijig; thingummy; the t'ingy; what-d'ye-call-it; what's-it; whatchama-callit.

whistle, to wet one's: to damp one's mug; to (have a) gargle; to have a lotion; to have a wet; to sluice one's ivories; to wash one's neck.

wide-awake, to be: all there; an art-ful dodger; a clever Dick; cute; a cute one; as sharp as a pickled herring; dodgy; fly; to get (*or* to be) hep (*or* hip); to get on the ball; to get wise; a groover; to have been around; to have been through the mill; to have plenty of gumption; ikey; in the know; to know all the answers (*or* all the tricks of the trade *or* how many beans make five); to know it all; to know it backwards; to know it inside out; to know one's book (*or* one's onions *or* the ropes *or* the score or one's stuff *or* a thing or two *or* the time of day *or* a trick or two *or* one's way about *or* what's what); to be knowing; to be a knowing card (*or* a knowing one *or* a know-all); to be leary (*or* leery); a live wire; an old hand (at the game); a smart Alec(k);

a smart guy; a smarty; spry; trendy; up to scratch *or* up to snuff *or* up to all the dodges *or* up to all the tricks; up to a move (*or* a thing) or two; up to every move; to be wide (*or* a wide boy); a wily old bird; a wise guy; wised-up; to be 'with it'.

wife my: my ball and chain; my bet-ter half; the little woman; the missus; the missis; my old Dutch; my old girl; my old lady; my old woman; my sparring partner; my trouble and strife (*R.S.*).

win easily, to: (*in a race*) to doddle it; to leave the others standing; to romp home; to romp in; to walk it; to win by a street; to win hands down; to win in a (common) canter; to piss (through) it.

woman: (*pej.*) old bag; baggage; biddy; bint; bird; broad; dame; donah; faggot; floozey; floosie; floosy; Jane; moll; mot; skirt; tart; trollop.

work hard (at), to: to drudge; to fag; to graft; to grub along; to keep one's nose to the grindstone; to peg away; to pitch into; to plod (away); to plug away; to slave (away); to slog (away); to steam ahead; to steam away; to sweat; to toil (and moil); to wear oneself out (to a shadow); to work like stink (*or* like a horse *or* like a nigger). *See also* **study hard (at), to.**

worthless, to be (absolutely): an also-ran; a (no-good) bum; crap; crappy; duff; measly; mouldy; no cop; not much cop; no great shakes; not worth shucks; not to be worth a bean (*or* a brass farthing *or* a conti-nental *or* a cuss *or* a halfpenny *or* a hang *or* one's salt *or* a rap *or* a scrap *or* a sausage *or* a straw *or* a tinker's cuss *or* a (tinker's) damn *or* a tuppenny damn); punk; a stumer; tin-pot; tup-penny-ha'penny; trashy; a dead loss; a washout.